# COUNTERTERRORISM LAW

Aspen Publishers
Attn: Permissions Department
76 Ninth Avenue, 7th Floor
New York, NY 10011-5201

To contact Customer Care, e-mail customer.care@aspenpublishers.com, call 1-800-234-1660, fax 1-800-901-9075, or mail correspondence to:

Aspen Publishers
Attn: Order Department
PO Box 990
Frederick, MD 21705

Printed in the United States of America.

1 2 3 4 5 6 7 8 9 0

ISBN 978-0-7355-6559-3

**Library of Congress Cataloging-in-Publication Data**

Dycus, Stephen.
    Counterterrorism law / Stephen Dycus, William C. Banks, Peter Raven-Hansen.
      p. cm.
    Includes index.
    ISBN 978-0-7355-6559-3
    1. Terrorism—United States. 2. Terrorism—United States—Prevention. 3. National security—Law and legislation—United States. 4. Intelligence service—Law and legislation—United States. 5. Terrorism—Prevention—International cooperation. 6. Terrorists. 7. Data mining. I. Banks, William C. II. Raven-Hansen, Peter, 1946- III. Title.

KF9430.D93 2006
345.73'02—dc22

2007019857

ASPEN PUBLISHERS

# COUNTERTERRORISM LAW

**Stephen Dycus**
*Professor of Law*
*Vermont Law School*

**William C. Banks**
*Laura J. and L. Douglas Meredith Professor*
*Syracuse University*

**Peter Raven-Hansen**
*Glen Earl Weston Research Professor of Law*
*George Washington University*

 Wolters Kluwer
Law & Business

AUSTIN   BOSTON   CHICAGO   NEW YORK   THE NETHERLANDS

# About Wolters Kluwer Law & Business

Wolters Kluwer Law & Business is a leading provider of research information and workflow solutions in key specialty areas. The strengths of the individual brands of Aspen Publishers, CCH, Kluwer Law International and Loislaw are aligned within Wolters Kluwer Law & Business to provide comprehensive, in-depth solutions and expert-authored content for the legal, professional and education markets.

**CCH** was founded in 1913 and has served more than four generations of business professionals and their clients. The CCH products in the Wolters Kluwer Law & Business group are highly regarded electronic and print resources for legal, securities, antitrust and trade regulation, government contracting, banking, pensions, payroll, employment and labor, and healthcare reimbursement and compliance professionals.

**Aspen Publishers** is a leading information provider for attorneys, business professionals and law students. Written by preeminent authorities, Aspen products offer analytical and practical information in a range of specialty practice areas from securities law and intellectual property to mergers and acquisitions and pension/benefits. Aspen's trusted legal education resources provide professors and students with high-quality, up-to-date and effective resources for successful instruction and study in all areas of the law.

**Kluwer Law International** supplies the global business community with comprehensive English-language international legal information. Legal practitioners, corporate counsel and business executives around the world rely on the Kluwer Law International journals, loose-leafs, books and electronic products for authoritative information in many areas of international legal practice.

**Loislaw** is a premier provider of digitized legal content to small law firm practitioners of various specializations. Loislaw provides attorneys with the ability to quickly and efficiently find the necessary legal information they need, when and where they need it, by facilitating access to primary law as well as state-specific law, records, forms and treatises.

Wolters Kluwer Law & Business, a unit of Wolters Kluwer, is headquartered in New York and Riverwoods, Illinois. Wolters Kluwer is a leading multinational publisher and information services company.

*To our teachers*

# SUMMARY OF CONTENTS

# CONTENTS

## Chapter 19.  *Trying Suspected Terrorists as "special Interest" Immigrants*          601

## PART VI.  *MANAGING TERRORIST ATTACKS*          627

## Chapter 20.  *Responding to a WMD Attack*          629

*Chapter 21.* ***The Military's***
              ***Domestic Role in***
              ***Counterterrorism***                                    **669**

## PART VII.   *NONCRIMINAL SANCTIONS AGAINST TERRORISTS AND THEIR SPONSORS*                                   **701**

## Chapter 22.   *Public Sanctions Against Terrorists and Their Sponsors*                                   **703**

## *Chapter 23.*    *Suing Terrorists and Their Sponsors*    **733**

# PREFACE

Throughout our history this nation has faced a variety of serious threats. The asymmetric threat of international terrorism is only the latest. This book addresses the relatively recent development of law and policy concerning counterterrorism, part of the larger field of national security law.

The law of counterterrorism was not invented after September 11, 2001, however. Even in 1990, when we published the first edition of *National Security Law* (with Arthur L. Berney), we addressed the military retaliation for the terrorist bombing of a Berlin night club in 1986, the use of classified evidence in criminal cases, the government's powers of detention, "civil defense," foreign intelligence surveillance, and a domestic military response to a terrorist incident. The bombing of the World Trade Center in 1993 and of the Alfred P. Murrah Building in Oklahoma City in 1995 led to revisions in the FBI Guidelines for investigation and helped spur enactment of the Anti-Terrorism and Effective Death Penalty Act of 1996, Pub. L. No. 104-132, 110 Stat. 1214. Each of these developments was treated in the second edition of *National Security Law*, which appeared in 1997.

Before 9/11, however, counterterrorism law was still too immature to form a coherent intellectual discipline. The field has only taken shape in the years since the attacks on the World Trade Center and the Pentagon. And while counterterrorism law continues to evolve at a rapid pace, we believe it has advanced enough to warrant separate treatment. In this book we provide both an analytical framework and content to give teachers and students a good grounding in this still-maturing field.

In the developments in counterterrorism law since 9/11, we can identify several basic themes. The most important is the continuing primacy of checks and balances in our government. We see persistent evidence of the distinction Justice Jackson drew in *The Steel Seizure Case* between "the President's power to act without congressional authority [and to] . . . act contrary to an Act of Congress." Youngstown Sheet & Tube Co. v. Sawyer, 343 U.S. 579, 635 n.2 (1952) (Jackson, J., concurring). After a period of hesitancy, the courts have reasserted their role in interpreting the law, increasingly affording access to the judicial process, insisting on due process, and recognizing the primacy of statutory law — even in this field so closely tied to national security. Congress has also awakened to a more aggressive role in overseeing and regulating counterterrorist efforts. The shifting balance of executive "law" and execution, statutory law and oversight, and judicial gatekeeping and interpretation offers deep insights into the way law can work to protect us from terrorists without sacrificing the very values of liberty and democracy that terrorists seek to destroy. Users of the casebook will find these broad themes reflected in every chapter.

This study of counterterrorism law is both comprehensive and self-contained. We have organized the materials in this book into functional categories in order to facilitate study and to help put new developments in the field into perspective. This is not a "how-to-do-it" course, however. Rather, it is a collection of resources to help bright students and citizens reflect intensively on how to protect national security under the rule of law; whether civil rights and liberties must be traded for security, and, if so, how much; and what roles each of the three branches of government should play in making these decisions and trade-offs. A key to using this casebook successfully is therefore not mastery of the nuances of each functional subject but recognition of the themes they share.

Another key to success is active incorporation of new materials as they are reported in the media and a growing number of online sources that monitor the field. Given the dynamic quality of counterterrorism law, it is virtually certain that breaking news will supply opportunities to rehearse and apply principles addressed in the book. To aid in this effort the authors will provide significant new teaching materials — judicial opinions, statutes, executive orders, and the like — on a Web site maintained by Aspen Publishers.

The materials presented in this book and the issues they raise are as challenging as they are important. A comprehensive Teacher's Manual, available to adopters in late 2007, will provide helpful analysis, as well as guidance in planning courses.

Finally, we remind readers that counterterrorism law is only a subset of the larger and equally dynamic field of national security law. That broader field includes war, foreign affairs, covert operations, emergency powers, and the protection of state secrets. While this book focuses strictly on counterterrorism law, we hope that you will explore the larger and, in many ways, even richer subject of national security law as well.

Our most important goal is to encourage you to help find new ways to make this nation both secure and free under law. These materials are designed to advance that goal. We hope you find them interesting and provocative, and we welcome your comments.

*Stephen Dycus*
*William C. Banks*
*Peter Raven-Hansen*

May 2007

# *ACKNOWLEDGMENTS*

This book builds on work the authors began together in the late 1980s with Arthur L. Berney, now Professor Emeritus at Boston College Law School. It owes a great debt to friends, colleagues, and professionals in the national security field who have shared their ideas and experience in the years since. This is also a better book because of the contributions of several generations of law students who, in and out of the classroom, have taught us a lot about teaching.

Stephen Dycus is especially grateful to the late Reverend William Sloane Coffin Jr., whose stubborn patriotism and generosity inspired so many. Special thanks are due as well to my wife Elizabeth for her unflagging patience and support. I appreciate the encouragement of my Dean, Geoffrey B. Shields, and my other colleagues at Vermont Law School. I also want to recognize the contributions of a long succession of bright, energetic research assistants. Those involved most recently in the completion of this book are Pamela I. Lundquist, William L. (Trey) Martin, Catherine Rawson, Nathaniel Shoaff, and Rebecca Turner. Finally, I am grateful for the opportunity to undertake this work with two wonderful coauthors, whose brilliance, dedication, and sense of humor have made it all possible.

William Banks continues to recognize the memory of Brady Howell, a former National Security Law student and victim of the September 11 attack on the Pentagon. I also thank the Syracuse University law and graduate students who tested these materials in draft form. I am grateful to Deans Hannah Arterian and Mitchell Wallerstein for their generous support of this project, and to Cheryl Ficarra for her patience and support through many seven-day work weeks. My most recent research assistants, Laura Pierce and Jesse Blinick, were immensely helpful and supportive along the way. Finally, I want to thank my friends Steve Dycus and Peter Raven-Hansen for their commitment to excellence, dedication, and good humor through this remarkable project. Their intelligence and commitment to exploring this emerging new field continue to be an invaluable source of inspiration to me.

Peter Raven-Hansen expresses his thanks to current and former George Washington University Law School students Justin T. Ryan, who provided timely assistance with many last-minute tasks in getting this book ready for publication, and Alexis Victoria Chapin, Rachel Kramer, Stephan Rice, and Kelly Rich, who helped with the underlying research and editing. Thanks once again to my co-authors for life, Bill Banks and Steve Dycus, for their hard work, inspiration, and sense of humor, and to Steve Dycus also for once again leading the march through drafts, page proofs, and publication with unflagging and patient insistence on accuracy and consistency. Finally, but most importantly, thanks to my wife Winnie for putting up with back-to-back-to-back book projects.

Together, the authors wish to express their gratitude for the continuing support and encouragement of the staff at Aspen, especially Carol McGeehan, Melody Davies, Eric Holt, John Devins, Peter Skagestad, and Michael Gregory, as well as our marvelous copy editor, Barbara Rappaport.

The authors also gratefully acknowledge permission to reprint excerpts from the following:

Carroll Publishing, chart on organization of the intelligence community (2005). Reprinted by permission of Carroll Publishing.

Philip Heymann & Juliette Kayyem, Protecting Liberty in an Age of Terror 65 (MIT Press 2005). Reprinted by permission of the MIT Press.

Thomas V. Inglesby, Rita Grossman & Tara O'Toole, A Plague on Your City: Observations from TOPOFF, 32 Clinical Infectious Diseases 436 (2001). Copyright © 2001 by The University of Chicago Press. Reprinted by permission of The University of Chicago Press.

Peter M. Shane, chart, The Bureaucratic Due Process of Government Watch Lists, 75 Geo. Wash. L. Rev. (forthcoming 2007). Reprinted by permission of the author.

# EDITORS' NOTE

In general we have adhered to the rules for citation of authority followed by most lawyers and courts. They are set out in The Bluebook: A Uniform System of Citation (18th ed. 2005). For reasons of economy we have omitted without notation many citations within excerpted materials, and we have removed almost all parallel citations. We have, on the other hand, sought to provide citations that will enable readers to locate and review original sources. To make it easier to refer back to materials where they were originally published, we have preserved original footnote numbers in all excerpted materials. Editors' footnotes are numbered consecutively throughout each chapter. Additions to quoted or excerpted materials are enclosed in brackets.

# COUNTERTERRORISM LAW

# INTRODUCTION

# CHAPTER 1

# DEFINING TERRORISM AND COUNTERTERRORISM

Terrorism is a phenomenon that is easier to describe than to define. It is the unlawful use or threat of violence against persons or property to further political or social objectives. It is generally intended to intimidate or coerce a government, individuals, or groups to modify their behavior or policies.

Some experts see terrorism as the lower end of the warfare spectrum, a form of low-intensity, unconventional aggression. . . .

. . . Americans . . . realize that terrorism needs an audience; that it is propaganda designed to shock and stun them; that it is behavior that is uncivilized and lacks respect for human life. They also believe that terrorism constitutes a growing danger to our system, beliefs, and policies worldwide. [*Public Report of the Vice President's Task Force on Combating Terrorism* 1, 21 (1986).]

Unlike war, terrorism often deliberately targets noncombatants. Unlike the ordinary murderer or mugger, who directs his violence against the victim alone without wanting to alert others, a terrorist uses violence "to instill fear in the targeted population . . . [in a] deliberate evocation of dread." Jessica Stern, *The Ultimate Terrorists* 11 (1999).

This chapter introduces the book and our study of the role of law in countering terrorism. We first provide a short survey of terrorism in the United States — its history and our approaches to defining what it is. Among the thorny questions introduced here is whether terrorism should be treated as a crime, as a species of war, or as some combination of the two. The answer to this question matters in sorting out the legal bases for responding to terrorism. Later in the chapter we offer two compelling and contrasting judicial decisions that question the existence of a consensus in the international community as to whether an act of terrorism violates international law. Finally, with some understanding of the definitional difficulties in hand, we provide a road map for the study of counterterrorism that follows.

## A.   SEEKING A DEFINITION OF TERRORISM: A BRIEF SKETCH

Terrorism has ancient roots. At least since the first century A.D., terrorists have wrought destruction in furtherance of religious or secular ends. Sometimes by assassinating individual targets, at other times by fomenting mass uprisings or forming marauding bands of roving thugs, early terrorists probably inflicted more harm than any equivalent modern group. *See* Stern, *supra,* at 15. In the United States, where terrorism is generally considered a modern phenomenon, terrorist acts have in fact occurred throughout our history. From presidential and other political assassinations, to Civil War–related terrorist violence, to anarchist and other radical group actions, our nation has experienced its share of lethal and usually politically motivated terrorism. *Id.* at 17.

Still, terrorism has emerged as a central national security concern in the United States only since the end of the Cold War. At first, the vulnerability of U.S. interests abroad dominated the policy agenda. Not long after terrorist Abu Nidal killed 19 tourists at airports in Rome and Vienna in December 1985, however, President Reagan issued NSDD-207, establishing a comprehensive counterterrorism policy for the United States and noting that terrorists use or threaten violence against innocents "to achieve a political objective through coercion or intimidation of an audience beyond the immediate victims." NSDD-207 (Jan. 20, 1986) (partly classified), *reprinted in* Christopher Simpson, *National Security Directives of the Reagan & Bush Administrations* 656 (1995). The bombings of the World Trade Center in 1993 and the Oklahoma City federal building in 1995, along with the 1995 Aum Shinrikyo nerve gas attack in Tokyo, shifted attention toward homeland security and domestic terrorist threats. In 1994, President Clinton found "that the proliferation of nuclear, biological, and chemical weapons ('weapons of mass destruction'), and of the means for delivering such weapons, constitutes an unusual and extraordinary threat to the national security," and he declared "a national emergency to deal with that threat." Exec. Order No. 12,938, 59 Fed. Reg. 58,099 (Nov. 14, 1994). After the September 11, 2001, attacks on the World Trade Center and the Pentagon, President George W. Bush also declared a national emergency, citing "the continuing and immediate threat of further attacks on the United States." Proclamation No. 7463, 66 Fed. Reg. 48,199 (Sept. 14, 2001).

Beginning in the 1990s, terrorism changed in important ways:

> As the 1990s began, the conventional wisdom that terrorists employed violence in discriminate and proportionate ways was called into question. A new, more ruthless breed of terrorists began to leave its mark on the world. The first sharp departure from their predecessors was that many terrorists who became active in this time period did not necessarily espouse political causes or aim to take power. The second distinguishing feature was that a fair share of 1990s terrorists were intent on harming a maximum number of people. Instead of kidnaping an ambassador, the 1990s-vintage terrorists took a whole embassy hostage. Rather than hijack an aircraft, terrorists plotted to blow planes out of the sky. Terrorists upped the ante from pipe bombs to truck bombs capable of

blowing up entire buildings, peppering the decade with headlines about the World Trade Center in 1993, the Murrah Federal Building in Oklahoma City in 1995, the Khobar Towers barracks in Saudi Arabia in 1997, and U.S. embassies in Kenya and Tanzania in 1998. [Amy E. Smithson, *Grounding the Threat in Reality*, in *Ataxia: The Chemical and Biological Terrorism Threat and the U.S. Response* 15 (Amy E. Smithson & Leslie-Anne Levy eds., Henry L. Stimson Center 2000).]

The September 11 attacks vividly displayed these terrorism trends and catapulted the United States into what the Bush administration has called a "global war on terror." Six years of sustained efforts to combat al Qaeda "have degraded the ability of the core [al Qaeda] leadership group . . . to mount global acts of terrorism. . . . [However,] terrorists continue[] to attempt to adapt to improved countermeasures and evolve new approaches in response to a less permissive operating environment." U.S. Dept. of State, *Country Reports on Terrorism 2005* 11-12 (2006). Although al Qaeda and its affiliates remain the most prominent terrorist threat, the general trends in terrorism show that micro-actors — small autonomous cells and individuals enabled by technologies and international commerce — are increasingly worrisome and difficult to counter. *Id.* at 11. Some of these small groups are ethnically defined, others are mixed, and some meet and organize virtually, using the Internet for training and communications. *Id.* at 13. Trends also point toward ever-greater sophistication by terrorists in using global mechanisms to share "information, finance, and ideas [and] improved . . . technological sophistication across many areas of operational planning, communications, targeting, and propaganda," *id.*, while the same groups may overlap in their planning and operations with transnational crime. *Id.* The Department of State concluded in 2006 that al Qaeda, although weakened, is "adaptive and resilient," and that "we are still in the first phase of a potentially long war." *Id.* at 14-15.

Exactly what is terrorism? Before we can be confident of the scope of our subject — counterterrorism law — we need to know what it is that we are countering. Although everyone who uses the term today agrees that terrorism is bad, the inevitable politicization of terrorism renders any search for a consensus definition futile. Because polemicists have used the term in a variety of self-serving ways over the years, "terrorism" might be used today to describe any disfavored action taken in response to another's policies.

After attempting to distinguish terrorists from other criminals and from irregular armed forces, political scientist Bruce Hoffman defines "terrorism" as "the deliberate creation and exploitation of fear through violence or the threat of violence in pursuit of political change." *See* Bruce Hoffman, *Inside Terrorism* 40 (rev. ed. 2006). In its capacity as record keeper of incidents of international terrorism, the State Department defines "terrorism" as "premeditated, politically motivated violence perpetrated against noncombatant targets by subnational groups or clandestine agents." *Country Reports on Terrorism, supra*, at 9. *See also* 22 U.S.C. §2656f(d)(2) (Supp. IV 2004). However, the State Department definition is only one in hundreds of federal statutes and regulations that address terrorism in some way, ranging from the Justice Department's "Victims of Crime Act Compensation Grant Program," to Commerce Department export controls, to FBI requirements that banks disclose financial information on terrorists to the Bureau, to a law waiving limits on the liability of government and nonprofit volunteers who have committed terrorist acts. *See* Elizabeth Martin, *"Terrorism" and Related Terms in Statute and Regulation: Selected Language* 1 (Cong. Res. Serv. RS21021), Dec. 5, 2006; Nicholas J. Perry, *The Numerous Federal Legal Definitions of Terrorism: The Problem of Too Many Grails*, 30 J. Legis. 249 (2004).

Inspired by international political implications, the U.N. General Assembly devoted considerable energy during the 1970s to avoiding application of the term "terrorists" to groups that might instead be called "national liberation movements," "urban guerrillas," or "freedom fighters." In the summer of 2005, after ten years of negotiations, it appeared that the United Nations might reach agreement on a definition of "terrorism" in anticipation of the adoption of a Comprehensive Convention on International Terrorism. A draft of the Convention contained this statement: "The targeting and deliberate killing of civilians and non-combatants cannot be justified or legitimized by any cause or grievance." *See Advanced Unedited Version*, Aug. 5, 2005, *at* http://www.un.org/ga/59/hlpm_rev.2.pdf. The U.S. ambassador urged that the words "by terrorists" be inserted between "killing" and "of." *See* Letter from John R. Bolton (n.d.), *at* http://www.un.int/usa/reform-un-jrb-ltr-terror-8-05.pdf. Some governments, however, sought to exclude from the definition of "terrorism" actions that are taken in "resistance to occupation" and to add language that would reach collateral damage caused by military action. When government leaders gathered in September, they approved an agenda-setting document in anticipation of the 60th session of the General Assembly that avoided these controversies by simply deleting all of the definitional language. *See Draft Outcome Document*, Sept. 13, 2005, *at* http://www.un.org/summit2005/Draft_Outcome130905.pdf. One year later, a General Assembly resolution aimed at promoting adoption of a comprehensive convention still lacked a definition of the contentious term. Instead, the resolution declared that member states "consistently, unequivocally and strongly condemn terrorism in all its forms and manifestations, committed by whomever, wherever and for whatever purposes, as it constitutes one of the most serious threats to international peace and security." *United Nations Global Counter-Terrorism Strategy*, G.A. Res. 60/288, U.N. Doc. A/RES/60/288 (Sept. 20, 2006). See *infra* p. 705.

Although defining "terrorism" is difficult, it is legally important. As one federal appeals court has explained:

> Under the Anti-Terrorism and Effective Death Penalty Act of 1996, 8 U.S.C. §1189, the Secretary of State is empowered to designate an entity as a "foreign terrorist organization." The consequences of designation are dire. The designation by the Secretary results in blocking any funds which the organization has on deposit with any financial institution in the United States. 18 U.S.C. §2339B(a)(2). Representatives and certain members of the organization are barred from entry into the United States. 8 U.S.C. §1182(a)(3)(B)(i)(IV & V). Perhaps most importantly, all persons within or subject to jurisdiction of the United States are forbidden from "knowingly providing material support or

resources" to the organization. 18 U.S.C. §2339B(a)(1). [National Council of Resistance of Iran v. Department of State, 251 F.3d 192, 196 (D.C. Cir. 2001).]

Such knowing provision of material support or resources is a crime punishable by up to ten years' imprisonment.

Under the 1996 statute, the Secretary may designate an organization as a terrorist organization if it engages in "terrorist activity" that threatens "the security of United States nationals or the national security of the United States." 8 U.S.C. §1189(a)(1) (2000). Under a different part of the statute, an alien is deemed inadmissible to the United States if he engages in "terrorist activity," defined as activity that is

unlawful . . . where it is committed . . . and which involves any of the following:

(I) The hijacking or sabotage of any conveyance . . . .

(II) The seizing or detaining, and threatening to kill, injure, or continue to detain, another individual in order to compel a third person (including a governmental organization) to do or abstain from doing any act as an explicit or implicit condition for the release of the individual seized or detained.

(III) A violent attack upon an internationally protected person . . . or upon the liberty of such a person.

(IV) An assassination.

(V) The use of any—

(a) biological agent, chemical agent, or nuclear weapon or device, or

(b) explosive, firearm, or other weapons or dangerous device (other than for mere personal monetary gain),

with intent to endanger, directly or indirectly, the safety of one or more individuals or to cause substantial damage to property.

(VI) A threat, attempt, or conspiracy to do any of the foregoing.

[8 U.S.C. §1182(a)(3)(B)(iii) (2000 & Supp. IV 2004).]

A different federal statute provides criminal sanctions for "international terrorism," defined as activities that—

(A) involve violent acts or acts dangerous to human life that are a violation of the criminal laws of the United States or of any State, or that would be a criminal violation if committed within the jurisdiction of the United States or of any State;

(B) appear to be intended—

(i) to intimidate or coerce a civilian population;

(ii) to influence the policy of a government by intimidation or coercion; or

(iii) to affect the conduct of a government by mass destruction, assassination or kidnaping; and

(C) occur primarily outside the territorial jurisdiction of the United States, or transcend national boundaries in terms of the means by which they are accomplished, the persons they appear intended to intimidate or coerce, or the locale in which their perpetrators operate or seek asylum. [18 U.S.C. §2331(1) (2000 & Supp. IV 2004).]

*See also* 18 U.S.C. §2332b(g)(5) (2000 & Supp. IV 2004), as amended by Pub. L. No. 109-177, §§110(b)(3)(A), 112(a) and (b), 120 Stat. 192, 208, 209 (2006) (defining "Federal crime of terrorism"). In addition, if the Secretary of State finds that a country has "repeatedly provided support for acts of international terrorism," she is required to cut off U.S. foreign aid to the offending country. 22 U.S.C. §2371(a) (2000). Criminal, economic, and other sanctions are addressed in greater detail in later chapters.

The USA Patriot Act, passed in response to the September 11 attacks, borrows from the foregoing definition of "international terrorism" to define as "domestic terrorism" such acts that occur primarily *within* the jurisdiction of the United States. Pub. L. No. 107-56, §802(5), 115 Stat. 560 (2001) (codified at 18 U.S.C. §2331(5) (Supp. IV 2004)). The same definition is used (with one change) to identify permissible targets of electronic surveillance or surreptitious physical searches under the Foreign Intelligence Surveillance Act. 50 U.S.C. §1801(c) (2000). See Chapter 5.

## NOTES AND QUESTIONS

1. *One Definition?* How would you rate the chances of arriving at a single definition of "terrorism" on which everyone could agree? Bearing in mind our desire to be clear about our subject matter in this book, is it wise to even attempt a single consensus definition?

2. *Terrorism as Crime?* Is terrorism a crime and therefore best viewed as a matter to be addressed by law enforcement agencies? What are the legal and practical implications of characterizing terrorism as part of the criminal law? Consider this observation:

> Since 1986, presidents have taken international terrorism, drug-trafficking, and international organized crime out of the law enforcement closet of ordinary crimes and relabeled them as "national security threats." "Threats" must be prevented, not just detected and prosecuted like ordinary crimes. To prevent them, law enforcement must conduct the open-ended collection of intelligence, instead of just the more focused and close-ended assembly of criminal evidence. Furthermore, law enforcement cannot do it alone. Both the intelligence community and the military are therefore now tasked to participate, breaching the walls that society (and, some would have said, our Constitution) has traditionally maintained between civilian law enforcement and military or intelligence operations.
>
> In short, under the twin banners of the war on terrorism and international crime . . . federal *law enforcement* is metamorphosing into *security enforcement* in the new national security state. [Peter Raven-Hansen, *Security's Conquest of Law Enforcement*, in *In Democracy's Shadow* 217 (Marcus G. Raskin & A. Carl Levin eds., 2005).]

What considerations prompt government to lump international terrorism together with other, more traditional law enforcement problems? Can you see the value in doing so? What legal issues are likely to arise with a policy of security enforcement that includes international terrorism? *See also* Tyler Raimo, *Winning at the Expense of Law: The Ramifications of Expanding Counter-Terrorism Law Enforcement Jurisdiction Overseas*, 14 Am. U. Intl. L. Rev. 1473, 1481-1485 (1999).

The State Department definition noted above describes terrorism as "premeditated, politically motivated violence perpetrated against noncombatant targets by subnational groups or clandestine agents." *Country Reports on Terrorism, supra* p. 5, at 9. *See also* 22 U.S.C. §2656f(d)(2) (Supp. IV 2004). The first two qualifiers—premeditation and political motivation—are well-suited to the evidentiary intent requirements of criminal law. What is there about the intent to commit terrorist violence that distinguishes it from other violent crimes? If political motivation is central to terrorism and if the motivation includes some deep grievance against a government and its policies, is it possible that terrorism is not appropriately understood as a crime?

3. *Terrorism and Spreading the Message of Fear.* Recall Jessica Stern's evocation, *supra* p. 3, of the terrorist's aim to instill fear in the target population. In this respect, the threat of terrorism can be terrorism. Do criminal laws offer a good remedy to counter the threat of terrorism?

In order to instill the desired fear, terrorists seek to exploit available media to communicate news of the actual or threatened violence to the widest possible audience. Whether through traditional broadcast or cable services or through their own television, radio, and Internet media outlets, as Brian Jenkins observed more than 30 years ago, "terrorism is theater." Brian M. Jenkins, *International Terrorism: A New Mode of Conflict*, in *International Terrorism and World Security* 16 (David Carlton & Carlo Schaerf eds., 1975).

What legal mechanisms are capable of countering this aspect of terrorism? How should they be employed?

4. *Terrorism as War?* In an October 31, 2003, speech, then-National Security Adviser Condoleezza Rice stated that "Iraq is the central front in the war on Terror." Remarks by National Security Adviser Dr. Condoleezza Rice to the National Legal Center for the Public Interest, *available at* http://www.whitehouse.gov/news/releases/2003/10/20031031-5.html. In the same week, former National Security Adviser Zbigniew Brzezinski argued that the "war on terrorism" is a misleading phrase, because its abstractness obscures the nature of the enemy: "[T]errorism is a technique for killing people. That doesn't tell us who the enemy is. It's as if we said that World War II was not against the Nazis but against the blitzkrieg." Zbigniew Brzezinski, Remarks, New American Strategies for Security and Peace Conference, Oct. 28, 2003, *available at* http://www.prospect.org/webfeatures/2003/10/brzezinski-z-10-31.html.

What harm could there be in affixing the "war" label to terrorism? The State Department definition quoted *supra* p. 5 points out that terrorists deliberately attack those who cannot shoot back. Does this definition — which distinguishes terrorism from traditional military operations — suggest a limit to the terrorism/war metaphor? Does the reference to "subnational groups or clandestine agents" distinguish terrorism from war?

Do you see any downside to defining "terrorism" as a crime for law enforcement purposes, or as war where a military response is desirable?

5. ***Guerrilla War vs. Insurgency vs. Terrorism.*** Insurgents and guerrillas may share goals with terrorists, such as changing a government or political system. They also may use the same tactics, such as assassinations or bombings in public places, for similar purposes — to cause fear that leads to a change in government. The similarities do not end there. The three types of violent individuals also do not wear uniforms or other insignia that would distinguish them from noncombatant civilians. *See* Hoffman, *supra* p. 5, at 35.

While it may be accurate in some colloquial sense to lump the three types together as "irregulars," their differences may be more important for our purposes. NATO defines "insurgency" as "an organized movement aimed at the overthrow of a constituted government through the use of subversion and armed conflict," while "guerrilla warfare" is "military and paramilitary operations conducted in enemy-held or hostile territory by irregular, predominantly indigenous forces." U.S. Army Training and Doctrine Command, *A Military Guide to Terrorism in the Twenty-First Century (Version 3.0)* 1-7 (Aug. 15, 2005). On the basis of these definitions can you see how terrorism differs?

Some terrorist groups, such as Hezbollah, FARC (Revolutionary Armed Forces of Colombia), and the LTTE (Liberation Tigers of Tamil Eelam), are sometimes called guerrilla movements because they control a territory and its people, and they are large movements. Hoffman, *supra*, at 35. Hoffman estimates that about one-third of the 37 groups designated as "foreign terrorist organizations" by the State Department could be described as guerrilla movements. *Id.* at 35-36. Does the fuzziness of this distinction present any legal difficulties that you can see in countering the terrorism that such groups practice?

6. ***Defining Terrorism by What It Does.*** Most of the definitions offered by scholars follow the State Department determination to focus on the premeditated political motivation of the violence or threat of violence as central to the act of terrorism. In view of the seemingly futile quest for a consensus definition, would it be prudent to focus on the nature of the terrorist act, rather than its purpose? Consider this view:

> The early American experience with terrorism — the post-Civil War phenomenon of the Ku Klux Klan — indicates that the most salient defining characteristic of terrorism is not the purpose of the terrorist but the threat level represented by the terrorist. It is the level of threat, and the organized nature of the perpetrators, rather than their political motive, that should drive the distinction between terrorism and more common violence. [Wayne McCormack & Jeffrey Breinholt, *Defining Terrorism: Perfection as Enemy of the Possible*, Intl. Assessment and Strategy Center, Jan. 17, 2007, *available at* http://www.strategycenter.net/printVersion/print_pub.asp?pubID=141.]

If political motivation is eliminated from the definition of "terrorism," what would be included? What would be left out? Would national armed forces potentially become terrorists under such a definition? What factors distinguish the violence produced by regular national armies from that caused by terrorists?

7. ***Differences in Statutory Definitions.*** How do the statutory definitions of "terrorism" excerpted above differ? Why do you think they are different? One possibility is that the definitions reflect the emphases or concerns of the institutions they represent. Is there any harm in the State Department's defining "terrorism" to suit its purposes, or in the Defense Department or Department of Justice doing the same?

8. ***Domestic Terrorism.*** Note that by adapting the definition of "international terrorism" to acts that occur primarily inside the United States, the USA Patriot Act defines as "domestic terrorism" some acts attributed to Operation Rescue (an anti-abortion group), the Environmental Liberation Front, Greenpeace, and PETA (People for the Ethical Treatment of Animals). Should members of these groups be defined as terrorists? What legal issues would arise if a member of one of those groups were charged with "domestic terrorism"?

9. ***The Politics of Labeling.*** Do any of the definitions of "terrorism" set out above permit us to distinguish among the following: the attack on the World Trade Center on September 11, 2001; the attack on the Pentagon on the same day; the 1995 bombing of the federal building in Oklahoma City; acts of violence by Nelson Mandela and the ANC — carried out for the political purpose of fighting apartheid; the 1946 bombing for political purposes of the King David Hotel, which housed civilian as well as military guests, by Menachem Begin (later prime minister of Israel); and the 2001 Palestinian suicide bombing that killed more than a dozen Israeli teenagers at a discotheque to avenge Israeli attacks on other Palestinians who allegedly had participated in bombings?

Could you argue that some of these acts were not terrorism? Which ones, and why not? Note that our courts have sometimes refused to extradite members of the IRA who have killed British troops in Northern Ireland on grounds that they were engaged in "political" acts. See *infra* p. 514.

Does it matter that Mandela and Begin succeeded in their political purposes, while the Palestinians have not? *See Symposium, Post-Cold War International Security Threats: Terrorism, Drugs, and Organized Crime*, 21 Mich. J. Intl. L. 527, 569 (2000) (so suggesting).

Is it legally significant for this purpose that we have a political relationship with South Africa and Israel that is different from the one we have with the Palestinian Authority? Does the electoral victory of Hamas in the January 2006 elections in the Palestinian Authority permit, or even require, the United States to designate the Palestinian Authority as a state supporter of terrorism? *See* Michael Herzog, *Can Hamas Be Tamed?* Foreign Aff., Mar.-Apr. 2006, at 83. How should the law and politics of designation account for participation by designated terrorist organizations in democratic processes? Does politics alone account for the Bush administration's reported reluctance, during its effort to build an anti-terrorist coalition after the September 11 attacks, to include Syria on the list of countries that support terrorism? *See* Karen DeYoung, *Definitions of Terrorism Dog U.S. Officials*, Wash. Post, Oct. 25, 2001, at A9.

10. *State Sponsorship of Terrorism.* How do the lawful options for countering terrorism change when governments provide support to non-state terrorist organizations? The State Department currently lists Cuba, Iran, North Korea, Sudan, and Syria as state sponsors of terrorism. U.S. Dept. of State, *State Sponsors of Terrorism* (n.d.), *available at* http://www.state.gov/s/ct/c14151.htm. Legal responses to state-sponsored terrorism are assessed in Chapter 23.

## B. THE PROCESS OF LABELING TERRORISTS AND TERRORIST ORGANIZATIONS

The consequences of designating an individual as an "enemy combatant" or an organization as "terrorist" or of identifying a sovereign state as a sponsor of terrorism may be dire. (We address these consequences in some detail later in the book.) Therefore, when we use these labels, it is important to get it right — not only as a matter of basic fairness, but also because mistakes could be very counterproductive. Equally important, when labeling affects the property or liberty interests of a person or organization entitled to constitutional protection, the procedures followed in attaching these labels must satisfy requirements of due process.

The labels, like the contexts in which they are used, vary. The procedures for their use also vary considerably. While we focus here on just one such procedure, the designation of "foreign terrorist organizations," the practical and constitutional questions analyzed here also arise in other settings. See for example, pp. 349-398 (military detention of "enemy combatants") and pp. 557-600 (trial by military commission of "enemy combatants").

A portion of the Antiterrorism and Effective Death Penalty Act of 1996, §302(a), Pub. L. No. 104-132, 110 Stat. 1214, 1248 (codified as amended at 8 U.S.C. §1189(a) (Supp. IV 2004)), authorizes the Secretary of State to designate an entity as a "foreign terrorist organization" (FTO).

### §1189. Designation of foreign terrorist organizations

(a) Designation

(1) In general. The Secretary is authorized to designate an organization as a foreign terrorist organization in accordance with this subsection if the Secretary finds that —

(A) the organization is a foreign organization;

(B) the organization engages in terrorist activity (as defined in section 1182(a)(3)(B) of this title) or terrorism (as defined in section 2656f(d)(2) of Title 22), or retains the capability and intent to engage in terrorist activity or terrorism; and

(C) the terrorist activity or terrorism of the organization threatens the security of United States nationals or the national security of the United States. . . .

By late 2005, 42 organizations were on the FTO list (including Hamas, Hizballah, Liberation Tigers of Tamil Eelam, Mujahedin-e Khalq (also called People's Mojahedin Organization of Iran), al-Qa'ida, Real IRA, and Shining Path). Office of Counterterrorism, U.S. Dept. of State, *Fact Sheet: Foreign Terrorist Organizations (FTOs)*, Oct. 11, 2005.

Does the Due Process Clause of the Fifth Amendment require that designees be given advance notice and an opportunity to be heard? The answer for foreign entities not connected to the United States is no. "A foreign entity without property or presence in this country has no constitutional rights, under the due process clause or otherwise." People's Mojahedin Organization of Iran v. United States Department of State, 182 F.3d 17, 22 (D.C. Cir. 1999). A fortiori, no foreign state is entitled to any process before it is listed as a country that supports terrorism and is therefore cut off from foreign aid. "No one would suppose that a foreign nation had a due process right to notice and a hearing before the Executive imposed an embargo on it for the purpose of coercing a change in policy." *Id.*

But entities and persons with substantial connections to the United States stand on a different constitutional footing. They are, for example, entitled to due process before their property or liberty rights can be curtailed by the government. National Council of Resistance of Iran v. Department of State, 251 F.3d 192, 203 (D.C. Cir. 2001).

The following cases examine several constitutional concerns.

## PEOPLE'S MOJAHEDIN ORGANIZATION OF IRAN V. DEPARTMENT OF STATE

United States Court of Appeals, District of Columbia Circuit, 2003
327 F.3d 1238

SENTELLE, Circuit Judge. The People's Mojahedin Organization of Iran ("PMOI" or "Petitioner") seeks review of 1999 and 2001 decisions of the Secretary of State . . . designating Petitioner as a foreign terrorist organization. . . .

### I. Background

We note at the outset that this is PMOI's third petition to this court to review designations of the PMOI as a foreign terrorist organization. *See* People's Mojahedin Org. of Iran v. Dep't. of State, 182 F.3d 17 (D.C. Cir. 1999) (*"PMOI"*); Nat'l Council of Resistance of Iran v. Dep't. of State, 251 F.3d 192 (D.C. Cir. 2001) (*"NCOR"*). . . .

### II. Analysis

#### A. Due Process and Sufficiency of Evidence

Petitioner raises several arguments. First, it contends that its redesignation as a terrorist organization under 8 U.S.C. §1189 is unconstitutional under the Due Process Clause of the Fifth Amendment of the Constitution because the statute permitted the Secretary to rely upon secret evidence — the classified information that respondents refused to disclose and against which PMOI could therefore not effectively defend. We reject this contention. . . . [T]hat statute authorizes designation of a foreign terrorist organization when the Secretary finds three elements. As to the first, that is that the organization is a foreign organization, there is not and cannot be any dispute. The People's Mojahedin is so assuredly a foreign organization that until the Secretary's designation of the NCOR as its alias, it could not even establish a presence in the United States. Nothing has changed in that regard since our prior decisions on the subject.

As to the second element, the PMOI advances a colorable argument: that the Secretary was able under §1189(a)(3)(B) to "consider classified information in making [this designation]" and that the classified information was not "subject to disclosure" except to the court ex parte and in camera for purposes of this judicial review. Petitioner contends that this violates the due process standard set forth in Abourezk v. Reagan, 785 F.2d 1043, 1061 (D.C. Cir. 1986), "that a court may not dispose of the merits of a case on the basis of ex parte, in camera submissions." While colorable, this argument will not carry the day.

First, we have already set forth in *NCOR* the due process standards that the Secretary must meet in making designations under the statute. We held that the Constitution requires the Secretary in designating foreign terrorist organizations to provide to the potential designees, "notice that the designation is impending." *NCOR*, 251 F.3d at 208. We further required that the Secretary must afford the potential designee an "opportunity to be heard at a meaningful time and in a meaningful manner." *Id.* at 209. The record reflects that the Secretary complied with our instructions.

Granted, petitioners argue that their opportunity to be heard was not meaningful, given that the Secretary relied on secret information to which they were not afforded access. The response to this is twofold. We already decided in *NCOR* that due process required the disclosure of only the unclassified portions of the administrative record. 251 F.3d at 207-09. We made that determination informed by the historically recognized proposition that under the separation of powers created by the United States Constitution, the Executive Branch has control and responsibility over access to classified information and has "'compelling interest' in withholding national security information from unauthorized persons in the course of executive business." Dep't. of the Navy v. Egan, 484 U.S. 518, 527 (1988) (quoting Snepp v. United States, 444 U.S. 507, 509 n.3 (1980)). In the context of another statutory scheme involving classified information, we noted the courts are often ill-suited to determine the sensitivity of classified information. United States v. Yunis, 867 F.2d 617, 623 (D.C. Cir. 1989) ("Things that did not make sense to [a judge] would make all too much sense to a foreign counter intelligence specialist. . . ."). The Due Process Clause requires only that process which is due under the circumstances of the case. We have already established in *NCOR* the process which is due under the circumstances of this sensitive matter of classified intelligence in the effort to combat foreign terrorism. The Secretary has complied with the standard we set forth therein, and nothing further is due.

However, even if we err in describing the process due, even had the Petitioner been entitled to have its counsel or itself view the classified information, the breach of that entitlement has caused it no harm. This brings us to Petitioner's statutory objection. Petitioner argues that there is not adequate record support for the Secretary's determination that it is a foreign terrorist organization under the statute. However, on this element, even the unclassified record taken alone is quite adequate to support the Secretary's determination. Indeed, as to this element — that is, that the organization engages in terrorist activities — the People's Mojahedin has effectively admitted not only the adequacy of the unclassified record, but the truth of the allegation. . . .

By its own admission, the PMOI has

(1) attacked with mortars the Islamic Revolutionary Prosecutor's Office; (2) assassinated a former Iranian prosecutor and killed his security guards; (3) killed the Deputy Chief of the Iranian Joint Staff Command, who was the personal military adviser to Supreme Leader Khamenei; (4) attacked with mortars the Iranian Central Command Headquarters of the Islamic Revolutionary Guard Corps and the Defense Industries Organization in Tehran; (5) attacked and targeted with mortars the offices of the Iranian Supreme Leader Khamenei, and of the head of the State Exigencies Council; (6) attacked with mortars the central headquarters of the Revolutionary Guards; (7) attacked with mortars two Revolutionary Guards Corps headquarters; and (8) attacked the headquarters of the Iranian State Security Forces in Tehran.

Were there no classified information in the file, we could hardly find that the Secretary's determination that the Petitioner engaged in terrorist activities is "lacking substantial support in the administrative record taken as a whole," even without repairing to the "classified information submitted to the court." 8 U.S.C. §1189(b)(3)(D). . . .

The remaining element under §1189(a)(1) is that "the terrorist activity or terrorism of the organization threatens the security of United States nationals or the national security of the United States." *Id.* §1189(a)(1)(C). The thrust of Petitioner's argument is that its allegedly terrorist acts were not acts of terrorism under the statute, because they do not meet the requirement of subsection (C). Petitioner argues that the attempt to overthrow the despotic government of Iran, which itself remains on the State Department's list of state sponsors of terrorism, is not "terrorist activity," or if it is, that it does not threaten the security of the United States or its nationals. We cannot review that claim. In *PMOI* we expressly held that that finding "is nonjusticiable." 182 F.3d at 23. As we stated in that decision, "it is beyond the judicial function for a court to review foreign policy decisions of the Executive Branch." *Id.* (citing Chicago & Southern Air Lines v. Waterman Steamship Corp., 333 U.S. 103, 111 (1948)). . . . In short, we find neither statutory nor due process errors in the Secretary's designation of petitioner as a foreign terrorist organization.

## B. Petitioner's Other Claims

Petitioner raises several other arguments to the effect that the designation violates its constitutional rights. Those warranting separate discussion fall under the general heading of First Amendment claims. Petitioner's argument that its First Amendment rights have been violated rests on the consequences of the designation. Petitioner argues that by forbidding all persons within or subject to the jurisdiction of the United States from "knowingly provid[ing] material support or resources," 18 U.S.C. §2339B(a)(1), to it as a designated foreign terrorist organization, the statute violates its rights of free speech and association guaranteed by the First Amendment. We disagree.

As the Ninth Circuit held in Humanitarian Law Project v. Reno, 205 F.3d 1130, 1135 (9th Cir. 2000) [*infra* p. 480], the statute "is not aimed at interfering with the expressive component of [the organization's] conduct but at stopping aid to terrorist groups." It is conduct and not communication that the statute controls. We join the Ninth Circuit in observing that "there is no constitutional right to facilitate terrorism by giving terrorists the weapons and explosives with which to carry out their grisly missions. Nor, of course, is there a right to provide resources with which terrorists can buy weapons and explosives." *Id.* at 1133. . . .

### III. Conclusion

For the reasons set forth above, we conclude that in the designation and redesignation of the People's Mojahedin of Iran as a foreign terrorist organization, the Secretary of State afforded all the process that the organization was due, and that this designation violated neither statutory nor constitutional rights of the Petitioner. We therefore deny the petitions for review.

So ordered.

[The concurring opinion of EDWARDS, J., is omitted.]

## UNITED STATES v. AFSHARI

United States Court of Appeals, Ninth Circuit, 2006
446 F.3d 915

Before ANDREW J. KLEINFELD, KIM MCLANE WARDLAW, and WILLIAM A. FLETCHER, Circuit Judges. [Defendants were charged with knowingly and willfully conspiring to provide material support to a designated terrorist organization, in violation of 18 U.S.C. §2339B(a)(1). See *infra* p. 479. The district court dismissed the indictment on the ground that the terrorist designation statute was unconstitutional, and the court of appeals reversed.] The petition for rehearing and the petition for rehearing en banc are DENIED.

KOZINSKI, Circuit Judge, with whom Judges PREGERSON, REINHARDT, THOMAS and PAEZ join, dissenting from denial of rehearing en banc. It goes without saying that the United States government may prohibit donations to terrorist organizations. As we explained in *Humanitarian Law Project v. Reno*, 205 F.3d 1130, 1133 (9th Cir. 2000) [*infra* p. 480], money is fungible; if an organization engages in terrorism, it can channel money donated to it for humanitarian and advocacy purposes to promote its grisly agenda. At the same time, however, giving money to a political organization that is *not* engaged in terrorist activities is constitutionally protected. The determination of whether or not an organization is engaged in terrorism is therefore crucial, because it distinguishes activities that can be criminalized from those that are protected by the First Amendment.

This case concerns the manner in which this distinction is drawn. . . .

. . . A foreign "terrorist organization" is defined as any organization so designated by the Secretary of State under 8 U.S.C. §1189(a)(1).[2]

Roya Rahmani was indicted under 18 U.S.C. §2339B for making monetary contributions to the Mujahedin-e-Khalq (MEK), also known as the People's Mojahedin Organization for Iran, between 1997 and 2001. *See United States v. Rahmani, sub nom. United States v. Afshari,* 426 F.3d 1150, 1152 (9th Cir. 2005). MEK is opposed to the current fundamentalist regime in Iran. *See People's Mojahedin Org. of Iran v. Dep't of State,* 182 F.3d 17, 20-21 (D.C. Cir. 1999) (*"PMOI I"*). It was first designated a terrorist organization in 1997, and was re-designated in 1999 and 2001. *See id.* at 18; *Nat'l Council of Resistance of Iran v. Dep't of State,* 251 F.3d 192, 197 (D.C. Cir. 2001) (*"PMOI II"*); *People's Mojahedin Org. of Iran v. Dep't of State,* 327 F.3d 1238, 1241 (D.C. Cir. 2003) (*"PMOI III"*); *cf.* 8 U.S.C. §1189(a)(4) (requiring re-designation every two years).

Rahmani argues that MEK is not a terrorist organization, but the crime isn't defined as providing support to an organization that *is* terrorist, only to one that is *designated* as such under 8 U.S.C. §1189. Further, she is statutorily barred from arguing that the organization is not terrorist in nature, and therefore that her contribution is constitutionally protected. *See* 8 U.S.C. §1189(a)(8). Not to worry, says the panel; the organization itself can challenge the designation, so Rahmani's First Amendment rights are adequately protected.

The organization's challenges in this case, however, proved futile. MEK brought a legal challenge each time it was designated, under the judicial review provision of the governing statute: "The [D.C. Circuit] Court shall hold unlawful and set aside a designation the court finds to be . . . contrary to constitutional right, power, privilege, or immunity." 8 U.S.C. §1189(b)(3)(B). When the D.C. Circuit reviewed MEK's 1997 designation, however, it found the organization lacked due process rights and thus could not challenge the designation. *See PMOI I,* 182 F.3d at 22, 25. When MEK was re-designated in 1999 and challenged its new designation, the D.C. Circuit reached the merits and found that the designation *violated due process* because the government did not provide MEK with notice or an opportunity to be heard. *See PMOI II,* 251 F.3d at 196, 208-09. But, instead of setting the designation aside as the statute requires, *see* 8 U.S.C. §1189(b)(3)(B), the court left the designation in place and remanded the case to the Secretary of State for further proceedings, *see PMOI II,* 251 F.3d at 209. On remand, the Secretary promptly re-designated MEK a terrorist organization *retroactively* for the two-year period ending in 2001. *See PMOI III,* 327 F.3d at 1241. The D.C. Circuit did not uphold this retroactive designation until 2003. *See id.* at 1245.

It is these designations — one of which was found to be unreviewable, one of which was found to be unconstitutional, and the last of which was adopted retroactively — that form the basis of the government's prosecution of Rahmani.

---

2. All references to 8 U.S.C. §1189 are to the version in place before the 2001 and 2004 amendments.

## Discussion

It is firmly established that monetary contributions to political organizations are a form of "speech" protected by the First Amendment. . . . In *Humanitarian Law Project,* 205 F.3d at 1133, we held that giving money to a designated terrorist organization is not protected speech. But if the organization is *not* a designated terrorist organization, then monetary contributions to it *are* protected by the First Amendment — maybe not to the same degree as pure speech, but protected nonetheless. A terrorist designation is thus a type of prior restraint on speech, because it criminalizes monetary contributions that would otherwise be protected by the First Amendment.

The panel dismisses Rahmani's First Amendment arguments with conclusory statements that the money here is being given to a *terrorist* organization, and is therefore a completely unprotected form of expression. But this begs the question. The crux of the case — the issue the panel has elided in each iteration of its opinion — is the *process* by which the designation was made. If the designation process does not comply with constitutional standards, then the designation is invalid and Rahmani's donations are protected by the First Amendment. . . .

1. "[A]ny system of prior restraints of expression comes to this Court bearing a heavy presumption against its constitutional validity." *Freedman* [v. Maryland, 380 U.S. 51 (1965)], at 57. In *Freedman,* the Supreme Court detailed the "procedural safeguards" that must accompany prior restraints on speech, setting a high hurdle for the government to clear before a restraint can be held constitutional. *Id.* at 58. *Freedman* concluded that "only a *judicial determination* in an *adversary proceeding* ensures the necessary sensitivity to freedom of expression, [thus] only a procedure requiring a *judicial* determination suffices to impose a valid final restraint." *Id.* (emphasis added). The panel ignores *Freedman* entirely, upholding a prior restraint on speech that contains not a single one of *Freedman's* procedural safeguards.

In *Freedman,* the Supreme Court struck down a Maryland censorship scheme in which theaters were banned — on penalty of criminal prosecution — from showing films designated as obscene:

> It is readily apparent that the Maryland procedural scheme does not satisfy [constitutional] criteria. *First,* once the censor disapproves the film, *the exhibitor must assume the burden of instituting judicial proceedings and of persuading the courts that the film is protected expression. Second,* once the Board has acted against a film, *exhibition is prohibited pending judicial review, however protracted.* . . . *Third,* it is abundantly clear that the Maryland statute provides *no assurance of prompt judicial determination.* . . . The Maryland scheme fails to provide adequate safeguards against undue inhibition of protected expression. . . .

*Id.* at 59-60 (emphasis added).

The procedure for designating a foreign terrorist organization has all of the deficiencies identified by the Supreme Court in *Freedman,* and then some. First, once the Secretary of State makes the designation, the prohibition on monetary contributions takes effect immediately, *see* 8 U.S.C. §1189(a)(2)(B)(i), and "the burden of instituting judicial proceedings and of persuading the courts" that the designation was improper, *Freedman,* 380 U.S. at 60, falls on the organization. *See* 8 U.S.C. §1189(b)(1).

Second, monetary contributions to a designated organization are prohibited even while judicial review is pending. *See id.* §§1189(a)(2)(B)(i), (b)(4) ("The pendency of an action for judicial review of a designation shall not affect the application of this section, unless the court issues a final order setting aside the designation."). . . . Third, "it is abundantly clear that the . . . statute provides no assurance of prompt judicial determination." [*Freedman,* 380 U.S. at 60.] To the contrary, the statute seems to discourage any judicial determination at all, giving the organization only 30 days to challenge its designation. *See* [8 U.S.C.] §1189(b)(1). What's more, the panel concedes that the D.C. Circuit has found foreign entities have no due process rights: "MEK was a 'foreign entity without . . . presence in this country' and thus 'ha[d] no constitutional rights under the due process clause.' Therefore, the MEK was not entitled to notice and a hearing." *Rahmani,* 426 F.3d at 1153 (quoting *PMOI I,* 182 F.3d at 22). In other words, the only entity that is statutorily eligible to challenge the terrorist designation — the organization being designated — will ordinarily be unable to bring any kind of meaningful challenge.

Even when an organization can avail itself of the full "judicial review" prescribed by the statute, *see id.* §§1189(b)(2) & (3), such review comes nowhere near what *Freedman* requires. The statute uses "APA-like language" barring the D.C. Circuit from overturning the Secretary's designation unless, for example, it lacks substantial evidence or is arbitrary and capricious. *See* 8 U.S.C. §1189(b)(3). As the D.C. Circuit noted, under the statute's judicial review provisions, the designated organization "does not have the benefit of meaningful adversary proceedings . . . other than procedural shortfalls so obvious a Secretary of State is not likely to commit them." *PMOI II,* 251 F.3d at 197. But *Freedman* explicitly requires a *"judicial* determination in an *adversary* proceeding" on the merits, not merely a court's cursory check that the agency followed its own procedures. 380 U.S. at 58 (emphasis added). And *Freedman* underscores the inadequacy of *any* agency for making such a judicial determination: "[T]here inheres the danger that [an agency] may well be less responsive than a court — part of an independent branch of government — to the constitutionally protected interests in free expression." *Id.* at 57-58. . . .

The procedural history of this case perfectly illustrates the patent unconstitutionality of the terrorist organization designation process: Rahmani was indicted for sending money to MEK from 1997 to 2001, the *very years* during which the designation was admittedly unconstitutional.[5] Had the D.C. Circuit

---

5. Only the 1999 designation was declared unconstitutional by the D.C. Circuit. *See PMOI II,* 251 F.3d at 197. But the 1999 designation "extended the . . . 1997 designation," the constitutionality of which the court never reached in *PMOI I. See id.* The process by which the organization was designated had not changed from 1997 to 1999, so if one was unconstitutional then the other was as well. After *PMOI II* was decided, the designation process was amended to redress the due process problems identified by the court. *See* USA PATRIOT Act §411(c) [requiring publication of a designation in the *Federal Register* and forbidding deportation of an alien for activity with respect to a group at a time when the group was not a terrorist organization designated by the Secretary of State]; *PMOI II,* 251 F.3d at 208-09.

followed the letter of the statute, it would have struck down the designation, *see* 8 U.S.C. §1189(b)(3)(B), and Rahmani could not have been charged with a crime. The State Department could, of course, have re-designated MEK in 2001 using constitutional procedures, but it could not have *retroactively* designated it to criminalize Rahmani's donations.[6] *See* U.S. Const. art. I, §9, cl. 3 (Ex Post Facto Clause).

No "judicial determination" upheld MEK's designation on its merits until two years *after* Rahmani made her allegedly criminal monetary contributions. The panel thus condones a uniquely unconstitutional (and oxymoronic) practice: an *ex post facto prior restraint.* The simple fact is that Rahmani is being prosecuted — and will surely be sent to prison for up to 10 years — for giving money to an organization that no one other than some obscure mandarin in the bowels of the State Department had determined to be a terrorist organization. . . .

I can understand the panel's reticence to interfere with matters of national security, but the entire purpose of the terrorist designation process is to determine *whether* an organization poses a threat to national security. Under the Constitution, the State Department does not have carte blanche to label any organization it chooses a foreign terrorist organization and make a criminal out of anyone who donates money to it. Far too much political activity could be suppressed under such a regime. . . .

## NOTES AND QUESTIONS

1. *Process Without Access?* If an organization is entitled to the protections of the Due Process Clause, how can the process due not include a right of access to the evidence upon which its designation is based? Is there any way to describe such a process as "meaningful"? Upon what basis did the *PMOI* court approve a process that relied on ex parte consideration of classified information?

   Would you say that the outcome in *PMOI* was determined primarily by the State Department, by Congress, or by the court? Does it really matter who makes the determination?

2. *Justiciability of the Exercise of Statutory Authority?* The ability of the Secretary of State to designate an organization as an FTO depends on her finding that "the terrorist activity or terrorism of the organization threatens the security of United States nationals or the national security of the United States." 8 U.S.C. §1189(a)(1)(C). The statute provides no guidance for the Secretary in making this required finding. Can you guess how she does it? The *PMOI* court, refusing to second-guess the Secretary on this point, ruled that "it is beyond the judicial function for a court to review foreign policy decisions of the Executive Branch." 327 F.3d at 1244. If a court will not intervene, are there thus no constraints on the Secretary when she exercises her discretion in finding the predicate threat? Can you think of any way to reduce the (at least theoretical) potential for abuse of that discretion?

---

6. In crafting its remand to the Secretary of State, the D.C. Circuit did not seem to be aware of the effect the designation plays in criminal prosecutions. *See PMOI II,* 251 F.3d at 209. . . .

3. ***First Amendment Issues.*** Linking due process and First Amendment concerns, the dissenters in *Afshari* argued that the heavy presumption against what amounts to a prior restraint on speech can only be overcome by a "judicial determination" in an "adversary proceeding." 446 F.3d at 918. Was either of these requirements met by the court's review of the FTO designation in *PMOI*? Do you agree with the dissenters that the burden of a judicial test, however meaningful, of the designation should fall on the government rather than on the organization, and that there ought to be a "prompt" judicial determination?

Should the statute be amended to address the dissenters' concerns? Can you draft the amendment?

4. ***Efficacy of FTO Designations.*** Not everyone believes that a ban on material support for designated organizations is necessarily an effective tool in fighting terrorism. *See, e.g.,* Peter Margulies, *Laws of Unintended Consequences: Terrorist Financing Restrictions and Transitions to Democracy,* 20 N.Y. Intl. L. Rev. (forthcoming 2007) (arguing that while "[r]estrictions on funding for terrorist organizations are an important element of a coordinated strategy in the war on terror . . . [a] rigid, absolutist approach to financing restrictions . . . may be counterproductive"). Can you describe other legal and political elements of a "coordinated strategy"? Does the efficacy of restrictions on material support have any bearing on the constitutionality of such restrictions? If so, who should determine that the restrictions are sufficiently efficacious to make them constitutional?

## C.   DEFINING TERRORISM IN INTERNATIONAL LAW

### ALMOG V. ARAB BANK, PLC

United States District Court, Eastern District of New York, 2007
471 F. Supp. 2d 257

GERSHON, J. . . . [More than 1,600 United States and foreign national plaintiffs alleged that the defendant Arab Bank was part of a formalized system of financing that the Islamic Resistance Movement (HAMAS), the Palestinian Jihad (PIJ), the Al Aqsa Martyrs' Brigade (AAMB), and the Popular Front for the Liberation of Palestine (PFLP) used to sponsor suicide bombings and other murderous attacks on innocent civilians in Israel. The foreign nationals asserted violations of the law of nations, basing jurisdiction on the Alien Tort Claims Act (or Alien Tort Statute ("ATS")), 28 U.S.C. §1350 (2000). The Bank moved to dismiss the amended complaints for lack of subject matter jurisdiction and for failure to state a claim.]

### III. Alien Tort Claims Act Claims

The ATS provides that "[t]he district courts shall have original jurisdiction of any civil action by an alien for a tort only, committed in violation of the law of nations or a treaty of the United States." 28 U.S.C. §1350. On its face, the statute requires that plaintiffs must 1) be aliens, 2) claiming damages for a tort only, 3) resulting from a violation of the law of nations or a treaty of the United States. Arab Bank moves to dismiss the claims of the foreign nationals brought under the ATS, arguing that this court lacks jurisdiction and that plaintiffs have failed to state a claim because plaintiffs have failed to plead a violation of the law of nations. Neither the Almog nor the Afriat-Kurtzer plaintiffs assert that the torts they allege are in violation of a treaty of the United States; rather, they assert a violation of the law of nations. The essential issues in contention are therefore whether plaintiffs have pled a violation of the law of nations that should be recognized by this court under the ATS, and whether Arab Bank can be liable for aiding and abetting those violations.

Any discussion of the ATS must begin with the Supreme Court's recent decision in Sosa v. Alvarez-Machain, 542 U.S. 692 (2004). Humberto Alvarez-Machain, the plaintiff in *Sosa*, was a Mexican national who had been indicted for the torture and murder of an agent of the United States Drug Enforcement Agency (the "DEA"). *Id.* at 697-98. The DEA authorized a plan whereby a group of Mexican nationals, including Jose Francisco Sosa, seized Alvarez-Machain and brought him back to the United States for trial. *Id.* Alvarez-Machain brought a civil action against Sosa, among others, seeking damages under the ATS for a violation of the law of nations, namely, arbitrary arrest and detention. *Id.* at 699. The defendant argued that the ATS provides courts only with subject matter jurisdiction and neither creates nor authorizes a court to recognize a cause of action for an alleged violation of the law of nations. *Id.* at 712.

The Supreme Court, in *Sosa*, stated that, "although the ATS is a jurisdictional statute creating no new causes of action . . . [t]he jurisdictional grant is best read as having been enacted on the understanding that the common law would provide a cause of action for the modest number of international law violations with a potential for personal liability at the time" the ATS was enacted. *Id.* at 724. Thus, under the ATS, courts can hear a limited category of claims "defined by the law of nations and recognized at common law." *Sosa*, 542 U.S. at 712. . . . The Court assumed that the "First Congress understood that the district courts would recognize private causes of action for certain torts in violation of the law of nations. . . ." *Id.* at 724. In particular, the Court stated, "[i]t would take some explaining to say now that federal courts must avert their gaze entirely from any international norm intended to protect individuals." *Id.* at 730. . . .

Having held that, under the ATS's jurisdictional grant, federal courts can recognize a cause of action that arose after enactment of the ATS, the *Sosa* Court set out the standard for doing so: "federal courts should not recognize private claims under federal common law for violations of any international law norm with less definite content and acceptance among civilized nations than the historical paradigms familiar when §1350 was enacted." 542 U.S. at 732. The norm of international law may not be merely aspirational; rather, it must be specific and well-defined. *Id.* at 738. . . .

*Sosa* instructs that courts consider the *current* state of the law of nations in deciding whether to recognize a claim under the ATS. *Id.* at 733. . . .

. . . First, then, in order for a rule to become a norm of international law, States must universally abide by or accede to it. Flores [v. S. Peru Copper Corp.,

414 F.3d 233, 248 (2d Cir. 2003)]; Filartiga [v. Pena-Irala, 630 F.2d 876, 881 (2d Cir. 1980)] ("The requirement that a rule command the 'general assent of civilized nations' to become binding upon them all is a stringent one."). The question is not one of whether the rule is often violated, but whether virtually all States recognize its validity. *Filartiga,* 630 F.2d at 884 (citing the Department of State, Country Reports on Human Rights for 1979, published as Joint Comm. Print, House Comm. on Foreign Affairs, and Senate Comm. on Foreign Relations, 96th Cong., 2d Sess. (Feb. 4, 1980), Introduction at 1). Thus, that a norm of international law is honored in the breach does not diminish its binding effect as a norm of international law. *Filartiga,* 630 F.2d at 884 n.15; *cf. Sosa,* 542 U.S. at 738 n.29.

Second, States must abide by or accede to the rule from a sense of *legal obligation* and not for moral or political reasons. *Flores,* 414 F.3d at 248. Whether States abide by or accede to a rule out of a sense of legal obligation is shown by, among other things, state practice.

Third, "[i]t is only where the nations of the world have demonstrated that the wrong is of *mutual,* and not merely *several,* concern, by means of express international accords, that a wrong generally recognized becomes an international law violation within the meaning of the statute." *Filartiga,* 630 F.2d at 888 (emphasis added). Matters of "mutual" concern are those involving States' actions performed with regard to each other. *Flores,* 414 F.3d at 249. Matters of "several" concern are "matters in which States are separately and independently interested." *Id.* "[O]ffenses that may be purely intra-national in their execution, such as official torture, extrajudicial killings, and genocide, do violate customary international law because the nations of the world have demonstrated that such wrongs are of mutual concern and capable of impairing international peace and security." *Id.* (internal quotation marks, citations, and alterations omitted). . . .

Finally, under *Sosa,* in deciding whether to recognize a claim under the ATS, a court must consider the practical consequences of making the claim available to litigants in the federal courts. 542 U.S. at 732-33. For instance, there may be collateral consequences, such as implications on foreign relations, that advise against recognizing a claim. *Id.* at 727. The Court in *Sosa* also cautioned courts to tread lightly in exercising their discretion because courts generally have to look for "legislative guidance before exercising innovative authority over substantive law" and because the "decision to create a private right of action is one better left to legislative judgment in the great majority of cases." *Id.* at 726, 727.

It is against this backdrop and mindful of *Sosa*'s direction that the court's "judicial power should be exercised on the understanding that the door is still ajar subject to vigilant doorkeeping, and thus open to a narrow class of international norms today," *Sosa,* 542 U.S. at 729, that I address the motion to dismiss the ATS claims. . . .

## A. Violation of the Law of Nations

### 1. Genocide and crimes against humanity

Acts of genocide and crimes against humanity violate the law of nations and these norms are of sufficient specificity and definiteness to be recognized under the ATS. *See Flores,* 414 F.3d at 244 n.18 ("Customary international law rules proscribing crimes against humanity, including genocide, and war crimes, have been enforceable against individuals since World War II."); Kadic v. Karadzic, 70 F.3d 232, 241-42 (2d Cir. 1995) ("In 1946, the General Assembly of the United Nations declared that genocide is a crime under international law that is condemned by the civilized world, whether the perpetrators are private individuals, public officials or statesmen." (internal quotation marks omitted)).

Defendant does not contest the availability of genocide or crimes against humanity claims under the ATS but argues that plaintiffs have not sufficiently pled a claim for genocide and crimes against humanity. The Convention on the Prevention and Punishment of the Crime of Genocide ("Genocide Convention") defines genocide as:

> any of the following acts committed with intent to destroy, in whole or in part, a national, ethnical, racial or religious group, as such:
>
>   (a) Killing members of the group;
>
>   (b) Causing serious bodily or mental harm to members of the group;
>
>   (c) Deliberately inflicting on the group conditions of life calculated to bring about its physical destruction in whole or in part;
>
>   (d) Imposing measures intended to prevent births within the group;
>
>   (e) Forcibly transferring children of the group to another group.

Genocide Convention, art. 2, Dec. 9, 1948, 78 U.N.T.S. 227, *implemented in* Genocide Convention Implementation Act of 1987 (the Proxmire Act), 18 U.S.C. §1091 (2000). The Second Circuit has found a violation of the international norm proscribing genocide where the plaintiffs alleged that the defendant "personally planned and ordered a campaign of murder, rape, forced impregnation, and other forms of torture designed to destroy the religious and ethnic groups of Bosnian Muslims and Bosnian Croats." *Kadic,* 70 F.3d at 242.

Article 7 of the Rome Statute of the International Criminal Court (the "Rome Statute"), defines crimes against humanity:

> 1. For the purpose of this Statute, "crime against humanity" means any of the following acts when committed as part of a *widespread or systematic attack directed against any civilian population,* with knowledge of the attack:
>
>   (a) Murder;
>
>   (b) Extermination; . . .
>
>   (h) Persecution against any identifiable group or collectivity on political, racial, national, ethnic, cultural, religious, gender . . . or other grounds that are universally recognized as impermissible under international law, in connection with any act referred to in this paragraph or any crime within the jurisdiction of the Court; . . .
>
>   (k) Other inhumane acts of a similar character intentionally causing great suffering, or serious injury to body or to mental or physical health.

2. For the purpose of paragraph 1:

(a) "Attack directed against any civilian population" means a course of conduct involving the multiple commission of acts referred to in paragraph 1 against any civilian population, pursuant to or in furtherance of a State or organizational policy to commit such attack;

(b) "Extermination" includes the intentional infliction of conditions of life, inter alia the deprivation of access to food and medicine, calculated to bring about the destruction of part of a population. . . .

July 17, 1998, 37 I.L.M. 999, 1004-05 (emphasis added).

"Customary international law defines 'widespread' as 'massive, frequent, large scale action, carried out collectively with considerable seriousness and directed against a multiplicity of victims,' and 'systematic' as 'thoroughly organised action, following a regular pattern on the basis of a common policy and involving substantial public or private resources.'" Wiwa [v. Royal Dutch Petroleum Co., No. 96-CIV-8386, 2002 WL 319887, at *10 (S.D.N.Y. Feb. 28, 2002)] (quoting *Prosecutor v. Rutaganda,* Case No. ICTR-96-3-T, 69 (Dec. 6, 1999)). To be a crime against humanity, the emphasis must not be on the individual but rather on the collective — the individual is victimized not because of his or her individual attributes but because of membership in a targeted civilian population. *Id.* Although the requirement of widespread or systematic action ensures that a plaintiff must allege not just one act but, instead, a course of conduct, "a single act by a perpetrator, taken within the context of a widespread or systematic attack against a civilian population entails individual criminal responsibility and an individual perpetrator need not commit numerous offences to be held liable." *Id.*

Applying the standards provided in the Genocide Convention and the Rome Statute to the facts alleged here, plaintiffs have successfully stated claims for genocide and crimes against humanity. The amended complaints allege that HAMAS, the PIJ, the AAMB, and the PFLP act with the united purpose and shared mission to eradicate the State of Israel, murder or throw out the Jews, and liberate the area by replacing it with an Islamic or Palestinian State through the use of suicide bombings and other shockingly egregious violent acts. These goals reflect an intent to target people based on criteria prohibited by both the Genocide Convention and the Rome Statute.

Plaintiffs allege that the terrorist organizations seek to accomplish their shared goal by cooperating in the planning and commission of suicide bombings and other murderous attacks using explosives, incendiary weapons, and lethal devices in public places, which has resulted in the systematic and continuous killing and injury of thousands of unarmed innocent civilians in Israel, the West Bank, and the Gaza Strip. These are precisely the sorts of acts proscribed in both the Genocide Convention and the Rome statute.

Plaintiffs also allege that the terrorist organizations have developed and implemented a sophisticated financial structure through which they seek to accomplish their goals. The amended complaints describe dozens upon dozens of instances in which hundreds of innocent civilians were killed, and countless others injured, in attacks caused by individuals sponsored by the terrorist organizations. The acts as alleged constitute the "widespread" and "systematic" action necessary for claims of genocide and crimes against humanity. Even the acts other than suicide bombings, specifically those that defendant contends are nothing more than street crimes, may be sufficient for liability if plaintiffs can prove they were committed as part of a genocidal scheme or crimes against humanity.

### 2. Suicide bombings and other murderous attacks on innocent civilians intended to intimidate or coerce a civilian population

The third international norm which plaintiffs allege Arab Bank has violated is the financing of suicide bombings and other murderous attacks on innocent civilians which are intended to intimidate or coerce a civilian population. The underlying norm thus differs from the genocide norm with respect to the purpose of the perpetrators, and it differs from the more general crimes against humanity norm in that it specifically condemns bombings and other attacks intended to coerce or intimidate a civilian population. . . .

In 1997, the United Nations General Assembly adopted the International Convention for the Suppression of Terrorist Bombings ("Bombing Convention"). G.A. Res. 52/164, 1, U.N. Doc A/RES/52/164 (Dec. 15, 1997). The Bombing Convention states in pertinent part:

#### Article 2

1. Any person commits an offence within the meaning of this Convention if that person unlawfully and intentionally delivers, places, discharges or detonates an explosive or other lethal device in, into or against a place of public use, a State or government facility, a public transportation system or an infrastructure facility:

(a) With the intent to cause death or serious bodily injury; or

(b) With the intent to cause extensive destruction of such a place, facility or system, where such destruction results in or is likely to result in major economic loss. . . .

#### Article 5

Each State Party shall adopt such measures as may be necessary, including, where appropriate, domestic legislation, to ensure that criminal acts within the scope of this Convention, in particular where they are intended or calculated to provoke a state of terror in the general public or in a group of persons or particular persons, are under no circumstances justifiable by considerations of a political, philosophical, ideological, racial, ethnic, religious or other similar nature and are punished by penalties consistent with their grave nature.

Dec. 15, 1997, S. Treaty Doc. No. 106-6 (1998), *implemented in* 18 U.S.C. §2332f, Pub. L. No. 107-197, 116 Stat. 721 (2002). This Convention focuses on the principal method of attacking civilians alleged in the amended complaints in that it specifically makes it an offense to bomb public places or public transportation systems with the intent to cause death or serious bodily harm. The Bombing Convention particularly condemns such acts when they are, as alleged here, intended to provoke a state of terror in the general public or a group of persons. It specifies that such acts are not justifiable by any racial, ethnic, religious, political, or other similar considerations. In terms of its evidentiary weight, the Bombing Convention is significant. It has been ratified by over 120 United Nations Member States, including the United States (June 26, 2002). *Cf. Kadic,* 70 F.3d at 241 (noting that the Genocide Convention "has been ratified by more than 120 nations, including the United States. . . ."). In addition, the United States has implemented the Bombing Convention in the Terrorist Bombings Convention Implementation Act of 2002. *See* Pub. L. No. 107-197, 116 Stat. 721 (2002), *enacting* 18 U.S.C. §2332f.

Two years after the Bombing Convention was adopted by the General Assembly, the International Convention for the Suppression of the Financing of Terrorism ("Financing Convention") was also adopted by the General Assembly of the United Nations. G.A. Res. 54/109, U.N. Doc. A/RES/54/109 (Dec. 9, 1999 *infra* p. 712). It has been ratified by over 130 countries, including the United States (June 26, 2002). The United States implemented the Financing Convention via the Suppression of the Financing of Terrorism Convention Implementation Act of 2002. *See* 18 U.S.C. §2339C. The Convention makes it an offense to finance certain acts, including those proscribed in the Bombing Convention. Article 2 of the Financing Convention states:

> 1. Any person commits an offence within the meaning of this Convention if that person by any means, directly or indirectly, unlawfully and wilfully, provides or collects funds with the intention that they should be used or in the knowledge that they are to be used, in full or in part, in order to carry out:
>    (a) An act which constitutes an offence within the scope of and as defined in [the Bombing Convention]; or
>    (b) Any other act intended to cause death or serious bodily injury to a civilian, or to any other person not taking an active part in the hostilities in a situation of armed conflict, when the purpose of such act, by its nature or context, is to intimidate a population, or to compel a Government or an international organization to do or to abstain from doing any act.

Dec. 9, 1999, S. Treaty Doc. No. 106-49 (2000). Thus, the Financing Convention, along with the Bombing Convention, specifically condemns suicide bombings and other murderous attacks against innocent civilians intended to intimidate or coerce a population. Once again, this Convention provides that such acts "are under no circumstances justifiable by considerations of a political, philosophical, ideological, racial, ethnic, religious or other similar nature." Financing Convention, art. 6.

The prohibition against attacks on innocent civilians that is reflected in both of these Conventions is not a new one. The three-century-old "principle of distinction," which requires parties to a conflict to at all times distinguish between civilians and combatants, forbids the deliberate attacking of civilians. State practice establishes the principle of distinction as a long-established norm of the customary law of armed conflict. This principle is also reflected in Common Article 3 of the Geneva Conventions of 1949 (the "Geneva Conventions"), which provides in pertinent part:

> In the case of armed conflict not of an international character occurring in the territory of one of the High Contracting Parties, each Party to the conflict shall be bound to apply, as a minimum, the following provisions:
>
> (1) *Persons taking no active part in the hostilities,* including members of armed forces who have laid down their arms and those placed *hors de combat* by sickness, wounds, detention, or any other cause, *shall in all circumstances be treated humanely, without any adverse distinction founded on race, colour, religion or faith, sex, birth or wealth, or any other similar criteria.*
>
> To this end the following acts are and shall remain prohibited at any time and in any place whatsoever with respect to the above-mentioned persons:
>
> (a) violence to life and person, in particular murder of all kinds, mutilation, cruel treatment and torture; . . .

Geneva Convention for the Amelioration of the Condition of the Wounded and Sick in Armed Forces in the Field, Aug. 12, 1949, 6 U.S.T. 3316; Geneva Convention for the Amelioration of the Condition of Wounded, Sick and Shipwrecked Members of Armed Forces at Sea, Aug. 12, 1949, 6 U.S.T. 3316; Geneva Convention Relative to the Treatment of Prisoners of War, Aug. 12, 1949, 6 U.S.T. 3316; Geneva Convention Relative to the Protection of Civilian Persons in Time of War, art. III, Aug. 12, 1949, 6 U.S.T. 3316 (emphasis added).

Under the customary law of armed conflict, as reflected in the Geneva Conventions, all "parties" to a conflict, including insurgent military groups, must adhere to these most fundamental requirements. *Kadic,* 70 F.3d at 243. While the principle of distinction and the Geneva Conventions apply expressly only in situations of armed conflict, their long-standing existence supports the conclusion, made explicit in the Bombing and Financing Conventions, that attacks against innocent civilians of the type alleged here are condemned by international law.

United Nations Security Council Resolution 1566 also supports this conclusion. It states, in pertinent part, that the Security Council:

> 3. *Recalls* that criminal acts, including against civilians, committed with the intent to cause death or serious bodily injury, or taking of hostages, with the purpose to provoke a state of terror in the general public or in a group of persons or particular persons, intimidate a population or compel a government or an international organization to do or to abstain from doing any act, which constitute offences within the scope of and as defined in the international conventions and protocols relating to terrorism, are under no circumstances justifiable by considerations of a political, philosophical, ideological, racial, ethnic, religious or other

similar nature, and *calls upon* all States to prevent such acts and, if not prevented, to ensure that such acts are punished by penalties consistent with their grave nature.

S.C. Res. 1566, ¶3, U.N. Doc. S/RES/1566 (Oct. 8, 2004). Resolution 1566 specifically condemns attacks against civilians intended to intimidate a civilian population, regardless of who commits the attacks or what the motivation behind such attacks may be. While such resolutions cannot be relied on as a sole source of international law, they are informative as to what the current state of international law is. *See Filartiga,* 630 F.2d at 882 n.9 (observing that non-self-executing agreements serve as evidence of binding principles of international law and relying on several United Nations General Assembly Resolutions).

In the face of all these sources evidencing universal condemnation of the types of acts alleged here, Arab Bank does not address the actual conduct condemned by these sources. Rather, it argues that the underlying suicide bombings and other murderous acts alleged in Count Three, which it says are "commonly referred to as terrorism," cannot be a violation of the law of nations because there is no consensus on the meaning of "terrorism." In support of its argument, Arab Bank relies on United States v. Yousef, a pre-*Sosa* case, in which the court stated that "customary international law currently does not provide for the prosecution of 'terrorist' acts under the universality principle, in part due to the failure of States to achieve anything like consensus on the definition of terrorism." 327 F.3d 56, 97 (2d Cir. 2003) (per curiam).

Arab Bank's reliance on *Yousef* is misplaced. First, the court in *Yousef* was reviewing whether the district court had criminal jurisdiction under the universality principle[1] and not whether the district court should recognize a claim under the civil jurisdictional grant of the ATS. The *Yousef* Court held that "the universality principle permits jurisdiction over only a limited set of crimes that *cannot be expanded judicially*" whereas *Sosa* held, with regard to the ATS, that federal courts *can* recognize new causes of action, albeit with restraint, under the ATS. *Compare Yousef,* 327 F.3d at 103 (emphasis added), *with Sosa,* 542 U.S. at 725.

Second, the court in *Yousef,* in addressing the issue as framed by the parties, whether "terrorism" was a violation of the law of nations, criticized the lower court's reliance on the Restatement (Third) of the Foreign Relations Law of the United States, a non-authoritative source, for the finding that "terrorism" violates international law. 327 F.3d at 98-103 n.37. The parties in *Yousef* had not addressed specific international law sources, and the district court relied, not on such sources, but on the Restatement. The appellate briefs also did not address accepted sources of international law. The court in *Yousef* emphasized that the proper sources for determining international law are the

---

[1. Customary international law imposes an obligation on states to detain, extradite, or prosecute those within its territory or control who are reasonably accused of committing war crimes, genocide, or other acts that violate peremptory norms, wherever they are committed. *See* Jordan Paust, *International Law as Law of the United States* 405 (1996).]

sources described in *Kadic* and *Filartiga,* that is, the sources this court relies on here. *See id.*

Defendant also errs in relying on the following language in *Yousef:* "nor have we shaken ourselves free of the cliché that 'one man's terrorist is another man's freedom fighter.'" *Id.* at 107. This court does not accept that the Court of Appeals, in referring to this cliché, was accepting . . . this . . . principle. On the contrary, if anything, the Court of Appeals seemed concerned that defining terrorism in a way that would receive international agreement could exclude outrageous conduct that should properly be condemned. *See, e.g., id.* at 108 n.42 ("This attempt to distinguish 'terrorists' from 'freedom fighters' potentially could legitimate as non-terrorist certain groups nearly universally recognized as terrorist, including the Irish Republican Army, Hezbollah, and Hamas.").

In any event, in this case, there is no need to resolve any definitional disputes as to the scope of the word "terrorism," for the Conventions expressing the international norm provide their own specific descriptions of the conduct condemned. Although the Conventions refer to such acts as "terrorism," the pertinent issue here is only whether the acts as alleged by plaintiffs violate a norm of international law, however labeled. *See Sosa,* 542 U.S. at 738 (examining whether the specific conduct alleged by plaintiff violated a norm of international law). In exploring that question, this court has examined the very sources of international law found to be valid by the Second Circuit in *Kadic, Filartiga* and *Yousef,* and by the Supreme Court in *Sosa.* These authoritative sources establish that the specific conduct alleged — organized, systematic suicide bombings and other murderous attacks on innocent civilians intended to intimidate or coerce a civilian population — are universally condemned.

In a similar way, the *Yousef* court, after holding that there was no jurisdiction under the universality principle, held that there was jurisdiction in the district court to try the defendant for bombing a Philippines Airlines flight under the Montreal Convention, which expressly addresses offenses against aircraft. 327 F.3d at 108-110. It did so because it found that the conduct charged, "whether it is termed 'terrorist' — constitutes the core conduct proscribed by the Montreal Convention and its implementing legislation." *Id.* at 97-98. In sum, regardless of whether there is universal agreement as to the precise scope of the word "terrorism," the conduct involved here is specifically condemned in the Conventions upon which this court relies.

Arab Bank attempts to undermine the weight of the international sources discussed above by arguing that state practice does not support the existence of a universal norm. The basis for this argument is that "some 80 nations in Africa, in the Arab world and elsewhere expressly exempt from the definition of terrorism conduct that they believe furthers the rights of self-determination of a people." To begin with, Arab Bank ignores that the international sources relied upon here themselves evidence state practice. As stated in *Flores,* 414 F.3d at 256, treaties evidence the "customs and practices" of the States that ratify them. This is so because ratification of a treaty that embodies specific norms of conduct evidences a State's acceptance of the norms as legal obligations. Here, the international sources specifically articulate a universal standard that condemns the conduct alleged.

In addition, Arab Bank's state practice argument is based upon a flawed premise and is devoid of factual support. As for the premise, Arab Bank's argument is that the acts alleged here — organized, systematic suicide bombings and other murderous acts intended to intimidate a civilian population — are viewed by some States as acceptable acts in furtherance of the right to self-determination. However, Arab Bank offers no authority for the proposition that the right to self-determination can be effectuated in violation of the law of nations. . . . Indeed, the Bombing Convention, the Financing Convention and Resolution 1566 all expressly acknowledge that violation of the principles embodied in those documents are under no circumstances justifiable by political, philosophical, ideological, racial, ethnic, or religious considerations. Moreover, there have been no formal reservations to either of the Conventions purporting to assert that a right to self-determination justifies committing otherwise condemned acts. On the contrary, even the statements relied upon, which are made by officials of varying official stature, never expressly state that the type of conduct alleged here is a legitimate means of asserting the right to self-determination.

Turning to the lack of factual support for defendant's state practice argument, it is significant that the United States prohibits the specific conduct alleged in the cases at hand. *See* 18 U.S.C. §2332f (implementing the Bombing Convention); 18 U.S.C. §2339C (implementing the Financing Convention); *see also* 18 U.S.C. §§2331 *et seq.* (setting forth the criminal penalties and civil remedies for enforcement of these laws); *cf. Flores,* 414 F.3d at 257 n.33 (citing *Yousef,* 327 F.3d at 92 n.25 ("While it is not possible to claim that the practice or policies of any one country, including the United States, has such authority that the contours of customary international law may be determined by reference only to that country, it is highly unlikely that a purported principle of customary international law in direct conflict with the recognized practices and customs of the United States and/or other prominent players in the community of States could be deemed to qualify as a *bona fide* customary international principle.")). Arab Bank has offered no evidence that it is lawful in any State to engage in organized, systematic murderous attacks on civilians for the purpose of coercing or intimidating the civilian population. *Cf. Filartiga,* 630 F.2d at 884 ("We have been directed to no assertion by any contemporary state of a right to torture its own or another nation's citizens."). Both sides to this litigation note that the Palestinian Authority has explicitly condemned suicide bombings and that it "arrests, convicts, and sentences to imprisonment terrorists who kill Israeli citizens in the occupied territories." The international sources cited above, coupled with the fact that no State has expressly stated that such conduct would be legal in its country, provide further support for the conclusion that the alleged conduct violates a norm of international law. *Cf. Filartiga,* 630 F.2d at 880 ("In light of the universal condemnation of torture in numerous international agreements, and the renunciation of torture as an instrument of official policy by virtually all of the nations of the world (in principle if not in practice), we find that an act of torture committed by a state official against one held in detention violates established norms of the international law of human rights, and hence the law of nations.").

The next issue to be addressed is whether the international norm is of mutual, and not merely several, concern. [The court held that the suicide bombings are of mutual concern.] . . .

Finally, the collateral consequences about which the *Sosa* Court expressed concern seem limited here. . . . Based upon all of the factors set forth above, organized, systematic suicide bombings and other murderous attacks against innocent civilians for the purpose of intimidating a civilian population are a violation of the law of nations for which this court can and does recognize a cause of action under the ATS.

[The court also found that similar principles of the law of nations extend secondary liability under the ATS to Arab Bank for its conduct aiding and abetting the suicide bombings and other attacks.] . . .

### SAPERSTEIN V. THE PALESTINIAN AUTHORITY

United States District Court, Southern District of Florida, 2006
2006 WL 3804718

SEITZ, J. . . . [Foreign national plaintiffs alleged that the Palestinian Authority (PA) and Palestine Liberation Organization (PLO), as the *de jure* and *de facto* rulers of territories in the Gaza Strip and West Bank, sponsored and executed acts of violence and terrorism against Jewish civilians in Israel, Gaza, and the West Bank, and granted financial support to the families of members of the Al Aqsa Brigade who had been captured or killed while carrying out acts of terrorist violence. The court sought to determine whether the Alien Tort Claims Act (or Alien Tort Statute (ATS)), 28 U.S.C. §1350 (2000), provides subject matter jurisdiction over claims based on the non-state, private actions of the PA and PLO and, if so, whether the claims described constitute violations of the law of nations.]

### 2. Tel-Oren v. Libyan Arab Republic

In Tel-Oren v. Libyan Arab Republic, 726 F.2d 774 (D.C. Cir. 1984), *cert. denied*, 470 U.S. 1003 (1985), victims of a 1978 terrorist attack in Israel sued a number of parties, including several private organizations, for violations of the law of nations under the ATS. The terrorists seized a civilian bus, a taxi, a passing car, and subsequently a second civilian bus and took the passengers hostage. *Id.* at 776. The terrorists tortured, shot, wounded and murdered many of the hostages. *Id.* A three-judge panel unanimously dismissed the case with three separate opinions. Judge Edwards gave the ATS the broadest reach, generally agreeing with the decision in *Filartiga* that acts of official torture violate the law of nations. *Id.* at 791. Judge Edwards, however, found no consensus that private actors are bound by the law of nations with regard to torture. *Id.* at 791-95. Only a year later, the court of appeals addressed the issue again in Sanchez-Espinoza v. Reagan, 770 F.2d 202 (D.C. Cir. 1985), a case involving allegations of "execution, murder, abduction, torture, rape, [and] wounding" by the Nicaraguan Contras. In *Sanchez-Espinoza,* the appellate court stated quite clearly that the law of nations "does not reach private, non-state conduct of this sort" for the reasons stated by Judge Edwards and Judge Bork in *Tel-Oren. Id.* at 205-207.

In *Tel-Oren,* Judge Edwards undertook an in-depth analysis of whether to stretch *Filartiga's* reasoning to incorporate torture perpetuated by a party other than a recognized state or one of its officials. *Tel Oren,* 726 F.2d at 792-95. Judge Edwards observed that the extension would necessarily require the court to venture out of the realm of established international law in which states are the actors and would mandate an assessment of the extent to which international law imposes not only rights but also obligations on individuals.[9] *Id.* at 792. He concluded his analysis saying that he "was not prepared to extend the definition of the 'law of nations' absent direction from the Supreme Court." *Id.*

Judge Edwards also examined the question of whether terrorism in and of itself was a law of nations violation, regardless of whether it is conducted by a state or private actor. *Id.* at 795-96. In finding that condemnation of terrorism was not universal, he stated that "the nations of the world are so divisively split on the legitimacy of such aggression as to make it impossible to pinpoint an area of harmony or consensus."[10] *Id.* Thus, he concluded that the law of nations, defined as the principles and rules that states feel themselves bound to observe, did not outlaw politically motivated terrorism. *Id.*

### 3. Kadic v. Karadzic

The 1995 Kadic v. Karadzic decision is the most recent circuit court opinion thoroughly analyzing those actions for which international law imposes individual liability. 70 F.3d 232 (2nd Cir. 1995). In *Kadic,* the plaintiffs, Croat and Muslim citizens of Bosnia-Herzegovina, sued the president of the self-proclaimed Bosnian-Serb republic within Bosnia-Herzegovina. 70 F.3d at 237. Plaintiffs asserted causes of action for various atrocities at the hands of the Bosnian-Serb republic including, genocide, rape, forced prostitution and impregnation, torture, and other cruel, inhuman and degrading treatment such as assault and battery, sex and ethnic inequality, summary execution and wrongful death. *Id.* The district court dismissed the case finding that defendant was not a state actor for purposes of the ATS but the court of appeals reversed. *Id.* at 239. In so doing, the Second Circuit found that the law of nations, as understood in the modern era, did not confine its reach to state

---

9. Judge Edwards highlighted some of the ramifications of extending the *Filartiga* reasoning to the actions of private entities, stating: "[i]t would require a determination of where to draw a line between persons or groups who are or are not bound by dictates of international law, and what the groups look like. Would the terrorists be liable, because numerous international documents recognize their existence and proscribe their acts?" He further asked, "would all organized political entities be obliged to abide by the law of nations? Would everybody be liable? As firmly established as is the core principle binding states to customary international obligations, these fringe areas are only gradually emerging and offer, as of now, no obvious stopping point." *Tel-Oren,* 726 F.2d 59.

10. As support for the proposition that terrorism is not a violation of the law of nations, Judge Edwards referenced documents of the United Nations. He contends that they demonstrate that to some states acts of terrorism, in particular those with political motives, are legitimate acts of aggression and are therefore immune from condemnation. As an example, Judge Edwards points to a resolution entitled "Basic principles of the legal status of the combatants struggling against colonial and alien domination and racist regimes," G.A. Res. 3103, 28 U.N. GAOR at 512, U.N. Doc. A/9102 (1973), which declared, "The struggle of peoples under colonial and alien domination and racist regimes for the implementation of their right to self-determination and independence is legitimate and in full accordance with principles of international law."

action. *Id.* The court of appeals held that "certain forms of conduct violate the laws of nations whether undertaken by those acting under the auspices of a state or only as a private individuals, such as piracy, slave-trading, aircraft hijacking, genocide, and war crimes." *Id.* at 240-43. The Second Circuit, however, held that torture and summary execution, when not perpetrated in the course of genocide or war crimes, are proscribed by international law only when committed by state officials under color of law. *Id.* at 243.

These cases reflect the trend toward finding that certain conduct violates the law of nations whether committed by a state or a private actor, however, which conduct falls into this realm has not been completely defined. Plaintiffs contend that a violation of the "law of war" now called "international humanitarian law" is recognized as a breach of the law of nations and the actions alleged in the TAC [third amended complaint] constitute such violations. . . .

With this legal landscape in mind and noting the Supreme Court's cautionary advice regarding the creation of new offenses in the law of nations in *Sosa,* the Court turns to the Plaintiffs' allegations.

### C. Plaintiffs Fail to Plead a Violation of the Law of Nations Sufficient to Invoke the Court's Subject Matter Jurisdiction.

To resolve Defendants' motion, it is necessary to determine if the Plaintiffs' TAC allegations fit the categories of conduct that prior courts have found constitute a violation of the law of nations, even when carried out by a private actor. The conduct in *Tel-Oren* is substantially similar to the conduct in the present case. Judge Edwards, in *Tel-Oren,* made it abundantly clear that politically motivated terrorism has not reached the status of a violation of the law of nations. In their own words, Plaintiffs describe Defendants' conduct as terrorism. Beginning with their introduction, Plaintiffs state that they bring this action for damages caused by Defendants' "acts of terrorism as defined in federal law, and by reason of related tortious terrorist behavior." Further, Plaintiffs specifically allege that the PA and PLO failed to "denounce and condemn acts of terror, apprehend, prosecute and imprison persons involved directly, and/or indirectly in acts of terrorism and outlaw and dismantle the infrastructure of terrorist organizations." Thus, if the conduct of the Defendants is construed as terrorism, then Plaintiffs have not alleged a violation of the law of nations.

Plaintiffs attempt to get around such facts in their response to Defendants' motion to dismiss by characterizing the allegations in the TAC as a "murder of [a] civilian[ ] in the course of an armed conflict," or a war crime. In doing this, Plaintiffs are grasping at the *Kadic* decision and attempting to bring the alleged conduct within the language of Common Article 3. Plaintiffs' strategy in this regard is certainly obvious, as the Second Circuit in *Kadic* based much of its analysis of the definition of "war crimes" on Common Article 3. *Kadic,* 70 F.3d at 242-43. However, Plaintiffs then make the overreaching leap by stating that if the conduct falls within Common Article 3 and is prohibited thereby, then they have sufficiently alleged a violation of the law of nations for purposes of the ATS. Essentially, Plaintiffs are saying that if they allege a murder of an innocent person during an armed conflict, then they have alleged a per se violation of the law of nations and federal courts have subject matter jurisdiction over the dispute under the ATS. No court has so held. In fact, as discussed above, international customary law is not taken from one source but rather is "discerned from [a] myriad of decisions made in numerous and varied international and domestic arenas." *See Flores,* 343 F.3d at 154.

Further, while Plaintiffs' reliance on the *Kadic* decision's references to Common Article 3 is understandable, the severe and horrendous conduct alleged in that case, including "brutal acts of rape, forced prostitution, forced impregnation, torture and summary execution" against an entire class of citizens, differentiate[s] it from this case. Unlike the conduct alleged here, the abominate actions the Croat and Muslim plaintiffs asserted in *Kadic* did not require the same extent of canvassing of international law to determine if the prohibition of such conduct was "universally recognized." Thus, the Second Circuit's reliance on Common Article 3 was sufficient to ascertain a consensus in customary international law. In fact, the appellate court specifically directed [its] decision to the particular horrendous allegations by stating that the "offenses alleged by the [plaintiffs], if proved, would violate the most fundamental norms of the law of war embodied in common article 3." *See Kadic,* 73 F.2d at 243. The court of appeals did not make a blanket holding that any alleged violation of Common Article 3 would be sufficient for the purposes of the ATS.

Further, two practical considerations highlight the flaws in Plaintiffs' desired expansion of the law of nations. First, if it were accepted that any alleged violation of Common Article 3 was sufficient for subject matter jurisdiction under the ATS, then a violation of any provision in the Article would yield the same result. This includes such unspecific conduct as "violence to life," "cruel treatment" and "outrages upon personal dignity." For federal courts to interpret such ambiguous standards to assess its own subject matter jurisdiction would pose problems for federal courts and would not meet the defined standards of specificity that *Sosa* requires. Second, if Plaintiffs' specific allegation, i.e., the murder of an innocent civilian during an armed conflict, was sufficient for the purposes of the ATS, then whenever an innocent person was murdered during an "armed conflict" anywhere in the world, whether it be Bosnia, the Middle East or Darfur, Sudan, the federal courts would have subject matter jurisdiction over the dispute. Clearly, such an interpretation would not only make district courts international courts of civil justice, it would be in direct contravention of the Supreme Court's specific prudential guidance admonishing lower courts to be cautious in creating new offenses under the law of nations. *See Sosa,* 542 U.S. 725. For the foregoing reasons, Plaintiffs do not sufficiently allege a violation of the law of nations and, thus, this Court lacks subject matter jurisdiction. . . .

## NOTES AND QUESTIONS

1. ***Reconciling the Cases.*** In light of the factually similar bases for the claims in *Almog* and *Saperstein*, what best explains their different outcomes in finding a law of nations violation? Is it that the *Almog* plaintiffs argue genocide, while the *Saperstein* plaintiffs make claims for victims of terrorism?

Are you persuaded, based on the sources discussed in the cases, that genocide but not terrorism violates the law of nations? If there is another basis for explaining the different outcomes of the cases, what is it?

Do you agree that the differences between the ethnic cleansing chronicled in the *Kadic* decision and the suicide attacks and bombings complained of in *Saperstein* justify a finding that there was no violation of the law of nations in the latter? What is the utility of Common Article 3 of the Geneva Conventions in this regard? Should Judge Seitz's worry that district courts might become "international courts of civil justice" stand in the way of a finding that the terrorism complained of in *Saperstein* violates the law of nations?

2. ***Genocide and Crimes Against Humanity.*** Consider the terms of the Genocide Convention and Rome Statute quoted in *Almog*. Are you satisfied that the attacks alleged to have been carried out or supported by the Palestinian defendants meet the requirements of these instruments? Do they also constitute terrorism? If so, what is the value of the labels?

3. ***The Financing Convention, the Bombing Convention, and United Nations Resolutions.*** Compare the terms of the U.N. Conventions and Resolutions with the Genocide Convention and the Rome Statute, and then with the U.S. statutory definitions set out earlier in the chapter. What are the common and distinct elements of each? How do you explain the different approaches taken by the United Nations in General Assembly Resolution 3103 and Security Council Resolution 1566? How much weight should these various instruments have in determining the current state of international law?

4. ***Consensus on the Meaning of "Terrorism"?*** Are you persuaded by Judge Gershon's response to the defendants' argument in *Almog* that the actions alleged cannot be a violation of the law of nations because there is no consensus on the meaning of the term "terrorism"? Do you agree with Judge Gershon that the reasoning in *Yousef*, upon which the *Almog* defendants rely, was distinguishable as a criminal prosecution in which the government sought jurisdiction under the universality principle? Was Judge Seitz on firmer ground in *Saperstein* in finding that the 1985 *Tel-Oren* decision shows a lack of consensus about the illegality of terrorism?

The cliché, "one man's terrorist is another man's freedom fighter," lives on. In Cheema v. Ashcroft, 383 F.3d 848 (9th Cir. 2004), *infra* p. 603, the court reversed a Board of Immigration Appeals order denying asylum and directing deportation of an Indian Sikh alien. The court rejected the Board's determination that "a person engaged in extra-territorial or resistance activities — even militant activities — is necessarily a security threat to the United States. One country's terrorist can often be another country's freedom fighter." *Id.* at 858. The court recounted the terrorist tactics employed by Contras in Nicaragua in an attempt to overthrow the Sandinista government during a period when the United States was providing financial and other support to the Contras. *Id.* It also offered the heroic example of Nelson Mandela, whose paramilitary branch of the African National Congress conducted guerrilla warfare against the ruling white government in South Africa. *Id.* at 859. Do these examples add support to the cliché? Do they describe terrorism as we understand it today?

Does consensus on one or more definitions matter if the Conventions provide sufficient descriptions of the conduct condemned to permit claims to go forward? Are you persuaded by Judge Gershon's conclusion that Arab Bank's state practice argument is based on a flawed premise and lacks factual support? Upon what basis does Judge Seitz come to a different conclusion?

## D.   DEFINING COUNTERTERRORISM: A ROAD MAP TO THIS BOOK

In this chapter we have begun the process of defining terrorism. As we have seen, this is more than just an intellectual exercise. The labeling also furnishes a predicate for civil and criminal liability. And it affects the movement of money, the movements of immigrants across our borders, and relations among nations.

While the use of force against terrorists abroad might be viewed by some as a last resort, and thus the logical last subject in a sequential study of counterterrorism, we take up that subject in Part II. That is because the rhetoric of war, the relevant constitutional framework, and the scope of statutory authorizations for the use of force affect most, if not all, of the less extreme counterterrorism measures that we address later in the book. The balance of the book explores such measures functionally, from prevention of terrorism by investigation, detention, and interrogation, to arrest, trial, and removal, to management of terrorist attacks, and finally to non-criminal legal sanctions against terrorists and their supporters.

In Part III we address the growing array of legal concerns that arise in attempting to detect and prevent terrorism through surveillance, data collection, and screening. This part builds upon consideration of the core constitutional powers of the executive branch and the Fourth and First Amendment rights that protect against misuse of those powers. Building on this foundation, we examine Congress's prescriptions for counterterrorism surveillance and collection, and for mining of third party records, then review screening mechanisms developed by federal, state, and local governments. Because so many players are involved in counterterrorism detection and prevention, we next consider how the government organizes and coordinates its intelligence gathering activities. Part III concludes by extending our study to U.S. counterterrorism investigations abroad.

Part IV explores several controversial aspects of the detention and treatment of terrorist suspects who have been taken into custody. The first three chapters treat the legal parameters of civil and military detention of terrorist suspects, including suspension of the privilege of the writ of habeas corpus. The last two chapters examine in some detail the domestic and incorporated international law respecting interrogation of terrorist suspects, as well as the "extraordinary" rendition of suspects to third countries where they may be subjected to coercive treatment not permitted in the United States.

In Part V we examine various methods for adjudicating terrorist suspects. The first chapter in this part explores a range of constitutional issues that attend the criminalization of terrorism. The remaining chapters address legal limits on apprehending terrorists, as well as the problems that arise in trying accused terrorists as criminals, as "unlawful enemy combatants," or as "special interest" immigrants.

In Part VI of the book we consider what to do when all of our efforts to prevent an attack fail. We first explore legal problems that arise in planning for and responding to a terrorist attack using a weapon of mass destruction. We then turn to the military's domestic role in counterterrorism, from intelligence collection and support of civil authorities to, in the worst case, the imposition of martial law.

To conclude our study, in Part VII we examine the legal bases for imposing sanctions against terrorists and their sponsors outside the criminal justice system. One chapter explores sanctions that the international community and individual governments may employ to dissuade and punish terrorist activities, and a final chapter considers prospects for gaining relief through civil litigation against terrorists and their supporters.

# PART II

# ATTACKING TERRORISTS ABROAD

# *2*

# *WAGING WAR ON TERRORISTS*

Shortly after the terrorist bombings of U.S. embassies in East Africa in 1998, and again following the September 11, 2001, attacks on the World Trade Center and the Pentagon, U.S. authorities determined that al Qaeda was responsible for planning and carrying out the attacks. Was the President authorized to order a military response against al Qaeda—and possibly other terrorist groups—without the approval of Congress? If Congress had a role to play, how extensive was that role, and what form should its approval have taken?

Answers to these questions begin with the text and history of the Constitution. At the Constitutional Convention, the delegates substituted "declare" for "make" in the Declare War Clause of Article I, section 8, "leaving to the Executive the power to repel sudden attacks," according to Madison's notes. 2 Max Farrand, *The Records of the Federal Convention of 1787* (rev. ed. 1937) (hereinafter *Records*), at 318-319. The implication is that the President has some inherent constitutional power to respond to terrorist attacks without prior statutory authorization—what we shall call his defensive war power. Alternatively, he could ask Congress to declare war or, as we shall see, to give him statutory authorization for the use of military force.

In Part A of this chapter, we explore the origins and scope of the President's defensive war power. In Part B, we consider express and implied statutory authorizations for the use of military force, and we ask whether other forms of congressional action can supply whatever authority is necessary. In Part C, we apply the analysis in the first two parts to the use of military force against al Qaeda, both before and after the 9/11 attacks.

## A. THE PRESIDENT'S DEFENSIVE WAR POWER

At the Constitutional Convention, the Committee on Detail prepared a draft Constitution vesting "The Executive Power of the United States . . . in a . . . President," who would be "Commander in Chief of the Army and Navy of the United States, and of the Militia of the several States." 2 *Records, supra*, at 171-172. It gave Congress the power to "make war," to appropriate funds, and "to call for the aid of the militia, in order to execute the laws of the Union, enforce treaties, suppress insurrections, and repel invasions." *Id.* at 168.

In the ensuing debates on the draft, Charles Pinckney of South Carolina complained that requiring the whole Congress to declare war would be cumbersome:

> Mr. Pinckney. . . . Its proceedings were too slow. It wd. meet but once a year. The Hs. of Reps. would be too numerous for such deliberations. The Senate would be the best depositary, being more acquainted with foreign affairs, and most capable of proper resolutions. If the States are equally represented in Senate, so as to give no advantage to large States, the power will notwithstanding be safe, as the small have their all at stake in such cases as well as the large States. It would be singular for one authority to make war, and another peace.
>
> Mr. Butler. The Objections agst the Legislature lie in a great degree agst the Senate. He was for vesting the power in the President, who will have all the requisite qualities, and will not make war but when the Nation will support it.
>
> Mr. M(adison) and Mr. Gerry moved to insert "*declare*," striking out "*make*" war; leaving to the Executive the power to repel sudden attacks.
>
> Mr. Sharman thought it stood very well. The Executive shd. be able to repel and not to commence war. "Make" better than "declare" the latter narrowing the power too much.
>
> Mr. Gerry never expected to hear in a republic a motion to empower the Executive alone to declare war.
>
> Mr. Elseworth. there is a material difference between the cases of making *war*, and making *peace*. It shd. be more easy to get out of war, than into it. War also is a simple and overt declaration. peace attended with intricate & secret negociations.
>
> Mr. Mason was agst giving the power of war to the Executive, because not (safely) to be trusted with it; or to the Senate, because not so constructed as to be entitled to it. He was for clogging rather than facilitating war; but for facilitating peace. He preferred "*declare*" to "*make*." [*Id.* at 318-319.]

In support of Madison's motion, Rufus King of Massachusetts argued "that 'make' war might be understood to 'conduct' it which was an Executive function." *Id.* at 319.

Eventually, Pinckney's motion to vest the war power solely in the Senate was overwhelmingly rejected, and Madison's motion was approved. As for military action short of declared war, the Committee on Detail did not include in the list of powers given to the new legislature the power to issue letters of marque and reprisal, which the old Congress enjoyed under the Articles. Such letters had traditionally been used as public commissions for privateers to raid and capture merchant vessels of an enemy state — typically in response to the unlawful acts of the enemy state — but gradually had come to "signify any intermediate or low-intensity hostility short of declared war that utilized public *or* private forces, although the emphasis on the use of private forces remained." Jules Lobel, *Covert War and Congressional Authority: Hidden War and Forgotten Power*, 134 U. Pa. L. Rev. 1035, 1045 (1986) (emphasis in original). At Pinckney's request the "Marque and Reprisal" language was added and approved without discussion. 2 *Records, supra*, at 324, 326.

It was not until the Civil War that the federal courts had occasion to consider the President's implied power to repel attack. Then, of course, the "attack" was the insurrection of the Confederate states commenced by the bombing of Fort Sumter. President Lincoln responded by imposing an armed blockade on the Confederacy, prompting the following challenge.

## THE PRIZE CASES

United States Supreme Court, 1863
67 U.S. (2 Black) 635

Mr. Justice GRIER. . . . [At the beginning of the Civil War, during a congressional recess, President Lincoln issued a proclamation by which he "deemed it advisable to set on foot a blockade of the ports within [certain of the Confederate states], in pursuance of the laws of the United States and of the law of nations. . . . If, therefore, with a view to violate such blockade, a vessel shall approach or shall attempt to leave either of said ports, she will be duly warned by the commander of one of the blockading vessels, who will endorse on her register the fact and date of such warning, and if the same vessel shall again attempt to enter or leave the blockaded port, she will be captured and sent to the nearest convenient port for such proceedings against her and her cargo, as prize, as may be deemed advisable." The owners of vessels that were captured as prizes during the blockade brought this action challenging the legality of the President's proclamation.]

Had the President a right to institute a blockade of ports in possession of persons in armed rebellion against the Government, on the principles of international law, as known and acknowledged among civilized States? . . .

The right of prize and capture has its origin in the "*jus belli,*" and is governed and adjudged under the law of nations. To legitimate the capture of a neutral vessel or property on the high seas, a war must exist *de facto,* and the neutral must have a knowledge or notice of the intention of one of the parties belligerent to use this mode of coercion against a port, city, or territory, in possession of the other.

Let us enquire whether, at the time this blockade was instituted, a state of war existed which would justify a resort to these means of subduing the hostile force.

War has been well defined to be, "That state in which a nation prosecutes its right by force." . . .

By the Constitution, Congress alone has the power to declare a national or foreign war. It cannot declare war against a State, or any number of States, by virtue of any clause in the Constitution. The Constitution confers on the President the whole Executive power. He is bound to take care that the laws be faithfully executed. He is Commander-in-Chief of the Army and Navy of the United States, and of the militia of the several States when called into the actual service of the United States. He has no power to initiate or declare a war either against a foreign nation or a domestic State. But by the Acts of Congress of February 28th, 1795, and 3d of March, 1807, he is authorized to call out the militia and use the military and naval forces of the United States in case of invasion by foreign nations, and to suppress insurrection against the government of a State or of the United States.

If a war be made by invasion of a foreign nation, the President is not only authorized but bound to resist force by force. He does not initiate the war, but is bound to accept the challenge without waiting for any special legislative authority. And whether the hostile party be a foreign invader, or States organized in rebellion, it is none the less a war, although the declaration of it be "*unilateral.*" Lord Stowell (1 Dodson, 247) observes, "It is not the less a war on *that account,* for war may exist without a declaration on either side. It is so laid down by the best writers on the law of nations. A declaration of war by one country only, is not a mere challenge to be accepted or refused at pleasure by the other." . . .

This greatest of civil wars was not gradually developed by popular commotion, tumultuous assemblies, or local unorganized insurrections. However long may have been its previous conception, it nevertheless sprung forth suddenly from the parent brain, a Minerva in the full panoply of *war.* The President was bound to meet it in the shape it presented itself, without waiting for Congress to baptize it with a name; and no name given to it by him or them could change the fact. . . .

Whether the President in fulfilling his duties, as Commander-in-Chief, in suppressing an insurrection, has met with such armed hostile resistance, and a civil war of such alarming proportions as will compel him to accord to them the character of belligerents, is a question to be decided *by him,* and this Court must be governed by the decisions and acts of the political department of the Government to which this power was entrusted. "He must determine what degree of force the crisis demands." The proclamation of blockade is itself official and conclusive evidence to the Court that a state of war existed which demanded and authorized a recourse to such a measure, under the circumstances peculiar to the case. . . .

If it were necessary to the technical existence of a war, that it should have a legislative sanction, we find it in almost every act passed at the extraordinary session of the Legislature of 1861, which was wholly employed in enacting laws to enable the Government to prosecute the war with vigor and efficiency. And finally, in 1861, we find Congress "*ex majore cautela*" [out of caution] and in anticipation of such astute objections, passing an act "approving, legalizing, and making valid all the acts, proclamations, and orders of the President, &c., as if they had been *issued and done under the previous express authority* and direction of the Congress of the United States."

Without admitting that such an act was necessary under the circumstances, it is plain that if the President had in any manner assumed powers which it was necessary should have the authority or sanction of Congress, that on the well known principle of law, "*omnis ratihabitio retrotrahitur et mandato equiparatur*" [ratifications relate back and are the equivalent of prior authority] this ratification has operated to perfectly cure the defect. . . .

The objection made to this act of ratification, that it is *ex post facto,* and therefore unconstitutional and void, might possibly have some weight on the trial of an indictment in a criminal Court. But precedents from that source cannot be received as authoritative in a tribunal administering public and international law.

On this first question therefore we are of the opinion that the President had a right, *jure belli,* to institute a blockade of ports in possession of the States in rebellion, which neutrals are bound to regard. . . .

Mr. Justice NELSON, dissenting [in an opinion in which Chief Justice TANEY and Justices CATRON and CLIFFORD concurred]. . . . It is not to be denied . . . that if a civil war existed between that portion of the people in organized insurrection to overthrow this Government at the time this vessel and cargo were seized, and if she was guilty of a violation of the blockade, she would be lawful prize of war. But before this insurrection against the established Government can be dealt with on the footing of a civil war, within the meaning of the law of nations and the Constitution of the United States, and which will draw after it belligerent rights, it must be recognized or declared by the war-making power of the Government. No power short of this can change the legal status of the Government or the relations of its citizens from that of peace to a state of war, or bring into existence all those duties and obligations of neutral third parties growing out of a state of war. The war power of the Government must be exercised before this changed condition of the Government and people and of neutral third parties can be admitted. . . .

. . . [W]e find there that to constitute a civil war in the sense in which we are speaking, before it can exist, in contemplation of law, it must be recognized or declared by the sovereign power of the State, and which sovereign power by our Constitution is lodged in the Congress of the United States — civil war, therefore, under our system of government, can exist only by an act of Congress, which requires the assent of two of the great departments of the Government, the Executive and Legislative. . . .

. . . But we are asked, what would become of the peace and integrity of the Union in case of an insurrection at home or invasion from abroad if this power could not be exercised by the President in the recess of Congress, and until that body could be assembled?

The framers of the Constitution fully comprehended this question, and provided for the contingency. Indeed, it would have been surprising if they had not, as a rebellion had occurred in the State of Massachusetts while the Convention was in session, and which had become so general that it was quelled only by calling upon the military power of the State. The Constitution declares that Congress shall have power "to provide for calling forth the militia to execute the laws of the Union, suppress insurrections, and repel invasions." Another clause, "that the President shall be Commander-in-chief of the Army and Navy of the United States, and of the Militia of the several States when called into the actual service of the United States;" and, again: "He shall take care that the laws shall be faithfully executed." Congress passed laws on this subject in 1792 and 1795. 1 United States Laws, pp. 264, 424. [It also passed a law on the subject in 1807. Act of Mar. 3, 1807, ch. 39, 2 Stat. 443.] . . .

The Acts of 1795 and 1807 did not, and could not under the Constitution, confer on the President the power of declaring war against a State of this Union, or of deciding that war existed, and upon that ground authorize the capture and confiscation of the property of every citizen of the State whenever it was found on the waters. The laws of war, whether the war be civil or *inter gentes,* as we have seen, convert every citizen of the hostile State into a public enemy, and treat him accordingly, whatever may have been his previous conduct. This great power over the business and property of the citizen is reserved to the legislative department by the express words of the Constitution. It cannot be delegated or surrendered to the Executive. Congress alone can determine whether war exists or should be declared; and until they have acted, no citizen of the State can be punished in his person or property, unless he has committed some offence against a law of Congress passed before the act was committed, which made it a crime, and defined the punishment. The penalty of confiscation for the acts of others with which he had no concern cannot lawfully be inflicted. . . .

. . . [C]onsequently, . . . the President had no power to set on foot a blockade under the law of nations, and . . . the capture of the vessel and cargo in this case, and in all cases before us in which the capture occurred before the 13th of July, 1861 [the date on which Congress first authorized a naval blockade of the Confederacy], for breach of blockade, or as enemies' property, are illegal and void, and . . . the decrees of condemnation should be reversed and the vessel and cargo restored.

## NOTES AND QUESTIONS

1. *Inherent Defensive War Power.* The legal challenge to the naval blockade of the South in *The Prize Cases* presented the Supreme Court for the first time with the question whether the President has the inherent power to repel attacks — to conduct defensive war — without prior congressional authorization. What answer did the Court give? Why did the Court take such pains to define "war"? On September 12, 2001, President George W. Bush declared that the terrorist attacks on the World Trade Center and the Pentagon were "acts of war." Remarks by the President in Photo Opportunity with the National Security Team, Sept. 12, 2001, *at* http://www.whitehouse.gov/news/releases/2001/09/20010912-4.html. Did the circumstances that day or since fit the Court's definition of "war"?

Is there any danger that a President might *create* the conditions said to warrant a military response? Consider Lincoln's warning in 1846 about the President's invocation of the repel-attack authority to fight the undeclared Mexican War:

Allow the President to invade a neighboring nation, whenever he shall deem it necessary to repel an invasion and you allow him to do so, whenever he may choose to say he deems it necessary for such purpose, and you allow him to make war at pleasure. Study to see if you can fix any limit to his power in this respect, after you have given him so much as you propose. [2 Abraham Lincoln, *The Writings of Abraham Lincoln* 51 (Arthur Brooks Lapsley ed., 1906).]

Could the Court in *The Prize Cases* have upheld the President's actions on any narrower ground? Can you argue that it did so? *See generally* Ludwell H. Johnson III, *Abraham Lincoln and the Development of Presidential War-Making Powers: Prize Cases (1863) Revisited*, 35 Civil War Hist. 208 (1989).

The dissenters in *The Prize Cases* did not contest the proposition that a civil war places the nation *in extremis*. Why then did they find the blockade unlawful? Did they conclude that the President's actions were forbidden by Congress? That they exceeded a congressional grant of authority? That the President lacked any inherent authority to order the blockade?

2. ***Defensive War or Just Defense?*** The *Prize Cases* involved the President's authority to respond to force with force in a war. Does the opinion support the same authority to respond immediately to attack, even when the attack is not part of a larger conflict? By the logic of the Court, is the President constitutionally empowered to meet *any* violent threat with as much force as he determines, without awaiting congressional authorization? What answer does the "sudden attack" language in Madison's notes of the framing of the Declaration Clause suggest? How important is "sudden"? How far can the President go beyond immediate self-defense?

3. ***Executive Practice and Congressional Acquiescence.*** In *Youngstown Sheet & Tube Co. v. Sawyer*, 343 U.S. 579, 610-611 (1952), Justice Felix Frankfurter wrote:

> The Constitution is a framework for Government. Therefore the way the framework has consistently operated fairly establishes that it has operated according to its true nature. Deeply embedded traditional ways of conducting government cannot supplant the Constitution or legislation, but they give meaning to the words of a text or supply them. It is an inadmissibly narrow conception of American constitutional law to confine it to the words of the Constitution and to disregard the gloss which life has written upon them. In short, a systematic, unbroken, executive practice, long pursued to the knowledge of the Congress and never before questioned, engaged in by presidents who have also sworn to uphold the Constitution, making as it were such exercise of power part of the structure of our Government, may be treated as a gloss on "executive Power" vested in the President by §1 of Art. II. . . .

In other words, Congress may by its *inaction* (or by collateral legislation) *acquiesce* in a long-standing executive practice or policy of which it is aware, and thus suggest a kind of customary legal authority in the executive to engage in the practice.

Although we have formally declared war only 11 times in our history, we had used armed force abroad on more than 300 occasions through 2004, most of them well-known to Congress. *See* Richard F. Grimmett, *Instances of Use of United States Armed Forces Abroad, 1798–2004* (Cong. Res. Serv. RL30172), Oct. 5, 2004. Does this history indicate that the President may use armed force whenever he thinks it necessary to protect national security? That argument was made to support the legality of U.S. participation in the Vietnam War. The Legal Adviser to the State Department inferred from 125 prior congressionally unauthorized uses of armed force abroad that the President has the "power to deploy American forces abroad and commit them to military operations when . . . [he] deems such action necessary to maintain the security and defense of the United States. . . ."

Leonard C. Meeker, *The Legality of United States Participation in the Defense of Viet-Nam*, 75 Yale L.J. 1085, 1100-1101 (1966); *see also* J. Terry Emerson, *War Powers Resolution*, 74 W. Va. L. Rev. 53, App. A (1971) (citing usage for the same proposition). Is this inference supported by the theory of customary law suggested by Justice Frankfurter?

Or does history suggest a narrower claim of presidential war power: that the President has acquired *particular* customary war powers with congressional acquiescence? For example, he has occasionally ordered military force to protect or rescue American nationals and their property from foreign threats of violence. *See* Francis D. Wormuth & Edwin B. Firmage, *To Chain the Dog of War* 145-151 (2d ed. 1989) (listing some uses of force for rescue and protection). Not only was Congress generally aware of such uses of force, but it has given strong evidence of acquiescing in these uses. *See* Peter Raven-Hansen, *Constitutional Constraints: The War Clause*, in *The U.S. Constitution and the Power to Go to War* 38-39 (Gary M. Stern & Morton H. Halperin eds., 1994). On the other hand, according to one view any resulting customary

> rescue/protection authority ... must be confined to cases of actual or reasonably imminent risk to Americans. In addition, its logical limit is its immediate object: rescue and protection. Once American nationals are evacuated out of harm's way or otherwise secured, the authority is exhausted. Neither customary law demarcated by the practice that Congress understood and acquiesced to, nor international law ... permits the President to order reprisals on his own initiative. [*Id.* at 40-41.]

The constitutional assignment of the power to "grant letters of Marque and Reprisal" to Congress may suggest that the Framers meant for Congress, not the President alone, to decide on reprisals taken in response to unlawful acts against us, at least when there is time to choose among responses.

A mid-nineteenth-century opinion indicated in dicta that the President has customary authority to use force to rescue American nationals taken hostage by terrorists. *See* Durand v. Hollins, 8 F. Cas. 111, 112 (No. 4186) (S.D.N.Y. 1860) (". . . as it respects the interposition of the executive abroad, for the protection of the lives and property of the citizen, the duty must, of necessity, rest in the discretion of the president."). Do you think that authority extends to counterterrorist military operations?

4. ***Anticipatory Self-Defense?*** Does the President's defensive war power also include the power to use military force against *suspected* terrorists? Consider Secretary of State Daniel Webster's classic statement that under the law of nations, a valid plea of anticipatory self-defense must rest on a showing of "a necessity of self-defense, instant, overwhelming, leaving no choice of means, no moment for deliberation." VI *The Works of Daniel Webster* 261 (1851).

If so, has the advent of suicide terrorism, with surprise attacks in which the terrorists intentionally perish, changed the meaning of "no moment for deliberation"? An immediate response to a terrorist attack is often impossible. Terrorist attacks are unpredictable and therefore it is difficult to protect the targets, and attribution of responsibility is typically problematic and time-consuming. *See* David Turndorf, *The U.S. Raid on Libya: A Forceful Response to Terrorism,* 14 Brook. J. Intl. L. 187, 216 (1988). Consequently, as a practical matter, the best defense against a terrorist attack may be to attack the terrorists first. *See Durand, supra,* at 112 ("Acts of lawless violence, or of threatened violence to the citizen or his property, cannot be anticipated and provided for; and the protection, to be effectual or of any avail, may, not infrequently, require the most prompt and decided action.").

In other words, does the President's defensive war power include "anticipatory self-defense"? If so, what is the scope of anticipatory self-defense? How, if at all, can you distinguish between anticipatory self-defense and reprisal, assuming that reprisal requires congressional authorization?

5. ***The Evidentiary Standard for Anticipatory Self-Defense.*** When a state defends itself against ongoing attack, "the factual predicate for self-defense is clear and observable." Jules Lobel, *The Use of Force to Respond to Terrorist Attacks: The Bombing of Sudan and Afghanistan,* 24 Yale J. Intl. L. 537, 543 (1999). But when a state uses force in anticipatory self-defense against a stateless terrorist group operating abroad or against a state that gives such a group sanctuary, the factual predicate is more ambiguous. If unsubstantiated self-serving claims by the counterterrorist state are not deemed sufficient justification, what sort of proof must be supplied, and to whom?

Some scholars have argued that, because death may ensue from such attacks, the appropriate evidentiary standard is a criminal one — beyond a reasonable doubt. *See id.* at 551; Sara N. Scheideman, *Standards of Proof in Forcible Responses to Terrorism,* 50 Syracuse L. Rev. 249 (2000). That is, the preemptively attacking state must make public for international scrutiny evidence that shows beyond a reasonable doubt that the targeted group was responsible for terrorist attacks or that the state attacked knowingly harbored the group. Another scholar suggests instead that responsible decision makers must consider a host of "prudential considerations," including

> whether [the use of force] will make a martyr of the leader of the target organization, or deeply offend good relations with affected countries, or waste military assets that are not limitless . . . , whether the use of force will save the lives of victims and prevent future attacks; whether the only realistic way to achieve deterrence is to signal that the responsible country will strike back hard; and whether a leader who has come to power by brutal means is likely to scoff at words and remonstrations that are not backed by force. [Ruth Wedgwood, *Responding to Terrorism: The Strikes Against bin Laden,* 24 Yale J. Intl. L. 559, 563 (1999).]

Wedgwood notes that the counterterrorist state will often be unable to disclose its evidence in public without compromising its intelligence sources, but that sometimes it may take this risk to influence world opinion or to obtain foreign support. *Id.* at 574.

Which of these standards is more appropriate?

## B.  STATUTORY AUTHORIZATION AND LIMITS

The Framers assigned Congress both the power to "declare War" and the power to "grant letters of Marque and Reprisal." U.S. Const. art. I, §8, cl. 11. Although the constitutional debates shed little light on the meaning of "declare," contemporaneous writings indicate that a nation could "declare war" "not only by formal announcement, but also by an act of hostility." Michael D. Ramsey, *Textualism and War Powers*, 69 U. Chi. L. Rev. 1543, 1590 (2002). As John Locke wrote, a "state of War" could be "declar[ed] by Word or Action. . . ." Locke, *Two Treatises of Government* 278 (Peter Laslett ed., 1967). While in our system of divided powers Congress could not itself engage in an act of hostility, it could pass a law to authorize the President to act. In fact, that is precisely what Congress did in the so-called Quasi-War with France, as the following case points out.

### Bas v. Tingy

United States Supreme Court, 1800
4 U.S. (4 Dall.) 37

[As relations between France and the United States deteriorated between 1798 and 1800, Congress enacted a succession of measures approving naval actions against France. Initially, Congress authorized U.S. armed vessels of the recently established navy to capture French vessels that had "committed depredations" on U.S.-owned vessels or that were "found hovering" off U.S. coasts for that purpose. Act of May 28, 1798, ch. 48, 1 Stat. 561. When this measure did not adequately protect U.S. merchants on the high seas, Congress next authorized such merchants to defend themselves against "any search, restraint or seizure" by vessels operating under French colors. Act of June 25, 1798, ch. 60, 1 Stat. 572. This act also provided for the recapture of U.S.-owned vessels from the French and their restoration to their former owners upon payment of salvage value. Three days later Congress passed another act that provided for the judicial condemnation of captured vessels and for the return of recaptured vessels to their owners for a salvage payment of one-eighth the full value. Act of June 28, 1798, ch. 62, 1 Stat. 574. Eventually, Congress authorized U.S. public and private armed vessels to take any French armed vessels found on the high seas. Act of July 9, 1798, ch. 68, 1 Stat. 578.

The next year Congress passed a set of rules and regulations for its infant navy. This act provided:

> That for the ships or goods belonging to the citizens of the United States, or to the citizens or subjects of any nation, in amity with the United States, if retaken from the enemy within twenty-four hours, the owners are to allow one eighth part of the whole value for salvage, if after twenty-four hours, and under forty-eight, one fifth thereof, if above that and under ninety-six hours, one third part thereof, and if above that, one half, all of which is to be paid without any deduction whatsoever. . . . [Act of Mar. 2, 1799, ch. 24, §7, 1 Stat. 709, 716.]

On April 21, 1799, Captain Tingy, commander of the public armed ship *Ganges,* recaptured the *Eliza,* which belonged to John Bas and had been captured by a French privateer on the high seas on March 31, 1799. After he returned the vessel to Bas, Tingy brought an action in libel for salvage. The question in the case was whether Tingy was entitled to one-eighth the value of the *Eliza,* as provided by the 1798 act, or one-half, as provided by the 1799 act. The lower courts ruled that Tingy was entitled to half the value. On appeal to the Supreme Court, the Justices delivered their opinions seriatim. The opinion of Justice MOORE in favor of affirmance is omitted.]

WASHINGTON, Justice. . . . 1st. [The 1798 Act] relates to re-captures from *the French,* and [the 1799 Act] relates to re-captures from *the enemy;* and, it is said, that "the enemy" is not descriptive of France, or of her armed vessels, according to the correct and technical understanding of the word.

The decision of this question must depend upon another; which is, whether, at the time of passing the act of congress of the 2d of March 1799, there subsisted a state of war between the two nations? It may, I believe, be safely laid down, that every contention by force between two nations, in external matters, under the authority of their respective governments, is not only war, but public war. If it be declared in form, it is called *solemn,* and is of the perfect kind; because one whole nation is at war with another whole nation; and *all* the members of the nation declaring war, are authorised to commit hostilities against all the members of the other, in every place, and under every circumstance. In such a war all the members act under a general authority, and all the rights and consequences of war attach to their condition.

But hostilities may subsist between two nations more confined in its nature and extent; being limited as to places, persons, and things; and this is more properly termed *imperfect war*; because not solemn, and because those who are authorised to commit hostilities, act under special authority, and can go no farther than to the extent of their commission. Still, however, it is *public war*, because it is an external contention by force, between some of the members of the two nations, authorised by the legitimate powers. It is a war between the two nations, though all the members are not authorised to commit hostilities such as in a solemn war, where the government restrain the general power.

Now, if this be the true definition of war, let us see what was the situation of the United States in relation to France. In March 1799, congress had raised an army; stopped all intercourse with France; dissolved our treaty; built and equipt ships of war; and commissioned private armed ships; enjoining the former, and authorising the latter, to defend themselves against the armed ships of France, to attack them on the high seas, to subdue and take them as prize, and to re-capture armed vessels found in their possession. Here, then, let me ask, what were the technical characters of an American and French armed vessel, combating on the high seas, with a view the one to subdue the other, and to make prize of his property? They certainly were not friends, because there was a contention by force; nor were they private enemies, because the contention was external, and authorised by the legitimate authority of the two governments. If they were not our enemies, I know not what constitutes an enemy.

2d. But, secondly, it is said, that a war of the imperfect kind, is more properly called acts of hostility, or reprizal, and that congress did not mean to consider the hostility subsisting between France and the United States, as constituting a state of war.

In support of this position, it has been observed, that in no law prior to March 1799, is France styled our enemy, nor are we said to be at war. This is true; but neither of these things were necessary to be done: because as to France, she was sufficiently described by the title of the French republic; and as to America, the degree of hostility meant to be carried on, was sufficiently described without declaring war, or declaring that we were at war. Such a declaration by congress, might have constituted a perfect state of war, which was not intended by the government. . . .

. . . [T]herefore, in my opinion, the decree of the Circuit Court ought to be affirmed.

CHASE, Justice. . . . Congress is empowered to declare a general war, or congress may wage a limited war; limited in place, in objects, and in time. If a general war is declared, its extent and operations are only restricted and regulated by the *jus belli*, forming a part of the law of nations; but if a partial war is waged, its extent and operation depend on our municipal laws.

What, then, is the nature of the contest subsisting between America and France? In my judgment, it is a limited, partial, war. Congress has not declared war in general terms; but congress has authorized hostilities on the high seas by certain persons in certain cases. There is no authority given to commit hostilities on land; to capture unarmed French vessels, nor even to capture French armed vessels lying in a French port; and the authority is not given, indiscriminately, to every citizen of America, against every citizen of France; but only to citizens appointed by commissions, or exposed to immediate outrage and violence. So far it is, unquestionably, a partial war; but, nevertheless, it is a public war, on account of the public authority from which it emanates.

There are four acts, authorised by our government, that are demonstrative of a state of war. A belligerent power has a right, by the law of nations, to search a neutral vessel; and, upon suspicion of a violation of her neutral obligations, to seize and carry her into port for further examination. But by the acts of congress, an American vessel is authorised: 1st. To resist the search of a French public vessel: 2d. To capture any vessel that should attempt, by force, to compel submission to a search: 3d. To re-capture any American vessel seized by a French vessel: and 4th. To capture any French armed vessel wherever found on the high seas. This suspension of the law of nations, this right of capture and re-capture, can only be authorized by an act of the government, which is, in itself, an act of hostility. But still it is a restrained, or limited, hostility; and there are, undoubtedly, many rights attached to a general war, which do not attach to this modification of the powers of defence and aggression. . . .

The acts of congress have been analyzed to show, that a war is not openly denounced against France, and that France is no where expressly called the enemy of America: but this only proves the circumspection and prudence of the legislature. Considering our national prepossessions in favour of the French republic, congress had an arduous task to perform, even in preparing for necessary defence, and just retaliation. As the temper of the people rose, however, in resentment of accumulated wrongs, the language and the measures of the government became more and more energetic and indignant; though hitherto the popular feeling may not have been *ripe* for a solemn declaration of war; and an active and powerful opposition in our public councils, has postponed, if not prevented that decisive event, which many thought would have best suited the interest, as well as the honour of the United States. The progress of our contest with France, indeed, resembles much the progress of our revolutionary contest; in which, watching the current of public sentiment, the patriots of that day proceeded, step by step, from the supplicatory language of petitions for a redress of grievances, to the bold and noble declaration of national independence.

Having, then, no hesitation in pronouncing, that a partial war exists between America and France, and that France was an enemy, within the meaning of the act of March 1799, my voice must be given for affirming the decree of the Circuit Court.

PATERSON, Justice. As the case appears on the record, and has been accurately stated by the counsel, and by the judges, who have delivered their opinions, it is not necessary to recapitulate the facts. My opinion shall be expressed in a few words. The United States and the French republic are in a qualified state of hostility. An imperfect war, or a war, as to certain objects, and to a certain extent, exists between the two nations; and this modified warfare is authorized by the constitutional authority of our country. It is a war *quoad hoc* [to this extent]. As far as congress tolerated and authorized the war on our part, so far may we proceed in hostile operations. It is a maritime war; a war at sea as to certain purposes. The national armed vessels of France attack and capture the national armed vessels of the United States; and the national armed vessels of the United States are expressly authorized and directed to attack, subdue, and take, the national armed vessels of France, and also to re-capture American vessels. It is therefore a public war between the two nations, qualified, on our part, in the manner prescribed by the constitutional organ of our country. In such a state of things, it is scarcely necessary to add, that the term "enemy," applies; it is the appropriate expression, to be limited in its signification, import, and use, by the qualified nature and operation of the war on our part. The word enemy proceeds the full length of the war, and no farther. . . .

By the COURT: Let the decree of the Circuit Court be affirmed.

## NOTES AND QUESTIONS

1. *The Obsolescent Declaration of War?* Increasing state sensitivity to public diplomacy and world opinion, as well as the decline of opportunities for the lawful use of force occasioned by the proliferation of treaties and the evolution of customary international law, have long made declarations of war impolitic. As a consequence, "[a]lthough conflicts between and among

states continue, no state has issued a formal declaration of war [since the 1948 Arab-Israeli War]. Indeed, some argue that a declaration of war today would constitute prima facie evidence of illegal aggression." Robert F. Turner, *The War Powers Resolution: Its Implementation in Theory and Practice* 25 (1983).

In fact, there is evidence that the declaration of war was already obsolete in 1789, by which date the concept of "defensive war" had taken such firm root in the law of nations that it was widely understood that war could be started without the formality of a declaration. *See, e.g., The Federalist No. 25*, at 165 (Alexander Hamilton) (Clinton Rossiter ed., 1961); Turner, *supra*, at 16 nn.45-57 (citing sources). In this light, is it likely that the Framers intended to vest Congress with only the increasingly anachronistic formal declaration power, *see* J. Gregory Sidak, *To Declare War*, 41 Duke L.J. 27 (1991) (supplying reasons for such an intent), and no other constitutional means to choose war? What answer did the members of the Court give in *Bas*? Regardless of the framing history or current geopolitical realities, does the advent of non-state enemies, such as non-state-sponsored terrorists, now make formal declarations of war obsolete?

2. ***Expressly Authorizing War Without Declaring It.*** How did Congress express its decision to make war on France at the end of the eighteenth century? How broad was the resulting authority in the President as Commander in Chief? Could he have deployed land forces to invade France or French possessions? Could he have deployed the Navy to take the war to French ports? *See* Little v. Barreme, 6 U.S. (2 Cranch) 170 (1804) (finding that when Congress had specified by statute that U.S. ships could intercept vessels heading *to* French ports, a presidential order was ineffective to legalize interception of vessels coming *from* French ports).

Less than a year after *Bas,* the Court was again called upon to decide rights of salvage during the naval war with France. Writing for the Court, Chief Justice Marshall concluded that "[t]he whole powers of war being, by the constitution of the United States, vested in congress, the acts of that body can alone be resorted to as our guides in this enquiry." Talbot v. Seeman, 5 U.S. (1 Cranch) 1, 28 (1801). The Court unanimously found that Congress had authorized "partial hostilities" against France.

Do the Quasi-War cases (*Bas, Talbot, Little*) tell us anything about whether the President could have ordered similar hostilities without any congressional authorization at all? *Compare* J. Gregory Sidak, *The Quasi-War Cases — and Their Relevance to Whether "Letters of Marque and Reprisal" Constrain Presidential War Powers*, 28 Harv. J.L. & Pub. Poly. 465, 482, 486 (2005) (asserting that the answer is no, because the cases do not address "how the Constitution divides between Congress and the President the power to commit the nation to waging a limited war"), *with* Campbell v. Clinton, 203 F.3d 19, 30 n.7 (D.C. Cir. 2000) (Randolph, J., concurring) (citing *Little* for the proposition that executive power in war "was constrained by an absence of legislation"), and 38 (Tatel, J., concurring) (citing *Talbot* for the proposition that Congress possesses the "whole powers of war").

3. ***Impliedly Authorizing War by Statute.*** Must Congress *expressly* authorize the use of force? In Orlando v. Laird, 443 F.2d 1039 (2d Cir. 1971), the

court found congressional authorization for the Vietnam War in, *inter alia*, military appropriations and selective service statutes. It did not cite *Bas*. Is there a difference between the form of authorization found in *Bas* and authorization by appropriation for counterterrorist strike forces or selective service legislation? If Congress can indirectly authorize war by appropriating money for it, is there any constitutional or practical limit on the form of war authorization?

4. *Impliedly Authorizing War Without a Statute?* Does Congress even need to use a statute? Could Congress authorize war by separate and substantively different actions in each House? Single-chamber resolutions ("simple resolutions") do not have bicameral approval and are not presented to the President for his signature. Conceding that such separate actions by each House lack the force and effect of statutes, Charles Tiefer nonetheless argues that

> [a]ctions by Congress short of enactment may elucidate the intent of congressional appropriations. . . . Formal and express presidential requests for congressional approval [to use military force] . . . may [also] bestow or confirm the legal significance of the corresponding congressional "partial" approval actions. Finally, Congress may take legally significant positions, even apart from a presidential request. [Charles Tiefer, *War Decisions in the Late 1990s by Partial Congressional Declaration*, 36 San Diego L. Rev. 1, 105 (1999).]

Is this theory of "partial congressional declaration" supported by any constitutional text or framing history? If you are skeptical, is the theory strengthened if we require that *each* House pass a "partial declaration" to support military action even though the resulting simple resolutions do not match?

Finally, does either House need to do anything at all to approve war? May Congress authorize war silently by acquiescence in a conflict started by the Executive? See *supra* p. 47.

5. *The Legal Domino Effects of War.* A formal declaration of war by Congress gives notice to neutrals of the existence of hostilities and of the identity of the belligerents, and it activates certain rights and obligations of neutrals and belligerents alike under international law. It also triggers approximately 30 standby statutory authorities that would not otherwise be available to the President. For example, under the Alien Enemy Act, 50 U.S.C. §21 (2000), "whenever there is a declared war between the United States and any foreign nation or government," citizens of "the hostile nation or government" who are not naturalized are subject to summary arrest, internment, and deportation when the President so proclaims.

More than 170 other standby authorities are triggered "in time of war" or "when war is imminent," without requiring a declaration of war. *See generally* David M. Ackerman & Richard F. Grimmett, *Declarations of War and Authorizations for the Use of Military Force: Historical Background and Legal Implications* (Cong. Res. Serv. RL31133), Jan. 14, 2003; J. Gregory Sidak, *War, Liberty, and Enemy Aliens*, 67 N.Y.U. L. Rev. 1402, 1430 & nn.138-145 (1992). These authorize the President to take land for military purposes; commandeer private production lines for war manufacturing; take control of private transportation for war transport; and sequester, hold, and dispose of enemy property, among other powers.

Do these differences between declarations of war and non-declaratory statutory authorizations help explain why Congress did not declare war on France during the Quasi-War? What explanation does Justice Chase give? Do they provide any guidance for whether the United States *should* declare war on terrorists today?

If you have concluded that Congress can impliedly authorize the use of force, what, if any, domino effects does an implied authorization have? It is partly the domino effects, as well as the need for accountability for war decisions, that have caused some scholars to insist on the formality of a declaration as a predicate for war. *See* Sidak, *supra* Note 1. Tiefer, in response, notes that the interaction between a President who requests approval for the use of force and the houses of Congress that respond separately but approvingly "cranks up an elaborate machinery for the democratic inclusion of the nation in the military commitment decision," including "[h]earings, news coverage, briefings, disputes over conditions or demands for assurances, and floor debate." Tiefer, *supra*, at 125. Does this machinery satisfy the need for accountability?

6. *Area and Use Limitations in War.* The congressional authorizations for the Quasi-War with France established limitations on both the area of hostilities and the types of forces that could be used. In Little v. Barreme, 6 U.S. (2 Cranch) 170 (1804), the Court effectively enforced a use limitation (permitting naval vessels to intercept vessels going to, but not coming from, French ports) over a presidential order to the contrary.

On the other hand, most scholars agree that Congress could not under the guise of a statutory use limitation direct Platoon Alpha to seize the third house from the corner on Baghdad Boulevard during an authorized war. The Framers vested such real-time tactical decisions in the Commander in Chief, partly because they remembered the unhappy experience of command by committee during the Revolutionary War. The Commander in Chief Clause assured not only civilian control of the military and unity of command, but also efficiency in such decisions. "As commander in chief," the Court has emphasized, "[the President] is authorized to direct the movements of the naval and military forces placed by law at his command, and to employ them in the manner he may deem most effectual to harass and conquer and subdue the enemy." Fleming v. Page, 50 U.S. (9 How.) 603, 614-615 (1851).

Could Congress authorize counterterrorist operations subject to area and use limitations: "no attacks in civilian areas using unmanned Predator aircraft," or "no more than 5,000 active duty troops in counterterrorist operations in Afghanistan"? Would it make any difference that a limitation is framed as an appropriations rider ("No funds authorized or appropriated pursuant to this [appropriation] or any other Act may be used to finance the use of the U.S. armed forces for. . . .")? *See* U.S. Const. art. I, §9, cl. 7. Or would such a limitation amount to unconstitutional micromanaging of hostilities in violation of the Commander in Chief Clause? Recognizing that there is no bright-line test, one scholar has suggested that the constitutionality of a congressional area or use limitation depends in part on its "intrusiveness as to the monopoly of command itself" (i.e., its impact on civilian control and unity of command), and the "generality" of the limitation (i.e., whether it lays down a "general rule" addressing "overall structure and relations of the components of the armed forces" or operates instead as an order "direct[ed] . . . toward a particular operation or mission"). *See* Charles Tiefer, *Can Appropriations Riders Speed Our Exit From Iraq?*, 42 Stan. J. Intl. L. 291, 320-323 (2006). How would the proposed counterterrorist limitations fare by this analysis?

7. ***Command Authority Revisited.*** Consider this summary of the President's powers as Commander in Chief in time of war:

> The President, not Congress, makes all day-to-day tactical decisions in the combat deployment of armed forces. Indeed, even when it ends a use of force by cutting off funds, Congress cannot constitutionally interfere with the Commander in Chief's tactical decisions for the safe withdrawal of the armed forces. But as powerful as the command authority is, the framers still intended that the Commander in Chief "would amount to nothing more than the supreme command and direction of the military and naval forces, as first General and Admiral of the Confederacy . . . ," as Alexander Hamilton explained in the *Federalist Papers*. By making the President the Commander in Chief in Article II, the framers addressed what they recognized as a defect in the conduct of the Revolutionary War. They did not compromise their insistence in Article I on collective judgment in the decision for war.
>
> Nor did they give the Commander in Chief any constitutional right to ignore the terms of a congressional authorization for the use of force. When Congress gives the President the authority to conduct war, he or she must conduct it within that authority, just as the President must follow any law that is constitutionally made. [*Deciding to Use Force Abroad: War Powers in a System of Checks and Balances* 15 (The Constitution Project) (Peter Raven-Hansen rptr., 2005).]

Do you think congressional constraints have the same force when the President is fighting a war thrust upon us by attack as when he is fighting one authorized by Congress? Put another way, are you clear about precisely which Commander in Chief powers are exclusive? *See generally* Louis Fisher, *Presidential War Power* (2d rev. ed. 2004).

## C. DEFENDING AGAINST AL QAEDA — 1998 AND 2001[1]

On August 7, 1998, truck bombs exploded at the U.S. embassies in Kenya and Tanzania killing nearly 300 people, including 12 Americans. Two weeks

---

1. Except as otherwise noted, background information on the 1998 cruise missile attacks on Sudan and Afghanistan is drawn from Scheideman, *supra* p. 49; Sean Murphy, *Contemporary Practice of the United States Relating to International Law*, 93 Am. J. Intl. L. 161-166 (1999);

later, on August 20, the United States launched 79 Tomahawk cruise missiles against terrorist training camps in Afghanistan and a Sudanese pharmaceutical plant that the United States alleged to be a chemical weapons facility. President Clinton explained that he ordered the attacks because "we have convincing evidence that [Islamic terrorist groups, including that of Osama bin Laden] . . . played the key role in the Embassy bombings . . . and compelling information that they were planning additional terrorist attacks against our citizens. . . ." He had notified certain congressional leaders on August 19 that the attacks were coming and sent Congress a letter the day after the attacks reporting, "consistent with the War Powers Resolution," that

> [t]he United States acted in exercise of our inherent right of self-defense consistent with Article 51 of the United Nations Charter.[2] These strikes were a necessary and proportionate response to the imminent threat of further terrorist attacks against U.S. personnel and facilities. These strikes were intended to prevent and deter additional attacks by a clearly identified terrorist threat. [Letter to Congressional Leaders Reporting on Military Action Against Terrorist Sites in Afghanistan and Sudan, 34 Weekly Comp. Pres. Doc. 1650 (Aug. 21, 1998).]

The President's National Security Adviser explained that it was "appropriate" not only under Article 51 but also "under a 1996 statute in Congress, for us to try to disrupt and destroy those kinds of military terrorist targets." The statute referred to apparently was the Antiterrorism and Effective Death Penalty Act of 1996 (AEDPA), Pub. L. No. 104-132, 110 Stat. 1214. In the AEDPA, Congress prohibited various kinds of assistance to countries that sponsor or harbor terrorists. In the preamble to these prohibitions, Congress made the following "finding," among others: "the President should use all necessary means, including covert action and military force, to disrupt, dismantle, and destroy international infrastructure used by international terrorists, including overseas terrorist training facilities and safe havens." *Id.* §324(4). The finding was not codified, but it appears instead in the annotations to a codified prohibition on assistance to countries that aid terrorist states. 22 U.S.C. §2377 note (2000).

Reports on the results of the attacks varied. A spokesman for bin Laden reported that 28 people were killed in the attacks on the camps. Sudan reported that ten were injured in the attack on the pharmaceutical plant. The U.S. government subsequently asserted that a soil sample from the plant revealed the presence of a precursor chemical for the production of VX, a nerve agent.

---

Lobel, *supra* p. 49; Wedgwood, *supra* p. 49; William C. Banks, *To "Prevent and Deter" International Terrorism: The U.S. Response to the Kenya and Tanzania Embassy Bombings* (National Security Studies CS 0699-12, 1999).

[2. Article 51 provides, "Nothing in the present charter shall impair the inherent right of individual and collective self-defense if an armed attack occurs against a Member of the United Nations, until the Security Council has taken measures necessary to maintain international peace and security. . . ."]

Other evidence suggested that the plant was an unguarded pharmaceutical factory, which had often been visited by foreign dignitaries, and that the soil sample contained a chemical structure resembling an agricultural insecticide. It was subsequently reported that the Defense Intelligence Agency had reviewed the evidence and concluded that the attack was based on bad intelligence and bad science. *See Last Summer's Attack in the Sudan, Was It Based on Faulty Evidence?*, ABC World News Tonight, Feb. 10, 1999, *available at* 1999 WL 6800665. *But see* Daniel Benjamin & Steven Simon, *A Failure of Intelligence?*, N.Y. Rev. of Books, Dec. 20, 2001, at 7 (asserting that the attack was correctly based on classified evidence).

Three years later, hijackers flew commercial airliners into the World Trade Center towers and the Pentagon. Congress quickly took up bills to authorize military force against those who were involved in the September 11, 2001, attacks or who gave them support or sanctuary. The White House reportedly first proposed a joint resolution that would have authorized force against those involved in the attacks "*and* to deter and preempt any future acts of terrorism and aggression against the United States." David Abramowitz, *The President, the Congress and Use of Force: Legal and Political Considerations in Authorizing Use of Force Against International Terrorism,* 43 Harv. Intl. L.J. 71 (2002) (emphasis added). Instead, Congress passed the following resolution and the President signed it into law on September 18, 2001.

## AUTHORIZATION FOR USE OF MILITARY FORCE

Pub. L. No. 107-40, 115 Stat. 224 (2001)

Joint Resolution To authorize the use of United States Armed Forces against those responsible for the recent attacks launched against the United States.

Whereas, on September 11, 2001, acts of treacherous violence were committed against the United States and its citizens; and

Whereas, such acts render it both necessary and appropriate that the United States exercise its rights to self-defense and to protect United States citizens both at home and abroad; and

Whereas, in light of the threat to the national security and foreign policy of the United States posed by these grave acts of violence; and

Whereas, such acts continue to pose an unusual and extraordinary threat to the national security and foreign policy of the United States; and

Whereas, the President has authority under the Constitution to take action to deter and prevent acts of international terrorism against the United States:

Now, therefore, be it resolved by the Senate and House of Representatives of the United States of America in Congress assembled,

### SECTION 1. SHORT TITLE.

This joint resolution may be cited as the "Authorization for Use of Military Force."

**SECTION 2. AUTHORIZATION FOR USE OF UNITED STATES ARMED FORCES.**

(a) IN GENERAL. — That the President is authorized to use all necessary and appropriate force against those nations, organizations, or persons he determines planned, authorized, committed, or aided the terrorist attacks that occurred on September 11, 2001, or harbored such organizations or persons, in order to prevent any future acts of international terrorism against the United States by such nations, organizations or persons.

(b) War Powers Resolution Requirements —

(1) SPECIFIC STATUTORY AUTHORIZATION. — Consistent with section 8(a)(1) of the War Powers Resolution, the Congress declares that this section is intended to constitute specific statutory authorization within the meaning of section 5(b) of the War Powers Resolution.

(2) APPLICABILITY OF OTHER REQUIREMENTS. — Nothing in this resolution supercedes any requirement of the War Powers Resolution.

## NOTES AND QUESTIONS

1. *Express(?) Congressional Authorization for the 1998 Attacks.* Did either law cited by the administration supply authority for the 1998 attacks? Would either one support the invasion of Afghanistan? A continuing campaign against al Qaeda camps and host regimes in Sudan, Somalia, Afghanistan, and Iraq?

   Would either law authorize an attack against bin Laden himself? See Chapter 3 for a discussion of targeted killing.

2. *Congressional Acquiescence in Counterterrorism Strikes?* In April 1986, the United States conducted an air strike against Libya in response to its alleged involvement in a terrorist bombing in Berlin that took the life of an American soldier. Does this earlier attack suggest any other source of authority for the 1998 strikes? Consider this testimony by the Legal Adviser to the State Department in support of the 1986 air strike:

   > It is also important to note, in this regard, that the President is not simply acting alone, under this inherent constitutional author-ity, when taking the types of actions we are discussing today. The Congress has, over the years, learned of, considered, and effec-tively endorsed in principle the use of U.S. forces for a variety of purposes through its adoption of laws and other actions. Most sig-nificantly, Congress has authorized and appropriated money for creation of forces specifically designed for anti-terrorist tasks. For example, Section 1453 of the 1986 Department of Defense Authori-zation Act specifically states that it is the duty of the government to safeguard the safety and security of U.S. citizens against a rapidly increasing terrorist threat, and that U.S. special operations forces provide the immediate and primary capability to respond to

such terrorism; and the Congress has appropriated funds for the specific purpose of improving U.S. capabilities to carry out such oper-ations. . . . In this sense, Congress has participated in the creation and maintenance of the forces whose function, at least in part, is to defend Americans from terrorism through the measured use of force. The President has openly discussed and explained the need for and propriety of these uses of force, which he has correctly assumed are widely supported by Congress and the American people. All of the actions undertaken were clearly signaled well in advance, and there-fore posed no threat to the role of Congress under the Constitution in military and foreign affairs. . . . [*War Powers, Libya, and State-Spon-sored Terrorism: Hearing Before the Subcomm. on Arms Control, Intl. Security and Science of the H. Comm. on Foreign Aff.*, 99th Cong. 26-31 (1986) (hereinafter *Libya Hearings*) (statement of Abraham D. Sofaer, Legal Adviser to the Department of State).]

What theory of legal authority was the Legal Adviser invoking? Was he right?

3. ***Striking First or Striking Back: Does It Make a Legal Difference?*** The 1998 attacks can be characterized either as striking first (in anticipatory self-defense) or striking back (in reprisal). Assuming that there was no prior congressional authorization for the attacks, does the proper character-ization of them make any difference to their legality? *See* U.S. Const. art. I, §8, cl.11.

Professor Bowett has argued that, "coming after the event and when the harm has already been inflicted, reprisals cannot be characterized as a means of protection." D. Bowett, *Reprisals Involving Recourse to Armed Force*, 66 Am. J. Intl. L. 1, 3 (1972). Recall also Daniel Webster's statement of the conditions for anticipatory self-defense. See *supra* p. 48. If you con-clude that the attacks were not self-defense under international law, does that conclusion affect their legality under U.S. law?

4. ***Anticipatory Self-Defense.*** Recall the proposed evidentiary standards for anticipatory self-defense. How would the conflicting standards apply to the 1998 attacks on Sudan and Afghanistan? Bin Laden and several of his associ-ates were eventually indicted for the embassy bombings. The indictment alleged that these defendants, "together with other members and associates of al Qaeda and others known and unknown to the Grand Jury, unlawfully, willfully, and knowingly combined, conspired, confederated and agreed to kill nationals of the United States," including those who served in the U.S. embassies in Tanzania and Kenya. *See* Murphy, *supra* p. 57 at 166. Although bin Laden was not apprehended, the defendants who were tried were all convicted of various crimes and sentenced to life in prison without the pos-sibility of parole. The convictions came, however, after lengthy trials and almost three years after the embassy bombings.

5. ***Applicability of the War Powers Resolution.*** The War Powers Resolu-tion (WPR), 50 U.S.C. §§1541-1548 (2000), was enacted over President Richard Nixon's veto in 1973 in response to the Viet Nam War. By the

WPR Congress required the administration to report to Congress within 48 hours of introducing "United States armed forces into hostilities or into situations where imminent involvement in hostilities is clearly indicated by the circumstances"; "into the territory, airspace, or waters of a foreign nation, while equipped for combat, except for deployments which relate solely to supply, replacement, repair, or training of such forces"; or "in numbers which substantially enlarge United States Armed Forces equipped for combat already located in a foreign nation." *Id.* §1543(a). Within 60 days after a report of a "hostilities" deployment is made or required to be made, the WPR requires the President to terminate the deployment unless he obtains a declaration of war or specific statutory authorization for the deployment. *Id.* §1544(b). Was the 1998 attack on bin Laden's terrorist training camps in Afghanistan subject to the WPR?

Professor Archibald Cox has suggested that the WPR does not apply to military action to "directly repel immediate acts of terrorists and promptly capture terrorists without encounter with the armed forces of a *de jure* [or] *de facto* government." *See Libya Hearings, supra* p. 61, at 247. According to the Legal Adviser to the State Department:

> We have substantial doubt that the Resolution should, in general, be construed to apply to the deployment of . . . antiterrorist units, where operations of a traditional military character are not contemplated and where no confrontation is expected between our units and forces of another state. To be sure, the language of the resolution makes no explicit exception for activities of this kind, but such units can reasonably be distinguished from "forces equipped for combat" and their actions against terrorists differ greatly from the "hostilities" contemplated by the Resolution.
>
> Nothing in the legislative history indicated, moreover, that the Congress intended the Resolution to cover deployments of such antiterrorist units. These units are not conventional military forces. A rescue effort or an effort to capture or otherwise deal with terrorists, where the forces of a foreign nation are not involved, is not a typical military mission, and our *antiterrorist forces are not equipped to conduct sustained combat with foreign armed forces.* Rather, these units operate in secrecy to carry out precise and limited tasks designed to liberate U.S. citizens from captivity or to attack terrorist kidnappers and killers. *When used, these units are not expected to confront the military forces of a sovereign state.* In a real sense, therefore, action by an antiterrorist unit constitutes a use of force that is more analogous to law enforcement activity by police in the domestic context than it is to the "hostilities" between states contemplated by the War Powers Resolution. [*Id.* at 20-21 (statement of Abraham D. Sofaer, Legal Adviser to the Department of State) (emphasis in original).]

Do you agree? Can you find these distinctions in the Constitution? In the quoted language of the WPR? Suppose bin Laden and his network were intertwined with the Taliban (which ruled most of Afghanistan before the September 11 attacks), sharing resources and engaging in joint planning and defense. On this supposition, were the attackers stateless or state-sponsored? Should the President's legal authority for attacks in anticipatory self-defense turn on nice distinctions about the sponsorship of the terrorists?

6. ***Declaring War on al Qaeda?*** Formal declarations of war have always named belligerents that were sovereign states. Following the September 2001 terrorist attacks on the World Trade Center and the Pentagon, however, a newspaper columnist wrote and some members of Congress reportedly agreed that "Congress . . . should immediately declare war. It does not have to name a country. It can declare war against those who carried out [the] attack. . . ." Robert Kagan, *We Must Fight This War*, Wash. Post, Sept. 12, 2001, at A31. May Congress declare war on a group of people? May it declare war without naming any enemy at all? Should Congress have declared war on al Qaeda or on international terrorists after September 11?

7. ***The September 18, 2001, Resolution.*** How is the September 18 Authorization for Use of Military Force (generally referred to as AUMF) different from the bill the White House proposed? Does the AUMF's scope match the administration's rhetorical commitment to combating terrorists wherever they can be found and the states that give them support? Does its last clause serve as a limitation on the authority it bestows?

Is there any important difference between this law and a formal declaration of war against al Qaeda? Do these two different forms of legislative authority affect U.S. relations with other nations differently? Or the domestic powers of the President? Or the legal "dominoes" discussed *supra*?

8. ***The AUMF and the Invasion of Iraq.*** President George W. Bush and members of his administration asserted, or at least strongly suggested, that there was a link between Saddam Hussein and al Qaeda, and even that Saddam bore some responsibility for the 9/11 attacks. *See, e.g.*, State of the Union Address (Jan. 28, 2003) ("Saddam Hussein aids and protects terrorists, including members of al Qaeda"); remarks of National Security Adviser Condoleeza Rice, on Morning Show, CBS, Nov. 28, 2003 ("Oh, indeed there is a tie between Iraq and what happened on 9/11."). Examining the 2001 AUMF, can you see how such claims could be used to build a legal case for the invasion of Iraq, even without the passage of a later resolution specifically naming Iraq? How would you rebut that case?

3

# *TARGETED KILLING*

[A]ssassination, poison, perjury. . . . All these were considered legitimate principles in the dark ages which intervened between ancient and modern civilizations, but exploded and held in just horror in the 18th Century.

Thomas Jefferson[1]

I can assure you that no constitutional questions are raised here [referring to targeted killing by a U.S. unmanned aerial vehicle of senior al Qaeda official in Yemen and four others, including a U.S. citizen]. There are authorities that the president can give to officials [and] he's well within the balance of accepted practice and the letter of his constitutional authority.

Condoleezza Rice, National Security Adviser[2]

One hopes that each time you get a success like that [referring to the same attack], not only to have gotten rid of somebody dangerous, but to have imposed changes in their tactics and operations.

Paul Wolfowitz, U.S. Under Secretary of Defense for Policy[3]

On November 3, 2002, video feeds from television cameras on a 27-foot-long unmanned aerial vehicle with a 49-foot wingspan, called a Predator, flying slowly ten to fifteen thousand feet above the Marib province in Yemen, showed an RV speeding through the desert. A joint Yemeni and American intelligence team had for days been tracing cell phone calls by an al Qaeda leader named al-Harethi, and the team determined that he was in the car. Al-Harethi was a prime suspect in the suicide bombing of the USS *Cole*, which had killed 17 U.S. sailors. Using a joystick to control the Predator remotely, a U.S. operator fired a Hellfire missile from the plane, striking the RV dead center and killing all five of its passengers. Yemeni security officials later took the bodies to a hospital in Yemen's capital, where U.S. officials obtained DNA samples. They confirmed that the Predator attack had "taken out" al-Harethi. The officials also identified

---

1. Letter from Thomas Jefferson to James Madison, Aug. 28, 1789, 5 *Works of Thomas Jefferson* 264 (Paul Leicester Ford ed., 1905).
2. *Quoted in* Eblen Kaplan, *Targeted Killings* 2 (Council on Foreign Rel. Mar. 2, 2006).
3. *Quoted in US Still Opposes Targeted Killings,* BBC News, Nov. 6, 2002, *at* http://news.bbc.co.uk/2/hi/middle_east/2408031.stm.

one of the other victims as Kamal Derwish, a U.S. citizen who grew up near Buffalo and who reportedly recruited American Muslims for training in al Qaeda camps. *See* Seymour M. Hersh, *Manhunt*, New Yorker, Dec. 23, 2002, at 66.

The United States had conducted a targeted killing in the war on terrorism, a selective extra-judicial killing. Was it an assassination? If so, is assassination or targeted killing a "legitimate principle" today, after it had been discredited in the eighteenth century? Is such killing now "well within the balance of accepted practice and the letter of [the President's] constitutional authority"? The letter or spirit of incorporated international law? Legalities aside, was the targeted killing a "success" in the broader sense that its benefits exceed its costs?

This chapter addresses these issues. We begin with a background look at the law and practice of assassination before turning to a fuller account of targeted killings by the United States using the Predator and the legal and policy questions they raise.

## A.   LAW AND PRACTICE OF ASSASSINATION

In 1976, a congressional committee found evidence of CIA involvement in assassination plots against foreign leaders (including President Ngo Dinh Diem of South Vietnam, who was murdered in a coup, and General Rene Schneider of Chile, who died in a kidnapping attempt in an effort to prevent a change of government), but the committee was unable to determine whether such involvement had been approved by senior officials. *See* Select Comm. to Study Governmental Operations with Respect to Intelligence Activities (Church Comm.), *Alleged Assassination Plots Involving Foreign Leaders: An Interim Report*, 94th Cong. (1976) (*Church Comm. Report*). The CIA acknowledged, however, that it subsequently made payments to the Schneider kidnappers. *See* Central Intelligence Agency, *CIA Activities in Chile*, Sept. 18, 2000, *at* https://www.cia.gov/cia/reports/chile/index.html#15. When the Church Committee proposed legislation to forbid political assassinations, the Ford administration pre-emptively promulgated its own prohibition by executive order. The prohibition was carried forward, with slight modifications, in Executive Order No. 12,333, 46 Fed. Reg. 59,941 (Dec. 4, 1981), which remains in effect at this writing (2007):

> 2.11 Prohibition on Assassination. No person employed by or acting on behalf of the United States Government shall engage in, or conspire to engage in, assassination.
>
> 2.12 Indirect Participation. No agency of the Intelligence Community shall participate in or request any person to undertake activities forbidden by this Order. . . .

Partly owing to this prohibition, military actions against terrorists or their supporters before 1998 took pains to avoid any appearance of targeting specific persons.

Following the al Qaeda attacks on U.S. embassies in Kenya and Tanzania in 1998, however, President William Clinton reportedly made a secret presidential finding[4] authorizing lethal force in self-defense in connection with missile attacks against al Qaeda training camps in Afghanistan, described in Chapter 2. Three years later, following the September 11, 2001, attacks, President George W. Bush reportedly made another finding that authorized the CIA to target al Qaeda leaders anywhere in the world. The CIA had by then acquired a number of Predators, which it controlled remotely in cooperation with military commanders in the military campaign then starting in Afghanistan.

## W. HAYS PARKS, MEMORANDUM OF LAW: EXECUTIVE ORDER 12333 AND ASSASSINATION

Department of the Army Pamphlet 27-50-204, from Army Law. 4 (Dec. 1989)

1. *Summary.* Executive Order 12333 prohibits assassination as a matter of national policy, but does not expound on its meaning or application. This memorandum explores the term and analyzes application of the ban to military operations at three levels: (a) conventional military operations; (b) counterinsurgency operations; and (c) peacetime counterterrorist operations. It concludes that the clandestine, low visibility, or overt use of military force against legitimate targets in time of war, or against similar targets in time of peace where such individuals or groups pose an immediate threat to United States citizens or the national security of the United States, as determined by competent authority, does not constitute assassination or conspiracy to engage in assassination, and would not be prohibited by the proscription in EO 12333 or by international law. . . .

3. a. *Assassination in General.* . . . While assassination generally is regarded as an act of murder for political reasons, its victims are not necessarily limited to persons of public office or prominence. The murder of a private person, if carried out for political purposes, may constitute an act of assassination. For example, the 1978 "poisoned-tip umbrella" killing of Bulgarian defector Georgi Markov by Bulgarian State Security agents on the streets of London falls into the category of an act of murder carried out for political purposes, and constitutes an assassination. In contrast, the murder of Leon Klinghoffer, a private citizen, by the terrorist Abu el Abbas during the 1985 hijacking of the Italian cruise ship *Achille Lauro*, though an act of murder for political purposes, would not constitute an assassination. The distinction lies not merely in the purpose of the act and/or its intended victim, but also under certain circumstances in its covert nature.[1] Finally, the killings of Martin Luther

---

4. Intelligence oversight legislation requires the President, in order to authorize covert actions, to make a written finding that such action is "necessary to support identifiable foreign policy objectives of the United States and is important to the national security." 50 U.S.C. §413b(a) (2000). A finding may not authorize action "that would violate the Constitution or any statute of the United States," *id.* §413b(a)(5), and it must ordinarily be reported to the Intelligence Committees or at least a small circle of congressional leaders. *Id.* §413b(c).

1. *Covert operations* are defined as "operations which are planned and executed so as to conceal the identity of or permit plausible denial by the sponsor. They differ from clandestine operations in that emphasis is placed on concealment of identity of [the] sponsor rather than on concealment of the operation." In contrast, low visibility operations are . . . undertaken with the knowledge that the action and or sponsorship of the operation may preclude plausible denial by the initiating power. JCS Pub. 1, *Dictionary of Military and Associated Terms* (1 June 1987).

King and Presidents Abraham Lincoln, James A. Garfield, William McKinley and John F. Kennedy generally are regarded as assassination because each involved the murder of a public figure or national leader for political purposes accomplished through a surprise attack.

b. *Assassination in Peacetime.* In peacetime, the citizens of a nation — whether private individuals or public figures — are entitled to immunity from intentional acts of violence by citizens, agents, or military forces of another nation. Article 2(4) of the Charter of the United Nations provides that all Member States

> shall refrain in their international relations from the threat or use of force against the territorial integrity or political independence of any state, or in any manner inconsistent with the Purpose of the United Nations.

Peacetime assassination, then, would seem to encompass the murder of a private individual or public figure for political purposes, and in some cases also require that the act constitute a covert activity, particularly when the individual is a private citizen. Assassination is unlawful killing, and would be prohibited by international law even if there were no executive order proscribing it.

c. *Assassination in Wartime.* . . . In wartime the role of the military includes the legalized killing (as opposed to murder) of the enemy, whether lawful combatants or unprivileged belligerents, and may include in either category civilians who take part in the hostilities.

The term *assassination* when applied to wartime military activities against enemy combatants or military objectives does not preclude acts of violence involving the element of surprise. Combatants are liable to attack at any time or place, regardless of their activity when attacked. . . . An individual combatant's vulnerability to lawful targeting (as opposed to assassination) is not dependent upon his or her military duties, or proximity to combat as such. Nor does the prohibition on assassination limit means that otherwise would be lawful; no distinction is made between an attack accomplished by aircraft, missile, naval gunfire, artillery, mortar, infantry assault, ambush, land mine or boobytrap, a single shot by a sniper, a commando attack, or other, similar means. All are lawful means for attacking the enemy and the choice of one vis-a-vis another has no bearing on the legality of the attack. If the person attacked is a combatant, the use of a particular lawful means for attack (as opposed to another) cannot make an otherwise lawful attack either unlawful or an assassination.

Likewise, the death of noncombatants ancillary to the lawful attack of a military objective is neither assassination nor otherwise unlawful. Civilians and other noncombatants who are within or in close proximity to a military objective assume a certain risk through their presence in or in proximity to such targets. . . .

The scope of assassination in the U.S. military was first outlined in U.S. Army General Orders No. 100 (1863). Paragraph 148 states

> Assassination. The law of war does not allow proclaiming either an individual belonging to the hostile army, or a citizen, or a subject of the hostile

government, an outlaw, who may be slain without trial by any captor, any more than the modern law of peace allows such international outlawry; on the contrary, it abhors such outrage. . . .

This provision, consistent with the earlier writings of Hugo Grotius (Cf. Bk. III, Sec. XXXVIII(4)), has been continued in U.S. Army Field Manual 27-10, *The Law of Land Warfare* (1956), which provides (paragraph 31):

> (Article 23b, Annex to Hague Convention IV, 1907) is construed as prohibiting assassination, proscription, or outlawry of an enemy, or putting a price upon an enemy's head, as well as offering reward for an enemy "dead or alive." . . .

[4] *Conventional War.* . . . [An] unresolved issue concerns which civilians may be regarded as combatants, and therefore subject to lawful attack. While there is general agreement among the law of war experts that civilians who participate in hostilities may be regarded as combatants, there is no agreement as to the degree of participation necessary to make an individual civilian a combatant. . . . There is a lack of agreement on this matter, and no existing law of war treaty provides clarification or assistance. Historically, however, the decision as to the level at which civilians may be regarded as combatants or "quasi-combatants" and thereby subject to attack generally has been a policy rather than legal matter. . . .

[5] *Counterinsurgency.* Guerrilla warfare is particularly difficult to address because a guerrilla organization generally is divided into political and guerrilla (military) cadre, each garbed in civilian attire in order to conceal their presence or movement from the enemy. . . .

Just as members of conventional military units have an obligation to wear uniforms in order to distinguish themselves from the civilian population, civilians have an obligation to refrain from actions that might place the civilian population at risk. A civilian who undertakes military activities assumes a risk of attack, and efforts by military forces to capture or kill that individual would not constitute assassination.

The wearing of civilian attire does not make a guerrilla immune from lawful attack, and does not make a lawful attack on a guerrilla an act of assassination. As with the attack of civilians who have combatant responsibilities in conventional war, the difficulty lies in determining where the line should be drawn between guerrillas/combatants and the civilian population in order to provide maximum protection from intentional attack to innocent civilians. The law provides no precise answer to this problem, and one of the most heated debates arising during and after the U.S. war in Vietnam surrounded this issue. As with conventional war, however, ultimately the issue is settled along policy rather than legal lines. If a member of a guerrilla organization falls above the line established by competent authority for combatants, a military operation to capture or kill an individual designated as a combatant would not be assassination.

[6] *Peacetime operations.* The use of force in peacetime is limited by the previously cited article 2(4) of the Charter of the United Nations. However, article 51 of the Charter of the United Nations recognizes the inherent right of self defense of nations. Historically the United States has resorted to the use

of military force in peacetime where another nation has failed to discharge its international responsibilities in protecting U.S. citizens from acts of violence originating in or launched from its sovereign territory, or has been culpable in aiding and abetting international criminal activities. For example:

- 1804-1805: Marine First Lieutenant Presley O'Bannon led an expedition into Libya to capture or kill[6] the Barbary pirates.
- 1916: General "Blackjack" Pershing led a year-long campaign into Mexico to capture or kill the Mexican bandit Pancho Villa following Villa's attack on Columbus, New Mexico.
- 1928-1932: U.S. Marines conducted a successful campaign to capture or kill the Nicaraguan bandit leader Augusto Cesar Sandino.
- 1967: U.S. Army personnel assisted the Bolivian Army in its campaign to capture or kill Ernesto "Che" Guevara.
- 1985: U.S. naval forces were used to force an Egypt Air airliner to land at Sigonella, Sicily, in an attempt to prevent the escape of the *Achille Lauro* hijackers.
- 1986: U.S. naval and air forces attacked terrorist-related targets in Libya in response to the Libyan government's continued employment of terrorism as a foreign policy means.

Hence there is historical precedent for the use of military force to capture or kill individuals whose peacetime actions constitute a direct threat to U.S. citizens or national security.

The Charter of the United Nations recognizes the inherent right of self defense and does not preclude unilateral action against an immediate threat.

In general terms, the United States recognizes three forms of self defense:

a. Against an actual use of force, or hostile act.
b. Preemptive self defense against an imminent use of force.
c. Self defense against a continuing threat.[8]

A national decision to employ military force in self defense against a legitimate terrorist or related threat would not be unlike the employment of force in response to a threat by conventional forces; only the nature of the threat has changed, rather than the international legal right of self defense. The terrorist organizations envisaged as appropriate to necessitate or warrant an armed

---

6. In the employment of military force, the phrase "capture or kill" carries the same meaning or connotation in peacetime as it does in wartime. There is no obligation to capture rather than attack an enemy. In some cases, it may be preferable to utilize ground forces to capture (*e.g.*) a known terrorist. However, where the risk to U.S. forces is deemed too great, if the President has determined that the individual(s) pose such a threat to U.S. citizens as to require the use of military force, it would be legally permissible to employ (*e.g.*) an air strike against that individual or group rather than attempt his, her, or their capture, and would not constitute assassination.

8. . . . This right of self defense would be appropriate to the attack of terrorist leaders where their actions pose a continuing threat to U.S. citizens or the national security of the United States. As with an attack on a guerrilla infrastructure, the level to which attacks could be carried out against individuals within a terrorist infrastructure would be a policy rather than a legal decision.

response by U.S. military forces are well-financed, highly-organized paramilitary structures engaged in the illegal use of force.[9] . . .

# B.  TARGETED KILLING BY PREDATOR[5]

In October 2001, on the first night of the campaign against al Qaeda and the Taliban authorized by Congress after the September 11 attacks, a Predator deployed over southern Afghanistan apparently identified Taliban leader Mullah Mohammed Omar in a convoy of cars fleeing Kabul. Following its agreement with military commanders, the CIA operators sought approval from the United States Central Command in Tampa to launch a Hellfire missile at Omar, who by then had sought cover in a building with an estimated 100 guards. General Tommy Franks declined to give approval based on on-the-spot advice of his military lawyer. Other reports suggest that, in light of the number of possible casualties, he sought approval from the President, who personally approved the strike. But the resulting delay apparently allowed Omar to escape.

In February 2002, another Predator filmed a very tall man being greeted effusively by villagers. Osama bin Laden is said to be about six feet five inches tall. The order was quickly given to fire, but by that time the group had disbanded, and the Predator captured another image of a tall man and two others emerging from a wooded area. The Hellfire was launched, killing all three. Journalists later reported that they were locals who had been scavenging for wood. Bin Laden was not among them.

The abortive targeted killing of Mullah Omar reportedly prompted then-Secretary of Defense Donald Rumsfeld to order Special Operations units to prepare a plan for "hunter killer teams," who were ordered not just to "grab and snatch" terror suspects, but to kill them. Secretary Rumsfeld wanted to cut through the bureaucracy to be able to process kill orders "in minutes and hours, not days and weeks." When asked later about the factual basis for pre-emptive military actions, Rumsfeld gave an answer that could apply as well to targeted killings:

> We all would like perfection. We'd like all the dots connected for us with a ribbon wrapped around it. [Americans] want evidence beyond a reasonable doubt. You want to be able to be certain that you know before anyone's punished. My point is, this isn't punishment. We've got the wrong model in our minds if we're thinking about punishment. We're not. This isn't retaliation or retribution. [U.S. Dept. of Defense, *Secretary Rumsfeld's Media Roundtable with the BBC and Voice of America*, Nov. 16, 2002, *available at* http://www.defenselink.mil/Transcripts/Transcript.aspx?TranscriptID = 3652.]

---

9. In a conventional armed conflict, such individuals would be regarded as unprivileged belligerents, subject to attack, but not entitled to prisoner of war protection or exemption from prosecution for their crimes. Employment of military force against terrorists does not bestow prisoner of war protection upon members of the terrorist organization.

5. This brief report is drawn from William C. Banks, *The Predator* (Maxwell School of Citizenship & Pub. Affairs, Syracuse Univ., CS 0603-32, 2003); Kristen Eichensehr, *On the Offensive: Assassination Policy Under International Law*, 25 Harv. Intl. Rev. 1 (Fall 2003), *available at* http://hir.harvard.edu/articles/1149/3/; Hersh, *supra* p. 66, at 74; and Kaplan, *supra* p. 65.

Since September 11, 2001, Predators have reportedly been used at least 19 times to fire on targets in Afghanistan, Iraq, and elsewhere. A number of senior al Qaeda operatives have been killed in these attacks, including al Qaeda's reputed chief of military operations, Mohammed Atef. But mistakes continue to be made. On January 13, 2006, for example, a CIA-operated Predator fired on a target in Damadola in northern Pakistan, having apparently identified bin Laden deputy Ayman al-Zawahiri. When the dust cleared, 18 civilians were found dead, but al-Zawahiri was not among them. The attack set off angry anti-American demonstrations across northern Pakistan.

## NOTES AND QUESTIONS

1. *The Origins of the Executive Order Ban on Assassination.* As noted above, in 1976 the Church Committee proposed to criminalize the assassi-nation or attempted assassination of "any foreign official because of such official's political views, actions, or statements, while such official is outside the United States." *Church Comm. Report, supra* p. 66, at App. A. "Foreign official" was defined as "Chief of State or the political equivalent . . . of a foreign government . . . or of a foreign political group, party, military force, movement or other association with which the United States is not at war pursuant to a declaration of war or against which the United States Armed Forces have not been introduced into hostilities or situations pur-suant to the provisions of the War Powers Resolution." *Id.*

However, President Ford headed off such legislation by adopting Executive Order No. 11,905, 41 Fed. Reg. 7703 (Feb. 19, 1976), prohibiting U.S. employees from engaging in "political assassination." In 1978, President Carter replaced this order with Executive Order No. 12,036, 43 Fed. Reg. 3674 (Jan. 26, 1978), which expanded the prohibition to include agents of the United States, and which dropped, without explanation, the modifier "politi-cal." President Reagan retained Carter's language as sections 2.11 and 2.12 in the still-current Executive Order No. 12,333, set out above. *See generally* William C. Banks & Peter Raven-Hansen, *Targeted Killing and Assassination: The U.S. Legal Framework*, 37 U. Rich. L. Rev. 667, 717-726 (2003); Jonathan M. Fredman, *Covert Action, Loss of Life, and the Prohibition on Assassination*, 1 Studies in Intelligence 15 (1997 unclassified ed.).

2. *The Applicability of the Executive Order Prohibition.*

a. Would the executive order have barred the killing of Saddam Hussein, leader of Iraq, in 1991 during the first Gulf War, or in 2003, during the invasion of Iraq? *See* Stuart Taylor Jr., *Should We Just Kill Saddam?*, Legal Times, Feb. 4, 1991.

b. Would the prohibition have applied to General Manuel Antonio Noriega, leader of Panama? In 1989 the CIA was approached for help by Panamanian military officers who proposed a coup against Noriega after he nullified a national election that he had lost. The officers sought non-lethal assistance in the form of money and equipment, but they admitted that Noriega might be killed in the coup. Could the United States have legally furnished assistance? *See* David B. Ottaway & Don Oberdorfer,

*Administration Alters Assassination Ban,* Wash. Post, Nov. 4, 1989, at A1; David B. Ottaway, *CIA Aides Call Hill Rules No Hindrance,* Wash. Post, Oct. 18, 1989, at A14.

c. How about targeting Columbian drug trafficker Pablo Escobar, who reportedly conducted a campaign of narco-terror and assassination against the government of Columbia, and who was indicted in the United States for drug trafficking and multiple drug-related murders? *See* Mark Bowden, *Killing Pablo* (2001) (asserting that U.S. Special Forces were actively involved in his death).

d. After the September 11 terrorist attacks, President Bush stated that Osama bin Laden, who was alleged to have been behind both the 1998 embassy bombings and the September 11 attacks, should be taken "dead or alive." *Guard and Reserves "Define Spirit of America": Remarks by the President to Employees at the Pentagon,* Sept. 17, 2001. Could President Bush legally order the killing of bin Laden? *See, e.g.,* Robert F. Turner, *In Self-Defense, U.S. Has Right to Kill Terrorist bin Laden,* USA Today, Oct. 26, 1998, at 17A. In this regard, consider the following recommendation:

> The United States should adopt a[n assassination] program aimed not only at the heads of the [terrorist] networks, but also at the arms and the fingers. It should locate and assassinate the killers, the planners, and the trainers. It should go beyond the organizations to target those who finance them and those who tend to communications and logistics. The program should target officials of the governments that give terrorists shelter. None should feel safe who knowingly aid these organizations — whether they launder their money or their clothes. [Lawrence J. Siskind, *Our Killer Instinct,* Legal Times, Oct. 8, 2001.]

Would such a program be lawful under the executive order? Would it be wise, now that we have learned that the "arms and fingers" of the group that executed the September 11 attacks apparently made significant preparations in Germany and that they had financing from institutions in Switzerland and Saudi Arabia? *See* Barton Gellman, *CIA Weighs "Targeted Killing" Missions,* Wash. Post, Oct. 28, 2001, at A01 (reporting that senior managers in CIA's Directorate of Operations urged targeting not just al Qaeda's commanders, but also its financiers — "the Gucci guys, the guys who write the checks," because they are easier to find and because "it would have a tremendously chilling effect"). *See* Daniel Byman, *Do Targeted Killings Work?* 85 Foreign Aff. 95 (Mar./Apr. 2006).

3. ***Force and Effect of the Executive Order Ban.*** How do you think the legal force of the executive order ban was affected by President Reagan's secret intelligence findings authorizing lethal operations against Libyan leader Muammar al-Qadhafi (*see* Bob Woodward & Walter Pincus, *1984 Order Gave CIA Latitude; Reagan's Secret Move to Counter Terrorists Called "License to Kill,"* Wash. Post, Oct. 5, 1988, at A1), or by President Clinton's (*see* James Risen, *Bin Laden Was Target of Afghan Raid, U.S. Confirms,* N.Y. Times, Nov. 14, 1998, at A3) and President George W. Bush's findings authorizing lethal operations against bin Laden? *See* Memorandum from

Acting Asst. Attorney General Randolph D. Moss to the President, *Legal Effectiveness of a Presidential Directive as Compared to an Executive Order*, Jan. 29, 2000 (concluding that presidential directives — and, by implication, findings — can have the same substantive legal effect as an executive order, and that any such presidential decision, however it is memorialized, remains effective upon a change in administration and until subsequent presidential action is taken). *See also* Banks & Raven-Hansen, *supra* p. 72, at 725-726.

In the wake of the September 11 attacks, Representative Bob Barr introduced the Terrorist Elimination Act of 2001, which provided that sections 2.11 and 2.12 of Executive Order No. 12,333 "shall have no further force or effect." H.R. 19, 107th Cong. (2001). Is such a law necessary to permit the military to use military strikes to remove a terrorist leader, as the bill's proposed findings indicate? Would it be constitutional? *See* Banks & Raven-Hansen, *supra*, at 745-747.

4. *Targeted Killing and International Law.* The Parks memorandum suggests that assassination in peacetime is unlawful at international law, but that the use of military force in self-defense arguably is not. *See generally* Vincent-Joël Proulx, *If the Hat Fits, Wear It, If the Turban Fits, Run for Your Life: Reflections on the Indefinite Detention and Targeted Killing of Suspected Terrorists*, 56 Hastings L.J. 801 (2005); Jami Melissa Jackson, *The Legality of Assassination of Independent Terrorist Leaders: An Examination of National and International Implications*, 24 N.C. J. Intl. & Com. Reg. 669 (1999); Michael N. Schmitt, *State-Sponsored Assassination in International and Domestic Law*, 17 Yale J. Intl. L. 609 (1992); Patricia Zengel, *Assassination and the Law of Armed Conflict*, 43 Mercer L. Rev. 615 (1992). The analysis under international law may turn on whether the "war on terror" is really a law enforcement operation, to which the law of human rights applies, or an armed conflict, to which humanitarian law applies.

a. *Law Enforcement Model.* The law enforcement model rests on a presumption of innocence, a preference for arrest and detention by due process, and an insistence on credible evidence and fair trial before judicial punishment. *See generally* David Kretzmer, *Targeted Killing of Suspected Terrorists: Extra-Judicial Executions or Legitimate Means of Defence?*, 16 Eur. J. Intl. L. 171 (2005). Although law enforcement officials can use lethal force without a trial, the circumstances under which such use is lawful are extremely limited. Thus, a 1990 U.N. report concludes:

> Law enforcement officials shall not use firearms except in self-defence or defence of others against the imminent threat of death or serious injury to prevent the perpetration of a particularly serious crime involving grave threat to life, to arrest a person presenting such a danger and resisting their authority, or to prevent his or her escape, and only when less extreme means are insufficient to achieve these objectives. In any event, the lethal use of firearms may only be made when strictly unavoidable in order to protect life. [Eighth United Nations Congress on the Prevention of Crime and

the Treatment of Offenders, Havana, Cuba, Aug. 27-Sept. 7, 1990, *Basic Principles on the Use of Force and Firearms by Law Enforcement Officials*, U.N. Doc. A/CONF.144/28/Rev.1, at 112 ¶9 (1990).]

In effect, the imminence of the threat provides the evidence needed to justify the use of lethal force and obviates any need to prove the target's intention. Kretzmer, *supra*, at 182. But unless the strict requirements of imminence and necessity through unavailability of other means are satisfied, the use of lethal force by law enforcement officers would deny a suspected terrorist basic due process, "preventing the target from contesting the determination that he or she is a terrorist, and imposing a unilateral death penalty." Proulx, *supra*, at 889. Thus, "the very purpose of international human rights is defeated, whether through the violation of the right to a fair trial, the absolute circumvention of the right to liberty, or the disregard of the inherent right to life." *Id.* at 889-890.

If you adopt the view that counterterrorist efforts are law enforcement, how would you judge the U.S. Predator strike on al-Harethi in Yemen? The U.N. Special Rapporteur to the Commission on Human Rights reported his opinion that "the attack in Yemen constitutes a clear case of extrajudicial killing." U.N. Economic and Social Council, *Civil and Political Rights, Including the Questions of Disappearances and Summary Executions, submitted to Comm. on Human Rights*, U.N. Doc. E/CN.4/2003/3 (Jan. 13, 2003). The Swedish Foreign Minister reached a similar conclusion, calling the attack "a summary execution that violates human rights. Terrorists must be treated according to international law. Otherwise, any country can start executing those whom they consider terrorists." *Quoted in* Hersh, *supra* p. 66, at 4. Do you agree? Does it matter whether the targeted killing is in the relatively lawless northern tribal region of Pakistan or in Somalia — or in Germany? Note that although Yemeni officials apparently cooperated in the targeted killing of al-Harethi, they had previously failed to apprehend him and may have been reluctant to do so because of a perceived debt owed to bin Laden, who had assisted the Yemeni president in putting down a separatist movement in 1994. Should the availability of the "normal judicial channels" that the law enforcement advocates urge make a difference in the law enforcement analysis? Should it matter that one of the persons in the RV in Yemen was an American?

b. *The War Model.* As the Parks memo suggests, under the law of armed conflict and international humanitarian law, the legality of a targeted killing depends on the status of the target rather than on his actions. *See also* Kretzmer, *supra*, at 190. Combatants are fair game (and the "legality of an attack on a military unit is not dependent on the imminence of military action by that unit"), *id.* at 191, but civilians cannot be the object of attack "unless and for such time as they take a direct part in hostilities." Protocol Additional (No. 1) to the Geneva Conventions of Aug. 12, 1949, and Relating to the Protection of Victims of International Armed Conflicts, §51(3), June 8, 1977, 1125 U.N.T.S. 3. Although the United States is not a party to this protocol, this principle has been characterized as customary international law. *See, e.g.,* HCJ 769/02 Public Comm. Against Torture in Israel v. Government of Israel [2005] IsrSC, at 21 (favorably citing "position of the Red Cross"), *available at* http://elyon1.court.gov.il/Files_ENG/02/690/007/a34/02007690.a34.pdf.

This principle of "distinction" between combatants and noncombatant civilians poses a difficult classification problem when terrorists are targets. Are they enemy combatants, civilians who have lost their immunity from attack by virtue of their direct part in hostilities, or "unlawful combatants" (in effect outlaws), a new category unknown to the traditional law of war or humanitarian law?

Calling them enemy combatants makes it lawful to kill them without any imminence requirement, as the Parks memo suggests, but it may also entitle them to combatant rights, including rights of prisoners of war.

Calling them civilians who have taken a direct part in hostilities presents a further definitional problem. It is easy enough to identify hostilities, but which civilians take a "direct part" in them? Adopting this definition of terrorists for purposes of judging targeted killings, the Israeli Supreme Court found that persons taking a "direct part" include:

> a person who collects intelligence on the army . . . ; a person who transports unlawful combatants to or from the place where the hostilities are taking place; a person who operates weapons which unlawful combatants use, or supervises their operation, or provides service to them, be the distance from the battlefield as it may. . . . However, a person who sells food or medicine to an unlawful combatant is not taking a direct part, rather than an indirect part in the hostilities. The same is the case regarding a person who aids the unlawful combatants by general strategic analysis, and grants them logistical, general support, including monetary aid. The same is the case regarding a person who distributes propaganda supporting these unlawful combatants. . . .
>
> . . . What says the law about those who enlist him to take a direct part in the hostilities, and those who send him to commit hostilities? Is there a difference between his direct commanders and those responsible for them? Is the "direct" part taken only by the last terrorist in the chain of command, or by the entire chain? In our opinion, the "direct" character of the part taken should not be narrowed merely to the person committing the physical act of attack. Those who have sent him, as well, take "a direct part." The same goes for the person who decided upon the act, and the person who planned it. It is not to be said about them that they are taking an indirect part in the hostilities. Their contribution is direct (and active). [*Id.* at 26-27.]

By this standard, which of the targets listed in Note 2, above, could properly be characterized as civilians who take a "direct part"?

Even if targets do fall into this category, they are lawful targets only for "such time" as they take a direct part. A civilian who takes a direct part but then separates himself from hostilities regains his immunity from targeted killing. But what of a terrorist who only involves himself in attacks from time to time? The Israeli Supreme Court concluded that

> a civilian who has joined a terrorist organization which has become his "home," and in the framework of his role in that organization he commits a chain of hostilities, with short periods of rest between them, loses his immunity from attack "for such time" as he is committing the chain of acts. Indeed, regarding such a civilian, the rest between hostilities is nothing other than preparation for the next hostility. [*Id.* at 28.]

c. *Proportionality.* Even for targets who meet these standards, international law still requires "proportionality"—that the destruction of civilian lives and property from the attack ("collateral damage") be proportional to its military benefits. *Id.* at 30-31 (setting out authorities). An attack on terrorists violates this principle "if it 'may be expected to cause incidental loss of civilian life, injury to civilians, damage to civilian objects, or a combination thereof, which would be excessive in relation to the concrete and direct military advantage anticipated.'" Kretzmer, *supra*, at 200 (quoting Judith Gail Gardam, *Proportionality and Force in International Law*, 87 Am. J. Intl. L. 391 (1993)). The principle of proportionality also requires consideration of whether there is a less harmful alternative to targeted killing, such as arrest, that can achieve the same benefits.

By these standards of international humanitarian law, how would you judge the Predator attacks described above?

d. *Incorporation as U.S. Law?* Even if a particular targeted killing is unlawful under international law, would that make it unlawful under our law? *See* U.S. Const. art. VI. Suppose the President has ordered it? *See supra* pp. 47-48 (discussing the President's authority in relation to customary international law).

5. **Target Selection.** The brief report, above, on the use of the Predator noted several reported presidential findings authorizing targeted killing of al Qaeda operatives. But the intelligence oversight legislation requires such findings only for "covert actions." 50 U.S.C. §413b(a) (2000). Does it apply to targeted killings by Predators? If the Predators are operated by military pilots and the killing decision is made by military commanders, do intelligence oversight requirements applicable to the intelligence community even apply? *See generally* Philip B. Heymann & Juliette N. Kayyem, *Protecting Liberty in an Age of Terror* 59-68 (2005).

Whether they do or not, what evidentiary standard, if any, should the administration use in deciding on a targeted killing? *See* Byman, *supra* p. **73**, at 108 (faulting the United States for the absence of "clear, transparent, and legitimate procedures for deciding when targeted killings are appropriate"). Since the decision is to kill someone, is the appropriate standard the one that is used in a capital criminal case: beyond a reasonable doubt? Recall Secretary Rumsfeld's response, *supra* p. 71. A student has argued that "[t]argeted killings *do not* substitute for apprehension, prosecution, and court-ordered punishment . . . [;] they substitute for *overt use of military or paramilitary force.*" Brian P. Finnegan, *Assassination, U.S. Law, and the International Use of Lethal Force* 33 (Nov. 17, 2000) (on file with authors) (emphasis in original).

On the other hand, our experience with the Predator highlights the potential for mistakes. One scholar argues that the potential is so great that "in many regards, the practice of targeted killing is often an indiscriminate attack by definition." Proulx, *supra,* at 888. The Israeli Supreme Court has therefore insisted on "well based . . . thoroughly verified information" regarding the identity, activity, and therefore proper categorization of the intended target *before* the decision is made, as well as "a thorough investigation regarding the precision of the identification of the target and the circumstances of the attack upon him" *after* the attack. *Public Comm. Against Torture, supra* p. 76, at 29. Should the standard also include the gravity of the risk posed by the target? Would your answer change if targeted killing were used as a tool of policy not just against terrorists but also against other transnational criminals, such as drug-traffickers? How thorough can pre-attack verification be if the decision has to be made in "minutes and hours," as Secretary Rumsfeld said, and not days?

6. ***Costs and Benefits of Targeted Killing.*** As our opening quotation from Undersecretary of Defense Wolfowitz suggested, targeted killing of the leaders of a terrorist group can change the group's organizational behavior. Constant elimination of its leaders can cause confusion and disarray; successors become paranoid and secretive, impeding their ability to communicate with their members; and members become fearful about communicating even with one another. The terrorists spend more and more of their time protecting themselves, with correspondingly less time to attack others. *See, e.g.,* Byman, *supra* p. 73, at 102-104 (reporting significant drop-off in Israeli civilian deaths from terrorist attacks "partly because Israel's targeted killings have shattered Palestinian terrorist groups and made it difficult for them to conduct effective operations"); Gal Luft, *The Logic of Israel's Targeted Killing,* 10 Middle East Q. 1 (Winter 2003). Lives are saved by attacks averted. In addition, the targeted killing of a suspected terrorist may cause fewer casualties (and lower costs) among counterterrorist forces than seeking to make an arrest in hostile territory, let alone invading to destroy the terrorist's group. *See* Eichensehr, *supra* p. 71, at 4. For example, 17 U.S. Army Rangers and hundreds of Somalis lost their lives during an unsuccessful U.S. effort on behalf of the United Nations to arrest a Somali war lord in Mogadishu in 1993. *See* Stephen Dycus et al., *National Security Law* 329 (4th ed. 2007). Furthermore, extradition and prosecution may not be viable alternatives to the use of force when the terrorists take refuge in failed or sympathetic states. Finally, targeted killing satisfies domestic demands for the government to "do something" after a society has suffered terrorist attacks. *See* Byman, *supra,* at 102. Can you identify other benefits from targeted killing?

On the other hand, targeted killings carry significant costs as well. *See generally id.* at 100, 106; Eichensehr, *supra,* at 4; Luft, *supra,* at 4. Terrorist groups adjust to decapitations; their decentralization largely negates the disruptive effect by creating many, or no, leaders. Successful targeted killing requires a heavy investment in real-time continuing intelligence and surveillance as well as rapid response capability. Byman, *supra*, at 100 (quoting a former Israeli intelligence director as saying, "When a Palestinian child draws a picture of the sky, he doesn't draw it without a helicopter."). Even a successful killing may only create a martyr for the terrorists and perversely help them to recruit others, and it will often prompt retaliation. Finally, as the discussion of international law should suggest, targeted killing carries serious diplomatic costs, not just for negotiations to end the terrorism or to coordinate allies in the counterterrorist effort, but also for diplomatic efforts to condemn targeted killing by other states. Can you think of other costs of targeted killing? Should we include a moral cost in the calculus?

How would you balance costs and benefits of targeted killings by the United States in Afghanistan? In Northern Pakistan? In Italy?

7. ***Targeted Killing at Home?*** It is important to keep in mind that the executive order and all the discussion about it contemplate only targeted killings or assassinations of foreign persons *abroad*. A variety of laws, in addition to ordinary criminal laws, seemingly prohibit the use of such tools against any person in the United States. *See, e.g.,* U.S. Const. amend. V (providing that "no person" shall be deprived of life "without due process of law"); Posse Comitatus Act, 18 U.S.C. §1385 (2000), *infra* p. 671 (prohibiting the U.S. Army or Air Force from executing the laws without express constitutional or statutory authority); National Security Act of 1947, 50 U.S.C.A. §403-4a(d) (2003 & West Supp. 2006) (prohibiting the CIA from performing "internal security functions"); Idaho v. Horiuchi, 253 F.3d 359, 377 (9th Cir. 2001) (asserting, in a suit growing out of the Ruby Ridge killing by an FBI sharpshooter, that "wartime rules" of engagement permitting the targeting of suspects who pose no "immediate threat . . . [are] patently unconstitutional for a police action"), *vacated as moot*, 266 F.3d 986 (9th Cir. 2001).

Even assuming that the President could disregard these authorities, would a targeted killing of José Padilla as he stepped off the plane in Chicago meet *any* of the standards discussed in these notes?

8. ***Recommendations for Targeted Killing.*** Two scholars have suggested that targeted killing should be confined to "a designated zone of active combat" designated by the President "as constituting a theater of military operations" in connection with a declared war "or other armed conflict" between the United States and a foreign state, organization, or defined class of individuals or within occupied territory or territory in which the United States has been asked to assist with suppression of an armed insurrection. Heymann & Kayyem, *supra*, at 62-63, 65. Within that zone, they would permit targeted killing in compliance with the following proposed statutory standards:

**II.  Targeted Killing Outside a Designated Zone of Active Combat**

A. In all situations and locations outside designated zones of active combat, any targeted killing must be pursuant to procedures outlined in legislation detailing the conditions for such an action.

### III. Standards for the Use of Targeted Killing

A. Any such authorization of targeting a particular individual outside a zone of active combat must be justified as necessary to prevent a greater, reasonably imminent harm or in defense against a reasonably imminent threat to the life of one or more persons.

1. To be "necessary" there must be no reasonable alternative such as arrest or capture followed by detention.

2. To be "reasonably imminent" there must be a real risk that any delay in the hope of developing an alternative would result in a significantly increased risk of the lethal attack.

3. Retribution for past events, as opposed to prevention of future attacks, cannot justify a targeted killing.

B. Under familiar rules applicable to military action under the laws of war, the action taken must be proportionate to the objective to be obtained, and the selection of the time, place and means employed must avoid to the extent reasonably possible harm to innocent persons.

C. Even when these conditions are met, there shall be no targeted killing of:

1. A U.S. person,

2. Any person found in the United States, or

3. An individual found in any state that has previously agreed to and displayed a willingness to try, extradite, or otherwise incapacitate those reasonably suspected of planning terrorist attacks on U.S. citizens and facilities.

D. Any decision to target an identified individual for killing must be approved by the President of the United States in a finding, provided to appropriate committees of the Congress, and setting forth:

1. The evidence on which the necessary conclusion of imminent danger has been made,

2. The alternatives considered and the basis for rejecting them and

3. The reasons for concluding that the conditions of Sections III. A-C have been met.

E. The President shall promulgate detailed procedures for making these findings reliably and for maintaining a permanent record, available to appropriate committees of Congress, of any such decision.

F. The rules described in Section III.E shall be made public. Particular findings in any individual case and the fact that such targeting was approved by the President need not be made public, but must be provided to appropriate committees of the Congress. [Adapted from Heymann & Kayyem, *supra* p. 77, at 59-61.]

How would these standards fare according to the international law summarized above? According to U.S. constitutional law? How would you change them?

# PART III

# DETECTING AND PREVENTING TERRORISM

# CHAPTER 4

# THE FOURTH AMENDMENT AND COUNTERTERRORISM

Since the birth of our nation, Americans have worried about espionage committed by hostile foreign agents. In recent times, we have also become the target of violent terrorist acts at home and abroad. To gather information about these threats to national security, we have employed many of the same techniques that are used in ordinary criminal investigations, including wiretaps; undercover agents and informants; physical searches of persons and places; and, more recently, sophisticated computer technologies, including e-mail intercepts and data mining.

In almost every instance, these measures have succeeded in protecting the American people from harm. In the process, however, government officials have occasionally lost sight of their mission, or strayed from it, and have violated individual privacy rights, just as in any criminal investigation gone awry. Where the subject of a probe is a possible terrorist act, which may be politically motivated, First Amendment freedoms of assembly and expression may be implicated as well. Special care is thus required in sorting out protected activities from those that could lead to violence or serious disruption of society and in selecting appropriate investigative techniques for each.

This sorting-out process is often complicated by a lack of information about the exact nature of suspected threats. While no one argues that a mere hunch about anticipated violent acts or subversion will justify surveillance of potential targets, something less than a completed illegal act must suffice. Thus, the development of standards for approval of investigations into national security threats is a critical legal issue.

In this and the succeeding five chapters we focus on intelligence collection operations within the United States and abroad—electronic surveillance; physical searches; infiltration of groups by informants; the collection of tangible and electronic transactional records, such as travel records, telephone dialing and billing information, bank records, and library records; and data mining of the resulting databases, among others. In this chapter, we start with a short primer on the Fourth Amendment, then examine the Supreme Court's seminal analysis of the President's claim of inherent authority to conduct warrantless electronic surveillance in domestic security investigations. We then consider subsequent lower court case law exploring the contours of an inherent executive authority for such surveillance in foreign intelligence investigations. In Chapter 5, we turn to statutory authority for electronic foreign intelligence surveillance in the Foreign Intelligence Surveillance Act (FISA) and related legislation. In Chapter 6, we take up statutory authority for investigatory collection of tangible and electronic transactional records from third parties, using court orders, national security letters, and subpoenas. In Chapter 7, we consider a range of other surveillance and collection techniques used to profile and "watchlist" terrorist suspects and to screen access to transportation systems, critical infrastructure, and other possible targets for terrorism. In Chapter 8, we assess self-imposed executive branch rules for internal security investigations, and we examine how counterterrorism investigations are coordinated among various agencies and overseen by Congress and the Executive. Our primary focus throughout the foregoing chapters is on domestic surveillance, but the "Global War on Terror" is, as its name suggests, also conducted abroad. In Chapter 9, we therefore turn to the U.S. law, if any, governing national security surveillance abroad.

## A. DETECTION OF TERRORIST THREATS

### WILLIAM C. BANKS & M.E. BOWMAN, EXECUTIVE AUTHORITY FOR NATIONAL SECURITY SURVEILLANCE

50 Am. U. L. Rev. 1, 92-94 (2001)

Terrorism presents a unique set of challenges in the United States. First, current criminal laws and traditional law enforcement processes cannot provide absolute protection against terrorist acts. While arrest, prosecution, and incarceration serve well to help prevent most crimes from occurring, the risk of catastrophic harm from terrorist attacks forces us to consider other means of prevention. Moreover, traditional Fourth Amendment requirements may thwart many investigations of terrorism, which depend on stealth to prevent terrorist plans before they are carried out.

Second, while terrorism is at its core a national security problem, it represents an unusual confluence of phenomena for the investigative community — the primary purpose of the investigation may be simultaneously and in equal measure law enforcement and national security. With few exceptions, the rules for gathering intelligence about terrorism in the United States are no different from the rules for ordinary criminal investigations.

Third, most prognostications are for more threats of terrorism in the United States in coming years, largely due to the perception that our defenses against conventional attacks are so formidable. Greater threats thus place an additional premium on greater intelligence resources and successes.

The tradition of liberty in the United States casts a shadow over all national security surveillance, and is an overriding problem in addressing terrorism concerns. The core openness of our society permits all of us, including the potential terrorist, considerable freedom to move about, to associate with others, and to act in furtherance of political aims. As recent terrorist incidents in the United States have created a sense of urgency among citizens and government officials to find better preventive strategies, reflection has also reminded us that hasty actions to thwart terrorism may threaten the freedoms that permit an open society. Thus, in seeking ways to investigate potential terrorist activity, just as in fashioning better responses to terrorist incidents, the measures adopted must not undermine our basic freedoms.

## STATEMENT OF JOHN ASHCROFT, ATTORNEY GENERAL, U.S. FEDERAL EFFORTS TO COMBAT TERRORISM

Hearing Before the Subcomm. on Commerce, Justice, and State, the Judiciary, and Related Agencies of the S. Comm. on Appropriations, 107th Cong. (2001)

... The Department of Justice is responsible for the investigation and prosecution of terrorist acts that violate U.S. law, wherever they occur. It has been involved in responding to overseas terrorist acts against U.S. interests for more than a decade and a half and has been involved in addressing terrorist acts at home for an even longer period. While we continue to make adjustments designed to improve our law enforcement response and to prepare for the challenges presented by the evolving nature of terrorist activity, the fact is that the Department's enforcement program related to terrorism is one which has had an opportunity to be fine tuned through experience. ...

It goes without saying that the paramount objective of U.S. counterterrorism policy is the prevention of terrorist acts. This requires both intelligence and investigative capabilities working together to detect and react effectively to incipient terrorist threats. By making effective use of intelligence information, we seek to involve the FBI in the investigation of terrorist plots as early in the chain of conspiratorial events as possible. In this way, the terrorist plot can not only be disrupted, but the conspirators can also be apprehended, preventing them from recycling their terrorist plans for use at some unknown future time and place.

This objective of preventing terrorist acts before they occur requires the collection and effective use of foreign intelligence and foreign counterintelligence to detect and to react to terrorist threats before they occur. The Department of Justice supports the collection efforts of U.S. intelligence agencies by representing them at the Foreign Intelligence Surveillance Court and obtaining the necessary warrants under the Foreign Intelligence Surveillance Act (FISA). In addition, under Executive Order 12333, the Attorney General approves the proposals of U.S. intelligence agencies to collect against U.S. persons overseas who are suspected of international terrorist activities. To enable effective use of the intelligence collected on terrorists under FISA and the Executive Order, the Attorney General also approves the passage of such intelligence to authorities in a position to prevent the planning, movement, or other actions of terrorists. ...

Some of our successes in prevention must necessarily remain secret. But some can be described. Several international terrorist plots have been prevented through effective law enforcement efforts.

1. For example, overseas, the Department worked with other U.S. agencies and our foreign counterparts to disrupt a bomb plot in 1995 which, if carried to

completion, would have resulted in the destruction of a dozen U.S. commercial jumbo jets flying Asian-Pacific routes. Three terrorists involved in the plot were arrested in distant countries, brought to the U.S., and convicted in federal court.

2. Within the United States, investigative efforts resulted in the arrest, and subsequent conviction, of Sheik Omar Abdel Rahman and a number of his followers in 1993 before they could carry out a deadly plot to bomb buildings, tunnels, and a bridge in Manhattan. Prevention of these two terrorist plots alone probably averted the death or serious injury of tens of thousands of Americans.

3. More recently, on December 14, 1999, Ahmed Ressam was arrested entering the United States from Canada with powerful explosives and timing devices. He has just been convicted of all counts of a nine count indictment, including the charge of an act of terrorism transcending national boundaries.

Similarly, a number of potentially deadly terrorist acts planned by domestic terrorists have been prevented. . . .

## FACT SHEET: PLOTS, CASINGS, AND INFILTRATIONS REFERENCED IN PRESIDENT BUSH'S REMARKS ON THE WAR ON TERROR

Oct. 6, 2005

Overall, the United States and our partners have disrupted at least ten serious al-Qaida terrorist plots since September 11 — including three al-Qaida plots to attack inside the United States. We have stopped at least five more al-Qaida efforts to case targets in the United States or infiltrate operatives into our country.

### 10 Plots

*The West Coast Airliner Plot*: In mid-2002 the U.S. disrupted a plot to attack targets on the West Coast of the United States using hijacked airplanes. The plotters included at least one major operational planner involved in planning the events of 9/11.

*The East Coast Airliner Plot*: In mid-2003 the U.S. and a partner disrupted a plot to attack targets on the East Coast of the United States using hijacked commercial airplanes.

*The Jose Padilla Plot*: In May 2002 the U.S. disrupted a plot that involved blowing up apartment buildings in the United States. One of the plotters, Jose Padilla, also discussed the possibility of using a "dirty bomb" in the U.S.

*The 2004 UK Urban Targets Plot*: In mid-2004 the U.S. and partners disrupted a plot that involved urban targets in the United Kingdom. These plots involved using explosives against a variety of sites.

*The 2003 Karachi Plot*: In the Spring of 2003 the U.S. and a partner disrupted a plot to attack Westerners at several targets in Karachi, Pakistan.

*The Heathrow Airport Plot*: In 2003 the U.S. and several partners disrupted a plot to attack Heathrow Airport using hijacked commercial airliners. The planning for this attack was undertaken by a major 9/11 operational figure.

*The 2004 UK Plot*: In the Spring of 2004 the U.S. and partners, using a combination of law enforcement and intelligence resources, disrupted a plot to conduct large-scale bombings in the UK.

*The 2002 Arabian Gulf Shipping Plot*: In late 2002 and 2003 the U.S. and a partner nation disrupted a plot by al-Qaida operatives to attack ships in the Arabian Gulf.

*The 2002 Straits of Hormuz Plot*: In 2002 the U.S. and partners disrupted a plot to attack ships transiting the Straits of Hormuz.

*The 2003 Tourist Site Plot*: In 2003 the U.S. and a partner nation disrupted a plot to attack a tourist site outside the United States.

### 5 Casings and Infiltrations

*The U.S. Government & Tourist Sites Tasking*: In 2003 and 2004, an individual was tasked by al-Qaida to case important U.S. Government and tourist targets within the United States.

*The Gas Station Tasking*: In approximately 2003, an individual was tasked to collect targeting information on U.S. gas stations and their support mechanisms on behalf of a senior al-Qaida planner.

*Iyman Faris & the Brooklyn Bridge*: In 2003, and in conjunction with a partner nation, the U.S. government arrested and prosecuted Iyman Faris, who was exploring the destruction of the Brooklyn Bridge in New York. Faris ultimately pleaded guilty to providing material support to al-Qaida and is now in a federal correctional institution.

*2001 Tasking*: In 2001, al-Qaida sent an individual to facilitate post-September 11 attacks in the U.S. U.S. law enforcement authorities arrested the individual.

*2003 Tasking*: In 2003, an individual was tasked by an al-Qaida leader to conduct reconnaissance on populated areas in the U.S.

# B. THE FOURTH AMENDMENT FRAMEWORK

WILLIAM C. BANKS & M.E. BOWMAN, EXECUTIVE AUTHORITY FOR NATIONAL SECURITY SURVEILLANCE

50 Am. U. L. Rev. 1, 2-4 (2001)

The British general warrant was a search tool employed without limitation on location, and without any necessity to precisely describe the object or person sought. British authorities were simply given license to "break into any shop or place suspected" wherever they chose. With that kind of unfettered discretion, the general warrant could be, and often was, used to intimidate. General warrants executed during the reign of Charles I sought to intimidate dissidents, authors, and printers of seditious material by ransacking homes and seizing personal papers. In 1765, the courts declared general warrants illegal, and Parliament followed a year later.

In the colonies, complaints that royal officials were violating the privacy of colonists through the use of writs of assistance, equivalent to general warrants, grew. Because English law did not, as yet, recognize a right of personal privacy, the crown's abuses in the colonies were not remediable at law. It was thus no surprise that the new American Constitution and the government it created would respect a series of individual freedoms. . . .

Although the Fourth Amendment eliminated the abuses of general warrants, its commands remain unclear, especially in the face of technological progress. Moreover, the Fourth Amendment was designed to protect against overreaching in investigations of criminal enterprises. Investigations of politically motivated threats to our national security, such as terrorism or espionage, were simply not contemplated.

-------

The Fourth Amendment to the United States Constitution provides:

The right of the people to be secure in their persons, houses, papers, and effects, against unreasonable searches and seizures shall not be violated, and no Warrants shall issue, but upon probable cause, supported by Oath or affirmation, and particularly describing the place to be searched, and the persons or things to be seized.

The Fourth Amendment limits government authority to conduct searches for various purposes, from criminal law enforcement to safety and health inspections of homes and businesses. The Fourth Amendment concern in this chapter arises because the techniques used in enforcing the criminal laws are also used in gathering intelligence for national security or counterterrorism, and because some such intelligence is obtained for use in criminal prosecutions. In this setting, most Fourth Amendment challenges to intelligence gathering concern electronic surveillance or the physical entry required for the installation of electronic, audio, or video equipment.

Apart from the fact that the Framers could not have foreseen problems of adapting the Amendment to electronic communication, the Fourth Amendment's two clauses—the protection against "unreasonable searches and seizures" and the warrant requirement—present a threshold problem of interpretation. Is a warrantless search *per se* unreasonable? In 1967, the Supreme Court held that warrantless searches "are *per se* unreasonable — subject only to a few specifically established and well-delineated exceptions." Katz v. United States, 389 U.S. 347, 357 (1967). Thus, exceptions are recognized for searches incident to arrest, *see, e.g.*, United States v. Robinson, 414 U.S. 218 (1973); automobile searches, Michigan v. Long, 463 U.S. 1032 (1983); "stop and frisk" searches, Terry v. Ohio, 392 U.S. 1 (1968); searches of persons and things entering and leaving the United States, United States v. Montoya de Hernandez, 473 U.S. 531 (1985), United States v. Duncan, 693 F.2d 971 (9th Cir. 1982); searches of boats on navigable waters, United States v. Villamonte-Marquez, 462 U.S. 579 (1983); and searches of airplanes, United States v. Nigro, 727 F.2d 100 (6th Cir. 1984) (*en banc*). The Supreme Court has also maintained that warrantless searches may be conducted to prevent railroad accidents that cause "great human loss," Skinner v. Railway Labor Executives' Assn., 489 U.S. 602, 628 (1989), or to address the potential spread of disease or contamination during a public health crisis, Camara v. Municipal Court, 387 U.S. 523, 539 (1967).

In view of the devastation wrought by the airline hijackings on September 11, 2001, any effort to defend warrantless preboarding airplane searches appears almost prosaic:

> When the risk is the jeopardy to hundreds of human lives and millions of dollars of property inherent in the pirating or blowing up of a large airplane, that danger alone meets the test of reasonableness, so long as the search is con- ducted in good faith for the purpose of preventing hijacking or like damage and with reasonable scope, and the passenger has been given notice of his liability to such a search so that he can avoid it by choosing not to travel by air. [United States v. Edwards, 498 F.2d 496, 500 (2d Cir. 1974).]

*See also* John Rogers, *Bombs, Borders, and Boarding: Combating International Terrorism at United States Airports and the Fourth Amendment*, 20 Suffolk Transnatl. L. Rev. 501 (1997); *infra* Chapter 7.

The reasoning in the decisions noted above might be thought to excuse the warrant requirement for surveillance in other kinds of cases implicating national security. It might, for example, be used to justify warrantless elec- tronic surveillance of Americans suspected in some way of being connected to terrorist threats. Or it might provide the basis for video surveillance of streets, parks, and other public places. But if there is an exception to the warrant requirement when surveillance involves national security concerns, what pro- cedures should substitute for the warrant process? The existence of a possible national security exception to the warrant requirement, and the effects of new technologies on this constitutional doctrine, are the primary issues explored in the following section.

# C.   A NATIONAL SECURITY EXCEPTION?

## FOREIGN INTELLIGENCE SURVEILLANCE ACT OF 1977

S. Rep. No. 95-604, at 9-12 (1977) [hereinafter *Senate Report No. 604*]

. . . In 1928, the Supreme Court in Olmstead v. United States [277 U.S. 468] held that wiretapping was not within the coverage of the Fourth Amendment. Three years later, Attorney General William D. Mitchell authorized telephone wiretapping, upon the personal approval of bureau chiefs, of syndicated bootleggers and in "exceptional cases where the crimes are substantial and serious, and the necessity is great and [the bureau chief and the Assistant Attorney General] are satisfied that the persons whose wires are to be tapped are of the criminal type." These general guidelines governed the Department's practice through the thirties and telephone wiretapping was considered to be an important law enforcement tool.

Congress placed the first restrictions on wiretapping in the Federal Communications Act of 1934, which made it a crime for any person "to intercept and divulge or publish the contents of wire and radio communications." [48 Stat. 1103.] The Supreme Court construed this section to apply to Federal agents and held that evidence obtained from the interception of wire and radio communications and the fruits of the evidence, were inadmissible to court. [Nardone v. United States, 302 U.S. 379 (1937); 308 U.S. 338 (1939).] However, the Justice Department did not interpret the Federal Communications Act or the *Nardone* decision as prohibiting the interception of wire communications per se; rather only the interception and divulgence of their contents outside the Federal establishment was considered to be unlawful. Thus, the Justice Department found continued authority for its national security wiretaps.

In 1940, President Roosevelt issued a memorandum to the Attorney General stating his view that electronic surveillance would be proper under the Constitution where "grave matters involving defense of the nation" were involved. The President authorized and directed the Attorney General "to secure information by listening devices [directed at] the conversation or other communications of persons suspected of subversive activities against the Government of the United States, including suspected spies." The Attorney General was requested "to limit these investigations so conducted to a minimum and to limit them insofar as possible to aliens."

This practice was continued in successive administrations. . . .

In the early fifties, however, Attorney General J. Howard McGrath took the position that he would not approve or authorize the installation of microphone surveillances by means of trespass. This policy was quickly reversed by Attorney General Herbert Brownell in 1954 in a sweeping memorandum to FBI Director Hoover instructing him that the Bureau was indeed authorized to conduct such trespassory surveillances regardless of the fact of surreptitious entry, and without the need to first acquire the Attorney General's authorization. Such surveillance was simply authorized whenever the Bureau concluded that the "national interest" so required. . . .

In Katz v. United States, 389 U.S. 347 (1967), the Supreme Court finally discarded the *Olmstead* doctrine and held that the Fourth Amendment's warrant provision did apply to electronic surveillance. The Court explicitly declined, however, to extend its holding to cases "involving the national security." 389 U.S. at 358 n.23. The next year, Congress followed suit: responding to the *Katz* case, Congress enacted the Omnibus Crime Control and Safe Streets Act (18 U.S.C. §§2510-2520). Title III of that Act established a procedure for the judicial authorization of electronic surveillance for the investigation and prevention of specified types of serious crimes and the use of the product of such surveillance in court proceedings. It prohibited wiretapping and electronic surveillance by persons other than duly authorized law enforcement officers, personnel of the Federal Communications Commission, or communication common carriers monitoring communications in the normal course of their employment.

Title III, however, disclaimed any intention of legislating in the national security area. . . .

# UNITED STATES V. UNITED STATES DISTRICT COURT (*KEITH*)[1]

United States Supreme Court, 1972
407 U.S. 297

Mr. Justice POWELL delivered the opinion of the Court. The issue before us is an important one for the people of our country and their Government. It involves the delicate question of the President's power, acting through the Attorney General, to authorize electronic surveillance in internal security matters without prior judicial approval. . . . This case brings the issue here for the first time. Its resolution is a matter of national concern, requiring sensitivity both to the Government's right to protect itself from unlawful subversion and attack and to the citizen's right to be secure in his privacy against unreasonable Government intrusion.

This case arises from a criminal proceeding in the United States District Court for the Eastern District of Michigan, in which the United States charged three defendants with conspiracy to destroy Government property in violation of 18 U.S.C. §371. One of the defendants, Plamondon, was charged with the dynamite bombing of an office of the Central Intelligence Agency in Ann Arbor, Michigan.

During pretrial proceedings, the defendants moved to compel the United States to disclose certain electronic surveillance information and to conduct a hearing to determine whether this information "tainted" the evidence on which the indictment was based or which the Government intended to offer at trial. In response, the Government filed an affidavit of the Attorney General, acknowledging that its agents had overheard conversations in which Plamondon had participated. The affidavit also stated that the Attorney General approved the wiretaps "to gather intelligence information deemed necessary to protect the nation from attempts of domestic organizations to attack and subvert the existing structure of the Government." The logs of the surveillance were filed in a sealed exhibit for in camera inspection by the District Court.

On the basis of the Attorney General's affidavit and the sealed exhibit, the Government asserted that the surveillance was lawful, though conducted without prior judicial approval, as a reasonable exercise of the President's power (exercised through the Attorney General) to protect the national security. The District Court held that the surveillance violated the Fourth Amendment, and ordered the Government to make full disclosure to Plamondon of his overheard conversations.

. . . [T]he Court of Appeals for the Sixth Circuit . . . held that the surveillance was unlawful and that the District Court had properly required disclosure of the overheard conversations. . . .

## I

Title III of the Omnibus Crime Control and Safe Streets Act, 18 U.S.C. §§2510-2520, authorizes the use of electronic surveillance for classes of crimes

---

[1. This case is commonly referred to by the name of the district court judge who first heard it, Damon J. Keith.]

carefully specified in 18 U.S.C. §2516. Such surveillance is subject to prior court order. Section 2518 sets forth the detailed and particularized application necessary to obtain such an order as well as carefully circumscribed conditions for its use. The Act represents a comprehensive attempt by Congress to promote more effective control of crime while protecting the privacy of individual thought and expression. Much of Title III was drawn to meet the constitutional requirements for electronic surveillance enunciated by this Court in Berger v. New York, 388 U.S. 41 (1967), and Katz v. United States, 389 U.S. 347 (1967).

Together with the elaborate surveillance requirements in Title III, there is the following proviso, 18 U.S.C. §2511(3):

> Nothing contained in this chapter or in section 605 of the Communications Act of 1934 (48 Stat. 1143; 47 U.S.C. 605) shall limit the constitutional power of the President to take such measures as he deems necessary to protect the Nation against actual or potential attack or other hostile acts of a foreign power, to obtain foreign intelligence information deemed essential to the security of the United States, or to protect national security information against foreign intelligence activities. *Nor shall anything contained in this chapter be deemed to limit the constitutional power of the President to take such measures as he deems necessary to protect the United States against the overthrow of the Government by force or other unlawful means, or against any other clear and present danger to the structure or existence of the Government.* The contents of any wire or oral communication intercepted by authority of the President in the exercise of the foregoing powers may be received in evidence in any trial hearing, or other proceeding only where such interception was reasonable, and shall not be otherwise used or disclosed except as is necessary to implement that power. (Emphasis supplied.)

The Government relies on §2511(3). It argues that "in excepting national security surveillances from the Act's warrant requirement Congress recognized the President's authority to conduct such surveillances without prior judicial approval." The section thus is viewed as a recognition or affirmance of a constitutional authority in the President to conduct warrantless domestic security surveillance such as that involved in this case.

We think the language of §2511(3), as well as the legislative history of the statute, refutes this interpretation. The relevant language is that: "Nothing contained in this chapter . . . shall limit the constitutional power of the President to take such measures as he deems necessary to protect . . ." against the dangers specified. At most, this is an implicit recognition that the President does have certain powers in the specified areas. Few would doubt this, as the section refers — among other things — to protection "against actual or potential attack or other hostile acts of a foreign power." But so far as the use of the President's electronic surveillance power is concerned, the language is essentially neutral.

Section 2511(3) certainly confers no power, as the language is wholly inappropriate for such a purpose. It merely provides that the Act shall not be interpreted to limit or disturb such power as the President may have under the Constitution. In short, Congress simply left presidential powers where it found them. . . .

... [I]t would have been incongruous for Congress to have legislated with respect to the important and complex area of national security in a single brief and nebulous paragraph. This would not comport with the sensitivity of the problem involved or with the extraordinary care Congress exercised in drafting other sections of the Act. We therefore think the conclusion inescapable that Congress only intended to make clear that the Act simply did not legislate with respect to national security surveillances. ...

... [V]iewing §2511(3) as a congressional disclaimer and expression of neutrality, we hold that the statute is not the measure of the executive authority asserted in this case. Rather, we must look to the constitutional powers of the President.

## II

It is important at the outset to emphasize the limited nature of the question before the Court. This case raises no constitutional challenge to electronic surveillance as specifically authorized by Title III of the Omnibus Crime Control and Safe Streets Act of 1968. Nor is there any question or doubt as to the necessity of obtaining a warrant in the surveillance of crimes unrelated to the national security interest. Further, the instant case requires no judgment on the scope of the President's surveillance power with respect to the activities of foreign powers, within or without this country. The Attorney General's affidavit in this case states that the surveillances were "deemed necessary to protect the nation from attempts of *domestic organizations* to attack and subvert the existing structure of Government" (emphasis supplied). There is no evidence of any involvement, directly or indirectly, of a foreign power.[8]

Our present inquiry, though important, is therefore a narrow one. It addresses a question left open by *Katz*: "Whether safeguards other than prior authorization by a magistrate would satisfy the Fourth Amendment in a situation involving the national security. ..." The determination of this question requires the essential Fourth Amendment inquiry into the "reasonableness" of the search and seizure in question, and the way in which that "reasonableness" derives content and meaning through reference to the warrant clause.

... [T]he President of the United States has the fundamental duty, under Art. II, §1, of the Constitution, to "preserve, protect and defend the Constitution

---

8. Section 2511(3) refers to "the constitutional power of the President" in two types of situations: (i) where necessary to protect against attack, other hostile acts or intelligence activities of a "foreign power"; or (ii) where necessary to protect against the overthrow of the Government or other clear and present danger to the structure or existence of the Government. Although both of the specified situations are sometimes referred to as "national security" threats, the term "national security" is used only in the first sentence of §2511(3) with respect to the activities of foreign powers. This case involves only the second sentence of §2511(3), with the threat emanating — according to the Attorney General's affidavit — from "domestic organizations." Although we attempt no precise definition, we use the term "domestic organization" in this opinion to mean a group or organization (whether formally or informally constituted) composed of citizens of the United States and which has no significant connection with a foreign power, its agents or agencies. No doubt there are cases where it will be difficult to distinguish between "domestic" and "foreign" unlawful activities directed against the Government of the United States where there is collaboration in varying degrees between domestic groups or organizations and agents or agencies of foreign powers. But this is not such a case.

of the United States." Implicit in that duty is the power to protect our Government against those who would subvert or overthrow it by unlawful means. In the discharge of this duty, the President—through the Attorney General—may find it necessary to employ electronic surveillance to obtain intelligence information on the plans of those who plot unlawful acts against the Government. The use of such surveillance in internal security cases has been sanctioned more or less continuously by various Presidents and Attorneys General since July 1946. . . .

Though the Government and respondents debate their seriousness and magnitude, threats and acts of sabotage against the Government exist in sufficient number to justify investigative powers with respect to them. The covertness and complexity of potential unlawful conduct against the Government and the necessary dependency of many conspirators upon the telephone make electronic surveillance an effective investigatory instrument in certain circumstances. The marked acceleration in technological developments and sophistication in their use have resulted in new techniques for the planning, commission, and concealment of criminal activities. It would be contrary to the public interest for Government to deny to itself the prudent and lawful employment of those very techniques which are employed against the Government and its law-abiding citizens. . . .

But a recognition of these elementary truths does not make the employment by Government of electronic surveillance a welcome development—even when employed with restraint and under judicial supervision. There is, understandably, a deep-seated uneasiness and apprehension that this capability will be used to intrude upon cherished privacy of law-abiding citizens. We look to the Bill of Rights to safeguard this privacy. Though physical entry of the home is the chief evil against which the wording of the Fourth Amendment is directed, its broader spirit now shields private speech from unreasonable surveillance. Our decision in *Katz* refused to lock the Fourth Amendment into instances of actual physical trespass. Rather, the Amendment governs "not only the seizure of tangible items, but extends as well to the recording of oral statements . . . without any 'technical trespass under . . . local property law.'" . . . *Katz,* supra, at 353. . . .

National security cases, moreover, often reflect a convergence of First and Fourth Amendment values not present in cases of "ordinary" crime. Though the investigative duty of the executive may be stronger in such cases, so also is there greater jeopardy to constitutionally protected speech. "Historically the struggle for freedom of speech and press in England was bound up with the issue of the scope of the search and seizure power," Marcus v. Search Warrant, 367 U.S. 717, 724 (1961). History abundantly documents the tendency of Government—however benevolent and benign its motive—to view with suspicion those who most fervently dispute its policies. Fourth Amendment protections become the more necessary when the targets of official surveillance may be those suspected of unorthodoxy in their political beliefs. The danger to political dissent is acute where the Government attempts to act under so vague a concept as the power to protect "domestic security." Given the difficulty of defining the domestic security interest, the danger of abuse in acting to protect that interest becomes apparent. . . .

# III

As the Fourth Amendment is not absolute in its terms, our task is to examine and balance the basic values at stake in this case: the duty of Government to protect the domestic security, and the potential danger posed by unreasonable surveillance to individual privacy and free expression. If the legitimate need of Government to safeguard domestic security requires the use of electronic surveillance, the question is whether the needs of citizens for privacy and free expression may not be better protected by requiring a warrant before such surveillance is undertaken. We must also ask whether a warrant requirement would unduly frustrate the efforts of Government to protect itself from acts of subversion and overthrow directed against it.

Though the Fourth Amendment speaks broadly of "unreasonable searches and seizures," the definition of "reasonableness" turns, at least in part, on the more specific commands of the warrant clause. . . .

. . . [W]here practical, a governmental search and seizure should represent both the efforts of the officer to gather evidence of wrongful acts and the judgment of the magistrate that the collected evidence is sufficient to justify invasion of a citizen's private premises or conversation. Inherent in the concept of a warrant is its issuance by a "neutral and detached magistrate." The further requirement of "probable cause" instructs the magistrate that baseless searches shall not proceed.

These Fourth Amendment freedoms cannot properly be guaranteed if domestic security surveillances may be conducted solely within the discretion of the Executive Branch. . . . The historical judgment, which the Fourth Amendment accepts, is that unreviewed executive discretion may yield too readily to pressures to obtain incriminating evidence and overlook potential invasions of privacy and protected speech.

It may well be that, in the instant case, the Government's surveillance of Plamondon's conversations was a reasonable one which readily would have gained prior judicial approval. But this Court "has never sustained a search upon the sole ground that officers reasonably expected to find evidence of a particular crime and voluntarily confined their activities to the least intrusive means consistent with that end." *Katz,* supra, at 356-357. The Fourth Amendment contemplates a prior judicial judgment, not the risk that executive discretion may be reasonably exercised. This judicial role accords with our basic constitutional doctrine that individual freedoms will best be preserved through a separation of powers and division of functions among the different branches and levels of Government. The independent check upon executive discretion is not satisfied, as the Government argues, by "extremely limited" post-surveillance judicial review. Indeed, post-surveillance review would never reach the surveillances which failed to result in prosecutions. . . .

It is true that there have been some exceptions to the warrant requirement. But those exceptions are few in number and carefully delineated; in general, they serve the legitimate needs of law enforcement officers to protect their own wellbeing and preserve evidence from destruction. Even while carving out those exceptions, the Court has reaffirmed the principle that the "police must, whenever practicable, obtain advance judicial approval of searches and seizures through the warrant procedure," Terry v. Ohio, [392 U.S. 1, 20 (1968)].

The Government argues that the special circumstances applicable to domestic security surveillances necessitate a further exception to the warrant requirement. It is urged that the requirement of prior judicial review would obstruct the President in the discharge of his constitutional duty to protect domestic security. We are told further that these surveillances are directed primarily to the collecting and maintaining of intelligence with respect to subversive forces, and are not an attempt to gather evidence for specific criminal prosecutions. It is said that this type of surveillance should not be subject to traditional warrant requirements which were established to govern investigation of criminal activity, not ongoing intelligence gathering.

The Government further insists that courts "as a practical matter would have neither the knowledge nor the techniques necessary to determine whether there was probable cause to believe that surveillance was necessary to protect national security." These security problems, the Government contends, involve "a large number of complex and subtle factors" beyond the competence of courts to evaluate.

As a final reason for exemption from a warrant requirement, the Government believes that disclosure to a magistrate of all or even a significant portion of the information involved in domestic security surveillances "would create serious potential dangers to the national security and to the lives of informants and agents. . . . Secrecy is the essential ingredient in intelligence gathering; requiring prior judicial authorization would create a greater 'danger of leaks . . . because in addition to the judge, you have the clerk, the stenographer and some other officer like a law assistant or bailiff who may be apprised of the nature' of the surveillance." . . .

. . . There is, no doubt, pragmatic force to the Government's position.

But we do not think a case has been made for the requested departure from Fourth Amendment standards. . . . Security surveillances are especially sensitive because of the inherent vagueness of the domestic security concept, the necessarily broad and continuing nature of intelligence gathering, and the temptation to utilize such surveillances to oversee political dissent. We recognize, as we have before, the constitutional basis of the President's domestic security role, but we think it must be exercised in a manner compatible with the Fourth Amendment. In this case we hold that this requires an appropriate prior warrant procedure.

We cannot accept the Government's argument that internal security matters are too subtle and complex for judicial evaluation. Courts regularly deal with the most difficult issues of our society. There is no reason to believe that federal judges will be insensitive to or uncomprehending of the issues involved in domestic security cases. . . . If the threat is too subtle or complex for our senior law enforcement officers to convey its significance to a court, one may question whether there is probable cause for surveillance.

Nor do we believe prior judicial approval will fracture the secrecy essential to official intelligence gathering. The investigation of criminal activity has long involved imparting sensitive information to judicial officers who have respected the confidentialities involved. Judges may be counted upon to be especially conscious of security requirements in national security cases. Title III of the Omnibus Crime Control and Safe Streets Act already has imposed this responsibility on the judiciary in connection with such crimes as espionage, sabotage, and treason, §2516(1)(a) and (c), each of which may involve domestic as well as foreign security threats. Moreover, a warrant application involves no public or adversary proceedings: it is an *ex parte* request before a magistrate or judge. Whatever security dangers clerical and secretarial personnel may pose can be minimized by proper administrative measures, possibly to the point of allowing the Government itself to provide the necessary clerical assistance.

Thus, we conclude that the Government's concerns do not justify departure in this case from the customary Fourth Amendment requirement of judicial approval prior to initiation of a search or surveillance. Although some added burden will be imposed upon the Attorney General, this inconvenience is justified in a free society to protect constitutional values. Nor do we think the Government's domestic surveillance powers will be impaired to any significant degree. A prior warrant establishes presumptive validity of the surveillance and will minimize the burden of justification in post-surveillance judicial review. By no means of least importance will be the reassurance of the public generally that indiscriminate wiretapping and bugging of law-abiding citizens cannot occur.

## IV

. . . [W]e do not hold that the same type of standards and procedures prescribed by Title III are necessarily applicable to this case. We recognize that domestic security surveillance may involve different policy and practical considerations from the surveillance of "ordinary crime." The gathering of security intelligence is often long range and involves the interrelation of various sources and types of information. The exact targets of such surveillance may be more difficult to identify than in surveillance operations against many types of crime specified in Title III. Often, too, the emphasis of domestic intelligence gathering is on the prevention of unlawful activity or the enhancement of the Government's preparedness for some possible future crisis or emergency. Thus, the focus of domestic surveillance may be less precise than that directed against more conventional types of crime.

Given these potential distinctions between Title III criminal surveillances and those involving the domestic security, Congress may wish to consider protective standards for the latter which differ from those already prescribed for specified crimes in Title III. Different standards may be compatible with the Fourth Amendment if they are reasonable both in relation to the legitimate need of Government for intelligence information and the protected rights of our citizens. For the warrant application may vary according to the governmental interest to be enforced and the nature of citizen rights deserving protection. . . .

. . . We . . . hold . . . that prior judicial approval is required for the type of domestic security surveillance involved in this case and that such approval may be made in accordance with such reasonable standards as the Congress may prescribe.

## V

As the surveillance of Plamondon's conversations was unlawful, because conducted without prior judicial approval, the courts below correctly held that

Alderman v. United States, 394 U.S. 165 (1969), is controlling and that it requires disclosure to the accused of his own impermissibly intercepted conversations. As stated in *Alderman,* "the trial court can and should, where appropriate, place a defendant and his counsel under enforceable orders against unwarranted disclosure of the materials which they may be entitled to inspect." 394 U.S. at 185.

The judgment of the Court of Appeals is hereby affirmed.

The Chief Justice concurs in the result.

[The concurring opinions of DOUGLAS and WHITE, JJ., are omitted.]

## NOTES AND QUESTIONS

1. *The Nature of the Privacy Interest.* Has your phone ever been tapped, or have you ever suspected that it was? Ever had your mail opened? Your e-mail or the history of your Internet use read by others without your permission? How did you feel (or how do you think you would feel) upon discovering such an intrusion? Would you feel better knowing that a judge had issued a warrant to authorize it?

   While acknowledging that "physical entry of the home is the chief evil" addressed by the Fourth Amendment, the Court found in *Keith*, as it had in *Katz,* that the "broader spirit" of the amendment protects telephone conversations as well. But what is it about electronic surveillance that the Court found objectionable? Is it that a "search" of private conversations is being conducted, or is it the "convergence of First and Fourth Amendment values"?

   Arguably, a physical search may be less intrusive than a wiretap, especially if the electronic surveillance continues for weeks or months after the initial intrusion. *See* Olmstead v. United States, 277 U.S. 438, 473 (1928) (Brandeis, J., dissenting); Berger v. New York, 388 U.S. 41, 60 (1967).

   Why is this form of privacy important to individuals? What purpose does it serve in society? *See generally* Alan Westin, *Privacy and Freedom* (1967); Daniel J. Solove, *A Taxonomy of Privacy*, 154 U. Pa. L. Rev. 477 (2006).

2. *Inherent Surveillance Authority?* Does Article II, §1 implicitly authorize the President to conduct electronic surveillance? *See* Letter from William E. Moschella, Asst. Attorney General, to the Honorable Pat Roberts, Chairman, Senate Select Committee on Intelligence et al. (Dec. 22, 2005), *available at* http://www.fas.org/irp/agency/doj/fisa/doj122205.pdf (arguing that the President has inherent constitutional authority to direct the NSA to engage in warrantless electronic surveillance); *see also* In re Sealed Case, 310 F.3d 717, 742 (FISA Ct. Rev. 2002). Both the Moschella letter and In re Sealed Case are reproduced *infra* pp. 157, 145. Does Article II distinguish between domestic and foreign national security threats?

   If the President possesses some independent constitutional authority to engage in domestic electronic surveillance, why, according to the Court, is an exception to the warrant requirement not appropriate? Assuming that there is some constitutional authority to undertake warrantless surveillance, does

Congress have the constitutional authority to limit the exercise of that authority?

3. ***Balancing Away the Warrant Requirement.***  Does the warrant clause of the Fourth Amendment adequately protect privacy interests? What is the function of a "neutral and detached magistrate" in a warrant proceeding? Why did the government object to the warrant procedure for electronic surveillance in *Keith*?

How did the Supreme Court balance the President's Article II powers against the Fourth Amendment warrant requirement for domestic subjects? Did the Court fairly reconcile "the Government's right to protect itself from unlawful subversion and attack" with "the citizen's right to be secure in his privacy against unreasonable Government intrusion"? Should the Court have attached more importance to the fact that a magistrate's role could be performed more efficiently by after-the-fact judicial review where surveillance abuses are alleged?

In December 2005, the New York Times revealed the existence of a four-year, large-scale warrantless electronic surveillance program that intercepted communications of some U.S. citizens. James Risen & Eric Lichtblau, *Bush Lets U.S. Spy on Callers Without Courts*, N.Y. Times, Dec. 16, 2005, at A1. At a White House press conference, President Bush offered this explanation for the warrantless surveillance:

> We know that a two-minute phone conversation between somebody linked to al Qaeda here and an operative overseas could lead directly to the loss of thousands of lives. To save American lives, we must be able to act fast and to detect these conversations so that we can prevent new attacks.
>
> So, consistent with U.S. law and the Constitution, I authorized the interception of international communications of people with known links to al Qaeda and related terrorist organizations. . . .
>
> . . . I've reauthorized this program more than 30 times since the September 11th attacks, and I intend to do so for so long as our nation . . . faces the continuing threat of an enemy that wants to kill American citizens. [Press Conference of the President, Dec. 19, 2005.]

Assuming, arguendo, that Congress has enacted no applicable statute, would you agree, based on *Keith*, that the program described by the President is constitutional? Other aspects of this program are considered in Chapter 5.

4. ***Domestic vs. Foreign Surveillance.***  Justice Powell's interpretation of §2511(3) may have been crucial to the outcome of the case. His willingness to draw a sharp distinction between a "domestic organization" and "foreign" activities in the United States became the predicate for establishing the Fourth Amendment warrant requirement for "domestic" national security investigations. Why is the power to protect "domestic security" viewed with greater skepticism by the Court than the power to protect against foreign perils? Are the two concepts really different? Does §2511(3) clearly reflect such a sharp distinction in the origin of national security threats?

Justice Powell also concluded that §2511(3) "is essentially neutral" regarding presidential power. Do you agree?

5. ***Title III (Ordinary Criminal) Electronic Surveillance.*** Title III requires that an application for authorization to conduct electronic surveillance contain detailed information about the alleged criminal offense, the facilities and communication sought to be intercepted, the identity of the target (if known), the period of time sought for surveillance, and an explanation of whether other investigative methods have failed or why they are unlikely to succeed or are too dangerous. 18 U.S.C. §2518(1)(b)-(d) (2000). A court may issue an order for electronic surveillance only if it finds probable cause that communications related to the commission of a crime will be obtained through the surveillance. *Id.* §2518(3)(b). Can you see why intelligence agencies would seek to avoid the strictures of Title III in conducting electronic surveillance for intelligence purposes?

   Title III also requires a warrant before the government may obtain access to stored communications, such as electronic mail, during the first 180 days of storage. 18 U.S.C. §2703(a) (2000 & Supp. IV 2004). After 180 days, the government may obtain access to stored communications pursuant to a search warrant or, after notice to the subscriber, pursuant to an administrative or grand jury subpoena or a court order. *Id.* §2703; see Chapter 6. Likewise, cellular phones, display pagers, and voice pagers are protected by Title III. 18 U.S.C. §2510(1), (12) (2000 & Supp. IV 2004).

6. ***Post-Keith Case Law on Warrantless Foreign Intelligence Surveillance.*** Several lower courts have taken up the important question, reserved by the Supreme Court in *Keith,* of surveillance to obtain foreign intelligence.

> The Fifth Circuit in United States v. Brown, 484 F.2d 418 (5th Cir. 1973), *cert. denied,* 415 U.S. 960 (1974), upheld the legality of a surveillance in which the defendant, an American citizen, was incidentally overheard as a result of a warrantless wiretap authorized by the Attorney General for foreign intelligence purposes. The court found that on the basis of "the President's constitutional duty to act for the United States in the field of foreign affairs, and his inherent power to protect national security in the conduct of foreign affairs . . . the President may constitutionally authorize warrantless wiretaps for the purpose of gathering foreign intelligence." [484 F.2d at 426.]
>
> In United States v. Butenko, 494 F.2d 593 (3d Cir. 1974) (en banc), *cert. denied sub nom.* Ivanov v. United States, 419 U.S. 881 (1974), the Third Circuit similarly held that electronic surveillance conducted without a warrant would be lawful so long as the primary purpose was to obtain foreign intelligence information. The court found that such surveillance would be reasonable under the Fourth Amendment without a warrant even though it might involve the overhearing of conversations.
>
> However, in Zweibon v. Mitchell, 516 F.2d 594 (D.C. Cir. 1975), *cert. denied,* 425 U.S. 944 (1976), the Circuit Court of Appeals for the District of Columbia, in the course of an opinion requiring that a warrant must be obtained before a wiretap is installed on a domestic

organization that is neither the agent of, nor acting in collaboration with, a foreign power, questioned whether any national security exception to the warrant requirement would be constitutionally permissible.

Although the holding of *Zweibon* was limited to the case of a domestic organization without ties to a foreign power, the plurality opinion of the court — in legal analysis closely patterned on *Keith* — concluded "that an analysis of the policies implicated by foreign security surveillance indicates that, absent exigent circumstances, all warrantless electronic surveillance is unreasonable and therefore unconstitutional." [*Senate Report No. 604, supra* p. 89, at 14, 15.]

Note that the Supreme Court declined to decide the appeals in the above cases.

*Zweibon* was a suit for damages by members of the Jewish Defense League (JDL) for unlawful electronic surveillance. Although the JDL is a U.S. organization, JDL protest actions directed against Soviet facilities inside the United States risked a significant foreign relations problem with the Soviet Union. Despite the fact that "Soviet officials vigorously and continuously protested these activities, for which they held the United States Government responsible," 516 F.2d at 608, 609, the D.C. Circuit refused to rule that this foreign affairs tension was cause to waive the Fourth Amendment warrant requirement. 516 F.2d at 614. A similar result was reached in Berlin Democratic Club v. Rumsfeld, 410 F. Supp. 144 (D.D.C. 1976), where a warrant was required to wiretap Americans living in West Germany despite Department of Defense arguments about dangers to United States forces and to American foreign policy. *Id.* at 157.

7. *Implications of Keith?*  In the principal case, Justice Powell suggested that national security wiretaps may not have to meet all the Fourth Amendment requirements applicable in criminal investigations, but he did not specify what alternative processes might be appropriate in such cases. Nor did the Court refer to the constitutional requirements for other forms of surveillance, such as searches of the home and person. Meanwhile, the agencies within the intelligence community had, since their inception after World War II, been developing their own guidelines for national security surveillance. A post-Watergate investigation revealed widespread abuses within the intelligence community and prompted significant reform efforts by Congress and the executive branch. Part D examines some of these abuses.

# D.   A FOREIGN INTELLIGENCE EXCEPTION?

### SELECT COMMITTEE TO STUDY GOVERNMENTAL OPERATIONS WITH RESPECT TO INTELLIGENCE ACTIVITIES (CHURCH COMMITTEE), INTELLIGENCE ACTIVITIES AND THE RIGHTS OF AMERICANS

S. Rep. No. 94-755, Book III, at 355 (1976)

... Before 1966, the FBI conducted over two hundred "black bag jobs." These warrantless surreptitious entries were carried out for intelligence purposes *other than* microphone installation, such as physical search and photographing or seizing documents.

. . . [T]here is no indication that the FBI informed any Attorney General about its use of "black bag jobs."

Surreptitious entries were performed by teams of FBI agents with special training in subjects such as "lock studies." Their missions were authorized in writing by FBI Director Hoover or his deputy, Clyde Tolson. A "Do Not File" procedure was utilized, under which most records of surreptitious entries were destroyed soon after an entry was accomplished.

The use of surreptitious entries against domestic targets dropped drastically after J. Edgar Hoover banned "black bag jobs" in 1966. . . .

## UNITED STATES V. EHRLICHMAN

United States District Court, District of Columbia, 1974
376 F. Supp. 29, *aff'd*, 546 F.2d 910 (D.C. Cir. 1976), *cert. denied*,
429 U.S. 1120 (1977)

GESELL, J. Five defendants stand indicted for conspiring to injure a Los Angeles psychiatrist [Dr. Lewis Fielding] in the enjoyment of his Fourth Amendment rights by entering his offices without a warrant for the purpose of obtaining the doctor's medical records relating to one of his patients, a Daniel Ellsberg, then under Federal indictment for revealing top secret documents. They now claim that broad pretrial discovery into the alleged national security aspects of this case is essential to the presentation of their defense, in that it will establish (1) that the break-in was legal under the Fourth Amendment because the President authorized it for reasons of national security, and (2) that even in the absence of such authorization the national security information available to the defendants at that time led them to the good-faith, reasonable belief that the break-in was legal and justified in the national interest. The Court has carefully considered these assertions, which have been fully briefed and argued over a two-day period, and finds them to be unpersuasive as a matter of law. . . .

The Fourth Amendment protects the privacy of citizens against unreasonable and unrestrained intrusion by Government officials and their agents. It is not theoretical. It lies at the heart of our free society. As the Supreme Court recently remarked, "no right is held more sacred." Terry v. Ohio, 392 U.S. 1, 9 (1968). Indeed, the American Revolution was sparked in part by the complaints of the colonists against the issuance of writs of assistance, pursuant to which the King's revenue officers conducted unrestricted, indiscriminate searches of persons and homes to uncover contraband. James Otis' famous argument in Lechmere's Case, challenging the writ as a "monster of oppression" and a "remnant of Star Chamber tyranny," sowed one of the seeds of the coming rebellion. The Fourth Amendment was framed against this background; and every state in the Union, by its own constitution, has since reinforced the protections and the security which that Amendment was designed to achieve.

Thus the security of one's privacy against arbitrary intrusion by governmental authorities has proven essential to our concept of ordered liberty. When officials have attempted to justify law enforcement methods that ignore the strictures of this Amendment on grounds of necessity, such excuses have proven fruitless, for the Constitution brands such conduct as lawless, irrespective of the end to be served. Throughout the years the Supreme Court of the United States, regardless of changes in its composition or contemporary issues, has steadfastly applied the Amendment to protect a citizen against the warrantless invasion of his home or office, except under carefully delineated emergency circumstances. No right so fundamental should now, after the long struggle against governmental trespass, be diluted to accommodate conduct of the very type the Amendment was designed to outlaw.

The break-in charged in this indictment involved an unauthorized entry and search by agents of the Executive branch of the Federal Government. It is undisputed that no warrant was obtained and no Magistrate gave his approval. Moreover, none of the traditional exceptions to the warrant requirement are claimed and none existed; however desirable the break-in may have appeared to its instigators, there is no indication that it had to be carried out quickly, before a warrant could have been obtained. On the contrary, it had been meticulously planned over a period of more than a month. The search of Dr. Fielding's office was therefore clearly illegal under the unambiguous mandate of the Fourth Amendment.

Defendants contend that even though the Fourth Amendment would ordinarily prohibit break-ins of this nature, the President has the authority, by reason of his special responsibilities over foreign relations and national defense, to suspend its requirements, and that he did so in this case. Neither assertion is accurate. Many of the landmark Fourth Amendment cases in this country and in England concerned citizens accused of disloyal or treasonous conduct, for history teaches that such suspicions foster attitudes within a government that generate conduct inimical to individual rights. See United States v. United States District Court, 407 U.S. 297, 314 (1972). The judicial response to such Executive overreaching has been consistent and emphatic: the Government must comply with the strict constitutional and statutory limitations on trespassory searches and arrests even when known foreign agents are involved. To hold otherwise, except under the most exigent circumstances, would be to abandon the Fourth Amendment to the whim of the Executive in total disregard of the Amendment's history and purpose.

Defendants contend that, over the last few years, the courts have begun to carve out an exception to this traditional rule for purely intelligence-gathering searches deemed necessary for the conduct of foreign affairs. However, the cases cited are carefully limited to the issue of wiretapping, a relatively nonintrusive search, United States v. Butenko, 494 F.2d 593 (3d Cir. 1974); United States v. Brown, 484 F.2d 418 (5th Cir. 1973); Zweibon v. Mitchell, 363 F. Supp. 936 (D.D.C. 1973), and the Supreme Court has reserved judgment in this unsettled area. United States v. United States District Court, 407 U.S. 297, 322 n.20 (1972). The Court cannot find that this recent, controversial judicial response to the special problem of national security wiretaps indicates an intention to obviate the entire Fourth Amendment whenever the President determines that an American citizen, personally innocent of wrongdoing, has in his possession information that may touch upon foreign policy concerns.[4] Such a doctrine, even in the context of purely information-gathering searches, would give the Executive a blank check to disregard the very heart and core of the Fourth Amendment and the vital privacy interests that it protects. . . .

The facts presented pretrial lead the Court to conclude as a matter of law that the President not only lacked the authority to authorize the Fielding break-in but also that he did not in fact give any specific directive permitting national security break-ins, let alone this particular intrusion. The President has repeatedly and publicly denied prior knowledge or authorization of the Fielding break-in, and the available transcripts of the confidential tape recordings support that claim. . . . [The evidence reflected] intense Presidential concern with the need to plug the national security leaks and a belief that Dr. Ellsberg might be involved, but no specific reference either to Dr. Fielding or to trespassory searches. . . .

Defendants adopt the fall-back position that even if the President did not specifically authorize the Fielding break-in, he properly delegated to one or more of the defendants or unindicted co-conspirators the authority to approve national security break-ins. Of course, since the President had no such authority in the first place, he could not have delegated it to others. Beyond this, however, the Court rejects the contention that the President could delegate his alleged power to suspend constitutional rights to non-law enforcement officers in the vague, informal, inexact terms noted above. Even in the wiretap cases the courts have stressed the fact that the President had specifically delegated the authority over "national security" wiretaps to his chief legal officer, the Attorney General, who approved each such tap. See, e.g., Katz v. United States, 389 U.S. 347, 364 (1967) (White, J., concurring). Whatever accommodation is required between the guarantees of the Fourth Amendment and the conduct of foreign affairs, it cannot justify a casual, ill-defined assignment to White House aides and part-time employees granting them an uncontrolled discretion to select, enter and search the homes and offices of innocent American citizens without a warrant. Cf. Ex parte Milligan, 71 U.S. (4 Wall.) 2 (1866); Ex parte Merryman, 17 Fed. Cas. p. 144, 151 (No. 9,487) (C.C. Md. 1861). . . .

## NOTES AND QUESTIONS

1. ***Comparing Searches and Electronic Surveillance.*** Is physical entry of the home more threatening to civil liberties than a wiretap? Microphone surveillance requires entry to install the device, which will, like a wiretap,

---

4. The doctrine of the President's inherent authority as "the sole organ of the nation in its external relations," 10 Annals of Cong. 613 (1800) (remarks of John Marshall), has been developed by a series of Supreme Court decisions dealing with the President's power to enter into international agreements and to prohibit commercial contracts which impede American foreign policy. United States v. Curtiss-Wright Export Corp., 299 U.S. 304 (1936). None of these cases purport to deal with the constitutional rights of American citizens or with Presidential action in defiance of congressional legislation. When such issues have arisen, Executive assertions of inherent authority have been soundly rejected. See Kent v. Dulles, 357 U.S. 116 (1958); Youngstown Sheet & Tube Co. v. Sawyer, 343 U.S. 579 (1952).

transmit all conversations, including those not subject to the investigation. If a physical search is controlled, it will take less time and may focus only on material relevant to the investigation. Yet for many of us, invasion of our physical space is more threatening than the prospect of electronic surveillance. Why is that so?

2. *Accountability for the Exception.* While the D.C. Circuit Court affirmed the conviction in United States v. Ehrlichman, 546 F.2d 910 (1976), *cert. denied*, 429 U.S. 1120 (1977), the panel was more circumspect than Judge Gesell. The court merely held that no "national security" exception to the warrant requirement could be invoked without specific authorization by the President or Attorney General. *Id.* at 925. Judge Wilkey elaborated:

> The danger of leaving delicate decisions of propriety and probable cause to those actually assigned to ferret out "national security" information is patent, and is indeed illustrated by the intrusion undertaken in this case, without any more specific Presidential direction than that ascribed to Henry II vexed with Becket.[68] As a constitutional matter, if Presidential approval is to replace judicial approval for foreign intelligence gathering, the personal authorization of the President — or his alter ego for these matters, the Attorney General — is necessary to fix accountability and centralize responsibility for insuring the least intrusive surveillance necessary and preventing zealous officials from misusing the President's prerogative. [*Id.* at 926.]

3. *Executive Approval as a Warrant Substitute?* Would the substitution of the President's or Attorney General's approval for a search compensate for the loss of the warrant procedure? The Attorney General at the time of the Fielding break-in was John N. Mitchell, who was subsequently sent to prison for perjury and conspiracy in connection with efforts to cover up the burglary of the Democratic National Committee headquarters at the Watergate in Washington. The President was Richard M. Nixon, who was named an unindicted co-conspirator in the same affair. *See* United States v. Haldeman, 559 F.2d 31, 51 (D.C. Cir. 1976).

4. *A Domestic Intelligence Exception?* At the time of the break-in, Ellsberg had been indicted for disclosing the *Pentagon Papers* (a classified account of American involvement in the Vietnam War) to reporters. *See* Daniel Ellsberg, *Secrets: A Memoir of Vietnam and the Pentagon Papers* (2002). Ehrlichman and his codefendants argued that "the search was legal because [it was] undertaken pursuant to a delegated Presidential power to authorize such a search in the field of foreign affairs." *Ehrlichman*, 546 F.2d at 913. However, there was no accusation that Ellsberg or his psychiatrist had any relationship to a foreign power. What does Judge Wilkey's dictum, *supra* Note 2, suggest about the parameters of any such "national security" exception to the warrant requirement?

Consider again the warrantless surveillance program described by President Bush, *supra* p. 99. Does the *Ehrlichman* decision change your

---

68. Attributed as "Who will free me from this turbulent priest?"

view about the constitutionality of the more recent surveillance program, again assuming no controlling legislative authority?

5. ***Applying the Exception to Other Searches.*** If there is some "national security" exception to the warrant requirement, is there a principled basis for limiting the exception to electronic surveillance? *See* United States v. Ehrlichman, 546 F.2d at 938 (Leventhal, J., concurring); David S. Eggert, Note, *Executive Order 12,333: An Assessment of the Validity of Warrantless National Security Searches*, 1983 Duke L.J. 611, 627-628. *See also* Banks & Bowman, *supra* p. 84, at 67 ("In light of the potentially greater intrusiveness of electronic surveillance, it may be reasonable to expect greater executive discretion to conduct warrantless searches than warrantless wiretaps."). In addition to the degree of intrusion, what factors should be taken into account in deciding whether the warrant requirement applies? *See id.* at 67-68.

6. ***Search or Seizure?*** Computer searches "challenge several of the basic assumptions underlying Fourth Amendment doctrine. Computers are like containers in a physical sense, homes in a virtual sense, and vast warehouses in an informational sense." Orin S. Kerr, *Searches and Seizures in a Digital World*, 119 Harv. L. Rev. 531, 533 (2005). Which perspective do you find most helpful in thinking about application of the Fourth Amendment to Internet and computer searches?

Computer searches may involve the remote collection of digital electronic data. By copying the data, the government arguably deprives the owner of the ability to delete or alter the data once they have been placed in government files. Should such a search therefore be regarded as a seizure, since it involves the deprivation of a property interest as well as a violation of privacy? *See* Paul Ohm, *The Olmsteadian Seizure Clause*, 2007 Stan. Tech. L. Rev. (forthcoming). Does the Fourth Amendment "protect[] privacy *by protecting property*"? Ricardo J. Bascuas, *Fourth Amendment Lessons from the Highway and the Subway: A Principled Approach to Suspicionless Searches*, 38 Rutgers L.J. (forthcoming 2007). If we characterize these digital surveillance methods as "seizures" rather than "searches," should the Fourth Amendment apply differently to them?

---

## UNITED STATES v. TRUONG DINH HUNG

United States Court of Appeals, Fourth Circuit, 1980
629 F.2d 908, *cert. denied,* 454 U.S. 1144 (1982)

WINTER, J. Truong Dinh Hung, more familiarly known as David Truong, and Ronald Humphrey were convicted of espionage, conspiracy to commit espionage and several espionage-related offenses for transmitting classified United States government information to representatives of the government of the Socialist Republic of Vietnam. In these appeals, they seek reversal of their convictions because of warrantless surveillance and searches. . . .

We hold that the warrantless searches and surveillance did not violate the Fourth Amendment. . . .

David Truong, a Vietnamese citizen and son of a prominent Vietnamese political figure, came to the United States in 1965. At least since his arrival in the United States, Truong has pursued an active scholarly and political interest in Vietnam and the relationship between Vietnam and the United States. In 1976, Truong met Dung Krall, a Vietnamese-American, the wife of an American Naval Officer, who had extensive contacts among the Vietnamese community in Paris. Truong persuaded Krall to carry packages for him to Vietnamese in Paris. The recipients were representatives of the Socialist Republic of Vietnam at the time of the 1977 Paris negotiations between that country and the United States. The packages contained copies of diplomatic cables and other classified papers of the United States government dealing with Southeast Asia. Truong procured the copies from Ronald Humphrey, an employee of the United States Information Agency, who obtained the documents surreptitiously, copied them, removed their classification markings and furnished the copies to Truong. In a statement given after his arrest, Humphrey said that his motive was to improve relations between the North Vietnamese government and the United States so that he could be reunited with a woman whom he loved who was a prisoner of the North Vietnamese government.

Unknown to Truong, Krall was a confidential informant employed by the CIA and the FBI. Krall kept these agencies fully informed of Truong's activities and presented the packages Truong had given her to the FBI for inspection, copying and approval before she carried the documents to Paris. The FBI permitted this operation to continue, while monitoring it closely, from approximately September, 1976, until January 31, 1978.

When the intelligence agencies first learned that Truong was transmitting classified documents to Paris, they were understandably extremely anxious to locate Truong's source for his data. Toward that end, the government conducted a massive surveillance of Truong. Truong's phone was tapped and his apartment was bugged from May, 1977 to January, 1978. The telephone interception continued for 268 days and every conversation, with possibly one exception, was monitored and virtually all were taped. The eavesdropping device was operative for approximately 255 days and it ran continuously. No court authorization was ever sought or obtained for the installation and maintenance of the telephone tap or the bug. The government thus ascertained that Humphrey was providing Truong with the copies of secret documents. This leak of sensitive information of course ceased when Truong and Humphrey were arrested on January 31, 1978. . . .

The defendants raise a substantial challenge to their convictions by urging that the surveillance conducted by the FBI violated the Fourth Amendment and that all the evidence uncovered through that surveillance must consequently be suppressed. As has been stated, the government did not seek a warrant for the eavesdropping on Truong's phone conversations or the bugging of his apartment. Instead, it relied upon a "foreign intelligence" exception to the Fourth Amendment's warrant requirement. In the area of foreign intelligence, the government contends, the President may authorize surveillance without seeking a judicial warrant because of his constitutional prerogatives in the area of foreign affairs. On this basis, the FBI sought and received approval for the surveillance from the President's delegate, the Attorney General. This approval alone, according to the government, is constitutionally sufficient to authorize foreign intelligence surveillance such as the surveillance of Truong. . . .

. . . Although the Supreme Court has never decided the issue which is presented to us, it formulated the analytical approach which we employ here in an analogous case, United States v. United States District Court (*Keith*), 407 U.S. 297 (1972). . . .

For several reasons, the needs of the executive are so compelling in the area of foreign intelligence, unlike the area of domestic security, that a uniform warrant requirement would, following *Keith*, "unduly frustrate" the President in carrying out his foreign affairs responsibilities. First of all, attempts to counter foreign threats to the national security require the utmost stealth, speed, and secrecy. A warrant requirement would add a procedural hurdle that would reduce the flexibility of executive foreign intelligence initiatives, in some cases delay executive response to foreign intelligence threats, and increase the chance of leaks regarding sensitive executive operations.

More importantly, the executive possesses unparalleled expertise to make the decision whether to conduct foreign intelligence surveillance, whereas the judiciary is largely inexperienced in making the delicate and complex decisions that lie behind foreign intelligence surveillance. The executive branch, containing the State Department, the intelligence agencies, and the military, is constantly aware of the nation's security needs and the magnitude of external threats posed by a panoply of foreign nations and organizations. On the other hand, while the courts possess expertise in making the probable cause determination involved in surveillance of suspected criminals, the courts are unschooled in diplomacy and military affairs, a mastery of which would be essential to passing upon an executive branch request that a foreign intelligence wiretap be authorized. Few, if any, district courts would be truly competent to judge the importance of particular information to the security of the United States or the "probable cause" to demonstrate that the government in fact needs to recover that information from one particular source.

Perhaps most crucially, the executive branch not only has superior expertise in the area of foreign intelligence, it is also constitutionally designated as the pre-eminent authority in foreign affairs. The President and his deputies are charged by the constitution with the conduct of the foreign policy of the United States in times of war and peace. See United States v. Curtiss-Wright Corp., 299 U.S. 304 (1936). Just as the separation of powers in *Keith* forced the executive to recognize a judicial role when the President conducts domestic security surveillance, so the separation of powers requires us to acknowledge the principal responsibility of the President for foreign affairs and concomitantly for foreign intelligence surveillance. . . .

However, because individual privacy interests are severely compromised any time the government conducts surveillance without prior judicial approval, this foreign intelligence exception to the Fourth Amendment warrant requirement must be carefully limited to those situations in which the interests of the executive are paramount. First, the government should be relieved of seeking a warrant only when the object of the search or the surveillance is a foreign power, its agent or collaborators. In such cases, the government has the greatest need for speed, stealth, and secrecy, and the surveillance in such cases is most likely to call into play difficult and subtle judgments about foreign and military affairs. When there is no foreign connection, the executive's needs become less compelling; and the surveillance more closely resembles the surveillance of suspected criminals, which must be authorized by warrant. Thus, if the government wishes to wiretap the phone of a government employee who is stealing sensitive documents for his personal reading or to leak to a newspaper, for instance, the absence of a foreign connection and the importance of individual privacy concerns contained within the Fourth Amendment lead to a requirement that the executive secure advance judicial approval for surveillance. . . .

Second . . . the executive should be excused from securing a warrant only when the surveillance is conducted "primarily" for foreign intelligence reasons. We think that the district court adopted the proper test, because once surveillance becomes primarily a criminal investigation, the courts are entirely competent to make the usual probable cause determination, and because, importantly, individual privacy interests come to the fore and government foreign policy concerns recede when the government is primarily attempting to form the basis for a criminal prosecution. We thus reject the government's assertion that, if surveillance is to any degree directed at gathering foreign intelligence, the executive may ignore the warrant requirement of the Fourth Amendment.

The defendants urge that the "primarily" test does not go far enough to protect privacy interests. They argue that the government should be able to avoid the warrant requirement only when the surveillance is conducted "solely" for foreign policy reasons. The proposed "solely" test is unacceptable, however, because almost all foreign intelligence investigations are in part criminal investigations. Although espionage prosecutions are rare, there is always the possibility that the targets of the investigation will be prosecuted for criminal violations. Thus, if the defendants' "solely" test were adopted, the executive would be required to obtain a warrant almost every time it undertakes foreign intelligence surveillance, and, as indicated above, such a requirement would fail to give adequate consideration to the needs and responsibilities of the executive in the foreign intelligence area.

In this case, the district court concluded that on July 20, 1977, the investigation of Truong had become primarily a criminal investigation. Although the Criminal Division of the Justice Department had been aware of the investigation from its inception, until summer the Criminal Division had not taken a central role in the investigation. On July 19 and July 20, however, several memoranda circulated between the Justice Department and the various intelligence and national security agencies indicating that the government had begun to assemble a criminal prosecution. . . .

Therefore, because there was more than enough evidence to indicate that Truong had collaborated with the Vietnamese government and because the district court did not err in choosing July 20 as the date when the investigation became primarily a criminal investigation, we do not disturb the decision of the district court to exclude all evidence obtained through the surveillance after July 20 but to permit the government to introduce evidence secured through the surveillance before July 20.

Because the Fourth Amendment warrant requirement is a critical constitutional protection of individual privacy, this discussion should conclude by underscoring the limited nature of this foreign intelligence exception to the warrant requirement which we recognize in the instant case. The exception applies only to foreign powers, their agents, and their collaborators. Moreover, even these actors receive the protection of the warrant requirement if the government is primarily attempting to put together a criminal prosecution. . . .

## NOTES AND QUESTIONS

1. *Deciding Reasonableness.* The court found that intercepting Truong's phone calls and listening to conversations with visitors to Truong's apartment were "reasonable" efforts to locate the source of the purloined documents. 629 F.2d at 916-917. In light of the court's conclusion that no warrant was required for the surveillance, does it necessarily follow that the surveillance was reasonable? According to what criteria should reasonableness be determined?

2. *Package Searches.* Although the discussion of surveillance in *Truong* is not specifically directed to either electronic or non-electronic surveillance as such, the court did independently consider the constitutionality of the searches of packages Truong sent to Paris with Krall. Search of a letter and package with executive authorization but without a warrant before July 20, at which date the surveillance became, in the Court's view, criminal in nature, were treated as governed by a foreign intelligence exception to the warrant requirement. *Id.* at 917 n.8. Another package search during the same period without either the authorization of the Attorney General or a warrant was not covered by a foreign intelligence exception to the warrant requirement but was nonetheless constitutional, according to the court, because Truong had no reasonable expectation of privacy in the package, since it was "poorly wrapped and because it was destined for foreign delivery." *Id.* at 917.

3. *Reconciling the Cases?* Is there any way to square the reasoning of the court in *Truong* with the holding of the Supreme Court in *Keith*? With the holding by Judge Gesell in *Ehrlichman*? Does the *Truong* court's reasoning apply equally to inspection of sealed parcels and to installation of surveillance cameras in a target's workplace or home?

4. *The "Primary Purpose" Doctrine.* At what point in a counterterrorism investigation would you advise the Attorney General to seek a Title III warrant? Recall that the court in *Truong* concluded that the standard for deciding the constitutionality of warrantless foreign intelligence surveillance that eventually became a criminal investigation was whether the "primary purpose" of the search was in fact to obtain foreign intelligence information. At what point does an investigation change from "primarily" foreign intelligence to "primarily" law enforcement? Does the "primary purpose" rule adequately accommodate the competing interests? The "primary purpose" problem also arises in connection with statutory authorization for intelligence surveillance. See Chapter 5.

# 5

# CONGRESS AND COUNTERTERRORISM INTELLIGENCE: THE FOREIGN INTELLIGENCE SURVEILLANCE ACT (FISA)

Communications technology has undergone explosive growth since the digital and dot-com revolutions of the 1980s and 1990s. Both ordinary and Internet communications can be intercepted, and cell phone calls can be traced to the phone's location. Hidden recorders may preserve conversations, while parabolic microphones can capture conversations at long distances. Video surveillance cameras permit government officials to monitor public areas by closed-circuit television. Computer-driven scanners can search through millions of e-mail messages in a heartbeat.

By providing the means to watch and listen to people and to trace their movements, electronic surveillance can help to detect and prevent terrorism. Surveillance may also help to find those responsible for terrorism-related crimes after the fact.

Yet unlike physical searches for particular information or things, electronic surveillance records everything a target says or does. Especially when undertaken over a long period on a 24/7 basis, electronic surveillance casts a wide and open-ended net, capturing data that may be at best irrelevant and at worst deeply personal.

The Constitution contains two provisions that can guard against government abuses of such advanced technology. The Fourth Amendment was included in our Bill of Rights to counter any tendency government might have toward the kind of intimidation practiced by the English Crown against its citizens. The First Amendment was added as a bulwark against government intrusions that could dampen political expression.

This chapter extends our review, begun in Chapter 4, of the evolution of Fourth Amendment and electronic surveillance law in the courts, turning here to legislative efforts in this field. In the aftermath of the Vietnam War, there was widespread concern about reports of government abuses of warrantless electronic surveillance that targeted civil rights leaders, war protesters, and political opponents. Congress responded by enacting measures that regulate the approval of such surveillance. Yet it remained for the courts to explore the scope of constitutional privacy protection recognized in Katz v. United States, 389 U.S. 347 (1967), and Justice Harlan's concurrence in that case. In what settings and under which circumstances is there a reasonable expectation of privacy? More recent litigation testing statutory requirements also examines more closely the meaning of the Fourth Amendment's protection against unreasonable searches, taking into account the separation of powers and the troublesome distinction between law enforcement and counterterrorism.

## A.  THE SCOPE OF FOURTH AMENDMENT PROTECTION

### SMITH v. MARYLAND

United States Supreme Court, 1979
442 U.S. 735

Mr. Justice BLACKMUN delivered the opinion of the Court. This case presents the question whether the installation and use of a pen register[1] constitutes a "search" within the meaning of the Fourth Amendment, made applicable to the States through the Fourteenth Amendment.

On March 5, 1976, in Baltimore, Md., Patricia McDonough was robbed. She gave the police a description of the robber and of a 1975 Monte Carlo automobile she had observed near the scene of the crime. After the robbery, McDonough began receiving threatening and obscene phone calls from a man identifying himself as the robber. On one occasion, the caller asked that she step out on her front porch; she did so, and saw the 1975 Monte Carlo she had earlier described to police moving slowly past her home. On March 16, police spotted a man who met McDonough's description driving a 1975 Monte Carlo in her neighborhood. By tracing the license plate number, police learned that the car was registered in the name of petitioner, Michael Lee Smith.

The next day, the telephone company, at police request, installed a pen register at its central offices to record the numbers dialed from the telephone at petitioner's home. The police did not get a warrant or court order before having the pen register installed. The register revealed that on March 17 a call was placed from petitioner's home to McDonough's phone. On the basis of this and other evidence, the police obtained a warrant to search petitioner's residence. The search revealed that a page in petitioner's phone book was

---

1. "A pen register is a mechanical device that records the numbers dialed on a telephone by monitoring the electrical impulses caused when the dial on the telephone is released. It does not overhear oral communications and does not indicate whether calls are actually completed." United States v. New York Tel. Co., 434 U.S. 159, 161 n.1 [(1977)]. A pen register is "usually installed at a central telephone facility [and] records on a paper tape all numbers dialed from [the] line" to which it is attached. United States v. Giordano, 416 U.S. 505, 549 n.1 (1974).

turned down to the name and number of Patricia McDonough; the phone book was seized. Petitioner was arrested, [convicted, and sentenced to six years' imprisonment.] . . .

. . . In determining whether a particular form of government-initiated electronic surveillance is a "search" within the meaning of the Fourth Amendment, our lodestar is *Katz v. United States*, 389 U.S. 347 (1967). . . .

In applying the *Katz* analysis to this case, it is important to begin by specifying precisely the nature of the state activity that is challenged. The activity here took the form of installing and using a pen register. Since the pen register was installed on telephone company property at the telephone company's central offices, petitioner obviously cannot claim that his "property" was invaded or that police intruded into a "constitutionally protected area." Petitioner's claim, rather, is that, notwithstanding the absence of a trespass, the State, as did the Government in *Katz*, infringed a "legitimate expectation of privacy" that petitioner held. Yet a pen register differs significantly from the listening device employed in *Katz,* for pen registers do not acquire the *contents* of communications. This Court recently noted:

> Indeed, a law enforcement official could not even determine from the use of a pen register whether a communication existed. These devices do not hear sound. They disclose only the telephone numbers that have been dialed — a means of establishing communication. Neither the purport of any communication between the caller and the recipient of the call, their identities, nor whether the call was even completed is disclosed by pen registers. *United States v. New York Tel. Co.*, 434 U.S. 159, 167 (1977).

Given a pen register's limited capabilities, therefore, petitioner's argument that its installation and use constituted a "search" necessarily rests upon a claim that he had a "legitimate expectation of privacy" regarding the numbers he dialed on his phone.

This claim must be rejected. First, we doubt that people in general entertain any actual expectation of privacy in the numbers they dial. All telephone users realize that they must "convey" phone numbers to the telephone company, since it is through telephone company switching equipment that their calls are completed. All subscribers realize, moreover, that the phone company has facilities for making permanent records of the numbers they dial, for they see a list of their long-distance (toll) calls on their monthly bills. In fact, pen registers and similar devices are routinely used by telephone companies "for the purposes of checking billing operations, detecting fraud and preventing violations of law." *United States v. New York Tel. Co.*, 434 U.S. at 174-175. . . .

. . . Most phone books tell subscribers, on a page entitled "Consumer Information," that the company "can frequently help in identifying to the authorities the origin of unwelcome and troublesome calls." Telephone users, in sum, typically know that they must convey numerical information to the phone company; that the phone company has facilities for recording this information; and that the phone company does in fact record this information for a variety of legitimate business purposes. Although subjective expectations cannot be scientifically gauged, it is too much to believe that telephone subscribers, under these circumstances, harbor any general expectation that the numbers they dial will remain secret. . . .

. . . [E]ven if petitioner did harbor some subjective expectation that the phone numbers he dialed would remain private, this expectation is not "one that society is prepared to recognize as 'reasonable.'" This Court consistently has held that a person has no legitimate expectation of privacy in information he voluntarily turns over to third parties. E.g., *United States v. Miller*, 425 U.S. [435 (1976)], at 442-444. In *Miller,* for example, the Court held that a bank depositor has no "legitimate 'expectation of privacy'" in financial information "voluntarily conveyed to . . . banks and exposed to their employees in the ordinary course of business." 425 U.S. at 442. The Court explained:

> The depositor takes the risk, in revealing his affairs to another, that the information will be conveyed by that person to the Government. . . . This Court has held repeatedly that the Fourth Amendment does not prohibit the obtaining of information revealed to a third party and conveyed by him to Government authorities, even if the information is revealed on the assumption that it will be used only for a limited purpose and the confidence placed in the third party will not be betrayed. *Id*. at 443.

Because the depositor "assumed the risk" of disclosure, the Court held that it would be unreasonable for him to expect his financial records to remain private.

This analysis dictates that petitioner can claim no legitimate expectation of privacy here. When he used his phone, petitioner voluntarily conveyed numerical information to the telephone company and "exposed" that information to its equipment in the ordinary course of business. In so doing, petitioner assumed the risk that the company would reveal to police the numbers he dialed. The switching equipment that processed those numbers is merely the modern counterpart of the operator who, in an earlier day, personally completed calls for the subscriber. Petitioner concedes that if he had placed his calls through an operator, he could claim no legitimate expectation of privacy. We are not inclined to hold that a different constitutional result is required because the telephone company has decided to automate. . . .

. . . We therefore conclude that petitioner in all probability entertained no actual expectation of privacy in the phone numbers he dialed, and that, even if he did, his expectation was not "legitimate." The installation and use of a pen register, consequently, was not a "search," and no warrant was required. . . .

Mr. Justice POWELL took no part in the consideration or decision of this case.

Mr. Justice STEWART, with whom Mr. Justice BRENNAN joins, dissenting. . . . The numbers dialed from a private telephone—although certainly more prosaic than the conversation itself—are not without "content." Most private telephone subscribers may have their own numbers listed in a publicly distributed directory, but I doubt there are any who would be happy to have broadcast to the world a list of the local or long distance numbers they have called. This is not because such a list might in some sense be incriminating, but because it easily could reveal the identities of the persons and the places called, and thus reveal the most intimate details of a person's life. . . .

Mr. Justice MARSHALL, with whom Mr. Justice BRENNAN joins, dissenting.
. . . [E]ven assuming . . . that individuals "typically know" that a phone company monitors calls for internal reasons, it does not follow that they expect this information to be made available to the public in general or the government in particular. Privacy is not a discrete commodity, possessed absolutely or not at all. Those who disclose certain facts to a bank or phone company for a limited business purpose need not assume that this information will be released to other persons for other purposes.

The crux of the Court's holding, however, is that whatever expectation of privacy petitioner may in fact have entertained regarding his calls, it is not one "society is prepared to recognize as 'reasonable.'" In so ruling, the Court determines that individuals who convey information to third parties have "assumed the risk" of disclosure to the government. This analysis is misconceived in two critical respects.

Implicit in the concept of assumption of risk is some notion of choice. At least in the third-party consensual surveillance cases, which first incorporated risk analysis into Fourth Amendment doctrine, the defendant presumably had exercised some discretion in deciding who should enjoy his confidential communications. By contrast here, unless a person is prepared to forgo use of what for many has become a personal or professional necessity, he cannot help but accept the risk of surveillance. It is idle to speak of "assuming" risks in contexts where, as a practical matter, individuals have no realistic alternative.

More fundamentally, to make risk analysis dispositive in assessing the reasonableness of privacy expectations would allow the government to define the scope of Fourth Amendment protections. For example, law enforcement officials, simply by announcing their intent to monitor the content of random samples of first-class mail or private phone conversations, could put the public on notice of the risks they would thereafter assume in such communications. Yet, although acknowledging this implication of its analysis, the Court is willing to concede only that, in some circumstances, a further "normative inquiry would be proper." No meaningful effort is made to explain what those circumstances might be, or why this case is not among them.

In my view, whether privacy expectations are legitimate within the meaning of *Katz* depends not on the risks an individual can be presumed to accept when imparting information to third parties, but on the risks he should be forced to assume in a free and open society. . . .

The use of pen registers, I believe, constitutes such an extensive intrusion. To hold otherwise ignores the vital role telephonic communication plays in our personal and professional relationships, as well as the First and Fourth Amendment interests implicated by unfettered official surveillance. Privacy in placing calls is of value not only to those engaged in criminal activity. The prospect of unregulated governmental monitoring will undoubtedly prove disturbing even to those with nothing illicit to hide. Many individuals, including members of unpopular political organizations or journalists with confidential sources, may legitimately wish to avoid disclosure of their personal contacts. Permitting governmental access to telephone records on less than probable cause may thus impede certain forms of political affiliation and journalistic endeavor that are the hallmark of a truly free society. Particularly given the Government's previous reliance on warrantless telephonic surveillance to trace reporters' sources and monitor protected political activity, I am unwilling to insulate use of pen registers from independent judicial review. . . .

## NOTES AND QUESTIONS

1. *Pen Registers and Trap and Trace vs. Wiretaps.* What is it about a pen register or trap and trace device that makes it so different from a wiretap? Should the differences have such constitutional significance? Consider the analogy to a mailed letter. The letter contains protected content, while the envelope contains only the mailing and return addresses and postage information. Thus, the contents of the letter deserve protection, but the envelope does not. *See* Orin S. Kerr, *Internet Surveillance Law After the USA Patriot Act: The Big Brother That Isn't*, 97 Nw. U. L. Rev. 607, 611-616 (2003). Does the same contents/envelope distinction fit the pen register/trap and trace scenarios? Consider the views of Justices Stewart and Marshall. What "content" is arguably revealed by a pen register? *See* Daniel J. Solove, *Reconstructing Electronic Surveillance Law*, 72 Geo. Wash. L. Rev. 1264, 1286-1287 (2004).

2. *Comparing Katz.* Is the privacy interest recognized by the Court in *Katz* different in any appreciable way from the interest asserted in *Smith*? If the telephone company had the technical means to listen in on the phone calls in both cases, why protect one caller but not the other? Are the phone numbers dialed private? Should they be? *See* Patricia Bellia, *Surveillance Law Through Cyberlaw's Lens*, 72 Geo. Wash. L. Rev. 1375, 1405 (2004). Why should providing that information to a private third party matter so much in deciding what information the government can acquire? When you provide phone numbers to the phone company, do you expect that the company will turn them over to Big Brother? Have you knowingly and willingly "assumed the risk" of such disclosure?

   Alternately, is the outcome in *Smith* best understood as reflecting a judgment that it doesn't really matter much, because the phone numbers were not of much value to the individual? *See* Daniel J. Solove, *Digital Dossiers and the Dissipation of the Fourth Amendment Privacy*, 75 S. Cal. L. Rev. 1083 (2002).

3. *A Statutory Remedy?* After *Smith*, Congress enacted the Pen Register Act, 18 U.S.C. §§3121-3127 (2000 & Supp. IV 2004). The Act imposes a warrant requirement before the government may obtain a pen register. *Id.* §3121(a). However, in contrast to a traditional Fourth Amendment warrant based on probable cause, the government may obtain an order for a pen register simply by showing that its use is "relevant to an ongoing investigation." *Id.* §3123(a).

4. *Extending Smith to the Internet.* Is *Smith* authority for searching e-mail subject lines and URLs without a warrant? The USA Patriot Act extended

the pen register and trap and trace authorities to addressing information on e-mail and to ISP and URL addresses. Pub. L. No. 107-56, §216, 115 Stat. 272, 288-290 (2001) (amending 18 U.S.C. §3127(3), (4)). Is this statutory provision constitutional?

5. ***Location, Location, Location.*** First and Fourth Amendment interests have not always received such extensive judicial protection where arguably less intrusive information collection techniques are employed. For example, in an area that is open to visual surveillance, the monitoring of beeper signals from a radio transmitter placed in contraband material and picked up by a police radio receiver does not trigger Fourth Amendment protections, because the target has no legitimate expectation of privacy. United States v. Knotts, 460 U.S. 276, 284-285 (1983). The same result applies when the police use the beeper signal to monitor movements, so long as visual surveillance could have performed the monitoring. *Id.* at 285.

   Does this extension of *Katz* imply that someone who "knowingly exposes" her movements to others in a public place has no reasonable expectation of privacy when others, including police or intelligence officials, take note of or record those movements? Katz v. United States, 389 U.S. 347, 351 (1967). In many cities today, public cameras are ubiquitous, and video surveillance in stores, banks, mass transit facilities, and other places where crowds gather is now commonplace. Do individuals who enter places with surveillance cameras have any protectable privacy interests that are threatened by the surveillance? Does your answer depend on whether the place is truly "public"? Can you define "public" for this purpose? Does knowledge of the surveillance equal consent?

6. ***Who's Listening?*** Does the application of the Fourth Amendment in a public place depend on who is conducting the surveillance or perhaps on who ends up with a record of the surveillance? In Laird v. Tatum, 408 U.S. 1, 10 (1972), the Supreme Court dismissed on standing grounds a complaint against an Army program that investigated civil disturbances by collecting personal information about individuals and organizations. See *infra* p. 682. *See also* Socialist Workers Party v. Attorney General, 510 F.2d 253 (2d Cir. 1974) (approving undercover FBI surveillance of convention of Young Socialists of America). *But see* Philadelphia Yearly Meeting of the Religious Society of Friends v. Tate, 519 F.2d 1335 (3d Cir. 1975) (approving photography and compilation of records on political demonstrators, but not the sharing of information with private employers or broadcasters).

   In 2007, a federal court ruled that the New York City Police Department could not engage in routine videotaping of people at public gatherings unless there is some indication that unlawful activity may occur. Handschu v. Special Services Division, 475 F. Supp. 2d 331 (S.D.N.Y. 2007). After reviewing two events in 2005 — a march in Harlem and a demonstration by homeless people in front of the Mayor's residence — the court found that there was "no reason to suspect or anticipate that unlawful or terrorist activity might occur" or that "pertinent information" of such activity might be obtained by filming the participants. *Id.* at 351. What do you suppose police officials would have to show before such surveillance would be lawful? *See* Blitz, *supra*, 82 Tex. L. Rev. at 1406-1407.

Constitutional protections generally have not been extended to investigations based on the use of informants and the examination of financial records. *See* John Elliff, *The Attorney General's Guidelines for FBI Investigations*, 69 Cornell L. Rev. 785, 788-789 (1984). Should the courts be more solicitous of individual rights in these cases?

7. ***Effect of New Technologies on Fourth Amendment Law.*** Evolving surveillance technologies continue to raise civil liberties concerns. In Kyllo v. United States, 533 U.S. 27 (2001), the police used thermal imaging technology to measure the heat radiating from the exterior walls of a private home to verify suspicions that high-intensity lamps were being used indoors to grow marijuana. Because the sense-enhancing technology permitted intrusion into the home that would not otherwise have been possible without physical intrusion, and because the thermal imaging technique is not in general public use, the Court found that the homeowner had a reasonable expectation of privacy that was violated. *Id.* at 34-35. Although the Court has declined to speculate generally about the effects of changing technologies on Fourth Amendment protections, it has noted that expectations of privacy changed dramatically when air flight permitted new forms of observation. *See* Dow Chemical Co. v. United States, 476 U.S. 227, 234-235 (1986) (advanced aerial photography of business activities not a "search" for Fourth Amendment purposes).

Do these developments insulate from constitutional challenge the use of evolving technologies such as GPS tracking devices; radio frequency identification (RFID) chips in passports and consumer goods; iris, gait, face recognition, and other biometric surveillance; even whole-body backscatter x-ray in public places? *See* Marc Jonathan Blitz, *Video Surveillance and the Constitution of Public Space: Fitting the Fourth Amendment to a World That Tracks Image and Identity*, 82 Tex. L. Rev. 1349, 1375-1398 (2004). Has an individual's reasonable expectation of privacy necessarily changed because she now "risks" not merely observation but also recognition (and perhaps much more) whenever she goes into a public place? Consider Justice Marshall's observation that it is "idle to speak of 'assuming' risks in contexts where, as a practical matter, individuals have no practical alternative." Smith v. Maryland, 442 U.S. 735, 750 (1979) (Marshall, J., dissenting). If you think the relentless development of new surveillance technologies and their increasingly ubiquitous official use might effectively "allow the government to define the scope of Fourth Amendment protections," *id.*, how would you propose to limit such use?

8. ***Comparing Keith.*** *Smith* is like United States v. United States District Court (*Keith*), 407 U.S. 297 (1972), *supra* p. 91, in that both decisions of the Court prompted federal legislation. Recall, however, that the problem addressed in *Keith* was wiretapping for domestic security investigations. Although Justice Powell's opinion for the Court suggested that something other than traditional law enforcement warrant requirements might be appropriate for such investigations, the Court did not suggest what a satisfactory judicial approval scheme might look like. When Congress responded with legislation a few years later, the resulting statute did nothing to guide domestic intelligence investigations. Instead, Congress created a scheme for the collection of foreign intelligence inside the United States.

# B. CONGRESSIONAL AUTHORITY FOR SURVEILLANCE: THE FOREIGN INTELLIGENCE SURVEILLANCE ACT (FISA)

The Supreme Court's decision in the *Keith* case, *supra* p. 91, was only one part of a unique set of circumstances that led to the enactment in 1978 of the Foreign Intelligence Surveillance Act (FISA), 50 U.S.C.A §§1801-1862 (West 2003 & Supp. 2006). In addition to the Watergate scandal, the early 1970s saw startling revelations of illegal spying and other activities by U.S. intelligence agencies, including the FBI and CIA, and by the IRS and the military. These agencies sought to target and disrupt politically active domestic groups (principally civil rights and anti-war organizations), and they engaged in widespread warrantless surveillance. The Senate Select Committee to Study Government Operations with Respect to Intelligence Activities, known as the Church Committee, for its chairman Senator Frank Church, summarized the effects of these domestic intelligence abuses in a 1976 report:

> FBI headquarters alone has developed over 500,000 domestic intelligence files, and these have been augmented by additional files at FBI Field Offices. The FBI opened 65,000 of these domestic intelligence files in 1972 alone. In fact, substantially more individuals and groups are subject to intelligence scrutiny than the number of files would appear to indicate, since typically, each domestic intelligence file contains information on more than one individual or group, and this information is readily retrievable through the FBI General Name Index.
>
> The number of Americans and domestic groups caught in the domestic intelligence net is further illustrated by the following statistics:
>
> • Nearly a quarter of a million first class letters were opened and photographed in the United States by the CIA between 1953-1973, producing a CIA computerized index of nearly one and one-half million names.
> • At least 130,000 first class letters were opened and photographed by the FBI between 1940-1966 in eight U.S. cities.
> • Some 300,000 individuals were indexed in a CIA computer system and separate files were created on approximately 7,200 Americans and over 100 domestic groups during the course of CIA's Operation CHAOS (1967-1973).
> • Millions of private telegrams sent from, to, or through the United States were obtained by the National Security Agency from 1947 to 1975 under a secret arrangement with three United States telegraph companies.
> • An estimated 100,000 Americans were the subjects of United States Army intelligence files created between the mid-1960's and 1971.
> • Intelligence files on more than 11,000 individuals and groups were created by the Internal Revenue Service between 1969 and 1973 and tax investigations were started on the basis of political rather than tax criteria.
> • At least 26,000 individuals were at one point catalogued on an FBI list of persons to be rounded up in the event of a "national emergency."
>
> [Select Committee to Study Government Operations with Respect to Intelligence Activities (Church Committee), *Intelligence Activities and the Rights of Americans,* S. Rep. No. 94-755, Book II, at 6-7 (1976).]

Two years later, Congress enacted FISA. Consider how that statute applied to the defendants in the following case and whether it is constitutional.

## UNITED STATES V. ROSEN

United States District Court,
Eastern District of Virginia, 2006
447 F. Supp. 2d 538

ELLIS, District Judge. Defendants, Steven J. Rosen and Keith Weissman, are charged . . . with one count of conspiring to communicate national defense information to persons not entitled to receive it, in violation of 18 U.S.C. §793(d), (e) and (g). More specifically, Count One . . . alleges that between April 1999 and continuing until August 2004, Rosen and Weissman along with alleged co-conspirator Lawrence Franklin, then an employee of the Department of Defense ("DOD"), were engaged in a conspiracy to communicate information relating to the national defense to those not entitled to receive it. According to the superseding indictment, Franklin and certain other unnamed government officials with authorized possession of classified national defense information communicated that information to Rosen and Weissman, who were employed at the time as lobbyists for the American-Israel Public Affairs Committee (AIPAC). It is further alleged that Rosen and Weissman then communicated the information received from their government sources to members of the media, other foreign policy analysts, and certain foreign officials, none of whom were authorized to receive this information. . . .

In the course of its investigation of the alleged conspiracy, the government sought and obtained orders issued by the Foreign Intelligence Surveillance Court ("FISC") pursuant to the Foreign Intelligence Surveillance Act ("FISA"), 50 U.S.C. §1801 *et seq.*, authorizing certain physical searches and electronic surveillance. As the investigation pertained to national security, these applications and orders were classified. Because the government intends to offer evidence obtained or derived from physical searches and electronic surveillance authorized by these orders, defendants seek by motion (1) to obtain disclosure of the classified applications submitted to the FISC, the FISC's orders, and related materials, and/or (2) to suppress the evidence obtained or derived from any searches or surveillance conducted pursuant to the issued FISA orders. . . .

### I.

FISA, enacted in 1978, was Congress's response to three related concerns: (1) the judicial confusion over the existence, nature and scope of a foreign intelligence exception to the Fourth Amendment's warrant requirement that arose in the wake of the Supreme Court's 1972 decision in United States v. United States District Court, 407 U.S. 297 (1972); (2) the Congressional concern over perceived Executive Branch abuses of such an exception;[2] and (3) the felt need to provide the Executive Branch with an appropriate means to investigate and counter foreign intelligence threats.[3] FISA accommodates these concerns by establishing a detailed process the Executive Branch must follow to obtain orders allowing it to collect foreign intelligence information "without violating the rights of citizens of the United States." United States v. Hammoud, 381 F.3d 316, 332 (4th Cir. 2004) (en banc), *vacated on other grounds,* 543 U.S. 1097 (2005), *reinstated in pertinent part,* 405 F.3d 1034 (2005). Although originally limited to electronic surveillance, FISA's coverage has now been expanded to include physical searches, as well. Thus, the detailed FISA process applicable to electronic surveillance relating to foreign intelligence also applies now to physical searches.[4]

FISA's detailed procedure for obtaining orders authorizing electronic surveillance or physical searches of a foreign power or an agent of a foreign power begins with the government's filing of an *ex parte,* under seal application with the FISC.[5] Such an application must be approved by the Attorney General and must include certain specified information. *See* 50 U.S.C. §§1804(a) and 1823(a). A FISC judge considering the application may also require the submission of additional information necessary to make the requisite findings under §§1805(a) and 1824(a).

After review of the application, a single judge of the FISC must enter an *ex parte* Order granting the government's application for electronic surveillance or a physical search of a foreign power or an agent of a foreign power provided the judge makes certain specific findings, including most importantly, that on the basis of the facts submitted by the applicant there is probable cause to believe that—

> (1) the target of the electronic surveillance or physical search is a foreign power or an agent of a foreign power, except that no United States person may be considered a foreign power or an agent of a foreign power solely upon the basis of activities protected by the First Amendment to the Constitution of the United States; and
> (2) for electronic surveillance, each of the facilities or places at which the electronic surveillance is directed is being used, or is about to be used, by a foreign power or an agent of a foreign power; or

---

2. *See* S. Rep. No. 95-604(I), at 7, 1978 U.S.C.C.A.N. 3904, 3908 [hereinafter S. Judiciary Comm. Rep.] ("This legislation is in large measure a response to the revelations that warrantless electronic surveillance in the name of national security has been seriously abused.").

3. *See generally* William C. Banks and M.E. Bowman, *Executive Authority for National Security Surveillance,* 50 Am. U. L. Rev. 1, 75-76 (2000) (describing the impetus for FISA).

4. *See* Intelligence Authorization Act for Fiscal Year 1995, Pub. L. No. 103-359, 108 Stat. 3443 (1994) (codified as amended at 50 U.S.C. §1821 *et seq.*). And, in 1998, Congress further amended FISA to create slightly different procedures for authorizing the use of pen registers and trap and trace devices for foreign intelligence information, *see* Intelligence Authorization Act for Fiscal Year 1999, Pub. L. No. 105-272, 112 Stat. 2405 (1998) (codified as amended at 50 U.S.C. §1841 *et seq.*), and to allow the executive branch access to business records for foreign intelligence and international terrorism investigations. *See* 18 U.S.C. §§1861-63. The parties' dispute involves only electronic surveillance and physical searches conducted pursuant to FISA.

5. The FISC consists of eleven district court judges selected by the Chief Justice from at least seven judicial circuits and serving staggered seven year terms. *See* 50 U.S.C. §1803(a). At least three of the FISC's judges must reside within twenty miles of Washington, D.C. *Id.* In the unlikely event that a FISA application is denied by a judge of the FISC, the government may seek review of such denial in the Foreign Intelligence Surveillance Court of Review (FISCR), and if necessary, in the Supreme Court of the United States. *See* 50 U.S.C. §1803(b).

(3) for physical searches, the premises or property to be searched is owned, used, possessed by, or is in transit to or from an agent of a foreign power or a foreign power.

*See* 50 U.S.C. §§1805(a) and 1823(a).[6] If the FISC judge's findings reflect that the government has satisfied the statute's requirements, the judge must issue an order approving the surveillance or search. Such an order must describe the target, the information sought, and the means of acquiring such information. *See* 50 U.S.C. §§1805(c)(1) and 1824(c)(1). The order must also set forth the period of time during which the electronic surveillance or physical searches are approved, which is generally ninety days or until the objective of the electronic surveillance or physical search has been achieved. *See* 50 U.S.C. §§1805(e)(1) and 1824(d)(1). Applications for a renewal of the order must generally be made upon the same basis as the original application and require the same findings by the FISC. *See* 50 U.S.C. §§1805(e)(2) and 1824(d)(2).

Although FISA is chiefly directed to obtaining "foreign intelligence information,"[7] the Act specifically contemplates cooperation between federal authorities conducting electronic surveillance and physical searches pursuant to FISA and federal law enforcement officers investigating clandestine intelligence activities. In this respect, FISA explicitly allows the use of evidence derived from FISA surveillance and searches in criminal prosecutions. *See* 50 U.S.C. §§1806(k) and 1825(k).

If the Attorney General approves the use of evidence collected pursuant to FISA in a criminal prosecution, and the government intends to use or disclose FISA evidence at the trial of an "aggrieved person,"[8] the government must first

---

6. In addition to these probable cause findings, the FISC judge must also find that: (1) the President has authorized the Attorney General to approve applications for electronic surveillance or physical searches for foreign intelligence information; (2) that the application has been made by a Federal officer and approved by the Attorney General; (3) that the proposed minimization procedures meet the respective definitions of minimization procedures for electronic surveillance and physical searches; and (4) that the application contains all statements and certifications required by 50 U.S.C. §1804 for electronic surveillance and 50 U.S.C. §1823 for physical searches and, if the target is a United States person, the certification or certifications are not clearly erroneous on the basis of the statement made under sections 1804(a)(7)(E) and 1823(a)(7)(E) of title 18 and any other information furnished under sections 1804(d) and 1823(c) of this title. *See* 50 U.S.C. §§1805(a) and 1823(a).

7. FISA defines "foreign intelligence information" as —

(1) information that relates to, and if concerning a United States person is necessary to, the ability of the United States to protect against —
    (A) actual or potential attack or other grave hostile acts of a foreign power or an agent of a foreign power;
    (B) sabotage or international terrorism by a foreign power or an agent of a foreign power; or
    (C) clandestine intelligence activities by an intelligence service or network of a foreign power or by an agent of a foreign power; or
(2) information with respect to a foreign power or foreign territory that relates to, and if concerning a United States person is necessary to —
    (A) the national defense or the security of the United States; or
    (B) the conduct of the foreign affairs of the United States.

50 U.S.C. §1801(e).

8. FISA defines an "aggrieved person" with respect to electronic surveillance as "a person who is the target of an electronic surveillance or any other person whose communications or activities were subject to electronic surveillance." 50 U.S.C. §1801(k). With respect to physical searches, FISA

notify the aggrieved person and the district court that the government intends to disclose or use the FISA evidence. *See* 50 U.S.C. §§1806(c) and 1825(d). On receiving such notification, an aggrieved person may seek to suppress any evidence derived from FISA surveillance or searches on the grounds that: (1) the evidence was unlawfully acquired; or (2) the electronic surveillance or physical search was not conducted in conformity with the Order of authorization or approval. *See* 50 U.S.C. §§1806(e) and 1825(f). And, if an aggrieved person moves to suppress FISA evidence or to obtain FISA material, then upon the filing of an affidavit by the Attorney General stating under oath that disclosure of such material would harm national security, the district court must review the FISA warrant applications and related materials *in camera* and *ex parte* to determine whether the surveillance or search "of the aggrieved person was lawfully authorized and conducted." 50 U.S.C. §§1806(f) and 1825(g).

This review is properly *de novo,* especially given that the review is *ex parte* and thus unaided by the adversarial process. Thus, the government's contention here that a reviewing district court must accord the FISC's probable cause determination "substantial deference" cannot be sustained in light of the Fourth Circuit's clear contrary statement on the issue. But the government is correct that the certifications contained in the applications should be "presumed valid." *See* 50 U.S.C. §1805(a)(5) (applying "clearly erroneous" standard to factual averments contained in certification when the target is a United States person). . . .

## II.

At the threshold, defendants seek disclosure of the FISA applications, orders, and related materials at issue in this case so they may effectively participate in the review process. On this point FISA is clear: It allows a reviewing court to disclose such materials "only where such disclosure is necessary to make an accurate determination of the legality of the surveillance." 50 U.S.C. §1806(f). Defendants claim this condition is met, by arguing (1) that the FISC's determination that they were agents of a foreign power was surely wrong; and (2) that evidence of the government's evident failure to comply with FISA's minimization procedures requires disclosure. Neither argument is persuasive. . . .

Review of the FISA applications, orders and other materials in this case presented none of the concerns that might warrant disclosure to defendants. The FISA dockets contained no facial inconsistencies, nor did they disclose any reason to doubt any of the representations made by the government in its applications. Likewise, the targets of the surveillance are precisely defined. Finally, although defendants claim that the discovery obtained from the government contains a significant amount of non-foreign intelligence information, this contention relies upon an inordinately narrow view of what constitutes foreign intelligence information, and therefore is unavailing. For these reasons,

---

similarly defines an "aggrieved person" as a "person whose premises, property, information, or material is the target of physical search or any other person whose premises, property, information, or material was subject to physical search." 50 U.S.C. §1821(2).

and given the government's legitimate national security interest in maintaining the secrecy of the information contained in the FISA applications, disclosure of the FISA materials to defendants is not warranted in this case.

## III. ....

Defendants' attack on the lawfulness of the FISA surveillance in this case focuses chiefly on two issues: (1) whether the FISC had probable cause to believe that the targets of the sanctioned surveillance were "agents of a foreign power," as required by FISA, and (2) whether there was proper compliance with the minimization procedures subsequent to the surveillance. Review of the FISA material confirms that both of these issues must be resolved in favor of the lawfulness of the surveillance.

Defendants' necessarily speculative contention that the FISC must have erred when it found probable cause to believe that the targets are agents of a foreign power is without merit. An agent of a foreign power is defined by the statute, in pertinent part, as any person who —

(A) knowingly engages in clandestine intelligence gathering activities for or on behalf of a foreign power, which activities involve or may involve a violation of the criminal statutes of the United States;

(B) pursuant to the direction of an intelligence service or network of a foreign power, knowingly engages in any other clandestine intelligence activities for or on behalf of such power, which activities involve or are about to involve a violation of the criminal statutes of the United States; ... or

(E) knowingly aids or abets any person in the conduct of activities described in [the subparagraphs above] or knowingly conspires with any person to engage in activities described in [the subparagraphs above].

50 U.S.C. §1801(b)(2). Although the phrase "clandestine intelligence gathering activities" is not defined in FISA, the legislative history demonstrates that the drafters viewed these "activities" in light of the criminal espionage laws, including 18 U.S.C. §§793 and 794, and considered that such "activities" would include, for example, "collection or transmission of information or material that is not generally available to the public." *See* S. Rep. No. 95-701, at 21-22 (1978), 1978 U.S.C.C.A.N. 3973, 3990-91 [hereinafter S. Intelligence Rep.]. ...

Importantly, FISA is clear that in determining whether there is probable cause to believe that a potential target of FISA surveillance or a FISA search is an agent of a foreign power, the FISC judge may not consider a United States person an agent of a foreign power "*solely* upon the basis of activities protected by the First Amendment." 50 U.S.C. §1805(a) (emphasis added). From this plain language, it follows that the probable cause determination may rely in part on activities protected by the First Amendment, provided the determination also relies on activities not protected by the First Amendment. This issue received extensive treatment in the legislative history, which, consistent with the statute's plain language, makes clear that First Amendment activities cannot form the *sole* basis for concluding a U.S. person is an agent of a foreign power. The following excerpt from the legislative history illustrates this point:

> The Bill is not intended to authorize electronic surveillance when a United States person's activities, even though secret and conducted for a foreign power, consist entirely of lawful acts such as lobbying or the use of confidential contacts to influence public officials, directly or indirectly, through the dissemination of information. Individuals exercising their right to lobby public officials or to engage in political dissent from official policy may well be in contact with representatives of foreign governments and groups when the issues concern foreign affairs or international economic matters.
>
> They must continue to be free to communicate about such issues and to obtain information or exchange views with representatives of foreign governments or with foreign groups, free from any fear that such contact might be the basis for probable cause to believe they are acting at the direction of a foreign power thus triggering the government's power to conduct electronic surveillance.

*See* S. Intelligence Rep. at 29.

The legislative history makes equally clear, however, that this protection extends only to the "*lawful* exercise of First Amendment rights of speech, petition, assembly and association." *Id.* (emphasis added). Similarly, the House Report (Intelligence Committee) emphasized that FISA "would not authorize surveillance of ethnic Americans who *lawfully* gather political information and perhaps even *lawfully* share it with the foreign government of their national origin." *See* In re Sealed Case, 310 F.3d 717, 739 (FISCR 2002) (emphasis added) (quoting H. Rep. No. 95-1283, at 40). For example, electronic surveillance might be appropriate if there is probable cause to believe that —

> foreign intelligence services [are] hid[ing] behind the cover of some person or organization in order to influence American political events and deceive Americans into believing that the opinions or influence are of domestic origin and initiative and such deception is willfully maintained in violation of the Foreign Agents Registration Act.

S. Intelligence Rep. at 29. Thus, if the FISC judge has probable cause to believe that the potential target is engaged in *unlawful* activities in addition to those protected by the First Amendment, the FISC may authorize surveillance of a U.S. person.

In this respect, it is important to emphasize the significant difference between FISA's probable cause requirement and the government's ultimate burden to prove the existence of criminal activity beyond a reasonable doubt. Indeed, the Fourth Circuit has described probable cause in this context as "a fluid concept — turning on the assessment of probabilities in particular factual contexts — not readily, or even usefully, reduced to a neat set of rules." United States v. Hammoud, 381 F.3d [316 (4th Cir. 2004),] at 332 (upholding probable cause finding that Hammoud was an agent of Hizballah). Furthermore, "[i]n evaluating whether probable cause exists, it is the task of the issuing judge 'to make a practical, common-sense decision, whether, given all the circumstances set forth in the affidavit, there is a fair probability' that the search will be fruitful." *Id.* (quoting Illinois v. Gates, 462 U.S. 213, 238 (1983)); *see also* Mason v. Godinez, 47 F.3d 852, 855 (7th Cir. 1995) ("Probable cause means more than bare suspicion but less than absolute certainty that a search will be fruitful."). And, in making the probable cause determination, FISA permits a judge to "consider past activities of the target, as well as facts and circumstances relating to current or future activities of the target." 50 U.S.C. §1805(b). Furthermore, with respect to those U.S. persons suspected of involvement in clandestine intelligence activities, the probable cause determination "does not necessarily require a showing of an imminent violation of criminal law" because "Congress clearly intended a lesser showing of probable cause for these activities than that applicable to ordinary cases." In re Sealed Case, 310 F.3d at 738. Illustrative of this intent is FISA's description of clandestine intelligence activities as those that "involve or *may* involve a violation of the criminal statutes of the United States." 50 U.S.C. §1801(b)(2)(A); *see* In re Sealed Case, 310 F.3d at 738. As FISA's drafters made clear: "The term 'may involve' not only requires less information regarding the crime involved, but also permits electronic surveillance at some point prior to the time when a crime sought to be prevented, as for example, the transfer of classified documents, actually occurs." In re Sealed Case, 310 F.3d at 738 (quoting H. Rep. No. 95-1283, at 40). Thus, while the statute is intended to avoid permitting electronic surveillance solely on the basis of First Amendment activities, it plainly allows a FISC judge to issue an order allowing the surveillance or physical search if there is probable cause to believe that the target, even if engaged in First Amendment activities, may also be involved in unlawful clandestine intelligence activities, or in knowingly aiding and abetting such activities. In these circumstances, the fact that a target is also involved in protected First Amendment activities is no bar to electronic surveillance pursuant to FISA.

A thorough review of the FISA dockets in issue confirms that the FISC had ample probable cause to believe that the targets were agents of a foreign power quite apart from their First Amendment lobbying activities. While the defendants' lobbying activities are generally protected by the First Amendment, willful violations of §793 are not, and as is demonstrated by the allegations contained in the superseding indictment, the FISC had probable cause to believe that such violations had occurred in this case.

Defendants' second argument in support of their motion is that the government failed to follow the applicable minimization procedures. In this regard, it is true that once the electronic surveillance or the physical search has been approved, the government must apply the specific minimization procedures contained in the application to the FISC. These minimization procedures are "designed to protect, as far as reasonable, against the acquisition, retention, and dissemination of nonpublic information which is not foreign intelligence information." In re Sealed Case, 310 F.3d 717, 731 (FISCR 2002). While the specific minimization procedures for each application are classified, they must meet the definition of minimization procedures under §1801(h) for electronic surveillance and §1821(4) for physical searches. FISA minimization procedures include, in pertinent part—

(1) specific procedures adopted by the Attorney General that are reasonably designed in light of the purpose and technique of the particular

surveillance or search, to minimize the acquisition and retention, and prohibit the dissemination, of nonpublicly available information concerning unconsenting United States persons consistent with the need of the United States to obtain, produce, and disseminate foreign intelligence information;

(2) procedures that require that nonpublicly available information, which is not foreign intelligence information, shall not be disseminated in a manner that identifies any United States person, without such person's consent, unless such person's identity is necessary to understand foreign intelligence information or assess its importance;

(3) notwithstanding paragraphs (1) and (2), procedures that allow for the retention and dissemination of information that is evidence of a crime which has been, is being, or is about to be committed and that is to be retained or disseminated for law enforcement purposes.

*See* 50 U.S.C. §§1801(h) and 1821(4). Congress intended these minimization procedures to act as a safeguard for U.S. persons at the acquisition, retention and dissemination phases of electronic surveillance and searches. *See* S. Intelligence Rep. at 39. Thus, for example, minimization at the acquisition stage is designed to insure that the communications of non-target U.S. persons who happen to be using a FISA target's telephone, or who happen to converse with the target about non-foreign intelligence information, are not improperly disseminated. *See id.* Similarly, minimization at the retention stage is intended to ensure that "information acquired, which is not necessary for obtaining, producing, or disseminating foreign intelligence information, be destroyed where feasible." *See* In re Sealed Case, 310 F.3d at 731 (quoting H. Rep. No. 95-1283, at 56). Finally, the dissemination of foreign intelligence information "needed for an approved purpose . . . should be restricted to those officials with a need for such information." *Id.* As the Foreign Intelligence Surveillance Court of Review has recently made clear, these procedures do not prohibit the sharing of foreign intelligence information between FBI intelligence officials and criminal prosecutors when there is evidence of a crime. *Id.*

FISA's minimization procedures are meant to parallel the minimization procedures of Title III, which courts have sensibly construed as not requiring the total elimination of innocent conversation. *See* S. Intelligence Rep. at 39 (citing United States v. Bynum, 485 F.2d 490, 500 (2d Cir. 1973), *cert. denied*, 423 U.S. 952 (1975)).[15] On the contrary, "[i]n assessing the minimization effort, the Court's role is to determine whether 'on the whole the agents have shown a high regard for the right of privacy and have done all they reasonably could to avoid unnecessary intrusion.'" *Id.* at 39-40 (quoting United States v. Tortorello, 480 F.2d 764 (2d Cir.), *cert. denied*, 414 U.S. 866 (1973)). Thus, "[a]bsent a charge that the minimization procedures have been disregarded completely,

---

15. Title III's minimization procedures provide, in pertinent part, that:

Every order and extension thereof shall contain a provision that the authorization to intercept shall be executed as soon as practicable, shall be conducted in such a way as to minimize the interception of communications not otherwise subject to interception under this chapter, and must terminate upon attainment of the authorized objective, or in any event in thirty days.

*See* 18 U.S.C. §2518(5).

the test of compliance is 'whether a good faith effort to minimize was attempted.'" *Id.* (quoting United States v. Armocida, 515 F.2d 29, 44 (3d Cir. 1975)).

Obviously, the extent of the government's minimization will depend largely on its construction of the term "foreign intelligence information." And in this respect, "foreign intelligence information" includes, among other things, "information that relates to, and if concerning a United States person is necessary to, the ability of the United States to protect against . . . clandestine intelligence activities by an intelligence service or network of a foreign power or by an agent of a foreign power." 50 U.S.C. §1801(e). Acknowledging the inherent difficulty in determining whether something is related to clandestine activity, courts have construed "foreign intelligence information" broadly and sensibly allowed the government some latitude in its determination of what is foreign intelligence information. As the Fourth Circuit pointed out, "[i]t is not always immediately clear" whether a particular conversation must be minimized because "[a] conversation that seems innocuous on one day may later turn out to be of great significance, particularly if the individuals involved are talking in code." *Hammoud,* 381 F.3d at 334. For this reason, "when the government eavesdrops on clandestine groups . . . investigators often find it necessary to intercept all calls in order to record possible code language or oblique references to the illegal scheme." United States v. Truong, 629 F.2d 908, 917 (4th Cir. 1980). This latitude was intended by FISA's drafters who understood that it may be necessary to "acquire, retain and disseminate information concerning . . . the known contacts" of a U.S. person engaged in clandestine intelligence activities even though some of those contacts will invariably be innocent of any wrong-doing. H. Rep. No. 95-1283, at 58.

Given the breadth of the term "foreign intelligence information" in the context of investigating clandestine intelligence activities and the rule of reason that applies to the government's obligation to minimize non-pertinent information, defendants' motion to suppress for failure to properly minimize must be denied. The *ex parte, in camera* review of the FISA dockets discloses that any failures to minimize properly the electronic surveillance of the defendants were (i) inadvertent, (ii) disclosed to the FISC on discovery, and (iii) promptly rectified.

Yet, this does not end the analysis as the defendants also point to certain publicly available materials bearing on the FBI's general compliance with FISA during the period of this investigation. Specifically, defendants refer to (1) certain previously classified FBI documents, obtained by the media via the Freedom of Information Act, 5 U.S.C. §552, detailing violations of minimization procedures in certain unrelated cases, and (2) a March 8, 2006 Department of Justice, Office of the Inspector General Report to Congress on Implementation of Section 1001 of the USA Patriot Act describing certain failures of the FBI to adhere to FISA's requirements. These documents are general assessments and do not specifically address the integrity of the minimization effort that occurred here. As such, they are no more probative of a failure of minimization in this case than a general study of errors committed over a period of years in baseball would be probative of whether errors occurred in a specific game.

No doubt anticipating this, defendants also cite pre-indictment media reports of the charges eventually brought against Rosen, Weissman and alleged co-conspirator Franklin. In defendants' view these media reports are evidence of an intentional disregard for minimization requirements because the information in these reports could only have come from FISA surveillance. . . .

Even assuming these media reports came from a FISA minimization breach — other plausible explanations exist — a single unauthorized leak does not establish a complete disregard of the minimization requirements sufficient to warrant suppression of the entire investigation. FISA's minimization requirements were designed to protect the privacy interests of FISA targets, but these requirements are subject to a rule of reason and were not intended to invest a rogue official with the power to undermine a lengthy investigation. This sensible point was well-recognized by FISA's drafters who found persuasive the analogous Title III case law.[19] Accordingly, these news reports do not suffice on this record to warrant suppression of the FISA surveillance and an appropriate order will enter. This order will also grant defendants leave to renew this motion on this ground alone should the results of an investigation of the leak, which will be separately ordered, warrant doing so. . . .

## NOTES AND QUESTIONS

After reading *Rosen*, would you say that FISA supplies a constitutionally adequate substitute for the traditional law enforcement warrant? What advantages does FISA provide for intelligence officials? What drawbacks are there to the FISA process, from the investigators' point of view? If FISA had not been enacted, how and pursuant to what authority would investigators have learned about the alleged criminal activities of the co-conspirators charged in *Rosen*? To what extent does the legality of FISA surveillance turn on whether the objective of the investigation is a criminal prosecution?

### a.  The Mechanics of FISA

1. *Information Subject to FISA Surveillance.* Review the definition of "foreign intelligence information" quoted in *Rosen*. "International terrorism," which forms part of that definition, is itself defined in FISA to include activities that —

> (1) involve violent acts or acts dangerous to human life that . . . would be a criminal violation if committed within the jurisdiction of the United States or any State;
> (2) appear to be intended

---

19. *See* S. Intelligence Rep. at 39 ("Absent a charge that the minimization procedures have been disregarded completely, the test of compliance is 'whether a good faith effort to minimize was attempted.'") (quoting United States v. Armocida, 515 F.2d 29, 44 (3d Cir. 1975)). *See also* In re Sealed Case, 310 F.3d 717, 731 (2002) ("minimization procedures are designed to protect, *as far as reasonable,* against the acquisition, retention, and dissemination of nonpublic information which is not foreign intelligence information.") (emphasis added).

(A) to intimidate or coerce a civilian population;

(B) to influence the policy of a government by intimidation or coercion; or

(C) to affect the conduct of a government by assassination or kidnapping; and

(3) occur totally outside the United States, or transcend national boundaries in terms of the means by which they are accomplished, the persons they appear intended to coerce or intimidate, or the locale in which their perpetrators operate or seek asylum. [50 U.S.C. §1801(c).]

Can you think of some kinds of information that investigators of possible terrorism would be interested in having that could not be collected pursuant to FISA?

### 2. Surveillance Methods

a. *Electronic Surveillance.* The form of the electronic surveillance in *Rosen* was not specified. However, FISA defines four categories of electronic surveillance, some of which go beyond conventional telephone wiretaps and hidden microphones:

(f) "Electronic surveillance" means —

(1) the acquisition by an electronic, mechanical, or other surveillance device of the contents of any wire or radio communication sent by or intended to be received by a particular, known United States person who is in the United States, if the contents are acquired by intentionally targeting that United States person, under circumstances in which a person has a reasonable expectation of privacy and a warrant would be required for law enforcement purposes;

(2) the acquisition by an electronic, mechanical, or other surveillance device of the contents of any wire communication to or from a person in the United States, without the consent of any party thereto, if such acquisition occurs in the United States . . .

(3) the intentional acquisition by an electronic, mechanical, or other surveillance device of the contents of any radio communication, under circumstances in which a person has a reasonable expectation of privacy and a warrant would be required for law enforcement purposes, and if both the sender and all intended recipients are located within the United States; or

(4) the installation or use of an electronic, mechanical, or other surveillance device in the United States for monitoring to acquire information, other than from a wire or radio communication, under circumstances in which a person has a reasonable expectation of privacy and a warrant would be required for law enforcement purposes. [50 U.S.C. §1801(f)(1)-(4).]

Does this definition cover surveillance by hidden microphones installed in a person's home or office? What about a listening device in a person's car? Is video surveillance covered? *See* United States v. Koyomejian, 946 F.2d 1450, 1451 (9th Cir. 1991), *aff'd in part, rev'd in part*, 970 F.2d 536 (9th Cir. 1992) (en banc), *cert. denied,* 506 U.S. 1005 (1992) (yes).

b. *Traditional Pen Registers and Trap and Trace Devices and Access to Business Records*. Can you see why investigators might wish to employ FISA procedures for pen register or trap and trace devices, or to obtain access to business records? The pen register and trap and trace authorities were amended within weeks of the September 11, 2001, terrorist attacks when Congress enacted the USA Patriot Act, Pub. L. No. 107-56, 115 Stat. 272 (2001). First, the definitions of "pen register" and "trap and trace device" were changed to include "dialing, routing, addressing, or signaling information transmitted by an instrument or facility from which a wire or electronic communication is transmitted, provided . . . that such information shall not include the contents of any communication." *Id.* §216(c), 115 Stat. 290 (amending 18 U.S.C. §3127(3), (4)). What new forms of communication do these provisions reach?

The 2001 amendments also provided authorization under FISA for orders for the production of "any tangible things (including books, records, papers, documents, and other items)." USA Patriot Act §215, 115 Stat. 287. Concerning the collection of business records and other information held by third parties, see generally Chapter 6.

c. *Internet and E-mail Intercepts*. In Internet or e-mail communications, trap and trace and pen register devices record the e-mail or Web page addresses of incoming and outgoing communications of the surveillance target. Does FISA's "contents" restriction really protect the substantive content of these communications? If the FBI can record search terms used at a given Web site visited by the target, how will it sort "addressing" information from contents? Is government access to e-mail and Web addresses any more threatening to privacy interests than access to telephone numbers? How so?

d. *Physical Searches*. The substantive provisions for physical searches track those for electronic surveillance. The procedures are somewhat different. A physical search may be approved "for the period necessary to achieve its purpose, or for 90 days, whichever is less." 50 U.S.C. §1824(d)(1). But a search may continue for up to one year if it is directed against a foreign power or up to 120 days if the target is an agent of a foreign power who is not a U.S. person. *Id.* Unlike the usual procedure for a search pursuant to a warrant, FISA does not require that agents knock before entry, supply notice of the search, particularize the object of the search, or inventory what is found for the target. The difference is based on practical considerations:

Physical searches to gather foreign intelligence information depend upon stealth. If the targets of such searches discover that the United States Government had obtained significant information about their activities, those activities would likely be altered, rendering the information useless. [William F. Brown & Americo R. Cinquegrana, *Warrantless Physical Searches for Foreign Intelligence Purposes: Executive Order 12,333 and the Fourth Amendment,* 35 Cath. L. Rev. 97, 131 (1985).]

Does this explanation provide constitutional justification for either the FISA procedure or for a wholly untethered warrantless search? *See* Daniel J. Malooly, *Physical Searches Under FISA: A Constitutional Analysis*, 35 Am. Crim. L. Rev. 411, 420-423 (1998).

3. ***The Geographical Scope of FISA Surveillance.*** Are there geographical limits to the communications subject to FISA electronic surveillance? See the definition of "electronic surveillance," *supra* Note 2a. Does FISA cover the surveillance of communications from Afghanistan to the United States? From the United States to Afghanistan? From one city to another within Afghanistan? If not the last, why do you think Congress did not require FISA authorization for such communications?

4. ***Who May Be Targeted?*** In an espionage prosecution, it may be easy to see how the target of FISA surveillance falls within the definition of "agent of a foreign power." How do you suppose these determinations are made in counterterrorism investigations? In addition to the portions of definitions reproduced in *Rosen*, FISA sets out several categories of potential targets:

### §1801. Definitions.

As used in this subchapter:
   (a) "Foreign power" means—
      (1) a foreign government or any component thereof, whether or not recognized by the United States;
      (2) a faction of a foreign nation or nations, not substantially composed of United States persons;
      (3) an entity that is openly acknowledged by a foreign government or governments to be directed and controlled by such foreign government or governments;
      (4) a group engaged in international terrorism or activities in preparation therefor;
      (5) a foreign-based political organization, not substantially composed of United States persons; or
      (6) an entity that is directed and controlled by a foreign government or governments.
   (b) "Agent of a foreign power" means—
      (1) any person other than a United States person, who—
         (A) acts in the United States as an officer or employee of a foreign power, or as a member of a foreign power as defined in subsection (a)(4) of this section;
         (B) acts for or on behalf of a foreign power which engages in clandestine intelligence activities in the United States contrary to the interests of the United States, when the circumstances of such person's presence in the United States

> indicate that such person may engage in such activities in the United States, or when such person knowingly aids or abets any person in the conduct of such activities or knowingly conspires with any person to engage in such activities; or
>
> (C) engages in international terrorism or activities in preparation therefore [sic]; or
>
> (2) any person who— . . .
>
> (C) knowingly engages in sabotage or international terrorism, or activities that are in preparation therefor, for or on behalf of a foreign power;
>
> (D) knowingly enters the United States under a false or fraudulent identity for or on behalf of a foreign power or, while in the United States, knowingly assumes a false or fraudulent identity for or on behalf of a foreign power. . . .

Can you now describe the categories of targets that may be subjected to electronic surveillance or a physical search pursuant to FISA? Can you think of examples of a "foreign power" or "agent of foreign power"? Under what circumstances could a "United States person" be treated as an agent of a foreign power? Does the availability of wiretaps for some categories of targets threaten constitutional freedom? Alternately, do the prescribed categories of targets unreasonably limit needed flexibility for the intelligence agencies to conduct investigations?

The so-called "lone wolf" provision, 50 U.S.C. §1801(b)(1)(C), was added by §6001 of the Intelligence Reform and Terrorism Prevention Act of 2004, Pub. L. No. 108-458, 118 Stat. 3638, 3742. Like several other Patriot Act changes, this lone wolf authority was set to expire at the end of 2005. If the lone wolf need not be linked in any way to a foreign power, has the "foreign agent" requirement effectively been eliminated for foreign intelligence surveillance? Is the lone wolf provision constitutional? Why would the lone wolf provision have been sought by the government? Can you identify any downside risks to the expanded definition? *See* Patricia L. Bellia, *The "Lone Wolf" Amendment and the Future of Foreign Intelligence Surveillance Law*, 50 Vill. L. Rev. 425, 428-429, 455-456 (2005); Elizabeth B. Bazan, *Intelligence Reform and Terrorism Prevention Act of 2004: "Lone Wolf" Amendment to the Foreign Intelligence Surveillance Act* (Cong. Res. Serv. RS22011), Dec. 29, 2004. After short-term extensions were approved in December 2005 and January 2006, in March 2006 Congress enacted the USA Patriot Improvement and Reauthorization Act of 2005, Pub. L. No. 109-177, 120 Stat. 192 (2006), extending the sunset date for the lone wolf provision to December 31, 2009, but permitting its continued application to investigations begun or offenses or potential offenses committed before that date. *Id.* §103, 120 Stat. 195. Why has Congress again "sunsetted" this provision?

How would investigators make a "foreign agency" determination before seeking FISA surveillance? May the FBI make such a determination without the surveillance permitted by FISA? See *infra* pp. 242-252.

5. ***The Special Court.*** Congress relied on its Article III power to "ordain and establish" the lower federal courts when it created the Foreign Intelligence Surveillance Court (FISC). For background on the FISC and its procedures, see Elizabeth B. Bazan, *The U.S. Foreign Intelligence Surveillance Court and the U.S. Foreign Intelligence Surveillance Court of Review: An Overview* (Cong. Res. Serv. RL 33833), Jan. 24, 2007; *Foreign Intelligence Surveillance Court, Rules of Procedure*, Feb. 17, 2006, *available at* http://www.fas.org/irp/agency/doj/fisa/fiscrules.pdf.

6. ***What Must an Application Contain?*** What are the essential components of an application for FISA surveillance? How do they differ from the elements of an application for a traditional warrant for law enforcement purposes?

In addition to the requirements summarized in *Rosen*, the Attorney General must find that the information sought "cannot reasonably be obtained by normal investigative techniques." 50 U.S.C. §1804(a)(7)(C). The application also must describe any past surveillance involving the target, the surveillance devices to be employed, the means of installation (including whether physical entry will be required), and the period of time for conducting the surveillance. *Id.* §1804(a)(8), (9), (10).

In 2000, FISA was amended to require the Attorney General personally to review and to justify in writing any decision not to approve an application for a FISA order. Pub. L. No. 106-567, §§602(a), 603(b), 114 Stat. 2831, 2851-2853 (amending 50 U.S.C. §1804(e)(2)(A)). What is the likely purpose of this change? What is likely to be its effect?

In 2002, the presiding judge of the FISC complained that several applications to the court contained factual inaccuracies. In re All Matters Submitted to the Foreign Intelligence Surveillance Court, 218 F. Supp. 2d 611 (FISA Ct. 2002), noted *infra* p. 145. In response, the FBI developed FISA verification procedures (the so-called Woods Procedures, named for their author, FBI lawyer Michael J. Woods) to better ensure the accuracy of the facts in each FISA application, particularly concerning what FISA calls "probable cause," and the existence and nature of any parallel criminal processes or prior or ongoing asset relationship involving the target. The procedures include FBI computer database searches and requirements to check the status of the proposed target with the Asset and Informant Unit and Criminal Division. The Woods Procedures were declassified in 2002 and are available at http://www.fas.org/irp/agency/doj/fisa/woods/pdf. Are these likely to improve the accuracy of the FISA process? How will Congress or the public know of their success or failure?

FBI Director Robert Mueller responded to Senate Judiciary Committee questions about the new procedures in August 2003. He stated that FBI field offices had, among other things, mistakenly reported that there were no criminal investigations ongoing concerning a target when in fact there were, and that the Bureau had failed to report that a proposed FISA target was also an FBI informant. *See* Written Questions of Senator Leahy to the Honorable Robert S. Mueller III, Aug. 29, 2003, *at* http://www.fas.org/irp/agency/doj/fisa/fbi082903.pdf. Responding to a Freedom of Information Act (FOIA) request, in October 2005 the FBI released documents detailing hundreds of instances over three years in which procedural requirements of FISA may not have been met. Dan Eggen, *FBI Papers Indicate Intelligence Violations; Secret Surveillance Lacked Oversight*, Wash. Post, Oct. 24, 2005, at A1; Eric Lichtblau, *Tighter Oversight of F.B.I. Is Urged After Investigation Lapses*, N.Y. Times, Oct. 25, 2005, at A16. A March 2006 report by the Department of Justice (DOJ) confirmed that the FBI had violated its own procedures in conducting electronic surveillance and other intelligence activities, including wiretaps that were broader in scope and longer in duration than approved by a court. Eric Lichtblau, *Justice Dept. Report Cites Intelligence-Rule Violations by F.B.I.*, N.Y. Times, Mar. 9, 2006, at A21.

**7. *The FISA Order.***

a. *Probable Cause.* The general standard for searches in criminal investigations is set out in Federal Rule of Criminal Procedure 41. Among other things, Rule 41 permits warrants for a search and seizure of property that constitutes evidence of or is related to the commission of a crime.

Is the FISA standard quoted in *Rosen* a more onerous or a less onerous probable cause standard than the general criminal standard? For probable cause, both FISA and federal criminal laws require something like the probability of a certain fact. But unlike Title III warrants, FISA orders are based "upon the probability of a possibility; the probability to believe that the foreign target of the order *may* engage in spying, or the probability to believe that the American target of the order *may* engage in criminal spying activities." Charles Doyle, *Memorandum to Senate Select Committee On Intelligence, Probable Cause, Reasonable Suspicion, and Reasonableness Standards in the Context of the Fourth Amendment and the Foreign Intelligence Surveillance Act* (Cong. Res. Serv.), Jan. 30, 2006. Under what circumstances and according to what standard may the FISC question the determinations made in the application for surveillance? *See* William C. Banks & M.E. Bowman, *Executive Authority for National Security Surveillance*, 50 Am. U. L. Rev. 1, 83 (2001); Brown & Cinquegrana, *supra* p. 132, at 129-131.

Rule 41 also requires that the target receive a copy of the warrant and an inventory of seized property and that the investigator show "reasonable cause" for serving the warrant at night rather than in daylight. Would such requirements make sense in national security investigations? Under FISA, notice to the target of surveillance is not required until the government determines to introduce intelligence gathered through FISA surveillance in a judicial or other proceeding, 50 U.S.C. §1806(c)-(d), or if the Attorney General approves emergency surveillance and a court later denies a request for an order. *Id.* §1806(j).

b. *Relevancy to a Terrorism Investigation.* FISA "probable cause" is not required for an order for pen registers or trap and trace devices, as now broadly defined in FISA. Instead, the 2001 amendments to FISA require only a certification by the applicant

> that the information likely to be obtained is foreign intelligence
> information not concerning a United States person or is relevant
> to an ongoing investigation to protect against international terror-
> ism or clandestine intelligence activities, provided that such inves-
> tigation of a United States person is not conducted solely upon the
> basis of activities protected by the first amendment. . . . [USA
> Patriot Act §214(a)(2), 115 Stat. 286.]

How is the "relevant" standard different from FISA "probable cause"? Does
the "relevant" standard satisfy constitutional requirements?

The amendment was made at the same time that language was deleted
that had required an investigation to be in pursuit of "foreign intelligence
information or information concerning international terrorism," substituting
a requirement that the investigation serve instead "to obtain foreign intelligence information not concerning a United States person or to protect against
international terrorism or clandestine intelligence activities. . . ." *Id.*
§214(a)(1). Can you see what operational effect the changed targeting
language will have? Who may be targeted by pen register or trap and trace
devices now?

c. *Intelligence Collection vs. Law Enforcement.* What justifies the
lesser probable cause requirement in FISA? The purpose of law enforcement is to prosecute those guilty of committing a crime, while intelligence
investigations have a broader scope and seek to protect the nation from
foreign enemies. Foreign intelligence investigations are often more open-
ended. Consider this comparison:

> The hallmarks of a law enforcement investigation are repeated
> conferences with the appropriate criminal prosecutor, concerted
> efforts to acquire specific information needed to prove each element
> of every charged offense at trial, and the deliberate collection of the
> evidence required to sustain the prosecutorial theory of the case. In
> contrast, the primary use of counterintelligence information is the
> conduct of United States foreign and national defense policies.
> [Louis A. Chiarella & Michael A. Newton, *So Judge, How Do I
> Get That FISA Warrant?: The Policy and Procedure for Conducting
> Electronic Surveillance*, Army Law. 25, 27 (Oct. 1997).]

Do these differences justify the FISA probable cause standard? What are the
legal implications if law enforcement and intelligence surveillance objectives blur or even merge when intelligence information produces evidence
that is used in a criminal prosecution? What answer does *Rosen* suggest?

d. *Keeping Up with Technology.* Among the many changes in surveillance authorities wrought by the 2001 USA Patriot Act, Federal Rule of
Criminal Procedure 41(a) was amended to permit a single law enforcement
warrant to be used "in any district in which activities related to the terrorism may have occurred" in conducting "an investigation of domestic

terrorism or international terrorism." USA Patriot Act §219, 115 Stat. 291. Can you see why this change was sought?

FISA was also amended in 2001 to permit the FISC to order so-called "roving wiretaps." A roving wiretap permits investigators to listen in on any phone a target might use. If the judge "finds that the actions of the target of the application may have the effect of thwarting" the ability of the investigators to identify a specific communications carrier, Internet service provider, or other person needed to assist in the effective and secret execution of the surveillance, the order may authorize such assistance from multiple parties. USA Patriot Act §206, 115 Stat. 282 (amending 50 U.S.C. §1805(c)(2)(B)).

The FISA requirement that the FISC "specify . . . the nature and location of each of the facilities or places at which the electronic surveillance will be directed" was also amended by adding "if known" at the end. Intelligence Authorization Act for Fiscal Year 2002, Pub. L. No. 107-108, §314(a)(2)(A), 115 Stat. 1394, 1402 (amending 50 U.S.C. §1805(c)(1)(B)). Why was this change needed?

These provisions do not require that investigators first determine that the target is using the phone to be tapped. Does this authority permit investigators to tap a homeowner's phone if the target enters the home? Could they monitor the Internet use at the public library if the target enters the library?

In the USA Patriot Improvement and Reauthorization Act of 2005, Congress added a provision for orders when the "nature and location of . . . the facilities or places at which the surveillance will be directed is unknown." Within ten days after surveillance begins, investigators must provide the FISC with a description of the facility or place brought under surveillance, the reasons to believe that it is being used by the target, and any necessary minimization procedures. Pub. L. No. 109-177, §108, 120 Stat. 192, 203 (2006) (amending 50 U.S.C. §1805(c)).

8. *Minimization Requirements.* Do you agree with the *Rosen* court that the potential minimization breach in this investigation does not justify suppressing the FISA-derived evidence? Does the "rule of reason" standard adopted by the court adequately safeguard personal information?

The minimization procedures are classified, "although the internal review mechanisms include standard goals for all applications, as well as for situation-specific assessments for individual applications." Banks & Bowman, *supra* p. 135, at 89. *See also* James E. Meason, *The Foreign Intelligence Surveillance Act: Time for Reappraisal*, 24 Intl. Law. 1043, 1048-1050 (1990) (describing the review process).

9. *Provisions for Emergency Surveillance.* FISA authorizes electronic surveillance without a court order in certain emergency circumstances. Such surveillance is permitted for up to a year when directed solely at communications between or among foreign powers or focused on their property, when there is "no substantial likelihood" that a communication involving a U.S. person will be acquired. 50 U.S.C.A. §1802 (West 2003 & Supp. 2006).

More important, FISA includes this provision:

[W]hen the Attorney General reasonably determines that—

(1) an emergency situation exists with respect to the employment of electronic surveillance to obtain foreign intelligence information before an order authorizing such surveillance can with due diligence be obtained; and

(2) the factual basis for issuance of an order under this subchapter to approve such surveillance exists;

he may authorize the emergency employment of electronic surveillance if a judge [of the FISC] is informed by the Attorney General or his designee at the time of such authorization that the decision has been made to employ emergency electronic surveillance and if an application in accordance with this subchapter is made to that judge as soon as practicable, but not more than 72 hours after the Attorney General authorizes such surveillance. If the Attorney General authorizes such emergency employment of electronic surveillance, he shall require that the minimization procedures required by this subchapter for the issuance of a judicial order be followed. In the absence of a judicial order approving such electronic surveillance, the surveillance shall terminate when the information sought is obtained, when the application for the order is denied, or after the expiration of 72 hours from the time of authorization by the Attorney General, whichever is earliest. In the event that such application for approval is denied, or in any other case where the electronic surveillance is terminated and no order is issued approving the surveillance, no information obtained or evidence derived from such surveillance shall be received in evidence or otherwise disclosed in any trial, hearing, or other proceeding in or before any court, grand jury, department, office, agency, regulatory body, legislative committee, or other authority of the United States, a State, or political subdivision thereof, and no information concerning any United States person acquired from such surveillance shall subsequently be used or disclosed in any other manner by Federal officers or employees without the consent of such person, except with the approval of the Attorney General if the information indicates a threat of death or serious bodily harm to any person. . . . [50 U.S.C. §1805(f)].

Provision for physical searches in emergency circumstances is made on a basis parallel to that for electronic surveillance; the authority lasts for up to 72 hours, by which time an application for approval must be made to the FISC. 50 U.S.C. §§1822(a), 1824(e), (f). *See also* 50 U.S.C. §§1843(a), (b) (pen register and trap and trace devices).

Between FISA's enactment in 1978 and September 11, 2001, Attorneys General issued 47 emergency authorizations under FISA. In the 18 months after September 11, 2001, the Attorney General authorized more than 170 emergency wiretaps and/or physical searches under FISA. Dan Eggen & Robert O'Harrow Jr., *U.S. Steps Up Secret Surveillance*, Wash. Post, Mar. 23, 2003, at A1.

Are you troubled by the absence of a prior judicial check on these executive decisions? How can responsible officials be certain that these decisions satisfy statutory and constitutional norms?

Given the availability of these FISA emergency provisions, can you envision any emergency that would justify foreign intelligence surveillance in the United States without complying with FISA? This question is addressed *infra* p. 157.

The Homeland Security Act authorizes law enforcement officials to use pen registers and trap and trace devices without seeking a court order in emergencies involving "an immediate threat to a national security interest." Pub. L. No. 107-296, §225(i)(3), 116 Stat. 2135, 2158 (2002) (amending 18 U.S.C. §3125). It also allows an Internet service provider (ISP) to disclose the content of electronic communications to any government agency if the ISP in "good faith" believes that the communication relates to information that involves the risk of death or serious physical injury. *Id*. §225(d)(1)(D) (amending 18 U.S.C. §2702).

10. ***Judicial Review of FISA Surveillance.*** The *Rosen* defendants learned that FISA surveillance of their activities had been conducted only when the government notified them that evidence from the surveillance would be introduced at their criminal trial. If no criminal prosecution is initiated following FISA surveillance, how would an individual subjected to unlawful surveillance under FISA be able to challenge the illegal conduct in court? The FISC does not publish its decisions, and its orders are sealed. Proceedings are ex parte and are thus normally not known to the targets of surveillance. 50 U.S.C. §§1802(a)(3), 1806(f)-(g). As the *Rosen* defendants learned, even if targets of surveillance do find out, they may not be able to examine materials related to the surveillance if the Attorney General files a claim of privilege under FISA §1806(f).

Do you think the *Rosen* defendants can participate effectively in the review process, given their limited access to FISA materials? Can you see why FISA permits the government to withhold the applications and accompanying affidavits and certifications from discovery in an adversarial proceeding? If the reviewing judge exercises his statutory discretion not to disclose portions of the documents, how will the targets of surveillance be able to appeal the judge's decision? On what basis could a court of appeals overturn the nondisclosure decision? *See* ACLU v. Barr, 952 F.2d 457 (D.C. Cir. 1991) (reviewing court may overturn a nondisclosure decision if the certifications of compliance with FISA requirements are clearly erroneous). *See also* United States v. Rahman, 189 F.3d 88 (2d Cir. 1999), *cert. denied*, 528 U.S. 982 (2000).

### b.   Constitutional Concerns

1. ***Article III Case or Controversy?*** The FISC receives applications and issues orders solely on an ex parte basis without any adversarial proceedings. Do such matters meet the Article III case or controversy requirements? United States v. Megahey, 553 F. Supp. 1180 (E.D.N.Y. 1982), held that

FISA proceedings before the FISC "involve concrete questions respecting the application of the Act and are in a form such that a judge is capable of acting on them." 553 F. Supp. at 1197. *See also* United States v. Johnson, 952 F.2d 565 (2d Cir. 1991), *cert. denied*, 506 U.S. 816 (1992);United States v. Cavanaugh, 807 F.2d 787 (9th Cir. 1987); In re Kevork, 788 F.2d 566 (9th Cir. 1986); United States v. Falvey, 540 F. Supp. 1306, 1313 (E.D.N.Y. 1982).

2. *Political Question Doctrine.* The courts that have reviewed challenges to FISA surveillance orders have not been persuaded that their review itself is barred by the political question doctrine on the theory that the surveillance decision is for the President alone to make. *See, e.g.*, United States v. Duggan, 743 F.2d 59, 74-75 (2d Cir. 1984) (limited judicial role in determining whether the target of a warrant is properly subject to the prescribed procedure does not threaten political question values and does not inject courts into the making of foreign policy).

3. *Does FISA Occupy the Field?* In an effort to prevent the executive branch from bypassing the FISA procedures, in 1988 Congress enacted an amendment to Title III expressly eliminating the §2511(3) disclaimer that was central to the *Keith* decision and stating that FISA and Title III are intended to be "the exclusive means" for the conduct of electronic surveillance by the government. 18 U.S.C. §2511(2)(f) (2000 & Supp. IV 2004). Is Congress empowered to so restrict the President's conduct of national security surveillance? If it is, does the 1988 provision affect the constitutionality of surveillance undertaken outside the prescriptions of FISA? The exclusivity of FISA and Title III are considered in a case study of warrantless surveillance *infra* p. 157.

After September 11, the Department of Justice maintained that "FISA . . . is not required by the Constitution." Letter from Daniel J. Bryant, Asst. Attorney General, to Senator Bob Graham, Chairman, S. Select Comm. on Intelligence (Aug. 6, 2002) (copy on file with authors). Do you agree?

4. *Confrontation.* Did the *Rosen* court's refusal to disclose the FISA materials to the defendants violate their due process confrontation rights? Although the Supreme Court has never decided a FISA appeal, the Court did deny review in a challenge to the government's refusal to disclose materials that supported an application for FISA surveillance. In United States v. Squillicote, 221 F.3d 542 (4th Cir. 2000), *cert. denied,* 532 U. S. 971 (2001), a married couple were convicted of conspiring to commit espionage on behalf of East Germany, the Soviet Union, Russia, and South Africa. The FBI obtained 20 separate FISA orders for surveillance that lasted 550 days. Based almost exclusively on the FISA-derived evidence, the parties were sentenced to 22 and 17 years in prison, respectively. Although FISA and the Due Process Clause entitled the accused to question the basis for the government's surveillance, counsel for the accused spies were never permitted to see the underlying documentation that supported the applications for surveillance because the government invoked §1806(f) and filed a claim of privilege. Does §1806(f) comply with the Due Process Clause? Why do you think that the Supreme Court has declined to review a conviction on this basis?

5. *Fourth Amendment.* In United States v. Duggan, 743 F.2d 59 (2d Cir. 1984), alleged members of the Provisional Irish Republican Army (PIRA) faced a number of charges relating to export, transportation, and delivery

of explosives and firearms. Some of the evidence against them was derived from electronic surveillance pursuant to FISA. Defendants contended that FISA is unconstitutional on grounds that it violates the probable cause requirement of the Fourth Amendment. The court rejected their argument:

> . . . Congress passed FISA to settle what it believed to be the unresolved question of the applicability of the Fourth Amendment warrant requirement to electronic surveillance for foreign intelligence purposes, and to "remove any doubt as to the lawfulness of such surveillance." H.R. Rep. 1283, pt. I, 95th Cong., 2d Sess. 25 (1978) ("House Report"). FISA reflects both Congress's "legislative judgment" that the court orders and other procedural safeguards laid out in the Act "are necessary to insure that electronic surveillance by the U.S. Government within this country conforms to the fundamental principles of the fourth amendment," S. Rep. No. 701, 95th Cong., 2d Sess. 13, *reprinted in* 1978 U.S. Code Cong. & Ad. News 3973, 3982 ("Senate Report 95-701"), and its attempt to fashion a "secure framework by which the Executive Branch may conduct legitimate electronic surveillance for foreign intelligence purposes within the context of this Nation's commitment to privacy and individual rights." S. Rep. No. 604, 95th Cong., 1st Sess. 15, *reprinted in* 1978 U.S. Code Cong. & Ad. News 3904, 3916. In constructing this framework, Congress gave close scrutiny to departures from those Fourth Amendment doctrines applicable in the criminal-investigation context in order

>> to ensure that the procedures established in [FISA] are reasonable in relation to legitimate foreign counterintelligence requirements and the protected rights of individuals. Their reasonableness depends, in part, upon an assessment of the difficulties of investigating activities planned, directed, and supported from abroad by foreign intelligence services and foreign-based terrorist groups. The differences between ordinary criminal investigations to gather evidence of specific crimes and foreign counterintelligence investigations to uncover and monitor clandestine activities have been taken into account. Other factors include the international responsibilities of the United States, the duties of the Federal Government to the States in matters involving foreign terrorism, and the need to maintain the secrecy of lawful counterintelligence sources and methods. Senate Report 95-701, at 14-15, *reprinted in* 1978 U.S. Code Cong. & Ad. News 3973, 3983.

> We regard the procedures fashioned in FISA as a constitutionally adequate balancing of the individual's Fourth Amendment rights against the nation's need to obtain foreign intelligence information. The governmental concerns . . . make reasonable the adoption of prerequisites to surveillance that are less stringent than those precedent to the issuance of a warrant for a criminal investigation. . . .

We conclude that these requirements provide an appropriate balance between the individual's interest in privacy and the government's need to obtain foreign intelligence information, and that FISA does not violate the probable cause requirement of the Fourth Amendment.

Nor is there any merit to defendants' contention that the national security interests of the United States are not implicated by acts of terrorism directed wholly outside the United States. The government points out that if other nations were to harbor terrorists and give them safe haven for staging terrorist activities against the United States, United States national security would be threatened. As a reciprocal matter, the United States cannot afford to give safe haven to terrorists who seek to carry out raids against other nations. Thus, international terrorism conducted from the United States, no matter where it is directed, may well have a substantial effect on United States national security and foreign policy. In recognition of these considerations, Senate Report 95-701 noted:

> The committee intends that terrorists and saboteurs acting for foreign powers should be subject to surveillance under this bill when they are in the United States, even if the target of their violent acts is within a foreign country and therefore outside actual Federal or State jurisdiction. This departure from a strict criminal standard is justified by the international responsibility of government to prevent its territory from being used as a base for launching terrorist attacks against other countries. We demand that other countries live up to this responsibility and it is important that in our legislation we demonstrate a will to do so ourselves. Senate Report 95-701, at 30, *reprinted in* 1978 U.S. Code Cong. & Ad. News 3973, 3999.

We find highly persuasive the conclusions of Congress and the executive branch, the two branches most often concerned with foreign intelligence and national security questions, that international terrorist organizations are legitimate and important targets for foreign intelligence surveillance. [*Duggan*, 743 F.2d at 73-74.]

Although the Supreme Court has not considered the constitutionality of FISA, the lower courts have uniformly followed *Duggan* in upholding the FISA procedures. *See, e.g.,* United States v. Johnson, 952 F.2d 565, 575 (1st Cir. 1991) (FISA satisfies Fourth Amendment requirements); United States v. Pelton, 835 F.2d 1067, 1075 (4th Cir. 1987) (same); United States v. Ott, 827 F.2d 473, 475-477 (9th Cir. 1987) (ex parte review procedures do not violate Fourth or Fifth Amendments); *Cavanaugh, supra,* 807 F.2d at 790 (FISA satisfies the Fourth Amendment). Do you agree that FISA provides a "constitutionally adequate" substitute for a criminal warrant?

One of us has written that "FISA was the product of a set of compromises unique to their time. . . . While . . . suspicion of criminal activity was an essential part of . . . FISA, . . . Congress did not intend for FISA to authorize surveillance for the purpose of enforcing the criminal laws." William C. Banks, *The Death of FISA*, 91 Minn. L. Rev. (forthcoming 2007). How does this "FISA as compromise" view compare to your understanding of the constitutionality of FISA?

6. **First Amendment.** What protections does FISA provide against surveillance that would burden expressive freedoms? What is meant by the prohibition against finding a U. S. person to be an agent of a foreign power "solely upon the basis of activities protected by the first amendment"? 50 U.S.C. §1805(a)(3)(A). The 1978 Senate Judiciary Committee report on FISA stated that activities protected by the First Amendment may not "form *any part* of the basis" for identifying a FISA target. *See Foreign Intelligence Surveillance Act of 1978: Hearing Before the Subcomm. on Criminal Laws and Procedures of the S. Comm. on the Judiciary*, 95th Cong. 23 (1977) (emphasis added). Did the *Rosen* court take this legislative history into account in evaluating the rules for identifying a potential FISA target?

Did the *Rosen* court fairly separate the defendants' activities that might be protected from those that are not so protected? What other information could be available to investigators that would permit the application to go forward without being "solely" based on protected First Amendment activities?

Review the definition of "agent of a foreign power" set out *supra* p. 132. Could the FISC grant a surveillance order based on an investigator's assessment that advocacy or fund-raising on the part of a potential target constitutes "activities that are in preparation" for terrorism? Problems of profiling targets on the basis of their expressive activities are considered *infra* p. 207.

## C.   FISA, LAW ENFORCEMENT, AND "THE WALL"

The defendants in United States v. Duggan, noted above, contended that the FISA surveillance of one defendant's telephone was not lawful because the information was sought as part of a criminal investigation. The government answered that the investigators sought foreign intelligence information. Is it possible, indeed likely, that both sides are correct? Given the role allegedly played by the *Duggan* defendants in the PIRA, it is hard to muster much enthusiasm for their argument that the FISA requirements were not met. However, if, as the *Duggan* court concluded, "otherwise valid FISA surveillance is not tainted" simply because the government anticipates that its fruits may be used in a criminal prosecution, it may be difficult for judges to determine that the government has not used FISA as an end run around Rule 41. *See* United States v. Rahman, 861 F. Supp. 247 (S.D.N.Y. 1994), *aff'd*, 189 F.2d 88 (2d Cir. 1999).

Before 2002, courts followed United States v. Truong Dinh Hung, 629 F.2d 908 (4th Cir. 1980), *supra* p. 106, and allowed evidence gathered during FISA surveillance to support a criminal conviction only after finding that intelligence was the "primary" purpose of the surveillance, United States v. Johnson, 952 F.2d 565 (1st Cir. 1991), *cert. denied*, 506 U.S. 816 (1992), or at least a purpose (not necessarily primary), United States v. Sarkissian, 841 F.2d 959, 964 (9th Cir. 1988). The assumption seemed to be that if the original purpose of the surveillance was intelligence gathering, there was no reason not to use the information collected in a criminal prosecution. But the assumption raises some important issues, one of which is the ability of officials who authorize surveillance to verify its intelligence purpose. Another is the obligation of such officials to do so. Consider this observation:

> The net effect of FISA has been to confuse intelligence gathering with criminal law, and to enmesh intelligence in procedures which are wholly inappropriate to it. In law enforcement the purpose of surveillance is to prosecute the guilty. In intelligence, the purpose of surveillance is to gather information which should not be used for or against any individual, but to safeguard the country from foreign enemies. The proper cure for abuses of surveillance for purposes of intelligence is examination after the fact, and punishment of those who abuse their trust. But it is nonsense to think one can draw up a formula beforehand which will ensure that everyone is surveilled who should be. [S. Select Comm. on Intelligence, *Implementation of the Foreign Intelligence Surveillance Act of 1978,* S. Rep. No. 97-691, at 9-10 (1982) (supp. views of Sen. Wallop).]

In the days and weeks after the September 11, 2001, terrorist attacks, it was widely reported that an investigative failure may have permitted a twentieth hijacker to escape pre-attack detection because of a concern based on "primary purpose." Zacarias Moussaoui was arrested on immigration charges a few weeks before the attacks. Officials at a flight training school had grown suspicious when Moussaoui said that he wanted to learn to fly large jet aircraft, but that he had no interest in becoming a commercial pilot. At about the same time, a French intelligence agency warned the FBI in a classified cable that Moussaoui had "Islamic extremist beliefs." David Johnston & Philip Shenon, *F.B.I. Curbed Scrutiny of Man Now a Suspect in Attacks,* N.Y. Times, Oct. 6, 2001, at A1. When FBI field agents sought headquarters approval for a FISA search, they were turned down, apparently because there was insufficient indication that Moussaoui was an agent of a foreign power. The field agents then also failed to persuade headquarters to open a criminal investigation that would have employed grand jury subpoenas and law enforcement warrants to examine Moussaoui's computer and telephone records. Apparently, this request was denied because senior FBI officials worried that an open criminal investigation might thwart a later FISA application by defeating the primary purpose requirement. FISC Chief Judge Royce Lamberth had recently questioned the candor of Justice Department officials who sought FISA orders for targets who were already the subjects of criminal investigations. A criminal case was eventually opened and a FISA order was obtained, but only after the September 11 attacks. *Id.*

The belief that a full investigation of Moussaoui before September 11 might have led to exposure of the hijackers' plot helped spur enactment of the USA Patriot Act and, three years later, the lone wolf provision in the Intelligence Reform and Terrorism Prevention Act of 2004. See *supra* p. 133. The criminal prosecution of Moussaoui is considered *infra* p. 547.

Concerns about the primary purpose requirement produced an amendment to FISA in the USA Patriot Act, which led in turn to the following case.

# IN RE: SEALED CASE NOS. 02-001, 02-002

Foreign Intelligence Surveillance Court of Review, 2002
310 F.3d 717

GUY, Senior Circuit Judge, presiding; SILBERMAN and LEAVY, Senior Circuit Judges.

PER CURIAM: This is the first appeal from the Foreign Intelligence Surveillance Court to the Court of Review since the passage of the Foreign Intelligence Surveillance Act (FISA), 50 U.S.C. §§1801-1862 (West 1991 and Supp. 2002), in 1978. The appeal is brought by the United States from a FISA court surveillance order which imposed certain restrictions on the government. . . .

## I.

The court's decision from which the government appeals imposed certain requirements and limitations accompanying an order authorizing electronic surveillance of an "agent of a foreign power" as defined in FISA. There is no disagreement between the government and the FISA court as to the propriety of the electronic surveillance. . . . [T]he court ordered that

> law enforcement officials shall not make recommendations to intelligence officials concerning the initiation, operation, continuation or expansion of FISA searches or surveillances. Additionally, the FBI and the Criminal Division [of the Department of Justice] shall ensure that law enforcement officials do not direct or control the use of the FISA procedures to enhance criminal prosecution, and that advice intended to preserve the option of a criminal prosecution does not inadvertently result in the Criminal Division's directing or controlling the investigation using FISA searches and surveillances toward law enforcement objectives.

To ensure the Justice Department followed these strictures the court also fashioned what the government refers to as a "chaperone requirement"; that a unit of the Justice Department, the Office of Intelligence Policy and Review (OIPR) (composed of 31 lawyers and 25 support staff), "be invited" to all meetings between the FBI and the Criminal Division involving consultations for the purpose of coordinating efforts "to investigate or protect against foreign attack or other grave hostile acts, sabotage, international terrorism, or clandestine intelligence activities by foreign powers or their agents." If representatives of OIPR are unable to attend such meetings, "OIPR shall be appri[s]ed of the substance of the meetings forthwith in writing so that the Court may be notified at the earliest opportunity."

These restrictions are not original to the order appealed. They were actually set forth in an opinion written by the former Presiding Judge of the FISA court on May 17 of this year. [*See* In re All Matters Submitted to the Foreign Intelligence Surveillance Court, 218 F. Supp. 2d 611 (2002).] . . .

## II.

The government makes two main arguments. The first . . . is that the supposed pre-Patriot Act limitation in FISA that restricts the government's intention to use foreign intelligence information in criminal prosecutions is an illusion; it finds no support in either the language of FISA or its legislative history. The government does recognize that several courts of appeals, while upholding the use of FISA surveillances, have opined that FISA may be used only if the government's primary purpose in pursuing foreign intelligence information is not criminal prosecution, but the government argues that those decisions, which did not carefully analyze the statute, were incorrect in their statements, if not incorrect in their holdings.

Alternatively, the government contends that even if the primary purpose test was a legitimate construction of FISA prior to the passage of the Patriot Act, that Act's amendments to FISA eliminate that concept. And as a corollary, the government insists the FISA court's construction of the minimization procedures is far off the mark both because it is a misconstruction of those provisions *per se*, as well as an end run around the specific amendments in the Patriot Act designed to deal with the real issue underlying this case. The government, moreover, contends that the FISA court's restrictions, which the court described as minimization procedures, are so intrusive into the operation of the Department of Justice as to exceed the constitutional authority of Article III judges.

The government's brief, and its supplementary brief requested by this court, also set forth its view that the primary purpose test is not required by the Fourth Amendment. . . .

### The 1978 FISA

We turn first to the statute as enacted in 1978. . . . [The court reviewed the definitions of "foreign intelligence information" and "agent of a foreign power" and noted that each is concerned with national security crimes.]

In light of these definitions, it is quite puzzling that the Justice Department, at some point during the 1980s, began to read the statute as limiting the Department's ability to obtain FISA orders if it intended to prosecute the targeted agents—even for foreign intelligence crimes. To be sure, section 1804, which sets forth the elements of an application for an order, required a national security official in the Executive Branch—typically the Director of the FBI—to certify that "the purpose" of the surveillance is to obtain foreign intelligence information (amended by the Patriot Act to read "a significant purpose"). But as the government now argues, the definition of foreign intelligence information includes evidence of crimes such as espionage, sabotage or terrorism. Indeed, it is virtually impossible to read the 1978 FISA to exclude from its purpose the prosecution of foreign intelligence crimes, most importantly because, as we have noted, the definition of an agent of a foreign power—if he or she is a U.S. person—is grounded on criminal conduct. . . .

The government argues persuasively that arresting and prosecuting terrorist agents of, or spies for, a foreign power may well be the best technique to prevent them from successfully continuing their terrorist or espionage activity. The government might wish to surveil the agent for some period of time to discover other participants in a conspiracy or to uncover a foreign power's plans, but typically at some point the government would wish to apprehend the agent and it might be that only a prosecution would provide sufficient incentives for the agent to cooperate with the government. . . .

Congress was concerned about the government's use of FISA surveillance to obtain information not truly intertwined with the government's efforts to protect against threats from foreign powers. Accordingly, the certification of purpose under section 1804(a)(7)(B) served to

> prevent the practice of targeting, for example, a foreign power for electronic surveillance when the true purpose of the surveillance is to gather information about an individual for other than foreign intelligence purposes. It is also designed to make explicit that the sole purpose of such surveillance is to secure "foreign intelligence information," as defined, and not to obtain some other type of information.

[H.R. Rep. No. 95-1283 (hereinafter "H. Rep.")] at 76; *see also* [S. Rep. No. 95-701] at 51. But Congress did not impose any restrictions on the government's use of the foreign intelligence information to prosecute agents of foreign powers for foreign intelligence crimes. . . .

The origin of what the government refers to as the false dichotomy between foreign intelligence information that is evidence of foreign intelligence crimes and that which is not appears to have been a Fourth Circuit case decided in 1980. United States v. Truong Dinh Hung, 629 F.2d 908 (4th Cir. 1980). That case, however, involved an electronic surveillance carried out prior to the passage of FISA and predicated on the President's executive power. In approving the district court's exclusion of evidence obtained through a warrantless surveillance subsequent to the point in time when the government's investigation became "primarily" driven by law enforcement objectives, the court held that the Executive Branch should be excused from securing a warrant only when "the object of the search or the surveillance is a foreign power, its agents or collaborators," and "the surveillance is conducted 'primarily' for foreign intelligence reasons." *Id.* at 915. . . .

. . . [S]ome time in the 1980s—the exact moment is shrouded in historical mist—the Department [of Justice] applied the *Truong* analysis to an interpretation of the FISA statute. What is clear is that in 1995 the Attorney General adopted "Procedures for Contacts Between the FBI and the Criminal Division Concerning Foreign Intelligence and Foreign Counterintelligence Investigations."

Apparently to avoid running afoul of the primary purpose test used by some courts, the 1995 Procedures limited contacts between the FBI and the Criminal Division in cases where FISA surveillance or searches were being conducted by the FBI for foreign intelligence (FI) or foreign counterintelligence (FCI) purposes. The procedures state that "the FBI and Criminal Division should ensure that advice intended to preserve the option of a criminal prosecution does not inadvertently result in either the fact or the appearance of the Criminal Division's *directing or controlling* the FI or FCI investigation toward law enforcement objectives." 1995 Procedures at 2, ¶6 (emphasis added). Although these procedures provided for significant information sharing and coordination between criminal and FI or FCI investigations, based at least in part on the "directing or controlling" language, they eventually came to be narrowly interpreted within the Department of Justice, and most particularly by OIPR, as requiring OIPR to act as a "wall" to prevent the FBI intelligence officials from communicating with the Criminal Division regarding ongoing FI or FCI investigations. . . .

### The Patriot Act and the FISA Court's Decision

The passage of the Patriot Act altered and to some degree muddied the landscape. In October 2001, Congress amended FISA to change "the purpose" language in 1804(a)(7)(B) to "a significant purpose." It also added a provision allowing "Federal officers who conduct electronic surveillance to acquire foreign intelligence information" to "consult with Federal law enforcement officers to coordinate efforts to investigate or protect against" attack or other grave hostile acts, sabotage or international terrorism, or clandestine intelligence activities, by foreign powers or their agents. 50 U.S.C. §1806(k)(1). And such coordination "shall not preclude" the government's certification that a significant purpose of the surveillance is to obtain foreign intelligence information, or the issuance of an order authorizing the surveillance. *Id.* §1806(k)(2). Although the Patriot Act amendments to FISA expressly sanctioned consultation and coordination between intelligence and law enforcement officials, in response to the first applications filed by OIPR under those amendments, in November 2001, the FISA court for the first time adopted the 1995 Procedures, as augmented by the January 2000 and August 2001 Procedures, as "minimization procedures" to apply in all cases before the court.

The Attorney General interpreted the Patriot Act quite differently. On March 6, 2002, the Attorney General approved new "Intelligence Sharing Procedures" to implement the Act's amendments to FISA. The 2002 Procedures supersede prior procedures and were designed to permit the complete exchange of information and advice between intelligence and law enforcement officials. They eliminated the "direction and control" test and allowed the exchange of advice between the FBI, OIPR, and the Criminal Division regarding "the initiation, operation, continuation, or expansion of FISA searches or surveillance." On March 7, 2002, the government filed a motion with the FISA court, noting that the Department of Justice had adopted the 2002 Procedures and proposing to follow those procedures in all matters before the court. The government also asked the FISA court to vacate its orders adopting the prior procedures as minimization procedures in all cases and imposing special "wall" procedures in certain cases.

Unpersuaded by the Attorney General's interpretation of the Patriot Act, the court ordered that the 2002 Procedures be adopted, *with modifications*, as minimization procedures to apply in all cases. The court emphasized that the definition of minimization procedures had not been amended by the Patriot Act, and reasoned that the 2002 Procedures "cannot be used by the government to amend the Act in ways Congress has not." . . .

Undeterred, the government submitted the application at issue in this appeal on July 19, 2002, and expressly proposed using the 2002 Procedures *without modification*. In an order issued the same day, the FISA judge hearing the application granted an order for surveillance of the target but modified the 2002 Procedures consistent with the court's May 17, 2002 *en banc* order. It is the July 19, 2002 order that the government appeals. . . .

Essentially, the FISA court took portions of the Attorney General's augmented 1995 Procedures — adopted to deal with the primary purpose standard—and imposed them generically as minimization procedures. In doing so, the FISA court erred. . . .

The minimization procedures allow . . . the retention and dissemination of non-foreign intelligence information which is evidence of *ordinary crimes* for preventative or prosecutorial purposes. *See* 50 U.S.C. §1801(h)(3). Therefore, if through interceptions or searches, evidence of "a serious crime totally unrelated to intelligence matters" is incidentally acquired, the evidence is "*not* . . . required to be destroyed*." H. Rep. at 62 (emphasis added). As we have explained, under the 1978 Act, "evidence of certain crimes like espionage would itself constitute 'foreign intelligence information,' as defined, because it is necessary to protect against clandestine intelligence activities by foreign powers or their agents." H. Rep. at 62; *see also id.* at 49. In light of these purposes of the minimization procedures, there is simply no basis for the FISA court's reliance on section 1801(h) to limit criminal prosecutors' ability to advise FBI intelligence officials on the initiation, operation, continuation, or expansion of FISA surveillances to obtain foreign intelligence information, even if such information includes evidence of a foreign intelligence crime. . . .

We also think the refusal by the FISA court to consider the legal significance of the Patriot Act's crucial amendments was error. The government, in order to avoid the requirement of meeting the "primary purpose" test, specifically sought an amendment to section 1804(a)(7)(B) which had required a certification "that the purpose of the surveillance is to obtain foreign intelligence information" so as to delete the article "the" before "purpose" and replace it with "a." The government made perfectly clear to Congress why it sought the legislative change. Congress, although accepting the government's explanation for the need for the amendment, adopted language which it perceived as not giving the government quite the degree of modification it wanted. Accordingly, section 1804(a)(7)(B)'s wording became "that a *significant* purpose of the surveillance is to obtain foreign intelligence information" (emphasis added). There is simply no question, however, that Congress was keenly aware that this amendment relaxed a requirement that the government show that its primary purpose was other than criminal prosecution. . . .

Accordingly, the Patriot Act amendments clearly disapprove the primary purpose test. And as a matter of straightforward logic, if a FISA application can be granted even if "foreign intelligence" is only a significant—not a primary—purpose, another purpose can be primary. One other legitimate purpose that could exist is to prosecute a target for a foreign intelligence crime. . . .

. . . [I]t is our task to do our best to read the statute to honor congressional intent. The better reading, it seems to us, excludes from the purpose of gaining foreign intelligence information a sole objective of criminal prosecution. We therefore reject the government's argument to the contrary. Yet this may not make much practical difference. Because, as the government points out, when it commences an electronic surveillance of a foreign agent, typically it will not have decided whether to prosecute the agent (whatever may be the subjective intent of the investigators or lawyers who initiate an investigation). So long as the government entertains a realistic option of dealing with the agent other than through criminal prosecution, it satisfies the significant purpose test.

The important point is—and here we agree with the government—the Patriot Act amendment, by using the word "significant," eliminated any justification for the FISA court to balance the relative weight the government places on criminal prosecution as compared to other counterintelligence responses. If the certification of the application's purpose articulates a broader objective than criminal prosecution—such as stopping an ongoing conspiracy—and includes other potential non-prosecutorial responses, the government meets the statutory test. Of course, if the court concluded that the government's sole objective was merely to gain evidence of past criminal conduct—even foreign intelligence crimes—to punish the agent rather than halt ongoing espionage or terrorist activity, the application should be denied.

. . . It can be argued, however, that by providing that an application is to be granted if the government has only a "significant purpose" of gaining foreign intelligence information, the Patriot Act allows the government to have a primary objective of prosecuting an agent for a non-foreign intelligence crime. Yet we think that would be an anomalous reading of the amendment. For we see not the slightest indication that Congress meant to give that power to the Executive Branch. Accordingly, the manifestation of such a purpose, it seems to us, would continue to disqualify an application. That is not to deny that ordinary crimes might be inextricably intertwined with foreign intelligence crimes. For example, if a group of international terrorists were to engage in bank robberies in order to finance the manufacture of a bomb, evidence of the bank robbery should be treated just as evidence of the terrorist act itself. But the FISA process cannot be used as a device to investigate wholly unrelated ordinary crimes.

One final point; we think the government's purpose as set forth in a section 1804(a)(7)(B) certification is to be judged by the national security official's articulation and not by a FISA court inquiry into the origins of an investigation nor an examination of the personnel involved. It is up to the Director of the FBI, who typically certifies, to determine the government's national security purpose, as approved by the Attorney General or Deputy Attorney General. This is not a standard whose application the FISA court legitimately reviews by seeking to inquire into which Justice Department officials were instigators of an investigation. . . .

### III.

Having determined that FISA, as amended, does not oblige the government to demonstrate to the FISA court that its primary purpose in conducting electronic surveillance is not criminal prosecution, we are obliged to consider whether the statute as amended is consistent with the Fourth Amendment. . . . The FISA court indicated that its disapproval of the Attorney General's 2002 Procedures was based on the need to safeguard the "privacy of Americans in these highly intrusive surveillances and searches," which implies the invocation of the Fourth Amendment. The government, recognizing the Fourth Amendment's shadow effect on the FISA court's opinion, has affirmatively argued that FISA is constitutional. . . .

The FISA court expressed concern that unless FISA were "construed" in the fashion that it did, the government could use a FISA order as an improper substitute for an ordinary criminal warrant under Title III. That concern seems to suggest that the FISA court thought Title III procedures are constitutionally mandated if the government has a prosecutorial objective regarding an agent of a foreign power. But in United States v. United States District Court (*Keith*), 407 U.S. 297, 322 (1972) — in which the Supreme Court explicitly declined to consider foreign intelligence surveillance — the Court indicated that, even with respect to domestic national security intelligence gathering for prosecutorial purposes where a warrant was mandated, Title III procedures were not constitutionally required: "[W]e do not hold that the same type of standards and procedures prescribed by Title III are necessarily applicable to this case. We recognize that domestic security surveillance may involve different policy and practical considerations from the surveillance of 'ordinary crime.'" Nevertheless, in asking whether FISA procedures can be regarded as reasonable under the Fourth Amendment, we think it is instructive to compare those procedures and requirements with their Title III counterparts. Obviously, the closer those FISA procedures are to Title III procedures, the lesser are our constitutional concerns.

### Comparison of FISA Procedures with Title III

. . . [W]hile Title III contains some protections that are not in FISA, in many significant respects the two statutes are equivalent, and in some, FISA contains additional protections. Still, to the extent the two statutes diverge in constitutionally relevant areas — in particular, in their probable cause and particularity showings — a FISA order may not be a "warrant" contemplated by the Fourth Amendment. . . . We do not decide the issue but note that to the extent a FISA order comes close to meeting Title III, that certainly bears on its reasonableness under the Fourth Amendment.

### Did Truong Articulate the Appropriate Constitutional Standard?

Ultimately, the question becomes whether FISA, as amended by the Patriot Act, is a reasonable response based on a balance of the legitimate need of the government for foreign intelligence information to protect against national security threats with the protected rights of citizens. . . .

It will be recalled that the case that set forth the primary purpose test *as constitutionally required* was *Truong*. The Fourth Circuit thought that *Keith*'s balancing standard implied the adoption of the primary purpose test. We reiterate that *Truong* dealt with a pre-FISA surveillance based on the President's constitutional responsibility to conduct the foreign affairs of the United States. 629 F.2d at 914. Although *Truong* suggested the line it drew was a constitutional minimum that would apply to a FISA surveillance, *see id.* at 914 n.4, it had no occasion to consider the application of the statute carefully. The *Truong* court, as did all the other courts to have decided the issue, held that the President did have inherent authority to conduct warrantless searches to obtain foreign intelligence information. It was incumbent upon the court, therefore, to determine the boundaries of that constitutional authority in the case before it. We take for granted that the President does have that authority and, assuming that is so, FISA could not encroach on the President's constitutional power. The question before us is the reverse, does FISA amplify the President's power by providing a mechanism that at least approaches a classic warrant and which therefore supports the government's contention that FISA searches are constitutionally reasonable.

The district court in the *Truong* case had excluded evidence obtained from electronic surveillance after the government's investigation — the court found — had converted from one conducted for foreign intelligence reasons to one conducted primarily as a criminal investigation. . . . The court of appeals endorsed that approach, stating:

> We think that the district court adopted the proper test, because once surveillance becomes primarily a criminal investigation, the courts are entirely competent to make the usual probable cause determination, and because, importantly, individual privacy interests come to the fore *and government foreign policy concerns recede* when the government is primarily attempting to form the basis of a criminal prosecution.

*Id.* at 915 (emphasis added).

That analysis, in our view, rested on a false premise and the line the court sought to draw was inherently unstable, unrealistic, and confusing. The false premise was the assertion that once the government moves to criminal prosecution, its "foreign policy concerns" recede. As we have discussed in the first part of the opinion, that is simply not true as it relates to counterintelligence. In that field the government's primary purpose is to halt the espionage or terrorism efforts, and criminal prosecutions can be, and usually are, interrelated with other techniques used to frustrate a foreign power's efforts. . . .

### Supreme Court's Special Needs Cases

The distinction between ordinary criminal prosecutions and extraordinary situations underlies the Supreme Court's approval of entirely warrantless and even suspicionless searches that are designed to serve the government's "special needs, beyond the normal need for law enforcement." Vernonia School Dist. 47J v. Acton, 515 U.S. 646, 653 (1995) (quoting Griffin v. Wisconsin, 483 U.S. 868, 873 (1987) (internal quotation marks omitted)) (random drug-testing of student athletes). Apprehending drunk drivers and securing the border constitute such unique interests beyond ordinary, general law enforcement. *Id.* at 654 (citing Michigan Dep't of State Police v. Sitz, 496 U.S. 444 (1990), and United States v. Martinez-Fuerte, 428 U.S. 543 (1976)).

A recent case, City of Indianapolis v. Edmond, 531 U.S. 32 (2000), is relied on by both the government and amici. In that case, the Court held that a highway check point designed to catch drug dealers did not fit within its special needs exception because the government's "primary purpose" was merely "to uncover evidence of ordinary criminal wrongdoing." *Id.* at 41-42. The Court rejected the government's argument that the "severe and intractable nature of the drug problem" was sufficient justification for such a dragnet seizure lacking any individualized suspicion. *Id.* at 42. *Amici* particularly rely on the Court's statement that "the gravity of the threat alone cannot be dispositive of questions concerning what means law enforcement officers may employ to pursue a given purpose." *Id.*

But by "purpose" the Court makes clear it was referring not to a subjective intent, which is not relevant in ordinary Fourth Amendment probable cause analysis, but rather to a programmatic purpose. The Court distinguished the prior check point cases *Martinez-Fuerte* (involving checkpoints less than 100 miles from the Mexican border) and *Sitz* (checkpoints to detect intoxicated motorists) on the ground that the former involved the government's "longstanding concern for the protection of the integrity of the border," *id.* at 38 (quoting United States v. Montoya de Hernandez, 473 U.S. 531, 538 (1985)), and the latter was "aimed at reducing the immediate hazard posed by the presence of drunk drivers on the highways." *Id.* at 39. The Court emphasized that it was decidedly not drawing a distinction between suspicionless seizures with a "non-law-enforcement primary purpose" and those designed for law enforcement. *Id.* at 44 n.1. Rather, the Court distinguished general crime control programs and those that have another particular purpose, such as protection of citizens against special hazards or protection of our borders. The Court specifically acknowledged that an appropriately tailored road block could be used "to thwart an imminent terrorist attack." *Id.* at 44. The nature of the "emergency," which is simply another word for threat, takes the matter out of the realm of ordinary crime control.

### *Conclusion*

FISA's general programmatic purpose, to protect the nation against terrorists and espionage threats directed by foreign powers, has from its outset been distinguishable from "ordinary crime control." After the events of September 11, 2001, though, it is hard to imagine greater emergencies facing Americans than those experienced on that date.

We acknowledge, however, that the constitutional question presented by this case — whether Congress's disapproval of the primary purpose test is consistent with the Fourth Amendment — has no definitive jurisprudential answer. The Supreme Court's special needs cases involve random stops (seizures) not electronic searches. In one sense, they can be thought of as a greater encroachment into personal privacy because they are not based on any particular suspicion. On the other hand, wiretapping is a good deal more intrusive than an automobile stop accompanied by questioning.

. . . Our case may well involve the most serious threat our country faces. Even without taking into account the President's inherent constitutional authority to conduct warrantless foreign intelligence surveillance, we think the procedures and government showings required under FISA, if they do not meet the minimum Fourth Amendment warrant standards, certainly come close. We, therefore, believe firmly, applying the balancing test drawn from *Keith*, that FISA as amended is constitutional because the surveillances it authorizes are reasonable.

Accordingly, we reverse the FISA court's orders in this case to the extent they imposed conditions on the grant of the government's applications, vacate the FISA court's Rule 11, and remand with instructions to grant the applications as submitted and proceed henceforth in accordance with this opinion.

## NOTES AND QUESTIONS

1. *Defending the FISC (and the Public?) on Appeal.* No target of a FISC surveillance order ever learns about the issuance of the order, unless the information collected is later used in a criminal prosecution, such as in *Rosen,* or turns up in a FOIA or Privacy Act request. *See* Stephen Dycus et al., *National Security Law* 989-1014 (4th ed. 2007). As a practical matter, therefore, there was no one who could assert a legally protected interest to process an appeal of the *FISCR* decision to the Supreme Court. Nonetheless, public interest groups led by the ACLU filed a petition for leave to intervene and a petition for certiorari in the Supreme Court. Can you outline their likely positions, both on their right to intervene and on the merits? On March 24, 2003, the Supreme Court dismissed the petition. American Civil Liberties Union v. United States, 538 U.S. 920 (2003) (mem.). *See* Linda Greenhouse, *Opponents Lose Challenge to Government's Broader Use of Wiretaps to Fight Terrorism,* N.Y. Times, Mar. 25, 2003, at A12.

   Should Congress amend FISA to provide for public and FISC representation on appeals to the FISCR?

2. *The Holding.* What is the holding of the *FISCR* decision? Is the holding based on FISA, on the Constitution, or both? Can you reconcile the holding in the *FISCR* decision with *Keith*? With *Truong*?

3. *Purpose vs. Use.* Are the FISA limits addressed in the principal case concerned with the objective of the surveillance or with the nature and subsequent uses of the information to be obtained? The *FISCR* decision emphasized the importance of preserving the foreign intelligence objectives of FISA. In view of those objectives, on what basis did the FISCR object to forbidding the Criminal Division from directing or controlling the use of FISA procedures? Is the alleged flaw in the FISC order based on the Patriot Act amendments to FISA, or would the infirmity have been present even if FISA had not been amended?

   Is the FBI now permitted to conduct a secret search or wiretap for the primary purpose of investigating a crime even though there is no probable cause to suspect the commission of a crime? Although terrorism itself is criminal, terrorists may also engage in common criminal activities — credit card fraud, for example. If the primary purpose standard is still followed in criminal investigations, the existence of an ongoing credit card investigation might make it difficult to obtain a FISA order for surveillance of the same targets, even if there were some indication of plans for a terrorist act. If the Patriot Act amendment makes it easier for the FBI to manage parallel criminal and intelligence investigations, is the gain in effectiveness worth the risk of misuse of the process? Who will ensure that the FISA process is not employed as an end-run around Title III? Does the amendment "have the effect of changing the statute to more closely track the constitution"? *See* Letter from Daniel J. Bryant, *supra* p. 140 (arguing that it does). If so, is it because the constitutional "track" changed after September 11? *See id.* (arguing that it did); *see also* Banks, *supra* p. 143 (arguing that it shouldn't have).

   Can you now describe the significance of the Patriot Act amendment to the "purpose" requirement? Did the information-sharing additions to

FISA in the Patriot Act contribute to the result? If so, how? Should Congress revisit the "purpose" standard in FISA? If so, should Congress codify the "primary purpose" requirement, or should it more clearly abandon any required foreign intelligence objectives in shaping requests to the FISC?

Absent intervention by Congress, do you think the *FISCR* decision represents the last word on the issues it addresses? Can you see how these same issues might be addressed by other courts in the future?

4. ***The Minimization Requirements.*** Why did the FISC err in relying on the minimization requirements of FISA to justify its order? Do the minimization procedures imply a "wall" between law enforcement and intelligence investigators? Does the approach to minimization taken by the *Rosen* court support the FISCR or the FISC?

5. ***The "Special Needs" Precedents.*** Are you persuaded that the Supreme Court's "special needs" cases are based on considerations analogous to the Justice Department procedures at issue in the principal case?

6. ***The Aftermath.*** Approximately six months after the *FISCR* decision, Justice Department officials reported to the House Judiciary Committee that the procedures approved by the FISCR have

> allowed the Department of Justice to investigate cases in a more orderly, efficient, and knowledgeable way, and ha[ve] permitted all involved personnel, both law enforcement and intelligence, to discuss openly legal, factual, and tactical issues arising during the course of investigations. . . . The Department has developed counterterrorism tools and methods that plainly would not have been possible under the previous standards. [Letter from Jamie E. Brown, Acting Asst. Attorney General, Off. of Legis. Affairs, U.S. Dept. of Justice, to F. James Sensenbrenner Jr., Chair, H. Comm. on the Judiciary, May 13, 2003, at 15-16.]

The Department also reported that approximately 4,500 open intelligence files were shared with criminal prosecutors since October 2002 to allow the law enforcement personnel to determine whether criminal investigations of any of those intelligence targets should be initiated. *Id.*

In 2003, the FBI issued a classified field directive to further dismantle the wall between law enforcement and intelligence investigations. The directive spells out the Model Counterterrorism Investigations Strategy (MCIS) and new requirements that criminal and intelligence investigators physically work as part of the same teams investigating terrorism. All terrorism investigations are now treated as intelligence investigations, are formally run by the counterterrorism division at FBI headquarters, and will be able to use FISA procedures and methods. Dan Eggen, *FBI Applies New Rules to Surveillance*, Wash. Post, Dec. 13, 2003, at A1. FBI officials stated that the new system will deemphasize criminal prosecution in favor of longer-term intelligence surveillance. When a criminal case is brought, however, prosecutors will be able to use the FISA-derived evidence at trial. *Id.* Does the MCIS satisfy the requirements outlined in the *FISCR* decision? Is the new strategy constitutional?

## D.  FISA TRENDS

The FISC has been active. More than 14,000 applications for surveillance or searches have been approved by the FISC since 1979. Brief annual FISA reports from the Attorney General, including the volume of applications approved for the year, are posted at http://www.usdoj.gov/oipr/readingroom/2006fisa-ltr.pdf. During calendar year 2006, 2181 applications were made, and 2176 were approved by the FISC. Five applications were withdrawn by the government prior to a FISC ruling. The FISC denied one application submitted by the government in 2006. By comparison, an average of about 1,100 requests for electronic surveillance are submitted by law enforcement officials under 18 U.S.C. §2518 annually. What do the numbers suggest?

Section 6002 of the Intelligence Reform and Terrorism Prevention Act of 2004, Pub. L. No. 108-458, 118 Stat. 3742, expanded the reporting under FISA to require semiannual reports to the intelligence and judiciary committees of the House and Senate that include the aggregate number of persons targeted and breakdowns for electronic surveillance, physical searches, pen registers, access to records, and lone wolf orders. The new reports must also indicate the number of times the Attorney General has approved the use in criminal proceedings of information derived from FISA surveillance, provide summaries of significant legal interpretations of FISA by DOJ before the FISC or FISCR, and include copies of all decisions or opinions of the FISC or FISCR that include "significant construction or interpretation" of FISA. *Id.* During 2006, the government made 43 applications for business records, including requests for pen registers. Four proposed orders were modified substantively by the FISC, but none were denied. In the same period, the government issued approximately 19,000 national security letters. *See* U.S. Department of Justice, Office of the Inspector General, *A Review of the Federal Bureau of Investigation's Use of National Security Letters* 120 (March 2007), *available at* http://www.usdoj.gov/oig/special/s0703b/final. pdf. (National security letters are addressed in Chapter 6.) No mention was made of lone wolf orders, and none of the other information mentioned above was included. Why do you suppose the record is incomplete?

Notwithstanding the ever-increasing use of FISA and the FISC, foreign intelligence surveillance of suspected terrorists under the terms and conditions of FISA has not been a panacea. In part, this is because

> experience demonstrates three harsh realities: first, it is often difficult to isolate U.S. persons from one or more foreign surveillance targets in a place or through electronic monitoring; second, it is often impossible to determine the relationship of a potential terrorist to a foreign power early in an investigation; and third . . . U.S. persons are as capable as any other of wreaking catastrophic havoc. [Banks & Bowman, *supra* p. 135, at 95.]

The lone wolf provision, *supra* p. 133, is supposed to address the second of these concerns.

Enactment of the Intelligence Reform and Terrorism Prevention Act of 2004, *supra*, affected FISA in a number of ways. In addition to the lone wolf and reporting provisions noted above, the new Director of National Intelligence

(DNI) was given responsibility "to establish requirements and priorities for foreign intelligence information to be collected" under FISA and assist the Attorney General to ensure that FISA intelligence "may be used efficiently and effectively for foreign intelligence purposes, except that the Director shall have no authority to direct, manage, or undertake" surveillance or search operations under FISA "unless otherwise authorized by statute or Executive order." *Id.* §102(A)(f)(6), 118 Stat. 3650. Another section of the Intelligence Reform Act provides that "[n]othing in this act shall be construed as affecting the role of the Department of Justice or the Attorney General with respect to applications under" FISA. *Id.* §102(A)(f)(8), 118 Stat. 3650. The authorities and duties of the DNI generally are considered in Dycus, *supra* p. 154, at 363-368. The precise role of this new player in the FISA processes is not yet clear. Neither is it clear what legal issues might be raised by an executive order authorizing the DNI to direct or undertake FISA surveillance.

### CASE STUDY: THE TERRORIST SURVEILLANCE PROGRAM

On December 16, 2005, the New York Times reported that, according to government officials, "President Bush secretly authorized the National Security Agency to eavesdrop on Americans and others inside the United States to search for evidence of terrorist activity without the court-approved warrants ordinarily required for domestic spying." James Risen & Eric Lichtblau, *Bush Lets U.S. Spy on Callers Without Courts*, N.Y. Times, Dec. 16, 2005, at A1. Pursuant to a still-secret executive order signed by the President in 2002, the NSA has without warrants monitored the telephone and e-mail communications of thousands of persons inside the United States where one end of the communication is outside the United States in an effort to learn more about possible terrorist plots. *Id.* Later called the Terrorist Surveillance Program (TSP) by the Administration, the NSA surveillance created a major controversy, drawing out prominent critics and proponents alike, provoking hearings in Congress, prompting lawsuits by civil liberties organizations and by defendants in criminal cases who challenged their previous pleas or convictions, and generating countless op-ed pieces, blog debates, and comments.

The Bush administration vigorously defended the TSP. The Justice Department's Office of Legislative Affairs immediately prepared a letter for congressional leaders summarizing its legal rationale for the NSA surveillance. Soon thereafter lawsuits were filed challenging the TSP on statutory and constitutional grounds. Excerpts from the Justice Department letter and from one of the lawsuits follow.

### LETTER FROM WILLIAM E. MOSCHELLA, ASST. ATTORNEY GENERAL, TO THE HONORABLE PAT ROBERTS, CHAIRMAN, SENATE SELECT COMMITTEE ON INTELLIGENCE ET AL.

Dec. 22, 2005, *available at* http://www.fas.org/irp/agency/doj/fisa/doj122205.pdf

As you know, in response to unauthorized disclosures in the media, the President has described certain activities of the National Security Agency

("NSA") that he has authorized since shortly after September 11, 2001. As described by the President, the NSA intercepts certain international communications into and out of the United States of people linked to al Qaeda or an affiliated terrorist organization. The purpose of these intercepts is to establish an early warning system to detect and prevent another catastrophic terrorist attack on the United States. The President has made clear that he will use his constitutional and statutory authorities to protect the American people from further terrorist attacks, and the NSA activities the President described are part of that effort. Leaders of the Congress were briefed on these activities more than a dozen times.

The purpose of this letter is to provide an additional brief summary of the legal authority supporting the NSA activities described by the President.

As an initial matter, I emphasize a few points. The President stated that these activities are "crucial to our national security." The President further explained that "the unauthorized disclosure of this effort damages our national security and puts our citizens at risk. Revealing classified information is illegal, alerts our enemies, and endangers our country." These critical national security activities remain classified. All United States laws and policies governing the protection and nondisclosure of national security information, including the information relating to the activities described by the President, remain in full force and effect. The unauthorized disclosure of classified information violates federal criminal law. The Government may provide further classified briefings to the Congress on these activities in an appropriate manner. Any such briefings will be conducted in a manner that will not endanger national security.

Under Article II of the Constitution, including in his capacity as Commander in Chief, the President has the responsibility to protect the Nation from further attacks, and the Constitution gives him all necessary authority to fulfill that duty. *See, e.g., Prize Cases,* 67 U.S. (2 Black) 635, 668 (1863) (stressing that if the Nation is invaded, "the President is not only authorized but bound to resist by force . . . without waiting for any special legislative authority"); *Campbell v. Clinton*, 203 F.3d 19, 27 (D.C. Cir. 2000) (Silberman, J., concurring) ("[T]he *Prize Cases* . . . stand for the proposition that the President has independent authority to repel aggressive acts by third parties even without specific congressional authorization, and courts may not review the level of force selected."); *id.* at 40 (Tatel, J., concurring). The Congress recognized this constitutional authority in the preamble to the Authorization for the Use of Military Force ("AUMF") of September 18, 2001, 115 Stat. 224 (2001) ("[T]he President has authority under the Constitution to take action to deter and prevent acts of international terrorism against the United States."), and in the War Powers Resolution, *see* 50 U.S.C. §1541(c) ("The constitutional powers of the President as Commander in Chief to introduce United States Armed Forces into hostilities [] . . . [extend to] a national emergency created by attack upon the United States, its territories or possessions, or its armed forces.").

This constitutional authority includes the authority to order warrantless foreign intelligence surveillance within the United States, as all federal appellate courts, including at least four circuits, to have addressed the issue have concluded. *See, e.g., In re Sealed Case*, 310 F.3d 717, 742 (FISA Ct. of Rev. 2002)

("[A]ll the other courts to have decided the issue [have] held that the President did have inherent authority to conduct warrantless searches to obtain foreign intelligence information. . . . We take for granted that the President does have that authority. . . ."). The Supreme Court has said that warrants are generally required in the context of purely *domestic* threats, but it expressly distinguished *foreign* threats. *See United States v. United States District Court*, 407 U.S. 297, 308 (1972). As Justice Byron White recognized almost 40 years ago, Presidents have long exercised the authority to conduct warrantless surveillance for national security purposes, and a warrant is unnecessary "if the President of the United States or his chief legal officer, the Attorney General, has considered the requirements of national security and authorized electronic surveillance as reasonable." *Katz v. United States*, 389 U.S. 347, 363-364 (1967) (White, J., concurring).

The President's constitutional authority to direct the NSA to conduct the activities he described is supplemented by statutory authority under the AUMF. The AUMF authorizes the President "to use all necessary and appropriate force against those nations, organizations, or persons he determines planned, authorized, committed, or aided the terrorists attacks of September 11, 2001, . . . in order to prevent any future acts of international terrorism against the United States." §2(a). The AUMF clearly contemplates action within the United States, *see also id.* pmbl. (the attacks of September 11 "render it both necessary and appropriate that the United States exercise its rights to self-defense and to protect United States citizens both at home and abroad"). The AUMF cannot be read as limited to authorizing the use of force against Afghanistan, as some have argued. Indeed, those who directly "committed" the attacks of September 11 resided in the United States for months before those attacks. The reality of the September 11 plot demonstrates that the authorization of force covers activities both on foreign soil and in America.

In *Hamdi v. Rumsfeld*, 542 U.S. 507 (2004), the Supreme Court addressed the scope of the AUMF. At least five Justices concluded that the AUMF authorized the President to detain a U.S. citizen in the United States because "detention to prevent a combatant's return to the battlefield is a fundamental incident of waging war" and is therefore included in the "necessary and appropriate force" authorized by the Congress. *Id.* at 518-519 (plurality opinion of O'Connor, J.); *see id.* 587 (Thomas, J., dissenting). These five Justices concluded that the AUMF "clearly and unmistakably authorize[s]" the "fundamental incident[s] of waging war." *Id.* at 518-19 (plurality opinion); *see id.* at 587 (Thomas, J., dissenting).

Communications intelligence targeted at the enemy is a fundamental incident of the use of military force. Indeed, throughout history, signals intelligence has formed a critical part of waging war. In the Civil War, each side tapped the telegraph lines of the other. In the World Wars, the United States intercepted telegrams into and out of the country. The AUMF cannot be read to exclude this long-recognized and essential authority to conduct communications intelligence targeted at the enemy. We cannot fight a blind war. Because communications intelligence activities constitute, to use the language of *Hamdi*, a fundamental incident of waging war, the AUMF *clearly and unmistakably authorizes* such activities directed against the communications of our enemy. Accordingly, the President's "authority is at its maximum." *Youngstown Sheet & Tube Co. v. Sawyer*, 343 U.S. 579, 635 (1952) (Jackson, J., concurring); *see Dames & Moore v. Regan*, 453 U.S. 654, 668 (1981); *cf. Youngstown*, 343 U.S. at 585 (noting the absence of a statute "from which [the asserted authority] c[ould] be fairly implied").

The President's authorization of targeted electronic surveillance by the NSA is also consistent with the Foreign Intelligence Surveillance Act ("FISA"). Section 2511(2)(f) of title 18 provides, as relevant here, that the procedures of FISA and two chapters of title 18 "shall be the exclusive means by which electronic surveillance . . . may be conducted." Section 109 of FISA, in turn, makes it unlawful to conduct electronic surveillance, "except as authorized by statute." 50 U.S.C. §1809(a)(1). Importantly, section 109's exception for electronic surveillance "authorized by statute" is broad, especially considered in the context of surrounding provisions. *See* 18 U.S.C. §2511(1) ("Except as otherwise specifically provided *in this chapter* any person who — (a) intentionally intercepts . . . any wire, oral or electronic communication [] . . . shall be punished. . . .") (emphasis added); *id.* §2511(2)(e) (providing a defense to liability to individuals "conduct[ing] electronic surveillance, . . . as authorized by *that Act [FISA]*") (emphasis added).

By expressly and broadly excepting from its prohibition electronic surveillance undertaken "as authorized by statute," section 109 of FISA permits an exception to the "procedures" of FISA referred to in U.S.C. §2511(2)(f) where authorized by another statute, even if the other authorizing statute does not specifically amend section 2511(2)(f). The AUMF satisfies section 109's requirement for statutory authorization of electronic surveillance, just as a majority of the Court in *Hamdi* concluded that it satisfies the requirement in 18 U.S.C. §4001(a) that no U.S. citizen be detained by the United States "except pursuant to an Act of Congress." *See Hamdi*, 542 U.S. at 519 (explaining that "it is of no moment that the AUMF does not use specific language of detention"); *see id.* at 587 (Thomas, J., dissenting).

Some might suggest that FISA could be read to require that a subsequent statutory authorization must come in the form of an amendment to FISA itself. But under established principles of statutory construction, the AUMF and FISA must be construed in harmony to avoid any potential conflict between FISA and the President's Article II authority as Commander in Chief. *See, e.g., Zadvydas v. Davis*, 533 U.S. 678, 689 (2001); *INS v. St. Cyr*, 533 U.S. 289, 300 (2001). Accordingly, any ambiguity as to whether the AUMF is a statute that satisfies the requirements of FISA and allows electronic surveillance in the conflict with al Qaeda without complying with FISA procedures must be resolved in favor of an interpretation that is consistent with the President's long-recognized authority.

The NSA activities described by the President are also consistent with the Fourth Amendment and the protection of civil liberties. The Fourth Amendment's "central requirement is one of reasonableness." *Illinois vs. McArthur*, 531 U.S. 326, 330 (2001) (internal quotation marks omitted). For searches conducted in the course of ordinary criminal law enforcement, reasonableness generally requires securing a warrant. *See Bd. of Educ. v. Earls*, 536 U.S. 822, 828 (2002). Outside the ordinary criminal law enforcement context, however, the Supreme Court has, at times, dispensed with the warrant, instead adjudging the reasonableness of a search under the totality of circumstances. *See United States v. Knights*, 534 U.S. 112, 118 (2001). In particular, the Supreme Court has long recognized that "special needs, beyond the normal need for law enforcement," can justify departure from the usual warrant requirement. *Vernonia School Dist. 47J v. Acton*, 515 U.S. 646, 653 (1995); *see also City of Indianapolis v. Edmond*, 531 U.S. 32, 41-42 (2000) (striking down checkpoint where "primary purpose was to detect evidence of ordinary criminal wrongdoing").

Foreign intelligence collection, especially in the midst of an armed conflict in which the adversary has already launched catastrophic attacks within the United States, fits squarely within the "special needs" exception to the warrant requirement. Foreign intelligence collection undertaken to prevent further devastating attacks on our Nation serves the highest purpose through means other than traditional law enforcement. *See In re Sealed Case*, 310 F.3d at 745; *United States v. Duggan*, 743 F.2d 59, 72 (2d Cir. 1984) (recognizing that the Fourth Amendment implications of foreign intelligence surveillance are far different from ordinary wiretapping, because they are not principally used for criminal prosecution).

Intercepting communications into and out of the United States of persons linked to al Qaeda in order to detect and prevent a catastrophic attack is clearly *reasonable*. Reasonableness is generally determined by "balancing the nature of the intrusion on the individual's privacy against the promotion of legitimate governmental interests." *Earls*, 536 U.S. at 829. There is undeniably an important and legitimate privacy interest at stake with respect to the activities described by the President. That must be balanced, however, against the Government's compelling interest in the security of the Nation, *see, e.g., Haig v. Agee*, 453 U.S. 280, 307 (1981) ("It is obvious and unarguable that no governmental interest is more compelling than the security of the Nation.") (citation and quotation marks omitted). The fact that the NSA activities are reviewed and reauthorized approximately every 45 days to ensure that they continue to be necessary and appropriate further demonstrates the reasonableness of these activities.

As explained above, the President determined that it was necessary following September 11 to create an early warning system. FISA could not have provided the speed and agility required for the early warning detection system. In addition, any legislative change, other than the AUMF, that the President might have sought specifically to create such an early warning system would have been public and would have tipped off our enemies concerning our intelligence limitations and capabilities. Nevertheless, I want to stress that the United States makes full use of FISA to address the terrorist threat, and FISA has proven to be a very important tool, especially in longer-term investigations. In addition, the United States is constantly assessing all available legal options, taking full advantage of any developments in the law.

We hope this information is helpful.

Sincerely,
*William E. Moschella*
Assistant Attorney General

## AMERICAN CIVIL LIBERTIES UNION v. NATIONAL SECURITY AGENCY

United States District Court, Eastern District of Michigan, 2006
438 F. Supp. 2d 754

ANNA DIGGS TAYLOR, District Judge.

### I. Introduction

This is a challenge to the legality of a secret program (hereinafter "TSP") undisputedly inaugurated by the National Security Agency (hereinafter "NSA") at least by 2002 and continuing today, which intercepts without benefit of warrant or other judicial approval, prior or subsequent, the international telephone and internet communications of numerous persons and organizations within this country. The TSP has been acknowledged by this Administration to have been authorized by the President's secret order during 2002 and reauthorized at least thirty times since.

Plaintiffs are a group of persons and organizations who, according to their affidavits, are defined by the Foreign Intelligence Surveillance Act (hereinafter "FISA") as "U.S. persons." They conducted regular international telephone and internet communications for various uncontestedly legitimate reasons including journalism, the practice of law, and scholarship. Many of their communications are and have been with persons in the Middle East. Each Plaintiff has alleged a "well founded belief" that he, she, or it, has been subjected to Defendants' interceptions, and that the TSP not only injures them specifically and directly, but that the TSP substantially chills and impairs their constitutionally protected communications. Persons abroad who before the program spoke with them by telephone or internet will no longer do so.

Plaintiffs have alleged that the TSP violates their free speech and associational rights, as guaranteed by the First Amendment of the United States Constitution; their privacy rights, as guaranteed by the Fourth Amendment of the United States Constitution; the principle of the Separation of Powers because the TSP has been authorized by the President in excess of his Executive Power under Article II of the United States Constitution, and that it specifically violates the statutory limitations placed upon such interceptions by the Congress in FISA because it is conducted without observation of any of the procedures required by law, either statutory or Constitutional. . . .

### II. State Secrets Privilege

Defendants argue that the state secrets privilege[1] bars Plaintiffs' claims because Plaintiffs cannot establish standing or a *prima facie* case for any of their claims without the use of state secrets. Further, Defendants argue that they cannot defend this case without revealing state secrets. . . .

. . . It is undisputed that Defendants have publicly admitted to the following: (1) the TSP exists; (2) it operates without warrants; (3) it targets

---

[1. The state secrets privilege is an evidentiary privilege that operates to foreclose relief for violations of rights that may have occurred by foreclosing the discovery of evidence that they did occur. *See* Dycus, *supra* p. 154, at 1037-1050.]

communications where one party to the communication is outside the United States, and the government has a reasonable basis to conclude that one party to the communication is a member of al Qaeda, affiliated with al Qaeda, or a member of an organization affiliated with al Qaeda, or working in support of al Qaeda. As the Government has on many occasions confirmed the veracity of these allegations, the state secrets privilege does not apply to this information.

Contrary to Defendants' arguments, the court is persuaded that Plaintiffs are able to establish a *prima facie* case based solely on Defendants' public admissions regarding the TSP. Plaintiffs' declarations establish that their communications would be monitored under the TSP. Further, Plaintiffs have shown that because of the existence of the TSP, they have suffered a real and concrete harm. Plaintiffs' declarations state undisputedly that they are stifled in their ability to vigorously conduct research, interact with sources, talk with clients and, in the case of the attorney Plaintiffs, uphold their oath of providing effective and ethical representation of their clients. In addition, Plaintiffs have the additional injury of incurring substantial travel expenses as a result of having to travel and meet with clients and others relevant to their cases. Therefore, the court finds that Plaintiffs need no additional facts to establish a *prima facie* case for any of their claims questioning the legality of the TSP.

The court, however, is convinced that Plaintiffs cannot establish a *prima facie* case to support their datamining claims without the use of privileged information and further litigation of this issue would force the disclosure of the very thing the privilege is designed to protect. Therefore, the court grants Defendants' motion for summary judgment with respect to this claim.

Finally, Defendants assert that they cannot defend this case without the exposure of state secrets. This court disagrees. The Bush Administration has repeatedly told the general public that there is a valid basis in law for the TSP. Further, Defendants have contended that the President has the authority under the AUMF and the Constitution to authorize the continued use of the TSP. Defendants have supported these arguments without revealing or relying on any classified information. Indeed, the court has reviewed the classified information and is of the opinion that this information is not necessary to any viable defense to the TSP. Defendants have presented support for the argument that "it . . . is well-established that the President may exercise his statutory and constitutional authority to gather intelligence information about foreign enemies." Defendants cite to various sources to support this position. Consequently, the court finds Defendants' argument that they cannot defend this case without the use of classified information to be disingenuous and without merit. . . .

### III. Standing

Defendants argue that Plaintiffs do not establish their standing. They contend that Plaintiffs' claim here is merely a subjective fear of surveillance which falls short of the type of injury necessary to establish standing. They argue that Plaintiffs' alleged injuries are too tenuous to be recognized, not "distinct and palpable" nor "concrete and particularized." . . .

This court finds that the injuries alleged by Plaintiffs are "concrete and particularized," and not "abstract or conjectural." The TSP is not hypothetical, it is an actual surveillance program that was admittedly instituted after September 11, 2001, and has been reauthorized by the President more than thirty times since the attacks. The President has, moreover, emphasized that he intends to continue to reauthorize the TSP indefinitely. Further, the court need not speculate upon the kind of activity the Plaintiffs want to engage in — they want to engage in conversations with individuals abroad without fear that their First Amendment rights are being infringed upon. Therefore, this court concludes that Plaintiffs have satisfied the requirement of alleging "actual or threatened injury" as a result of Defendants' conduct. . . .

Although this court is persuaded that Plaintiffs have alleged sufficient injury to establish standing, it is important to note that if the court were to deny standing based on the unsubstantiated minor distinctions drawn by Defendants, the President's actions in warrantless wiretapping, in contravention of FISA, Title III, and the First and Fourth Amendments, would be immunized from judicial scrutiny. It was never the intent of the Framers to give the President such unfettered control, particularly where his actions blatantly disregard the parameters clearly enumerated in the Bill of Rights. The three separate branches of government were developed as a check and balance for one another. It is within the court's duty to ensure that power is never "condense[d] . . . into a single branch of government." *Hamdi v. Rumsfeld,* 542 U.S. 507, 536 (2004) (plurality opinion). We must always be mindful that "[w]hen the President takes official action, the Court has the authority to determine whether he has acted within the law." *Clinton v. Jones,* 520 U.S. 681 (1997). "It remains one of the most vital functions of this Court to police with care the separation of the governing powers. . . . When structure fails, liberty is always in peril." *Public Citizen v. U.S. Dept. of Justice,* 491 U.S. 440, 468 (1989) (Kennedy, J., concurring). . . .

### V. The Fourth Amendment . . .

[The court quotes the Fourth Amendment and the *Keith* case, *supra* p. 91, then provides the following analysis.]

Accordingly, the Fourth Amendment, about which much has been written, in its few words requires reasonableness in all searches. It also requires prior warrants for any reasonable search, based upon prior-existing probable cause, as well as particularity as to persons, places, and things, and the interposition of a neutral magistrate between Executive branch enforcement officers and citizens.

In enacting FISA, Congress made numerous concessions to stated executive needs. They include delaying the applications for warrants until after surveillance has begun for several types of exigencies, reducing the probable cause requirement to a less stringent standard, provision of a single court of judicial experts, and extension of the duration of approved wiretaps from thirty days (under Title III) to a ninety day term.

All of the above Congressional concessions to Executive need and to the exigencies of our present situation as a people, however, have been futile. The wiretapping program here in litigation has undisputedly been continued for at least five years, it has undisputedly been implemented without regard to FISA and of course the more stringent standards of Title III, and obviously in violation of the Fourth Amendment.

The President of the United States is himself created by that same Constitution.

## VI. The First Amendment . . .

Judge Wright, in *Zweibon* [v. Mitchell, 516 F.2d 594 (D.C. Cir. 1975, *cert. denied*, 425 U.S. 944 (1976), noted *supra* p. 100], noted that the tapping of an organization's office phone will provide the membership roster of that organization, as forbidden by *Bates v. City of Little Rock,* 361 U.S. 516 (1960); thereby causing members to leave that organization, and thereby chilling the organization's First Amendment rights and causing the loss of membership. *Zweibon,* 516 F.2d at 634.

A governmental action to regulate speech may be justified only upon showing of a compelling governmental interest; and that the means chosen to further that interest are the least restrictive of freedom of belief and association that could be chosen. *Clark v. Library of Congress,* 750 F.2d 89, 94 (D.C. Cir. 1984).

It must be noted that FISA explicitly admonishes that ". . . no United States person may be considered . . . an agent of a foreign power solely upon the basis of activities protected by the First Amendment to the Constitution of the United States." 50 U.S.C. §1805(a)(3)(A). See also *United States v. Falvey,* 540 F. Supp. at 1310.

Finally, as Justice Powell wrote for the Court in the *Keith* case:

> National security cases, moreover, often reflect a convergence of First and Fourth Amendment values not present in cases of "ordinary" crime. Though the investigative duty of the executive may be stronger in such cases, so also is there greater jeopardy to constitutionally protected speech. "Historically the struggle for freedom of speech and press in England was bound up with the issue of the scope of the search and seizure power," (citation omitted). History abundantly documents the tendency of Government—however benevolent and benign its motives—to view with suspicion those who most fervently dispute its policies. Fourth Amendment protections become the more necessary when the targets of official surveillance may be those suspected of unorthodoxy in their political beliefs. *U.S. v. U.S. District Court,* 407 U.S. at 313-314.

The President of the United States, a creature of the same Constitution which gave us these Amendments, has undisputedly violated the Fourth in failing to procure judicial orders as required by FISA, and accordingly has violated the First Amendment Rights of these Plaintiffs as well.

## VII. The Separation of Powers

The Constitution of the United States provides that "[a]ll legislative Powers herein granted shall be vested in a Congress of the United States. . . ." It further provides that "[t]he executive Power shall be vested in a President of the United States of America." And that ". . . he shall take care that the laws be faithfully executed. . . ."

Our constitution was drafted by founders and ratified by a people who still held in vivid memory the image of King George III and his General Warrants.

The concept that each form of governmental power should be separated was a well-developed one. James Madison wrote that:

> The accumulation of all powers, legislative, executive, and judiciary, in the same hands, whether of one, a few, or many, and whether hereditary, self-appointed, or elective, may justly be pronounced the very definition of tyranny. *The Federalist No. 47*, at 301 (James Madison).

The seminal American case in this area, and one on which the government appears to rely, is that of *Youngstown Sheet & Tube v. Sawyer,* 343 U.S. 579 (1952). . . .

In this case, if the teachings of *Youngstown* are law, the separation of powers doctrine has been violated. The President, undisputedly, has violated the provisions of FISA for a five-year period. Justice Black wrote, in *Youngstown:*

> Nor can the seizure order be sustained because of the several constitutional provisions that grant executive power to the President. In the framework of our Constitution, the President's power to see that the laws are faithfully executed refutes the idea that he is to be a lawmaker. The Constitution limits his functions in the lawmaking process to the recommending of laws he thinks wise and the vetoing of laws he thinks bad. And the Constitution is neither silent nor equivocal about who [shall] make laws which the President is to execute. The first section of the first article says that "All legislative powers herein granted shall be vested in a Congress of the United States * * *"
>
> The President's order does not direct that a congressional policy be executed in a manner prescribed by Congress — it directs that a presidential policy be executed in a manner prescribed by the President. . . . The Constitution did not subject this law-making power of Congress to presidential or military supervision or control. *Youngstown,* 343 U.S. at 587-588.

These secret authorization orders must, like the executive order in that case, fall. They violate the Separation of Powers ordained by the very Constitution of which this President is a creature.

### VIII. The Authorization for Use of Military Force . . .

The Government argues here that it was given authority by that resolution to conduct the TSP in violation of both FISA and the Constitution.

First, this court must note that the AUMF says nothing whatsoever of intelligence or surveillance. The government argues that such authority must be implied. Next it must be noted that FISA and Title III, are together by their terms denominated by Congress as the exclusive means by which electronic surveillance may be conducted. Both statutes have made abundantly clear that prior warrants must be obtained from the FISA court for such surveillance, with limited exceptions, none of which are here even raised as applicable. Indeed, the government here claims that the AUMF has by implication granted its TSP authority for more than five years, although FISA's longest exception, for the Declaration of War by Congress, is only fifteen days from date of such a Declaration.

FISA's history and content, detailed above, are highly specific in their requirements, and the AUMF, if construed to apply at all to intelligence is utterly general. In *Morales v. TWA, Inc.,* 504 U.S. 374 (1992), the Supreme Court taught us that "it is a commonplace of statutory construction that the specific governs the general." *Id.* at 384. The implication argued by Defendants, therefore, cannot be made by this court. . . .

[In *Hamdi,*] Justice O'Connor concluded that . . . a citizen must be given Fifth Amendment rights to contest his classification [as an enemy combatant], including notice and the opportunity to be heard by a neutral decisionmaker. *Hamdi,* 542 U.S. at 533 (citing *Cleveland Board of Education v. Loudermill,* 470 U.S. 532 (1985)). Accordingly, her holding was that the Bill of Rights of the United States Constitution must be applied despite authority granted by the AUMF.

She stated that:

> It is during our most challenging and uncertain moments that our Nation's commitment to due process is most severely tested; and it is in those times that we must preserve our commitment at home to the principles for which we fight abroad. . . .
>
> . . . Any process in which the Executive's factual assertions go wholly unchallenged or are simply presumed correct without any opportunity for the alleged combatant to demonstrate otherwise falls constitutionally short. *Hamdi,* 542 U.S. at 532, 537.

Under *Hamdi,* accordingly, the Constitution of the United States must be followed.

The AUMF resolution, if indeed it is construed as replacing FISA, gives no support to Defendants here. Even if that Resolution superceded all other statutory law, Defendants have violated the Constitutional rights of their citizens including the First Amendment, Fourth Amendment, and the Separation of Powers doctrine.

## IX. Inherent Power . . .

The Government appears to argue here that, pursuant to the penumbra of Constitutional language in Article II, and particularly because the President is designated Commander in Chief of the Army and Navy, he has been granted the inherent power to violate not only the laws of the Congress but the First and Fourth Amendments of the Constitution, itself.

We must first note that the Office of the Chief Executive has itself been created, with its powers, by the Constitution. There are no hereditary Kings in America and no powers not created by the Constitution. So all "inherent powers" must derive from that Constitution.

We have seen in *Hamdi* that the Fifth Amendment of the United States Constitution is fully applicable to the Executive branch's actions and therefore it can only follow that the First and Fourth Amendments must be applicable as well. In the *Youngstown* case the same "inherent powers" argument was raised and the Court noted that the President had been created Commander in Chief of only the military, and not of all the people, even in time of war. Indeed, since

*Ex Parte Milligan,* we have been taught that the "Constitution of the United-States is a law for rulers and people, equally in war and in peace. . . ." *Ex Parte Milligan,* 71 U.S. (4 Wall.) 2, 120 (1866). Again, in *Home Building & Loan Ass'n v. Blaisdell* [290 U.S. 398 (1934)], we were taught that no emergency can create power.

Finally, although the Defendants have suggested the unconstitutionality of FISA, it appears to this court that that question is here irrelevant. Not only FISA, but the Constitution itself has been violated by the Executive's TSP. As the court states in *Falvey,* even where statutes are not explicit, the requirements of the Fourth Amendment must still be met. And of course, the *Zweibon* opinion of Judge Skelly Wright plainly states that although many cases hold that the President's power to obtain foreign intelligence information is vast, none suggest that he is immune from Constitutional requirements.

The argument that inherent powers justify the program here in litigation must fail.

## X. Practical Justifications for Exemption

First, it must be remembered that both Title III and FISA permit delayed applications for warrants, after surveillance has begun. Also, the case law has long permitted law enforcement action to proceed in cases in which the lives of officers or others are threatened in cases of "hot pursuit," border searches, school locker searches, or where emergency situations exist. See generally *Warden v. Hayden,* 387 U.S. 294 (1967); *Vernonia School District v. Acton,* 515 U.S. 646 (1995); and *Michigan Department of State Police v. Sitz,* 496 U.S. 444 (1990).

Indeed, in *Zweibon,* Judge Wright enumerates a number of Defendants' practical arguments here (including judicial competence, danger of security leaks, less likelihood of criminal prosecution, delay, and the burden placed upon both the courts and the Executive branch by compliance) and finds, after long and careful analysis, that none constitutes adequate justification for exemption from the requirements of either FISA or the Fourth Amendment. *Zweibon,* 516 F.2d at 641. It is noteworthy, in this regard, that Defendants here have sought no Congressional amendments which would remedy practical difficulty.

As long ago as the *Youngstown* case, the Truman administration argued that the cumbersome procedures required to obtain warrants made the process unworkable. The *Youngstown* court made short shift of that argument and, it appears, the present Defendants' need for speed and agility is equally weightless. The Supreme Court in the *Keith* as well as the *Hamdi* cases, has attempted to offer helpful solutions to the delay problem, all to no avail.

## XI. Conclusion

For all of the reasons outlined above, this court is constrained to grant to Plaintiffs the Partial Summary Judgment requested, and holds that the TSP violates the APA; the Separation of Powers doctrine; the First and Fourth Amendments of the United States Constitution; and the statutory law.

Defendants' Motion to Dismiss the final claim of data-mining is granted, because litigation of that claim would require violation of Defendants' state secrets privilege.

The Permanent Injunction of the TSP requested by Plaintiffs is granted inasmuch as each of the factors required to be met to sustain such an injunction have undisputedly been met. The irreparable injury necessary to warrant injunctive relief is clear, as the First and Fourth Amendment rights of Plaintiffs are violated by the TSP. See *Dombrowski v. Pfister,* 380 U.S. 479 (1965). The irreparable injury conversely sustained by Defendants under this injunction may be rectified by compliance with our Constitution and/or statutory law, as amended if necessary. Plaintiffs have prevailed, and the public interest is clear, in this matter. It is the upholding of our Constitution.

As Justice Warren wrote in *U.S. v. Robel,* 389 U.S. 258 (1967):

> Implicit in the term "national defense" is the notion of defending those values and ideas which set this Nation apart. . . . It would indeed be ironic if, in the name of national defense, we would sanction the subversion of . . . those liberties . . . which makes the defense of the Nation worthwhile. *Id.* at 264.

*It is so ordered.*

## NOTES AND QUESTIONS

1. ***Nature of the Terrorist Surveillance Program.*** What is the NSA actually doing, as best you can tell from the DOJ letter? Are there any internal procedural controls? If so, what are they? Do they adequately safeguard any privacy rights that may be implicated?
2. ***The Predicate Legal Standard for Surveillance.*** As indicated in the Justice Department letter, the TSP conducts surveillance of persons "linked to al Qaeda or an affiliated terrorist organization." How do you suppose it is determined whether a person fits that description? What legal standard would govern such a decision? In written answers to questions raised by Senators at a July 26, 2006, Senate Judiciary Committee hearing, NSA Director Keith B. Alexander stated that

> professional intelligence officers at [NSA], with the assistance of other elements of the Intelligence Community and subject to appropriate and vigorous oversight by the NSA Inspector General and General Counsel, among others, would rely on the best available intelligence information to determine whether there are reasonable grounds to believe that a party to an international communication is affiliated with al Qaeda. [Senator Edward M. Kennedy, *FISA for the 21st Century: Questions for Lt. General Keith B. Alexander,* July 26, 2006, *available at* http://www.fas.org/irp/congress/2006_hr/alexander-qfr.pdf.]

Do you see any legal shortcomings in this description of the decision process and legal standard for implementing TSP surveillance?
3. ***Applicability of FISA.*** Although FISA's scope is summarized in *Rosen* and the Notes and Questions following that case, in considering the applicability of FISA to this program you will want to look in particular at the language of

§1801(f), quoted *supra* p. 130. Consider also the complete text of 18 U.S.C. §2511(2)(e) and (f), governing ordinary criminal warrants:

(e) Notwithstanding any other provision of this title or section 705 or 706 of the Communications Act of 1934, it shall not be unlawful for an officer, employee, or agent of the United States in the normal course of his official duty to conduct electronic surveillance, as defined in section 101 of the Foreign Intelligence Surveillance Act of 1978, as authorized by that Act.

(f) Nothing contained in this chapter or chapter 121 or 206 of this title, or section 705 of the Communications Act of 1934, shall be deemed to affect the acquisition by the United States Government of foreign intelligence information from international or foreign communications, or foreign intelligence activities conducted in accordance with otherwise applicable Federal law involving a foreign electronic communications system, utilizing a means other than electronic surveillance as defined in section 101 [50 U.S.C. §1801] of the Foreign Intelligence Surveillance Act of 1978, and procedures in this chapter or chapter 121 and the Foreign Intelligence Surveillance Act of 1978 shall be the exclusive means by which electronic surveillance, as defined in §101 of such Act, and the interception of domestic wire, oral, and electronic communications may be conducted.

Finally, consider §1809(a)(1) of FISA (making unauthorized electronic surveillance a criminal offense):

A person is guilty of an offense if he intentionally —
(1) engages in electronic surveillance under color of law except as authorized by statute; or
(2) discloses or uses information obtained under color of law by electronic surveillance, knowing or having reason to know that the information was obtained through electronic surveillance not authorized by statute. [50 U.S.C. §1809(a)(1).]

Are you persuaded by the DOJ analysis that FISA is inapplicable to the TSP? Did Judge Taylor adequately answer the DOJ position?

4. *Why Not FISA?* The government has an enviable track record in the Foreign Intelligence Surveillance Court. See *supra* p. 156. Why did it not seek a FISA order(s) for the TSP? In a January 2006 address, Attorney General Alberto R. Gonzales defended the decision not to rely on FISA:

We have to remember that we're talking about a wartime foreign intelligence program. It is an "early warning system" with only one purpose: To detect and prevent the next attack on the United States from foreign agents hiding in our midst. It is imperative for national security that we can detect RELIABLY, IMMEDIATELY, and WITHOUT DELAY whenever communications associated with al Qaeda enter or leave the United States. That may be the only way to alert us to the presence of an al Qaeda agent in our country and to the existence of an unfolding plot.

Consistent with the wartime intelligence nature of this program, the optimal way to achieve the necessary speed and agility is to leave the decisions about particular intercepts to the judgment of professional intelligence officers, based on the best available intelligence information. They can make that call quickly. If, however, those same intelligence officers had to navigate through the FISA process for each of these intercepts, that would necessarily introduce a significant factor of DELAY, and there would be critical holes in our early warning system.

Some have pointed to the provision in FISA that allows for so-called "emergency authorizations" of surveillance for 72 hours without a court order. There's a serious misconception about these emergency authorizations. People should know that we do not approve emergency authorizations without knowing that we will receive court approval within 72 hours. FISA requires the Attorney General to determine IN ADVANCE that a FISA application for that particular intercept will be fully supported and will be approved by the court before an emergency authorization may be granted. That review process can take precious time. Thus, to initiate surveillance under a FISA emergency authorization, it is not enough to rely on the best judgment of our intelligence officers alone. Those intelligence officers would have to get the sign-off of lawyers at the NSA that all provisions of FISA have been satisfied, then lawyers in the Department of Justice would have to be similarly satisfied, and finally as Attorney General, I would have to be satisfied that the search meets the requirements of FISA. And we would have to be prepared to follow up with a full FISA application within the 72 hours. [*Prepared Remarks for Attorney General Alberto R. Gonzales,* Georgetown University Law Center, Jan. 24, 2006, *available at* http://www. usdoj.gov/ag/speeches/2006/ag_speech_0601241.html.]

In evaluating the Attorney General's statement, consider FISA's emergency surveillance provisions, quoted *supra* p. 138. Do you believe he was justified in bypassing the FISA procedures?

5. ***The AUMF and the Clear Statement Requirement.*** The September 18, 2001, Authorization for the Use of Military Force is set forth *supra* p. 59. Did it authorize the TSP? (The Supreme Court's construction of the AUMF appears in the *Hamdi* case, *infra* p. 359.) Is it relevant to your answer that in the USA Patriot Act, enacted in October 2001, Congress amended FISA by, *inter alia*, extending the period of emergency surveillance from 24 hours to 72 hours, or that it left in place the following FISA provision?

Notwithstanding any other law, the President, through the Attorney General, may authorize electronic surveillance without a court order under this subchapter to acquire foreign intelligence information for a period not to exceed fifteen calendar days following a declaration of war by the Congress. [50 U.S.C. §1811 (2000).]

In light of the comprehensive scheme detailed in FISA, should the more open-ended grant of authority in the AUMF be read to authorize the TSP? In *Greene v. McElroy*, 360 U.S. 474 (1959), the Supreme Court declined to find authority for security clearance procedures employed by the executive in the absence of explicit authorization for the clearance program from either the President or Congress. *See also* Kent v. Dulles, 357 U.S. 116 (1958) (declining to find statutory authority for the Secretary of State to restrict the right of travel absent explicit delegation from Congress). *But see* Haig v. Agee, 453 U.S. 280 (1981) (inferring authority to restrict the right of travel from congressional acquiescence in State Department policy). The *Greene* Court cited Ex parte Endo, 323 U.S. 283, 303 n.24 (1944), in which the Court said that to authorize or ratify executive action an appropriation must "plainly show a purpose to bestow the precise authority which is claimed." There the Court found no authorization for the continued detention of loyal Japanese-Americans during World War II "where a lump appropriation was made for the overall program of the [War Relocation] Authority and no sums were earmarked for the single phase of the total program [there] involved." *Id.*

Should the "clear statement" requirement apply to limit the value of the AUMF as authority for the TSP?

6. ***Inherent Constitutional Authority?*** In light of all the foregoing, does President Bush have inherent constitutional authority to order the TSP? Consider the President's exchange with a reporter at a December 19, 2005, press conference:

> *Q* . . . [W]hy did you skip the basic safeguards of asking courts for permission for the intercepts?
>
> *THE PRESIDENT:* First of all, I — right after September the 11th, I knew we were fighting a different kind of war. And so I asked people in my administration to analyze how best for me and our government to do the job people expect us to do, which is to detect and prevent a possible attack. That's what the American people want. We looked at the possible scenarios. And the people responsible for helping us protect and defend came forth with the current program, because it enables us to move faster and quicker. And that's important. We've got to be fast on our feet, quick to detect and prevent.
>
> We use FISA still — you're referring to the FISA court in your question — of course, we use FISAs. But FISA is for long-term monitoring. What is needed in order to protect the American people is the ability to move quickly to detect.
>
> Now, having suggested this idea, I then, obviously, went to the question, is it legal to do so? I am — I swore to uphold the laws. Do I have the legal authority to do this? And the answer is, absolutely. As I mentioned in my remarks, the legal authority is derived from the Constitution, as well as the authorization of force by the United States Congress.

Are you persuaded by the President's statement? Consider the arguments made in the Justice Department letter and the opinion of Judge Taylor. If you think there is a clash between the President's claim of authority and the statutes—placing the program in Justice Jackson's third category—how should we resolve it?

7. *The Fourth Amendment.* If the President has inherent constitutional authority for the TSP, notwithstanding any statute, does he also escape the strictures of the Fourth Amendment? If not, is the program constitutional?

8. *The End of TSP?* On January 17, 2007, Attorney General Gonzales wrote to Senators Leahy and Specter of the Senate Judiciary Committee and advised them that on January 10 a FISC judge "issued orders authorizing the Government to target for collection international communications into or out of the United States where there is probable cause to believe that one of the communicants is a member or agent of al Qaeda or an associated terrorist organization." Letter from the Attorney General, Alberto R. Gonzales, *available at* http://www.fas.org/irp/congress/2007_cr/fisa011707.html. According to the Attorney General, these orders "will allow the necessary speed and agility" and, accordingly, all surveillance previously occurring under the TSP will now be conducted with the approval of the FISC. Gonzales concluded by stating that the President would not reauthorize the TSP when its current authorization expires. *Id*. At this writing, the FISC orders have not been publicly released.

Why would the President have chosen to discontinue the TSP? Did he decide to end the program because he came to realize that he lacked the necessary legal authority? Did he end the TSP because he was able to obtain the functional equivalent of the TSP through orders from the FISC? Review §§1804 and 1805 of FISA, described in *Rosen* and in the Notes and Questions that follow it. Can you imagine what the FISC orders say? Whatever their content, do these orders end the controversy over the TSP?

On October 4, 2006, a three-judge panel of the Sixth Circuit stayed Judge Taylor's ruling pending consideration of the government's appeal. On January 24, 2007, the government moved to dismiss the case as moot. *Government's Supplemental Submission Discussing the Implications of the Intervening FISA Court Orders of January 10, 2007* at 8-15, American Civil Liberties Union v. National Security Agency (No. 06-CV-10204). What arguments can you think of on both sides of the mootness claim? If this lawsuit is moot, does that mean that all suits against the TSP are moot? See below.

9. *Amending FISA.* Before the January 2007 FISC orders and the end of the TSP were announced, some argued that FISA should be amended "to provide for programmatic approvals of cutting-edge technologies—including automated monitoring of suspected terrorist communications." K.A. Taipale & James Jay Carafano, *Fixing Surveillance*, Wash. Times, Jan. 25, 2006, at A15. Taipale went further and asserted that FISA *must* be amended to permit orders for "electronic surveillance" to capture the data and voice communications inside modern networks:

> Thirty years ago . . . it made sense to speak exclusively about the interception of targeted communication—one in which there were usually two known ends and a dedicated ("circuit-based")

communication channel that could be "tapped." In modern networks, however, data and increasingly voice communications are
broken into discrete packets that travel along independent routes
between point of origin and destination where these fragments are
then reassembled into the original whole message. Not only is
there no longer a dedicated circuit, but individual packets from
the same communication may take completely different paths to
their destination. To intercept these kinds of communications, fil-
ters ("packet-sniffers") and search strategies are deployed at various
communication nodes to scan and filter all passing traffic with the
hope of finding and extracting those packets of interest and reassem-
bling them into a coherent message. . . . Were FISA to be applied
strictly according to its terms prior to any "electronic surveillance"
of foreign communication flows passing through the US or where
there is a substantial likelihood of intercepting US persons, then no
automated monitoring of any kind could occur. [K.A. Taipale, *Whispering Wires and Warrantless Wiretaps: Data Mining and Foreign
Intelligence Surveillance*, 8 N.Y.U. Rev. L. & Security 3 (2006).]

How would you respond to this claim? Are the FISA definitions of "electronic
surveillance," limitations regarding "U.S. persons," and inapplicability to
international communications relics that simply fail to reflect changing technologies and realities? Taipale also maintains that the retroactive warrant
procedures in FISA could not provide a remedy for these problems because
the communications intercepted would not meet the probable cause predicate in FISA. *Id.* How do you suppose the recommended pre-approved monitoring programs would operate? What legal issues would remain unresolved
and what new legal issues would arise if such a change were enacted?

   Taipale also argues that the automated monitoring conducted in TSP for
the purpose of identifying potential threats should be authorized by Congress to permit

some limited follow-up . . . to determine if the initial indicia of
suspicion are justified. If so, then existing FISA procedures can be
followed to "target" that U.S. person or source. What is needed, then,
is the electronic surveillance equivalent of a *Terry* stop — in this case
an authorized period for follow up monitoring or investigation of
initial suspicion derived from automated monitoring. [*Id.* at 5-6.]

The initial automated monitoring presumably consists of collecting
telephone numbers and analyzing patterns of their use. Neither it nor the
follow-up investigation would, according to Taipale's proposal, be subject to
FISA procedures or would collect "content" for Fourth Amendment purposes.
Terry v. Ohio, 392 U.S. 1 (1968), held that police may detain a suspect for a
brief period based on reasonable suspicion that a crime has been committed.
Do you think the *Terry* case is analogous? Can you see the value of granting
officials the discretion to make the follow-up monitoring Taipale advocates?
What downside risks could you imagine in giving legal sanction to this form
of *Terry* stop? Are you persuaded that Congress should enact these reforms?

# CHAPTER 6

# THIRD-PARTY RECORDS
# AND DATA MINING

The conventional wisdom after 9/11 was that U.S. national security agencies failed to "connect the dots" before the attacks. But some experts have noted that while there "certainly was a lack of dot-connecting before September 11," the more critical failure was that "[t]here were too few useful dots." Robert Bryant et al., *America Needs More Spies*, The Economist, July 12, 2003, at 30. In this chapter, we explore both parts of this insight.

We first consider how so-called "national security letters" and FISA "Section 215 orders" are used to collect dots in quantity — transactional data — from third-party record holders like banks, telephone companies, Internet service providers, and travel agencies. Later in the chapter we look at how dots are connected by computer "data mining" to perform link analysis or pattern recognition.

## A.  FINDING THE DOTS — THIRD-PARTY RECORDS

### 1.  EXPECTATIONS OF PRIVACY REGARDING TRANSACTIONAL DATA

As we saw in the last chapter, in Smith v. Maryland, 442 U.S. 735 (1979), *supra* p. 112, the Supreme Court reasoned that people have no "legitimate expectation of privacy" in telephone numbers they dial — merely "numerical information" they "voluntarily convey[] . . . to the phone company in the normal course of business." *Id*. at 735, 744. It therefore rejected a Fourth Amendment challenge to evidence obtained by police use of a pen register on Smith's phone (recording the numbers of outgoing calls) and laid the legal foundation for both pen registers and trap and trace devices as police investigatory tools.

But *Smith* laid the foundation for more than just pen registers. If people have no legitimate expectation of privacy in information they voluntarily convey to the phone company in the normal course of business, then they also arguably have no such expectation in the transactional information they convey to hundreds of other third parties in the ordinary course of business. Congress therefore authorized the Foreign Intelligence Surveillance Court (FISC) to issue so-called

"§215 Orders" for transactional records pursuant to the Foreign Intelligence Surveillance Act (FISA), and it enacted several statutes authorizing the FBI to obtain transactional data by issuing national security letters (NSLs) to third-party record holders without prior court order. The government initially reported that in calendar year 2005 it obtained 155 §215 orders and issued 9,254 NSLs related to U.S. persons (excluding NSLs for subscriber information). Letter from William E. Moschella (Asst. Attorney General, Dept. of Justice) to J. Dennis Hastert (Speaker, House of Representatives), April 28, 2006. The media then claimed that the FBI issues more than 30,000 NSLs a year. Barton Gellman, *The FBI's Secret Scrutiny*, Wash. Post, Nov. 6, 2005, at A1. Subsequently, the Justice Department's Inspector General reported that the FBI issued 19,000 NSLs in 2005. The IG found "that the FBI used NSLs in violation of applicable NSL statutes, Attorney General Guidelines, and internal FBI policies" and that "in a few . . . instances, the FBI sought or obtained telephone toll billing records in the absence of a national security investigation." U.S. Department of Justice, Office of the Inspector General, *A Review of the Federal Bureau of Investigation's Use of National Security Letters* 120, 124 (March 2007), *available at* http://www.usdoj.gov/oig/special/s0703b/final.pdf.

We begin here by exploring further the scope and implications of *Smith*. Then, after reviewing a redacted NSL, we consider one of two 2004 court decisions declaring parts of the NSL statutes unconstitutional. In response to these decisions, Congress amended the NSL statutes when it passed the USA Patriot Improvement and Reauthorization Act of 2005, Pub. L. No. 109-177, 120 Stat. 192 (2006) (hereinafter "Patriot Improvement Act"), *see generally* Brian T. Yeh, *USA Patriot Improvement and Reauthorization Act of 2005: A Legal Analysis* (Cong. Res. Serv. RL33332), Dec. 15, 2006, relevant parts of which are described in the Notes and Questions at the end of the chapter.

## SMITH V. MARYLAND

United States Supreme Court, 1979
442 U.S. 735

[The opinion is set forth *supra* p. 112.]

## NOTES AND QUESTIONS

1. *Some of the Dots: Transactional Data.* "Transactional information broadly describes information that documents financial or communications transactions without necessarily revealing the substance of those transactions." Michael J. Woods, *Counterintelligence and Access to Transactional Records: A Practical History of USA Patriot Act Section 215*, 1 J. Natl. Security L. & Poly. 37, 41 (2005). Such information includes telephone billing records that list numbers dialed, an Internet service provider's records

showing a customer's Internet use, records of banking transactions and money transfers, credit card records, and travel records. It has proven invaluable in counterterrorist investigations. Terrorists can try to encrypt or otherwise disguise the substance of their communications, but "[i]t is far more difficult for them to cover their transactional footsteps." *Id.* at 41-42. Counterterrorist analysts can use transactional information to perform "link analysis" to tie suspects together and thus help identify terror cells. *See* McCormick Tribune Foundation, *Counterterrorism Technology and Privacy* (Cantigny Conf. Rpt.) 53 (Patrick J. McMahon rep., 2005). An example is the retrospective link analysis of the 9/11 hijackers. Woods, *supra*, at 42. It can also be used for pattern recognition and data matching to identify suspects. See *infra* pp. 201-202.

2. *The Expectation of Privacy in Transactional Records.* In United States v. Miller, 425 U.S. 435 (1976), the Court held that police seizure of bank records under a defective subpoena duces tecum was lawful because the depositor had no protected Fourth Amendment privacy interest in checks, deposit slips, and other financial information that she voluntarily conveyed to banks. "The depositor takes the risk, in revealing his affairs to another, that the information will be conveyed by that person to the Government." *Id.* at 443. The Court used the same logic three years later in Smith v. Maryland, 442 U.S. 735 (1979).

Is this logic sound? Do you, subjectively, have any expectation of privacy when you convey data to a bank or commercial vendor, dial a telephone number, or transmit an e-mail message? Of course, you do not expect to keep the information private from the bank, vendor, phone company, or Internet service provider. The entities with which you deal directly need the data to complete the transaction that you initiate. But do you also expect those entities to share the information with others? In fact, don't some vendors promise you just the opposite, sometimes even providing a box to check or button to indicate whether you want such data to be shared?

Under Katz v. United States, 389 U.S. 347 (1967), a subjective expectation of privacy for Fourth Amendment purposes is legitimate — protectible — only if it is also "one that society is prepared to recognize as 'reasonable.'" *Id.* at 361. If your expectation is that transactional information will be disclosed by the bank, vendor, or phone company only as needed to complete a transaction, would society recognize it as reasonable? In the late 1970s, the Court thought not. Have the dramatic changes in patterns of commercial activity and communications in the decades since then also made such an expectation reasonable? *See* Christopher Slobogin & Joseph E. Schumacher, *Reasonable Expectations of Privacy and Autonomy in Fourth Amendment Cases: An Empirical Look at "Understandings Recognized and Permitted by Society,"* 42 Duke L.J. 727 (1993) (reporting a survey suggesting that the public finds government perusal of bank records highly invasive). Was the reasonableness of such an expectation altered by the events of September 11, 2001?

## 2. TECHNIQUES AND AUTHORITIES FOR COLLECTION OF TRANSACTIONAL DATA

Building on the privacy theory of *Smith*, Congress enacted several statutes that authorized the FBI to use NSLs—issued without any prior judicial order—to obtain transactional records from third-party record holders. Here is a redacted example of such a letter, followed by a judicial decision in a case testing its legitimacy.

SECRET

 ALL INFORMATION CONTAINED
HEREIN IS UNCLASSIFIED EXCEPT
WHERE SHOWN OTHERWISE

U.S. Department of Justice

Federal Bureau of Investigation

In Reply, Please Refer to
File No

[Drafting] Field Division
[Street Address]
[City, State, Zip]

[Month Date, Year]

[Mr /Mrs.] [COMPANY POINT OF CONTACT]
[TITLE]
[COMPANY]
[STREET ADDRESS]
[CITY, STATE No Zip Code]

Dear [Mr /Mrs ] [LAST NAME]:

Under the authority of Executive Order 12333, dated
December 4, 1981, and pursuant to Title 18, United States Code
(U S.C ), Section 2709 (as amended, October 26, 2001), you are
hereby directed to provide the Federal Bureau of Investigation

b2-2
b7E-1

In accordance with Title 18, U.S.C., Section 2709(b), I
certify that the information sought is relevant to an authorized
investigation to protect against international terrorism or
clandestine intelligence activities, and that such an
investigation of a United States person is not conducted solely
on the basis of activities protected by the first amendment of
the Constitution of the United States

You are further advised that Title 18, U.S C , Section
2709(c), prohibits any officer, employee or agent of yours from
disclosing to any person that the FBI has sought or obtained
access to information or records under these provisions.

b2-2
b7E-1

CLASSIFIED DECISIONS FINALIZED BY
DEPARTMENT REVIEW COMMITTEE (DRC)
DATE: 07-01-2004
CA# 03-2522

CLASSIFIED BY 65179 dmk/bce/amw    6/5/2004
REASON: 1.4 (c)
DECLASSIFY ON: X 6/5/2029

Patriot Act II-828

SECRET

DECLASSIFIED BY 65179 dmk/bce/amw
ON 8/3/2004

SECRET

---

[Mr /Mrs ] [COMPANY POINT OF CONTACT]

Your cooperation in this matter is greatly appreciated

Sincerely,

[ADIC/SAC Name]
Assistant Director/Special

Agent in Charge

CLASSIFIED DECISIONS FINALIZED BY
DEPARTMENT REVIEW COMMITTEE (DRC)
DATE: 5T-01-2004

CA# 03-2522

ALL INFORMATION CONTAINED
HEREIN IS UNCLASSIFIED EXCEPT
WHERE SHOWN OTHERWISE

CLASSIFIED BY 65/79 dnh/bc4/smw  6/30/2004
REASON: 1.4 (c)
DECLASSIFY ON: 6/30/2029

2

Patriot Act II-829

SECRET

DECLASSIFIED BY 65/29 dmh/bc4/smw

ON 8/3/2004

# DOE v. ASHCROFT (*DOE I*)

United States District Court, Southern District of New York, 2004
334 F. Supp. 2d 471, *vacated and remanded sub nom.* Doe v. Gonzales,
449 F.3d 415 (2d Cir. 2006)

MARRERO, J. . . .

## I. Introduction

Plaintiffs in this case challenge the constitutionality of 18 U.S.C. §2709 ("§2709").[1] That statute authorizes the Federal Bureau of Investigation ("FBI") to compel communications firms, such as internet service providers ("ISPs") or telephone companies, to produce certain customer records whenever the FBI certifies that those records are "relevant to an authorized investigation to protect against international terrorism or clandestine intelligence activities." [*Id.*] The FBI's demands under §2709 are issued in the form of national security letters ("NSLs"), which constitute a unique form of administrative subpoena cloaked in secrecy and pertaining to national security issues. The statute bars all NSL recipients from ever disclosing that the FBI has issued an NSL.

The lead plaintiff, called "John Doe" ("Doe") for purposes of this litigation, is described in the complaint as an internet access firm that received an NSL. . . .

## II. Background . . .

### A. Doe's Receipt of an NSL

After receiving a call from an FBI agent informing him that he would be served with an NSL, Doe received a document, printed on FBI letterhead, which stated that, "pursuant to Title 18, United States Code (U.S.C.), Section 2709" Doe was "directed" to provide certain information to the Government. As required by the terms of §2709, in the NSL the FBI "certif[ied] that the information sought [was] relevant to an authorized investigation to protect against international terrorism or clandestine intelligence activities." Doe was "further advised" that §2709(c) prohibited him, or his officers, agents, or employees, "from disclosing to *any person* that the FBI has sought or obtained access to information or records under these provisions." Doe was "requested to provide records responsive to [the] request *personally*" to a designated individual, and to not transmit the records by mail or even mention the NSL in *any* telephone conversation. . . .

. . . Doe has not complied with the NSL request, and has instead engaged counsel to bring the present lawsuit.

### B. §2709 in General

As stated above, §2709 authorizes the FBI to issue NSLs to compel communications firms to produce certain customer records whenever the FBI certifies that those records are relevant to an authorized international terrorism

---

[1. This section was amended by the Patriot Improvement Act in 2006, *supra* p. 176, as explained in the following Notes and Questions.]

or counterintelligence investigation, and the statute also categorically bars NSL recipients from disclosing the inquiry. In relevant part, it states:

>  (a) Duty to provide. — A wire or electronic communication service provider shall comply with a request for subscriber information and toll billing records information, or electronic communication transactional records in its custody or possession made by the Director of the Federal Bureau of Investigation under subsection (b) of this section.
>  (b) Required certification. — The Director of the Federal Bureau of Investigation, or his designee in a position not lower than Deputy Assistant Director at Bureau headquarters or a Special Agent in Charge in a Bureau field office designated by the Director, may —
>    (1) request the name, address, length of service, and local and long distance toll billing records of a person or entity if the Director (or his designee) certifies in writing to the wire or electronic communication service provider to which the request is made that the name, address, length of service, and toll billing records sought are relevant to an authorized investigation to protect against international terrorism or clandestine intelligence activities, provided that such an investigation of a United States person is not conducted solely on the basis of activities protected by the first amendment to the Constitution of the United States. . . .
>  (c) Prohibition of certain disclosure. — No wire or electronic communication service provider, or officer, employee, or agent thereof, shall disclose to any person that the Federal Bureau of Investigation has sought or obtained access to information or records under this section. . . .

Section 2709 is one of only a handful of statutes authorizing the Government to issue NSLs. The other NSL statutes authorize the Government to compel disclosure of certain financial and credit records which it certifies are relevant to international terrorism or counter-intelligence investigations, and to compel disclosure of certain records of current or former government employees who have (or have had) access to classified information.[17]

## C. Legislative History

Section 2709 was enacted as part of Title II of the Electronic Communications Privacy Act of 1986 ("ECPA"),[19] which sought to "protect privacy interests" in "stored wire and electronic communications" while also "protecting the Government's legitimate law enforcement needs."[20] . . .

. . . As first enacted, §2709 required electronic communication service providers to produce subscriber information," "toll billing records information," or

---

17. See 12 U.S.C. §3414 (financial records); 15 U.S.C. §§1681u, 1681v (credit records); 50 U.S.C. §436 (government employee records).

19. Pub. L. No. 99-508, §201, 100 Stat. 1848, 1867 (1986).

20. S. Rep. No. 99-541, at 3 (1986), *reprinted* in 1986 U.S.C.C.A.N. 3555, 3557.

"electronic communication transactional records," upon the FBI's internal certification that (1) the information was "relevant to an authorized foreign counterintelligence investigation" and that (2) there were "specific and articulable facts giving reason to believe that the person or entity to whom the information sought pertains [was] a foreign power or an agent of a foreign power." . . .

The . . . most recent major revision to §2709 occurred in October 2001,[2] as part of the USA Patriot Act of 2001 ("Patriot Act").[39] In short, the Patriot Act removed the previous requirement that §2709 inquiries have a nexus to a foreign power, replacing that prerequisite with a broad standard of relevance to investigations of terrorism or clandestine intelligence activities. In hearings before the House Judiciary Committee on September 24, 2001, the Administration submitted the following explanation for the proposed change:

> NSL authority requires both a showing of relevance and a showing of links to an "agent of a foreign power." In this respect, [it is] substantially more demanding than the analogous criminal authorities, which require only a certification of relevance. Because the NSLs require documentation of the facts supporting the "agent of a foreign power" predicate and because they require the signature of a high-ranking official at FBI headquarters, they often take months to be issued. This is in stark contrast to criminal subpoenas, which can be used to obtain the same information, and are issued rapidly at the local level. In many cases, counter-intelligence and counterterrorism investigations suffer substantial delays while waiting for NSLs to be prepared, returned from headquarters, and served. The section would streamline the process of obtaining NSL authority. . . .

The House Judiciary Committee agreed that "[s]uch delays are unacceptable" and stated in its October 11, 2001, report that the Patriot Act would "harmonize[ ]" §2709 "with existing criminal law where an Assistant United States Attorney may issue a grand jury subpoena for all such records in a criminal case."

### D.  NSLs and Other Information-Gathering Authority

It is instructive to place the Government's NSL authority in the context of other means by which the Government gathers information of the type covered by §2709 because Congress (in passing and amending the NSL statutes) and the parties here (in contesting §2709's constitutionality) have drawn analogies to those other authorities as grounds for or against its validity. The relationship of §2709 to other related statutes supplies a backdrop for assessing congressional intent and judging the validity of the law on its face and as applied. In addition, an analysis of these analogous information-gathering methods indicates that NSLs such as the ones authorized by §2709 provide fewer procedural protections to the recipient than any other information-gathering technique the Government employs to procure information similar to that which it obtains pursuant to §2709.

---

[2. The statute was amended again in 2006 by the Patriot Improvement Act, *supra* p. 176, as explained in the following Notes and Questions.]

39. See Pub. L. No. 107-56, §505, 115 Stat. 272, 365 (2001). . . .

### 1. Administrative subpoenas

The most important set of statutes relevant to this case are those authorizing federal agencies to issue administrative subpoenas for the purpose of executing the particular agency's function. Ordinary administrative subpoenas, which are far more common than NSLs, may be issued by most federal agencies, as authorized by the hundreds of applicable statutes in federal law. For example, the Internal Revenue Service (IRS) may issue subpoenas to investigate possible violations of the tax code, and the Securities Exchange Commission (SEC) may issue subpoenas to investigate possible violations of the securities laws. . . .

There is a wide body of law which pertains to administrative subpoenas generally. According to the Government's central theory in this case, those standing rules would presumably also apply to NSLs, even if not so explicitly stated in the text of the statute. Where an agency seeks a court order to enforce a subpoena against a resisting subpoena recipient, courts will enforce the subpoena as long as: (1) the agency's investigation is being conducted pursuant to a legitimate purpose, (2) the inquiry is relevant to that purpose, (3) the information is not already within the agency's possession, and (4) the proper procedures have been followed. The Second Circuit has described these standards as "minimal." Even if an administrative subpoena meets these initial criteria to be enforceable, its recipient may nevertheless affirmatively challenge the subpoena on other grounds, such as an allegation that it was issued with an improper purpose or that the information sought is privileged.

Unlike the NSL statutes, most administrative subpoena laws either contain no provision requiring secrecy, or allow for only limited secrecy in special cases. For example, some administrative subpoena statutes permit the investigating agency to apply for a court order to temporarily bar disclosure of the inquiry, generally during specific renewable increments or for an appropriate period of time fixed by the court, where such disclosure could jeopardize the investigation. . . .

### 2. Subpoena authority in the criminal context

In its role as a party to a federal criminal proceeding (including a grand jury proceeding), the Government has broad authority to issue a subpoena to obtain witness testimony or "*any* books, papers, documents, data, or other objects the subpoena designates."[52] Although such subpoenas "are issued in the name of the district court over the signature of the clerk, they are issued pro forma and in blank to anyone requesting them," and the "court exercises no prior control whatsoever upon their use."[53]

The court becomes involved in the subpoena process only if the subpoenaed party moves to quash the request as "unreasonable or oppressive,"[54] or if the Government seeks to compel compliance with the subpoena. The reasonableness of a subpoena depends on the context. For example, to survive a motion to quash, a subpoena issued in connection with a criminal

---

52. Fed. R. Crim. P. 17(a), (c)(1) (emphasis added).
53. In re Grand Jury Proceedings, 486 F.2d 85, 90 (3d Cir. 1973).
54. Fed. R. Crim. P. 17(c)(2).

trial "must make a reasonably specific request for information that would be both relevant and admissible at trial."[55] By contrast, a grand jury subpoena is generally enforced as long as there is a "reasonable possibility that the category of materials the Government seeks will produce information relevant to the general subject of the grand jury's investigation."[56] Considering the grand jury's broad investigatory power and minimal court supervision, it is accurate to observe, as the Second Circuit did long ago, that "[b]asically the grand jury is a law enforcement agency."[57]

While materials presented in a criminal trial setting are generally public, the federal rules impose stringent secrecy requirements on certain grand jury participants, including the attorneys, court reporters, and grand jurors.[59] ...

In certain contexts, the Government may issue subpoenas related to criminal investigations even without initiating a formal criminal proceeding. For example, the United States Attorney General is authorized to issue administrative subpoenas, without convening a grand jury, to investigate federal narcotics crimes, racketeering crimes, health care related crimes, and crimes involving the exploitation of children. In each of these instances, the administrative process is governed by the general rules described above, providing safeguards of judicial review.

### 3. Background rules governing disclosure of stored electronic communications

Title II of the ECPA [also called the Stored Communications Act], in which §2709 was enacted, sets forth an intricate framework by which electronic communications providers, such as ISPs and phone companies, may be compelled to disclose stored electronic information to the Government. The framework described below operates independently of the rules governing NSLs issued pursuant to §2709, but may aid with interpretation of §2709.

The Government may obtain basic subscriber information[69] merely by issuing an authorized administrative subpoena, trial subpoena, or grand jury subpoena, and the Government need not notify the subscriber of the request.

If the Government gives prior notice to the subscriber, or otherwise complies with certain delayed notice procedures, the Government may also subpoena the *contents* of electronic communications which are either (1) retained on a system for storage purposes (*e.g.*, opened email which remains on an ISP's server), or (2) retained, for more than 180 days, in intermediate or temporary storage (*e.g.*, unopened email on an ISP's server). For the Government to obtain the contents of electronic communications kept for 180 days

---

55. United States v. R. Enters., Inc., 498 U.S. 292, 299 (1991) (*citing* United States v. Nixon, 418 U.S. 683, 700 (1974)).

56. *Id.* at 301.

57. United States v. Cleary, 265 F.2d 459, 461 (2d Cir. 1959).

59. See Fed. R. Crim. P. 6(e).

69. Basic subscriber information includes: (1) a subscriber's name and (2) address; (3) the subscriber's local and long distance telephone connection records, or records of session times and durations; (4) the subscriber's length of service and types of service he has utilized; (5) any telephone or instrument number or other subscriber number or identity, including any temporarily assigned network address; and (6) the subscriber's means and source of payment for the service. See 18 U.S.C. §2703(c)(2).

or less in intermediate or temporary storage (*e.g.,* unopened email on an ISP's server), it must obtain a search warrant under Federal Rule of Criminal Procedure 41, or the state equivalent. In other words, the Government would have to appear before a neutral magistrate and make a showing of probable cause. The Government may also obtain a court order requiring an electronic communications service provider to turn over transactional and content information by setting forth "specific and articulable facts showing that there are reasonable grounds to believe that" the information sought is "relevant and material to an ongoing criminal investigation."[75]

The ECPA permits the Government to seek a court order prohibiting the communications provider from revealing the Government's inquiry "for such period as the court deems appropriate" if the court determines that such disclosure, among other things, would result in "destruction of or tampering with evidence" or "seriously jeopardizing an investigation or unduly delaying a trial."[76]

### 4. Mail

Government law enforcement agencies are authorized to request the Postal Inspector to initiate a so-called "mail cover" to obtain any information appearing on the outside of a particular piece of mail.[77] Among other grounds, the law enforcement agency can obtain a mail cover by "specify[ing] the reasonable grounds to demonstrate the mail cover is necessary" to "[p]rotect the national security" or to "[o]btain information regarding the commission or attempted commission of a crime." There is no requirement that the mail sender or recipient be notified of the mail cover.

The Government must obtain a warrant based upon probable cause to open and inspect sealed mail because the contents of mail are protected by the Fourth Amendment. As the Supreme Court established long ago: "Whilst in the mail, [a person's papers] can only be opened and examined under like warrant, issued upon similar oath or affirmation, particularly describing the thing to be seized, as is required when papers are subjected to search in one's own household."[80]

### 5. Pen registers and trap and trace devices

Pen registers and trap and trace devices record certain electronic communications data indicating the origins and destinations of various "dialing, routing, addressing, or signaling information," *e.g.,* the phone numbers dialed to and from a telephone.[81] In criminal investigations, the Government must apply for a court order, renewable in 60-day increments, to install or collect data from such devices, though the standard for issuing such an order is relatively low. The Government need only show that "the information likely to be obtained by such installation and use is relevant to an ongoing criminal investigation."[83]

---

75. 18 U.S.C. §2703(d).
76. *Id.* §2705(b).
77. *See* 39 C.F.R. §233.3.
80. *See* Ex Parte Jackson, 96 U.S. 727, 733 (1877).
81. *See* 18 U.S.C. §3127(3)-(4).
83. *Id.* §3123(a).

The person owning the communications device is prohibited, unless otherwise directed by court order, from disclosing the fact that a pen register or trap and trace device is in effect.

### 6. Wiretaps and electronic eavesdropping

The Fourth Amendment protects against warrantless Government wiretapping. Federal legislation specifies the procedures by which law enforcement officials may obtain a court order to conduct wiretaps and other forms of electronic eavesdropping. The requirements are rigorous. Among other things, the Government must show that: (1) "there is probable cause for belief that an individual is committing, has committed, or is about to commit" one of a list of enumerated crimes; (2) "there is probable cause for belief that particular communications concerning that offense will be obtained through such interception"; and (3) "normal investigative procedures have been tried and have failed or reasonably appear to be unlikely to succeed if tried or to be too dangerous."[87] Such orders are not available "for any period longer than is necessary to achieve the objective of the authorization," subject to a renewable maximum of 30 days.[88] The communications provider is prohibited from disclosing that a wiretap or electronic surveillance is in place, "except as may otherwise be required by legal process and then only after prior notification" to the appropriate law enforcement authorities.[89]

### 7. Foreign Intelligence Surveillance Act . . .

[The court summarized the procedures for obtaining an order from the Foreign Intelligence Surveillance Court for electronic surveillance under FISA.]

The FISA also authorizes the Government to apply to the FISA court "for an order requiring the production of any tangible things (including books, records, papers, documents, and other items) for an investigation to obtain foreign intelligence information not concerning a United States person or to protect against international terrorism or clandestine intelligence activities. . . ."[99] Such an application need only specify that the inquiry is part of an authorized investigation and in accordance with the appropriate guidelines. Recipients of such an order are prohibited from disclosing to anyone (except those whose assistance is necessary to comply with the subpoena) that the inquiry was made.

Finally, FISA authorizes the Government to apply to the FISA court for a an order, renewable in 90-day increments, to install a pen register or trap and trace device as part of "any investigation to obtain foreign intelligence information not concerning a United States person or to protect against

---

87. *Id.* §2518(3).
88. *Id.* §2518(5).
89. *Id.* §2511(2)(a)(ii).
99. 50 U.S.C. §1861(a). [This authority was added by §215 of the USA Patriot Act, Pub. L. No. 107-108, §215, 115 Stat. 272, 287-288 (2001), and is therefore sometimes called a "Section 215 Order." This authority was amended by the Patriot Improvement Act, as explained in the Notes and Questions that follow this decision.]

international terrorism or clandestine intelligence activities." The Government need only certify to the court that it will likely obtain information relevant to a proper inquiry. Just as in the criminal context, the person owning the communications device is prohibited, unless otherwise directed by court order, from disclosing the fact that a pen register or trap and trace device is in effect. . . .

## IV.  Discussion . . .

## B.  As Applied Here, Section 2709 Lacks Procedural Protections Necessary to Vindicate Constitutional Rights

### 1. Section 2709 and the Fourth Amendment[118] . . .

. . . The Fourth Amendment's protection against unreasonable searches applies to administrative subpoenas, even though issuing a subpoena does not involve a literal physical intrusion or search. In so doing, the Supreme Court explained that the Fourth Amendment is not "confined literally to searches and seizures as such, but extends as well to the orderly taking under compulsion of process."[122]

However, because administrative subpoenas are "at best, constructive searches," there is no requirement that they be issued pursuant to a warrant or that they be supported by probable cause. Instead, an administrative subpoena needs only to be "reasonable," which the Supreme Court has interpreted to mean that (1) the administrative subpoena is "within the authority of the agency;" (2) that the demand is "not too indefinite;" and (3) that the information sought is "reasonably relevant" to a proper inquiry.[124]

While the Fourth Amendment reasonableness standard is permissive in the context of administrative subpoenas, the constitutionality of the administrative subpoena is predicated on the availability of a neutral tribunal to determine, after a subpoena is issued, whether the subpoena actually complies with the Fourth Amendment's demands. In contrast to an actual physical search, which must be justified by the warrant and probable cause requirements occurring *before* the search, an administrative subpoena "is regulated by, and its justification derives from, [judicial] process" available *after* the subpoena is issued.[125]

---

118. To be clear, the Fourth Amendment rights at issue here belong to the person or entity receiving the NSL, not to the person or entity to whom the subpoenaed records pertain. Individuals possess a limited Fourth Amendment interest in records which they voluntarily convey to a third party. *See* [Smith v. Maryland, 442 U.S. 735, 742-746 (1979), *supra* p. 112; United States v. Miller, 425 U.S. 435, 440-443 (1976)]. Nevertheless, as discussed below, many potential NSL recipients may have particular interests in resisting an NSL, *e.g.*, because they have contractually obligated themselves to protect the anonymity of their subscribers or because their own rights are uniquely implicated by what they regard as an intrusive and secretive NSL regime. For example, since the definition of "wire or electronic communication service provider," 18 U.S.C. §2709(a), is so vague, the statute could (and may currently) be used to seek subscriber lists or other information from an association that also provides electronic communication services (e.g., email addresses) to its members, or to seek records from libraries that many, including the amici appearing in this proceeding, fear will chill speech and use of these invaluable public institutions. . . .

122. [See United States v. Morton Salt Co., 338 U.S. 632, 651-652 (1950)].

124. *Id.* at 652.

125. United States v. Bailey (In re Subpoena Duces Tecum), 228 F.3d 341, 348 (4th Cir. 2000).

Accordingly, the Supreme Court has held that an administrative subpoena "may not be made and enforced" by the administrative agency; rather, the subpoenaed party must be able to "obtain judicial review of the reasonableness of the demand prior to suffering penalties for refusing to comply."[126] In sum, longstanding Supreme Court doctrine makes clear that an administrative subpoena statute is consistent with the Fourth Amendment when it is subject to "judicial supervision" and "surrounded by every safeguard of judicial restraint."[127]

Plaintiffs contend that §2709 violates this Fourth Amendment process-based guarantee because it gives the FBI alone the power to issue as well as enforce its own NSLs, instead of contemplating some form of judicial review. Although Plaintiffs appear to concede that the statute does not authorize the FBI to literally enforce the terms of an NSL by, for example, unilaterally seizing documents or imposing fines, Plaintiffs contend that §2709 has the *practical* effect of coercing compliance. . . .

The crux of the problem is that the form NSL, like the one issued in this case, which is preceded by a personal call from an FBI agent, is framed in imposing language on FBI letterhead and which, citing the authorizing statute, orders a combination of disclosure *in person* and in complete secrecy, essentially coerces the reasonable recipient into immediate compliance. Objectively viewed, it is improbable that an FBI summons invoking the authority of a certified "investigation to protect against international terrorism or clandestine intelligence activities," and phrased in tones sounding virtually as biblical commandment, would not be perceived with some apprehension by an ordinary person and therefore elicit passive obedience from a reasonable NSL recipient. The full weight of this ominous writ is especially felt when the NSL's plain language, in a measure that enhances its aura as an expression of public will, prohibits disclosing the issuance of the NSL to "any person." Reading such strictures, it is also highly unlikely that an NSL recipient reasonably would know that he may have a right to contest the NSL, and that a process to do so may exist through a judicial proceeding.

Because neither the statute, nor an NSL, nor the FBI agents dealing with the recipient say as much, all but the most mettlesome and undaunted NSL recipients would consider themselves effectively barred from consulting an attorney or anyone else who might advise them otherwise, as well as bound to absolute silence about the very existence of the NSL. . . .

The evidence in this case bears out the hypothesis that NSLs work coercively in this way. The ACLU obtained, via the Freedom of Information Act ("FOIA"), and presented to the Court in this proceeding, a document listing all the NSLs the Government issued from October 2001 through January 2003. Although the entire substance of the document is redacted, it is apparent that hundreds of NSL requests were made during that period. Because §2709 has been available to the FBI since 1986 (and its financial records counterpart in RFPA since 1978), the Court concludes that there must have been hundreds

---

126. See v. City of Seattle, 387 U.S. 541, 544-45 (1967); *see also* Oklahoma Press [Pub. Co. v. Walling, 327 U.S. 186, 217 (1946)].

127. *Oklahoma Press*, 327 U.S. at 217.

more NSLs issued in that long time span. The evidence suggests that, until now, none of those NSLs was ever challenged in any court. . . .

. . . The Court thus concludes that in practice NSLs are essentially unreviewable because, as explained, given the language and tone of the statute as carried into the NSL by the FBI, the recipient would consider himself, in virtually every case, obliged to comply, with no other option but to immediately obey and stay quiet. . . .

Accordingly, the Court concludes that §2709, as applied here, must be invalidated because in all but the exceptional case it has the effect of authorizing coercive searches effectively immune from any judicial process, in violation of the Fourth Amendment. . . .

### 2. NSLs may violate ISP subscribers' rights

Plaintiffs have focused on the possibility that §2709 could be used to infringe subscribers' First Amendment rights of anonymous speech and association. Though it is not necessary to precisely define the scope of ISP subscribers' First Amendment rights, the Court concludes that §2709 may, in a given case, violate a subscriber's First Amendment privacy rights, as well as other legal rights, if judicial review is not readily available to an ISP that receives an NSL. . . .

The Supreme Court has recognized the First Amendment right to anonymous speech at least since *Talley v. California*,[161] which invalidated a California law requiring that handbills distributed to the public contain certain identifying information about the source of the handbills. The Court stated that the "identification requirement would tend to restrict freedom to distribute information and thereby freedom of expression."[162] The Supreme Court has also invalidated identification requirements pertaining to persons distributing campaign literature, persons circulating petitions for state ballot initiatives, and persons engaging in door-to-door religious advocacy.

In a related doctrine, the Supreme Court has held that "compelled disclosure of affiliation with groups engaged in advocacy" amounts to a "restraint on freedom of association" where disclosure could expose the members to "public hostility."[166] Laws mandating such disclosures will be upheld only where the Government interest is compelling.

The Court concludes that such First Amendment rights may be infringed by application of §2709 in a given case. For example, the FBI theoretically could issue to a political campaign's computer systems operator a §2709 NSL compelling production of the names of all persons who have email addresses through the campaign's computer systems. The FBI theoretically could also issue an NSL under §2709 to discern the identity of someone whose anonymous online web log, or "blog," is critical of the Government. Such inquiries might be beyond the permissible scope of the FBI's power under §2709 because the targeted information might not be relevant to an authorized investigation to protect against international terrorism or clandestine intelligence activities, or because the inquiry might be conducted solely on the basis of activities

---

161. 362 U.S. 60 (1960).
162. *Id.* at 64.
166. NAACP v. State of Alabama ex rel. Patterson, 357 U.S. 449, 462 (1958).

protected by the First Amendment. These prospects only highlight the potential danger of the FBI's self-certification process and the absence of judicial oversight.

Other rights may also be violated by the disclosure contemplated by the statute; the statute's reference to "transactional records" creates ambiguity regarding the scope of the information required to be produced by the NSL recipient. If the recipient — who in the NSL is called upon to exercise judgment in determining the extent to which complying materials constitute transactional records rather than content — interprets the NSL broadly as requiring produc-tion of all e-mail header information, including subject lines, for example, some disclosures conceivably may reveal information protected by the subscriber's attorney-client privilege, *e.g.,* a communication with an attorney where the subject line conveys privileged or possibly incriminating information. Indeed, the practical absence of judicial review may lead ISPs to disclose information that is protected from disclosure by the NSL statute itself, such as in a case where the NSL was initiated solely in retaliation for the subscriber's exercise of his First Amendment rights, as prohibited by §2709(b)(1)-(2). Only a court would be able to definitively construe the statutory and First Amendment rights at issue in the "First Amendment retaliation" provision of the statute, and to strike a proper balance among those interests.

The Government asserts that disclosure of the information sought under §2709 could not violate a subscriber's rights (and thus demands no judicial process) because the information which a §2709 NSL seeks has been voluntar-ily conveyed to the ISP who receives the NSL. According to the Government, an internet speaker relinquishes any interest in any anonymity, and any pro-tected claim to that information, as soon as he releases his identity and other information to his ISP. In support of its position, the Government cites the Supreme Court's holding [in *Smith* and *Miller*] that, at least in the Fourth Amendment context involving the Government installing a pen register or obtaining bank records, when a person voluntarily conveys infor-mation to third parties, he assumes the risk that the information will be turned over to the Government. . . .

The evidence on the record now before this Court demonstrates that the information available through a §2709 NSL served upon an ISP could easily be used to disclose vast amounts of anonymous speech and associational activ-ity. For instance, §2709 imposes a duty to provide "electronic communication transactional records," a phrase which, though undefined in the statute, certainly encompasses a log of email addresses with whom a subscriber has corresponded and the web pages that a subscriber visits. Those transactional records can reveal, among other things, the anonymous message boards to which a person logs on or posts, the electronic newsletters to which he sub-scribes, and the advocacy websites he visits. Moreover, §2709 imposes a duty on ISPs to provide the names and addresses of subscribers, thus enabling the Government to specifically identify someone who has written anonymously on the internet.[175] As discussed above, given that an NSL recipient is directed by

---

175. NSLs can potentially reveal far more than constitutionally-protected associational activ-ity or anonymous speech. By revealing the websites one visits, the Government can learn, among

the FBI to turn over all information *"which you consider to be* an electronic communication transactional record," the §2709 NSL could also reasonably be interpreted by an ISP to require, at minimum, disclosure of all e-mail header information, including subject lines.

In stark contrast to this potential to compile elaborate dossiers on internet users, the information obtainable by a pen register is far more limited. As the Supreme Court in *Smith* was careful to note:

> [Pen registers] disclose only the telephone numbers that have been dialed — a means of establishing communication. Neither the purport of any communication between the caller and the recipient of the call, their identities, nor whether the call was even completed is disclosed by pen registers.[177]

The Court doubts that the result in *Smith* would have been the same if a pen register operated as a key to the most intimate details and passions of a person's private life.

The more apt Supreme Court case for evaluating the assumption of risk argument at issue here is *Katz v. United States*,[178] the seminal decision underlying both *Smith* and *Miller*. *Katz* held that the Fourth Amendment's privacy protections applied where the Government wiretapped a telephone call placed from a public phone booth. Especially noteworthy and pertinent to this case is the Supreme Court's remark that: "The Government's activities in electronically listening to and recording the petitioner's words violated the privacy upon which he justifiably relied while using the telephone booth and thus constituted a 'search and seizure' within the meaning of the Fourth Amendment."[180] The Supreme Court also stated that a person entering a phone booth who "shuts the door behind him" is "surely entitled to assume that the words he utters into the mouthpiece will not be broadcast to the world," and held that, "[t]o read the Constitution more narrowly is to ignore the vital role that the public telephone has come to play in private communication."[181]

Applying that reasoning to anonymous internet speech and associational activity is relatively straightforward. A person who signs onto an anonymous forum under a pseudonym, for example, is essentially "shut[ting] the door behind him," and is surely entitled to a reasonable expectation that his speech, whatever form the expression assumes, will not be accessible to the Government to be broadcast to the world absent appropriate legal process. To hold otherwise would ignore the role of the internet as a remarkably powerful forum for private communication and association. Even the Government concedes here that the internet is an "important vehicle for the free exchange of ideas and facilitates associations."

---

many other potential examples, what books the subscriber enjoys reading or where a subscriber shops. As one commentator has observed, the records compiled by ISPs can "enable the government to assemble a profile of an individual's finances, health, psychology, beliefs, politics, interests, and lifestyle." Daniel J. Solove, *Digital Dossiers and the Dissipation of Fourth Amendment Privacy*, 75 S. Cal. L. Rev. 1083, 1084 (2002).

177. *Smith*, 442 U.S. at 741 (citation omitted).
178. 389 U.S. 347 (1967).
180. *Id.* at 353.
181. *Id.* at 352.

To be sure, the Court is keenly mindful of the Government's reminder that the internet may also serve as a vehicle for crime. The Court equally recognizes that circumstances exist in which the First Amendment rights of association and anonymity must yield to a more compelling Government interest in obtaining records from internet firms. To this end, the Court re-emphasizes that it does not here purport to set forth the scope of these First Amendment rights in general, or define them in this or any other case. The Court holds only that such fundamental rights are certainly implicated in some cases in which the Government may employ §2709 broadly to gather information, thus requiring that the process incorporate the safeguards of some judicial review to ensure that if an infringement of those rights is asserted, they are adequately protected through fair process in an independent neutral tribunal. Because the necessary procedural protections are wholly absent here, the Court finds on this ground additional cause for invalidating §2709 as applied.

### C. Constitutionality of the Non-Disclosure Provision

Finally, the Court turns to the issue of whether the Government may properly enforce §2709(c), the non-disclosure provision, against Doe or any other person who has previously received an NSL. Section 2709(c) states: "No wire or electronic communication service provider, or officer, employee, or agent thereof, shall disclose to any person that the Federal Bureau of Investigation has sought or obtained access to information or records under this section."

A threshold question concerning this issue is whether, as Plaintiffs contend, §2709(c) is subject to strict scrutiny as either a prior restraint on speech or a content-based speech restriction, or whether, as the Government responds, §2709(c) is subject to the more relaxed judicial review of intermediate scrutiny. The difference is crucial. A speech restriction which is either content-based or which imposes a prior restraint on speech is presumed invalid and may be upheld only if it is "narrowly tailored to promote a compelling Government interest." If "less restrictive alternatives would be at least as effective in achieving the legitimate purpose that the statute was enacted to serve," then the speech restriction is not narrowly tailored and may be invalidated. Under intermediate scrutiny, a speech restriction may be upheld as long as "it advances important governmental interests unrelated to the suppression of free speech and does not burden substantially more speech than necessary to further those interests."

The Court agrees with Plaintiffs that §2709(c) works as both a prior restraint on speech and as a content-based restriction, and hence, is subject to strict scrutiny. First, axiomatically the categorical non-disclosure mandate embodied in §2709(c) functions as prior restraint because of the straightforward observation that it prohibits speech before the speech occurs. As the Supreme Court articulated the threshold inquiry: "The relevant question is whether the challenged regulation authorizes suppression of speech in advance of its expression. . . ."[189] . . .

---

189. Ward v. Rock Against Racism, 491 U.S. 781, 795 n.5 (1989) (emphasis omitted).

Second, the Court considers §2709(c) to be a content-based speech restriction. . . .

The Government . . . argues that §2709(c) is content-neutral because it prohibits certain disclosures irrespective of any particular speaker's views on NSLs, terrorism, or anything else. . . .

The Government's argument is unpersuasive. It fails to recognize that even a *viewpoint*-neutral restriction can be *content*-based, if the restriction pertains to an entire category of speech. . . .

The Government's claim to perpetual secrecy surrounding the FBI's issuance of NSLs, by its theory as advanced here an authority neither restrained by the FBI's own internal discretion nor reviewable by any form of judicial process, presupposes a category of information, and thus a class of speech, that, for reasons not satisfactorily explained, must forever be kept from public view, cloaked by an official seal that will always overshadow the public's right to know. In general, as our sunshine laws and judicial doctrine attest, democracy abhors undue secrecy, in recognition that public knowledge secures freedom. Hence, an unlimited government warrant to conceal, effectively a form of secrecy *per se*, has no place in our open society. Such a claim is especially inimical to democratic values for reasons borne out by painful experience. Under the mantle of secrecy, the self-preservation that ordinarily impels our government to censorship and secrecy may potentially be turned on ourselves as a weapon of self-destruction. When withholding information from disclosure is no longer justified, when it ceases to foster the proper aims that initially may have supported confidentiality, a categorical and uncritical extension of non-disclosure may become the cover for spurious ends that government may then deem too inconvenient, inexpedient, merely embarrassing, or even illicit to ever expose to the light of day. At that point, secrecy's protective shield may serve not as much to secure a safe country as simply to save face. . . .

. . . Section 2709(c) does not countenance the possibility that the FBI could permit modification of the NSL's no-disclosure order even in those or any other similar situations no longer implicating legitimate national security interests and presenting factual or legal issues that any court could reasonably adjudicate. Bluntly stated, the statute simply does not allow for that balancing of competing public interests to be made by an independent tribunal at any point. In this regard, it is conceivable that "less restrictive alternatives would be at least as effective in achieving the legitimate purpose that the statute was enacted to serve." For instance, Congress could require the FBI to make at least *some* determination concerning need before requiring secrecy, and ultimately it could provide a forum and define at least *some* circumstances in which an NSL recipient could ask the FBI or a court for a subsequent determination whether continuing secrecy was still warranted. . . .

In this Court's judgment, . . . authorities persuasively confirm that the Government should be accorded a due measure of deference when it asserts that secrecy is necessary for national security purposes in a *particular situation* involving *particular persons* at a *particular time*. Here, however, the Government cites no authority supporting the open-ended proposition that it may universally apply these general principles to impose perpetual secrecy upon an entire category of future cases whose details are unknown and whose particular twists and turns may not justify, for all time and all places, demanding unremitting concealment and imposing a disproportionate burden on free speech. . . .

## VI. Conclusion

To summarize, the Court concludes that the compulsory, secret, and unreviewable production of information required by the FBI's application of 18 U.S.C. §2709 violates the Fourth Amendment, and that the non-disclosure provision of 18 U.S.C. §2709(c) violates the First Amendment. The Government is therefore enjoined from issuing NSLs under §2709 or from enforcing the non-disclosure provision in this or any other case, but enforcement of the Court's judgment will be stayed pending appeal, or if no appeal is filed, for 90 days. . . .

---

A different district court also found that the nondisclosure provisions of the NSL legislation violated the First Amendment. Doe v. Gonzales, 386 F. Supp. 2d 66 (D. Conn. 2004) (*Doe II*).

## DOE v. GONZALES

United States Court of Appeals for the Second Circuit, 2006
449 F.3d 415

[While consolidated appeals from the two district court cases were pending in the Second Circuit, Congress passed the Patriot Improvement Act, *supra* p. 176, and the government inadvertently revealed the names of the plaintiffs in *Doe II*. The Court of Appeals, in a per curiam opinion, dismissed *Doe II* as moot and vacated *Doe I* in part as moot, and remanded the remainder for reconsideration in light of the Patriot Improvement Act. Judge Cardamone concurred in the following separate opinion.]

CARDAMONE, Circuit Judge, concurring: . . . A permanent ban on speech seems highly unlikely to survive the test of strict scrutiny, one where the government must show that the statute is narrowly tailored to meet a compelling government interest.

It seems to me that courts resolve the tension between the government's interest in maintaining the integrity of its investigative process and the First Amendment in favor of the government so long as the ban on disclosure is limited. The cases also hold that a ban on speech is not constitutionally permissible once the investigation ends. . . .

The government advanced the "mosaic theory" as one of the reasons to support a permanent ban on speech. That theory envisions thousands of bits and pieces of apparently innocuous information, which when properly assembled create a picture. At bottom the government's assertion is simply that antiterrorism investigations are different from other investigations in that they are derivative of prior or concurrent investigations. Thus, permanent non-disclosure is necessary because, implicitly in the government's view, all terrorism investigations are permanent and unending.

The government's urging that an endless investigation leads logically to an endless ban on speech flies in the face of human knowledge and common sense: witnesses disappear, plans change or are completed, cases are closed, investigations terminate. Further, a ban on speech and a shroud of secrecy in perpetuity are antithetical to democratic concepts and do not fit comfortably with the fundamental rights guaranteed American citizens. Unending secrecy of actions taken by government officials may also serve as a cover for possible official misconduct and/or incompetence.

Moreover, with regard to having something be secret forever, most Americans would agree with Benjamin Franklin's observation on our human inability to maintain secrecy for very long. He wrote "three may keep a secret, if two of them are dead." Benjamin Franklin, Poor *Richard's Almanack* 8 (Dean Walley ed., Hallmark 1967) (1732). In fact, what happened in the Connecticut case bears out Franklin's astute observation. While striving to keep the identities of the Connecticut plaintiffs secret, the government inadvertently revealed their identities through public court filings. This revelation was widely reported in the media. Thus, the case assumed the awkward posture where the identities of the Connecticut plaintiffs were published, yet the government continued to insist that the Connecticut plaintiffs may not identify themselves and that their identities must still be kept secret. This is like closing the barn door after the horse has already bolted.

Since the passage of the [Patriot Improvement Act, *supra* p. 176], the government asserts that we should vacate the District of Connecticut's preliminary injunction rather than leaving it unreviewed on appeal. To me, the government's request for vacatur in the Connecticut case is not surprising, but right in line with the pervasive climate of secrecy. It sought to prevent, through §2709(c), the Doe plaintiffs from ever revealing that they were subjects of an NSL, effectively keeping that fact secret forever. Then, by requesting vacatur of the decision below, the government attempts to purge from the public record the fact that it had tried and failed to silence the Connecticut plaintiffs.

While everyone recognizes national security concerns are implicated when the government investigates terrorism within our Nation's borders, such concerns should be leavened with common sense so as not *forever* to trump the rights of the citizenry under the Constitution. . . .

Although I concur in the *per curiam* that declines to resolve the novel First Amendment issue before us on this appeal, that does not mean I think that issue unworthy of comment. Hence, this concurrence.

## NOTES AND QUESTIONS

1. *Matching Legal Thresholds and Processes with Government Surveillance and Collection Techniques.* Professor Orin Kerr identifies the following legal thresholds (standards for obtaining the information) and attendant processes (administrative or judicial or both) for government surveillance, in ascending order of strictness:

a. No standard or legal process. The government just gets the information it seeks.

b. Internal administrative process. There is no bifurcation between the issuing and enforcing authority.

c. Grand jury or administrative subpoena. The issuing and enforcing authority are bifurcated.

d. Certification court order. The government needs a court order, but gets it simply by certifying relevancy. The court does not decide whether the certification is justified.

e. Articulable facts court order. The government needs a court order and must offer specific and articulable facts to establish relevancy.

f. Probable cause search warrant. The traditional criminal law standard and the predicate preferred by the Fourth Amendment.

g. "Super" search warrant. Same, but government must first exhaust all other investigatory techniques or meet some other "plus" requirement beyond showing probable cause.

h. Prohibition. The government is forbidden from getting the information.

*Adapted from* Orin S. Kerr, *Internet Surveillance Law After the USA Patriot Act: The Big Brother That Isn't,* 97 Nw. U. L. Rev. 607, 620-621 (2003). Match one of these thresholds to each of the surveillance and collection techniques catalogued in Doe v. Ashcroft.

Recall that FISA electronic surveillance has its own unique threshold. See *supra* p. 135. Where would you place it in the hierarchy of thresholds? What about the threshold for national security surveillance ordered by the President on the basis of his own claimed unilateral authority? See *supra* p. 169. You may need to prepare a table of techniques and standards to do this exercise. Is there any logic or pattern to the matches reflected in your table?

Should one have to make a table to figure all this out? Looking just at electronic surveillance techniques, Professor Daniel Solove remarks, "The intricacy of electronic surveillance law is remarkable because it is supposed to apply not just to the FBI, but to state and local police — and even to private citizens. Given its complexity, however, it is unfair to expect these varying groups to comprehend what they can and cannot do." Daniel J. Solove, *Reconstructing Electronic Surveillance Law,* 72 Geo. Wash. L. Rev. 1264, 1293 (2004). If you agree, and if you believe that inclusion of non-electronic surveillance techniques only compounds the complexity, should the law be simplified? How?

2. *The Relevancy Standard.* Prior to the USA Patriot Act, FISA orders for selected business records required a showing of a counterintelligence purpose and of "specific and articulable facts giving reason to believe that the person to whom the records pertain is a foreign power or agent of a foreign power." Pub. L. No. 105-272, §602, 112 Stat. 2396, 2411. The USA Patriot Act broadened eligible information to "tangible things," and substituted a showing that the production was for an authorized investigation to protect against international terrorism and that such an investigation of a U.S. person was not based solely upon activities protected by the First Amendment. USA Patriot Act, Pub. L. No. 107-56, §215, 115 Stat.

287. *See supra* p. 131. This was effectively a relevancy standard. The same criteria were adopted for NSLs. USA Patriot Act, §214, 115 Stat. 286. See *supra* p. 182.

How did the substitution of the relevancy standard for the FISA probable cause standard affect the scope of government surveillance authority? Consider the following assessment.

> Previously, the FBI could get the credit card records of anyone suspected of being a foreign agent. Under the PATRIOT Act, broadly read, the FBI can get the entire database of the credit card company. Under prior law, the FBI could get library borrowing records only with a subpoena in a criminal investigation, and generally had to ask for the records of a specific patron. Under the PATRIOT Act, broadly read, the FBI can go into a public library and ask for the records on everybody who ever used the library, or who used it on a certain day, or who checked out certain kinds of books. It can do the same at any bank, telephone company, hotel or motel, hospital, or university—merely upon the claim that the information is . . . sought for . . . an investigation to protect against international terrorism or clandestine intelligence activities. [*Terrorism Investigations and the Constitution: Hearing Before the Subcomm. on the Constitution of the H. Comm. on the Judiciary*, 108th Cong. (2003) (statement of James X. Dempsey, Exec. Director, Center for Democracy & Technology), *available at* 2003 WL 21153545.]

The relevancy standard has been defended on the basis of the Supreme Court's reasoning in *Smith* and *Miller* that a person who voluntarily conveys information to a third party to consummate a transaction has no legitimate privacy interest in the information. Section 215, however, is not on its face limited to transactional information; it applies to "any tangible things (including books, records, papers, documents, and other items). . . ." 50 U.S.C. §1861(a)(1). Does the Court's reasoning, even if correct, support the full breadth of §215? Suppose you entrust your personal diary to your brother. Would a §215 order to your brother be supported by the Court's reasoning?

3. ***Tightening the Relevancy Standard?*** Although FISA §215 requires a prior FISC order for FBI access to "tangible things," its relevancy standard is so low that the order is arguably boilerplate. The government itself has suggested that the FISC's role is simply to ascertain that the government has made the required certification of relevancy, not to determine that the certification is justified. *See* Letter from Jamie E. Brown, Acting Asst. Attorney General, Off. of Legislative Affairs, U.S. Dept. of Justice, to F. James Sensenbrenner Jr., Chair, House Comm. on the Judiciary, May 13, 2003.

In the Patriot Improvement Act, *supra* p. 176, §106, Congress amended FISA §215 to clarify the relevancy standard. The government must now supply a "statement of facts" demonstrating that there are "reasonable grounds" to believe that the order is relevant to a counterterrorist investigation, although a requested order is deemed "presumptively relevant" to an authorized foreign intelligence or counterterrorist investigation if the government can show that the tangible things pertain to a foreign power or agent or suspected agent of a foreign power under FISA, or to "an individual in contact with, or known to, a suspected agent of a foreign power who is the subject of such authorized investigation." *Id.* The request must also provide a particularized description of the records sought. *Id.* Does this amendment make it easier or harder for the government to obtain a §215 order?

4. ***Judicial Review of NSLs.*** NSLs have been described as "the intelligence corollary to . . . administrative subpoena[s]." Lee S. Strickland, *New Information-Related Laws and the Impact on Civil Liberties*, Bull. Am. Socy. for Info. Sci. & Tech., Feb./Mar. 2002, *at* http://www.asis.org/Bulletin/Mar-02/strickland2.html. Neither administrative subpoenas nor NSLs require a prior court order. *See* Charles Doyle, *Administrative Subpoenas in Criminal Investigations: A Brief Legal Analysis* (Cong. Res. Serv. RL33321), Mar. 17, 2006; Charles Doyle, *Administrative Subpoenas and National Security Letters in Criminal and Foreign Intelligence Investigations: Background and Proposed Adjustments* (Cong. Res. Serv. RL 32880), Apr. 15, 2005. Why are the former lawful under the Fourth Amendment, but not the latter, according to the court in Doe v. Ashcroft? How, if at all, can the infirmity of NSLs be cured without compromising national security?

In the Patriot Improvement Act, *supra* p. 176, §115, Congress for the first time authorized a recipient of an NSL to petition a federal court to modify or set aside the letter "if compliance would be unreasonable, oppressive, or otherwise unlawful." (It also authorized the government to seek enforcement of an NSL from a federal court.) Does the opportunity for judicial review now afforded the NSL recipient satisfy the Fourth Amendment concern identified in the principal case? The plaintiffs there seemingly thought so; they abandoned their Fourth Amendment claims, mooting that part of the case on appeal. Doe v. Gonzales, 449 F.3d at 418.

5. ***First Amendment Issues.*** In Doe v. Ashcroft, the court found that NSLs for electronic communications records may impermissibly infringe First Amendment rights. Whose rights? (Hint: more than one category of person.) How are they infringed? How is this infringement different from that resulting from pen registers? How, if at all, could this infirmity be cured without compromising national security?

A former chief of the FBI's National Security Law Unit writes that the pre-9/11 "regulatory scheme governing counterintelligence, the higher legal standards for counter-intelligence authorities, and even the 'wall' separating intelligence and criminal law enforcement have all functioned to counterbalance and contain a tendency toward excessive secrecy in this area." Woods, *supra* p. 134, at 67. Does the post-9/11 lowering of the legal standards and dismantling of the wall, see *supra* pp. 145-153, upset that balance, supporting the conclusion that the nondisclosure provisions of the NSL statutes fail strict scrutiny? What answer does Judge Cardamone suggest?

In partial response to *Doe I* and *Doe II*, in §§115-116 of the Patriot Improvement Act Congress authorized a recipient of a national security letter to disclose the letter for the purpose of obtaining legal advice regarding her response and to petition a court to challenge the NSL, as noted above. A recipient also may seek a judicial order setting aside the nondisclosure requirement by showing "that there is no reason to believe that disclosure may endanger the national security of the United States, interfere with a criminal, counterterrorism, or counterintelligence investigation, interfere with diplomatic relations, or endanger the life or physical safety of any person." The government's certification to the contrary is conclusive, however. If, on the other hand, the petition is filed more than a year after the NSL is delivered, then the government must permit disclosure within 90 days unless it recertifies that disclosure would so endanger or interfere. A recertification is also treated as conclusive.

The *Doe I* plaintiffs did not think that this amendment laid the First Amendment issues to rest, and the Court of Appeals remanded for further consideration in light of the Patriot Improvement Act. What First Amendment arguments would you make for the plaintiffs on remand? Does the "conclusive" treatment of government certifications render this First Amendment protection toothless? *See* Yeh, *supra* p. 176, at 14.

6. *Library Records.* You have to tell the library what book you are borrowing. Do you intend that the library, in turn, will tell the government? Although as of April 2005, the government denied having yet used NSLs for library records, *see Attorney General Defends Patriot Act*, CNN.com, Apr. 5, 2005, *at* http://www.cnn.com/2005/POLITICS/04/05/Patriot.act/, "John Doe II" turned out to be four Connecticut librarians who had received an NSL demanding library records. American Library Assn., *Library Connection is "John Doe"—Board Speaks About NSL Order for Library Records*, May 30, 2006, *available at* http://www.ala.org/PrinterTemplate.cfm?Template=/ContentManagement/HTMLDisplay.cfm&ContentID=128280.

No potential application of §215 has drawn more criticism than its possible use to obtain library records. Can you guess why? Do you think the Fourth Amendment and/or the First Amendment are implicated? If library records enjoy a distinct First Amendment protection, should they be excluded from §215 authority?

In 2006, Congress excluded libraries from the definition of "wire or electronic communication service provider" for purposes of NSLs issued to obtain subscriber information and toll billing records information or electronic communication transactional records. Pub. L. No. 109-178, §§4(b) and 5, 120 Stat. 280, 281 (2006), *codified at* 18 U.S.C. §2709(f). *See* Yeh, *supra*, at 14-15 (describing dispute over construction of library exemption from "ISP" definition). It left them subject to §215 orders, however, although it also limited the number of FBI officials who could approve §215 applications for library records, as well as "book sales records, book customer lists, firearms sales records, tax return records, educational records, or medical records containing information that would identify a person." Patriot Improvement Act §106, *supra* p. 176. Do all of these different kinds of information present the same constitutional issues?

7. *SWIFT Records.* More than 2,200 leading international banks and financial institutions co-own and operate a Brussels-based organization called the Society for Worldwide Interbank Financial Telecommunication (SWIFT). SWIFT is a hub for about 11 million cross-border (not purely in-country) funds transfers each day and maintains records of the names, addresses,

and account numbers of senders and receivers of such wire transfers. In June 2006, the New York Times revealed that the Department of Treasury's Terrorist Finance Tracking Program had secretly subpoenaed and obtained SWIFT records to facilitate FBI investigation of thousands of transactions by particular persons or organizations. Eric Lichtblau & James Risen, *Bank Data Sifted by U.S. to Block Terror*, N.Y. Times, June 23, 2006, at A1.

Treasury officials claimed that SWIFT was not subject to U.S. bank secrecy laws as a messaging service; it was not a financial institution. They also invoked the International Emergency Economic Powers Act, 50 U.S.C. §§1701-1707 (2000 & Supp. III 2003), as amended by Pub. L. No. 109-177, §402, 120 Stat. 192, 243 (2006), which, *inter alia*, authorizes the President, in response to "an unusual and extraordinary threat," to "investigate" transactions involving property in which foreign states or nationals have an interest. Pursuant to the Act, the President had issued Executive Order No. 13,224, 66 Fed. Reg. 49,079 (Sept. 25, 2001). *See generally* Jennifer K. Elsea & M. Maureen Murphy, *Treasury's Terrorist Finance Program's Access to Information Held by the Society for Worldwide Interbank Financial Telecommunication (SWIFT)* (Cong. Res. Serv. RS22469), July 7, 2006 (identifying these and other legal authorities). Treasury officials also asserted that "[p]eople do not have a privacy interest in their international wire transactions." *See* Lichtblau & Risen, *supra*, quoting Treasury Under Secretary Stuart Levey.

SWIFT officials' unease about sharing data with the U.S. government eventually led to imposition of several safeguards, including employment of an outside auditing firm to verify that searches are based on intelligence leads about suspected terrorists, as well as the preservation of records of every search. The SWIFT data collection reportedly has resulted in identifying previously unknown terrorists and in bolstering the evidence against suspected terrorists.

News of the FBI's access to SWIFT records could cause terrorists to change the way they move funds around. Was the *New York Times* decision to print the story justified? The House of Representatives thought not and passed a resolution condemning the disclosure and calling on the media not to expose other classified intelligence programs. H.R. Res. 895, 109th Cong. (2006). What is your opinion? Does your answer depend on whether the access program was legally authorized? Can you describe such authority?

8. ***Internet Surveillance.*** As *Doe I* indicates, an important legal framework for Internet surveillance is the Electronic Communications Privacy Act of 1986 (ECPA), Pub. L. No. 99-508, 100 Stat. 1848, in addition to the pen register provisions of FISA. See *supra* p. 131. ECPA's intricacies are reviewed in Kerr, *supra* p. 196.

## B.   CONNECTING THE DOTS — DATA MINING

In May 2006, a news article asserted that the National Security Agency (NSA) had been secretly collecting telephone call data (external or "envelope" data, but not internal or "content" data) on "tens of millions of Americans" in order (in the words of an anonymous source) to "create a database of every call ever made" within the nation's borders. Leslie Cauley, *NSA Has Massive Database of Americans' Phone Calls*, USA Today, May 11, 2006. *See generally* Francesca Bignami, *European Versus American Liberty: A Comparative Privacy Analysis of Anti-Terrorism Data-Mining,* 48 B.C. L. Rev. (forthcoming 2007). The "call details records" may include calling and called phone numbers, dates, times, and perhaps lengths of completed calls. Although the records apparently do not include names, street addresses, or other personal information, phone numbers can easily be cross-checked with other databases to obtain such data. The details are unknown at this writing, but the records may be used in programs that identify patterns of calling that could indicate activity of particular interest to investigators ("traffic analysis"). For example, a computer using these programs to search phone calls by members of the Yemeni immigrant community in Buffalo might identify several phone numbers of interest. The calling records of these numbers would then be searched, yielding perhaps 100 other numbers with which each phone number of interest had repeated contact.

> If we began with 100 interesting phone numbers from the community under inspection, we now have 10,000 active phone taps. Everything is computer-driven so far, and a single workday at Fort Meade is not yet over. . . .
> Social nets of people whom the computers think make "interesting phone calls" to each other are defined and stored, presumably forever, as persons of interest. Computers compare these government lists to others. . . .
> Establishing the social networks within communities and among individuals requires tapping phones without probable cause. Computers must be free to crawl through their databases and open every phone line along the way. Of necessity, many phone taps are brief and will be discarded.
> Finding groups (e.g., everyone in a charity, all active contributors to a cause) is a good way to find conspiracies. Unfortunately and despite attempts to be selective, a system with geometrical expansion will yield many false positives. After all, only four "degrees of separation" will get you to all 100 million households in the United States when each phone has 100 contacts, all of them available in phone bill records. At some point, therefore, human analysts inspect the computer harvest we have been discussing. It is possible that a court might be asked for a paper-based search warrant. . . . [J.I. Nelson, *How the NSA Warrantless Wiretap System Works: An Educated Guess,* revised Sept. 26, 2006, *available at* http://wiretapfacts.notlong.com/.]

This outline of a massive domestic intelligence program, including warrantless wiretaps, is, of course, simply an educated guess, as its author acknowledges. The government has not yet admitted the existence of the NSA call detail records program, much less its details.

The use of pen registers and trap and trace devices contemplated in Smith v. Maryland represents a relatively limited, "retail" form of surveillance. The NSA call-records program, by contrast, apparently involves a "wholesale" collection effort to create a megadatabase of domestic calls by everyone in the United States. Such a database can be analyzed or "mined" to create new, more useful sets of information.

> Data mining involves the use of sophisticated data analysis tools to discover previously unknown, valid patterns and relationships in large data sets. . . .
> . . . Data mining applications can use a variety of parameters to examine the data. They include association (patterns where one event is connected to another event, such as purchasing a pen and purchasing paper), sequence or path analysis (patterns where one event leads to another event, such as the birth of a child and purchasing diapers), classification (identification of new patterns, such as coincidences between duct tape purchases and plastic sheeting purchases), clustering (finding and visually documenting groups of previously unknown facts, such as geographic location and brand preferences), and forecasting (discovering patterns from which one can make reasonable predictions regarding future activities, such as the prediction that people who join an athletic club may take exercise classes). [Jeffrey W. Seifert, *Data Mining and Homeland Security: An Overview* (Cong. Res. Serv. RL 31798) 1, Jan. 27, 2006.]

Data mining is widely used in the private sector as a means for fraud detection, risk assessment, and product retailing. The credit card industry uses it, for example, to detect fraud by revealing unusual patterns of credit card use. *See* Peter P. Swire, *Privacy and Information Sharing in the War on Terrorism*, 51 Vill. L. Rev. 951 (2006).

In a counterterrorism effort, "data mining can be a potential means to identify terrorist activities, such as money transfers and communications, and to identify and track individual terrorists themselves, such as through travel and immigration records." Seifert, *supra*, summary. *See generally* K.A. Taipale, *Data Mining and Domestic Security: Connecting the Dots to Make Sense of Data*, 5 Colum. Sci. & Tech. L. Rev. 2 (2003) (describing and assessing the technology). The NSA call-records program is only the latest example of data mining for counterterrorism purposes. Data mining has also likely been conducted on the real-time data obtained in the Terrorist Surveillance Program, see *supra* pp. 157-174, by automated analysis of data flows. *See generally* K.A. Taipale, *Whispering Wires and Warrantless Wiretaps: Data Mining and Foreign Intelligence Surveillance*, 8 N.Y.U. Rev. L. & Security 3 (2006). The following data-mining programs have also come to light:

- *The FBI database.* The FBI recently reported assembly of a database with more than 659 million records, about a quarter of which come from FBI records and criminal case files and the rest from suspicious financial activity reports, no-fly lists, airline passenger records, and lost and stolen passport data. Ellen Nakashima, *FBI Shows Off Counterterrorism Database*, Wash. Post, Aug. 30, 2006, at A6. Presumably, records from the NSA call-records program, as well as transactional data from the SWIFT program, could be added to this database. The FBI explained that an agent can now run 1,000 names through the database in 30 minutes or less, a search that would have taken 32,222 hours prior to 2002. A privacy lawyer commented that the database "appears to be the largest collection of personal data ever amassed by the federal government," and noted also that the *Federal Register* contained no record of the creation of such a system, as required by the Privacy Act, 5 U.S.C. §552a (2000 & Supp. IV 2004). *Id.*, quoting David Sobel, senior counsel of the Electronic Frontier

Foundation. *But cf.* Bignami, *supra* p. 201, at 17-18 (Privacy Act is "riddled with exceptions," and the call-records database may not even qualify as a "system of records" subject to the Act).

- *The Total (later Terrorist) Information Awareness Program (TIA).* This was a research project of the Defense Advanced Research Projects Agency (DARPA) in 2002 to develop technology programs to "counter asymmetric threats by achieving *total information awareness* useful for preemption, national security warning, and national security decision making." Dept. of Defense, *Report to Congress Regarding the Terrorism Information Awareness Program, Detailed Information* 1, May 20, 2003 (emphasis added), *available at* http://www.eff.org/Privacy/TIA/TIA-report.pdf. Serious public relations mistakes (placing TIA under the direction of a principal in the Iran-Contra scandal and adopting a logo with an all-seeing eye atop a pyramid over the globe with the motto "*scientia est potentia*" (knowledge is power)), *see* http://www.richardgingras.com/tia/, contributed to Congress's decision to cut off funding for TIA in its original form. *See generally* Seifert, *supra*, at 5-7; Gina Marie Stevens, *Privacy: Total Information Awareness Programs and Related Information Access* (Cong. Res. Serv. RL31730), Mar. 21, 2003.

- *Computer-Assisted Passenger Prescreening System (CAPPS II).* CAPPS II was an airline passenger prescreening program that used computer-generated profiles to select passengers for additional security screening — technically, data matching. It would have relied on commercial data to calculate "scores" for passengers. In fact, the Transportation Security Administration obtained such data from at least four airlines and two travel companies. But litigation made airlines wary of voluntarily sharing such data, the European Union objected, and Congress became concerned about false positives and a lack of procedures for correcting errors. In 2005, Congress prohibited the use of appropriated funds for CAPPS II or its successor, Secure Flight, until the Government Accountability Office certified that the system met certain privacy requirements. Seifert, *supra*, at 7-11; Office of Inspector General Audit Division, Dept. of Justice, *Review of the Terrorist Screening Center's Efforts to Support the Secure Flight Program* (Aug. 2005), *available at* http://www.usdoj.gov/oig/reports/FBI/a0534/final.pdf.

- *Multistate Anti-Terrorism Information Exchange (MATRIX) Pilot Project.* A private contractor developed MATRIX, a query-based search system that used a dynamic database of over 3.9 billion public records collected from thousands of sources, including FAA pilot licenses and aircraft ownership records, property ownership records, state sexual offender lists, corporation filings, criminal history information, driver's license information and photo images, motor vehicle registration information, bankruptcy filings, and information from commercial sources that "are generally available to the public or legally permissible under federal law." Seifert, *supra*, at 12 (quoting Web site no longer available). Although initially as many as sixteen states were reported as participating or considering participation in MATRIX, after critics raised concerns about law enforcement actions being taken on the basis of data mining performed privately without public or legislative input, only four states remained as participants as of April 2005. The pilot project was then reportedly discontinued. *See generally id.* at 11-15; William J. Krouse, *Multi-State Anti-Terrorism Information Exchange (MATRIX) Pilot Project* (Cong. Res. Serv. RL 32536), Aug. 18, 2004.

## NOTE AND QUESTIONS

1. *Just Finding Clues?* Police investigators have always conducted "link analysis" when they interview witnesses who saw a crime committed or who know the victim, then looked for connections in the information obtained in the interviews. "Data mining is no more than the computational automation of traditional investigative skills — that is, the intelligent analysis of myriad 'clues' in order to develop a theory of the case." Taipale, *Data Mining and Domestic Security, supra* p. 202, at 21. Does it follow that "using computers to analyze data is similar to a police officer examining the same information and does not violate personal privacy"? *Counterterrorism Technology and Privacy, supra* p. 177, at 27. Do the two processes have different implications for personal privacy or expectations of privacy? Should we distinguish, for example, between subject-specific searches and generalized undirected data mining to derive or to match patterns? If so, how is computerized pattern matching different, from a privacy perspective, from a police officer's observation of a masked individual running on a public street? *See* Taipale, *supra*, at 64.

2. *The Question the Smith and Miller Cases Did Not Ask.* Attorney General Alberto R. Gonzales defended the NSA call-records program without admitting its existence. He argued that "[t]here is no reasonable expectation of privacy in those kinds of records," citing *Smith*. Walter Pincus, *Gonzales Defends Phone-Data Collection*, Wash. Post, May 24, 2006, at A6. But the Supreme Court focused in *Smith* and *Miller* on the surveillance and collection techniques (pen registers recording dialed numbers and subpoenas for bank records), not on what became of the information they yielded. The Court's focus was understandable from the perspective of traditionally reactive "retail" criminal law enforcement, which builds one case at a time.

But in the fight against terrorism, reactive law enforcement has given way to proactive and preventive law enforcement. *See* Peter Raven-Hansen, *Security's Conquest of Law Enforcement*, in *In Democracy's Shadow* ch. 12 (Marcus G. Raskin & A. Carl LeVan eds., 2005); Daniel J. Steinbock, *Data Matching, Data Mining, and Due Process*, 40 Ga. L. Rev. 1, 16-17 (2005). Data are collected and stored in databases, perhaps indefinitely, for the continuing "wholesale" preventive effort. Even if they are not immediately archived with other data, they can be "virtually aggregated" at any moment to create a dynamic megadatabase. *See* Taipale, *supra*, at 42.

Does the prospect of such indefinite retention and aggregation have any bearing on the expectation of privacy? Do you have a greater expectation of privacy in your aggregated data than in their parts? For example, are you willing to risk that airlines will disclose your travel plans to the government, yet not want those data linked to your other consumer and credit information? Should courts gauge the legitimacy of privacy expectations in each collected item of personal information by the possibility that it will be aggregated for data mining to establish personal behavior patterns and profiles? Does your answer depend on the length of time that information may be maintained by a government agency? On the purpose for which the information was originally collected? *See* Laurence H. Tribe, Op-Ed., *Bush Stomps on Fourth Amendment*, Boston Globe, May 16, 2006, at A15 ("Even if one trusts the president's promise not to connect all the dots to the degree the technology permits, the act of collecting all those dots in a form that *permits* their complete connection at his whim is a 'search,'" and "[d]oing it to all Americans . . . is an 'unreasonable search' if those Fourth Amendment words have any meaning at all.").

In United States Dept. of Justice v. Reporters Comm. for Freedom of the Press, 489 U.S. 749 (1989), Justice Stevens, writing for the Court, acknowledged that even public personal data enjoy a certain "practical obscurity" that may be altered by its aggregation into an easily searched database. Posing the issue as "whether the compilation of otherwise hard-to-obtain information alters the privacy interest implicated by disclosure of that information," he asserted that "there is a vast difference between the public records" accessible by diligent effort in sundry locations throughout the country and "a computerized summary located in a single clearinghouse of information." *Id.* at 764. But today many public records exist in easily searchable computer databases. Are any computerized records still "practically obscure," in the same sense that hard copy records at the courthouse or land office once were? Does the ever-increasing use of data mining — in both the public and private sectors — suggest a diminishing expectation of privacy in data? *See* Kyllo v. United States, 533 U.S. 27, 34 (2001) (finding that the use of heat-sensing technology was an unreasonable search, "*at least where (as here) the technology in question is not in general public use*") (emphasis added).

3. ***Legal Authority for the NSA Call-Records Program.*** What arguments would you make for the President's authority to order the NSA call-records program? *See* Elizabeth B. Bazan et al., *Government Access to Phone Calling Activity and Related Records: Legal Authorities* (Cong. Res. Serv. RL33424), Jan. 25, 2007. Recall the arguments made in support of the Terrorist Surveillance Program, *supra* pp. 157-174. Are the arguments to support the call-records program stronger or weaker? *See* Bignami, *supra* p. 201, at 16-17 (stronger).

The Privacy Act, 5 U.S.C. §552a (2000 & Supp. IV 2004), limits the authority of federal agencies to collect, retain, or use personally identifiable information about individuals, including, presumably, the sort of data involved in the NSA call-records program. An agency may "maintain in its records only such information about an individual as is relevant and necessary to accomplish a purpose of the agency required to be accomplished by statute or by executive order of the President," *id.* §552a(e)(1), and it may "maintain no record describing how any individual exercises rights guaranteed by the First Amendment unless expressly authorized by statute or by the individual about whom the record is maintained or unless pertinent to and within the scope of an authorized law enforcement activity." *Id.*

§552a(e)(7). Data properly collected and held by an agency apparently may, however, be subjected to a "matching program" — a "computerized comparison of two or more automated systems of records . . . for foreign counterintelligence purposes." *Id.* §552a(a)(8). Do you think the Privacy Act restricts the President's authority to conduct the NSA call-records program?

As of January 2007, 42 actions challenging the legality of the NSA call-records program had been consolidated in one federal court and were pending. Bazan, *supra.* That court had previously rejected the government's motion to dismiss one such action based on invocation of the state secrets privilege, reasoning that enough about the program had been publicly disclosed to allow the action to proceed, Hepting v. AT&T Corp., 439 F. Supp. 2d 974 (N.D. Cal. 2006), but another court applied the privilege to bar discovery, without which the plaintiffs were unable to demonstrate standing. Terkel v. AT&T Corp., 441 F. Supp. 2d 899 (N.D. Ill. 2006).

4. ***False Positives.***  Credit card data have several attributes that contribute to the success of data mining: a large number of valid transactions, a large number of fraudulent transactions, repetitive fraudulent use that generates common data patterns, and a relatively low cost to "false positives" — valid purchases that are incorrectly flagged as fraudulent — since they usually simply trigger a confirming phone call to the credit card holder. *See* Swire, *supra* p. 202, at 964-965. In contrast, the number of terrorist attacks is extremely low, terrorist attacks are far less likely to be repetitive rather than one-of-a-kind, and the cost of false positives is far higher, both to the falsely identified innocent person and to the government, which must use substantial resources to investigate that person. *Id. But see* Paul Rosenzweig, *Proposals for Implementing the Terrorist Information Awareness System* (Heritage Found. Legal Memorandum), Aug. 7, 2003, at 4 (suggesting that costs of false positives are "relatively modest"), *available at* http://www.heritage.org/Research/HomelandDefense/lm8.cfm. These differences do not rule out data mining for counterterrorism purposes, but they might suggest the need for special rules for dealing with false positives. *See* Rosenzweig, *supra* (suggesting that "robust" mechanisms to correct false positives from counterterrorist data mining would make the high false positive rate acceptable in light of the consequences of failing to mine data); Steinbock, *supra* p. 201 (suggesting due process protections for persons against whom government action will be taken because of data matching, such as persons denied boarding because of a match on a terrorist watch list). Can you think of special rules to address these differences?

5. ***Mission Creep.***  CAPPS II ran afoul, in part, of a fear of mission creep. Originally justified as a screening device for foreign terrorists, CAPPS II could also be used to identify individuals with outstanding federal or state arrest warrants or linked to the U.S. Visitor and Immigrant Status Indicator Technology to identify illegal or out-of-status aliens. Seifert, *supra* p. 202, at 10. Presumably, with a little tweaking, it could also be used to identify deadbeat dads or tax delinquents. So what? If the decision to use data mining involves a balancing of privacy interests in the data against security concerns, then the balance shifts with each intended use of the data. Americans who are willing to give up privacy to protect against terrorism may feel

differently about giving it up to track scofflaws who refuse to pay parking tickets.

But mission creep can be deadly serious. In Nazi Germany, the authorities used IBM Hollerith punchcards for pre-computer data mining to identify Jews for asset confiscation, ghettoization, deportation, arrest and detention, and, ultimately, extermination, as well as to identify, track, and manage slave labor. The Nazis conducted card-sorting operations in every major concentration camp. *See* Edwin Black, *IBM and the Holocaust* 8-10 (2002). In Norway in World War II, the German Army was prevented from using the government's meticulous population files to identify Norwegian men to conscript into the German Army only by the Norwegian Resistance's destruction of the only file-sorting machinery then available. *See* Bignami, *supra*, p. 201, at 1-2.

6. ***Profiling.*** A Department of Defense report suggests that concerns about mission creep may extend beyond privacy if information is used for "targeting an individual solely on the basis of religion or expression, or . . . in a way that would violate the constitutional guarantee against self-incrimination." Technology and Privacy Advisory Comm., Dept. of Defense, *Safeguarding Privacy in the Fight Against Terrorism* 39 (Mar. 2004). After all, pattern matching *is* profiling of a sort when it is used predictively. Racial and ethnic profiling is discussed *infra* pp. 228-238.

7. ***Statutory Protection?*** In Whalen v. Roe, 429 U.S. 589 (1977), the Court upheld a state law requiring disclosure of certain prescription information to the state, which could enter it into an electronic database. The Court stated, however,

> We are not unaware of the threat to privacy implicit in the accumulation of vast amounts of personal information in computerized data banks or other massive government files. . . . The right to collect and use such data for public purposes is typically accompanied by a concomitant statutory or regulatory duty to avoid unwarranted disclosures. Recognizing that in some circumstances that duty arguably has its roots in the Constitution, nevertheless New York's statutory scheme, and its implementing administrative procedures, evidence a proper concern with, and protection of, the individual's interest in privacy. [*Id.* at 605.]

Congress has required inter-agency agreements for computer matching among federal agencies, *see* Computer Matching and Privacy Protection Act of 1988, Pub. L. No. 100-153, §1, 102 Stat. 2507 (1988), but Congress has also enacted Privacy Act exemptions for computer matching and inter-agency data sharing for national security and law enforcement purposes. *See* 5 U.S.C. §§552a(a)(8)(B)(vi), 552a(b)(7), 552a(j) (2000). Numerous other statutes regulate particular databases, usually with broad exemptions for law enforcement. *See* Taipale, *Data Mining and Domestic Security, supra* p. 202, at 53 n.223.

In 2006, Congress deferred regulating data mining and instead required the Attorney General to provide a report on any initiatives to "develop pattern-based data-mining technology." Patriot Improvement Act, *supra* p. 176, §126(b)(1), 120 Stat. 228. The Act defined data mining as a query or search or other analysis of one or more electronic databases, where at least one of the databases was obtained from or remains under the control of a non-Federal entity, or the information was acquired initially by another department or agency of the Federal Government for purposes other than intelligence or law enforcement; the search does not use personal identifiers of a specific individual or does not utilize inputs that appear on their face to identify or be associated with a specified individual to acquire information; and a department or agency of the Federal Government is conducting the query or search or other analysis to find a pattern indicating terrorist or other criminal activity. [*Id.*]

How much counterterrorist data mining falls outside this definition? The definition expressly excludes "telephone directories, information publicly available via the Internet or available by any other means to any member of the public, any databases maintained, operated, or controlled by a State, local, or tribal government (such as a State motor vehicle database), or databases of judicial and administrative opinions." *Id.* Even for what remains within the definition, however, Congress merely required the executive branch to give it a report.

What protections, if any, should Congress enact with respect to data mining by the government for counterterrorism purposes? *See Report of the Technology and Privacy Advisory Comm., supra* p. 207 (recommending, *inter alia,* that Congress authorize the FISC to oversee government data mining, but excluding data mining not involving U.S. persons or based on particularized suspicion); Rosenzweig, *supra* p. 206.

# CHAPTER 7

# SCREENING FOR SECURITY

On September 11, 2001, Mohamed Atta and Abdul Aziz al Omari boarded a 6 A.M. flight from Portland, Maine, to Boston's Logan International Airport to catch a connecting flight bound for Los Angeles.[1] A computerized prescreening system known as CAPPS (see *supra* p. 203) selected Atta for special security measures, which consisted at the time of holding his checked bags until he was on board the airplane. At Logan, Atta and al Omari, and eight colleagues who joined them, went through security checkpoints at which they were screened by metal detectors calibrated to detect items with at least the metal content of a .22-caliber handgun. Some of these men are now thought to have carried box cutters or pocket utility knives (defined as having blades less than four inches long and permitted on flights at the time).

In the meantime, as they were en route to board a flight bound for Los Angeles, four more colleagues were flagged by CAPPS at Dulles International Airport. Two of them—brothers—were selected for extra scrutiny by the airline customer representative at the check-in counter because one of the brothers lacked a photo identification and could not speak English, and they seemed suspicious. Both brothers had dark hair and swarthy complexions, and one had a dark mustache. Again, the consequence was that their bags were held until they were on board the airplane. Several of the men at Dulles set off the metal detectors at the security checkpoint and were hand-wanded before being passed. One had his carry-on bag swiped by an explosive trace detector. All were videotaped at the checkpoint.

Of the 19 men who eventually boarded the fateful flights on September 11 in this fashion, 7 used Virginia drivers' licenses as their identification at check-in. None of them lived in Virginia. They had obtained the licenses there because they had learned that one can get a genuine driver's license in Virginia in one day for approximately $100 cash with no questions asked.

---

1. These and other details in this introduction are drawn from *Final Report of the National Commission on Terrorist Attacks Upon the United States* (2004) (*9/11 Report*) and *Protecting Our National Security From Terrorist Attacks: A Review of Criminal Terrorism Investigations and Prosecutions: Hearing Before the S. Comm. on the Judiciary*, 108th Cong. (2003) (statement of Paul McNulty, U.S. Attorney, E.D. Va.).

The *9/11 Commission Report* tells the rest of the story.

> The 19 men were aboard four transcontinental flights. They were planning to hijack these planes and turn them into large guided missiles, loaded with up to 11,400 gallons of jet fuel. By 8:00 A.M. on the morning of Tuesday, September 11, 2001, they had defeated all the security layers that America's civil aviation system then had in place to prevent a hijacking. [*9/11 Report,* at 4 (footnotes omitted).]

This chapter explores some of the legal issues raised by this defeat of what was and still is essentially a system designed to screen terrorists from entry to transportation systems and other high-risk targets. In Part A we explore issues of checkpoint searches. In Part B we consider the narrower concerns of identification and watch list screening. Finally, in Part C we examine the difficult question of profiling.

## A. CHECKPOINT SEARCHES

The government has been screening persons seeking entry into this country since the first Congress passed a customs statute exempting border searches from probable cause requirements. *See* 5 Wayne R. LaFave, *Search and Seizure* §10.5(a) (4th ed. 2004), *citing* Act of July 31, 1789, ch. 5, 1 Stat. 29, 43 (1789). Border searches without warrants or probable cause have consistently been held reasonable as tools of national self-protection that are justified by "considerations specifically related to the need to police the border." City of Indianapolis v. Edmond, 531 U.S. 32, 38 (2000) (dictum). Such searches are often conducted at airports at which international carriers land.

Airplane hijacking — "skyjacking" — in the 1960s gave a reason to conduct searches of outbound, even domestic, air travelers. At first, passengers were selected for frisking if they fit a skyjacker profile and activated a metal detector. LaFave, *supra,* §10.6(a). Courts measured the reasonableness of this early selective screening program by balancing the probability that the selectee was armed and dangerous against the manner and extent of the intrusion on the passenger and the risk of air piracy if he slipped through. *Id.* §10(b) (citing Terry v. Ohio, 392 U.S. 1 (1968) (approving brief stop-and-frisk)).

But the selective screening program gave way after 1973 to a program requiring *all* passengers to go through a metal detector and to submit to a search and usually x-ray scan of all carry-on items. *See* United States v. Davis, 482 F.2d 893, 897-904 (9th Cir. 1973) (reciting history of airplane hijacking, early "profiling" by the FAA, and a 1972 order by the President for screening of passengers and inspection of carry-on baggage); LaFave, *supra,* §§10.6(a)-(b). The old balancing rationale could no longer be used to justify entirely suspicionless screening of all passengers. Instead, the courts justified the new all-passenger screening as an administrative or "regulatory" search.

> [S]creening searches of airline passengers are conducted as part of a general regulatory scheme in furtherance of an administrative purpose, namely, to

prevent the carrying of weapons or explosives aboard aircraft, and thereby to prevent hijackings. The essential purpose of the scheme is not to detect weapons or explosives or to apprehend those who carry them, but to deter persons carrying such material from seeking to board at all. [*Davis*, 482 F.2d at 908.]

The intrusiveness of the screening program had to match the administrative need, leading to the conclusion that there was no justification for compelled search of a person who elected not to board the plane. *Id. See generally* LaFave, *supra*, §10.6(c).

Entry control by screening is a counterterrorist tool that is not confined to airports alone. The following post-9/11 case concerns its use on subway passengers. Does the airport screening model fit the subway case? Could the law it discusses also be used to justify screening in government buildings and at national monuments?

## MacWade v. Kelly

United States Court of Appeals, Second Circuit, 2006
460 F.3d 260

[The New York City subway system, with 26 interconnected lines and 468 passenger stations operating 24 hours a day, is the most heavily used subway in the United States. Experts assert that transportation systems like it are attractive targets for terrorist bombings because they carry large numbers of people. An attack could produce huge casualties, as well as causing widespread economic consequences and public fear. Following the March 11, 2004, Madrid commuter train bombings that killed more than 200 persons, another 2004 train bombing in Moscow that killed 40, and the London subway bombings in July 2005 that killed 52 persons, the New York City subway system adopted a random "container inspection program" to address the threat of an explosive device being taken into the subway in a carry-on container or backpack.]

STRAUB, Circuit Judge. We consider whether the government may employ random, suspicionless container searches in order to safeguard mass transportation facilities from terrorist attack. The precise issue before us is whether one such search regime, implemented on the New York City subway system, satisfies the special needs exception to the Fourth Amendment's usual requirement of individualized suspicion. We hold that it does. . . .

### Background

**I. The Subway System and the Container Inspection Program** . . .

. . . A "checkpoint" consists of a group of uniformed police officers standing at a folding table near the row of turnstiles disgorging onto the train platform. At the table, officers search the bags of a portion of subway riders entering the station.

In order to enhance the Program's deterrent effect, the NYPD selects the checkpoint locations "in a deliberative manner that may appear random, undefined, and unpredictable." In addition to switching checkpoint locations, the NYPD also varies their number, staffing, and scheduling so that the "deployment patterns . . . are constantly shifting." While striving to maintain the veneer of random deployment, the NYPD bases its decisions on a sophisticated host of criteria, such as fluctuations in passenger volume and threat level, overlapping coverage provided by its other counter-terrorism initiatives, and available manpower.

The officers assigned to each checkpoint give notice of the searches and make clear that they are voluntary. Close to their table they display a large poster notifying passengers that "backpacks and other containers [are] subject to inspection." The Metropolitan Transportation Authority, which operates the subway system, makes similar audio announcements in subway stations and on trains. A supervising sergeant at the checkpoint announces through a bullhorn that all persons wishing to enter the station are subject to a container search and those wishing to avoid the search must leave the station. Although declining the search is not by itself a basis for arrest, the police may arrest anyone who refuses to be searched and later attempts to reenter the subway system with the uninspected container.

Officers exercise virtually no discretion in determining whom to search. The supervising sergeant establishes a selection rate, such as every fifth or tenth person, based upon considerations such as the number of officers and the passenger volume at that particular checkpoint. The officers then search individuals in accordance with the established rate only.

Once the officers select a person to search, they limit their search as to scope, method, and duration. As to scope, officers search only those containers large enough to carry an explosive device, which means, for example, that they may not inspect wallets and small purses. Further, once they identify a container of eligible size, they must limit their inspection "to what is minimally necessary to ensure that the . . . item does not contain an explosive device," which they have been trained to recognize in various forms. They may not intentionally look for other contraband, although if officers incidentally discover such contraband, they may arrest the individual carrying it.[1] Officers may not attempt to read any written or printed material. Nor may they request or record a passenger's personal information, such as his name, address, or demographic data.

The preferred inspection method is to ask the passenger to open his bag and manipulate his possessions himself so that the officer may determine, on a purely visual basis, if the bag contains an explosive device. If necessary, the officer may open the container and manipulate its contents himself. Finally, because officers must conduct the inspection for no "longer than necessary to

---

1. At oral argument counsel for defendants informed us that thus far there have been no arrests for general crimes stemming from the seizure of non-explosive contraband discovered during a search conducted pursuant to the Program.

ensure that the individual is not carrying an explosive device," a typical inspection lasts for a matter of seconds. . . .

## Discussion . . .

## II. The Special Needs Doctrine

. . . As the Fourth Amendment's text makes clear, the concept of reasonableness is the "touchstone of the constitutionality of a governmental search." Bd. of Educ. v. Earls, 536 U.S. 822, 828 (2002). "What is reasonable, of course, depends on all of the circumstances surrounding the search or seizure and the nature of the search or seizure itself." Skinner v. Railway Labor Exec. Ass'n, 489 U.S. 602 (1989) (internal quotation marks omitted). As a "general matter," a search is unreasonable unless supported "by a warrant issued upon probable cause. . . ." Nat'l Treasury Employees Union v. Von Raab, 489 U.S. 656, 665 (1989). However, "neither a warrant nor probable cause, nor, indeed, any measure of individualized suspicion, is an indispensable component of reasonableness in every circumstance." *Id.*

In light of those "longstanding" principles, *id.,* we upheld a program employing metal detectors and hand searches of carry-on baggage at airports. *See* United States v. Edwards, 498 F.2d 496, 500-501 (2d Cir. 1974). We determined that the "purpose" of the search program was not to serve "as a general means for enforcing the criminal laws" but rather to "prevent airplane hijacking" by "terrorists[.]" *Id.* at 500. We then dispensed with the traditional warrant and probable cause requirements and instead balanced "the need for a search against the offensiveness of the intrusion." *Id.* We concluded that,

> When the risk is the jeopardy to hundreds of human lives and millions of dollars of property inherent in the pirating or blowing up of a large airplane, the danger alone meets the test of reasonableness, so long as the search is conducted in good faith for the purpose of preventing hijacking or like damage and with reasonable scope and the passenger has been given advance notice of his liability to such a search so that he can avoid it by choosing not to travel by air.

*Id.* Although at the time we lodged our decision within the broad rubric of reasonableness, *id.* at 498 n.5, our reasoning came to be known as the "special needs exception" roughly one decade later. *See* New Jersey v. T.L.O., 469 U.S. 325, 351 (1985) (Blackmun, J., concurring) ("Only in those exceptional circumstances in which special needs, beyond the need for normal law enforcement, make the warrant and probable-cause requirement impracticable, is a court entitled to substitute its balancing of interests for that of the Framers."). . . .

The doctrine's central aspects are as follows. First, as a threshold matter, the search must "serve as [its] immediate purpose an objective distinct from the ordinary evidence gathering associated with crime investigation." Nicholas v. Goord, 430 F.3d 652, 663 (2d Cir. 2005). Second, once the government satisfies that threshold requirement, the court determines whether the search is reasonable by balancing several competing considerations. These balancing factors include (1) the weight and immediacy of the government interest, *Earls,* 536 U.S. at 834; (2) "the nature of the privacy interest allegedly compromised by" the search, *id.* at 830; (3) "the character of the intrusion imposed" by the search, *id.* at 832; and (4) the efficacy of the search in advancing the government interest.

### III. The Program is Constitutional . . .

#### A. *The special needs doctrine does not require that the subject of the search possess a diminished privacy interest*

Plaintiffs first raise the purely legal contention that, as a threshold matter, the special needs doctrine applies only where the subject of the search possesses a reduced privacy interest. While it is true that in most special needs cases the relevant privacy interest is somewhat "limited," *see Earls,* 536 U.S. at 832 (considering the privacy interest of public schoolchildren), the Supreme Court never has implied — much less actually held — that a reduced privacy expectation is a *sine qua non* of special needs analysis. . . .

Accordingly, to the extent that the principle needs clarification, we expressly hold that the special needs doctrine does not require, as a threshold matter, that the subject of the search possess a reduced privacy interest. Instead, once the government establishes a special need, the nature of the privacy interest is a factor to be weighed in the balance.

#### B. *The container inspection program serves a special need*

Plaintiffs next maintain that the District Court erred in concluding that the Program serves the special need of preventing a terrorist attack on the subway. . . .

As a factual matter, we agree with the District Court's conclusion that the Program aims to prevent a terrorist attack on the subway. Defendants implemented the Program in response to a string of bombings on commuter trains and subway systems abroad, which indicates that its purpose is to prevent similar occurrences in New York City. In its particulars, the Program seeks out explosives only: officers are trained to recognize different explosives, they search only those containers capable of carrying explosive devices, and they may not intentionally search for other contraband, read written or printed material, or request personal information. Additionally, the Program's voluntary nature illuminates its purpose: that an individual may refuse the search *provided* he leaves the subway establishes that the Program seeks to prevent a terrorist, laden with concealed explosives, from boarding a subway train in the first place.

As a legal matter, courts traditionally have considered special the government's need to "prevent" and "discover . . . latent or hidden" hazards, *Von Raab,* 489 U.S. at 668, in order to ensure the safety of mass transportation mediums, such as trains, airplanes, and highways. We have no doubt that concealed explosives are a hidden hazard, that the Program's purpose is prophylactic, and that the nation's busiest subway system implicates the public's safety. Accordingly, preventing a terrorist from bombing the subways constitutes a special need that is distinct from ordinary post hoc criminal investigation. Further, the fact that an officer incidentally may discover a different kind of contraband and arrest its possessor does not alter the Program's intended purpose.

Relying on dicta in *Edmond,* in which the Supreme Court struck down a drug interdiction checkpoint, plaintiffs urge the extraordinarily broad legal principle that a terrorist checkpoint serves a special need only in the face of an imminent attack. The *Edmond* Court merely remarked that under such dire circumstances, "[f]or example," a checkpoint regime "would almost certainly" be constitutional. *Edmond,* 531 U.S. at 44. . . . Where, as here, a search program is designed and implemented to seek out concealed explosives in order to safeguard a means of mass transportation from terrorist attack, it serves a special need.

### C. On balance, the Program is constitutional

Having concluded that the Program serves a special need, we next balance the factors set forth above to determine whether the search is reasonable and thus constitutional.

#### (i) The government interest is immediate and substantial

. . . In light of the thwarted plots to bomb New York City's subway system, its continued desirability as a target, and the recent bombings of public transportation systems in Madrid, Moscow, and London, the risk to public safety is substantial and real. . . .

#### (ii) A subway rider has a full expectation of privacy in his containers

. . . [A] person carrying items in a closed, opaque bag has manifested his subjective expectation of privacy by keeping his belongings from plain view and indicating "that, for whatever reason, [he] prefer[s] to keep [them] close at hand." [Bond v. United States, 529 U.S. 334, 338 (2000).] Further, the Supreme Court has recognized as objectively reasonable a bus rider's expectation that his bag will not be felt "in an exploratory manner" from the outside, *id.* at 338-39, let alone opened and its contents visually inspected or physically manipulated. Accordingly, a subway rider who keeps his bags on his person possesses an undiminished expectation of privacy therein. We therefore weigh this factor in favor of plaintiffs.

#### (iii) The search is minimally intrusive

Although a subway rider enjoys a full privacy expectation in the contents of his baggage, the kind of search at issue here minimally intrudes upon that interest. Several uncontested facts establish that the Program is narrowly tailored to achieve its purpose: (1) passengers receive notice of the searches and may decline to be searched so long as they leave the subway, (2) police search only those containers capable of concealing explosives, inspect eligible containers only to determine whether they contain explosives, inspect the containers visually unless it is necessary to manipulate their contents, and do not read printed or written material or request personal information, (4) uniformed personnel conduct the searches out in the open, which reduces the fear and stigma that removal to a hidden area can cause, and (5) police exercise no discretion in selecting whom to search, but rather employ a formula that ensures they do not arbitrarily exercise their authority. Although defendants need not employ "the least intrusive means" to serve the state interest, it appears they have approximated that model. Given the narrow tailoring that the Program achieves, this factor weighs strongly in favor of defendants, as the District Court properly concluded.

### (iv) The Program is reasonably effective

In considering the "degree to which the seizure advances the public interest," we must remember not to wrest "from politically accountable officials . . . the decision as to which among reasonable alternative law enforcement techniques should be employed to deal with a serious public danger." *Michigan Dep't of State Police v. Sitz,* 496 U.S. 444, 453-454 (1990) (internal quotation marks omitted). That decision is best left to those with "a unique understanding of, and responsibility for, limited public resources, including a finite number of police officers." *Id.* at 454. Accordingly, we ought not conduct a "searching examination of effectiveness." *Id.* at 454 (internal quotation marks omitted). Instead, we need only determine whether the Program is "a reasonably effective means of addressing" the government interest in deterring and detecting a terrorist attack on the subway system. *Earls,* 536 U.S. at 837. . . .

. . . [T]he expert testimony established that terrorists seek predictable and vulnerable targets, and the Program generates uncertainty that frustrates that goal, which, in turn, deters an attack. . . .

Plaintiffs further claim that the Program is ineffective because police notify passengers of the searches, and passengers are free to walk away and attempt to reenter the subway at another point or time. Yet we always have viewed notice and the opportunity to decline as beneficial aspects of a suspicionless search regime because those features minimize intrusiveness. *Edwards,* 498 F.2d at 500 (upholding suspicionless airport searches as reasonable "so long as . . . the passenger has been given advance notice of his liability to such a search so that he can avoid it by choosing not to travel by air"). Striking a search program as ineffective on account of its narrow tailoring would create a most perverse result: those programs "more pervasive and more invasive of privacy" more likely would satisfy the Fourth Amendment. *Von Raab,* 489 U.S. at 676-677 n.4 (internal quotation marks omitted).

Importantly, if a would-be bomber declines a search, he must leave the subway or be arrested — an outcome that, for the purpose of preventing subway bombings, we consider reasonably effective, especially since the record establishes that terrorists prize predictability. An unexpected change of plans might well stymie the attack, disrupt the synchronicity of multiple bombings, or at least reduce casualties by forcing the terrorist to detonate in a less populated location. . . .

## Conclusion

In sum, we hold that the Program is reasonable, and therefore constitutional, because (1) preventing a terrorist attack on the subway is a special need; (2) that need is weighty; (3) the Program is a reasonably effective deterrent; and (4) even though the searches intrude on a full privacy interest, they do so to a minimal degree. We thus Affirm the judgment of the District Court.

## NOTES AND QUESTIONS

1. *Consent.* Some of the airport screening cases argue that by electing to travel by air, after notice of the screening programs, a passenger impliedly consents to the screening. LaFave, *supra* p. 210, §10.6(g). If she consents, she waives her privacy interest. Is this logic compelling for subway travelers? For air travelers? *See* United States v. Davis, 482 F.2d at 905 (asserting that it would violate the principle that government cannot "avoid the restrictions of the Fourth Amendment by notifying the public that all telephone lines would be tapped or that all homes would be searched"); LaFave, *supra*, §10.6(g) (theory of implied consent "diverts attention from the more fundamental question of whether the nature of the regulation undertaken by the government is in fact reasonable under the Fourth Amendment"). Does *MacWade* rely on the consent theory?

2. *The Walk-Away Option.* Closely related to the consent theory is the logic that subway passengers have notice of the inspection and therefore can always refuse inspection and take alternative transportation. A few courts condition their finding that a screening program is reasonable upon the program's inclusion of this option. *See* United States v. Davis, 482 F.2d at 910. Does this logic take into account the impact of the walk-away option on the government's security interest? Some courts have reasoned that "such an option would constitute a one-way street for the benefit of a party planning airplane mischief, since there is no guarantee that if he were allowed to leave he might not return and be more successful" and that "the very fact that a safe exit is available if apprehension is threatened would, by diminishing risk, encourage attempts." United States v. Skipwith, 482 F.2d 1272, 1282 (5th Cir. 1973) (Aldrich, J., dissenting, but this discussion adopted by majority). Does the apparently heightened risk of terrorism to transportation systems after 9/11 now justify finding that a screening system without this option can still be reasonable? Then-Circuit Judge Alito, writing for the Third Circuit Court of Appeals, thought so in United States v. Hartwell, 436 F.3d 174, 182 (3d Cir. 2006) (upholding a nonconsensual hand-wanding of Hartwell after he set off the metal detector at an airport).

3. *Building Entry Screening.* The balancing test articulated in the airport screening cases and adapted for the container-inspection program in *MacWade* is fact-sensitive. Do the factors carry the same weight when the government screens people entering a building? How is that different? In Barrett v. Kunzig, 331 F. Supp. 266, 274 (M.D. Tenn. 1971), the court found

that "[w]hen the interest in protection of the government property and personnel from destruction is balanced against any invasion to the entrant's personal dignity, privacy, and constitutional rights, the government's substantial interest in conducting the cursory [article] inspection [at building entry] outweighs the personal inconvenience suffered by the individual." But there the court also emphasized the relatively unobtrusive nature of the article inspection and its neutral application to all entrants. Suppose the screening includes frisks? Body searches? Suppose, using a watch list, the security personnel select particular entrants for a second search? Does it matter whether the search is conducted at the Pentagon or the Smithsonian Museum of Natural History? Professor LaFave's answer is that "what is required is a judicial assessment of the magnitude of the danger and a judicial determination of what screening procedures will suffice to meet it." LaFave, *supra*, at §10.7(a). How would you perform this assessment for these building searches?

4. *Do Special Needs Tilt the Scales?*  One scholar has argued that the special needs exception tilts the scale in favor of government by focusing on the governmental policy objectives rather than on the specific facts of the case, and that it dilutes the Fourth Amendment by making its "requirements vary along with the difficulty government claims it encounters in detecting crime." Ricardo J. Bascuas, *Fourth Amendment Lessons From the Highway and the Subway: A Principled Approach to Suspicionless Searches*, 38 Rutgers L.J. (forthcoming 2007). Can you think of a checkpoint search to prevent terrorism that would fail the special needs test? Bascuas also cautions that special needs searches invite pretextual searches circumventing any requirement of individualized suspicion. *Id.* What features of the subway checkpoint searches, if any, address this concern?

## B.  IDENTIFICATION AND WATCH LISTING

Two of the 9/11 hijackers had been identified as possible terrorist suspects by the CIA before 9/11 and had been added to a State Department watch list of such suspects called "TIPOFF" on August 24, 2001. *9/11 Report, supra* p. 209 n.1, at 270. TIPOFF was intended primarily to keep terrorists from getting visas to the United States. It was not shared with the FAA, which maintained a separate no-fly list of persons banned for air travel because of the threat they were thought to pose to civil aviation, as well as an "Automatic Selectee" list of persons selected for further screening, such as hand-wanding and questioning. None of the hijackers was on either FAA list. *The 9/11 Investigations* 27 (Steve Strasser ed., 2004).

What authority does the government have to require identification in the screening process? The following case provides some answers, and subsequent Notes and Questions address the related question of whether we should adopt and require a national identifier. We also review a listing of currently known federal watch lists as a backdrop to discussing their creation and the problems they may pose of misidentification and other false positives.

## GILMORE V. GONZALES

United States Court of Appeals, Ninth Circuit, 2006
435 F.3d 1125, *cert. denied*, 127 S. Ct. 929 (2007)

PAEZ, Circuit Judge. John Gilmore ("Gilmore") sued Southwest Airlines and the United States Attorney General, Alberto R. Gonzales, among other defendants, alleging that the enactment and enforcement of the Government's civilian airline passenger identification policy is unconstitutional. The identification policy requires airline passengers to present identification to airline personnel before boarding or be subjected to a search that is more exacting than the routine search that passengers who present identification encounter. Gilmore alleges that when he refused to present identification or be subjected to a more thorough search, he was not allowed to board his flights to Washington, D.C. Gilmore asserts that because the Government refuses to disclose the content of the identification policy, it is vague and uncertain and therefore violated his right to due process. He also alleges that when he was not allowed to board the airplanes, Defendants violated his right to travel, right to be free from unreasonable searches and seizures, right to freely associate, and right to petition the government for redress of grievances. . . .

[The government contended that the Security Directive authorizing the Transportation Security Administration to require passenger identification as a condition of boarding was "sensitive security information" that could not be shown to Gilmore or disclosed to the public. The court accepted this claim, but reviewed the Directive in camera.]

### III. Right to Travel

Gilmore alleges that the identification policy violates his constitutional right to travel because he cannot travel by commercial airlines without presenting identification, which is an impermissible federal condition. We reject Gilmore's right to travel argument because the Constitution does not guarantee the right to travel by any particular form of transportation. . . .

. . . Gilmore does not possess a fundamental right to travel by airplane even though it is the most convenient mode of travel for him. Moreover, the identification policy's "burden" is not unreasonable. The identification policy requires that airline passengers either present identification or be subjected to a more extensive search. The more extensive search is similar to searches that we have determined were reasonable and "consistent with a full recognition of appellant's constitutional right to travel." United States v. Davis, 482 F.2d 893, 912-13 (9th Cir. 1973). . . .

. . . Additionally, Gilmore was free to decline both options and use a different mode of transportation. In sum, by requiring Gilmore to comply with the identification policy, Defendants did not violate his right to travel.

### IV. Fourth Amendment

Gilmore next alleges that both options under the identification policy— presenting identification or undergoing a more intrusive search—are subject to Fourth Amendment limitations and violated his right to be free from unreasonable searches and seizures.

### Request For Identification

Gilmore argues that the request for identification implicates the Fourth Amendment because "the government imposes a severe penalty on citizens who do not comply." Gilmore highlights the fact that he was once arrested at an airport for refusing to show identification and argues that the request for identification "[i]mposes the severe penalty of arrest." Gilmore further argues that the request for identification violates the Fourth Amendment because it constitutes "a warrantless general search for identification" that is unrelated to the goals of detecting weapons or explosives.

The request for identification, however, does not implicate the Fourth Amendment. "[A] request for identification by the police does not, by itself, constitute a Fourth Amendment seizure." INS v. Delgado, 466 U.S. 210, 216 (1984). Rather, "[a]n individual is seized within the meaning of the fourth amendment only if, in view of all of the circumstances surrounding the incident, a reasonable person would have believed that he was not free to leave." United States v. $25,000 U.S. Currency, 853 F.2d 1501, 1504 (9th Cir. 1988) (internal quotation marks omitted). In Delgado, the Supreme Court held that INS agents' questioning of factory workers about their citizenship status did not constitute a Fourth Amendment seizure. In $25,000 U.S. Currency, we held that a DEA agent's request for identification from a person waiting to board a flight was not a Fourth Amendment seizure.

Similarly, an airline personnel's request for Gilmore's identification was not a seizure within the meaning of the Fourth Amendment. Gilmore's experiences at the Oakland and San Francisco airports provide the best rebuttal to his argument that the requests for identification imposed a risk of arrest and were therefore seizures. Gilmore twice tried to board a plane without presenting identification, and twice left the airport when he was unsuccessful. He was not threatened with arrest or some other form of punishment; rather he simply was told that unless he complied with the policy, he would not be permitted to board the plane. There was no penalty for noncompliance.

### Request To Search

[The Court rejected the Fourth Amendment challenge to the selectee search option, relying on the balancing analysis of United States v. Davis, 482 F.2d 893 (9th Cir. 1973), noted *supra* p. 210.]

### Conclusion

In sum, we conclude that Defendants did not violate Gilmore's constitutional rights by adopting and implementing the airline identification policy. Therefore, his claims fail on the merits and we deny his petition for review. . . .

# Watch Lists Maintained by Federal Agencies

from Peter M. Shane, *The Bureaucratic Due Process of Government Watch Lists*,
75 Geo. Wash. L. Rev. (forthcoming 2007)

| Dept. | Agency | List | Purposes | Further Background |
|---|---|---|---|---|
| State | Bureau of Consular Affairs | Consular Lookout & Support System | Vetting foreign nationals seeking visas | Receives information from TIPOFF |
| | Bureau of Intelligence and Research | TIPOFF | Tracking known and suspected international terrorists | Created in 1987, transferred to NCTC in 2003, which plans to create new Terrorist Identities Datamart Identities watch list |
| Homeland Security | U.S. Customs and Border Protection | Interagency Border Inspection System | Primary database for border management and Customs law enforcement functions | Part of Treasury Enforcement Communications System (TECS) |
| | Transportation Security Agency | No-Fly List | Identify threats to civil aviation | |
| | | Automatic Selectee List | Selecting passengers for additional screening | |
| | U.S. Immigration and Customs Enforcement | National Automated Immigration Lookout System | Biographical and case date for aliens who may be inadmissible to US | Created originally by INS, now absorbed into DHS systems in 2005; also housed in the TECS |
| | | Automated Biometric Identification System | Tracking aliens entering US illegally or suspected of crimes | Created by INS, transferred to DHS |
| Justice | U.S Marshals Service | Warrant Information Network | Tracking persons with existing federal warrants | Does not perform any independent watch list function regarding terrorism |
| | FBI | Violent Gang and Terrorist Organization File | Tracking individuals associated with gangs, terrorist organizations | Created in 1995 as a component of the National Crime Information Center |
| | | Integrated Automated Fingerprint ID System | National fingerprint and criminal history database | |
| | U.S. National Central Bureau of Interpol | Interpol Terrorism Watch List | Assistance for global police operations | Created in 2002; contains about 100 names also in other watch lists |
| Defense | Air Force Office of Special Investigations | Top 10 Fugitive List | Retrieving Air Force fugitives | Performs no independent terrorist watch list function |

## NOTES AND QUESTIONS

### a. Identification Requirements

1. ***Identification for Screening Purposes and the Fourth Amendment.***
"Effective checking of names against watch lists . . . requires that every person carry an accurate and secure form of identification." Daniel J. Steinbock, *Designating the Dangerous: From Blacklists to Watch Lists*, 30 Seattle L. Rev. 65, 113 (2006). Watch-listing is thus linked closely to the asserted need for more secure identification and to more frequent identification stops or checkpoints. *Id.*

Identification is mandatory for boarding flights. As *Gilmore* suggests, the Fourth Amendment poses no barrier to suspicionless government requests for identification at check-in or the security checkpoint, provided that a reasonable requested person would feel free to terminate the encounter. Daniel J. Steinbock, *National Identity Cards: Fourth and Fifth Amendment Issues*, 56 Fla. L. Rev. 697, 711-714 (2004). Furthermore, the *MacWade* analysis suggests that "regulatory" (administrative) demands for identification at airport, transit system, and many building checkpoints would pass Fourth Amendment muster as well. *Id.* at 725-743. How would you apply that analysis to mandatory identification at the entrance to a federal building? What about a random demand for "your papers, please" made by police in a public street?

Of course, good identification serves not just a governmental interest, but also an individual interest in avoiding wrong matching. *See* Paul Rosenzweig & Jeff Jonas, *Correcting False Positives: Redress and the Watch List Conundrum*, 17 Legal Mem. 10-11 (Heritage Found. June 17, 2005), *available at* http://www.heritage.org/Research/HomelandDefense/lm17.cfm. For this reason in part, but more importantly as a personal convenience, most persons voluntarily provide identification. That is, we voluntarily show our government-issued identification — usually a driver's license — to cash checks, to register for classes, and to obtain other privileges. Such voluntary disclosure presents no Fourth Amendment concern. Why not?

2. ***A National Identity Card or Other Identifier?*** Some have argued that after 9/11, we need a national identity card system. *See* Alan Dershowitz, *Why Fear National ID Cards?*, N.Y. Times, Oct. 13, 2001, at A23. *See generally* Steinbock, *Designating the Dangerous, supra,* at 113 n.272 (citing proponents). An effective system "necessitates mandatory participation, both in the sense of having an identity within the system and in presenting identification when required." Steinbock, *National Identity Cards, supra,* at 708.

A mandatory national identifier requirement would pose at least three kinds of legal issues. First, there may be a Fourth Amendment question if identification is demanded randomly in some places, such as public streets, as suggested above. "[O]ne of the primary reasons that governments created passports and identity cards was to restrict movement, alter patterns of migration, and control the movements of poor people and others viewed as undesirable." Daniel J. Solove, *A Taxonomy of Privacy*, 154 U. Pa. L. Rev. 477, 514 n.183 (2006).

Second, the "main point of identity checking is to make a connection between the identified individual and collection of data." Steinbock, *National Identity Cards*, *supra*, at 699. A national identifier "would likely be but one component of a large and complex nationwide identity system, the core of which could be a database of personal information on the U.S. population." Computer Science and Telecommunications Board, National Research Council, *IDs—Not That Easy: Questions About Nationwide Identity Systems* 7 (Stephen T. Kent & Lynette I. Millet eds., 2002). The legality of a national identifier system thus turns in part on the legality of the associated database or watch list. *See infra* pp. 200-208.

Third, identity checking can also generate data that can be used to track movements and purchases (e.g., "subject was identified at 11:06 a.m. on June 20, 2006, at Constitution Ave. entrance to Department of Justice"). The use of such data in a computer database raises some of the same privacy concerns created by government access to and use of third-party records. See Chapter 6. By providing identification on demand, does a person waive her privacy interest in the data? *See* Steinbock, *National Identity Cards, supra*, at 748-752 (no, because identification is different from providing telephone numbers or banking information). Even if a single identification encounter does not offend privacy, does its aggregation into a database do so?

3. ***The Real ID Act—A Step in the Direction of a National ID Card?*** In 2005, Congress enacted the "Real ID" Act. Emergency Supplemental Appropriations Act for Defense, the Global War on Terror, and Tsunami Relief, Pub. L. No. 109-13, §202, 119 Stat. 231, 311 (codified at 49 U.S.C.A. §30301 note (West Supp. 2006)). The Real ID Act forbids any federal agency, three years after the Act's enactment, from accepting for any official purpose a state-issued driver's license or identification card unless it meets certain requirements. The identification must include name, address, date of birth, gender, a digital photo, signature, anti-tampering security features, and "[a] common machine-readable technology, with defined minimum data elements." In addition, the state must insist on and verify certain identifying information and evidence of lawful status to issue such an identification. Finally, each state must "provide electronic access to all other States to information contained in the motor vehicle database of the States," which must include, at a minimum, "all data fields printed on drivers' licenses and identification cards issued by the State." *Id.* How is the "Real ID" different from a national identity card? Which poses the larger privacy concern, the Real ID or the database the Act requires? In Whalen v. Roe, 429 U.S. 589 (1977), noted *supra* p. 207, the Supreme Court found reasonable a mandatory prescription reporting system tied to a centralized database, but only because the system limited access to the database and criminalized unauthorized disclosures. What protections, if any, are necessary to make the motor vehicle database contemplated by the Real ID Act reasonable?

## b. Watch Lists and Other Identification-Related Databases

1. *Blacklists and Watch Lists.* Watch lists are automated databases used to identify individuals or entities for consequences (such as denial of entry or boarding) based solely on their inclusion ("listing") in the database. *See* Government Accounting Office, *Terrorist Watch Lists Should Be Consolidated to Promote Better Integration and Sharing* (GAO-03-322) 3, Apr. 15, 2003; Steinbock, *Designating the Dangerous, supra* p. 222, at 66. Their use did not start with the counterterrorist efforts of the 1990s and later. The infamous "blacklists" of the McCarthy Era — listing "known" communists and their "fellow travelers" — are a disturbing antecedent. Professor Steinbock summarizes the blacklists and the loyalty screening programs with which they were associated as follows:

> Little or no effort was made to identify particular workers whose presence would actually pose some realistic threat to national security. Because Communist Party membership or "sympathetic association" with "subversive organizations," even long in the past, were deemed to be adequate proxies for dangerousness, large numbers of people were labeled disloyal or security threats who factually were not. In practice these programs often amounted, instead, to widespread punishment for the exercise of rights of belief, speech, and association. More broadly, they were also about public shaming and enforcing ideological conformity. [*Id.* at 77.]

Some procedural protections were eventually required by the courts or by Congress to protect victims of blacklisting and loyalty screening programs. Remarkably, "even [these] are wholly absent from twenty-first century listing. The result [today], in all likelihood, is a glut of both false positives and false negatives. . . ." *Id.* at 99. See *infra* p. 225.

2. *Generating Watch Lists.* Although the process obviously varies with the watch list, potential terrorists are "nominated" for what is now supposed to be a consolidated "Terrorist Screening Database" by various contributing governmental agencies through the National Counterterrorism Center (NCTC) and the Terrorist Watch and Warning Unit (TWWU) of the FBI, often based on intelligence. Nominee names are then forwarded to the Terrorist Screening Center (TSC), the agency established in 2003 for consolidating the 12 original watch lists. *See generally* William J. Krouse & Bart Elias, *Terrorist Watchlist Checks and Air Passenger Pre-screening* (Cong. Res. Serv. RL33645), Sept. 6, 2006. The NCTC codes each name to specify how the individual is associated with international terrorism. *See* Steinbock, *Designating the Dangerous, supra,* at 81. The standards applied are not public, although some anecdotal evidence suggests that they are at least partly subjective, can rest on indirect and possibly innocent connections to suspected terrorists as well as informant information of doubtful reliability, and err on the side of inclusion. *Id.* at 82.

3. *Mission Creep?* Watch lists are already used to control visa eligibility, entry, and departure, to screen airline passengers, to screen employees for sensitive jobs, and to trigger surveillance. *See id.* at 88-89. "Mission creep" — using lists for more and more purposes, including ordinary criminal and regulatory purposes, such as denial of firearms purchases — is a continuing risk. The Japanese-American internment experience suggests a more frightening mission — preventive detention in a perceived emergency. Indeed, the Japanese-Americans who were detained in World War II were selected from a "custodial detention list" prepared by the FBI. *Id.* at 89. See also *supra* pp. 206-207, Note 5. The FBI also prepared lists for use under the Emergency Detention Act of 1950, Pub. L. No. 81-831, 64 Stat. 1019. See *infra* pp. 303-304. By 1966, the FBI's "Security Index" had grown to 26,000 names. Steinbock, *Designating the Dangerous, supra* p. 222, at 89. Does the reasonableness of a watch list turn in part on some statutory control of the purposes for which it may be used? *See* Whalen v. Roe, 429 U.S. 589 (1977), *supra* p. 207; Solove, *supra* p. 223, at 520-522.

4. *False Positives and Protected Interests.* When an innocent person is erroneously included on a watch list or has the same name as someone on the list, the listing generates a "false positive." With approximately 8 percent of all air travelers being stopped each day and an estimated 70 million secondary screening searches being conducted annually, even a small rate of false positives will snare many innocent travelers. *See* Rosenzweig & Jonas, *supra* p. 222, at 2 n.3.

Does a person have a right to due process in the no-fly decision, or, more plausibly, in the making or correction of the no-fly list? To establish a claim to due process, a person must first show that the challenged government action deprives her of life or a constitutionally protected liberty or property interest. *See* American Manufacturers Mutual Insurance Co. v. Sullivan, 526 U.S. 40, 59 (1999). The Supreme Court has held that something more than a mere reputational injury or "stigma" from the government action is required to make out a liberty interest. It requires "stigma-plus," the "plus" being some tangible burden such as loss of employment or of the opportunity to purchase alcohol. *See* Wisconsin v. Constantineau, 400 U.S. 433 (1971); Paul v. Davis, 424 U.S. 693 (1976). Does a person who is singled out for further screening or barred from boarding by his identification on a no-fly list meet the requirement? The court in Green v. Transportation Security Administration, 351 F. Supp. 2d 1119 (W.D. Wash. 2005), held no.

> As Plaintiffs point out, there can be little doubt that association with a government terrorist watch-list "might seriously damage [Plaintiffs'] standing and associations in [their] community," Vanelli [v. Reynolds Sch. Dist. No. 7, 667 F.2d 773, 777 n.5 (9th Cir. 1982)], and Defendants have not argued otherwise.
>
> However, Plaintiffs fail to satisfy the "plus" prong of the stigma-plus doctrine. . . .
>
> Plaintiffs, in the present matter, argue that their status has been altered because they are no longer able to travel like other airline passengers because of their alleged association with the

No-Fly List. While Plaintiffs have a right to travel throughout the United States "uninhibited by statutes, rules, and regulations which unreasonably burden or restrict movement," Saenz v. Roe, 526 U.S. 489, 499 (1999), it is also true that "burdens on a single mode of transportation do not implicate the right to interstate travel." Miller v. Reed, 176 F.3d 1202, 1205 [(9th Cir. 1999)]. Thus, Plaintiffs do not have a right to travel without any impediments whatsoever. Indeed, Plaintiffs do not allege that they have suffered impediments different than the general traveling public.

Plaintiffs also argue that their status has been altered because they have been publicly associated with the No-Fly List in full view of co-workers and the general traveling public. However, "injury to reputation alone is insufficient to establish a deprivation of a liberty interest protected by the Constitution." Ulrich [v. City and County of San Francisco, 308 F.3d 968, 982 (9th Cir. 2002)]. Plaintiffs have not alleged any tangible harm to their personal or professional lives that is attributable to their association with the No-Fly List, and which would rise to the level of a Constitutional deprivation of a liberty right. Furthermore, Plaintiffs have not alleged any injury to a property interest as a result of the disclosure of allegedly stigmatizing statements. Plaintiffs have not plead[ed] any tangible harm that satisfies the "plus" prong. Therefore, Plaintiffs have failed to state a stigma-plus Fifth Amendment claim. [*Id.* at 1129-1130.]

Do you agree? If you are denied boarding on a transcontinental flight by your misidentification on a no-fly list, have you suffered any tangible burden? Suppose you have to get to the other coast as quickly as possible to see a dying relative. Is the court confusing the right to travel with the burden constituting a "plus factor"? *See* Shane, *supra* p. 221 ("court's analysis seems flatly wrong"); Justin Florence, Note, *Making the No Fly List: A Due Process Model for Terrorist Watchlists,* 115 Yale L.J. 2148, 2161 (2006) (asserting that the right to travel by plane is a liberty interest).

5. ***Process Due in Watch List Making or Correction.*** If, notwithstanding the *Green* decision, you think a watch-listed traveler has a constitutionally protected liberty interest, what process is due her? *See* Matthews v. Eldridge, 424 U.S. 319 (1976) (which is discussed so often in national security cases, see *infra* pp. 364, 611 n.3, that we do not describe it further here.)

Critics of watch lists have suggested several procedural fixes for false positives and misidentification. A "front-end" fix is to institute more careful vetting procedures for placing a name on the list and tighter, more transparent standards. *See* Shane, *supra* p. 221, at 19-26. Professor Steinbock, however, raises the question whether the cost of such additional procedure and/or higher evidentiary standards for watch-listing may be too high for effective prevention of terrorist entry. Given the magnitude of the risk, shouldn't doubts be resolved in favor of inclusion? *See* Steinbock, *Designating the Dangerous, supra* p. 222, at 107-108.

Another fix is "back-end": providing some procedure for the victim of misidentification or other false positive to clear his name from the list. *See* Rosenzweig & Jonas, *supra* p. 222 (suggesting administrative procedures for deciding passenger complaints, with a right of appeal to federal court, as well as "wrong matching" procedures for full attribution of list entries and for a wrongly matched person to supply additional information to correct an error); Shane, *supra*, at 31; Florence, *supra*, at 2166-2178 (suggesting that passengers be given "advance notice" of watch-listing on inquiry and a right to an administrative hearing about the alleged listing error through a government-appointed and security-cleared "compensatory counsel"). Professor Steinbock suggests a different and simpler kind of back-end protection: restricting the consequences of being listed just to selection for further investigation, thus "putting the *watch* back in watch lists." Steinbock, *Designating the Dangerous*, *supra*, at 110.

Congress has conditioned implementation of "Secure Flight," a new watch list-based passenger screening program, on development of procedures for protecting privacy and providing redress for victims of false positives. Department of Homeland Security Appropriations Act of 2006, Pub. L. No. 109-90, Tit. XLIX, §518(a)-(e), 119 Stat. 2064. *See generally* Office of Inspector General, Dept. of Justice, *Review of the Terrorist Screening Center's Efforts to Support the Secure Flight Program* (Aug. 2005), *available at* http://www.usdoj.gov/oig/reports/FBI/a0534/index.htm.

### c.   Transparency of Screening Law

*Secret Screening Law?* Congress has generally authorized screening of airline passengers and baggage. *See* 49 U.S.C. §§114(h)(1)-(3), 44901 (2000 & Supp. III 2003). In *Gilmore*, the government asserted that it had implemented that authority by an unpublished Security Directive requiring Gilmore to show a government-issued identification but refused to show the directive to him or make it public. Instead, the government showed the directive to the court in camera. The court rejected Gilmore's due process challenge to this secret law by finding that he had "actual notice" of the identification rule because airline personnel told him it was the rule and because he "saw a sign in front of United Airlines' ticketing counter that read 'PASSENGERS MUST PRESENT IDENTIFICATION UPON INITIAL CHECK-IN.'" 435 F.3d at 1136. It also found that the Security Directive embodied clear standards applicable to all passengers, which prevented its arbitrary application.

Why should such a rule be secret? What are the dangers, if any, of keeping it secret from the public? Should both identification and watch-list law (though not necessarily every particular of watch-list standards) be made with public participation and transparency—if not by Congress as part of the normal legislative process, then by agencies with public participation in notice-and-comment rulemaking?

## C.  PROFILING

### GUIDANCE REGARDING THE USE OF RACE BY FEDERAL LAW ENFORCEMENT AGENCIES [*DOJ GUIDANCE*]

U.S. Department of Justice, Civil Rights Division (June 2003)

#### The Constitutional Framework

"[T]he Constitution prohibits selective enforcement of the law based on considerations such as race." *Whren v. United States*, 517 U.S. 806, 813 (1996). Thus, for example, the decision of federal prosecutors "whether to prosecute may not be based on 'an unjustifiable standard such as race, religion, or other arbitrary classification.'"[4] *United States v. Armstrong*, 517 U.S. 456, 464 (1996) (quoting *Oyler v. Boles*, 368 U.S. 448, 456 (1962)). The same is true of Federal law enforcement officers. Federal courts repeatedly have held that any general policy of "utiliz[ing] impermissible racial classifications in determining whom to stop, detain, and search" would violate the Equal Protection Clause. *Chavez v. Illinois State Police*, 251 F.3d 612, 635 (7th Cir. 2001). As the Sixth Circuit has explained, "[i]f law enforcement adopts a policy, employs a practice, or in a given situation takes steps to initiate an investigation of a citizen based solely upon that citizen's race, without more, then a violation of the Equal Protection Clause has occurred." *United States v. Avery*, 137 F.3d 343, 355 (6th Cir. 1997). "A person cannot become the target of a police investigation solely on the basis of skin color. Such selective law enforcement is forbidden." *Id.* at 354.

As the Supreme Court has held, this constitutional prohibition against selective enforcement of the law based on race "draw[s] on 'ordinary equal protection standards.'" *Armstrong*, 517 U.S. at 465 (quoting *Wayte v. United States*, 470 U.S. 598, 608 (1985)). Thus, impermissible selective enforcement based on race occurs when the challenged policy has "'a discriminatory effect and . . . was motivated by a discriminatory purpose.'" *Id.* (quoting *Wayte*, 470 U.S. at 608). Put simply, "to the extent that race is used as a proxy" for criminality, "a racial stereotype requiring strict scrutiny is in operation." *Cf. Bush v. Vera*, 517 U.S. [952 (1996),] at 968 (plurality).

#### I. Guidance for Federal Officials Engaged in Law Enforcement Activities

#### A. Routine or Spontaneous Activities in Domestic Law Enforcement

**In making routine or spontaneous law enforcement decisions, such as ordinary traffic stops, Federal law enforcement officers may not use race or ethnicity to any degree, except that officers may rely on race and ethnicity in a specific suspect description. This prohibition**

---

4. These same principles do not necessarily apply to classifications based on alienage. For example, Congress, in the exercise of its broad powers over immigration, has enacted a number of provisions that apply only to aliens, and enforcement of such provisions properly entails consideration of a person's alien status.

**applies even where the use of race or ethnicity might otherwise be lawful.** . . .

Some have argued that overall discrepancies in certain crime rates among racial groups could justify using race as a factor in general traffic enforcement activities and would produce a greater number of arrests for non-traffic offenses (e.g., narcotics trafficking). We emphatically reject this view. The President has made clear his concern that racial profiling is morally wrong and inconsistent with our core values and principles of fairness and justice. Even if there were overall statistical evidence of differential rates of commission of certain offenses among particular races, the affirmative use of such generalized notions by federal law enforcement officers in routine, spontaneous law enforcement activities is tantamount to stereotyping. It casts a pall of suspicion over every member of certain racial and ethnic groups without regard to the specific circumstances of a particular investigation or crime, and it offends the dignity of the individual improperly targeted. Whatever the motivation, it is patently unacceptable and thus prohibited under this guidance for Federal law enforcement officers to act on the belief that race or ethnicity signals a higher risk of criminality. This is the core of "racial profiling" and it must not occur.

The situation is different when an officer has specific information, based on trustworthy sources, to "be on the lookout" for specific individuals identified at least in part by race or ethnicity. In such circumstances, the officer is not acting based on a generalized assumption about persons of different races; rather, the officer is helping locate specific individuals previously identified as involved in crime. . . .

## B. Law Enforcement Activities Related to Specific Investigations

**In conducting activities in connection with a specific investigation, Federal law enforcement officers may consider race and ethnicity only to the extent that there is trustworthy information, relevant to the locality or time frame, that links persons of a particular race or ethnicity to an identified criminal incident, scheme, or organization. This standard applies even where the use of race or ethnicity might otherwise be lawful.**

As noted above, there are circumstances in which law enforcement activities relating to particular identified criminal incidents, schemes or enterprises may involve consideration of personal identifying characteristics of potential suspects, including age, sex, ethnicity or race. Common sense dictates that when a victim describes the assailant as being of a particular race, authorities may properly limit their search for suspects to persons of that race. Similarly, in conducting an ongoing investigation into a specific criminal organization whose membership has been identified as being overwhelmingly of one ethnicity, law enforcement should not be expected to disregard such facts in pursuing investigative leads into the organization's activities.

Reliance upon generalized stereotypes is absolutely forbidden. Rather, use of race or ethnicity is permitted only when the officer is pursuing a specific lead concerning the identifying characteristics of persons involved in an *identified* criminal activity. The rationale underlying this concept carefully limits its reach. . . .

## II. Guidance for Federal Officials Engaged in Law Enforcement Activities Involving Threats to National Security or the Integrity of the Nation's Borders

**In investigating or preventing threats to national security or other catastrophic events (including the performance of duties related to air transportation security), or in enforcing laws protecting the integrity of the Nation's borders, Federal law enforcement officers may not consider race or ethnicity except to the extent permitted by the Constitution and laws of the United States.**

. . . "It is 'obvious and unarguable' that no governmental interest is more compelling than the security of the Nation." *Haig v. Agee*, 453 U.S. 280, 307 (1981) (quoting *Aptheker v. Secretary of State*, 378 U.S. 500, 509 (1964)).

The Constitution prohibits consideration of race or ethnicity in law enforcement decisions in all but the most exceptional instances. Given the incalculably high stakes involved in such investigations, however, federal law enforcement officers who are protecting national security or preventing catastrophic events (as well as airport security screeners) may consider race, ethnicity, and other relevant factors to the extent permitted by our laws and the Constitution. Similarly, because enforcement of the laws protecting the Nation's borders may necessarily involve a consideration of a person's alienage in certain circumstances, the use of race or ethnicity in such circumstances is properly governed by existing statutory and constitutional standards. *See, e.g., United States v. Brignoni-Ponce*, 422 U.S. 873, 886-87 (1975). This policy will honor the rule of law and promote vigorous protection of our national security.

As the Supreme Court has stated, all racial classifications by a governmental actor are subject to the "strictest judicial scrutiny." *Adarand Constructors, Inc. v. Pena*, 515 U.S. 200, 224-25 (1995). The application of strict scrutiny is of necessity a fact-intensive process. *Id.* at 236. Thus, the legality of particular, race-sensitive actions taken by Federal law enforcement officials in the context of national security and border integrity will depend to a large extent on the circumstances at hand. In absolutely no event, however, may Federal officials assert a national security or border integrity rationale as a mere pretext for invidious discrimination. Indeed, the very purpose of the strict scrutiny test is to "smoke out" illegitimate use of race, *Adarand*, 515 U.S. at 226 (quoting *Richmond v. J.A. Croson Co.*, 488 U.S. 469, 493 (1989)), and law enforcement strategies not actually premised on *bona fide* national security or border integrity interests therefore will not stand. . . .

*Example:* The FBI receives reliable information that persons affiliated with a foreign ethnic insurgent group intend to use suicide bombers to assassinate that country's president and his entire entourage during an official visit to the United States. Federal law enforcement may appropriately focus investigative attention on identifying members of that ethnic insurgent group who may be present and active in the United States and who, based on other available information, might conceivably be involved in planning some such attack during the state visit.

*Example:* U.S. intelligence sources report that terrorists from a particular ethnic group are planning to use commercial jetliners as weapons by hijacking them at an airport in California during the next week. Before allowing men of that ethnic group to board commercial airplanes in California airports during the next week, Transportation Security Administration personnel, and other federal and state authorities, may subject them to heightened scrutiny.

Because terrorist organizations might aim to engage in unexpected acts of catastrophic violence in any available part of the country (indeed, in multiple places simultaneously, if possible), there can be no expectation that the information must be specific to a particular locale or even to a particular identified scheme.

Of course, as in the example below, reliance solely upon generalized stereotypes is forbidden.

*Example:* At the security entrance to a Federal courthouse, a man who appears to be of a particular ethnicity properly submits his briefcase for x-ray screening and passes through the metal detector. The inspection of the briefcase reveals nothing amiss, the man does not activate the metal detector, and there is nothing suspicious about his activities or appearance. In the absence of any threat warning, the federal security screener may not order the man to undergo a further inspection solely because he appears to be of a particular ethnicity.

## NOTES AND QUESTIONS

1. *Fourth Amendment Analysis: Mere "Relevance"?* The Fourth Amendment "special needs" (administrative search) analysis of racial profiling in security screening asks whether the race or ethnic factor in the profile is "clearly . . . relevant to the law enforcement need to be served." *See* United States v. Martinez-Fuerte, 428 U.S. 543, 564 n.17 (1976). That it may constitute purposeful discrimination does not make the search or seizure unreasonable under the Fourth Amendment. Whren v. United States, 517 U.S. 806, 813 (1996). Thus, the Supreme Court has upheld secondary screening of persons at a border checkpoint made largely on the basis of apparent Mexican ancestry. United States v. Martinez-Fuerte, 428 U.S. 543, 563 (1976). The Court relied in part on its earlier decision in United States v. Brignoni-Ponce, 422 U.S. 873 (1975), where it noted that "[t]he likelihood that any given person of Mexican ancestry is an alien is high enough to make Mexican appearance a relevant factor. . . ." *Id.* at 886-887. In *Brignoni-Ponce*, however, the Court held that apparent Mexican ancestry could not *alone* create the reasonable suspicion required for a roving-patrol stop. *Id.* The *Martinez-Fuerte* Court also noted that "[d]ifferent

considerations would arise if . . . reliance were put on apparent Mexican ancestry at a checkpoint operated near the Canadian border." 428 U.S. at 564.

2. ***Equal Protection Analysis: Stricter Scrutiny and Necessity?*** Given the foregoing analysis, the constitutional basis for challenges to racial profiling is the Equal Protection Clause rather than the Fourth Amendment. *Id.* The former subjects purposeful race discrimination to a probing strict scrutiny form of judicial review. At least as early as 1944, the Supreme Court declared that "all legal restrictions which curtail the rights of a single racial group are immediately suspect" and therefore subject to the "most rigid scrutiny." Korematsu v. United States, 323 U.S. 214, 216 (1944), noted *infra* p. 391. The scrutiny actually applied by the Court, however, did not overturn the government's program to intern 120,000 Japanese-Americans following the attack on Pearl Harbor. Although the Court acknowledged that "[n]othing short of apprehension by the proper military authorities of the gravest imminent danger to the public safety can constitutionally justify" racially based confinement or exclusion, the Court deferred to the judgment of such military authorities and found that exclusion of Japanese-Americans from threatened areas "has a definite and close relationship to the prevention of crime and sabotage." 323 U.S. at 218.

Since *Korematsu*, the Court has refined equal protection analysis. When government action is challenged on equal protection grounds, "the issue is whether the government can identify a sufficiently important objective for its discrimination. What is a sufficient justification depends entirely on the type of discrimination." Erwin Chemerinsky, *Constitutional Law* 669-670 (3d ed. 2006). When the government discriminates on the basis of race, national origin, or, for some actions, alienage, its justification will be subject to "strict scrutiny" and upheld only "if it is proven necessary to achieve a compelling government purpose." *Id.* at 529 (footnote omitted). Other classifications may require only "rational basis" review, under which the law need only be rationally related to a legitimate government purpose, or "intermediate scrutiny." *Id.*

The *DOJ Guidance* apparently authorizes airport screening selection based on "ethnic selection" and alienage. Can you formulate an argument for the legality of such profiling under modern equal protection analysis? Can you justify the selection of the two brothers at Logan Airport for further screening on September 11? Could you justify that selection if it had been based only on the gate agent's suspicion of their "Middle Eastern" appearance? See *supra* p. 209. If your answers to these questions differ, can you see how the difference helps explain the final example given in the *DOJ Guidance*? Assuming that the computerized CAPPS air passenger screening system described in Part B profiles using both racial or ethnic characteristics *and* behavioral factors, would it satisfy the equal protection analysis? *See* Sharon L. Davies, *Profiling Terror*, 1 Ohio St. J. Crim. L. 45, 60-61 (2003) (noting that courts have required profiles to be based on more than racial or ethnic elements alone to withstand equal protection challenge).

3. **The Easy Case: Individualized Description.** The *DOJ Guidance* reflects general agreement that law enforcement agents may use race or an ethnic characteristic when it is part of the description of a particular suspect. *See* Davies, *supra*, at 54 & n.38 (citing decisions). "To act on the basis of a particular suspect's description as belonging to a given race is certainly to take race into account," Professor Ellmann explains, "but it is not to take *generalizations* about race into account." Stephen J. Ellmann, *Racial Profiling and Terrorism*, 46 N.Y.L. Sch. L. Rev. 675, 676 n.4 (2003). But the *DOJ Guidance*'s approval of profiling in some counterterrorism investigations may suggest how easily "the identification of a group of offenders by race tends to transform the physical description into a negative predictor and then into a mark of social status." Albert W. Alshuler, *Racial Profiling and the Constitution*, 2002 U. Chi. Legal F. 163, 265-266. Is being on the lookout for "Middle Eastern men" in their early twenties merely taking into account the fact that the original al Qaeda membership seems overwhelmingly to have included such men, or is it also a prediction that they are more likely to commit future terrorist acts than are Swedish grandmothers? And does the "look-out" profile stigmatize all Middle Eastern men?

4. **What Is "Race"?** In Saint Francis College v. Al Khazraji, 481 U.S. 604 (1987), the Supreme Court's earlier construction of 42 U.S.C. §1981 as forbidding all "racial" discrimination in the making of private and public contracts, *see* Runyon v. McCrary, 427 U.S. 160, 168 (1976), was extended to protect a citizen of the United States born in Iraq. The Court conceded that "a variety of ethnic groups, including Arabs, are now considered to be within the Caucasian race." *Id.* at 610. When §1981 became law in the nineteenth century, however, it was clear that "Congress intended to protect from discrimination identifiable classes of persons who are subjected to intentional discrimination solely because of their ancestry or ethnic characteristics." *Id.* at 613. Although *Saint Francis College* did not involve a constitutional claim, the Court's discussion of the concept of "race" is instructive, particularly because it relates to a statute that was enacted at about the same time as the adoption of the Fourteenth Amendment. Does "race" for equal protection purposes now encompass the "ethnic" characteristics mentioned by the *DOJ Guidance* in its examples of permissible counterterrorist discrimination?

5. **Applying Racial and Ethnic Classifications in Screening.** The *DOJ Guidance* is (calculatingly?) vague about the classification for profiling in counterterrorism cases; it refers simply to "ethnic groups." But "defenses of racial and ethnic profiling depend upon the ability of law enforcement officers to do it — to distinguish racial and ethnic groups from one another." Alschuler, *supra*, at 224. Doesn't the legality depend partly on how the "ethnic group" is described and what discretion that leaves checkpoint screeners or law enforcement officers?

One prominent conservative journalist has characterized *MacWade*'s random container inspection as an "obvious absurdity" and an "appalling waste of effort." Charles Krauthammer, *Give Grandma a Pass: Politically Correct Screening Won't Catch Jihadists*, Wash. Post, July 29, 2005, at A23. Since "jihadist terrorism has been carried out . . . by young Muslim men,"

he reasons, we should give "special scrutiny to young Islamic men." *Id.
See also* Milton Hirsch & David O. Markus, *Fourth Amendment Forum*,
27 Champion 34 (March 2003) ("since 9/11 attacks were perpetrated by
"Arab Muslim men," there "exists a demonstrable, verifiable nexus
between" such characteristics when used to select travelers for high-level
screening "and conduct that American officials have a public duty to
interdict").

Could you explain to subway security officers how to identify "Islamic
men" or "Muslim men"? What about persons "of Middle Eastern appearance"? *See* John Derbyshire, *At First Glance: Racial Profiling, Burning
Hotter*, Natl. Rev. Online, Oct. 5, 2001, *at* http://www.nationalreview.
com/derbyshire/derbyshire100501.shtml. What about "Arab-looking"? *See*
Stuart Taylor Jr., *D.C. Dispatch: Politically Incorrect Profiling: A Matter of
Life or Death*, Natl. J., Nov. 6, 2001. *See* Davies, *supra* p. 232, at 51 n.29
("It is a common misconception that all Arabs are racially identifiable by
their darker skin. In fact, Arabs may have white skin and blue eyes, olive or
dark skin and brown eyes, and hair in a variety of textures.").

One danger of vague classifications is that they leave the screeners too
much discretion, creating space for the screeners' conscious or unconscious
application of the their own classifications. The same may be true even of
profiling that includes behavioral factors, such as unusual passenger ner-
vousness or sweating or failure to make eye contact, in a profile together
with racial or ethnic factors. After 9/11, for example, the American Civil
Liberties Union reported that 67 percent of airline passengers subjected to
personal searches on entering the United States were people of color; black
and Latino Americans were four to nine times as likely as white Americans
to be x-rayed after being frisked or patted down; and black women were
more likely than any other U.S. citizens to be strip-searched. *See* R.
Spencer McDonald, Note, *Rational Profiling in America's Airports*, 17
BYU J. Pub. L. 113, 136 (2002) (citing American Civil Liberties Union
press release, Mar. 26, 2002). Is this kind of profiling justified under the
*DOJ Guidance*? If not, does it simply illustrate the need for closer supervision of the TSA security personnel or an inherent risk of racial or ethnic
screening profiles? Does the container inspection program in *MacWade*
avoid this danger?

6. *Empirical Nexus?* In United States v. Lopez, 328 F. Supp. 1077 (E.D.N.Y.
1971), the court initially upheld the use of a passenger profile in the pre-
1973 selective anti-skyjacking screening program and follow-up frisk. But
when discovery revealed that the airline had unilaterally eliminated one
element of the FAA-established profile and added "an ethnic element for
which there was no experimental basis, thus raising serious equal protection problems," the court suppressed the evidence from the frisk. *Id.* at
1101. "The approved [FAA] system survives constitutional scrutiny only
by its careful adherence to absolute objectivity and neutrality," the court
explained. "When elements of discretion and prejudice are interjected it
becomes constitutionally impermissible." *Id.*

Does this mean that any ethnic, religious, or national origin element of
a screening profile must have at least "an experimental basis" finding a

nexus between the element and the probability of a terrorist act? If so, does "Islamic men" or "Middle Eastern appearance" have such a nexus to terrorism in light of the fact that the 19 9/11 hijackers were apparently Muslims from the Middle East? *Compare* Thomas W. Joo, *Presumed Disloyal: Executive Power, Judicial Deference, and the Construction of Race Before and After September 11*, 34 Colum. Hum. Rts. L. Rev. 1, 41-42 (2002) (the "categories of 'Arab' and 'Muslim' are simply too broad"; "even if a man of Arab descent is relatively more likely to be a terrorist than a non-Arab, the likelihood that any given Arab man is a terrorist remains negligible"), *with* Ellmann, *supra* p. 233, at 698 ("People sharing all of Al Qaeda's background characteristics still seem more likely to be our adversaries than most of the people who share none of them — even though the great majority of people sharing all of these characteristics have no connection to terrorism whatsoever.").

Professor Alshuler suggests that "when a police practice systematically subjects the members of a race to searches and seizures at a higher rate than their rate of offending, a court should hold the practice unconstitutional unless it is appropriately tailored to advance a significant state interest." Alshuler, *supra* p. 233, at 223. Would profiling of "Middle Eastern men" satisfy this test? *See id.* at 265 ("special screening of people of Arab ethnicity at airports . . . should be impermissible"). How would we measure their "rate of offending"?

Professor Harcourt suggests that the success and justification of profiling depends on more than "identifying a stable group trait that correlates with higher offending." It also depends on "how responsive different groups are to the targeted policing and whether they engage in forms of substitution" by recruiting from nonprofiled groups or substituting different types of attacks that are more immune to profiling. *See* Bernard E. Harcourt, *Muslim Profiles Post 9/11: Is Racial Profiling an Effective Counterterrorist Measure and Does It Violate the Right to Be Free From Discrimination?*, Univ. of Chicago Law School, John M. Olin Law & Economics Working Paper No. 288 (2d Series), at 9-10 (March 2006), *available at* http://ssrn.com/abstract=893905.

> The central question [is] whether racial profiling of young Muslim men in the New York subways will likely detect a terrorist attack or instead lead to the recruitment of non-profiled persons and the substitution of other acts for subway attacks — in other words, whether profiling will detect or increase terrorist attacks. The answer to this question is pure speculation. In the end, then, there is no need or reason to engage in a rights trade-off by racial profiling as part of any subway screening. [*Id.* at 27-28.]

That is, without empirical evidence that racial profiling works, there is no need for it. Do you agree?

7. ***Costs and Benefits of Profiling.*** Proponents of counterterrorism profiling have argued that the cost to a victim of frequent false positives "is minuscule," while the cost to society of a false negative (letting a terrorist

through) could be enormous, and have concluded that racial profiling is justified by a cost-benefit analysis. *See* LaFave, *supra* p. 210 (so summarizing arguments of some proponents); Ellmann, *supra* p. 233, at 698-707. Does this analysis consider all the costs? What about the risk that al Qaeda will respond to the profile by selecting terrorists who do not look "Islamic" or "Middle Eastern" (if you can figure out what this means), including Americans like Jose Padilla (see *infra* p. 380), thus increasing the rate of false negatives? What about the cost of creating hostility and anxiety in the U.S. community of persons from the Middle East, thus discouraging its members from voluntary cooperation? *See generally* Ellmann, *supra*, at 705-707; Davies, *supra* p. 232, at 73-74. How would you inventory and balance all the benefits and costs of racial profiling in security screening and counterterrorism investigations?

8. ***National Origin Profiling of Post-9/11 Detainees and Interviewees.*** Following the September 11 attacks, law enforcement and immigration authorities detained more than 1,100 persons as part of their investigation. *See generally* Chapter 10. On November 27, 2001, the Bush administration provided a breakdown of some 600 persons still being held. According to the report, 548 detained on immigration charges hailed from 47 countries, including more than 200 from Pakistan, and smaller numbers from Egypt, Turkey, Yemen, and India. Dan Eggen, *About 600 Still Held in Connection with Attacks, Ashcroft Says*, Wash. Post, Nov. 28, 2001, at A15. An earlier newspaper investigation of 235 detainees found that the largest numbers were from Saudi Arabia, Egypt, and Pakistan, and that almost all of them were men in their twenties and thirties. Amy Goldstein, *A Deliberate Strategy of Disruption*, Wash. Post, Nov. 4, 2001, at A1. When these figures were reported, none of the detainees had been charged with any terrorist activity. Subsequently, the Administration conducted "voluntary" interviews targeting 5,000 mostly Middle Eastern aliens holding tourist, student, or business visas. *See* Allan Lengel, *Arab Men in Detroit to Be Asked to See U.S. Attorney*, Wash. Post, Nov. 27, 2001, at A5.

Did these actions constitute constitutionally suspect profiling? *Compare* Davies, *supra*, at 80-81, *and* Ellmann, *supra*, at 726-727 (because mass interviews were based on stigmatizing racial generalization that promoted public stereotypes, created great resentment in the targeted community, and probably generated few, if any leads, they were "unjustifiable discrimination"), *with* Samuel R. Gross & Debra Livingston, *Racial Profiling Under Attack*, 102 Colum. L. Rev. 1413, 1436 (2002) (concluding that the interview campaign was profiling to the extent that the FBI assumed that Middle Eastern men were more likely than others to commit acts of terror, but was not to the extent that FBI agents were "pursuing case-specific information about the September 11 attacks, albeit in dragnet fashion"). Does it matter? Professors Gross and Livingston suggest that how the FBI selects its interviewees matters less than how they carry out the interviews. *Id.* at 1436-1437 ("Are the interviews conducted respectfully . . . ?"). Do you agree?

A court has refused to dismiss equal protection and First Amendment (freedom of religion) challenges to the pretextual post-9/11 detentions of Muslim men arrested for nonterrorist criminal offenses. *See* Elmaghraby

v. Ashcroft, 2005 WL 2375202, at *28-29 (E.D.N.Y. 2005). But the same court dismissed claims by Muslim men that they had been selectively detained for immigration violations and identified as persons of "high interest" (to the 9/11 investigation) based on their national origin. The court explained:

> As a tool fashioned by the executive branch to ferret out information to prevent additional terrorist attacks, this approach may have been crude, but it was not so irrational or outrageous as to warrant judicial intrusion into an area in which courts have little experience and less expertise. See [Reno v. American-Arab Anti-Discrimination Committee, 525 U.S. 471, 490-491 (1999); Mathews v. Diaz, 426 U.S. 67, 81-82 (1976)] ("The reasons that preclude judicial review of political questions also dictate a narrow standard of review of decisions made by the Congress or the President in the area of immigration and naturalization."); see also Zadvydas [v. Davis, 533 U.S. 678, 696 (2001)] (stating that "terrorism" might warrant "special arguments" for "heightened deference to the judgments of the political branches with respect to matters of national security"). I note, however, that the extraordinary circumstances of September 11 are by no means a prerequisite to the deference owed the political branches in this area. Such national emergencies are not cause to relax the rights guaranteed in our Constitution. Yet regarding immigration matters such as this, the Constitution assigns to the political branches all but the most minimal authority in making the delicate balancing judgments that attend all difficult constitutional questions; "nothing in the structure of our Government or the text of our Constitution would warrant judicial review by standards which would require [courts] to equate [their] political judgment with that of" the executive or the Congress. Harisiades [v. Shaughnessy, 342 U.S. 580, 590 (1952)]. [Turkmen v. Ashcroft, 2006 WL 1662663, at *43 (E.D.N.Y. 2006).]

Can you articulate the difference between the claims in the two cases? *See DOJ Guidance, supra* p. 228 n.4. (Of course, profiling in terrorism investigations did not begin with the 9/11 attacks. *See* William C. Banks, *The "L.A. Eight" and Investigation of Terrorist Threats in the United States*, 31 Colum. Hum. Rts. L. Rev. 481 (2000).)

9. *Behavioral Profiling—An Improvement?* Criticism of identity-based profiling has prompted some to call for behavior-based profiling instead. Thus, the United States-based International Association of Chiefs of Police has promoted a checklist of "Suicide Bomber Preincident Indicators" that include:

> wearing loose or bulky clothing in summer;
> pacing back and forth;
> fidgeting with something beneath one's clothing;
> failure to make eye contact;
> being in a drug-induced state;

strange hair coloring;

wearing too much cologne;

the smell of scented water (for ritual purification);

mumbling (prayer);

sudden changes in behavior—for example, a fanatically religious person visiting sex clubs (or the reverse);

a fresh shave;

wearing talcum powder; and

being overly protective of one's baggage. [*See* Center for Human Rights and Global Justice, *Irreversible Consequences: Racial Profiling and Lethal Force in the "War on Terror"* 7, 29 (May 2006).]

Consider whether using this checklist or behavioral profile would have helped identify any of the 9/11 hijackers at the gate. Is it just behavioral, or does the checklist implicitly target religious or ethnic groups? The explanation of "fresh shave," for example, is that "a male with a fresh shave and lighter skin on his lower face may be a religious Muslim zealot who has just shaved his beard so as not to attract attention and to blend in better with other people in the vicinity." *Id.* at 29. Do the religion-oriented factors heighten the danger that all the factors will be read in non-neutral ways to target Muslims? *Id.* at 29-30 (so arguing).

10. ***Profiling and National Identity Cards.*** One commentator has argued that "[a] national identity card could facilitate greater civil liberties for groups targeted by racial and ethnic stereotyping and profiling. Membership would alleviate harassment because presentation of the card would result in an immediate check of one's identity with the national computerized data system." John Dwight Ingram, *Racial and Ethnic Profiling*, 29 T. Marshall L. Rev. 55, 83 (2003). Do you agree?

# CHAPTER 8

# ORGANIZING AND COORDINATING COUNTERTERRORISM INVESTIGATIONS

The constitutional and statutory framework established by the judiciary and by Congress in the Foreign Intelligence Surveillance Act (FISA) and other statutes tells only part of the legal story of counterterrorism investigations. Particularly for investigative techniques other than electronic surveillance and physical searches, the discretion in the executive branch to initiate and then conduct investigations is largely governed by executive branch rules, not by statute, and the courts have had little to say to provide guidance for these investigations.

Nevertheless, important legal determinations must be made — such as whether to approve an agent's request to follow the daily routine of a potential suspected terrorist, whether sufficient suspicion exists to launch even a preliminary investigation, and when informants may be placed inside a targeted organization. Once intelligence is collected — for example, by the FBI — under what circumstances should the information be shared, and with what other agencies?

In this chapter we first probe the executive branch organization for counterterrorism investigations. An executive order supplies an overarching template for the conduct of intelligence operations by executive agencies, including the FBI and CIA. Then we explore the rules that govern how the FBI — the principal federal intelligence agency for countering terrorism — conducts its terrorism detection activities. Post-September 11 evaluations by the Department of Justice have produced important revisions to longstanding FBI Guidelines governing a range of investigative activities.

Second, it is now common knowledge that some of the September 11 hijackers lived openly in the United States when their names or names of their close associates were on intelligence "watch lists." The watch-list information was not shared in a timely fashion with the FBI or state and local law enforcement agencies, which might have been able to detect the hijackers' plot before it was implemented. Because intelligence about would-be terrorists might be obtained by the FBI, CIA, NSA, or agencies inside the Defense Department, or by a state or local law enforcement agency, the challenges of sharing intelligence are staggering. Moreover, the FBI, long embedded in its role as the federal government's law enforcement agency, has struggled to reshape its mission to incorporate a vigorous counterterrorism component. How should information classified by one agency be shared with another agency? How should a federal agency share with a state or local agency? How can information be shared in a secure way without jeopardizing the privacy interests of those identified in the intelligence? Here we survey the efforts toward information sharing that have been made in the counterterrorism area, and we examine briefly the state of reforms at the FBI.

## A. EXECUTIVE AUTHORITY FOR COUNTERTERRORISM INVESTIGATIONS

The Attorney General is expressly vested with "primary investigative authority for all Federal crimes of terrorism." 18 U.S.C. §2332b(f) (2000 & Supp. IV 2004). The FBI, in contrast, has scant statutory authority to carry out its mission. Lacking a legislative charter, the FBI operates on the basis of the Attorney General's authority found in 28 U.S.C. §533 (2000 & Supp. IV 2004) to appoint officials:

(1) to detect and prosecute crimes against the United States;
(2) to assist in the protection of the person of the President; and . . .
(4) to conduct such other investigations regarding official matters under the control of the Department of Justice and the Department of State as may be directed by the Attorney General.

The FBI also draws investigative authority from statutes such as FISA.

All FBI investigations are conducted according to guidelines promulgated by the Attorney General and a 1981 executive order that directs the activities of all the agencies that make up the intelligence community. The *Attorney General's Guidelines on General Crimes, Racketeering Enterprise and Domestic Security/Terrorism Investigations*, Mar. 7, 1983, 32 Crim. L. Rep. 3087, "provide guidance for all investigations by the FBI of crimes and crime-related activities." *Id.*, Preamble. On May 30, 2002, the FBI issued three new sets of guidelines for investigations that significantly revise the 1983 *Domestic Security Guidelines*. They are the *Attorney General's Guidelines on General Crimes, Racketeering Enterprise and Terrorism Enterprise Investigations* (hereinafter *Domestic Security Guidelines*); the *Attorney General's Guidelines on the Use of Confidential Informants*; and the *Attorney General's Guidelines on Federal Bureau of Investigation Undercover Operations, available at* http://www.usdoj. gov/olp/index.html#agguide. The 1983 *Attorney General Foreign Counterintelligence (FCI) Guidelines* were replaced on November 5, 2003, by the *Attorney General's Guidelines for FBI National Security Investigations and Foreign Intelligence Collection (NSI Guidelines)*. These guidelines support FBI collection of foreign intelligence and national security information. Excerpts of the current guidelines, as revised, along with a portion of Executive Order No. 12,333, are set out below.

## EXECUTIVE ORDER NO. 12,333

46 Fed. Reg. 59,941 (Dec. 4, 1981)

Timely and accurate information about the activities, capabilities, plans, and intentions of foreign powers, organizations, and persons and their agents, is essential to the national security of the United States. All reasonable and lawful means must be used to ensure that the United States will receive the best intelligence available. For that purpose, by virtue of the authority vested in me by the Constitution and statutes of the United States of America, including the National Security Act of 1947, as amended, and as President of the United States of America, in order to provide for the effective conduct of United States intelligence activities and the protection of constitutional rights, it is hereby ordered as follows: . . .

1.8 The Central Intelligence Agency. All duties and responsibilities of the CIA shall be related to the intelligence functions set out below. As authorized by this Order; the National Security Act of 1947, as amended; the CIA Act of 1949, as amended; appropriate directives or other applicable law, the CIA shall:

(a) Collect, produce and disseminate foreign intelligence and counterintelligence, including information not otherwise obtainable. The collection of foreign intelligence or counterintelligence within the United States shall be coordinated with the FBI as required by procedures agreed upon by the [DCI] and the Attorney General; . . .

(c) Conduct counterintelligence activities outside the United States and, without assuming or performing any internal security functions, conduct counterintelligence activities within the United States in coordination with the FBI as required by procedures agreed upon by the [DCI] and the Attorney General; . . .

2.3 Collection of Information. Agencies within the Intelligence Community are authorized to collect, retain or disseminate information concerning United States persons only in accordance with procedures established by the head of the agency concerned and approved by the Attorney General. . . . Those procedures shall permit collection, retention and dissemination of the following types of information: . . .

(b) Information constituting foreign intelligence or counter-intelligence, including such information concerning corporations or other commercial organizations. Collection within the United States of foreign intelligence not otherwise obtainable shall be undertaken by the FBI or, when significant foreign intelligence is sought, by other authorized agencies of the Intelligence Community, provided that no foreign intelligence collection by such agencies may be undertaken for the purpose of acquiring information concerning the domestic activities of United States persons; . . .

2.5 Attorney General Approval. The Attorney General hereby is delegated the power to approve the use for intelligence purposes, within the United States or against a United States person abroad, of any technique for which a warrant would be required if undertaken for law enforcement purposes, provided that such techniques shall not be undertaken unless the Attorney General has determined in each case that there is probable cause to believe that the technique is directed against a foreign power or an agent of a foreign power. Electronic surveillance, as defined in the Foreign Intelligence Surveillance Act of 1978, shall be conducted in accordance with that Act, as well as this Order.

2.6 Assistance to Law Enforcement Authorities. Agencies within the Intelligence Community are authorized to: . . .

(b) Unless otherwise precluded by law or this Order, participate in law enforcement activities to investigate or prevent clandestine intelligence activities by foreign powers, or international terrorist or narcotics activities; . . .

2.8 Consistency With Other Laws. Nothing in this Order shall be construed to authorize any activity in violation of the Constitution or statutes of the United States.

2.9 Undisclosed Participation in Organizations Within the United States. No one acting on behalf of agencies within the Intelligence Community may join or otherwise participate in any organization in the United States on behalf of any agency within the Intelligence Community without disclosing his intelligence affiliation to appropriate officials of the organization, except in accordance with procedures established by the head of the agency concerned and approved by the Attorney General. Such participation shall be authorized only if it is essential to achieving lawful purposes as determined by the agency head or designee. No such participation may be undertaken for the purpose of influencing the activity of the organization or its members except in cases where:

(a) The participation is undertaken on behalf of the FBI in the course of a lawful investigation; or

(b) The organization concerned is composed primarily of individuals who are not United States persons and is reasonably believed to be acting on behalf of a foreign power. . . .

## ATTORNEY GENERAL'S GUIDELINES ON GENERAL CRIMES, RACKETEERING ENTERPRISE AND TERRORISM ENTERPRISE INVESTIGATIONS [DOMESTIC SECURITY GUIDELINES]

Department of Justice, May 2002
http://www.usdoj.gov/olp/index.html#agguide

### I. General Principles

Preliminary inquiries and investigations governed by these Guidelines are conducted for the purpose of preventing, detecting, or prosecuting violations of federal law. The FBI shall fully utilize the methods authorized by these Guidelines to maximize the realization of these objectives. . . .

All preliminary inquiries shall be conducted pursuant to the General Crime Guidelines. There is no separate provision for preliminary inquiries under the Criminal Intelligence guidelines. . . . A preliminary inquiry shall be promptly terminated when it becomes apparent that a full investigation is not warranted. If, on the basis of information discovered in the course of a preliminary inquiry an investigation is warranted, it may be conducted as a general crimes investigation, or a criminal intelligence investigation, or both. All such investigations, however, shall be based on a reasonable factual predicate and shall have a valid law enforcement purpose.

In its efforts to anticipate or prevent crime, the FBI must at times initiate investigations in advance of criminal conduct. It is important that such investigations not be based solely on activities protected by the First Amendment or on the lawful exercise of any other rights secured by the Constitution or laws of the United States. When, however, statements advocate criminal activity or indicate an apparent intent to engage in crime, particularly crimes of violence, an investigation under these Guidelines may be warranted unless it is apparent, from the circumstances or the context in which the statements are made, that there is no prospect of harm. . . .

## II. General Crimes Investigations . . .

### B. Preliminary Inquiries

(1) On some occasions the FBI may receive information or an allegation not warranting a full investigation—because there is not yet a "reasonable indication" of criminal activities—but whose responsible handling requires some further scrutiny beyond the prompt and extremely limited checking out of initial leads. In such circumstances, though the factual predicate for an investigation has not been met, the FBI may initiate an "inquiry" involving some measured review, contact, or observation activities in response to the allegation or information indicating the possibility of criminal activity.

This authority to conduct inquiries short of a full investigation allows the government to respond in a measured way to ambiguous or incomplete information and to do so with as little intrusion as the needs of the situation permit. This is especially important . . . when an allegation or information is received from a source of unknown reliability. . . .

(2) The FBI supervisor authorizing an inquiry shall assure that the allegation or other information which warranted the inquiry has been recorded in writing. . . .

(4) The choice of investigative techniques in an inquiry is a matter of judgment, which should take account of: (i) the objectives of the inquiry and available investigative resources, (ii) the intrusiveness of a technique, considering such factors as the effect on the privacy of individuals and potential damage to reputation, (iii) the seriousness of the possible crime, and (iv) the strength of the information indicating its existence or future commission. Where the conduct of an inquiry presents a choice between the use of more or less intrusive methods, the FBI should consider whether the information could be obtained in a timely and effective way by the less intrusive means. The FBI should not hesitate to use any lawful techniques consistent with these Guidelines in an inquiry, even if intrusive, where the intrusiveness is warranted in light of the seriousness of

the possible crime or the strength of the information indicating its existence or future commission. This point is to be particularly observed in inquiries relating to possible terrorist activities.

(5) All lawful investigative techniques may be used in an inquiry except:

(a) Mail openings; and

(b) Nonconsensual electronic surveillance or any other investigative technique covered by chapter 119 of title 18, United States Code (18 U.S.C. 2510-2522).

(6) The following investigative techniques may be used in an inquiry without any prior authorization from a supervisory agent:

(a) Examination of FBI indices and files;

(b) Examination of records available to the public and other public sources of information;

(c) Examination of available federal, state and local government records;

(d) Interview of the complainant, previously established informants and confidential sources;

(e) Interview of the potential subject;

(f) Interview of persons who would readily be able to corroborate or deny the truth of the allegation, except this does not include pretext interviews or interviews of a potential subject's employer or co-workers unless the interviewee was the complainant;

(g) Physical or photographic surveillance of any person.

The use of any other lawful investigative technique in an inquiry shall require prior approval by a supervisory agent, except in exigent circumstances. . . .

(7) Where a preliminary inquiry fails to disclose sufficient information to justify an investigation, the FBI shall terminate the inquiry and make a record of the closing. . . .

### III. Terrorism Enterprise Investigations

This section authorizes the FBI to conduct criminal intelligence investigations of certain enterprises who seek either to obtain monetary or commercial gains or profits through racketeering activities or to further political or social goals through activities that involve criminal violence. These investigations differ from general crimes investigations, authorized by Section II, in several important respects. As a general rule, an investigation of a completed criminal act is normally confined to determining who committed that act and with securing evidence to establish the elements of the particular offense. It is, in this respect, self-defining. An intelligence investigation of an ongoing criminal enterprise must determine the size and composition of the group involved, its geographic dimensions, its past acts and intended criminal goals, and its capacity for harm. While a standard criminal investigation terminates with the decision to prosecute or not to prosecute, the investigation of a criminal enterprise does not necessarily end, even though one or more of the participants may have been prosecuted. . . .

## B. Domestic Security/Terrorism Investigations . . .

### 1. General authority

a. A terrorism enterprise investigation may be initiated when facts or circumstances reasonably indicate that two or more persons are engaged in an enterprise for the purpose of: (i) furthering political or social goals wholly or in part through activities that involve force or violence and a violation of federal criminal law, (ii) engaging in terrorism as defined in 18 U.S.C. 2331(1) or (5) that involves a violation of federal criminal law, or (iii) committing any offense described in 18 U.S.C. 2332b(g)(5)(B). A terrorism enterprise investigation may also be initiated when facts or circumstances reasonably indicate that two or more persons are engaged in a pattern of racketeering activity as defined in the RICO statute, 18 U.S.C. 1961(5), that involves an offense or offenses described in 18 U.S.C. 2332b(g)(5)(B). The standard of "reasonable indication" is identical to that governing the initiation of a general crimes investigation under Part II. In determining whether an investigation should be conducted, the FBI shall consider all of the circumstances including: (i) the magnitude of the threatened harm; (ii) the likelihood it will occur; (iii) the immediacy of the threat; and (iv) any danger to privacy or free expression posed by an investigation. . . .

c. Mere speculation that force or violence might occur during the course of an otherwise peaceable demonstration is not sufficient grounds for initiation of an investigation under this Subpart, but where facts or circumstances reasonably indicate that a group or enterprise has engaged or aims to engage in activities involving force or violence or other criminal conduct described in paragraph (1)(a) in a demonstration, an investigation may be initiated in conformity with the standards of that paragraph. . . . This does not limit the collection of information about public demonstrations by enterprises that are under active investigation pursuant to paragraph (1)(a) above. . . .

### 4. Authorization and renewal

a. A terrorism enterprise investigation may be authorized by the Special Agent in Charge, with notification to FBIHQ, upon a written recommendation setting forth the facts or circumstances reasonably indicating the existence of an enterprise as described in paragraph (1)(a). . . .

## IV. Investigative Techniques

A. When conducting investigations under these guidelines the FBI may use any lawful investigative technique. . . . When the conduct of an investigation presents a choice between the use of more or less intrusive methods, the FBI should consider whether the information could be obtained in a timely and effective way by less intrusive means. . . .

B. All requirements for use of a technique set by statute, Department regulations and policies, and Attorney General Guidelines must be complied with. The investigative techniques listed below are subject to the noted restrictions:

   1. Informants and confidential sources must be used in compliance with the Attorney General's Guidelines on the Use of Informants and Confidential Sources;

2. Undercover operations must be conducted in compliance with the Attorney General's Guidelines of FBI Undercover Operations; . . .

4. Nonconsensual electronic surveillance must be conducted pursuant to the warrant procedures and requirements of Title III. . . .

7. Consensual electronic monitoring must be authorized pursuant to Department policy. . . .

8. Searches and seizures must be conducted under the authority of a valid warrant unless the search or seizure comes within a judicially recognized exception to the warrant requirements. . . .

### V. Dissemination of Information

A. The FBI may disseminate information during investigations conducted pursuant to these guidelines to another Federal agency or to a State or local criminal justice agency when such information:

1. falls within the investigative or protective jurisdiction or litigative responsibility of the agency;

2. may assist in preventing a crime or the use of violence or any other conduct dangerous to human life; . . .

3. is required to be disseminated by statute, interagency agreement approved by the Attorney General, or Presidential Directive;

and to other persons and agencies as permitted by Sections 552 and 552a of Title V, U.S.C. . . .

### VI. Counterterrorism Activities and Other Authorizations

### A. Counterterrorism Activities

#### 1. Information systems

The FBI is authorized to operate and participate in identification, tracking, and information systems for the purpose of identifying and locating terrorists. . . . Systems within the scope of this paragraph may draw on and retain pertinent information from any source permitted by law, including information derived from past or ongoing investigative activities; other information collected or provided by governmental entities, such as foreign intelligence information and lookout list information; publicly available information, whether obtained directly or through services or resources (whether nonprofit or commercial) that compile or analyze such information; and information voluntarily provided by private entities. Any such system operated by the FBI shall be reviewed periodically for compliance with all applicable statutory provisions, Department regulations and policies, and Attorney General Guidelines.

#### 2. Visiting public places and events

For the purpose of detecting or preventing terrorist activities, the FBI is authorized to visit any place and attend any event that is open to the public, on the same terms and conditions as members of the public generally.

No information obtained from such visits shall be retained unless it relates to potential criminal or terrorist activity.

### VII. Reservation . . .

C. These guidelines are set forth solely for the purpose of internal Department of Justice guidance. They are not intended to, do not, and may not be relied upon to create any rights, substantive or procedural, enforceable at law by any party in any manner, civil or criminal, nor do they place any limitation on otherwise lawful investigative and litigative prerogatives of the Department of Justice.

## ATTORNEY GENERAL'S GUIDELINES FOR FBI NATIONAL SECURITY INVESTIGATIONS AND FOREIGN INTELLIGENCE COLLECTION (U)[1] [*NSI GUIDELINES*]

Department of Justice, Oct. 2003
http://www.usdoj.gov/olp/nsiguidelines.pdf

### Introduction (U)

. . . These Guidelines generally authorize investigation by the FBI of threats to the national security of the United States; investigative assistance by the FBI to state, local, and foreign governments in relation to matters affecting the national security; the collection of foreign intelligence by the FBI; the production of strategic analysis by the FBI; and the retention and dissemination of information resulting from the foregoing activities. This includes guidance for the activities of the FBI pursuant to Executive Order 12333, "United States Intelligence Activities" (Dec. 4, 1981). (U)

The general objective of these Guidelines is the full utilization of all authorities and investigative techniques, consistent with the Constitution and laws of the United States, so as to protect the United States and its people from terrorism and other threats to the national security. (U) . . .

The activities of the FBI under these Guidelines are part of the overall response of the United States to threats to the national security, which includes cooperative efforts and sharing of information with other agencies, including other entities in the Intelligence Community and the Department of Homeland Security. The overriding priority in these efforts is preventing, preempting, and disrupting terrorist threats to the United States. In some cases, this priority will dictate the provision of information to other agencies even where doing so may affect criminal prosecutions or ongoing law enforcement or intelligence operations. To the greatest extent possible that is consistent with this overriding priority, the FBI shall also act in a manner to protect other significant interests, including the protection of intelligence and sensitive law enforcement sources and methods, other classified information, and sensitive operational and prosecutorial information. (U)

---

[1. The guidelines are partly classified. "(U)" means that a particular provision is unclassified.]

## A. National Security Investigations (U)

. . . The investigations authorized by these Guidelines serve to protect the national security by providing the basis for, and informing decisions concerning, a variety of measures to deal with threats to the national security. These measures may include, for example, recruitment of double agents and other assets; excluding or removing persons involved in terrorism or espionage from the United States; freezing assets of organizations that engage in or support terrorism; securing targets of terrorism or espionage; providing threat information and warnings to other federal agencies and officials, state and local governments, and private entities; diplomatic or military actions; and actions by other intelligence agencies to counter international terrorism or other national security threats. In addition, the matters identified by these Guidelines as threats to the national security, including international terrorism and espionage, almost invariably involve possible violations of criminal statutes. Detecting, solving, and preventing these crimes — and in many cases, arresting and prosecuting the perpetrators — are crucial objectives of national security investigations under these Guidelines. Thus, these investigations are usually both "counterintelligence" investigations and "criminal" investigations. (U)

The authority to conduct national security investigations under these Guidelines does not supplant or limit the authority to carry out activities under other Attorney General guidelines or pursuant to other lawful authorities of the FBI. (U) . . .

Part II of these Guidelines authorizes three levels of investigative activity in national security investigations: (1) threat assessments, (2) preliminary investigations, and (3) full investigations: (U)

> (1) *Threat assessments.* To carry out its central mission of preventing the commission of terrorist acts against the United States and its people, the FBI must proactively draw on available sources of information to identify terrorist threats and activities. It cannot be content to wait for leads to come in through the actions of others, but rather must be vigilant in detecting terrorist activities to the full extent permitted by law, with an eye towards early intervention and prevention of acts of terrorism before they occur. (U)
>
> Part II.A of these Guidelines accordingly authorizes the proactive collection of information concerning threats to the national security, including information on individuals, groups, and organizations of possible investigative interest, and information on possible targets of international terrorist activities or other national security threats (such as infrastructure and computer systems vulnerabilities). (U) . . .
>
> In addition to allowing proactive information collection for national security purposes, the authority to conduct threat assessments may be used in cases in which information or an allegation concerning possible terrorist (or other national security-threatening) activity by an individual, group, or organization is received, and the matter can be checked out promptly through the relatively non-intrusive techniques authorized in threat assessments. This can avoid the need to open a

formal preliminary or full investigation, if the threat assessment indicates that further investigation is not warranted. In this function, threat assessments under these Guidelines are comparable to the checking of initial leads in ordinary criminal investigations. (U)

(2) *Preliminary investigations.* . . . Preliminary investigations may relate to individuals, groups, organizations, and possible criminal violations, as specified in Part II.B. . . .

(3) *Full investigations.* Like preliminary investigations, full investigations may relate to individuals, groups, or organizations and possible criminal violations, as specified in Part II.B. . . .

Part II.E. of these Guidelines sets out conditions and approval requirements for extraterritorial activities. As provided in Part II.E, these activities require a request from or approval of the Director of Central Intelligence or a designee. This requirement ensures that extraterritorial activities under these Guidelines are properly coordinated with other agencies in the Intelligence Community, so that their authorities and capabilities are also brought to bear as appropriate to protect the national security, consistent with Executive Order 12333 or a successor order.

The FBI may also provide assistance to state and local governments, and to foreign law enforcement, intelligence, and security agencies, in investigations relating to threats to the national security. Part III of these Guidelines specifies standards and procedures for the provision of such assistance. (U) . . .

## B. Foreign Intelligence Collection (U)

The FBI's functions pursuant to Executive Order 12333 §§1.6, 1.14, 2.3, and 2.4 include engaging in foreign intelligence collection and providing operational support for other components of the U.S. Intelligence Community. This role is frequently critical in collecting foreign intelligence within the United States because the authorized domestic activities of other intelligence agencies are more constrained than those of the FBI under applicable statutory law and Executive Order 12333. (U) . . .

## I. General Authorities and Principles (U)

### A. General Authorities (U)

1. The FBI is authorized to conduct investigations to obtain information concerning or to protect against threats to the national security, including investigations of crimes involved in or related to threats to the national security, as provided in Parts II and V of these Guidelines. Threats to the national security are:

a. International terrorism.
b. Espionage and other intelligence activities, sabotage, or assassination, conducted by, for, or on behalf of foreign powers, organizations, or persons.
c. Foreign computer intrusions.
d. Other matters as determined by the Attorney General, consistent with Executive Order 12333 or a successor order. (U) . . .

## B. Use of Authorities and Method (U) . . .

### 2. Choice of methods (U)

The conduct of investigations and other activities authorized by these Guidelines may present choices between the use of information collection methods that are more or less intrusive, considering such factors as the effect on the privacy of individuals, and potential damage to reputation. As Executive Order 12333 §2.4 provides, "the latest intrusive collection techniques feasible" are to be used in such situations. It is recognized, however, that the choice of techniques is a matter of judgment. The FBI shall not hesitate to use any lawful techniques consistent with these Guidelines, even if intrusive, where the degree of intrusiveness is warranted in light of the seriousness of a threat to the national security or the strength of the information indicating its existence. This point is to be particularly observed in investigations relating to terrorism. (U)

### 3. Respect for legal rights (U)

These Guidelines do not authorize investigating or maintaining information on United States persons solely for the purpose of monitoring activities protected by the First Amendment or the lawful exercise of other rights secured by the Constitution or laws of the United States. Rather, all activities under these Guidelines must have a valid purpose consistent with these Guidelines, and must be carried out in conformity with the Constitution and all applicable statutes, executive orders, Department of Justice regulations and policies, and Attorney General Guidelines. . . .

## C. Determination of United States Person Status (U) . . .

### 3. Determination whether certain groups are substantially composed of United States persons (U)

In determining whether a group or organization in the United States that is affiliated with a foreign-based international organization is substantially composed of United States persons, the relationship between the two shall be considered. If the U.S.-based group or organization operates directly under the control of the international organization and has no independent program or activities in the United States, the membership of the entire international organization shall be considered in determining if it is substantially composed of United States persons. If, however, the U.S.-based group or organization has programs or activities separate from, or in addition to, those directed by the international organization, only its membership in the United States shall be considered in determining whether it is substantially composed of United States persons. (U)

## D. Nature and Application of the Guidelines (U)

### 1. Status as internal guidance (U)

These Guidelines are set forth solely for the purpose of internal Department of Justice guidance. They are not intended to, do not, and may not be relied upon to create any rights, substantive or procedural, enforceable by law by any party in any matter, civil or criminal, nor do they place any limitation on otherwise lawful investigative and litigative prerogatives of the Department of Justice. (U)

### 2. *Departures from the Guidelines (U)*

Departures from these Guidelines must be approved by the Attorney General, the Deputy Attorney General, or an official designated by the Attorney General. If a departure from these Guidelines is necessary without such prior approval because of the immediacy or gravity of a threat to the national security or to the safety of persons or property and the need to take immediate action to protect against such a threat, the Attorney General, the Deputy Attorney General, or an official designated by the Attorney General shall be notified as soon thereafter as practicable. The FBI shall provide timely written notice of departures from these Guidelines to the Office of Intelligence Policy and Review. Notwithstanding this paragraph, all activities in all circumstances must be carried out in a manner consistent with the Constitution and laws of the United States. (U) . . .

## II. National Security Investigations (U) . . .

## B. Common Provisions for Preliminary and Full Investigations (U) . . .

### 3. *Investigations of groups and organizations (U)*

    a. Preliminary and full investigations of groups and organizations should focus on activities related to threats to the national security, not on unrelated First Amendment activities. . . .

## E. Extraterritorial Operations (U)

1. The FBI may conduct investigations abroad, participate with foreign officials in investigations abroad, or otherwise conduct activities outside the United States with the written request or approval of the Director of Central Intelligence and the Attorney General or their designees. . . . The involvement of the Director of Central Intelligence or designee in the authorization of these extraterritorial activities reflects the coordinating and liaison roles of the Director of Central Intelligence and the Central Intelligence Agency in this area in accordance with the National Security Act of 1947 and Executive Order 12333, including §§1.5(e), 1.8(c)-(d), 1.14(b) of that Order, and helps to ensure that the collective resources and capabilities of the broader Intelligence Community will be used in the most effective manner to protect the national security. . . .

## IV. Foreign Intelligence Collection and Assistance to Intelligence Agencies (U)

## A. Foreign Intelligence Collection (U)

1. The FBI may collect foreign intelligence in response to requirements of topical interest published by an entity authorized by the Director of Central Intelligence to establish such requirements, including, but not limited to, the National HUMINT Requirements Tasking Center. When approved by the Attorney General, the Deputy Attorney General, or an official designated by the Attorney General, the FBI may collect other foreign intelligence in response to tasking specifically levied on the FBI by an official of the Intelligence

Community designated by the President. Upon a request by an official of the Intelligence Community designated by the President, the FBI may also collect foreign intelligence to clarify or complete foreign intelligence previously disseminated by the FBI. Copies of such requests shall be provided to the Office of Intelligence Policy and Review. (U)

2. The FBI may also collect foreign intelligence, if consistent with Executive Order 12333 or a successor order, as directed by the Attorney General, the Deputy Attorney General, or an official designated by the Attorney General. (U) . . .

### B. Operational Support (U)

1. When approved by the Attorney General, the Deputy Attorney General, or an official designated by the Attorney General, the FBI may provide operational support to authorized intelligence activities of other entities of the Intelligence Community upon a request made or confirmed in writing by an official of the Intelligence Community designated by the President. The request shall describe the type and duration of support required, the reasons why the FBI is being requested to furnish the assistance, and the techniques that are expected to be utilized, and shall certify that such assistance is necessary to an authorized activity of the requesting entity. (U)

2. The support may include techniques set forth in the approved request and, with the approval of FBI headquarters, any other technique that does not substantially alter the character of the support. The FBI shall promptly notify the Office of Intelligence Policy and Review of the utilization of any such additional techniques. (U)

3. The FBI may recruit new assets to obtain information or services needed to furnish the requested support, subject to the same standards and procedures applicable to other FBI assets. (U) . . .

### VII. Retention and Dissemination Of Information . . .

### B. Information Sharing (U)

Legal rules and Department of Justice policies regarding information sharing and interagency coordination have been significantly modified since the September 11, 2001, terrorist attack by statutory reforms and new Attorney General guidelines. The general principle reflected in current laws and policies is that information should be shared as consistently and fully as possible among agencies with relevant responsibilities to protect the United States and its people from terrorism and other threats to the national security, except as limited by specific constraints on such sharing. Under this general principle, the FBI shall provide information expeditiously to other agencies in the Intelligence Community, so that these agencies can take action in a timely manner to protect the national security in accordance with their lawful functions. (U) . . .

## NOTES AND QUESTIONS

### a.  Executive Order No. 12,333

1. *Investigatory Authorizations Under Executive Order No. 12,333.* The preamble to Executive Order No. 12,333 is directed at intelligence

information about "foreign powers, organizations, and persons and their agents" and its importance to national security. What is the legal significance of the preamble's description of the scope of the order? Preamble language typically sets forth the presumed authority for the prescriptions that follow. Precisely what constitutional or statutory authority empowers the President to promulgate this executive order?

What constitutes a "lawful" FBI investigation within the meaning of Executive Order No. 12,333? What are the likely elements of a probable cause determination under §2.5? How does such a probable cause decision differ from those made pursuant to either FISA or Federal Rule of Criminal Procedure 41? See *supra* pp. 135.

According to the executive order, the most important factor in assessing executive power to conduct national security investigations is the presence or absence of a connection between the target of surveillance and a foreign power. To this extent, the executive order tracks FISA. The 1994 amendments to FISA extended the FISA procedures to applications for a physical search for foreign intelligence information where the target is a foreign power or agent of a foreign power. In Executive Order No. 12,949, 60 Fed. Reg. 8169 (Feb. 9, 1995), President Clinton updated Executive Order No. 12,333 to authorize the Attorney General to approve applications to the Foreign Intelligence Surveillance Court (FISC) for physical searches for foreign intelligence purposes, following the certifications required by FISA. *Id.* §2. Bearing in mind the provisions of FISA, what "technique[s] for which a warrant would be required if undertaken for law enforcement purposes" (§2.5) continue to be governed by Executive Order No. 12,333 and FBI guidelines?

2. ***Executive Order No. 12,333 and the National Security Act of 1947.*** The National Security Act of 1947, Pub. L. No. 80-253, 61 Stat. 495 (codified as amended in scattered sections of 10 & 50 U.S.C.) authorizes the Director of the CIA to collect intelligence "through human sources and by other appropriate means." 50 U.S.C. §403-4a(d)(1). The Act also authorizes the Director to "perform such other functions and duties related to intelligence affecting the national security as the President or the Director of National Intelligence may direct." *Id.* §403-4a(d)(4). The Act provides, however, that the Director "shall have no police, subpoena, or law enforcement powers or internal security functions." *Id.* §403-4a(d)(1). Apart from Executive Order 12,333, what law governs CIA intelligence collection?

Compare §§1.8 and 2.3(b) of Executive Order No. 12,333, *supra*, to the National Security Act of 1947. Does the order adequately respect the statutory mandate that the CIA not engage in "internal security functions"? How may the CIA "conduct counterintelligence activities within the United States in coordination with the FBI" without performing any "internal security functions"?

3. ***Infiltration.*** Is CIA or FBI infiltration of domestic organizations permitted by Executive Order No. 12,333? On the basis of what information will the "agency head or designee" determine that infiltration is "essential to achieving lawful purposes"? If infiltration is authorized outside the limits of the order, what redress would be available to aggrieved persons? *See* Seth

Kreimer, *Watching the Watchers: Surveillance, Transparency, and Political Freedom in the War on Terror,* 7 U. Pa. J. Const. L. 133 (2004).

4. ***Making of Guidelines for Investigation.*** Several sections of Executive Order No. 12,333 provide that procedures for intelligence collection are to be independently established by each agency, subject to approval by the Attorney General. Should the public be able to participate in setting such procedures? Where would they be published?

### b.  Domestic Security Guidelines

1. ***Authority for Guidelines.*** Does the FBI have statutory authority to promulgate the guidelines set out above? In addition to the authority granted by 28 U.S.C. §533, the Attorney General "may from time to time make such provisions as he considers appropriate authorizing the performance by any other officer, employee, or agency of the Department of Justice of any function of the Attorney General." *Id.* §510. Do you think Congress should provide more explicit statutory authority for the FBI to conduct national security investigations? *See* Tom Lininger, *Sects, Lies, and Videotape: The Surveillance and Infiltration of Religious Groups,* 89 Iowa L. Rev. 1201 (2004).

2. ***The Guidelines and FISA.*** What purposes are served by these guidelines that are not met by FISA? Can you see where the prescriptions in FISA end and those of the two sets of guidelines begin?

3. ***Application.*** Compare the coverage of the two sets of guidelines. How can you tell which set applies to a potential investigation?

4. ***Preliminary Investigation.*** Are the standards for beginning a preliminary inquiry in the domestic security setting clear? What purpose is served by the preliminary inquiry? Can you predict when agents might opt for a preliminary inquiry instead of a full investigation? Are the rights of the targets of an inquiry safeguarded adequately by the *Domestic Security Guidelines*?

The Introduction to the 2002 *Domestic Security Guidelines* describes and explains the checking of leads and preliminary inquiries:

> The lowest level of investigative activity is the "prompt and extremely limited checking out of initial leads," which should be undertaken whenever information is received of such a nature that some follow-up as to the possibility of criminal activity is warranted. This limited activity should be conducted with an eye toward promptly determining whether further investigation (either a preliminary inquiry or a full investigation) should be conducted.
>
> The next level of investigative activity, a preliminary inquiry, should be undertaken when there is information or an allegation which indicates the possibility of criminal activity and whose responsible handling requires some further scrutiny beyond checking initial leads. This authority allows FBI agents to respond to information that is ambiguous or incomplete. Even where the available information meets only this threshold, the range of available investigative techniques is broad. . . .

Whether it is appropriate to open a preliminary inquiry immediately, or instead to engage first in a limited checking out of leads, depends on the circumstances presented. If, for example, an agent receives an allegation that an individual or group has advocated the commission of criminal violence, and no other facts are available, an appropriate first step would be checking out of leads to determine whether the individual, group, or members of the audience have the apparent ability or intent to carry out the advocated crime. A similar response would be appropriate on the basis of non-verbal conduct of an ambiguous character — for example, where a report is received that an individual has accumulated explosives that could be used either in a legitimate business or to commit a terrorist act. Where the limited checking out of leads discloses a possibility or reasonable indication of criminal activity, a preliminary inquiry or full investigation may then be initiated. However, if the available information shows at the outset that the threshold standard for a preliminary inquiry or full investigation is satisfied, then the appropriate investigative activity may be initiated immediately, without progressing through more limited investigative stages.

The application of these Guidelines' standards for inquiries merits special attention in cases that involve efforts by individuals or groups to obtain, for no apparent reason, biological, chemical, radiological, or nuclear materials whose use or possession is constrained by such statutes as 18 U.S.C. 175, 229, or 831. For example, FBI agents are not required to possess information relating to an individual's intended criminal use of dangerous biological agents or toxins prior to initiating investigative activity. On the contrary, if an individual or group has attempted to obtain such materials, or has indicated a desire to acquire them, and the reason is not apparent, investigative action, such as conducting a checking out of leads or initiating a preliminary inquiry, may be appropriate to determine whether there is a legitimate purpose for the possession of the materials by the individual or group. Likewise, where individuals or groups engage in efforts to acquire or show an interest in acquiring, without apparent reason, toxic chemicals or their precursors or radiological or nuclear materials, investigative action to determine whether there is a legitimate purpose may be justified.

Upon what authority do FBI agents check leads or conduct preliminary inquiries? Do you see a risk that this authority could be exercised in a way that burdens constitutional liberties?

5. *Full Investigation.* How would you describe the threshold test for initiating a full investigation under the *Domestic Security Guidelines*? The guidelines define "reasonable indication" as: "substantially lower than probable cause. . . . [T]he standard does require specific facts or circumstances indicating a post, current, or impending violation. There must be an objective, factual basis for initiating the investigation; a mere hunch is insufficient."

*Domestic Security Guidelines,* §II.C.1. Does the definition clarify or muddy "reasonable indication"? The 2002 guidelines add that a full investigation "may be conducted to prevent, solve, or prosecute" criminal activity. *Id.* Does the "reasonable indication" standard continue to provide an adequate benchmark for preserving privacy or First Amendment interests?

6. ***Informants.*** Compare the provisions for the use of informants in the executive order with those in the *Domestic Security Guidelines.* While interviews and photographic surveillance in a domestic security investigation do not require prior authorization, the use of an informant to infiltrate a group "in a manner that may influence the exercise of rights protected by the First Amendment" must be approved by FBI headquarters with notice to the Department of Justice. *Domestic Security Guidelines* §IV.B.3. By contrast, during a preliminary "inquiry," informants and infiltrators may be used based on uncorroborated allegations; no reasonable suspicion of an illegal act is required. *Id.* §§I, IIB. What accounts for the differing treatment of the use of informants in these rules? Do the guidelines provide sufficient protection for individual liberties in this respect?

The 2002 guidelines change the "undisclosed participation" strictures, providing instead that any such investigation that could raise "potential constitutional concerns relating to activities of the organization protected by the First Amendment" must comply with the *Attorney General's Guidelines on FBI Undercover Operations* and the *Attorney General's Guidelines Regarding the Use of Informants. Domestic Security Guidelines* §IV.B.3.

An undercover operation uses a government employee whose relationship with the FBI is concealed from third parties in the course of an investigation, *Undercover Operations Guidelines, supra,* §§II.B, C, while a confidential informant is any person who provides useful and credible information. *Confidential Informants Guidelines* §I.B.6. The *Confidential Informants Guidelines* do not mention the First Amendment interests of groups that may be infiltrated by an informant or undercover agent, and the *Undercover Operations Guidelines* simply say that any official empowered to authorize an undercover operation should give "careful consideration" to the "risk of invasion of privacy or interference with privileged or confidential relationships and any potential constitutional concerns or other legal concerns" in deciding whether to approve an application. *Undercover Operations Guidelines* §IV.A.(3). Do you think that these provisions are constitutional?

7. ***Mail Covers and New Techniques.*** The 2002 *Domestic Security Guidelines* removed mail covers from the list of forbidden techniques during preliminary inquiries. §II.B.5. Mail covers consist of viewing and recording information on the outside covers of mail. The Postal Inspector is authorized by regulation to initiate a mail cover at the request of a law enforcement agency. 39 C.F.R. §233.3 (2006). Is this change lawful? The 2002 guidelines also added potentially important and constitutionally controversial new authority for FBI investigations in counterterrorism in reaction to September 11 and the continuing threat of terrorism. Three broad investigative activities are authorized: (1) surfing the Internet to identify Web sites,

bulletin boards, chat rooms, and the like where terrorist or other criminal activities might be detected; (2) attending public events and visiting public places for the purpose of detecting terrorist activity; and (3) using data-mining services to search for terrorists and terrorist activities. *See Domestic Security Guidelines* §§VI.A.1, 2; VI.B. According to DOJ officials, the decision to spell out the authorities in these three areas was based on the fact that the prior guidelines were widely regarded as exclusive: if something was not explicitly permitted, it was viewed as barred. *See New Rules Allow FBI Greater Use of Web, Visits to Public Places in Terrorism Probes*, 70 U.S.L.W. 2779 (June 11, 2002). What are the implications of the DOJ explanation for the scope and meaning of the new guidelines?

Some groups reacted by claiming that the new authorities would permit "fishing expeditions" and would chill protected expression in places like mosques, libraries, and Internet chat rooms, and at public gatherings in support of Palestinian or Islamic causes. *See* Center for Democracy & Technology, *CDT's Analysis of New FBI Guidelines*, May 30, 2002, *available at* http://www.cdt.org/wiretap/020530guidelines.shtml; Adam Liptak, *Changing the Standard: Despite Civil Liberties Fears, FBI Faces No Legal Obstacles on Domestic Spying*, N.Y. Times, May 31, 2002, at A1.

Section VI.B of the 2002 *Domestic Security Guidelines* authorizes the FBI to carry out "general topical research" online, defined as

> concerning subject areas that are relevant for the purpose of facilitation or supporting the discharge of investigative responsibilities . . . [but] does not include online searches for information by individuals' names or other individual identifiers, except where such searches are incidental to topical research, such as searching to locate writings on a topic by searching under the names of authors who write on the topic, or searching by the name of a party to a case in conducting legal research.

But if a private citizen can search the Internet using someone's name, why can't the FBI?

8. ***Pretext Interviews?*** In advance of the 2004 Republican and Democratic party conventions in New York and Boston, the FBI interviewed dozens of members of antiwar groups. Although the Attorney General declared publicly that the interviews were based on specific threat information about planned violent disruptions, a subsequently disclosed and heavily redacted FBI field office memorandum characterized the effort as "pretext interviews to gain general information concerning possible criminal activity at the upcoming political conventions and presidential election." *See* Dan Eggen, *FBI Memos Show Agents Conducting "Pretext Interviews,"* Wash. Post, May 18, 2005, at A4. If the interviews were "pretext interviews," do they suggest that the FBI was treating political dissent as terrorism, as some critics asserted? *Id.* An internal Justice Department review concluded that the interviews were conducted for legitimate law enforcement purposes, not to inhibit the exercise of First Amendment rights. Inspector General, U.S. Dept. of Justice, *A Review of the FBI's Investigative Activities at the 2004 Democratic and Republican National*

*Political Conventions*, Apr. 27, 2006. On what authority would these "pretext interviews" have been conducted?

What constitutes a legitimate law enforcement purpose? In 2007, a federal court in New York City ruled that the New York Police Department could not engage in routine videotaping of people at public gatherings unless there is some indication that unlawful activity may occur. Handschu v. Special Services Div., 475 F. Supp. 2d 331 (S.D.N.Y. 2007). After reviewing two events in 2005 — a march in Harlem and a demonstration by homeless people in front of the Mayor's residence — the court found that there was "no reason to suspect or anticipate that unlawful or terrorist activity might occur" or that "pertinent information" of such activity might be obtained by filming the participants. *Id.* at 351.

9. ***Enforceability of Guidelines.*** The *Domestic Security Guidelines* explain that they are "solely for the purpose of internal Department of Justice guidelines" and are thus not judicially enforceable. §VII.C. If the guidelines are not judicially enforceable, do they serve any useful purpose? Would they have any importance in a judicial proceeding?

### c. NSI Guidelines

1. ***Comparing the Guidelines.*** What are the principal differences between the *Domestic Security Guidelines* and *NSI Guidelines*? What best explains the need for a separate set of *NSI Guidelines*? What guidance to investigators is supplied by the *NSI Guidelines* that is not already available under Executive Order No. 12,333, FISA, other statutes, and the Constitution?

2. ***Threat Assessments.*** The authorization for conducting threat assessments is new in the 2003 *NSI Guidelines*. Roughly equivalent to the checking of leads in the *Domestic Security Guidelines*, the threat assessment activity is designed to permit early intervention and prevention of terrorist attacks. The authorization for "proactive collection" of publicly available information was not part of the previous *FCI Guidelines*. Why do you think the *Guidelines* were changed in this way? The predicate criteria for conducting threat assessments are redacted from the *Guidelines*, as is the threshold for initiating such an assessment. Can you imagine what the redactions say?

3. ***Initiating and Conducting NSI Investigations.*** Like the prior *FCI Guidelines*, significant portions of the *NSI Guidelines* are classified. Review the threshold for opening and the techniques for conducting an investigation under the *Domestic Security Guidelines*. Based on those guidelines and what you know from FISA and Executive Order No. 12,333, can you predict the triggering requirements for opening an NSI investigation? Can you say what techniques are permitted or foreclosed?

4. ***Choice of Methods.*** Note that the *NSI Guidelines* contain language roughly similar to the *Domestic Security Guidelines*, which state that the FBI should "not hesitate to use any lawful techniques" if warranted by the circumstances. Of what value is such an instruction?

5. ***United States Persons.*** What is the idea behind the presumption that the entire membership of an international organization with no independent activities in the United States be counted in determining whether the

organization is substantially composed of U.S. persons? Why is making the "U.S. persons" determination important under the *NSI Guidelines*?

6. ***Extraterritorial Investigations.*** Why is the written request or approval of the Director of the CIA and the Attorney General required before the FBI conducts investigations abroad? Does Executive Order No. 12,333 further prescribe the standards for extraterritorial investigations by the FBI? If not, what limits are there on such investigations? See generally Chapter 9.

7. ***CIA and DOD Activities in the United States?*** One entirely redacted section in the *NSI Guidelines* is entitled "Central Intelligence Agency and Department of Defense [DOD] Activities Within the United States." In light of the National Security Act and Executive Order No. 12,333, can you imagine what the redacted language says? What DOD intelligence activities would be legally permissible in the United States? See *infra* pp. 682-691.

8. ***Enforceability.*** Like the *Domestic Security Guidelines*, the *NSI Guidelines* state that they are not judicially enforceable. Do the *NSI Guidelines* serve any useful purpose? Would they ever be relevant in a judicial proceeding?

9. ***Departures.*** What is the purpose of providing a process for exceeding the authority given by the Guidelines? What is the legal effect, if any, of a departure that is approved by or noticed to the Attorney General?

# B. INFORMATION SHARING AND AGENCY REFORMS

## 1. BRIDGING THE LAW ENFORCEMENT/INTELLIGENCE COLLECTION DIVIDE

The chapters in this part of the book have traced the increased intermingling of intelligence and law enforcement activities in support of counterterrorism objectives. While the FBI has expanded its extraterritorial role to acquire information about transnational threats, the CIA and agencies inside the Departments of Homeland Security and Defense have also stepped up their efforts in support of counterterrorism. In theory, at least, law enforcement and intelligence collection roles, activities, and methods had been legally and functionally separated to protect the integrity of their tasks and to protect the civil liberties of those targeted for investigation by the government. *See* Jonathan M. Fredman, *Intelligence Agencies, Law Enforcement, and the Prosecution Team*, 16 Yale L. & Poly. Rev. 331, 336-337 (1998). Intelligence gathering for counterterrorism must anticipate threats before they are carried out, while law enforcement typically reacts after the event. However, because terrorism and international crime pose national security threats that transcend both national borders *and* the borders between law enforcement and intelligence collection, coordination and cooperation are required among intelligence agencies and between the intelligence and law enforcement arms of the FBI.

The National Security Act of 1947 declares that the CIA shall have no "internal security" functions. See *supra* p. 253. It was thus determined by Congress that the already functioning FBI would continue to serve as the nation's domestic security agency. At the same time, it was understood early on that the "internal security" prohibition in the 1947 Act would not forbid the CIA from coordinating or collecting *foreign* intelligence information in the United States. However, there was nothing in the Act to provide for CIA and FBI coordination, and there were no rules to say when the CIA could play a counterintelligence role in the United States. Thus, the 1947 Act "cut the man down the middle . . . between domestic and foreign counterespionage." Mark Riebling, *Wedge: The Secret War Between the FBI and CIA* 78 (1994).

The 1947 Act also calls on the Director of the CIA to take any actions necessary to "protect intelligence sources and methods from unauthorized disclosure." In addition, the CIA is to "perform such other functions and duties related to intelligence affecting the national security as the President or the National Security Council may direct." See *supra* p. 253. According to Mark Riebling, this language provided "a pair of operational baggy pants," while CIA Counsel Scott Breckinridge called the "other functions" language a "banana-peel clause." Riebling, *supra*, at 79. In fact, efforts to coordinate FBI and CIA operations within the United States occurred from the beginning, with several high and low points in the decades since 1947.

In addition to the 1947 Act, Executive Order No. 12,333 explicitly confirms FBI and CIA joint authority over counterintelligence operations, *id.* §1.8(a), while it sustains the notion of divided FBI and CIA roles by charging the CIA with conducting counterintelligence activities within the United States "without assuming or performing any internal security functions." *Id.* §1.8(c). In spite of continuing efforts at coordinating counterintelligence, the agencies have frequently been at bureaucratic loggerheads. *See The Intelligence Community's Involvement in the Banca Nazionale del Lavoro (BNL) Affair*, S. Prt. No. 103-12, at 27 (1993).

The Aldrich Ames spy scandal prompted serious consideration of counterintelligence reform. Ames, a CIA employee since 1962, was recruited by the Soviet KGB while trying to turn Soviet agents toward the United States. Despite a series of suspicious developments dating from at least 1985 — U.S. agents exposed and killed in the Soviet Union, lavish spending by Ames and his wife, a failed 1991 polygraph test — the CIA declined for years to involve the FBI in a counterintelligence inquiry, and the FBI was not able to open a formal investigation of Ames until May 1993. Riebling, *supra*, at 430-431. Although the CIA had clearly violated a 1988 memorandum of understanding promising that CIA suspicions would be passed along to the Bureau in a timely fashion, CIA officials defended their actions. A Bureau search of Ames's CIA office, followed by telephone taps, mail opening, and various other bugging and surveillance methods, finally led to his arrest in February 1994. *Id.* at 431-433, 441-444.

The spectacle of an open and angry feud between the CIA and the FBI over the handling of the Ames investigation prompted passage of the Counterintelligence and Security Enhancements Act of 1994, Pub. L. No. 103-359, §§801-811, 108 Stat. 3423, amending the National Security Act of 1947. The measure made several changes in the way access to classified information is determined for federal employees. The Act also expanded the ability of federal investigators to gain access to financial and credit information, consumer reports, and travel records "as may be necessary to conduct any authorized law enforcement investigation, counterintelligence inquiry, or security determination." Pub. L. No. 103-359, §802(a). Investigations may be commenced concerning any executive branch employee as a condition of access to classified information. *Id.* The predicate for initiating such an investigation is that "there are reasonable grounds to believe, based on credible information, that the person is, or may be, disclosing classified information in an unauthorized manner to a foreign power or agent of a foreign power." *Id.*

In addition, the Act established a Counterintelligence Policy Board to report to the President through the National Security Council (NSC). *Id.* §811(a). *See Intelligence Authorization Act for Fiscal Year 1995,* H.R. Conf. Rep. No. 103-753, at 35 (1994). The Act provides that

> the head of each department or agency within the executive branch shall ensure that . . . the [FBI] is advised immediately of any information, regardless of its origin, which indicates that classified information is being, or may have been, disclosed in an unauthorized manner to a foreign power or an agent of a foreign power.

Pub. L. No. 103-359, §811(c)(1)(A). Following such a report to the FBI, the Bureau must be "consulted with respect to all subsequent actions" taken by the affected agency, and "given complete and timely access to the employees and records" of the affected agency. *Id.* §811(c)(1)(B), (C).

Another action taken partly in response to the Ames investigation was the establishment by the Attorney General in July 1995 of policies and procedures for internal DOJ coordination of FBI counterintelligence investigations with the Criminal Division. Although additional coordination procedures were promulgated in January 2000, problems persist. *See* General Accounting Office, *FBI Intelligence Investigations: Coordination Within Justice on Counterintelligence Criminal Matters Is Limited* (GAO-01-780) (2001). As with the "primary purpose" doctrine, see *supra* p. 110, limits on cooperation between law enforcement and intelligence gathering reflect a fear that investigators might characterize a law enforcement investigation as a purely intelligence operation in order to avoid the stricter investigative rules that attend the criminal laws, and that a judge could exclude evidence from a criminal trial based on that possibility. *Id.* at 3. Just such a cautionary stance may have thwarted an investigation that could have tipped off officials to the September 11, 2001, attacks before they occurred. See *supra* p. 144. Yet because counterterrorism investigations now regularly become law enforcement and intelligence investigations simultaneously, sorting out the problems of cooperation and coordination remains crucial. See *supra* p. 259. The perception that the "primary purpose" standard had made threat detection and interdiction more difficult before September 11 led to an amendment to FISA in the USA Patriot Act requiring that the intelligence purpose of an investigation be "a significant" purpose rather than "the" purpose. The "wall" between intelligence collection and law enforcement was effectively torn down by the Patriot Act, as construed by the Foreign Intelligence Surveillance Court of Review in In re Sealed Case. See *supra* p. 145.

Another USA Patriot Act provision authorizes a greater degree of interagency cooperation and sharing of information than was permitted previously.

The Act permits, "[n]otwithstanding any other provision of law . . . foreign or counterintelligence . . . information obtained as part of a criminal investigation to be disclosed to any Federal law enforcement, intelligence, protective, immigration, national defense, or national security official in order to assist the official receiving that information in the performance of his official duties." Pub. L. No. 107-56, §203(d)(1), 115 Stat. 272, 281 (2001), amending 50 U.S.C. §403-5(d). The same discretion is given for the sharing of grand jury information. *Id.* §203(a)(1), 115 Stat. 278-279, amending 18 U.S.C. §6(e)(3)(C). In addition, the USA Patriot Act amended FISA as follows:

> (1) Federal officers who conduct electronic surveillance [or a physical search] to acquire foreign intelligence information under this title may consult with Federal law enforcement officers to coordinate efforts to investigate or protect against —
>> a. actual or potential attack or other grave hostile acts of a foreign power or an agent of a foreign power;
>> b. sabotage or international terrorism by a foreign power or an agent of a foreign power;
>> c. clandestine intelligence activities by an intelligence service or network of a foreign power or by an agent of a foreign power.
> (2) Coordination authorized [above] shall not preclude the certification required by [FISA] or the entry of an order. . . . [*Id.* §504(a), (b), 115 Stat. 364-365, amending 50 U.S.C. §1825.]

The Homeland Security Act further amended FISA by permitting intelligence officers to consult with state and local law enforcement officers regarding foreign intelligence information. Pub. L. No. 107-296, §898, 116 Stat. 2258 (2002), amending 50 U.S.C. §1806(k)(1).

Likewise, the USA Patriot Act amended the National Security Act of 1947 to require the Director of Central Intelligence to "establish requirements and priorities" for disseminating foreign intelligence information collected under FISA, Pub. L. No. 107-56, §901, 115 Stat. 387, and to direct the Attorney General to disclose to the Director of the CIA foreign intelligence acquired by the Department of Justice in the course of a criminal investigation. *Id.* §905(a)(2), 115 Stat. 389. Exceptions to disclosure for classes, matters, or targets of foreign intelligence may be determined by the Attorney General in consultation with the Director of the CIA. *Id.* The same officials are obligated to develop guidelines to help inform the Director of the CIA "within a reasonable period of time" of a determination by the Department of Justice whether a foreign intelligence source will be subject to a criminal investigation. *Id.* §905(b), 115 Stat. 389.

Among the reforms recommended by the 9/11 Commission, *supra* p. 209, was creation of a national counterterrorism center. In August 2004, President Bush adopted the recommendation by executive order. Executive Order No. 13,354, *National Counterterrorism Center*, 69 Fed. Reg. 53,589 (August 27, 2004). A few months later, in the Intelligence Reform and Terrorism Prevention Act of 2004 (IRTPA), Pub. L. No. 108-458, 118 Stat. 3638, Congress created a National Counterterrorism Center (NCTC). *Id.* §1021, 118

Stat. 3672. The Senate-confirmed Director of the NCTC reports to the DNI generally, but to the President on the planning and implementation of joint counterterrorism operations. *Id.* In turn, IRTPA vests in the DNI the "principal authority to ensure maximum availability of and access to intelligence information within the intelligence community consistent with national security." *Id.* §1011(a), 118 Stat. 3650. IRTPA also requires a "coordinated environment" in which intelligence information can be "provided in its more shareable form." *Id.* §1016(b)(2), (d)(1), 118 Stat. at 3665-3666. This Information Sharing Environment (ISE) is supposed to combine policies, procedures, and technologies to link information collectors and users. A November 2006 implementation plan for the ISE includes procedures for sharing information among agencies at all levels of government. The plan also contains procedures for protecting information privacy and civil liberties. *See Information Sharing Environment Implementation Plan, available at* http://www.ise.gov/docs/ISE-impplan-200611.pdf. Privacy advocates noted that the new guidelines lack specificity and fail to match the protections offered by the Privacy Act of 1974 (see *supra* p. 205). Ellen Nakashima, *Civil Libertarians Protest Privacy Policy: New Guidelines Do Little to Protect Established Rights, White House Board Told*, Wash. Post, Dec. 6, 2006, at A11.

In December 2005, the 9/11 Commission, reincarnated as the Public Discourse Project, issued its *Final Report on 9/11 Commission Recommendations*, Dec. 5, 2005, *available at* http://www.9-11pdp.org. The Report gave a grade of "B" to the NCTC, noting that "shared analysis and evaluation of threat information is in progress; joint operational planning is beginning," but that insufficient resources are available to fulfill the intelligence and planning role envisioned.

The NCTC runs three video teleconferences (VTCs) on a daily basis, and its staff posts intelligence on a Web site, classified but accessible to about 5,000 analysts. The NCTC operates alongside the Counterterrorist Center (CTC) at the CIA, in addition to Information Analysis and Infrastructure Protection (IAIP) Directorate at the Department of Homeland Security (DHS). The CTC and NCTC have considerable overlap—pursuing al Qaeda operatives worldwide and providing strategic operational planning for counterterrorism activities. Scott Shane, *Year Into Revamped Spying, Troubles and Some Progress*, N.Y. Times, Feb. 28, 2006, at A12. Former National Intelligence Council vice chairman Gregory Treverton described the NCTC-CTC relationship as a "food fight" and called the relationship between federal officials and state and local law enforcement "a complete mess." *Id.*

## 2.   REFORMING THE FBI

Owing at least in part to its longstanding tradition of performing the federal law enforcement role, FBI intelligence collection and analysis efforts were long regarded inside the Bureau as of secondary importance. Even as additional resources and staff were devoted to intelligence collection and analysis inside the FBI during the 1990s, the intelligence function was still not central to the FBI mission. In addition to the perception among many that engaging heavily in intelligence work would only compromise the effectiveness of FBI law enforcement, the Bureau's reluctance to embrace an intelligence mission wholeheartedly was also due in part to our nation's cultural and historical antipathy to a domestic intelligence service. Images of the sinister omnipresence of the German Gestapo and the Soviet KGB were firmly etched into the public consciousness.

A few months after Congress created a revised intelligence community structure in December 2004, President Bush issued an order creating a new national security division within the FBI that will be subject to the overall direction of the DNI. *See* Douglas Jehl, *Bush to Create New Unit in F.B.I. for Intelligence*, N.Y. Times, June 30, 2005, at A1. The restructuring was designed to break down historic barriers between the FBI and the CIA while elevating the relative importance of the intelligence mission inside the FBI. *Id.* The new division, called the National Security Service, includes counterterrorism and counterintelligence divisions and an intelligence directorate. A new position of assistant attorney general for national security matters, in charge of counterterrorism, counterintelligence, and the Office of Intelligence Policy Review, was approved by Congress in the USA Patriot Improvement and Reauthorization Act of 2005, Pub. L. No. 109-177, §506(a), 120 Stat. 192, 247 (2006).

## NOTES AND QUESTIONS

1. *Organizing the Intelligence Sharing Network.* IRTPA places the Director of National Intelligence (DNI) at the head of the National Intelligence Program and vests in him authority to task intelligence agencies and shape their budgets and spending. *See* 50 U.S.C. §403(b). The Act does not, however, prescribe how to organize a network for sharing information or provide much detail concerning the rules for its implementation. How would you advise the DNI to shape an effective information-sharing network that ensures efficient sharing of information while protecting both the security of the information and the rights of those targeted? One model that is different in some important ways from the ISE was proposed in 2003 by the Markle Foundation Task Force, *Creating a Trusted Information Network for Homeland Security* (2003), *available at* http://www.markletaskforce.org/reports/TFNS_Master.pdf (proposing a decentralized network of information sharing and analysis around presidential guidelines shaped by public debate on how to achieve security and liberty).

2. *Separate Agencies for Domestic and Foreign Intelligence Activities?* Should there be a strict legal requirement that separate agencies gather intelligence inside and outside the United States? What is the value of such a requirement? Is it required by the Constitution? To the extent that such separation exists, are the inevitable compromises in information sharing worth the benefits?

3. *Utility of the Information-Sharing Requirements.* Are the USA Patriot Act and IRTPA information-sharing provisions clearly advisable? Do these provisions raise the possibility that the CIA will collect information in the United States about Americans? In light of the complexities of mounting an

effective counterterrorism strategy, can you think of any good alternatives to these information-sharing mechanisms? Can you think of ways to create greater accountability for their use?

Is the NCTC likely to promote effective information sharing? How will the Center discourage agencies from hoarding their own intelligence leads? Is the placement of the NCTC just below the DNI a good idea, or is the NCTC simply another layer of bureaucracy, this time at the top? The Public Discourse Project gave a "D" grade to the information-sharing efforts to date by Congress and the Administration and commented that "many complaints about lack of information sharing between federal authorities and state and local level officials" remain. *Final Report, supra,* at 3. What legal measures might improve information sharing across these jurisdictional lines? Between agencies? *See* Peter P. Swire, *Privacy and Information Sharing in the War on Terrorism,* 51 Vill. L. Rev. 951 (2006) (suggesting a due diligence checklist for information-sharing projects).

4. *9/11 Commission Report Card on the FBI Reorganization.* The Public Discourse Project *Final Report* issued a "C" grade on implementing the FBI national security division and commented that the FBI "shift to a counter-terrorism posture is far from institutionalized. . . . Unless there is improvement in a reasonable period of time, Congress will have to look at alternatives." *Final Report, supra,* at 3.

5. *Checks and Balances vs. Efficiency.* Is competition between the CIA and the FBI inevitable? If the coordination and competition problems *can* be solved, *should* they be solved? Or is it part of our nation's character "to chafe at bureaucratic inefficiency . . . [but] to distrust the centralization of power needed to correct it"? Riebling, *supra* p. 260, at 460. Are the agencies' missions so different that their work cannot be coordinated? Is the reluctance to vest one agency with both foreign and domestic security responsibility a sign of healthy skepticism about the dangers of the accumulation of power in one entity? In the end, is the foreign/domestic dichotomy that continues to dominate the law of internal security workable? Is it constitutionally defensible? Is the better dividing line one between intelligence collection and law enforcement?

6. *Oversight.* Can oversight of intelligence agencies and their information-sharing activities help safeguard the civil liberties that might otherwise be at risk? Oversight might be performed outside the intelligence community—through the intelligence and appropriations committees in Congress—or internally—by agency overseers, inspectors general, or presidential advisory groups such as the White House privacy board. *See* Nakashima, *supra.* How do you think the oversight function should be organized? How should it be codified? What agencies and congressional committees would have an interest in this question? What are the implications for democratic government?

# CHAPTER 9

# *INVESTIGATING ABROAD*

The policy of countering terrorism by detecting and then preventing terrorist acts targeting the United States has as its first line of defense the investigation of terrorism abroad. Indeed, the United States has long conducted law enforcement and intelligence investigations overseas. This chapter examines the question whether, when U.S. investigators go abroad, the Constitution travels with them to limit their activities and, if so, to what extent. It also asks whether any constitutional protections for U.S. citizens abroad extend equally to noncitizens, and how U.S. investigations outside the United States may be constrained by international law. Finally, in this chapter we consider how rules governing such investigations can be implemented practically.

## REID V. COVERT

United States Supreme Court, 1957
354 U.S. 1

[Mrs. Covert killed her husband, a U.S. Air Force sergeant, at an airbase in England. Pursuant to a "status-of-forces" executive agreement with that country, she was tried and convicted by U.S. court-martial without a jury trial under the Uniform Code of Military Justice (UCMJ). On a petition for a writ of habeas corpus, she attacked her conviction on the grounds that it violated her Fifth and Sixth Amendment rights to be tried by a jury after indictment by a grand jury. The District Court granted the petition, and this appeal followed. Mrs. Covert's appeal was consolidated with a like appeal by Mrs. Smith, who had been tried and convicted in similar fashion in Japan.]

Mr. Justice BLACK announced the opinion of the Court and delivered an opinion, in which The CHIEF JUSTICE, Mr. Justice DOUGLAS, and Mr. Justice BRENNAN join. . . . At the beginning we reject the idea that when the United States acts against citizens abroad it can do so free of the Bill of Rights. The United States is entirely a creature of the Constitution. Its power and authority have no other source. It can only act in accordance with all the limitations imposed by the Constitution. When the Government reaches out to punish a citizen who is abroad, the shield which the Bill of Rights and other parts of the Constitution provide to protect his life and liberty should not be stripped away just because he happens to be in another land. . . .

The rights and liberties which citizens of our country enjoy are not protected by custom and tradition alone, they have been jealously preserved from the encroachments of Government by express provisions of our written Constitution.

Among those provisions, Art. III, §2 and the Fifth and Sixth Amendments are directly relevant to these cases. Article III, §2 lays down the rule that:

> "The Trial of all Crimes, except in Cases of Impeachment, shall be by Jury; and such Trial shall be held in the State where the said Crimes shall have been committed; but when not committed within any State, the Trial shall be at such Place or Places as the Congress may by Law have directed."

The Fifth Amendment declares:

> "No person shall be held to answer for a capital, or otherwise infamous crime, unless on a presentment or indictment of a Grand Jury, except in cases arising in the land or naval forces, or in the Militia, when in actual service in time of War or public danger; . . ."

And the Sixth Amendment provides:

> "In all criminal prosecutions, the accused shall enjoy the right to a speedy and public trial, by an impartial jury of the State and district wherein the crime shall have been committed. . . ."

The language of Art. III, §2 manifests that constitutional protections for the individual were designed to restrict the United States Government when it acts outside of this country, as well as here at home. After declaring that all criminal trials must be by jury, the section states that when a crime is "not committed within any State, the Trial shall be at such Place or Places as the Congress may by Law have directed." If this language is permitted to have its obvious meaning, §2 is applicable to criminal trials outside of the States as a group without regard to where the offense is committed or the trial held. From the very first Congress, federal statutes have implemented the provisions of §2 by providing for trial of murder and other crimes committed outside the jurisdiction of any State "in the district where the offender is apprehended, or into which he may first be brought." The Fifth and Sixth Amendments, like Art. III, §2, are also all inclusive with their sweeping references to "no person" and to "all criminal prosecutions."

This Court and other federal courts have held or asserted that various constitutional limitations apply to the Government when it acts outside the continental United States. While it has been suggested that only those constitutional rights which are "fundamental" protect Americans abroad, we can find no warrant, in logic or otherwise, for picking and choosing among the remarkable collection of "Thou shalt nots" which were explicitly fastened on all departments and agencies of the Federal Government by the Constitution and its Amendments. Moreover, in view of our heritage and the history of the adoption of the Constitution and the Bill of Rights, it seems peculiarly anomalous to say that trial before a civilian judge and by an independent jury picked from the common citizenry is not a fundamental right. . . . Trial by jury in a court of law and in accordance with traditional modes of procedure after an indictment by grand jury has served and remains one of our most vital barriers to governmental arbitrariness. These elemental procedural safeguards were embedded in our Constitution to secure their inviolateness and sanctity against the passing demands of expediency or convenience. . . .

The [holding in In re Ross, 140 U.S. 453 (1891)] that the Constitution has no applicability abroad has long since been directly repudiated by numerous cases. That approach is obviously erroneous if the United States Government, which has no power except that granted by the Constitution, can and does try citizens for crimes committed abroad. . . . At best, the *Ross* case should be left as a relic from a different era.

[Last term the Court] relied on the "Insular Cases" to support its conclusion that Article III and the Fifth and Sixth Amendments were not applicable to the trial of Mrs. Smith and Mrs. Covert. We believe that reliance was misplaced. The "Insular Cases," which arose at the turn of the century, involved territories which had only recently been conquered or acquired by the United States. These territories, governed and regulated by Congress under Art. IV, §3, had entirely different cultures and customs from those of this country. . . .

Moreover, it is our judgment that neither the cases nor their reasoning should be given any further expansion. The concept that the Bill of Rights and other constitutional protections against arbitrary government are inoperative when they become inconvenient or when expediency dictates otherwise is a very dangerous doctrine and if allowed to flourish would destroy the benefit of a written Constitution and undermine the basis of our government. If our foreign commitments become of such nature that the Government can no longer satisfactorily operate within the bounds laid down by the Constitution, that instrument can be amended by the method which it prescribes. But we have no authority, or inclination, to read exceptions into it which are not there. . . .

Mr. Justice HARLAN, concurring in the result. . . . As I have already stated, I do not think that it can be said that these safeguards of the Constitution are never operative without the United States, regardless of the particular circumstances. On the other hand, I cannot agree with the suggestion that every provision of the Constitution must always be deemed automatically applicable to American citizens in every part of the world. For *Ross* and the *Insular Cases* do stand for an important proposition, one which seems to me a wise and necessary gloss on our Constitution. The proposition is, of course, not that the Constitution "does not apply" overseas, but that there are provisions in the Constitution which do not *necessarily* apply in all circumstances in every foreign place. . . . In other words, what *Ross* and the *Insular Cases* hold is that the particular local setting, the practical necessities, and the possible alternatives are relevant to a question of judgment, namely, whether jury trial should be deemed a necessary condition of the exercise of Congress' power to provide for the trial of Americans overseas. . . .

And so I agree with my brother Frankfurter that, in view of *Ross* and the *Insular Cases*, we have before us a question analogous, ultimately, to issues of due process; one can say, in fact, that the question of which specific safeguards of the Constitution are appropriately to be applied in a particular context overseas can be reduced to the issue of what process is "due" a defendant in the particular circumstances of a particular case.

On this basis, I cannot agree with the sweeping proposition that a full Article III trial, with indictment and trial by jury, is required in every case for the trial of a civilian dependent of a serviceman overseas. The Government, it seems to me, has made an impressive showing that at least for the run-of-the-mill offenses committed by dependents overseas, such a requirement would be as impractical and anomalous as it would have been to require jury trial for Balzac in Porto Rico. . . .

So far as capital cases are concerned, I think they stand on quite a different footing than other offenses. In such cases the law is especially sensitive to demands for that procedural fairness which inheres in a civilian trial where the judge and trier of fact are not responsive to the command of the convening authority. I do not concede that whatever process is "due" an offender faced with a fine or a prison sentence necessarily satisfies the requirements of the Constitution in a capital case. . . . The number of such cases would appear to be so negligible that the practical problems of affording the defendant a civilian trial would not present insuperable problems.

On this narrow ground I concur in the result in these cases.

[The opinions of FRANKFURTER, J., concurring, and of CLARK, J., dissenting, are omitted.]

## UNITED STATES v. VERDUGO-URQUIDEZ

United States Supreme Court, 1990
494 U.S. 259

[Respondent Rene Martin Verdugo-Urquidez was a citizen and resident of Mexico who was apprehended by Mexican police and delivered to U.S. border authorities in response to a U.S. warrant for his arrest on drug-smuggling charges. Following his arrest, and while he was incarcerated in the United States, DEA agents searched Verdugo-Urquidez's property in Mexico with the approval of Mexican authorities but without a U.S. warrant, and seized certain documents that were subsequently offered as evidence against him. The defendant sought to have that evidence excluded.]

Chief Justice REHNQUIST delivered the opinion of the Court. The question presented by this case is whether the Fourth Amendment applies to the search and seizure by United States agents of property that is owned by a nonresident alien and located in a foreign country. We hold that it does not. . . .

The Fourth Amendment provides:

"The right of the people to be secure in their persons, houses, papers, and effects, against unreasonable searches and seizures, shall not be violated, and no Warrants shall issue, but upon probable cause, supported by Oath or affirmation, and particularly describing the place to be searched, and the persons or things to be seized."

That text, by contrast with the Fifth and Sixth Amendments, extends its reach only to "the people." Contrary to the suggestion of *amici curiae* that the Framers used this phrase "simply to avoid [an] awkward rhetorical redundancy," "the people" seems to have been a term of art employed in select parts of the Constitution. The Preamble declares that the Constitution is ordained and established by "the People of the United States." The Second Amendment protects "the right of the people to keep and bear Arms," and the Ninth and Tenth Amendments provide that certain rights and powers are retained by and reserved to "the people." See also U.S. Const., Amdt. 1 ("Congress shall make no law . . . abridging . . . *the right of the people* peaceably to assemble") (emphasis added); Art. I, §2, cl. 1 ("The House of Representatives shall be composed of Members chosen every second Year *by the People of the several States*") (emphasis added). While this textual exegesis is by no means conclusive, it suggests that "the people" protected by the Fourth Amendment, and by the First and Second Amendments, and to whom rights and powers are reserved in the Ninth and Tenth Amendments, refers to a class of persons who are part of a national community or who have otherwise developed sufficient connection with this country to be considered part of that community. The language of these Amendments contrasts with the words "person" and "accused" used in the Fifth and Sixth Amendments regulating procedure in criminal cases.

What we know of the history of the drafting of the Fourth Amendment also suggests that its purpose was to restrict searches and seizures which might be conducted by the United States in domestic matters. . . . The available historical data show, therefore, that the purpose of the Fourth Amendment was to protect the people of the United States against arbitrary action by their own Government; it was never suggested that the provision was intended to restrain the actions of the Federal Government against aliens outside of the United States territory.

There is likewise no indication that the Fourth Amendment was understood by contemporaries of the Framers to apply to activities of the United States directed against aliens in foreign territory or in international waters. Only seven years after the ratification of the Amendment, French interference with American commercial vessels engaged in neutral trade triggered what came to be known as the "undeclared war" with France. In an Act to "protect the Commerce of the United States" in 1798, Congress authorized President Adams to "instruct the commanders of the public armed vessels which are, or which shall be employed in the service of the United States, to subdue, seize and take any armed French vessel, which shall be found within the jurisdictional limits of the United States, or elsewhere, on the high seas." §1 of An Act Further to Protect the Commerce of the United States, ch. 68, 1 Stat. 578. . . . Some commanders were held liable by this Court for unlawful seizures because their actions were beyond the scope of the congressional grant of authority, *see, e. g.*, Little v. Barreme, 2 Cranch 170, 177-178 (1804); *cf.* Talbot v. Seeman, 1 Cranch 1, 31 (1801) (seizure of neutral ship lawful where American captain had probable cause to believe vessel was French), but it was never suggested that the Fourth Amendment restrained the authority of congress or of United States agents to conduct operations such as this.

The global view taken by the Court of Appeals of the application of the Constitution is also contrary to this Court's decisions in the *Insular Cases*, which held that not every constitutional provision applies to governmental activity even where the United States has sovereign power. In Dorr v. United States, 195 U.S. 138 (1904), we declared the general rule that in an unincorporated territory—one not clearly destined for statehood—Congress was not required to adopt "a system of laws which shall include the right of trial by jury, and that *the Constitution does not, without legislation and of its own force, carry such right to territory so situated*." 195 U.S. at 149 (emphasis added). Only "fundamental" constitutional rights are guaranteed to inhabitants of those territories. . . . [C]ertainly, it is not open to us in light of the *Insular Cases* to endorse the view that every constitutional provision applies wherever the United States Government exercises its power.

Indeed, we have rejected the claim that aliens are entitled to Fifth Amendment rights outside the sovereign territory of the United States. In Johnson v. Eisentrager, 339 U.S. 763 (1950), the Court held that enemy aliens arrested in China and imprisoned in Germany after World War II could not obtain writs of habeas corpus in our federal courts on the ground that their convictions for war crimes had violated the Fifth Amendment and other constitutional provisions. The *Eisentrager* opinion acknowledged that in some cases constitutional provisions extend beyond the citizenry; "[t]he alien . . . has been accorded a generous and ascending scale of rights as he increases his identity with our society." *Id.*, at 770. But our rejection of extraterritorial application of the Fifth Amendment was emphatic:

> "Such extraterritorial application of organic law would have been so significant an innovation in the practice of governments that, if intended or apprehended, it could scarcely have failed to excite contemporary comment. Not one word can be cited. No decision of this Court supports such a view. *Cf.* Downes v. Bidwell, 182 U.S. 244 [(1901)]. None of the learned commentators on our Constitution has even hinted at it. The practice of every modern government is opposed to it." *Id.*, at 784.

If such is true of the Fifth Amendment, which speaks in the relatively universal term of "person," it would seem even more true with respect to the Fourth Amendment, which applies only to "the people."

To support his all-encompassing view of the Fourth Amendment, respondent points to language from the plurality opinion in Reid v. Covert, 354 U.S. 1 (1957). . . . Four Justices "reject[ed] the idea that when the United States acts *against citizens* abroad it can do so free of the Bill of Rights." *Id.*, at 5 (emphasis added). The plurality went on to say:

> "The United States is entirely a creature of the Constitution. Its power and authority have no other source. It can only act in accordance with all the limitations imposed by the Constitution. When the Government reaches out to punish *a citizen* who is abroad, the shield which the Bill of Rights and other parts of the Constitution provide to protect his life and liberty should not be stripped away

just because he happens to be in another land." *Id.*, at 5-6 (emphasis added; footnote omitted).

Respondent urges that we interpret this discussion to mean that federal officials are constrained by the Fourth Amendment wherever and against whomever they act. But the holding of *Reid* stands for no such sweeping proposition: it decided that United States citizens stationed abroad could invoke the protection of the Fifth and Sixth Amendments. The concurring opinions by Justices Frankfurter and Harlan in *Reid* resolved the case on much narrower grounds than the plurality and declined even to hold that United States citizens were entitled to the full range of constitutional protections in all overseas criminal prosecutions. *See id.*, at 75 (Harlan, J., concurring in result) ("I agree with my brother Frankfurter that . . . we have before us a question analogous, ultimately, to issues of due process; one can say, in fact, that the question of which specific safeguards of the Constitution are appropriately to be applied in a particular context overseas can be reduced to the issue of what process is 'due' a defendant in the particular circumstances of a particular case"). Since respondent is not a United States citizen, he can derive no comfort from the *Reid* holding.

Verdugo-Urquidez also relies on a series of cases in which we have held that aliens enjoy certain constitutional rights. *See, e.g.*, Plyler v. Doe, 457 U.S. 202, 211-212 (1982) (illegal aliens protected by Equal Protection Clause); Kwong Hai Chew v. Colding, 344 U.S. 590, 596 (1953) (resident alien is a "person" within the meaning of the Fifth Amendment); Bridges v. Wixon, 326 U.S. 135, 148 (1945) (resident aliens have First Amendment rights); Russian Volunteer Fleet v. United States, 282 U.S. 481 (1931) (just Compensation Clause of Fifth Amendment); Wong Wing v. United States, 163 U.S. 228, 238 (1896) (resident aliens entitled to Fifth and Sixth Amendment rights); Yick Wo v. Hopkins, 118 U.S. 356, 369 (1886) (Fourteenth Amendment protects resident aliens). These cases, however, establish only that aliens receive constitutional protections when they have come within the territory of the United States and developed substantial connections with this country. Respondent is an alien who has had no previous significant voluntary connection with the United States, so these cases avail him not. . . .

Not only are history and case law against respondent, but as pointed out in Johnson v. Eisentrager, 393 U.S. 763 (1950), the result of accepting his claim would have significant and deleterious consequences for the United States in conducting activities beyond its boundaries. The rule adopted by the Court of Appeals would apply not only to law enforcement operations abroad, but also to other foreign policy operations which might result in "searches or seizures." The United States frequently employs armed forces outside this country — over 200 times in our history — for the protection of American citizens or national security. Congressional Research Service, *Instances of Use of United States Armed Forces Abroad, 1798–1989* (E. Collier ed. 1989). Application of the Fourth Amendment to those circumstances could significantly disrupt the ability of the political branches to respond to foreign situations involving our national interest. Were respondent to prevail, aliens with no attachment to this country might well bring actions for damages to remedy claimed violations of the Fourth

Amendment in foreign countries or in international waters. *See* Bivens v. Six Unknown Federal Narcotics Agents, 403 U.S. 388 (1971). . . . The Members of the Executive and Legislative Branches are sworn to uphold the Constitution, and they presumably desire to follow its commands. But the Court of Appeals' global view of its applicability would plunge them into a sea of uncertainty as to what might be reasonable in the way of searches and seizures conducted abroad. Indeed, the Court of Appeals held that absent exigent circumstances, United States agents could not effect a "search or seizure" for law enforcement purposes in a foreign country without first obtaining a warrant — which would be a dead letter outside the United States — from a magistrate in this country. Even if no warrant were required, American agents would have to articulate specific facts giving them probable cause to undertake a search or seizure if they wished to comply with the Fourth Amendment as conceived by the Court of Appeals. . . .

For better or for worse, we live in a world of nation-states in which our Government must be able to "function effectively in the company of sovereign nations." Perez v. Brownell, 356 U.S. 44, 57 (1958). Some who violate our laws may live outside our borders under a regime quite different from that which obtains in this country. Situations threatening to important American interests may arise halfway around the globe, situations which in the view of the political branches of our Government require an American response with armed force. If there are to be restrictions on searches and seizures which occur incident to such American action, they must be imposed by the political branches through diplomatic understanding, treaty, or legislation.

The judgment of the Court of Appeals is accordingly

*Reversed.*

Justice KENNEDY, concurring. . . . I take it to be correct, as the plurality opinion in Reid v. Covert sets forth, that the Government may act only as the Constitution authorizes, whether the actions in question are foreign or domestic. *See* 354 U.S., at 6. But this principle is only a first step in resolving this case. The question before us then becomes what constitutional standards apply when the Government acts, in reference to an alien, within its sphere of foreign operations. . . . [Various cases], as well as United States v. Curtiss-Wright Export Corp., 299 U.S. 304, 318 (1936), stand for the proposition that we must interpret constitutional protections in light of the undoubted power of the United States to take actions to assert its legitimate power and authority abroad. Justice Harlan made this observation in his opinion concurring in the judgment in Reid v. Covert:

> "I cannot agree with the suggestion that every provision of the Constitution must always be deemed automatically applicable to American citizens in every part of the world. For *Ross* and the *Insular Cases* do stand for an important proposition, one which seems to me a wise and necessary gloss on our Constitution. The proposition is, of course, not that the Constitution 'does not apply' overseas, but that there are provisions in the Constitution which do not *necessarily* apply in all circumstances in every foreign place. In other words, it seems to me that the basic teaching of *Ross* and the *Insular Cases* is that there is no

rigid and abstract rule that Congress, as a condition precedent to exercising power over Americans overseas, must exercise it subject to all the guarantees of the Constitution, no matter what the conditions and considerations are that would make adherence to a specific guarantee altogether impracticable and anomalous." 354 U.S., at 74.

The conditions and considerations of this case would make adherence to the Fourth Amendment's warrant requirement impracticable and anomalous. . . . The absence of local judges or magistrates available to issue warrants, the differing and perhaps unascertainable conceptions of reasonableness and privacy that prevail abroad, and the need to cooperate with foreign officials all indicate that the Fourth Amendment's warrant requirement should not apply in Mexico as it does in this country. For this reason, in addition to the other persuasive justifications stated by the Court, I agree that no violation of the Fourth Amendment has occurred in the case before us. The rights of a citizen, as to whom the United States has continuing obligations, are not presented by this case.

I do not mean to imply, and the Court has not decided, that persons in the position of the respondent have no constitutional protection. The United States is prosecuting a foreign national in a court established under Article III, and all of the trial proceedings are governed by the Constitution. All would agree, for instance, that the dictates of the Due Process Clause of the Fifth Amendment protect the defendant. Indeed, as Justice Harlan put it, "the question of which specific safeguards . . . are appropriately to be applied in a particular context . . . can be reduced to the issue of what process is 'due' a defendant in the particular circumstances of a particular case." *Reid, supra*, at 75. Nothing approaching a violation of due process has occurred in this case.

[The opinion of Justice STEVENS, concurring in the judgment on the grounds that, although the Fourth Amendment applied, the search was reasonable, is omitted.]

Justice BRENNAN, with whom Justice MARSHALL joins, dissenting. . . . The Court today creates an antilogy: the Constitution authorizes our Government to enforce our criminal laws abroad, but when Government agents exercise this authority, the Fourth Amendment does not travel with them. This cannot be. At the very least, the Fourth Amendment is an unavoidable correlative of the Government's power to enforce the criminal law. . . .

When we tell the world that we expect all people, wherever they may be, to abide by our laws, we cannot in the same breath tell the world that our law enforcement officers need not do the same. Because we cannot expect others to respect our laws until we respect our Constitution, I respectfully dissent.

Justice BLACKMUN, dissenting. I cannot accept the Court of Appeals' conclusion, echoed in some portions of Justice Brennan's dissent, that the Fourth Amendment governs every action by an American official that can be characterized as a search or seizure. American agents acting abroad generally do not purport to exercise sovereign authority over the foreign nationals with whom they come in contact. The relationship between these agents and foreign nationals is therefore fundamentally different from the relationship between United States officials and individuals residing within this country.

I am inclined to agree with Justice Brennan, however, that when a foreign national is held accountable for purported violations of United States criminal laws, he has effectively been treated as one of "the governed" and therefore is entitled to Fourth Amendment protections. . . . I agree with the Government, however, that an American magistrate's lack of power to authorize a search abroad renders the Warrant Clause inapplicable to the search of a noncitizen's residence outside this country.

The Fourth Amendment nevertheless requires that the search be "reasonable." And when the purpose of a search is the procurement of evidence for a criminal prosecution, we have consistently held that the search, to be reasonable, must be based upon probable cause. Neither the District Court nor the Court of Appeals addressed the issue of probable cause, and I do not believe that a reliable determination could be made on the basis of the record before us. I therefore would vacate the judgment of the Court of Appeals and remand the case for further proceedings.

## NOTES AND QUESTIONS

1. *Does Verdugo Limit Reid?* Are *Reid* and *Verdugo* consistent? The *Verdugo* majority argues that *Reid*'s holding is limited to the proposition that U.S. citizens stationed abroad may invoke the protections of the Fifth and Sixth Amendments. But does this invalidate *Reid*'s broader proposition (dictum or not) that the Constitution travels with agents of the U.S. government because they and their government are "entirely a creature of the Constitution"? How can FBI, DEA, or INS agents ever act abroad without drawing their authority and limitations on that authority from the Constitution?
2. *To Which Persons Does the Fourth Amendment Apply?* *Verdugo* indicates that the Fourth Amendment is inapplicable to persons who lack a substantial connection to the United States. Is that conclusion consistent with Justice Kennedy's concurring opinion? Or with Justice Harlan's concurring opinion in *Reid*? Which understanding of the Constitution is more persuasive?
3. *Substantially Connected Aliens.* What is a "substantial connection" to the United States? Could the connection required to invoke the Fourth Amendment be greater than that required by the Due Process Clause for a U.S. criminal court to exercise jurisdiction over a defendant? Verdugo-Urquidez's actual connections were deemed insufficient by the majority. Other cases are inconsistent: one found a two-year illegal stay in the United States insufficient; another found several voluntary trips to negotiate an employment relation sufficient; and a third found that illegal drug trafficking to the United States was sufficient. *See generally* Douglas I. Koff, *Post-Verdugo-Urquidez: The Sufficient Connection Test — Substantially Ambiguous, Substantially Unworkable*, 25 Colum. Hum. Rts. L. Rev. 435, 455-465 (1994). The resulting ambiguity makes it difficult for U.S. officials engaged in overseas surveillance of aliens to know how to proceed. The differentiation among aliens also means that disparate standards may apply to

codefendants engaged in the same conduct, suspected of the same crimes, and subjected to the same search. Should courts draw a brighter line, and, if so, what should it be? *Compare* Randall K. Miller, *The Limits of U.S. International Law Enforcement After Verdugo-Urquidez: Resurrecting Rochin*, 58 U. Pitt. L. Rev. 867, 885 n.88 (1997) (drawing the line at the border, thus denying Fourth Amendment protections to all aliens searched abroad regardless of their connection to the United States), *with* Koff, *supra*, at 485 (extending Fourth Amendment protections to all persons except nonresident enemy aliens searched incident to a military confrontation).

4. ***Handicapping the Use of Force Abroad?*** The *Verdugo* majority worries that extension of Fourth Amendment protections to someone like Verdugo-Urquidez would have made unlawful U.S. naval searches and seizures on the high seas during the Quasi-War with France, and even that it "could significantly disrupt the ability of the political branches to respond to foreign situations" with armed force. Are the three kinds of operations truly analogous? Does Johnson v. Eisentrager, cited by the majority, suggest one answer? Does Bas v. Tingy, *supra* p. 50? Or can the approach urged by Justice Kennedy in *Verdugo* and by Justice Harlan in *Reid* be adapted to these situations?

5. ***Applying Verdugo to Torture.*** Suppose the DEA beats and tortures an "unconnected" alien abroad to force him to reveal the location of invoices, which are then seized and used against him at trial. How, if at all, would you distinguish *Verdugo* in arguing to suppress this evidence on the alien's behalf?

In Harbury v. Deutch, 233 F.3d 596 (D.C. Cir. 2000), the plaintiff alleged that the CIA conspired with its "assets" in Guatemala to violate her Guatemalan husband's substantive due process rights by psychologically abusing and physically torturing him for 18 months before executing him. Acknowledging that the alleged conduct "shocks the conscience," the court concluded that the Fifth Amendment does not prohibit torture by the CIA or its assets of nonresident foreign nationals living abroad. In support of its decision, the court quoted *Verdugo* and the discussion of *Eisentrager* in that case, *supra* p. 272. Can you distinguish *Verdugo*? What about *Eisentrager*, insofar as it is quoted in *Verdugo*? If the torture victim in *Harbury* had survived, could statements obtained from him under duress have been used in evidence against him in a criminal trial?

In 2005, Congress enacted the Detainee Treatment Act (DTA), National Defense Authorization Act for Fiscal Year 2006, Pub. L. No. 109-163, §§1401-1406, 119 Stat. 3136, 3474-3480 (2006). It provides, in part, "No individual in the custody or under the physical control of the United States Government, regardless of nationality or physical location, shall be subject to cruel, inhuman, or degrading treatment or punishment." *Id.* §1403(a). How important is the "regardless of nationality or physical location" language in determining the scope of the government's investigative authority and the rights of the detainee? The DTA is considered in greater detail *infra* pp. 443-444.

The Military Commissions Act of 2006, Pub. L. No. 109-366, 120 Stat. 2600, declares that statements obtained from a defendant by coercion not amounting to torture may be used against him in a trial before a military commission if the degree of coercion is disputed, provided the military judge finds that "(1) the totality of the circumstances renders the statement reliable and possessing sufficient probative value," and "(2) the interests of justice would best be served by admission of the statement into evidence." *Id.* §3(a)(1), 120 Stat. 2607, adding 10 U.S.C. §948r(c) and (d). Evidence obtained by "cruel, inhuman, or degrading treatment or punishment" is barred only if it was obtained after the effective date of the DTA. *Id.* §948r(d). Do you think these provisions will survive a Fourth Amendment challenge if the coercive interrogation was conducted abroad? The Military Commissions Act is examined extensively *infra* pp. 587-600.

The subject of coercive interrogation generally is analyzed in depth in Chapter 13.

## UNITED STATES V. BIN LADEN

United States District Court, Southern District of New York, 2000
126 F. Supp. 2d 264

SAND, District Judge. The Defendants are charged with numerous offenses arising out of their alleged participation in an international terrorist organization [al Qaeda] led by Defendant Usama Bin Laden and that organization's alleged involvement in the August 1998 bombings of the United States Embassies in Nairobi, Kenya and Dar es Salaam, Tanzania. Presently before the Court are Defendant El-Hage's motions which seek the following: suppression of evidence seized from the search of his residence in Nairobi, Kenya in August 1997 and suppression of evidence obtained from electronic surveillance, conducted from August 1996 to August 1997, of four telephone lines in Nairobi, Kenya.

### Background . . .

By the late spring of 1996, the United States intelligence community ("Intelligence Community") became aware that persons associated with Bin Laden's organization had established an al Qaeda presence in Kenya. In addition, the Intelligence Community had isolated and identified five telephone numbers which were being used by persons associated with al Qaeda. All five of these phone lines were monitored by the Intelligence Community from August 1996 through August 1997. One of these phone lines was located in an office in the same building where the Defendant, El-Hage, and his family resided. (El-Hage, an American citizen, and his family lived in Nairobi from 1994 to 1997.) Another of the phone lines was a cellular phone used by El-Hage and others.

On April 4, 1997, the Attorney General authorized the collection of intelligence specifically targeting El-Hage. This authorization was renewed on July 3, 1997. On August 21, 1997, American and Kenyan officials conducted a search of the Defendant's residence. The Defendant's wife (the Defendant was not present during the search) was shown a document which was identified as a Kenyan warrant authorizing a search for "stolen property." The American officials who participated in the search did not, however, "rely upon the Kenyan warrant as the legal authority for the search." At the end of the search, the Defendant's wife was given an inventory by one of the Kenyan officers present which enumerated the items which had been seized during the search.

## Analysis . . .

El-Hage's suppression motion raises significant issues of first impression concerning the applicability of the full panoply of the Fourth Amendment to searches conducted abroad by the United States for foreign intelligence purposes and which are directed at an American citizen believed to be an agent of a foreign power. . . .

## I. Application of the Fourth Amendment Overseas

Before proceeding to that Fourth Amendment analysis, it is necessary to ascertain whether the Amendment applies in this situation. El-Hage is an American citizen and the searches at issue were conducted in Kenya. . . .

The Supreme Court cases on point suggest that the Fourth Amendment applies to United States citizens abroad. See Reid v. Covert, 354 U.S. 1, 5-6 (1957) (plurality opinion) (stating, in a case involving the Fifth and Sixth Amendments, that the "shield" provided to an American citizen by the Bill of Rights "should not be stripped away just because he happens to be in another land"). . . . Thus, this Court finds that even though the searches at issue in this case occurred in Kenya, El-Hage can bring a Fourth Amendment challenge. However, the extent of the Fourth Amendment protection, in particular the applicability of the Warrant Clause, is unclear.

## II. An Exception to the Warrant Requirement for Foreign Intelligence Searches

. . . According to the Government, searches conducted for the purpose of foreign intelligence collection which target persons who are agents of a foreign power do not require a warrant. . . .

The question, for this Court, is twofold. First, it is necessary to evaluate whether there is an exception to the warrant requirement for searches conducted abroad for purposes of foreign intelligence collection. Second, if such an exception exists, the Court must evaluate whether the searches conducted in this case properly fall within the parameters of that exception.

### A. The constitutional and practical bases for the exception . . .

#### 1. The President's power over foreign affairs

In all of the cases finding an exception to the warrant requirement for foreign intelligence collection, a determinative basis for the decision was the constitutional grant to the Executive Branch of power over foreign affairs. . . .

Warrantless foreign intelligence collection has been an established practice of the Executive Branch for decades. . . . Congress has legislated with respect to domestic incidents of foreign intelligence collection, see FISA, 50 U.S.C. §§1801 et. seq. (1978), but has not addressed the issue of foreign intelligence collection which occurs abroad. The Supreme Court has remained, in the three decades since *Keith* [United States v. United States District Court, 407 U.S. 297 (1972), *supra* p. 91], essentially silent on both aspects of the issue. . . . While the fact of this silence is not dispositive of the question before this Court, it is by no means insignificant. . . .

### 2. The costs of imposing a warrant requirement

It is generally the case that imposition of a warrant requirement better safeguards the Fourth Amendment rights of citizens in the Defendant's position. But several cases direct that when the imposition of a warrant requirement proves to be a disproportionate and perhaps even disabling burden on the Executive, a warrant should not be required. *See* [United States v. Truong Dinh Hung, 629 F.2d 908, 913 (4th Cir. 1980), *supra* p. 106] (finding that a requirement that officials secure a warrant before these types of searches "would 'unduly frustrate' the President in carrying out his foreign affairs responsibilities"); *Keith*, 407 U.S. at 315 ("We must also ask whether a warrant requirement would unduly frustrate the efforts of Government to protect itself from acts of subversion and overthrow directed against it."). For several reasons, it is clear that imposition of a warrant requirement in the context of foreign intelligence searches conducted abroad would be a significant and undue burden on the Executive.

It has been asserted that the judicial branch is ill-suited to the task of overseeing foreign intelligence collection. Foreign affairs decisions, it has been said, are often particularly complex. *See* Chicago & Southern Airlines [v. Waterman S.S. Corp., 333 U.S. 103, 111 (1948)] (explaining that foreign affairs decisions are "of a kind for which the Judiciary has neither aptitude, facilities nor responsibility"). These arguments have, to some extent, been undercut by both the Supreme Court, in *Keith*, and Congress, in FISA. On the other hand, neither *Keith* nor FISA addresses the particular difficulties attendant to *overseas* foreign intelligence collection. In fact, as mentioned previously, it was precisely these peculiarities which caused Congress to restrain the reach of FISA to domestic searches. The Government makes several persuasive points about the intricacies of foreign intelligence collection conducted abroad. First, the Government cautions that a court would have greater difficulty (than in the domestic context) predicting "the international consequences flowing from a decision on the merits regarding Executive Branch foreign policy decisions." Often these decisions have significant impacts on the essential cooperative relationships between United States officials and foreign intelligence services. In addition, when some members of the government of the country in which the searches are sought to be conducted are perceived as hostile to the United States or sympathetic to the targets of the search, a procedure requiring notification to that government could be self-defeating. The Government also explains that too much involvement could place American courts in an "institutionally untenable position" when the operations which are authorized are violative of foreign law.

These concerns about the complexity of foreign intelligence decisions should not be taken to mean that the judiciary is not capable of making these judgments. Judges will, of course, be called on to assess the constitutionality of these searches ex post. Requiring judicial approval in advance, however, would inevitably mean costly increases in the response time of the Executive Branch. . . .

In addition to concerns about the impact of a warrant requirement on the speed of the executive response, there is an increased possibility of breaches of security when the Executive is required to take the Judiciary into its confidence. The Government emphasizes the detrimental impact that the existence of a warrant requirement for foreign intelligence searches might have on the cooperative relationships which are integral to overseas foreign intelligence collection efforts. As the Government explains, "[t]he mere *perception* that inadvertent disclosure is more likely is sufficient to obstruct the intelligence collection imperative." The United States' heightened dependence on foreign governments for assistance in overseas foreign intelligence collection is a concern that was not addressed by the circuit courts that considered an exception to the warrant requirement for foreign intelligence collection within this country.

### 3. The absence of a warrant procedure

The final consideration which persuades the Court of the need for an exception to the warrant requirement for foreign intelligence collection conducted overseas is that there is presently no statutory basis for the issuance of a warrant to conduct searches abroad. In addition, existing warrant procedures and standards are simply not suitable for foreign intelligence searches. . . .

. . . As an additional point, the people and agencies upon whom the Executive relies in the foreign intelligence context for information and cooperation would undoubtedly be wary of any warrant procedures that did not adequately protect sensitive foreign intelligence information.

### B. Adoption of the foreign intelligence exception to the warrant requirement

In light of the concerns outlined here, the Court finds that the power of the Executive to conduct foreign intelligence collection would be significantly frustrated by the imposition of a warrant requirement in this context. Therefore, this Court adopts the foreign intelligence exception to the warrant requirement for searches targeting foreign powers (or their agents) which are conducted abroad. . . .

At the same time, the Court is mindful of the importance of the Fourth Amendment interests at stake. In keeping with the precedents reviewed above, the warrant exception adopted by this Court is narrowly drawn to include only those overseas searches, authorized by the President (or his delegate, the Attorney General), which are conducted primarily for foreign intelligence purposes and which target foreign powers or their agents. . . . All warrantless searches are still governed by the reasonableness requirement and can be challenged in ex post criminal or civil proceedings.

### C. Application of the exception

Before the Court can find that the exception applies to this case, it is necessary to show, first, that Mr. El-Hage was an agent of a foreign power; second, that the searches in question were conducted "primarily" for foreign intelligence purposes; and finally, that the searches were authorized by the President or the Attorney General.

### 1. Agent of a foreign power

It is clear from the Court's review of the evidence contained in the classified DCI declaration and in the materials considered by the Attorney General in issuing authorization for the post-April 4, 1997 surveillance and the August 21, 1997 search of El-Hage's residence that there was probable cause to suspect that El-Hage was an agent of a foreign power. The Court is also persuaded that al Qaeda was properly considered a foreign power. In reaching this conclusion, the Court relies on the definitions of "foreign power" and "agent of a foreign power" which were incorporated by Congress into FISA. *See* 50 U.S.C. §1801(a)-(b) [*supra* p. 132].

### 2. Primarily for foreign intelligence purposes

This exception to the warrant requirement applies until and unless the primary purpose of the searches stops being foreign intelligence collection. *See Truong*, 629 F.2d at 915. If foreign intelligence collection is merely *a* purpose and not the *primary* purpose of a search, the exception does not apply. Similarly, if a reviewing judge finds that the Government officials were "looking for evidence of criminal conduct *unrelated* to the foreign affairs needs of a President, then he would undoubtedly hold the surveillances to be illegal and take appropriate measures." [United States v. Butenko, 494 F.2d 593, 606 (3d Cir. 1974) (en banc), *cert. denied sub nom.* Ivanov v. United States, 419 U.S. 881 (1974) (emphasis added)]. . . .

The Government's submissions establish persuasively that the purpose, throughout the entire electronic surveillance of El-Hage and during the physical search of his Nairobi residence, was primarily the collection of foreign intelligence information about the activities of Usama Bin Laden and al Qaeda. There was no FBI participation in the electronic surveillance that took place. Although there was an FBI agent present during the search of El-Hage's residence, the Court does not find that foreign intelligence collection ceased to be the primary purpose of that search. The Court's determination about the purpose of the residential search is, in part, dependent upon the Government's classified submissions. For that reason, further analysis of this question is included in Classified Appendix A.

In particular, the Government explained that the purpose of its efforts was "to gather intelligence about al Qaeda, including the status of the Kenyan cell, the points of contact for other al Qaeda cells around the world, as well as any indications of the future terrorist plans of al Qaeda." The searches yielded important foreign intelligence information. The electronic surveillance that was conducted revealed that al Qaeda persons in Kenya "were heavily involved in: providing passports and other false documentation to various al Qaeda associates . . . ; passing messages to al Qaeda members and associates . . . ; passing coded telephone numbers to and from al Qaeda headquarters; . . . and passing warnings when al Qaeda members and associates were compromised by authorities." Similarly, the Government asserts that the physical search "recovered documents of great intelligence value from el Hage's computer, including a report in which el Hage's close associate Harun made an explicit admission that the Kenyan cell of Bin Laden's group were responsible for the American military personnel killed in Somalia in 1993." The Court is satisfied that the facts presented here, while perhaps suggestive of an investigation that was driven by multiple motives, clearly establish that the primary purpose of the searches at issue was, from start to finish, foreign intelligence collection.

### 3. Authorization from the President or the Attorney General

Finally, to apply the exception to the warrant requirement for foreign intelligence searches conducted abroad against an agent of a foreign power, the Court must find that the searches in question were directly authorized by the President or the Attorney General. On April 4, 1997 (and again on July 3, 1997), the Attorney General gave her express authorization for the foreign intelligence collection techniques (including the post-April 4, 1997 electronic surveillance and the August 21, 1997 physical search) that were employed. . . .

The electronic surveillance conducted from August 1996 until April 4, 1997 is, however, not embraced by the foreign intelligence exception to the warrant requirement. The Government does not rely on the foreign intelligence exception and seeks, instead, to distinguish the pre-authorization surveillance by emphasizing that it was directed at the activities of al Qaeda, generally, and not at El-Hage. In the Government's words, although "incidental" interception of El-Hage was "anticipated," he was not the "target" of the collection. For that reason, the Government believed that its only constitutional obligation was to "minimize interception of el-Hage." It is on this basis that the Government suggests that no Fourth Amendment violation occurred. . . .

In the cases which have rejected the Fourth Amendment claims of an incidental interceptee, though, the term "incidental" appears to be reserved for those situations where, at the time the wiretap order was sought, either the identity or the actual involvement of the interceptee was not known. . . .

Ultimately, the Court holds that with respect to the electronic surveillance of the home and cellular phones, El-Hage was not intercepted "incidentally" because he was not an unanticipated user of those telephones and because he was believed to be a participant in the activities being investigated. The Court finds that El-Hage had a reasonable expectation of privacy in his home and cellular phones and the Government should have obtained approval from either the President or the Attorney General before undertaking the electronic surveillance on those phone lines in August 1996.

### III. The Exclusionary Rule

Despite the fact that this electronic surveillance was unlawful, the Court finds that exclusion of this evidence would be inappropriate because it would not have the deterrent effect which the exclusionary rule requires and because the surveillance was undertaken in good faith. . . .

### A. Deterrence

. . . [T]he main purpose of the exclusionary rule is deterrence. . . .

The Court is satisfied that the goal of the intelligence collection, "to neutralize the Bin Laden threat to national security," overwhelmingly dominated the electronic surveillance conducted prior to April 4, 1997. There was no FBI participation in that surveillance and the Court believes that the surveillance would have been conducted even if there had been an awareness that the material recorded would be inadmissible at a future criminal trial of El-Hage. Although El-Hage suggests that suppression would have the effect of deterring the Government "from improperly merging 'foreign-intelligence gathering' and criminal investigations," the Court did not find that there was any evidence of an impermissible merger in this case. . . .

### B. Good faith

One offshoot of the deterrence analysis has been the development of an exception to the exclusionary rule that is derived from the "good faith" of the officials involved in a particular search.

. . . The Court is persuaded that the officials who conducted the electronic surveillance operated under an actual and reasonable belief that Attorney General approval was not required prior to April 4, 1997, when El-Hage was specifically identified by the Government as a target of foreign intelligence collection. The surveillance was also conducted in a good faith attempt to conform to the Government's perception of what the law allowed. The Court finds that the officials' interpretation of the caselaw which informs this analysis was reasonable even if in the end it was incorrect. Therefore, the exclusionary rule should not be applied.

## IV. The Reasonableness Requirement

Even if the Government was not required to secure a warrant in advance of the searches, the Fourth Amendment still requires that the searches be reasonable. . . .

### A. The physical search of the residence

All of the cases which have established the existence of a foreign intelligence exception to the warrant requirement (and which are relied upon by the Government) arose in the context of electronic surveillance. El-Hage also notes, correctly, that "[n]one of the other 'foreign intelligence-gathering' cases involved a residential search." It is therefore necessary to assess whether the precedents reviewed apply with equal force to a physical search of the home.

The proposition that searches of the home have always merited rigorous Fourth Amendment scrutiny is unassailable. At the same time, numerous cases have emphasized the highly intrusive nature of electronic surveillance. These cases, considering the relative intrusiveness of residential searches and electronic surveillance, generally seem to conclude that neither automatically merits greater protection from the Fourth Amendment.

. . . For these reasons, the Court finds that the foreign intelligence exception to the warrant requirement applies with equal force to residential searches. El-Hage's argument that the search of his residence was *per se* unreasonable is therefore rejected.

In addition, the limited scope and overall nature of the search indicate that the search was executed in a reasonable manner and was not, as El-Hage alleges, "conducted as if pursuant to a 'general warrant.'" The Government and the Defendant both state that the search was conducted during the daytime, an inventory of the items seized was left at the residence and that an American official was present for the search (and "identified himself . . . in true name"). The scope of the search was limited to those items which were believed to have foreign intelligence value and retention and dissemination of the evidence acquired during the search were minimized. Therefore, the items seized during the physical search of El-Hage's Kenya residence are not suppressed.

## B. The electronic surveillance

The Defendant argues that the electronic surveillance undertaken in this case is unreasonable because there were no reasonable durational limits on the surveillance: "the Government continuously and without interruption intercepted any and all of Mr. El-Hage's and his family's telephone conversations and facsimiles from July 1996 through September 1997." Although the excessive length of an electronic surveillance can be a factor tending toward unreasonableness, courts will consider the duration and the continuity within the context of a particular case. As the Government notes, more extensive monitoring and "greater leeway" in minimization efforts are permitted in a case like this given the "world-wide, covert and diffuse nature of the international terrorist group(s) targeted."

In addition, the Government emphasizes that the recorded conversations were conducted in a foreign language and that there was a high likelihood that some of the seemingly innocuous conversations were in code. The Government minimized the electronic surveillance by limiting the conversations for which verbatim transcripts were prepared and by disseminating the Defendant's name only where necessary for foreign intelligence purposes.

Finally, the Government's surveillance was reasonable in light of the use to which the telephones in question were put. Here the Government's assertion that these were "communal" phones which were regularly used by al Qaeda associates is highly relevant. For these reasons this Court finds that the automated recording of the phone lines was not unreasonable. . . .

## Conclusion

For the foregoing reasons, El-Hage's motion to suppress evidence from the physical search of his Kenya residence and electronic surveillance is denied without a hearing.

*So ordered.*

## Declassified Appendix A

As outlined in the opinion, the Court finds that the search of El-Hage's residence was undertaken primarily for the purpose of foreign intelligence collection. The mere fact that FBI Agent Coleman [*redacted*] was present during the residential search does not mean that law enforcement displaced foreign intelligence collection as the primary purpose of the search. Coleman's presence was intended to ensure that "if anything of evidentiary value for law enforcement was found, [he] could testify to a chain of custody without involving covert [*redacted*] employees." ([*Name redacted*] Decl. ¶ 65.) Although [*redacted*] has, at times, "attempted to accommodate law enforcement . . . the primary focus has been collection, disruption, and dissemination of intelligence" on Bin Laden and his organization. (*Id.* ¶ 38.) The intelligence objective, [*redacted*] was at all times overriding, (*Id.* ¶ 59.) It was also believed that evidence gleaned from El-Hage's computer would provide [*redacted*] "insight into the Bin Laden infrastructure." (*Id.*) The Government's assertion that [*redacted*] actions were primarily for the purpose of foreign intelligence collection is reinforced by the fact that foreign intelligence collection against Bin Laden and al Qaeda "continues today." (*Id.* ¶ 38.) As is clear from the [*name redacted*] Declaration, the search of El-Hage's residence yielded important intelligence information about Bin Laden's organization. (¶ 67.) Finally, in disseminating the information discovered during the search, [*redacted*] followed minimization procedures (*Id.* ¶ 68).

## NOTES AND QUESTIONS

1. ***Impracticality of Warrants for Searches Abroad.*** Before reaching the "foreign intelligence exception" to the warrant requirement, the court concludes that such a requirement is impractical for searches conducted abroad. Do you agree? How would a warrant requirement be implemented for such searches? *See* Justin M. Sandberg, *The Need for Warrants Authorizing Foreign Intelligence Searches of American Citizens Abroad: A Call for Formalism*, 69 U. Chi. L. Rev. 403 (2002) (urging judicial creation of warrant requirement); Carrie Truehart, Comment, *United States v. Bin Laden and the Foreign Intelligence Exception to the Warrant Requirement for Searches of "United States Persons" Abroad*, 82 B.U. L. Rev. 555 (2002) (urging statutory implementation of asserted constitutional warrant requirement). The USA Patriot Act, enacted shortly after the September 11, 2001, terrorist attacks, now authorizes a federal magistrate "in any district in which activities related to terrorism may have occurred" to issue a warrant for a search of property or a person "within or outside the district." Pub. L. No. 107-56, §219, 115 Stat. 272, 291 (2001). In view of the impracticality of warrants for searches abroad, should this provision be interpreted to reach searches abroad?

2. ***Foreign Intelligence Exception.*** Even if the warrant requirement otherwise applied, the court adopts a foreign intelligence exception. How are its requirements satisfied in *Bin Laden*? Isn't foreign intelligence collection always a continuing purpose of any overseas surveillance of suspected terrorists? How and when, if ever, would it become a secondary purpose? Suppose several of El-Hage's at-large associates were secretly indicted with him, and surveillance of them continued until they were apprehended. Would the fruits of that surveillance also fall within the foreign intelligence exception?

3. ***Reasonableness of Searches Abroad.*** The court holds that even though the warrant requirement is inapplicable, searches conducted abroad still

must be reasonable. How does it test for reasonableness? Can you derive a general test from its analysis?

In United States v. Barona, 56 F.3d 1087 (9th Cir. 1995), a divided court came up with different tests for reasonableness of warrantless surveillance of U.S. citizens abroad in a drug-smuggling investigation. The majority looked to good faith compliance with the law of the foreign country where the surveillance was conducted, absent conduct that shocks the conscience. *Id.* at 1103. In fact, the United States has entered into a growing number of bilateral mutual legal assistance treaties (MLATs) that independently require U.S. officials operating abroad to comply with the law of the foreign state. *See, e.g.,* Treaty Between the United States and the Government of Mexico on Mutual Legal Assistance in Criminal Matters, Dec. 9, 1987, U.S.-Mex., art. 12, 1987 U.S.T. LEXIS 208 ("A request for search, seizure, and delivery of any object acquired thereby to the requesting State shall be executed if it includes the information justifying such action *under the laws of the requested Party.*") (emphasis supplied). Such treaties confer no private rights, but their very existence may support the *Barona* court's incorporation of a compliance-with-foreign-law requirement into the Fourth Amendment's reasonableness standard. (They also create formal methods for U.S. law enforcement authorities to obtain help with investigations abroad.)

Judge Reinhardt dissented vigorously. Under the majority's reasoning, he argued, Americans are not only relegated to the "vagaries of foreign law," they are given

> *even less* protection than foreign law since . . . the Constitution does not even require foreign officials to comply with their own law; all that is required is that American officials have a good faith belief that they did so. . . . [W]hen Americans enter Iraq, Iran, Singapore, Kuwait, China, or other similarly inclined foreign lands, they can be treated by the United States government exactly the way those foreign nations treat their own citizens — at least for Fourth Amendment purposes. [56 F.3d at 1101.]

Instead, Judge Reinhardt argued, the government still must have probable cause for a foreign search, even if a warrant is impractical. On a motion to suppress, a court would make a post hoc determination of probable cause based on the government's explanation of why it initiated the search. "Because judicial scrutiny of the search will always take place *after* it has been conducted, there is no conceivable way that imposing such a requirement would hinder law enforcement efforts abroad — except to the extent that those efforts violate our own Constitution." *Id.* at 1102.

Why do you suppose the government expressly declined to rely on its compliance with a Kenyan warrant as legal authority for the search against El-Hage? If it had not declined, how would that surveillance fare under the two standards set out in *Barona*, based on the facts given and on what those facts reasonably imply? Which of these tests for reasonableness — the *Bin Laden* test, the *Barona* test, or Judge Reinhardt's test — is most nearly faithful to Fourth Amendment values?

4. ***The Good Faith Exception.*** No matter which test for reasonableness a court employs, it may still decline to exclude evidence by finding that the law enforcement officers made a "good faith" mistake. How did the court apply the good faith exception in *Bin Laden*?

5. ***The Silver Platter Doctrine.*** Suppose the Kenyan police *alone* had conducted the warrantless surveillance of El-Hage without probable cause and in flagrant violation of their own laws. Should a U.S. court suppress the fruits of such a foreign police surveillance? With two exceptions noted below, the courts have uniformly held no. Because the Bill of Rights does not protect Americans from the acts of foreign sovereigns, and because applying the exclusionary rule to such acts would not deter them, such evidence can be turned over to U.S. law enforcement officials on a "silver platter" and admitted in U.S. criminal prosecutions. *See generally* Eric Bentley, *Toward an International Fourth Amendment: Rethinking Searches and Seizures After Verdugo-Urquidez*, 27 Vand. J. Transnatl. L. 329, 374-375 (1994); Robert L. King, *The International Silver Platter and the "Shocks the Conscience" Test: U.S. Law Enforcement Overseas*, 67 Wash. U. L.Q. 489, 511 (1989); Steven H. Theisen, *Evidence Seized in Foreign Searches: When Does the Fourth Amendment Exclusionary Rule Apply?*, 25 Wm. & Mary L. Rev. 161 (1983).

6. ***The Joint Venture Exception.*** Courts have recognized an exception to the silver platter doctrine for searches that are "joint ventures" between U.S. and foreign officials. Such searches are deemed the acts of the U.S. officials and subject to whatever limitations apply to U.S. searches abroad. Unfortunately, the courts are not agreed on what constitutes a "joint venture." Most agree that it is not a joint venture for U.S. agents merely to provide a tip to foreign police, and many hold it insufficient for U.S. agents just to request, be present during, or even participate in the search as long as they did not initiate and control it. *See* Bentley, *supra*, at 400 nn.297-314; Koff, *supra* p. 276, at 492 n.19. The *Restatement* simply restates the question by requiring application of the exclusionary rule only where "the participation of United States law enforcement officers in the investigation, arrest, search, or interrogation through which the evidence was obtained was so substantial as to render the action that of the United States." *Restatement (Third) of Foreign Relations Law of the United States* §433(3) (1987). A comment explains that such participation is lacking when U.S. officers "only assist, advise, or observe"; they must be "predominantly involved." *Id.* comment a. The Second Circuit has cut its own path, asking whether foreign police are acting as agents of the United States or whether U.S. law enforcement agents are evading our law by using foreign police. *See* United States v. Maturo, 982 F.2d 57, 61 (2d Cir. 1992). How would a court apply this standard? Apparently, U.S. participation in the Kenyan search was so substantial that the government did not contest responsibility. Related questions about the U.S. practice of rendering terrorist suspects to a third country for interrogation (and likely harsh treatment) by that country's police or intelligence officials are considered in Chapter 14.

7. ***The Shocks-the-Conscience Exception.*** A second exception to the silver platter doctrine exists for conduct that shocks the conscience. It was

articulated in United States v. Toscanino, 500 F.2d 267 (2d Cir. 1974), a forcible abduction case. But while it has been paid lip service in multiple opinions since then, it apparently has been applied to exclude evidence only in United States v. Fernandez-Caro, 677 F. Supp. 893 (S.D. Tex. 1987):

> The Defendant's undisputed evidence is that the [Mexican Federal Judicial Police] threatened to kill him, beat him about the face and body, poured water through his nostrils while he was stripped, bound, and gagged, and applied electrical shocks to his wet body, among other things. The [U.S.] Government does not dispute this evidence. Indeed, Agent Garza confirmed that when the Defendant was physically delivered to American officials by Mexican officials, physical signs of abuse were readily apparent on Defendant's body. Under these circumstances, the motion [to suppress evidence that was the fruit of a confession obtained by the torture conducted by the Mexican police] is easily resolved. . . . The conduct of the Mexican police officials violated even minimal standards of decency expected in a civilized society. Certainly the abuse of Defendant exceeded the conduct which "shocked the conscience" of the United States Supreme Court in Rochin v. California, 342 U.S. 165 (1952). Even more than in *Rochin*, the methods employed here were "too close to the rack and the screw" to be acceptable. [*Id.* at 894-895, quoting *Rochin*, 343 U.S. at 172.]

Exclusion of such evidence is "not based on our Fourth Amendment jurisprudence," said the majority in *Barona*, "but rather on the recognition that we may employ our supervisory powers when absolutely necessary to preserve the integrity of the criminal justice system." 56 F.3d at 1091. Such forced confessions may be excluded even when obtained by foreign officials not acting as agents of the United States. *Maturo, supra*, 982 F.2d at 60-61. *See also* United States v. Nagelberg, 434 F.2d 585, 587 n.1 (2d Cir. 1970) (suggesting that a foreign officer's "rubbing pepper in the eyes" of a prisoner might require exclusion of the prisoner's statement).

The reason the exception has not been applied more often is probably *not* that there are few investigations that could qualify. Many foreign police use investigatory methods that might shock the conscience of a U.S. court. *See, e.g.*, Kevin Sullivan, *Mexico Pledges an End to Torture of Suspects*, Wash. Post, Mar. 6, 2001, at A18. The more likely reason is serious doctrinal confusion in the courts about the shocks-the-conscience exception. After *Verdugo*, for example, does it apply at all to unconnected aliens?

There is also confusion about the constitutional basis for the exception. Is the exception grounded in the Fourth Amendment or in the Fifth Amendment's guarantee of substantive due process or protection against compelled self-incrimination? The Supreme Court has asserted that "[w]here a particular Amendment provides an explicit textual source of constitutional protection against a particular source of government behavior, that Amendment, not the more generalized notion of substantive due process, must be the guide for analyzing these claims." Graham v. Connor, 490 U.S. 386, 395 (1989) (internal quotation marks omitted). It is unclear whether this confines the shocks-the-conscience test to Fourth Amendment analysis. Moreover, the Supreme Court is deeply divided about whether substantive due process questions in general should be resolved by reference to "our Nation's history, legal traditions, and practices," Washington v. Glucksberg, 521 U.S. 702, 736 (1997), or to "the contemporary conscience [and] an understanding of contemporary practice." Sacramento v. Lewis, 523 U.S. 833, 847 n.8 (1998). Justice Scalia has ridiculed "th' ol' 'shocks-the-conscience' test" in other settings as "the *ne plus ultra*, the Napoleon Brandy, the Mahatma Ghandi, the Celophane of subjectivity." *Id.* at 861 (Scalia, J., concurring in judgment).

Finally, despite the court's statement in *Barona, supra*, there is confusion about the prudential basis for an exclusionary rule aimed at shocking conduct by foreign police. Such a rule would probably have no deterrent effect on the offending police. United States courts have no authority to exercise supervisory power over foreign courts, and, some scholars argue, no reason to exercise it over their own system when the shocking conduct was perpetrated by foreign officials. *See* Theisen, *supra*, at 168 (arguing that because an offending foreign official is incapable of violating the U.S. Constitution, the admission of evidence seized by him does not impair U.S. courts' integrity).

**8. *International Prohibitions on Shocking Investigative Conduct.*** Arguments against the shocks-the-conscience exception may be unduly parochial. The prohibition against torture is a peremptory norm of international law, or *jus cogens*. See *infra* p. 436. In addition, the United States has ratified the Convention Against Torture and Other Cruel, Inhuman or Degrading Treatment or Punishment, Dec. 10, 1984, S. Treaty Doc. No. 100-20 (1988), 1465 U.N.T.S. 85, which requires states to adopt measures to prevent acts of "torture," defined in relevant part as

> any act by which severe pain or suffering, whether physical or mental, is intentionally inflicted on a person *for such purposes as obtaining from him or a third person information or a confession* . . . when such pain or suffering is inflicted by or at the instigation of or with the consent or acquiescence of a public official or other person acting in an official capacity. [*Id.* art. 1(1) (emphasis added).]

Congress has included a similar definition in the Torture Victim Protection Act, 28 U.S.C. §1350 note (2000), creating a civil cause of action for victims of torture, and in legislation implementing the Convention, 18 U.S.C. §§2340-2340B (2000 & Supp. IV 2004), which criminalizes acts of torture. The laws prohibiting torture are considered in greater detail *infra* pp. 443-451.

Thus, sanctions against torture are already part of our law. Excluding evidence obtained by torture — no matter which officials committed the acts — would vindicate international law and "demonstrate that no civilized nations should countenance violations of fundamental human rights." Stephen Saltzburg, *The Reach of the Bill of Rights Beyond the Terra Firma of the United States*, 20 Va. J. Intl. L. 741, 775 (1980). Do you think such exclusions by U.S. courts might even deter foreign police from violating peremptory international law?

9. ***Statutory Endorsements of the Silver Platter Doctrine?*** Six years after *Verdugo*, Congress authorized the intelligence community to collect information outside the United States against non-U.S. persons at the request of law enforcement agencies, "notwithstanding that the law enforcement agency intends to use the information collected for purposes of a law enforcement investigation or counterintelligence investigation." 50 U.S.C. §403-5a(a) (2000). Does the act impliedly approve the admission of such information into evidence however it was obtained? *See* Thomas Cooperstein, *The Emerging Interplay Between Law Enforcement and Intelligence Gathering*, Intl. & Natl. Security L. News 3, 9 (1997). Should the Act be read to prevail over inconsistent international law forbidding the use of torture to obtain information? See *infra* pp. 434-443.

What effect, if any, does the DTA prohibition of cruel, inhuman, or degrading treatment, *supra* p. 277, have on intelligence collection abroad? Do you think the admissibility of evidence obtained by coercive interrogation in trials before military commissions, as authorized by the Military Commissions Act of 2006, *supra* p. 277, will have any practical effect on intelligence collection abroad? At least within the context in which the 2006 Act applies, has Congress effectively repealed the exceptions to the silver platter doctrine? Could it do so consistent with the Fourth Amendment?

10. ***An International Fourth Amendment?*** No clear international standard has yet emerged for government searches and seizures, although the International Covenant on Civil and Political Rights, which the United States ratified in 1992, provides that "[n]o one shall be subjected to arbitrary or unlawful interference with his privacy, family, home or correspondence. . . . Everyone has the right to the protection of the law against such interference or attacks." International Covenant on Civil and Political Rights, Dec. 16, 1966, art. 17, 999 U.N.T.S. 171. Do you think a U.S. court would ever find, based on the Covenant, that a search that complied with foreign law was "arbitrary and unlawful," that probable cause should have been shown, or that a warrant was required? Would a U.S. court ever find that evidence produced by such a search should be excluded?

# DETAINING AND INTERROGATING TERRORIST SUSPECTS

# 10
# CIVIL DETENTION OF TERRORIST SUSPECTS

Investigation of the September 11 terrorist attacks (dubbed the PENTTBOM investigation)[1] began even before the last plane crashed, but not simply to identify, apprehend, and convict the perpetrators in the time-honored fashion of criminal investigations. Assistant Attorney General Michael Chertoff explained:

> In past terrorist investigations, you usually had a defined event and you're investigating it after the fact. That's not what we had here. . . . From the start, there was every reason to believe that there [was] more to come. . . . So we thought that we were getting information to prevent more attacks, which was even more important than trying any case that came out of the attacks. [*Quoted in* Toobin, *supra* note 1.]

The FBI immediately checked passenger manifests, airport terminal and parking garage videotapes, car rental agreements, credit card receipts, telephone records, and numerous other data sources to help identify the hijackers. It then extended its investigation to persons who lived or worked with the hijackers or otherwise crossed paths with them.

Most of those interviewed were foreign nationals. The FBI itself detained some or had state and local authorities detain them on suspicion of committing a variety of minor crimes. In addition, it detained a few persons as "material witnesses." The Bureau asked the INS to detain many others who were in technical violation of their immigration status ("out-of-status" immigrants).

---

1. Background about the investigation has been drawn from The Constitution Project, *Report on Post-9/11 Detentions*, June 2, 2004; Amnesty International, *United States of America: Amnesty International's Concerns Regarding Post September 11 Detentions in the USA* (AMR 51/044/2002), Mar. 14, 2002; Jeffrey Rosen, *Holding Pattern*, New Republic, Dec. 10, 2001, at 17; *Hearing on DOJ Oversight: Preserving Our Freedom While Defending Against Terrorism, Before the S. Comm. on the Judiciary*, 107th Cong. (2001) (statements of John Ashcroft, Attorney General, and Michael Chertoff, Asst. Attorney General); Dan Eggen, *Many Held on Tenuous Ties to Sept. 11*, Wash. Post, Nov. 29, 2001; Dept. of Justice, *Attorney General Ashcroft Provides Total Number of Federal Criminal Charges and INS Detainees*, Nov. 27, 2001; Jeffrey Toobin, *Crackdown*, New Yorker, Nov. 5, 2001, at 56; Amy Goldstein, *A Deliberate Strategy of Disruption; Massive, Secretive Detention Effort Aimed Mainly at Preventing More Terror*, Wash. Post, Nov. 4, 2001, at A1.

"We're clearly not standing on ceremony, and if there is a basis to hold them we're going to hold them," Chertoff said in reference to the detentions. *Id.* Attorney General Ashcroft was even more blunt: "We have waged a deliberate campaign of arrest and detention to remove suspected terrorists who violate the law from our streets." *Hearing on DOJ Oversight, supra* note 1.

Within weeks, the media reported that more than 1,100 persons had been or were being detained by law enforcement authorities. Although the government declined to release a breakdown of this number, a newspaper investigation of 235 detainees whom it could identify indicated that the largest number were from Egypt, Saudi Arabia, and Pakistan. By the end of November, federal criminal charges had been brought against 104 individuals (most relating to possession of false identification or other fraud), of whom 55 were then in custody, while the INS had detained 548 persons for immigration violations.

In January 2002, the government initiated the "Absconder Apprehension Initiative" to locate and deport 6,000 Arabs and Muslims with outstanding deportation orders (among more than 300,000 foreign nationals subject to similar orders). As of May 2003, another 2,747 noncitizens were detained as part of a Special Registration Program directed at Arabs and Muslims.

The following affidavit of an FBI agent, opposing an immigrant detainee's bond request, offers a rare insight into the otherwise secretive investigative process.

## AFFIDAVIT OF MICHAEL E. ROLINCE, U.S. DEPT. OF JUSTICE, EXEC. OFFICE FOR IMMIGRATION REVIEW, IMMIGRATION COURT

*Reprinted in* Human Rights Watch, *Presumption of Guilt: Human Rights Abuses of Post-September 11 Detainees,* App. B (Aug. 2002) *available at* http://www.hrw.org/reports/2002/us911/USA0802.pdf

In Bond Proceedings
RE: ALI ABUBAKR ALI AL-MAQTARI

Pursuant to 28 U.S.C. §1736, I, Michael E. Rolince, hereby declare as follows:

1. I have been employed by the Federal Bureau of Investigation (FBI) since September 1974 as a Special Agent, and since August 1998, I have been the Section Chief of the Counterterrorism Division's International Terrorism Operations Section (ITOS) at FBI Headquarters in Washington D.C. . . .

3. As the ITOS Section Chief, I am personally involved in and have significant supervisory responsibilities for the nationwide FBI investigation initiated in response to a series of deadly terrorist attacks which occurred on September 11, 2001. As such, I am privy both to the broad scope of and to particular details from the investigation. . . .

5. The FBI has identified nineteen suspected hijackers, some of whose legal immigration status had expired. Based on a review of intelligence and other source information, the FBI has reason to believe that the hijackers were associated with al Qaeda, aka "the Base," an international network of terrorist cells controlled by Osama bin Laden, which has been formally designated by the Department of State as a foreign terrorist organization since October 8, 1999.

Prior to the September 11, 2001 attacks, Osama bin Laden was being sought by the FBI in connection with the August 7, 1998 bombings of the United States embassies in Dar es Salaam, Tanzania, and Nairobi, Kenya, which killed over 200 individuals.

6. At the direction of President George W. Bush and Attorney General John Ashcroft, the FBI has initiated a nationwide investigation to identify and apprehend individuals involved in the hijackings and to prevent future acts of terrorism within the United States. To date the FBI has received or generated more than 250,000 leads from its web site, special hot line, a toll-free WATTS line, and in the FBI field offices, and additional leads are coming in every day. The investigation has yielded over 300 searches, and more than 100 court orders and 3000 subpoenas. There is still a great deal of information to be collected before the FBI will be in a position to determine the full scope of the terrorist conspiracy and to determine the full extent of damage that the terrorists intended to cause.

7. The FBI has come to believe that associates of the hijackers with connections to foreign terrorist organizations may still be in the United States. The tips received and the leads developed in our field offices have enabled the FBI to identify individuals who may have information about these associates, or, in fact, be among the participants. As explained below, the number of people of interest to the FBI is constantly changing as leads are followed and more information is obtained.

8. Information available to the FBI indicates a potential for additional terrorist incidents. As a result, the FBI has requested that all law enforcement agencies nationwide be on heightened alert. When there is threat information about a specific target, the FBI shares that information with appropriate state and local authorities. Several city and state officials have been contacted over the last few weeks to alert them to potential threats.

9. On September 23, 2001, the FBI issued a nationwide alert based on information indicating the possibility of attacks using crop-dusting aircraft. The FBI assesses the uses of this type of aircraft to distribute chemical or biological weapons of mass destruction as potential threats to Americans. At this point, there is no clear indication of the intended time or place of any such attack. The FBI has confirmed that Mohammed Atta, one of the suspected hijackers, was acquiring knowledge of crop-dusting aircraft prior to the attacks on September 11th. . . .

10. The investigation has also uncovered several individuals, including individuals who may have links to the hijackers, who fraudulently have obtained, or attempted to obtain, licenses to transport hazardous material.

11. In the context of this terrorism investigation, the FBI identified individuals whose activities warranted further inquiry. When such individuals were identified as aliens who were believed to have violated their immigration status, the FBI notified the Immigration and Naturalization Service (INS). The INS detained such aliens under the authority of the Immigration and Nationality Act. At this point, the FBI must consider the possibility that these aliens are somehow linked to, or may possess knowledge useful to the investigation of, the terrorist attacks on the World Trade Center and the Pentagon. The respondent, Ali Abubakr Ali Al-Maqtari (AL-MAQTARI) is one such individual.

12. As a result of a search previously described to the court, the FBI continues to download the hard drive of a computer. (The computer was found in a car belonging to Al-Maqtari's wife.) When interviewed by the FBI, Al-Maqtari said he had not used the laptop but purchased it used for $250 from a customer at the convenience store where he works. Al-Maqtari said that the customer obtained the computer from a third party. At present, the download of the hard drive is still running. Once this process is completed, the FBI will need several days to review the information obtained.

13. The FBI continues to actively pursue this investigation.

14. The business of counterterrorism intelligence gathering in the United States is akin to the construction of a mosaic. At this stage of the investigation, the FBI is gathering and processing thousands of bits and pieces of information that may seem innocuous at first glance. We must analyze all that information, however, to see if it can be fit into a picture that will reveal how the unseen whole operates. The significance of one item of information may frequently depend upon knowledge of many other items of information. What may seem trivial to some may appear of great moment to those within the FBI or the intelligence community who have a broader context within which to consider a questioned item or isolated piece of information. At the present stage of this vast investigation, the FBI is gathering and culling information that may corroborate or diminish our current suspicions of the individuals that have been detained. The Bureau is approaching that task with unprecedented resources and a nationwide urgency. In the meantime, the FBI has been unable to rule out the possibility that respondent is somehow linked to, or possesses knowledge of, the terrorist attacks on the World Trade Center and the Pentagon. To protect the public, the FBI must exhaust all avenues of investigation while ensuring that critical information does not evaporate pending further investigation.

I declare under penalty of perjury that the foregoing is true and correct. Executed on October 11, 2001, in Washington, D.C.

*Michael E. Rolince*
Federal Bureau of Investigation

## OFFICE OF THE INSPECTOR GENERAL, DEPARTMENT OF JUSTICE, PRESS RELEASE, THE SEPTEMBER 11 DETAINEES: A REVIEW OF THE TREATMENT OF ALIENS HELD ON IMMIGRATION CHARGES IN CONNECTION WITH THE INVESTIGATION OF THE SEPTEMBER 11 ATTACKS

June 2, 2003
http://www.usdoj.gov/oig/special/0306/press.pdf

After the September 11 terrorist attacks, the Department of Justice (Department) used federal immigration laws to detain aliens in the United States who were suspected of having ties to the attacks or connections to terrorism, or who were encountered during the course of the Federal Bureau of Investigation's (FBI) investigation into the attacks. In the 11 months after the attacks, 762 aliens were detained in connection with the FBI terrorism investigation for various immigration offenses, including overstaying their visas and entering the country illegally.

The Office of the Inspector General (OIG) examined the treatment of these detainees, including their processing, bond decisions related to them, the timing of their removal from the United States or their release from custody, their access to counsel, and their conditions of confinement. . . .

Among the specific findings in the OIG's report:

### Arrest, Charging & Assignment to a Detention Facility

- The FBI in New York City made little attempt to distinguish between aliens who were subjects of the FBI terrorism investigation (called "PENTTBOM") and those encountered coincidentally to a PENTTBOM lead. The OIG report concluded that, even in the chaotic aftermath of the September 11 attacks, the FBI should have expended more effort attempting to distinguish between aliens who it actually suspected of having a connection to terrorism from [sic] those aliens who, while possibly guilty of violating federal immigration law, had no connection to terrorism but simply were encountered in connection with a PENTTBOM lead.

- The INS did not consistently serve the September 11 detainees with notice of the charges under which they were being held within the INS's stated goal of 72 hours. The review found that some detainees did not receive these charging documents (called a "Notice to Appear" or NTA) for more than a month after being arrested. This delay affected the detainees' ability to understand why they were being held, obtain legal counsel, and request a bond hearing. . . .

- The Department instituted a policy that all aliens in whom the FBI had an interest in connection with the PENTTBOM investigation required clearance by the FBI of any connection to terrorism before they could be removed or released. Although not communicated in writing, this "hold until cleared" policy was clearly understood and applied throughout the Department. The policy was based on the belief—which turned out to be erroneous—that the FBI's clearance process would proceed quickly. FBI agents responsible for clearance investigations often were assigned other duties and were not able to focus on the detainee cases. The result was that detainees remained in custody—many in extremely restrictive conditions of confinement—for weeks and months with no clearance investigations being conducted. The OIG review found that, instead of taking a few days as anticipated, the FBI clearance process took an average of 80 days, primarily because it was understaffed and not given sufficient priority by the FBI.

### Bond and Removal Issues

- The Department instituted a "no bond" policy for all September 11 detainees as part of its effort to keep the detainees confined until the FBI could complete its clearance investigations. The OIG review found that the INS raised concerns about this blanket "no bond" policy, particularly when it became clear that the FBI's clearance process was much slower than anticipated and the INS had little information in many individual cases on which to base its continued opposition to bond in immigration hearings. INS officials also were concerned about continuing to hold detainees while the FBI conducted clearance investigations where detainees had received a final removal or voluntary departure order. The OIG review found that the INS and the Department did not timely address conflicting interpretations of federal immigration law about detaining aliens with final orders of removal who wanted and were able to leave the country, but who had not been cleared by the FBI.

- In January 2002, when the FBI brought the issue of the extent of the INS's detention authority to the Department's attention, the Department abruptly changed its position as to whether the INS should continue to hold aliens after they had received a final departure or removal order until the FBI had completed the clearance process. After this time, the Department allowed the INS to remove aliens with final orders without FBI clearance. In addition, in many cases the INS failed to review the detainees' custody determination as required by federal regulations.

The FBI's initial assessment of the September 11 detainees' possible connections to terrorism and the slow pace of the clearance process had significant ramifications on the detainees' conditions of confinement. Our review found that 84 September 11 detainees were housed at the MDC [Metropolitan Detention Center] in Brooklyn under highly restrictive conditions. These conditions included "lock down" for at least 23 hours per day; escort procedures that included a "4-man hold" with handcuffs, leg irons, and heavy chains any time the detainees were moved outside their cells; and a limit of one legal telephone call per week and one social call per month.

Among the OIG review's findings regarding the treatment of detainees held at the MDC and Passaic are:

### Conditions of Confinement

- BOP officials imposed a communications blackout for September 11 detainees immediately after the terrorist attacks that lasted several weeks. After the blackout period ended, the MDC's designation of the September 11 detainees as "Witness Security" inmates frustrated efforts by detainees' attorneys, families, and even law enforcement officials, to determine where the detainees were being held. We found that MDC staff frequently — and mistakenly — told people who inquired about a specific September 11 detainee that the detainee was not held at the facility when, in fact, the opposite was true.

- The MDC's restrictive and inconsistent policies on telephone access for detainees prevented some detainees from obtaining legal counsel in a timely manner. Most of the September 11 detainees did not have legal representation prior to their detention at the MDC. Consequently, the policy developed by the MDC that permitted detainees one legal call per week — while complying with broad BOP national standards — severely limited the detainees' ability to obtain and consult with legal counsel. In addition, we found that in many instances MDC staff did not ask detainees if they wanted their one legal call each week. We also found that the list of pro bono attorneys provided to the detainees contained inaccurate and outdated information.

- With regard to allegations of abuse at the MDC, the evidence indicates a pattern of physical and verbal abuse by some correctional officers at the MDC against some September 11 detainees, particularly during the first months after the attacks and during intake and movement of prisoners. Although the allegations of abuse have been declined for criminal prosecution, the OIG is continuing to investigate these matters administratively.

- The OIG review found that certain conditions of confinement at the MDC were unduly harsh, such as subjecting the September 11 detainees to having two lights illuminated in their cells 24 hours a day for several months longer than necessary, even after electricians rewired the cellblock to allow the lights to be turned off individually. We also found that MDC staff failed to inform MDC detainees in a timely manner about the process for filing formal complaints about their treatment.

- By contrast, the OIG review found that the detainees confined at Passaic had much different, and significantly less harsh, experiences than the MDC detainees. According to INS data, Passaic housed 400 September 11 detainees from the date of the terrorist attacks through May 30, 2002, the largest number of September 11 detainees held at any single U.S. detention facility. Passaic detainees housed in the general population were treated like "regular" INS detainees who also were held at the facility. Although we received some allegations of physical and verbal abuse, we did not find the evidence indicated a pattern of abuse at Passaic. However, the INS did not conduct sufficient and regular visits to Passaic to ensure the September 11 detainees' conditions of confinement were appropriate.

"The Justice Department faced enormous challenges as a result of the September 11 terrorist attacks, and its employees worked with dedication to meet these challenges," [Inspector General] Fine said. "The findings of our review should in no way diminish their work. However, while the chaotic situation and the uncertainties surrounding the detainees' connections to terrorism explain some of the problems we found in our review, they do not explain them all," Fine said. . . .

## NON-DETENTION ACT

18 U.S.C. §4001(a) (2000)

No citizen shall be imprisoned or otherwise detained by the United States except pursuant to an Act of Congress.

## NOTES AND QUESTIONS

### a. Constitutional and Statutory Limits on Detention

1. ***The Constitutional Standard for Detention.*** Generally, the Fourth Amendment requires police, before making an arrest, to have probable cause to believe that a suspect has committed a crime. However, they are allowed to stop a person when there is an "articulable suspicion that the person has been, is, or is about to be engaged in criminal activity." United States v. Place, 462 U.S. 696, 703 (1983). *See* Terry v. Ohio, 392 U.S. 1, 9 (1968). Nevertheless, "reasonable suspicion of criminal activity," short of probable cause, only "warrants a temporary seizure for the purpose of questioning limited to the purpose of the stop." Florida v. Royer, 460 U.S. 491, 498 (1983).

   The INS may stop and detain persons for questioning about their citizenship upon a reasonable suspicion that they are illegal aliens. United States v. Brignoni-Ponce, 422 U.S. 873, 882-883 (1975). Congress has authorized the arrest and detention of such aliens pending a decision about their removal. 8 U.S.C. §1226 (2000). The Supreme Court has ruled that after a decision to remove, continued indefinite detention would present a serious due process issue, at least as to aliens already in the country, who enjoy Fifth Amendment protection. Zadvydas v. Davis, 533 U.S. 678 (2001).

   *Zadvydas*, however, did not involve an alien suspected of terrorism. The Court emphasized that the detention there at issue "did not apply narrowly to 'a small segment of particularly dangerous individuals,' say suspected terrorists." *Id.* at 691 (quoting Kansas v. Hendricks, 521 U.S. 346, 368 (1997) (involving preventive detention of convicted sexual predator until he is no longer dangerous)). "Neither do we consider terrorism or other special circumstances," it added, "where special arguments might be made for forms of preventive detention and for heightened deference to the judgments of the political branches with respect to matters of national security." *Zadvydas, supra*, 533 U.S. at 696.

   Is the Court suggesting a "national security exception" to the Fifth Amendment guarantee of due process? In the same vein, could there be such an exception to the Fourth Amendment's protection against unreasonable seizure? (Recall that, before enactment of the Foreign Intelligence Surveillance Act in 1978, some lower courts found a national security exception to the warrant requirement for some kinds of searches and electronic surveillance. See *supra* pp. 101-110.) How would you define such an exception? What limitations, if any, would the Fourth or Fifth Amendments place on the preventive detention of suspected alien terrorists in the United States?

2. ***The Burden of Proof.*** In the final analysis, the FBI affidavit sought to justify the detention of Al-Maqtari on the basis that the Bureau was "unable to rule out the possibility that respondent is somehow linked to, or possesses knowledge of, the terrorist attacks on the World Trade Center and the Pentagon." Rolince Aff. ¶14. Is this rationale consistent with the Fourth Amendment? With a presumption of innocence? Or was the FBI suggesting a new standard or presumption for detentions intended to prevent terrorist attacks?

**3.** *Due Process Requirements for Statutory Detention.* In Denmore v. Hyung Joon Kim, 538 U.S. 510 (2003), Justice Souter summarized the due process requirements for preventive detention as follows:

> [D]ue process requires a "special justification" for physical detention that "outweighs the individual's constitutionally protected interest in avoiding physical restraint" as well as "adequate procedural protections." "There must be a 'sufficiently compelling' governmental interest to justify such an action, usually a punitive interest in imprisoning the convicted criminal or a regulatory interest in forestalling danger to the community." The class of persons subject to confinement must be commensurately narrow and the duration of confinement limited accordingly. . . . Finally, procedural due process requires, at a minimum, that a detainee have the benefit of an impartial decisionmaker able to consider particular circumstances on the issue of necessity. [*Id.* at 557 (Souter, J., concurring in part and dissenting in part).]

Applying similar standards in United States v. Salerno, 481 U.S. 739 (1987), a divided Supreme Court upheld the provisions of the Bail Reform Act of 1984, 18 U.S.C. §3142(e) (2000), which authorized preventive detention (denial of bail) of arrestees on the grounds of flight risk or future dangerousness. The majority found that the Act authorized a "regulatory," rather than punitive, detention that was reasonably related to compelling government interests. The Court noted that regulatory interests in community safety can outweigh an individual's liberty interest, "[f]or example, in times of war and insurrection." 481 U.S. at 748. But it emphasized that the Bail Reform Act authorized detention of an arrestee only when: (a) he has been arrested and indicted on probable cause of having committed one or more specified extremely dangerous offenses, (b) a court conducts a full-blown adversary hearing on the denial of bail, at which the arrestee is entitled to be represented by his own counsel, (c) the government persuades the court by clear and convincing evidence that no conditions of release can assure the presence of the arrestee or the safety of the community, and (d) the arrestee is given a right of appeal from the court's decision.

Do the post-September 11 detentions described above satisfy the Court's due process standards? Even if they do, does the Bail Reform Act occupy the field of preventive detention (leaving aside immigration detentions)?

**4.** *Cold War Detentions and the Non-Detention Act.* In 1950, Congress passed, over President Truman's veto, the Emergency Detention Act, Pub. L. No. 81-831, 64 Stat. 1019. Following a lengthy litany of the dangers of a "world communist movement," it authorized the President to declare an "Internal Security Emergency" in the event of an invasion, declaration of war by Congress, or "Insurrection within the United States in aid of a foreign enemy." *Id.* §102(a). In such an emergency, the President, acting through the Attorney General, was empowered to "apprehend and by order detain . . . each person as to whom there is reasonable ground to believe that such person probably will engage in, or probably will conspire with others to engage in, acts of espionage or of sabotage." *Id.* §103(a). The Justice

Department constructed a half-dozen detention "camps" around the country pursuant to the Act, and during the Vietnam era it was suggested that a war protest might be regarded for purposes of the Act as an "Insurrection within the United States in aid of a foreign enemy." *See* Alan M. Dershowitz, *The Role of Law During Times of Crisis: Would Liberty Be Suspended?*, in *Civil Disorder and Violence* 140-141 (Harry M. Cloor ed., 1972).

The Act was repealed unused by Pub. L. No. 92-129, 85 Stat. 348 (1971). The legislative history of the repealer cites First and Fifth Amendment violations and declares that "the concentration camp implications of the legislation render it abhorrent." H.R. Rep. No. 92-116, at 4 (1971), *reprinted in* 1971 U.S.C.C.A.N. 1438. But does the threat of further terrorist attacks after September 11, 2001, justify reenactment of the measure or one like it that permits preventive detention of citizens and noncitizens alike, as a counterterrorist measure? *See* Thomas F. Powers, *When to Hold 'Em*, Legal Aff. (Sept./Oct. 2004) (yes).

At the same time that it repealed the Emergency Detention Act, Congress adopted the Non-Detention Act, 18 U.S.C. §4001(a) (2000), set forth above. Does this Act apply to the detention of suspected terrorists? *See* Louis Fisher, *Detention of U.S. Citizens* (Cong. Res. Serv. RS22130), Apr. 28, 2005 (concluding from legislative history of the Non-Detention Act that Congress "intended the statutory language to restrict all detentions by the executive branch, not merely those by the Attorney General"). *See also* Howe v. Smith, 452 U.S. 473, 479 n.3 (1981) (the Act proscribes "detention of *any kind* by the United States, absent a congressional grant of authority to detain") (emphasis in original). Application of the Non-Detention Act was considered in two recent cases, set out *infra* pp. 359 and 383.

### b. "Spitting on the Sidewalk"

1. *"Spitting on the Sidewalk" Detentions.* Explaining the detentions, Attorney General Ashcroft likened some of the arrests for minor crimes to Attorney General Robert Kennedy's policy of "arrest[ing] mobsters [for] spitting on the sidewalk if it would help in the battle against organized crime." Goldstein, *supra* p. 295 n.1. Identity fraud, credit card fraud, forgery, and larceny were among the criminal charges brought against some of the detainees. One difficulty with the spitting-on-the-sidewalk policy, however, is that persons charged with such minor offenses are usually released on bail. Indeed, even *conviction* on such a charge often yields no term of imprisonment. Rising to the occasion, however, one federal magistrate denied bail for an immigrant from El Salvador who had allegedly helped some of the September 11 hijackers obtain false identity papers (apparently without knowing that they were terrorists), explaining that "[o]ne of the unspoken issues today is, after the events of September 11, is it going to be business as usual? I suspect not. The defendant, either wittingly or unwittingly, certainly contributed to [the attacks]." T.R. Reid & Allen Lengel, *Scotland Yard Says Hijackers May Have Trained in Britain; Terror Suspects Arrested in Spain, Holland*, Wash. Post, Sept. 27, 2001, at A18.

**2. *PENTTBOM Convictions.*** In mid-2005, the Administration asserted that terrorism investigations had resulted in charges against more than 400 suspects, half of whom were convicted. A Washington Post study of the Department of Justice's own list of prosecutions, however, indicated that only 39 of these convictions were for crimes related to terrorism or national security. Dan Eggen & Julie Tate, *U.S. Campaign Produces Few Convictions of Terrorism Charges*, Wash. Post, June 12, 2005, at A1. The majority were for minor crimes such as fraud, making false statements, and passport violations, for which the median sentence was just eleven months.

The Justice Department defended the numbers by arguing that many defendants were prosecuted for such crimes in exchange for nonpublic information that was valuable in other terrorism probes. *Id.* The former Associate Attorney General who headed the Office of Legal Policy had an additional explanation: "You're talking about a violation of law that may or may not rise to the level of what might usually be called a federal case. But the calculation does not happen in isolation; you are not just talking about the [minor] crime itself, but the suspicion of terrorism. . . . That skews the calculation in favor of prosecution." *Id.* (quoting Viet D. Dinh). In other words, the Post paraphrased, "the primary strategy is to use 'prosecutorial discretion' to detain suspicious individuals by charging them with minor crimes." *Id.* Replied a defense attorney, "That's fine if you take it as a given that you have the devil there," citing Al Capone (who was eventually prosecuted for income tax evasion) as an example, but "the problem is . . . [that] you're going to make mistakes and you're going to hurt innocent people." *Id.*

### c.  Material Witness Detentions

**1. *Detaining Material Witnesses.*** The material witness statute, 18 U.S.C. §3144 (2000), has been employed extensively by the government in the fight against terrorism. It provides as follows:

> If it appears from an affidavit filed by a party that the testimony of a person is material in a criminal proceeding, and if it is shown that it may become impracticable to secure the presence of the person by subpoena, a judicial officer may order the arrest of the person and treat the person in accordance with the provisions of section 3142 of this title [governing release on bond and requiring a judicial hearing]. No material witness may be detained because of inability to comply with any condition of release if the testimony of such witness can adequately be secured by deposition, and if further detention is not necessary to prevent a failure of justice. Release of a material witness may be delayed for a reasonable period of time until the deposition of the witness can be taken pursuant to the Federal Rules of Criminal Procedure.

The statute apparently was first used in a terrorism investigation to detain Terry Nichols, who was eventually convicted in connection with the Oklahoma City bombing. *See* United States v. McVeigh, 940 F. Supp. 1541, 1562 (D. Colo. 1996) (finding that Nichols' renunciation of U.S. citizenship and his association with Timothy McVeigh sufficiently showed probable cause to believe that it "may become impracticable" to rely on a subpoena to secure his testimony).

2. ***Material Witness Detentions in PENTTBOM.*** Although the government has not disclosed exactly how many persons it has held as material witnesses in the PENTTBOM and subsequent counterterrorist investigations, Human Rights Watch reported that its research had identified 70 such individuals as of June 2005. Human Rights Watch, *Witness to Abuse: Human Rights Abuses Under the Material Witness Law Since September 11*, 17 Hum. Rts. Watch 1, June 2005, at 2. What aspect of the procedure for detaining material witnesses might deter the government from making wider use of this legal basis for detention? On the other hand, in view of the fact that criminal arrests require probable cause and that immigration detentions apply only to aliens, when might material witness detention appeal to the government?

3. ***Applicability to Grand Jury Investigations.*** A Second Circuit Court of Appeals panel rejected a challenge to one of the PENTTBOM detentions, finding that it was lawful to detain a material witness in connection with a grand jury investigation, and not just for trial, as the challenger had argued. United States v. Awadallah, 349 F.3d 42, 52 (2d Cir. 2003), *cert. denied*, 543 U.S. 1056 (2005). At the same time, however, the court cautioned that "it would be improper for the government to use [material witness detention] for other ends, such as the detention of persons suspected of criminal activity for which probable cause has not yet been established." *Id.* at 59.

Human Rights Watch found, nevertheless, that fewer than half of the 9/11 material witnesses were ever brought before a grand jury or court to testify; many were apparently held as suspects rather than witnesses. *Witness to Abuse, supra*, at 2. Yet the government has not been shy about explaining this use of the statute. For example, after acknowledging that the United States has no general preventive detention law, one architect of the post-9/11 detention policy said that "the material witness statute *gives the government effectively the same power. . . .* To the extent that it is a suspect involved in terror, you hold them on a material witness warrant, and you get the information until you find out what's going on." *Id.* at 19 (quoting Mary Jo White, former U.S. Attorney for the Southern District of New York) (emphasis added). In another case in which the material witness's lawyer argued that the government was holding his client as a criminal suspect, not as a witness, the government responded, "Based on evidence collected to date, the government cannot exclude the possibility that [the detainee] was criminally, rather than innocently, involved in how his fingerprint got to Spain." *Quoted in* Ricardo J. Bascuas, *The Unconstitutionality of "Hold Until Clear": Reexamining Material Witnesses Detentions in the Wake of the September 11th Dragnet*, 58 Vand. L. Rev. 677, 679 (2005) (citation omitted).

Is the use of the statute to detain suspects, rather than witnesses, consistent with the Second Circuit dictum? With the Constitution? *See* Bascuas, *supra*, at 732-736 (no; section 3144 is "facially unconstitutional" and unprecedented for permitting arrests without probable cause or even individualized suspicion of criminal conduct). Is the probable cause standard for arrest satisfied by probable cause to believe that the material witness statute's standards are satisfied? *See id.* at 717 ("[P]robable cause cannot be redefined with reference to a statute or rule to suit whatever ends the government wishes to accomplish in any given time or circumstance." It must have a fixed meaning: "cause to believe the individual to be seized is involved in the commission of a crime").

4. ***Testimony: A Key to the Material Witness's Jail Cell?*** The Second Circuit panel also found that the material witness statute made a deposition available as an alternative to detention for obtaining grand jury testimony, effectively giving the detainee a key to his jail cell. *Awadallah*, 349 F.3d at 52. Human Rights Watch reports, however, that the government has consistently opposed depositions or stalled taking them, citing national security reasons. *Witness to Abuse, supra*, at 79. Moreover, the government reportedly failed to advise many detainees of the reasons for their arrests, of their right to an attorney and to have an attorney present at their interrogations, and of their right to remain silent. *Id.* at 4.

### d.   Immigration Detentions

1. ***Immigration Detentions.*** Aliens who have been found either inadmissible or removable for terrorist activity are subject to mandatory detention under the immigration laws until their removal can be effected. 8 U.S.C. §§1182(a)(3)(B), 1227(a)(4)(B) (2000). *See generally* 8 Charles Gordon et al., *Immigration Law and Procedure* §108.02[2][b] (2001). Most of the September 11 detainees, however, were not charged with terrorist activity. For example, as the Rolince affidavit, *supra* p. 296, suggests, at ¶11, Al-Maqtari was arrested for a minor immigration violation: overstaying his visa. *See* Goldstein, *supra* p. 295 n.1.

Prolonged detention for minor "overstays" is highly unusual, according to immigration lawyers. Pat Leisner, *Detention After Attacks Challenged*, AP Online, Dec. 1, 2001. INS regulations before the September 11 attacks provided that persons suspected of immigration violations could be held for 24 hours before being charged. After the attacks, the Department of Justice lengthened the period to 48 hours, then authorized the Attorney General to stay for ten days the release of immigrants granted bond in order to allow the government to appeal. 66 Fed. Reg. 54,909 (Oct. 31, 2001). Asked to explain what standard he used for staying releases ordered by immigration judges, Attorney General Ashcroft testified that "if the attorney general develops an understanding that it's against the national interest and would in some way potentially violate or jeopardize the national security, then those orders are overruled." *Hearing on DOJ Oversight, supra* p. 295. *See also* 66 Fed. Reg. 56,967 (Nov. 14, 2001) (providing for indefinite detention of suspected terrorist aliens after expiration of removal period); Jess Bravin, *U.S. Issues Rules to Indefinitely Detain Illegal Aliens Who Are Potentially Terrorists*, Wall St. J., Nov. 15, 2001, at A18. Authorities explained that immigration charges are a good way to detain persons suspected of terrorism connections when the government lacks sufficient evidence to prove the connections. *Id.*

Since March 2003, the government has filed immigration charges against more than 500 people who were under scrutiny in terrorism investigations. Mary Beth Sheridan, *Immigration Law as an Anti-Terrorism Tool*, Wash. Post, June 13, 2005, at A1. The Washington Post reports that 768 suspects were "secretly processed on immigration charges" in the 9/11 investigations, most being deported after being cleared of terrorism connections. *Id.*

2. ***Pretextual Immigration Detention.*** In Turkmen v. Ashcroft, No. 02-CV-2307(JG), 2006 WL 1662663 (E.D.N.Y. June 14, 2006), a group of post-9/11 immigration detainees, all but one of whom were Muslims of Middle Eastern origin, challenged their detention in part on the Fourth Amendment ground that they were really detained for criminal investigation without probable cause. The court rejected the challenge:

> [P]laintiffs' entire detention was authorized by the postremoval period [immigration] detention statute [8 U.S.C. §1231(a)(2)]. That the government may have been motivated by a desire to keep terrorism suspects in jail pending further investigation does not alter the legality of the detention. It is well-established that the government's "[s]ubjective intent . . . does not make otherwise lawful conduct illegal or unconstitutional." Whren v. United States, 517 U.S. 806, 813 (1996) (internal quotation marks omitted). Accordingly, even accepting as true plaintiffs' allegations regarding defendants' motives, the detention of plaintiffs was authorized pursuant to the post-removal detention statute and thus did not violate the Fourth Amendment. [*Turkmen, supra*, slip op. at *41.]

The court's rejection of the detainees' Equal Protection claim is discussed *supra* p. 237.

3. ***The USA Patriot Act Preventive Detention Provision.*** Immediately after the 9/11 attacks, Attorney General Ashcroft asked Congress for authority to hold suspected alien terrorists indefinitely. Bravin, *supra* p. 307. Would such legislation be constitutional? Congress rebuffed this request, providing instead in the USA Patriot Act that the INS could hold immigrants for up to seven days before charging them and then hold them while immigration proceedings were pending if the Attorney General certified, at least every six months, that their release would threaten national security. Pub. L. No. 107-56, §412, 115 Stat. 272, 350-351 (2001). How, if at all, might you argue that this legislation affected the legality of subsequent immigration detentions in the PENTTBOM investigation?

4. ***The Ethics of Immigration Bond Hearings.*** As the OIG report suggests, immigration laws, like the Bail Reform Act, see *supra* p. 303, authorize immigration judges to deny bond for a detained immigrant if the government provides evidence of flight risk or dangerousness. The FBI, however, provided no information to sustain such determinations in many cases. Nevertheless, INS lawyers were apparently ordered to argue the "no bond" position in court without any evidence, using "boilerplate" language like that in the Rolince affidavit, *supra* p. 296. *See The September 11 Detainees: A Review of the Treatment of Aliens Held on Immigration Charges, supra*

p. 298, at 78-80. Was this ethical? *See id.* at 79, 81. In some cases, the alien succeeded in obtaining a bond order and in posting bond, but the INS, without appealing the order, continued to hold him anyway. Was this lawful? *See id.* at 87 (reporting that one INS official admitted not knowing what to tell the immigrant's lawyer, "because I cannot bring myself to say that the INS no longer feels compelled to obey the law"). How far may a government lawyer go in defending preventive detention if she is instructed that it is essential to a terrorism investigation?

5. *The Length of Immigration Detentions.* In Denmore v. Hyung Joon Kim, 538 U.S. 510 (2003), the Supreme Court revisited the issue of immigration detention, this time considering a statutory provision for mandatory detention of criminal aliens pending their removal hearings. Admitting that individualized bond hearings might be feasible, the majority nevertheless concluded that "when the Government deals with deportable aliens, the Due Process Clause does not require it to employ the least burdensome means to accomplish its goal." *Id.* at 528. The Court therefore upheld the mandatory detention law but emphasized that such detentions pending removal were for less than 90 days in the majority of cases. Joining in the opinion, Justice Kennedy noted that if the removal proceedings were unreasonably delayed, "it could become necessary then to inquire whether the detention is not to facilitate deportation, or to protect against risk of flight or dangerousness, but to incarcerate for other reasons." *Id.* at 532-533 (Kennedy, J., concurring). How would the post-September 11 immigration detentions described in the OIG report fare by these standards?

6. *Rights of Detainees.* Ordinarily, immigrant detainees have a due process right to counsel at their own expense. *See generally* Gordon, *supra* p. 307, §108.04[2][b]. The Department of Justice said it afforded the September 11 detainees that right, although some detainees reportedly found it difficult to exercise it. *See, e.g., Hearing on DOJ Oversight, supra* p. 295 n.1 (questions by Senator Feingold to Attorney General Ashcroft); Amnesty International, *supra* p. 295 n.1, at 4-6 (reporting that many detainees were effectively denied access to a lawyer for substantial periods). Shortly after publication of the OIG report, a divided panel of the D.C. Circuit Court of Appeals found that various public interest groups had no right under the Freedom of Information Act or First Amendment to assorted information about the post-September 11 detentions, which they sought in part to ascertain the legality of the detentions and conditions of confinement. Center for National Security Studies v. United States Dept. of Justice, 331 F.3d 918 (D.C. Cir. 2003), *cert. denied,* 540 U.S. 1104 (2004). Based presumably on the government's representations, a majority of the panel assumed that the immigrant detainees "have had access to counsel, and the INS has provided detainees with lists of attorneys willing to represent them. . . . They have also been free to disclose their names to the public." *Id.* In light of the OIG report, were these assumptions warranted?

7. *International Legal Rights of Alien Detainees.* Detainees also have rights under international law. The Vienna Convention on Consular Relations, April 24, 1963, 21 U.S.T. 77, 596 U.N.T.S. 261, which the United States has ratified, gives a foreign arrestee the right to have his government

notified of his arrest. *Id.* art. 361(b). *See* Sanchez-Llamas v. Oregon, 126 S. Ct. 2669 (2006) (assuming, without deciding, that the Convention grants individuals enforceable rights, violations will not be enforced by applying an exclusionary rule, and enforceability is conditioned on compliance with state procedural rules). What purpose do you think this right serves? State law enforcement authorities have notoriously disregarded this right, *see* Sean D. Murphy, *United States Practice in International Law 1999–2000* (2002), at 39 & n.1, despite the primacy of the Convention under the Supremacy Clause. Apart from the Supremacy Clause, can you think of any policy reason why the United States should honor the Convention's notification requirement?

The International Covenant on Civil and Political Rights art. 9, Dec. 16, 1966, 999 U.N.T.S. 171, ratified by the United States in 1992, states that "[n]o one shall be subjected to arbitrary arrest or detention," and that "[a]nyone who is deprived of his liberty by arrest or detention shall be entitled to take proceedings before a court, in order that that court may decide without delay on the lawfulness of his detention." Were these provisions violated by the PENTTBOM detentions?

### e.  Military Detentions

The USA Patriot Act was not the last word in preventive detention of immigrants. On November 13, 2001, President Bush claimed by "Military Order" the very detention authority he had unsuccessfully sought from Congress. 66 Fed. Reg. 57,833 (Nov. 13, 2001). See *infra* p. 559. The Military Order directs the Secretary of Defense to detain without time limit any alien whom the President has "reason to believe" is a member of al Qaeda, is involved in international terrorism, or has knowingly harbored such members or terrorists. *Id.* §3. Is the Military Order's detention provision consistent with the USA Patriot Act? If not, which prevails? Is the Military Order's detention provision constitutional? Military detention of both citizen and noncitizen "enemy combatants" is discussed in Chapter 12.

### f.  Profiling?

Even the incomplete numbers reflect the fact that the PENTTBOM detentions have overwhelmingly targeted Arabs and Muslims. The immigration crackdown did the same. Indeed, civil rights lawyers allege that immigration laws are being selectively enforced against Muslims and Arabs and largely ignored with respect to the rest of the immigrant population. "The approach is basically to target the Muslim and Arab community with a kind of zero-tolerance immigration policy. No other community is treated to zero-tolerance enforcement," said Professor David Cole. Sheridan, *supra* p. 308. We addressed the legality of "profiling" in Chapter 7.

# 11

# *SUSPENDING THE GREAT WRIT*

A case in which an "enemy combatant" held by the United States petitioned a federal court for a writ of habeas corpus prompted the following account of the writ by Justice Scalia:

The very core of liberty secured by our Anglo-Saxon system of separated powers has been freedom from indefinite imprisonment at the will of the Executive. Blackstone stated this principle clearly:

"Of great importance to the public is the preservation of this personal liberty: for if once it were left in the power of any, the highest, magistrate to imprison arbitrarily whomever he or his officers thought proper . . . there would soon be an end of all other rights and immunities. . . . To bereave a man of life, or by violence to confiscate his estate, without accusation or trial, would be so gross and notorious an act of despotism, as must at once convey the alarm of tyranny throughout the whole kingdom. But confinement of the person, by secretly hurrying him to gaol, where his sufferings are unknown or forgotten; is a less public, a less striking, and therefore a more dangerous engine of arbitrary government. . . .

"To make imprisonment lawful, it must either be, by process from the courts of judicature, or by warrant from some legal officer, having authority to commit to prison; which warrant must be in writing, under the hand and seal of the magistrate, and express the causes of the commitment, in order to be examined into (if necessary) upon a *habeas corpus*. If there be no cause expressed, the gaoler is not bound to detain the prisoner. For the law judges in this respect, . . . that it is unreasonable to send a prisoner, and not to signify withal the crimes alleged against him." 1 W. Blackstone, Commentaries on the Laws of England 132-133 (1765).

These words were well known to the Founders. Hamilton quoted from this very passage in The Federalist No. 84, p. 444 (G. Carey & J. McClellan eds., 2001). The two ideas central to Blackstone's understanding—due process as the right secured, and habeas corpus as the instrument by which due process could be insisted upon by a citizen illegally imprisoned—found expression in the Constitution's Due Process and Suspension Clauses. See Amdt. 5; Art. I, §9, cl. 2.

The gist of the Due Process Clause, as understood at the founding and since, was to force the Government to follow those common-law procedures traditionally deemed necessary before depriving a person of life, liberty, or property. When a citizen was deprived of liberty because of alleged criminal conduct, those procedures typically required committal by a magistrate followed by indictment and trial. . . . [Hamdi v. Rumsfeld, 542 U.S. 507, 554-556 (2004) (Scalia, J., dissenting), *infra* p. 359.]

The Great Writ, as it is called, is mentioned in Article I, §9 of the U.S. Constitution: "The Privilege of the Writ of Habeas Corpus shall not be suspended, unless when in Cases of Rebellion or Invasion the public Safety may require it." Despite this seemingly restrictive language, Congress has long limited the availability of the writ by statute.

We begin this chapter with a look at the statutory basis for habeas corpus jurisdiction in federal courts. We next examine how the writ is suspended or restricted. In the final parts of the chapter we consider the availability and suspension of the writ for nonresident aliens.

## A. STATUTORY BASIS FOR HABEAS CORPUS

### HABEAS CORPUS

28 U.S.C.A. §§2241-2255 (West 2006) & Pub. L. No. 109-163, §1405(e)(1), 119 Stat. 3136, 3477 (2006)

### §2241. Power to Grant Writ

(a) Writs of habeas corpus may be granted by the Supreme Court, any justice thereof, the district courts and any circuit judge within their respective jurisdictions. The order of a circuit judge shall be entered in the records of the district court of the district wherein the restraint complained of is had.

(b) The Supreme Court, any justice thereof, and any circuit judge may decline to entertain an application for a writ of habeas corpus and may transfer the application for hearing and determination to the district court having jurisdiction to entertain it.

(c) The writ of habeas corpus shall not extend to a prisoner unless —

(1) He is in custody under or by color of the authority of the United States or is committed for trial before some court thereof; or

(2) He is in custody for an act done or omitted in pursuance of an Act of Congress, or an order, process, judgment or decree of a court or judge of the United States; or

(3) He is in custody in violation of the Constitution or laws or treaties of the United States; or

(4) He, being a citizen of a foreign state and domiciled therein is in custody for an act done or omitted under any alleged right, title, authority, privilege, protection, or exemption claimed under the commission, order or sanction of any foreign state, or under color thereof, the validity and effect of which depend upon the law of nations; or

(5) It is necessary to bring him into court to testify or for trial. . . .

### §2243.  Issuance of Writ; Return; Hearing; Decision

A court, justice or judge entertaining an application for a writ of habeas corpus shall forthwith award the writ or issue an order directing the respondent to show cause why the writ should not be granted, unless it appears from the application that the applicant or person detained is not entitled thereto.

The writ, or order to show cause shall be directed to the person having custody of the person detained. It shall be returned within three days unless for good cause additional time, not exceeding twenty days, is allowed.

The person to whom the writ or order is directed shall make a return certifying the true cause of the detention.

When the writ or order is returned a day shall be set for hearing, not more than five days after the return unless for good cause additional time is allowed.

Unless the application for the writ and the return present only issues of law the person to whom the writ is directed shall be required to produce at the hearing the body of the person detained.

The applicant or the person detained may, under oath, deny any of the facts set forth in the return or allege any other material facts. . . .

The court shall summarily hear and determine the facts, and dispose of the matter as law and justice require.

## B.  SUSPENDING THE WRIT FOR U.S. PERSONS

Although the Suspension Clause appears in that part of the Constitution devoted to an enumeration of legislative powers, there is no other textual clue about who possesses the power to suspend the writ. The question arose in an early Civil War era case, Ex parte Merryman, 17 F. Cas. 144 (C.C.D. Md. 1861) (No. 9487), when Chief Justice Taney, sitting as a circuit court judge, ordered the release of a Southern sympathizer imprisoned at Fort McHenry. Merryman had been seized after President Lincoln signed an order authorizing suspension of the writ of habeas corpus. Said the Chief Justice, "I had supposed it to be one of those points of constitutional law upon which there was no difference of opinion . . . that the privilege of the writ could not be suspended, except by act of congress." *Id.* at 148. However, Taney's decree was ignored by the President, and Merryman remained in prison for a time. A month later, in a message to a special session of Congress, Lincoln remarked that Taney's interpretation of the constitutional requirement would allow

> all the laws, but one, to go unexecuted, and the government itself go to pieces, lest that one be violated. . . . [T]he Constitution itself, is silent as to which, or who, is to exercise the power; and as the provision was plainly made for a dangerous emergency, it cannot be believed the framers of the instrument intended, that in every case, the danger should run its course, until Congress could be called together; the very assembling of which might be prevented, as was intended in this case, by the rebellion. [4 *The Collected Works of Abraham Lincoln* 430-431 (Roy P. Basler ed., 1953).]

Five years later, the full Supreme Court made it clear that under some circumstances the writ can properly be suspended.

## EX PARTE MILLIGAN

United States Supreme Court, 1866
71 U.S. (4 Wall.) 2

[Lambdin P. Milligan, a resident of Indiana, was not a member of the armed forces. Nevertheless, on October 5, 1864, he was arrested at his home by order of General Alvin P. Hovey, commander of the military district of Indiana, and held in close confinement. He was then brought before a military tribunal in Indianapolis, tried on charges ranging from conspiracy against the government to inciting insurrection, found guilty, and sentenced to be hanged.

Subsequently, on January 2, 1865, the United States Circuit Court for Indiana met at Indianapolis and empanelled a grand jury to inquire whether any laws of the United States had been broken by anyone, and to make presentments. The grand jury did not find any bill of indictment or make any presentment against Milligan, and on January 27 the court adjourned after discharging the grand jury from further service. Milligan later petitioned the Circuit Court for his release, arguing that the military tribunal had no jurisdiction to try him.]

Mr. Justice DAVIS delivered the opinion of the court. . . . The importance of the main question presented by this record cannot be overstated; for it involves the very framework of the government and the fundamental principles of American liberty.

During the late wicked Rebellion, the temper of the times did not allow that calmness in deliberation and discussion so necessary to a correct conclusion of a purely judicial question. *Then*, considerations of safety were mingled with the exercise of power; and feelings and interests prevailed which are happily terminated. *Now* that the public safety is assured, this question, as well as all others, can be discussed and decided without passion or the admixture of any element not required to form a legal judgment. . . .

. . . Milligan claimed his discharge from custody by virtue of the act of Congress "relating to *habeas corpus* and regulating judicial proceedings in certain cases," approved March 3d, 1863.[1] Did that act confer jurisdiction on the Circuit Court of Indiana to hear this case?

In interpreting a law, the motives which must have operated with the legislature in passing it are proper to be considered. This law was passed in a time of great national peril, when our heritage of free government was in danger. An armed rebellion against the national authority, of greater proportions than history affords an example of, was raging; and the public safety required

---

[1. The Suspension Act of 1863, Act of Mar. 3, 1863, ch. 81, §1, 12 Stat. 755, 755, was the first statute authorizing suspension. *See* Amanda L. Tyler, *Is Suspension a Political Question?*, 59 Stan. L. Rev. 333, 345 (2006). Union forces detained thousands of individuals during the Civil War, both under the Act and under prior unilateral suspensions by President Lincoln. *Id.* at 344-345.]

that the privilege of the writ of *habeas corpus* should be suspended. The President had practically suspended it, and detained suspected persons in custody without trial; but his authority to do this was questioned. It was claimed that Congress alone could exercise this power; and that the legislature, and not the President, should judge of the political considerations on which the right to suspend it rested. The privilege of this great writ had never before been withheld from the citizen; and as the exigence of the times demanded immediate action, it was of the highest importance that the lawfulness of the suspension should be fully established. It was under these circumstances, which were such as to arrest the attention of the country, that this law was passed. The President was authorized by it to suspend the privilege of the writ of *habeas corpus,* whenever, in his judgment, the public safety required; and he did, by proclamation, bearing date the 15th of September, 1863, reciting, among other things, the authority of this statute, suspend it. The suspension of the writ does not authorize the arrest of any one, but simply denies to one arrested the privilege of this writ in order to obtain his liberty.

It is proper, therefore, to inquire under what circumstances the courts could rightfully refuse to grant this writ, and when the citizen was at liberty to invoke its aid.

The second and third sections of the law are explicit on these points. The language used is plain and direct, and the meaning of the Congress cannot be mistaken. The public safety demanded, if the President thought proper to arrest a suspected person, that he should not be required to give the cause of his detention on return to a writ of *habeas corpus*. But it was not contemplated that such person should be detained in custody beyond a certain fixed period, unless certain judicial proceedings, known to the common law, were commenced against him. . . .

Milligan, in his application to be released from imprisonment, averred the existence of every fact necessary under the terms of this law to give the Circuit Court of Indiana jurisdiction. If he was detained in custody by the order of the President, otherwise than as a prisoner of war; if he was a citizen of Indiana and had never been in the military or naval service, and the grand jury of the district had met, after he had been arrested, for a period of twenty days, and adjourned without taking any proceedings against him, *then* the court had the right to entertain his petition and determine the lawfulness of his imprisonment. . . .

Why was he not delivered to the Circuit Court of Indiana to be proceeded against according to law? No reason of necessity could be urged against it; because Congress had declared penalties against the offences charged, provided for their punishment, and directed that court to hear and determine them. And soon after this military tribunal was ended, the Circuit Court met, peacefully transacted its business, and adjourned. It needed no bayonets to protect it, and required no military aid to execute its judgments. It was held in a state, eminently distinguished for patriotism, by judges commissioned during the Rebellion, who were provided with juries, upright, intelligent, and selected by a marshal appointed by the President. The government had no right to conclude that Milligan, if guilty, would not receive in that court merited punishment; for its records disclose that it was constantly engaged in the trial of similar offences, and was never interrupted in its administration of criminal justice. If it was dangerous, in the distracted condition of affairs, to leave Milligan unrestrained of his liberty because he "conspired against the government, afforded aid and comfort to rebels, and incited the people to insurrection," the *law* said arrest him, confine him closely, render him powerless to do further mischief; and then present his case to the grand jury of the district, with proofs of his guilt, and, if indicted, try him according to the course of the common law. If this had been done, the Constitution would have been vindicated, the law of 1863 enforced, and the securities for personal liberty preserved and defended. . . .

. . . When peace prevails, and the authority of the government is undisputed, there is no difficulty of preserving the safeguards of liberty; for the ordinary modes of trial are never neglected, and no one wishes it otherwise; but if society is disturbed by civil commotion — if the passions of men are aroused and the restraints of law weakened, if not disregarded — these safeguards need, and should receive, the watchful care of those intrusted with the guardianship of the Constitution and laws. In no other way can we transmit to posterity unimpaired the blessings of liberty, consecrated by the sacrifices of the Revolution. . . .

This nation, as experience has proved, cannot always remain at peace, and has no right to expect that it will always have wise and humane rulers, sincerely attached to the principles of the Constitution. Wicked men, ambitious of power, with hatred of liberty and contempt of law, may fill the place once occupied by Washington and Lincoln; and if this right is conceded, and the calamities of war again befall us, the dangers to human liberty are frightful to contemplate. If our fathers had failed to provide for just such a contingency, they would have been false to the trust reposed in them. They knew — the history of the world told them — the nation they were founding, be its existence short or long, would be involved in war; how often or how long continued, human foresight could not tell; and that unlimited power, wherever lodged at such a time, was especially hazardous to freemen. For this, and other equally weighty reasons, they secured the inheritance they had fought to maintain, by incorporating in a written constitution the safeguards which *time* had proved were essential to its preservation. Not one of these safeguards can the President, or Congress, or the Judiciary disturb, except the one concerning the writ of *habeas corpus*.

It is essential to the safety of every government that, in a great crisis, like the one we have just passed through, there should be a power somewhere of suspending the writ of *habeas corpus*. In every war, there are men of previously good character, wicked enough to counsel their fellow-citizens to resist the measures deemed necessary by a good government to sustain its just authority and overthrow its enemies; and their influence may lead to dangerous combinations. In the emergency of the times, an immediate public investigation according to law may not be possible; and yet, the peril to the country may be too imminent to suffer such persons to go at large. Unquestionably, there is then an exigency which demands that the government, if it should see fit in the exercise of a proper discretion to make arrests, should not be required to produce the persons arrested in answer to a writ of *habeas corpus*. The Constitution goes no further. It does not say after a writ of *habeas corpus* is denied a citizen, that he shall be tried otherwise than by the course of the common law. . . .

[The Court then addressed this question: "Upon the *facts* stated in Milligan's petition, and the exhibits filed, had the military commission mentioned in it *jurisdiction,* legally, to try and sentence him?" We explore this aspect of the case *infra* pp. 349-353.]

## NOTES AND QUESTIONS

1. *Presidential Authority to Suspend the Writ?* Although the privilege of the writ has been suspended on a number of other occasions, the question raised by *Merryman* has not yet reached the full Supreme Court. *But see* Ex parte Bollman, 8 U.S. (4 Cranch) 75, 1010 (1807) ("If at any time the public safety should require the suspension of the powers vested by this act in the courts of the United States, it is for the legislature to say so. That question depends on political considerations, on which the legislature is to decide."). Do you see any danger in allowing the President, acting alone, to suspend the writ, as Lincoln did initially? *See* Michael Stokes Paulsen, *The Merryman Power and the Dilemma of Autonomous Executive Branch Interpretation,* 15 Cardozo L. Rev. 81, 88-99 (1993); (Chief Justice) William H. Rehnquist, *All the Laws But One: Civil Liberties in Wartime* 11-45 (1998) (criticizing Chief Justice Taney); Harold C. Relyea, *National Emergency Powers: A Brief Overview of Presidential Suspensions of the Habeas Corpus Privilege and Invocations of Martial Law* (Cong. Res. Serv.), Sept. 20, 1976; John T. Sharer, *Power, Idealism, and Compromise: The Coordinate Branches and the Writ of Habeas Corpus,* 26 Emory L.J. 149 (1977); and Martin S. Sheffer, *Presidential Power to Suspend Habeas Corpus: The Taney-Bates Dialogue and Ex parte Merryman,* 11 Okla. City U. L. Rev. 1 (1986). Is there a danger in not allowing the President, acting alone, to suspend? How, if at all, could the Suspension Clause be interpreted to balance the dangers?

2. *Congress's Authority to Suspend, Delegate, or Regulate?* Given the placement of the Suspension Clause in Article I, it appears that Congress can suspend the writ under the conditions stated. Does it follow that Congress can delegate the suspension decision to the President? Would such a delegation help to lessen the dangers suggested in the last Note? Does *Milligan* suggest any answer to the delegation question?

    May Congress restrict or condition the President's authority to suspend the writ? Did the *Milligan* decision shed any light on this question?

3. *The Courts' Authority to Review Suspension?* The "purpose of suspension is to permit Congress to override core due process safeguards during time of crisis." Tyler, *supra* p. 314 n.1, at 386. When Congress suspends habeas and thus switches due process rights "off," does it also effectively switch off judicial review of the suspension itself? How would the courts decide whether there has been a "Case[] of Rebellion or Invasion," let alone whether the "public Safety . . . require[s] it"? Are these "political questions," inappropriate for judicial review (in part, because there is no judicially manageable standard for their decision) and therefore left to be resolved in the political process? *See, e.g.,* Luther v. Borden, 48 U.S. (7 How.) 1 (1849) (holding that whether the government of Rhode Island violated the Republican Form of

Government Clause, U.S. Const., art. IV, §4, was a political question textually committed to Congress and for which the courts lacked judicially manageable standards). *See generally* Erwin Chemerinsky, *Federal Jurisdiction* §2.6 (4th ed. 2003). In other words, is suspension justiciable?

Reasoning in part that due process leaves no choice and in part from cases in which the courts have decided war powers questions (see Chapter 2), one scholar concludes that the Rebellion or Invasion question is justiciable, though not the "public Safety" question. *See* Tyler, *supra*, at 360, 367. Under the contrary view — that suspension is nonjusticiable — by *"any* act of suspension (whether following from lawful premises or not), Congress effectively can switch 'off' the guarantee of due process and shield this fundamental individual right from judicial protection." *Id.* at 386.

Even if elements of suspension were nonjusticiable, a court could still decide whether the suspension power is vested exclusively or partially in Congress; whether Congress has, in fact, exercised the suspension authority; and, as *Milligan* shows, whether any congressional limitations on suspension have been met. *See* David L. Shapiro, *Habeas Corpus, Suspension, and Detention: Another View*, 82 Notre Dame L. Rev. 59, 78 (2006).

4. ***Construing to Avoid the Constitutional Question.*** By the usual rules of statutory construction, courts should construe legislation or executive orders, when "fairly possible," to avoid significant constitutional questions. *See* Immigration & Naturalization Serv. v. St. Cyr, 533 U.S. 289, 299-300 (2001). It may be especially desirable to avoid having to decide whether the executive alone may cut off access to the courts or whether suspension is justiciable because, "[a]t its historical core, the writ of habeas corpus has served as a means of reviewing the legality of executive detention, and it is in that context that its protections have been the strongest." *Id.* at 301. Thus, in *St. Cyr*, the Court construed a statute to allow access to the courts even though the statute was entitled "Elimination of Custody Review by Habeas Corpus." The Court insisted that any effort to restrict the privilege of seeking the writ must be clearly stated! *See also* Tyler, *supra*, at 390.

5. ***Congressional Limits on Appeals.*** Could Congress, exercising its authority under Article III, §2 of the Constitution, limit judicial scrutiny of a suspension of the writ either by Congress or by the President? After the *Milligan* decision, Congress expressly provided for appeals to the Supreme Court from lower federal court decisions in habeas corpus proceedings. Act of Feb. 5, 1867, 14 Stat. 385. When a Southern newspaper editor was arrested and held for trial by a military commission on charges of libel and inciting insurrection, he applied for a writ of habeas corpus first to a federal circuit court and then to the Supreme Court. During the pendency of his appeal, Congress repealed the appellate jurisdiction of the Supreme Court under the 1867 Act. 15 Stat. 44 (1868). This apparent end run around *Milligan* was upheld in Ex parte McCardle, 74 U.S. (7 Wall.) 506 (1868), although the Court noted an alternate route to Supreme Court review. The Court then granted a petition for a writ of certiorari in another case involving the trial of a civilian in a military court. Ex parte Yerger, 75 U.S. (8 Wall.) 85 (1868). It based its decision on the appellate jurisdiction conferred on the Supreme Court by

the Judicial Act of 1789 and by the Constitution to hear petitions for writs of habeas corpus. *Id.* at 96-106.

These cases, and the linkage of habeas to due process, have led most scholars to conclude that, even without expressly suspending the writ, Congress can effectively supplant habeas review with an adequate and effective substitute — another avenue for judicial review of the legality of detention. *See, e.g.*, Henry M. Hart Jr., *The Power of Congress to Limit the Jurisdiction of Federal Courts: An Exercise in Dialectic*, 66 Harv. L. Rev. 1362, 1366-1367 (1953). As one scholar explains it, "Precedent supports the common sense proposition that the substitution of a reasonable alternative remedy for the traditional writ does not constitute an invalid suspension. . . ." Shapiro, *supra*, at 76. Uncertainty about the constitutional necessity for an avenue of appeal to the Supreme Court is explored in William W. Van Alstyne, *A Critical Guide to Ex Parte McCardle,* 15 Ariz. L. Rev. 229 (1973); and Leonard G. Ratner, *Congressional Power Over the Appellate Jurisdiction of the Supreme Court,* 109 U. Pa. L. Rev. 157 (1960).

6. ***Habeas Corpus After September 11.*** In the massive PENTTBOM investigation that followed the terrorist attacks on September 11, 2001, the Justice Department extended by regulation from 24 to 48 hours the time that an alien suspected of an immigration violation could be held without criminal charges and provided for indefinite detention of suspected terrorist aliens. See *supra* p. 307. Do you think any of the several hundred persons detained for questioning for an extended period was entitled to a writ of habeas corpus? Reportedly, a secret first draft of the administration's post-9/11 anti-terrorism bill contained a section entitled "Suspension of the Writ of Habeas Corpus." *See* Tyler, *supra*, at 347 n.80. What findings should such a law have contained?

7. ***Habeas for U.S. Citizens Detained Abroad.*** Shawqi Ahmad Omar is a U.S. citizen captured and detained in Iraq by U.S. military forces. *See* Omar v. Harvey, 479 F.3d 1 (D.C. Cir. 2007). He was declared an "enemy combatant" by military authorities and had been held for over two years, without legal process or meaningful access to counsel, when the government decided to transfer him to Iraqi authorities for trial on terrorism charges. After Omar's family filed a habeas petition in the federal District Court in the District of Columbia, that court issued a preliminary injunction barring his transfer in order to preserve its jurisdiction to entertain the habeas petition. Distinguishing precedent in which habeas relief was denied a U.S. citizen who had been tried by an international tribunal abroad, the Court of Appeals found that, unlike a citizen who is detained as a consequence of judicial process, Omar had yet to receive any. "[W]here, as here, the Executive detains an individual without trial, the risk of unlawful incarceration is at its apex." *Id.* at 8. The court also rejected the government's claim that Omar's petition presented political questions and found instead that claims that his detention violated due process and that his impending transfer lacked treaty or statutory authorization were clearly justiciable. *Id.* at 9-11.

In a variant on *Omar*, Ahmed Omar Abu Ali, a U.S. citizen studying in Saudi Arabia, was detained by Saudi security officers, allegedly at the request of the United States. *See* Abu Ali v. Ashcroft, 350 F. Supp. 2d 28 (D.D.C. 2004). Ali filed a habeas petition directed to U.S. officials in the District of Columbia contending that his arrest and detention had been sought by the U.S. government. The government made no rebuttal; instead, it argued that a federal court "has no jurisdiction to consider the habeas petition of a United States citizen if he is in the hands of a foreign state." *Id.* at 31. Is this a sufficient response? Is any answer suggested by the "joint venture" exception to the silver platter doctrine in Fourth Amendment law? See *supra* p. 288. The court refused to dismiss the petition, concluding that "the United States may not avoid the habeas jurisdiction of the federal courts by enlisting a foreign ally as an intermediary to detain [a U.S.] citizen." *Abu Ali, supra*, at 41. The government then brought Abu Ali back to the United States, where he was indicted for providing material support to al Qaeda and plotting to assassinate the President. *See* Jerry Markon & Dana Priest, *Terrorist Plot to Kill Bush Alleged*, Wash. Post, Feb. 23, 2005, at A1. *See generally* Daniel J. Taylor, *The Ancient Writ in a New Kind of War: Is Habeas Corpus Relief Available to U.S. Citizens Detained Abroad in the War on Terrorism?*, Geo. Wash. Student Legal Writing Rev. 55 (2006).

## C. AVAILABILITY OF THE WRIT TO NONRESIDENT ALIENS

During World War II, the government had to decide what to do with eight German saboteurs who were caught in the United States. President Roosevelt opted to try them by military commission (a panel of military officers operating under military rules) in Washington, D.C., because a commission could impose death sentences, unlike the civilian courts at the time. *See* David J. Danelski, *The Saboteurs' Case*, 1 J. S. Ct. Hist. 61 (1996). But he also told his Attorney General, "I won't hand them over to any United States marshal armed with a writ of habeas corpus. Understand?" *Id.* The presidential proclamation establishing the military commission dealt with this eventuality by providing that defendants "shall not be privileged to seek any remedy or maintain any proceeding directly or indirectly, or to have any such remedy or proceeding brought on their behalf, in the courts of the United States," except under such regulations as the Attorney General might issue. Proclamation No. 2561, 7 Fed. Reg. 5101 (July 2, 1942).

This transparent attempt to suspend the writ ultimately fared poorly in court, however. The Supreme Court concluded that nothing in the proclamation "foreclose[d] consideration by the courts of petitioners' contentions that the Constitution and the laws of the United States constitutionally enacted forbid their trial by military commission." Ex parte Quirin, 317 U.S. 1, 25 (1942), *infra* p. 353.

In a later World War II case involving a military commission, the Court added that the Congress "has not withdrawn, and the Executive branch of the Government could not, unless there was suspension of the writ, withdraw from the courts the duty and power to make such inquiry into the authority of the commission as may be made by habeas corpus." Application of Yamashita,

327 U.S. 1, 9 (1946). Indeed, Justice Murphy characterized the claim that courts could not make such inquiries as an "obnoxious doctrine," which he said the Court "rejected fully and unquestionably." *Id.* at 30. In both *Quirin* and *Yamashita*, however, the Justices unanimously agreed that habeas corpus was available only to test the legal authority for trial by military commission, not to question the correctness of a commission's decisions.

Citing this precedent, 21 German nationals filed a habeas petition after the war to test the legality of their confinement by the United States in a German prison following trial and sentencing by a U.S. military commission. (We explore the legality of trial by military commission in Chapter 18.) More than half a century later, alien detainees in the war on terrorism again sought the writ to challenge their detention at Guantanamo Bay. Are the resulting decisions reconcilable?

## JOHNSON V. EISENTRAGER

United States Supreme Court, 1950
339 U.S. 763

Mr. Justice JACKSON delivered the opinion of the Court. The ultimate question in this case is one of jurisdiction of civil courts of the United States vis-a-vis military authorities in dealing with enemy aliens overseas. . . .

[U.S. armed forces captured twenty-one German nationals in service of German armed forces in China. They were tried and convicted by a U.S. military commission sitting in China of violating laws of war by engaging in, permitting, or ordering continued military activity against the United States after the surrender of Germany and before the surrender of Japan. After conviction, their sentences were reviewed and approved by military reviewing authority. They were then repatriated to the U.S.-run Landsberg Prison in Germany to serve their sentences.

They filed a petition for a writ of habeas corpus in the District of Columbia, naming the Secretary of Defense, among others, and asserting that their trial, conviction, and imprisonment violated Articles I and III of the Constitution, the Fifth Amendment, and provisions of the Geneva Convention governing the treatment of prisoners of war.]

We are cited to no instance where a court, in this or any other country where the writ is known, has issued it on behalf of an alien enemy who, at no relevant time and in no stage of his captivity, has been within its territorial jurisdiction. Nothing in the text of the Constitution extends such a right, nor does anything in our statutes. . . .

### I.

Modern American law has come a long way since the time when outbreak of war made every enemy national an outlaw, subject to both public and private slaughter, cruelty and plunder. But even by the most magnanimous view, our law does not abolish inherent distinctions recognized throughout the civilized world between citizens and aliens, nor between aliens of friendly and of enemy allegiance, nor between resident enemy aliens who have submitted themselves to our laws and nonresident enemy aliens who at all times have remained with, and adhered to, enemy governments.

With the citizen we are now little concerned, except to set his case apart as untouched by this decision and to take measure of the difference between his status and that of all categories of aliens. . . .

The alien, to whom the United States has been traditionally hospitable, has been accorded a generous and ascending scale of rights as he increases his identity with our society. Mere lawful presence in the country creates an implied assurance of safe conduct and gives him certain rights. . . .

But, in extending constitutional protections beyond the citizenry, the Court has been at pains to point out that it was the alien's presence within its territorial jurisdiction that gave the Judiciary power to act. In the pioneer case of Yick Wo v. Hopkins, the Court said of the Fourteenth Amendment, "These provisions are universal in their application, to all persons within the territorial jurisdiction, without regard to any differences of race, of color, or of nationality; * * *." 118 U.S. 356, 369. . . .

Since most cases involving aliens afford this ground of jurisdiction, and the civil and property rights of immigrants or transients of foreign nationality so nearly approach equivalence to those of citizens, courts in peace time have little occasion to inquire whether litigants before them are alien or citizen.

It is war that exposes the relative vulnerability of the alien's status. The security and protection enjoyed while the nation of his allegiance remains in amity with the United States are greatly impaired when his nation takes up arms against us. While his lot is far more humane and endurable than the experience of our citizens in some enemy lands, it is still not a happy one. But disabilities this country lays upon the alien who becomes also an enemy are imposed temporarily as an incident of war and not as an incident of alienage. . . .

. . . [T]he nonresident enemy alien, especially one who has remained in the service of the enemy, does not have even this qualified access to our courts, for he neither has comparable claims upon our institutions nor could his use of them fail to be helpful to the enemy. Our law on this subject first emerged about 1813 when the Supreme Court of the State of New York had occasion, in a series of cases, to examine the foremost authorities of the Continent and of England. It concluded the rule of the common law and the law of nations to be that alien enemies resident in the country of the enemy could not maintain an action in its courts during the period of hostilities. This Court has recognized that rule, and it continues to be the law throughout this country and in England.

## II.

The foregoing demonstrates how much further we must go if we are to invest these enemy aliens, resident, captured and imprisoned abroad, with standing to demand access to our courts.

We are here confronted with a decision whose basic premise is that these prisoners are entitled, as a constitutional right, to sue in some court of the United States for a writ of habeas corpus. To support that assumption we must hold that a prisoner of our military authorities is constitutionally entitled to the writ, even though he (a) is an enemy alien; (b) has never been or resided in the United States; (c) was captured outside of our territory and there held in military custody as a prisoner of war; (d) was tried and convicted by a Military Commission sitting outside the United States; (e) for offenses against laws of war committed outside the United States; (f) and is at all times imprisoned outside the United States.

We have pointed out that the privilege of litigation has been extended to aliens, whether friendly or enemy, only because permitting their presence in the country implied protection. No such basis can be invoked here, for these prisoners at no relevant time were within any territory over which the United States is sovereign, and the scenes of their offense, their capture, their trial and their punishment were all beyond the territorial jurisdiction of any court of the United States.

Another reason for a limited opening of our courts to resident aliens is that among them are many of friendly personal disposition to whom the status of enemy is only one imputed by law. But these prisoners were actual enemies, active in the hostile service of an enemy power. . . .

A basic consideration in habeas corpus practice is that the prisoner will be produced before the court. This is the crux of the statutory scheme established by the Congress; indeed, it is inherent in the very term "habeas corpus." . . . To grant the writ to these prisoners might mean that our army must transport them across the seas for hearing. This would require allocation of shipping space, guarding personnel, billeting and rations. It might also require transportation for whatever witnesses the prisoners desired to call as well as transportation for those necessary to defend legality of the sentence. The writ, since it is held to be a matter of right, would be equally available to enemies during active hostilities as in the present twilight between war and peace. Such trials would hamper the war effort and bring aid and comfort to the enemy. They would diminish the prestige of our commanders, not only with enemies but with wavering neutrals. It would be difficult to devise more effective fettering of a field commander than to allow the very enemies he is ordered to reduce to submission to call him to account in his own civil courts and divert his efforts and attention from the military offensive abroad to the legal defensive at home. Nor is it unlikely that the result of such enemy litigiousness would be a conflict between judicial and military opinion highly comforting to enemies of the United States. . . .

## III.

The Court of Appeals dispensed with all requirement of territorial jurisdiction based on place of residence, captivity, trial, offense, or confinement. It could not predicate relief upon any intraterritorial contact of these prisoners with our laws or institutions. Instead, it gave our Constitution an extraterritorial application to embrace our enemies in arms. Right to the writ, it reasoned, is a subsidiary procedural right that follows from possession of substantive constitutional rights. These prisoners, it considered, are invested with a right of personal liberty by our Constitution and therefore must have the right to the remedial writ. The court stated the steps in its own reasoning as follows: "First. The Fifth Amendment, by its terms, applies to 'any person'. Second. Action of Government officials in violation of the Constitution is void. This is the ultimate essence of the present controversy. Third. A basic and inherent function of the judicial branch of a government built upon a constitution is to set aside void action by government officials, and so to restrict executive action to the confines of the constitution. In our jurisprudence, no Government action which is void under the Constitution is exempt from judicial power. Fourth. The writ of habeas corpus is the established, time-honored process in our law for testing the authority of one who deprives another of his liberty, — 'the best and only sufficient defense of personal freedom.' * * *" 174 F.2d 961, 963-964. . . .

When we analyze the claim prisoners are asserting and the court below sustained, it amounts to a right not to be tried at all for an offense against our armed forces. If the Fifth Amendment protects them from military trial, the Sixth Amendment as clearly prohibits their trial by civil courts. The latter requires in all criminal prosecutions that "the accused" be tried "by an impartial jury of the State and district wherein the crime shall have been committed, which district shall have been previously ascertained by law." And if the Fifth be held to embrace these prisoners because it uses the inclusive term "no person," the Sixth must, for it applies to all "accused." No suggestion is advanced by the court below or by prisoners of any constitutional method by which any violations of the laws of war endangering the United States forces could be reached or punished, if it were not by a Military Commission in the theatre where the offense was committed. . . .

If this Amendment invests enemy aliens in unlawful hostile action against us with immunity from military trial, it puts them in a more protected position than our own soldiers. American citizens conscripted into the military service are thereby stripped of their Fifth Amendment rights and as members of the military establishment are subject to its discipline, including military trials for offenses against aliens or Americans. . . .

If the Fifth Amendment confers its rights on all the world except Americans engaged in defending it, the same must be true of the companion civil-rights Amendments, for none of them is limited by its express terms, territorially or as to persons. Such a construction would mean that during military occupation irreconcilable enemy elements, guerrilla fighters, and "were-wolves" [German nationals trained to conduct terrorist activities in postwar Germany] could require the American Judiciary to assure them freedoms of speech, press, and assembly as in the First Amendment, right to bear arms as in the Second, security against "unreasonable" searches and seizures as in the Fourth, as well as rights to jury trial as in the Fifth and Sixth Amendments.

Such extraterritorial application of organic law would have been so significant an innovation in the practice of governments that, if intended or apprehended, it could scarcely have failed to excite contemporary comment. Not one word can be cited. No decision of this Court supports such a view. None of the learned commentators on our Constitution has ever hinted at it. The practice of every modern government is opposed to it.

We hold that the Constitution does not confer a right of personal security or an immunity from military trial and punishment upon an alien enemy engaged in the hostile service of a government at war with the United States. . . .

## V. . . .

Since in the present application we find no basis for invoking federal judicial power in any district, we need not debate as to where, if the case were otherwise, the petition should be filed.

For reasons stated, the judgment of the Court of Appeals is reversed and the judgment of the District Court dismissing the petition is affirmed.

*Reversed.*

Mr. Justice BLACK, with whom Mr. Justice DOUGLAS and Mr. Justice BURTON concur, dissenting. . . . In Parts I, II, and III of its opinion, the Court apparently holds that no American court can even consider the jurisdiction of the military tribunal to convict and sentence these prisoners for the alleged crime. . . . [T]his holding . . . is based on the facts that (1) they were enemy aliens who were belligerents when captured, and (2) they were captured, tried, and imprisoned outside our realm, never having been in the United States.

The contention that enemy alien belligerents have no standing whatever to contest conviction for war crimes by habeas corpus proceedings has twice been emphatically rejected by a unanimous Court [citing Ex parte Quirin and Re Yamashita]. . . . That we went on to deny the requested writ [in both cases] in no way detracts from the clear holding that habeas corpus jurisdiction is available even to belligerent aliens convicted by a military tribunal for an offense committed in actual acts of warfare.

. . . Does a prisoner's right to test legality of a sentence then depend on where the Government chooses to imprison him? Certainly the Quirin and Yamashita opinions lend no support to that conclusion, for in upholding jurisdiction they place no reliance whatever on territorial location. The Court is fashioning wholly indefensible doctrine if it permits the executive branch, by deciding where its prisoners will be tried and imprisoned, to deprive all federal courts of their power to protect against a federal executive's illegal incarcerations.

If the opinion thus means, and it apparently does, that these petitioners are deprived of the privilege of habeas corpus solely because they were convicted and imprisoned overseas, the Court is adopting a broad and dangerous principle. . . .

. . . It has always been recognized that actual warfare can be conducted successfully only if those in command are left the most ample independence in the theatre of operations. Our Constitution is not so impractical or inflexible that it unduly restricts such necessary independence. It would be fantastic to suggest that alien enemies could hail our military leaders into judicial tribunals to account for their day to day activities on the battlefront. Active fighting forces must be free to fight while hostilities are in progress. But that undisputable axiom has no bearing on this case or the general problem from which it arises. . . .

The question here involves a far narrower issue. Springing from recognition that our government is composed of three separate and independent branches, it is whether the judiciary has power in habeas corpus proceedings to test the legality of criminal sentences imposed by the executive through military tribunals in a country which we have occupied for years. . . .

Though the scope of habeas corpus review of military tribunal sentences is narrow, I think it should not be denied to these petitioners and others like them. We control that part of Germany we occupy. These prisoners were convicted by our own military tribunals under our own Articles of War, years after hostilities had ceased. However illegal their sentences might be, they can expect no relief from German courts or any other branch of the German Government we permit to function. Only our own courts can inquire into the legality of their imprisonment. Perhaps, as some nations believe, there is merit in leaving the administration of criminal laws to executive and military agencies completely free from judicial scrutiny. Our Constitution has emphatically expressed a contrary policy. . . .

. . . Our nation proclaims a belief in the dignity of human beings as such, no matter what their nationality or where they happen to live. Habeas corpus, as an instrument to protect against illegal imprisonment, is written into the Constitution. Its use by courts cannot in my judgment be constitutionally abridged by Executive or by Congress. I would hold that our courts can exercise it whenever any United States official illegally imprisons any person in any land we govern. . . .

## RASUL v. BUSH

United States Supreme Court, 2004
542 U.S. 466

Justice STEVENS delivered the opinion of the Court. These two cases present the narrow but important question whether United States courts lack jurisdiction to consider challenges to the legality of the detention of foreign nationals captured abroad in connection with hostilities and incarcerated at the Guantanamo Bay Naval Base, Cuba.

### I . . .

. . . Acting pursuant to [statutory] authorization [*supra* p. 59], the President sent U.S. Armed Forces into Afghanistan [in late 2001] to wage a military campaign against al Qaeda and the Taliban regime that had supported it.

Petitioners in these cases are 2 Australian citizens and 12 Kuwaiti citizens who were captured abroad during hostilities between the United States and the Taliban. Since early 2002, the U.S. military has held them — along with, according to the Government's estimate, approximately 640 other non-Americans captured abroad — at the Naval Base at Guantanamo Bay. The United States occupies the Base, which comprises 45 square miles of land and water along the southeast coast of Cuba, pursuant to a 1903 Lease Agreement executed with the newly independent Republic of Cuba in the aftermath of the Spanish-American War. Under the Agreement, "the United States recognizes the continuance of the ultimate sovereignty of the Republic of Cuba over the [leased areas]," while "the Republic of Cuba consents that during the period of the occupation by the United States . . . the United States shall exercise complete jurisdiction and control over and within said areas."[2] In 1934, the parties entered into a treaty providing that, absent an agreement to modify or abrogate the lease, the lease would remain in effect "[s]o long as the United States of America shall not abandon the . . . naval station of Guantanamo."[3] . . .

[Petitioners filed various actions in the U.S. District Court for the District of Columbia challenging the legality of their detention and/or seeking to be informed of the charges against them, to be allowed to meet with their families and with counsel, and to have access to the courts or some other impartial tribunal, and claiming that denial of these rights violated the Constitution, international law, and treaties of the United States.]

Construing all three actions as petitions for writs of habeas corpus, the District Court dismissed them for want of jurisdiction. The court held, in reliance on our opinion in *Johnson v. Eisentrager,* 339 U.S. 763 (1950), that "aliens detained outside the sovereign territory of the United States [may not] invok[e] a petition for a writ of habeas corpus." 215 F. Supp. 2d 55, 68 (D.D.C. 2002). The Court of Appeals affirmed. . . .

## II

Congress has granted federal district courts, "within their respective jurisdictions," the authority to hear applications for habeas corpus by any person who claims to be held "in custody in violation of the Constitution or laws or treaties of the United States." 28 U.S.C. §§2241(a), (c)(3). . . .

Habeas corpus is, however, "a writ antecedent to statute, . . . throwing its root deep into the genius of our common law." *Williams v. Kaiser,* 323 U.S. 471, 484 n.2 (1945) (internal quotation marks omitted). The writ appeared in English law several centuries ago, became "an integral part of our common-law heritage" by the time the Colonies achieved independence, *Preiser v. Rodriguez,* 411 U.S. 475, 485 (1973), and received explicit recognition in the Constitution, which forbids suspension of "[t]he Privilege of the Writ of Habeas Corpus . . . unless when in Cases of Rebellion or Invasion the public Safety may require it," Art. I, §9, cl. 2.

As it has evolved over the past two centuries, the habeas statute clearly has expanded habeas corpus "beyond the limits that obtained during the 17th and 18th centuries." *Swain v. Pressley,* 430 U.S. 372, 380 n.13 (1977). But "[a]t its historical core, the writ of habeas corpus has served as a means of reviewing the legality of Executive detention, and it is in that context that its protections have been strongest." *INS v. St. Cyr,* 533 U.S. 289, 301 (2001). As Justice Jackson wrote in an opinion respecting the availability of habeas corpus to aliens held in U.S. custody:

"Executive imprisonment has been considered oppressive and lawless since John, at Runnymede, pledged that no free man should be imprisoned,

---

2. Lease of Lands for Coaling and Naval Stations, Feb. 23, 1903, U.S.-Cuba, Art. III, T.S. No. 418 (hereinafter 1903 Lease Agreement). . . .

3. Treaty Defining Relations with Cuba, May 29, 1934, U. S.-Cuba, Art. III, 48 Stat. 1683, T. S. No. 866 (hereinafter 1934 Treaty).

dispossessed, outlawed, or exiled save by the judgment of his peers or by the law of the land. The judges of England developed the writ of habeas corpus largely to preserve these immunities from executive restraint." *Shaughnessy v. United States ex rel. Mezei,* 345 U.S. 206, 218-219 (1953) (dissenting opinion).

Consistent with the historic purpose of the writ, this Court has recognized the federal courts' power to review applications for habeas relief in a wide variety of cases involving Executive detention, in wartime as well as in times of peace. The Court has, for example, entertained the habeas petitions of an American citizen who plotted an attack on military installations during the Civil War, *Ex parte Milligan,* 4 Wall. 2 (1866), and of admitted enemy aliens convicted of war crimes during a declared war and held in the United States, *Ex parte Quirin,* 317 U.S. 1 (1942), and its insular possessions, *In re Yamashita,* 327 U.S. 1 (1946).

The question now before us is whether the habeas statute confers a right to judicial review of the legality of Executive detention of aliens in a territory over which the United States exercises plenary and exclusive jurisdiction, but not "ultimate sovereignty."

## III

Respondents' primary submission is that the answer to the jurisdictional question is controlled by our decision in *Eisentrager.* . . .

Petitioners in these cases differ from the *Eisentrager* detainees in important respects: They are not nationals of countries at war with the United States, and they deny that they have engaged in or plotted acts of aggression against the United States; they have never been afforded access to any tribunal, much less charged with and convicted of wrongdoing; and for more than two years they have been imprisoned in territory over which the United States exercises exclusive jurisdiction and control.

Not only are petitioners differently situated from the *Eisentrager* detainees, but the Court in *Eisentrager* made quite clear that all six of the facts critical to its disposition were relevant only to the question of the prisoners' *constitutional* entitlement to habeas corpus. [*Eisentrager,* 339 U.S.] at 777. The Court had far less to say on the question of the petitioners' *statutory* entitlement to habeas review. Its only statement on the subject was a passing reference to the absence of statutory authorization: "Nothing in the text of the Constitution extends such a right, nor does anything in our statutes." *Id.* at 768. . . .

[Here the Court notes that the *Eisentrager* Court relied on an earlier decision, *Ahrens v. Clark,* 335 U.S. 188 (1948), holding that the habeas statute did not permit a district court to issue the writ for a detainee outside the court's territorial jurisdiction. However, *Ahrens* was overruled by *Braden v. 30th Judicial Circuit Court of Ky.,* 410 U.S. 484, 495 (1973), in which the Court held that because "the writ of habeas corpus does not act upon the prisoner who seeks relief, but upon the person who holds him in what is alleged to be unlawful custody," a district court acts "within [its] respective jurisdiction" within the meaning of §2241 as long as "the custodian can be reached by service of process." *Id.* at 494-495.]

Because *Braden* overruled the statutory predicate to *Eisentrager*'s holding, *Eisentrager* plainly does not preclude the exercise of §2241 jurisdiction over petitioners' claims.

## IV

Putting *Eisentrager* and *Ahrens* to one side, respondents contend that we can discern a limit on §2241 through application of the "longstanding principle of American law" that congressional legislation is presumed not to have extraterritorial application unless such intent is clearly manifested. *EEOC v. Arabian American Oil Co.,* 499 U.S. 244, 248 (1991). Whatever traction the presumption against extraterritoriality might have in other contexts, it certainly has no application to the operation of the habeas statute with respect to persons detained within "the territorial jurisdiction" of the United States. *Foley Bros., Inc. v. Filardo,* 336 U.S. 281, 285 (1949). By the express terms of its agreements with Cuba, the United States exercises "complete jurisdiction and control" over the Guantanamo Bay Naval Base, and may continue to exercise such control permanently if it so chooses. 1903 Lease Agreement, Art. III; 1934 Treaty, Art. III. Respondents themselves concede that the habeas statute would create federal-court jurisdiction over the claims of an American citizen held at the base. Considering that the statute draws no distinction between Americans and aliens held in federal custody, there is little reason to think that Congress intended the geographical coverage of the statute to vary depending on the detainee's citizenship. Aliens held at the base, no less than American citizens, are entitled to invoke the federal courts' authority under §2241.

Application of the habeas statute to persons detained at the base is consistent with the historical reach of the writ of habeas corpus. At common law, courts exercised habeas jurisdiction over the claims of aliens detained within sovereign territory of the realm, as well as the claims of persons detained in the so-called "exempt jurisdictions," where ordinary writs did not run, and all other dominions under the sovereign's control. . . .

In the end, the answer to the question presented is clear. Petitioners contend that they are being held in federal custody in violation of the laws of the United States.[15] No party questions the District Court's jurisdiction over petitioners' custodians. Cf. *Braden,* 410 U.S. at 495. Section 2241, by its terms, requires nothing more. We therefore hold that §2241 confers on the District Court jurisdiction to hear petitioners' habeas corpus challenges to the legality of their detention at the Guantanamo Bay Naval Base.

## V

In addition to invoking the District Court's jurisdiction under §2241, the . . . complaint invoked the court's jurisdiction under 28 U.S.C. §1331, the federal question statute, as well as §1350, the Alien Tort Statute. The Court of

---

15. Petitioners' allegations — that, although they have engaged neither in combat nor in acts of terrorism against the United States, they have been held in Executive detention for more than two years in territory subject to the long-term, exclusive jurisdiction and control of the United States, without access to counsel and without being charged with any wrongdoing — unquestionably describe "custody in violation of the Constitution or laws or treaties of the United States." 28 U.S.C. §2241(c)(3).

Appeals, again relying on *Eisentrager,* held that the District Court correctly dismissed the claims founded on §1331 and §1350 for lack of jurisdiction, even to the extent that these claims "deal only with conditions of confinement and do not sound in habeas," because petitioners lack the "privilege of litigation" in U.S. courts. 321 F.3d at 1144 (internal quotation marks omitted). . . .

. . . But . . . nothing in *Eisentrager* or in any of our other cases categorically excludes aliens detained in military custody outside the United States from the "'privilege of litigation'" in U.S. courts. 321 F.3d at 1139. The courts of the United States have traditionally been open to nonresident aliens. And indeed, 28 U.S.C. §1350 explicitly confers the privilege of suing for an actionable "tort . . . committed in violation of the law of nations or a treaty of the United States" on aliens alone. The fact that petitioners in these cases are being held in military custody is immaterial to the question of the District Court's jurisdiction over their nonhabeas statutory claims.

## VI

Whether and what further proceedings may become necessary after respondents make their response to the merits of petitioners' claims are matters that we need not address now. What is presently at stake is only whether the federal courts have jurisdiction to determine the legality of the Executive's potentially indefinite detention of individuals who claim to be wholly innocent of wrongdoing. Answering that question in the affirmative, we reverse the judgment of the Court of Appeals and remand for the District Court to consider in the first instance the merits of petitioners' claims.

*It is so ordered.*

Justice KENNEDY, concurring in the judgment. The Court is correct, in my view, to conclude that federal courts have jurisdiction to consider challenges to the legality of the detention of foreign nationals held at the Guantanamo Bay Naval Base in Cuba. While I reach the same conclusion, my analysis follows a different course. . . . In my view, the correct course is to follow the framework of *Eisentrager.* . . .

The decision in *Eisentrager* indicates that there is a realm of political authority over military affairs where the judicial power may not enter. The existence of this realm acknowledges the power of the President as Commander in Chief, and the joint role of the President and the Congress, in the conduct of military affairs. A faithful application of *Eisentrager,* then, requires an initial inquiry into the general circumstances of the detention to determine whether the Court has the authority to entertain the petition and to grant relief after considering all of the facts presented. A necessary corollary of *Eisentrager* is that there are circumstances in which the courts maintain the power and the responsibility to protect persons from unlawful detention even where military affairs are implicated. See also *Ex parte Milligan,* 4 Wall. 2 (1866).

The facts here are distinguishable from those in *Eisentrager* in two critical ways, leading to the conclusion that a federal court may entertain the petitions. First, Guantanamo Bay is in every practical respect a United States territory, and it is one far removed from any hostilities. . . .

The second critical set of facts is that the detainees at Guantanamo Bay are being held indefinitely, and without benefit of any legal proceeding to determine their status. In *Eisentrager,* the prisoners were tried and convicted by a military commission of violating the laws of war and were sentenced to prison terms. Having already been subject to procedures establishing their status, they could not justify "a limited opening of our courts" to show that they were "of friendly personal disposition" and not enemy aliens. 339 U.S., at 778. Indefinite detention without trial or other proceeding presents altogether different considerations. It allows friends and foes alike to remain in detention. It suggests a weaker case of military necessity and much greater alignment with the traditional function of habeas corpus. Perhaps, where detainees are taken from a zone of hostilities, detention without proceedings or trial would be justified by military necessity for a matter of weeks; but as the period of detention stretches from months to years, the case for continued detention to meet military exigencies becomes weaker.

In light of the status of Guantanamo Bay and the indefinite pretrial detention of the detainees, I would hold that federal-court jurisdiction is permitted in these cases. This approach would avoid creating automatic statutory authority to adjudicate the claims of persons located outside the United States, and remains true to the reasoning of *Eisentrager.* For these reasons, I concur in the judgment of the Court.

Justice SCALIA, with whom the CHIEF JUSTICE and Justice THOMAS join, dissenting. . . . Today, the Court springs a trap on the Executive, subjecting Guantanamo Bay to the oversight of the federal courts even though it has never before been thought to be within their jurisdiction — and thus making it a foolish place to have housed alien wartime detainees.

## II

In abandoning the venerable statutory line drawn in *Eisentrager,* the Court boldly extends the scope of the habeas statute to the four corners of the earth. . . .

The consequence of this holding, as applied to aliens outside the country, is breathtaking. It permits an alien captured in a foreign theater of active combat to bring a §2241 petition against the Secretary of Defense. Over the course of the last century, the United States has held millions of alien prisoners abroad. A great many of these prisoners would no doubt have complained about the circumstances of their capture and the terms of their confinement. The military is currently detaining over 600 prisoners at Guantanamo Bay alone; each detainee undoubtedly has complaints — real or contrived — about those terms and circumstances. The Court's unheralded expansion of federal-court jurisdiction is not even mitigated by a comforting assurance that the legion of ensuing claims will be easily resolved on the merits. To the contrary, the Court says that the "[p]etitioners' allegations . . . unquestionably describe 'custody in violation of the Constitution or laws or treaties of the United States.'" Ante, n.15. From this point forward, federal courts will entertain petitions from these prisoners, and others like them around the world, challenging actions and events far away, and forcing the courts to oversee one aspect of the Executive's conduct of a foreign war.

Today's carefree Court disregards, without a word of acknowledgment, the dire warning of a more circumspect Court in *Eisentrager*. . . . These results should not be brought about lightly, and certainly not without a textual basis in the statute and on the strength of nothing more than a decision dealing with an Alabama prisoner's ability to seek habeas in Kentucky.

## III

Part IV of the Court's opinion, dealing with the status of Guantanamo Bay, is a puzzlement. . . .

The Court gives only two reasons why the presumption against extraterritorial effect does not apply to Guantanamo Bay. First, the Court says (without any further elaboration) that "the United States exercises 'complete jurisdiction and control' over the Guantanamo Bay Naval Base [under the terms of a 1903 lease agreement], and may continue to exercise such control permanently if it so chooses [under the terms of a 1934 Treaty]." But that lease agreement explicitly recognized "the continuance of the ultimate sovereignty of the Republic of Cuba over the [leased areas]," Lease of Lands for Coaling and Naval Stations, Feb. 23, 1903, U.S.-Cuba, Art. III, T.S. No. 418, and the Executive Branch — whose head is "exclusively responsible" for the "conduct of diplomatic and foreign affairs," *Eisentrager, supra*, at 789 — affirms that the lease and treaty do not render Guantanamo Bay the sovereign territory of the United States.

The Court does not explain how "complete jurisdiction and control" without sovereignty causes an enclave to be part of the United States for purposes of its domestic laws. Since "jurisdiction and control" obtained through a lease is no different in effect from "jurisdiction and control" acquired by lawful force of arms, parts of Afghanistan and Iraq should logically be regarded as subject to our domestic laws. Indeed, if "jurisdiction and control" rather than sovereignty were the test, so should the Landsberg Prison in Germany, where the United States held the *Eisentrager* detainees.

The second and last reason the Court gives for the proposition that domestic law applies to Guantanamo Bay is the Solicitor General's concession that there would be habeas jurisdiction over a United States citizen in Guantanamo Bay. "Considering that the statute draws no distinction between Americans and aliens held in federal custody, there is little reason to think that Congress intended the geographical coverage of the statute to vary depending on the detainee's citizenship." But the reason the Solicitor General conceded there would be jurisdiction over a detainee who was a United States citizen had *nothing to do* with the special status of Guantanamo Bay: "Our answer to that question, Justice Souter, is that citizens of the United States, because of their constitutional circumstances, may have greater rights with respect to the scope and reach of the Habeas Statute as the Court has or would interpret it." And *that* position — the position that United States citizens throughout the world may be entitled to habeas corpus rights — is precisely the position that this Court adopted in *Eisentrager*, see 339 U.S., at 769-770, even while holding that aliens abroad *did not have* habeas corpus rights. Quite obviously, the Court's second reason has no force whatever. . . .

In sum, the Court's treatment of Guantanamo Bay, like its treatment of §2241, is a wrenching departure from precedent. . . .

Departure from our rule of *stare decisis* in statutory cases is always extraordinary; it ought to be unthinkable when the departure has a potentially harmful effect upon the Nation's conduct of a war. The Commander in Chief and his subordinates had every reason to expect that the internment of combatants at Guantanamo Bay would not have the consequence of bringing the cumbersome machinery of our domestic courts into military affairs. Congress is in session. If it wished to change federal judges' habeas jurisdiction from what this Court had previously held that to be, it could have done so. And it could have done so by intelligent revision of the statute, instead of by today's clumsy, countertextual reinterpretation that confers upon wartime prisoners greater habeas rights than domestic detainees. The latter must challenge their present physical confinement in the district of their confinement, see *Rumsfeld v. Padilla*, [542 U.S. 426 (2004)], whereas under today's strange holding Guantanamo Bay detainees can petition in any of the 94 federal judicial districts. The fact that extraterritorially located detainees lack the district of detention that the statute requires has been converted from a factor that precludes their ability to bring a petition at all into a factor that frees them to petition wherever they wish — and, as a result, to forum shop. For this Court to create such a monstrous scheme in time of war, and in frustration of our military commanders' reliance upon clearly stated prior law, is judicial adventurism of the worst sort. I dissent.

## NOTES AND QUESTIONS

1. *Military Order of November 13, 2001.* Following the September 11 attacks, President George W. Bush issued Military Order of November 13, 2001, *Detention, Treatment, and Trial of Certain Non-Citizens in the War Against Terrorism*, 66 Fed. Reg. 57,833 (Nov. 13, 2001) (see *infra* pp. 559-563.) Applicable only to noncitizens whom the President designates, §7 provides, in part,

> (B) With respect to any individual
> subject to this order —
> > (1) military tribunals shall have exclusive jurisdiction with respect to offenses by the individual; and
> > (2) the individual shall not be privileged to seek any remedy or maintain any proceeding, directly or indirectly, or to have any such remedy or proceeding sought on the individual's behalf, in
> > > (i) any court of the United States, or any State thereof,
> > > (ii) any court of any foreign nation, or
> > > (iii) any international tribunal. . . .

Assuming that some of the petitioners in *Rasul* were detained pursuant to the Military Order, why didn't §7(b) of the order cut off their access to the courts? First, consider whether, in light of §7(b)'s pedigree and its language (as compared to the Suspension Clause itself), it was intended to suspend the writ. *See* Alberto R. Gonzales, Op-Ed., *Martial Justice, Full and Fair*, N.Y. Times, Nov. 30, 2001, at A27 (denying such intent). Next, if it was so intended, consider whether, in light of the clear statement rule declared in *St. Cyr, supra* p. 318, the intent was stated with the required clarity. Finally, if the answer to the first two questions is yes, was the suspension authorized under the Suspension Clause?

2. ***Eisentrager's "Dire Warning."*** Justice Scalia cites *Eisentrager's* "dire warning" to suggest that the Court's ruling in *Rasul* will open the floodgates to habeas petitions by enemy aliens after we capture large numbers in battle. Indeed, alien detainees at Guantánamo quickly pressed habeas petitions in U.S. courts. *See* In re Guantanamo Detainee Cases, 355 F. Supp. 2d 443 (D.D.C. 2005) (reporting that 13 cases involving more than 60 detainees had been filed as of July 2004).

   Does the Court have any answer to this concern? *Milligan* and the statute it applied in 1866 supply one answer. What is it? *See, e.g.,* Detainee Treatment Act of 2005, *infra* p. 335. Another is suggested by the first sentence of part VI of the opinion for the Court. What is it? How might the "further proceedings" in the habeas court, or prior proceedings by the military itself, affect the floodgates claim?

3. ***Combatant Status Review Tribunals (CSRTs).*** In an apparent effort to control the floodgates, the Pentagon announced shortly after the Supreme Court's decision in *Rasul* that it was creating a Combatant Status Review Tribunal (CSRT), to be staffed by military officers, before which detainees could contest their combatant status. Memorandum from the Deputy Secretary of Defense to the Secretary of the Navy, *Order Establishing Combatant Status Review Tribunal*, July 7, 2004, *available at* http://www.defenselink.mil/news/Jul2004/d20040707review.pdf. Detainees would have the assistance of a "personal representative" assigned by the government, but not a lawyer, and they would have to overcome a "rebuttable presumption in favor of the government's evidence." *Id.* ¶¶c. & g.(12). Subsequently, Congress provided statutory authority for CSRTs by passing the Detainee Treatment Act of 2005, §1005, Pub. L. No. 109-148, 119 Stat. 2680 (2005) (DTA). Do you think this program will satisfy Justice Stevens's concerns? Justice Scalia's?

   In December 2006, an analysis of CSRT proceedings based on Defense Department documents characterized them as "no-hearing hearings." Mark Denbeaux & Joshua W. Denbeaux, *No-Hearing Hearings — CSRT: The Modern Habeas Corpus?*, Seton Hall Pub. L. Res. Paper No. 951245 (Dec. 2006), *available at* http://papers.ssrn.com/sol3/papers.cfm?abstract_id=951245. The analysis found, *inter alia*, that

   - the government produced no witnesses in any hearing and presented no documentary evidence to the detainee prior to the hearing in 96% of the cases;
   - the detainee's only knowledge of the reasons the government considered him to be an enemy combatant was from what the CSRTs themselves called a "conclusory" summary of classified evidence, which nevertheless was presumed to be reliable and valid;
   - 55% of the detainees sought to inspect the classified evidence and all were turned down;
   - detainees' requests for witnesses detained in Guantanamo were denied in 74% of the cases;

- detainees' requests to produce documentary evidence were denied in 60% of the cases;
- detainees were assigned, instead of a lawyer, a "personal representative" whose role was minimal and who, in 78% of the cases, met only once with the detainee, and in 98% of the cases failed to exercise his right to comment on the decision at the end of the hearing. *Id.*

If these conclusions are accurate, is the CSRT an adequate substitute for habeas review and a habeas hearing?

4. *Footnote 15.* Another way to close the floodgates would be to hear an alien detainee's habeas petition but then simply deny it on the grounds that the detainees have no cognizable constitutional or international rights. Would such an approach be consistent with *Rasul*? *See* footnote 15 therein. With *Eisentrager*?

5. *The Inner Realm of Military Affairs: What's Left of Eisentrager?* Judge Kennedy joined in the judgment by preserving part of *Eisentrager*. He found that it approved of "a realm of political authority over military affairs where the judicial power may not enter," but also that the Guantánamo Bay detentions, far removed from hostilities and attended by no status-determining procedures, even by the military, fell outside that realm. How does he define that realm? What detainees from the U.S. military operations in Afghanistan would fall within it? More generally, reading the opinion for the Court and Justice Kennedy's opinion together, what is left of *Eisentrager*?

# D.  SUSPENDING THE WRIT FOR ALIENS?

*Rasul* started a minuet between the federal courts and the Congress. First, as noted above, Congress responded to *Rasul* by passing the DTA. The DTA added a new subsection (e) to 28 U.S.C. §2241, part of the habeas statute set out *supra* p. 312, restricting jurisdiction over detainee habeas petitions "except as provided" in subsections 1005(e)(2) and (e)(3) of the DTA, which authorized limited scope judicial review of CSRT determinations and military commission decisions exclusively in the D.C. Circuit. *See* DTA §1005(e)(2), (e)(3).

Next, the Supreme Court decided in *Hamdan v. Rumsfeld,* 126 S. Ct. 2749 (2006) (*infra* p. 563), that the DTA did not strip federal courts of jurisdiction over habeas cases *pending* at the time of the DTA's enactment.

Congress responded again, this time passing the Military Commissions Act of 2006, Pub. L. No. 109-366, 120 Stat. 2600 (2006) (MCA). Section 7(a) of the MCA replaced subsection (e) of 28 U.S.C. §2241, just months after it was added by the DTA, with the following language:

> (e)(1) No court, justice, or judge shall have jurisdiction to hear or consider an application for a writ of habeas corpus filed by or on behalf of an alien detained by the United States who has been determined by the United States to have been properly detained as an enemy combatant or is awaiting such determination.
>
> (2) Except as provided in paragraphs (2) and (3) of section 1005(e) of the Detainee Treatment Act of 2005 (10 U.S.C. 801 note), no court,

justice, or judge shall have jurisdiction to hear or consider any other action against the United States or its agents relating to any aspect of the detention, transfer, treatment, trial, or conditions of confinement of an alien who is or was detained by the United States and has been determined by the United States to have been properly detained as an enemy combatant or is awaiting such determination. [MCA §7(a), 120 Stat. 2636.]

Section 7(b) of the Military Commissions Act adds:

The amendment made by subsection (a) shall take effect on the date of the enactment of this Act, and shall apply to *all cases, without exception, pending on or after the date of the enactment* of this Act which relate to any aspect of the detention, transfer, treatment, trial, or conditions of detention of an alien detained by the United States since September 11, 2001. [MCA §7(b), 120 Stat. 2636 (emphasis added).]

Did this do the job—if the job was suspending habeas for Guantánamo detainees?

## BOUMEDIENE V. BUSH

United States Court of Appeals, District of Columbia Circuit, 2007
476 F.3d 981, *cert. denied*, 127 S. Ct. 1478 (2007)

RANDOLPH, Circuit Judge. Do federal courts have jurisdiction over petitions for writs of habeas corpus filed by aliens captured abroad and detained as enemy combatants at the Guantanamo Bay Naval Base in Cuba? . . .

The first question is whether the MCA applies to the detainees' habeas petitions. If the MCA does apply, the second question is whether the statute is an unconstitutional suspension of the writ of habeas corpus.

### I. . . .

Everyone who has followed the interaction between Congress and the Supreme Court knows full well that one of the primary purposes of the MCA was to overrule *Hamdan* [v. Rumsfeld, 542 U.S. 507 (2006)]. Everyone, that is, except the detainees. Their cases, they argue, are not covered. The arguments are creative but not cogent. To accept them would be to defy the will of Congress. Section 7(b) could not be clearer. It states that "the amendment made by subsection (a)" — which repeals habeas jurisdiction — applies to "all cases, without exception" relating to any aspect of detention. It is almost as if the proponents of these words were slamming their fists on the table shouting "When we say 'all,' we mean all—**without exception!**" . . .

### II.

This brings us to the constitutional issue: whether the MCA, in depriving the courts of jurisdiction over the detainees' habeas petitions, violates the Suspension Clause of the Constitution, U.S. Const. art. I, §9, cl. 2, which states that

"The Privilege of the Writ of Habeas Corpus shall not be suspended, unless when in Cases of Rebellion or Invasion the public Safety may require it."

The Supreme Court has stated the Suspension Clause protects the writ "as it existed in 1789," when the first Judiciary Act created the federal courts and granted jurisdiction to issue writs of habeas corpus. [INS v.] *St. Cyr,* 533 U.S. [289 (2001),] at 301. . . .

. . . The detainees cite no case and no historical treatise showing that the English common law writ of habeas corpus extended to aliens beyond the Crown's dominions. Our review shows the contrary. . . .

*Johnson v. Eisentrager,* 339 U.S. 763 (1950), ends any doubt about the scope of common law habeas. "We are cited to no instance where a court, in this or any other country where the writ is known, has issued it on behalf of an alien enemy who, at no relevant time and in no stage of his captivity, has been within its territorial jurisdiction. Nothing in the text of the Constitution extends such a right, nor does anything in our statutes." *Id.* at 768. The detainees claim they are in a different position than the prisoners in *Eisentrager,* and that this difference is material for purposes of common law habeas.[8] They point to dicta in *Rasul* [v. Bush], 542 U.S. [466 (2004),] at 481-82, in which the Court discussed English habeas cases and the "historical reach of the writ." *Rasul* refers to several English and American cases involving varying combinations of territories of the Crown and relationships between the petitioner and the country in which the writ was sought. *See id.* But as Judge Robertson found in *Hamdan,* "[n]ot one of the cases mentioned in *Rasul* held that an alien captured abroad and detained outside the United States — or in 'territory over which the United States exercises exclusive jurisdiction and control,' *Rasul,* 542 U.S. at 475 — had a common law or constitutionally protected right to the writ of habeas corpus." *Hamdan v. Rumsfeld,* 464 F. Supp. 2d. 9, 17 (D.D.C. 2006). Justice Scalia made the same point in his *Rasul* dissent, *see Rasul,* 542 U.S. at 502-05 & n.5 (Scalia, J., dissenting) (noting the absence of "a single case holding that aliens held outside the territory of the sovereign were within reach of the writ"), and the dissent acknowledges it here. We are aware of no case prior to 1789 going the detainees' way, and we are convinced that the writ in 1789 would not have been available to aliens held at an overseas military base leased from a foreign government.

The detainees encounter another difficulty with their Suspension Clause claim. Precedent in this court and the Supreme Court holds that the Constitution does not confer rights on aliens without property or presence within the United States. As we explained in *Al Odah* [v. United States], 321 F.3d [1134, 1140-41 (D.C. Cir. 2003), *rev'd sub nom. Rasul v. Bush,* 542 U.S. 466 (2004)], the controlling case is *Johnson v. Eisentrager.* . . . [There] [t]he Supreme Court rejected the proposition "that the Fifth Amendment confers rights upon all persons, whatever their nationality, wherever they are located and whatever their offenses," 339 U.S. at 783. . . .

---

8. The detainees are correct that they are not "enemy aliens." That term refers to citizens of a country with which the United States is at war. But under the common law, the dispositive fact was not a petitioner's enemy alien status, but his lack of presence within any sovereign territory.

Later Supreme Court decisions have followed *Eisentrager*. In 1990, for instance, the Court stated that *Eisentrager* "rejected the claim that aliens are entitled to Fifth Amendment rights outside the sovereign territory of the United States." *United States v. Verdugo-Urquidez,* 494 U.S. 259, 269 (1990). . . . A decade after *Verdugo-Urquidez,* the Court — again citing *Eisentrager* — found it "well established that certain constitutional protections available to persons inside the United States are unavailable to aliens outside of our geographic borders." *Zadvydas v. Davis,* 533 U.S. 678, 693 (2001).[10] . . . .

As against this line of authority, the dissent offers the distinction that the Suspension Clause is a limitation on congressional power rather than a constitutional right. But this is no distinction at all. Constitutional rights are rights against the government and, as such, *are* restrictions on governmental power. Consider the First Amendment. (In contrasting the Suspension Clause with provisions in the Bill of Rights, the dissent is careful to ignore the First Amendment.) Like the Suspension Clause, the First Amendment is framed as a limitation on Congress: "Congress shall make no law. . . ." Yet no one would deny that the First Amendment protects the rights to free speech and religion and assembly. . . .

Why is the dissent so fixated on how to characterize the Suspension Clause? The unstated assumption must be that the reasoning of our decisions and the Supreme Court's in denying constitutional rights to aliens outside the United States would not apply if a constitutional provision could be characterized as protecting something other than a "right." On this theory, for example, aliens outside the United States are entitled to the protection of the Separation of Powers because they have no individual rights under the Separation of Powers. Where the dissent gets this strange idea is a mystery, as is the reasoning behind it.

### III.

Federal courts have no jurisdiction in these cases. . . . Our only recourse is to vacate the district courts' decisions and dismiss the cases for lack of jurisdiction.

*So ordered.*

ROGERS, Circuit Judge, dissenting. I can join neither the reasoning of the court nor its conclusion that the federal courts lack power to consider the detainees' petitions. While I agree that Congress intended to withdraw federal jurisdiction through the [MCA], the court's holding that the MCA is consistent with the Suspension Clause of Article I, section 9, of the Constitution does not withstand analysis. By concluding that this court must reject "the detainees' claims to constitutional rights," the court fundamentally misconstrues the nature of suspension: Far from conferring an individual right that might pertain only to persons substantially connected to the United States, *see United*

---

10. The *Rasul* decision, resting as it did on statutory interpretation, could not possibly have affected the constitutional holding of *Eisentrager*. Even if *Rasul* somehow calls *Eisentrager*'s constitutional holding into question, as the detainees suppose, we would be bound to follow *Eisentrager*.

*States v. Verdugo-Urquidez,* 494 U.S. 259, 271 (1990), the Suspension Clause is a limitation on the powers of Congress. Consequently, it is only by misreading the historical record and ignoring the Supreme Court's well-considered and binding dictum in *Rasul v. Bush,* 542 U.S. 466, 481-82 (2004), that the writ at common law would have extended to the detainees, that the court can conclude that neither this court nor the district courts have jurisdiction to consider the detainees' habeas claims.

A review of the text and operation of the Suspension Clause shows that, by nature, it operates to constrain the powers of Congress. Prior to the enactment of the MCA, the Supreme Court acknowledged that the detainees held at Guantanamo had a statutory right to habeas corpus. *Rasul,* 542 U.S. at 483-84. The MCA purports to withdraw that right but does so in a manner that offends the constitutional constraint on suspension. The Suspension Clause limits the removal of habeas corpus, at least as the writ was understood at common law, to times of rebellion or invasion unless Congress provides an adequate alternative remedy. The writ would have reached the detainees at common law, and Congress has neither provided an adequate alternative remedy, through the [DTA], nor invoked the exception to the Clause by making the required findings to suspend the writ. The MCA is therefore void and does not deprive this court or the district courts of jurisdiction. . . .

## I. . . .

### A.

The court holds that Congress may suspend habeas corpus as to the detainees because they have no individual rights under the Constitution. It is unclear where the court finds that the limit on suspension of the writ of habeas corpus is an individual entitlement. The Suspension Clause itself makes no reference to citizens or even persons. Instead, it directs that "[t]he Privilege of the Writ of Habeas Corpus shall not be suspended, unless when in Cases of Rebellion or Invasion the public Safety may require it." U.S. Const. art. I, §9, cl. 2. This mandate appears in the ninth section of Article I, which enumerates those actions expressly excluded from Congress's powers. Although the Clause does not specifically say so, it is settled that only Congress may do the suspending. *Ex parte Bollman,* 8 U.S. (4 Cranch) 75, 101 (1807); *see Hamdi v. Rumsfeld,* 542 U.S. 507, 562 (2004) (Scalia, J., dissenting); *Ex parte Merryman,* 17 F. Cas. 144, 151-152 (No. 9487) (Taney, Circuit Justice, C.C.D. Md. 1861). In this manner, by both its plain text and inclusion in section 9, the Suspension Clause differs from the Fourth Amendment, which establishes a "right of the people," the Fifth Amendment, which limits how a "person shall be held," and the Sixth Amendment, which provides rights to "the accused." These provisions confer rights to the persons listed.

The other provisions of Article I, section 9, indicate how to read the Suspension Clause. The clause immediately following provides that "[n]o Bill of Attainder or ex post facto Law shall be passed." The Supreme Court has construed the Attainder Clause as establishing a "category of Congressional actions which the Constitution barred." *United States v. Lovett,* 328 U.S. 303, 315, (1946). . . . So too, in *Weaver v. Graham,* 450 U.S. 24, 28-29 & n.10 (1981), where the Court noted that the ban on *ex post facto* legislation "restricts governmental power by restraining arbitrary and potentially vindictive legislation" and acknowledged that the clause "confin[es] the legislature to penal decisions with prospective effect." For like reasons, any act in violation of the Suspension Clause is void, *cf. Lovett,* 328 U.S. at 316, and cannot operate to divest a court of jurisdiction. . . .

The court appears to believe that the Suspension Clause is just like the constitutional amendments that form the Bill of Rights. It is a truism, of course, that individual rights like those found in the first ten amendments work to limit Congress. However, individual rights are merely a subset of those matters that constrain the legislature. These two sets cannot be understood as coextensive unless the court is prepared to recognize such awkward individual rights as Commerce Clause rights, *see* U.S. Const. art. I, §8, cl. 3, or the personal right not to have a bill raising revenue that originates in the Senate, *see* U.S. Const. art. I, §7, cl. 1; *see also Schlesinger v. Reservists Comm. to Stop the War,* 418 U.S. 208, 224 (1974) (finding no individual right under the Ineligibility Clause). . . .

The court also alludes to the idea that the Suspension Clause cannot apply to foreign military conflicts because the exception extends only to cases of "Rebellion or Invasion." The Framers understood that the privilege of the writ was of such great significance that its suspension should be strictly limited to circumstances where the peace and security of the Nation were jeopardized. Only after considering alternative proposals authorizing suspension "on the most urgent occasions" or forbidding suspension outright did the Framers agree to a narrow exception upon a finding of rebellion or invasion. *See* 2 The Records of the Federal Convention of 1787, *supra,* at 438. Indeed, it would be curious if the Framers were implicitly sanctioning Executive-ordered detention abroad without judicial review by limiting suspension — and by the court's reasoning therefore limiting habeas corpus — to domestic events. . . .

## C.

The question, then, is whether by attempting to eliminate all federal court jurisdiction to consider petitions for writs of habeas corpus, Congress has overstepped the boundary established by the Suspension Clause. The Supreme Court has stated on several occasions that "*at the absolute minimum,* the Suspension Clause protects the writ 'as it existed in 1789.'" *St. Cyr,* 533 U.S. at 301 (quoting *Felker v. Turpin,* 518 U.S. 651, 663-64 (1996)) (emphasis added). Therefore, at least insofar as habeas corpus exists and existed in 1789, Congress cannot suspend the writ without providing an adequate alternative except in the narrow exception specified in the Constitution. This proscription applies equally to removing the writ itself and to removing all jurisdiction to issue the writ. *See United States v. Klein,* 80 U.S. (13 Wall.) 128 (1872). *See generally* Erwin Chemerinsky, Federal Jurisdiction §3.2 (4th ed. 2003). . . .

### 1. . . .

. . . In *Rasul,* the Supreme Court stated that "[a]pplication of the habeas statute to persons detained at the [Guantánamo] base is consistent with the historical reach of the writ of habeas corpus." 542 U.S. at 481. By reaching a contrary conclusion, the court ignores the settled principle that "carefully considered language of the Supreme Court, even if technically dictum, generally must be treated as authoritative." *Sierra Club v. EPA,* 322 F.3d 718, 724 (D.C. Cir. 2003) (quoting *United States v. Oakar,* 111 F.3d 146, 153 (D.C. Cir. 1997)) (internal quotation marks omitted). Even setting aside this principle, the court offers no convincing analysis to compel the contrary conclusion. . . .

Finally, the court reasons that *Eisentrager* requires the conclusion that there is no constitutional right to habeas for those in the detainees' posture. In *Eisentrager,* the detainees claimed that they were "entitled, as a constitutional right, to sue in some court of the United States for a writ of *habeas corpus.*" 339 U.S. at 777. Thus *Eisentrager* presented a far different question than confronts this court. The detainees do not here contend that the Constitution accords them a positive right to the writ but rather that the Suspension Clause restricts Congress's power to eliminate a preexisting statutory right. To answer that question does not entail looking to the extent of the detainees' ties to the United States but rather requires understanding the scope of the writ of habeas corpus at common law in 1789. The court's reliance on *Eisentrager* is misplaced.

### 2.

This brings me to the question of whether, absent the writ, Congress has provided an adequate alternative procedure for challenging detention. If it so chooses, Congress may replace the privilege of habeas corpus with a commensurate procedure without overreaching its constitutional ambit. However, as the Supreme Court has cautioned, if a subject of Executive detention "were subject to any substantial procedural hurdles which ma[k]e his remedy . . . less swift and imperative than federal habeas corpus, the gravest constitutional doubts would be engendered [under the Suspension Clause]." *Sanders v. United States*, 373 U.S. 1, 14 (1963). . . .

. . . As the Supreme Court has stated, "[a]t its historical core, the writ of habeas corpus has served as a means of reviewing the legality of Executive detention, and it is in that context that its protections have been strongest." *St. Cyr*, 533 U.S. at 301. With this in mind, the government is mistaken in contending that the combatant status review tribunals ("CSRTs") established by the DTA suitably test the legitimacy of Executive detention. Far from merely adjusting the mechanism for vindicating the habeas right, the DTA imposes a series of hurdles while saddling each Guantanamo detainee with an assortment of handicaps that make the obstacles insurmountable. . . .

[First, Judge Rogers noted that, contrary to habeas practice, CSRTs place on the detainee the burden of producing evidence to show why he should not be detained. In discharging that burden, he is not entitled to be informed of the basis for his detention and must proceed without benefit of counsel. Second, the limited judicial review allowed by the DTA is no cure, because it is narrower than the scope of traditional habeas review. Third, the government can justify continued detention on the basis of evidence resulting from torture. Fourth, the CSRT protocol does not guarantee release even of a detainee who meets its standards.]

*3.*

Therefore, because Congress in enacting the MCA has revoked the privilege of the writ of habeas corpus where it would have issued under the common law in 1789, without providing an adequate alternative, the MCA is void unless Congress's action fits within the exception in the Suspension Clause: Congress may suspend the writ "when in Cases of Rebellion or Invasion the public Safety may require it." U.S. Const. art. I, §9, cl. 2. However, Congress has not invoked this power.

Suspension has been an exceedingly rare event in the history of the United States. On only four occasions has Congress seen fit to suspend the writ. These examples follow a clear pattern: Each suspension has made specific reference to a state of "Rebellion" or "Invasion" and each suspension was limited to the duration of that necessity. In 1863, recognizing "the present rebellion," Congress authorized President Lincoln during the Civil War "whenever, in his judgment, the public safety may require it, . . . to suspend the writ of habeas corpus." Act of Mar. 3, 1863, ch. 81, §1, 12 Stat. 755, 755 [discussed in *Milligan*, *supra* p. 314]. As a result, no writ was to issue "so long as said suspension by the President shall remain in force, and said rebellion continue." *Id.* In the Ku Klux Klan Act of 1871, Congress agreed to authorize suspension whenever "the unlawful combinations named [in the statute] shall be organized and armed, and so numerous and powerful as to be able, by violence, to either overthrow or set at defiance the constituted authorities of such State, and of the United States within such State," finding that these circumstances "shall be deemed a rebellion against the government of the United States." Act of Apr. 20, 1871, ch. 22, §4, 17 Stat. 13, 14-15. Suspension was also authorized "when in cases of rebellion, insurrection, or invasion the public safety may require it" in two territories of the United States: the Philippines, Act of July 1, 1902, ch. 1369, §5, 32 Stat. 691, 692, and Hawaii, Hawaiian Organic Act, ch. 339, §67, 31 Stat. 141, 153 (1900); *see Duncan v. Kahanamoku*, 327 U.S. 304, 307-08 (1946).

Because the MCA contains neither of these hallmarks of suspension, and because there is no indication that Congress sought to avail itself of the exception in the Suspension Clause, its attempt to revoke federal jurisdiction that the Supreme Court held to exist exceeds the powers of Congress. The MCA therefore has no effect on the jurisdiction of the federal courts to consider these petitions and their related appeals.

## II. . . .

The fundamental question presented by a petition for a writ of habeas corpus is whether Executive detention is lawful. . . .

The Supreme Court in *Rasul* did not address "whether and what further proceedings may become necessary after respondents make their responses to the merits of petitioners' claims," 542 U.S. at 485. The detainees cannot rest on due process under the Fifth Amendment. . . . [T]he Supreme Court in *Eisentrager* held that the Constitution does not afford rights to aliens in this context. Although in *Rasul* the Court cast doubt on the continuing vitality of *Eisentrager,* absent an explicit statement by the Court that it intended to overrule *Eisentrager*'s constitutional holding, that holding is binding on this court. Rather, the process that is due inheres in the nature of the writ and the inquiry it entails. The Court in *Rasul* held that federal court jurisdiction under 28 U.S.C. §2241 is permitted for habeas petitions filed by detainees at Guantanamo, and this result is undisturbed because the MCA is void. . . .

Therefore, I would hold that on remand the district courts shall follow the return and traverse procedures of 28 U.S.C. §2241 *et seq.* . . .

Accordingly, I respectfully dissent from the judgment vacating the district courts' decisions and dismissing these appeals for lack of jurisdiction.

## BOUMEDIENE V. BUSH

Supreme Court of the United States, 2007
127 S.Ct. 1478

Statement of Justice STEVENS and Justice KENNEDY respecting the denial of certiorari. The petitions for writs of certiorari are denied. Despite the obvious importance of the issues raised in these cases, we are persuaded that traditional rules governing our decision of constitutional questions, see *Ashwander v. TVA*, 297 U.S. 288, 341 (1936) (Brandeis, J., concurring), and our practice of requiring the exhaustion of available remedies as a precondition to accepting jurisdiction over applications for the writ of habeas corpus, cf. *Ex parte Hawk*, 321 U.S. 114 (1944) *(per curiam),* make it appropriate to deny these petitions at this time. However, "[t]his Court has frequently recognized that the policy underlying the exhaustion-of-remedies doctrine does not require the exhaustion of inadequate remedies." *Marino v. Ragen,* 332 U.S. 561, 570 n.12 (1947) (Rutledge, J., concurring). If petitioners later seek to establish that the Government has unreasonably delayed proceedings under the Detainee Treatment Act of 2005, Tit. X, 119 Stat. 2739, or some other and ongoing injury, alternative means exist for us to consider our jurisdiction over the allegations made by petitioners before the Court of Appeals. See 28 U.S.C. §§1651(a), 2241. Were the Government to take additional steps to prejudice the position of petitioners in seeking review in this Court, "courts of competent jurisdiction," including this Court, "should act promptly to ensure that the office and purposes of the writ of habeas corpus are not compromised." *Padilla v. Hanft,* 547 U.S. 1062, 1064 (2006) (Kennedy, J., concurring in denial of certiorari). And as always, denial of certiorari does not constitute an expression of any opinion on the merits. See *Rasul v. Bush,* 542 U.S. 466, 480-481 (2004) (majority opinion of Stevens, J.); *id.,* at 487 (Kennedy, J., concurring in judgment).

Justice BREYER, with whom Justice SOUTER joins, and with whom Justice GINSBURG joins as to Part I, dissenting from the denial of certiorari. I would grant the petitions for certiorari and expedite argument in these cases.

## I

Petitioners, foreign citizens imprisoned at Guantanamo Bay, Cuba, raise an important question: whether the Military Commissions Act of 2006, Pub. L. 109-366, 120 Stat. 2600, deprives courts of jurisdiction to consider their habeas claims, and, if so, whether that deprivation is constitutional. I believe these questions deserve this Court's immediate attention.

First, the "province" of the Great Writ, "shaped to guarantee the most fundamental of all rights, is to provide an effective *and speedy* instrument by which judicial inquiry may be had into the legality of the detention of a person." *Carafas v. LaVallee,* 391 U.S. 234, 238 (1968) (emphasis added and footnote omitted). Yet, petitioners have been held for more than five years. They have not obtained judicial review of their habeas claims. If petitioners are right about the law, immediate review may avoid an additional year or more of imprisonment. If they are wrong, our review is nevertheless appropriate to help establish the boundaries of the constitutional provision for the writ of habeas corpus. Cf. *Carafas, supra.* Finally, whether petitioners are right or wrong, our prompt review will diminish the legal "uncertainty" that now "surrounds" the application to Guantanamo detainees of this "fundamental constitutional principle." Brief for Senator Arlen Specter as *Amicus Curiae* 19; see generally *ibid.* (favoring expedited consideration of these cases). Doing so will bring increased clarity that in turn will speed review in other cases.

Second, petitioners plausibly argue that the lower court's reasoning is contrary to this Court's precedent. This Court previously held that federal jurisdiction lay to consider petitioners' habeas claims. *Rasul v. Bush,* 542 U.S. 466, 485 (2004) (providing several of these petitioners with the right to habeas review under law as it then stood). Our analysis proceeded under the then-operative statute, but petitioners urge that our reasoning applies to the scope of the constitutional habeas right as well. In holding that the writ extended to the petitioners in *Rasul,* we said that Guantanamo was under the complete control and jurisdiction of the United States. *Id.,* at 480-481; *id.,* at 487 (Kennedy, J., concurring in judgment) ("Guantanamo Bay is in every practical respect a United States territory"). We then observed that the writ at common law would have extended to petitioners:

> "Application of the habeas statute to persons detained at the base is consistent with the historical reach of the writ of habeas corpus. At common law, courts exercised habeas jurisdiction over the claims of aliens detained within sovereign territory of the realm, as well as the claims of persons detained in the so-called exempt jurisdictions, where ordinary writs did not run, and all other dominions under the sovereign's control. . . . [E]ven if a territory was not part of the realm, there was no doubt as to the court's power to issue writs of habeas corpus if the territory was under the subjection of the Crown." *Id.,* at 481-482 (internal quotation marks and footnotes omitted).

Our reasoning may be applicable here. The lower court's holding, petitioners urge, disregards these statements and reasoning.

Further, petitioners in *Boumediene* are natives of Algeria, and citizens of Bosnia, seized in Bosnia. Other detainees, including several petitioners in *Al Odah,* also are citizens of friendly nations, including Australia, Canada, Kuwait, Turkey, and the United Kingdom; and many were seized outside of any theater of hostility, in places like Pakistan, Thailand, and Zambia. It is possible that these circumstances will make a difference in respect to our resolution of the constitutional questions presented. Cf. *Hamdi v. Rumsfeld,* 542

U.S. 507, 509, 514, 521 (2004) (plurality opinion of O'Connor, J., joined by Rehnquist, C. J., and Kennedy and Breyer, JJ.) (holding military had authority to detain United States citizen "enemy combatant," captured in a *"zone of active combat* in a foreign theater of conflict," specifically Afghanistan, and stressing, in a "narrow" holding, that *"[a]ctive combat operations against Taliban fighters . . . [were] ongoing in Afghanistan"* (emphasis added)).

The Government, of course, contests petitioners' arguments on the merits. But I do not here say petitioners are correct; I say only that the questions presented are significant ones warranting our review.

If petitioners have the right of access to habeas corpus in the federal courts, this Court would then have to consider whether Congress' provision in the Detainee Treatment Act of 2005 (DTA), Tit. X, 119 Stat. 2739, providing for review in the Court of Appeals for the D.C. Circuit of those proceedings, is a constitutionally adequate substitute for habeas corpus. The Government argues that we should therefore wait for a case where, unlike petitioners here, the detainee seeking certiorari has actually sought and received review under these alternative means. Petitioners respond, however, that further proceedings in the Court of Appeals under the DTA could not possibly remedy a constitutional violation. The lower court expressly indicated that *no constitutional rights* (not merely the right to habeas) extend to the Guantanamo detainees. 476 F.3d, at 991-992 (rejecting petitioners' arguments under this Court's precedent that fundamental rights afforded by the Constitution extend to Guantanamo, and noting that "[p]recedent in this circuit also forecloses the detainees' claims to constitutional rights"). Therefore, it is irrelevant, to petitioners, that the DTA provides for review in the D.C. Circuit of any constitutional infirmities in the proceedings under that Act, §1005(e)(2)(C)(ii), 119 Stat. 2742; the lower court has already rendered that provision a nullity.

Nor will further percolation of the question presented offer elucidation as to either the threshold question whether petitioners have a right to habeas, or the question whether the DTA provides a constitutionally adequate substitute. It is unreasonable to suggest that the D.C. Circuit in future proceedings under the DTA will provide review that affords petitioners the rights that the Circuit has already concluded they do not have. Ordinarily, habeas petitioners need not exhaust a remedy that is inadequate to vindicate the asserted right.

The Government, in *Hamdan v. Rumsfeld,* [126 S. Ct. 2749] (2006), similarly argued for delay. That case, too, presented questions of the scope of the Guantanamo detainees' right to federal-court review of DTA-authorized procedures. We there rejected the Government's argument for delay as unsound.

Here, as in *Hamdan,* petitioners argue that the tribunals to which they have already been subjected were infirm (by, *inter alia,* denying Petitioners counsel and access to evidence). Here, as in *Hamdan,* petitioners assert that these procedural infirmities cannot be corrected by review under the DTA which provides for no augmentation of the record on appeal and, as noted above, will provide no remedy for any constitutional violation. See DTA §1005(e)(2)(C), 119 Stat. 2742; 476 F.3d, at 1005 (Rogers, J., dissenting). Here, as in *Hamdan,* petitioners have a compelling interest in assuring in advance that the procedures to which they are subject are lawful. And here, *unlike Hamdan,* the military tribunals in Guantanamo have completed their work; all that remains are the appeals. For all these reasons, I would grant the petitions.

## II

Moreover, I would expedite our consideration. In the past, this Court has expedited other cases where important issues and a need for speedy consideration were at stake. In *Ex parte Quirin,* 317 U.S. 1 (1942), the Court decided that it should grant expedited consideration,

> "[i]n view of the public importance of the questions raised by [the] petitions and of the duty which rests on the courts, in time of war as well as in time of peace, to preserve unimpaired the constitutional safeguards of civil liberty, and because in our opinion the public interest required that we consider and decide those questions without any avoidable delay." *Id.,* at 19.

For these reasons, I would grant the petitions for certiorari and the motions to expedite the cases in accordance with the schedule deemed acceptable (in the alternative) by the Government.

## NOTES AND QUESTIONS

1. ***Does Habeas Extend to Aliens Held Abroad?*** All members of the *Boumediene* D.C. Circuit panel agreed that Congress had finally satisfied any clear statement requirement by its jurisdiction-stripping provision of the MCA, and that it applied to the pending cases. The issue then was whether Congress had withdrawn federal jurisdiction consistently with the Suspension Clause, which, all agree, protects the writ at least as it existed in 1789.

   For the Court of Appeals majority, the answer was simple: the writ did not extend to aliens abroad in 1789, so Congress had not violated the Suspension Clause. They added that *Eisentrager* established that the Constitution does not confer "rights" on aliens without property or presence in the United States. How did they distinguish the holding in *Rasul*? What about the dictum in *Rasul*?

   Judge Rogers, dissenting, obviously read the history — and *Rasul*'s take on the history — differently. What was the dissent's response to the aliens-have-no-constitutional-rights argument? Why was the dissent "fixated," in the majority's pejorative term, on how to characterize the Suspension Clause? Is footnote 15 in *Rasul* relevant? How did the dissent distinguish *Eisentrager*?

2. ***"Commensurate" Alternatives?*** If aliens abroad do have some right to habeas corpus that Congress has suspended, the next question for the dissent is whether Congress has provided — or whether there otherwise is available — "an adequate alternative procedure for challenging detention." Congress, after all, did not cut off all federal jurisdiction in the DTA and the MCA. It preserved limited scope judicial review of both CSRT decisions and

eventual decisions of military commissions. See *supra* p. 335. Why, according to Judge Rogers, is this not enough? What did the dissenters in the Supreme Court have to say on this matter?

One commentator has observed that while under the DTA the Court of Appeals for the D.C. Circuit cannot engage in *de novo* review of a CSRT decision, "it *can* require the CSRTs to conform their own standards to all statutory, constitutional, law-of-war, and even, perhaps, treaty-based requirements." Marty Lederman, *What Now at GTMO?*, Apr. 2, 2007 (emphasis in original), *available at* http://balkin.blogspot.com/2007/04/what-now-at-gtmo.html. Yet he speculates that this review might not satisfy all constitutional requirements, because, for example, the Constitution might require "some sort of factual review of the basis for detention *by an independent adjudicator* outside the executive branch. . . ." *Id.* (emphasis in original).

Whatever the scope of the review, according to Lederman, it might simply come too late. *Id.* (quoting Preiser v. Rodriguez, 411 U.S. 475, 494 (1973) ("[S]peedy review of [a prisoner's] grievance . . . is so often essential to any effective redress.")). At this writing, some of the detainees are well into their sixth year of detention. How did the Supreme Court dissenters address this concern? How did Justices Stevens and Kennedy respond? What "additional steps" by the government would provoke the Court to "act promptly to ensure that the office and purposes of habeas corpus are not compromised"?

3. ***Satisfying the Suspension Clause.*** If the alternatives provided by Congress in the DTA and MCA are insufficient, we finally reach the question whether the resulting suspension of the writ of habeas corpus satisfies the requirements of the Suspension Clause. What are those requirements? As we noted above, no court has ever squarely ruled on their justiciability. If Congress had found, as a predicate to the DTA and MCA, that the public safety required suspension for aliens held abroad following the "invasion" of the United States on September 11 by al Qaeda, by what standard would a court decide whether we had suffered an "invasion" within the meaning of the Suspension Clause, and, if so, whether the "public Safety" now required suspension? If your answer is that there is no such standard and that these questions are nonjusticiable, how could a *U.S. citizen* detainee challenge a suspension based on the same statutory predicate? How did the dissent in *Boumediene* deal with these issues?

4. ***The Remedy.*** When, on a habeas challenge, the government is unable to prove a lawful justification for detention, the judicial remedy is an order for release of the habeas petitioner. Why didn't the dissent propose this remedy? If the dissent had prevailed, what kind of showing do you suppose the government would make on remand?

5. ***The Minuet Continues?*** At this writing, a Democratic Congress is reconsidering the MCA and discussing various habeas "restoration" bills. What is the habeas right of aliens held abroad that would be "restored"? If "restored" is just political rhetoric, what should a habeas right of such detainees look like? Can you craft a bill that would preserve some right to judicial review of CSRT status determinations without opening the proverbial floodgates to

hundreds, if not thousands, of alien detainee (including enemy combatant) habeas petitions?

Alternatively, if you believe that such detainees deserve no U.S. forum for challenging the legality of their detention, can you formulate a suspension provision that would meet the test that the *Boumediene* dissent finds in the Suspension Clause?

*12*

# *MILITARY DETENTION OF TERRORIST SUSPECTS*

During war, national security may require the detention of both noncombatants and combatants for the duration of hostilities, and the military may participate in the detention. Here we consider the law governing such detentions as it applies in the "war on terrorism." We postpone the overlapping topic of military trial until Chapter 18. Part A of this chapter sets out two seminal pre-9/11 cases regarding military authority over putative combatants. Although these cases deal primarily with military trials rather than detention, their reasoning has influenced the law of military detention and military trials alike because detention is a predicate for trial. Part B considers military detention of U.S. citizens after 9/11. Finally, Part C discusses military detention of aliens after 9/11, briefly noting some applicable international laws of war in the process.

## A. WARTIME DETENTION OF COMBATANTS BEFORE 9/11

### EX PARTE MILLIGAN

United States Supreme Court, 1866
71 U.S. (4 Wall.) 2

[The facts of the case are set forth *supra* p. 314.]

MR. JUSTICE DAVIS delivered the opinion of the court. . . . The controlling question in the case is this: Upon the *facts* stated in Milligan's petition, and the exhibits filed, had the military commission mentioned in it *jurisdiction*, legally, to try and sentence him? . . .

No graver question was ever considered by this court, nor one which more nearly concerns the rights of the whole people; for it is the birthright of every American citizen when charged with crime, to be tried and punished according to law. The power of punishment is, alone through the means which the laws have provided for that purpose, and if they are ineffectual, there is an immunity from punishment, no matter how great an offender the individual may be, or how much his crimes may have shocked the sense of justice of the country, or endangered its safety. By the protection of the law human rights are secured; withdraw that protection, and they are at the mercy of wicked rulers, or the clamor of an excited people. If there was law to justify this military trial, it is not our province to interfere; if there was not, it is our duty to declare the nullity of the whole proceedings. The decision of this question does not depend on argument or judicial precedents, numerous and highly illustrative as they are. These precedents inform us of the extent of the struggle to preserve liberty and to relieve those in civil life from military trials. The founders of our government were familiar with the history of that struggle; and secured in a written constitution every right which the people had wrested from power during a contest of ages. By that Constitution and the laws authorized by it this question must be determined. The provisions of that instrument on the administration of criminal justice are too plain and direct, to leave room for misconstruction or doubt of their true meaning. Those applicable to this case are found in that clause of the original Constitution which says, "That the trial of all crimes, except in case of impeachment, shall be by jury;" and in the fourth, fifth, and sixth articles of the amendments. The fourth proclaims the right to be secure in person and effects against unreasonable search and seizure; and directs that a judicial warrant shall not issue "without proof of probable cause supported by oath or affirmation." The fifth declares "that no person shall be held to answer for a capital or otherwise infamous crime unless on presentment by a grand jury, except in cases arising in the land or naval forces, or in the militia, when in actual service in time of war or public danger, nor be deprived of life, liberty, or property, without due process of law." And the sixth guarantees the right of trial by jury, in such manner and with such regulations that with upright judges, impartial juries, and an able bar, the innocent will be saved and the guilty punished. . . .

Time has proven the discernment of our ancestors; for even these provisions, expressed in such plain English words, that it would seem the ingenuity of man could not evade them, are *now*, after the lapse of more than seventy years, sought to be avoided. Those great and good men foresaw that troublous times would arise, when rulers and people would become restive under restraint, and seek by sharp and decisive measures to accomplish ends deemed just and proper; and that the principles of constitutional liberty would be in peril, unless established by irrepealable law. The history of the world had taught them that what was done in the past might be attempted in the future. The Constitution of the United States is a law for rulers and people, equally in war and in peace, and covers with the shield of its protection all classes of men, at all times, and under all circumstances. No doctrine, involving more pernicious consequences, was ever invented by the wit of man than that any of its provisions can be suspended during any of the great exigencies of government. Such a doctrine leads directly to anarchy and despotism, but the theory of necessity on which it is based is false; for the government, within the Constitution, has all the powers granted to it, which are necessary to preserve its existence; as has been happily proved by the result of the great effort to throw off its just authority.

Have any of the rights guaranteed by the Constitution been violated in the case of Milligan? and if so, what are they?

Every trial involves the exercise of judicial power; and from what source did the military commission that tried him derive their authority? Certainly no part of the judicial power of the country was conferred on them; because the Constitution expressly vests it "in one supreme court and such inferior courts as the Congress may from time to time ordain and establish," and it is not pretended that the commission was a court ordained and established by Congress. They cannot justify on the mandate of the President; because he is controlled by law, and has his appropriate sphere of duty, which is to execute, not to make, the laws; and there is "no unwritten criminal code to which resort can be had as a source of jurisdiction."

But it is said that the jurisdiction is complete under the "laws and usages of war."

It can serve no useful purpose to inquire what those laws and usages are, whence they originated, where found, and on whom they operate; they can never be applied to citizens in states which have upheld the authority of the government, and where the courts are open and their process unobstructed. This court has judicial knowledge that in Indiana the Federal authority was always unopposed, and its courts always open to hear criminal accusations and redress grievances; and no usage of war could sanction a military trial there for any offence whatever of a citizen in civil life, in nowise connected with the military service. Congress could grant no such power; and to the honor of our national legislature be it said, it has never been provoked by the state of the country even to attempt its exercise. One of the plainest constitutional provisions was, therefore, infringed when Milligan was tried by a court not ordained and established by Congress, and not composed of judges appointed during good behavior. . . .

It is claimed that martial law covers with its broad mantle the proceedings of this military commission. The proposition is this: that in a time of war the commander of an armed force (if in his opinion the exigencies of the country demand it, and of which he is to judge), has the power, within the lines of the military district, to suspend all civil rights and their remedies, and subject citizens as well as soldiers to the *rule* of his will; and in the exercise of his lawful authority cannot be restrained, except by his superior officer or the President of the United States.

If this position is sound to the extent claimed, then when war exists, foreign or domestic, and the country is subdivided into military departments for mere convenience, the commander of one of them can, if he chooses, within his limits, on the plea of necessity, with the approval of the Executive, substitute military force for and to the exclusion of the laws, and punish all persons, as he thinks right and proper, without fixed or certain rules.

The statement of this proposition shows its importance; for, if true, republican government is a failure, and there is an end of liberty regulated by law. Martial law, established on such a basis, destroys every guarantee of the Constitution, and effectually renders the "military independent of and superior to the civil power" — the attempt to do which by the King of Great Britain was deemed by our fathers such an offence, that they assigned it to the world as one of the causes which impelled them to declare their independence. Civil liberty and this kind of martial law cannot endure together; the antagonism is irreconcilable; and, in the conflict, one or the other must perish. . . .

It will be borne in mind that this is not a question of the power to proclaim martial law, when war exists in a community and the courts and civil authorities are overthrown. Nor is it a question what rule a military commander, at the head of his army, can impose on states in rebellion to cripple their resources and quell the insurrection. The jurisdiction claimed is much more extensive. The necessities of the service, during the late Rebellion, required that the loyal states should be placed within the limits of certain military districts and commanders appointed in them; and, it is urged, that this, in a military sense, constituted them the theatre of military operations; and, as in this case, Indiana had been and was again threatened with invasion by the enemy, the occasion was furnished to establish martial law. The conclusion does not follow from the premises. If armies were collected in Indiana, they were to be employed in another locality, where the laws were obstructed and the national authority disputed. On *her* soil there was no hostile foot; if once invaded, that invasion was at an end, and with it all pretext for martial law. Martial law cannot arise from a *threatened* invasion. The necessity must be actual and present; the invasion real, such as effectually closes the courts and deposes the civil administration.

It is difficult to see how the *safety* for the country required martial law in Indiana. If any of her citizens were plotting treason, the power of arrest could secure them, until the government was prepared for their trial, when the courts were open and ready to try them. It was as easy to protect witnesses before a civil as a military tribunal; and as there could be no wish to convict, except on sufficient legal evidence, surely an ordained and established court was better able to judge of this than a military tribunal composed of gentlemen not trained to the profession of the law.

It follows, from what has been said on this subject, that there are occasions when martial rule can be properly applied. If, in foreign invasion or civil war, the courts are actually closed, and it is impossible to administer criminal justice according to law, *then*, on the theatre of active military operations, where war really prevails, there is a necessity to furnish a substitute for the civil authority, thus overthrown, to preserve the safety of the army and society; and as no power is left but the military, it is allowed to govern by martial rule until the laws can have their free course. As necessity creates the rule, so it limits its duration; for, if this government is continued *after* the courts are reinstated, it is a gross usurpation of power. Martial rule can never exist where the courts are open, and in the proper and unobstructed exercise of their jurisdiction. It is also confined to the locality of actual war. Because, during the late Rebellion it could have been enforced in Virginia, where the national authority was overturned and the courts driven out, it does not follow that it should obtain in Indiana, where that authority was never disputed, and justice was always administered. And so in the case of a foreign invasion, martial rule may become a necessity in one state, when, in another, it would be "mere lawless violence." . . .

If the military trial of Milligan was contrary to law, then he was entitled, on the facts stated in his petition, to be discharged from custody by the terms of the act of Congress of March 3d, 1863. . . .

The CHIEF JUSTICE delivered the following opinion [in which WAYNE, SWAYNE, and MILLER, JJ., concurred]. . . . [The Chief Justice agreed that the military commission was without lawful jurisdiction to try Milligan.] But the opinion which has just been read goes further; and as we understand it, asserts not only that the military commission held in Indiana was not authorized by Congress, but that it was not in the power of Congress to authorize it. . . .

We think that Congress had power, though not exercised, to authorize the Military Commission which was held in Indiana. . . .

. . . Congress cannot direct the conduct of campaigns, nor can the President, or any commander under him, without the sanction of Congress, institute tribunals for the trial and punishment of offences, either of soldiers or civilians, unless in cases of a controlling necessity, which justifies what it compels, or at least insures acts of indemnity from the justice of the legislature.

We by no means assert that Congress can establish and apply the laws of war where no war has been declared or exists.

Where peace exists the laws of peace must prevail. What we do maintain is, that when the nation is involved in war, and some portions of the country are invaded, and all are exposed to invasion, it is within the power of Congress to determine in what states or district such great and imminent public danger exists as justifies the authorization of military tribunals for the trial of crimes and offences against the discipline or security of the army or against the public safety. . . .

## EX PARTE QUIRIN

United States Supreme Court, 1942
317 U.S. 1

[After war was declared between the United States and Germany, seven German nationals, and Herbert Hans Haupt, a dual U.S.-German national, were trained at a German sabotage school near Berlin. German submarines then carried the saboteurs with a supply of explosives to the United States. They landed on U.S. beaches wearing German Marine Infantry uniforms, which they immediately buried. Before they could engage in any act of sabotage, however, they were betrayed to the FBI by one of their number.

After their arrest, President Roosevelt issued an order establishing a military commission and proclaimed its jurisdiction to try nationals of enemy states or those who act under their direction for sabotage, espionage, or "violations of the law of war." Proclamation 2561, 7 Fed. Reg. 5101 (1942). The Military Commission conducted a secret 18-day trial of the saboteurs. Toward the end of the trial, the Supreme Court decided in an extraordinary expedited summer session to hear argument on the saboteurs' appeal from refusal of the lower courts to entertain their petitions for writs of habeas corpus. Less than 24 hours after argument, it ruled *per curiam* that the military commission was lawfully constituted and authorized to try the saboteurs, promising a full opinion later. Six of the saboteurs were executed eight days after the Supreme Court's *per curiam* ruling (Roosevelt commuted the sentences of the others to imprisonment). The Court issued its full opinion three months later.]

Mr. Chief Justice STONE delivered the opinion of the Court. . . . We are not here concerned with any question of the guilt or innocence of petitioners. Constitutional safeguards for the protection of all who are charged with offenses are not to be disregarded in order to inflict merited punishment on some who are guilty. Ex parte Milligan, [71 U.S. (4 Wall.) 2 (1866)]. But the detention and trial of petitioners — ordered by the President in the declared exercise of his powers as Commander in Chief of the Army in time of war and of grave public danger — are not to be set aside by the courts without the clear conviction that they are in conflict with the Constitution or laws of Congress constitutionally enacted.

Congress and the President, like the courts, possess no power not derived from the Constitution. But one of the objects of the Constitution, as declared by its preamble, is to "provide for the common defence." . . .

[The Court then catalogued first Congress's, then the President's, national security authorities under the Constitution.]

The Constitution thus invests the President as Commander in Chief with the power to wage war which Congress has declared, and to carry into effect all laws passed by Congress for the conduct of war and for the government and regulation of the Armed Forces, and all laws defining and punishing offences against the law of nations, including those which pertain to the conduct of war.

By the Articles of War, 10 U.S.C. §§1471-1593, Congress has provided rules for the government of the Army. . . . But the Articles also recognize the "military commission" appointed by military command as an appropriate tribunal for the trial and punishment of offenses against the law of war not ordinarily tried by court martial. See Arts. 12, 15. Articles 38 and 46 authorize the President, with certain limitations, to prescribe the procedure for military commissions. Articles 81 and 82 authorize trial, either by court martial or military commission, of those charged with relieving, harboring or corresponding with the enemy and those charged with spying. And Article 15 declares that "the provisions of these articles conferring jurisdiction upon courts-martial shall not be construed as depriving military commissions . . . or other military tribunals of concurrent jurisdiction in respect of offenders or offenses that by statute or by the law of war may be triable by such military commissions . . . or other military tribunals." . . .

From the very beginning of its history this Court has recognized and applied the law of war as including that part of the law of nations which prescribes, for the conduct of war, the status, rights and duties of enemy nations as well as of enemy individuals. By the Articles of War, and especially Article 15, Congress has explicitly provided, so far as it may constitutionally do so, that military tribunals shall have jurisdiction to try offenders or offenses against the law of war in appropriate cases. . . .

An important incident to the conduct of war is the adoption of measures by the military command not only to repel and defeat the enemy, but to seize and subject to disciplinary measures those enemies who in their attempt to thwart or impede our military effort have violated the law of war. It is unnecessary for present purposes to determine to what extent the President as Commander in Chief has constitutional power to create military commissions without the support of Congressional legislation. For here Congress has authorized trial of offenses against the law of war before such commissions. . . . We may assume that there are acts regarded in other countries, or by some writers on international law, as offenses against the law of war which would not be triable by military tribunal here, either because they are not recognized by our courts as violations of the law of war or because they are of that class of offenses constitutionally triable only by a jury. It was upon such grounds that the Court denied the right to proceed by military tribunal in Ex parte Milligan, supra. But as we shall show, these petitioners were charged with an offense against the law of war which the Constitution does not require to be tried by jury. . . .

. . . [B]y the reference in the 15th Article of War to "offenders or offenses that . . . by the law of war may be triable by such military commissions," Congress has incorporated by reference, as within the jurisdiction of military commissions, all offenses which are defined as such by the law of war, and which may constitutionally be included within that jurisdiction. Congress had the choice of crystallizing in permanent form and in minute detail every offense against the law of war, or of adopting the system of common law applied by military tribunals so far as it should be recognized and deemed applicable by the courts. It chose the latter course.

By universal agreement and practice the law of war draws a distinction between the armed forces and the peaceful populations of belligerent nations and also between those who are lawful and unlawful combatants. Lawful combatants are subject to capture and detention as prisoners of war by opposing military forces. Unlawful combatants are likewise subject to capture and detention, but in addition they are subject to trial and punishment by military tribunals for acts which render their belligerency unlawful. The spy who secretly and without uniform passes the military lines of a belligerent in time of war, seeking to gather military information and communicate it to the enemy, or an enemy combatant who without uniform comes secretly through the lines for the purpose of waging war by destruction of life or property, are familiar examples of belligerents who are generally deemed not to be entitled to the status of prisoners of war, but to be offenders against the law of war subject to trial and punishment by military tribunals. . . .

Specification 1 states that petitioners "being enemies of the United States and acting for . . . the German Reich, a belligerent enemy nation, secretly and covertly passed, in civilian dress, contrary to the law of war, through the military and naval lines and defenses of the United States . . . and went behind such lines, contrary to the law of war, in civilian dress . . . for the purpose of committing . . . hostile acts, and, in particular, to destroy certain war industries, war utilities and war materials within the United States."

This specification . . . plainly alleges violation of the law of war. . . .

Citizenship in the United States of an enemy belligerent does not relieve him from the consequences of a belligerency which is unlawful because in violation of the law of war. Citizens who associate themselves with the military arm of the enemy government, and with its aid, guidance and direction enter this country bent on hostile acts are enemy belligerents within the meaning of the Hague Convention and the law of war. It is as an enemy belligerent that petitioner Haupt is charged with entering the United States, and unlawful belligerency is the gravamen of the offense of which he is accused. . . .

But petitioners insist that even if the offenses with which they are charged are offenses against the law of war, their trial is subject to the requirement of the Fifth Amendment that no person shall be held to answer for a capital or otherwise infamous crime unless on a presentment or indictment of a grand jury, and that such trials by Article III, §2, and the Sixth Amendment must be by jury in a civil court. . . .

Presentment by a grand jury and trial by a jury of the vicinage where the crime was committed were at the time of the adoption of the Constitution familiar parts of the machinery for criminal trials in the civil courts. But they were procedures unknown to military tribunals, which are not courts in the sense of the Judiciary Article, and which in the natural course of events are usually called upon to function under conditions precluding resort to such procedures. . . .

. . . [W]e must conclude that §2 of Article III and the Fifth and Sixth Amendments cannot be taken to have extended the right to demand a jury to trials by military commission, or to have required that offenses against the law of war not triable by jury at common law be tried only in the civil courts. . . .

Petitioners, and especially petitioner Haupt, stress the pronouncement of this Court in the *Milligan* case that the law of war "can never be applied to citizens in states which have upheld the authority of the government, and where the courts are open and their process unobstructed." Elsewhere in its opinion, the Court was at pains to point out that Milligan, a citizen twenty years resident in Indiana, who had never been a resident of any of the states in rebellion, was not an enemy belligerent either entitled to the status of a prisoner of war or subject to the penalties imposed upon unlawful belligerents. We construe the Court's statement as to the inapplicability of the law of war to Milligan's case as having particular reference to the facts before it. From them the Court concluded that Milligan, not being a part of or associated with the armed forces of the enemy, was a non-belligerent, not subject to the law of war save as — in circumstances found not there to be present and not involved here — martial law might be constitutionally established.

The Court's opinion is inapplicable to the case presented by the present record. We have no occasion now to define with meticulous care the ultimate boundaries of the jurisdiction of military tribunals to try persons according to the law of war. It is enough that petitioners here, upon the conceded facts, were plainly within those boundaries, and were held in good faith for trial by military commission, charged with being enemies who, with the purpose of destroying war materials and utilities, entered or after entry remained in our territory without uniform — an offense against the law of war. We hold only that those particular acts constitute an offense against the law of war which the Constitution authorizes to be tried by military commission. . . .

It follows that the orders of the District Court should be affirmed, and that leave to file petitions for habeas corpus in this Court should be denied.

Mr. Justice Murphy took no part in the consideration or decision of these cases.

## NOTES AND QUESTIONS

1. *Military Necessity.* In Reid v. Covert, 354 U.S. 1, 21 (1957), the Court emphasized that

> the jurisdiction of military tribunals is a very limited and extraordinary jurisdiction derived from the cryptic language of Art. I, §8, and, at most, was intended to be only a narrow exception to the normal and preferred method of trial in courts of law. Every extension of military jurisdiction is an encroachment on the jurisdiction of the civil courts, and, more important, acts as a deprivation of the right to jury trial and of other treasured constitutional protections.

At the same time, it found that the "exigencies which have required military rule on the battlefront are not present . . . where no conflict exists. Military trial of civilians 'in the field' is an extraordinary jurisdiction and it should not be expanded at the expense of the Bill of Rights." *Id.* at 35.

The exception to the "preferred" method of civilian trial is thus justified by necessity. Military commissions were historically used in the field or theater of military operations or in occupied territory. *See* Edmund M. Morgan, *Court-Martial Jurisdiction Over Non-Military Persons Under the Articles of War*, 4 Minn. L. Rev. 79, 107 & n.100 (1920). In such cases, loyal civilian courts were unavailable and it was difficult to collect admissible evidence and to preserve chains of custody for evidence.

If military necessity is the predicate for military commissions, what is the necessity for military detention? When and where does necessity justify military detention, rather than arrest pursuant to judicially issued arrest warrants?

2. *Law of War Authority?* *Quirin* suggests in several places that there was statutory authority for the commission that tried the German saboteurs. Indeed, articles 81 and 82 of the Articles of War, which it cites, seemed to authorize the trial of spies, at least, by military commission. When the Articles of War were generally replaced by the Uniform Code of Military Justice in 1956, however, articles 81 and 82 were dropped. But the decision places chief reliance on article 15, which it quotes *supra* p. 354. Does article 15, which is now 10 U.S.C. §821 (2000), expressly authorize military commissions, or is it merely a savings clause? If it is a savings clause, what authority does it save? In another World War II case involving military commissions, Application of Yamashita, 327 U.S. 1 (1946), the Supreme Court explained that "[b]y thus recognizing military commissions in order to preserve their traditional jurisdiction over enemy combatants unimpaired by the Articles, Congress gave sanction, as we held in Ex parte Quirin, to any use of the military commission contemplated by the *common law of war*." *Id.* at 20 (emphasis added).

The law of war also authorizes military detention of combatants and some civilians. *See, e.g.*, International & Operational Law Dept., U.S. Army Judge Advocate General's School, *Law of War Handbook* 80, 263-267 (2005) (describing prisoners of war; civilian detainees interned during armed conflict or occupation for security reasons, their own protection, or for offense against the detaining power; and other persons captured or detained by armed forces); Dept. of Army, *Enemy Prisoners of War, Civilian Internees and Detained Persons* (FM 19-40) (Feb. 1976). Assuming law of war authorization, is §821 or any statute necessary to authorize military detention as long as we are at war? *Cf.* Hamdan v. Rumsfeld, 126 S. Ct., 2749, 2774 (2006), *infra* p. 566 (refraining from deciding analogous question for military commissions). Could Congress by statute regulate or prohibit such detentions? On what specific constitutional authority would Congress rely for such a statute?

3. ***Declared War?*** If military detention is authorized by the common law of war, must war be declared for the Commander in Chief to exercise that authority? War had, of course, been declared before *Quirin* and *Yamashita* were decided. One advantage of requiring a declared war to authorize military detention is that the authority then has a temporal limit. *See Yamashita*, 327 U.S. at 11-12 (asserting that military commissions can be used "so long as a state of war exists from its declaration until peace is proclaimed"). "A declaration of war draws clear lines. It defines (or at least has traditionally done so) who the enemy is: another state and all the nationals of that state. It marks a clear beginning, and (again traditionally) an end, with some act or instrument marking its conclusion." American Bar Assn. Task Force on Terrorism and the Law, *Report and Recommendations on Military Commissions* 5 (Jan. 4, 2002) (*ABA Task Force Report*). *See also* David B. Rivkin Jr., Lee A. Casey & Darin R. Bartram, *Bringing Al-Qaeda to Justice — The Constitutionality of Trying Al-Qaeda Terrorists in the Military Justice System* 12 (Heritage Found. Legal Mem., Nov. 5, 2001) (concluding that a formal declaration of war should be sought before military commissions are used to try al Qaeda members).

But we have seen that Congress can authorize "imperfect" war without a formal declaration. See Chapter 2. Writing of one such war (the Quasi-War with France) in Talbot v. Seeman, 5 U.S. 1 (1801), Chief Justice Marshall observed that "congress may authorize general hostilities, in which case the general laws of war apply to our situation; or partial hostilities, in which case the laws of war, so far as they actually apply to our situation, must be noticed." Military detention and military commissions were also widely used in the field and in occupied Confederate states during the undeclared Civil War.

Yet even those states of war each had a defined and discernible end. Does a war on terrorists have a discernible end? If a state of war triggers common law of war authority, did the 2001 Authorization for the Use of Military Force, Pub. L. No. 107-40, 115 Stat. 224 (AUMF), reproduced *supra* p. 59, which approves the use of force against the perpetrators of the September 11 attacks, authorize a state of war permitting the President to order military detention and the use of military commissions? *See* Hamdan v. Rumsfeld, 126 S. Ct. 2749, 2775 (2006), *infra* p. 563 (finding that it did authorize the President to use statutory authority to convene such commissions, but that it did not expand that authority). War against whom? Does this state of war draw clear lines for the duration or scope of military detention?

4. ***Reconciling Milligan and Quirin.*** Although Attorney General Biddle at first asked the Court in *Quirin* to overrule *Milligan*, he later backed off from this demand in his oral argument and asserted that it could uphold the use of

the military commission to try the saboteurs "without touching a hair of the *Milligan* case." George Lardner Jr., *Nazi Saboteurs Captured!*, Wash. Post, Jan. 13, 2002, Magazine, at 23. How *did* the Court distinguish *Milligan*? Did it distinguish the case by Milligan's citizenship? *See* Mudd v. Caldera, 134 F. Supp. 2d 138 (D.D.C. 2001) (citizens and noncitizens alike may be subject to the jurisdiction of a military commission for violating the laws of war). By his acts? (Recall that he was charged with "Violation of the laws of war.")

   *Quirin* suggests that *Milligan* should be limited to its facts. On the other hand, Justice Black wrote the other Justices in *Quirin* that "[i]n this case I want to go no further than to declare that these particular defendants are subject to the jurisdiction of a military tribunal because of the circumstances." *See* Evan P. Schultz, *Now and Later*, Legal Times, Dec. 24, 2001, at 54. Accordingly, the opinion for the Court stated, "We hold only that these particular facts constitute an offense against the law of nations which the Constitution authorizes to be tried by military commission." *Quirin*, 317 U.S. at 20. Do "these particular facts" include the fact of declared war with its attendant limits (including identification of combatants)? If *Quirin* is limited to *its* facts, could a military commission constitutionally try a terrorist apprehended in the United States while civilian courts are open?

   If these cases also provide law by analogy for military detention, could the military detain a suspected terrorist apprehended in the United States when the civilian courts are open (and thus able to issue an arrest warrant)? A suspected terrorist apprehended in Afghanistan during hostilities? Apprehended there, but then transported under restraints to Guantánamo or to a military brig in the United States?

## B.  DETENTION OF U.S. CITIZENS AS COMBATANTS AFTER 9/11

After 9/11, the government placed two U.S. citizens in military detention, citing Ex parte Quirin as authority. We consider first the case of Yaser Hamdi, who reportedly was captured on the battlefield in Afghanistan and then transported to Guantánamo Bay before being brought to the United States. We then turn to the military detention of José Padilla, who originally was arrested in Chicago as a material witness, then designated an "enemy combatant" by President George W. Bush and transferred to military custody.

### HAMDI v. RUMSFELD

United States Supreme Court, 2004
542 U.S. 507

   Justice O'CONNOR announced the judgment of the Court and delivered an opinion, in which THE CHIEF JUSTICE, Justice KENNEDY, and Justice BREYER join. . . .

   [During the U.S. military operations in Afghanistan that followed the 9/11 terrorist attacks, petitioner Hamdi was captured by Afghan Northern

Alliance forces. He was subsequently transferred to U.S. military custody in Afghanistan and sent to Guantánamo. When it was discovered that he had been born in Louisiana, making him a U.S. citizen, he was transferred to the United States as an "enemy combatant" and detained at a Navy brig in Charleston, South Carolina. Hamdi's father filed this habeas petition on behalf of his son under 28 U.S.C. §2241, alleging that the government held him in violation of the Fifth and Fourteenth Amendments. In the ensuing proceeding, the government filed an affidavit by Department of Defense official Michael Mobbs setting forth the foregoing facts as hearsay.]

## II

The threshold question before us is whether the Executive has the authority to detain citizens who qualify as "enemy combatants." There is some debate as to the proper scope of this term, and the Government has never provided any court with the full criteria that it uses in classifying individuals as such. It has made clear, however, that, for purposes of this case, the "enemy combatant" that it is seeking to detain is an individual who, it alleges, was "part of or supporting forces hostile to the United States or coalition partners" in Afghanistan and who "engaged in an armed conflict against the United States" there. We therefore answer only the narrow question before us: whether the detention of citizens falling within that definition is authorized.

The Government maintains that no explicit congressional authorization is required, because the Executive possesses plenary authority to detain pursuant to Article II of the Constitution. We do not reach the question whether Article II provides such authority, however, because we agree with the Government's alternative position, that Congress has in fact authorized Hamdi's detention, through the AUMF [Authorization for Use of Military Force, Pub. L. No. 107-40, 115 Stat. 224 (2001), *supra* p. 59].

Our analysis on that point, set forth below, substantially overlaps with our analysis of Hamdi's principal argument for the illegality of his detention. He posits that his detention is forbidden by 18 U.S.C. §4001(a) [*supra* p. 301]. Section 4001(a) states that "[n]o citizen shall be imprisoned or otherwise detained by the United States except pursuant to an Act of Congress." Congress passed §4001(a) in 1971 as part of a bill to repeal the Emergency Detention Act of 1950, 50 U.S.C. §811 *et seq.*, which provided procedures for executive detention, during times of emergency, of individuals deemed likely to engage in espionage or sabotage. Congress was particularly concerned about the possibility that the Act could be used to reprise the Japanese internment camps of World War II. The Government again presses two alternative positions. First, it argues that §4001(a), in light of its legislative history and its location in Title 18, applies only to "the control of civilian prisons and related detentions," not to military detentions. Second, it maintains that §4001(a) is satisfied, because Hamdi is being detained "pursuant to an Act of Congress"—the AUMF. Again, because we conclude that the Government's second assertion is correct, we do not address the first. In other words, for the reasons that follow, we conclude that the AUMF is explicit congressional authorization for the detention of individuals in the narrow category we describe (assuming, without deciding, that such authorization is required), and that the AUMF satisfied

§4001(a)'s requirement that a detention be "pursuant to an Act of Congress" (assuming, without deciding, that §4001(a) applies to military detentions).

The AUMF authorizes the President to use "all necessary and appropriate force" against "nations, organizations, or persons" associated with the September 11, 2001, terrorist attacks. 115 Stat. 224. There can be no doubt that individuals who fought against the United States in Afghanistan as part of the Taliban, an organization known to have supported the al Qaeda terrorist network responsible for those attacks, are individuals Congress sought to target in passing the AUMF. We conclude that detention of individuals falling into the limited category we are considering, for the duration of the particular conflict in which they were captured, is so fundamental and accepted an incident to war as to be an exercise of the "necessary and appropriate force" Congress has authorized the President to use.

The capture and detention of lawful combatants and the capture, detention, and trial of unlawful combatants, by "universal agreement and practice," are "important incident[s] of war." *Ex parte Quirin*, 317 U.S. [1 (1942)], at 28. The purpose of detention is to prevent captured individuals from returning to the field of battle and taking up arms once again.

There is no bar to this Nation's holding one of its own citizens as an enemy combatant. In *Quirin*, one of the detainees, Haupt, alleged that he was a naturalized United States citizen. 317 U.S., at 20. We held that "[c]itizens who associate themselves with the military arm of the enemy government, and with its aid, guidance and direction enter this country bent on hostile acts, are enemy belligerents within the meaning of . . . the law of war." *Id.*, at 37-38. While Haupt was tried for violations of the law of war, nothing in *Quirin* suggests that his citizenship would have precluded his mere detention for the duration of the relevant hostilities. See *id.*, at 30-31. Nor can we see any reason for drawing such a line here. A citizen, no less than an alien, can be "part of or supporting forces hostile to the United States or coalition partners" and "engaged in an armed conflict against the United States"; such a citizen, if released, would pose the same threat of returning to the front during the ongoing conflict.

In light of these principles, it is of no moment that the AUMF does not use specific language of detention. Because detention to prevent a combatant's return to the battlefield is a fundamental incident of waging war, in permitting the use of "necessary and appropriate force," Congress has clearly and unmistakably authorized detention in the narrow circumstances considered here. . . .

Hamdi contends that the AUMF does not authorize indefinite or perpetual detention. Certainly, we agree that indefinite detention for the purpose of interrogation is not authorized. Further, we understand Congress' grant of authority for the use of "necessary and appropriate force" to include the authority to detain for the duration of the relevant conflict, and our understanding is based on longstanding law-of-war principles. If the practical circumstances of a given conflict are entirely unlike those of the conflicts that informed the development of the law of war, that understanding may unravel. But that is not the situation we face as of this date. Active combat operations against Taliban fighters apparently are ongoing in Afghanistan. The United States may detain, for the duration of these hostilities, individuals legitimately determined to be

Taliban combatants who "engaged in an armed conflict against the United States." If the record establishes that United States troops are still involved in active combat in Afghanistan, those detentions are part of the exercise of "necessary and appropriate force," and therefore are authorized by the AUMF.

*Ex parte Milligan*, [71 U.S. (4 Wall.) 2 (1866)], does not undermine our holding about the Government's authority to seize enemy combatants, as we define that term today. In that case, the Court made repeated reference to the fact that its inquiry into whether the military tribunal had jurisdiction to try and punish Milligan turned in large part on the fact that Milligan was not a prisoner of war, but a resident of Indiana arrested while at home there. *Id.*, at 118, 131. That fact was central to its conclusion. Had Milligan been captured while he was assisting Confederate soldiers by carrying a rifle against Union troops on a Confederate battlefield, the holding of the Court might well have been different. The Court's repeated explanations that Milligan was not a prisoner of war suggest that had these different circumstances been present he could have been detained under military authority for the duration of the conflict, whether or not he was a citizen. . . .

## III

Even in cases in which the detention of enemy combatants is legally authorized, there remains the question of what process is constitutionally due to a citizen who disputes his enemy-combatant status. . . .

## A

Though they reach radically different conclusions on the process that ought to attend the present proceeding, the parties begin on common ground. All agree that, absent suspension, the writ of habeas corpus remains available to every individual detained within the United States. U.S. Const., Art. I, §9, cl. 2 ("The Privilege of the Writ of Habeas Corpus shall not be suspended, unless when in Cases of Rebellion or Invasion the public Safety may require it"). Only in the rarest of circumstances has Congress seen fit to suspend the writ. . . . All agree suspension of the writ has not occurred here. Thus, it is undisputed that Hamdi was properly before an Article III court to challenge his detention under 28 U.S.C. §2241. Further, all agree that §2241 and its companion provisions provide at least a skeletal outline of the procedures to be afforded a petitioner in federal habeas review. Most notably, §2243 provides that "the person detained may, under oath, deny any of the facts set forth in the return or allege any other material facts," and §2246 allows the taking of evidence in habeas proceedings by deposition, affidavit, or interrogatories.

The simple outline of §2241 makes clear both that Congress envisioned that habeas petitioners would have some opportunity to present and rebut facts and that courts in cases like this retain some ability to vary the ways in which they do so as mandated by due process. The Government recognizes the basic procedural protections required by the habeas statute, but asks us to hold that, given both the flexibility of the habeas mechanism and the circumstances presented in this case, the presentation of the Mobbs Declaration to the habeas court completed the required factual development. It suggests two separate reasons for its position that no further process is due.

## B

First, the Government urges the adoption of the Fourth Circuit's holding below—that because it is "undisputed" that Hamdi's seizure took place in a combat zone, the habeas determination can be made purely as a matter of law, with no further hearing or factfinding necessary. This argument is easily rejected. As the dissenters from the denial of rehearing en banc noted, the circumstances surrounding Hamdi's seizure cannot in any way be characterized as "undisputed," as "those circumstances are neither conceded in fact, nor susceptible to concession in law, because Hamdi has not been permitted to speak for himself or even through counsel as to those circumstances." 337 F.3d 335, 357 (Luttig, J., dissenting from denial of rehearing en banc). Further, the "facts" that constitute the alleged concession are insufficient to support Hamdi's detention. Under the definition of enemy combatant that we accept today as falling within the scope of Congress' authorization, Hamdi would need to be "part of or supporting forces hostile to the United States or coalition partners" and "engaged in an armed conflict against the United States" to justify his detention in the United States for the duration of the relevant conflict. The habeas petition states only that "[w]hen seized by the United States Government, Mr. Hamdi resided in Afghanistan." An assertion that one *resided* in a country in which combat operations are taking place is not a concession that one was "*captured* in a zone of active combat operations in a foreign theater of war," 316 F.3d, at 459 (emphasis added), and certainly is not a concession that one was "part of or supporting forces hostile to the United States or coalition partners" and "engaged in an armed conflict against the United States." Accordingly, we reject any argument that Hamdi has made concessions that eliminate any right to further process.

## C

The Government's second argument requires closer consideration. This is the argument that further factual exploration is unwarranted and inappropriate in light of the extraordinary constitutional interests at stake. Under the Government's most extreme rendition of this argument, "[r]espect for separation of powers and the limited institutional capabilities of courts in matters of military decision-making in connection with an ongoing conflict" ought to eliminate entirely any individual process, restricting the courts to investigating only whether legal authorization exists for the broader detention scheme. At most, the Government argues, courts should review its determination that a citizen is an enemy combatant under a very deferential "some evidence" standard. [Brief for Respondents] 34 ("Under the some evidence standard, the focus is exclusively on the factual basis supplied by the Executive to support its own determination" (citing *Superintendent, Mass. Correctional Institution at Walpole v. Hill*, 472 U.S. 445, 455-457 (1985) (explaining that the some evidence standard "does not require" a "weighing of the evidence," but rather calls for assessing "whether there is any evidence in the record that could support the conclusion")). Under this review, a court would assume the accuracy of the Government's articulated basis for Hamdi's detention, as set forth in the Mobbs Declaration, and assess only whether that articulated basis was a legitimate one.

In response, Hamdi emphasizes that this Court consistently has recognized that an individual challenging his detention may not be held at the will of the Executive without recourse to some proceeding before a neutral tribunal to determine whether the Executive's asserted justifications for that detention have basis in fact and warrant in law. See, *e.g., Zadvydas v. Davis*, 533 U.S. 678, 690 (2001). . . .

. . . The ordinary mechanism that we use for balancing such serious competing interests, and for determining the procedures that are necessary to ensure that a citizen is not "deprived of life, liberty, or property, without due process of law," U.S. Const., Amdt. 5, is the test that we articulated in *Mathews v. Eldridge*, 424 U.S. 319 (1976). *Mathews* dictates that the process due in any given instance is determined by weighing "the private interest that will be affected by the official action" against the Government's asserted interest, "including the function involved" and the burdens the Government would face in providing greater process. 424 U.S., at 335. The *Mathews* calculus then contemplates a judicious balancing of these concerns, through an analysis of "the risk of an erroneous deprivation" of the private interest if the process were reduced and the "probable value, if any, of additional or substitute safeguards." *Ibid.* We take each of these steps in turn.

### 1

It is beyond question that substantial interests lie on both sides of the scale in this case. Hamdi's "private interest . . . affected by the official action," *ibid.*, is the most elemental of liberty interests — the interest in being free from physical detention by one's own government. "In our society liberty is the norm," and detention without trial "is the carefully limited exception." [United States v. Salerno, 481 U.S. 739 (1987)], at 755. . . .

Nor is the weight on this side of the *Mathews* scale offset by the circumstances of war or the accusation of treasonous behavior, for "[i]t is clear that commitment for *any* purpose constitutes a significant deprivation of liberty that requires due process protection," *Jones v. United States*, 463 U.S. 354, 361 (1983) (emphasis added; internal quotation marks omitted), and at this stage in the *Mathews* calculus, we consider the interest of the *erroneously* detained individual. Indeed, as *amicus* briefs from media and relief organizations emphasize, the risk of erroneous deprivation of a citizen's liberty in the absence of sufficient process here is very real. See Brief for AmeriCares et al. as *Amici Curiae* 13-22 (noting ways in which "[t]he nature of humanitarian relief work and journalism present a significant risk of mistaken military detentions"). Moreover, as critical as the Government's interest may be in detaining those who actually pose an immediate threat to the national security of the United States during ongoing international conflict, history and common sense teach us that an unchecked system of detention carries the potential to become a means for oppression and abuse of others who do not present that sort of threat. . . .

### 2

On the other side of the scale are the weighty and sensitive governmental interests in ensuring that those who have in fact fought with the enemy during a war do not return to battle against the United States. As discussed above, the law of war and the realities of combat may render such detentions both necessary and appropriate, and our due process analysis need not blink at those realities. Without doubt, our Constitution recognizes that core strategic matters of warmaking belong in the hands of those who are best positioned and most politically accountable for making them. *Department of Navy v. Egan*, 484 U.S. 518, 530 (1988) (noting the reluctance of the courts "to intrude upon the authority of the Executive in military and national security affairs"); *Youngstown Sheet & Tube Co. v. Sawyer*, 343 U.S. 579, 587 (1952) (acknowledging "broad powers in military commanders engaged in day-to-day fighting in a theater of war").

The Government also argues at some length that its interests in reducing the process available to alleged enemy combatants are heightened by the practical difficulties that would accompany a system of trial-like process. In its view, military officers who are engaged in the serious work of waging battle would be unnecessarily and dangerously distracted by litigation half a world away, and discovery into military operations would both intrude on the sensitive secrets of national defense and result in a futile search for evidence buried under the rubble of war. To the extent that these burdens are triggered by heightened procedures, they are properly taken into account in our due process analysis.

### 3

Striking the proper constitutional balance here is of great importance to the Nation during this period of ongoing combat. But it is equally vital that our calculus not give short shrift to the values that this country holds dear or to the privilege that is American citizenship. It is during our most challenging and uncertain moments that our Nation's commitment to due process is most severely tested; and it is in those times that we must preserve our commitment at home to the principles for which we fight abroad.

With due recognition of these competing concerns, we believe that neither the process proposed by the Government nor the process apparently envisioned by the District Court below strikes the proper constitutional balance when a United States citizen is detained in the United States as an enemy combatant. That is, "the risk of erroneous deprivation" of a detainee's liberty interest is unacceptably high under the Government's proposed rule, while some of the "additional or substitute procedural safeguards" suggested by the District Court are unwarranted in light of their limited "probable value" and the burdens they may impose on the military in such cases. *Mathews*, 424 U.S., at 335.

We therefore hold that a citizen-detainee seeking to challenge his classification as an enemy combatant must receive notice of the factual basis for his classification, and a fair opportunity to rebut the Government's factual assertions before a neutral decisionmaker. "For more than a century the central meaning of procedural due process has been clear: 'Parties whose rights are to be affected are entitled to be heard; and in order that they may enjoy that right they must first be notified.' It is equally fundamental that the right to notice and an opportunity to be heard 'must be granted at a meaningful time and in a meaningful manner.'" *Fuentes v. Shevin*, 407 U.S. 67, 80 (1972). These essential constitutional promises may not be eroded.

At the same time, the exigencies of the circumstances may demand that, aside from these core elements, enemy combatant proceedings may be tailored to alleviate their uncommon potential to burden the Executive at a time of ongoing military conflict. Hearsay, for example, may need to be accepted as the most reliable available evidence from the Government in such a proceeding. Likewise, the Constitution would not be offended by a presumption in favor of the Government's evidence, so long as that presumption remained a rebuttable one and fair opportunity for rebuttal were provided. Thus, once the Government puts forth credible evidence that the habeas petitioner meets the enemy-combatant criteria, the onus could shift to the petitioner to rebut that evidence with more persuasive evidence that he falls outside the criteria. A burden-shifting scheme of this sort would meet the goal of ensuring that the errant tourist, embedded journalist, or local aid worker has a chance to prove military error while giving due regard to the Executive once it has put forth meaningful support for its conclusion that the detainee is in fact an enemy combatant. In the words of *Mathews*, process of this sort would sufficiently address the "risk of erroneous deprivation" of a detainee's liberty interest while eliminating certain procedures that have questionable additional value in light of the burden on the Government. 424 U.S., at 335.

We think it unlikely that this basic process will have the dire impact on the central functions of warmaking that the Government forecasts. The parties agree that initial captures on the battlefield need not receive the process we have discussed here; that process is due only when the determination is made to *continue* to hold those who have been seized. The Government has made clear in its briefing that documentation regarding battlefield detainees already is kept in the ordinary course of military affairs. Any factfinding imposition created by requiring a knowledgeable affiant to summarize these records to an independent tribunal is a minimal one. Likewise, arguments that military officers ought not have to wage war under the threat of litigation lose much of their steam when factual disputes at enemy-combatant hearings are limited to the alleged combatant's acts. This focus meddles little, if at all, in the strategy or conduct of war, inquiring only into the appropriateness of continuing to detain an individual claimed to have taken up arms against the United States. While we accord the greatest respect and consideration to the judgments of military authorities in matters relating to the actual prosecution of a war, and recognize that the scope of that discretion necessarily is wide, it does not infringe on the core role of the military for the courts to exercise their own time-honored and constitutionally mandated roles of reviewing and resolving claims like those presented here. Cf. *Korematsu v. United States*, 323 U.S. 214, 233-234 (1944) (Murphy, J., dissenting) ("[L]ike other claims conflicting with the asserted constitutional rights of the individual, the military claim must subject itself to the judicial process of having its reasonableness determined and its conflicts with other interests reconciled"); *Sterling v. Constantin*, 287 U.S. 378, 401 (1932) ("What are the allowable limits of military discretion, and whether or not they have been overstepped in a particular case, are judicial questions").

In sum, while the full protections that accompany challenges to detentions in other settings may prove unworkable and inappropriate in the enemy-combatant setting, the threats to military operations posed by a basic system of independent review are not so weighty as to trump a citizen's core rights to challenge meaningfully the Government's case and to be heard by an impartial adjudicator.

## D

In so holding, we necessarily reject the Government's assertion that separation of powers principles mandate a heavily circumscribed role for the courts in such circumstances. Indeed, the position that the courts must forgo any examination of the individual case and focus exclusively on the legality of the broader detention scheme cannot be mandated by any reasonable view of separation of powers, as this approach serves only to *condense* power into a single branch of government. We have long since made clear that a state of war is not a blank check for the President when it comes to the rights of the Nation's citizens. *Youngstown Sheet & Tube*, 343 U.S., at 587. Whatever power the United States Constitution envisions for the Executive in its exchanges with other nations or with enemy organizations in times of conflict, it most assuredly envisions a role for all three branches when individual liberties are at stake. *Mistretta v. United States*, 488 U.S. 361, 380 (1989) (it was "the central judgment of the Framers of the Constitution that, within our political scheme, the separation of governmental powers into three coordinate Branches is essential to the preservation of liberty"); *Home Building & Loan Assn. v. Blaisdell*, 290 U.S. 398, 426 (1934) (The war power "is a power to wage war successfully, and thus it permits the harnessing of the entire energies of the people in a supreme cooperative effort to preserve the nation. But even the war power does not remove constitutional limitations safeguarding essential liberties"). Likewise, we have made clear that, unless Congress acts to suspend it, the Great Writ of habeas corpus allows the Judicial Branch to play a necessary role in maintaining this delicate balance of governance, serving as an important judicial check on the Executive's discretion in the realm of detentions. See *INS v. St. Cyr*, 533 U.S. 289, 301 (2001) ("At its historical core, the writ of habeas corpus has served as a means of reviewing the legality of Executive detention, and it is in that context that its protections have been strongest"). Thus, while we do not question that our due process assessment must pay keen attention to the particular burdens faced by the Executive in the context of military action, it would turn our system of checks and balances on its head to suggest that a citizen could not make his way to court with a challenge to the factual basis for his detention by his government, simply because the Executive opposes making available such a challenge. Absent suspension of the writ by Congress, a citizen detained as an enemy combatant is entitled to this process.

Because we conclude that due process demands some system for a citizen detainee to refute his classification, the proposed "some evidence" standard is inadequate. Any process in which the Executive's factual assertions go wholly unchallenged or are simply presumed correct without any opportunity for the alleged combatant to demonstrate otherwise falls constitutionally short. As the

Government itself has recognized, we have utilized the "some evidence" standard in the past as a standard of review, not as a standard of proof. That is, it primarily has been employed by courts in examining an administrative record developed after an adversarial proceeding — one with process at least of the sort that we today hold is constitutionally mandated in the citizen enemy-combatant setting. This standard therefore is ill suited to the situation in which a habeas petitioner has received no prior proceedings before any tribunal and had no prior opportunity to rebut the Executive's factual assertions before a neutral decisionmaker.

Today we are faced only with such a case. Aside from unspecified "screening" processes, and military interrogations in which the Government suggests Hamdi could have contested his classification, Hamdi has received no process. An interrogation by one's captor, however effective an intelligence-gathering tool, hardly constitutes a constitutionally adequate factfinding before a neutral decisionmaker. Compare Brief for Respondents 42-43 (discussing the "secure interrogation environment," and noting that military interrogations require a controlled "interrogation dynamic" and "a relationship of trust and dependency" and are "a critical source" of "timely and effective intelligence") with *Concrete Pipe* [and Products of California, Inc. v. Construction Laborers Pension Trust], 508 U.S. 602, 617-618 (1993) ("one is entitled as a matter of due process of law to an adjudicator who is not in a situation which would offer a possible temptation to the average man as a judge . . . which might lead him not to hold the balance nice, clear and true" (internal quotation marks omitted)). That even purportedly fair adjudicators "are disqualified by their interest in the controversy to be decided is, of course, the general rule." *Tumey v. Ohio*, 273 U.S. 510, 522 (1927). Plainly, the "process" Hamdi has received is not that to which he is entitled under the Due Process Clause.

There remains the possibility that the standards we have articulated could be met by an appropriately authorized and properly constituted military tribunal. Indeed, it is notable that military regulations already provide for such process in related instances, dictating that tribunals be made available to determine the status of enemy detainees who assert prisoner-of-war status under the Geneva Convention. See Enemy Prisoners of War, Retained Personnel, Civilian Internees and Other Detainees, Army Regulation 190-8, §1-6 (1997). In the absence of such process, however, a court that receives a petition for a writ of habeas corpus from an alleged enemy combatant must itself ensure that the minimum requirements of due process are achieved. . . . As we have discussed, a habeas court in a case such as this may accept affidavit evidence like that contained in the Mobbs Declaration, so long as it also permits the alleged combatant to present his own factual case to rebut the Government's return. We anticipate that a District Court would proceed with the caution that we have indicated is necessary in this setting, engaging in a factfinding process that is both prudent and incremental. We have no reason to doubt that courts faced with these sensitive matters will pay proper heed both to the matters of national security that might arise in an individual case and to the constitutional limitations safeguarding essential liberties that remain vibrant even in times of security concerns.

## IV

Hamdi asks us to hold that the Fourth Circuit also erred by denying him immediate access to counsel upon his detention and by disposing of the case without permitting him to meet with an attorney. Since our grant of certiorari in this case, Hamdi has been appointed counsel, with whom he has met for consultation purposes on several occasions, and with whom he is now being granted unmonitored meetings. He unquestionably has the right to access to counsel in connection with the proceedings on remand. No further consideration of this issue is necessary at this stage of the case. . . .

The judgment of the United States Court of Appeals for the Fourth Circuit is vacated, and the case is remanded for further proceedings.

*It is so ordered.*

Justice SOUTER, with whom Justice GINSBURG joins, concurring in part, dissenting in part, and concurring in the judgment. . . . The plurality rejects [the government's "some evidence"] limit on the exercise of habeas jurisdiction and so far I agree with its opinion. The plurality does, however, accept the Government's position that if Hamdi's designation as an enemy combatant is correct, his detention (at least as to some period) is authorized by an Act of Congress as required by §4001(a), that is, by the Authorization for Use of Military Force, 115 Stat. 224 (hereinafter Force Resolution). Here, I disagree and respectfully dissent. . . .

## II

The threshold issue is how broadly or narrowly to read the Non-Detention Act, the tone of which is severe: "No citizen shall be imprisoned or otherwise detained by the United States except pursuant to an Act of Congress." . . . For a number of reasons, the prohibition within §4001(a) has to be read broadly to accord the statute a long reach and to impose a burden of justification on the Government.

First, the circumstances in which the Act was adopted point the way to this interpretation. The provision superseded a cold-war statute, the Emergency Detention Act of 1950, which had authorized the Attorney General, in time of emergency, to detain anyone reasonably thought likely to engage in espionage or sabotage. That statute was repealed in 1971 out of fear that it could authorize a repetition of the World War II internment of citizens of Japanese ancestry; Congress meant to preclude another episode like the one described in *Korematsu v. United States*, 323 U.S. 214 (1944). . . .

. . . To appreciate what is most significant, one must only recall that the internments of the 1940's were accomplished by Executive action. Although an Act of Congress ratified and confirmed an Executive order authorizing the military to exclude individuals from defined areas and to accommodate those it might remove, see *Ex parte Endo*, 323 U.S. 283, 285-288 (1944), the statute said nothing whatever about the detention of those who might be removed; internment camps were creatures of the Executive, and confinement in them rested on assertion of Executive authority. When, therefore, Congress repealed the 1950 Act and adopted §4001(a) for the purpose of avoiding another *Korematsu*, it intended to preclude reliance on vague congressional authority (for example, providing "accommodations" for those subject to removal) as authority for detention or imprisonment at the discretion of the Executive (maintaining detention camps of American citizens, for example). In requiring that any Executive detention be "pursuant to an Act of Congress," then, Congress necessarily meant to require a congressional enactment that clearly authorized detention or imprisonment.

Second, when Congress passed §4001(a) it was acting in light of an interpretive regime that subjected enactments limiting liberty in wartime to the requirement of a clear statement and it presumably intended §4001(a) to be read accordingly. This need for clarity was unmistakably expressed in *Ex parte Endo, supra*, decided the same day as *Korematsu*. . . . The petitioner was held entitled to habeas relief in an opinion that set out this principle for scrutinizing wartime statutes in derogation of customary liberty:

> "In interpreting a wartime measure we must assume that [its] purpose was to allow for the greatest possible accommodation between . . . liberties and the exigencies of war. We must assume, when asked to find implied powers in a grant of legislative or executive authority, that the law makers intended to place no greater restraint on the citizen than was clearly and unmistakably indicated by the language they used." *Id.*, at 300.

Congress's understanding of the need for clear authority before citizens are kept detained is itself therefore clear, and §4001(a) must be read to have teeth in its demand for congressional authorization.

Finally, even if history had spared us the cautionary example of the internments in World War II, even if there had been no *Korematsu*, and *Endo* had set out no principle of statutory interpretation, there would be a compelling reason to read §4001(a) to demand manifest authority to detain before detention is authorized. The defining character of American constitutional government is its constant tension between security and liberty, serving both by partial helpings of each. In a government of separated powers, deciding finally on what is a reasonable degree of guaranteed liberty whether in peace or war (or some condition in between) is not well entrusted to the Executive Branch of Government, whose particular responsibility is to maintain security. For reasons of inescapable human nature, the branch of the Government asked to counter a serious threat is not the branch on which to rest the Nation's entire reliance in striking the balance between the will to win and the cost in liberty on the way to victory; the responsibility for security will naturally amplify the claim that security legitimately raises. A reasonable balance is more likely to be reached on the judgment of a different branch, just as Madison said in remarking that "the constant aim is to divide and arrange the several offices in such a manner as that each may be a check on the other — that the private interest of every individual may be a sentinel over the public rights." The Federalist No. 51, p. 349 (J. Cooke ed.1961). Hence the need for an assessment by Congress before citizens are subject to lockup, and likewise the need for a clearly expressed congressional resolution of the competing claims.

## III

Under this principle of reading §4001(a) robustly to require a clear statement of authorization to detain, none of the Government's arguments suffices to justify Hamdi's detention.

### A

First, there is the argument that §4001(a) does not even apply to wartime military detentions, a position resting on the placement of §4001(a) in Title 18 of the United States Code, the gathering of federal criminal law.... [The] legislative history indicates that Congress was aware that §4001(a) would limit the Executive's power to detain citizens in wartime to protect national security, and it is fair to say that the prohibition was thus intended to extend not only to the exercise of power to vindicate the interests underlying domestic criminal law, but to statutorily unauthorized detention by the Executive for reasons of security in wartime, just as Hamdi claims.[2]

### B

Next, there is the Government's claim, accepted by the Court, that the terms of the Force Resolution are adequate to authorize detention of an enemy combatant under the circumstances described,[3] a claim the Government fails to support sufficiently to satisfy §4001(a) as read to require a clear statement of authority to detain. Since the Force Resolution was adopted one week after the attacks of September 11, 2001, it naturally speaks with some generality, but its focus is clear, and that is on the use of military power. It is fairly read to authorize the use of armies and weapons, whether against other armies or individual terrorists. But, like the statute discussed in *Endo*, it never so much as uses the word detention, and there is no reason to think Congress might have perceived any need to augment Executive power to deal with dangerous citizens within the United States, given the well-stocked statutory arsenal of defined criminal offenses covering the gamut of actions that a citizen sympathetic to terrorists might commit. See, *e.g.*, 18 U.S.C. §2339A (material support for various terrorist acts); §2339B (material support to a foreign terrorist organization); §2332a (use of a weapon of mass destruction, including conspiracy and attempt); §2332b(a)(1) (acts of terrorism "transcending national boundaries," including threats, conspiracy, and attempt); 18 U.S.C.A. §2339C (financing of certain terrorist acts); see also 18 U.S.C. §3142(e) (pretrial detention).

---

2. Nor is it possible to distinguish between civilian and military authority to detain based on the congressional object of avoiding another *Korematsu v. United States*, 323 U.S. 214 (1944). Although a civilian agency authorized by Executive order ran the detention camps, the relocation and detention of American citizens was ordered by the military under authority of the President as Commander in Chief. See *Ex parte Endo*, 323 U.S. 283, 285-288 (1944). The World War II internment was thus ordered under the same Presidential power invoked here and the intent to bar a repetition goes to the action taken and authority claimed here.

3. ... [T]he Government argues that a required Act of Congress is to be found in a statutory authorization to spend money appropriated for the care of prisoners of war and of other, similar prisoners, 10 U.S.C. §956(5). It is enough to say that this statute is an authorization to spend money if there are prisoners, not an authorization to imprison anyone to provide the occasion for spending money.

## C

Even so, there is one argument for treating the Force Resolution as sufficiently clear to authorize detention of a citizen consistently with §4001(a). Assuming the argument to be sound, however, the Government is in no position to claim its advantage.

Because the Force Resolution authorizes the use of military force in acts of war by the United States, the argument goes, it is reasonably clear that the military and its Commander in Chief are authorized to deal with enemy belligerents according to the treaties and customs known collectively as the laws of war. Accordingly, the United States may detain captured enemies, and *Ex parte Quirin*, 317 U.S. 1 (1942), may perhaps be claimed for the proposition that the American citizenship of such a captive does not as such limit the Government's power to deal with him under the usages of war. Thus, the Government here repeatedly argues that Hamdi's detention amounts to nothing more than customary detention of a captive taken on the field of battle: if the usages of war are fairly authorized by the Force Resolution, Hamdi's detention is authorized for purposes of §4001(a). . . .

By holding him incommunicado, however, the Government obviously has not been treating him as a prisoner of war, and in fact the Government claims that no Taliban detainee is entitled to prisoner of war status. This treatment appears to be a violation of the Geneva Convention provision that even in cases of doubt, captives are entitled to be treated as prisoners of war "until such time as their status has been determined by a competent tribunal." Art. 5, 6 U.S.T., at 3324. . . .

Whether, or to what degree, the Government is in fact violating the Geneva Convention and is thus acting outside the customary usages of war are not matters I can resolve at this point. What I can say, though, is that the Government has not made out its claim that in detaining Hamdi in the manner described, it is acting in accord with the laws of war authorized to be applied against citizens by the Force Resolution. I conclude accordingly that the Government has failed to support the position that the Force Resolution authorizes the described detention of Hamdi for purposes of §4001(a).

It is worth adding a further reason for requiring the Government to bear the burden of clearly justifying its claim to be exercising recognized war powers before declaring §4001(a) satisfied. Thirty-eight days after adopting the Force Resolution, Congress passed the statute entitled Uniting and Strengthening America by Providing Appropriate Tools Required to Intercept and Obstruct Terrorism Act of 2001 (USA PATRIOT ACT), 115 Stat. 272; that Act authorized the detention of alien terrorists for no more than seven days in the absence of criminal charges or deportation proceedings, 8 U.S.C. §1226a(a)(5) (2000 ed., Supp. I). It is very difficult to believe that the same Congress that carefully circumscribed Executive power over alien terrorists on home soil would not have meant to require the Government to justify clearly its detention of an American citizen held on home soil incommunicado.

## D

Since the Government has given no reason either to deflect the application of §4001(a) or to hold it to be satisfied, I need to go no further; the Government hints of a constitutional challenge to the statute, but it presents none here. I will, however, stray across the line between statutory and constitutional territory just far enough to note the weakness of the Government's mixed claim of inherent, extrastatutory authority under a combination of Article II of the Constitution and the usages of war. It is in fact in this connection that the Government developed its argument that the exercise of war powers justifies the detention, and what I have just said about its inadequacy applies here as well. Beyond that, it is instructive to recall Justice Jackson's observation that the President is not Commander in Chief of the country, only of the military. *Youngstown Sheet & Tube Co. v. Sawyer*, 343 U.S. 579, 643-644 (1952) (concurring opinion); see also *id.*, at 637-638 (Presidential authority is "at its lowest ebb" where the President acts contrary to congressional will).

There may be room for one qualification to Justice Jackson's statement, however: in a moment of genuine emergency, when the Government must act with no time for deliberation, the Executive may be able to detain a citizen if there is reason to fear he is an imminent threat to the safety of the Nation and its people (though I doubt there is any want of statutory authority). This case, however, does not present that question, because an emergency power of necessity must at least be limited by the emergency; Hamdi has been locked up for over two years. Cf. *Ex parte Milligan*, 4 Wall. 2, 127 (1866) (martial law justified only by "actual and present" necessity as in a genuine invasion that closes civilian courts). . . .

## IV . . .

It should go without saying that in joining with the plurality to produce a judgment, I do not adopt the plurality's resolution of constitutional issues that I would not reach. It is not that I could disagree with the plurality's determinations (given the plurality's view of the Force Resolution) that someone in Hamdi's position is entitled at a minimum to notice of the Government's claimed factual basis for holding him, and to a fair chance to rebut it before a neutral decision maker; nor, of course, could I disagree with the plurality's affirmation of Hamdi's right to counsel. On the other hand, I do not mean to imply agreement that the Government could claim an evidentiary presumption casting the burden of rebuttal on Hamdi, or that an opportunity to litigate before a military tribunal might obviate or truncate enquiry by a court on habeas.

Subject to these qualifications, I join with the plurality in a judgment of the Court vacating the Fourth Circuit's judgment and remanding the case.

Justice SCALIA, with whom Justice STEVENS joins, dissenting. . . . Where the Government accuses a citizen of waging war against it, our constitutional tradition has been to prosecute him in federal court for treason or some other crime. Where the exigencies of war prevent that, the Constitution's Suspension Clause, Art. I, §9, cl. 2, allows Congress to relax the usual protections temporarily. Absent suspension, however, the Executive's assertion of military exigency has not been thought sufficient to permit detention without charge. No one contends that the congressional Authorization for Use of Military Force, on which the Government relies to justify its actions here, is an implementation of the Suspension Clause. Accordingly, I would reverse the decision below.

## I

The very core of liberty secured by our Anglo-Saxon system of separated powers has been freedom from indefinite imprisonment at the will of the Executive. Blackstone stated this principle clearly:

> "Of great importance to the public is the preservation of this personal liberty: for if once it were left in the power of any, the highest, magistrate to imprison arbitrarily whomever he or his officers thought proper . . . there would soon be an end of all other rights and immunities. . . . To bereave a man of life, or by violence to confiscate his estate, without accusation or trial, would be so gross and notorious an act of despotism, as must at once convey the alarm of tyranny throughout the whole kingdom. But confinement of the person, by secretly hurrying him to gaol, where his sufferings are unknown or forgotten; is a less public, a less striking, and therefore a more dangerous engine of arbitrary government. . . .
>
> "To make imprisonment lawful, it must either be, by process from the courts of judicature, or by warrant from some legal officer, having authority to commit to prison; which warrant must be in writing, under the hand and seal of the magistrate, and express the causes of the commitment, in order to be examined into (if necessary) upon a *habeas corpus*. If there be no cause expressed, the gaoler is not bound to detain the prisoner. For the law judges in this respect, . . . that it is unreasonable to send a prisoner, and not to signify withal the crimes alleged against him." 1 W. Blackstone, Commentaries on the Laws of England 132-133 (1765) (hereinafter Blackstone).

These words were well known to the Founders. Hamilton quoted from this very passage in The Federalist No. 84, p. 444 (G. Carey & J. McClellan eds. 2001). The two ideas central to Blackstone's understanding — due process as the right secured, and habeas corpus as the instrument by which due process could be insisted upon by a citizen illegally imprisoned — found expression in the Constitution's Due Process and Suspension Clauses. See Amdt. 5; Art. I, §9, cl. 2.

The gist of the Due Process Clause, as understood at the founding and since, was to force the Government to follow those common-law procedures traditionally deemed necessary before depriving a person of life, liberty, or property. When a citizen was deprived of liberty because of alleged criminal conduct, those procedures typically required committal by a magistrate followed by indictment and trial. . . .

## II

The allegations here, of course, are no ordinary accusations of criminal activity. Yaser Esam Hamdi has been imprisoned because the Government believes he participated in the waging of war against the United States. The relevant question, then, is whether there is a different, special procedure for imprisonment of a citizen accused of wrongdoing *by aiding the enemy in wartime*.

### A

Justice O'CONNOR writing for a plurality of this Court, asserts that captured enemy combatants (other than those suspected of war crimes) have traditionally been detained until the cessation of hostilities and then released. That is probably an accurate description of wartime practice with respect to enemy *aliens*. The tradition with respect to American citizens, however, has been quite different. Citizens aiding the enemy have been treated as traitors subject to the criminal process. . . .

The modern treason statute is 18 U.S.C. §2381; it basically tracks the language of the constitutional provision. Other provisions of Title 18 criminalize various acts of warmaking and adherence to the enemy. The only citizen other than Hamdi known to be imprisoned in connection with military hostilities in Afghanistan against the United States *was* subjected to criminal process and convicted upon a guilty plea. See *United States v. Lindh*, 212 F. Supp. 2d 541 (E.D. Va. 2002) (denying motions for dismissal).

## B

There are times when military exigency renders resort to the traditional criminal process impracticable. English law accommodated such exigencies by allowing legislative suspension of the writ of habeas corpus for brief periods. Blackstone explained:

> "And yet sometimes, when the state is in real danger, even this [*i.e.*, executive detention] may be a necessary measure. But the happiness of our constitution is, that it is not left to the executive power to determine when the danger of the state is so great, as to render this measure expedient. For the parliament only, or legislative power, whenever it sees proper, can authorize the crown, by suspending the *habeas corpus* act for a short and limited time, to imprison suspected persons without giving any reason for so doing. . . . In like manner this experiment ought only to be tried in case of extreme emergency; and in these the nation parts with it[s] liberty for a while, in order to preserve it for ever." 1 Blackstone 132. . . .

Our Federal Constitution contains a provision explicitly permitting suspension, but limiting the situations in which it may be invoked: "The privilege of the Writ of Habeas Corpus shall not be suspended, unless when in Cases of Rebellion or Invasion the public Safety may require it." Art. I, §9, cl. 2. Although this provision does not state that suspension must be effected by, or authorized by, a legislative act, it has been so understood, consistent with English practice and the Clause's placement in Article I.

The Suspension Clause was by design a safety valve, the Constitution's only "express provision for exercise of extraordinary authority because of a crisis," *Youngstown Sheet & Tube Co. v. Sawyer*, 343 U.S. 579, 650 (1952) (Jackson, J., concurring). . . .

## III . . .

Writings from the founding generation also suggest that, without exception, the only constitutional alternatives are to charge the crime or suspend the writ. In 1788, Thomas Jefferson wrote to James Madison questioning the need for a Suspension Clause in cases of rebellion in the proposed Constitution. His letter illustrates the constraints under which the Founders understood themselves to operate:

> "Why suspend the Hab. corp. in insurrections and rebellions? The parties who may be arrested may be charged instantly with a well defined crime. Of course

the judge will remand them. If the publick safety requires that the government should have a man imprisoned on less probable testimony in those than in other emergencies; let him be taken and tried, retaken and retried, while the necessity continues, only giving him redress against the government for damages." 13 Papers of Thomas Jefferson 442 (July 31, 1788) (J. Boyd ed.1956). . . .

Further evidence comes from this Court's decision in *Ex parte Milligan*, [71 U.S. (4 Wall.) 2] (1866). There, the Court issued the writ to an American citizen who had been tried by military commission for offenses that included conspiring to overthrow the Government, seize munitions, and liberate prisoners of war. The Court rejected in no uncertain terms the Government's assertion that military jurisdiction was proper "under the 'laws and usages of war,'" *id.*, at 121:

> "It can serve no useful purpose to inquire what those laws and usages are, whence they originated, where found, and on whom they operate; they can never be applied to citizens in states which have upheld the authority of the government, and where the courts are open and their process unobstructed." *Ibid.*[1]

*Milligan* is not exactly this case, of course, since the petitioner was threatened with death, not merely imprisonment. But the reasoning and conclusion of *Milligan* logically cover the present case. The Government justifies imprisonment of Hamdi on principles of the law of war and admits that, absent the war, it would have no such authority. But if the law of war cannot be applied to citizens where courts are open, then Hamdi's imprisonment without criminal trial is no less unlawful than Milligan's trial by military tribunal.

*Milligan* responded to the argument, repeated by the Government in this case, that it is dangerous to leave suspected traitors at large in time of war:

> "If it was dangerous, in the distracted condition of affairs, to leave Milligan unrestrained of his liberty, because he 'conspired against the government, afforded aid and comfort to rebels, and incited the people to insurrection,' the *law* said arrest him, confine him closely, render him powerless to do further mischief; and then present his case to the grand jury of the district, with proofs of his guilt, and, if indicted, try him according to the course of the common law. If this had been done, the Constitution would have been vindicated, the law of 1863 enforced, and the securities for personal liberty preserved and defended." *Id.*, at 122.

Thus, criminal process was viewed as the primary means — and the only means absent congressional action suspending the writ — not only to punish traitors, but to incapacitate them.

---

1. As I shall discuss presently, the Court purported to limit this language in *Ex parte Quirin*, 317 U.S. 1, 45 (1942). Whatever *Quirin's* effect on *Milligan's* precedential value, however, it cannot undermine its value as an indicator of original meaning. Cf. *Reid v. Covert*, 354 U.S. 1, 30 (1957) (plurality opinion) (*Milligan* remains "one of the great landmarks in this Court's history").

The proposition that the Executive lacks indefinite wartime detention authority over citizens is consistent with the Founders' general mistrust of military power permanently at the Executive's disposal. In the Founders' view, the "blessings of liberty" were threatened by "those military establishments which must gradually poison its very fountain." The Federalist No. 45, p. 238 (J. Madison). No fewer than 10 issues of the Federalist were devoted in whole or part to allaying fears of oppression from the proposed Constitution's authorization of standing armies in peacetime. Many safeguards in the Constitution reflect these concerns. Congress's authority "[t]o raise and support Armies" was hedged with the proviso that "no Appropriation of Money to that Use shall be for a longer Term than two Years." U.S. Const., Art. 1, §8, cl. 12. Except for the actual command of military forces, all authorization for their maintenance and all explicit authorization for their use is placed in the control of Congress under Article I, rather than the President under Article II. . . . A view of the Constitution that gives the Executive authority to use military force rather than the force of law against citizens on American soil flies in the face of the mistrust that engendered these provisions.

## IV

The Government argues that our more recent jurisprudence ratifies its indefinite imprisonment of a citizen within the territorial jurisdiction of federal courts. It places primary reliance upon *Ex parte Quirin*, 317 U.S. 1 (1942), a World War II case upholding the trial by military commission of eight German saboteurs, one of whom, Hans Haupt, was a U.S. citizen. The case was not this Court's finest hour. The Court upheld the commission and denied relief in a brief *per curiam* issued the day after oral argument concluded; a week later the Government carried out the commission's death sentence upon six saboteurs, including Haupt. The Court eventually explained its reasoning in a written opinion issued several months later.

Only three paragraphs of the Court's lengthy opinion dealt with the particular circumstances of Haupt's case. The Government argued that Haupt, like the other petitioners, could be tried by military commission under the laws of war. In agreeing with that contention, *Quirin* purported to interpret the language of *Milligan* quoted above (the law of war "can never be applied to citizens in states which have upheld the authority of the government, and where the courts are open and their process unobstructed") in the following manner:

> "Elsewhere in its opinion . . . the Court was at pains to point out that Milligan, a citizen twenty years resident in Indiana, who had never been a resident of any of the states in rebellion, was not an enemy belligerent either entitled to the status of a prisoner of war or subject to the penalties imposed upon unlawful belligerents. We construe the Court's statement as to the inapplicability of the law of war to Milligan's case as having particular reference to the facts before it. From them the Court concluded that Milligan, not being a part of or associated with the armed forces of the enemy, was a non-belligerent, not subject to the law of war. . . ." 317 U.S., at 45.

In my view this seeks to revise *Milligan* rather than describe it. *Milligan* had involved (among other issues) two separate questions: (1) whether the military trial of Milligan was justified by the laws of war, and if not (2) whether the President's suspension of the writ, pursuant to congressional authorization, prevented the issuance of habeas corpus. The Court's categorical language about the law of war's inapplicability to citizens where the courts are open (with no exception mentioned for citizens who were prisoners of war) was contained in its discussion of the first point. See 4 Wall., at 121. The factors pertaining to whether Milligan could reasonably be considered a belligerent and prisoner of war, while mentioned earlier in the opinion, were made relevant and brought to bear in the Court's later discussion of whether Milligan came within the statutory provision that effectively made an exception to Congress's authorized suspension of the writ for (as the Court described it) "all parties, not prisoners of war, resident in their respective jurisdictions, . . . who were citizens of states in which the administration of the laws in the Federal tribunals was unimpaired," *id.* at 116. *Milligan* thus understood was in accord with the traditional law of habeas corpus I have described: Though treason often occurred in wartime, there was, absent provision for special treatment in a congressional suspension of the writ, no exception to the right to trial by jury for citizens who could be called "belligerents" or "prisoners of war."

But even if *Quirin* gave a correct description of *Milligan*, or made an irrevocable revision of it, *Quirin* would still not justify denial of the writ here. In *Quirin* it was uncontested that the petitioners were members of enemy forces. They were "*admitted* enemy invaders," 317 U.S., at 47 (emphasis added), and it was "undisputed" that they had landed in the United States in service of German forces, *id.*, at 20. The specific holding of the Court was only that, "upon the *conceded* facts," the petitioners were "plainly within [the] boundaries" of military jurisdiction, *id.*, at 46 (emphasis added). But where those jurisdictional facts are *not* conceded — where the petitioner insists that he is *not* a belligerent — *Quirin* left the pre-existing law in place: Absent suspension of the writ, a citizen held where the courts are open is entitled either to criminal trial or to a judicial decree requiring his release.

## V

It follows from what I have said that Hamdi is entitled to a habeas decree requiring his release unless (1) criminal proceedings are promptly brought, or (2) Congress has suspended the writ of habeas corpus. A suspension of the writ could, of course, lay down conditions for continued detention, similar to those that today's opinion prescribes under the Due Process Clause. But there is a world of difference between the people's representatives' determining the need for that suspension (and prescribing the conditions for it), and this Court's doing so.

The plurality finds justification for Hamdi's imprisonment in the Authorization for Use of Military Force, 115 Stat. 224. . . . This is not remotely a congressional suspension of the writ, and no one claims that it is. Contrary to the plurality's view, I do not think this statute even authorizes detention of a citizen with the clarity necessary to satisfy the interpretive canon that statutes should be construed so as to avoid grave constitutional concerns; with the clarity necessary to comport with cases such as *Ex parte Endo*, 323 U.S. 283, 300 (1944), and *Duncan v. Kahanamoku*, 327 U.S. 304, 314-316, 324 (1946); or with the clarity necessary to overcome the statutory prescription that "[n]o citizen shall be imprisoned or otherwise detained by the United States except pursuant to an Act of Congress." 18 U.S.C. §4001(a).[5] But even if it did, I would not permit it to overcome Hamdi's entitlement to habeas corpus relief. The Suspension Clause of the Constitution, which carefully circumscribes the conditions under which the writ can be withheld, would be a sham if it could be evaded by congressional prescription of requirements *other than the common-law requirement of committal for criminal prosecution* that render the writ, though available, unavailing. If the Suspension Clause does not guarantee the citizen that he will either be tried or released, unless the conditions for suspending the writ exist and the grave action of suspending the writ has been taken; if it merely guarantees the citizen that he will not be detained unless Congress by ordinary legislation says he can be detained; it guarantees him very little indeed.

It should not be thought, however, that the plurality's evisceration of the Suspension Clause augments, principally, the power of Congress. As usual, the major effect of its constitutional improvisation is to increase the power of the Court. Having found a congressional authorization for detention of citizens where none clearly exists; and having discarded the categorical procedural protection of the Suspension Clause; the plurality then proceeds, under the guise of the Due Process Clause, to prescribe what procedural protections *it* thinks appropriate. . . .

. . . This judicial remediation of executive default is unheard of. The role of habeas corpus is to determine the legality of executive detention, not to supply the omitted process necessary to make it legal. . . .

There is a certain harmony of approach in the plurality's making up for Congress's failure to invoke the Suspension Clause and its making up for the Executive's failure to apply what it says are needed procedures — an approach that reflects what might be called a Mr. Fix-it Mentality. The plurality seems to view it as its mission to Make Everything Come Out Right, rather than merely to decree the consequences, as far as individual rights are concerned, of the other two branches' actions and omissions. Has the Legislature failed to suspend the writ in the current dire emergency? Well, we will remedy that failure by prescribing the reasonable conditions that a suspension should have included. And has the Executive failed to live up to those reasonable conditions? Well, we will ourselves make that failure good, so that this dangerous fellow (if he is dangerous) need not be set free. The problem with this approach is not only that it steps out of the courts' modest and limited role in a democratic society; but that by repeatedly doing what it thinks the political branches ought to do it encourages their lassitude and saps the vitality of government by the people.

---

5. The plurality rejects any need for "specific language of detention" on the ground that detention of alleged combatants is a "fundamental incident of waging war." Its authorities do not support that holding in the context of the present case. Some are irrelevant because they do not address the detention of *American citizens*. The plurality's assertion that detentions of citizen and alien combatants are equally authorized has no basis in law or common sense. Citizens and noncitizens, even if equally dangerous, are not similarly situated. See, *e.g., Milligan, supra; Johnson v. Eisentrager*, 339 U.S. 763 (1950); Rev. Stat. 4067, 50 U.S.C. §21 (Alien Enemy Act). That captivity may be consistent with the principles of international law does not prove that it also complies with the restrictions that the Constitution places on the American Government's treatment of its own citizens. . . .

## VI

Several limitations give my views in this matter a relatively narrow compass. They apply only to citizens, accused of being enemy combatants, who are detained within the territorial jurisdiction of a federal court. This is not likely to be a numerous group; currently we know of only two, Hamdi and Jose Padilla. Where the citizen is captured outside and held outside the United States, the constitutional requirements may be different. Cf. *Johnson v. Eisentrager*, 339 U.S. 763, 769-771 (1950); *Reid v. Covert*, 354 U.S. 1, 74-75 (1957) (Harlan, J., concurring in result); *Rasul v. Bush*, [542 U.S. 466 (2004)] (Scalia, J., dissenting). Moreover, even within the United States, the accused citizen-enemy combatant may lawfully be detained once prosecution is in progress or in contemplation. . . .

. . . If the situation demands it, the Executive can ask Congress to authorize suspension of the writ—which can be made subject to whatever conditions Congress deems appropriate, including even the procedural novelties invented by the plurality today. To be sure, suspension is limited by the Constitution to cases of rebellion or invasion. But whether the attacks of September 11, 2001, constitute an "invasion," and whether those attacks still justify suspension several years later, are questions for Congress rather than this Court. . . .

Justice THOMAS, dissenting. The Executive Branch, acting pursuant to the powers vested in the President by the Constitution and with explicit congressional approval, has determined that Yaser Hamdi is an enemy combatant and should be detained. This detention falls squarely within the Federal Government's war powers, and we lack the expertise and capacity to second-guess that decision. As such, petitioners' habeas challenge should fail, and there is no reason to remand the case. . . . I do not think that the Federal Government's war powers can be balanced away by this Court. Arguably, Congress could provide for additional procedural protections, but until it does, we have no right to insist upon them. But even if I were to agree with the general approach the plurality takes, I could not accept the particulars. The plurality utterly fails to account for the Government's compelling interests and for our own institutional inability to weigh competing concerns correctly. I respectfully dissent. . . .

### ORDER BY PRESIDENT GEORGE W. BUSH TO THE SECRETARY OF DEFENSE

June 9, 2002
Appendix A, Padilla v. Rumsfeld, 352 F.3d 695 (2d Cir. 2003)

TO THE SECRETARY OF DEFENSE:

Based on the information available to me from all sources,
REDACTED
In accordance with the Constitution and consistent with the laws of the United States, including the Authorization for Use of Military Force Joint Resolution (Public Law 107-40);

I, GEORGE W. BUSH, as President of the United States and Commander in Chief of the U.S. armed forces, hereby DETERMINE for the United States of America that:

(1) Jose Padilla, who is under the control of the Department of Justice and who is a U.S. citizen, is, and at the time he entered the United States in May 2002 was, an enemy combatant;

(2) Mr. Padilla is closely associated with al Qaeda, an international terrorist organization with which the United States is at war;

(3) Mr. Padilla engaged in conduct that constituted hostile and war-like acts, including conduct in preparation for acts of international terrorism that had the aim to cause injury to or adverse effects on the United States;

(4) Mr. Padilla possesses intelligence, including intelligence about personnel and activities of al Qaeda, that, if communicated to the U.S., would aid U.S. efforts to prevent attacks by al Qaeda on the United States or its armed forces, other governmental personnel, or citizens;

(5) Mr. Padilla represents a continuing, present and grave danger to the national security of the United States, and detention of Mr. Padilla is necessary to prevent him from aiding al Qaeda in its efforts to attack the United States or its armed forces, other governmental personnel, or citizens;

(6) it is in the interest of the United States that the Secretary of Defense detain Mr. Padilla as an enemy combatant; and

(7) it is REDACTED consistent with U.S. law and the laws of war for the Secretary of Defense to detain Mr. Padilla as an enemy combatant.

Accordingly, you are directed to receive Mr. Padilla from the Department of Justice and to detain him as an enemy combatant.

------

Padilla challenged his detention by filing a habeas petition in the Southern District of New York. The District Court held that the government was authorized to detain him if it could adduce "some evidence" that he was an enemy combatant but that he was entitled to an evidentiary hearing in court on that question and to have access to counsel in order to participate meaningfully in such hearing. Padilla *ex rel.* Newman v. Bush, 233 F. Supp. 2d 564 (S.D.N.Y. 2002).

In a decision reached before the Supreme Court decided *Hamdi*, the Second Circuit Court of Appeals reversed on the merits. Padilla v. Rumsfeld, 352 F.3d 695 (2d Cir. 2003), *rev'd and remanded for lack of jurisdiction*, 542 U.S. 426 (2004). It found that the President "lacks inherent constitutional authority as Commander-in-Chief to detain American citizens on American soil outside a zone of combat." 352 F.3d at 712. It reasoned that the Constitution's explicit grant of powers to Congress by the Offenses Clause, U.S. Const. art. II, §8, cl. 10, the Suspension Clause (which it found to lodge the suspension power only in Congress), and the Third Amendment is "a powerful indication that, absent express congressional authorization, the President's Commander-in-Chief powers do not support Padilla's confinement." *Id.* at 715. *Quirin* was not to the contrary, it explained, because there Congress had authorized the military detention and trial of the saboteurs. Finally, the Court found that the 2001 AUMF did not meet the clear statement standard of the Non-Detention Act, 18 U.S.C. §4001(a), to authorize "the detention of an American citizen already held in a federal correctional institution and not 'arrayed against our troops' in the field of battle." *Id.* at 723. Is this reasoning invalidated by the subsequent decision in *Hamdi*?

The Supreme Court reversed on jurisdictional grounds by a 5-4 vote, ruling that Padilla had chosen the wrong court for filing his habeas petition. The following is an excerpt of the dissenting opinion from that decision.

## RUMSFELD v. PADILLA

United States Supreme Court, 2004
542 U.S. 426

Justice STEVENS, with whom Justice SOUTER, Justice GINSBURG, and Justice BREYER join, dissenting. . . . In sum, respondent properly filed his petition against Secretary Rumsfeld in the Southern District of New York.

### III

Whether respondent is entitled to immediate release is a question that reasonable jurists may answer in different ways.[8] There is, however, only one possible answer to the question whether he is entitled to a hearing on the justification for his detention.[9]

At stake in this case is nothing less than the essence of a free society. Even more important than the method of selecting the people's rulers and their successors is the character of the constraints imposed on the Executive by the rule of law. Unconstrained Executive detention for the purpose of investigating and preventing subversive activity is the hallmark of the Star Chamber. Access to counsel for the purpose of protecting the citizen from official mistakes and mistreatment is the hallmark of due process.

Executive detention of subversive citizens, like detention of enemy soldiers to keep them off the battlefield, may sometimes be justified to prevent persons from launching or becoming missiles of destruction. It may not, however, be justified by the naked interest in using unlawful procedures to extract information. Incommunicado detention for months on end is such a procedure.

---

8. Consistent with the judgment of the Court of Appeals, I believe that the Non-Detention Act, 18 U.S.C. §4001(a), prohibits — and the Authorization for Use of Military Force Joint Resolution, 115 Stat. 224, adopted on September 18, 2001, does not authorize — the protracted, incommunicado detention of American citizens arrested in the United States.

9. Respondent's custodian has been remarkably candid about the Government's motive in detaining respondent: "'[O]ur interest really in his case is not law enforcement, it is not punishment because he was a terrorist or working with the terrorists. Our interest at the moment is to try and find out everything he knows so that hopefully we can stop other terrorist acts.'" 233 F. Supp. 2d 564, 573-574 (S.D.N.Y. 2002) (quoting News Briefing, Dept. of Defense (June 12, 2002), 2002 WL 22026773).

Whether the information so procured is more or less reliable than that acquired by more extreme forms of torture is of no consequence. For if this Nation is to remain true to the ideals symbolized by its flag, it must not wield the tools of tyrants even to resist an assault by the forces of tyranny.

I respectfully dissent.

---

Taking into account this dissent, as well as the lineup of the Justices in *Hamdi*, how many votes would you count for finding that the military detention of Padilla was unlawful? (Of course, the Court's composition has since changed.)

After the Supreme Court's decision, Padilla filed a new habeas petition in the proper federal court in South Carolina. The District Court granted the petition, and the government appealed to the Fourth Circuit Court of Appeals, with the following result.

## PADILLA v. HANFT

United States Court of Appeals, Fourth Circuit, 2005
423 F.3d 386, *cert. denied*, 126 S. Ct. 1649 (2006)

LUTTIG, Circuit Judge. . . . The exceedingly important question before us is whether the President of the United States possesses the authority to detain militarily a citizen of this country who is closely associated with al Qaeda, an entity with which the United States is at war; who took up arms on behalf of that enemy and against our country in a foreign combat zone of that war; *and* who thereafter traveled to the United States for the avowed purpose of further prosecuting that war on American soil, against American citizens and targets.

We conclude that the President does possess such authority pursuant to the Authorization for Use of Military Force Joint Resolution enacted by Congress in the wake of the attacks on the United States of September 11, 2001. Accordingly, the judgment of the district court is reversed.

### I.

Al Qaeda operatives recruited Jose Padilla, a United States citizen, to train for jihad in Afghanistan in February 2000, while Padilla was on a religious pilgrimage to Saudi Arabia.[1] Subsequently, Padilla met with al Qaeda operatives in Afghanistan, received explosives training in an al Qaeda-affiliated camp, and served as an armed guard at what he understood to be a Taliban outpost. When United States military operations began in Afghanistan, Padilla and other al Qaeda operatives moved from safehouse to safehouse to evade bombing or capture. Padilla was, on the facts with which we are presented, "armed and present in a combat zone during armed conflict between al Qaeda/Taliban forces and the armed forces of the United States."

---

1. For purposes of Padilla's summary judgment motion, the parties have stipulated to the facts as set forth by the government. It is only on these facts that we consider whether the President has the authority to detain Padilla.

Padilla eventually escaped to Pakistan, armed with an assault rifle. Once in Pakistan, Padilla met with Khalid Sheikh Mohammad, a senior al Qaeda operations planner, who directed Padilla to travel to the United States for the purpose of blowing up apartment buildings, in continued prosecution of al Qaeda's war of terror against the United States. After receiving further training, as well as cash, travel documents, and communication devices, Padilla flew to the United States in order to carry out his accepted assignment.

Upon arrival at Chicago's O'Hare International Airport on May 8, 2002, Padilla was detained by FBI agents, who interviewed and eventually arrested him pursuant to a material witness warrant issued by the district court for the Southern District of New York in conjunction with a grand jury investigation of the September 11 attacks. Padilla was transported to New York, where he was held at a civilian correctional facility until, on June 9, 2002, the President designated him an "enemy combatant" against the United States and directed the Secretary of Defense to take him into military custody. Since his delivery into the custody of military authorities, Padilla has been detained at a naval brig in South Carolina. . . .

## II.

### A.

The Authorization for Use of Military Force Joint Resolution (AUMF), upon which the President explicitly relied in his order that Padilla be detained by the military and upon which the government chiefly relies in support of the President's authority to detain Padilla, was enacted by Congress in the immediate aftermath of the September 11, 2001, terrorist attacks on the United States. It provides as follows:

> [T]he President is authorized to use all necessary and appropriate force against those nations, organizations, or persons he determines planned, authorized, committed, or aided the terrorist attacks that occurred on September 11, 2001, or harbored such organizations or persons, in order to prevent any future acts of international terrorism against the United States by such nations, organizations or persons.

Pub. L. No. 107-40, §2(a), 115 Stat. 224 (September 18, 2001). . . .

As the AUMF authorized Hamdi's detention by the President, so also does it authorize Padilla's detention. Under the facts as presented here, Padilla unquestionably qualifies as an "enemy combatant" as that term was defined for purposes of the controlling opinion in *Hamdi*. Indeed, under the definition of "enemy combatant" employed in *Hamdi*, we can discern no difference in principle between Hamdi and Padilla. Like Hamdi, Padilla associated with forces hostile to the United States in Afghanistan. And, like Hamdi, Padilla took up arms against United States forces in that country in the same way and to the same extent as did Hamdi. Because, like Hamdi, Padilla is an enemy combatant, and because his detention is no less necessary than was Hamdi's in order to prevent his return to the battlefield, the President is authorized by the AUMF to detain Padilla as a fundamental incident to the conduct of war.

Our conclusion that the AUMF as interpreted by the Supreme Court in *Hamdi* authorizes the President's detention of Padilla as an enemy combatant is reinforced by the Supreme Court's decision in *Ex parte Quirin*, 317 U.S. 1 (1942), on which the plurality in *Hamdi* itself heavily relied. In *Quirin*, the Court held that Congress had authorized the military trial of Haupt, a United States citizen who entered the country with orders from the Nazis to blow up domestic war facilities but was captured before he could execute those orders. The Court reasoned that Haupt's citizenship was no bar to his military trial as an unlawful enemy belligerent, concluding that "[c]itizens who associate themselves with the military arm of the enemy government, and with its aid, guidance and direction enter this country bent on hostile acts, are enemy belligerents within the meaning of . . . the law of war."

Like Haupt, Padilla associated with the military arm of the enemy, and with its aid, guidance, and direction entered this country bent on committing hostile acts on American soil. Padilla thus falls within *Quirin*'s definition of enemy belligerent, as well as within the definition of the equivalent term accepted by the plurality in *Hamdi*. Compare *Quirin*, 317 U.S. at 37-38 (holding that "[c]itizens who associate themselves with the military arm of the enemy government, and with its aid, guidance and direction enter this country bent on hostile acts, are enemy belligerents within the meaning of . . . the law of war"), *with Hamdi*, 124 S. Ct. at 2639 (accepting for purposes of the case the government's definition of "enemy combatants" as those who were "'part of or supporting forces hostile to the United States or coalition partners' in Afghanistan and who 'engaged in an armed conflict against the United States' there").

We understand the plurality's *reasoning* in *Hamdi* to be that the AUMF authorizes the President to detain all those who qualify as "enemy combatants" within the meaning of the laws of war, such power being universally accepted under the laws of war as necessary in order to prevent the return of combatants to the battlefield during conflict. Given that Padilla qualifies as an enemy combatant under both the definition adopted by the Court in *Quirin* and the definition accepted by the controlling opinion in *Hamdi*, his military detention as an enemy combatant by the President is unquestionably authorized by the AUMF as a fundamental incident to the President's prosecution of the war against al Qaeda in Afghanistan.

**B. . . .**

*1.*

Recognizing the hurdle to his position represented by the Supreme Court's decision in *Hamdi*, Padilla principally argues that his case does not fall within the "narrow circumstances" considered by the Court in that case because, although he too stood alongside Taliban forces in Afghanistan, he was seized on American soil, whereas Hamdi was captured on a foreign battlefield. In other words, Padilla maintains that capture on a foreign battlefield was one of the "narrow circumstances" to which the plurality in *Hamdi* confined its opinion. We disagree. When the plurality articulated the "narrow question" before it, it referred simply to the permissibility of detaining "an individual who . . . was 'part of or supporting forces hostile to the United States or coalition partners' in Afghanistan and who 'engaged in an armed conflict against the United States' there." Nowhere in its framing of the "narrow question" presented did the plurality even mention the locus of capture.

The actual reasoning that the plurality thereafter employed is consistent with the question having been framed so as to render locus of capture irrelevant. That reasoning was that Hamdi's detention was an exercise of "necessary and appropriate force" within the meaning of the AUMF because "detention to prevent a combatant's return to the battlefield is a fundamental incident of waging war." *Id.* at 2641. This reasoning simply does not admit of a distinction between an enemy combatant captured abroad and detained in the United States, such as Hamdi, and an enemy combatant who escaped capture abroad but was ultimately captured domestically and detained in the United States, such as Padilla. As we previously explained, Padilla poses the same threat of returning to the battlefield as Hamdi posed at the time of the Supreme Court's adjudication of Hamdi's petition. Padilla's detention is thus "necessary and appropriate" to the same extent as was Hamdi's. . . .

Our conclusion that the reasoning in *Hamdi* does not support a distinction based on the locus of capture is buttressed by the plurality's analysis of *Quirin*. Although at issue in *Quirin* was the authority of the President to subject a United States citizen who was also an enemy combatant to military trial, the plurality in *Hamdi* went to lengths to observe that Haupt, *who had been captured domestically*, could instead have been permissibly *detained* for the duration of hostilities. That analysis strongly suggests, if it does not confirm, that the plurality did not regard the locus of capture (within or without the United States) as relevant to the President's authority to detain an enemy combatant who is also a citizen, and that it believed that the detention of such a combatant is not more or less a necessary incident of the President's power to wage war depending upon the locus of eventual capture. . . .

### 2.

Padilla also argues, and the district court held, that Padilla's military detention is "neither necessary nor appropriate" because he is amenable to criminal prosecution. . . .

As to the fact that Padilla can be prosecuted, the availability of criminal process does not distinguish him from Hamdi. If the mere availability of criminal prosecution rendered detention unnecessary within the meaning of the AUMF, then Hamdi's detention would have been unnecessary and therefore unauthorized, since he too was detained in the United States and amenable to criminal prosecution. We are convinced, in any event, that the availability of criminal process cannot be determinative of the power to detain, if for no other reason than that criminal prosecution may well not achieve the very purpose for which detention is authorized in the first place — the prevention of return to the field of battle. Equally important, in many instances criminal prosecution would impede the Executive in its efforts to gather intelligence from the detainee and to restrict the detainee's communication with confederates so as to ensure that the detainee does not pose a continuing threat to national security even as he is confined — impediments that would render military detention not only an appropriate, but also the necessary, course of action to be taken in the interest of national security. . . .

### 3.

Padilla, citing *Ex parte Endo*, 323 U.S. 283 (1944), and relying upon *Quirin*, next argues that only a clear statement from Congress can authorize his detention, and that the AUMF is not itself, and does not contain, such a clear statement.

In *Endo*, the Court did state that, when asked to find implied powers in a wartime statute, it must assume that "the law makers intended to place no greater restraint on the citizen than was clearly and unmistakably indicated by the language [the law makers] used." The Court almost immediately thereafter observed, however, that the "fact that the Act" at issue was "silent on detention [did] not of course mean that any power to detain [was] lacking," an observation that proves that the Court did not adopt or even apply in that case a "clear statement" rule of the kind for which Padilla argues.

Padilla contends that *Quirin* also supports the existence of a clear statement rule. However, in no place in *Quirin* did the Court even purport to establish a clear statement rule. In its opinion, the Court did note that Congress had "explicitly" authorized Haupt's military trial. But to conclude from this passing note that the Court required a clear statement as a matter of law would be unwarranted. In fact, to the extent that *Quirin* can be understood to have addressed the need for a clear statement of authority from Congress at all, the rule would appear the opposite:

> [T]he detention and trial of petitioners—ordered by the President in the declared exercise of his powers as Commander in Chief of the Army in time of war and of grave public danger—are not to be set aside by the courts without the clear conviction that they are in conflict with the Constitution or laws of Congress constitutionally enacted.

Of course, even were a clear statement by Congress required, the AUMF constitutes such a clear statement according to the Supreme Court. In *Hamdi*, stating that "it [was] of no moment that the AUMF does not use specific language of detention," the plurality held that the AUMF "clearly and unmistakably authorized" Hamdi's detention. Nothing in the AUMF permits us to conclude that the Joint Resolution clearly and unmistakably authorized Hamdi's detention but not Padilla's. To the contrary, read in light of its purpose clause ("in order to prevent any future acts of international terrorism against the United States") and its preamble (stating that the acts of 9/11 "render it both necessary and appropriate . . . to protect United States citizens both at home and abroad"), the AUMF applies even more clearly and unmistakably to Padilla than to Hamdi. Padilla, after all, in addition to supporting hostile forces in Afghanistan and taking up arms against our troops on a battlefield in that country like Hamdi, *also* came to the United States in order to commit future acts of terrorism against American citizens and targets. . . .

**4.**

Finally, Padilla argues that, even if his detention is authorized by the AUMF, it is unlawful under *Ex parte Milligan*, 71 U.S. (4 Wall.) 2 (1866). In *Milligan*, the Supreme Court held that a United States citizen associated with an anti-Union secret society but unaffiliated with the Confederate army could not be tried by a military tribunal while access to civilian courts was open and unobstructed. *Milligan* purported to restrict the power of Congress as well as the power of the President. ("[N]o usage of war could sanction a military trial . . . for any offence whatever of a citizen in civil life, in nowise connected with the military service. Congress could grant no such power. . . ."). *Quirin*, however, confirmed that *Milligan* does not extend to enemy combatants. As the Court in *Quirin* explained, the *Milligan* Court's reasoning had "particular reference to the facts before it," namely, that Milligan was not "a part of or associated with the armed forces of the enemy." The *Hamdi* plurality in turn reaffirmed this limitation on the reach of *Milligan*, emphasizing that *Quirin*, a unanimous opinion, "both postdates and clarifies *Milligan*." Thus confined, *Milligan* is inapposite here because Padilla, unlike Milligan, associated with, and has taken up arms against the forces of the United States on behalf of, an enemy of the United States. . . .

**III.** . . .

The detention of petitioner being fully authorized by Act of Congress, the judgment of the district court that the detention of petitioner by the President of the United States is without support in law is hereby reversed.

*Reversed.*

## NOTES AND QUESTIONS

1. ***Hamdi After Remand.*** After the Supreme Court remanded, Hamdi and the government negotiated an agreement for his release to his family in Saudi Arabia. The government asserted that he no longer had any intelligence value and posed no threat. Under the agreement, Hamdi gave up his U.S. citizenship, renounced terrorism, waived any civil claim he had for his detention, and accepted certain travel restrictions, including a ten-year ban on returning to the United States. *See* Motion to Stay Proceedings, Hamdi v. Rumsfeld, No. 2:02CV439 (E.D. Va. Sept. 24, 2004), *available at* http://notablecases.vaed.uscourts.gov/2:02-cv-00439/docs/70223/0.pdf.

2. ***The Greater Includes the Lesser?*** In both *Hamdi* and *Padilla* the courts assume that Supreme Court precedents concerning trial by military commission, especially *Quirin*, are apposite to the legality of military detention. *Quirin* did say that both lawful and unlawful combatants "are subject to capture and *detention*," and that unlawful combatants are additionally subject to military trial and punishment. *Supra* p. 355 (emphasis supplied). This the lower court in *Padilla* understood to reflect the Supreme Court's belief that "detention alone . . . [is] certainly the lesser of the consequences an unlawful combatant could face." Padilla *ex*

*rel.* Newman v. Bush, 233 F. Supp. 2d 564, 595 (S.D.N.Y. 2002), *rev'd*, 352 F.3d 685 (2d Cir. 2003), *rev'd and remanded*, 542 U.S. 426 (2004).

But is that always true? The unlawful combatant who is tried at least will see a resolution of his status. *See Rasul, supra* p. 326 (Kennedy, J., concurring in judgment) (distinguishing *Eisentrager*, involving aliens being detained after having been convicted by military commission, from *Rasul*, involving aliens "being held indefinitely, and without benefit of any legal proceeding to determine their status"). What about the combatant who is detained indefinitely by the military without trial or even charges, or until the political branches determine that the war is over? If detention is not the "lesser" consequence for such a combatant, is case law establishing the legality of a military *trial* really apposite to the legality of *detention*?

3. ***Necessity for Military Detention in Hamdi.*** Detention under the law of war is based on military necessity, a premise echoed in the AUMF authorization for use of "*necessary* and appropriate force." *See* §2(a), *supra* p. 59 (emphasis supplied). What is that necessity?

"The purpose of detention is to prevent captured individuals from returning to the field of battle and taking up arms once again," Justice O'Connor noted in *Hamdi*. They are detained, in other words, both to enable U.S. forces to carry out their mission and to provide force protection. In addition, such individuals are detained to obtain operational intelligence by interrogation. Indeed, their detention may itself be instrumental to a successful interrogation, because the isolation of the detainees and their consequent dependence on their captors may induce them to talk. Bringing such persons before a judge, or even holding some kind of hearing, may be impracticable in the midst of hostilities, while the bullets are flying. Moving detainees back from the front lines may not be a cure, because it is often still impractical to withdraw troops from the front to give testimony or to preserve evidence during the fighting. *Cf.* Odah v. United States, 321 F.3d 1134, 1150 (D.C. Cir. 2003) (Randolph, J., concurring) (asserting with respect to military detainees at Camp X-Ray in Guantánamo Naval Base, Cuba, that "[t]he historical meaning of 'in the field' was not restricted to the field of battle. It applied as well to 'organized camps stationed in remote places where civil courts did not exist.'"), *rev'd and remanded by* Rasul v. Bush, 542 U.S. 466 (2004), *supra* p. 326.

How, if at all, did the Court in *Hamdi* respond to such arguments of military necessity? Do you agree? Would it make a difference whether Hamdi—a U.S. citizen allegedly fighting alongside the enemy—was one of a kind or one of a thousand?

4. ***Necessity for Military Detention in Padilla.*** If the arguments of necessity apply to Hamdi, do they also apply to Padilla? What if the government believes Padilla to be an imminent threat to set off a dirty bomb but lacks probable cause to arrest him? What response does Justice Souter suggest for such an emergency? Here is the District Court's answer, after Padilla refiled his habeas petition on remand from the Supreme Court:

Simply stated, this is a law enforcement matter, not a military matter. . . . At the time that [Padilla] was arrested pursuant to the material arrest warrant, any alleged terrorist plans that he harbored were thwarted. From then on, he was available to be questioned — and was indeed questioned — just like any citizen accused of criminal conduct. . . .

There can be no debate that this country's laws amply provide for the investigation, detention and prosecution of citizen and non-citizen terrorists alike. . . .

> . . . The difference between invocation of the criminal process and the power claimed by the President here, however, is one of accountability. The criminal justice system requires that defendants and witnesses be afforded access to counsel, imposes judicial supervision over government action, and places congressionally imposed limits on incarceration.

[Padilla v. Hanft, 389 F. Supp. 2d 678, 691-692 (D.S.C.), *rev'd*, 423 F.3d 387 (4th Cir. 2005), *cert. denied*, 126 S. Ct. 1649 (2006) (mem.) (quoting *amici curiae* in Rumsfeld v. Padilla, 542 U.S. 426 (2004).]

As the principal case shows, the Fourth Circuit Court of Appeals disagreed. Barely three weeks later and just two business days before the government's brief in response to Padilla's petition for certiorari was due to be filed in the Supreme Court of the United States, however, the government announced Padilla's indictment on charges considerably less serious than those for which he had been militarily detained. It then moved to transfer him to civilian custody.

The Court of Appeals, in an opinion by the obviously angry author of the earlier opinion, which had accepted the government's claim of military necessity in upholding the military detention, denied the motion and refused to vacate its decision. Padilla v. Hanft, 432 F.3d 582 (4th Cir. 2005). The court asserted that the timing of the indictment gave an appearance that it had been driven by the government's desire to avoid consideration of the Fourth Circuit's favorable decision by the Supreme Court, *id.* at 585, and stated that the issues raised by Padilla's military detention were sufficiently important to warrant consideration by the Supreme Court. *Id.* at 587. As to claims of military necessity, the Court of Appeals commented:

> [A]s the government surely must understand, although the various facts it has asserted are not necessarily inconsistent or without basis, its actions have left not only the impression that Padilla may have been held for these years, even if justifiably, by mistake — an impression we would have thought the government could ill afford to leave extant. They have left the impression that the government may even have come to the belief that the principle in reliance upon which it has detained Padilla for this time, that the President possesses the authority to detain enemy combatants who enter into this country for the purpose of attacking America and its citizens from within, can, in the end, yield to expediency with little or no cost to its conduct of the war against terror — an impression we would have thought the government likewise could ill afford to leave

extant. And these impressions have been left, we fear, at what may ultimately prove to be substantial cost to the government's credibility before the courts, to whom it will one day need to argue again in support of a principle of assertedly like importance and necessity to the one that it seems to abandon today. While there could be an objective that could command such a price as all of this, it is difficult to imagine what that objective would be. [*Id.* at 587.]

5. *Military Necessity Redux.* In Korematsu v. United States, 323 U.S. 214 (1944), the government also claimed military necessity to exclude persons of Japanese ancestry, including U.S. citizens, from much of the West Coast during World War II, citing "evidence of disloyalty on the part of some" and the danger of invasion. *Id.* at 223. The Supreme Court accepted the claim and upheld the legality of this racially targeted military order. Years later, a federal court set aside Korematsu's conviction for violating the exclusion orders, finding that "the government knowingly withheld information from the courts when they were considering the critical question of military necessity in this case." Korematsu v. United States, 584 F. Supp. 1406, 1417-1419 (N.D. Cal. 1984). The District Court stated that *Korematsu* "stands as a caution that in times of stress the shield of military necessity and national security must not be used to protect governmental actions from close scrutiny and accountability." *Id.* at 1420.

Do the 1984 *Korematsu* decision and the last Court of Appeals decision in *Padilla* cast any doubt on the wisdom of judicial deference to executive claims of military necessity for military detention? If so, how should the courts view such claims? How would you reframe the authority for military detention to confine it strictly to situations of bona fide military necessity? Does the length of the detention affect the necessity? If so, how would you factor this consideration into your specification of detention authority?

The issue of necessity again figured prominently in the Supreme Court's 2006 decision about the jurisdiction of a military commission to try an alien charged with violations of the law of war. *See* Hamdan v. Rumsfeld, 126 S. Ct. 2749, 2777 (2006), *infra* p. 563.

6. *The Non-Detention Act — Section 4001(a).* A plurality in *Hamdi* assumes, but does not decide, that §4001(a) applies to military detentions and then finds it satisfied by the AUMF. If §4001(a) does apply, and the AUMF is invoked as a statutory exception within its contemplation, should we apply the clear statement requirement to the AUMF, as Justices Souter and Ginsburg insist in *Hamdi* and the Second Circuit did in *Padilla*? Why does the Fourth Circuit not apply that rule? Who was right about the application of the clear statement rule — the Fourth Circuit or the Second Circuit?

On the other hand, even without insisting on a clear statement, does a natural reading of the AUMF embrace uses of force (and, by implication, military detention) *within* the United States, or just in Afghanistan or wherever else the armed forces are deployed in combat? *See* Stephen I. Vladeck, Comment, *A Small Problem of Precedent: 18 U.S.C. §4001(a) and the Detention of U.S. Citizen "Enemy Combatants,"* 112 Yale L.J. 961, 967 (2003) (arguing that the AUMF fails to satisfy §4001(a)).

7. *"Plenary" Military Authority.* In *Hamdi*, the government argued that the executive has plenary authority under Article II to detain "enemy combatants," presumably a "war power" of the Commander in Chief. Though the plurality did not reach this claim, it agreed that the capture and military detention of combatants are " 'important incident[s] of war," quoting *Quirin*, and Justice Thomas dissented on the ground that Hamdi's "detention falls squarely within the Federal Government's war powers" vested in the executive branch. This assertion of war power presents several thorny questions.

First, if the war power presupposes a war, is a state of war as the Supreme Court defined that term in *The Prize Cases, supra* p. 43, sufficient, or must the war be expressly authorized by Congress? Was a war authorized by the AUMF, *supra* p. 59? If so, what is its scope, both geographical and temporal? Does the AUMF trigger all the war powers of the President, or just some of them?

Second, how should we define "enemy combatants" subject to military detention under the law of war? How does the *Hamdi* Court define them? Recall the differences in the status of Milligan and of Quirin. Is Hamdi more like Milligan or like Quirin? In this regard, note that the saboteurs in *Quirin*, unlike Hamdi, did not contest their status as enemy soldiers. (This was one basis on which the Second Circuit distinguished *Quirin*. Another was that *Quirin* was decided before the Non-Detention Act.) What about Padilla? What definition of "enemy combatant" would you construct from *Milligan*, *Quirin*, and *Hamdi*? One scholar has argued that "enemy combatant" is not a legal term of art; rather, it is a term contrived by the government for skirting the law of war in the war on terrorism. *See* Peter Jan Honigsberg, *Chasing "Enemy Combatants" and Circumventing International Law: A License for Sanctioned Abuse*," 12 UCLA J. Intl. L. & For. Aff. (forthcoming 2007).

Or are we looking in the wrong place? If war is authorized by declaration or by a use-of-force statute, shouldn't we also look to that authorization for a definition of the enemy? Suppose Congress had not authorized the use of force against terrorist organizations like al Qaeda, but the President had gone ahead anyway on the theory of repelling attack. Would military detention of combatants in that war be authorized? How would they be defined? What about persons detained as terrorists generally in an undeclared "war on terrorism"?

Third, even if the AUMF suffices to authorize military detention in the field, does it apply in the United States? The Fourth Circuit reasoned that the "locus of capture [is] irrelevant" to the military necessity for Padilla's detention. Should the court have considered the availability of criminal law and open civilian courts to that end, or considered the constitutional authorities that the Second Circuit identified as vesting explicit legislative power in Congress?

8. *Determining the Combatant Status of U.S. Citizens.* The plurality in *Hamdi* decided what procedures were required for determining his status by conducting a due process balancing. To test your understanding of where they came out, consider the alternatives.

First, why was combatant status not an issue in *Quirin*? All are agreed that the answer is that the German saboteurs admitted their status. If there is no factual dispute, then even a due process balancing presumably does not require any procedure to decide that status. Why did the Court reject the government's argument that Hamdi's status was undisputed?

If the detainee's combatant status *is* disputed and he is entitled to petition for a writ of habeas corpus, then the habeas corpus statute, 28 U.S.C. §2243, *supra* p. 312, itself suggests some evidentiary proceeding. Can you see why from examining the statute?

But what evidence and what kind of proceeding? The government suggested that "some evidence" would suffice, a conclusion reached by the district court in *Padilla* as well. The government therefore argued that the court's role in a habeas corpus proceeding was only to decide whether the evidence stated in the Mobbs declaration was sufficient standing alone. Is that consistent with the habeas corpus statute? Or with due process?

The Court rejected the "some evidence" standard partly on the grounds that "it primarily has been employed by courts in examining an administrative record developed after an adversarial proceeding. . . ." But the government has asserted that it *has* developed an administrative record after an elaborate internal process for determining combatant status of U.S. citizens that incorporated information developed by the Department of Defense, the Central Intelligence Agency, and the Department of Justice, written assessments by the same agencies, a formal legal opinion by the Office of Legal Counsel, recommendations by the Attorney General and the Secretary of Defense, and a final recommendation to and briefing for the President by the White House Counsel.[2] If such procedures were actually used to designate Hamdi and Padilla as enemy combatants and to generate the factual predicates for their military detention, why isn't the "some evidence" standard sufficient?

Finally, consider the procedures that the plurality in *Hamdi* found were required by a due process balancing. Are these sufficient to reduce the risk of inaccuracy in light of the interests at stake? What more would Justices Souter and Ginsburg require if they found that Congress had authorized military detention? What would you find necessary if you performed the balancing?

In light of the foregoing, are Justices Scalia and Stevens right — is this a job for Congress? If so, what procedures would you recommend that Congress require?

9. ***The Right to Assistance of Counsel.*** Is any proceeding for determining a detainee's status fair without his input? May he give that input without a lawyer? Many have argued that the right to assistance of counsel is the most important right of a person detained or prosecuted by the government because it is essential to effectively asserting every other right.

---

2. Alberto R. Gonzales, Counsel to the President, Remarks at the American Bar Assn. Standing Comm. on Law and Natl. Security (Feb. 24, 2004) (transcript *available at* http://www.fas.org/irp/news/2004/02/Gonzales.pdf) (asserting also, however, that neither these procedures nor any other specific procedures were required by law, but that they were simply adopted by administrative grace).

The government responded to such concerns by insisting that "[t]he rights the Constitution affords persons in the criminal justice system simply do not apply in the context of detention of enemy combatants." Letter from Daniel J. Bryant (Asst. Attorney General, U.S. Dept. of Justice) to Carl Levin (Chairman of the Senate Committee on Armed Services), Nov. 26, 2002, at 4. But doesn't this beg the question whether a detainee *is* an "enemy combatant"? Even if military detention and trial operate in some legal universe parallel to the Constitution, does it follow that the President alone is gatekeeper to that universe? If the court has some gatekeeping function as well, how can it fulfill that function without help from the detainee through his counsel?

Consider the following recommendations from the American Bar Association Task Force on Treatment of Enemy Combatants:

> RESOLVED, That the American Bar Association urges that U.S. citizens and residents who are detained within the United States based on their designation as "enemy combatants" be afforded the opportunity for meaningful judicial review of their status, under a standard according such deference to the designation as the review court determines to be appropriate to accommodate the needs of the detainee and the requirements of national security; and
>
> FURTHER RESOLVED, That the American Bar Association urges that U.S. citizens and residents who are detained within the United States based on their designations as "enemy combatants" not be denied access to counsel in connection with the opportunity for such review, subject to appropriate conditions as may be set by the court to accommodate the needs of the detainee and the requirements of national security. . . . [ABA Task Force on Treatment of Enemy Combatants, *Report to the House of Delegates* (2003).]

Shortly before the argument in the Supreme Court in *Hamdi*, but not earlier, Hamdi was permitted to meet with counsel appointed to represent him. The timing of the government's action suggested to some a desire to avoid a ruling by the high court on this issue. The Court asserted that Hamdi "unquestionably has the right to access to counsel in connection with proceedings on remand. No further consideration of this issue is necessary at this stage of the case." 542 U.S. at 539. Did the plurality decide that access to counsel is part of the procedure owed Hamdi by due process? How would you decide that question?

## C. MILITARY DETENTION OF ALIEN ENEMY COMBATANTS AFTER 9/11

The decisions in *Hamdi* and *Padilla* might suggest that the military detention of *alien* enemy combatants after 9/11 would be comparatively less controversial, as least as a matter of domestic law. First, aliens outside the United States have fewer, if any, constitutional rights. *See, e.g.*, United States v. Verdugo-Urquidez, 494 U.S. 259 (1990), *supra* p. 270. Second, the Non-Detention Act, *supra* p. 301, does not apply to them.

President George W. Bush presumably was so advised when, two months after the 9/11 attacks, he issued a military order authorizing military detention of aliens whom he believed to be members of al Queda or who have "engaged in, aided or abetted, or conspired to commit, acts of international terrorism, or acts in preparation therefor" directed at the United States or its people. Military Order of November 13, 2001, *Detention, Treatment, and Trial of Certain Non-Citizens in the War Against Terrorism*, 66 Fed. Reg. 57,833 (Nov. 13, 2001), *infra* p. 559. When military operations in Afghanistan began to yield captives in the fall of 2001, the government decided to transfer many of them to a detention facility at the U.S. Naval Base at Guantánamo Bay, Cuba, pursuant to the military order.

Applications for writs of habeas corpus, as well as other suits, soon followed, leading to the decision in Rasul v. Bush, 542 U.S. 466 (2004), *supra* p. 326, holding that the federal courts had statutory "jurisdiction to determine the legality of the Executive's potentially indefinite detention of individuals [including Rasul and other alien detainees held at Guantánamo Bay] who claim to be wholly innocent of wrongdoing." 542 U.S. at 485.

The *Rasul* ruling paved the way for conflicting decisions in the lower courts. In Hamdan v. Rumsfeld, 344 F. Supp. 2d 152 (D.D.C. 2004), *rev'd*, 435 F.3d 582 (D.C. Cir. 2005), *rev'd*, 126 S. Ct. 2749 (2006), *infra* p. 563, the District Court found that the proposed trial of a Guantánamo Bay detainee by military commission pursuant to the military order violated the Geneva Conventions. In In re Guantánamo Detainee Cases, 355 F. Supp. 2d 443 (D.D.C. 2005), *vacated sub nom.* Boumediene v. Bush, 476 F.3d 981 (D.C. Cir. 2007) *cert. denied*, 127 S. Ct. 1478 (2007), a different district court adopted the lower court's reasoning in *Hamdan* to find that the Geneva Conventions applied to fighters for the Taliban and then held that the Conventions were not satisfied by the hearings held by Combatant Status Review Tribunals (CSRTs) to determine whether detainees were enemy combatants. In addition, relying on footnote 15 in *Rasul, supra* p. 329, the court held that detainees had stated valid claims under the Fifth Amendment when they asserted that the procedures used by the CSRTs violated due process. However, a third district court reached the opposite conclusions in Khalid v. Bush, 355 F. Supp. 2d 311 (D.D.C. 2005), *vacated sub nom.* Boumediene v. Bush, *supra*. Reasoning that *Rasul* decided only the jurisdictional question and not the question whether detainees in Guantánamo Bay have constitutional rights, the *Khalid* court found that they did not, relying on *Eisentrager*. The *Boumediene* court also held that the detention and treatment of individuals held at Guantánamo Bay violated no U.S. laws and that international laws were either inapplicable or not privately enforceable.

Both of the decisions were appealed. While the appeal was pending, the Supreme Court decided Hamdan v. Rumsfeld, 126 S. Ct. 2749 (2006) (*infra* p. 563), ruling that the trial of an enemy combatant by a military commission violated applicable statutes. Congress then passed the Military Commissions Act of 2006 (MCA), Pub. L. No. 109-366, 120 Stat. 2600, *infra* p. 587. As we saw in Chapter 11, the MCA purports to strip courts of jurisdiction to hear habeas petitions "by or on behalf of an alien detained by the United States who has been determined by the United States to have been properly detained as an enemy combatant or is awaiting such a determination." MCA §7(a), amending 28 U.S.C. §2241(e). It leaves intact the provision in the Detainee Treatment Act of 2005 (DTA), National Defense Authorization Act for Fiscal Year 2006, Pub. L. No. 109-163, §1405(e)(1), 119 Stat. 3136, 3477 (2006), directing limited review of such a determination—now made by CSRTs—to the Court of Appeals for the D.C. Circuit. *Id.* These limitations on judicial review of alien enemy combatant determinations were upheld and applied to the pending appeals in Boumediene v. Bush, *supra*, which therefore vacated both lower court decisions.

## NOTES AND QUESTIONS

1. *Constitutional Rights of Alien Detainees?* Recall *Eisentrager, supra* p. 321, and, if necessary, reread *Verdugo-Urquidez, supra* p. 270. It held that alien Verdugo-Urquidez had no constitutional protection under the Fourth Amendment from a warrantless search of his property in Mexico. Why didn't that decision resolve the question of the constitutional rights of aliens generally? If that question was left open after these cases, does *Rasul* shed light on the substantive constitutional rights of the alien detainees, or is it just a jurisdictional ruling on their access to statutory habeas corpus? On the other hand, if they have no substantive rights, is such a procedural right a cruel hoax? *See* Amnesty International, *Guantánamo and Beyond: The Continuing Pursuit of Unchecked Executive Power*, May 13, 2005, at 46 (characterizing the government's claim that *Rasul* conferred only "procedural rights" on alien detainees as an argument that "the detainees could file *habeas corpus* petitions, but only in order to have them necessarily dismissed"), *available at* http://web.amnesty.org/library/Index/ENGAMR510632005?open&of=ENG-USA. What other rights could they assert in their petition?

   Al-Marri v. Hanft, 378 F. Supp. 2d 673 (D.S.C. 2005), may help put some of these questions into sharper relief. Al-Marri is a Qatari national who earned a bachelor's degree during the 1990s from Bradley University in Illinois, and who legally returned to the United States with his family to pursue a master's degree from the same university. Unfortunately for him, he returned on September 10, 2001, and he was subsequently arrested on December 12 as a material witness and later indicted for making false statements and for credit card fraud before being designated an enemy combatant by President Bush on June 23, 2003. The criminal case was dismissed with prejudice, and al-Marri was transferred to military detention at the Naval Consolidated Brig in South Carolina.

   Does al-Marri have any constitutional rights that he can assert to challenge his military detention? Is he differently situated from the Guantánamo detainees? The court that rejected his petition for a writ of habeas corpus cited *Eisentrager* in concluding that the Supreme Court had limited "a resident alien enemy's use of our courts . . . 'as necessary to prevent use of the courts to accomplish a purpose which might hamper our own war efforts or to give aid to the enemy.'" *Id.* at 678 (quoting *Eisentrager*, 339 U.S. at 776 (internal citation omitted)). Should the court have discussed *Rasul*?

2. *CSRTs and the Value of Due Process.* Between August 2004 and March 2005, CSRTs reviewed the status of 558 detainees and deemed 520 to be enemy combatants. *See Combatant Status Review Summary*, Mar. 29, 2005 (reporting review by Convening Authority Rear Adm. James M. McGarrah), *available at* http://www.dod.mil/news/Mar2005/d20050329csrt.pdf. As we have seen, *supra* pp. 334-335, analysis of the public records of the hearings raises substantial doubts about their fairness and, therefore, in some cases, their accuracy.

   Thirty-two of the 38 CSRT decisions that rejected that designation were decided *after* the decision in In re Guantanamo Detainee Cases. *See* Amnesty International, *supra*, at 50. However, it is not clear whether these results reflect a change in procedures or the way in which procedures were applied.

   Do you think that additional procedures in the CSRTs would make a difference in the outcomes? If alien detainees at Guantánamo Bay have a right to due process, what procedures would be required beyond those described in *Boumediene, supra* p. 336 and p. 334 Note 3?

3. *The Alien Enemy Act.* The Alien Enemy Act, 50 U.S.C. §21 (2000), provides:

   > Whenever there is a declared war between the United States and any foreign nation or government, or any invasion or predatory incursion is perpetrated, attempted, or threatened against the territory of the United States by any foreign nation or government, and the President makes public proclamation of the event, all natives, citizens, denizens, or subjects of the hostile nation or government, being of the age of fourteen years and upward, who shall be within the United States and not actually naturalized, shall be liable to be apprehended, restrained, secured, and removed as alien enemies. . . .

   Why wasn't this Act invoked to justify the detention of suspected alien terrorists after September 11? The *Al-Marri* court reasoned that the Act confirmed that during war even resident enemy aliens receive protections different from those enjoyed by citizens, although the court conceded that the Act had no direct application. 378 F. Supp. 2d at 679. What contrary argument could you make based upon the existence of that Act?

4. *A New Detention Paradigm?* Do the foregoing cases suggest that the threat of terrorism requires a new model for detention? One scholar has suggested detention for "dangerousness," by extrapolating from civil detention law for dangerous individuals. *See* Tung Yin, *Ending the War on Terrorism One Terrorist at a Time: A Noncriminal Detention Model for Holding and Releasing Guantanamo Bay Detainees*, 29 Harv. J.L. & Pub. Poly. 149 (2005). See also *supra* p. 302, Note 1 (describing civilian "dangerousness" cases). Dangerousness would be determined by the amount of training the detainee has received, his expressed willingness to engage in

terrorism, the detainee's prior violent conduct, and the detainee's age. *Id.* at 199. Professor Yin also suggests that experts could play a role in dangerousness hearings. *Id.* at 200. What procedural requirements do you think would be necessary for this model to work? *See id.* at 202-207.

5. ***Synthesis?*** The cases in this chapter present the following variables, among others:

- citizen or alien?
- admitted "enemy combatant" or contested?
- detention in the mainland United States or at Guantánamo Bay Naval Base?
- capture on the Afghan battlefield or in the United States?
- member of al Qaeda or fighter for the Taliban?

Can you distinguish the outcomes of the cases using these variables or others? Can you synthesize the cases to state the present law of military detention in the war on terrorism? If not, do you think this is an appropriate issue for resolution by the courts rather than by the political branches? Do the courts have a choice?

# CHAPTER 13

# *INTERROGATING TERRORIST SUSPECTS*

As early as December 2002, U.S. military and civilian interrogators are reported to have abused individuals captured and detained in the war on terrorism by beating them and subjecting them to prolonged sleep and sensory deprivation, as well as to sexual humiliation. The abuse began in Afghanistan, then migrated to Guantánamo Bay, Cuba, and other offshore U.S. interrogation centers, and later to Iraq. Several investigations of these abuses revealed that serious injuries and deaths occurred among the detainees.

Our objective in this chapter is to tell the interrogation story from September 11 to the present, then to introduce the legal regime for U.S. interrogation and treatment of detainees abroad. We consider both the sources of applicable rules and the limits those rules impose on interrogation techniques. We also try to determine whether the President enjoys constitutional or other powers that would excuse him from compliance with the rules. The raw materials for this analysis — internal government legal memoranda — provide a remarkable view of the work of lawyers in a wartime executive branch.

## A. THE EVOLVING HISTORY OF DETAINEE INTERROGATION IN THE WAR ON TERRORISM

In October 1996, Secretary of Defense William Perry spoke at a meeting of Western Hemisphere defense ministers in Argentina. Responding to criticisms of so-called "torture manuals" used to train Latin American intelligence officers at the U.S. Army School of the Americas in the 1980s, and to a 1996 Intelligence Oversight Board report describing intelligence activities in Latin America, Perry said he was shocked when he found out about the manuals. He declared that the Defense Department would never again advocate torture or other inhumane treatment in its training programs.[1]

Secretary Perry's assertion could not have taken into account September 11 and the war on terrorism. According to Cofer Black, former director of the CIA's

---

1. Linda D. Kozaryn, *Perry Bans U.S. Training in Inhumane Techniques*, American Forces Information Serv., Oct. 9, 1996, *available at* http://www.defenselink.mil/news/Oct1996/n10091996_9610095.html.

counterterrorism unit, "after 9/11, the gloves came off."[2] Beginning with the capture in Afghanistan of senior al Qaeda operatives, the Bush administration had to determine how best to extract intelligence information from individuals detained by U.S. forces. "Setting" the methods and parameters of interrogation thus became an integral part of counterterrorism planning. Should al Qaeda figures be questioned by the FBI using traditional methods? By military interrogators following service branch rules? By the CIA, perhaps using harsher techniques in secret locations?

The Bush administration decided early on to detain indefinitely a number of persons seized in Afghanistan and elsewhere, and to create a new detention facility at the U.S. base at Guantánamo Bay to hold at least some of them. The first detainees taken there in January 2002 were designated "unlawful combatants" by President Bush.

Initially, the Administration contended that Taliban and al Qaeda fighters held at Guantánamo were not eligible for the protections of the Geneva Conventions, the principal set of international legal norms for wartime detainees created by the international community after World War II. The internal debate attending this decision is reflected in memoranda from the Justice Department, the White House Counsel, and the State Department excerpted *infra* pp. 404-414. The Administration eventually decided that captured Taliban fighters would be protected by the Third Geneva Convention, although not as "prisoners of war." Captured members of al Qaeda would be treated "humanely," although the Geneva Conventions would not apply to them. In any case, according to the Defense Department, at least until December 2002 interrogations at Guantánamo were conducted in accordance with rules set out in Department of the Army, *Intelligence Interrogation* (FM 34-52) (1992).[3]

In the summer of 2002, however, the Justice Department was asked to advise what interrogation techniques would violate U.S. or international law. In August, the Office of Legal Counsel (OLC) opined that

> for an act to constitute torture as defined in [the Torture Statute], it must inflict pain that is difficult to endure. Physical pain amounting to torture must be equivalent in intensity to the pain accompanying serious physical injury, such as organ failure, impairment of bodily function, or even death. For purely mental pain or suffering to amount to torture . . . it must result in significant psychological harm of significant duration, e.g., lasting for months or even years. We conclude that the mental harm also must result from one of the predicate acts listed in the statute, namely: threats of imminent death; threats of the infliction of the kind of pain that would amount to physical torture; infliction of such physical pain as a means of psychological torture; use of drugs or other procedures designed to deeply disrupt the senses, or fundamentally alter an individual's personality; or threatening to do any of these things to a third party.[4]

---

2. John Barry, Michael Hirsh & Michael Isikoff, *The Roots of Terror*, Newsweek, May 24, 2004.

3. Dept. of Defense News Release, *DoD Provides Details on Interrogation Process,* June 22, 2004, *at* http://www.defenselink.mil/releases/2004/nr20040622-0930.html.

4. Office of Legal Counsel, U.S. Dept. of Justice, *Memorandum for Alberto R. Gonzales, Counsel to the President, Re: Standards of Conduct for Interrogation Under 18 U.S.C. §§2340-2340A*, Aug. 1, 2002 (commonly referred to as the Bybee Memo, for Asst. Atty. General Jay S. Bybee, who signed it), at 1, *available at* http://www.gwu.edu/~nsarchiv/NSAEBB/NSAEBB127/02.08.01.pdf. The "organ failure" passage relies on public health statutes of questionable applicability to the interrogation setting.

The memorandum suggested that a one-time kick to a prisoner's stomach with military boots while forcing him into a kneeling position would not amount to "torture" that would be subject to prosecution. The OLC memorandum even concluded that torture might be justified in some circumstances.[5]

Reacting to what was characterized as "tenacious resistance by some detainees to existing interrogation techniques,"[6] in October 2002 the commander at Guantánamo Bay sought permission to use new interrogation techniques that were more coercive than those authorized in the Army field manual, including the "use of stress positions (like standing), for a maximum of four hours"; isolation for up to 30 days; "deprivation of light and auditory stimuli"; hooding; removal of clothing; "forced grooming (shaving of facial hair, etc.)"; and using "fear of dogs . . . to induce stress."[7] A separate legal opinion by Army Lt. Col. Diane Beaver evaluated a range of even more aggressive techniques — from exposure to cold weather or water to threats of death or severe pain to inducing the "misperception of asphyxiation" and "mild noninjurious physical contact."[8] Lt. Col. Beaver found that these techniques were consistent with existing legal standards if they could "plausibly have been thought necessary . . . to achieve a legitimate governmental objective," and the force was applied "in a good faith effort and not maliciously or sadistically for the very purpose of causing harm."[9]

By December 2002, the media began reporting that so-called "stress and duress" tactics or "high pressure methods" were being used in secret detention centers overseas by Defense Department and CIA interrogators in pursuit of "actionable intelligence." Those methods included forcing detainees to stand or kneel for hours in black hoods or spray-painted goggles, bombarding the detainees with lights 24 hours a day, withholding painkillers from wounded detainees, confining them in tiny rooms or binding them in painful positions, subjecting them to loud noises, and depriving them of sleep.[10] A June 2004 statement from the Department of Defense confirmed that similarly harsh interrogation techniques were approved by Defense Secretary Donald Rumsfeld on December 2, 2002, for use in Guantánamo but were rescinded on January 15, 2003.[11] An August 2004 Army report found that interrogators in Afghanistan employed similar techniques beginning in December 2002.[12]

---

5. The memo took the position that the statutory prohibition on torture cannot be applied to actions taken by the President as Commander in Chief. *Id*. at 33-39.

6. *Final Report of the Independent Panel to Review DoD Detention Operations* 35, Aug. 24, 2004 [hereinafter *Schlesinger Report*], at http://www.dod.gov/news/Aug2004/d20040824finalreport.pdf.

7. Memorandum for Chairman of the Joint Chiefs of Staff from James T. Hill, General, U.S. Army, *Counter-Resistance Techniques*, Oct. 25, 2002, *available at* http://www.gwu.edu/~nsarchiv/ NSAEBB/NSAEBB127/02.10.25.pdf. The techniques were outlined in Diane E. Beaver, Joint Task Force 170, Dept. of Defense, *Legal Brief on Proposed Counter-Resistance Strategies*, Oct. 11, 2002, *available at* http://www.gwu.edu/~nsarchiv/NSAEBB/NSAEBB127/02.10.11.pdf.

8. Beaver, *supra* note 7.

9. *Id*.

10. *See* Dana Priest & Barton Gellman, *U.S. Decries Abuse But Defends Interrogations*, Wash. Post, Dec. 26, 2002, at A1.

11. Dept. of Defense News Release, *DoD Provides Details on Interrogation Process*, June 22, 2004, *available at* http://www.defenselink.mil/releases/release.aspx?releaseid=7487.

12. Maj. Gen. George R. Fay, *AR 15-6 Investigation of the Abu Ghraib Prison and 205th Military Intelligence Brigade* 29, Aug. 25, 2004 [hereinafter *Fay Report*], at http://www.dod.gov/news/Aug2004/d20040825fay.pdf.

By early 2003, the apparent failure to obtain useful information from certain detainees at Guantánamo led Secretary Rumsfeld to charge an "Interrogation Working Group" of senior Defense Department lawyers to develop guidance on parameters for interrogation. In April 2003, the Working Group advised that the President as Commander in Chief could authorize torture despite legal prohibitions. Excerpts from the Working Group's report are set forth *infra* p. 414. Based at least in part on advice in the report, Secretary Rumsfeld approved interrogation techniques that included reversing detainees' sleep patterns, exposing them to heat, cold, loud noise, and bright lights, and extending interrogation sessions to 20 hours or more.[13] In June 2004, however, the Defense Department stated:

> It is the policy and practice of the Department of Defense to treat detainees in the War on Terrorism humanely and, to the extent appropriate and consistent with military necessity, in a manner consistent with the principles of the Geneva Convention.
>
> No procedures approved for use ordered, authorized, permitted, or tolerated torture. Individuals who have abused the trust and confidence placed in them will be held accountable.[14]

After the United States and its allies invaded Iraq in March 2003, there reportedly was widespread confusion there about permissible techniques for interrogating prisoners. The U.S. command authority initially ordered that standard FM 34-52 rules be followed. In August 2003, however, Secretary Rumsfeld sent the military overseer of interrogation at Guantánamo, Major General Geoffrey Miller, to Iraq to "rapidly exploit internees for actionable intelligence."[15] General Miller brought with him the list of techniques approved by Secretary Rumsfeld for Guantánamo, although he noted that the Geneva Conventions were supposed to apply in Iraq. In September, the military commander in Iraq approved a policy on interrogation that included portions of the Guantánamo policy and elements of policies then used by special forces.[16] Central Command disapproved the September policy, however, and in October approved rules that mirrored an outdated version of FM 34-52, permitting interrogators to control "lighting and heating, as well as food, clothing, and shelter given to detainees."[17] The policy on interrogation in Iraq changed again in October, the third amendment in less than 30 days.[18]

In January 2004, following public reports of detainee abuse, Lieutenant General Ricardo S. Sanchez, Commander of Combined Joint Task Force Seven in Iraq, requested an investigation of the operations of the 800th Military

---

13. *See* Jess Bravin, *Pentagon Report Set Framework for Use of Torture*, Wall St. J., June 7, 2004.

14. *DoD Provides Details on Interrogation Process, supra* note 11.

15. General Antonio M. Taguba, *Article 15-6 Investigation of the 800th Military Police Brigade* [hereinafter *Taguba Report*], Jan. 31, 2004, at 7, *available at* http://news.findlaw.com/hdocs/docs/iraq/tagubarpt.html.

16. Subsequent investigators described a migration to Iraq of Guantánamo techniques — such as the use of dogs and forced nudity to intimidate and dehumanize detainees. *See Schlesinger Report, supra* note 6, at 36; *Fay Report, supra* note 12, at 10.

17. *Schlesinger Report, supra* note 6, at 37-38; *see* Dept. of the Army, *Intelligence Interrogation* (FM 34-52), Sept. 28, 1992, at ch. 3.

18. *Fay Report, supra* note 12, at 28.

Police Brigade, the unit in charge of Abu Ghraib prison near Baghdad. Major General Antonio M. Taguba, who was appointed to conduct the investigation, found "numerous incidents of sadistic, blatant, wanton criminal abuses" at the prison "intentionally perpetrated by several members of the military police guard force." The abuses included "punching, slapping, and kicking detainees," a litany of sexual and vulgar insults and attacks, and threats with loaded weapons.[19] In February 2004, the International Committee of the Red Cross (ICRC) issued a report detailing a number of serious human rights abuses by coalition forces in Iraq between March and November 2003.[20] Finally, in May 2004, public attention focused on Abu Ghraib after graphic photos of prisoner abuse were exposed by the media.[21]

A July 2004 Army report found 94 cases of "confirmed or possible abuse" in Iraq.[22] The report determined that the abuses "resulted from the failure of individuals to follow known standards of discipline and Army values and, in some cases, the failure of a few leaders to enforce those standards of discipline."[23] The Army decided not to charge any of those leaders with wrongdoing, however, finding some senior officers "responsible" but not "culpable."[24] By contrast, an investigation led by former Defense Secretary Schlesinger found that the abuses were "more than the failure of a few leaders to enforce proper discipline. There is both institutional and personal responsibility at higher levels."[25]

On March 22, 2006, an Army spokesman reported more than 600 accusations of detainee abuse in Iraq and Afghanistan since October 2001, and disciplinary actions against 251 soldiers. Only 11 soldiers had been convicted on criminal charges, the highest-ranking an Army captain.[26] Four of the five officers investigated by the Army for their role in the Abu Ghraib abuses were cleared; Brig. Gen. Janis Karpinski, Commander of the 800th Military Police Brigade, was demoted to the rank of colonel.[27] No one has been criminally prosecuted in U.S. civilian courts for detainee abuse.

The following materials trace this tangled history. They include portions of the legal memorandum prepared in early 2002 by Justice Department lawyers that purports to spell out legal requirements for interrogation and treatment of al Qaeda and Taliban detainees. Also included is follow-on correspondence from the White House Counsel, the Attorney General, and the Legal Adviser to the Department of State, along with part of an April 2003 memorandum from the

---

19. *Taguba Report, supra* note 15.

20. *Report of the International Committee of the Red Cross (ICRC) on the Treatment by the Coalition Forces of Prisoners of War and Other Protected Persons by the Geneva Conventions in Iraq During Arrest, Internment and Interrogation,* Feb. 2004, *available at* http://www.informationclearinghouse.info/pdf/icrc_iraq.pdf.

21. The Abu Ghraib photos are collected at http://www.salon.com/news/abu_ghraib/2006/03/14/introduction.

22. Inspector General, Dept. of the Army, *Detainees Operation Inspection Report,* July 21, 2004, at foreword, *at* http://www4.army.mil/ocpa/reports/ArmyIGDetaineeAbuse/index.html.

23. *Id.*

24. Josh White & Thomas E. Ricks, *Officers Won't Be Charged in Prison Scandal,* Wash. Post, Aug. 27, 2004, at A17.

25. *Schlesinger Report, supra* note 6, at 5.

26. Eric Schmitt, *Iraq Abuse Trial Is Again Limited to Lower Ranks,* N.Y. Times, Mar. 23, 2006, at A1; Eric Schmitt, *Army Dog Handler Is Convicted in Detainee Abuse at Abu Ghraib,* N.Y. Times, Mar. 22, 2006, at A1.

27. U.S. Army News Release, *Army Releases Findings in Detainee Abuse Investigations,* May 5, 2005, *at* http://www4.army.mil/ocpa/read.php?story_id_key=7293.

Defense Department "Interrogation Working Group" and portions of another April 2003 memorandum from Defense Secretary Rumsfeld expanding the permissible interrogation techniques at Guantánamo. These materials are followed in turn by extensive notes and questions.

## B.  THE LEGAL STANDARDS AND THEIR APPLICATION

### APPLICATION OF TREATIES AND LAWS TO AL QAEDA AND TALIBAN DETAINEES

U.S. Department of Justice, Office of Legal Counsel, January 9, 2002
http://www.gwu.edu/~nsarchiv/NSAEBB/NSAEBB127/02.01.09.pdf

Memorandum for: William J. Haynes II, General Counsel,
                Department of Defense

From: John Yoo, Deputy Asst. Attorney General
      Robert J. Delahunty, Special Counsel

You have asked for our Office's views concerning the effect of international treaties and federal laws on the treatment of individuals detained by the U.S. Armed Forces during the conflict in Afghanistan. In particular, you have asked whether the laws of armed conflict apply to the conditions of detention and the procedures for trial of members of al Qaeda and the Taliban militia. We conclude that these treaties do not protect members of the al Qaeda organization, which as a non-State actor cannot be a party to the international agreements governing war. We further conclude that these treaties do not apply to the Taliban militia. This memorandum expresses no view as to whether the President should decide, as a matter of policy, that the U.S. Armed Forces should adhere to the standards of conduct in those treaties with respect to the treatment of prisoners.

We believe it most useful to structure the analysis of these questions by focusing on the War Crimes Act, 18 U.S.C. §2441 (Supp. III 1997) ("WCA"). The WCA directly incorporates several provisions of international treaties governing the laws of war into the federal criminal code. Part I of this memorandum describes the WCA and the most relevant treaties that it incorporates: the four 1949 Geneva Conventions, which generally regulate the treatment of non-combatants, such as prisoners of war ("POWs"), the injured and sick, and civilians.[1]

Part II examines whether al Qaeda detainees can claim the protections of these agreements. Al Qaeda is merely a violent political movement or

---

1. The four Geneva Conventions for the Protection of Victims of War, dated August 12, 1949, were ratified by the United States on July 14, 1955. These are the Convention for the Amelioration of the Condition of the Wounded and Sick in Armed Forces in the Field, 6 U.S.T. 3115 ("Geneva Convention I"); the Convention for the Amelioration of the Condition of Wounded, Sick and Shipwrecked Members of the Armed Forces at Sea, 6 U.S.T. 3219 ("Geneva Convention II"); the Convention Relative to the Treatment of Prisoners of War, 6 U.S.T. 3517 ("Geneva Convention III"); and the Convention Relative to the Protection of Civilian Persons in Time of War, 6 U.S.T. 3317 ("Geneva Convention IV").

organization and not a nation-state. As a result, it is ineligible to be a signatory to any treaty. Because of the novel nature of this conflict, moreover, we do not believe that al Qaeda would be included in non-international forms of armed conflict to which some provisions of the Geneva Conventions might apply. Therefore, neither the Geneva Conventions nor the WCA regulate[s] the detention of al Qaeda prisoners captured during the Afghanistan conflict.

Part III discusses whether the same treaty provisions, as incorporated through the WCA, apply to the treatment of captured members of the Taliban militia. We believe that the Geneva Conventions do not apply for several reasons. First, the Taliban was not a government and Afghanistan was not — even prior to the beginning of the present conflict — a functioning State during the period in which they engaged in hostilities against the United States and its allies. Afghanistan's status as a failed state is ground alone to find that members of the Taliban militia are not entitled to enemy POW status under the Geneva Conventions. Further, it is clear that the President has the constitutional authority to suspend our treaties with Afghanistan pending the restoration of a legitimate government capable of performing Afghanistan's treaty obligations. Second, it appears from the public evidence that the Taliban militia may have been so intertwined with al Qaeda as to be functionally indistinguishable from it. To the extent that the Taliban militia was more akin to a non-governmental organization that used military force to pursue its religious and political ideology than a functioning government, its members would be on the same legal footing as al Qaeda.

In Part IV, we address the question whether any customary international law of armed conflict might apply to the al Qaeda or Taliban militia members detained during the course of the Afghanistan conflict. We conclude that customary international law, whatever its source and content, does not bind the President, or restrict the actions of the United States military, because it does not constitute federal law recognized under the Supremacy Clause of the Constitution. The President, however, has the constitutional authority as Commander in Chief to interpret and apply the customary or common laws of war in such a way that they would extend to the conduct of members of both al Qaeda and the Taliban, and also to the conduct of the U.S. Armed Forces towards members of those groups taken as prisoners in Afghanistan.

### I.   Background and Overview of the War Crimes Act and the Geneva Conventions

. . . We believe that the WCA provides a useful starting point for our analysis of the application of the Geneva Conventions to the treatment of detainees captured in the Afghanistan theater of operations.[4] Section 2441 of Title 18 renders certain acts punishable as "war crimes." The statute's definition of that term incorporates, by reference, certain treaties or treaty provisions relating to the laws of war, including the Geneva Conventions.

---

4. The rule of lenity requires that the WCA be read so as to ensure that prospective defendants have adequate notice of the nature of the acts that the statute condemns. *See, e.g.,* Castillo v. United States, 530 U.S. 120, 131 (2000). In those cases in which the application of a treaty incorporated by the WCA is unclear, therefore, the rule of lenity requires that the interpretative issue be resolved in the defendant's favor.

## A. Section 2441: An Overview

Section 2441 reads in full as follows:

*War crimes*

(a) Offense. — Whoever, whether inside or outside the United States, commits a war crime, in any of the circumstances described in subsection (b), shall be fined under this title or imprisoned for life or any term of years, or both, and if death results to the victim, shall also be subject to the penalty of death.

(b) Circumstances. — The circumstances referred to in subsection (a) are that the person committing such war crime or the victim of such war crime is a member of the Armed Forces of the United States or a national of the United States. . . .

(c) Definition. — As used in this section the term "war crime" means any conduct —

(1) defined as a grave breach in any of the international conventions signed at Geneva 12 August 1949, or any protocol to such convention to which the United States is a party;

(2) prohibited by Article 23, 25, 27, or 28 of the Annex to the Hague Convention IV, Respecting the Laws and Customs of War on Land, signed 18 October 1907;

(3) which constitutes a violation of common Article 3 of the international conventions signed at Geneva, 12 August 1949, or any protocol to such convention to which the United States is a party and which deals with non-international armed conflict; or

(4) of a person who, in relation to an armed conflict and contrary to the provisions of the Protocol on Prohibitions or Restrictions on the Use of Mines, Booby-Traps and Other Devices as amended at Geneva on 3 May 1996 (Protocol II as amended on 3 May 1996), when the United States is a party to such Protocol, willfully kills or causes serious injury to civilians.

18 U.S.C. §2441.

. . . A House Report states that the original legislation "carries out the international obligations of the United States under the Geneva Conventions of 1949 to provide criminal penalties for certain war crimes." H.R. Rep. No. 104-698 at 1 (1996), *reprinted in* 1996 U.S.C.C.A.N. 2166, 2166. Each of those four conventions includes a clause relating to legislative implementation and to criminal punishment.[5]

---

5. That common clause reads as follows:

The [signatory Nations] undertake to enact any legislation necessary to provide effective penal sanctions for persons committing, or ordering to be committed, any of the grave breaches of the present Convention. . . . Each [signatory nation] shall be under the obligation to search for persons alleged to have committed, or to have ordered to be committed, such grave breaches, and shall bring such persons, regardless of their nationality, before its own courts. . . . It may also, if it prefers, . . . hand such persons over for trial to another [signatory nation], provided such [nation] has made out a *prima facie* case.

Geneva Convention I, art. 49; Geneva Convention II, art. 50; Geneva Convention III, art. 129; Geneva Convention IV, art. 146.

In enacting section 2441, Congress also sought to fill certain perceived gaps in the coverage of federal criminal law. The main gaps were thought to be of two kinds: subject matter jurisdiction and personal jurisdiction. First, Congress found that "[t]here are major gaps in the prosecutability of individuals under federal criminal law for war crimes committed against Americans." H.R. Rep. No. 104-698 at 6, *reprinted in* 1996 U.S.C.C.A.N. at 2171. For example, "the simple killing of a[n American] prisoner of war" was not covered by any existing Federal statute. *Id.* at 5, *reprinted in* 1996 U.S.C.C.A.N. at 2170.[6] Second, Congress found that "[t]he ability to court martial members of our armed services who commit war crimes ends when they leave military service. [Section 2441] would allow for prosecution even after discharge." *Id.* at 7, *reprinted in* 1996 U.S.C.C.A.N. at 2172.[7] Congress considered it important to fill this gap, not only in the interest of the victims of war crimes, but also of the accused. "The Americans prosecuted would have available all the procedural protections of the American justice system. These might be lacking, if the United States extradited the individuals to their victims' home countries for prosecution." *Id.*[8] Accordingly, Section 2441 criminalizes forms of conduct in which a U.S. national or a member of the Armed Forces may be either a victim or a perpetrator.

## B. Grave Breaches of the Geneva Conventions ...

The Geneva Conventions ... structure legal relationships between Nation States, not between Nation States and private, subnational groups or organizations. All four Conventions share the same Article 2, known as "common Article 2." It states:

> In addition to the provisions which shall be implemented in peacetime, the present Convention shall apply to all cases of declared war or of any other armed conflict *which may arise between two or more of the High Contracting Parties*, even if the state of war is not recognized by one of them.
>
> The Convention shall also apply to all cases of partial or total occupation of the territory of a High Contracting Party, even if the said occupation meets with no armed resistance.
>
> Although one of the Powers in conflict may not be a party to the present Convention, the Powers who are parties thereto shall remain bound by it in their mutual relations. They shall furthermore be bound by the Convention in relation to the said Power, if the latter accepts and applies the provisions thereof.

(Emphasis added.)

---

6. In projecting our criminal law extraterritorially in order to protect victims who are United States nationals, Congress was apparently relying on the international law principle of passive personality. . . .

7. In *United States ex rel. Toth v. Quarles*, 350 U.S. 11 (1955), the Supreme Court had held that a former serviceman could not constitutionally be tried before a court martial under the Uniform Code for Military Justice (the "UCMJ") for crimes he was alleged to have committed while in the armed services.

8. The principle of nationality in international law recognizes that (as Congress did here) a State may criminalize acts performed extraterritorially by its own nationals. *See, e.g, Skiriotes v. Florida*, 313 U.S. 69, 73 (1941); *Steele v. Bulova Watch Co.*, 344 U.S. 280, 282 (1952).

As incorporated by §2441(c)(1), the four Geneva Conventions similarly define "grave breaches." Geneva Convention III on POWs defines a grave breach as:

> willful killing, torture or inhuman treatment, including biological experiments, willfully causing great suffering or serious injury to body or health, compelling a prisoner of war to serve in the forces of the hostile Power, or willfully depriving a prisoner of war of the rights of fair and regular trial prescribed in this Convention.

Geneva Convention III, art. 130. . . .

Thus, the WCA does not criminalize all breaches of the Geneva Conventions. Failure to follow some of the regulations regarding the treatment of POWs, such as difficulty in meeting all of the conditions set forth for POW camp conditions, does not constitute a grave breach within the meaning of Geneva Convention III, art. 130. Only by causing great suffering or serious bodily injury to POWs, killing or torturing them, depriving them of access to a fair trial, or forcing them to serve in the Armed Forces, could the United States actually commit a grave breach. Similarly, unintentional, isolated collateral damage on civilian targets would not constitute a grave breach within the meaning of Geneva Convention IV, art. 147. Article 147 requires that for a grave breach to have occurred, destruction of property must have been done "wantonly" and without military justification, while the killing or injury of civilians must have been "wilful."

### D. Common Article 3 of the Geneva Conventions

Section 2441(c)(3) also defines as a war crime conduct that "constitutes a violation of common Article 3" of the Geneva Conventions. Article 3 is a unique provision that governs the conduct of signatories to the Conventions in a particular kind of conflict that is *not* one between High Contracting Parties to the Conventions. Thus, common Article 3 may require the United States, as a High Contracting Party, to follow certain rules even if other parties to the conflict are not parties to the Conventions. On the other hand, Article 3 requires state parties to follow only certain minimum standards of treatment toward prisoners, civilians, or the sick and wounded, rather than the Conventions as a whole.

Common Article 3 reads in relevant part as follows:

> In the case of armed conflict not of an international character occurring in the territory of one of the High Contracting Parties, each Party to the conflict shall be bound to apply, as a minimum, the following provisions:
>
> (1) Persons taking no active part in the hostilities, including members of armed forces who have laid down their arms and those placed *hors de combat* by sickness, wounds, detention, or any other cause, shall in all circumstances, be treated humanely, without any adverse distinction founded on race, color, religion or faith, sex, birth or wealth, or any other similar criteria.

To this end, the following acts are and shall remain prohibited at any time and in any place whatsoever with respect to the above-mentioned persons:

(a) violence to life and person, in particular murder of all kinds, mutilation, cruel treatment and torture;

(b) taking of hostages;

(c) outrages upon personal dignity, in particular humiliating and degrading treatment;

(d) the passing of sentences and the carrying out of executions without previous judgment pronounced by a regularly constituted court, affording all the judicial guarantees which are recognized as indispensable by civilized peoples. . . .

The application of the preceding provisions shall not affect the legal status of the Parties to the conflict.

Common Article 3 complements common Article 2. Article 2 applies to cases of declared war or of any other armed conflict that may arise between two or more of the High Contracting Parties, even if the state of war is not recognized by one of them. Common Article 3, however, covers "armed conflict not of an international character"—a war that does not involve cross-border attacks—that occurs within the territory of one of the High Contracting Parties. There is substantial reason to think that this language refers specifically to a condition of civil war, or a large-scale armed conflict between a State and an armed movement within its own territory.

To begin with, Article 3's text strongly supports the interpretation that it applies to large-scale conflicts between a State and an insurgent group. First, the language at the end of Article 3 states that "[t]he application of the preceding provisions shall not affect the legal status of the Parties to the conflict." This provision was designed to ensure that a Party that observed Article 3 during a civil war would not be understood to have granted the "recognition of the insurgents as an adverse party." Frits Kalshoven, *Constraints on the Waging of War* 59 (1987). Second, Article 3 is in terms limited to "armed conflict . . . occurring *in the territory of one of the High Contracting Parties*" (emphasis added). This limitation makes perfect sense if the Article applies to civil wars, which are fought primarily or solely within the territory of a single state. The limitation makes little sense, however, as applied to a conflict between a State and a transnational terrorist group, which may operate from different territorial bases, some of which might be located in States that are parties to the Conventions and some of which might not be. In such a case, the Conventions would apply to a single armed conflict in some scenes of action but not in others—which seems inexplicable. . . .

Analysis of the background to the adoption of the Geneva Conventions in 1949 confirms our understanding of common Article 3. It appears that the drafters of the Conventions had in mind only the two forms of armed conflict that were regarded as matters of general *international* concern at the time: armed conflict between Nation States (subject to Article 2), and large-scale civil war within a Nation State (subject to Article 3). . . .

### DECISION RE APPLICATION OF THE GENEVA CONVENTION ON PRISONERS OF WAR TO THE CONFLICT WITH AL QAEDA AND THE TALIBAN

January 25, 2002
http://www.gwu.edu/~nsarchiv/NSAEBB/NSAEBB127/02.01.25.pdf

Memorandum for: The President

From: Alberto R. Gonzales [Counsel to the President]

#### Purpose

On January 18, I advised you that the Department of Justice had issued a formal legal opinion concluding that the Geneva Convention III on the Treatment of Prisoners of War (GPW) does not apply to the conflict with al Qaeda. I also advised you that DOJ's opinion concludes that there are reasonable grounds for you to conclude that GPW does not apply with respect to the conflict with the Taliban. I understand that you decided that GPW does not apply and, accordingly, that al Qaeda and Taliban detainees are not prisoners of war under the GPW.

The Secretary of State has requested that you reconsider that decision.[28] Specifically, he has asked that you conclude that GPW does apply to both al Qaeda and the Taliban. I understand, however, that he would agree that al Qaeda and Taliban fighters could be determined not to be prisoners of war (POWs) but only on a case-by-case basis following individual hearings before a military board.

This memorandum outlines the ramifications of your decision and the Secretary's request for reconsideration. . . .

#### Ramifications of Determination that GPW Does Not Apply

The consequences of a decision to adhere to what I understood to be your earlier determination that the GPW does not apply to the Taliban include the following:

#### Positive:

Preserves flexibility:

- As you have said, the war against terrorism is a new kind of war. It is not the traditional clash between nations adhering to the laws of war that formed the backdrop for GPW. The nature of the new war places a high premium on other factors, such as the ability to quickly obtain information from captured terrorists and their sponsors in order to avoid further atrocities against American civilians, and the need to try terrorists for war crimes such as wantonly killing civilians. In my judgment, this new paradigm renders obsolete Geneva's strict limitations on questioning of enemy prisoners and renders quaint some of its provisions requiring that

---

[28. Gonzales was reacting to an earlier Department of State memorandum, the essence of which is contained in the memorandum from State Department Legal Adviser William H. Taft IV, *infra* p. 413.]

captured enemy be afforded such things as commissary privileges, scrip (i.e., advances of monthly pay), athletic uniforms, and scientific instruments.

- Although some of these provisions do not apply to detainees who are not POWs, a determination that GPW does not apply to al Qaeda and the Taliban eliminates any argument regarding the need for case-by-case determinations of POW status. It also holds open options for the future conflicts in which it may be more difficult to determine whether an enemy force as a whole meets the standard for POW status.
- By concluding that GPW does not apply to al Qaeda and the Taliban, we avoid foreclosing options for the future, particularly against nonstate actors.

Substantially reduces the threat of domestic criminal prosecution under the War Crimes Act (18 U.S.C. 2441)

- . . . A determination that the GPW is not applicable to the Taliban would mean that Section 2441 would not apply to actions taken with respect to the Taliban.
- Adhering to your determination that GPW does not apply would guard effectively against misconstruction or misapplication of Section 2441 for several reasons.
  - First, some of the language of the GPW is undefined (it prohibits, for example, "outrages upon personal dignity" and "inhuman treatment"), and it is difficult to predict with confidence what actions might be deemed to constitute violations of the relevant provisions of GPW.
  - Second, it is difficult to predict the needs and circumstances that could arise in the course of the war on terrorism.
  - Third, it is difficult to predict the motives of prosecutors and independent counsels who may in the future decide to pursue unwarranted charges based on Section 2441. Your determination would create a reasonable basis in law that Section 2441 does not apply, which would provide a solid defense to any future prosecution.

### Negative:

On the other hand, the following arguments would support reconsideration and reversal of your decision that the GPW does not apply to either al Qaeda or the Taliban:

- Since the Geneva Conventions were concluded in 1949, the United States has never denied their applicability to either U.S. or opposing forces engaged in armed conflict, despite several opportunities to do so. During the last Bush Administration, the United States stated that it "has a policy of applying the Geneva Conventions of 1949 whenever armed hostilities occur with regular foreign armed forces, even if arguments could be made that the threshold standards for the applicability of the Conventions . . . are not met."

- The United States could not invoke the GPW if enemy forces threatened to mistreat or mistreated U.S. or coalition forces captured during operations in Afghanistan, or if they denied Red Cross access or other POW privileges.
- The War Crimes Act could not be used against the enemy, although other criminal statutes and the customary law of war would still be available.
- Our position would likely provoke widespread condemnation among our allies and in some domestic quarters, even if we make clear that we will comply with the core humanitarian principles of the treaty as a matter of policy.
- Concluding that the Geneva Convention does not apply may encourage other countries to look for technical "loopholes" in future conflicts to conclude that they are not bound by GPW either.
- Other countries may be less inclined to turn over terrorists or provide legal assistance to us if we do not recognize a legal obligation to comply with the GPW.
- A determination that GPW does not apply to al Qaeda and the Taliban could undermine U.S. military culture which emphasizes maintaining the highest standards of conduct in combat, and could introduce an element of uncertainty in the status of adversaries.

### Response to Arguments for Applying GPW to the Al Qaeda and the Taliban

On balance, I believe that the arguments for reconsideration and reversal are unpersuasive.

- The argument that the U.S. has never determined that GPW did not apply is incorrect. In at least one case (Panama in 1989) the U.S. determined that GPW did not apply even though it determined for policy reasons to adhere to the convention. More importantly, as noted above, this is a new type of warfare — one not contemplated in 1949 when the GPW was framed — and requires a new approach in our actions towards captured terrorists. Indeed, as the statement quoted from the administration of President George Bush makes clear, the U.S. will apply GPW "whenever hostilities occur *with regular foreign armed forces.*" By its terms, therefore, the policy does not apply to a conflict with terrorists, or with irregular forces, like the Taliban, who are armed militants that oppressed and terrorized the people of Afghanistan.
- In response to the argument that we should decide to apply GPW to the Taliban in order to encourage other countries to treat captured U.S. military personnel in accordance with the GPW, it should be noted that your policy of providing humane treatment to enemy detainees gives us the credibility to insist on like treatment for our soldiers. Moreover, even if GPW is not applicable, we can still bring war crimes charges against anyone who mistreats U.S. personnel. Finally, I note that our adversaries in several recent conflicts have not been deterred by GPW in their mistreatment of captured U.S. personnel, and terrorists will not follow GPW rules in any event.

- The statement that other nations would criticize the U.S. because we have determined that GPW does not apply is undoubtedly true. It is even possible that some nations would point to that determination as a basis for failing to cooperate with us on specific matters in the war against terrorism. On the other hand, some international and domestic criticism is already likely to flow from your previous decision not to treat the detainees as POWs. And we can facilitate cooperation with other nations by reassuring them that we fully support GPW where it is applicable and by acknowledging that in this conflict the U.S. continues to respect other recognized standards.
- In the treatment of detainees, the U.S. will continue to be constrained by (i) its commitment to treat the detainees humanely and, to the extent appropriate and consistent with military necessity, in a manner consistent with the principles of GPW, (ii) its applicable treaty obligations, (iii) minimum standards of treatment universally recognized by the nations of the world, and (iv) applicable military regulations regarding the treatment of detainees.
- Similarly, the argument based on military culture fails to recognize that our military remain bound to apply the principles of GPW because that is what you have directed them to do.

## COMMENTS ON YOUR PAPER ON THE GENEVA CONVENTION

February 2, 2002
http://www.fas.org/sgp/othergov/taft.pdf

Memorandum to: Counsel to the President

From: William H. Taft, IV [Legal Adviser, Department of State]

The paper should make clear that the issue for decision by the President is whether the Geneva Conventions apply to the conflict in Afghanistan in which U.S. armed forces are engaged. The President should know that a decision that the Conventions do apply is consistent with the plain language of the Conventions and the unvaried practice of the United States in introducing its forces into conflict over fifty years. It is consistent with the advice of DOS lawyers and, as far as is known, the position of every other party to the Conventions. It is consistent with UN Security Council Resolution 1193 affirming that "All parties to the conflict [in Afghanistan] are bound to comply with their obligations under international humanitarian law and in particular the Geneva Conventions. . . ." It is not inconsistent with the DOJ opinion that the Conventions generally do not apply to our world-wide effort to combat terrorism and to bring al Qaeda members to justice.

From a policy standpoint, a decision that the Conventions apply provides the best legal basis for treating the al Qaeda and Taliban detainees in the way we intend to treat them. It demonstrates that the United States bases its conduct not just on its policy preference but on its international legal obligations. Agreement by all lawyers that the War Crimes Act does not apply to our conduct means that the risk of prosecution under that statute is negligible. Any small benefit from reducing it further will be purchased at the expense of the men and women in our armed forces that we send into combat. A decision that the Conventions do not apply to the conflict in Afghanistan in which our armed forces are engaged deprives our troops there of any claim to the protection of the Convention in the event they are captured and weakens the protections afforded by the Conventions to our troops in future conflicts.

The structure of the paper suggesting a distinction between our conflict with al Qaeda and our conflict with the Taliban does not conform to the structure of the Conventions. The Conventions call for a decision whether they apply to the conflict in Afghanistan. If they do, their provisions are applicable to all persons involved in that conflict — al Qaeda, Taliban, Northern Alliance, U.S. troops, civilians, etc. If the Conventions do not apply to the conflict, no one involved in it will enjoy the benefit of their protections as a matter of law. . . .

## Working Group Report On Detainee Interrogations in the Global War on Terrorism[29]

April 4, 2003
http://www.defenselink.mil/news/Jun2004/d20040622doc8.pdf

### II. International Law . . .

### B. The 1994 Convention Against Torture

(U)[30] The United States' primary obligation concerning torture and related practices derives from the Convention Against Torture and Other Cruel, Inhuman, or Degrading Treatment or Punishment (commonly referred to as "the Torture Convention"). The United States ratified the Convention in 1994, but did so with a variety of Reservations and Understandings.

(U) Article 1 of the Convention defines the term "torture" for purpose of the treaty.[3] The United States conditioned its ratification of the treaty on an understanding that:

> . . . in order to constitute torture, an act must be specifically intended to inflict severe physical or mental pain or suffering and that mental pain or suffering refers to prolonged mental harm caused by or resulting from (1) the intentional infliction or threatened infliction of severe physical pain or suffering; (2) the

---

[29. The Working Group, consisting of Defense Department officials, was tasked to prepare this report in a January 15, 2003, order from Secretary Donald Rumsfeld.]

[30. The expression "(U)" means that the adjacent material is unclassified.]

3. (U) Article 1 provides: "For the purposes of this Convention, the term 'torture' means any act by which severe pain or suffering, whether physical or mental, is intentionally inflicted on a person for such purposes as obtaining from him or a third person information or a confession, punishing him for an act he or a third person has committed or is suspected of having committed, or intimidating or coercing him or a third person, or for any reason based on discrimination of any kind, when such pain or suffering is inflicted by or at the instigation of or with the consent or acquiescence of a public official acting in an official capacity. It does not include pain or suffering arising only from, inherent in or incidental to lawful sanctions."

administration or application, or threatened administration or application, of mind altering substances or other procedures calculated to disrupt profoundly the senses or the personality; (3) the threat of imminent death; or (4) the threat that another person will imminently be subjected to death, severe physical pain or suffering, or the administration or application of mind altering substances or other procedures calculated to disrupt profoundly the senses or personality.[4]

(U) Article 2 of the Convention requires the Parties to "take effective legislative, administrative, judicial and other measures to prevent acts of torture in any territory under its jurisdiction." The U.S. Government believed existing state and federal criminal law was adequate to fulfill this obligation, and did not enact implementing legislation. Article 2 also provides that acts of torture cannot be justified on the grounds of exigent circumstances, such as a state of war or public emergency, or on orders from a superior officer or public authority.[5] The United States did not have an Understanding or Reservation relating to this provision (however the U.S. issued a Declaration stating that Article 2 is not self-executing).

(U) Article 3 of the Convention contains an obligation not to expel, return, or extradite a person to another state where there are "substantial grounds" for believing that the person would be in danger of being subjected to torture. The U.S. understanding relating to this article is that it only applies "if it is more likely than not" that the person would be tortured.

(U) Under Article 5, the Parties are obligated to establish jurisdiction over acts of torture when committed in any territory under its jurisdiction or on board a ship or aircraft registered in that state, or by its nationals wherever committed. The U.S. has criminal jurisdiction over territories under U.S. jurisdiction and onboard U.S. registered ships and aircraft by virtue of the special maritime and territorial jurisdiction of the United States (the "SMTJ") established under 18 U.S.C. §7. Acts that would constitute torture are likely to be criminal acts under the SMTJ. . . . Accordingly, the U.S. has satisfied its obligation to establish jurisdiction over such acts in territories under U.S. jurisdiction or on board a U.S. registered ship or aircraft. However, the additional requirement of Article 5 concerning jurisdiction over acts of torture by U.S. nationals "wherever committed" needed legislative implementation. Chapter 113C of Title 18 of the U.S. Code provides federal criminal jurisdiction over an extraterritorial act or attempted act of torture if the offender is a U.S. national. The statute defines "torture" consistent with the U.S. Understanding on Article 1 of the Torture Convention.

(U) The United States is obligated under Article 10 of the Convention to ensure that law enforcement and military personnel involved in interrogations are educated and informed regarding the prohibition against torture. Under Article 11, systematic reviews of interrogation rules, methods, and practices are also required.

---

4. 18 U.S.C. §2340 tracks this language. For a further discussion of the U.S. understandings and reservations, see the Initial Report of the U.S. to the U.N. Committee Against Torture, dated October 15, 1999.

5. (U) See discussion in the Domestic Law section on the necessity defense.

(U) In addition to torture, the Convention prohibits cruel, inhuman and degrading treatment or punishment within territories under a Party's jurisdiction (Art 16). Primarily because the meaning of the term "cruel, inhuman and degrading treatment or punishment" was vague and ambiguous, the United States imposed a Reservation on this article to the effect that it is bound only to the extent that such treatment or punishment means the cruel, unusual and inhuman treatment or punishment prohibited by the 5th, 8th, and 14th Amendments to the U.S. Constitution. . . .

(U) An additional treaty to which the United States is a party is the International Covenant on Civil and Political Rights, ratified by the United States in 1992. Article 7 of this treaty provides that "No one shall be subjected to torture or to cruel, inhuman or degrading treatment or punishment." The United States' ratification of the Covenant was subject to a Reservation that "the United States considers itself bound by Article 7 only to the extent that cruel, inhuman, or degrading treatment or punishments means the cruel and unusual treatment or punishment prohibited by the Fifth, Eighth, and/or Fourteenth Amendments to the Constitution of the United States." Under this treaty, a "Human Rights Committee" may, with the consent of the Party in question, consider allegations that such Party is not fulfilling its obligations under the Covenant. The United States has maintained consistently that the Covenant does not apply outside the United States or its special maritime and territorial jurisdiction, and that it does not apply to operations of the military during an international armed conflict. . . .

### III. Domestic Law

## A. Federal Criminal Law

### 1. Torture Statute

(U) 18 U.S.C. §2340 defines as torture any "*act committed by a person acting under the color of law specifically intended to inflict severe physical or mental pain. . . .*" The intent required is the intent to inflict severe physical or mental pain. 18 U.S.C. §2340A requires that the offense occur "outside the United States." Jurisdiction over the offense extends to any national of the United States or any alleged offender present in the United States, and could, therefore, reach military members, civilian employees of the United States, or contractor employees.[8] The "United States" is defined to include all areas under the jurisdiction of the United States, including the special maritime and territorial jurisdiction (SMTJ) of the United States. SMTJ is a statutory creation[9] that extends the criminal jurisdiction of the United States for designated crimes to defined areas.[10] The effect is to grant federal court criminal jurisdiction for the specifically identified crimes. . . .

---

8. (U) Section 2340A provides, "*Whoever outside* the United States commits or attempts to commit torture shall be fined or imprisoned. . . ." (emphasis added).

9. (U) 18 USC §7, "Special maritime and territorial jurisdiction of the United States" includes any lands under the exclusive or concurrent jurisdiction of the United States.

10. (U) Several paragraphs of 18 USC §7 are relevant to the issue at hand. Paragraph 7(3) provides: [SMTJ includes:] "Any lands reserved or acquired for the use of the United States, and under the exclusive or concurrent jurisdiction thereof, or any place. . . ." Paragraph 7(7) provides:

(U) By its terms, the plain language of new subsection 9 includes Guantanamo Bay Naval Station (GTMO) within the definition of the SMTJ, and accordingly makes GTMO within the United States for purposes of §2340. As such, the Torture Statute does not apply to the conduct of U.S. personnel at GTMO. Prior to passage of the Patriot Act in 2001, GTMO was still considered within the SMTJ as manifested by (i) the prosecution of civilian dependents and employees living in GTMO in Federal District Courts based on SMTJ jurisdiction, and (ii) a Department of Justice opinion[11] that effect. . . .

(U) Although Section 2340 does not apply to interrogations at GTMO, it could apply to U.S. operations outside U.S. jurisdiction, depending on the facts and circumstances of each case involved. The following analysis is relevant to such activities.

(U) To convict a defendant of torture, the prosecution must establish that: (1) the torture occurred outside the United States; (2) the defendant acted under color of law; (3) the victim was within the defendant's custody or physical control; (4) the defendant specifically intended to cause severe physical or mental pain or suffering; and (5) that the act inflicted severe physical or mental pain or suffering. *See also* S. Exec. Rep. No. 101-30, at 6 (1990). . . .

### 3. *Legal doctrines under the Federal Criminal Law that could render specific conduct, otherwise criminal, not unlawful* . . .

#### a. *Commander-in-Chief authority*

(U) As the Supreme Court has recognized, and as we will explain further below, the President enjoys complete discretion in the exercise of his Commander-in-Chief authority including in conducting operations against hostile forces. Because both "[t]he executive power and the command of the military and naval forces [are] vested in the President," the Supreme Court has unanimously stated that it is *the President alone* who is constitutionally invested with the *entire charge of hostile operations.*" *Hamilton v. Dillin*, 88 U.S. (21 Wall.) 73, 87 (1874) (emphasis added).

(U) In light of the President's complete authority over the conduct of war, without a clear statement otherwise, criminal statutes are not read as infringing on the President's ultimate authority in these areas. The Supreme Court has established a canon of statutory construction that statutes are to be construed in a manner that avoids constitutional difficulties so long as a reasonable alternative construction is available. *See, e.g., Edward J. DeBartolo Corp. v. Florida Gulf Coast Bldg. & Constr. Trades Council*, 485 U.S. 568, 575 (1988)

---

[SMTJ includes:] "Any place outside the jurisdiction of any nation to an offense by or against a national of the United States. Similarly, paragraphs 7(1) and 7(5) extend SMTJ jurisdiction to, "the high seas, any other waters within the admiralty and maritime jurisdiction of the United States and out of the jurisdiction of any particular state, and any vessel belonging in whole or in part to the United States . . ." and to "any aircraft belonging in whole or in part to the United States . . . while such aircraft is in flight over the high seas, or over any other waters within the admiralty and maritime jurisdiction of the United States and out of the jurisdiction of any particular State."

11. (U) 6 Op. OLC 236 (1982). The issue was the status of GTMO for purposes of a statute banning slot machines on "any land where the United States government exercises exclusive or concurrent jurisdiction."

(citing *NLRB v. Catholic Bishop of Chicago*, 440 U.S. 490, 499-501, 504 (1979)) ("[W]here an otherwise acceptable construction of a statute would raise serious constitutional problems, [courts] will construe [a] statute to avoid such problems unless such construction is plainly contrary to the intent of Congress."). This canon of construction applies especially where an act of Congress could be read to encroach upon powers constitutionally committed to a coordinate branch of government. . . .

(U) In the area of foreign affairs, and war powers in particular, the avoidance canon has special force. *See, e.g., Dept of Navy v. Egan*, 484 U.S. 518, 530 (1988) ("unless Congress specifically has provided otherwise, courts traditionally have been reluctant to intrude upon the authority of the Executive in military and national security affairs."); *Japan Whaling Ass'n v. American Cetacean Socy*, 478 U.S. 221, 232-33 (1986) (construing federal statutes to avoid curtailment of traditional presidential prerogatives in foreign affairs). It should not be lightly assumed that Congress has acted to interfere with the President's constitutionally superior position as Chief Executive and Commander-in-Chief in the area of military operations. *See Egan*, 484 U.S. at 529 (quoting *Haig v. Agee*, 1453 U.S. 280, 293-94 (1981)[)]. *See also Agee*, 453 U.S. at 291 (deference to Executive Branch is "especially" appropriate "in the area of national security").

(U) In order to respect the President's inherent constitutional authority to manage a military campaign, 18 U.S.C. §2340A (the prohibition against torture) as well as any other potentially applicable statute must be construed as inapplicable to interrogations undertaken pursuant to his Commander-in-Chief authority. Congress lacks authority under Article I to set the terms and conditions under which the President may exercise his authority as Commander-in-Chief to control the conduct of operations during a war. The President's power to detain and interrogate enemy combatants arises out of his constitutional authority as Commander-in-Chief. A construction of Section 2340A that applied the provision to regulate the President's authority as Commander-in-Chief to determine the interrogation and treatment of enemy combatants would raise serious constitutional questions. Congress may no more regulate the President's ability to detain and interrogate enemy combatants than it may regulate his ability to direct troop movements on the battlefield. Accordingly, we would construe Section 2340A to avoid this constitutional difficulty and conclude that it does not apply to the President's detention and interrogation of enemy combatants pursuant to his Commander-in-Chief authority. . . .

(U) One of the core functions of the Commander in Chief is that of capturing, detaining, and interrogating members of the enemy. It is well settled that the President may seize and detain enemy combatants, at least for the duration of the conflict, and the laws of war make clear that prisoners may be interrogated for information concerning the enemy, its strength, and its plans. Numerous Presidents have ordered the capture, detention, and questioning of enemy combatants during virtually every major conflict in the Nation's history, including recent conflicts in Korea, Vietnam, and the Persian Gulf. Recognizing this authority, Congress has never attempted to restrict or interfere with the President's authority on this score.

(U) Any effort by Congress to regulate the interrogation of unlawful combatants would violate the Constitution's sole vesting of the Commander-in-Chief authority in the President. There can be little doubt that intelligence operations, such as the detention and interrogation of enemy combatants and leaders, are both necessary and proper for the effective conduct of a military campaign. Indeed, such operations may be of more importance in a war with an international terrorist organization than one with the conventional armed forces of a nation-state, due to the former's emphasis on secret operations and surprise attacks against civilians. It may be the case that only successful interrogations can provide the information necessary to prevent the success of covert terrorist attacks upon the United States and its citizens. . . .

### b. Necessity

(U) The defense of necessity could be raised, under the current circumstances, to an allegation of a violation of a criminal statute. Often referred to as the "choice of evils" defense, necessity has been defined as follows:

> Conduct that the actor believes to be necessary to avoid a harm or evil to himself or to another is justifiable, provided that:
>
> (a) the harm or evil sought to be avoided by such conduct is greater than that sought to be prevented by the law defining the offense charged; and
>
> (b) neither the Code nor other law defining the offense provides exceptions or defenses dealing with the specific situation involved; and
>
> (c) a legislative purpose to exclude the justification claimed does not otherwise plainly appear.

Model Penal Code §3.02. *See also* Wayne R. LaFave & Austin W. Scott, 1 Substantive Criminal Law §5.4 at 627 (1986 & 2002 supp.) ("LaFave & Scott"). Although there is no federal statute that generally establishes necessity or other justifications as defenses to federal criminal laws, the Supreme Court has recognized the defense. *See United States v. Bailey*, 444 U.S. 394, 410 (1980) (relying on LaFave & Scott and Model Penal Code definitions of necessity defense). . . .

(U) Legal authorities identify an important exception to the necessity defense. The defense is available "only in situations wherein the legislature has not itself, in its criminal statute, made a determination of values." [LaFave & Scott] at 629. Thus, if Congress explicitly has made clear that violation of a statute cannot be outweighed by the harm avoided, courts cannot recognize the necessity defense. LaFave and Israel provide as an example an abortion statute that made clear that abortions even to save the life of the mother would still be a crime; in such cases the necessity defense would be unavailable. *Id.* at 630. Here, however, Congress has not explicitly made a determination of values vis-à-vis torture. In fact, Congress explicitly removed efforts to remove torture from the weighing of values permitted by the necessity defense.[21]

### c. Self-defense

(U) Even if a court were to find that necessity did not justify the violation of a criminal statute, a defendant could still appropriately raise a claim of self-defense. The right to self-defense, even when it involves deadly force, is deeply embedded in our law, both as to individuals and as to the nation as a whole. . . . Self-defense is a common-law defense to federal criminal law offenses, and nothing in the text, structure or history of Section 2340A precludes its application to a charge of torture. In the absence of any textual provision to the contrary, we assume self-defense can be an appropriate defense to an allegation of torture. . . .

(U) There can be little doubt that the nation's right to self-defense has been triggered under our law. The Constitution announces that one of its purposes is "to provide for the common defense." U.S. Const., Preamble. Article I, §8 declares that Congress is to exercise its powers to "provide for the common defense." *See also* 2 Pub. Papers of Ronald Reagan 920, 921 (1988-89) (right to self-defense recognized by Article 51 of the U.N. Charter). The President has particular responsibility and power to take steps to defend the nation and its people. *In re Neagle*, 135 U.S. at 64. *See also* U.S. Const. art. IV, §4 ("The United States shall . . . protect [each of the States] against Invasion"). As Commander-in-Chief and Chief Executive, he may use the Armed Forces to protect the nation and its people. *See, e.g., United States v. Verdugo-Urquidez*, 494 U.S. 259, 273 (1990). And he may employ secret agents to aid in his work as Commander-in-Chief. *Totten v. United States*, 92 U.S. 105, 106 (1876). As the Supreme Court observed in *The Prize Cases*, 67 U.S. (2 Black) 635 (1862), in response to an armed attack on the United States "the President is not only authorized but bound to resist force by force . . . without waiting for any special legislative authority." *Id.* at 668. The September 11 events were a direct attack on the United States, and as we have explained above, the President has authorized the use of military force with the support of Congress.

(U) As DOJ has made clear in opinions involving the war on al Qaida, the nation's right to self-defense has been triggered by the events of September 11. If a government defendant were to harm an enemy combatant during an

---

21. In the CAT [Convention Against Torture], torture is defined as the intentional infliction of severe pain or suffering "for such purposes as obtaining from him or a third person information or a confession." CAT art 1.1. One could argue that such a definition represented an attempt to indicate that the good of obtaining information — no matter what the circumstances — could not justify an act of torture. In other words, necessity would not be a defense. In enacting Section 2340, however, Congress removed the purpose element in the definition of torture, evidencing an intention to remove any fixing of values by statute. By leaving Section 2340 silent as to the harm done by torture in comparison to other harms, Congress allowed the necessity defense to apply when appropriate.

Further, the CAT contains an additional provision that "no exceptional circumstances whatsoever, whether a state of war or a threat of war, internal political instability or any other public emergency, may be invoked as a justification of torture," CAT art. 2.2. Aware of this provision of the treaty and of the definition of the necessity defense that allows the legislature to provide *for* an exception to the defense, see Model Penal Code §3.02(b), Congress did not incorporate CAT article 2.2 into Section 2-4. Given that Congress omitted CAT's effort to bar a necessity or wartime defense, Section 2340 could be read as permitting the defense.

interrogation in a manner that might arguably violate criminal prohibition, he would be doing so in order to prevent further attacks on the United States by the al Qaida terrorist network. In that case, DOJ believes that he could argue that the executive branch's constitutional authority to protect the nation from attack justified his actions. This national and international version of the right to self-defense could supplement and bolster the government defendant's individual right. . . .

## B. Federal Civil Statutes

### 1. 28 U.S.C. §1350

(U) 28 U.S.C. §1350 extends the jurisdiction of the U.S. District Courts to *"any civil action by an alien for a tort only, committed in violation of the law of nations or a treaty of the United States."*[33] Section 1350 is a vehicle by which victims of torture and other human rights violations by their native government and its agents have sought judicial remedy for the wrongs they've suffered. However, all the decided cases we have found involve foreign nationals suing in U.S. District Courts for conduct by foreign actors/governments.[34] The District Court for the District of Columbia has determined that section 1350 actions, by the GTMO detainees, against the United States or its agents acting within the scope of employment fail. This is because (1) the United States has not waived sovereign immunity to such suits like those brought by the detainees, and (2) the *Eisentrager* doctrine barring habeas access also precludes other potential avenues of jurisdiction.[35] This of course leaves interrogators vulnerable in their individual capacity for conduct a court might find to constitute torture. Assuming a court would take jurisdiction over the matter and grant standing to the detainee,[36] it is possible that this statute would provide an avenue of relief for actions of the United States or its agents found to violate customary international law. . . .

### 2. Torture Victims Protection Act (TVPA)

(U) In 1992, President Bush signed into law the Torture Victims Protection Act of 1991.[37] Appended to the U.S. Code as a note to section 1350, the TVPA specifically creates a cause of action for individuals (or their successors) who have been subjected to torture or extra-judicial killing by "an individual who, under actual or apparent authority, or color of law, *of any foreign nation* — (1) subjects an individual to torture shall, in a civil action, be liable for damages to that individual; or (2) subjects an individual to extra-judicial killing shall, in a

---

33. (U) 28 U.S.C. §1350, the Alien Tort Claim Act (ATCA).

34. (U) See, for example, *Abebe-Jira v. Negewo*, No. 93-9133, United States Court of Appeals, Eleventh Circuit, Jan. 10, 1996. In this case the 11th Circuit concluded, "the Alien Tort Claims Act establishes a federal forum where courts may fashion domestic common law remedies to give effect to violations of customary international law."

35. (U) *Al Odah v. United States* (D.D.C., 2002).

36. (U) *Filartiga v. Pena-Irala*, 630 F.2d 876 (2nd Cir. 1980) 885, note 18, "conduct of the type alleged here [torture] would be actionable under 42 U.S.C. §1983, or undoubtedly the Constitution, if performed by a government official."

37. Pub. L. No. 102-256, 106 Stat. 73, 28 U.S.C. §1350 (note).

civil action, be liable for damages. . . ." (emphasis added).[38] Thus, the TVPA does not apply to the conduct of U.S. agents acting under the color of law. . . .

## COUNTER-RESISTANCE TECHNIQUES IN THE WAR ON TERRORISM

April 16, 2003
http://www.defenselink.mil/news/Jun2004/d20040622doc9.pdf

Memorandum for the Commander, US Southern Command

From: Donald Rumsfeld, Secretary of Defense

(U) I have considered the report of the Working Group that I directed be established on January 15, 2003.

(U) I approve the use of specified counter-resistance techniques, subject to the following:

(U) a.   The techniques I authorize are those lettered A-X, at Tab A.

(U) b.   These techniques must be used with all the safeguards described at Tab B.

(U) c.   Use of these techniques is limited to interrogations of unlawful combatants held at Guantanamo Bay, Cuba.

(U) d.   Prior to the use of these techniques, the Chairman of the Working Group on Detainee Interrogations in the Global War on Terrorism must brief you and your staff.

(U) I reiterate that US Armed Forces shall continue to treat detainees humanely and, to the extent appropriate and consistent with military necessity, in a manner consistent with the principles of the Geneva Conventions. In addition, if you intend to use techniques B, I, O, or X, you must specifically determine that military necessity requires its use and notify me in advance.

(U) If, in your view, you require additional interrogation techniques for a particular detainee, you should provide me, via the Chairman of the Joint Chiefs of Staff, a written request describing the proposed technique, recommended safeguards, and the rationale for applying it with an identified detainee.

(U) Nothing in this memorandum in any way restricts your existing authority to maintain good order and discipline among detainees.

---

38. (U) The definition of torture used in PL 102-256 is: "any act, directed against an individual in the offender's custody or physical control, by which severe pain or suffering (other than pain or suffering arising only from or inherent in, or incidental to lawful sanctions) whether physical or mental, is intentionally inflicted on that individual for such purposes as obtaining from that individual or a third person information or a confession, punishing that individual for an act that individual or a third person has committed or is suspected of having committed, intimidating or coercing that individual or a third person, or for any reason based on discrimination of any kind." This is similar, but broader, than the definition in the Torture Statute. The definition of mental pain and suffering is the same as in the Torture Statute.

# TAB A
## INTERROGATION TECHNIQUES

(U) The use of techniques A-X is subject to the general safeguards as provided below as well as specific implementation guidelines to be provided by the appropriate authority. Specific implementation guidance with respect to techniques A-Q is provided in Army Field Manual 34-52. Further implementation guidance with respect to techniques R-X will need to be developed by the appropriate authority.

(U) Of the techniques set forth below, the policy aspects of certain techniques should be considered to the extent those policy aspects reflect the views of other major U.S. partner nations. Where applicable, the description of the technique is annotated to include a summary of the policy issues that should be considered before application of the technique.

A. (U) Direct: Asking straightforward questions.

B. (U) Incentive/Removal of Incentive: Providing a reward or removing a privilege, above and beyond those that are required by the Geneva Convention, from detainees. (Caution: Other nations that believe that detainees are entitled to POW protections may consider that provision and retention of religious items (e.g., the Koran) are protected under international law (see, Geneva III, Article 34). Although the provisions of the Geneva Convention are not applicable to the interrogation of unlawful combatants, consideration should be given to these views prior to the application of the technique.)

C. (U) Emotional Love: Playing on the love a detainee has for an individual or group.

D. (U) Emotional Hate: Playing on the hatred a detainee has for an individual or group.

E. (U) Fear Up Harsh: Significantly increasing the fear level in a detainee.

F. (U) Fear Up Mild: Moderately increasing the fear level in a detainee.

G. (U) Reduced Fear: Reducing the fear level in a detainee.

H. (U) Pride and Ego Up: Boosting the ego of a detainee.

I. (U) Pride and Ego Down: Attacking or insulting the ego of a detainee, not beyond the limits that would apply to a POW. (Caution: Article 17 of the Geneva III provides, "Prisoners of war who refuse to answer may not be threatened, insulted, or exposed to any unpleasant or disadvantageous treatment of any kind." Other nations that believe that detainees are entitled to POW protections may consider this technique inconsistent with the provisions of Geneva. Although the provisions of Geneva are not applicable to the interrogation of unlawful combatants, consideration should be given to these views prior to application of the technique.)

J. (U) Futility: Invoking the feeling of futility of a detainee.

K. (U) We Know All: Convincing the detainee that the interrogator knows the answer to questions he asks the detainee.

L. (U) Establish Your Identity: Convincing the detainee that the interrogator has mistaken the detainee for someone else.

M. (U) Repetition Approach: Continuously repeating the same question to the detainee within interrogation periods of normal duration.

N. (U) File and Dossier: Convincing the detainee that the interrogator has a damning and inaccurate file, which must be fixed.

O. (U) Mutt and Jeff: A team consisting of a friendly and harsh interrogator. The harsh interrogator might employ the Pride and Ego Down technique. (Caution: Other nations that believe that POW protections apply to detainees may view this technique as inconsistent with the Geneva III, Article 13 which provides that POWs must be protected against acts of intimidation. Although the provisions of Geneva are not applicable to the interrogation of unlawful combatants, consideration should be given to these views prior to application of the technique.)

P. (U) Rapid Fire: Questioning in rapid succession without allowing detainee to answer.

Q. (U) Silence: Staring at the detainee to encourage discomfort.

R. (U) Change of Scenery Up: Removing the detainee from the standard interrogation setting (generally to a location more pleasant, but no worse).

S. (U) Change of Scenery Down: Removing the detainee from the standard interrogation setting and placing him in a setting that may be less comfortable; would not constitute a substantial change in environmental quality.

T. (U) Dietary Manipulation: Changing the diet of a detainee; no intended deprivation of food or water; no adverse medical or cultural effect and without intent to deprive subject of food or water, e.g., hot rations to MREs.

U. (U) Environmental Manipulation: Altering the environment to create moderate discomfort (e.g., adjusting temperature or introducing an unpleasant smell). Conditions would not be such that they would injure the detainee. Detainee would be accompanied by interrogator at all times. (Caution: Based on court cases in other countries, some nations may view application of this technique in certain circumstances to be inhumane. Consideration of these views should be given to use of this technique.)

V. (U) Sleep Adjustment: Adjusting the sleeping times of the detainee (e.g., reversing sleep cycles from night to day.) This technique is NOT sleep deprivation.

W. (U) False Flag: Convincing the detainee that individuals from a country other than the United States are interrogating him.

X. (U) Isolation: Isolating the detainee from other detainees while still complying with basic standards of treatment. (Caution: The use of isolation as an interrogation technique requires detailed implementation instructions, including specific guidelines regarding the length of isolation, medical and psychological review, and approval for extensions of the length of isolation by the appropriate level in the chain of command. This technique is not known to have been generally used for interrogation purposes for longer than 30 days. Those nations that believe detainees are subject to POW protections may view use of this technique as inconsistent with the requirements of Geneva III, Article 13 which provides that POWs must be protected against acts of intimidation; Article 14 which provides that POWs are entitled to respect for their person; Article 34 which prohibits coercion and Article 126 which ensures access and basic standards of treatment. Although the provisions of Geneva are not applicable to the interrogation of unlawful combatants, consideration should be given to these views prior to application of the technique.)

**TAB B**
**GENERAL SAFEGUARDS**

(U) Application of these interrogation techniques is subject to the following general safeguards: (i) limited to use only at strategic interrogation facilities; (ii) there is a good basis to believe that the detainee possesses critical intelligence; (iii) the detainee is medically and operationally evaluated as suitable (considering all techniques to be used in combination); (iv) interrogators are specifically trained for the technique(s); (v) a specific interrogation plan (including reasonable safeguards, limits on duration, intervals between applications, termination criteria and the presence or availability of qualified medical personnel) has been developed; (vi) there is appropriate supervision; and (vii) there is appropriate specified senior approval for use with any specific detainee (after considering the foregoing and receiving legal advice). . . .

## NOTES AND QUESTIONS

### a.  Torture in General

1. *Detainee Investigations.* Several collections of documents relating to U.S. interrogation of its detainees may be found online. Among the most extensive are New York Times, *A Guide to the Memos on Torture* (n.d.), *at* http://www.nytimes.com/ref/international/24MEMO-GUIDE.html; National Security Archive, *Interrogation Documents: Debating U.S. Policy and Methods* (updated July 13, 2004), *at* http://www.gwu.edu/~nsarchiv/NSAEBB/NSAEBB127; and American Civil Liberties Union, *Government Documents on Torture* (n.d.), *at* http://action.aclu.org/torturefoia/links.html. The Department of Defense Web site also provides links to DOD reports, independent panel and inspector general reports, briefing transcripts, and news releases and articles, *at* http://www.defenselink.mil/news/detainee_investigations.html. Many of the key documents are collected in Mark Danner, *Torture and Truth: America, Abu Ghraib, and the War on Terror* (2004); and *The Torture Papers: the Road to Abu Ghraib* (Karen J. Greenberg & Joshua L. Dratel eds., 2005).

A February 2006 U.N. report on the Guantánamo Bay detentions, compiled by U.N. envoys who interviewed former detainees, their families, and their lawyers, along with U.S. officials, concluded that U.S. treatment of detainees there violated the detainees' rights to physical and mental health and, in some cases, constituted torture. United Nations Commission on Human Rights, *Situation of Detainees at Guantanamo Bay*, Feb. 15, 2006, *available at* http://www.ohchr.org/english/bodies/chr/docs/62chr/E.CN.4.2006.120_.pdf. Similar conclusions were reached in Center for Constitutional Rights, *Report on Torture and Cruel, Inhuman, and Degrading Treatment of Prisoners at Guantanamo Bay, Cuba*, July 2006, *available at* http://www.ccr-ny.org/v2/reports/docs/Torture_Report_Final_version.pdf. The United States replied to the U.N. report with a factual and legal defense, *Reply of the Government of the United States of America to the Report of the Five UNCHR Special Rapporteurs on Detainees in Guantanamo Bay, Cuba*, Mar. 10, 2006, *available at* http://www.asil.org/pdfs/ilib0603212.pdf.

2. *Definitions.* What constitutes "torture"? Not surprisingly, torture is forbidden by a number of written treaties and international conventions, by customary international law, and by U.S. statutory and constitutional law. There is, however, no universally accepted definition of "torture." Torture may be physical or psychological, and a variety of interrogation techniques may be forbidden as torture.

What are the elements of the Torture Convention's definition of "torture"? See *supra* p. 414. Of the U.S. understanding upon ratification? See *supra* p. 414. Do any of the techniques in Defense Secretary Rumsfeld's April 16, 2003, memo on Guantánamo Bay exceed the limits set out in either? See *supra* pp. 422-425. Which techniques? Would the same methods be lawful in Iraq? At some undisclosed offshore location?

The Torture Statute, 18 U.S.C. §§2340-2340B, is supposed to implement the Torture Convention. *See* Working Group Report, *supra* p. 414 (noting that the statute tracks the U.S. reservation to Article 1 the Torture Convention). Recall that in August 2002, the Justice Department's Office of Legal Counsel (OLC) offered a very narrow definition of "torture," see *supra* p. 400, and argued that the President could authorize torture. It also indicated that interrogation activities "may be cruel, inhuman, or degrading, but still not produce pain and suffering of the requisite intensity" to violate §2340. Bybee Memo, *supra* p. 400 n.4, at 1. The memorandum also asserted that a specific intent to torture is required to violate the torture statute. *Id.* at 4. How would you rate this definition of the key terms against those set out in the Torture Convention and the U.S. understanding? According to some commentators, the interpretations of relevant law by Defense Department and Justice Department lawyers amounted to endorsements of what has been referred to as "torture lite." *See* Seth F. Kreimer, *"Torture Light," "Full Bodied" Torture, and the Insulation of Legal Conscience*, 1 J. Natl. Security L. & Poly. 187 (2005); Duncan Campbell, *U.S. Interrogators Turn to "Torture Lite,"* The Guardian, Jan. 25, 2003, at 17.

Two months after the public disclosure of abuses at Abu Ghraib, the August 2002 memorandum was withdrawn by OLC head Jack Goldsmith, and a new opinion superseding it was delivered to the new Deputy Attorney General for the OLC on December 30, 2004. Memorandum for James B. Comey, Deputy Atty. General, from Daniel Levin, Acting Asst. Atty.

General, *Legal Standards Applicable Under 18 U.S.C. 2340-2340A*, Dec. 30, 2004, *at* http://www.usdoj.gov/olc/18usc23402340a2.htm. The new memorandum questioned "the appropriateness and relevance of the non-statutory discussion . . . and various aspects of the statutory analysis" in the earlier memo; namely, the assertion that torture required organ failure, impaired bodily function, or death. *Id*. at 1-2. However, the new memorandum did not disagree with any substantive conclusions offered by the 2002 memorandum. *Id*. at 2 n.8. The 2004 memorandum continued to maintain that it was unlikely that a person who "acted in good faith, and only after reasonable investigation establishing that his conduct would not inflict severe physical or mental pain or suffering," would possess the specific intent required to violate the torture statute. *Id*. at 17. Do you agree? *See* Manfred Nowak, *What Practices Constitute Torture?: US and UN Standards*, 28 Hum. Rts. Q. 809 (2006).

Would a universal definition of the key terms be a good idea? Would it matter? *See* Oren Gross, *Are Torture Warrants Warranted? Pragmatic Absolutism and Official Disobedience*, 88 Minn. L. Rev. 101, 109 (2004) ("preventive interrogational torture is far too complex to be addressed by definitional juggling"); Jeremy Waldron, *Torture and Positive Law: Jurisprudence for the White House*, 105 Colum. L. Rev. 1681, 1698 (2005) (A precise definition of "torture" is advisable, because "if the terms are . . . indeterminate, the person to whom the prohibition is addressed may not know exactly what is required of him".). *Compare* John T. Parry, *"Just For Fun": Understanding Torture and Understanding Abu Ghraib*, 1 J. Natl. Security L. & Poly. 253, 262-270 (2005) (asserting that the U.S. and other nations play a "definitional game" where governments parse language and deny responsibility for conduct that goes too far).

Do you think the legal ambiguities described here contributed to abuses at Abu Ghraib or elsewhere?

3. *Assigning Responsibility.* Guidance for interrogations at Abu Ghraib prison came from three different sources at different times — from Army field manuals, from personnel who had worked earlier in Afghanistan, and from Guantánamo. Craig Gordon, *High-Pressure Tactics: Critics Say Bush Policies — Post 9/11 — Gave Interrogators Leeway to Push Beyond Normal Limits*, Newsday, May 23, 2004, at A5. General Taguba found that operating procedures and copies of the Geneva Conventions were not distributed to the guards handling the prisoners. To complicate matters, senior military commanders called for interrogators to isolate and manipulate detainees who might have "significant intelligence value." R. Jeffrey Smith, *Memo Gave Intelligence Bigger Role: Increased Pressure Sought on Prisoners*, Wash. Post, May 21, 2004, at A17.

The overall detention and interrogation picture that has emerged from official statements and documents reveals "a trail of fitful ad hoc policymaking" where interrogation techniques were authorized, then rescinded or modified, at times leading to decisions made in the field or at the Pentagon on a case-by-case basis. Dana Priest & Bradley Graham, *U.S. Struggled Over How Far to Push Tactics*, Wash. Post, June 24, 2004, at A1. Unlike CIA requests for expanded interrogation authority that were reviewed by the

Department of Justice and the National Security Council, Defense Department interrogation policy decisions were not subjected to outside review. *Id.*

A March 2004 classified report by the CIA Inspector General, however, concluded that some of the interrogation techniques approved for CIA use by the Department of Justice in 2002 may violate the Convention Against Torture prohibition on "cruel, inhuman, or degrading" treatment. Douglas Jehl, *Report Warned on CIA's Tactics in Interrogation*, N.Y. Times, Nov. 9, 2005, at A1. A March 2006 news story described the existence of a temporary, top-secret detention site at Camp Nana, near Baghdad, that since early 2004 included a "Black Room" where placards posted by soldiers stated, "No blood, no foul." Eric Schmitt & Carolyn Marshall, *In Secret Unit's "Black Room," a Grim Portrait of U.S. Abuse*, N.Y. Times, Mar. 19, 2006, at A1. Detainee abuse attributed to the Special Operations unit at Camp Nana reflected "confusion over and, in some cases, disregard for" interrogation rules and standards for treatment of detainees. *Id.*

The Army announced in April 2005 that it was preparing to issue a new field manual to replace *Intelligence Interrogation* (FM 34-52), Sept. 28, 1992. The new manual was finally released more than a year later. Headquarters, Dept. of the Army, *Human Intelligence Collector Operations*, FM 2-22.3 (FM 34-52), Sept. 2006, *available at* http://www.fas.org/irp/doddir/army/fm2-22-3. pdf. The new manual states that "no person in the custody or under the control of DOD, regardless of nationality or physical location, shall be subject to torture or cruel, inhuman, or degrading treatment or punishment, in accordance with and as defined by U.S. law." *Id.* at 5-20. The manual also states that all intelligence interrogations must be conducted in accordance with applicable law and policy, including "relevant international law." *Id.* The manual notes that torture "is a poor technique that yields unreliable results, may damage subsequent collection efforts, and can induce the source to say what he thinks the HUMINT collector wants to hear." *Id.* at 5-21. In addition, it specifically prohibits the harsh techniques that came to light in the Abu Ghraib scandal, including waterboarding, forced nakedness or sexual acts, hooding, and the use of working dogs. *Id.* Does the new manual provide adequate legal guidance to all U.S. personnel?

In June 2005 the Defense Department promoted or nominated for promotion the former deputy commander of U.S. forces in Iraq and the senior military lawyer for the U.S. command in Baghdad. Both of them were involved in overseeing or advising detention and interrogation operations during the Abu Ghraib scandal. The top intelligence officer in Iraq at that time was promoted earlier in the year. Eric Schmitt, *Army Moves to Advance 2 Linked to Abu Ghraib*, N.Y. Times, June 29, 2005, at A20. The *Schlesinger Report, supra* p. 401 n.6, found those officers to be among those responsible for the abuses at Abu Ghraib, and the Fay Report, *supra* p. 401 n.12, faulted the commanders for issuing and revising the interrogation rules three times in 30 days, and their legal staff for giving bad legal advice — not warning that practices permitted at Guantánamo and in Afghanistan might not be lawful in Iraq. Nevertheless, the Army Inspector General cleared the commanders of any wrongdoing. Inspector General, Dept. of the Army, *Detainee*

*Operations Inspection*, July 21, 2004, *at* http://www4.army.mil/ocpa/reports/ ArmyIGDetaineeAbuse/index.html.

Thus far, with one exception, only low-level interrogators and handlers have been disciplined for interrogation abuses in Afghanistan and at Guantánamo. In April 2006, Lt. Col. Steven L. Jordan, former head of interrogation operations at Abu Ghraib, was charged with a series of UCMJ violations, including failure to train and supervise subordinates regarding interrogation policy, and failure to obtain permission from superior officers to use certain interrogation techniques, including the use of dogs. *See* Mark Benjamin, *First Officer Is Charged in Abu Ghraib Scandal*, Salon, Apr. 29, 2006. The Army Charge Sheet may be viewed at http://balkin. blogspot.com/ucmj.Jordan.chargesheet.pdf. A review by Air Force Lt. Gen. Randall M. Schmidt of three years' practice and over 24,000 interrogations at Guantánamo led to a recommendation of reprimand for Army Maj. Gen. Geoffrey C. Miller, commander of the Guantánamo facility in 2002 and 2003, for failing to oversee the interrogation of a high-value detainee who was subjected to abusive treatment. *Army Regulation 15-6: Final Report, Investigation into FBI Allegations of Detainee Abuse at Guantanamo Bay, Cuba Detention Facility*, Apr. 1, 2005, amended June 9, 2005. Nevertheless, the Army's Inspector General decided that Miller had not violated the law or Defense Department policy. *See* David S. Cloud, *Guantanamo Reprimand Was Sought, An Aide Says*, N.Y. Times, July 13, 2005, at A16. General Miller retired from the Army in July 2006 and received the Distinguished Service Medal at his retirement ceremony. *See* Thom Shanker, *General in Abu Ghraib Case Retires After Forced Delay*, N.Y. Times, Aug. 1, 2006, at A13. Miller had planned to retire sooner, but his initial refusal to testify at the court-martial trial of a dog handler at Abu Ghraib prompted some members of the Senate Armed Services Committee to ask Army officials to postpone his retirement until he appeared before the committee. Miller then testified at a second court-martial for another dog handler, where he stated that he never suggested that dogs be used to intimidate prisoners in Iraq. *Id.*

One suggested reason for the failure to hold senior officials accountable is the lack of an independent prosecutor inside the military, equivalent to a district attorney, who would have command authority to investigate up the chain of command. Eric Schmitt, *Iraq Abuse Trial Is Again Limited to Lower Ranks*, N.Y. Times, March 23, 2006, A1.

At a news conference called in response to the Abu Ghraib publicity in June 2004, White House Counsel Alberto Gonzales denied that "the president . . . authorized ordered or directed" violations of "the standards of the torture conventions or the torture statute." *Transcript of Press Briefing by Alberto Gonzales*, June 22, 2004. What legal wiggle room does the Gonzales statement leave for the President? Does it mean that President Bush was not responsible for the reported abuses?

Who do you think is responsible for the abuses at Abu Ghraib and Camp Nana? If you are unsure of the answer, how do you think it will be possible to find out?

4. ***Who Decides What Interrogation Conduct Is Unlawful?*** The official policy of the United States is to condemn and prohibit torture. *See generally* U.S. Dept. of State, *Initial Report of the United States of America to the UN Committee Against Torture,* Oct. 15, 1999, *available at* http://www.state.gov/www/global/human_rights/torture_intro.html ("Torture is prohibited by law throughout the United States. It is categorically denounced as a matter of policy and as a tool of state authority."); *Second Periodic Report of the United States of America to the Committee Against Torture,* May 6, 2005, *available at* http://www.state.gov/g/drl/rls/45738.htm ("United States is unequivocally opposed to the use and practice of torture. . . . No circumstance whatsoever . . . may be invoked as a justification for or defense to committing torture."). Who decides how to translate the policy into enforceable rules?

5. ***Hiding Torture?*** Article 49 of the Fourth Geneva Convention prohibits "the deportations of protected persons from occupied territory." Such a deportation or transfer or unlawful confinement of a protected person is a "grave breach" of the convention. Art. 147. On March 19, 2004, the OLC drafted a memo indicating that the CIA could transfer detainees out of Iraq for interrogation, despite the Geneva Convention, by construing the ban not to apply to illegal aliens who have no legal right to remain in Iraq. The memo concluded that the temporary relocation of persons not charged with a crime to face interrogation at another location outside Iraq is not akin to the wartime practices the Geneva Convention provision was designed to forbid. Draft Memorandum from Jack Goldsmith, Asst. Attorney General, to Alberto R. Gonzales, Counsel to the President, *Permissibility of Relocating Certain "Protected Persons" From Occupied Iraq,* Mar. 19, 2004, *reprinted in The Torture Papers, supra* p. 425. The CIA then transported as many as a dozen detainees from Iraq to other countries between March and October of 2004. *See* Dana Priest, *Memo Lets CIA Take Detainees Out of Iraq,* Wash. Post, Oct. 24, 2004, at A1. (The practice of "extraordinary rendition" is addressed in Chapter 14.)

In June or July 2003, Hiwa Abdul Rahman Rashul, a suspected member of the Iraqi Al-Ansar terrorist group who was nicknamed "Triple X" by CIA and military officials, was captured by Kurdish fighters. He was turned over to the CIA, which rendered him to Afghanistan for interrogation, then brought him back to Iraq. Then-DCI George Tenet asked Defense Secretary Rumsfeld not to give Rashul a prisoner number and to hide him from the Red Cross. Rashul was then lost in the Iraqi prison system for seven months. When asked about the legal basis for hiding Rashul, Rumsfeld replied, "We know from our knowledge that [Tenet] has authority to do this." *Id.*; Eric Schmitt & Thom Shanker, *Rumsfeld Issued an Order to Hide Detainee in Iraq,* N.Y. Times, June 17, 2004, at A1.

What could be wrong with hiding a detainee in this fashion? How would you respond to the OLC's legal justification for rendering "ghost detainees"?

6. ***The Moral Dimension.*** What *should* the U.S. position on torture be? One perspective emphasizes a range of practical problems that seriously limit the value of information obtained through torture. *See* Jeannine Bell, *One Thousand Shades of Gray: The Effectiveness of Torture,* Ind.

U. Sch. of Law-Bloomington Res. Paper No. 37, Oct. 2005, *available at* http://ssrn.com/abstract=820467. Still, there is an undoubted and morally complex tension between the need to obtain information that could save many lives through coercive interrogation of a suspect and the condoning of torture.

Is it *ever* justifiable to torture a detainee? Assume that authorities have in custody someone whom they are certain has placed an especially destructive explosive device somewhere in a large shopping mall. The explosive may go off at any time, and there may not be enough time to evacuate the mall. If the bomb detonates, thousands will die. The detainee is the only person with knowledge of the bomb, and he will not talk. Should the interrogators torture the detainee in hopes of learning the location of the bomb before it is too late? *Compare* Alan Dershowitz, *Why Terrorism Works* 142-149 (2002) (torture techniques may be morally and legally justified in some circumstances), *with* Assn. of the Bar of the City of New York, Comm. on Intl. Human Rights, Comm. on Military Affairs and Justice, *Human Rights Standards Applicable to the United States' Interrogation of Detainees*, Apr. 30, 2004, at 8-9, *available at* http://www.abcny.org/pdf/HUMANRIGHTS.pdf ("Condoning torture under any circumstances erodes one of the most basic principles of international law and human rights and contradicts our values as a democratic state"), *and* David Luban, *Liberalism, Torture, and the Ticking Bomb*, 91 Va. L. Rev. 1425 (2005) (ticking-bomb scenarios may be used to rationalize institutionalized practices and procedures of torture). *See also* Kim Lane Scheppele, *Hypothetical Torture in the "War on Terrorism,"* 1 J. Natl. Security L. & Poly. 285 (2005) (taking a "hard line" against torture on sociological grounds). The Convention Against Torture, to which the United States is a party, says torture can never be justified. See *supra* p. 414.

A 2006 study sponsored by U.S. intelligence agencies concluded that there is little systematic knowledge of what interrogation methods best protect national security. *See* Intelligence Science Board, *Educing Information — Interrogation: Science and Art: Foundations for the Future*, Dec. 2006, *available at* http://www.fas.org/irp/dni/educing.pdf.

7. ***Torture Warrants?*** Professor Dershowitz would recognize a qualified prohibition on torture. He suggests a form of judicial "torture warrant" before permitting torture of suspected terrorists in interrogations. Dershowitz, *supra,* at 148-149, 158-163. What might be the criteria for issuing such warrants? Should a judge, for example, try to balance the credibility or gravity of a threat against the suffering or injury to be inflicted on the recalcitrant detainee? Can you articulate a process that would be helpful to the court in doing that?

Another approach to making exceptions to a ban on torture has been recommended by Professors Philip Heymann and Juliette Kayyem. They advocate an "emergency exception" to a ban on torture, based on a written finding by the President of "an urgent and extraordinary need" reported "within a reasonable period" to appropriate congressional committees, stating the reason to believe that the information is known by the person to be interrogated, that it "concerns a specific plan that threatens U.S. lives," and that there are "no reasonable alternatives to save the lives in question." Philip B. Heymann & Juliette N. Kayyem, *Long-Term Strategy Project for*

*Preserving Security and Democratic Freedoms in the War on Terrorism* 25-26 (2004). Is this "findings" approach preferable in the ticking-bomb case to a torture warrant?

Professor Jeremy Waldron would not allow the authorization of torture even in the ticking-bomb scenario. Waldron argues that a line on what techniques are permitted has to be drawn "somewhere, and I say we should draw it where the law requires it, and where the human rights tradition has insisted that it should be drawn." Waldron, *supra*, at 1715.

Alternatively, should we expect government officials confronted with the ticking-bomb case to engage in a form of official disobedience, hoping for ratification of the disobedient conduct after the fact? *See* Gross, *supra* p. 427, at 107. Could Congress or the President make lawful through ratification torture that was undertaken in disobedience of the law?

Which of these approaches is best? If you think torture might be permissible in some circumstances, can you think of other methods for keeping its "qualified" use in check?

8. ***Defenses of Torture Offered by the Government***
   a. ***Necessity.*** Bush administration lawyers argued that self-defense and necessity may legitimate torture. Does the presence of an arguable defense to an act of torture nullify the requirement that the torture be legally authorized? *See* William C. Banks & Peter Raven-Hansen, *Targeted Killing and Assassination: The U.S. Legal Framework*, 37 U. Richmond L. Rev. 667, 668 (2003) (basic rule of law requires positive legal authority for government actions). Would a necessity defense be available even where Congress clearly proscribed the conduct so defended? *See* Wayne R. LaFave & Austin W. Scott, I *Substantive Criminal Law* §5.4 (1986), at 629. Might a defense be available to someone charged with carrying out even a specious legal authorization of torture? *See* Public Committee Against Torture in Israel v. State of Israel, H.C. 5100/94, 53(4) P.D. 817 (1999).
   b. ***Self-Defense.*** The criminal law doctrine of self-defense permits the use of force to prevent harm to another person. Does that doctrine apply in this setting to exculpate otherwise unlawful torture or inhumane treatment by an interrogator of a prisoner? Is an individual claim of self-defense portable to the executive branch in the war on terrorism? How would you rebut the argument made by the Working Group, *supra* p. 414, that the Commander in Chief's defensive war powers legitimate what might otherwise be proscribed as torture? Unlike the Bybee Memo, *supra* p. 400 n.4, the December 30, 2004, OLC memo, *supra* p. 426, made no mention of the constitutional authority of the President to disregard statutory or treaty obligations regarding torture. Of what significance is the revision?
   c. ***Article II as a Trump Card?*** The January 2002 OLC memo, *supra* p. 404, at 36, 39, asserted that "Congress can no more interfere with the President's conduct of the interrogation of enemy combatants than it can dictate strategic or tactical decisions on the battlefield." In what particular settings is the Article II argument most persuasive? *See*

Michael D. Ramsey, *Torturing Executive Power*, 93 Geo. L.J. 1213 (2005). Compare detention and on-the-spot interrogations of those seized on the battlefield during combat with long-term detentions in remote locations away from the battle. Al Qaeda reportedly continues to plan and carry out terrorist acts that threaten national security. Does that ongoing threat give the Commander in Chief a tactical choice to capture and interrogate al Qaeda operatives using torture?

If you agree that there is a constitutional limit to the authority of Congress to regulate interrogation, can you construe the laws reviewed in this section to avoid the potential constitutional problem? Did the Working Group Report persuasively apply the avoidance canon? Can Congress prohibit at least some particular interrogatory techniques?

9. *Lawyers and Their Role.* Many of the legal opinions in the Justice Department and Defense Department memoranda excerpted above are highly controversial. Some commentators argue that the memoranda were designed primarily to protect potentially culpable officials from prosecution for interrogation abuses. See *Lawyers' Statement on Bush Administration's Torture Memos*, Aug. 4, 2004, *at* http://www.afj.org/spotlight/0804statement. pdf (letter signed by about 130 prominent lawyers); *Letter Sent to the United States Congress Regarding Recent Human Rights Issues in Iraq*, June 16, 2004, *at* http://www.lawprofessorblogs.com/taxprof/linkdocs/ harvardimpeach.pdf#search=iraqletter.com (letter signed by more than 500 university professors). Others, including Defense Department investigators of detention and interrogation practices, found that the confusion and ambiguity fostered by these memoranda may have contributed to the abusive practices, or to a "permissive climate in which abuses were more likely." Richard B. Bilder & Detlev F. Vagts, *Speaking Law to Power: Lawyers and Torture*, 98 Am. J. Intl. L. 689, 691 (2004) (citing, e.g., John Barry, Michael Hirsh & Michael Isikoff, *The Roots of Torture*, Newsweek, May 24, 2004, at 28). What are the legal and ethical responsibilities of government lawyers in the war on terror? *See* Bilder & Vagts, *supra*, at 691-695; *Symposium: Lawyers' Roles and the War on Terror*, 1 J. Natl. Security L. & Poly. 357 (2005).

The *Schlesinger Report, supra* p. 401 n.6, found that in the development of Defense Department detention and interrogation policies in 2002 and 2003 "the legal resources of the Services' Judge Advocate General (JAG) and General Counsels were not utilized to their full potential. Had the Secretary of Defense had a wider range of legal opinions and more robust debate regarding detainee policies and operations," the frequent policy changes between December 2002 and April 2003 might have been avoided. *Id.* at 8. Why would the Secretary not have sought more advice from JAG lawyers and General Counsels? What would have been gained by their perspectives?

At a Senate hearing in July 2005, the JAGs for the Army, Air Force, and Marines stated that they complained about the Justice Department's definition of "torture" and how it would be applied in the Working Group process early in 2003. Their objections apparently were overruled by the Defense

Department General Counsel's office. Neil A. Lewis, *Military's Opposition to Harsh Interrogation Is Outlined*, N.Y. Times, July 28, 2005, at A21; Josh White, *Military Lawyers Fought Policy on Interrogations, JAGs Recount Objections to Definition of Torture*, Wash. Post, July 15, 2005, at A1. Why do you think the Secretary failed to heed the advice that was offered?

Apparently, on March 17, 2005, the General Counsel of the Defense Department wrote a memo that rescinded the Working Group Report and concluded that the report "does not reflect now-settled executive branch views of the relevant law. . . . [T]he [report] is to be considered a historical document with no standing in policy, practice, or law." White, *supra*. What do you suppose happened between April 2003 and March 2005 to change the executive branch's views of the relevant law? In what specific ways is the new understanding different from the old one?

### b. (Incorporated?) International Law on Torture

1. ***International Law as Law of the United States.*** Charging a grand jury in a 1793 national security case, our first Chief Justice asserted that "the laws of the United States admit of being classed under the three heads of descriptions. 1st. All treaties made under the authority of the United States. 2d. The laws of nations. 3dly. The constitution, and statutes of the United States." Trial of Gideon Henfield (C.C.D. Pa. 1793) (charge to the grand jury by Jay, C.J.), *reprinted in* Wharton, *State Trials of the United States During the Administrations of Washington and Adams* 49, 52-53 (1849). John Jay thus implied that some international agreements and customary international laws are part of our domestic law. But what part? What is their effect in United States law?

2. ***Treaties as Law of the United States.*** The Supremacy Clause seems to supply one answer to the question of the domestic effect of international law by providing that "all Treaties made, or which shall be made, under the Authority of the United States, shall be the supreme Law of the Land. . . ." U.S. Const. art. VI. But this only restates Jay's assertion about treaties. It does not explain the effect of a treaty that requires domestic legislation for its execution or that is inconsistent with a statute, let alone the effect of executive agreements or customary international law. Treaties are, of course, subject to the Bill of Rights and to other constitutional limits and requirements. Even so, "failure of the United States to carry out an obligation on the ground of its unconstitutionality will not relieve the United States of responsibility under international law." *Restatement (Third) of Foreign Relations Law of the United States* §111 cmt. a (1987). Conversely, an international treaty has no status as law in the United States if the treaty is invalid or has been terminated or suspended in United States law. *See id*, cmt. b; Goldwater v. Carter, 617 F.2d 697 (D.C. Cir. 1979), *vacated and remanded*, 444 U.S. 996 (1979).

   a. ***Self-Executing and Non-Self-Executing Treaties.*** The *Head Money Cases*, 112 U.S. 580, 598-599 (1884), supports the proposition that a treaty is the legal equivalent of a statute "whenever its provisions prescribe a rule by which the rights of the private citizen or subject may be determined." Chief Justice John Marshall asserted the same proposition more fully:

> Our constitution declares a treaty to be the law of the land. It is, consequently, to be regarded in courts of justice as equivalent to an act of the legislature, whenever it operates of itself, without the aid of any legislative provision. But when the terms of the stipulation import a contract, when either of the parties engages to perform a particular act, the treaty addresses itself to the political, not the judicial department; and the legislature must execute the contract before it can become the rule for the court. [Foster v. Neilson, 27 U.S. (2 Pet.) 253, 314 (1829).]

Whether a treaty or a provision thereof is "self-executing" is therefore significant not only for deciding its enforceability in U.S. courts, but also for deciding whether it authorizes the President to act alone, without further legislation. *See generally* Carlos M. Vazquez, *The Four Doctrines of Self-Executing Treaties*, 89 Am. J. Intl. L. 695 (1995). How can you tell if a treaty is self-executing? *See Restatement, supra*, §111(4) (asserting that an international agreement of the United States is non-self-executing if the treaty so indicates by its terms, if the Senate in consenting to a treaty or the Congress by resolution requires implementing legislation, or "if implementing legislation is constitutionally required").

b. *Last-in-Time Rule.* If a particular international agreement is the legal equivalent of a statute, it is logical, as a matter of domestic law, that it can be modified or superseded by statute. *Lex posterior* — the last-in-time — controls. *Restatement, supra*, §115. *See, e.g.*, Whitney v. Robertson, 124 U.S. 190, 193-194 (1888); *The Chinese Exclusion Case*, 130 U.S. 581, 600 (1889). *But see* Jordan J. Paust, *Rediscovering the Relationship Between Congressional Power and International Law: Exceptions to the Last in Time Rule and the Primacy of Custom*, 28 Va. J. Intl. L. 392 (1988) (noting case law exceptions to last-in-time rule). Does this mean that Congress can modify or repeal an international agreement? What is the international effect of a subsequent statutory repealer?

How should courts construe U.S. legislation in light of prior international agreements? Chief Justice Marshall stated that "an Act of Congress ought never to be construed to violate the law of nations if any other possible construction remains. . . ." Murray v. Schooner Charming Betsy, 6 U.S. (2 Cranch) 64, 118 (1804). *See Restatement, supra*, §114.

3. *Customary International Law as Law of the United States.* In The Paquete Habana, 175 U.S. 677, 700 (1900), the Court declared broadly that "international law is part of our law." The Court went on to indicate that "where there is no treaty, and no controlling executive or legislative act or judicial decision, resort must be had to the customs and usages of nations." *Id*. These statements had become virtual hornbook law, as reflected in

*Restatement* §111, cmt. d ("customary international law, while not mentioned explicitly in the Supremacy Clause, [is] also federal law. . . . Customary international law is considered to be like common law in the United States, but it is federal law."), before recent academic challenges to this conventional wisdom.

Notwithstanding the holding of The Paquete Habana, some scholars have complained that customary international law is so malleable that it is no more than "a matter of taste, . . . [and] [a]s such, . . . cannot function as a legitimate source of substantive legal norms." J. Patrick Kelly, *The Twilight of Customary International Law*, 40 Va. J. Intl. L. 449, 451 (2000). *See also* Jack L. Goldsmith & Eric A. Posner, *A Theory of Customary International Law*, 66 U. Chi. L. Rev. 1113 (1999).

How is customary international law made? *See Restatement, supra*, §102(2) ("Customary international law results from a general and consistent practice of states followed by them from a sense of legal obligation."). *See also* Jordan Paust, *International Law as Law of the United States* 1-5 (1995); Anthony D'Amato, *The Concept of Custom in International Law* (1971).

4. *Jus Cogens.* Some customary international norms are based neither on explicit agreements, such as treaties, nor on the implied consent of individual states to be bound. They are referred to as *jus cogens*, and they carry more weight than others. What is the difference between ordinary customary international law and *jus cogens*? In Siderman de Blake v. Republic of Argentina, 965 F.2d 699, 715 (9th Cir. 1992), the court explained it as follows:

> Customary international law, like international law defined by treaties and other international agreements, rests on the consent of states. A state that persistently objects to a norm of customary international law . . . is not bound. . . .
>
> In contrast, *jus cogens* "embraces customary laws considered binding on all nations" and is "derived from values taken to be fundamental by the international community, rather than from the fortuitous or self-interested choices of nations". . . . [T]he fundamental and universal norms constituting *jus cogens* transcend such consent, as exemplified by the theories underlying the judgments of the Nuremberg tribunals following World War II. [Citation omitted.]

The substantive content of customary international law in the area of torture is embodied in the Convention Against Torture and the International Covenant on Civil and Political Rights, described below, among other instruments. The torture prohibition is also part of *jus cogens* and is so recognized by U.S. courts. *See Restatement (Third) of Foreign Relations Law of the United States* §702 (1986). It remains unclear, however, whether the prohibition against cruel, inhuman, or degrading treatment is also part of *jus cogens*.

5. *The U.N. Convention Against Torture and Other Cruel, Inhuman, or Degrading Treatment or Punishment (CAT).* The instruments of ratification submitted by the United States for the CAT include a declaration

making it clear that it regards CAT Articles 1 through 16 as not self-executing. *See* Office of the High Commissioner for Human Rights, *Declarations and Reservations* (as of 23 April 2004) ("United States of America" at ¶III(1)), *at* http://www.unhchr.ch/html/menu2/6/cat/treaties/convention-reserv.htm. What is the legal significance of such a declaration?

The prohibitions against torture in the CAT, qualified by the various U.S. reservations, understandings, and declarations attached to it, have been implanted in domestic law in a range of settings, and its provisions underlie the Alien Tort Claims Act and Torture Victim Protection Act, both addressed *infra*. What are the important elements of "torture" as defined in the CAT? Does it apply to military and civilian interrogators? To private persons?

Recall that in ratifying the CAT the United States specified that "torture" as mental pain or suffering refers to

> prolonged mental harm caused by or resulting from: (1) the intentional infliction or threatened infliction of severe physical pain or suffering; (2) the administration or application, or threatened administration or application, of mind-altering substances or other procedures calculated to disrupt profoundly the senses or the personality; (3) the threat of imminent death; or (4) the threat that another person will imminently be subjected to death, severe physical pain or suffering, or the administration or application of mind-altering substances or other procedures calculated to disrupt profoundly the senses or personality. [*Id.* at ¶II(1)(a).]

What is the practical significance of this understanding? Consistent with this understanding, what interrogation techniques are permitted by the CAT? Sleep deprivation? Starvation? Sensory deprivation or bombardment? Do any of the techniques approved by the Secretary of Defense, *supra* p. 423, constitute "torture" or "cruel, inhuman, or degrading treatment" under the CAT?

Article 2(2) of the CAT provides that "[n]o exceptional circumstances whatsoever, whether a state of war or a threat of war, internal political instability, or any other public emergency, may be invoked as a justification of torture." What is the legal significance of this "no exceptions" provision?

Article 2(1) requires parties to take preventive measures "in any territory under its jurisdiction." How does extension of the CAT to the special maritime and territorial jurisdiction of the United States affect the rules for interrogation at Guantánamo? How do you think this Article 2 provision applies in Afghanistan or in Iraq?

6. *Cruel, Inhuman, or Degrading Treatment.* How does the prohibition against cruel, inhuman, or degrading treatment differ from the rule barring torture? As noted in the Working Group Report, the United States reserved its commitment to the prevention of "cruel, inhuman, or degrading treatment or punishment" under CAT Article 16 to acts that would be forbidden by the Fifth, Eighth, and/or Fourteenth Amendments. See *supra* p. 416. Why would the United States make such a reservation? Because the case law interpreting those amendments arises in domestic criminal justice

proceedings, how would you measure U.S. compliance with the "cruel, inhuman, or degrading" proviso? *See* Kreimer, *supra*, at 201-224. Do the techniques described in the *Taguba Report* or the Rumsfeld memorandum fall within the definition?

7. ***Criminalizing Torture Under the CAT.*** The criminal sanction in 18 U.S.C. §2340 was included to meet the CAT requirement that each ratifying country criminalize torture. Compare the definitions in the treaty and the Act, *supra* pp. 414-417. Do you see any important differences? In an August 1, 2002, letter to the White House Counsel, the OLC asserted that "interrogation methods that comply with Section 2340 would not violate our international obligations under the Torture Convention." Letter to Alberto R. Gonzales, Counsel to the President, from John C. Yoo, Deputy Asst. Atty. General, Aug. 1, 2002, at 1, *available at* http://www.gwu.edu/~nsarchiv/NSAEBB/NSAEBB127/02.08.01.pdf. If the measures of compliance with the CAT prohibition against "cruel, inhuman, or degrading treatment" are the Fifth, Eighth, and Fourteenth Amendments, do aliens held by the United States overseas have any protection from cruel, inhuman, or degrading treatment by U.S. officials under the CAT? Does the lack of domestic criminal enforcement authority extinguish U.S. obligations under the Torture Convention not to engage in "cruel, inhuman, and degrading treatment"? *See* Arar v. Ashcroft, 414 F. Supp. 2d 250 (E.D.N.Y. 2006), *infra* p. 453.

In 18 U.S.C. §2340 (2000), Congress forbade conduct that is "specifically intended to inflict severe physical or mental pain or suffering." Without further statutory definitions, how would you define the key words and phrases — "severe," "severe physical pain or suffering," "severe mental pain or suffering," and "specifically intended"? See *Memorandum for James B. Comey, supra* p. 426, at 5-17.

8. ***Application of the Geneva Conventions.*** Apply the language of the Geneva Conventions, as incorporated through the War Crimes Act (WCA), *supra* pp. 405-409, to the detentions and interrogation described in these materials. What threshold determinations must be made, and by whom?

   a. ***What Conflicts?*** Was the conflict with the Taliban and al Qaeda in Afghanistan covered by the Geneva Conventions? Do you agree with the January 9, 2002, OLC opinion, *supra* p. 409, that Geneva Convention III for the protection of POWs should not apply because Afghanistan was a "failed" state? Despite the Taliban's violent and harsh measures against Afghan citizens, its government controlled nearly all of Afghanistan when U.S. and British forces invaded that country in December 2001. *See* Hamdan v. Rumsfeld, 415 F.3d 33 (D.C. Cir. 2005), *rev'd*, 126 S.Ct. 2749 (2006). In *Hamdan*, a panel of the D.C. Circuit Court of Appeals ruled that the conflict was neither an international conflict between a signatory state and an opposing power that has accepted the provisions of the convention, nor an "armed conflict not of an international character occurring in the territory of one of the High Contracting Parties," because the President had determined that the conflict was "international in scope." Does this ruling affirm the OLC's analysis? Does it make sense? Is there a third category of conflict that falls outside the convention altogether, and which therefore escapes the convention rules?

What do you think was the effect, if any, of the election of the Karzai government in Afghanistan in June 2002? Before that date, the conflict arguably was subject to the Geneva Conventions by virtue of common Article 2, which provides that the conventions "apply to all cases of . . . armed conflict" between two or more parties to the Convention. Signatories are bound regardless of whether an additional party to the conflict is a signatory. After formation of the Karzai government, the conflict seemingly became internal, and U.S. and other foreign forces were present in Afghanistan with the consent of the government.

Whatever the applicability of Article 2, in Hamdan v. Rumsfeld, 126 S. Ct. 2749 (2006), the Supreme Court reversed the Court of Appeals and found that Common Article 3 affords some protection to persons who are not associated with a signatory or nonsignatory "Power" but who are involved in a conflict "in the territory of" a signatory. The Court construed the phrase "not of an international character" literally to distinguish conflicts between nations. The *Hamdan* decision is presented *infra* p. 563. In light of the Supreme Court's interpretation, what do you think of the OLC analysis of Common Article 3? *See* Waldron, *supra*, at 1694 (the OLC opinion "proceeds as though the methods of analogy, inference, and reasoned elaboration—the ordinary tools of our lawyerly trade—are utterly inappropriate in this case. . . . The Geneva Conventions . . . respond to a strongly felt and well-established sense that certain abuses are beyond the pale.").

Do you think it likely, as the Yoo/Delahunty memorandum argues, that the signers of the 1949 Geneva Conventions meant to exclude "small-scale" civil wars from their coverage? If so, was the conflict between U.S. and Taliban and al Qaeda forces "small-scale"?

b. ***Which Combatants?*** Can you say on what basis any persons detained during wartime are wholly outside the protections of the Geneva Conventions? *See* Sean D. Murphy, *Contemporary Practice of the United States Relating to International Law*, 96 Am. J. Intl. L. 461, 476-477 (2002).

The Bush administration first took the position that al Qaeda and Taliban prisoners are "unlawful combatants" and thus not protected at all by the conventions. The White House, President George W. Bush, *Memorandum to National Security Advisors Re: Humane Treatment of al Qaeda and Taliban Detainees*, Feb. 7, 2002, *available at* http://www.gwu.edu/~nsarchiv/NSAEBB/NSAEBB127/02.02.07.pdf. The Administration also reasoned that the Geneva Conventions have no application to non-state organizations such as al Qaeda, that the conflict was internal, and, further, that al Qaeda members failed to meet the criteria in Article 4 of Geneva Convention III. Under Article 4, combatants earn POW status if they are members of the armed forces other than medical or chaplain personnel. The general criteria include being subject to command authority, having a "fixed distinctive sign recognizable at a distance," carrying arms openly, and conducting operations in accordance with the laws and customs of war. The Taliban also were not entitled to Geneva Convention protections, according to the Administration, because Afghanistan was not a functioning state during the conflict and because the Taliban were not recognized as a legitimate government. *Id.*

After Secretary of State Powell objected and requested that the Administration reconsider its position, President Bush announced that Geneva Convention III was applicable to the Taliban, though not to al Qaeda. But because the Taliban violated the laws of war and associated with al Qaeda, he determined that Taliban detainees do not qualify as POWs. *See White House Fact Sheet: Status of Detainees at Guantanamo,* Feb. 7, 2002. Do you find support for the Administration's position in the memoranda excerpted here? If not, in what respects does the argument come up short? *Cf.* United States v. Lindh, 212 F. Supp. 2d 541 (E.D. Va. 2002) (concluding that the Taliban were not covered by Geneva Convention III because they had an insufficient internal system of military command, wore no distinctive sign, and regularly targeted civilian populations).

In cases of doubt, Article 5 of Geneva Convention III entitles detainees to a "competent tribunal" to determine their status. Does it offer a reasonable way to accommodate both sides in this debate? *See* Jennifer Elsea, *Treatment of "Battlefield Detainees" in the War on Terrorism* (Cong. Res. Serv. RL31367) 35, Jan. 13, 2005 (asserting that the United States has in the past required an individualized assessment of detainee status before denying POW status). Why do you suppose POW determination tribunals have not been established? Does the U.S. stance itself constitute a violation of the laws of war, thus providing an enemy with an argument for denying captured U.S. soldiers POW status?

The OLC asserted in a March 28, 2002, letter to the State Department Legal Adviser that there can be no doubt about the POW status of any individual affiliated with the Taliban, because the organization was found not to meet the requirements of Article 4. Letter to William H. Taft IV, Legal Adviser, Dept. of State, from John C. Yoo, Deputy Asst. Atty. General, Mar. 28, 2002, *available at* http://www.cartoonbank.com/newyorker/slideshows/05YooTaft.pdf. Does it necessarily follow that the categorical denial of POW status to a military organization makes any person allegedly a member of that organization ineligible for an Article 5 tribunal? *See* Waldron, *supra,* at 1695 (it is "discouraging . . . to see American lawyers arguing for the inapplicability of the Conventions on grounds that are strikingly similar . . . to those invoked by Germany" during World War II.).

c. *Which Other Persons?* Defense Secretary Rumsfeld acknowledged in early 2002 in comments about the detention facility at Guantánamo Bay that "[s]ometimes when you capture a big, large group there will be

someone who just happened to be in there that didn't belong in there."
*Secretary Rumsfeld Media Availability En Route to Camp X-Ray*, Jan.
27, 2002, *available at* http://www.defenselink.mil/transcripts/2002/
t01282002_t0127sd2.html. What rights do such innocent bystanders
have, once detained? Do Articles 4 and 5 of Geneva Convention III
and Geneva Convention IV apply? Does it matter for the purposes of
qualifying for Geneva Convention IV that a person may have unlawfully
participated in a conflict?

d. ***What Conduct Is Covered?*** What constitutes a "grave breach" under
the Geneva Conventions? If "torture or inhuman treatment" is such a
breach, what aspects of the conventions remain in dispute concerning
detainees in the war on terrorism? For POWs, Article 17 of Geneva
Convention III provides that "no physical or mental torture, nor any
other form of coercion, may be inflicted on prisoners of war to secure
from them information of any kind whatever." For protected civilians,
Article 31 of Geneva Convention IV provides that "[n]o physical or moral
coercion shall be exercised against [them], in particular to obtain information from them or from third parties." What interrogation techniques
would be proscribed by these rules? How do the techniques recommended by the Working Group and approved by Secretary Rumsfeld,
*supra* p. 422, measure up under the Geneva Conventions? *See* Jennifer
K. Elsea, *Lawfulness of Interrogation Techniques under the Geneva
Conventions* (Cong. Res. Serv. RL32567) 23-35, Sept. 8, 2004.

e. ***Liability for U.S. Personnel?*** The documents excerpted above expose
an underlying tension in setting the interrogation policy—providing
maximum flexibility to pressure detainees to talk while ensuring immunity from criminal sanctions if lawful boundaries are crossed. Compare
the arguments on the amenability of U.S. personnel to criminal prosecution in the OLC opinion of January 9, 2002, and by State Department
General Counsel Taft. Which side has the better view in light of the
Geneva Conventions?

f. ***Are the Conventions Judicially Enforceable?*** Salim Ahmed
Hamdan was captured by Afghan militia forces in November 2001. He
was turned over to the U.S. military and transported to Guantánamo
Bay. In July 2003, President Bush determined "that there was reason to
believe that [Hamdan] was a member of al Qaeda or was otherwise
involved in terrorism directed against the United States," and Hamdan
was designated for trial before a military commission. After Hamdan
filed a petition for habeas corpus in federal district court, he was charged
with a variety of terrorism-related offenses stemming from his alleged
role as the personal driver for Osama bin Laden. In November 2004, the
District Court granted Hamdan's petition in part, holding that he could
not be tried by a military commission unless a competent tribunal determined that he was not a POW under Geneva Convention III. Hamdan v.
Rumsfeld, 344 F. Supp. 2d 152 (D.D.C. 2004).

On July 15, 2005, a D.C. Circuit Court of Appeals panel reversed.
In Hamdan v. Rumsfeld, 415 F.3d 33, 40 (D.C. Cir. 2005), the court
found that Geneva Convention III confers upon Hamdan no right to

enforce its provisions in court. In 2006, the Supreme Court reversed the judgment of the Court of Appeals. In Hamdan v. Rumsfeld, 126 S. Ct. 2749, 2795 (2006), the Court found that Common Article 3 is applicable to the conflict with al Qaeda. Even though its protections fall "short of full protection under the Conventions," *id.* at 2796, Hamdan must be tried by a "'regularly constituted court affording all the judicial guarantees which are recognized as indispensable by civilized peoples.'" *Id.* at 2795, quoting from Common Article 3. What effect will the *Hamdan* decision likely have on future disputes about interrogation and treatment of detainees? *See infra* p. 563.

Shortly after the *Hamdan* decision in the Supreme Court, Congress enacted the Military Commissions Act of 2006, Pub. L. No. 109-366, 120 Stat. 2600. The Act states that a "military commission established under this chapter is a regularly constituted court, affording all the necessary 'judicial guarantees which are recognized as indispensable by civilized peoples' for purposes of common Article 3 of the Geneva Conventions." *Id.* §3(a)(1), 120 Stat. 2602 (adding 10 U.S.C. §948b(f)). The Act also asserts that "[n]o alien unlawful enemy combatant subject to trial by military commission under this chapter may invoke the Geneva Conventions as a source of rights." *Id.* §3(a)(1), 120 Stat. 2602 (adding 10 U.S.C. §948b(g)). Is the Act dispositive of Hamdan's ability to rely on the Geneva Conventions as a source of rights in litigation? May the President interpret the Military Commissions Act to preclude litigants from relying on the Geneva Conventions as a source of rights for other purposes?

In February 2006, a federal district court dismissed most of a lawsuit for damages brought by Guantánamo Bay detainees who alleged that they were tortured in violation of the Geneva Conventions, the law of nations, and the Constitution. Rasul v. Rumsfeld, 414 F. Supp. 2d 26 (D.D.C. 2006). The court held that sovereign immunity barred the law of nations and Geneva Conventions claims and that qualified immunity required dismissal of the constitutional claims because the rights at stake were not "clearly established." For sovereign immunity to apply to the international law claims, however, the court had to find that the defendants were acting within their scope of employment. How could U.S. officials act within their scope of employment when they torture detainees? The status of U.S. constitutional law regarding torture-related claims is assessed *infra* p. 446.

9. *The New Paradigm?* White House Counsel Gonzales argued that the "nature of the new war" and the "new paradigm render[] obsolete Geneva's strict limitations" on questioning and make other Geneva provisions "quaint." How would you rebut the Gonzales interpretation? Do Gonzales's arguments apply with equal force in Afghanistan and in Iraq? To detainees captured elsewhere? *See* Derek Jinks & David Sloss, *Is the President Bound by the Geneva Conventions?*, 90 Cornell L. Rev. 97 (2004) (concluding that he is). By contrast, the OLC argued that the Geneva Conventions are "quite clear," and that the President correctly determined that the Taliban and al Qaeda detainees cannot meet the clear

requirements of Geneva Convention III. *Letter to Taft from Yoo, supra* p. 440. Is the OLC position more or less persuasive than that of the former White House Counsel?

10. ***The International Covenant on Civil and Political Rights.*** The ICCPR, like the CAT, forbids torture and cruel, inhuman, and degrading conduct, and it was subject to Senate approval. The ICCPR is non-self-executing, and lower federal courts have found that the ICCPR creates no privately enforceable rights in U.S. courts. However, some courts cite the ICCPR as evidence that customary international law prohibits arbitrary arrest, prolonged detention, and torture. See *supra* p. 416. What is the legal basis for the Working Group position that the ICCPR does not apply to U.S. activities abroad during an armed conflict? *See* Elsea, *supra* p.441, at 12-13 (United States "has not officially proclaimed an emergency or named measures that would derogate from the ICCPR.").

### c. Domestic Law on Torture

1. *A Congressional Prohibition.* In 2005, over the strenuous objection of the Bush administration, Congress enacted the Detainee Treatment Act (DTA), part of the National Defense Authorization Act for Fiscal Year 2006, Pub. L. No. 109-163, §§1401-1406, 119 Stat. 3136, 3474-3480 (2006). It provides, in part:

> *Prohibition on Cruel, Inhuman, or Degrading Treatment or Punishment of Persons Under Custody or Control of the United States Government.*
>
> (a) In General—No individual in the custody or under the physical control of the United States Government, regardless of nationality or physical location, shall be subject to cruel, inhuman, or degrading treatment or punishment.
>
> (b) Construction—Nothing in this section shall be construed to impose any geographical limitation on the applicability of the prohibition against cruel, inhuman, or degrading treatment or punishment under this section.
>
> (c) Limitation on Supersedure. — The provisions of this section shall not be superseded, except by a provision of law enacted after the date of the enactment of this Act which specifically repeals, modifies, or supersedes the provisions of this section.
>
> (d) Cruel, Inhuman, or Degrading Treatment or Punishment Defined. — In this section, the term "cruel, inhuman, or degrading treatment or punishment" means the cruel, unusual, and inhumane treatment or punishment prohibited by the Fifth, Eighth, and Fourteenth Amendments to the Constitution of the United States, as defined in the United States Reservations, Declarations and Understandings to the United Nations Convention Against Torture and Other Forms of Cruel, Inhuman or Degrading Treatment or Punishment done at New York, December 10, 1984. [Pub. L. No. 109-163, §1403, 119 Stat. 3475.]

How does the DTA affect the availability of a necessity defense to a criminal charge under the Torture Statute, *supra* p. 416? *See* the Working Group Report, *supra* p. 414. How important is the "regardless of nationality or physical location" language in determining the scope of the government's investigative authority and the rights of the detainee? The definition of "cruel, inhuman, or degrading treatment" mirrors that stated in the U.S. reservation to Article 16 of the CAT and covers only acts prohibited by the Fifth, Eighth, and Fourteenth Amendments. Does the DTA thus require that persons (including aliens) in U.S. custody or control abroad not be subjected to treatment that would be unconstitutional if it occurred in the United States? If the meaning of the constitutional protections changes over time, the treatment forbidden by the Act presumably will change as well. How would you advise those responsible for supervising interrogations to keep abreast of their responsibilities?

The Detainee Treatment Act also forbids exposure of persons in the custody or under the effective control of DOD to any interrogation techniques not listed in the *Army Field Manual on Intelligence Interrogation*. Pub. L. No. 109-163, §1402(a), 119 Stat. 3475. What is the legal significance of limiting DOD interrogators to techniques in the *Army Field Manual*? Why do you suppose that non-DOD interrogators were not subject to the same or some similar restriction?

In a signing statement for the legislation containing the DTA, President Bush declared that he would construe the provisions set forth above

> in a manner consistent with the constitutional authority of the President to supervise the unitary executive branch and as Commander in Chief and consistent with the constitutional limitations on the judicial power, which will assist in achieving the shared objective of the Congress and the President . . . of protecting the American people from further terrorist attacks. [Statement on Signing the Department of Defense, Emergency Supplemental Appropriations to Address Hurricanes in the Gulf of Mexico, and Pandemic Influenza Act, 2006, 41 Weekly Comp. Pres. Doc. 1918, Jan. 2, 2006.]

Do you think this declaration qualifies the President's obligation to comply with the statute?

2. ***The Prohibition Modified.*** The Military Commissions Act of 2006 provides that statements obtained from a defendant through the use of coercion not amounting to torture may be used against him in a trial before a military commission in some circumstances and that evidence obtained by "cruel, inhuman, or degrading treatment or punishment" is barred only if it was obtained after the effective date of the DTA. Pub. L. No. 109-366, §3(a)(1), 120 Stat. 2600, 2607 (adding 10 U.S.C. §948r(c) and (d)). See *supra* p. 443. What are the likely practical and legal consequences of these provisions? The Military Commissions Act is examined in greater detail *infra* pp. 587-600.

3. ***Ghost Prisoners and Black Sites: Rules for the CIA?*** Although the broad prohibition on cruel, inhuman, and degrading treatment or punishment in the DTA applies to all U.S. government personnel, the Act does not

provide more detailed rules to guide interrogation practices by the CIA. A November 2005 news story described a global prison system set up by the CIA after September 11, reportedly including secret facilities ("black sites") in at least eight countries, including Thailand, Afghanistan, and "several democracies in Eastern Europe." Dana Priest, *CIA Holds Terror Suspects in Secret Prisons*, Wash. Post, Nov. 2, 2005, at A1. In late 2005, Human Rights Watch provided a list of 26 "ghost detainees" believed to be in U.S. custody. *U.S. Holding at Least Twenty-Six "Ghost Detainees,"* Dec. 1, 2005. One secret CIA prison is reportedly code-named Bright Light, where the most important al Qaeda detainees are held in an undisclosed location. *See* James Risen, *State of War: The Secret History of the CIA and the Bush Administration* 31 (2006). Soon thereafter, the allegations were corroborated by human rights organizations, and investigations were launched by European organizations. *See* Jennifer K. Elsea & Julie Kim, *Undisclosed U.S. Detention Sites Overseas: Background and Issues* 3 (Cong. Res. Serv. RL33643), Sept. 12, 2006. Controversy surrounding the black sites and ghost prisoners merged with parallel reports that the United States was engaging in the practice of "extraordinary rendition," transferring detainees to third countries for interrogation where it is more likely than not that the detainee will be subject to abusive treatment. The legal issues involved in extraordinary rendition are considered in Chapter 14.

Although U.S. officials would not confirm the existence of the secret prisons for nearly two years following their exposure in the media, President Bush announced on September 6, 2006, that 14 "high-value detainees" suspected of terrorist activity had been transferred from locations abroad to the U.S. detention facility at Guantánamo Bay. Elsea & Kim, *supra*, at 1. In a remarkable five-page statement, DNI John Negroponte described a CIA detention and interrogation program involving captured detainees "who have been in the inner circle" of al Qaeda and who "hold information that simply cannot be obtained from any other source." Office of the Director of National Intelligence, *Summary of the High Value Terrorist Detainee Program* (n.d.), *available at* http://www.dni.gov/announcements/content/TheHighValueDetaineeProgram.pdf. According to the statement, the CIA program "is designed to ensure that intelligence is collected in a manner that does not violate the Constitution, any US statute, or US treaty obligations." *Id.* at 2. The statement further asserts that the Justice Department "has reviewed the procedures proposed by the CIA on more than one occasion and determined them to be lawful." *Id.*

According to which laws would the Justice Department have determined that the CIA program was lawful?

One section of the Military Commissions Act apparently requires the President to establish rules and procedures to ensure compliance with the prohibition against cruel, inhuman, or degrading treatment or punishment. Pub. L. No. 109-366, §6(c)(3), 120 Stat. at 2635. As of March 2007, new rules had not been issued, apparently relegating CIA interrogators to procedures approved by the Department of Defense. *See* Mark Mazzetti, *C.I.A. Awaits Rules on Interrogation of Terror Suspects*, N.Y. Times, Mar. 25, 2007, at 1. What legal arguments can you make for and against interrogation rules and procedures for the CIA that are more permissive than those for Defense Department interrogators?

4. ***Applying the Constitution.*** The U.S. reservation to Article 16 of the CAT limits "cruel, inhuman or degrading conduct" to that which violates the Fifth, Eighth, and/or Fourteenth Amendments. What is the content of those constitutional protections? For contrasting views, see Seth F. Kreimer, *Too Close to the Rack and the Screw: Constitutional Constraints on Torture in the War on Terror*, 6 U. Penn. J. Constl. L. 278 (2003); and John T. Parry, *What Is Torture, Are We Doing It, and What If We Are?*, 64 U. Pitt. L. Rev. 237 (2003).

In Chavez v. Martinez, 538 U.S. 760 (2003), a badly fractured Supreme Court ruled on claims of liability asserted by a plaintiff who had been subjected to persistent police questioning while he was in the hospital incapacitated by extreme pain. Five Justices voted to remand the question whether the plaintiff could pursue a claim for violation of his substantive due process rights, but the Court could not agree about the scope and applicability of those rights or the related right against self-incrimination.

Three Justices joined in part of an opinion by Justice Thomas asserting that the interrogation was not egregious or conscience-shocking enough to violate the plaintiff's substantive due process rights. They reasoned that "freedom from unwanted police questioning is [not] a right so fundamental that it cannot be abridged absent a 'compelling state interest.'" *Id.* at 776. For these Justices, it was enough that the questioning was justified by *some* government interest — here the need to preserve critical evidence concerning a shooting by a police officer — and that it was not "conduct intended to injure in some way unjustifiable by any government interest." *Id.* at 774.

Justice Stevens concluded that "the interrogation of respondent was the functional equivalent of an attempt to obtain an involuntary confession from a prisoner by torturous methods," which is "a classic example of a violation of a constitutional right 'implicit in the concept of ordered liberty.'" *Id.* at 788 (Stevens, J., concurring in part, dissenting in part).

Justice Kennedy (joined on this point by Justices Stevens and Ginsburg) agreed that the use of investigatory torture violates a person's fundamental right to liberty but noted that interrogating suspects who are in pain or anguish is not necessarily torture when the police have "legitimate reasons, borne of exigency . . . [such as] [l]ocating the victim of a kidnapping, ascertaining the whereabouts of a dangerous assailant or accomplice, or determining whether there is a rogue police officer." *Id.* at 796 (Kennedy, J., concurring in part, dissenting in part). On the other hand, Justice Kennedy added, the police may not prolong or increase the suspect's suffering or threaten to do so to elicit a statement. The test for a constitutional violation, in Justice Kennedy's view, was whether the police "exploited" the suspect's pain to secure his statement. He found that the police had done so in *Chavez*.

Under any of the tests in *Chavez*, would torture in the United States of a suspected terrorist to obtain information about an imminent terrorist attack violate substantive due process? How about practices such as hooding and sleep deprivation? Do military or civilian investigators in the war on terrorism have broader authority than the police do to use coercive interrogation techniques because of their different goals in an interrogation? *See* Marcy Strauss, *Torture*, 48 N.Y.L. Sch. L. Rev. 201, 251 (2003) (maintaining that it is unclear whether torture used to gain information violates the Fifth Amendment privilege against self-incrimination if the information is not used in a criminal prosecution; if so used, the right is violated).

Does the Eighth Amendment ban on "cruel and unusual punishment" supply an interpretive standard in the coercive interrogation context? If no judicially imposed punishment is contemplated by the interrogators, does the Eighth Amendment even apply? *See* Ingraham v. Wright, 430 U.S. 651, 671 n.40 (1977) ("[T]he State does not acquire the power to punish with which the Eighth Amendment is concerned until after it has secured a formal adjudication of guilt in accordance with due process of law.").

5. ***Extraterritorial Application of the Constitution.*** Are U.S. interrogators in Iraq, Afghanistan, or elsewhere outside the United States subject to the same constitutional constraints on interrogation methods that limit their conduct in the United States? Are they subject to any U.S. laws? See *supra* pp. 434-436. If aliens held at Guantánamo have *some* U.S. constitutional rights, *see* Rasul v. Bush, 542 U.S. 466 (2004), *supra* p. 326, *but see* Boumediene v. Bush, 476 F.3d 981 (D.C. Cir.), *cert. denied*, 127 S. Ct. 1478 (2007), do aliens held by U.S. forces in Afghanistan or Iraq have *any*? If they do not, are U.S. interrogators therefore not constrained by Article 16 of the CAT? How, if at all, is your answer affected by the DTA, *supra* p. 443?

6. ***"Shocks the Conscience" Redux.*** Consider the "shocks the conscience" standard described *supra* p. 288. Applying this standard, would the most abusive techniques used at Abu Ghraib ever be permitted in the United States? How about in the ticking-bomb situation? Would your answer be different if the treatment occurred abroad? *See* Oren Gross, *The Prohibition on Torture and the Limits of the Law* 2 (2004).

7. ***Criminal Sanctions.*** The torture statute, 18 U.S.C. §§2340-2340B (2000 & Supp. IV 2004), imposes criminal sanctions for torture, purportedly in accordance with U.S. obligations under the Convention Against Torture. It applies, however, only to U.S. nationals or others present in the United States who commit or conspire to commit torture "outside the United States." The Working Group took pains to assert that Guantánamo is included within the special maritime jurisdiction of the United States and thus that the U.S. personnel conducting interrogations there are not subject to the torture statute. At the same time, the government rejected claims of sovereignty over Guantánamo for the purpose of federal court jurisdiction to hear claims by detainees held there. *See* Rasul v. Bush, 542 U.S. 466 (2004), *supra* p. 326. Can the two positions be reconciled?

The torture statute was amended in 2004 to extend the definition of "United States" to include the several states, the District of Columbia, and the commonwealths, territories, and possessions of the United States. Pub. L. No. 108-375, §1089, 118 Stat. 2067 (amending 18 U.S.C. §2340(3)). *See* Michael John Garcia, *U.N. Convention Against Torture (CAT): Overview and Application to Interrogation Techniques* (Cong. Res. Serv. RL34238) 11-12, Feb. 10, 2005.

In December 2006, federal prosecutors brought the first-ever indictment under the torture statute against the son of former Liberian President Charles Taylor for a brutal interrogation that took place in Liberia in 2002. Press Release, Dept. of Justice, *Roy Belfast Jr. AKA Chuckie Taylor Indicted on Torture Charges*, Dec. 6, 2006, *available at* http://www.usdoj.gov/criminal/ press_room/press_releases/2006_4878_1_12-06-06rbelfastcharge.pdf. Taylor and other Liberian security personnel allegedly poured boiling water on the victim, applied a hot iron, shocked the victim's genitals, applied salt to his wounds, and otherwise inflicted "severe physical pain or suffering." *Id.*

Why do you suppose Congress has not enacted a statute specifically outlawing torture within the United States?

The Uniform Code of Military Justice (UCMJ) provides for courts-martial to prosecute torture or inhumane acts committed within or outside the United States by members of the military and certain accompanying civilians. 10 U.S.C. §805 (UCMJ applies worldwide); *id.* §802 (to any service member); *id.* §802(a)(10) (to certain accompanying civilians); *id.* §818 (for an offense against the laws of war); *id.* §855 (torture or cruel or unusual punishment); *id.* §934 ("disorders and neglects to the prejudice of good order and discipline in the armed forces"). To date, ten low-ranking soldiers and one captain have been convicted under the UCMJ of abusing detainees at Abu Ghraib, while 251 other soldiers and officers have been punished in some way for detainee abuse in Iraq and Afghanistan. Eric Schmitt, *Iraq Abuse Trial Is Again Limited to Lower Ranks*, N.Y. Times, Mar. 23, 2006, at A1.

One part of the DTA, *supra* p. 443, provides a legal defense for U.S. personnel in any criminal or civil action brought against them based on their involvement in an authorized interrogation of suspected foreign terrorists. The defense exists when the U.S. interrogator "did not know that the [interrogation] practices were unlawful and a person of ordinary sense and understanding would not know the practices were unlawful." Pub. L. No. 109-148, §1004(a), 119 Stat. 2740; Pub. L. No. 109-163, §1404, 119 Stat. 3475-3476. A good faith reliance on the advice of counsel may be "an important factor" in measuring the accused's culpability. *Id.* Why do you think these provisions were added to the act? What is their likely impact?

8. ***Prosecuting Civilian Contractors.***  In June 2004 a federal grand jury in North Carolina indicted a contractor employed by the CIA on assault charges for allegedly beating a detainee in Afghanistan over two days in 2003. The detainee died the next day. Richard A. Oppel Jr. & Ariel Hart, *Contractor Indicted in Afghan Detainee's Beating*, N.Y. Times, June 17, 2004, at A1. The CIA refused to acknowledge whether the agency was aware that the accused had been arrested on felony assault charges before his employment by the Agency. *Id.* How might the War Crimes Act, 18 U.S.C. §2441, *supra* pp. 404-406, apply to the accused in this case?

Generally, the UCMJ has not been applied to civilians accompanying military units in peacetime. *See, e.g.,* Willenburg v. Neurauter, 48 M.J. 152, 157 (C.A.A.F. 1998). The Military Extraterritorial Jurisdiction Act of 2000 (MEJA), however, provides for federal jurisdiction over crimes committed abroad by civilians who are "accompanying or employed by" the U.S.

military. 18 U.S.C. §§3261-3267 (2000 & Supp. IV 2004). Still, after the *Taguba Report, supra* p. 402 n.15, named the contracting firms Titan Corporation and CACI International, Inc. as having provided translators and interrogators accused of engaging in detainee abuse at the Abu Ghraib prison, it appeared that the jurisdictional provisions of the MEJA would not reach the contractors that employed the accused individuals. Moreover, CACI's contract is with the Department of Interior rather than with the Department of Defense. Scott Shane, *Some U.S. Prison Contractors May Avoid Charges*, Balt. Sun, May 24, 2004, at A1. In response to this jurisdictional gap, the 2005 Defense Authorization Act broadened the range of potential defendants under the MEJA to include civilian employees, contractors or subcontractors, and their employees, of DOD or "any other Federal agency, or any provisional authority, to the extent such employment relates to supporting the mission of the Department of Defense overseas." Pub. L. No. 108-375, §1088, 118 Stat. 1811, 2066-2067 (2004). Do these amendments to the MEJA plug all the holes? Would it reach State Department or FBI contractors? CIA contractors? *See* Frederick A. Stein, *Have We Closed the Barn Door Yet? A Look at the Current Loopholes in the Military Extraterritorial Jurisdiction Act*, 27 Hous. J. Intl. L. 579 (2005).

Expressing frustration that contractors and other civilians were not being held accountable for wrongdoing while serving with U.S. forces in Iraq and Afghanistan, Congress added a provision to the 2007 Defense Authorization Act allowing the UCMJ to be applied to certain civilians during a "contingency operation," defined to include operations in Iraq and Afghanistan. National Defense Authorization Act for Fiscal Year 2007, Pub. L. No. 109-364, §552, 120 Stat. 2083, 2217. *See* Griff Witte, *New Law Could Subject Civilians to Military Trial*, Wash. Post, Jan. 15, 2007, at A1. Although sponsors of the measure say that the change was aimed at contractors, some observers suggested that it could be interpreted broadly to include a range of civilian government employees as well as reporters. *Id.* What legal problems will the new provision present?

The MEJA creates no substantive crimes but incorporates a range of existing offenses, such as murder, assault, sexual abuse, and deprivation of rights under color of law. What ordinary crimes might be charged against civilian contractors working in facilities like Abu Ghraib? Could CIA operatives engaged in interrogational torture while operating with military units be prosecuted under the UCMJ? Do these problems with the use of contractors suggest broader issues that should be considered in privatizing national security activities of the government? How might these issues be addressed? *See* Jon D. Michaels, *Beyond Accountability: The Constitutional, Democratic, and Strategic Problems with Privatizing War*, 82 Wash. U. L.Q. 1001 (2004).

A Justice Department team created in 2004 to investigate detainee abuse accusations against civilian government employees has not brought a single indictment in the nearly 20 cases that have been referred by the Department of Defense and the CIA, and the team has been plagued by difficulties in collecting evidence and by the fragmentary nature of some of the accusations. *See* David Johnston, *U.S. Inquiry Falters on Civilians*

*Accused of Abusing Detainees*, N.Y. Times, Dec. 19, 2006, at A1. What remedies are there for these problems of criminal investigation?

9. **Civil Sanctions.** The Foreign Claims Act (FCA), 10 U.S.C. §2734(a) (2000), permits recovery up to $100,000 from the United States for a claim brought by a resident of a foreign country where the injury occurred outside the United States "and is caused by, or is otherwise incident to [the] noncombat activities of" the U.S. military. *Id.* "Noncombat activity" is defined to include any "activity, other than combat, war or armed conflict, that is particularly military in character and has little parallel in the civilian community." 32 C.F.R. §842.41(c) (2006). Under the Act, claims commissions, consisting of commissioned officers, are established for each service branch and are in place wherever the military has a significant presence. However, experience with the FCA in Iraq suggests that complex procedures and stringent policies have prevented most injured Iraqis from obtaining compensation for their injuries. Scott Borrowman, *Sosa v. Alvarez-Machain and Abu Ghraib — Civil Remedies for Victims of Extraterritorial Torts by U.S. Military Personnel and Civilian Contractors*, 2005 B.Y.U. L. Rev. 371, 376 (2005).

The Alien Tort Statute (ATS), 28 U.S.C. §1350 (2000), confers jurisdiction on federal district courts over tort suits by aliens where a violation of the law of nations or a treaty of the United States is alleged. In Sosa v. Alvarez-Machain, 542 U.S. 692 (2004), the Supreme Court rejected the ATS as a basis for jurisdiction in the federal courts over a tort claim related to the abduction of Alvarez-Machain by a Mexican national who acted with the approval of the DEA. The Court reasoned that the ATS was intended to create jurisdiction to hear suits based on current international norms, but only those whose "content and acceptance among civilized nations" is no less definite than the small number of "historical paradigms" familiar when the statute was passed in 1789. *Id.* at 718. In the course of its opinion, however, the Court cited with evident approval the decision in Filartiga v. Peña-Irala, 630 F.2d 876 (2d Cir. 1980), noted *supra* p. 421, which applied the ATS in a torture case. Review the *Almog* and *Saperstein* decisions, *supra* pp. 21, 32. Can you predict whether ATS claims based on torture will be recognized by the federal courts?

The Torture Victim Protection Act (TVPA), Pub. L. No. 102-256, 106 Stat. 73 (1992) (codified at 28 U.S.C. §1350 note (2000)), provides a civil remedy in the federal courts for individuals, including U.S. persons, who have been victims of torture or extrajudicial killing. See *supra* p. 421. The TVPA thus may offer relief for U.S. persons that would be unavailable under the ATS. However, the TVPA only provides a cause of action for torture or extrajudicial killing "under color of law, of any foreign nation." *Id.* §2a. Do you think that the TVPA would support an action for improper removal by U.S. officials of an individual who might be subjected to torture abroad? Would it apply where U.S. officials allegedly direct foreign officials to carry out acts of torture against a non-U.S. citizen? *See* Arar v. Ashcroft, 414 F. Supp. 2d 250 (E.D.N.Y. 2006), *infra* p. 453.

What would be the measure of "torture" under these civil mechanisms? Relying on the ATS, in 2004 the Center for Constitutional Rights sued the two prime security contractors operating for the United States in Iraq—CACI International, Inc. and Titan Corp.—on behalf of Iraqi prisoners, alleging that the contractors conspired with government officials to abuse the detainees and failed adequately to supervise their employees. *See* Renae Merle, *CACI and Titan Sued Over Iraq Operations*, Wash. Post, June 10, 2004, at E3. The suit seeks damages and an injunction to prevent the contractors from obtaining new government contracts. What problems can you foresee for the plaintiffs in this lawsuit? *See* Saleh v. Titan Corp., 353 F. Supp. 2d 1087 (S.D. Ca. 2004); 361 F. Supp. 2d 1152 (S.D. Ca. 2005); *see also* Ibrahim v. Titan Corp., 391 F. Supp. 2d 10 (D.D.C. 2005). In other civil suits U.S. courts have found that defendants committed actionable torture by subjecting detainees to interrogation sessions lasting 14 hours, Xuncax v. Gramajo, 886 F. Supp. 162, 170 (D. Mass. 1995); beating with hands, Tachiaona v. Mugabe, 234 F. Supp. 2d 401, 420-423 (S.D.N.Y. 2002), *cert. denied*, 126 S. Ct. 2020 (2006) (mem.); striking with blunt objects and boots, Mehinovic v. Vuckovic, 198 F. Supp. 2d 1322 (N.D. Ga. 2002); threatening with death, Adebe-Jira v. Negewo, 72 F.3d 844, 845 (11th Cir. 1996), *cert. denied*, 519 U.S. 830 (1996); and using techniques to increase pain or injury. *Id.*

# CHAPTER 14

# *EXTRAORDINARY RENDITION*

Rendition is generally understood to be the surrender of a person from one state to another state that has requested him, typically pursuant to an agreement or extradition treaty, for the purpose of criminal prosecution. In recent years, however, the United States has begun transferring detainees to foreign countries without the request of the transferee country for detention and interrogation, sometimes in circumstances where it is possible that the individuals will be subjected to torture or to cruel, inhuman, or degrading treatment. The practice is called "irregular rendition" or "extraordinary rendition," because it involves no treaty or formal agreement and is attended by no judicial process. Whether authorized by secret presidential directive or simply done by government officials without authorization, extraordinary rendition has apparently been utilized as an integral adjunct to coercive interrogation in the war on terrorism.

## ARAR v. ASHCROFT

United States District Court, Eastern District of New York, 2006
414 F. Supp. 2d 250

TRAGER, District Judge. Plaintiff Maher Arar brings this action against defendants, U.S. officials, who allegedly held him virtually incommunicado for thirteen days at the U.S. border and then ordered his removal to Syria for the express purpose of detention and interrogation under torture by Syrian officials. He brings claims under the Torture Victim Prevention Act and the Fifth Amendment to the U.S. Constitution.

Defendants have filed motions to dismiss the complaint. . . . The questions presented by these motions are whether the facts alleged can give rise to any theory of liability under those provisions of law and, if so, whether those claims can survive on prudential grounds in light of the national-security and foreign policy issues involved.

### Background

All statements contained in parts (1) through (4) in this background section of the opinion are taken from the complaint, attached exhibits, or documents referred to in the complaint and are presumed true for the limited purposes of these motions to dismiss. . . .

(1) Plaintiff Maher Arar ("Arar" or "plaintiff") is a 33-year-old native of Syria who immigrated to Canada with his family when he was a teenager. He is a dual citizen of Syria and Canada and presently resides in Ottawa. In September 2002, while vacationing with family in Tunisia, he was called back to work by his employer to consult with a prospective client. He purchased a return ticket to Montreal with stops in Zurich and New York and left Tunisia on September 25, 2002.

On September 26, 2002, Arar arrived from Switzerland at John F. Kennedy Airport ("JFK Airport") in New York to catch a connecting flight to Montreal. Upon presenting his passport to an immigration inspector, he was identified as "the subject of a . . . lookout as being a member of a known terrorist organization." He was interrogated by various officials for approximately eight hours. The officials asked Arar if he had contacts with terrorist groups, which he categorically denied. Arar was then transported to another site at JFK Airport, where he was placed in solitary confinement. He alleges that he was transported in chains and shackles and was left in a room with no bed and with lights on throughout the night. . . .

[Arar was detained and interrogated for 13 days in the United States. He alleges that during that time he was physically and psychologically abused by U.S. officials.]

. . . [On] October 7, 2002, the INS Regional Director, J. Scott Blackman, determined from classified and unclassified information that Arar is "clearly and unequivocally" a member of al Qaeda and . . . "that there are reasonable grounds to believe that [Arar] is a danger to the security of the United States." At approximately 4:00 a.m. on October 8, 2002, Arar learned that, based on classified information, INS regional director Blackman had ordered that Arar be sent to Syria and that his removal there was consistent with Article 3 of the United Nations Convention Against Torture and Other Cruel, Inhuman, or Degrading Treatment or Punishment ("CAT"). Arar pleaded for reconsideration but was told by INS officials that the agency was not governed by the "Geneva Conventions." . . .

Later that day, Arar was taken in chains and shackles to a New Jersey airfield, where he boarded a small jet bound for Washington, D.C. From there, he was flown to Amman, Jordan, arriving there on October 9, 2002. He was then handed over to Jordanian authorities, who delivered him to the Syrians later that day. At this time, U.S. officials had not informed . . . Canadian Consulate official[s] . . . that Arar had been removed to Syria. Arar alleges that Syrian officials refused to accept Arar directly from the United States. . . .

(2) During his ten-month period of detention in Syria, Arar alleges that he was placed in a "grave" cell measuring six-feet long, seven feet high, and three feet wide. The cell was located within the Palestine Branch of the Syrian Military Intelligence ("Palestine Branch"). The cell was damp and cold, contained very little light, and was infested with rats, which would enter the cell through a small aperture in the ceiling. Cats would urinate on Arar through the aperture, and sanitary facilities were nonexistent. Arar was allowed to bathe himself in cold water once per week. He was prohibited from exercising and was provided

barely edible food. Arar lost forty pounds during his ten-month period of detention in Syria.

During his first twelve days in Syrian detention, Arar was interrogated for eighteen hours per day and was physically and psychologically tortured. He was beaten on his palms, hips and lower back with a two-inch-thick electric cable. His captors also used their fists to beat him on his stomach, face and back of his neck. He was subjected to excruciating pain and pleaded with his captors to stop, but they would not. He was placed in a room where he could hear the screams of other detainees being tortured and was told that he, too, would be placed in a spine-breaking "chair," hung upside down in a "tire" for beatings and subjected to electric shocks. To lessen his exposure to the torture, Arar falsely confessed, among other things, to having trained with terrorists in Afghanistan, even though he had never been to Afghanistan and had never been involved in terrorist activity.

Arar alleges that his interrogation in Syria was coordinated and planned by U.S. officials, who sent the Syrians a dossier containing specific questions. As evidence of this, Arar notes that the interrogations in the U.S. and Syria contained identical questions, including a specific question about his relationship with a particular individual wanted for terrorism. In return, the Syrian officials supplied U.S. officials with all information extracted from Arar; plaintiff cites a statement by one Syrian official who has publicly stated that the Syrian government shared information with the U.S. that it extracted from Arar.

**(3)** The Canadian Embassy contacted the Syrian government about Arar on October 20, 2002, and, the following day, Syrian officials confirmed that they were detaining him. At this point, the Syrian officials ceased interrogating and torturing Arar.

Canadian officials visited Arar at the Palestine Branch five times during his ten-month detention. Prior to each visit, Arar was warned not to disclose that he was being mistreated. He complied but eventually broke down during the fifth visit, telling the Canadian consular official that he was being tortured and kept in a grave. . . .

On October 5, 2003, Syria, without filing any charges against Arar, released him into the custody of Canadian Embassy officials in Damascus. He was flown to Ottawa the following day and reunited with his family.

Arar contends that he is not a member of any terrorist organization, including al Qaeda, and has never knowingly associated himself with terrorists, terrorist organizations or terrorist activity. . . .

Arar alleges that he continues to suffer adverse effects from his ordeal in Syria. He claims that he has trouble relating to his wife and children, suffers from nightmares, is frequently branded a terrorist and is having trouble finding employment due to his reputation and inability to travel in the United States.

**(4)** The complaint alleges on information and belief that Arar was removed to Syria under a covert U.S. policy of "extraordinary rendition," according to which individuals are sent to foreign countries to undergo methods of interrogation not permitted in the United States. The extraordinary rendition policy involves the removal of "non-U.S. citizens detained in this country and elsewhere and suspected — reasonably or unreasonably — of terrorist activity to countries, including Syria, where interrogations under torture are routine." Arar alleges on information and belief that the United States sends individuals "to countries like Syria precisely because those countries can and do use methods of interrogation to obtain information from detainees that would not be morally acceptable or legal in the United States and other democracies." . . .

This extraordinary rendition program is not part of any official or declared U.S. public policy; nevertheless, it has received extensive attention in the press, where unnamed U.S. officials and certain foreign officials have admitted to the existence of such a policy. . . .

Arar alleges that defendants directed the interrogations by providing information about Arar to Syrian officials and receiving reports on Arar's responses. Consequently, the defendants conspired with, and/or aided and abetted, Syrian officials in arbitrarily detaining, interrogating and torturing Arar. Plaintiff argues in the alternative that, at a minimum, defendants knew or at least should have known that there was a substantial likelihood that he would be tortured upon his removal to Syria.

(5) Arar's claim that he faced a likelihood of torture in Syria is supported by U.S. State Department reports on Syria's human rights practices. *See, e.g.,* Bureau of Democracy, Human Rights, and Labor, United States Department of State, 2004 Country Reports on Human Rights Practices (Released February 28, 2005) ("2004 Report"). According to the State Department, Syria's "human rights record remained poor, and the Government continued to commit numerous, serious abuses . . . includ[ing] the use of torture in detention, which at times resulted in death." 2004 Report at 1. . . .

[The court first held that Arar failed to show sufficient continuing injury to establish standing to sue for declaratory relief, and that the Torture Victim Protection Act, *supra* p. 450, does not create a private right of action for rendition leading to torture and, in any case, does not apply where U.S. officials are alleged to direct foreign officials to torture a non-U.S. citizen.]

### Due Process Claims for Detention and Torture in Syria

Counts 2 and 3 of plaintiff's complaint allege that defendants violated Arar's rights to substantive due process by removing him to Syria and subjecting him to both torture and coercive interrogation (Count 2) and arbitrary and indefinite detention (Count 3). He seeks damages under *Bivens v. Six Unknown Named Agents of Fed. Bureau of Narcotics,* 403 U.S. 388 (1971), claiming deprivation of Fifth Amendment due process rights.

*Bivens* establishes "that the victims of a constitutional violation by a federal agent have a right to recover damages against the official in federal court despite the absence of any statute conferring such a right." *Carlson v. Green,* 446 U.S. 14, 18 (1980). The threshold inquiry is whether Arar alleges a violation of federal law that can be vindicated in his *Bivens* claim. . . .

Arar argues that the treatment he allegedly suffered unquestionably constitutes a violation of substantive due process. However, defendants question whether robust Fifth Amendment protections can extend to someone like Arar, who, for juridical purposes, never actually entered the United States. Moreover, they cite precedent rejecting extraterritorial Fifth Amendment protections to non-U.S. citizens.

While one cannot ignore the "shocks the conscience" test established in *Rochin v. California,* 342 U.S. 165, 172-73 (1952), that case involved the question whether torture could be used to extract evidence for the purpose of prosecuting criminal conduct, a very different question from the one ultimately presented here, to wit, whether substantive due process would erect a *per se* bar to coercive investigations, including torture, for the purpose of preventing a terrorist attack. Whether the circumstances here ultimately cry out for immediate application of the Due Process clause, or, put differently, whether torture always violates the Fifth Amendment under established Supreme Court case law prohibiting government action that "shocks the conscience"—a question analytically prior to those taken up in the parties' briefing—remains unresolved from a doctrinal standpoint. Nevertheless, because both parties seem (at least implicitly) to have answered this question in the affirmative, it will be presumed for present purposes that the Due Process clause would apply to the facts alleged.

Defendants argue that Arar's claims alleging torture and unlawful detention in Syria are *per se* foreclosed under *Johnson v. Eisentrager,* 339 U.S. 763 (1950) [see *supra* p. 321], and its progeny. These cases, they claim, unequivocally establish that non-resident aliens subjected to constitutional violations on non-U.S. soil are prohibited from bringing claims under the Due Process clause. . . .

However, there are obvious distinctions between *Eisentrager* and the case at bar. The *Eisentrager* petitioners had a trial pursuant to the laws of war. Although that trial might not have afforded them the panoply of rights provided in the civilian context, one cannot say that the petitioners had no fair process. Moreover, the *Eisentrager* detainees had "never been or resided in the United States," were "captured outside of our territory and there held in military custody as [ ] prisoner[s] of war," were "tried by a Military Commission sitting outside the United States," and were "at all times imprisoned outside the United States." *Eisentrager,* 339 U.S. at 777. Arar, by contrast, was held virtually incommunicado—moreover, on U.S. soil—and denied access to counsel and process of any kind. Owing to these factual distinctions, *Eisentrager* is not squarely applicable to the case at bar.

Defendants also cite *United States v. Verdugo-Urquidez,* 494 U.S. 259 (1990) [see *supra* p. 270], in which the Supreme Court revisited the question of the extraterritoriality of the U.S. Constitution to non-U.S. citizens. . . . After foreclosing the possibility of any extraterritorial application of the Fourth Amendment, the *Verdugo-Urquidez* court explored in dicta the same question with regard to the Fifth Amendment. Relying on dicta in *Eisentrager,* the Supreme Court held that prior case law foreclosed such possibility. . . .

However, *Verdugo-Urquidez,* which involved a search and seizure of a home in Mexico, can be distinguished from the case at bar. As Justice Kennedy observed in his concurring opinion, Mexico's different legal regime compounded (and perhaps created) the Fourth Amendment violations. "The absence of local judges or magistrates available to issue warrants, the differing and perhaps unascertainable conceptions of reasonableness and privacy that prevail abroad, and the need to cooperate with foreign officials all indicate that the Fourth Amendment's warrant requirement should not apply in Mexico as it does in this country." *Verdugo-Urquidez,* 494 U.S. at 278 (Kennedy, J., concurring).

*Verdugo-Urquidez* is further distinguishable from the instant case by the fact that the defendant in that case was prosecuted in an Article III court, where "all of the trial proceedings are governed by the Constitution. All would agree, for instance, that the dictates of the Due Process Clause of the Fifth Amendment protect the defendant." *Id.* Thus, any anxiety over the lack of Fourth Amendment protection [was] minimized by the fact that the trial would ultimately proceed in accordance with Fifth Amendment guarantees.

After *Verdugo-Urquidez,* the Court of Appeals for the District of Columbia Circuit considered a case, more directly applicable to the facts at issue here, involving a Guatemalan citizen and high-ranking member of a Guatemalan rebel organization who was allegedly tortured in Guatemala at the behest of CIA officials, who had ordered and directed the torture and then engaged in an eighteen-month cover-up. *Harbury v. Deutch,* 233 F.3d 596 (D.C. Cir. 2000), *rev'd on other grounds sub nom. Christopher v. Harbury,* 536 U.S. 403 (2002) [see *supra* p. 277]. The constitutional violations at issue in *Harbury* included torture. Moreover, the torture was allegedly planned and orchestrated by U.S. officials acting within the United States. Thus, unlike *Eisentrager* and *Verdugo-Urquidez,* the factual background of *Harbury* is closely related to the case at bar.

The D.C. Circuit relied heavily on dicta in *Verdugo-Urquidez,* particularly its reading of *Eisentrager,* to ultimately hold that the decedent's wife (a U.S. citizen) could not bring a Fifth Amendment claim on his behalf for the torture he suffered in Guatemala. The D.C. Circuit noted, first, that *Verdugo-Urquidez* did not attach constitutional significance to the fact "that the search was both planned and ordered from within the United States. Instead, it focused on the location of the primary constitutionally significant conduct at issue: the search and seizure itself." *Harbury,* 233 F.3d at 603. Because of this, the D.C. Circuit found that "the primary constitutionally relevant conduct at issue here — [the deceased's] torture — occurred outside the United States." *Id.* at 603.

The D.C. circuit further noted that *Verdugo-Urquidez* read *Eisentrager* to "emphatically" reject the notion of any extraterritorial application of the Fifth Amendment. That language, although "dicta . . . is firm and considered dicta that binds this court." *Harbury,* 233 F.3d at 604.

Still, the case at bar, unlike *Harbury,* presents a claim of torture by an alien apprehended at the U.S. border and held here pending removal; furthermore, the fact that Arar's alleged torture began with his removal from the territory of the United States makes this case factually different from *Harbury.* Nevertheless, by answering the question "whether the Fifth Amendment prohibits torture of non-resident foreign nationals living abroad" in the negative, *id.* at 602, *Harbury* appears to have important implications for the case at bar.

However, in *Rasul v. Bush,* 542 U.S. 466 (2004) [*supra* p. 326], the Supreme Court issued a ruling potentially favorable to Arar. . . .

*Rasul* only considered the question "whether the federal courts have jurisdiction to determine the legality of the Executive's potentially indefinite detention of individuals who claim to be wholly innocent of wrongdoing." *Id.* at 485. Moreover, the Supreme Court reached its decision by noting that "the United States exercises 'complete jurisdiction and control' over the Guantanamo Bay Naval Base, and may continue to exercise such control permanently if it so chooses." *Id.* at 480.

To be sure, there is no argument that the United States exercises the same control over the Syrian officials alleged to have detained and tortured Arar as it does in the case of Guantanamo Bay. Nevertheless, one might read *Rasul* as extending habeas jurisdiction to a group of aliens with even less of a connection to the United States than Arar.

Defendants reject that contention, arguing that, in light of the above-cited cases, the substantive due process violations asserted in Arar's complaint "are predicated upon a constitutional protection that has never been extended to arriving aliens, much less aliens whom the executive has determined pursuant to legislative authorization have terrorist connections." But Arar — who received none of the procedural and substantive protections afforded the petitioners in *Eisentrager* — has a connection to the United States lacking in *Eisentrager, Verdugo-Urquidez, Harbury* and *Rasul*. All of Arar's claims against U.S. officials allegedly arise out of actions taken or initiated by them while Arar was on U.S. soil. Moreover, the factual scenario presented in this case makes it more difficult to simply apply the precedents established in the *Eisentrager* line of cases.

As already noted, the *Eisentrager* detainees had "never been or resided in the United States," were "captured outside of our territory and there held in military custody as [ ] prisoner[s] of war, were 'tried by a Military Commission sitting outside the United States'" and were "at all times imprisoned outside the United States." *Eisentrager,* 339 U.S. at 777. Arar, by contrast, was held virtually incommunicado in *this* country and denied access to counsel and a meaningful process of any kind. Moreover, as the *Rasul* court noted, the Guantanamo detainees "are not nationals of countries at war with the United States, and they deny that they have engaged in or plotted acts of aggression against the United States; they have never been afforded access to any tribunal, much less charged with and convicted of wrongdoing. . . ." *Id.* at 476.

Another difference between *Rasul* and the case at bar is that *Rasul* based its jurisdiction on the statutory habeas provision (28 U.S.C. §2241), not the U.S. Constitution. Arar, by contrast, alleges substantive constitutional claims not addressed in *Rasul. See In re Guantanamo Detainee Cases,* 355 F. Supp. 2d 443, 463 (D.D.C. 2005) (citing language in *Rasul* as "stand[ing] in sharp contrast to the declaration in *Verdugo-Urquidez* . . . that the Supreme Court's 'rejection of extraterritorial application of the Fifth Amendment [has been] emphatic'").

At this juncture, the question whether the Due Process Clause vests Arar with substantive rights is unresolved. Assuming, without resolving, the existence of some substantive protection, Arar's claims are foreclosed under an exception to the *Bivens* doctrine.

## Special Factors Counseling Hesitation

The substantive due process analysis notwithstanding, the Supreme Court's creation of a *Bivens* remedy for alleged constitutional violations by federal officials is subject to certain prudential limitations and exceptions. The Supreme Court has "expressly cautioned . . . that such a remedy will not be available when 'special factors counseling hesitation' are present." *Chappell v. Wallace,* 462 U.S. 296, 298 (1983) (quoting *Bivens,* 403 U.S. at 396). Those factors do not concern "the merits of the particular remedy [being] sought." *Bush v. Lucas,* 462 U.S. 367, 380 (1983). Rather, they involve "the question of who should decide whether such a remedy should be provided." *Id.* . . . Moreover, courts will refrain from extending a *Bivens* claim if doing so trammels upon matters best decided by coordinate branches of government. *See Lucas,* 462 U.S. at 378-80 (discussing case law according to which courts have deferred to coordinate branches). . . .

This case undoubtedly presents broad questions touching on the role of the Executive branch in combating terrorist forces — namely the prevention of future terrorist attacks within U.S. borders by capturing or containing members of those groups who seek to inflict damage on this country and its people. Success in these efforts requires coordination between law-enforcement and foreign-policy officials; complex relationships with foreign governments are also involved. In light of these factors, courts must proceed cautiously in reviewing constitutional and statutory claims in that arena, especially where they raise policy-making issues that are the prerogative of coordinate branches of government.

A number of considerations must be noted here. First, Article I, Section 8 of the U.S. Constitution places the regulation of aliens squarely within the authority of the Legislative branch. Congress has yet to take any affirmative position on federal-court review of renditions; indeed, by withholding any explicit grant of a private cause of action under the Torture Victim Protection Act to plaintiffs like Arar . . . the opposite is the more reasonable inference.

Second, this case raises crucial national-security and foreign policy considerations, implicating "the complicated multilateral negotiations concerning efforts to halt international terrorism." *Doherty v. Meese,* 808 F.2d 938, 943 (2d Cir. 1986). The propriety of these considerations, including supposed agreements between the United States and foreign governments regarding intelligence-gathering in the context of the efforts to combat terrorism, are most appropriately reserved to the Executive and Legislative branches of government. Moreover, the need for much secrecy can hardly be doubted. One need not have much imagination to contemplate the negative effect on our relations with Canada if discovery were to proceed in this case and were it to turn out that certain high Canadian officials had, despite public denials, acquiesced in Arar's removal to Syria. More generally, governments that do not wish to acknowledge publicly that they are assisting us would certainly hesitate to do so if our judicial discovery process could compromise them. Even a ruling sustaining state-secret-based objections to a request for interrogatories, discovery demand, or questioning of a witness could be compromising. Depending on the context it could be construed as the equivalent of a public admission that the alleged conduct had occurred in the manner claimed — to the detriment of our relations with foreign countries, whether friendly or not. Hence, extending a *Bivens* remedy "could significantly disrupt the ability of the political branches to respond to foreign situations involving our national interest." *Verdugo-Urquidez,* 494 U.S. 259, 273-274. It risks "produc[ing] what the Supreme Court has called in another context 'embarrassment of our government abroad' through 'multifarious pronouncements by various departments on one question.'" *Sanchez-Espinoza v. Reagan,* 770 F.2d 202, 208 (D.C. Cir. 1985) (Scalia, J.) (quoting *Baker v. Carr,* 369 U.S. 186, 226, 217 (1962)). . . .

Third, with respect to these coordinate branch concerns, there is a fundamental difference between courts evaluating the legitimacy of actions taken by federal officials in the domestic arena and evaluating the same conduct when taken in the international realm. In the former situation . . . judges have not only the authority vested under the Constitution to evaluate the decision-making of government officials that goes on in the domestic context, whether it be a civil or a criminal matter, but also the experience derived from living in a free and democratic society, which permits them to make sound judgments. In the international realm, however, most, if not all, judges have neither the experience nor the background to adequately and competently define and adjudge the rights of an individual vis-à-vis the needs of officials acting to defend the sovereign interests of the United States, especially in circumstances involving countries that do not accept our nation's values or may be assisting those out to destroy us. . . .

Accordingly, the task of balancing individual rights against national-security concerns is one that courts should not undertake without the guidance or the authority of the coordinate branches, in whom the Constitution imposes responsibility for our foreign affairs and national security. Those branches have the responsibility to determine whether judicial oversight is appropriate. Without explicit legislation, judges should be hesitant to fill an arena that, until now, has been left untouched — perhaps deliberately — by the Legislative and Executive branches. To do otherwise would threaten "our customary policy of deference to the President in matters of foreign affairs." [Jama v. Immigration and Customs Enforcement, 543 U.S. 335 (2005)], at 348. In sum, whether the policy be seeking to undermine or overthrow foreign governments, or rendition, judges should not, in the absence of explicit direction by Congress, hold officials who carry out such policies liable for damages even if such conduct violates our treaty obligations or customary international law.

For these reasons, I conclude that a remedy under *Bivens* for Arar's alleged rendition to Syria is foreclosed. Accordingly, Counts 2 and 3 of the complaint are dismissed. . . .

[The court also dismissed Arar's claim of substantive due process violations based on his treatment while in the United States, but the dismissal without prejudice allows Arar to refile and supply more detail concerning the physical mistreatment he alleges occurred.]

## NOTES AND QUESTIONS

1. ***Corroborating Arar's Story?***  On March 30, 2005, media sources reported the discovery of flight records that appear to corroborate at least part of Arar's story. *See* Scott Shane, Stephen Grey & Ford Fessenden, *Detainee's Suit Gains Support from Jet's Log*, N.Y. Times, Mar. 30, 2005, at A1. A year and a half later, a Canadian government Commission of Inquiry set up to investigate what happened to Arar released a three-volume report. Commission of Inquiry into the Actions of Canadian Officials in Relation to Maher Arar, *Report of the Events Relating to Maher Arar: Analysis and Recommendations*, Sept. 18, 2006. The Commission found no evidence that Arar committed any crime or that his activities threatened the security of Canada. *See* Press Release, *Arar Commission Releases Its Findings on the*

*Handling of the Maher Arar Case,* Sept. 18, 2006, *available at* http://www.ararcommission.ca/eng/ReleaseFinal_Sept18.pdf. It also found that Canadian investigators erroneously placed Arar and his wife on a "terrorist lookout" list, which in turn led the Mounted Police to include them in a database that alerts U.S. border officers to suspect individuals. The police falsely described them as "Islamic extremists suspected of being linked to the al Qaeda movement." Ian Austen, *Canadians Fault U.S. for Its Role in Torture Case*, N.Y. Times, Sept. 19, 2006, at A1.

While Arar was detained in New York, Canadian officials communicated to U.S. officials that they had been unable to find any connection between Arar and al Qaeda and that he would be subject to surveillance but not arrest if he returned home to Canada. Canadian officials were unaware that, at the time, U.S. officials were planning to render Arar to Syria. Despite the Canadian inquiry and subsequent Commission report, on January 16, 2007, Attorney General Gonzales and Homeland Security Secretary Michael Chertoff wrote a letter to the Canadian minister of public safety and concluded, after a re-examination of materials in the possession of the United States regarding Arar, that "continued watch-listing of Mr. Arar is appropriate." Scott Shane, *Canadian to Remain on U.S. Terrorist Watch List*, N.Y. Times, Jan. 23, 2007, at A1. How do you account for these very different positions on Arar by the two governments?

2. **Scope of the Operations.** No one knows for sure how many extraordinary renditions have occurred. Rendition of suspected terrorists to other nations apparently has been part of U.S. counterterrorism activities since the late 1990s, and perhaps since a directive from President Ronald Reagan in 1986. Some estimate that more than 100 persons have been thus rendered by the United States since the September 11 attacks. Dana Priest, *CIA's Assurances on Transferred Suspects Doubted*, Wash. Post, Mar. 17, 2005, at A1. Reported destinations for extraordinary rendition include Egypt, Jordan, Morocco, Saudi Arabia, Yemen, and Syria, all condemned by the U.S. State Department as employing torture in interrogation. *See* Jane Mayer, *Outsourcing Torture*, New Yorker, Feb. 14, 2005, at 106. In March 2005, it was reported that President Bush issued a classified directive following the September 11 attacks that broadened the CIA's authority to render suspected terrorists to other states. Eighteen months later, in September 2006, President Bush confirmed the existence of a previously classified CIA program to detain and interrogate suspected terrorists, reportedly created on September 17, 2001, by secret presidential directive. *See* David Johnston, *At a Secret Interrogation, Dispute Flares Over Tactics*, N.Y. Times, Sept. 10, 2006, at 1. There is also evidence that the Department of Defense has participated in these operations through the use of military aircraft and airbases, and that the FBI has joined in at least one interrogation session pursuant to one such rendition. *See* Margaret L. Satterthwaite, *Rendered Meaningless: Extraordinary Rendition and the Rule of Law*, 75 Geo. Wash. L. Rev. (forthcoming 2007). What are the likely authorities that each of these agencies would cite as legal justification for their participation in extraordinary rendition?

In June 2005, Italian police officials issued arrest warrants for 22 alleged U.S. intelligence operatives in connection with the rendering of an Islamic cleric from Italy to Egypt without the consent of the Italian government. Although some reported that Italian authorities knew of and consented to the rendition, the Italian government denied those reports. Craig Whitlock, *Italy Denies Complicity in Alleged CIA Action*, Wash. Post, July 1, 2005, at A14. In February 2007, an Italian judge issued indictments against 26 Americans, most of them CIA agents, and ordered their trial for their involvement in the 2003 kidnapping of the cleric. All of the agents have left Italy, and there is no indication that Italy will seek their extradition or that the United States would agree to such a request. *See* Ian Fisher, *Italy Indicts 26 Americans in C.I.A. Abduction Case*, N.Y. Times, Feb. 16, 2007, at A1. Other examples of alleged extraordinary renditions, compiled from news sources, are summarized in Comm. on Intl. Human Rts. of the Assn. of the Bar of the City of New York and Center for Human Rights and Global Justice, N.Y.U. School of Law, *Torture by Proxy: International and Domestic Law Applicable to "Extraordinary Renditions"* 9-13 (2004), *available at* http://www.nyuhr.org/docs/TortureByProxy.pdf. *See also* Amnesty Intl., *Below the Radar: Secret Flights to Torture and "Disappearance,"* Apr. 5, 2006, *available at* http://web.amnesty.org/library/Index/ENGAMR510512006.

3. ***CIA Charter Flights.*** Some extraordinary renditions have reportedly been carried out by the CIA pursuant to broadly worded findings approved by the President. Douglas Jehl & David Johnston, *Rule Change Lets CIA Freely Send Suspects Abroad to Jails*, N.Y. Times, Mar. 6, 2005, at A1. An apparently private charter company, Aero Contractors, is actually a domestic centerpiece of the CIA secret air service that conducts flights to render suspects abroad. *See* Scott Shane, *CIA Expanding Terror Battle Under Guise of Charter Flights*, N.Y. Times, May 31, 2005, at A1. One 2005 analysis of 26 planes operated by CIA companies showed 307 flights in Europe since September 2001. Ian Fisher, *Reports of Secret U.S. Prisons in Europe Draw Ire and Otherwise Red Faces*, N.Y. Times, Dec. 1, 2005, A14. Assuming that the President's findings complied with the National Security Act, which requires that the findings be reported to the intelligence committees of the Senate and House, 50 U.S.C. §413b, are the renditions lawful? Does it matter legally if Congress is not notified about individual cases?

4. ***Why Do It?*** Why would the United States sponsor or participate in extraordinary renditions? One unnamed official with experience in so rendering detainees explained: "We don't kick the [expletive] out of them. We send them to other countries so they can kick the [expletive] out of them." Dana Priest & Barton Gellman, *U.S. Decries Abuse but Defends Interrogations; "Stress and Duress" Tactics Used on Terrorism Suspects Held in Secret Overseas Facilities*, Wash. Post, Dec. 26, 2002, at A1. A former CIA agent put it this way:

> If you want a serious interrogation, you send a prisoner to Jordan.
> If you want them to be tortured, you send them to Syria. If you
> want someone to disappear — never to be seen again — you send
> them to Egypt. [Lily Rajiva, *The CIA's Rendition Flights to Secret*

*Prisons: The Torture-Go-Round*, Counterpunch, Dec. 5, 2005, *available at* http://www.counterpunch.org/rajival2052005.html.]

If the former CIA agent had been willing to make this statement in Arar's lawsuit, what impact would the testimony have had on the outcome?

5. ***Arar v. Ashcroft and the Availability of Judicial Remedies.*** In an omitted portion of Arar v. Ashcroft, the court ruled that the Torture Victim Protection Act (TVPA) creates no private right of action for rendition of a person who may be subjected to torture. Nor does the TVPA apply where U.S. officials allegedly direct foreign officials to torture a non-U.S. citizen. 414 F. Supp. 2d at 266. Of what value, then, is the TVPA to victims of torture?

Why did the court decline to decide Arar's claim for damages arising out of the alleged due process violations? What is the basis for the exception to the *Bivens* constitutional torts doctrine, where "foreign policy and national security" concerns suggest that the claims asserted should "be left to the political branches of government"? *Id.* at 283. Are the political branches better suited than the court to resolve Arar's dispute with the United States?

In El-Masri v. United States, 479 F.3d 296 (4th Cir. 2007), the Fourth Circuit affirmed a district court dismissal of a civil action by German citizen Khaled El-Masri against the CIA and corporate defendants for their part in a CIA rendition of El-Masri from Macedonia to Afghanistan, where he was detained, beaten, drugged, confined in a small unsanitary cell, interrogated several times, and prevented from communicating with his family or his government. El-Masri made claims of Fifth Amendment constitutional rights violations and Alien Tort Statute claims for prolonged detention and for cruel, inhuman, and degrading treatment. After the United States intervened as a defendant in the district court, it urged and the district court and court of appeals agreed that El-Masri's action could not proceed because it posed an unreasonable risk that state secrets would be disclosed. *Id.* at 301-313. The court rejected El-Masri's contention that by yielding to the government's state secrets claims, the court had abdicated its role:

> [I]t is the court, not the Executive, that determines whether the state secrets privilege has been properly invoked. In order to successfully claim the state secrets privilege, the Executive must satisfy the court that disclosure of the information sought to be protected would expose matters that, in the interest of national security, ought to remain secret. [*Id.* at 312.]

In January 2007, a German court issued an arrest warrant for 13 members of an alleged CIA "abduction team" that reportedly took part in rendering El-Masri. *See* Mark Landler, *German Court Seeks Arrest of 13 C.I.A. Agents*, N.Y. Times, Jan. 31, 2007, at A1.

6. ***Availability of Habeas Corpus.*** In Abu Ali v. Ashcroft, 350 F. Supp. 2d 28 (D.D.C. 2004), U.S. citizen Omar Abu Ali challenged his ongoing detention in a prison in Saudi Arabia allegedly at the direction and with the ongoing supervision of the United States. When Abu Ali's parents

sought habeas corpus for their son, the United States argued that the suit must be dismissed for lack of jurisdiction, "no matter how extensive a role the United States might have played and continues to play" in Abu Ali's detention, "for the sole reason that he is presently in a foreign prison." *Id.* at 40. The court held that the United States may not avoid habeas corpus jurisdiction by enlisting a foreign nation to detain an American citizen:

> This position is as striking as it is sweeping. The full contours of the position would permit the United States, at its discretion and without judicial review, to arrest a citizen of the United States and transfer her to the custody of allies overseas in order to avoid constitutional scrutiny; to arrest a citizen of the United States through the intermediary of a foreign ally and ask the ally to hold the citizen at a foreign location indefinitely at the direction of the United States; or even to deliver American citizens to foreign governments to obtain information through the use of torture. In short, the United States is in effect arguing for nothing less than the unreviewable power to separate an "American citizen from the most fundamental of his constitutional rights merely by choosing where he will be detained or who will detain him." [*Id.*]

How, if at all, does the court's answer to the government affect those in a situation similar to Arar's?

7. ***Due Process.*** If the court had reached the merits on Arar's due process claim, what should the outcome have been? Which precedents provide guideposts that are most portable to the *Arar* setting — Verdugo-Urquidez v. United States, *supra* p. 270, Johnson v. Eisentrager, *supra* p. 321, Harbury v. Deutch, noted *supra* p. 277, or Rasul v. Bush, *supra* p. 326?

8. ***The CAT and Implementing Legislation.*** Upon release of the Commission of Inquiry report concerning Maher Arar, a Justice Department spokesperson stated that the U.S. government "removed Mr. Arar in full compliance with the law and applicable treaties and conventions." The government also claimed to have "sought assurances with respect to Mr. Arar's treatment" in Syria. *See* Scott Shane, *Torture Victim Had No Terror Link, Canada Told U.S.*, N.Y. Times, Sept. 25, 2006, at A1. Review the discussion of the Convention Against Torture and its implementing legislation, *supra* pp. 414-417. CAT Article 3 provides that "[n]o State Party shall expel, return ('refouler') or extradite a person to another State where there are substantial grounds for believing that he would be in danger of being subjected to torture." An understanding attached to the convention by the Senate upon its advice and consent states that the requirement in Article 3 would apply when it is "more likely than not" that torture would follow such a rendition. Sen. Exec. Rpt. No. 101-30, *Resolution of Advice and Consent to Ratification* (1990), at ¶II(2).

What information should lawyers take into account when asked to advise on a "more likely than not" determination? On what basis would U.S. officials have obtained "assurances" from Syria regarding Arar's treatment? Of what value are such assurances? *See* Satterthwaite, *supra*.

The CAT lacks a parallel provision regarding cruel, inhuman, or degrading treatment. What is the legal significance of this omission? *See* Michael John Garcia, *Renditions: Constraints Imposed by Laws on Torture* (Cong. Res. Serv. RL32890) 8, Apr. 5, 2006.

In 1998, Congress approved legislation implementing Article 3 of the CAT. Pub. L. No. 105-277, §2242(a)-(b), 112 Stat. 2681, 2681-822. Although Congress gave immigration officials administrative discretion in excluding from CAT protection certain classes of aliens, current Department of Homeland Security regulations prohibit the removal of all persons to states where they more likely than not would be tortured. 8 C.F.R. §§208.16-18, 1208.16-18 (2006). CIA regulations concerning renditions, if any, are not publicly available. Garcia, *supra,* at 9.

The criminal sanctions implementing Articles 4 and 5 of the CAT forbid torture outside the United States. Review the specific intent required by the statute. See *supra* p. 414. Would the torturer be liable if the torture occurred, say, in Syria? How about the CIA official who arranged for the extraordinary rendition?

9. ***Official Policy?*** The Bush administration has not denied that persons have been rendered to foreign nations reputed to practice torture. However, officials have denied that renditions have occurred for the purpose of torture. *See* R. Jeffrey Smith, *Gonzales Defends Transfer of Detainees*, Wash. Post, Mar. 8, 2005, at A3 (quoting Attorney General Gonzales as stating that it is not U.S. policy to send persons "to countries where we believe or we know that they're going to be tortured"); Joel Brinkley, *U.S. Interrogations Are Saving European Lives, Rice Says*, N.Y. Times, Dec. 6, 2005, at A3 (quoting Secretary of State Condoleezza Rice as stating that "[t]he United States does not transport and has not transported detainees from one country to another for the purpose of interrogation using torture."). When President Bush reported the existence of the CIA detention and interrogation program in September 2006, he reiterated that "the United States does not torture." Jennifer K. Elsea & Julie Kim, *Undisclosed U.S. Detention Sites Overseas: Background and Legal Issues* 1 (Cong. Res. Serv. RL33643), Sept. 12, 2006. How much legal wiggle room do these statements preserve for the Administration? How, if at all, should these statements of U.S. policy affect Arar's likelihood of gaining relief in his lawsuit?

CAT Article 4 and its implementing legislation would, in any case, provide criminal penalties for U.S. officials who conspire with others to render a person to facilitate torture. Recall, however, Attorney General Gonzales's comment above. Would a mere belief that a suspect might be tortured in the destination state be sufficient to attach criminal responsibility to U.S. officials for any torture that occurs there?

10. ***Geneva Convention Limits on Rendition.*** An involuntary transfer of "protected persons" to another state is forbidden by Geneva Convention IV, Article 49. A violation constitutes a "grave breach" and is thus a war crime. *Id.* art. 147. Recall, from the last chapter, the Bush administration's arguments concerning the applicability of the Geneva Conventions in the post-September 11 campaign. Which persons in what places are protected from rendition under the Geneva Conventions? Would these provisions be helpful to Maher Arar in his lawsuit?

11. ***Effect of the Detainee Treatment Act.*** Review the language of the Detainee Treatment Act set forth *supra* p. 443. If this provision had been in effect when Arar was rendered to Syria, would the Act have been violated? Does the Act establish rights for detainees that they otherwise would not enjoy?

12. ***The High Value Terrorist Detainee Program.*** In September 2006, Director of National Intelligence (DNI) John Negroponte described a CIA detention and interrogation program involving captured detainees "who have been in the inner circle" of al Qaeda and who "hold information that simply cannot be obtained from any other source." Office of the Director of National Intelligence, *Summary of the High Value Terrorist Detainee Program* (n.d.), *available at* http://www.dni.gov/announcements/content/ TheHighValueDetaineeProgram.pdf. According to the statement, the CIA program "is designed to ensure that intelligence is collected in a manner that does not violate the Constitution, any US statute, or US treaty obligations." *Id.* at 2. The statement further asserts that the Justice Department "has reviewed the procedures proposed by the CIA on more than one occasion and determined them to be lawful." *Id.* CIA interrogation is considered in Chapter 13. If some of those detained and interrogated subject to this program were rendered by the United States to foreign countries as part of the program, does DNI Negroponte's assurance also apply to the renditions? How could his assertion be tested?

# PART V

# ARRESTING, PROSECUTING, AND REMOVING TERRORISTS

# CHAPTER 15

# CRIMINALIZING TREASON, TERRORISM, AND MATERIAL SUPPORT

Generally, First Amendment protections for freedom of speech, assembly, and association pose no obstacle to prosecution of terrorists for committing terrorist acts. Murder and maiming enjoy no constitutional protection. But the prosecution of such primary offenders — if they survive the terrorist attack and are successfully hunted down — comes too late to prevent the harm. Nor is such prosecution likely to deter others who are religiously or politically motivated to commit terrorist attacks. Counterterrorist criminal law therefore necessarily searches up the chain of causation for secondary defendants who aid and abet, conspire, harbor, or otherwise assist the terrorists. Prosecution of either primary or secondary defendants is complicated when their conduct takes place abroad, given the normal presumption against extraterritorial application of U.S. law.

In Part A of this chapter, we begin with a case that suggests that the hoary criminal laws of treason and sedition may be a poor fit for such prosecutions. In the 1990s, Congress therefore criminalized providing "material support" to terrorists or designated foreign terrorist organizations. See Chapters 1, 19, and 22 (describing other effects of designation). In Part B, we consider these laws and the issues they raise about criminalizing advocacy and association as well as personal guilt. Finally, in Part C we consider the extraterritorial application of these and other U.S. counterterrorism laws.

## A. TREASON AND SEDITION

### UNITED STATES V. RAHMAN

United States Court of Appeals, Second Circuit, 1999
189 F.3d 88

PER CURIAM: These are appeals by ten defendants convicted of seditious conspiracy and other offenses arising out of a wide-ranging plot to conduct a campaign of urban terrorism. Among the activities of some or all of the defendants were rendering assistance to those who bombed the World Trade Center, planning to bomb bridges and tunnels in New York City, murdering Rabbi Meir

Kahane, and planning to murder the President of Egypt. We affirm the convictions of all the defendants. . . .

The Government adduced evidence at trial showing the following: Abdel Rahman, a blind Islamic scholar and cleric, was the leader of the seditious conspiracy, the purpose of which was *"jihad,"* in the sense of a struggle against the enemies of Islam. Indicative of this purpose, in a speech to his followers Abdel Rahman instructed that they were to "do *jihad* with the sword, with the cannon, with the grenades, with the missile . . . against God's enemies." Abdel Rahman's role in the conspiracy was generally limited to overall supervision and direction of the membership, as he made efforts to remain a level above the details of individual operations. However, as a cleric and the group's leader, Abdel Rahman was entitled to dispense *"fatwas,"* religious opinions on the holiness of an act, to members of the group sanctioning proposed courses of conduct and advising them whether the acts would be in furtherance of *jihad.*

According to his speeches and writings, Abdel Rahman perceives the United States as the primary oppressor of Muslims worldwide, active in assisting Israel to gain power in the Middle East, and largely under the control of the Jewish lobby. Abdel Rahman also considers the secular Egyptian government of Mubarak to be an oppressor because it has abided Jewish migration to Israel while seeking to decrease Muslim births. Holding these views, Abdel Rahman believes that *jihad* against Egypt and the United States is mandated by the Qur'an. Formation of a *jihad* army made up of small "divisions" and "battalions" to carry out this *jihad* was therefore necessary, according to Abdel Rahman, in order to beat back these oppressors of Islam including the United States. . . .

## I. Constitutional Challenges

### A. Seditious Conspiracy Statute and the Treason Clause

Defendant Nosair (joined by other defendants) contends that his conviction for seditious conspiracy, in violation of 18 U.S.C. §2384, was illegal because it failed to satisfy the requirements of the Treason Clause of the U.S. Constitution, Art. III, §3.

Article III, Section 3 provides, in relevant part:

> Treason against the United States, shall consist only in levying War against them, or in adhering to their Enemies, giving them Aid and Comfort. No Person shall be convicted of Treason unless on the Testimony of two Witnesses to the same overt Act, or on Confession in open Court.

The seditious conspiracy statute provides:

> If two or more persons in any State or Territory, or in any place subject to the jurisdiction of the United States, conspire to overthrow, put down or to destroy by force the Government of the United States, or to levy war against them, or to oppose by force the authority thereof, or by force to prevent, hinder or delay the execution of any law of the United States, or by force to seize, take, or possess

any property of the United States contrary to the authority thereof, they shall each be fined under this title or imprisoned not more than twenty years, or both.

18 U.S.C. §2384.

Nosair contends that because the seditious conspiracy statute punishes conspiracy to "levy war" against the United States without a conforming two-witness requirement, the statute is unconstitutional. He further claims that because his conviction for conspiracy to levy war against the United States was not based on the testimony of two witnesses to the same overt act, the conviction violates constitutional standards.

It is undisputed that Nosair's conviction was not supported by two witnesses to the same overt act. Accordingly the conviction must be overturned if the requirement of the Treason Clause applies to this prosecution for seditious conspiracy.

The plain answer is that the Treason Clause does not apply to the prosecution. The provisions of Article III, Section 3 apply to prosecutions for "treason." Nosair and his co-appellants were not charged with treason. Their offense of conviction, seditious conspiracy under Section 2384, differs from treason not only in name and associated stigma, but also in its essential elements and punishment. . . .

Seditious conspiracy by levying war includes no requirement that the defendant owe allegiance to the United States, an element necessary to conviction of treason. *See* 18 U.S.C. §2381 (defining "allegiance to United States" as an element of treason). . . .

The reference to treason in the constitutional clause necessarily incorporates the elements of allegiance and betrayal that are essential to the concept of treason. . . . Nosair was thus tried for a different, and lesser, offense than treason. We therefore see no reasonable basis to maintain that the requirements of the Treason Clause should apply to Nosair's prosecution.

## B. Seditious Conspiracy Statute and the First Amendment

Abdel Rahman, joined by the other appellants, contends that the seditious conspiracy statute, 18 U.S.C. §2384, is an unconstitutional burden on free speech and the free exercise of religion in violation of the First Amendment. First, Abdel Rahman argues that the statute is facially invalid because it criminalizes protected expression and that it is overbroad and unconstitutionally vague. Second, Abdel Rahman contends that his conviction violated the First Amendment because it rested solely on his political views and religious practices.

### 1. Facial Challenge

**a. *Restraint on Speech*.** . . . As Section 2384 proscribes "speech" only when it constitutes an agreement to use force against the United States, Abdel Rahman's generalized First Amendment challenge to the statute is without merit. Our court has previously considered and rejected a First Amendment challenge to Section 2384. *See* United States v. Lebron, 222 F.2d 531, 536 (2d Cir. 1955). Although *Lebron*'s analysis of the First Amendment issues posed by Section 2384 was brief, the panel found the question was squarely controlled by the Supreme Court's then-recent decision in Dennis v. United States, 341 U.S. 494 (1951). In *Dennis*, the Court upheld the constitutionality of the Smith Act, which made it a crime to advocate, or to conspire to advocate, the overthrow of the United States government by force or violence. *See* 18 U.S.C. §2385; *Dennis*, 341 U.S. at 494. The *Dennis* Court concluded that, while the "element of speech" inherent in Smith Act convictions required that the Act be given close First Amendment scrutiny, the Act did not impermissibly burden the expression of protected speech, as it was properly "directed at advocacy [of overthrow of the government by force], not discussion." *See id.* at 502.

After *Dennis*, the Court broadened the scope of First Amendment restrictions on laws that criminalize subversive advocacy. It remains fundamental that while the state may not criminalize the expression of views — even including the view that violent overthrow of the government is desirable — it may nonetheless outlaw encouragement, inducement, or conspiracy to take violent action. Thus, in Yates v. United States, 354 U.S. 298, 318 (1957), overruled in part on other grounds, Burks v. United States, 437 U.S. 1, 7 (1978), the Court interpreted the Smith Act to prohibit only the advocacy of concrete violent action, but not "advocacy and teaching of forcible overthrow as an abstract principle, divorced from any effort to instigate action to that end." And in Brandenburg v. Ohio, 395 U.S. 444, 447 (1969) (per curiam), the Court held that a state may proscribe subversive advocacy only when such advocacy is directed towards, and is likely to result in, "imminent lawless action."

The prohibitions of the seditious conspiracy statute are much further removed from the realm of constitutionally protected speech than those at issue in *Dennis* and its progeny. To be convicted under Section 2384, one must conspire to *use* force, not just to *advocate* the use of force. We have no doubt that this passes the test of constitutionality. . . .

**b. *Vagueness and Overbreadth.*** Abdel Rahman also contends that Section 2384 is overbroad and void for vagueness.

**(i) *Overbreadth.*** A law is overbroad, and hence void, if it "does not aim specifically at evils within the allowable area of State control, but, on the contrary, sweeps within its ambit other activities that . . . constitute an exercise of freedom of speech or of the press." Thornhill v. Alabama, 310 U.S. 88, 97 (1940). . . .

We recognize that laws targeting "sedition" must be scrutinized with care to assure that the threat of prosecution will not deter expression of unpopular viewpoints by persons ideologically opposed to the government. But Section 2384 is drawn sufficiently narrowly that we perceive no unacceptable risk of such abuse.

Abdel Rahman argues that Section 2384 is overbroad because Congress could have achieved its public safety aims "without chilling First Amendment rights" by punishing only "substantive acts involving bombs, weapons, or other violent acts." One of the beneficial purposes of the conspiracy law is to permit arrest and prosecution before the substantive crime has been accomplished. The Government, possessed of evidence of conspiratorial planning, need not wait until buildings and tunnels have been bombed and people killed before arresting the conspirators. Accordingly, it is well established that the Government may criminalize certain preparatory steps towards criminal action, even when the crime consists of the use of conspiratorial or exhortatory words. Because Section 2384 prohibits only conspiratorial agreement, we are satisfied that the statute is not constitutionally overbroad.

(ii) *Vagueness.* Abdel Rahman also challenges the statute for vagueness. A criminal statute, particularly one regulating speech, must "define the criminal offense with sufficient definiteness that ordinary people can understand what conduct is prohibited and in a manner that does not encourage arbitrary and discriminatory enforcement." Kolender v. Lawson, 461 U.S. 352, 357 (1983). Abdel Rahman argues that Section 2384 does not provide "fair warning" about what acts are unlawful, leaving constitutionally protected speech vulnerable to criminal prosecution.

There is indeed authority suggesting that the word "seditious" does not sufficiently convey what conduct it forbids to serve as an essential element of a crime. *See* Keyishian v. Board of Regents, 385 U.S. 589, 598 (1967) (noting that "dangers fatal to First Amendment freedoms inhere in the word 'seditious,'" and invalidating law that provided, *inter alia,* that state employees who utter "seditious words" may be discharged). But the word "seditious" does not appear in the prohibitory text of the statute; it appears only in the caption. The terms of the statute are far more precise. The portions charged against Abdel Rahman and his co-defendants — conspiracy to levy war against the United States and to oppose by force the authority thereof — do not involve terms of such vague meaning. Furthermore, they unquestionably specify that agreement *to use force* is an essential element of the crime. Abdel Rahman therefore cannot prevail on the claim that the portions of Section 2384 charged against him criminalize mere expressions of opinion, or are unduly vague.

## 2. Application of Section 2384 to Abdel Rahman's Case

Abdel Rahman also argues that he was convicted not for entering into any conspiratorial agreement that Congress may properly forbid, but "solely for his religious words and deeds" which, he contends, are protected by the First Amendment. In support of this claim, Abdel Rahman cites the Government's use in evidence of his speeches and writings.

There are two answers to Abdel Rahman's contention. The first is that freedom of speech and of religion do not extend so far as to bar prosecution of one who uses a public speech or a religious ministry to commit crimes. Numerous crimes under the federal criminal code are, or can be, committed by speech alone. As examples: Section 2 makes it an offense to "counsel[ ]," "command[ ]," "induce[ ]" or "procure[ ]" the commission of an offense against the United States. 18 U.S.C. §2(a). Section 371 makes it a crime to "conspire . . . to commit any offense against the United States." 18 U.S.C. §371. Section 373, with which Abdel Rahman was charged, makes it a crime to "solicit[ ], command[ ], induce[ ], or otherwise endeavor[ ] to persuade" another person to commit a crime of violence. 18 U.S.C. §373(a). Various other statutes, like Section 2384, criminalize conspiracies of specified objectives, *see, e.g.*, 18 U.S.C. §1751(d) (conspiracy to kidnap); 18 U.S.C. §1951 (conspiracy to interfere with commerce through robbery, extortion, or violence); 21 U.S.C. §846 (conspiracy to violate drug laws). All of these offenses are characteristically committed through speech. Notwithstanding that political speech and religious exercise are among the activities most jealously guarded by the First Amendment, one is not immunized from prosecution for such speech-based offenses merely because one commits them through the medium of political speech or religious preaching. Of course, courts must be vigilant to insure that prosecutions are not improperly based on the mere expression of unpopular ideas. But if the evidence shows that the speeches crossed the line into criminal solicitation, procurement of criminal activity, or conspiracy to violate the laws, the prosecution is permissible.

The evidence justifying Abdel Rahman's conviction for conspiracy and solicitation showed beyond a reasonable doubt that he crossed this line. His speeches were not simply the expression of ideas; in some instances they constituted the crime of conspiracy to wage war on the United States under Section 2384 and solicitation of attack on the United States military installations, as well as of the murder of Egyptian President Hosni Mubarak under Section 373.

For example: Abdel Rahman told Salem he "should make up with God . . . by turning his rifle's barrel to President Mubarak's chest, and kill[ing] him." Tr. 4633.

On another occasion, speaking to Abdo Mohammed Haggag about murdering President Mubarak during his visit to the United States, Abdel Rahman told Haggag, "Depend on God. Carry out this operation. It does not require a fatwa. . . . You are ready in training, but do it. Go ahead." Tr. 10108.

The evidence further showed that Siddig Ali consulted with Abdel Rahman about the bombing of the United Nations Headquarters, and Abdel Rahman told him, "Yes, it's a must, it's a duty." Tr. 5527-5529.

On another occasion, when Abdel Rahman was asked by Salem about bombing the United Nations, he counseled against it on the ground that it would be "bad for Muslims," Tr. 6029, but added that Salem should "find a plan to destroy or to bomb or to . . . inflict damage to the American Army." Tr. 6029-6030.

Words of this nature — ones that instruct, solicit, or persuade others to commit crimes of violence — violate the law and may be properly prosecuted regardless of whether they are uttered in private, or in a public speech, or in administering the duties of a religious ministry. The fact that his speech or conduct was "religious" does not immunize him from prosecution under generally-applicable criminal statutes.

Abdel Rahman also protests the Government's use in evidence of his speeches, writings, and preachings that did not in themselves constitute the crimes of solicitation or conspiracy. He is correct that the Government placed in evidence many instances of Abdel Rahman's writings and speeches in which Abdel Rahman expressed his opinions within the protection of the First Amendment. However, while the First Amendment fully protects Abdel Rahman's right to express hostility against the United States, and he may not be prosecuted for so speaking, it does not prevent the use of such speeches or writings in evidence when relevant to prove a pertinent fact in a criminal prosecution. The Government was free to demonstrate Abdel Rahman's resentment and hostility toward the United States in order to show his motive for soliciting and procuring illegal attacks against the United States and against President Mubarak of Egypt.

Furthermore, Judge Mukasey properly protected against the danger that Abdel Rahman might be convicted because of his unpopular religious beliefs that were hostile to the United States. He explained to the jury the limited use it was entitled to make of the material received as evidence of motive. He instructed that a defendant could not be convicted on the basis of his beliefs or the expression of them — even if those beliefs favored violence. He properly instructed the jury that it could find a defendant guilty only if the evidence proved he committed a crime charged in the indictment.

We reject Abdel Rahman's claim that his conviction violated his rights under the First Amendment. . . .

## NOTES AND QUESTIONS

1. *Treason.* "Treason" is the only crime expressly identified in the Constitution, which states that "Treason against the United States, shall consist only in levying War against them, or in adhering to their Enemies, giving them Aid and Comfort." U.S. Const. art. III, §3. Furthermore, the text supplies a special evidentiary rule for treason prosecutions: "No Person shall be convicted of Treason unless on the Testimony of two Witnesses to the same overt Act, or on Confession in open Court." *Id.* Why did the Framers single out treason for special mention and write an evidentiary rule for treason prosecutions directly into the Constitution, yet leave other crimes to legislative definition and evidentiary rules to common law development?

The restrictive nature of the constitutional rule of evidence suggests an answer: the Framers feared that the state would use treason prosecutions to suppress dissent.

> The treason clause is a product of the awareness of the Framers of the "numerous and dangerous excrescences" which had disfigured the English law of treason and was therefore intended to put it beyond the power of Congress to "extend the crime and punishment of treason." The debate in the Convention, remarks in the ratifying conventions, and contemporaneous public comment make clear that a restrictive concept of the crime was imposed and that ordinary partisan divisions within political society were not to be escalated by the stronger into capital charges of treason, as so often had happened in England. [S. Doc. No. 92-82, Congressional Research Service, *The Constitution of the United States of America: Analysis and Interpretation* (1973) (citations omitted), *updated version available at* http://www.law.cornell.edu/anncon/html/art3frag60_user.html#art3_sec3.]

Indeed, the Framers provided additional protections for such partisan divisions by prohibiting Congress from enacting any law abridging freedom of speech, the press, assembly, petition, and (by judicial implication) association. U.S. Const. amend. I. *See* Ronald D. Rotunda & John E. Nowak, *Treatise on Constitutional Law* §20.41 (3d ed. Pocket Part 2005) (describing case law regarding freedom of association).

Why did Abdel Rahman argue that he was effectively convicted of treason? Did the court's answer to his claim bypass the protections that the Framers built into the Treason Clause?

2. **Inciting Imminent Harm.** The *Rahman* court's synopsis of the constitutional law governing advocacy of lawless action makes it sound more consistent than it is. *See, e.g.,* Christina E. Wells, *Fear and Loathing in Constitutional Decision-Making*, 2005 Wis. L. Rev. 115. In a World War I case under the 1918 Sedition Act, the Supreme Court declared that the government could constitutionally criminalize the utterance of "words . . . used in such circumstances . . . as to create a clear and present danger that they will bring about the substantive evils that Congress has a right to prevent." Schenck v. United States, 249 U.S. 47, 52 (1919). The Court seemed to relax the clear-and-present-danger test in Dennis v. United States, 341 U.S. 494 (1951), by finding that the harm from an overthrow of the government would be so grave that the government need not show its imminence or probability in order to punish advocacy of the overthrow. Dennis and his codefendants were convicted and sentenced to long prison terms for violating the Smith Act, which made it unlawful "to knowingly or willfully advocate, abet, advise, or teach the duty, necessity, desirability, or propriety of overthrowing or destroying any government in the United States by force or violence. . . ." Act of June 28, 1940, 54 Stat. 670, 671 (1940). What were their criminal acts? Apparently, according to the evidence adduced by the government, assembling to discuss and plan future teaching of books by Stalin, Marx and Engels, and Lenin. Finally, without disavowing these chilling precedents, the Court reversed a conviction for "criminal syndicalism" in Brandenberg v. Ohio, 395 U.S. 444 (1969). There, the defendant had given a racist and anti-Semitic speech at a Ku Klux Klan rally. The Court held that a State could not criminalize "advocacy of the use of force or violation of law except where such advocacy is directed to inciting or producing imminent lawless action *and* is *likely* to incite or produce such action." *Id.* at 447 (emphasis added).

How does Section 2384 fare under these tests? Did the *Rahman* court apply them correctly? *See* John Alan Cohan, *Seditious Conspiracy, the Smith Act, and Prosecution for Religious Speech Advocating the Violent Overthrow of Government*, 17 St. John's J.L. Comm. 199 (2003).

3. **Expression as Evidence.** Are not Rahman's religious expressions quoted in the case quintessentially protected speech? Why was it constitutional to base his criminal prosecution in part on them? *See generally id.*

## B. MATERIAL SUPPORT CRIMES

The material support statutes set out below have often been invoked in criminal prosecutions growing out of the war on terrorism. They have also been amended a number of times. Note that the italicized language was added by the Intelligence Reform and Terrorism Prevention Act of 2004, Pub. L. No. 108-458,

§6603(c)-(f), 118 Stat. 3638, 3763, *after* and partly in response to the decisions in the two cases that follow the statutory excerpts.

### 18 U.S.C. §2339A (2000 & Supp. IV 2004). Providing Material Support to Terrorists

(a) Offense. — Whoever provides material support or resources or conceals or disguises the nature, location, source, or ownership of material support or resources, knowing or intending that they are to be used in preparation for, or in carrying out, a violation of [various specific terrorist crimes] or in preparation for, or in carrying out, the concealment of an escape from the commission of any such violation, or attempts or conspires to do such an act, shall be fined under this title, imprisoned not more than 15 years, or both, and, if the death of any person results, shall be imprisoned for any term of years or for life. A violation of this section may be prosecuted in any Federal judicial district in which the underlying offense was committed, or in any other Federal judicial district as provided by law.

(b) Definitions. — As used in this section —

(1) the term "material support or resources" means *any property, tangible or intangible, or service, including* currency or monetary instruments or financial securities, financial services, lodging, training, expert advice or assistance, safehouses, false documentation or identification, communications equipment, facilities, weapons, lethal substances, explosives, personnel *(1 or more individuals who may be or include oneself)*, and transportation, except medicine or religious materials.

(2) *the term "training" means instruction or teaching designed to impart a specific skill, as opposed to general knowledge; and*

(3) *the term "expert advice or assistance" means advice or assistance derived from scientific, technical or other specialized knowledge.*

### 18 U.S.C. §2339B (2000 & Supp. IV 2004). Providing Material Support or Resources to Designated Foreign Terrorist Organizations

(a) Prohibited activities. —

(1) Unlawful conduct. — Whoever knowingly provides material support or resources to a foreign terrorist organization, or attempts or conspires to do so, shall be fined under this title or imprisoned not more than 15 years, or both, and, if the death of any person results, shall be imprisoned for any term of years or for life. *To violate this paragraph, a person must have knowledge that the organization is a designated terrorist organization . . . , that the organization has engaged or engages in terrorist activity . . . , or that the organization has engaged or engages in terrorism. . . .*

(g) Definitions. — As used in this section — . . .

(4) the term "material support or resources" has the same meaning given that term in section 2339A. . . .

(h) *Provision of personnel. —No person may be prosecuted under this section in connection with the term "personnel" unless that person has knowingly provided, attempted to provide, or conspired to provide a foreign terrorist organization with 1 or more individuals (who may be or include himself) to work under that terrorist organization's direction or control or to organize, manage, supervise, or otherwise direct the operation of that organization. Individuals who act entirely independently of the foreign terrorist organization to advance its goals or objectives shall not be considered to be working under the foreign terrorist organization's direction and control.*

(i) Rule of construction. —Nothing in this section shall be construed or applied so as to abridge the exercise of rights guaranteed under the First Amendment to the Constitution of the United States. . . .

## 18 U.S.C. §2339C (2000 & Supp. IV 2004). Prohibitions Against the Financing of Terrorism

(a) Offenses. —

(1) In general. —Whoever, in a circumstance described in subsection (b) [prescribing jurisdictional attributes of crime], by any means, directly or indirectly, unlawfully and willfully provides or collects funds with the intention that such funds be used, or with the knowledge that such funds are to be used, in full or in part, in order to carry out . . .

(B) any . . . act intended to cause death or serious bodily injury to a civilian, or to any other person not taking an active part in the hostilities in a situation of armed conflict, when the purpose of such act, by its nature or context, is to intimidate a population, or to compel a government or an international organization to do or to abstain from doing any act, shall be punished as prescribed in subsection (d)(1). . . .

## HUMANITARIAN LAW PROJECT v. RENO

United States Court of Appeals, Ninth Circuit, 2000
205 F.3d 1130 (*Humanitarian I*), cert. denied sub nom.
Humanitarian Law Project v. Ashcroft, 532 U.S. 904 (2001)

KOZINSKI, Circuit Judge: We consider whether Congress may, consistent with the First Amendment, prohibit contributions of material support to certain foreign terrorist organizations.

The Antiterrorism and Effective Death Penalty Act of 1996, Pub. L. No. 104-132, 110 Stat. 1214, known among the cognoscenti as AEDPA, authorizes the Secretary of State to "designate an organization as a foreign terrorist organization . . . if the Secretary finds that (A) the organization is a foreign organization; (B) the organization engages in terrorist activity . . . ; and (C) the terrorist activity of the organization threatens the security of United States nationals or the national security of the United States." AEDPA §302(a), 110 Stat. at 1248 (codified at 8 U.S.C. §1189(a)).

This provision has teeth. AEDPA decrees punishment by fine, imprisonment for up to 10 years or both on "[w]hoever, within the United States or subject to the jurisdiction of the United States, knowingly provides material support or resources to a foreign terrorist organization, or attempts or conspires to do so. . . ." AEDPA §303(a), 110 Stat. at 1250 (codified at 18 U.S.C. §2339B(a)(1)). The phrase "material support or resources" is broadly defined as "currency or other financial securities, financial services, lodging, training, safehouses, false documentation or identification, communications equipment, facilities, weapons, lethal substances, explosives, personnel, transportation, and other physical assets, except medicine or religious materials." AEDPA §323, 110 Stat. at 1255 (codified at 18 U.S.C. §2339A(b)).

Pursuant to those guidelines, the Secretary had, as of October 1997, designated 30 organizations as foreign terrorist organizations. Two such entities are the Kurdistan Workers' Party ("PKK") and the Liberation Tigers of Tamil Eelam ("LTTE"). Plaintiffs, six organizations and two United States citizens, wish to provide what they fear would be considered material support to the PKK and LTTE. Plaintiffs claim that such support would be directed to aid only the nonviolent humanitarian and political activities of the designated organizations. Being prohibited from giving this support, they argue, infringes their associational rights under the First Amendment. Because the statute criminalizes the giving of material support to an organization regardless of whether the donor intends to further the organization's unlawful ends, plaintiffs claim it runs afoul of the rule set forth in cases such as NAACP v. Claiborne Hardware Co., 458 U.S. 886 (1982). That rule, as succinctly stated in *Claiborne Hardware*, is "[f]or liability to be imposed by reason of association alone, it is necessary to establish that the group itself possessed unlawful goals and that the individual held a specific intent to further those illegal aims." *Id.* at 920. Plaintiffs further complain that AEDPA grants the Secretary unfettered and unreviewable authority to designate which groups are listed as foreign terrorist organizations, a violation of the First and Fifth Amendments. Lastly, plaintiffs maintain that AEDPA is unconstitutionally vague.

Plaintiffs sought a preliminary injunction barring enforcement of AEDPA against them. The district court denied the injunction, for the most part. However, it agreed with plaintiffs that AEDPA was impermissibly vague, specifically in its prohibition on providing "personnel" and "training." The court therefore enjoined the enforcement of those prohibitions. Each side appeals its losses.

**A.** Plaintiffs try hard to characterize the statute as imposing guilt by association, which would make it unconstitutional under cases such as *Claiborne Hardware*. But *Claiborne Hardware* and similar cases address situations where people are punished "by reason of association alone," *Claiborne Hardware*, 458 U.S. at 920 — in other words, merely for membership in a group or for espousing its views. AEDPA authorizes no such thing. The statute does not prohibit being a member of one of the designated groups or vigorously promoting and supporting the political goals of the group. Plaintiffs are even free to praise the groups for using terrorism as a means of achieving their ends. What AEDPA prohibits is the act of giving material support, and there is no constitutional right to facilitate terrorism by giving terrorists the weapons and explosives with which to carry out their grisly missions. Nor, of course, is there a right to provide resources with which terrorists can buy weapons and explosives.

**B.** Plaintiffs also insist that AEDPA is unconstitutional because it proscribes the giving of material support even if the donor does not have the specific intent to aid in the organization's unlawful purposes. They rely on American-Arab Anti-Discrimination Comm. v. Reno, 70 F.3d 1045 (9th Cir. 1995) (ADC I), where we declared that "[t]he government must establish a 'knowing affiliation' and a 'specific intent to further those illegal aims'" in order to punish advocacy. *Id.* at 1063 (quoting Healy v. James, 408 U.S. 169, 186 (1972)). But advocacy is far different from making donations of material support. Advocacy is always protected under the First Amendment whereas making donations is protected only in certain contexts. *See* Section C. *infra.* Plaintiffs here do not contend they are prohibited from advocating the goals of the foreign terrorist organizations, espousing their views or even being members of such groups. They can do so without fear of penalty right up to the line established by Brandenburg v. Ohio, 395 U.S. 444 (1969). . . .

Material support given to a terrorist organization can be used to promote the organization's unlawful activities, regardless of donor intent. Once the support is given, the donor has no control over how it is used. We therefore do not agree that the First Amendment requires the government to demonstrate a specific intent to aid an organization's illegal activities before attaching liability to the donation of funds.

**C.** Plaintiffs make a separate First Amendment argument based on the fact that the terrorist organizations in question also engage in political advocacy. Pointing to cases such as Buckley v. Valeo, 424 U.S. 1 (1976), and In re Asbestos Sch. Litig., 46 F.3d 1284 (3d Cir. 1994), plaintiffs argue that providing money to organizations engaged in political expression is itself both political expression and association. *See Buckley*, 424 U.S. at 44-45 ("[T]he constitutionality of [the restrictions on contributions to political candidates] turns on whether the government interests advanced in [their] support satisfy the exacting scrutiny applicable to limitations on core First Amendment rights of political expression."). However, the cases equating monetary support with expression involved organizations whose overwhelming function was political advocacy. *Buckley* is the quintessential example, where the contributions were made to candidates for political office for the purpose of helping them engage in electioneering. Under those circumstances, money, and the things money can buy, do indeed serve as a proxy for speech and demonstrate one's association with the organization. However, even in *Buckley*, the Court treated limits on donations differently from limits on candidates' expenditures of personal funds. While the First Amendment protects the expressive component of seeking and donating funds, expressive *conduct* receives significantly less protection than pure speech. *See* Texas v. Johnson, 491 U.S. 397, 406 (1989) ("The government generally has a freer hand in restricting expressive conduct than it has in restricting the written or spoken word.") (citing United States v. O'Brien, 391 U.S. 367, 376-377 (1968)).

The government may thus regulate contributions to organizations that engage in lawful — but non-speech related — activities. And it may certainly regulate contributions to organizations performing unlawful or harmful activities, even though such contributions may also express the donor's feelings about the recipient.

Contrary to plaintiffs' argument, the material support restriction here does not warrant strict scrutiny because it is not aimed at interfering with the expressive component of their conduct but at stopping aid to terrorist groups. *Compare O'Brien*, 391 U.S. at 376-377 (applying intermediate scrutiny to regulation prohibiting the burning of any draft card) with *Johnson*, 491 U.S. at 406 (applying strict scrutiny to law prohibiting only the burning of flags which offended witnesses). Intermediate scrutiny applies where, as here, "a regulation . . . serves purposes unrelated to the content of expression." *Ward v. Rock Against Racism*, 491 U.S. 781, 791 (1989).

When we review under the intermediate scrutiny standard, we must ask four questions: Is the regulation within the power of the government? Does it promote an important or substantial government interest? Is that interest unrelated to suppressing free expression? And, finally, is the incidental restriction on First Amendment freedoms no greater than necessary? *See O'Brien*, 391 U.S. at 377.

Here all four questions are answered in the affirmative. First, the federal government clearly has the power to enact laws restricting the dealings of United States citizens with foreign entities; such regulations have been upheld in the past over a variety of constitutional challenges. Second, the government has a legitimate interest in preventing the spread of international terrorism, and there is no doubt that that interest is substantial.[3] Third, this interest is unrelated to suppressing free expression because it restricts the actions of those who wish to give material support to the groups, not the expression of those who advocate or believe the ideas that the groups support.

So the heart of the matter is whether AEDPA is well enough tailored to its end of preventing the United States from being used as a base for terrorist fundraising. Because the judgment of how best to achieve that end is strongly bound up with foreign policy considerations, we must allow the political branches wide latitude in selecting the means to bring about the desired goal. . . .

Congress explicitly incorporated a finding into the statute that "foreign organizations that engage in terrorist activity are so tainted by their criminal conduct that any contribution to such an organization facilitates that conduct." AEDPA §301(a)(7), 110 Stat. at 1247. It follows that all material support given to such organizations aids their unlawful goals. Indeed, as the government points out, terrorist organizations do not maintain open books. Therefore, when someone makes a donation to them, there is no way to tell how the

---

3. Plaintiffs complain that the statute allows the designation not only of groups who threaten our "national defense," but also those groups that imperil our "foreign relations" or "economic interests." But "[p]rotection of the foreign policy of the United States is a governmental interest of great importance, since foreign policy and national security considerations cannot neatly be compartmentalized." *Haig v. Agee*, 453 U.S. 280, 307 (1981). The same, of course, is true of our economic interests.

donation is used. Further, as amicus Anti-Defamation League notes, even contributions earmarked for peaceful purposes can be used to give aid to the families of those killed while carrying out terrorist acts, thus making the decision to engage in terrorism more attractive. More fundamentally, money is fungible; giving support intended to aid an organization's peaceful activities frees up resources that can be used for terrorist acts. We will not indulge in speculation about whether Congress was right to come to the conclusion that it did. We simply note that Congress has the fact-finding resources to properly come to such a conclusion. Thus, we cannot say that AEDPA is not sufficiently tailored. . . .

**E.** Finally, Plaintiffs challenge AEDPA on vagueness grounds. . . . When a criminal law implicates First Amendment concerns, the law must be "sufficiently clear so as to allow persons of 'ordinary intelligence a reasonable opportunity to know what is prohibited.'" Foti v. City of Menlo Park, 146 F.3d 629, 638 (9th Cir. 1998) (quoting Grayned v. City of Rockford, 408 U.S. 104, 108 (1972)). It is easy to see how someone could be unsure about what AEDPA prohibits with the use of the term "personnel," as it blurs the line between protected expression and unprotected conduct. Someone who advocates the cause of the PKK could be seen as supplying them with personnel; it even fits under the government's rubric of freeing up resources, since having an independent advocate frees up members to engage in terrorist activities instead of advocacy. But advocacy is pure speech protected by the First Amendment.

In order to keep the statute from trenching on such advocacy, the government urges that we read into it a requirement that the activity prohibited be performed "under the direction or control" of the foreign terrorist organization. While we construe a statute in such a way as to avoid constitutional questions, *see* Crowell v. Benson, 285 U.S. 22, 62 (1932), we are not authorized to rewrite the law so it will pass constitutional muster. . . .

The term "training" fares little better. Again, it is easy to imagine protected expression that falls within the bounds of this term. For example, a plaintiff who wishes to instruct members of a designated group on how to petition the United Nations to give aid to their group could plausibly decide that such protected expression falls within the scope of the term "training." The government insists that the term is best understood to forbid the imparting of skills to foreign terrorist organizations through training. Yet, presumably, this definition would encompass teaching international law to members of designated organizations. The result would be different if the term "training" were qualified to include only military training or training in terrorist activities. Because plaintiffs have demonstrated that they are likely to succeed on the merits of their claim with respect to the terms "training" and "personnel," we conclude that the district court did not abuse its discretion in issuing its limited preliminary injunction.

The judgment of the district court is Affirmed.

## UNITED STATES V. AL-ARIAN

United States District Court, Middle District of Florida, 2004
308 F. Supp. 2d 1322

MOODY, J. . . .

### I. Background

#### A. Factual and Procedural Background

This is a criminal action against alleged members of the Palestinian Islamic Jihad-Shiqaqi Faction (the "PIJ") who purportedly operated and directed fundraising and other organizational activities in the United States for almost twenty years. The PIJ is a foreign organization that uses violence, principally suicide bombings, and threats of violence to pressure Israel to cede territory to the Palestinian people. On February 19, 2003, the government indicted the Defendants in a 50 count indictment that included counts for . . . (3) conspiracy to provide material support to or for the benefit of foreign terrorists (Counts 3 and 4). . . .

### II. Discussion . . .

#### A. Statutory Construction and Constitutional Issues

*1. Statutory Construction of AEDPA*[1] . . .

*b. Standards for interpreting a statute* . . .

In [*United States v.*] *X-Citement Video* [513 U.S. 64 (1994)], the Supreme Court faced almost the same statutory interpretation issues faced in this case. There, the Supreme Court considered the Protection of Children Against Sexual Exploitation Act, 18 U.S.C. §2252. 513 U.S. at 65-66. Section 2252 of that Act made it unlawful for any person to "knowingly" transport, ship, receive, distribute, or reproduce a visual depiction involving a "minor engaging in sexually explicit conduct." *Id.* at 68. The Ninth Circuit had interpreted "knowingly" to only modify the surrounding verbs, like transport or ship. *See id.* Under this construction, whether a defendant knew the minority of the performer(s) or even knew whether the material was sexually explicit was inconsequential. *See id.* at 68-69. The Supreme Court reversed, concluding that, while the Ninth Circuit's construction of Section 2252 complied with the plain meaning rule, the construction caused absurd results. *See id.* at 69. Under the Ninth Circuit's construction, the Court noted that a Federal Express courier who knew that there was film in a package could be convicted even though the courier had no knowledge that the film contained child pornography. *See id.* To avoid such results, the Court utilized the cannons of statutory construction to imply a "knowing" requirement to each element, including the age of the performers and the sexually explicit nature of the material. *See id.* at 70-78. The Court stated that in criminal statutes "the presumption in favor of a scienter requirement should apply to each of the statutory elements that criminalize otherwise innocent conduct." *Id.* at 72.

---

[1. Anti-Terrorism and Effective Death Penalty Act of 1996, Pub. L. No. 104-132.]

#### c. Statutory construction of AEDPA

Turning now to AEDPA, Section 2339B(a)(1) makes it unlawful for a person to "knowingly provide[ ] material support or resources to a foreign terrorist organization [FTO], or attempts or conspires to do so. . . ." 18 U.S.C. §2339B(a)(1). The Ninth Circuit has twice in a single case interpreted Section 2339B and found portions to be unconstitutionally vague as applied to the plaintiffs in that case. *See Humanitarian II* [Humanitarian Law Project v. United States Dep't of Justice, 352 F.3d 382 (9th Cir. 2003),] at 385, 393; *Humanitarian I* [Humanitarian Law Project v. Reno, 205 F.3d 1130 (9th Cir. 2000), *cert. denied sub nom.* Humanitarian Law Project v. Ashcroft, 532 U.S. 904 (2001),] at 1133-36. *Humanitarian* involved a civil action for declaratory and injunctive relief brought by six organizations and two United States citizens who wished to provide the Kurdistan Workers' Party (the "PKK") and the Liberation Tigers of Tamil Eelam (the "LTTE") with support for the political and non-violent humanitarian activities of each organization. . . .

On subsequent appeal in *Humanitarian II,* the Ninth Circuit reaffirmed its prior rulings on the plaintiffs' First Amendment arguments. 352 F.3d at 385, 393. However, the *Humanitarian II* panel faced a new Fifth Amendment challenge by the plaintiffs, who argued that the lack of personal guilt requirement in Section 2339B rendered it unconstitutional. *See id.* at 385. Therefore, the Ninth Circuit reconsidered its interpretation of the *mens rea* requirement in *Humanitarian I. See id.* Under its new interpretation, the Ninth Circuit concluded that Section 2339B also required proof that a person either knew: (a) that an organization was a FTO; or (b) of an organization's unlawful activities that caused it to be designated as a FTO. *See id.* at 400. The Ninth Circuit then reaffirmed its prior holding on the vagueness of "personnel" and "training" without analyzing how the change in the *mens rea* requirement affected its prior vagueness analysis. *See id.* at 403-05.

This Court agrees with the Ninth Circuit in *Humanitarian I* that a purely grammatical reading of the plain language of Section 2339B(a)(1) makes it unlawful for any person to knowingly furnish any item contained in the material support categories to an organization that has been designated a FTO. And like *Humanitarian II,* this Court agrees that this construction renders odd results and raises serious constitutional concerns. For example, under *Humanitarian I,* a donor could be convicted for giving money to a FTO without knowledge that an organization was a FTO or that it committed unlawful activities, and without an intent that the money be used to commit future unlawful activities.[28]

*Humanitarian II* attempted to correct this odd result and accompanying constitutional concerns by interpreting "knowingly" to mean that a person knew: (a) an organization was a FTO; or (b) an organization committed unlawful activities, which caused it to be designated a FTO. *See* 352 F.3d at 400. But, *Humanitarian II*'s construction of Section 2339B only cures some of the Fifth Amendment concerns. First, *Humanitarian II* fails to comply with *X-Citement Video*'s holding that a *mens rea* requirement "should apply to each of the statutory

---

28. Similarly, a bank teller who cashes the donor's check for a FTO could also be guilty despite a similar lack of knowledge.

elements that criminalize otherwise innocent conduct." 513 U.S. at 72. *Humanitarian II* implies only a *mens rea* requirement to the FTO element of Section 2339B(a)(1) and not to the material support element. Under *Humanitarian II*'s construction, a cab driver could be guilty for giving a ride to a FTO member to the UN, if he knows that the person is a member of a FTO or the member or his organization at some time conducted an unlawful activity in a foreign country. Similarly, a hotel clerk in New York could be committing a crime by providing lodging to that same FTO member under similar circumstances as the cab driver. Because the *Humanitarian II*'s construction fails to avoid potential Fifth Amendment concerns, this Court rejects its construction of Section 2339B.

Second, the *Humanitarian II* construction does not solve the constitutional vagueness concerns of Section 2339B(a)(1), which can be avoided by implying a *mens rea* requirement to the "material support or resources" element of Section 2339(B)(a)(1). If this Court accepted the *Humanitarian II* construction, it would likely have to declare many more categories of "material support" (in addition to "training" and "personnel" determined to be unconstitutionally vague in the *Humanitarian* cases) unconstitutionally vague for impinging on advocacy rights, including "financial services," "lodging," "safe houses," "communications equipment," "facilities," "transportation" and "other physical assets." Using the Ninth Circuit's vagueness example on "training,"[30] the statute could likewise punish other innocent conduct, such as where a person in New York City (where the United Nations is located) gave a FTO member a ride from the airport to the United Nations before the member petitioned the United Nations. Such conduct could be punished as providing "transportation" to a FTO under Section 2339B.[31] The end result of the Ninth Circuit's statutory construction in *Humanitarian II* is to render a substantial portion of Section 2339B unconstitutionally vague.

But, it is not necessary to do such serious damage to the statute if one follows the analysis used by the United States Supreme Court in *X-Citement Video*.[32] This Court concludes that it is more consistent with Congress's intent, which was to prohibit material support from FTOs to the "fullest possible basis," to imply a *mens rea* requirement to the "material support" element of Section 2339B(a)(1). Therefore, this Court concludes that to convict a defendant under Section 2339B(a)(1) the government must prove beyond a reasonable doubt that the defendant knew that: (a) the organization was a FTO or had committed unlawful activities that caused it to be so designated; and (b) what he was furnishing was

---

30. The Ninth Circuit utilized the example of "a plaintiff who wishes to instruct members of a designated group on how to petition the United Nations to give aid to their group. . . ." *Humanitarian I,* 205 F.3d at 1138.

31. Other examples of innocent conduct that could be prohibited include the same person allowing the FTO member to spend the night at his house, cashing a check, loaning the member a cell phone for use during the stay, or allowing the member to use the fax machine or laptop computer in preparing the petition. And, the additional phrase "expert advice or assistance" added by the Patriot Act in 2002 could also fail as unconstitutionally vague. *See, e.g., Humanitarian Law Project v. Ashcroft,* 2004 WL 112760, at *12-14 (C.D. Cal. Jan. 22, 2004) (holding that "expert advice or assistance" added by the Patriot Act to definition of "material support" was unconstitutionally vague).

32. The Supreme Court has repeatedly recognized that a *scienter* or *mens rea* requirement may mitigate a law's vagueness. *See, e.g., Posters 'N' Things, Ltd. v. United States,* 511 U.S. 513, 526 (1994).

"material support." To avoid Fifth Amendment personal guilt problems, this Court concludes that the government must show more than a defendant knew something was within a category of "material support" in order to meet (b). In order to meet (b), the government must show that the defendant knew (had a specific intent) that the support would further the illegal activities of a FTO.

This Court does not believe this burden is that great in the typical case.[34] Often, such an intent will be easily inferred. For example, a jury could infer a specific intent to further the illegal activities of a FTO when a defendant knowingly provides weapons, explosives, or lethal substances to an organization that he knows is a FTO because of the nature of the support. Likewise, a jury could infer a specific intent when a defendant knows that the organization continues to commit illegal acts and the defendant provides funds to that organization knowing that money is fungible and, once received, the donee can use the funds for any purpose it chooses. That is, by its nature, money carries an inherent danger for furthering the illegal aims of an organization. Congress said as much when it found that FTOs were "so tainted by their criminal conduct that any contribution to such an organization facilitates that conduct." Pub. L. No. 104-132, §301(a)(7).

This opinion in no way creates a safe harbor for terrorists or their supporters to try and avoid prosecution through utilization of shell "charitable organizations" or by directing money through the memo line of a check towards lawful activities.[35] This Court believes that a jury can quickly peer through such facades when appropriate. This is especially true if other facts indicate a defendant's true intent, like where defendants or conspirators utilize codes or unusual transaction practices to transfer funds. Instead, this Court's holding works to avoid potential constitutional problems and fully accomplish congressional intent. . . .

. . . Therefore, this Court denies Defendants' motions to dismiss the Indictment for alleged due process violations of the PIJ's rights. . . .

[The court denied defendants' motions to dismiss particular counts insofar as they were based on the aforementioned constitutional grounds and dismissed other counts on other grounds.]

## NOTES AND QUESTIONS

1. *The Anti-Terrorist Prosecutor's Weapon of Choice?* As we noted above, the apparent expansion of the suicide terrorist threat in the nineties and the difficulty of identifying and arresting would-be suicide terrorists in time, has caused the government to begin searching more vigorously up the chain of causation not only for those who plan but also for those who support acts of terrorism. Abdel Rahman's prosecution was a way station in this shift in

---

34. Indeed, Congress recently added 18 U.S.C. §2339C, which criminalized raising funds with the specific intent that the funds will be or are used to cause the death or serious bodily injury of a civilian with the purpose of intimidating the population or compelling a government to do or abstain from doing any act. *See* 18 U.S.C. §2339C.

35. For example, a donation to a suicide bomber's family given with the intent to encourage others to engage in such activities or support such activities would satisfy this specific intent requirement.

prosecutorial focus to "precursor crimes," because he was prosecuted for "overall supervision and direction of the membership," as the *Rahman* court put it, not for involvement in "individual operations." But the "seditious conspiracy" crime that the government there charged was anachronistic, notwithstanding the eventual success of the prosecution. *But see* Carlton F.W. Larson, *The Forgotten Constitutional Law of Treason and the Enemy Combatant Problem*, 154 U. Pa. L. Rev. 863 (2006) (urging prosecution of enemy combatants for treason and noting the historical applicability of the offense not just to citizens, but to anyone within the United States). Prosecutors needed a tool better suited to interdicting material support and, thereby, suicide terrorism.

When Congress responded by enacting the material support provision of AEDPA in 1996 and expanding material support liability in subsequent legislation, prosecutors used their new weapon enthusiastically. The material support charge is increasingly the government's weapon of choice against suspected terrorists. Data through October 2004 indicate that material support charges ranked second only to document fraud in charges and convictions in the war on terrorism. Center on Law and Security, *Terrorist Trials: A Report Card* 6-7, Feb. 2005, *available at* http://www.lawandsecurity.org/publications/TTRCComplete.pdf. See generally Norman Abrams, *The Material Support Terrorism Offenses: Perspectives Derived from the (Early) Model Penal Code*, 1 J. Natl. Security L. & Poly. 5 (2005); Robert M. Chesney, *The Sleeper Scenario: Terrorism-Support Laws and the Demands of Prevention*, 42 Harv. J. Legis. 1 (2005); Wayne McCormack, *Inchoate Terrorism: Liberalism Clashes With Fundamentalism*, 37 Geo. J. Intl. L. 1 (2005).

2. ***Constitutional Issues in Criminalizing Material Support: An Overview.*** When the government targets support, it risks hitting advocacy and association. The *Rahman* case foreshadowed the resulting constitutional issues, but they have since surfaced more fully in material support prosecutions.

*Vagueness and Overbreadth.* Vagueness is one issue: does the law give fair notice of the conduct it prohibits? Overbreadth is a related issue: does the law sweep so broadly that it may reach or at least chill activity that is protected by the First Amendment? Critics charge that " '[m]aterial support' has been used as a catch-all category in terrorism cases . . . and has failed to provide clarity or consistency as to the use of these statutes." Center on Law and Security, *supra*, at 2.

*Scienter.* The material support statutes carry different scienter requirements. This raises the further question whether they comport with the Fifth Amendment's implicit insistence on personal guilt for a criminal prosecution. These issues are complicated by their interaction, as *Al-Arian* suggests: a vague or overbroad statute may be saved by a narrow scienter requirement.

*Regulation of Protected Expression.* Of course, the material support provisions are *intended* to reach some activities usually protected by the First Amendment, such as fundraising, in order to achieve the government purpose of preventing terrorism. This poses an issue about the level of First

Amendment protection to which such activity is entitled and the corresponding level of judicial scrutiny of governmental regulation of the activity.

*Collateral Attack on FTO Designation.* Finally, 18 U.S.C. §2339B poses its own due process issue by criminalizing material support for an entity that has been designated an FTO. Does a criminal defendant have the right to mount a collateral challenge to the fairness or accuracy of the FTO designation in his criminal case?

Keeping in mind the interrelation of many of these problems, we treat them separately in the following notes.

3. *Vagueness and Overbreadth.* "Because First Amendment freedoms need breathing space to survive, government may regulate in the area only with narrow specificity." NAACP v. Button, 371 U.S. 415, 433 (1963). Criminal laws that impact such freedoms are therefore always subject to attack for vagueness or overbreadth. A law is unconstitutionally vague if a reasonable person cannot tell what expression is prohibited and what is permitted. A law is unconstitutionally overbroad if it "regulates substantially more speech than the Constitution allows to be regulated and a person to whom the law constitutionally can be applied can argue that it would be unconstitutional as applied to others." Erwin Chemerinsky, *Constitutional Law* 943 (3d ed. 2006). Because the overbreadth doctrine creates substantial social costs by prohibiting enforcement of a criminal statute even for behavior that it could otherwise constitutionally reach, the Supreme Court has "insisted that the law's application to protected speech be 'substantial,' not only in an absolute sense, but also relative to the scope of the law's plainly legitimate applications" for the statute to be struck down for overbreadth. Virginia v. Hicks, 539 U.S. 113, 119-120 (2003).

Applying just these principles for the moment, consider the case of a lawyer for a convicted terrorist who meets periodically with her client in prison and secretly conveys messages between him and his associates (including members of an FTO) outside of prison. Is this term unconstitutionally vague as applied to prosecute that lawyer for providing *herself* as "personnel" to a terrorist or FTO? *See* United States v. Sattar, 272 F. Supp. 2d 348, 360 (S.D.N.Y. 2003) (*Sattar I*) (yes; government's assertion in oral argument that "you know it when you see it" is an "insufficient guide by which a person can predict the legality of that person's conduct," whatever merit it may have as a way to identify obscenity). Is it too vague for prosecuting the lawyer for supplying *her client* as "personnel" to the FTO by making him "available" through communications that she conveys? *See* United States v. Sattar, 314 F. Supp. 2d 279, 300 (S.D.N.Y. 2004) (*Sattar II*) (no; "the 'provision' of 'personnel' — in this case, by making [the imprisoned] Sheik Abdel Rahman available as a co-conspirator in a conspiracy to kill and kidnap persons in a foreign country — is conduct that plainly is prohibited by the statute" with sufficient definiteness). How about a U.S. citizen who joins the Taliban to fight alongside al Qaeda fighters against U.S. armed forces in Afghanistan? *See* United States v. Lindh, 212 F. Supp. 2d 541, 574 (E.D. Va. 2002) (no; "personnel" is not unconstitutionally vague as applied to "employees" or "employee-like operatives" who were under the "direction and control" of an FTO). *See* James P. Fantetti, Comment, *John Walker Lindh, Terrorist?*

*Or Merely a Citizen Exercising His Constitutional Freedom: The Limits of the Freedom of Association in the Aftermath of September Eleventh,* 71 U. Cinn. L. Rev. 1373 (2003). Note that Congress amended the "personnel" definitions in the material support statute (as shown in italics *supra* p. 480) after the cases cited in this Note were decided.

Can you think of applications of the "training" or "expert advice or assistance" forms of material support that would invite vagueness or overbreadth challenges? In footnote 30 in *Al-Arian*, the court recalls the Ninth Circuit's characterization of "expert advice or assistance" as unconstitutionally vague if it applied to "a plaintiff who wishes to instruct members of a designated group on how to petition the United Nations to give aid to their group." But suppose this person styled himself a "trainer" in lobbying and called the instruction "Training in Dealing with the UN"? Has the vagueness problem been cured? Is it still vague if applied to a person who trains members of an FTO in car bomb assembly? In either case, is the problem vagueness or overbreadth? *See Humanitarian I*, 205 F.3d at 1138. *See generally* McCormack, *supra* p. 489, at 40-43.

4. ***Scienter and Guilt by Association?*** Congress has not made it a crime to be a member of an FTO. What legal reasons might explain why it has not?

In the Smith Act, Congress criminalized knowing membership in any organization that advocates the overthrow of the government by force or violence. 18 U.S.C. §2385 (2000). The Act came before the Supreme Court in Scales v. United States, 367 U.S. 203 (1961), in which the Court upheld a conviction for membership on proof of *knowing* membership or affiliation and *specific intent* to further the group's unlawful goals. The Court explained its insistence on these elements of proof by rejecting the concept of guilt by association:

> In our jurisprudence guilt is personal, and when the imposition of punishment on a status or on conduct can only be justified by reference to the relationship of that status or conduct to other concededly criminal activity (here advocacy of violent overthrow), that relationship must be sufficiently substantial to satisfy the concept of personal guilt in order to withstand attack under the Due Process Clause of the Fifth Amendment. [*Id.* at 224-225.]

Specific intent implements the requirement of personal guilt by "tying the imposition of guilt to an individually culpable act." David Cole, *Hanging With the Wrong Crowd: Of Gangs, Terrorists, and the Right of Association,* 1999 Sup. Ct. Rev. 203, 217. In First Amendment terms, the specific intent requirement "identifies the only narrowly tailored way to punish individuals for group wrongdoing (essentially by requiring evidence of individual wrongdoing), just as the *Brandenburg* test [*supra* p. 478] sets forth the narrowly tailored way to respond to advocacy of illegal conduct." Cole, *supra*, at 218.

But the material support statute does not criminalize membership in, or even support for the political goals of, an FTO. It criminalizes "the act of giving material support, and there is no constitutional right to facilitate terrorism by giving terrorists the weapons and explosives with which to carry out their grisly mission . . . [or] to provide resources with which terrorists can buy weapons and explosives." *Humanitarian I*, 205 F.3d at 1133. *Humanitarian II* did not read a specific intent requirement into the statute. The court found instead that knowledge of the FTO's designation or of its terrorist activities sufficed for criminal liability. The court in *Al-Arian*, on the other hand, thought a heightened scienter requirement was necessary to offset the vagueness of the material support definition. Other courts disagree. "The statute's vagueness as applied to the allegations in the Indictment concerning the provision of personnel is a fatal flaw that the Court cannot cure by reading into the statute a stricter definition of the material support provision than the statute itself provides." *Sattar I*, 272 F. Supp. 2d at 360.

Should the *Al-Arian* court have read 18 U.S.C. §§2339A, 2339B, and 2339C *in pari materia* in construing §2339B? What does such a reading suggest about the legislative intent regarding scienter? *See Sattar II*, 314 F. Supp. 2d at 301.

5. ***Humanitarian II or Al-Arian? Congress's Answer.***  Would applying the *Humanitarian II* scienter requirement to the hypotheticals set out by the court in *Al-Arian* in footnote 31 and the related text be consistent with "the concept of personal guilt" mentioned in *Scales* or the "presumption in favor of a scienter requirement" declared in *X-Citement Video*? In that regard, consider the fact that some FTOs engage in both terrorism and social work. *Cf.* Michael Whidden, Note, *Unequal Justice: Arabs in America and United States Antiterrorism in Legislation*, 69 Fordham L. Rev. 2825, 2873 (2001) (asserting that FTOs, Hamas, and Hezbollah operate orphanages, hospitals, schools, and medical clinics for indigent Palestinians in addition to conducting terrorist activities).

On the other hand, doesn't the court's solution in *Al-Arian* undercut congressional intent? *See Aiding Terrorists—An Examination of the Material Support Statute: Hearing Before the S. Judiciary Comm.*, 108th Cong. (May 5, 2004) (statement of Asst. Prof. Robert Chesney, Wake Forest Univ. School of Law), *available at* http://judiciary.senate.gov/print_testimony.cfm?id=1172&wit_id=3394 ("By interpreting the statute to require proof of specific intent to further the illegal ends of the recipient organization in all its applications, the district court in effect rejected the Congressional determination that all forms of support for a foreign terrorist organization, however well-intentioned, enhance the overall capacity of the organization to engage in activities harmful to U.S. national security and foreign policy."). Congress apparently thought so, because it amended §2339B(a)(1) after *Al-Arian* to add the italicized language *supra* p. 479. Does this solve the problem that *Al-Arian* identified?

6. ***Donating Money as Protected Expression.***  Donating money is not membership, but it is also unlike donating weapons, safe houses, or transportation. "The right to join together 'for the advancement of beliefs and ideas' is diluted," the Supreme Court explained, "if it does not include the right to pool money through contributions, for funds are often essential if 'advocacy' is to be truly or optimally 'effective.'" Buckley v. Valeo, 424 U.S. 1, 65-66 (1974) (quoting NAACP v. Alabama ex rel. Patterson, 357 U.S. 449, 460 (1958)). Why is donating money to an FTO not protected political expression?

One answer is that it *is* protected expression but that the protection is not absolute. What degree of scrutiny should a court then give to its regulation? *Compare* Cole, *supra*, at 237-238 (urging strict scrutiny — requiring a close relationship to a compelling government interest — when government's purpose is to regulate association as such), *with Al-Arian, supra* (apparently applying intermediate scrutiny — requiring a "sufficiently important government interest"). Does it matter, given the government interest in regulating material support? *See generally* Nina J. Crimm, *High Alert: The Government's War on the Financing of Terrorism and Implications for Donors, Domestic Charitable Organizations, and Global Philanthropy*, 45 Wm. & Mary L. Rev. 1341 (2004); David Cole, *The New McCarthyism: Repeating History in the War on Terrorism*, 38 Harv. C.R.-C.L. L. Rev. 1, 11 (2003).

7. ***Collaterally Challenging the FTO Designation.*** The D.C. Circuit has held that some FTOs have a due process right, in connection with their designation as FTOs, to notice, disclosure of at least unclassified parts of the administrative record underlying their designation, and an opportunity to be heard. *See generally* Sahar Aziz, *The Laws on Providing Material Support to Terrorist Organizations: Erosion of Constitutional Rights or a Legitimate Tool for Preventing Terrorism?*, 9 Tex. J. C.L. & C.R. 45 (2003). Is Al-Arian bound by the designation when he is prosecuted for violating §2339B, or can he then challenge its fairness or accuracy?

Congress has prohibited a material support defendant from raising "any question concerning the validity of the issuance of such designation as a defense or an objection at any trial or hearing." 8 U.S.C. §1189(a)(8) (2000 & Supp. IV 2004). But because Congress may not prohibit by statute what due process requires, the due process question remains. *See* United States v. Afshari, 412 F.3d 1071, 1076 (9th Cir. 2005). The *Al-Arian* court answered that question by finding that Al-Arian, as a stranger to the designation, lacked standing to challenge it, and that the designation itself had been made with due process. In any case, §2339B requires only that the recipient of the material support have been designated an FTO, not that the designation have been valid. *Accord, id.* at 1078; United States v. Hammoud, 381 F.3d 316, 331 (4th Cir. 2004) (en banc). *But see* United States v. Afshari, 446 F.3d 915, 920 (9th Cir. 2006) (Kozinski, J., dissenting from denial of rehearing en banc) ("The simple fact is that [defendant] is being prosecuted — and will surely be sent to prison for up to 10 years — for giving money to an organization that no one other than some obscure mandarin in the bowels of the State Department had determined to be a terrorist organization."). The designation process was examined in Chapter 1.

# C.  THE LONG ARM OF THE LAW: EXTRATERRITORIAL CRIMINAL JURISDICTION

Congress has enacted a variety of statutes aimed at international terrorism. *See, e.g.*, 18 U.S.C. §§31-32 (2000) (hijacking or sabotaging aircraft); *id.* §§175-178 (developing or possessing biological or toxin weapons); *id.* §§2331-2332 (killing or injuring U.S. citizens abroad); *id.* §2332a (directing weapons of mass destruction against Americans abroad or against anyone within the United States); *id.* §§2339A-2339C, *supra* pp. 478-480 (providing material support or financing for terrorists); and 49 U.S.C. §§46501-46507 (2000 & Supp. III 2003) (committing air piracy). Most of these are now expressly extraterritorial in application. For example, the material support statute, 18 U.S.C. §2339B (2000 & Supp. IV 2004), provides in relevant part:

> (d) Extraterritorial jurisdiction.—
>   (1) In general.—There is jurisdiction over an offense under subsection (a) if—
>     (A) an offender is a national of the United States (as defined in section 101(a)(22) of the Immigration and Nationality Act (8 U.S.C. 1101(a)(22))) or an alien lawfully admitted for permanent residence in the United States (as defined in section 101(a)(20) of the Immigration and Nationality Act (8 U.S.C. 1101(a)(20)));
>     (B) an offender is a stateless person whose habitual residence is in the United States;
>     (C) after the conduct required for the offense occurs an offender is brought into or found in the United States, even if the conduct required for the offense occurs outside the United States;
>     (D) the offense occurs in whole or in part within the United States;
>     (E) the offense occurs in or affects interstate or foreign commerce; or
>     (F) an offender aids or abets any person over whom jurisdiction exists under this paragraph in committing an offense under subsection (a) or conspires with any person over whom jurisdiction exists under this paragraph to commit an offense under subsection (a).
>   (2) Extraterritorial jurisdiction.—There is extraterritorial Federal jurisdiction over an offense under this section. . . .

But some older criminal statutes do not expressly apply extraterritorially. The following case discusses the interpretative principles governing extraterritorial application of U.S. criminal laws.

## UNITED STATES v. BIN LADEN

United States District Court, Southern District of New York, 2000
92 F. Supp. 2d 189

SAND, District Judge. The sixth superseding indictment in this case ("the Indictment") charges fifteen defendants with conspiracy to murder United States nationals, to use weapons of mass destruction against United States nationals, to destroy United States buildings and property, and to destroy United States defense utilities. The Indictment also charges defendants Mohamed Sadeek Odeh, Mohamed Rashed Daoud al-'Owhali, and Khalfan Khamis Mohamed, among others, with numerous crimes in connection with the August 1998 bombings of the United States Embassies in Nairobi, Kenya, and Dar es Salaam, Tanzania, including 223 counts of murder. . . .

## I. Extraterritorial Application

Odeh argues that Counts 5-8, 11-237, and 240-244 must be dismissed because (a) they concern acts allegedly performed by Odeh and his co-defendants outside United States territory, yet (b) are based on statutes that were not intended by Congress to regulate conduct outside United States territory. More specifically, Odeh argues that "the statutes that form the basis for the indictment fail clearly and unequivocally to regulate the conduct of foreign nationals for conduct outside the territorial boundaries of the United States". . . .

### A. General Principles of Extraterritorial Application

It is well-established that Congress has the power to regulate conduct performed outside United States territory. It is equally well-established, however, that courts are to presume that Congress has not exercised this power — i.e., that statutes apply only to acts performed within United States territory — unless Congress manifests an intent to reach acts performed outside United States territory. This "clear manifestation" requirement does not require that extraterritorial coverage should be found only if the statute itself explicitly provides for extraterritorial application. Rather, courts should consider "all available evidence about the meaning" of the statute, e.g., its text, structure, and legislative history.

Furthermore, the Supreme Court has established a limited exception to this standard approach for "criminal statutes which are, as a class, not logically dependent on their locality for the Government's jurisdiction, but are enacted because of the right of the Government to defend itself against obstruction, or fraud wherever perpetrated, especially if committed by its own citizens, officers, or agents." United States v. Bowman, 260 U.S. 94, 98 (1922). As regards statutes of this type, courts may infer the requisite intent "from the nature of the offense" described in the statute, and thus need not examine its legislative history.[3] *Id.* The Court further observed that "to limit the [ ] locus [of such a statute] to the strictly territorial jurisdiction [of the United States] would be greatly to curtail the scope and usefulness of the statute and leave open a large immunity for frauds as easily committed by citizens on the high seas and in foreign countries as at home. . . ."

Odeh argues that *Bowman* is "not controlling precedent" because it "involved the application of [a] penal statute[ ] to United States citizens," i.e., not to foreign nationals such as himself. This argument is unavailing. . . .

. . . Under international law, the primary basis of jurisdiction is the "subjective territorial principle," under which "a state has jurisdiction to prescribe law with respect to . . . conduct that, wholly or in substantial part, takes place

---

3. This is not necessarily to say, however, that legislative history is entirely irrelevant under the *Bowman* exception to the standard approach. Given that the *Bowman* rule is ultimately concerned with congressional intent, if the legislative history clearly indicates that Congress intended the statute in question to apply only within the United States, it would be inconsistent with *Bowman* to ignore this evidence, and conclude — in reliance on *Bowman* — that Congress intended the statute to apply extraterritorially. . . .

within its territory." Restatement (Third) of the Foreign Relations Law of the United States §402(1)(a)(1987). International law recognizes five other principles of jurisdiction by which a state may reach conduct *outside* its territory: (1) the objective territorial principle; (2) the protective principle; (3) the nationality principle; (4) the passive personality principle; and (5) the universality principle. The objective territoriality principle provides that a state has jurisdiction to prescribe law with respect to "conduct outside its territory that has or is intended to have substantial effect within its territory." Restatement §402(1)(c). The protective principle provides that a state has jurisdiction to prescribe law with respect to "certain conduct outside its territory by *persons not its nationals* that is directed against *the security of the state* or against a limited class of other state interests." *Id.* §402(3) (emphasis added). The nationality principle provides that a state has jurisdiction to prescribe law with respect to "the activities, interests, status, or relations of its nationals outside as well as within its territory." *Id.* §402(2). The passive personality principle provides that "a state may apply law — particularly criminal law — to an act committed outside its territory by a person not its national where the victim of the act was its national." *Id.* §402, cmt. g. The universality principle provides that, "[a] state has jurisdiction to define and prescribe punishment for certain offenses recognized by the community of nations as of universal concern, such as piracy, slave trade, attacks on or hijacking of aircraft, genocide, war crimes, and perhaps *certain acts of terrorism*," regardless of the locus of their occurrence. *Id.* §404 (emphasis added). Because Congress has the power to override international law if it so chooses, Restatement §402, cmt. I., none of these five principles places ultimate limits on Congress's power to reach extraterritorial conduct. At the same time, however, "[i]n determining whether a statute applies extraterritorially, [courts] presume that Congress does not intend to violate principles of international law. . . . [and] in the absence of an explicit Congressional directive, courts do not give extraterritorial effect to any statute that violates principles of international law." United States v. Vasquez-Velasco, 15 F.3d 833, 839 (9th Cir. 1994) (citing McCulloch v. Sociedad Nacional de Marineros de Honduras, 372 U.S. 10, 21-22 (1963)). Hence, courts that find that a given statute applies extraterritorially typically pause to note that this finding is consistent with one or more of the five principles of extraterritorial jurisdiction under international law.

The *Bowman* rule would appear to be most directly related to the protective principle, which, as noted, explicitly authorizes a state's exercise of jurisdiction over "conduct outside its territory *by persons not its nationals*." Restatement §402(3). Hence, an application of the *Bowman* rule that results in the extraterritorial application of a statute to the conduct of foreign nationals is consistent with international law. . . .

In light of the preceding general principles, we find that Congress intended each of the following statutory provisions to reach conduct by foreign nationals on foreign soil. . . .

The Indictment predicates Count 5 on 18 U.S.C. §§844(f) . . . Subsection 844(f)(1) provides:

> Whoever maliciously damages or destroys, or attempts to damage or destroy, by means of fire or an explosive, any building, vehicle, or other

personal or real property in whole or in part owned or possessed by, or leased to, the United States, or any department or agency thereof, shall be imprisoned for not less than 5 years and not more than 20 years, fined under this title, or both. [18 U.S.C. §844(f)(1).]

Given (i) that this provision is explicitly intended to protect United States property, (ii) that a significant amount of United States property is located outside the United States, and (iii) that, accordingly, foreign nationals are in at least as good a position as are United States nationals to damage such property, we find, under *Bowman*, that Congress intended Section 844(f)(1) to apply extraterritorially — irrespective of the nationality of the perpetrator. . . .

Odeh argues that the Counts based on 18 U.S.C. §§2332 and 2332a must be dismissed because these statutes are unconstitutional in that they exceed Congress's authority to legislate under the Constitution. As noted above, Subsection 2332(b) provides in relevant part that "[w]hoever outside the United States . . . engages in a conspiracy to kill[ ] a national of the United States shall [be punished as further provided]," 18 U.S.C. §2332(b); and Section 2332a(a) provides in relevant part that, "[a] person who . . . uses, threatens, or attempts or conspires to use, a weapon of mass destruction . . . (1) against a national of the United States while such national is outside of the United States; . . . or (3) against any property that is owned, leased or used by the United States . . . , whether the property is within or outside of the United States, shall [be punished as further provided]." 18 U.S.C. §2332a(a).

Odeh suggests that there is but one constitutional grant of authority to legislate that could support these two statutory provisions: Article I, Section 8, Clause 10. Clause 10 grants Congress the authority "[t]o define and punish Piracies and Felonies committed on the high Seas, and Offenses against the Law of Nations." U.S. Const. art. I, §8, cl. 10. Odeh argues that, as "[t]he acts described in these two statutes . . . are not widely regarded as offenses 'against the law of nations,'" these statutes exceed Congress's authority under Clause 10.

There are two problems with this argument. First, even assuming that the acts described in Sections 2332 and 2332a are not *widely* regarded as violations of international law, it does not necessarily follow that these provisions exceed Congress's authority under Clause 10. Clause 10 does not merely give Congress the authority to punish offenses against the law of nations; it also gives Congress the power to "define" such offenses. Hence, provided that the acts in question are recognized by at least some members of the international community as being offenses against the law of nations, Congress arguably has the power to criminalize these acts pursuant to its power *to define* offenses against the law of nations. *See* United States v. Smith, 18 U.S. (5 Wheat.) 153, 159 (1820) (Story, J.) ("Offenses . . . against the law of nations, cannot, with any accuracy, be said to be completely ascertained and defined in any public code recognized by the common consent of nations. . . . [T]herefore . . . , there is a peculiar fitness in giving the power to define as well as to punish.").

Second, and more important, it is not the case that Clause 10 provides the only basis for Sections 2332 and 2332a. The Supreme Court has recognized that, with regard to foreign affairs legislation, "investment of the federal Government with the powers of external sovereignty did not depend upon the affirmative grants of the Constitution." United States v. Curtiss-Wright Export Corp., 299 U.S. 304, 318 (1936). Rather, Congress's authority to regulate foreign affairs "exist[s] as inherently inseparable from the conception of nationality." *Id.* (citations omitted). More specifically, this "concept of essential sovereignty of a free nation clearly requires the existence and recognition of an inherent power in the state to protect itself from destruction." United States v. Rodriguez, 182 F. Supp. 479, 491 (S.D. Cal. 1960), *aff'd in part sub nom.* Rocha v. United States, 288 F.2d 545 (9th Cir.), *cert. denied,* 366 U.S. 948 (1961).

In penalizing extraterritorial conspiracies to kill nationals of the United States, Section 2332(b) is clearly designed to protect a vital United States interest. And, indeed, Congress expressly identified this protective function as the chief purpose of Section 2332. Therefore, we conclude, under *Curtiss-Wright,* that Congress acted within its authority in enacting these provisions. . . .

Odeh argues that interpreting Section 930(c)[2] to reach "the deaths of Kenyan and Tanzanian citizens [as opposed to United States citizens] would be contrary to established principles of international law." More specifically, Odeh advances the following two arguments. First, given (i) that "[u]nder 18 U.S.C. §930(c), the only arguable basis for jurisdiction over the deaths of foreign citizens is the principle of universality," (ii) that "[u]niversal jurisdiction results where there is *universal* condemnation of an offense, and a general interest in cooperating to suppress them, as reflected in *widely accepted* international agreements," and (iii) that "the universality principle does not encompass terrorist actions resulting in the deaths of individuals who are not diplomatic personnel," it follows that applying Section 930(c) to the deaths of "ordinary" foreign nationals on foreign soil would constitute a violation of international law.

There are two problems with this argument. First, because "universal jurisdiction is increasingly accepted for certain acts of terrorism, such as . . . indiscriminate violent assaults on people at large," Restatement §404, cmt. a, a plausible case could be made that extraterritorial application of Section 930(c) in this case *is* supported by the universality principle.

Second, it is not the case that the universality principle is the "only arguable basis for jurisdiction over the deaths of foreign citizens." As indicated by our conclusion . . . that Section 930(c) is designed to *protect* vital United States interests, the protective principle is also an "arguable basis" for the extraterritorial application of Section 930(c). . . . In providing for the death penalty where death results in the course of an attack on a Federal facility, Section 930(c) is clearly designed to deter attacks on Federal facilities. Given the likelihood that foreign nationals will be in or near Federal facilities located in foreign nations, this deterrent effect would be significantly diminished if Section 930(c) were limited to the deaths of United States nationals. . . .

Odeh argues, second, that, even if the universality principle (or one of the four other principles) did authorize the application of Section 930(c) to the

---

[2. 18 U.S.C. §930(c) provides that "[a] person who kills or attempts to kill any person in the course of a violation of subsection (a) or (b) [involving knowing possession of firearms or other dangerous weapons in a federal facility], or in the course of an attack on a Federal facility involving the use of a firearm or other dangerous weapon, shall be punished [as further provided]."]

deaths of ordinary foreign nationals on foreign soil, such application would violate international law nevertheless, because (i) "[e]ven where one of the principles authorizes jurisdiction, a nation is nevertheless precluded from exercising jurisdiction where jurisdiction would be 'unreasonable,'" and (ii) application of Section 930(c) to the deaths of ordinary foreign nationals on foreign soil would be unreasonable. *Id.* (citations omitted).

According to the Restatement, the following factors are to be taken into account for the purpose of determining whether exercise of extraterritorial jurisdiction is reasonable:

> (a) the link of the activity to the territory of the regulating state, i.e., the extent to which the activity takes place within the territory, or has substantial, direct, and foreseeable effect upon or in the territory;
>
> (b) the connections, such as nationality, residence, or economic activity, between the regulating state and the person principally responsible for the activity to be regulated, or between that state and those whom the regulation is designed to protect;
>
> (c) the character of the activity to be regulated, the importance of regulation to the regulating state, the extent to which other states regulate such activities, and the degree to which the desirability of such regulation is generally accepted;
>
> (d) the existence of justified expectations that might be protected or hurt by the regulation;
>
> (e) the importance of the regulation to the international political, legal, or economic system;
>
> (f) the extent to which the regulation is consistent with the traditions of the international system;
>
> (g) the extent to which another state may have an interest in regulating the activity; and
>
> (h) the likelihood of conflict with regulation by another state.

Restatement §403(2). Given that factor (a) alludes to the subjective territorial principle and the objective territorial principle, it is not especially relevant to a statute, such as Section 930(c), based primarily on the protective principle. Much the same can be said of factor (b), as it alludes to the nationality principle, the subjective territorial principle, and the objective territorial principle. Factor (c), in contrast, is highly relevant to Section 930(c). It is important both to the United States and other nations to prevent the destruction of their facilities — regardless of their location; and such regulation is accordingly widely accepted among the nations of the world. As for factor (d), Section 930(c) protects the expectation of foreign nationals that they will be free of harm while on the premises of United States facilities. We can think of no "justified" expectation, however, that would be hurt by the extraterritorial application of Section 930(c). As for factor (e), in light of the prominent role played by the United States in "the international political, legal, and economic systems," the protection of United States facilities — regardless of their location — is highly important to the stability of these systems. Turning to factor (f), as indicated by the preceding discussion of factor (c), most, if not all, nations are concerned about protecting their facilities, both at home and abroad. Hence, Section 930(c) is highly consistent "with the traditions of the international system."

As for (g), it must be acknowledged that when the United States facility is on foreign soil, and when the victims of the attack are nationals of the host nation, the host nation "has a keen interest in regulating and punishing [the] offenders." This is not to say, however, that the host nation has a greater interest than does the United States. Furthermore, even if it were the case that the host nation had a greater interest than the United States, this single factor would be insufficient to support the conclusion that application of Section 930(c) to the bombings of the two Embassies is unreasonable. Coming, finally, to factor (h), Odeh does not argue that application of Section 930(c) to the bombings would conflict with Kenyan and/or Tanzanian law, nor are we otherwise aware of such conflict. On the contrary, the Government informs the Court that "[t]he Kenyan Government voluntarily rendered Odeh (and [co-defendant] al-'Owhali) to the United States, and neither the Kenyan nor the Tanzanian Government has asserted any objection to the United States' exercise of jurisdiction in this case." Factor (h) thus counts in favor of the reasonableness of applying Section 930(c) to the bombings. . . .

## NOTES AND QUESTIONS

1. *Extraterritoriality and the Constitution.* No one questions a sovereign state's authority to prescribe laws for its own territory, and the Constitution quite clearly vests limited authority to do so in Congress. But may Congress constitutionally make laws that apply abroad? The Constitution is silent on this question, but Article III states that when a crime is "not committed within any State," trial for the crime shall be conducted where Congress directs. U.S. Const. art. III, §2, cl. 3. Thus, the Framers clearly contemplated criminal sanctions against acts committed outside any state of the union. Moreover, they vested Congress with the authority to define and punish "Offenses against the Law of Nations." *Id.* art. I, §8, cl. 10. Because such offenses may be committed abroad, this provision gives Congress extraterritorial lawmaking authority. On what basis does Odeh argue that 18 U.S.C. §§2332 and 2332a exceed Congress's lawmaking authority? Is the court's response consistent with a federal government of limited lawmaking authority?

   Assuming that Congress can enact laws with extraterritorial effect, does the Constitution place any limit on extraterritoriality? Civil procedure students may suspect that some "minimum contact" by the defendant or her acts with the United States might be required as a matter of due process. Beyond that, however, customary international law principles of prescriptive jurisdiction might also establish limits as a part of our federal common law. See *supra* pp. 435-436. Indeed, one commentator asserts that "[i]t is arguable that the Constitution permits Congress to make acts committed abroad crimes under United States law only to the extent permitted by international law." Andreas F. Lowenfeld, *U.S. Law Enforcement Abroad: The Constitution and International Law*, 83 Am. J. Intl. L. 880, 881 (1989). How does the *Bin Laden* court regard this assertion?

If international law does not limit extraterritorial lawmaking by Congress, what role, if any, does that law play, according to the court? What rule of statutory construction is implicated by applicable international laws?

2. ***Presumption Against Extraterritoriality.*** Why should the courts presume that a statute applies locally only unless Congress clearly manifests an intent to reach acts performed abroad? Sometimes such an intent is manifested by the plain language of the statute. The statute that makes it a crime to develop, produce, stockpile, transfer, acquire, retain, or possess any biological agent, toxin, or delivery system for use as a weapon, for example, expressly provides that "[t]here is extraterritorial Federal jurisdiction over an offense under this section committed by or against a national of the United States." 18 U.S.C. §175 (2000). Similarly, 18 U.S.C. §2332(b) (2000) expressly makes it a crime to engage in a conspiracy "outside the United States" to kill U.S. nationals. *Bowman* created an exception to the presumption against extraterritoriality. Why?

3. ***The Territoriality and Nationality Principles of Extraterritorial Jurisdiction.*** The court in *Bin Laden* catalogued principles of jurisdiction under customary international law, but such principles are not equally accepted by all nations, and they may not be helpful for other reasons. *See generally* Christopher L. Blakesley, *Extraterritorial Jurisdiction*, in II *International Criminal Law* 33 (M. Cherif Bassiouni ed., 2d ed. 1999). The territorial principle, for example, applies both to actors within a sovereign's territory ("subjective territoriality") and to effects in such territory resulting from acts abroad ("objective territoriality"), and it is reflected in *Restatement* §402(1). But while it is the most common and widely accepted principle of jurisdiction, it often will be unavailable for terrorist or other criminal acts performed abroad, including inchoate acts intended ultimately to cause injury in the United States. The nationality principle — allowing a sovereign to exercise jurisdiction over its nationals for their acts performed abroad — is also accepted by the practice of nations. Roman Boed, *United States Legislative Approach to Extraterritorial Jurisdiction in Connection with Terrorism*, in II *International Criminal Law*, *supra*, at 147. But international terrorists may not be U.S. nationals, just as most of the *Bin Laden* defendants were not.

4. ***The Protective Principle of Extraterritorial Jurisdiction.*** The protective principle is more likely to apply to acts of international terrorism, but it is limited to offenses against the security of the state or acts that threaten the integrity of governmental functions. *Restatement (Third) of Foreign Relations Law* §402(3) & cmt. f. (1981). It thus easily applied to the embassy bombings. Would it apply to terrorist acts committed against private U.S. nationals abroad? "The lack of definition of the range of conduct encompassed by the protective principle and the principle's malleability," Professor Boed worries, "could lead to the principle's justification of a wide-ranging exercise of extraterritorial jurisdiction." Boed, *supra*, at 148.

5. ***The Passive Personality Principle of Extraterritorial Jurisdiction.*** Even if the protective principle does not apply to terrorist acts against private U.S. nationals, such acts would clearly fall under the passive

personality principle. But this principle has not traditionally found wide support in the practice of states, Boed, *supra*, at 149, and it was squarely rejected by the United States until recently. *See* Blakesley, *supra*, at 69-70 ("The passive-personality theory traditionally has been anathema to U.S. law and practice.").

In the Omnibus Diplomatic Security and Antiterrorism Act of 1986, however, Congress made it a crime to kill or conspire to kill or cause physical violence to a U.S. national while such national is outside the United States. Pub. L. No. 99-399, §1202, 100 Stat. 853, 896, now codified at 18 U.S.C. §2332 (2000). The *Bin Laden* defendants were charged with this crime, and it would apply as well to acts of homicide or physical violence against private U.S. nationals traveling abroad. Does that mean that the United States could prosecute an Italian pickpocket for pushing a U.S. tourist in Rome as he extracted the tourist's wallet? Even Congress had doubts about reaching so far, so it added a limitation forbidding any prosecution except upon written certification by the Attorney General or his deputy that "such offense was intended to coerce, intimidate, or retaliate against a government or a civilian population." 18 U.S.C. §2332(d). Here Congress attempted to narrow the offenses to terrorist offenses without defining them and thus to avoid extending the statute to barroom brawls or ordinary street crimes. But what new problem does this provision arguably create? Who creates jurisdiction under this law, and when is it created? *See* Lowenfeld, *supra* p. 500, at 891 (opining that the statute is unconstitutional).

Congress came back to passive personality jurisdiction in the Antiterrorism and Effective Death Penalty Act of 1996. Pub. L. No. 104-132, 110 Stat. 1214 (1996). In a section of that act entitled "Clarification and Extension of Criminal Jurisdiction Over Certain Terrorism Offenses Overseas," Congress systematically amended multiple sections of the criminal code to supply the "clear manifestation" of extraterritoriality that is needed to overcome the presumption against extraterritoriality. *Id.* §721. These sections address aircraft piracy, destruction of aircraft, violence at international airports, murder of and threats and extortion against foreign officials and other persons, kidnapping of internationally protected persons, and developing or possessing biological weapons. *See* Boed, *supra* p. 501, at 159-173.

**6. *The Universality Principle of Extraterritorial Jurisdiction.*** Universality is perhaps the most controversial of the principles of extraterritorial jurisdiction, because it could theoretically result in a state prosecuting a non-national for acts performed abroad against other non-nationals. *See* Kenneth C. Randall, *Universal Jurisdiction Under International Law*, 66 Tex. L. Rev. 785 (1988). The principle rests on the assumption that there are some crimes so widely regarded as heinous that their perpetrators are enemies of mankind and are subject to prosecution the world over. The prosecuting nation acts for all nations to protect their collective interest. See *supra* p. 436 (discussing *jus cogens*).

To which crimes does this principle apply, according to the *Bin Laden* court? Do they include terrorism? In 1984, Judge Edwards of the D.C. Circuit Court of Appeals asserted that he was unable to conclude "that the law of nations . . . outlaws politically motivated terrorism, no matter how repugnant it might be to our legal system." Tel-Oren v. Libyan Arab Republic, 726 F.2d 774, 796 (D.C. Cir. 1984), *cert. denied*, 470 U.S. 1003 (1985). *But see* Almog v. Arab Bank, PLC, 471 F. Supp. 2d 257 (E.D.N.Y. 2007), *supra* p. 21 (holding that the intentional targeting of Jewish civilians violated the law of nations as genocide or a crime against humanity). Why do you suppose that the law of nations might not subject terrorism to universal jurisdiction? On the other hand, the law of nations is not static. *Restatement* §404 (quoted in *Bin Laden, supra* p. 496) would include "*perhaps* certain acts of terrorism" (emphasis supplied). Professor Blakesley argues that the law of nations has *already* condemned individual offenses (such as air piracy and hostage taking) for which "terrorism" is merely a composite term. Blakesley, *supra*, at 72. What was the *Bin Laden* court's conclusion in 2000?

7. ***The Rule of Reasonableness.*** The *Restatement* suggests that traditional principles of extraterritoriality are not to be mechanically applied; a court must always consider whether exercising jurisdiction in the particular circumstances would be reasonable. Indeed, the malleability and overlap of the traditional principles of extraterritorial jurisdiction under international law have caused some to suggest that reasonableness is today the overriding principle under which the availability or non-availability of the traditional principles is just a factor in the equation. Blakesley, *supra*, at 41. Is extraterritorial jurisdiction in *Bin Laden* reasonable? Why or why not?

8. ***"Substantial Nexus."*** We suggested that the civil procedure student might speculate whether the Due Process Clause imposes a "minimum contacts" requirement for extraterritorial jurisdiction. In fact, a few cases have spoken of the need for a substantial nexus between the defendant, or his acts, and the state exercising extraterritorial jurisdiction. *See, e.g.*, United States v. Davis, 905 F.2d 245 (9th Cir. 1990), *cert. denied*, 498 U.S. 1047 (1991). Most courts, however (including the *Bin Laden* court in a portion of the opinion not reproduced here), have concluded that if extraterritorial jurisdiction is justified by the international principles of extraterritorial jurisdiction, due process is satisfied. 905 F.2d at 249. This seems persuasive when jurisdiction is supported by the territoriality, nationality, or protective principle, because each presumes "contact." Can you explain how? But does it work for jurisdiction supported only by the passive personality or universality principle?

# 16

# *APPREHENDING TERRORISTS*

"Regular rendition of a person . . . occurs when an individual is surrendered by a requested country to a requesting state." Jordan Paust et al., *International Criminal Law* 436 (2d ed. 2000). Extradition is the most common method of regular rendition. A treaty creates a binding legal obligation of the requested state to extradite the suspect to the requesting state in accordance with procedures established by the treaty and the requested state's domestic laws. Extradition is discussed in Part A. States may also consent to surrender fugitives without formal extradition. By contrast, "[r]endition is irregular when [an] individual[] [is] taken from one country to another as a criminal suspect against [his] free will and without consent of the country from which [he is] taken." *Id. See also* A. John Radsan, *A More Regular Process for Irregular Rendition*, 37 Seton Hall L. Rev. 1, 8 (2006). The individual may be lured into custody by officials of the prosecuting state or, more rarely, abducted by force. (This process is not to be confused with "extraordinary" rendition, discussed in Chapter 14, in which the United States sends detainees to third countries for interrogation and detention.) In Part B, we discuss irregular rendition *to* the United States.

Sometimes deportation may be used as an alternative to extradition. Procedures for deportation—now called removal—of alleged terrorists from the United States are discussed in Chapter 19.

## A. EXTRADITION

### IN THE MATTER OF THE EXTRADITION OF MARZOOK

United States District Court, Southern District of New York, 1996
924 F. Supp. 565

DUFFY, District Judge. This is an extradition proceeding in which the Government of Israel seeks the extradition of Mousa Mohammed Abu Marzook ("Abu Marzook"), the admitted leader of the political wing of the Islamic Resistance Movement, known by its acronym "Hamas." According to Abu Marzook, Hamas seeks the establishment of a Palestinian identity and homeland, partly through a campaign of providing education, health care, and other social services, as well as political awareness of Palestinian issues. Admittedly, however, there is a "military wing" of Hamas, which engages in hostile activities in Israel. Israel alleges that the military wing of Hamas has engaged in a series of acts denominated as terrorist acts in Israel. Among these acts are the ones for which Israel seeks the extradition and trial of Abu Marzook.

Specifically, Israel charges Abu Marzook with crimes relating to the following ten incidents: (1) the bombing at a beach in Tel Aviv on July 28, 1990, which killed a Canadian tourist; (2) the stabbing deaths of three civilians working in a factory in Jaffa on December 14, 1990; (3) the January 1, 1992, shooting death of a civilian as he drove his car in Kfar Darom in Gaza; (4) the shooting death of a civilian as he drove his car in the Beit La'hiah region of Gaza on May 17, 1992; (5) the stabbing deaths of two civilians working at a packing plant in Sajaeya on June 25, 1992; (6) the gun-fire attack by three persons of a passenger bus in Jerusalem on July 1, 1993, in which two civilians were killed and others were injured; (7) the bombing of a passenger bus in Afula on April 6, 1994, which killed eight civilians and injured forty-six; (8) the bombing of a passenger bus in Hadera on April 13, 1994, which killed four civilians and injured twelve; (9) the machine-gun attack in a pedestrian mall in Jerusalem on October 9, 1994, which killed one civilian and injured eighteen; and (10) the bombing of a bus in Tel Aviv on October 19, 1994, which killed twenty-two civilians and injured forty-six. Israel has charged Abu Marzook with the following crimes: murder, attempted murder, manslaughter, causing harm with aggravating intent, harm and wounding under aggravating circumstances, and conspiracy to commit a felony.

This court's responsibility in the proceeding is governed by Title 18, United States Code, Section 3184, and by the Convention on Extradition, Dec. 10, 1962, U.S.-Isr., 14 UST 1707, 18 UST 382 (the "Convention"). Articles I and II, *inter alia,* of the Convention describe the responsibility of the United States to extradite an accused:

**Article I**
   Each Contracting Party agrees . . . to deliver up persons found in its territory who have been charged with . . . any of the offenses mentioned in Article II of the present convention committed within the territorial jurisdiction of the other. . . .

**Article II**
   Persons shall be delivered up according to the provisions of the present Convention for prosecution when they have been charged with . . . any of the following offenses:

1. Murder.
2. Manslaughter.
3. Malicious wounding; inflicting grievous bodily harm. . . .

Extradition shall also be granted for attempts to commit or conspiracy to commit any of the offenses mentioned in this Article provided such attempts or such conspiracy are punishable under the laws of both Parties by a term of imprisonment exceeding three years.

Where, as here, Israel has issued a criminal complaint and requested the extradition of a person, Title 18, Section 3184 requires a hearing so that "the evidence of criminality may be heard and considered." 18 U.S.C. §3184 (West Supp. 1995). If, after a consideration of such evidence, I find that there is probable cause to believe that Abu Marzook is criminally liable for the charged crimes, I must certify that finding to the Secretary of State. 18 U.S.C. §3184 (West Supp. 1995). . . .

Abu Marzook asserts that Section 3184 violates the principle of separation of powers because the Secretary of State may disregard, or even disagree with a court's determination that a person is extraditable. Abu Marzook also states that the Secretary may seek to extradite a person numerous times despite each court's determination that the person is not extraditable. Because the determination of the extradition court has no *res judicata* effect, Abu Marzook argues, the Executive Branch is given impermissible power over decisions of the Judicial Branch.

I must reject Abu Marzook's reasoning, as it inverts the proper analysis for a separation of powers argument. Abu Marzook assumes that no judicial pronouncement may ever be rejected by the Executive Branch. However, as described below, a separation of powers analysis is not so cut and dry. . . .

The concern of the separation of powers principle is the encroachment and aggrandizement of one branch at the expense of the other. In fact, the Supreme Court has "upheld statutory provisions that to some degree commingle the functions of the Branches, but that pose no danger of either aggrandizement or encroachment." [*Mistretta v. United States*, 488 U.S. 361, 382 (1989).]

In the case of Section 3184 extradition hearings, there is no impermissible encroachment or aggrandizement of power by either the Executive or Judicial Branch. Extradition is an Executive Branch function, not an Article III function of the judiciary. Section 3184 does not alter this balance, as the final decision of whether to extradite remains with the Executive.

The task of determining extraditability has been assigned to the courts by legislation in order to protect fundamental individual rights and liberty. The delegation of this task is not unconstitutional unless Congress has vested in the Judiciary "powers that are more appropriately performed by the other Branches." *See Mistretta,* 488 U.S. at 385. Abu Marzook does not claim that the Executive Branch is better suited to make a determination of whether probable cause exists. In fact, Federal courts have traditionally been charged with making probable cause determinations, whether for purposes of issuing an arrest warrant, for a preliminary examination, or for issuance of search warrants. The tasks performed by an extradition judge are primarily judicial and are ones that are performed daily by the courts. Section 3184 does not represent an improper aggrandizement of power to the Judicial Branch, but instead represents a realization by the Executive and Legislative Branches that the judiciary is better prepared to make such determinations.

Furthermore, the statutory scheme does not vest all aspects of extradition in the Judicial Branch. The Judiciary does not decide whether to extradite; that decision remains in the hands of the Executive Branch.[8] Were it the other way, an argument could be made that the statute improperly assigns foreign affairs powers to the Judiciary. In [*Chicago & Southern Air Lines, Inc. v. Waterman S.S. Corp.*, 333 U.S. 103, 111 (1948)], the Supreme Court explained that foreign affairs questions are not the province of the Judiciary, stating:

> the very nature of executive decisions as to foreign policy is political, not judicial. Such decisions are wholly confided by our Constitution to the political departments of the government, Executive and Legislative. . . . They are decisions of a kind for which the Judiciary has neither aptitude, facilities nor responsibility and have long been held to belong in the domain of political power *not subject to judicial intrusion or inquiry*.

*Id.* at 111 (citations omitted) (emphasis added). . . .

Because Section 3184 allows the Executive to exercise its foreign policy powers without interference from the Judiciary, there is no impermissible encroachment by the Judiciary upon executive functions. Having found that the statute in question is not unconstitutional, I find that this court has jurisdiction to hold the extradition hearing. . . .

### Scope of the Extradition Treaty

Abu Marzook argues that the Israeli warrant for his arrest does not charge him with an extraditable offense. The warrant charges him with, *inter alia,* "conspiracy to commit a felony," and with several substantive crimes of the conspiracy. According to Abu Marzook, however, conspiracy to commit a felony is not an extraditable crime under the Convention. Abu Marzook also argues that

> Israel originally charged Dr. Abu Marzook with conspiracy to commit murder, manslaughter — all crimes which were extraditable. Israel thereafter [in a superseding warrant] decided *not* to charge Dr. Abu Marzook with these crimes and instead a more generic, but distinct, criminal offense — conspiracy to commit a felony. The necessary implication is that the felony Dr. Abu Marzook has allegedly conspired to commit is not murder, manslaughter, or intentional harm but some other felony. What is clear is Israel has not specified which felony and, standing alone, Conspiracy to Commit a Felony is not an extraditable offense.

The extradition complaint makes clear that the conspiracy charged to Abu Marzook is the conspiracy to commit the enumerated crimes listed in the arrest warrant. The Israeli conspiracy statute is titled "Conspiracy to commit a felony or misdemeanor." Both the original and the superseding warrant charged Abu Marzook with conspiracy under this statute. . . .

---

8. The analogy to arrest warrants is especially strong. If a court issues an arrest warrant, it is the Executive which determines whether to prosecute. This happens every day, and yet it would be absurd to conclude that our entire criminal justice system violates the separation of powers principle.

... [The language of the Israeli conspiracy statute makes it] clear ... that by charging Abu Marzook with murder and conspiracy to commit a felony, Israel has charged him with conspiracy to commit murder. Since the Convention on Extradition covers conspiracy to commit murder, Abu Marzook has been charged with an extraditable offense. ...

### Political Offense Exception

Abu Marzook asserts that "the request for extradition must be denied as the acts charged in this case are of a political character outside the purview of the treaty of extradition." He also argues that the request for extradition has been made "with a view to trying and punishing him for an offense of a political character."

The political offense exception arises out of the Article VI language of the Convention on Extradition, which states:

> Extradition shall not be granted in any of the following circumstances: ...
> 4. When the offense is regarded by the requested Party as one of a political character or if the person sought proves that the request for his extradition has, in fact, been made with a view to trying or punishing him for an offense of a political character.

An offense falls within this exception if the offense was incidental to a severe political disturbance. *See, e.g., Ahmad v. Wigen,* 726 F. Supp. 389, 401 (E.D.N.Y. 1989), *aff'd,* 910 F.2d 1063 (2d Cir. 1990); *Sindona v. Grant,* 619 F.2d 167, 173 (2d Cir. 1980).

In a Memorandum dated April 11, 1996, I rejected Abu Marzook's offer of evidence on this issue. He contended that the proffered testimony would support his assertion that the charged offenses were incidental to the occurrence of a severe political disturbance and, therefore, would fall within the political offense exception to the Convention.

This approach, however, reverses the appropriate way of looking at the political offense exception. In my Memorandum, I held that if the act complained of is of such heinous nature that it is a crime against humanity, it is necessarily outside the political offense exception. Thus, if any of the charges against Abu Marzook are crimes abhorrent to human nature, the political offense exception will not lie in this case.

The charges leveled by Israel clearly bring this matter outside the realm of the political offense exception. The indiscriminate bombing of buses laden with civilians and other such types of attacks targeted at civilians do not advance any political motive other than as terrorist acts.[13] Such attacks have been universally condemned, even when they occur during a declared war, and clearly are less tolerable when committed by terrorists. *See* Convention Relative to the Protection of Civilian Persons in Time of War, *entered into force* Oct. 21, 1950, *for the United States* Feb. 2, 1956, 6 U.S.T. 3516, T.I.A.S.

---

13. One definition of terrorism is that it is indiscriminate violence toward civilians to terrorize the citizenship at large.

3365, 75 U.N.T.S. 287 [hereinafter "the Geneva Convention"]. Article 3 of the Geneva Convention states that

> Persons taking no active part in the hostilities . . . shall in all circumstances be treated humanely, . . .
>
> To this end, the following acts are and shall remain prohibited at any time and in any place whatsoever with respect to the above-mentioned persons:
>
> (a) violence to life and person, *in particular murder of all kinds, mutilation, cruel treatment and torture.*

*Id.* (emphasis added); *see also Kadic v. Karadzic,* 70 F.3d 232, 242-43 (2d Cir. 1995), *reh'g denied,* 74 F.3d 377 (1996).

Indeed, the Court of Appeals for this Circuit has rejected the political offense exception under facts similar to these. *Ahmad v. Wigen,* 910 F.2d 1063, 1066 (2d Cir. 1990) ("We agree that an attack on a commercial bus carrying civilian passengers on a regular route is not a political offense"). And, in a more recent decision, this Circuit reaffirmed the application of the Geneva Convention to acts of terrorism. *See Kadic,* 70 F.3d at 242-43 (stating that Article 3 "binds parties to internal conflicts regardless of whether they are recognized nations or roving hordes of insurgents").

Since the political offense exception will not lie in this case, the proffered testimony of Abu Marzook's proposed witnesses on this issue was not relevant and had to be rejected. The political offense exception is not available under the facts alleged here. . . .

Somewhat akin to the political offense exception argument, Abu Marzook also sought to make an issue of and to produce proof as to whether or not the Israeli legal system will give him "due process." . . .

. . . Judge Jack Weinstein conducted an extensive investigation into that question in the case of *Ahmad v. Wigen,* 726 F. Supp. 389, 409-20 (E.D.N.Y. 1989), *aff'd,* 910 F.2d 1063 (2d Cir. 1990). That case shows clearly that criminal defendants are accorded basic human rights, both in theory and in fact, by the Israelis. The theory is spelled out in detail by Judge Weinstein. The fact is that Ahmad was acquitted after his extradition to Israel. In any event, the law in this Circuit is that such an inquiry is improper for the extradition magistrate. *See Ahmad v. Wigen,* 910 F.2d at 1066-67 ("The interests of international comity are ill-served by requiring a foreign nation such as Israel to satisfy a United States district judge concerning the fairness of its laws and the manner in which they are enforced."); *see also Glucksman v. Henkel,* 221 U.S. 508 (1911) ("We are bound by the existence of an extradition treaty to assume that the trial will be fair.").

### Probable Cause

. . . The only remaining issue, therefore, is whether there is probable cause on any of the charged extraditable offenses. If so, I must certify Abu Marzook as extraditable. 18 U.S.C. §3184. Counsel for Abu Marzook urges me to adopt a legal standard that would require Israel to show probable cause beyond a reasonable doubt. This incomprehensible approach would go against the clear terms of the treaty and of Title 18, Section 3184. Indeed, the two standards of proof—"probable cause" and "beyond a reasonable doubt"—are at opposite ends of the spectrum. A finding of probable cause is appropriate if the evidence supports a reasonable belief that Abu Marzook is guilty of the crimes charged.

All extradition charges against Abu Marzook stem from terrorist activities conducted by Hamas. Abu Marzook admits that he is the leader of the political wing of Hamas and that he has raised money for Hamas. He further admits that there is a "propaganda apparatus" of Hamas which "was created to give a voice to the Palestinian movement toward self determination and that *one of its specific purposes was and is to disavow acts of violence committed by others but attributed to Hamas.*" The latter admission is important because there is no evidence that Hamas has disavowed any of the incidents set forth in the Request for Extradition, and there is evidence that Hamas has taken credit for many of the incidents.

Israel has charged Abu Marzook with responsibility for the following ten incidents. [The court lists details of the attacks described earlier, all of which were attributed to Hamas by the testimony of an attacker or by Hamas media. The court found that "[t]here is probable cause that the conspiracy known as Hamas is responsible for" each attack.] . . .

### Abu Marzook's Involvement

Since I have found there is probable cause to believe that the conspiracy known as Hamas is responsible for the ten incidents described above, I must now examine Abu Marzook's alleged involvement in the conspiracy. . . .

. . . The extradition complaint alleges that Abu Marzook

is the head of the political bureau of the Hamas Organization. . . . In addition to its other functions, this bureau has responsibility for directing and coordinating terrorist acts by Hamas against soldiers and civilians in Israel and the territories. In his role as head of the political bureau, Abu Marzook financed certain activities of the Hamas, including terrorist activities. In addition, he played an important role in organizing and structuring Hamas and in supervising the activities of the wing of Hamas responsible for the terrorist attacks [*i.e.* the military wing] and in appointing individuals to important leadership roles in the military wing.

To prove Abu Marzook's responsibility for the acts done by the Hamas conspiracy, Israel would not need to show that Abu Marzook knew of the specific acts committed in furtherance of the conspiracy, nor that he intended that they occur, nor that he even indirectly engaged in committing the specific crimes. Israel need only show that Abu Marzook was involved in an "agreement to accomplish an unlawful act," *United States v. Masotto,* 73 F.3d 1233, 1241 (2d Cir. 1996), and that the charged incidents were "reasonably foreseeable consequences" of the conspiracy. [Pinkerton v. United States, 328 U.S. 640, 643 (1946).] . . .

There is more than sufficient evidence to show that Abu Marzook was a member of the conspiracy known as Hamas and that the acts charged against him were foreseeable consequences of the conspiracy. [The court here reviews Marzook's multiple admissions of his leadership of Hamas and his knowledge of its military activities.] . . .

## Admissibility and Reliability of Evidence

In his memorandum opposing extradition, Abu Marzook argues that an "extradition complaint may not be founded purely upon multiple hearsay." However, the standard for admissibility of evidence in this hearing is not left to judicial discretion. Rather, Congress has determined that

> Depositions, warrants, or other papers or copies thereof offered in evidence upon the hearing of any extradition case *shall be received and admitted as evidence* on such hearing *for all purposes* of such hearing if they shall be properly and legally authenticated. . . .

18 U.S.C. §3190 (emphasis added). Since Israel has properly authenticated the documents submitted with the extradition complaint, I must consider them, regardless of their hearsay content.

In my Memorandum dated April 11, 1996, I held that the question of the weight or reliability of the evidence of the demanding country is not before me as an extradition magistrate. I must accept as true all of the statements and offers of proof by the demanding state. Accordingly, the testimony of Abu Marzook's proposed witnesses on this issue was deemed irrelevant to this proceeding. . . .

## Conclusion

. . . The documentary evidence, together with all transcripts of testimony and argument shall be certified to the Secretary of State, that a warrant may issue for the surrender of the accused, MOUSA MOHAMMED ABU MARZOOK, in accordance with the Convention on Extradition between the United States and Israel. The accused is hereby ordered committed to the Bureau of Prisons, Metropolitan Correction Center, New York, New York, there to remain until such surrender to the authorities of Israel when the appropriate diplomatic officials so designate.

*So ordered.*

## NOTES AND QUESTIONS

1. *Procedure.* The United States does not allow extradition without a treaty or "convention," 18 U.S.C. §3184 (2000), but it has enacted statutory procedures to supplement extradition treaties. *Id.* §§3184-3195. The exact procedures vary by treaty, but they typically begin with the requesting state's requisition to the Department of State to surrender a person. The United States then files a complaint with an appropriate judge or magistrate, and the court issues an arrest warrant for the fugitive. After the fugitive is apprehended, the court holds a hearing at which the requesting state may be privately represented. As *Marzook* shows, at the hearing the court must determine that the fugitive is the person sought, that a valid extradition treaty exists, that it allows extradition, and that the standard of proof set by that treaty (typically akin to probable cause in U.S. criminal law) is

satisfied. *See id.* §3184; Barry Carter & Phillip Trimble, *International Law* 795-796 (3d ed. 1999). Usually, as in *Marzook*, it is the last two issues that are contested. *See* Carter & Trimble, *supra*, at 795-796. If the court decides for extradition, it certifies the decision and the record to the Secretary of State, who makes the final determination. There is no appeal from the court's decision, although it can be tested in part by habeas corpus proceedings. When the Secretary of State approves extradition, she issues a warrant of surrender to a U.S. marshal. Most other countries also require a judicial decision on requisitions and retain some degree of executive discretion for the final decision. *See id.* at 797; *Restatement (Third) of Foreign Relations Law* §476 cmt. a. (1987).

2. ***Covered Offenses, Dual Criminality, and the Doctrine of Specialty.*** Whether a treaty allows extradition is initially a question of scope: is the offense for which extradition is sought covered by the treaty? Under the doctrine of *dual criminality*, the extradition offense must be a serious crime in both the requesting and the requested countries, *Restatement*, *supra*, §476, cmt. d. Were the offenses with which Marzook was charged covered by the treaty? What was his argument that they were not?

Criminal laws creating enterprise liability, especially the Racketeer Influenced and Corrupt Organizations Act, 18 U.S.C.A. §§1961-1968 (West 2000 & Supp. 2006), as amended, have been important weapons in the U.S. fight against organized crime, and they could be useful in the global war on terrorism. However, the United States is out in front of most other states in creating criminal enterprise liability, and that fact has sometimes presented an obstacle to extradition because of the dual criminality doctrine. *See* Ethan A. Nadelmann, *Cops Across Borders* 413 n.52 (1993); Michael J. Dinga, *Extradition of RICO Defendants to the United States Under Recent U.S. Extradition Treaties*, 7 B.U. Intl. L.J. 329 (1989); Barbara Sicalides, *RICO, CCE, and International Extradition*, 62 Temp. L. Rev. 1281 (1989). Similarly, although the United States has enacted a host of criminal laws directed at terrorism and support for terrorism, *see, e.g.*, Stephen C. Warneck, *A Preemptive Strike: Using RICO and the AEDPA to Attack the Financial Strength of International Terrorist Organizations*, 78 B.U. L. Rev. 177 (1998), these often have no counterpart in the laws of foreign states.

Of course, one way around the coverage problem would be to extradite for a covered offense and then add other uncovered offenses to the indictment after the fugitive has been apprehended. The difficulty with this strategy is the doctrine of *speciality,* by which a fugitive ordinarily can be prosecuted by the requesting state only for the offense for which he was extradited. *See* Eric P. Wempen, *United States v. Puentes: Re-Examining Extradition Law and the Specialty Doctrine*, 1 J. Intl. Legal Stud. 151 (1995).

Another solution is to renegotiate extradition treaties to eliminate the "listing" approach to covered offenses in favor of a more flexible "no-list" approach, which defines covered offenses by type of punishment. *See generally* Bruce Zagaris, *U.S. International Cooperation Against Transnational Organized Crime*, 44 Wayne L. Rev. 1401, 1422-1425 (1998).

3. ***The Political Offense Exception.*** Article VI of the treaty at issue in *Marzook* reflects an important exception to extradition that may seriously

curtail its utility in the fight against international terrorism. The *political offense* exception is grounded partly "in a belief that individuals have a 'right to resort to political activism to foster political change.'" Quinn v. Robinson, 783 F.2d 776, 793 (9th Cir. 1986) (quoting Note, *American Courts and Modern Terrorism: The Politics of Extradition*, 13 N.Y.U. J. Intl. L. & Pol. 617, 622 (1981)). Although the U.S. courts are divided, most have determined the applicability of this exception by the *incidence test*: whether the charged offenses were incident to or in furtherance of a contemporaneous uprising or other political disturbance. *See Quinn, supra*, at 794. Given the inability of states always to agree on a definition of "terrorism" (see *supra* pp. 21-37), this exception could thwart the extradition of fugitives whom the U.S. law enforcement authorities and courts regard as terrorists.

The exception has been applied by U.S. courts to block the extradition of Provisional Irish Republican Army (IRA) terrorists to the United Kingdom. In In re Doherty, 599 F. Supp. 270 (S.D.N.Y. 1984), Doherty was convicted *in absentia* by a British court of murder and firearms violations in connection with the killing of a British Army officer in an ambush on a British Army convoy. Citing the political offense exception to the extradition treaty between the United States and the United Kingdom, the U.S. court found that these acts had been committed for political purposes during an armed struggle. At the same time, it acknowledged that not every act committed for a political purpose should properly be regarded as a political offense, citing, as examples, the My Lai massacre (of Vietnamese by U.S. soldiers in Viet Nam), the Katyn Forest Massacre (of Polish officers by Soviet soldiers in Poland), and atrocities in Nazi death camps. *Id.* at 274. "[N]o act [should] be regarded as political [for the purpose of extradition]," the court concluded, "where the nature of the act is such as to be violative of international law, and inconsistent with international standards of civilized conduct." *Id.* The court then noted that Doherty's acts were committed against armed soldiers at the behest of an organized and disciplined command and were not directed at civilians, committed in a place other than where political change was sought, or aimed at helpless hostages, all circumstances that would render the political offense exception inapplicable. *Id.* at 275-276. Extradition was denied over the objection of the executive branch that the denial would jeopardize foreign relations. "The Treaty vests the determination of the . . . exception in the courts," the court responded. *Id.* at 277. The United States and the United Kingdom have since narrowed the political offense exception in a supplementary treaty. *See* Jordan J. Paust, *"Such a Narrow Approach" Indeed*, 29 Va. J. Intl. L. 413 (1989); Steven Lubet, *Taking the Terror Out of Political Terrorism: The Supplementary Treaty on Extradition Between the United States and the United Kingdom*, 19 Conn. L. Rev. 863 (1987). The *Restatement* reports that in response to terrorism other extradition treaties have also been narrowed since 1960. *Restatement, supra* p. 513, §476 note 5.

Given the highly political nature of the Palestinian-Israeli conflict, should the political offense exception have been applied to bar the extradition of Marzook? Note that after this case, Israel dropped its extradition request. Even though the United States had labeled Marzook a Specially Designated Global Terrorist in 1995, it reportedly made a deal with Jordan to take him, and he was deported to Jordan in 1997. *See Militant Ejected by U.S. Meets with Jordan King*, N.Y. Times, May 14, 1997, at A11. Does this development affect the applicability of the political offense exception to his case? Jordan, in turn, deported him in 1999 in a crackdown on Hamas. *See Mousa Abu Marzook*, Jewish Virtual Library (n.d.), *at* http://www.jewishvirtuallibrary. org/jsource/biography/marzook.html. In 2002, a federal grand jury in Dallas returned an indictment against Marzook for conspiring to provide material support to Hamas. *See* Dept. of Justice, *Senior Leader of Hamas and Texas Computer Company Indicted*, Dec. 18, 2002, *at* http://www.usdoj. gov/opa/pr/2002/December/02_crm_734.htm. Marzook was also indicted in 2004. *See Three Hamas Terrorists Indicted for Racketeering*, USINFO. STATE.GOV, Aug. 20, 2004, *at* http://usinfo.state.gov/xarchives/display.html? p=washfile-english&y=2004&m=August&x=20040820170346dmslahrellek 0.9784662. He is currently reported to be living in Syria, where he is active in Hamas activities. *See* Mousa Abu Marzook, *What Hamas Is Seeking*, Wash. Post, Jan. 31, 2006, at A17.

4. ***The Rule of Non-Inquiry.*** Another reason for the political offense exception is concern that "unsuccessful rebels should not be returned to countries where they may be subjected to unfair trials and punishments because of their political opinions." *Quinn, supra*, 783 F.2d at 793. To assess this concern, however, courts might need to inquire deeply into the legitimacy of the requesting state's judicial procedures and punishments, which could constitute an affront to comity. Consequently, U.S. and some foreign courts follow a "rule of non-inquiry," by which the legitimacy of such procedures is essentially presumed. *See* Rachel A. Van Cleave, *The Role of United States Federal Courts in Extradition Matters: The Rule of Non-Inquiry, Preventive Detention, and Comparative Legal Analysis*, 13 Temp. Intl. & Comp. L.J. 27 (1999). In part, the rule assumes that the Secretary of State's discretion in forwarding an extradition request, and (after a judicial hearing) in approving the request, is a sufficient safeguard against unfair procedures or punishment in the requesting country. How did the court in *Marzook* dispose of the due process attack on the Israeli legal system?

Many nations do inquire into the fairness of trial and punishments in a requesting state. What, if any, aspects of U.S. judicial procedures and criminal punishments might be found unfair in such an inquiry?

5. ***The Nationality and Other Exceptions.*** Most civil law jurisdictions will not extradite their own nationals, but they are typically authorized by their law to prosecute such nationals for breaking a foreign state's criminal laws. *See* Nadelmann, *supra* p. 513, at 399. Why might the United States prefer extradition to a requested state's prosecution of the fugitive? The United States has not refused to extradite its own nationals, and the Secretary of State is by law given the discretion to do so. 18 U.S.C. §3196 (2000).

# B.  IRREGULAR RENDITION

## UNITED STATES V. ALVAREZ-MACHAIN

United States Supreme Court, 1992
504 U.S. 655

Chief Justice REHNQUIST delivered the opinion of the Court. The issue in this case is whether a criminal defendant, abducted to the United States from a nation with which it has an extradition treaty, thereby acquires a defense to the jurisdiction of this country's courts. We hold that he does not, and that he may be tried in federal district court for violations of the criminal law of the United States.

Respondent, Humberto Alvarez-Machain, is a citizen and resident of Mexico. He was indicted for participating in the kidnap and murder of United States Drug Enforcement Administration (DEA) special agent Enrique Camarena-Salazar and a Mexican pilot working with Camarena, Alfredo Zavala-Avelar. The DEA believes that respondent, a medical doctor, participated in the murder by prolonging Agent Camarena's life so that others could further torture and interrogate him. On April 2, 1990, respondent was forcibly kidnaped from his medical office in Guadalajara, Mexico, to be flown by private plane to El Paso, Texas, where he was arrested by DEA officials. The District Court concluded that DEA agents were responsible for respondent's abduction, although they were not personally involved in it.[1]

Respondent moved to dismiss the indictment, claiming that . . . the District Court lacked jurisdiction to try him because he was abducted in violation of the extradition treaty between the United States and Mexico. [The district court agreed and the court of appeals affirmed.] We granted certiorari and now reverse.

Although we have never before addressed the precise issue raised in the present case, we have previously considered proceedings in claimed violation of an extradition treaty and proceedings against a defendant brought before a court by means of a forcible abduction. We addressed the former issue in United States v. Rauscher, 119 U.S. 407 (1886); more precisely, the issue whether the Webster-Ashburton Treaty of 1842, 8 Stat. 572, 576, which governed extraditions between England and the United States, prohibited the prosecution of defendant Rauscher for a crime other than the crime for which he had been extradited. Whether this prohibition, known as the doctrine of specialty, was an intended part of the treaty had been disputed between the two nations for some time. Justice Miller delivered the opinion of the Court, which carefully examined the terms and history of the treaty; the practice of nations in regards to extradition treaties; the case law from the States; and the writings of commentators, and reached the following conclusion:

> "[A] person who has been brought within the jurisdiction of the court *by virtue of proceedings under an extradition treaty*, can only be tried for one of the

---

[1. Apparently, DEA officials had attempted to gain respondent's presence in the United States through informal negotiations with Mexican officials, but were unsuccessful. DEA officials then, through a contact in Mexico, offered to pay a reward and expenses in return for the delivery of respondent to the United States.]

offences described in that treaty, and for the offence with which he is charged in the proceedings for his extradition, until a reasonable time and opportunity have been given him, after his release or trial upon such charge, to return to the country from whose asylum he had been forcibly taken under those proceedings."

*Id.* at 430 (emphasis added). . . .

In Ker v. Illinois, 119 U.S. 436 (1886), also written by Justice Miller and decided the same day as *Rauscher*, we addressed the issue of a defendant brought before the court by way of a forcible abduction. Frederick Ker had been tried and convicted in an Illinois court for larceny; his presence before the court was procured by means of forcible abduction from Peru. A messenger was sent to Lima with the proper warrant to demand Ker by virtue of the extradition treaty between Peru and the United States. The messenger, however, disdained reliance on the treaty processes, and instead forcibly kidnaped Ker and brought him to the United States. We distinguished Ker's case from *Rauscher*, on the basis that Ker was not brought into the United States by virtue of the extradition treaty between the United States and Peru, and rejected Ker's argument that he had a right under the extradition treaty to be returned to this country only in accordance with its terms. We rejected Ker's due process argument more broadly, holding in line with "the highest authorities" that "such forcible abduction is no sufficient reason why the party should not answer when brought within the jurisdiction of the court which has the right to try him for such an offence, and presents no valid objection to his trial in such court." *Ker, supra*, at 444.

In Frisbie v. Collins, 342 U.S. 519 (1952), we applied the rule in *Ker* to a case in which the defendant had been kidnaped in Chicago by Michigan officers and brought to trial in Michigan. We upheld the conviction over objections based on the Due Process Clause and the federal Kidnaping Act and stated:

> This Court has never departed from the rule announced in [*Ker*] that the power of a court to try a person for crime is not impaired by the fact that he had been brought within the court's jurisdiction by reason of a "forcible abduction." No persuasive reasons are now presented to justify overruling this line of cases. They rest on the sound basis that due process of law is satisfied when one present in court is convicted of crime after having been fairly apprized of the charges against him and after a fair trial in accordance with constitutional procedural safeguards. There is nothing in the Constitution that requires a court to permit a guilty person rightfully convicted to escape justice because he was brought to trial against his will. [*Frisbie (supra)*, at 522 (citation and footnote omitted).]

The only differences between *Ker* and the present case are that *Ker* was decided on the premise that there was no governmental involvement in the abduction; and Peru, from which Ker was abducted, did not object to his prosecution. Respondent finds these differences to be dispositive, . . . contending that they show that respondent's prosecution, like the prosecution of Rauscher, violates the implied terms of a valid extradition treaty. The Government, on the other hand, argues that *Rauscher* stands as an "exception" to the rule in *Ker* only when an extradition treaty is invoked, and the terms of the treaty provide that its breach will limit the jurisdiction of a court. Therefore, our first inquiry must be whether the abduction of respondent from Mexico violated the Extradition Treaty between the United States and Mexico. If we conclude that the Treaty does not prohibit respondent's abduction, the rule in *Ker* applies, and the court need not inquire as to how respondent came before it.

In construing a treaty, as in construing a statute, we first look to its terms to determine its meaning. The Treaty says nothing about the obligations of the United States and Mexico to refrain from forcible abductions of people from the territory of the other nation, or the consequences under the Treaty if such an abduction occurs. Respondent submits that Article 22(1) of the Treaty, which states that it "shall apply to offenses specified in Article 2 [including murder] committed before and after this Treaty enters into force," 31 U.S.T., at 5073-5074, evidences an intent to make application of the Treaty mandatory for those offenses. However, the more natural conclusion is that Article 22 was included to ensure that the Treaty was applied to extraditions requested after the Treaty went into force, regardless of when the crime of extradition occurred.

More critical to respondent's argument is Article 9 of the Treaty[2]. . . .

According to respondent, Article 9 embodies the terms of the bargain which the United States struck: If the United States wishes to prosecute a Mexican national, it may request that individual's extradition. Upon a request from the United States, Mexico may either extradite the individual or submit the case to the proper authorities for prosecution in Mexico. In this way, respondent reasons, each nation preserved its right to choose whether its nationals would be tried in its own courts or by the courts of the other nation. This preservation of rights would be frustrated if either nation were free to abduct nationals of the other nation for the purposes of prosecution. More broadly, respondent reasons, as did the Court of Appeals, that all the processes and restrictions on the obligation to extradite established by the Treaty would make no sense if either nation were free to resort to forcible kidnaping to gain the presence of an individual for prosecution in a manner not contemplated by the Treaty.

We do not read the Treaty in such a fashion. Article 9 does not purport to specify the only way in which one country may gain custody of a national of the other country for the purposes of prosecution. In the absence of an extradition treaty, nations are under no obligation to surrender those in their country to foreign authorities for prosecution. *Rauscher*, 119 U.S., at 411-412. Extradition treaties exist so as to impose mutual obligations to surrender individuals in certain defined sets of circumstances, following established procedures. The Treaty thus provides a mechanism which would not otherwise exist, requiring, under certain circumstances, the United States and Mexico to extradite individuals to the other country, and establishing the procedures to be followed when the Treaty is invoked. . . .

Thus, the language of the Treaty, in the context of its history, does not support the proposition that the Treaty prohibits abductions outside of its

---

[2. "Neither Contracting Party shall be bound to deliver up its own nationals, but the executive authority of the requested Party shall, if not prevented by the laws of that Party, have the power to deliver them up if, in its discretion, it be deemed proper to do so."]

terms. The remaining question, therefore, is whether the Treaty should be interpreted so as to include an implied term prohibiting prosecution where the defendant's presence is obtained by means other than those established by the Treaty.

Respondent contends that the Treaty must be interpreted against the backdrop of customary international law, and that international abductions are "so clearly prohibited in international law" that there was no reason to include such a clause in the Treaty itself. The international censure of international abductions is further evidenced, according to respondent, by the United Nations Charter and the Charter of the Organization of American States. Respondent does not argue that these sources of international law provide an independent basis for the right respondent asserts not to be tried in the United States, but rather that they should inform the interpretation of the Treaty terms. . . .

. . . [T]he difficulty with the support respondent garners from international law is that none of it relates to the practice of nations in relation to extradition treaties. In *Rauscher*, we implied a term in the Webster-Ashburton Treaty because of the practice of nations with regard to extradition treaties. In the instant case, respondent would imply terms in the Extradition Treaty from the practice of nations with regards to international law more generally. Respondent would have us find that the Treaty acts as a prohibition against a violation of the general principle of international law that one government may not "exercise its police power in the territory of another state." There are many actions which could be taken by a nation that would violate this principle, including waging war, but it cannot seriously be contended that an invasion of the United States by Mexico would violate the terms of the Extradition Treaty between the two nations.

In sum, to infer from this Treaty and its terms that it prohibits all means of gaining the presence of an individual outside of its terms goes beyond established precedent and practice. In *Rauscher*, the implication of a doctrine of specialty into the terms of the Webster-Ashburton Treaty, which, by its terms, required the presentation of evidence establishing probable cause of the crime of extradition before extradition was required, was a small step to take. By contrast, to imply from the terms of this Treaty that it prohibits obtaining the presence of an individual by means outside of the procedures the Treaty establishes requires a much larger inferential leap, with only the most general of international law principles to support it. The general principles cited by respondent simply fail to persuade us that we should imply in the United States-Mexico Extradition Treaty a term prohibiting international abductions.

Respondent and his *amici* may be correct that respondent's abduction was "shocking," and that it may be in violation of general international law principles. Mexico has protested the abduction of respondent through diplomatic notes, and the decision of whether respondent should be returned to Mexico, as a matter outside of the Treaty, is a matter for the Executive Branch. We conclude, however, that respondent's abduction was not in violation of the Extradition Treaty between the United States and Mexico, and therefore the rule of Ker v. Illinois is fully applicable to this case. The fact of respondent's forcible abduction does not therefore prohibit his trial in a court in the United States for violations of the criminal laws of the United States.

The judgment of the Court of Appeals is therefore reversed, and the case is remanded for further proceedings consistent with this opinion.

Justice STEVENS, with whom Justice BLACKMUN and Justice O'CONNOR join, dissenting. The Court correctly observes that this case raises a question of first impression. The case is unique for several reasons. It does not involve an ordinary abduction by a private kidnaper, or bounty hunter, as in Ker v. Illinois, 119 U.S. 436 (1886); nor does it involve the apprehension of an American fugitive who committed a crime in one State and sought asylum in another, as in Frisbie v. Collins, 342 U.S. 519 (1952). Rather, it involves this country's abduction of another country's citizen; it also involves a violation of the territorial integrity of that other country, with which this country has signed an extradition treaty. . . .

The extradition treaty with Mexico is a comprehensive document containing 23 articles and an appendix listing the extraditable offenses covered by the agreement. The parties announced their purpose in the preamble: The two governments desire "to cooperate more closely in the fight against crime and, to this end, to mutually render better assistance in matters of extradition."[4] From the preamble, through the description of the parties' obligations with respect to offenses committed within as well as beyond the territory of a requesting party, the delineation of the procedures and evidentiary requirements for extradition, the special provisions for political offenses and capital punishment, and other details, the Treaty appears to have been designed to cover the entire subject of extradition. . . .

The Government's claim that the Treaty is not exclusive, but permits forcible governmental kidnaping, would transform these, and other, provisions into little more than verbiage. For example, provisions requiring "sufficient" evidence to grant extradition (Art. 3), withholding extradition for political or military offenses (Art. 5), withholding extradition when the person sought has already been tried (Art. 6), withholding extradition when the statute of limitations for the crime has lapsed (Art. 7), and granting the requested Country discretion to refuse to extradite an individual who would face the death penalty in the requesting country (Art. 8), would serve little purpose if the requesting country could simply kidnap the person. . . .

It is true, as the Court notes, that there is no express promise by either party to refrain from forcible abductions in the territory of the other nation. Relying on that omission, the Court, in effect, concludes that the Treaty merely creates an optional method of obtaining jurisdiction over alleged offenders, and that the parties silently reserved the right to resort to self-help whenever they deem force more expeditious than legal process. If the United States, for example, thought it more expedient to torture or simply to execute a person rather than to attempt extradition, these options would be equally available because they, too, were not explicitly prohibited by the Treaty. That, however, is

---

4. . . . Extradition treaties prevent international conflict by providing agreed-upon standards so that the parties may cooperate and avoid retaliatory invasions of territorial sovereignty. . . . The object of reducing conflict by promoting cooperation explains why extradition treaties do not prohibit informal consensual delivery of fugitives, but why they do prohibit state-sponsored abductions.

a highly improbable interpretation of a consensual agreement, which on its face appears to have been intended to set forth comprehensive and exclusive rules concerning the subject of extradition.[14] In my opinion, "the manifest scope and object of the treaty itself," *Rauscher*, 119 U.S., at 422, plainly imply a mutual undertaking to respect the territorial integrity of the other contracting party. That opinion is confirmed by a consideration of the "legal context" in which the Treaty was negotiated. . . .

. . . It is shocking that a party to an extradition treaty might believe that it has secretly reserved the right to make seizures of citizens in the other party's territory. . . .

. . . [According to] the chief reporter for the American Law Institute's Restatement of Foreign Relations . . . :

> "When done without consent of the foreign government, abducting a person from a foreign country is a gross violation of international law and gross disrespect for a norm high in the opinion of mankind. It is a blatant violation of the territorial integrity of another state; it eviscerates the extradition system (established by a comprehensive network of treaties involving virtually all states)." . . .

As the Court observes at the outset of its opinion, there is reason to believe that respondent participated in an especially brutal murder of an American law enforcement agent. That fact, if true, may explain the Executive's intense interest in punishing respondent in our courts. Such an explanation, however, provides no justification for disregarding the Rule of Law that this Court has a duty to uphold.[33] That the Executive may wish to reinterpret the Treaty to allow for an action that the Treaty in no way authorizes should not influence this Court's interpretation. Indeed, the desire for revenge exerts "a kind of hydraulic pressure . . . before which even well settled principles of law will bend," but it is precisely at such moments that we should remember and be guided by our duty "to render judgment evenly and dispassionately according to

---

14. Mexico's understanding is that "[t]he extradition treaty governs comprehensively the delivery of all persons for trial in the requesting state 'for an offense committed outside the territory of the requesting Party.'" Brief for United Mexican States as Amicus Curiae, O.T. 1991, No. 91-670, p. 6. And Canada, with whom the United States also shares a large border and with whom the United States also has an extradition treaty, understands the treaty to be "the exclusive means for a requesting government to obtain . . . a removal" of a person from its territory, unless a nation otherwise gives its consent. Brief for Government of Canada as Amicus Curiae 4.

33. As Justice Brandeis so wisely urged:

> "In a government of laws, existence of the government will be imperilled if it fails to observe the law scrupulously. Our Government is the potent, the omnipresent teacher. For good or for ill, it teaches the whole people by its example. Crime is contagious. If the Government becomes a lawbreaker, it breeds contempt for law; it invites every man to become a law unto himself; it invites anarchy. To declare that in the administration of the criminal law the end justifies the means — to declare that the Government may commit crimes in order to secure the conviction of a private criminal — would bring terrible retribution. Against that pernicious doctrine this Court should resolutely set its face."

Olmstead v. United States, 277 U.S. 438, 485 (1928) (dissenting opinion) [the case in which the Supreme Court initially ruled that wiretapping was not within the scope of the Fourth Amendment's protections].

law, as each is given understanding to ascertain and apply it." The way that we perform that duty in a case of this kind sets an example that other tribunals in other countries are sure to emulate.

... As Thomas Paine warned, an "avidity to punish is always dangerous to liberty" because it leads a nation "to stretch, to misinterpret, and to misapply even the best of laws." To counter that tendency, he reminds us:

> "He that would make his own liberty secure must guard even his enemy from oppression; for if he violates this duty he establishes a precedent that will reach to himself."

I respectfully dissent.

## NOTES AND QUESTIONS

1. *Regular Rendition by "Informal Negotiations" and Less Regular Means.* The DEA had first attempted to apprehend Alvarez-Machain by "informal negotiations with the Mexican officials." See *supra* p. 516 n.1. Reportedly, Mexican officials wanted to make the arrangement "under the table" to avoid upsetting Mexican citizens, but the deal fell through when the Drug Enforcement Agency balked at paying them $50,000 up front for "transportation expenses." *See* United States v. Caro-Quintero, 745 F. Supp. 599, 602 (C.D. Cal. 1990). If these negotiations had succeeded, how might the officials have rendered Alvarez-Machain? In some cases, fugitives have simply been delivered by local authorities to U.S. law enforcement officials; in others, they have been deported to the requesting country or expelled with notice to the requesting country of the route of travel. Nadelmann, *supra* p. 513, at 437. For example, a terrorist who seized an airliner and systematically shot hostages, including three Americans, was later detained by Nigerian authorities after he landed there and was placed on a plane chartered by the FBI, which then carried him to the United States. *See* United States v. Rezaq, 899 F. Supp. 697 (D.D.C. 1995).

   The State Department reported that 13 terrorists brought to the United States for trial from 1993 to 1999 were rendered by means other than extradition. The State Department did not identify the rendering country in four of the listed cases. Why would a cooperating government not want to be publicly associated with the rendition? In other cases, *our* State Department and diplomats were "cut out of the loop" by U.S. law enforcement officials who arranged for irregular rendition of fugitives. Nadelmann, *supra*, at 443. Why would these officials want to keep such knowledge from our own diplomats?

2. *Luring Fugitives into U.S. Custody.* What if Alvarez-Machain had been tricked into coming to the United States instead of being taken by force? The *United States Attorneys' Manual* explains that "a lure involves using a subterfuge to entice a criminal defendant to leave a foreign country so that he or she can be arrested in the United States, in international waters or airspace, or in a third country for subsequent extradition, expulsion, or deportation to the United States." *United States Attorneys' Manual* §9-15.630 (1997).

One extraterritorial arrest of a suspected terrorist by U.S. law enforcement agents was accomplished by luring him on board a yacht in international waters off Cyprus with promises of a drug deal. *See* United States v. Yunis, 924 F.2d 1086 (D.C. Cir. 1991). Like the Supreme Court in *Alvarez-Machain*, the *Yunis* court cited the *Ker-Frisbie* doctrine in upholding the arrest, noting that arrests achieved by lures have been uniformly upheld. *Id.* at 1093. Should *Ker-Frisbie* apply equally to support abduction and trickery?

Other states are not in agreement: they view apprehension by luring as the equivalent of an unlawful abduction. *See* Paust et al., *supra* p.514, at 443-446. A meeting of the International Penal Law Association has adopted a resolution that "enticing a person under false pretenses to come voluntarily from another country in order to subject such a person to arrest and criminal prosecution is contrary to public international law and should not be tolerated. . . ." *Mutual Assistance in Criminal Matters: XVth Congress of International Penal Law Association Adopts Resolutions*, 10 Intl. Enforcement L. Rep. 383, 387 (1994). What are the pros and cons of luring fugitives into custody? Should it matter whether extradition is an available alternative or whether the United States first unsuccessfully seeks the cooperation of the asylum state?

3. *The U.S.-Mexico Extradition Treaty.* Now that you are familiar with the major provisions of the extradition treaty and the issues to which they relate, how convincing do you find the majority's reasoning in *Alvarez-Machain*? Why would either country bother with an extradition treaty, let alone with express detailed exceptions to it, if it could lawfully abduct suspects outside the treaty regime?

4. *International Law on Abduction.* The Supreme Court in *Alvarez-Machain* did not decide whether the abduction violated international law. From dicta in the majority opinion and in the dissent, however, can you divine what the Justices thought the relevant international law to be? Many academic commentators insist that the principles of sovereignty and human rights law coincide in disapproving abductions from sovereign foreign states, even if they are followed inconsistently. *See, e.g.,* Andreas F. Lowenfeld, *U.S. Law Enforcement Abroad: The Constitution and International Law, Continued*, 84 Am. J. Intl. L. 444, 472-474 (1990). The former principles are reflected in Article 2(4) of the United Nations Charter (a treaty that the United States has ratified), which provides:

> All members shall refrain in their international relations from the threat or use of force against the territorial integrity or political independence of any state, or in any other manner inconsistent with the purpose of the United Nations. [59 Stat. 1031, 1037, 3 Bevans 1153, 1155.]

The principle of territorial integrity, however, may carry a correlative duty of states to protect against harm from criminals operating within their territory. Professor Gurule argues that

> [i]t is abundantly clear that under international law a state is obligated to prosecute and punish criminal offenders within its

territorial boundaries; extradite foreign fugitives if it is unwilling or unable to prosecute; refrain from "organizing, instigating, assisting, or participating" in hostile attacks against another state or the nationals of that state; and take appropriate measures to prevent the commission of such hostile attacks. [Jimmy Gurule, *Terrorism, Territorial Sovereignty, and the Forcible Apprehension of International Terrorists Abroad*, 17 Hastings Intl. & Comp. L. Rev. 457, 477 (1994) (quoting Declaration on Principles of International Law Governing Friendly Relations and Co-operation Among States in Accordance with the Charter of the United Nations, G.A. Res. 2625, 25 U.N. GAOR Supp. No. 28 at 121, U.N. Doc. A/8028 (1971), *reprinted in* 9 I.L.M. 1292 (1970)).]

When an asylum state violates this duty, should the principle of territorial integrity be trumped by another state's proper exercise of "the inherent right of individual . . . self-defense"? *See* U.N. Charter, art. 51, *supra* p. 70. Can you apply this theory to the abduction of *Alvarez-Machain*? *See* Gurule, *supra*, at 485-489; *Authority of the Federal Bureau of Investigation to Seize Suspects Abroad, Hearings Before the Subcomm. on Civil and Constitutional Rights of the H. Comm. on the Judiciary*, 101st Cong. 34-35 (1989) (statement by Abraham D. Sofaer, Legal Adviser to the Department of State), *quoted in* Marian Nash Leich, *Contemporary Practice of the United States Relating to International Law*, 84 Am. J. Intl. L. 724, 725-729 (1990).

   For other academic commentary on the international law implications of *Alvarez-Machain*, see Gregory S. McNeal & Brian Field, *Snatch-and-Grab Ops: Justifying Extraterritorial Abduction*, 16 U. Iowa J. Trans. L. & Contemp. Probs. (forthcoming 2007), *available at* http://papers.ssrn.com/sol3/papers.cfm?abstract_id=961048; articles listed at Stephan Wilske & Teresa Schiller, *Jurisdiction Over Persons Abducted in Violation of International Law in the Aftermath of United States v. Alvarez-Machain*, 5 U. Chi. L. Sch. Roundtable 205, 233 n.136 (1998) (describing articles as "almost unanimously" condemning the opinion).

5. ***The Ker-Frisbie Doctrine.*** What is the doctrine? Professor Lowenfeld usefully capsulizes it by saying that "the exclusionary rule applies only to evidence, not to persons." Lowenfeld *supra*, p. 523, at 460. But another commentator has argued that "[r]efusing to exercise jurisdiction is far more drastic a step than, say, excluding evidence produced by the illegal arrest; it completely deprives the state of the opportunity to present its case." Comment, *United States v. Toscanino*, 88 Harv. L. Rev. 813, 816 (1975). Do you agree? Can you answer without weighing the risks and benefits of abduction? The *Restatement* reports that "nearly all states" adhere to a rule like the *Ker-Frisbie* doctrine, absent protest from other states. *Restatement, supra* p. 513, §433 note 2.

6. ***The Shocks-the-Conscience Exception.*** We saw in Chapter 9 that the silver platter doctrine, by which evidence collected abroad by foreign police may be used in U.S. prosecutions no matter how obtained, at least theoretically makes an exception for investigatory conduct that shocks the conscience of the U.S. court. See *supra* p. 288-289. In fact, the exception was

developed in an abduction case, United States v. Toscanino, 500 F.2d 267 (2d Cir. 1974), *reh'g denied*, 504 F.2d 1380 (2d Cir. 1974). There the court held that due process requires "a court to divest itself of jurisdiction over the person of a defendant where it has been acquired as the result of the government's deliberate, unnecessary, and unreasonable invasion of the accused's constitutional rights." *Id.* at 275. The continued vitality of *Toscanino*'s shock-the-conscience exception to the *Ker-Frisbie* doctrine, however, is drawn into question by the fact that the court held that it was "deliberate misconduct" for the United States to abduct Toscanino in violation of international treaty law. *Id.* at 276-279. Does any part of *Toscanino* survive *Alvarez-Machain*?

United States and foreign agents allegedly deprived Toscanino of sleep, kicked and beat him, pinched his fingers with metal pliers, flushed his eyes and body cavities with alcohol, and rendered him unconscious by sending jarring jolts of electricity through his body by electrodes attached to his earlobes, toes, and genitals. *Id.* at 270. In *Yunis, supra*, suspected terrorist Yunis was knocked to the deck of a yacht to which he had been lured, breaking his wrists, then was strip-searched, handcuffed, shackled with leg irons, and kept in a windowless room for four days while being transported to the United States. Declaring that *Toscanino* establishes "at best, only a very limited exception" to the *Ker-Frisbie* doctrine, the *Yunis* court found nothing suggesting "the sort of intentional, outrageous government conduct" needed to divest it of jurisdiction, even though that conduct was concededly not "picture perfect." *Id.* at 1092-1093. Alvarez-Machain maintained in court that he was punched in the stomach, forced to lie facedown in a car, shocked with an electric prod, and injected with a drug during his abduction. Does this treatment meet the *Toscanino* standard? Would the actions of U.S. agents in *Toscanino, Yunis*, and *Alvarez-Machain* violate the Detainee Treatment Act, *supra* p. 443, if those incidents occurred today?

7. ***Risks of Abduction.*** Professors Carter and Trimble report that after the Supreme Court's decision in *Alvarez-Machain*, the Iranian Parliament reportedly passed a law authorizing the President of Iran to arrest anywhere and bring to Iran for trial Americans who injure Iranian citizens or their property anywhere in the world. *See* Carter & Trimble, *supra* p. 513, at 794. If *Alvarez-Machain* was correctly decided, was the Iranian Parliament right, too? Abraham Sofaer, one-time Legal Adviser to the Department of State, warned that "we need to consider the fact that our legal position may be seized upon by other nations to engage in irresponsible conduct against our interests. Reciprocity is the heart of international law; all nations need to take into account the reactions of other nations to conduct which departs from accepted norms." Sofaer, *supra* p. 524, at 39-41, *quoted in* Leich, *supra* p. 524, at 727-728.

Mr. Sofaer also identified other "substantial risks to the U.S. agents involved" in overseas abductions.

> Apart from being killed in action, U.S. agents involved in such operations risk apprehension and punishment for their actions. Our agents would not normally enjoy immunity from prosecution or civil suit in the foreign country involved for any violations of local

law which occur. . . . Moreover, many states will not accord POW status to military personnel apprehended in support of an unconsented law enforcement action. The United States could also face requests from the foreign country for extradition of the agents. Obviously the United States would not extradite its agents for carrying out an authorized mission, but our failure to do so could lead the foreign country to cease extradition cooperation with us. Moreover, our agents would be vulnerable to extradition from third countries they visit.

Beyond the risks to our agents, the possibility also exists of suits against the United States in the foreign country's courts for illegal actions taken in that country. . . . The United States could also face challenges from such actions in international fora, including the International Court of Justice.

An unconsented, extraterritorial arrest would inevitably have an adverse impact on our bilateral relations with the country in which we act. Less obviously, such arrests could also greatly reduce law enforcement cooperation with that or other countries. . . . [*Id.*]

*See also* Abraham Abramovsky, *Extraterritorial Abductions: America's "Catch and Snatch" Policy Run Amok*, 31 Va. J. Intl. L. 151, 201-208 (1991).

Mr. Sofaer's predictions have come true. As we noted *supra* p. 464, a German court has issued arrest warrants for 13 members of an alleged CIA "abduction team" that seized a German citizen for irregular rendition from Macedonia to Afghanistan, and an Italian court has issued indictments against 26 Americans, most of them alleged CIA agents, for the 2003 kidnaping in Italy of an Egyptian cleric. See *supra* p. 463.

Argentina, Bolivia, Brazil, Canada, Chile, Columbia, Costa Rica, Jamaica, Paraguay, Peru, Spain, Switzerland, Uruguay, Venezuela, and, of course, Mexico have each protested or criticized *Alvarez-Machain*. Wilske & Schiller, *supra* p. 524, at 235-238. *See also* Mark S. Zaid, *Military Might Versus Sovereign Right: The Kidnaping of Dr. Humberto Alvarez-Machain and the Resulting Fallout*, 19 Hous. J. Intl. L. 829, 840-856 (1997).

8. ***Benefits of Abduction and Other Irregular Rendition.*** If the requested country refuses to extradite, or if its corrupt officials tip off the fugitive before trying to execute the extradition order, or if they fail in good faith to prosecute as an alternative to extradition, irregular rendition is the only way to apprehend a fugitive for trial in the United States. It is also often faster and less costly. *Cf.* Abramovsky, *supra*, at 155.

In 1994, the United States and Mexico signed a treaty effectively prohibiting future abductions. Treaty to Prohibit Transborder Abductions, Nov. 23, 1994, U.S.-Mex., 31 U.S.T. 5059. Mexico has, in turn, since found "exceptional circumstances" to disregard the nationality exception in its extradition law, which previously prevented extradition of Mexican nationals like Alvarez-Machain. *See* Argiro Kosmetatos, Comment, *U.S.-Mexican Extradition Policy: Were the Predictions Right About Alvarez?*, 22 Fordham Intl. L.J. 1064, 1102 (1999). Do these developments suggest another benefit of abduction?

**9.** *U.S. Policy Regarding Abduction.* Notwithstanding academic and international criticism of *Alvarez-Machain* and the risks of a policy of abduction, abduction remains official U.S. policy. A classified but inadvertently published part of Presidential Decision Directive 39, *U.S. Policy on Counterterrorism* (1995), warns that "[i]f we do not receive adequate cooperation from a state that harbors a terrorist whose extradition we are seeking, we shall take appropriate measures to induce cooperation. Return of suspects by force may be effected without the cooperation of the host government, consistent with the procedures outlined in NSD-77, which shall remain in effect." (NSD-77 is classified.)

# CHAPTER 17

# TRYING SUSPECTED TERRORISTS AS CRIMINALS

It is not just defining the crimes that poses legal problems in prosecuting terrorists; it is also the evidence. In 1996, Congress for the first time authorized the intelligence community, "upon the request of a United States law enforcement agency, [to] collect information outside the United States about individuals who are not United States persons . . . notwithstanding that the law enforcement agency intends to use the information collected for purposes of a law enforcement investigation or counterintelligence investigation." 50 U.S.C. §403-5a(a) (2000). Moreover, after 9/11, Congress expressly authorized and encouraged more sharing of information among intelligence and law enforcement agencies. See *supra* pp. 259-263. When intelligence agencies are tasked with information collection for law enforcement and those agencies share their information, the information collected may be used or sought in criminal prosecutions of alleged terrorists or their supporters. *See generally* Note, *Secret Evidence in the War on Terror*, 118 Harv. L. Rev. 1962 (2005). However, such use or access may compromise the security of the information itself, as well as the sources and methods by which it was collected.

In a criminal prosecution, the Sixth Amendment requires that the defendant "be informed of the nature and cause of the accusation [and] be confronted with the witnesses against him." U.S. Const. amend. VI. The amendment thus reinforces what the Supreme Court has characterized as an "immutable" principle of our legal system: that "the evidence used to prove the Government's case must be disclosed to the individual so that he has an opportunity to show that it is untrue." Greene v. McElroy, 360 U.S. 474, 496 (1959) (dictum). Accordingly, if the government needs to use secret information obtained by classified intelligence sources and methods to make its criminal case against a suspected terrorist, it must either disclose the information or drop the prosecution.

Even when the government decides that it has sufficient nonclassified information for a successful prosecution, however, a defendant may invoke her constitutional, statutory, and rule-based rights of discovery to gain access to classified information in government hands that she says she needs to defend herself. Alternatively, as a current or former government employee she may already possess classified information, and may threaten to use that information at trial to rebut or explain the charged conduct. In either case, the defendant may be in a position to "greymail" the government by forcing it into a disclose-or-dismiss dilemma.

It was partly to reduce the prospect of greymail in criminal cases that Congress enacted the Classified Information Procedures Act (CIPA) in 1980. We consider CIPA in Part A. We examine creative extensions of CIPA to deal with a defendant's right of confrontation in a suppression hearing in Part B, and with defendant's access to secret exculpatory testimony in Part C.

# A.  CLASSIFIED INFORMATION PROCEDURES ACT

## CLASSIFIED INFORMATION PROCEDURES ACT

18 U.S.C. App. 3 §§1-16 (2000 & Supp. IV 2004), as amended

### §4. Discovery of Classified Information by Defendants

The court, upon a sufficient showing, may authorize the United States to delete specified items of classified information from documents to be made available to the defendant through discovery under the Federal Rules of Criminal Procedure, to substitute a summary of the information for such classified documents, or to substitute a statement admitting relevant facts that the classified information would tend to prove. The court may permit the United States to make a request for such authorization in the form of a written statement to be inspected by the court alone. . . .

### §5. Notice of Defendant's Intention to Disclose Classified Information

(a) Notice by defendant. If a defendant reasonably expects to disclose or to cause the disclosure of classified information in any manner in connection with any trial or pretrial proceeding involving the criminal prosecution of such defendant, the defendant shall, within the time specified by the court or, where no time is specified, within thirty days prior to trial, notify the attorney for the United States and the court in writing. Such notice shall include a brief description of the classified information. Whenever a defendant learns of additional classified information he reasonably expects to disclose at any such proceeding, he shall notify the attorney for the United States and the court in writing as soon as possible thereafter and shall include a brief description of the classified information. . . .

### §6. Procedure for Cases Involving Classified Information

(a) Motion for hearing. Within the time specified by the court for the filing of a motion under this section, the United States may request the court to conduct a hearing to make all determinations concerning the use, relevance, or admissibility of classified information that would otherwise be made during the trial or pretrial proceeding. Upon such a request, the court shall conduct such a hearing. Any hearing held pursuant to this subsection (or any portion of such hearing specified in the request of the Attorney General) shall be held in camera if the Attorney General certifies to the court in such petition that a public proceeding may result in the disclosure of classified information. As to each item of classified information, the court shall set forth in writing the basis for its determination. Where the United States' motion under this subsection is filed prior to the trial or pretrial proceeding, the court shall rule prior to the commencement of the relevant proceeding.

(b) Notice.

(1) Before any hearing is conducted pursuant to a request by the United States under subsection (a), the United States shall provide the defendant with notice of the classified information that is at issue. Such notice shall identify the specific classified information at issue whenever that information previously has been made available to the defendant by the United States. When the United States has not previously made the information available to the defendant in connection with the case, the information may be described by generic category, in such form as the court may approve, rather than by identification of the specific information of concern to the United States.

(2) Whenever the United States requests a hearing under subsection (a), the court, upon request of the defendant, may order the United States to provide the defendant, prior to trial, such details as to the portion of the indictment or information at issue in the hearing as are needed to give the defendant fair notice to prepare for the hearing.

(c) Alternative procedure for disclosure of classified information.

(1) Upon any determination by the court authorizing the disclosure of specific classified information under the procedures established by this section, the United States may move that, in lieu of the disclosure of such specific classified information, the court order—

(A) the substitution for such classified information of a statement admitting relevant facts that the specific classified information would tend to prove; or

(B) the substitution for such classified information of a summary of the specific classified information.

The court shall grant such a motion of the United States if it finds that the statement or summary will provide the defendant with substantially the same ability to make his defense as would disclosure of the specific classified information. The court shall hold a hearing on any motion under this section. Any such hearing shall be held in camera at the request of the Attorney General.

(2) The United States may, in connection with a motion under paragraph (1), submit to the court an affidavit of the Attorney General certifying that disclosure of classified information would cause identifiable damage to the national security of the United States and explaining the basis for the classification of such information. If so requested by the United States, the court shall examine such affidavit in camera and ex parte. . . .

(e) Prohibition on disclosure of classified information by defendant, relief for defendant when United States opposes disclosure.

(1) Whenever the court denies a motion by the United States that it issue an order under subsection (c) and the United States files with the court an affidavit of the Attorney General objecting to disclosure of the

classified information at issue, the court shall order that the defendant not disclose or cause the disclosure of such information.

(2) Whenever a defendant is prevented by an order under paragraph (1) from disclosing or causing the disclosure of classified information, the court shall dismiss the indictment or information; except that, when the court determines that the interests of justice would not be served by dismissal of the indictment or information, the court shall order such other action, in lieu of dismissing the indictment or information, as the court determines is appropriate. Such action may include, but need not be limited to —

(A) dismissing specified counts of the indictment or information;

(B) finding against the United States on any issue as to which the excluded classified information relates; or

(C) striking or precluding all or part of the testimony of a witness. . . .

## UNITED STATES v. LEE

United States District Court, District of New Mexico, 2000
90 F. Supp. 2d 1324

CONWAY, Chief Judge. This matter came on for consideration of the Motion of Dr. Wen Ho Lee for a Declaration that Sections 5 and 6 of the Classified Information Procedures Act (CIPA) are Unconstitutional as Applied. . . . [Wen Ho Lee was being prosecuted on charges of espionage and mishandling of classified information at the Los Alamos National Laboratory.]

### I. CIPA Framework

The Classified Information Procedures Act (CIPA), 18 U.S.C. app. III §§1-16 (1988), provides for pretrial procedures to resolve questions of admissibility of classified information in advance of its use in open court.[1] Under CIPA procedures, the defense must file a notice briefly describing any classified information that it "reasonably expects to disclose or to cause the disclosure of" at trial. 18 U.S.C. app. III §5(a). Thereafter, the prosecution may request an *in camera* hearing for a determination of the "use, relevance and admissibility" of the proposed defense evidence. *Id.* at §6(a). If the Court finds the evidence admissible, the government may move for, and the Court may authorize, the substitution of unclassified facts or a summary of the information in the form of an admission by the government.[2] *See id.* at §6(c)(1). Such a motion may be granted if the Court finds that the statement or summary will provide the defendant with "substantially the same ability to make his defense as would disclosure of the specific classified information." *Id.* If the Court does not authorize the

---

1. Classified information is defined as including "information and material" subject to classification or otherwise requiring protection from public disclosure. *See* 18 U.S.C. app. III §1. Thus, CIPA applies to classified testimony as well as to classified documents.

2. If the court finds that the evidence is not admissible at trial, CIPA is no longer implicated. When determining the use, relevance and admissibility of the proposed evidence, the court may not take into account that the evidence is classified; relevance of classified information in a given case is governed solely by the standards set forth in the Federal Rules of Evidence.

substitution, the government can require that the defendant not disclose classified information. *See id.* at §6(e). However, under §6(e)(2), if the government prevents a defendant from disclosing classified information at trial, the court may: (A) dismiss the entire indictment or specific counts, (B) find against the prosecution on any issue to which the excluded information relates, or (C) strike or preclude the testimony of particular government witnesses. *See* 18 U.S.C. app. III §6(e)(2). Finally, CIPA requires that the government provide the defendant with any evidence it will use to rebut the defendant's revealed classified information evidence. *See id.* at §6(f).

## II. Constitutionality of CIPA

Defendant Lee contends that, as applied to him, the notice and hearing requirements of §5 and §6 of CIPA are unconstitutional. . . . Although I find Defendant's claims unjustified, I will nevertheless address them in turn.[3]

### A. Defendant's Privilege Against Self-Incrimination

Defendant Lee's first contention is that the notice and hearing requirements of §5 and §6 violate his Fifth Amendment privilege against self-incrimination because they force him to reveal classified aspects of his own trial testimony. Defendant argues that by forcing him to reveal portions of his potential testimony, CIPA unconstitutionally infringes upon his right to remain silent until and unless he decides to testify. Similarly, Defendant argues that if he chooses not to comply with the notice requirements, under the penalty of not being able to offer such testimony at trial, CIPA unconstitutionally denies him the right to testify on his own behalf. In either case, Defendant contends that CIPA forces him to pay a price in the form of a costly pretrial decision in order to preserve his constitutional rights at trial.

. . . CIPA does not require that a defendant specify whether or not he will testify or what he will testify about. Instead, CIPA requires "merely a general disclosure as to what classified information the defense expects to use at trial, regardless of the witness or the document through which that information is to be revealed." United States v. Poindexter, 725 F. Supp. 13, 33 (D.D.C. 1989). Therefore, Defendant's argument that if he discloses the classified information his right to remain silent has been compromised (or in the alternative that if he refuses to disclose the classified information his right to testify has been compromised) is misplaced. Despite CIPA's requirements, Defendant still has the option of not testifying. Similarly, if the defense does not disclose classified information as required by CIPA, the defendant retains the option of testifying, albeit with the preclusion of any classified information.

In addition, the pretrial disclosure of certain aspects of a criminal defense is hardly a novel concept. Examples of such requirements include Fed. R. Crim. P. 12.1 (alibi defense); Fed. R. Crim. P. 12.2 (insanity defense); Fed. R. Crim. P. 12.3 (public authority defense); and Fed. R. Crim. P. 16 (medical and scientific tests, and tangible objects and certain documents). Such provisions have consistently been held constitutional. . . . CIPA merely provides a mechanism

---

3. Other courts that have considered the constitutionality of CIPA are in accord. . . .

for determining the admissibility of classified information so that classified information is not inadvertently disclosed during open proceedings. Defendant still has the choice of presenting the evidence during trial or not, after it has been deemed admissible. "That the defendant faces . . . a dilemma demanding a choice between complete silence and presenting a defense has never been thought an invasion of the privilege against compelled self-incrimination." Williams v. Florida, 399 U.S. 78, 84 (1970).

Defendant also argues that the burdens placed upon him by CIPA unconstitutionally violate his Fifth Amendment rights in that they do not advance any interests related to the fairness and accuracy of the criminal trial. However, Defendant's argument is unconvincing. CIPA is designed to "assure the fairness and reliability of the criminal trial" while permitting the government to "ascertain the potential damage to national security of proceeding with a given prosecution before trial." See United States v. Ivy, 1993 WL 316215 at *4 (citations omitted). As the Supreme Court has noted, "it is obvious and unarguable that no governmental interest is more compelling than the security of the Nation." Poindexter, 725 F. Supp. at 34 (quoting Haig v. Agee, 453 U.S. 280, 307 (1981)). CIPA serves that interest "by providing a mechanism for protecting both the unnecessary disclosure of sensitive national security information and by helping to ensure that those with significant access to such information will not escape the sanctions of the law applicable to others by use of the greymail route."[5] Id. at 34. Accordingly, I find that CIPA does not violate Defendant's privilege against self-incrimination by infringing upon either his right to remain silent or his right to testify on his own behalf.

## B. Defendant's Right to Confront and Cross-Examine Witnesses

Defendant Lee next argues that §5 and §6 of CIPA violate his Sixth Amendment right to confront and cross-examine government witnesses by forcing him to notify the government pretrial (and explain the significance) of all the classified information he reasonably expects to elicit from prosecution witnesses on cross-examination and all such information that will be contained in defense counsel's questions to those witnesses.[6]

Defendant contends that under CIPA, the "prosecution can shape its case-in-chief to blunt the force of the defense cross examination" and that the advance notice under CIPA "will impede effective defense cross-examination." However, the Confrontation Clause does not guarantee the right to undiminished surprise with respect to cross-examination of prosecutorial witnesses. . . .

CIPA does not require that the defense reveal its plan of cross-examination to the government. CIPA also does not require that the defendant reveal what questions his counsel will ask, in which order, and to which witnesses. Likewise, the defendant need not attribute the information to any particular

---

5. Greymail refers to a tactic employed by a defendant who threatens to disclose classified information with the hopes that the prosecution will choose not to prosecute in order to keep the information protected.

6. Under the Sixth Amendment, a criminal defendant "shall enjoy the right . . . to be confronted with the witnesses against him." U.S. Const. amend. VI. Pursuant to the right to confront the witnesses against him, a criminal defendant has the "fundamental right" to cross examine witnesses for the prosecution.

witness. CIPA merely requires that the defendant identify the classified information he reasonably intends to use. Because the only cited tactical disadvantage that may accrue, minimization of surprise, is slight, Defendant has failed to demonstrate that the requirements under CIPA render his opportunity for cross-examination ineffective.

### C. Defendant's Right to Due Process

Defendant's due process argument is based on the contention that CIPA's disclosure requirements violate the Due Process Clause by imposing a one-sided burden on the defense, without imposing a mandatory reciprocal duty on the prosecution. However, due process is only denied where the balance of discovery is tipped against the defendant and in favor of the government. . . .

Here, the CIPA burdens are not one-sided. First, the government has already agreed to allow Defendant and his counsel access to all classified files at issue in the indictment. Second, the government must produce all discoverable materials before the defense is required to file a §5(a) notice. Third, before a §6 hearing is conducted, the government must reveal details of its case so as to give the defense fair notice to prepare for the hearing. See 18 U.S.C. app. III §6(b)(2). Specifically, the government must provide the defense with any portions of any material it may use to establish the "national defense" element of any charges against Lee. Fourth, under §6(f), the government is required to provide notice of any evidence it will use to rebut classified information that the court permits the defense to use at trial. Finally, in addition to the discovery obligations under §6 of CIPA, the government must also comply with the Federal Rules of Criminal Procedure and Brady v. Maryland, 373 U.S. 83 (1963).

Despite the fact that the government's reciprocal duties under CIPA are not triggered until it decides to request a §6 hearing, the overall balance of discovery is not tipped against Lee. . . .

### III. Conclusion

In summary, Defendant Lee has failed to show that the carefully balanced framework for determining the use of classified information by the defense set forth in CIPA violates his Fifth Amendment privilege against self-incrimination, his Fifth Amendment right to remain silent or his Fifth and Sixth Amendment rights to testify on his own behalf. Defendant has also failed to demonstrate that CIPA violates his Fifth Amendment right to due process of law or his Sixth Amendment right to confront and cross-examine witnesses.

## NOTES AND QUESTIONS

1. *The Decision to Prosecute.* As we noted above, when the government decides whether to mount a criminal prosecution or initiate an immigration proceeding against an alleged terrorist or international criminal, it must evaluate the risk that going forward will expose state secrets or classified information. Consequently, the Attorney General has instructed federal prosecutors, in deciding whether to prosecute, to weigh (a) the likelihood

of such exposure, (b) the resulting damage to national security, (c) the likelihood of success if the case is brought, and (d) the nature and importance of other federal interests that prosecution would promote. U.S. Dept. of Justice, *Attorney General's Guidelines for Prosecutions Involving Classified Information* 4-6 (1981). Sometimes this weighing will dictate not prosecuting. How, if at all, would the enactment of CIPA have affected this process? The decision to prosecute and the government's conduct of the trial of Wen Ho Lee are dealt with extensively in Dan Stober & Ian Hoffman, *A Convenient Spy: Wen Ho Lee and the Politics of Nuclear Espionage* (2001).

2. ***Is It Classified?*** How did the *Lee* court decide whether CIPA was applicable — that is, whether the information Wen Ho Lee was planning to use was "classified"? Must the court simply defer to the government's classification stamp? If so, "the government could make CIPA applicable whenever it suited its purpose simply by rubber-stamping documents that have no relevance to the national security." 26 Charles Alan Wright & Kenneth W. Graham Jr., *Federal Practice and Procedure* 748 (1992 & Supp. 2006).

3. ***Greymail.*** In United States v. Reynolds, 345 U.S. 1, 12 (1953), the Supreme Court said that "it is unconscionable to allow [the government] to undertake prosecution and then invoke its governmental privileges to deprive the accused of anything which might be material to his defense." Rejected Federal Rule of Evidence 509 therefore provided that when the state secrets privilege is sustained and a party is thereby deprived of material evidence, the court should make whatever orders "the interests of justice require, including striking the testimony of a witness, declaring a mistrial, finding against the government upon an issue as to which the evidence is relevant, or dismissing the action." 26 Wright & Graham, *supra*, at 417. *See generally* Louis Fisher, *In the Name of National Security: Unchecked Presidential Power and the Reynolds Case* (2006) (reviewing the history of the rule).

Can you see how these principles from civil litigation help set the stage for greymail in criminal trials? How does it work? Is it an unfair tactic by unscrupulous defendants or lawyers? Former Assistant Attorney General Philip Heymann has noted that "[i]t would be a mistake . . . to view the 'greymail' problem as limited to instances of unscrupulous or questionable conduct by defendants since wholly proper defense attempts to obtain or disclose classified information may present the government with the same 'disclose or dismiss' dilemma." S. Rep. No. 96-823, at 3 (1980), *reprinted in* 1980 U.S.C.C.A.N. 4294, 4296-4297. Into which category would the disclose-or-dismiss dilemma in the *Wen Ho Lee* case fall? *See* Bob Drogin, *Nuke Secrets Deemed Vital to Scientist's Case*, L.A. Times, June 16, 2000, at A28 (reporting that a member of Lee's legal team characterized as "graymailing the government" his request for complete computer records and 400,000 pages of classified data for nearly every U.S. nuclear weapon). Has the enactment of CIPA eliminated the possibility of greymail?

4. ***Prosecutor's Use of Secret Evidence?*** Look closely at the CIPA provisions. Do they permit the prosecutor to use classified information *to make the government's case* against the defendant, either secretly or in

substituted or summarized form? If you are not sure, how should we resolve any ambiguity? *See* Greene v. McElroy, 360 U.S. 474 (1959).

5. ***Defendant's Discovery in Criminal Cases.*** In criminal cases, defendants have certain limited rights to discovery. The Supreme Court has held that the prosecution must disclose evidence that is favorable to the defendant and "is material either to guilt or to punishment." Brady v. Maryland, 373 U.S. 83-87 (1963). Specific defense requests thus require the prosecution to turn over all exculpatory evidence, which may include classified information in national security prosecutions. *See* United States v. Rezaq, 156 F.R.D. 514, 516-517 (D.D.C. 1994). In addition, the Jencks Act, 18 U.S.C. §3500 (2000), requires the prosecution to produce statements in its possession by witnesses who have testified on direct examination at trial, in order to facilitate cross-examination by the defense. Such statements could include ones made by secret intelligence assets. For example, in the case that prompted enactment of the Act, the statements were confidential reports by paid government informants who were members of the Communist Party. Jencks v. United States, 353 U.S. 657 (1957). Finally, Federal Rule of Criminal Procedure 16(a)(1) permits criminal defendants to discover their own statements, as well as documents and tangible objects in the possession, custody, or control of the government that are material to defendant's defense, intended for use by government as evidence, or were obtained from or belong to the defendant. Here again, the documents or tangible objects might include classified information, or their disclosure might reveal intelligence courses and methods. *See generally* Jonathan M. Fredman, *Intelligence Agencies, Law Enforcement, and the Prosecution Team*, 16 Yale L. & Poly. Rev. 331 (1998).

Of course, intelligence agencies may hold back classified information or sources and methods and only provide unclassified information to the prosecution. Could the prosecution then argue that it had only the latter in its possession, custody, or control, thus avoiding discovery of classified information by the defense? The cases are neither clear nor consistent, but in general they hold that "federal discovery obligations extend to those government agencies that are so closely 'aligned' with the prosecution of a specific matter that justice requires their records be subject to the respective discovery obligations." *Id.* at 347. The *United States Attorneys' Manual* states that "an investigative or prosecutive agency becomes aligned with the government prosecutor when it becomes actively involved in the investigation or the prosecution of a particular case." *United States Attorneys' Manual* tit. 9-90.210(D)(1) (1997).

Does the tasking of an intelligence agency by the FBI under the 1996 law (quoted *supra* p. 529) constitute sufficient "active involvement" to align it with the prosecution? *See* Fredman, *supra*, at 364 (opining that "a court may well [so] conclude"). Suppose the intelligence community on its own initiative forwards to the FBI foreign surveillance information suggesting criminal wrongdoing. Has it thereby aligned itself with the prosecutors if a criminal prosecution results? *Id.* (Probably not.) The *United States Attorneys' Manual* suggests that its role must first "exceed the role of providing mere tips or leads based on information generated independently of the criminal case." *United States Attorneys' Manual* tit. 9-90.210(d)(1) (1997). The alignment described here is encouraged by a provision of the USA Patriot Act that amended the Foreign Intelligence Surveillance Act (FISA) to allow law enforcement officials to participate with intelligence agencies in, and even to direct, domestic surveillance under FISA that has a "significant" foreign intelligence purpose. See *supra* pp. 148, 155.

6. ***CIPA and Discovery.*** CIPA permits the government to argue ex parte against the discovery of classified information, 18 U.S.C. app. 3 §4, but the Act does not purport to change discovery standards. Nevertheless, some courts and commentators have read CIPA to narrow defendants' rights or balance them against governmental interests. *See* 26 Wright & Graham, *supra* p. 536, §5672. In United States v. Yunis, 867 F.2d 617 (D.C. Cir. 1989), for example, the court arguably crafted a new relevancy standard for discovery of classified information by holding that "mere . . . theoretical relevance" was not enough; the defendant was obliged to show that the information is "at least 'helpful to the defense of [the] accused.'" *Id.* at 623 (quoting Roviaro v. United States, 353 U.S. 53, 60-61 (1957) (involving informer's privilege)).

When a court, in a section 4 proceeding, does find that classified information is discoverable, the government is afforded the option of substituting a summary or a statement admitting relevant facts that the classified information would tend to prove. The courts have also inferred authority from CIPA to order defense counsel to obtain security clearances as a condition of seeing classified information or participating in hearings at which it may be disclosed. *See* United States v. Bin Laden, 58 F. Supp. 2d 113 (S.D.N.Y. 1999) (rejecting the claim that this requirement unconstitutionally interferes with defendant's choice of counsel).

7. ***CIPA Notice and the Admissibility Hearing.*** A defendant who wishes to disclose classified information in the case must give specific prior notice to the government pursuant to section 5, on penalty of having the court exclude any classified information omitted from the notice. 18 U.S.C. app. 3 §5. Why is it not unconstitutional to thus require a defendant to tip his hand, according to *Lee*?

Following a §5 notice, the government may request a hearing concerning the use, relevancy, or admissibility of the identified information. 18 U.S.C. app. 3 §6. This hearing is usually held in camera. CIPA's legislative history is quite clear that it was not intended to change existing rules of evidence applicable in this hearing. *See* 26 Wright & Graham, *supra*, §5672 (discussing history). Some courts have taken this history to heart and even stated that they must disregard the classified nature of the information in ruling on its relevancy and admissibility. Others — notably the Fourth Circuit — have found that CIPA established "a more strict rule of admissibility" for classified information. United States v. Smith, 780 F.2d 1102, 1105 (4th Cir. 1985). *See* Note, *United States v. Smith: Construing the Classified Information Procedures Act as Restricting the Admissibility of Evidence*, 44 Wash. & Lee L. Rev. 720 (1987). Moreover, other courts have obtained the same results as *Smith* by narrowly construing defenses, such as reliance on CIA authority (*see* United States v. Lopez-Lima, 738 F. Supp. 1404 (S.D. Fla. 1990), in order to rule the classified information irrelevant. *See* 26 Wright & Graham, *supra*, §5672.

8. *CIPA Substitution.* Courts may find classified information to be relevant and material. CIPA section 6 then affords the government the option of moving to substitute an unclassified statement of admissions or an unclassified summary for the classified information. The court must grant that motion "if it finds that the statement or summary will provide the defendant with substantially the same ability to make his defense as would disclosure." 18 U.S.C. app. 3 §6(c)(1).

9. *CIPA: Disclose or Dismiss.* If, on the other hand, the court denies the motion, then the Attorney General must decide whether to disclose the information. *Id.* §6(e)(1). If she decides against disclosure, the court may dismiss all or part of the indictment, find against the government on an issue to which the withheld information relates, or strike testimony. *Id.* §6(e)(2). In deciding among these alternatives, the court is not supposed to balance interests; it instead must take whatever action is necessary "to make the defendant whole again." S. Rep. No. 96-823, at 9 (1980). For example, in United States v. Fernandez, 913 F.2d 148 (4th Cir. 1990), a prosecution of the CIA station chief in Costa Rica growing out of the Iran-Contra Affair, the defendant sought to introduce classified documents purporting to show the truth of statements he had made concerning the CIA's role in the resupply of the Contras. Using CIPA procedures, the Independent Counsel proposed that an unclassified summary of evidence be used to substitute for the documents, but the court found that the summary would not provide Fernandez with substantially the same ability to make his defense as would disclosure of the classified information. When the Attorney General refused to declassify the information, the court dismissed the indictment over the strenuous objections of the Independent Counsel. The government also ended the Wen Ho Lee prosecution by accepting his plea to a single count of the multi-count indictment—partly, it is reported, because senior Energy Department officials feared that the judge would order disclosure of classified information to Lee for use in his defense. *See* Bob Drogin, *How FBI's Flawed Case Against Lee Unraveled*, L.A. Times, Sept. 13, 2000, at A1.

10. *Another Option: Lying?* In 1983, a former CIA officer named Edwin P. Wilson was tried and convicted for illegally exporting explosives to Libya. He claimed that he was still working for the Agency and acting on its authority. During Wilson's trial, the government introduced an affidavit from a high-ranking CIA official denying Wilson's continued employment. The affidavit was a deliberate falsehood. Before Wilson was sentenced, attorneys at the CIA and the Justice Department learned of the fabrication, yet they failed to inform either the trial court or the appellate court. When the truth came to light 20 years later, Wilson's conviction was vacated. United States v. Wilson, 289 F. Supp. 2d 801 (S.D. Tex. 2003). A clearly incensed judge wrote, "Honesty comes hard to the government." *Id.* at 809.

# B.  CONFRONTING SECRET WITNESSES

## United States v. Abu Marzook

United States District Court, Northern District of Illinois, 2006
412 F. Supp. 2d 913

St. Eve, District Judge. [Muhammad Hamid Khalil Salah ("Defendant" or "Salah") was indicted for providing material support to the designated foreign terrorist organization Hamas by recruiting and training new Hamas leaders and disbursing money to support Hamas activities. The government planned to introduce at trial statements Salah had made while in Israeli custody.] . . .

Defendant Salah has moved to suppress any written and oral statements that he allegedly made to agents of the Israeli government, including the Israeli police, interrogators of the GSS/ISA, and others working with these authorities. In support of his motion, Salah has submitted a sworn affidavit detailing the treatment he claims he received at the hands of his interrogators. Salah argues that he did not voluntarily give any of these statements. He contends that he involuntarily made such statements because Israeli authorities coerced and tortured him into making them. Given that Defendant Salah's affidavit makes a preliminary showing that a significant, disputed factual issue exists, the Court will hold an evidentiary hearing.

### III. The Hearing

The suppression hearing will commence with opening statements on March 3, 2006, and testimony on March 6, 2006. At the hearing, the government intends to call approximately six or seven witnesses to testify. Two of these witnesses will be agents of the ISA. The ISA is an intelligence agency for the State of Israel that provides for Israel's internal security. The government has moved the Court to close the hearing to the public when these ISA agents testify. It argues that a closed hearing is mandated by the Classified Information Procedures Act, and warranted to protect the safety of the ISA agents and the sanctity of the ISA's intelligence gathering methods. . . .

### Analysis

At the suppression hearing, the Court will determine whether Defendant Salah's alleged statements are admissible at trial. The government has moved to have the testimony of the ISA agents at the hearing conducted *in camera* for the Court to resolve questions regarding the use and admissibility of Salah's statements. The government argues, and has provided supporting evidence, that the substance of the ISA agents' testimony is classified and thus cannot be disclosed to the public. The government does not seek to have Defendant Salah and his attorneys excluded from this testimony because the Israeli authorities have agreed to waive the classification designation as to the majority of this information as to Salah and his counsel, as well as to

Co-Defendant Ashqar's counsel. Instead, the government seeks to have these agents testify outside the presence of the public because Israel has not waived the classification designation generally. Thus, the primary issue presented to the Court is whether the public can have access to the testimonial information deemed classified at the suppression hearing. . . .

CIPA defines classified information as "any information or material that has been determined by the United States Government pursuant to an Executive order, statute, or regulation, to require protection against unauthorized disclosure for reasons of national security. . . ." 18 U.S.C. App. 3, §1(a). "National security," under CIPA, "means the national defense and foreign relations of the United States." *Id.,* §1(b). . . .

## A. The Substance of the Testimony[3]

The ISA is a domestic intelligence agency for the State of Israel. By law, the ISA provides for the internal security of Israel. Israel is in a state of high risk given the terrorist operations working against Israel. Israel maintains the secrecy of the true identities of the ISA agents, as well as identifying characteristics. Given this secrecy and the ISA's safety concerns for its agents, Israel has never before permitted ISA agents to give live testimony in the United States. Although the Court cannot publicly disclose the substance of these agents' testimony in this case, generally speaking, these witnesses will testify regarding topics that are themselves classified, including the agents' work, work-related activities, procedures, interrogation techniques, investigative methods, and other counterintelligence and securities activities of the ISA. Defendant does not contradict the anticipated substance of the ISA agents' testimony. Based on the *in camera* submissions of the government, the Court finds that Israel has classified the substance of the testimony of these agents, as well as their true identities. As set forth below, the United States, in turn, treats this information as classified for purposes of CIPA.

## B. The Anticipated Testimony Is Classified by Executive Order

Pursuant to Executive Order 12958, issued on April 17, 1995, as further amended by Executive Order 13292, issued on March 25, 2003, "information provided to the United States Government by a foreign government . . . with the expectation that the information, the source of the information, or both, are to be held in confidence" or "information produced by the United States pursuant to or as a result of a joint arrangement with a foreign government . . . requiring that the information, the arrangement, or both, are to be held in confidence" constitutes "foreign government information." Exec. Order No. 12958, 60 Fed. Reg. 19825 (Apr. 17, 1995), §1.1(d). Moreover, "the unauthorized disclosure of foreign government information is presumed to cause damage to the national security." *Id.,* §1.1(c).

It is undisputed that Israel provided the substance of the testimony of the ISA agents to the United States with the expectation that it would be held in

---

3. The Court is precluded from providing details of the anticipated testimony given that it is covered by CIPA.

confidence. Given that Israel considers the true identities of the ISA agents and the substance of their testimony classified, American authorities have certified it as classified. Accordingly, the Court grants the government's request to close the hearing to the public when these agents testify because the Court finds that the agents' anticipated testimony falls within CIPA's scope. Defendant Salah and his counsel, as well as counsel for Co-Defendant Ashqar, may be present during this time. The Court will only permit those with the appropriate security clearance to remain in the courtroom during this testimony. . . .

### 2. Classified designation

Defendant also challenges the designation of the agents' testimony as "classified" based on Section 1.8 of Executive Order 12958. Section 1.8 provides that "[i]n no case shall information be classified in order to: . . . (2) prevent embarrassment to a person, organization, or agency." Exec. Order No. 12958, 60 Fed. Reg. 19825, §1.8(2). Defendant argues, without any supporting evidence, that Israel has improperly designated the testimony at issue classified in order to prevent embarrassment and "to conceal Israel's use of harsh and illegal interrogation methods which violate international law as well as the law of Israel and the United States." Defendant therefore asks the Court to deem the testimony not classified.

At lease [sic] one Circuit has held that a court cannot question the Executive's designation of material as classified. See, e.g., United States v. Smith, 750 F.2d 1215, 1217 (4th Cir. 1984) ("[T]he government . . . may determine what information is classified. A defendant cannot challenge this classification. A court cannot question it."). Although the Seventh Circuit has not addressed this precise issue in the context of CIPA, it has provided some guidance in the context of the Freedom of Information Act ("FOIA") where it has made clear that classification "decisions rest with the executive branch." Stein [v. Dept. of Justice & Fed. Bureau of Investigation, 662 F.2d 1245, 1259 (7th Cir. 1981)]. In Stein, the Seventh Circuit confronted whether the FBI had properly withheld certain documents under the classified documents exception to FOIA (codified at 5 U.S.C. §552(b)(1)). In this context, the Seventh Circuit addressed a court's in camera review of classified documents under the FOIA where the statute — in contrast to the CIPA statute — specifically provides for de novo review of classified documents. Stein, 662 F.2d at 1254. The Stein court noted that:

> It is a matter of conjecture whether the court performs any real judicial function when it reviews classified documents in camera. Without the illumination provided by adversarial challenge and with no expertness in the field of national security, the court has no basis on which to test the accuracy of the government's claims. The court is limited to determining that the documents are the kinds of documents described in the government's affidavit, that they have been classified in fact, and that there is a logical nexus between the information at issue and the claimed exemption. The court is in no position to second-guess either the agency's determination of the need for classification or the agency's prediction of harm should release be permitted. Even in those instances where the court might have its own view of the soundness of the original policy

decision, . . . it must defer to the agency's evaluation of the need to maintain the secrecy of the methods used to carry out such projects.

This does not mean, however, that such review does not further the purposes of the Act. Clearly, the prospect of having to justify its classification decisions before a neutral arbiter causes a more thorough and objective presubmission review by the agency than would otherwise be the case.

*Id. See also Braslavsky v. Fed. Bureau of Investigation,* 57 F.3d 1073, 1995 WL 341618 (7th Cir. 1995) ("As to the intelligence material, unchallenged declarations of government officers that the undisclosed information satisfies the procedural and substantive requirements of Executive Order 12356 and could be expected to cause damage to national security justifies withholding the information"). . . .

In any event, the Court need not resolve whether it can review the legitimacy of a classification designation in the context of CIPA where the statute does not provide for such review, because even if the Court had the authority to make such a determination, Defendant's challenge fails under the clear language of the Executive Order. The Court interprets Executive Orders in the same manner that it interprets statutes. Namely, the Court looks first to the text of the Executive Order. If the language is unambiguous, the inquiry ceases.

The classification exception upon which Defendant relies provides that information should not be classified in order to "prevent embarrassment to a person, organization, or agency." Under a plain reading of the Executive Order, the State of Israel does not constitute a person, organization, or agency. . . . Thus, even if Defendant's assertion is correct, the Executive Order does not preclude its classification.

Further, based on the submissions before the Court, there is simply no evidence that these materials are classified merely to prevent embarrassment to Israel. Moreover, the materials submitted to the Court support the classified designation of the anticipated testimony of these agents. . . .

## C. True Identities

The government also seeks to have the ISA agents' true names and identities remain undisclosed to the public, as well as Defendant Salah. The government does not even know their true identities. Instead, the government seeks to have these agents testify using the pseudonyms under which the ISA agents conduct all of their ISA affairs. Defendant objects to this procedure. . . .

In Israel, it is a criminal violation to disclose the true identity of an ISA agent because of the sensitive and dangerous nature of the agent's work. This Israeli law is similar to the law in this country which penalizes disclosure of identifying information of a covert agent. *See* 50 U.S.C. §421(a). Under Israeli law, the true identities of these agents — including their names, identifying information, and physical characteristics — are classified. Their names are therefore classified under Executive Order 12958. The government thus has met its burden of proving that these identities constitute classified information. Accordingly, the Court orders that the ISA agents may testify using pseudonyms, and they do not have to disclose their true identities in court.

Allowing the ISA agents to testify using pseudonyms does not deprive Defendant of his Sixth Amendment right to confront these witnesses. The Sixth Amendment's Confrontation Clause guarantees a criminal defendant the right "to be confronted with the witnesses against him." *United States v. McGee,* 408 F.3d 966, 974 (7th Cir. 2005), quoting U.S. CONST., amend. VI. "The clause protects the criminal defendant's right physically to face those who testify against him, and the right to conduct cross-examination." *Id.* (quotation and citation omitted). Defendant will be able to physically face each of the ISA witnesses and to cross examine them. Although he will not know their true identities, they will identify themselves by their pseudonyms that they use in connection with their work. Defendant has admitted that he never knew these individuals by their true identities, but only by the pseudonyms that they will use in court. Defendant remains free to cross examine these witnesses on the basis of their direct testimony or any other proper basis. *See Delaware v. Van Arsdall,* 475 U.S. 673, 679 (1986) (courts can "impose reasonable limits on such cross-examination based on concerns about, among other things, harassment, prejudice, confusion of the issues, the witness' safety, or interrogation that is repetitive or only marginally relevant."). The use of pseudonyms is also appropriate for the security of these witnesses. *See United States v. Watson,* 599 F.2d 1149, 1157 (2d Cir. 1979) (finding no Confrontation Clause violation: "given the seriousness of the threat and the extensiveness of the cross-examination that the court did permit, we believe that the judge acted within his discretion in limiting the scope of cross-examination so as to permit [witness who was in the Federal Witness Protection Program] to maintain his concealed identity"); *United States v. Abu Ali,* 395 F. Supp.2d 338, 344 (E.D. Va. 2005) (on motion to suppress, court considered testimony from witnesses who, for security reasons, used pseudonyms).

## D. Review of Transcripts

Under Section 6 of CIPA, review of testimony differs from review of documents. Unlike a document which is static and which the Court can review in its entirety, live testimony is dynamic—neither the Court nor the parties can anticipate every question that counsel will ask these ISA witnesses nor every answer they will provide. As discussed above, the government has properly invoked CIPA based on the anticipated substance of the ISA agents' testimony, and Assistant Attorney General Fisher has certified that a public proceeding of the ISA agents' testimony may result in disclosure of classified information.

In order to ensure that all of the received testimony is in fact classified, however, the Court directs the United States to conduct a post-hearing review of the actual testimony of these ISA agents to confirm whether the government deems the entirety of each ISA agent's testimony classified. The Court directs the government to conduct this review within seven business days from the issuance of the final transcript. If the government deems the testimony not classified, the Court will promptly make it part of the public filing. This expedited review of the testimony will ensure that any information that is not classified will be made available to the public in a timely manner.

Further, the Court directs the government to review any documents introduced into evidence during the testimony of these agents. To the extent these documents, or portions of them, are not classified, they will be available to the public no later than seven days from their admission into evidence.

## E. The First and Sixth Amendments

Because the government seeks to apply the agents' testimony to the merits of the suppression hearing and thus practically, the CIPA hearing will coincide with a portion of the suppression hearing, the government must establish that courtroom closure squares with the Constitution, even though CIPA independently covers the agents' testimony. Indeed, in assessing the merits of the government's motion and the motions to intervene, the Court is well aware that "[t]he First Amendment presumes that there is a right of access to proceedings and documents which have 'historically been open to the public' and where the disclosure would serve a significant role in the functioning of the process in question." . . .

Similarly, "the Sixth Amendment right of the accused [to a public trial] is no less protective of a public trial than the implicit First Amendment right of the press and public." [Waller v. Georgia, 467 U.S. 39, 46 (1984).] "[U]nder the Sixth Amendment any closure of a suppression hearing over the objections of the accused must meet the test set out in *Press-Enterprise* [Co. v. Superior Court, 464 U.S. 501 (1984)] and its predecessors." *Id.* at 47. Specifically, "[u]nder *Press-Enterprise,* the party seeking to close the hearing must advance an overriding interest that is likely to be prejudiced, the closure must be no broader than necessary to protect that interest, the trial court must consider reasonable alternatives to closing the proceeding, and it must make findings adequate to support the closure." *Id.* at 48.

[The court concluded that the presumption of public access to suppression hearings was overcome by the overriding government "interest in maintaining the agents' sensitive testimony . . . as classified in order to protect the national security of Israel and the relationship between Israel and the United States of sharing national security information," as well as the grave danger the agents would face if they were publicly identified. It also found that "[t]he closure of the courtroom is narrowly tailored to address the CIPA interest and the security concerns. The courtroom will only be closed to the public during the testimony of the ISA agents. The remaining witnesses, including the Israeli police officers whom the government anticipates calling at the hearing, will testify in an open courtroom, and the attorneys' opening and closing statements will be public." The right of public access to public adjudicative proceedings is explored more fully *infra* pp. 618-626.] . . .

## II. Other Security Measures

The government has requested other security measures for the ISA agents. It is clear that a "judge has wide discretion in determining what is necessary to maintain the security of the courtroom." *United States v. Brooks,* 125 F.3d 484, 502 (7th Cir.1997).

## A. Light Disguise

The government seeks permission to have the ISA agents testify in light disguise for "the protection of their identity, both for their ability to continue covert work as well as their safety and the safety of their families." Defendant opposes this measure.

The appearance of these agents presents legitimate security issues. Although light disguise would be appropriate in some circumstances, it is not necessary here where the courtroom will be closed to the public. The government contends that Defendant Salah and others in the courtroom will be able to publicly identify these agents if they do not wear light disguise. These are the same agents that previously questioned Defendant Salah. The government has not submitted any evidence or argument that these agents were in disguise at the time of such questioning, thus Salah presumably has already physically seen them at length. The only other individuals in the courtroom will be defense attorneys, court personnel who have security clearances, and federal agents. Without any evidence of why the extra precaution of light disguise is necessary in a closed courtroom, the Court denies the government's request without prejudice. The Court orders that no one present in the courtroom can disclose or describe the physical identity of these ISA agents.

## B. Non-Public Entrance

The ISA agent witnesses may, however, use a private entrance to the courthouse and the courtroom. *See United States v. George,* Crim. Nos. 91-0521(RCL), 92-0215(RCL), 1992 WL 200027, at *3 (D.D.C. July 29, 1992) (permitting undercover CIA witnesses to "enter and exit the courthouse and the courtroom without using the public entrances"). This procedure will assist in protecting the identity of these witnesses and ensuring their safety. Defendant does not object to this request. Accordingly, the Court grants the government's request for the ISA agents to use a private entrance to the courthouse and courtroom. . . .

## NOTES AND QUESTIONS

1. *Compromising the Immutable Principle?* At the start of this chapter, we noted the axiom that "the evidence used to prove the Government's case must be disclosed to the individual so that he has an opportunity to show that it is untrue." Greene v. McElroy, 360 U.S. 474, 496 (1959) (dictum). Was the axiom violated in *Marzook*? If not, what is the defendant's complaint? Is the result fair?

2. *Classified Testimony.* The court applies CIPA. Does it work as well for testimony as for documentary evidence? When the testimony has not yet been given and the witnesses not yet cross-examined, how do we know whether or how much of the testimony is classified? How does the court respond to this challenge?

3. *The Propriety of Classification.* Like *Lee, Marzook* poses the question of the court's role in testing the government's claim that information or testimony is properly classified. What is the *Marzook* court's answer? Is the court's deferential treatment of the government's claim sufficiently protective of Salah's rights? What are the alternatives? For a discussion, see Stephen Dycus et al., *National Security Law* 997-1014 (4th ed. 2007).

4. *Other Terrorism Trial Issues. Marzook* presents some largely managerial problems of terrorism trials with possible constitutional ramifications, but there are many more problems. May a defendant be excluded if he threatens to blurt out classified information or disrupt the trial? May he insist on

representing himself in order to make a public display of the trial? May a jury be disguised or isolated for its own protection? May the government require that defense counsel be cleared for security purposes? May the judge visit the CIA ex parte to hear firsthand its concerns about possible disclosures at trial? Must the judge and her clerks get security clearances? If the judge sees classified information in camera, may she show it to her clerk for help in writing an opinion? Must the opinion be published or can it operate as secret law? *See generally Symposium: Secret Evidence and the Courts in the Age of National Security*, 5 Cardozo Pub. L. Poly. & Ethics J. 1 (2006).

# C.   HANDLING SECRET EXCULPATORY TESTIMONY

## UNITED STATES v. MOUSSAOUI

United States Court of Appeals, 4th Circuit, 2004
365 F.3d 292, *amended on reh'g*, 382 F.3d 453, *cert. denied*, 544 U.S. 93 (2005)

[Zacarias Moussaoui was arrested before the 9/11 attacks, then later indicted for acts in connection with those attacks. The Government sought the death penalty on several of these charges. Subsequently, Witness * * * * (the asterisks are used by the court), a suspected member of al Qaeda, was captured by the United States. Moussaoui moved for access to Witness * * * *, asserting that the witness would be an important part of his defense. Ultimately, he sought access to two additional witnesses in U.S. custody. The government opposed these requests.

The District Court found that the requested witnesses were material witnesses who might support Moussaoui's claim that he was not involved in the 9/11 attacks and that he should not receive the death penalty if convicted. It ordered their deposition by remote video, but the government appealed. The Court of Appeals remanded for the District Court to determine whether any substitution existed that would place Moussaoui in substantially the same position as would a deposition. The District Court rejected the government's proposed substitutions and again ordered deposition of the witnesses. When the government refused to comply with this order, the District Court dismissed the death notice and prohibited the government "from making any argument, or offering any evidence, suggesting that the defendant had any involvement in, or knowledge of, the September 11 attacks." This appeal followed.]

WILLIAM W. WILKINS, Chief Judge: . . .

### III. . . .

#### A. Process Power

The Sixth Amendment guarantees that "[i]n all criminal prosecutions, the accused shall enjoy the right . . . to have compulsory process for obtaining witnesses in his favor." U.S. Const. amend. VI. The compulsory process right is circumscribed, however, by the ability of the district court to obtain the presence of a witness through service of process. The Government maintains that because the enemy combatant witnesses are foreign nationals outside the boundaries of the United States, they are beyond the process power of the district court and, hence, unavailable to Moussaoui. . . .

The Government's argument overlooks the critical fact that the enemy combatant witnesses are in the custody of an official of the United States Government. Therefore, we are concerned not with the ability of the district court to issue a subpoena to the witnesses, but rather with its power to issue a writ of habeas corpus *ad testificandum* ("testimonial writ") to the witnesses' custodian. . . .

[The court found that Secretary Rumsfeld was the proper custodian and that he was within the process power of the District Court.]

## IV.

The Government next argues that even if the district court would otherwise have the power to order the production of the witnesses, the January 30 and August 29 orders are improper because they infringe on the Executive's warmaking authority, in violation of separation of powers principles. . . .

### B. Governing Principles . . .

This is not a case involving arrogation of the powers or duties of another branch. The district court orders requiring production of the enemy combatant witnesses involved the resolution of questions properly — indeed, exclusively — reserved to the judiciary. Therefore, if there is a separation of powers problem at all, it arises only from the burden the actions of the district court place on the Executive's performance of its duties.

The Supreme Court has explained on several occasions that determining whether a judicial act places impermissible burdens on another branch of government requires balancing the competing interests. *See, e.g., Nixon v. Admin'r of Gen. Servs.,* 433 U.S. 425, 443 (1977). . . .

### C. Balancing

#### 1. The burden on the Government

The Constitution charges the Congress and the Executive with the making and conduct of war. It is not an exaggeration to state that the effective performance of these duties is essential to our continued existence as a sovereign nation. Indeed, "no governmental interest is more compelling than the security of the Nation." *Haig v. Agee,* 453 U.S. 280, 307 (1981). . . .

The Government alleges — and we accept as true — that * * * * the enemy combatant witnesses is critical to the ongoing effort to combat terrorism by al Qaeda. The witnesses are al Qaeda operatives * * * * Their value as intelligence sources can hardly be overstated. And, we must defer to the Government's assertion that interruption * * * * will have devastating effects on the ability to gather information from them. * * * *, it is not unreasonable to suppose that interruption * * * * could result in the loss of information that might prevent future terrorist attacks.

The Government also asserts that production of the witnesses would burden the Executive's ability to conduct foreign relations. The Government claims that if the Executive's assurances of confidentiality can be abrogated by the judiciary, the vital ability to obtain the cooperation of other governments will be devastated.

The Government also reminds us of the bolstering effect production of the witnesses might have on our enemies. . . . For example, al Qaeda operatives are trained to disrupt the legal process in whatever manner possible; indications that such techniques may be successful will only cause a redoubling of their efforts.

In summary, the burdens that would arise from production of the enemy combatant witnesses are substantial.

### 2. Moussaoui's interest

The importance of the Sixth Amendment right to compulsory process is not subject to question — it is integral to our adversarial criminal justice system:

> The need to develop all relevant facts in the adversary system is both fundamental and comprehensive. The ends of criminal justice would be defeated if judgments were to be founded on a partial or speculative presentation of the facts. The very integrity of the judicial system and public confidence in the system depend on full disclosure of all the facts, within the framework of the rules of evidence. To ensure that justice is done, it is imperative to the function of the courts that compulsory process be available for the production of evidence needed either by the prosecution or by the defense.

United States v. Nixon, 418 U.S. 683, 709 (1974).

The compulsory process right does not attach to any witness the defendant wishes to call, however. Rather, a defendant must demonstrate that the witness he desires to have produced would testify "in his favor." Thus, in order to assess Moussaoui's interest, we must determine whether the enemy combatant witnesses could provide testimony material to Moussaoui's defense.

In the CIPA context,[12] we have adopted the standard articulated by the Supreme Court in *Roviaro v. United States,* 353 U.S. 53 (1957), for determining whether the government's privilege in classified information must give way. Under that standard, a defendant becomes entitled to disclosure of classified information upon a showing that the information " 'is relevant and helpful to the defense . . . or is essential to a fair determination of a cause.' " [United States v. Smith, 780 F.2d 1102 (4th Cir. 1985)], at 1107 (quoting *Roviaro,* 353 U.S. at 60-61).

Because Moussaoui has not had — and will not receive — direct access to any of the witnesses, he cannot be required to show materiality with the

---

12. We adhere to our prior ruling that CIPA does not apply because the January 30 and August 29 orders of the district court are not covered by either of the potentially relevant provisions of CIPA: §4 (concerning deletion of classified information from *documents* to be turned over to the defendant during discovery) or §6 (concerning the disclosure of classified information by the defense during pretrial or trial proceedings). *See* [United States v. Moussaoui, 333 F.3d 509, 514-515 (4th Cir. 2003)]. Like the district court, however, we believe that CIPA provides a useful framework for considering the questions raised by Moussaoui's request for access to the enemy combatant witnesses.

degree of specificity that applies in the ordinary case. Rather, it is sufficient if Moussaoui can make a "plausible showing" of materiality. However, in determining whether Moussaoui has made a plausible showing, we must bear in mind that Moussaoui *does* have access to the * * * * summaries. . . .

. . . [T]he Government argues that even if the witnesses' testimony would tend to exonerate Moussaoui of involvement in the September 11 attacks, such testimony would not be material because the conspiracies with which Moussaoui is charged are broader than September 11. Thus, the Government argues, Moussaoui can be convicted even if he lacked any prior knowledge of September 11. This argument ignores the principle that the scope of an alleged conspiracy is a jury question, and the possibility that Moussaoui may assert that the conspiracy culminating in the September 11 attacks was distinct from any conspiracy in which he was involved. Moreover, even if the jury accepts the Government's claims regarding the scope of the charged conspiracy, testimony regarding Moussaoui's non-involvement in September 11 is critical to the penalty phase. If Moussaoui had no involvement in or knowledge of September 11, it is entirely possible that he would not be found eligible for the death penalty.

We now consider the rulings of the district court regarding the ability of each witness to provide material testimony in Moussaoui's favor.

******

The district court did not err in concluding that Witness * * * * could offer material evidence on Moussaoui's behalf. * * * * Several statements by Witness * * * * tend to exculpate Moussaoui. For example, the * * * * summaries state that * * * * This statement tends to undermine the theory (which the Government may or may not intend to advance at trial) that Moussaoui was to pilot a fifth plane into the White House. Witness * * * * has also * * * * This statement is significant in light of other evidence * * * * indicating that Moussaoui had no contact with any of the hijackers. * * * * This is consistent with Moussaoui's claim that he was to be part of a post-September 11 operation. . . .

. . . Moussaoui has made a sufficient showing that evidence from Witness * * * * would be more helpful than hurtful, or at least that we cannot have confidence in the outcome of the trial without Witness * * * * evidence. . . .

### 3. Balancing

Having considered the burden alleged by the Government and the right claimed by Moussaoui, we now turn to the question of whether the district court should have refrained from acting in light of the national security interests asserted by the Government. The question is not unique; the Supreme Court has addressed similar matters on numerous occasions. In all cases of this type — cases falling into "what might loosely be called the area of constitutionally guaranteed access to evidence," *Arizona v. Youngblood,* 488 U.S. 51, 55 (1988) (internal quotation marks omitted) — the Supreme Court has held that the defendant's right to a trial that comports with the Fifth and Sixth Amendments prevails over the governmental privilege. Ultimately, as these cases make clear, the appropriate procedure is for the district court to order production of the evidence or witness and leave to the Government the choice of whether to comply with that order. If the government refuses to produce the information at issue — as it may properly do — the result is ordinarily dismissal. . . .

In addition to the pronouncements of the Supreme Court in this area, we are also mindful of Congress' judgment, expressed in CIPA, that the Executive's interest in protecting classified information does not overcome a defendant's right to present his case. Under CIPA, once the district court determines that an item of classified information is relevant and material, that item must be admitted unless the government provides an adequate substitution. If no adequate substitution can be found, the government must decide whether it will prohibit the disclosure of the classified information; if it does so, the district court must impose a sanction, which is presumptively dismissal of the indictment.

In view of these authorities, it is clear that when an evidentiary privilege — even one that involves national security — is asserted by the Government in the context of its prosecution of a criminal offense, the "balancing" we must conduct is primarily, if not solely, an examination of whether the district court correctly determined that the information the Government seeks to withhold is material to the defense. We have determined that the enemy combatant witnesses can offer material testimony that is essential to Moussaoui's defense, and we therefore affirm the January 30 and August 29 orders. Thus, the choice is the Government's whether to comply with those orders or suffer a sanction.

## V.

As noted previously, the Government has stated that it will not produce the enemy combatant witnesses for depositions (or, we presume, for any other purpose related to this litigation). We are thus left in the following situation: the district court has the power to order production of the enemy combatant witnesses and has properly determined that they could offer material testimony on Moussaoui's behalf, but the Government has refused to produce the witnesses. Under such circumstances, dismissal of the indictment is the usual course. Like the district court, however, we believe that a more measured approach is required. Additionally, we emphasize that no punitive sanction is warranted here because the Government has rightfully exercised its prerogative to protect national security interests by refusing to produce the witnesses.

Although, as explained above, this is not a CIPA case, that act nevertheless provides useful guidance in determining the nature of the remedies that may be available. Under CIPA, dismissal of an indictment is authorized only if the government has failed to produce an adequate substitute for the classified information, and the interests of justice would not be served by imposition of a lesser sanction. CIPA thus enjoins district courts to seek a solution that neither disadvantages the defendant nor penalizes the government (and the public) for protecting classified information that may be vital to national security.

A similar approach is appropriate here. Under such an approach, the first question is whether there is any appropriate substitution for the witnesses' testimony. Because we conclude, for the reasons set forth below, that appropriate substitutions are available, we need not consider any other remedy. . . .

## C. Instructions

. . . [W]e conclude that the district court erred in ruling that any substitution for the witnesses' testimony is inherently inadequate to the extent it is derived from the * * * * reports. To the contrary, we hold that the * * * * summaries (which, as the district court determined, accurately recapitulate the * * * * reports) provide an adequate basis for the creation of written statements that may be submitted to the jury in lieu of the witnesses' deposition testimony.

The crafting of substitutions is a task best suited to the district court, given its greater familiarity with the facts of the case and its authority to manage the presentation of evidence. Nevertheless, we think it is appropriate to provide some guidance to the court and the parties.

First, the circumstances of this case — most notably, the fact that the substitutions may very well support Moussaoui's defense — dictate that the crafting of substitutions be an interactive process among the parties and the district court. Second, we think that accuracy and fairness are best achieved by crafting substitutions that use the exact language of the * * * * summaries to the greatest extent possible. We believe that the best means of achieving both of these objectives is for defense counsel to identify particular portions of the * * * * summaries that Moussaoui may want to admit into evidence at trial. The Government may then argue that additional portions must be included in the interest of completeness. . . . If the substitutions are to be admitted at all (we leave open the possibility that Moussaoui may decide not to use the substitutions in his defense), they may be admitted only by Moussaoui. Based on defense counsel's submissions and the Government's objections, the district court could then create an appropriate set of substitutions. . . .

As previously indicated, the jury must be provided with certain information regarding the substitutions. While we leave the particulars of the instructions to the district court, the jury must be informed, at a minimum, that the substitutions are what the witnesses would say if called to testify; that the substitutions are derived from statements obtained under conditions that provide circumstantial guarantees of reliability; that the substitutions contain statements obtained * * * *; and that neither the parties nor the district court has ever had access to the witnesses. . . .

*Affirmed in part, vacated in part, and remanded.*

[The opinions of WILLIAMS, Circuit Judge, and GREGORY, Circuit Judge, each concurring in part and dissenting in part, are omitted.]

## NOTES AND QUESTIONS

1. ***Guilty Plea and Sentence.*** On April 22, 2005, Moussaoui surprised everyone by pleading guilty to the key charges against him, while at the same time denying having any intention to commit mass murder. *See Moussaoui Pleads Guilty to Terror Charges*, CNN.com, Apr. 23, 2005, *at* http://www.cnn.com/ 2005/LAW/04/22/moussaoui/index.html. He was subsequently sentenced to

life in prison. United States v. Moussaoui, No. 1:01CR00455-001, Judgment in a Criminal Case at 2 (E.D. Va. May 14, 2006).

2. ***Deciding a Clash Between Branches: Formalism or Balancing?*** The court concluded that the appropriate separation of powers analysis required by Moussaoui's insistence on access to * * * * is balancing, as prescribed by Nixon v. Administrator of General Services, 433 U.S. 425, 443 (1977 (stating that "the proper inquiry focuses on the extent to which [the judicial act of ordering access in this instance] prevents the Executive Branch from accomplishing its constitutionally assigned functions, . . . [and whether] that impact is justified by an overriding need to promote objectives within the constitutional authority of [the court]"). But in Public Citizen v. United States Department of Justice, 491 U.S. 440, 485 (1989), Justice Kennedy indicated that there is "a line of cases of equal weight and authority, . . . where the Constitution by explicit text commits the power at issue to the exclusive control of the President, . . . [and the Court has] refused to tolerate *any* intrusion by [the courts]." Why isn't *Moussaoui* controlled by the latter line of cases? Doesn't the Commander in Chief Clause of Article II commit command of the armed forces in war to the President, and isn't the interrogation of enemy combatants in war part of that command? Does *Hamdi, supra* p. 359, or *Padilla, supra* p. 383, suggest any answers to these questions?

What other cases would you rely on in making the formalist argument for the government, or, by a balancing analysis, in arguing the extent to which court-ordered access to * * * * would prevent the President from conducting the war? In this regard, consider United States v. United States District Court (*Keith*), *supra* p. 91, and Zadvydas v. Davis, noted *supra* p. 302. If the *Moussaoui* jury had been the target of serious threats of harm, how would you balance his Sixth Amendment right to trial by jury against the government's interest in protecting the jurors by empaneling them secretly in a secure location to hear the trial by video?

3. ***CIPA by Analogy.*** In deciding the alternatives, the court determined that CIPA (see *supra* p. 530) did not apply but relied on it anyway for a "useful framework." *See also* United States v. Paracha, 2006 WL 12768 (S.D.N.Y. Jan. 3, 2006) (using CIPA by analogy to impose *Moussaoui*-type solution to terror defendant's demand for access to witnesses in U.S. custody in Afghanistan). Why did CIPA not apply? By what authority did the court undertake the relevance and balancing inquiries and order access to the summaries? Did the court, in effect, create a "wartime exception" to the Sixth Amendment after all? Is this another example of what Justice Scalia condemned as the "Mr. Fix-It Mentality" of courts? If CIPA is to be amended to cover the *Moussaoui* problem, why not leave that job to Congress?

4. ***Switching Fora?*** The District Court invited the government to "reconsider whether the civilian criminal courts are the appropriate fora" for trying someone like Moussaoui. United States v. Moussaoui, No. Cr-01-455-A, 2003 WL 21263699, at *6 (E.D. Va. Mar. 10, 2003). The alternative is trial by military commission, which we explore in Chapter 18. Indeed, even Moussaoui's standby counsel appears to have invited this alternative, gratuitously conceding that the government's authority to try enemy

combatants by military commission is "settled" and implying that the government can simply dismiss the criminal prosecution and proceed instead by a military commission to resolve the tension between Moussaoui's Sixth Amendment rights and the war powers. Brief of the Appellee at 3-4, United States v. Moussaoui, No. 03-4162 (4th Cir. May 13, 2003).

After you read the materials on military commissions, you can decide for yourself whether this was a wise concession. But do you agree with the apparent assumption on which it and the District Court's invitation rested — that the government can switch fora in midstream? Even assuming that the government could lawfully have tried Moussaoui by military commission *ab initio*, does it necessarily follow that it can start in a civilian court and then dismiss in favor of a military commission when it is unhappy with the civilian court's rulings? Would it matter how far the criminal prosecution had progressed beyond the indictment? If such a switch survived constitutional challenges, would it nevertheless violate the spirit of the law?

The government did, in fact, make a switch — actually a double-switch — in Al-Marri v. Hanft, 378 F. Supp. 2d 673 (D.S.C. 2005), noted *supra* p. 396. After Al-Marri lawfully entered the United States with his family to obtain a master's degree, he was initially arrested as a material witness in the 9/11 investigation. In the first switch, he was then rearrested and indicted for making false statements and for credit card fraud. More than two years later, President Bush interrupted the course of normal criminal proceedings (trial had not yet begun) by designating Al-Marri an enemy combatant, after which he was transferred to military detention in South Carolina. The government then successfully moved to drop the criminal indictment with prejudice. At this writing, Al-Marri remains in military detention without charges.

Al-Marri argued that his criminal detention was sufficient to thwart any terrorist acts and that there was no necessity for military detention. The District Court rejected his argument in part on the reasoning that when a federal investigation of criminal charges pending in state court reveals a federal crime, the state charges can be dismissed and the matter can be transferred to federal jurisdiction. *Id.* at 681. Is the analogy sound?

Al-Marri also protested that while he might have been acquitted of the criminal charges, he had no opportunity to prove his innocence in military detention. The court rejected this claim as well, reasoning that the purpose of military detention is preventive.

> This Court recognizes the natural response to this reasoning that, when a defendant is acquitted of criminal charges, society should not assume that he ever did nor that he will, in the future, engage in the activities for which he was charged. In this case, however, Petitioner was not charged with crimes of terrorism, and thus, an acquittal of various fraud charges does not lead to the conclusion that he will not, in the future, engage in acts of terrorism as alleged by the government.

*Id.* at 681 n.8. In a subsequent decision, the court ruled that the government had met its burden in Al-Marri's habeas challenge to provide credible evidence that he is an enemy combatant. Al-Marri v. Wright, 433 F. Supp. 2d 774 (D.S.C. 2006).

5. *A Military Brig—the Better Forum?* The following assessment was written before the conclusion of the Moussaoui trial.

> The United States should drop all criminal charges against Zacarias Moussaoui, not because he is innocent, but because he is a foreign citizen who is (or was) a terrorist bent on killing innocent Americans, destroying American property, and disrupting American society. For less than a nanosecond, Moussaoui should be a free man again. . . .
>
> Before the nanosecond of Moussaoui's freedom ends, he should be transferred to the custody of the United States Department of Defense. After that, based on recommendations coordinated by the National Security Council (NSC) for the President, the Executive Branch should implement a well-conceived decision about Moussaoui's next address. The NSC, rather than a particular United States agency, such as the Justice Department or the Defense Department, is the appropriate forum to vet such policies because they transcend the boundaries between domestic and international spheres, going beyond law enforcement and military issues. . . . The President, in making this decision on Moussaoui's next address, should consider our relations with foreign countries and the safety of our homeland. But whatever happens to Moussaoui, he did not — and does not — belong in criminal custody. [A. John Radsan, *The Moussaoui Case: The Mess From Minnesota,* 31 Wm. Mitchell L. Rev. 1417, 1417-1419 (2005).]

Do you agree? Or did the system work? Or was the system distorted to accommodate national security? If you think the system was distorted, is this an argument for trying Moussaoui and other terrorists by military commission? (We turn to this subject in the next chapter.)

# CHAPTER 18

# *TRYING SUSPECTED TERRORISTS AS UNLAWFUL ENEMY COMBATANTS*

Before deploying "necessary and appropriate force" against al Qaeda and the Taliban in Afghanistan in November 2001, the Administration had to decide what it would do with those whom U.S. forces and their allies captured in the fight. Apart from simply detaining them, one possibility was trying them in U.S. criminal courts. But the problems of secret evidence we explored in the previous chapter, not to mention concerns about security and efficiency, given the sheer numbers of anticipated captives, made this option impractical. A second option was trying them before some ad hoc international tribunal. The surrender of control that this would entail, coupled with the Administration's repudiation of the International Criminal Court, made this option unappealing. A third option was trying them by court-martial, using the same rules applicable to U.S. service personnel. This option would have used fair and time-tested procedures at the same time that it conformed with the laws of war. But the very fairness of the procedures may have been a strike against them; they may have seemed too fair and, partly as a result, too cumbersome for terrorists charged with horrific war crimes against civilians. *See* Remarks by Vice President Dick Cheney to the U.S. Chamber of Commerce, Nov. 14, 2001, *available at* http://www.whitehouse.gov/vicepresident/news-speeches/speeches/vp20011114-1.html ("They don't deserve the same guarantees and safeguards that would be used for an American citizen going through the normal judicial process. . . . We think [trial by military commission] guarantees that we'll have the kind of treatment of these individuals that we believe they deserve."). Conformity of such procedures with the laws of war could have been another strike against them, as long as the Administration insisted that such laws did not apply to terrorists. See *supra* Chapter 13.

Whatever the precise reasons, the Administration chose a fourth option: to try selected captives by "military commission" under procedures devised for the occasion. Military commissions are tribunals of military officers who sit as judge and jury. Historically, they have been used in the field to try spies, saboteurs, and others who violate the laws of war, and in occupied territories to try common crimes as well. In Chapter 12, we considered two pre-9/11 cases in reviewing the legal authority for *detention* by the military. In Part A of this chapter, we revisit these cases in exploring the historical legal authority for *trial* by military commission. In Part B, we examine the Military Order of November 13, 2001, which adopted the military commission option, and the procedures implementing it, before turning to the Supreme Court's 2006 decision about the legal authority for military commissions in Hamdan v. Rumsfeld. In Part C, we explore the Military Commissions Act of 2006 (MCA), Congress's response to *Hamdan*.

## A.  TRIAL BY MILITARY COMMISSION BEFORE 9/11

### Ex parte Milligan

United States Supreme Court, 1866
71 U.S. (4 Wall.) 2

[The opinion is set forth *supra* p. 349.]

### Ex parte Quirin

United States Supreme Court, 1942
317 U.S. 1

[The opinion is set forth *supra* p. 353.]

### NOTES AND QUESTIONS

[The Notes and Questions are set forth *supra* pp. 357-359.]

## B.  TRIAL BY MILITARY COMMISSION AFTER 9/11

By the following Military Order, President Bush authorized trial by military commissions of persons he designated. The order delegated to the Secretary of Defense the task of promulgating procedures for such trials. Secretary Rumsfeld and the Department of Defense subsequently issued a host of implementing orders and instructions, some of which were subsequently revised. *See* Dept. of Defense, *Military Commission Order No. 1*, Mar. 21, 2002; Dept. of Defense, *Military Commissions Instructions Nos. 1-10* (various dates). The flow chart *infra* p. 563 generally depicts the resulting military commission process before *Hamdan* and the enactment of the MCA, while the most relevant pre-MCA military commission procedures and characteristics are summarized in Hamdan v. Rumsfeld, 126 S. Ct. 2749, 2786-2787 (2006), *infra* p. 563, which follows the chart.

## MILITARY ORDER OF NOVEMBER 13, 2001
## DETENTION, TREATMENT, AND TRIAL OF CERTAIN
## NON-CITIZENS IN THE WAR AGAINST TERRORISM

66 Fed. Reg. 57,833 (Nov. 13, 2001)

By the authority vested in me as President and as Commander in Chief of the Armed Forces of the United States by the Constitution and the laws of the United States of America, including the Authorization for Use of Military Force Joint Resolution (Public Law 107-40, 115 Stat. 224) and sections 821 and 836 of title 10, United States Code, it is hereby ordered as follows:

### Section 1. Findings.

(a) International terrorists, including members of al Qaeda, have carried out attacks on United States diplomatic and military personnel and activities abroad and on citizens and property within the United States on a scale that has created a state of armed conflict that requires the use of the United States Armed Forces.

(b) In light of grave acts of terrorism and threats of terrorism, including the terrorist attacks on Sept. 11, 2001, on the headquarters of the United States Department of Defense in the national capital region, on the World Trade Center in New York, and on civilian aircraft such as in Pennsylvania, I proclaimed a national emergency on Sept. 14, 2001 (Proclamation 7463, Declaration of National Emergency by Reason of Certain Terrorist Attacks).

(c) Individuals acting alone and in concert involved in international terrorism possess both the capability and the intention to undertake further terrorist attacks against the United States that, if not detected and prevented, will cause mass deaths, mass injuries, and massive destruction of property, and may place at risk the continuity of the operations of the United States government.

(d) The ability of the United States to protect the United States and its citizens, and to help its allies and other cooperating nations protect their nations and their citizens, from such further terrorist attacks depends in significant part upon using the United States Armed Forces to identify terrorists and those who support them, to disrupt their activities, and to eliminate their ability to conduct or support such attacks.

(e) To protect the United States and its citizens, and for the effective conduct of military operations and prevention of terrorist attacks, it is necessary for individuals subject to this order pursuant to section 2 hereof to be detained, and, when tried, to be tried for violations of the laws of war and other applicable laws by military tribunals.

(f) Given the danger to the safety of the United States and the nature of international terrorism, and to the extent provided by and under this order, I find consistent with section 836 of title 10, United States Code, that it is not practicable to apply in military commissions under this order the principles of law and the rules of evidence generally recognized in the trial of criminal cases in the United States district courts.

(g) Having fully considered the magnitude of the potential deaths, injuries, and property destruction that would result from potential acts of terrorism against the United States, and the probability that such acts will occur, I have determined that an extraordinary emergency exists for national defense purposes, that this emergency constitutes an urgent and compelling government interest, and that issuance of this order is necessary to meet the emergency.

### Section 2.  Definition and Policy.

(a) The term "individual subject to this order" shall mean any individual who is not a United States citizen with respect to whom I determine from time to time in writing that:

(1) there is reason to believe that such individual, at the relevant times,

(i) is or was a member of the organization known as al Qaeda;

(ii) has engaged in, aided or abetted, or conspired to commit, acts of international terrorism, or acts in preparation therefor, that have caused, threaten to cause, or have as their aim to cause, injury to or adverse effects on the United States, its citizens, national security, foreign policy, or economy; or

(iii) has knowingly harbored one or more individuals described in subparagraphs (i) or (ii) of subsection 2(a)(1) of this order; and

(2) it is in the interest of the United States that such individual be subject to this order.

(b) It is the policy of the United States that the Secretary of Defense shall take all necessary measures to ensure that any individual subject to this order is detained in accordance with section 3, and, if the individual is to be tried, that such individual is tried only in accordance with section 4.

(c) It is further the policy of the United States that any individual subject to this order who is not already under the control of the Secretary of Defense but who is under the control of any other officer or agent of the United States or any state shall, upon delivery of a copy of such written determination to such officer or agent, forthwith be placed under the control of the Secretary of Defense.

### Section 3.  Detention Authority of the Secretary of Defense.

Any individual subject to this order shall be —

(a) detained at an appropriate location designated by the Secretary of Defense outside or within the United States;

(b) treated humanely, without any adverse distinction based on race, color, religion, gender, birth, wealth, or any similar criteria;

(c) afforded adequate food, drinking water, shelter, clothing, and medical treatment;

(d) allowed the free exercise of religion consistent with the requirements of such detention; and

(e) detained in accordance with such other conditions as the Secretary of Defense may prescribe.

## Section 4. Authority of the Secretary of Defense Regarding Trials of Individuals Subject to this Order.

(a) Any individual subject to this order shall, when tried, be tried by military commission for any and all offenses triable by military commission that such individual is alleged to have committed, and may be punished in accordance with the penalties provided under applicable law, including life imprisonment or death.

(b) As a military function and in light of the findings in section 1, including subsection (f) thereof, the Secretary of Defense shall issue such orders and regulations, including orders for the appointment of one or more military commissions, as may be necessary to carry out subsection (a) of this section.

(c) Orders and regulations issued under subsection (b) of this section shall include, but not be limited to, rules for the conduct of the proceedings of military commissions, including pretrial, trial, and post-trial procedures, modes of proof, issuance of process, and qualifications of attorneys, which shall at a minimum provide for—

(1) military commissions to sit at any time and any place, consistent with such guidance regarding time and place as the Secretary of Defense may provide;

(2) a full and fair trial, with the military commission sitting as the triers of both fact and law;

(3) admission of such evidence as would, in the opinion of the presiding officer of the military commission (or instead, if any other member of the commission so requests at the time the presiding officer renders that opinion, the opinion of the commission rendered at that time by a majority of the commission), have probative value to a reasonable person;

(4) in a manner consistent with the protection of information classified or classifiable under Executive Order 12958 of April 17, 1995, as amended, or any successor Executive Order, protected by statute or rule from unauthorized disclosure, or otherwise protected by law, (A) the handling of, admission into evidence of, and access to materials and information, and (B) the conduct, closure of, and access to proceedings;

(5) conduct of the prosecution by one or more attorneys designated by the Secretary of Defense and conduct of the defense by attorneys for the individual subject to this order;

(6) conviction only upon the concurrence of two-thirds of the members of the commission present at the time of the vote, a majority being present;

(7) sentencing only upon the concurrence of two-thirds of the members of the commission present at the time of the vote, a majority being present; and

(8) submission of the record of the trial, including any conviction or sentence, for review and final decision by me or by the Secretary of Defense if so designated by me for that purpose.

### Section 5. Obligation of Other Agencies to Assist the Secretary of Defense.

Departments, agencies, entities, and officers of the United States shall, to the maximum extent permitted by law, provide to the Secretary of Defense such assistance as he may request to implement this order.

### Section 6. Additional Authorities of the Secretary of Defense.

(a) As a military function and in light of the findings in section 1, the Secretary of Defense shall issue such orders and regulations as may be necessary to carry out any of the provisions of this order.

(b) The Secretary of Defense may perform any of his functions or duties, and may exercise any of the powers provided to him under this order (other than under section 4(c)(8) hereof) in accordance with section 113(d) of title 10, United States Code.

### Section 7. Relationship to Other Law and Forums.

(a) Nothing in this order shall be construed to —

(1) authorize the disclosure of state secrets to any person not otherwise authorized to have access to them;

(2) limit the authority of the President as Commander in Chief of the Armed Forces or the power of the President to grant reprieves and pardons; or

(3) limit the lawful authority of the Secretary of Defense, any military commander, or any other officer or agent of the United States or of any State to detain or try any person who is not an individual subject to this order.

(b) With respect to any individual subject to this order —

(1) military tribunals shall have exclusive jurisdiction with respect to offenses by the individual; and

(2) the individual shall not be privileged to seek any remedy or maintain any proceeding, directly or indirectly, or to have any such remedy or proceeding sought on the individual's behalf, in

(i) any court of the United States, or any State thereof,

(ii) any court of any foreign nation, or

(iii) any international tribunal.

(c) This order is not intended to and does not create any right, benefit, or privilege, substantive or procedural, enforceable at law or equity by any party, against the United States, its departments, agencies, or other entities, its officers or employees, or any other person.

(d) For purposes of this order, the term "state" includes any State, district, territory, or possession of the United States.

(e) I reserve the authority to direct the Secretary of Defense, at any time hereafter, to transfer to a governmental authority control of any individual subject to this order. Nothing in this order shall be construed to limit the authority of any such governmental authority to prosecute any individual for whom control is transferred.

### Section 8. Publication.

This order shall be published in the *Federal Register*.

*George W. Bush*

## Commission Process[1]

### HAMDAN v. RUMSFELD

United States Supreme Court, 2006
126 S. Ct. 2749

[Salim Ahmed Hamdan, a Yemeni national, was captured in November 2001 by militia forces in Afghanistan and turned over to the U.S. military. In June 2002, he was transported to the military prison at Guantánamo Bay, Cuba. On July 3, 2003, President Bush determined that Hamdan (and five other detainees at Guantánamo Bay) were subject to the Military Order of November 13, 2001, and therefore triable by military commission. Military counsel was appointed for him, and his counsel promptly filed demands for charges and for a

---

[1. U.S. Dept. of Defense, *Department of Defense Fact Sheet: Military Commission Procedures,* Aug. 2003. The appeals process depicted in the chart is substantially changed by the Military Commissions Act of 2006, Pub. L. No. 109-366, 120 Stat. 2600. See *infra* p. 587.]

speedy trial pursuant to the Uniform Code of Military Justice (UCMJ), 10 U.S.C. §801-946 (2000 & Supp. IV 2004). The demands were denied by a military official on the ground that Hamdan was not entitled to any of the protections of the UCMJ. On July 13, 2004, Hamdan was charged with conspiring with members of al Qaeda to commit the offenses of "attacking civilians; attacking civilian objects; murder by an unprivileged belligerent; and terrorism." Among the overt acts listed in the charges was the claim that Hamdan acted as Osama bin Laden's "bodyguard and personal driver."

Before his trial could begin, Hamdan challenged the legality of the commission by habeas and mandamus petitions. The district court granted his petition for a writ of habeas corpus, but the Court of Appeals, in an opinion by then-Judge Roberts, reversed. The Supreme Court granted certiorari and issued the following opinion.]

Justice STEVENS announced the judgment of the Court and delivered the opinion of the Court with respect to Parts I through IV, Parts VI through VI-D-iii, Part VI-D-v, and Part VII, and an opinion with respect to Parts V and VI-D-iv, in which Justice SOUTER, Justice GINSBURG, and Justice BREYER join. . . . [Hamdan] concedes that a court-martial constituted in accordance with the Uniform Code of Military Justice (UCMJ) would have authority to try him. His objection is that the military commission the President has convened lacks such authority, for two principal reasons: First, neither congressional Act nor the common law of war supports trial by this commission for the crime of conspiracy — an offense that, Hamdan says, is not a violation of the law of war. Second, Hamdan contends, the procedures that the President has adopted to try him violate the most basic tenets of military and international law, including the principle that a defendant must be permitted to see and hear the evidence against him. . . .

For the reasons that follow, we conclude that the military commission convened to try Hamdan lacks power to proceed because its structure and procedures violate both the UCMJ and the Geneva Conventions. Four of us also conclude, see Part V, *infra,* that the offense with which Hamdan has been charged is not an "offens[e] that by . . . the law of war may be tried by military commissions." 10 U.S.C. §821. . . .

## II

[The Court found that the Detainee Treatment Act, *supra* p. 335, did not preclude review.]

## III

[The Court refused to abstain pending completion of the military commission proceedings against Hamdan, noting that the comity considerations favoring abstention in Schlesinger v. Councilman, 420 U.S. 738 (1975), did not apply to Hamdan's case.] . . .

First, Hamdan is not a member of our Nation's Armed Forces, so concerns about military discipline do not apply. Second, the tribunal convened to try Hamdan is not part of the integrated system of military courts, complete with independent review panels, that Congress has established. Unlike the officer in *Councilman,* Hamdan has no right to appeal any conviction to the civilian judges of the Court of Military Appeals (now called the United States Court of Appeals for the Armed Forces, see Pub. L. 103-337, 108 Stat. 2831). Instead, under Dept. of Defense Military Commission Order No. 1 (Commission Order No. 1), which was issued by the President on March 21, 2002, and amended most recently on August 31, 2005, and which governs the procedures for Hamdan's commission, any conviction would be reviewed by a panel consisting of three military officers designated by the Secretary of Defense. Commission Order No. 1 §6(H)(4). Commission Order No. 1 provides that appeal of a review panel's decision may be had only to the Secretary of Defense himself, §6(H)(5), and then, finally, to the President, §6(H)(6).

We have no doubt that the various individuals assigned review power under Commission Order No. 1 would strive to act impartially and ensure that Hamdan receive all protections to which he is entitled. Nonetheless, these review bodies clearly lack the structural insulation from military influence that characterizes the Court of Appeals for the Armed Forces, and thus bear insufficient conceptual similarity to state courts to warrant invocation of abstention principles. . . .

## IV

The military commission, a tribunal neither mentioned in the Constitution nor created by statute, was born of military necessity. See W. Winthrop, Military Law and Precedents 831 (rev. 2d ed. 1920) (hereinafter Winthrop). . . .

As further discussed below, each aspect of that seemingly broad [military commission] jurisdiction was in fact supported by a separate military exigency. Generally, though, the need for military commissions during this period — as during the Mexican War — was driven largely by the then very limited jurisdiction of courts-martial: "The *occasion* for the military commission arises principally from the fact that the jurisdiction of the court-martial proper, in our law, is restricted by statute almost exclusively to members of the military force and to certain specific offences defined in a written code." *Id.,* at 831 (emphasis in original).

Exigency alone, of course, will not justify the establishment and use of penal tribunals not contemplated by Article I, §8 and Article III, §1 of the Constitution unless some other part of that document authorizes a response to the felt need. See *Ex parte Milligan,* [71 U.S.] 4 Wall. 2, 121 (1866) ("Certainly no part of the judicial power of the country was conferred on [military commissions]"). And that authority, if it exists, can derive only from the powers granted jointly to the President and Congress in time of war. See *In re Yamashita,* 327 U.S. 1, 11 (1946).

The Constitution makes the President the "Commander in Chief" of the Armed Forces, Art. II, §2, cl. 1, but vests in Congress the powers to "declare War . . . and make Rules concerning Captures on Land and Water," Art. I, §8, cl. 11, to "raise and support Armies," *id.,* cl. 12, to "define and punish . . . Offences against the Law of Nations," *id.,* cl. 10, and "To make Rules for the Government and Regulation of the land and naval Forces," *id.,* cl. 14. The interplay between these powers was described by Chief Justice Chase in the seminal case of *Ex parte Milligan:*

"The power to make the necessary laws is in Congress; the power to execute in the President. Both powers imply many subordinate and auxiliary powers. Each includes all authorities essential to its due exercise. But neither can the President, in war more than in peace, intrude upon the proper authority of Congress, nor Congress upon the proper authority of the President. . . . Congress cannot direct the conduct of campaigns, nor can the President, or any commander under him, without the sanction of Congress, institute tribunals for the trial and punishment of offences, either of soldiers or civilians, unless in cases of a controlling necessity, which justifies what it compels, or at least insures acts of indemnity from the justice of the legislature." 4 Wall., at 139-140.

Whether Chief Justice Chase was correct in suggesting that the President may constitutionally convene military commissions "without the sanction of Congress" in cases of "controlling necessity" is a question this Court has not answered definitively, and need not answer today. For we held in [Ex parte Quirin, 317 U.S. 1 (1942), *supra* p. 353] that Congress had, through Article of War 15, sanctioned the use of military commissions in such circumstances. 317 U.S., at 28 ("By the Articles of War, and especially Article 15, Congress has explicitly provided, so far as it may constitutionally do so, that military tribunals shall have jurisdiction to try offenders or offenses against the law of war in appropriate cases"). Article 21 of the UCMJ, the language of which is substantially identical to the old Article 15 and was preserved by Congress after World War II, reads as follows:

"Jurisdiction of courts-martial not exclusive.
    "The provisions of this code conferring jurisdiction upon courts-martial shall not be construed as depriving military commissions, provost courts, or other military tribunals of concurrent jurisdiction in respect of offenders or offenses that by statute or by the law of war may be tried by such military commissions, provost courts, or other military tribunals." 64 Stat. 115.

We have no occasion to revisit *Quirin*'s controversial characterization of Article of War 15 as congressional authorization for military commissions. Contrary to the Government's assertion, however, even *Quirin* did not view the authorization as a sweeping mandate for the President to "invoke military commissions when he deems them necessary." Rather, the *Quirin* Court recognized that Congress had simply preserved what power, under the Constitution and the common law of war, the President had had before 1916 to convene military commissions — with the express condition that the President and those under his command comply with the law of war. See 317 U.S., at 28-29.[23] That much is evidenced by the Court's inquiry, *following* its conclusion

---

23. Whether or not the President has independent power, absent congressional authorization, to convene military commissions, he may not disregard limitations that Congress has, in proper exercise of its own war powers, placed on his powers. See *Youngstown Sheet & Tube Co. v. Sawyer*, 343 U.S. 579, 637 (1952) (Jackson, J., concurring). The Government does not argue otherwise.

that Congress had authorized military commissions, into whether the law of war had indeed been complied with in that case.

The Government would have us dispense with the inquiry that the *Quirin* Court undertook and find in either the AUMF [Authorization for Use of Military Force, Pub. L. No. 107-40, 115 Stat. 224 (2001), *supra* p. 59] or the DTA [Detainee Treatment Act of 2005, Pub. L. 109-163, §§1401-1406, 119 Stat. 3136, 3474-3480 (2006), *supra* p. 335] specific, overriding authorization for the very commission that has been convened to try Hamdan. Neither of these congressional Acts, however, expands the President's authority to convene military commissions. First, while we assume that the AUMF activated the President's war powers, see *Hamdi v. Rumsfeld,* 542 U.S. 507 (2004) (plurality opinion), and that those powers include the authority to convene military commissions in appropriate circumstances, there is nothing in the text or legislative history of the AUMF even hinting that Congress intended to expand or alter the authorization set forth in Article 21 of the UCMJ.[24]

Likewise, the DTA cannot be read to authorize this commission. Although the DTA, unlike either Article 21 or the AUMF, was enacted after the President had convened Hamdan's commission, it contains no language authorizing that tribunal or any other at Guantanamo Bay. The DTA obviously "recognize[s]" the existence of the Guantanamo Bay commissions in the weakest sense because it references some of the military orders governing them and creates limited judicial review of their "final decision[s]," DTA §1005(e)(3), 119 Stat. 2743. But the statute also pointedly reserves judgment on whether "the Constitution and laws of the United States are applicable" in reviewing such decisions and whether, if they are, the "standards and procedures" used to try Hamdan and other detainees actually violate the "Constitution and laws."

Together, the UCMJ, the AUMF, and the DTA at most acknowledge a general Presidential authority to convene military commissions in circumstances where justified under the "Constitution and laws," including the law of war. Absent a more specific congressional authorization, the task of this Court is, as it was in *Quirin,* to decide whether Hamdan's military commission is so justified. It is to that inquiry we now turn.

## V

The common law governing military commissions may be gleaned from past practice and what sparse legal precedent exists. Commissions historically have been used in three situations. First, they have substituted for civilian courts at times and in places where martial law has been declared. Their use in these circumstances has raised constitutional questions, see *Duncan v. Kahanamoku,* 327 U.S. 304 (1946); *Milligan,* 4 Wall., at 121-122, but is well recognized. Second, commissions have been established to try civilians "as part of a temporary military government over occupied enemy territory or territory regained from

---

24. On this point, it is noteworthy that the Court in *Ex parte Quirin,* 317 U.S. 1 (1942), looked beyond Congress' declaration of war and accompanying authorization for use of force during World War II, and relied instead on Article of War 15 to find that Congress had authorized the use of military commissions in some circumstances. Justice Thomas' assertion that we commit "error" in reading Article 21 of the UCMJ to place limitations upon the President's use of military commissions ignores the reasoning in *Quirin.*

an enemy where civilian government cannot and does not function." *Duncan,* 327 U.S., at 314; see *Milligan,* 4 Wall., at 141-142 (Chase, C. J., concurring in judgment) (distinguishing "martial law proper" from "military government" in occupied territory). . . .

The third type of commission, convened as an "incident to the conduct of war" when there is a need "to seize and subject to disciplinary measures those enemies who in their attempt to thwart or impede our military effort have violated the law of war," *Quirin,* 317 U.S., at 28-29, has been described as "utterly different" from the other two. Not only is its jurisdiction limited to offenses cognizable during time of war, but its role is primarily a factfinding one — to determine, typically on the battlefield itself, whether the defendant has violated the law of war. The last time the U.S. Armed Forces used the law-of-war military commission was during World War II. In *Quirin,* this Court sanctioned President Roosevelt's use of such a tribunal to try Nazi saboteurs captured on American soil during the War. 317 U.S. 1. And in *Yamashita,* we held that a military commission had jurisdiction to try a Japanese commander for failing to prevent troops under his command from committing atrocities in the Philippines. 327 U.S. 1.

*Quirin* is the model the Government invokes most frequently to defend the commission convened to try Hamdan. That is both appropriate and unsurprising. Since Guantanamo Bay is neither enemy-occupied territory nor under martial law, the law-of-war commission is the only model available. At the same time, no more robust model of executive power exists; *Quirin* represents the high-water mark of military power to try enemy combatants for war crimes.

The classic treatise penned by Colonel William Winthrop, whom we have called "the 'Blackstone of Military Law,'" *Reid v. Covert,* 354 U.S. 1, 19, n. 38 (1957) (plurality opinion), describes at least four preconditions for exercise of jurisdiction by a tribunal of the type convened to try Hamdan. First, "[a] military commission, (except where otherwise authorized by statute), can legally assume jurisdiction only of offenses committed within the field of the command of the convening commander." Winthrop 836. The "field of command" in these circumstances means the "theatre of war." *Ibid.* Second, the offense charged "must have been committed within the period of the war." *Id.,* at 837. No jurisdiction exists to try offenses "committed either before or after the war." *Ibid.* Third, a military commission not established pursuant to martial law or an occupation may try only "[i]ndividuals of the enemy's army who have been guilty of illegitimate warfare or other offences in violation of the laws of war" and members of one's own army "who, in time of war, become chargeable with crimes or offences not cognizable, or triable, by the criminal courts or under the Articles of war." *Id.,* at 838. Finally, a law-of-war commission has jurisdiction to try only two kinds of offense: "Violations of the laws and usages of war cognizable by military tribunals only," and "[b]reaches of military orders or regulations for which offenders are not legally triable by court-martial under the Articles of war." *Id.,* at 839.

. . . The question is whether the preconditions designed to ensure that a military necessity exists to justify the use of this extraordinary tribunal have been satisfied here.

The charge against Hamdan . . . alleges a conspiracy extending over a number of years, from 1996 to November 2001.[30] All but two months of that more than 5-year-long period preceded the attacks of September 11, 2001, and the enactment of the AUMF—the Act of Congress on which the Government relies for exercise of its war powers and thus for its authority to convene military commissions.[31] Neither the purported agreement with Osama bin Laden and others to commit war crimes, nor a single overt act, is alleged to have occurred in a theater of war or on any specified date after September 11, 2001. None of the overt acts that Hamdan is alleged to have committed violates the law of war.

These facts alone cast doubt on the legality of the charge and, hence, the commission; as Winthrop makes plain, the offense alleged must have been committed both in a theater of war and *during,* not before, the relevant conflict. But the deficiencies in the time and place allegations also underscore—indeed are symptomatic of—the most serious defect of this charge: The offense it alleges is not triable by law-of-war military commission.

There is no suggestion that Congress has, in exercise of its constitutional authority to "define and punish . . . Offences against the Law of Nations," U.S. Const., Art. I, §8, cl. 10, positively identified "conspiracy" as a war crime. As we explained in *Quirin,* that is not necessarily fatal to the Government's claim of authority to try the alleged offense by military commission; Congress, through Article 21 of the UCMJ, has "incorporated by reference" the common law of war, which may render triable by military commission certain offenses not defined by statute. 317 U.S., at 30. When, however, neither the elements of the offense nor the range of permissible punishments is defined by statute or treaty, the precedent must be plain and unambiguous. To demand any less would be to risk concentrating in military hands a degree of adjudicative and punitive power in excess of that contemplated either by statute or by the Constitution. . . .

At a minimum, the Government must make a substantial showing that the crime for which it seeks to try a defendant by military commission is acknowledged to be an offense against the law of war. That burden is far from satisfied here. The crime of "conspiracy" has rarely if ever been tried as such in this country by any law-of-war military commission not exercising some other form of jurisdiction, and does not appear in either the Geneva Conventions or the Hague Conventions—the major treaties on the law of war. . . .

---

30. The elements of this conspiracy charge have been defined not by Congress but by the President. See Military Commission Instruction No. 2, 32 C.F.R. §11.6 (2005).

31. Justice Thomas would treat Osama bin Laden's 1996 declaration of jihad against Americans as the inception of the war. But even the Government does not go so far; although the United States had for some time prior to the attacks of September 11, 2001, been aggressively pursuing al Qaeda, neither in the charging document nor in submissions before this Court has the Government asserted that the President's *war powers* were activated prior to September 11, 2001. Justice Thomas' further argument that the AUMF is "backward looking" and therefore authorizes *trial by military commission* of crimes that occurred prior to the inception of war is insupportable. If nothing else, Article 21 of the UCMJ requires that the President comply with the law of war in his use of military commissions. As explained in the text, the law of war permits trial only of offenses "committed within the period of the war." Winthrop 837; see also *Quirin,* 317 U.S., at 28-29 (observing that law-of-war military commissions may be used to try "those enemies *who in their attempt to thwart or impede our military effort* have violated the law of war" (emphasis added)). . . .

. . . [T]he only "conspiracy" crimes that have been recognized by international war crimes tribunals (whose jurisdiction often extends beyond war crimes proper to crimes against humanity and crimes against the peace) are conspiracy to commit genocide and common plan to wage aggressive war, which is a crime against the peace and requires for its commission actual participation in a "concrete plan to wage war." 1 Trial of the Major War Criminals Before the International Military Tribunal: Nuremberg, 14 November 1945-1 October 1946, p. 225 (1947). . . .

In sum, the sources that the Government and Justice Thomas rely upon to show that conspiracy to violate the law of war is itself a violation of the law of war in fact demonstrate quite the opposite. Far from making the requisite substantial showing, the Government has failed even to offer a "merely colorable" case for inclusion of conspiracy among those offenses cognizable by law-of-war military commission. Cf. *Quirin,* 317 U.S., at 36. Because the charge does not support the commission's jurisdiction, the commission lacks authority to try Hamdan.

The charge's shortcomings are not merely formal, but are indicative of a broader inability on the Executive's part here to satisfy the most basic precondition — at least in the absence of specific congressional authorization — for establishment of military commissions: military necessity. Hamdan's tribunal was appointed not by a military commander in the field of battle, but by a retired major general stationed away from any active hostilities. Cf. *Rasul v. Bush,* 542 U.S., at 487 (Kennedy, J., concurring in judgment) (observing that "Guantanamo Bay is . . . far removed from any hostilities"). Hamdan is charged not with an overt act for which he was caught redhanded in a theater of war and which military efficiency demands be tried expeditiously, but with an *agreement* the inception of which long predated the attacks of September 11, 2001 and the AUMF. That may well be a crime,[41] but it is not an offense that "by the law of war may be tried by military commissio[n]." 10 U.S.C. §821. None of the overt acts alleged to have been committed in furtherance of the agreement is itself a war crime, or even necessarily occurred during time of, or in a theater of, war. Any urgent need for imposition or execution of judgment is utterly belied by the record; Hamdan was arrested in November 2001 and he was not charged until mid-2004. These simply are not the circumstances in which, by any stretch of the historical evidence or this Court's precedents, a military commission established by Executive Order under the authority of Article 21 of the UCMJ may lawfully try a person and subject him to punishment.

## VI

Whether or not the Government has charged Hamdan with an offense against the law of war cognizable by military commission, the commission

---

41. Justice Thomas' suggestion that our conclusion precludes the Government from bringing to justice those who conspire to commit acts of terrorism is therefore wide of the mark. That conspiracy is not a violation of the law of war triable by military commission does not mean the Government may not, for example, prosecute by court-martial or in federal court those caught "plotting terrorist atrocities like the bombing of the Khobar Towers."

lacks power to proceed. The UCMJ conditions the President's use of military commissions on compliance not only with the American common law of war, but also with the rest of the UCMJ itself, insofar as applicable, and with the "rules and precepts of the law of nations," *Quirin,* 317 U.S., at 28 — including, *inter alia,* the four Geneva Conventions signed in 1949. The procedures that the Government has decreed will govern Hamdan's trial by commission violate these laws.

## A

The commission's procedures are set forth in Commission Order No. 1, which was amended most recently on August 31, 2005 — after Hamdan's trial had already begun. Every commission established pursuant to Commission Order No. 1 must have a presiding officer and at least three other members, all of whom must be commissioned officers. §4(A)(1). The presiding officer's job is to rule on questions of law and other evidentiary and interlocutory issues; the other members make findings and, if applicable, sentencing decisions. §4(A)(5). The accused is entitled to appointed military counsel and may hire civilian counsel at his own expense so long as such counsel is a U.S. citizen with security clearance "at the level SECRET or higher." §§4(C)(2)-(3).

The accused also is entitled to a copy of the charge(s) against him, both in English and his own language (if different), to a presumption of innocence, and to certain other rights typically afforded criminal defendants in civilian courts and courts-martial. See §§5(A)-(P). These rights are subject, however, to one glaring condition: The accused and his civilian counsel may be excluded from, and precluded from ever learning what evidence was presented during, any part of the proceeding that either the Appointing Authority or the presiding officer decides to "close." Grounds for such closure "include the protection of information classified or classifiable . . . ; information protected by law or rule from unauthorized disclosure; the physical safety of participants in Commission proceedings, including prospective witnesses; intelligence and law enforcement sources, methods, or activities; and other national security interests." §6(B)(3). Appointed military defense counsel must be privy to these closed sessions, but may, at the presiding officer's discretion, be forbidden to reveal to his or her client what took place therein. *Ibid.*

Another striking feature of the rules governing Hamdan's commission is that they permit the admission of *any* evidence that, in the opinion of the presiding officer, "would have probative value to a reasonable person." §6(D)(1). Under this test, not only is testimonial hearsay and evidence obtained through coercion fully admissible, but neither live testimony nor witnesses' written statements need be sworn. See §§6(D)(2)(b), (3). Moreover, the accused and his civilian counsel may be denied access to evidence in the form of "protected information" (which includes classified information as well as "information protected by law or rule from unauthorized disclosure" and "information concerning other national security interests," §§6(B)(3), 6(D)(5)(a)(v)), so long as the presiding officer concludes that the evidence is "probative" under §6(D)(1) and that its admission without the accused's knowledge would not "result in the

denial of a full and fair trial." §6(D)(5)(b).[43] Finally, a presiding officer's determination that evidence "would not have probative value to a reasonable person"
may be overridden by a majority of the other commission members. §6(D)(1).

Once all the evidence is in, the commission members (not including the
presiding officer) must vote on the accused's guilt. A two-thirds vote will suffice
for both a verdict of guilty and for imposition of any sentence not including
death (the imposition of which requires a unanimous vote). §6(F). Any appeal
is taken to a three-member review panel composed of military officers and
designated by the Secretary of Defense, only one member of which need have
experience as a judge. §6(H)(4). The review panel is directed to "disregard any
variance from procedures specified in this Order or elsewhere that would not
materially have affected the outcome of the trial before the Commission." *Ibid.*
Once the panel makes its recommendation to the Secretary of Defense, the
Secretary can either remand for further proceedings or forward the record to
the President with his recommendation as to final disposition. §6(H)(5). The
President then, unless he has delegated the task to the Secretary, makes the
"final decision." §6(H)(6). He may change the commission's findings or sentence
only in a manner favorable to the accused. *Ibid.* . . .

**C**

In part because the difference between military commissions and courts-
martial originally was a difference of jurisdiction alone, and in part to protect
against abuse and ensure evenhandedness under the pressures of war, the
procedures governing trials by military commission historically have been
the same as those governing courts-martial.

The uniformity principle is not an inflexible one; it does not preclude all
departures from the procedures dictated for use by courts-martial. But any
departure must be tailored to the exigency that necessitates it. See Winthrop
835, n.81. That understanding is reflected in Article 36 of the UCMJ, which
provides:

> "(a) The procedure, including modes of proof, in cases before courts-martial,
> courts of inquiry, military commissions, and other military tribunals may be
> prescribed by the President by regulations which shall, so far as he considers
> practicable, apply the principles of law and the rules of evidence generally
> recognized in the trial of criminal cases in the United States district courts,
> but which may not be contrary to or inconsistent with this chapter.
>
> "(b) All rules and regulations made under this article shall be uniform
> insofar as practicable and shall be reported to Congress." 70A Stat. 50.

Article 36 places two restrictions on the President's power to promulgate
rules of procedure for courts-martial and military commissions alike. First, no
procedural rule he adopts may be "contrary to or inconsistent with" the

---

43. As the District Court observed, this section apparently permits reception of testimony from
a confidential informant in circumstances where "Hamdan will not be permitted to hear the testimony, see the witness's face, or learn his name. If the government has information developed by
interrogation of witnesses in Afghanistan or elsewhere, it can offer such evidence in transcript form,
or even as summaries of transcripts." 344 F. Supp. 2d 152, 168 (D.D.C. 2004).

UCMJ—however practical it may seem. Second, the rules adopted must be "uniform insofar as practicable." That is, the rules applied to military commissions must be the same as those applied to courts-martial unless such uniformity proves impracticable. . . .

Without reaching the question whether any provision of Commission Order No. 1 is strictly "contrary to or inconsistent with" other provisions of the UCMJ, we conclude that the "practicability" determination the President has made is insufficient to justify variances from the procedures governing courts-martial. Subsection (b) of Article 36 was added after World War II, and requires a different showing of impracticability from the one required by subsection (a). Subsection (a) requires that the rules the President promulgates for courts-martial, provost courts, and military commissions alike conform to those that govern procedures in *Article III courts,* "so far as *he considers* practicable." 10 U.S.C. §836(a) (emphasis added). Subsection (b), by contrast, demands that the rules applied in courts-martial, provost courts, and military commissions—whether or not they conform with the Federal Rules of Evidence—be "uniform *insofar as practicable.*" §836(b) (emphasis added). Under the latter provision, then, the rules set forth in the Manual for Courts-Martial must apply to military commissions unless impracticable.

The President here has determined, pursuant to subsection (a), that it is impracticable to apply the rules and principles of law that govern "the trial of criminal cases in the United States district courts," §836(a), to Hamdan's commission. We assume that complete deference is owed that determination. The President has not, however, made a similar official determination that it is impracticable to apply the rules for courts-martial. And even if subsection (b)'s requirements may be satisfied without such an official determination, the requirements of that subsection are not satisfied here.

Nothing in the record before us demonstrates that it would be impracticable to apply court-martial rules in this case. There is no suggestion, for example, of any logistical difficulty in securing properly sworn and authenticated evidence or in applying the usual principles of relevance and admissibility. Assuming *arguendo* that the reasons articulated in the President's Article 36(a) determination ought to be considered in evaluating the impracticability of applying court-martial rules, the only reason offered in support of that determination is the danger posed by international terrorism. Without for one moment underestimating that danger, it is not evident to us why it should require, in the case of Hamdan's trial, any variance from the rules that govern courts-martial.

The absence of any showing of impracticability is particularly disturbing when considered in light of the clear and admitted failure to apply one of the most fundamental protections afforded not just by the Manual for Courts-Martial but also by the UCMJ itself: the right to be present. See 10 U.S.C.A. §839(c) (Supp. 2006). Whether or not that departure technically is "contrary to or inconsistent with" the terms of the UCMJ, 10 U.S.C. §836(a), the jettisoning of so basic a right cannot lightly be excused as "practicable."

Under the circumstances, then, the rules applicable in courts-martial must apply. Since it is undisputed that Commission Order No. 1 deviates in many significant respects from those rules, it necessarily violates Article 36(b).

The Government's objection that requiring compliance with the court-martial rules imposes an undue burden both ignores the plain meaning of Article 36(b) and misunderstands the purpose and the history of military commissions. The military commission was not born of a desire to dispense a more summary form of justice than is afforded by courts-martial; it developed, rather, as a tribunal of necessity to be employed when courts-martial lacked jurisdiction over either the accused or the subject matter. See Winthrop 831. Exigency lent the commission its legitimacy, but did not further justify the wholesale jettisoning of procedural protections. That history explains why the military commission's procedures typically have been the ones used by courts-martial. That the jurisdiction of the two tribunals today may sometimes overlap does not detract from the force of this history. Article 21 did not transform the military commission from a tribunal of true exigency into a more convenient adjudicatory tool. Article 36, confirming as much, strikes a careful balance between uniform procedure and the need to accommodate exigencies that may sometimes arise in a theater of war. That Article not having been complied with here, the rules specified for Hamdan's trial are illegal.

### D

The procedures adopted to try Hamdan also violate the Geneva Conventions. The Court of Appeals dismissed Hamdan's Geneva Convention challenge on three independent grounds: (1) the Geneva Conventions are not judicially enforceable; (2) Hamdan in any event is not entitled to their protections; and (3) even if he is entitled to their protections, . . . abstention is appropriate. . . .

*i* . . .

We may assume that "the obvious scheme" of the 1949 Conventions is identical in all relevant respects to that of the 1929 Convention,[57] and even that that scheme would, absent some other provision of law, preclude Hamdan's invocation of the Convention's provisions as an independent source of law binding the Government's actions and furnishing petitioner with any enforceable right. For, regardless of the nature of the rights conferred on Hamdan, cf. *United States v. Rauscher,* 119 U.S. 407 (1886), they are, as the Government does not dispute, part of the law of war. And compliance with the law of war is the condition upon which the authority set forth in Article 21 is granted.

*ii* . . .

The conflict with al Qaeda is not, according to the Government, a conflict to which the full protections afforded detainees under the 1949 Geneva Conventions apply because Article 2 of those Conventions (which appears in all four Conventions) renders the full protections applicable only to "all cases of

---

57. But see, *e.g.,* 4 Int'l Comm. of Red Cross, Commentary: Geneva Convention Relative to the Protection of Civilian Persons in Time of War 21 (1958) (hereinafter GCIV Commentary) (the 1949 Geneva Conventions were written "first and foremost to protect individuals, and not to serve State interests"); GCIII Commentary 91 ("It was not . . . until the Conventions of 1949 . . . that the existence of 'rights' conferred in prisoners of war was affirmed").

declared war or of any other armed conflict which may arise between two or more of the High Contracting Parties." 6 U.S.T., at 3318. Since Hamdan was captured and detained incident to the conflict with al Qaeda and not the conflict with the Taliban, and since al Qaeda, unlike Afghanistan, is not a "High Contracting Party"—*i.e.,* a signatory of the Conventions, the protections of those Conventions are not, it is argued, applicable to Hamdan.[60]

We need not decide the merits of this argument because there is at least one provision of the Geneva Conventions that applies here even if the relevant conflict is not one between signatories. Article 3, often referred to as Common Article 3 because, like Article 2, it appears in all four Geneva Conventions, provides that in a "conflict not of an international character occurring in the territory of one of the High Contracting Parties, each Party to the conflict shall be bound to apply, as a minimum," certain provisions protecting "[p]ersons taking no active part in the hostilities, including members of armed forces who have laid down their arms and those placed *hors de combat* by . . . detention." *Id.,* at 3318. One such provision prohibits "the passing of sentences and the carrying out of executions without previous judgment pronounced by a regularly constituted court affording all the judicial guarantees which are recognized as indispensable by civilized peoples." *Ibid.*

The Court of Appeals thought, and the Government asserts, that Common Article 3 does not apply to Hamdan because the conflict with al Qaeda, being "'international in scope,'" does not qualify as a "'conflict not of an international character.'" That reasoning is erroneous. The term "conflict not of an international character" is used here in contradistinction to a conflict between nations. So much is demonstrated by the "fundamental logic [of] the Convention's provisions on its application." [415 F.3d 33, 44 (D.C. Cir. 2005) (Williams, J., concurring).] Common Article 2 provides that "the present Convention shall apply to all cases of declared war or of any other armed conflict which may arise between two or more of the High Contracting Parties." 6 U.S.T., at 3318 (Art. 2, ¶1). High Contracting Parties (signatories) also must abide by all terms of the Conventions vis-à-vis one another even if one party to the conflict is a nonsignatory "Power," and must so abide vis-à-vis the nonsignatory if "the latter accepts and applies" those terms. *Ibid.* (Art. 2, ¶3). Common Article 3, by contrast, affords some minimal protection, falling short of full protection under the Conventions, to individuals associated with neither a signatory nor even a nonsignatory "Power" who are involved in a conflict "in the territory of" a signatory. The latter kind of conflict is distinguishable from the conflict described in Common Article 2 chiefly because it does not involve a clash between nations (whether signatories or not). In context, then, the phrase "not of an international character" bears its literal meaning. See, *e.g.,* J. Bentham, Introduction to the Principles of Morals and Legislation 6, 296 (J. Burns & H. Hart eds. 1970) (using the term "international law" as a "new though not inexpressive appellation" meaning "betwixt nation and nation"; defining "international" to include "mutual transactions between sovereigns as such"). . . .

---

60. The President has stated that the conflict with the Taliban is a conflict to which the Geneva Conventions apply.

### iii

Common Article 3, then, is applicable here and, as indicated above, requires that Hamdan be tried by a "regularly constituted court affording all the judicial guarantees which are recognized as indispensable by civilized peoples." 6 U.S.T., at 3320 (Art. 3, ¶1(d)). While the term "regularly constituted court" is not specifically defined in either Common Article 3 or its accompanying commentary, other sources disclose its core meaning. The commentary accompanying a provision of the Fourth Geneva Convention, for example, defines "'regularly constituted'" tribunals to include "ordinary military courts" and "definitely exclud[e] all special tribunals." GCIV Commentary 340 (defining the term "properly constituted" in Article 66, which the commentary treats as identical to "regularly constituted"). . . .

The Government offers only a cursory defense of Hamdan's military commission in light of Common Article 3. As Justice Kennedy explains, that defense fails because "[t]he regular military courts in our system are the courts-martial established by congressional statutes." At a minimum, a military commission "can be 'regularly constituted' by the standards of our military justice system only if some practical need explains deviations from court-martial practice." As we have explained, see Part VI-C, *supra,* no such need has been demonstrated here.

### iv

Inextricably intertwined with the question of regular constitution is the evaluation of the procedures governing the tribunal and whether they afford "all the judicial guarantees which are recognized as indispensable by civilized peoples." 6 U.S.T., at 3320 (Art. 3, ¶1(d)). Like the phrase "regularly constituted court," this phrase is not defined in the text of the Geneva Conventions. But it must be understood to incorporate at least the barest of those trial protections that have been recognized by customary international law. . . .

We agree with Justice Kennedy that the procedures adopted to try Hamdan deviate from those governing courts-martial in ways not justified by any "evident practical need," and for that reason, at least, fail to afford the requisite guarantees. We add only that, as noted in Part VI-A, *supra,* various provisions of Commission Order No. 1 dispense with the principles, articulated in Article 75 [of Protocol I to the Geneva Conventions of 1949, June 8, 1977, 1125 U.N.T.S. 3, 16 I.L.M. 1391] and indisputably part of the customary international law, that an accused must, absent disruptive conduct or consent, be present for his trial and must be privy to the evidence against him. See §§6(B)(3), (D). That the Government has a compelling interest in denying Hamdan access to certain sensitive information is not doubted. But, at least absent express statutory provision to the contrary, information used to convict a person of a crime must be disclosed to him. . . .

### VII

We have assumed, as we must, that the allegations made in the Government's charge against Hamdan are true. We have assumed, moreover, the truth of the message implicit in that charge — viz., that Hamdan is a dangerous individual whose beliefs, if acted upon, would cause great harm and even death to innocent civilians, and who would act upon those beliefs if given the opportunity. It bears emphasizing that Hamdan does not challenge, and we do not today address, the Government's power to detain him for the duration of active hostilities in order to prevent such harm. But in undertaking to try Hamdan and subject him to criminal punishment, the Executive is bound to comply with the Rule of Law that prevails in this jurisdiction.

The judgment of the Court of Appeals is reversed, and the case is remanded for further proceedings.

*It is so ordered.*

The CHIEF JUSTICE took no part in the consideration or decision of this case.

Justice BREYER, with whom Justice KENNEDY, Justice SOUTER, and Justice GINSBURG join, concurring. The dissenters say that today's decision would "sorely hamper the President's ability to confront and defeat a new and deadly enemy." They suggest that it undermines our Nation's ability to "preven[t] future attacks" of the grievous sort that we have already suffered. That claim leads me to state briefly what I believe the majority sets forth both explicitly and implicitly at greater length. The Court's conclusion ultimately rests upon a single ground: Congress has not issued the Executive a "blank check." Cf. *Hamdi v. Rumsfeld,* 542 U.S. 507, 536 (2004) (plurality opinion). Indeed, Congress has denied the President the legislative authority to create military commissions of the kind at issue here. Nothing prevents the President from returning to Congress to seek the authority he believes necessary.

Where, as here, no emergency prevents consultation with Congress, judicial insistence upon that consultation does not weaken our Nation's ability to deal with danger. To the contrary, that insistence strengthens the Nation's ability to determine — through democratic means — how best to do so. The Constitution places its faith in those democratic means. Our Court today simply does the same.

Justice KENNEDY, with whom Justice SOUTER, Justice GINSBURG, and Justice BREYER join as to Parts I and II, concurring in part. Military Commission Order No. 1, which governs the military commission established to try petitioner Salim Hamdan for war crimes, exceeds limits that certain statutes, duly enacted by Congress, have placed on the President's authority to convene military courts. This is not a case, then, where the Executive can assert some unilateral authority to fill a void left by congressional inaction. It is a case where Congress, in the proper exercise of its powers as an independent branch of government, and as part of a long tradition of legislative involvement in matters of military justice, has considered the subject of military tribunals and set limits on the President's authority. Where a statute provides the conditions for the exercise of governmental power, its requirements are the result of a deliberative and reflective process engaging both of the political branches. Respect for laws derived from the customary operation of the Executive and Legislative Branches gives some assurance of stability in time of crisis.

The Constitution is best preserved by reliance on standards tested over time and insulated from the pressures of the moment. . . .

I join the Court's opinion, save Parts V and VI-D-iv. To state my reasons for this reservation, and to show my agreement with the remainder of the Court's analysis by identifying particular deficiencies in the military commissions at issue, this separate opinion seems appropriate.

## I

Trial by military commission raises separation-of-powers concerns of the highest order. Located within a single branch, these courts carry the risk that offenses will be defined, prosecuted, and adjudicated by executive officials without independent review. Concentration of power puts personal liberty in peril of arbitrary action by officials, an incursion the Constitution's three-part system is designed to avoid. It is imperative, then, that when military tribunals are established, full and proper authority exists for the Presidential directive. . . .

## II . . .

These structural differences between the military commissions and courts-martial — the concentration of functions, including legal decisionmaking, in a single executive official; the less rigorous standards for composition of the tribunal; and the creation of special review procedures in place of institutions created and regulated by Congress — remove safeguards that are important to the fairness of the proceedings and the independence of the court. Congress has prescribed these guarantees for courts-martial; and no evident practical need explains the departures here. For these reasons the commission cannot be considered regularly constituted under United States law and thus does not satisfy Congress' requirement that military commissions conform to the law of war.

Apart from these structural issues, moreover, the basic procedures for the commissions deviate from procedures for courts-martial, in violation of §836(b). As the Court explains, the Military Commission Order abandons the detailed Military Rules of Evidence, which are modeled on the Federal Rules of Evidence in conformity with §836(a)'s requirement of presumptive compliance with district-court rules. . . .

In sum, as presently structured, Hamdan's military commission exceeds the bounds Congress has placed on the President's authority in §§836 and 821 of the UCMJ. Because Congress has prescribed these limits, Congress can change them, requiring a new analysis consistent with the Constitution and other governing laws. At this time, however, we must apply the standards Congress has provided. By those standards the military commission is deficient.

## III

In light of the conclusion that the military commission here is unauthorized under the UCMJ, I see no need to consider several further issues addressed in the plurality opinion by Justice Stevens and the dissent by Justice Thomas. . . .

Justice SCALIA, with whom Justice THOMAS and Justice ALITO join, dissenting. . . . [Justice Scalia found that the DTA deprived the Court of jurisdiction to hear Hamdan's case at this time. He then considered, assuming that the Court had jurisdiction, whether it should abstain from exercising it.]

. . . The principal opinion on the merits makes clear that it does not believe that the trials by military commission involve any "military necessity" *at all:* "The charge's shortcomings . . . are indicative of a broader inability on the Executive's part here to satisfy the most basic precondition . . . for establishment of military commissions: military necessity." This is quite at odds with the views on this subject expressed by our political branches. Because of "military necessity," a joint session of Congress authorized the President to "use all necessary and appropriate force," including military commissions, "against those nations, organizations, or persons [such as petitioner] he determines planned, authorized, committed, or aided the terrorist attacks that occurred on September 11, 2001." Authorization for Use of Military Force, §2(a), 115 Stat. 224, note following 50 U.S.C. §1541 (2000 ed., Supp. III). In keeping with this authority, the President has determined that "[t]o protect the United States and its citizens, and for the effective conduct of military operations and prevention of terrorist attacks, it is necessary for individuals subject to this order . . . to be detained, and, when tried, to be tried for violations of the laws of war and other applicable laws by military tribunals." Military Order of Nov. 13, 2001, 3 C.F.R. §918(e) (2002). It is not clear where the Court derives the authority — or the audacity — to contradict this determination. If "military necessities" relating to "duty" and "discipline" required abstention in *Councilman, supra,* at 757, military necessities relating to the disabling, deterrence, and punishment of the mass-murdering terrorists of September 11 require abstention all the more here.

The Court further seeks to distinguish *Councilman* on the ground that "the tribunal convened to try Hamdan is not part of the integrated system of military courts, complete with independent review panels, that Congress has established." . . .

Even if we were to accept the Court's extraordinary assumption that the President "lack[s] the structural insulation from military influence that characterizes the Court of Appeals for the Armed Forces,"[8] the Court's description of the review scheme here is anachronistic. As of December 30, 2005, the "fina[l]" review of decisions by military commissions is now conducted by the D.C. Circuit pursuant to §1005(e)(3) of the DTA, and by this Court under 28 U.S.C. §1254(1). This provision for review by Article III courts creates, if anything, a review scheme *more* insulated from Executive control than that in *Councilman.* . . .

Moreover, a third consideration counsels strongly in favor of abstention in this case. . . . Here, apparently for the first time in history, a District Court enjoined ongoing military commission proceedings, which had been deemed "necessary" by the President "[t]o protect the United States and its citizens, and for the effective conduct of military operations and prevention of terrorist attacks." Military Order of Nov. 13, 3 C.F.R. §918(e). Such an order brings the

---

8. The very purpose of Article II's creation of a *civilian* Commander in Chief in the President of the United States was to generate "structural insulation from military influence." See The Federalist No. 28 (A. Hamilton); *id.,* No. 69 (same). We do not live under a military junta. It is a disservice to both those in the Armed Forces and the President to suggest that the President is subject to the undue control of the military.

Judicial Branch into direct conflict with the Executive in an area where the Executive's competence is maximal and ours is virtually nonexistent. We should exercise our equitable discretion to *avoid* such conflict. Instead, the Court rushes headlong to meet it. . . .

I would abstain from exercising our equity jurisdiction, as the Government requests. . . .

Justice THOMAS, with whom Justice SCALIA joins, and with whom Justice ALITO joins in all but parts I, II-C-1, and III-B-2, dissenting. . . . [T]he President's decision to try Hamdan before a military commission for his involvement with al Qaeda is entitled to a heavy measure of deference. In the present conflict, Congress has authorized the President "to use all necessary and appropriate force against those nations, organizations, or persons *he determines* planned, authorized, committed, or aided the terrorist attacks that occurred on September 11, 2001 . . . in order to prevent any future acts of international terrorism against the United States by such nations, organizations or persons." Authorization for Use of Military Force (AUMF) 115 Stat. 224, note following 50 U.S.C. §1541 (2000 ed., Supp. III) (emphasis added). As a plurality of the Court observed in *Hamdi*, the "capture, detention, and *trial* of unlawful combatants, by 'universal agreement and practice,' are 'important incident[s] of war,'" *Hamdi*, 542 U.S., at 518 (quoting *Quirin, supra*, at 28, 30; emphasis added), and are therefore "an exercise of the 'necessary and appropriate force' Congress has authorized the President to use." *Hamdi*, 542 U.S., at 518; *id.*, at 587 (Thomas, J., dissenting). *Hamdi*'s observation that military commissions are included within the AUMF's authorization is supported by this Court's previous recognition that "[a]n important incident to the conduct of war is the adoption of measures by the military commander, not only to repel and defeat the enemy, but to seize and subject to disciplinary measures those enemies who, in their attempt to thwart or impede our military effort, have violated the law of war." *In re Yamashita*, 327 U.S. 1, 11 (1946). . . .

Nothing in the language of Article 21 . . . suggests that it outlines the entire reach of congressional authorization of military commissions in all conflicts — quite the contrary, the language of Article 21 presupposes the existence of military commissions under an independent basis of authorization. Indeed, consistent with *Hamdi*'s conclusion that the AUMF itself authorizes the trial of unlawful combatants, the original sanction for military commissions historically derived from congressional authorization of "the initiation of war" with its attendant authorization of "the employment of all necessary and proper agencies for its due prosecution." W. Winthrop, Military Law and Precedents 831 (2d ed. 1920) (hereinafter Winthrop). Accordingly, congressional authorization for military commissions pertaining to the instant conflict derives not only from Article 21 of the UCMJ, but also from the more recent, and broader, authorization contained in the AUMF.[2] . . .

---

2. Although the President very well may have inherent authority to try unlawful combatants for violations of the law of war before military commissions, we need not decide that question because Congress has authorized the President to do so. Cf. *Hamdi v. Rumsfeld*, 542 U.S. 507, 587 (2004) (Thomas, J., dissenting) (same conclusion respecting detention of unlawful combatants).

## II . . .

### A

. . . [A] law-of-war military commission may only assume jurisdiction of "offences committed within the field of the command of the convening commander," and . . . such offenses "must have been committed within the period of the war." See *id.*, at 836, 837. Here, as evidenced by Hamdan's charging document, the Executive has determined that the theater of the present conflict includes "Afghanistan, Pakistan and other countries" where al Qaeda has established training camps, and that the duration of that conflict dates back (at least) to Usama bin Laden's August 1996 *"Declaration of Jihad Against the Americans."* Under the Executive's description of the conflict, then, every aspect of the charge, which alleges overt acts in "Afghanistan, Pakistan, Yemen and other countries" taking place from 1996 to 2001, satisfies the temporal and geographic prerequisites for the exercise of law-of-war military commission jurisdiction. And these judgments pertaining to the scope of the theater and duration of the present conflict are committed solely to the President in the exercise of his commander-in-chief authority. See [*The Prize Cases*, 67 U.S. (2 Black) 635, 670 (1863), *supra* p. 43] (concluding that the President's commander-in-chief judgment about the nature of a particular conflict was "a question to be decided *by him,* and this Court must be governed by the decisions and acts of the political department of the Government to which this power was entrusted"). . . .

. . . The starting point of the present conflict (or indeed any conflict) is not determined by congressional enactment, but rather by the initiation of hostilities. See *Prize Cases, supra,* at 668 (recognizing that war may be initiated by "invasion of a foreign nation," and that such initiation, and the President's response, usually *precedes* congressional action). Thus, Congress' enactment of the AUMF did not mark the beginning of this Nation's conflict with al Qaeda, but instead authorized the President to use force in the midst of an ongoing conflict. Moreover, while the President's "war powers" may not have been activated until the AUMF was passed, the date of such activation has never been used to determine the scope of a military commission's jurisdiction.[3] . . .

### C

[Justice Thomas also concluded that, under the law of war, Hamdan could properly be charged with membership in a war-criminal enterprise and with conspiracy to commit war crimes.]

---

3. Even if the formal declaration of war were generally the determinative act in ascertaining the temporal reach of the jurisdiction of a military commission, the AUMF itself is inconsistent with the plurality's suggestion that such a rule is appropriate in this case. The text of the AUMF is backward looking, authorizing the use of "all necessary and appropriate force against those nations, organizations, or persons he determines planned, authorized, committed, or aided the terrorist attacks that occurred on September 11, 2001." Thus, the President's decision to try Hamdan by military commission—a use of force authorized by the AUMF—for Hamdan's involvement with al Qaeda prior to September 11, 2001, fits comfortably within the framework of the AUMF. In fact, bringing the September 11 conspirators to justice is the *primary point* of the AUMF. By contrast, on the plurality's logic, the AUMF would not grant the President the authority to try Usama bin Laden himself for his involvement in the events of September 11, 2001.

*3*

Ultimately, the plurality's determination that Hamdan has not been charged with an offense triable before a military commission rests not upon any historical example or authority, but upon the plurality's raw judgment of the "inability on the Executive's part here to satisfy the most basic precondition . . . for establishment of military commissions: military necessity." This judgment starkly confirms that the plurality has appointed itself the ultimate arbiter of what is quintessentially a policy and military judgment, namely, the appropriate military measures to take against those who "aided the terrorist attacks that occurred on September 11, 2001." AUMF §2(a), 115 Stat. 224. The plurality's suggestion that Hamdan's commission is illegitimate because it is not dispensing swift justice on the battlefield is unsupportable. Even a cursory review of the authorities confirms that law-of-war military commissions have wide-ranging jurisdiction to try offenses against the law of war in exigent and nonexigent circumstances alike. Traditionally, retributive justice for heinous war crimes is as much a "military necessity" as the "demands" of "military efficiency" touted by the plurality, and swift military retribution is precisely what Congress authorized the President to impose on the September 11 attackers in the AUMF.

Today a plurality of this Court would hold that conspiracy to massacre innocent civilians does not violate the laws of war. This determination is unsustainable. The judgment of the political branches that Hamdan, and others like him, must be held accountable before military commissions for their involvement with and membership in an unlawful organization dedicated to inflicting massive civilian casualties is supported by virtually every relevant authority, including all of the authorities invoked by the plurality today. It is also supported by the nature of the present conflict. We are not engaged in a traditional battle with a nation-state, but with a worldwide, hydra-headed enemy, who lurks in the shadows conspiring to reproduce the atrocities of September 11, 2001, and who has boasted of sending suicide bombers into civilian gatherings, has proudly distributed videotapes of beheadings of civilian workers, and has tortured and dismembered captured American soldiers. But according to the plurality, when our Armed Forces capture those who are plotting terrorist atrocities like the bombing of the Khobar Towers, the bombing of the U.S.S. *Cole,* and the attacks of September 11—even if their plots are advanced to the very brink of fulfillment—our military cannot charge those criminals with any offense against the laws of war. Instead, our troops must catch the terrorists "redhanded" in the midst of *the attack itself,* in order to bring them to justice. Not only is this conclusion fundamentally inconsistent with the cardinal principal of the law of war, namely protecting non-combatants, but it would sorely hamper the President's ability to confront and defeat a new and deadly enemy. . . .

## III . . .

[Justice Thomas concluded that the Court should defer to the President's determination that court martial procedures are not "practicable" for military commissions and therefore reject any requirement for uniformity of procedures. He also concluded that Common Article 3 was not judicially enforceable; that, if it were, the Court should defer to the President's "reasonable" interpretation of Common Article 3 as inapplicable to the "international" conflict with al Qaeda; and, finally, that any claim Hamdan might have under Common Article 3 was not ripe.]

For these reasons, I would affirm the judgment of the Court of Appeals.

Justice ALITO, with whom Justices SCALIA and THOMAS join in parts I-III, dissenting. For the reasons set out in Justice Scalia's dissent, which I join, I would hold that we lack jurisdiction. On the merits, I join Justice Thomas' dissent with the exception of Parts I, II-C-1, and III-B-2, which concern matters that I find unnecessary to reach. . . .

### I . . .

In order to determine whether a court has been properly appointed, set up, or established, it is necessary to refer to a body of law that governs such matters. I interpret Common Article 3 as looking to the domestic law of the appointing country because I am not aware of any international law standard regarding the way in which such a court must be appointed, set up, or established, and because different countries with different government structures handle this matter differently. Accordingly, "a regularly constituted court" is a court that has been appointed, set up, or established in accordance with the domestic law of the appointing country. . . .

### III . . .
### A . . .

In sum, I believe that Common Article 3 is satisfied here because the military commissions (1) qualify as courts, (2) that were appointed and established in accordance with domestic law, and (3) any procedural improprieties that might occur in particular cases can be reviewed in those cases.

### B

The commentary on Common Article 3 supports this interpretation. The commentary on Common Article 3, ¶1(d) . . . states: . . . *"We must be very clear about one point: it is only 'summary' justice which it is intended to prohibit."* . . . GCIV Commentary 39 (emphasis added).

It seems clear that the commissions at issue here meet this standard. Whatever else may be said about the system that was created by Military Commission Order No. 1 and augmented by the Detainee Treatment Act, §1005(e)(1), 119 Stat. 2742, this system — which features formal trial procedures, multiple levels of administrative review, and the opportunity for review by a United States Court of Appeals and by this Court — does not dispense "summary justice." . . .

For these reasons, I respectfully dissent.

## NOTES AND QUESTIONS

1. *Holding?* What, precisely, did *Hamdan* hold? Note that Justice Kennedy's vote is necessary to form a majority. Which parts of the decision are those of

the plurality alone? Note also that the Chief Justice — who wrote the opinion for the Court of Appeals in *Hamdan* — did not participate. If he had, how might it have changed any of the Court's conclusions?

2. ***Military Necessity Redux.*** We saw in Chapter 12 that the military commission exception to the "preferred" method of civilian trial is justified by necessity. What is the necessity that the majority identified in *Hamdan*? Is it limited by time or place? Is it limited to acts for which a person is "caught redhanded in a theater of war and which military efficiency demands be tried expeditiously," as the plurality suggests? See *supra* p. 570. If so, is necessity a wasting justification? If necessity for trying Hamdan by military commission is no longer present, is there any necessity for continuing to detain him? What does the Court say and why? See *supra* p. 577.

Reread section 1 of the Military Order, especially section 1(e), *supra* p. 559. Hasn't the President already found military commissions necessary? Why doesn't the Court defer to his finding, as it did to the finding of military necessity in *Korematsu*, noted *supra* p. 391? Reread the AUMF, *supra* p. 59. Hasn't Congress found necessity and authorized the President to use all "necessary and appropriate force," as he determines? Why doesn't the Court defer to Congress? Which branch is best equipped to decide necessity?

When there is a "controlling necessity," does the President *need* any statutory authority to use military commissions? That is, does he have inherent authority to establish them? What does the majority say? Justice Thomas? If so, is there any limit on that authority?

3. ***Statutory Authority.*** The Court does not reach the question of inherent presidential authority for military commissions because it found that Article 21 preserved or incorporated the common law of war authority for military commissions.

Recall that the Court found that the AUMF authorized the military detention of Yaser Hamdi. *See* Hamdi v. Rumsfeld, 542 U.S. 507 (2004), *supra* p. 359. Why doesn't it also authorize trial of Hamdan by military commission, especially since it was enacted after Article 21? Alternatively, why doesn't the DTA authorize such a trial?

4. ***The Law-of-War Limits on Military Commissions.*** Article 21 is a two-headed coin: if it incorporates the common law of war and thus authorizes military commissions, it also incorporates any jurisdictional and procedural limits set by that law. What are they? By what constitutional authority can Congress directly, or by implication, impose any limits on the President's use of military commissions?

One law-of-war limit is temporal — military commission jurisdiction is only for charges for acts committed within the period of war. When did that period commence? If it commenced by attack, was the attack on 9/11 or on the earliest date that al Qaeda attacked U.S. persons or property? Is Justice Thomas correct in arguing that *The Prize Cases* commits this decision to the President's conclusive discretion? If Congress took a different view by enacting the AUMF and referring to the 9/11 attacks, which branch prevails? *See generally* Barbara Salazar Torreon, *Periods of War* (Cong. Res. Serv. RS21405), May 1, 2006.

Even if the AUMF controls, why doesn't its language targeting those whom the President "determines *planned*, authorized, committed, or *aided* the terrorist attacks that occurred on September 11, 2001," *supra* p. 59 (emphasis added), justify trying Hamdan by military commission for conspiracy? *See* Stephen J. Ellmann, *The "Rule of Law" and the Military Commission*, 51 N.Y.L. Sch. L. Rev. (forthcoming 2007), *available at* http://ssrn.com/abstract= 939603.

5. ***The UCMJ and the Uniformity Principle.*** Article 36 of the UCMJ authorizes the President to prescribe procedures for military commissions. *See generally* Jennifer Elsea, *The Department of Defense Rules for Military Commissions: Analysis of Procedural Rules and Comparison with Proposed Legislation and the Uniform Code of Military Justice* (Cong. Res. Serv. RL31600), Aug. 4, 2005. What two restrictions does it place on the President's procedural power? Why weren't these restrictions met by sections 1(f) and 1(g) of the Military Order of November 13, 2001? See *supra* pp. 559-560. If the President had simply added "or the procedures of courts-martial recognized by the UCMJ" at the end of section 1(f), would that have satisfied the restriction? If not, what else would he have to find?

6. ***The Geneva Conventions.*** International treaties also impose procedural law-of-war limitations on military commissions. The majority in *Hamdan* held that Common Article 3 of the Geneva Conventions of 1949 applied to the conflict with al Qaeda. It requires trial by a tribunal that is "regularly constituted. . . ." Why doesn't the majority think that a military commission established by the President's military order and operating under procedures promulgated with his authority is such a court? How are courts "regularly constituted" in the United States? Could a military commission ever be "regularly constituted"? What is Justice Alito's answer to these questions?

Common Article 3 also forbids "cruel treatment and torture," as well as "outrages upon personal dignity, in particular humiliating and degrading treatment." See *supra* p. 408. Does Common Article 3 now clearly govern investigatory torture of persons captured in the conflict against al Qaeda, or can you distinguish *Hamdan*?

7. ***Military Commission Procedures and Due Process.*** In In re Yamashita, 327 U.S. 1 (1946), a military commission gave General Yamashita less than three weeks to prepare for a massive trial that ultimately heard more than 200 witnesses. The commission permitted the government to add 59 new specifications to the 64 pending specifications just two days before trial, then denied Yamashita's defense any extra time to meet them; it denied him access to the Army's investigative reports that might have contained exculpatory materials; it admitted the rankest hearsay; and it even cut back cross-examination "as a means of saving time." *See* Stephen B. Ives Jr., *Vengeance Did Not Deliver Justice*, Wash. Post, Dec. 30, 2001, at B2. Most observers concluded that Yamashita did not receive a fair trial, but the Supreme Court refused to review the commission's rulings on the evidence or its conduct of the proceedings and therefore found it "unnecessary to consider what, in other situations, the Fifth Amendment might require." *Yamashita*, 327 U.S. at 23.

Justice Murphy dissented vehemently:

The immutable rights of the individual, including those secured by the due process clause of the Fifth Amendment, belong not alone to the members of those nations that excel on the battlefield or that subscribe to the democratic ideology. They belong to every person in the world, victor or vanquished, whatever may be his race, color or beliefs. They rise above any status of belligerency or outlawry. They survive any popular passion or frenzy of the moment. No court or legislature or executive, not even the mightiest army in the world, can destroy them. . . .

The failure of the military commission to obey the dictates of the due process requirements of the Fifth Amendment is apparent in this case. . . . No military necessity or other emergency demanded the suspension of the safeguards of due process. Yet petitioner was rushed to trial under an improper charge, given insufficient time to prepare an adequate defense, deprived of the benefits of some of the most elementary rules of evidence, and summarily sentenced to be hanged. [*Id.* at 27-28.]

Justice Rutledge agreed with Justice Murphy in dissent.

Does the Fifth Amendment apply to trial by military commission? Does it depend on where the defendant is captured or whether the military commission sits here or abroad? *See* Rasul v. Bush, 542 U.S. 466, 483 n.15 (2004), *supra* p. 326; Zadvydas v. Davis, 533 U.S. 678, 693 (2001) ("[T]he Due Process Clause applies to all 'persons' within the United States, including aliens, whether their presence here is lawful, temporary, or permanent."); *cf.* United States v. Verdugo-Urquidez, 494 U.S. 259 (1990), *supra* p. 270.

The District Court found it unnecessary to reach the question whether Hamdan has any constitutional rights, although it noted that the Supreme Court's decision in *Rasul* "may contain some hint that non-citizens held at Guantanamo Bay have some Constitutional protection." 344 F. Supp. 2d 152, 173 n.19 (D.D.C. 2004), *rev'd*, 415 F.3d 33 (D.C. Cir. 2005), *rev'd and remanded*, 126 S. Ct. 2749 (2006). The question of Hamdan's right to due process, if any, was therefore not before the Supreme Court.

In In re Guantanamo Detainee Cases, 355 F. Supp. 2d 443 (D.D.C. 2005), *vacated by* Boumediene v. Bush, 476 F.3d 981 (D.C. Cir.), *cert. denied*, 127 S. Ct. 1478 (2007), however, Judge Joyce Hens Green found that the Due Process Clause applied to the procedures followed in combatant status review tribunals (CSRTs) for detainees held at the Guantánamo Bay Naval Base. *Contra*, Khalid v. Bush, 355 F. Supp. 2d 311 (D.D.C. 2005), *vacated by* Boumediene v. Bush, *supra*. If Judge Green is right, would the Due Process Clause apply also to military commission trials held at Guantánamo Bay? She noted that the military commission procedures, unlike the CSRT procedures, authorize withholding of classified information only from the defendant, not from defense counsel. Would this difference save a commission hearing from a due process challenge, if due process applied to military commission proceedings?

A strict reading of the November 13 Military Order might suggest that military commissions could use information obtained through torture or coercion, if it "would have probative value to a reasonable person." Military Order of Nov. 13, 2001, §4(c)(3), *supra* p. 561. If a military commission relies on such evidence, would it violate due process?

8. ***Hampering the President.*** Does the Court's ruling undermine the nation's ability to prevent future attacks? *See* John Yoo, *How We Fight*, Legal Times, Feb. 5, 2007, at 44 (characterizing *Hamdan* as a "misguided effort[] to second-guess the president's wartime decisions," "an unprecedented attempt by the Court to rewrite the law of war and intrude into warfare policies and operations" that "ignored, creatively misread, or silently overruled the Court's World War II cases. . . ."). As we see below, Congress responded by passing the Military Commissions Act of 2006 (MCA), Pub. L. No. 109-366, 120 Stat. 2636. If the MCA gives the President what he wants, what, if anything, was accomplished by the *Hamdan* decision?

9. ***Steel Seizure for Our Times?*** What lesson does *Hamdan* teach for exercises of presidential power when Congress is silent or has legislated to the contrary? What lesson, if any, would you draw from *Hamdan* for executive assertions that the President can ignore statutory restrictions on the interrogation of detainees in the war on terror, see *supra* pp. 418, 444, or on the permissible scope of warrantless electronic surveillance of telephone calls by U.S. citizens from the United States abroad? See *supra* pp. 158-159. *See generally* Ellmann, *supra* p. 585.

# C.  THE MILITARY COMMISSIONS ACT OF 2006

Congress responded quickly to the *Hamdan* decision by enacting the following act.

## MILITARY COMMISSIONS ACT OF 2006

Pub. L. No. 109-366, 120 Stat. 2636 (codified in scattered sections of 10 U.S.C.)

**Section 1. Short Title.** . . .

(a) Short Title—This Act may be cited as the Military Commissions Act of 2006. . . .

**Sec. 2. Construction of Presidential Authority to Establish Military Commissions.**

The authority to establish military commissions under chapter 47A of title 10, United States Code, as added by section 3(a), may not be construed to alter or limit the authority of the President under the Constitution of the United States and laws of the United States to establish military commissions for areas declared to be under martial law or in occupied territories should circumstances so require.

**Sec. 3. Military Commissions.** . . .

[Amending Subtitle A of 10 U.S.C. to insert after Chapter 47 a new Chapter 47A, Military Commissions.]

## Chapter 47A—Military Commissions
## Subchapter I—General Provisions
### §948a. Definitions

In this chapter:

(1) Unlawful enemy combatant. —

(A) The term "unlawful enemy combatant" means—

(i) a person who has engaged in hostilities or who has purposefully and materially supported hostilities against the United States or its co-belligerents who is not a lawful enemy combatant (including a person who is part of the Taliban, al Qaeda, or associated forces); or

(ii) a person who, before, on, or after the date of the enactment of the Military Commissions Act of 2006, has been determined to be an unlawful enemy combatant by a Combatant Status Review Tribunal or another competent tribunal established under the authority of the President or the Secretary of Defense.

(B) Co-belligerent—In this paragraph, the term "co-belligerent," with respect to the United States, means any State or armed force joining and directly engaged with the United States in hostilities or directly supporting hostilities against a common enemy.

(2) Lawful enemy combatant. —The term "lawful enemy combatant" means a person who is—

(A) a member of the regular forces of a State party engaged in hostilities against the United States;

(B) a member of a militia, volunteer corps, or organized resistance movement belonging to a State party engaged in such hostilities, which are under responsible command, wear a fixed distinctive sign recognizable at a distance, carry their arms openly, and abide by the law of war; or

(C) a member of a regular armed force who professes allegiance to a government engaged in such hostilities, but not recognized by the United States.

(3) Alien. —The term "alien" means a person who is not a citizen of the United States. . . .

### §948b. Military commissions generally

(a) Purpose. —This chapter establishes procedures governing the use of military commissions to try alien unlawful enemy combatants engaged in hostilities against the United States for violations of the law of war and other offenses triable by military commission.

(b) Authority for Military Commissions under This Chapter. — The President is authorized to establish military commissions under this chapter for offenses triable by military commission as provided in this chapter[2]. . . .

(f) Status of Commissions under Common Article 3. — A military commission established under this chapter is a regularly constituted court, affording all the necessary "judicial guarantees which are recognized as indispensable by civilized peoples" for purposes of common Article 3 of the Geneva Conventions.

(g) Geneva Conventions Not Establishing Source of Rights. — No alien unlawful enemy combatant subject to trial by military commission under this chapter may invoke the Geneva Conventions as a source of rights.

### §948c. Persons subject to military commissions

Any alien unlawful enemy combatant is subject to trial by military commission under this chapter.

### §948d. Jurisdiction of military commissions

(a) Jurisdiction. — A military commission under this chapter shall have jurisdiction to try any offense made punishable by this chapter or the law of war when committed by an alien unlawful enemy combatant before, on, or after September 11, 2001.

(b) Lawful Enemy Combatants. — Military commissions under this chapter shall not have jurisdiction over lawful enemy combatants. . . .

(c) Determination of Unlawful Enemy Combatant Status Dispositive. — A finding, whether before, on, or after the date of the enactment of the Military Commissions Act of 2006, by a Combatant Status Review Tribunal or another competent tribunal established under the authority of the President or the Secretary of Defense that a person is an unlawful enemy combatant is dispositive for purposes of jurisdiction for trial by military commission under this chapter. . . .

### Subchapter III — Pre-Trial Procedure . . .

### §948r. Compulsory self-incrimination prohibited; treatment of statements obtained by torture and other statements

(a) In General. — No person shall be required to testify against himself at a proceeding of a military commission under this chapter.

(b) Exclusion of Statements Obtained by Torture. — A statement obtained by use of torture shall not be admissible in a military commission under this chapter, except against a person accused of torture as evidence that the statement was made.

(c) Statements Obtained before Enactment of Detainee Treatment Act of 2005. — A statement obtained before December 30, 2005 (the date of the enactment of the Defense [*sic*] Treatment Act of 2005) in which the degree of coercion is disputed may be admitted only if the military judge finds that —

---

[2. The President exercised this authority by Executive Order No. 13,425, *Trial of Alien Unlawful Enemy Combatants by Military Commission*, 72 Fed. Reg. 7737 (Feb. 14, 2007), superseding the provisions of the Military Order of Nov. 13, 2001, that relate to military commissions.]

(1) the totality of the circumstances renders the statement reliable and possessing sufficient probative value; and

(2) the interests of justice would best be served by admission of the statement into evidence.

(d) Statements Obtained after Enactment of Detainee Treatment Act of 2005. — A statement obtained on or after December 30, 2005 (the date of the enactment of the Defense [*sic*] Treatment Act of 2005) in which the degree of coercion is disputed may be admitted only if the military judge finds that —

(1) the totality of the circumstances renders the statement reliable and possessing sufficient probative value;

(2) the interests of justice would best be served by admission of the statement into evidence; and

(3) the interrogation methods used to obtain the statement do not amount to cruel, inhuman, or degrading treatment prohibited by section 1003 of the Detainee Treatment Act of 2005. . . .

## Subchapter IV — Trial Procedure

### §949a. Rules

(a) Procedures and Rules of Evidence. — Pretrial, trial, and post-trial procedures, including elements and modes of proof, for cases triable by military commission under this chapter may be prescribed by the Secretary of Defense, in consultation with the Attorney General. Such procedures shall, so far as the Secretary considers practicable or consistent with military or intelligence activities, apply the principles of law and the rules of evidence in trial by general courts-martial. Such procedures and rules of evidence may not be contrary to or inconsistent with this chapter.

(b) Rules for Military Commission. —

(1) Notwithstanding any departures from the law and the rules of evidence in trial by general courts-martial authorized by subsection (a), the procedures and rules of evidence in trials by military commission under this chapter shall include the following:

(A) The accused shall be permitted to present evidence in his defense, to cross-examine the witnesses who testify against him, and to examine and respond to evidence admitted against him on the issue of guilt or innocence and for sentencing, as provided for by this chapter.

(B) The accused shall be present at all sessions of the military commission (other than those for deliberations or voting), except when excluded under section 949d of this title.

(C) The accused shall receive the assistance of counsel. . . .

(D) The accused shall be permitted to represent himself. . . .

(2) In establishing procedures and rules of evidence for military commission proceedings, the Secretary of Defense may prescribe the following provisions:

(A) Evidence shall be admissible if the military judge determines that the evidence would have probative value to a reasonable person.

(B) Evidence shall not be excluded from trial by military commission on the grounds that the evidence was not seized pursuant to a search warrant or other authorization.

(C) A statement of the accused that is otherwise admissible shall not be excluded from trial by military commission on grounds of alleged coercion or compulsory self-incrimination so long as the evidence complies with the provisions of section 948r of this title. . . .

(E)(i) Except as provided in clause (ii), hearsay evidence not otherwise admissible under the rules of evidence applicable in trial by general courts-martial may be admitted in a trial by military commission if the proponent of the evidence makes known to the adverse party, sufficiently in advance to provide the adverse party with a fair opportunity to meet the evidence, the intention of the proponent to offer the evidence, and the particulars of the evidence (including information on the general circumstances under which the evidence was obtained). The disclosure of evidence under the preceding sentence is subject to the requirements and limitations applicable to the disclosure of classified information in section 949j(c) of this title. . . .

(ii) Hearsay evidence not otherwise admissible under the rules of evidence applicable in trial by general courts-martial shall not be admitted in a trial by military commission if the party opposing the admission of the evidence demonstrates that the evidence is unreliable or lacking in probative value.

(F) The military judge shall exclude any evidence the probative value of which is substantially outweighed —

(i) by the danger of unfair prejudice, confusion of the issues, or misleading the commission; or

(ii) by considerations of undue delay, waste of time, or needless presentation of cumulative evidence. . . .

## §949d. Sessions . . .

(d) Closure of Proceedings. —

(1) The military judge may close to the public all or part of the proceedings of a military commission under this chapter, but only in accordance with this subsection.

(2) The military judge may close to the public all or a portion of the proceedings under paragraph (1) only upon making a specific finding that such closure is necessary to —

(A) protect information the disclosure of which could reasonably be expected to cause damage to the national security, including intelligence or law enforcement sources, methods, or activities; or

(B) ensure the physical safety of individuals.

(3) A finding under paragraph (2) may be based upon a presentation, including a presentation ex parte or in camera, by either trial counsel or defense counsel.

(e) Exclusion of Accused from Certain Proceedings. — The military judge may exclude the accused from any portion of a proceeding upon a determination that, after being warned by the military judge, the accused persists in conduct that justifies exclusion from the courtroom —

(1) to ensure the physical safety of individuals; or

(2) to prevent disruption of the proceedings by the accused.

(f) Protection of Classified Information. —

(1) National security privilege. —

(A) Classified information shall be protected and is privileged from disclosure if disclosure would be detrimental to the national security. The rule in the preceding sentence applies to all stages of the proceedings of military commissions under this chapter.

(B) The privilege referred to in subparagraph (A) may be claimed by the head of the executive or military department or government agency concerned based on a finding by the head of that department or agency that —

(i) the information is properly classified; and

(ii) disclosure of the information would be detrimental to the national security. . . .

(2) Introduction of classified information. —

(A) Alternatives to disclosure. — To protect classified information from disclosure, the military judge, upon motion of trial counsel, shall authorize, to the extent practicable —

(i) the deletion of specified items of classified information from documents to be introduced as evidence before the military commission;

(ii) the substitution of a portion or summary of the information for such classified documents; or

(iii) the substitution of a statement of relevant facts that the classified information would tend to prove.

(B) Protection of sources, methods, or activities. — The military judge, upon motion of trial counsel, shall permit trial counsel to introduce otherwise admissible evidence before the military commission, while protecting from disclosure the sources, methods, or activities by which the United States acquired the evidence if the military judge finds that (i) the sources, methods, or activities by which the United States acquired the evidence are classified, and (ii) the evidence is reliable. The military judge may require trial counsel to present to the military commission and the defense, to the extent practicable and consistent with national security, an unclassified summary of the sources, methods, or activities by which the United States acquired the evidence.

(C) Assertion of national security privilege at trial — During the examination of any witness, trial counsel may object to any question, line of inquiry, or motion to admit evidence that would require the disclosure of classified information. Following such an objection, the military judge shall take suitable action to safeguard such classified information. Such action may include the review of trial counsel's claim of privilege by the military judge in camera and on an ex parte basis, and the delay of proceedings to permit trial counsel to consult with the department or agency concerned as to whether the national security privilege should be asserted.

(3) Consideration of privilege and related materials. — A claim of privilege under this subsection, and any materials submitted in support thereof, shall, upon request of the Government, be considered by the military judge in camera and shall not be disclosed to the accused. . . .

### §949j. Opportunity to obtain witnesses and other evidence

(a) Right of Defense Counsel. — Defense counsel in a military commission under this chapter shall have a reasonable opportunity to obtain witnesses and other evidence as provided in regulations prescribed by the Secretary of Defense.

(b) Process for Compulsion. — Process issued in a military commission under this chapter to compel witnesses to appear and testify and to compel the production of other evidence —

(1) shall be similar to that which courts of the United States having criminal jurisdiction may lawfully issue; and

(2) shall run to any place where the United States shall have jurisdiction thereof.

(c) Protection of Classified Information. —

(1) With respect to the discovery obligations of trial counsel under this section, the military judge, upon motion of trial counsel, shall authorize, to the extent practicable —

(A) the deletion of specified items of classified information from documents to be made available to the accused;

(B) the substitution of a portion or summary of the information for such classified documents; or

(C) the substitution of a statement admitting relevant facts that the classified information would tend to prove.

(2) The military judge, upon motion of trial counsel, shall authorize trial counsel, in the course of complying with discovery obligations under this section, to protect from disclosure the sources, methods, or activities by which the United States acquired evidence if the military judge finds that the sources, methods, or activities by which the United States acquired such evidence are classified. The military judge may require trial counsel to provide, to the extent practicable, an unclassified summary of the sources, methods, or activities by which the United States acquired such evidence.

(d) Exculpatory Evidence. —

(1) As soon as practicable, trial counsel shall disclose to the defense the existence of any evidence known to trial counsel that reasonably tends to exculpate the accused. Where exculpatory evidence is classified,

the accused shall be provided with an adequate substitute in accordance with the procedures under subsection (c).

(2) In this subsection, the term "evidence known to trial counsel," in the case of exculpatory evidence, means exculpatory evidence that the prosecution would be required to disclose in a trial by general court-martial under chapter 47 of this title. . . .

### Subchapter VI—Post-Trial Procedure and Review of Military Commissions . . .

### §950b. Review by the convening authority . . .

[The MCA authorizes the convening authority to reconsider the findings and sentence of the military commission, but prohibits it from reconsidering findings of not guilty or increasing the severity of a sentence.]

### §950c. Appellate referral; waiver or withdrawal of appeal

(a) Automatic Referral for Appellate Review. — Except as provided under subsection (b), in each case in which the final decision of a military commission (as approved by the convening authority) includes a finding of guilty, the convening authority shall refer the case to the Court of Military Commission Review. Any such referral shall be made in accordance with procedures prescribed under regulations of the Secretary. . . .

### §950f. Review by Court of Military Commission Review

(a) Establishment. — The Secretary of Defense shall establish a Court of Military Commission Review which shall be composed of one or more panels, and each such panel shall be composed of not less than three appellate military judges. For the purpose of reviewing military commission decisions under this chapter, the court may sit in panels or as a whole in accordance with rules prescribed by the Secretary. . . .

(c) Cases to Be Reviewed. — The Court of Military Commission Review, in accordance with procedures prescribed under regulations of the Secretary, shall review the record in each case that is referred to the Court by the convening authority under section 950c of this title with respect to any matter of law raised by the accused.

(d) Scope of Review — In a case reviewed by the Court of Military Commission Review under this section, the Court may act only with respect to matters of law.

### §950g. Review by the United States Court of Appeals for the District of Columbia Circuit and the Supreme Court

(a) Exclusive Appellate Jurisdiction. —

(1)(A) Except as provided in subparagraph (B), the United States Court of Appeals for the District of Columbia Circuit shall have exclusive jurisdiction to determine the validity of a final judgment rendered by a military commission (as approved by the convening authority) under this chapter. . . .

(b) Standard for Review. — In a case reviewed by it under this section, the Court of Appeals may act only with respect to matters of law.

(c) Scope of Review. — The jurisdiction of the Court of Appeals on an appeal under subsection (a) shall be limited to the consideration of —

(1) whether the final decision was consistent with the standards and procedures specified in this chapter; and

(2) to the extent applicable, the Constitution and the laws of the United States.

(d) Supreme Court. — The Supreme Court may review by writ of certiorari the final judgment of the Court of Appeals pursuant to section 1257 of title 28. . . .

### §950j. Finality or proceedings, findings, and sentences . . .

(b) Provisions of Chapter Sole Basis for Review of Military Commission Procedures and Actions. — Except as otherwise provided in this chapter and notwithstanding any other provision of law (including section 2241 of title 28 or any other habeas corpus provision), no court, justice, or judge shall have jurisdiction to hear or consider any claim or cause of action whatsoever, including any action pending on or filed after the date of the enactment of the Military Commissions Act of 2006, relating to the prosecution, trial, or judgment of a military commission under this chapter, including challenges to the lawfulness of procedures of military commissions under this chapter.

### Subchapter VII. Punitive Matters

### §950p. Statement of substantive offenses

(a) Purpose. — The provisions of this subchapter codify offenses that have traditionally been triable by military commissions. This chapter does not establish new crimes that did not exist before its enactment, but rather codifies those crimes for trial by military commission. . . .

### §950v. Crimes triable by military commissions . . .

(b) Offenses. — The following offenses shall be triable by military commission under this chapter at any time without limitation: . . .

(2) Attacking civilians. — Any person subject to this chapter who intentionally engages in an attack upon a civilian population as such, or individual civilians not taking active part in hostilities, shall be punished, if death results to one or more of the victims, by death or such other punishment as a military commission under this chapter may direct, and, if death does not result to any of the victims, by such punishment, other than death, as a military commission under this chapter may direct.

(3) Attacking civilian objects. — Any person subject to this chapter who intentionally engages in an attack upon a civilian object that is not a

military objective shall be punished as a military commission under this chapter may direct. . . .

(24) Terrorism.—Any person subject to this chapter who intentionally kills or inflicts great bodily harm on one or more protected persons, or intentionally engages in an act that evinces a wanton disregard for human life, in a manner calculated to influence or affect the conduct of government or civilian population by intimidation or coercion, or to retaliate against government conduct, shall be punished, if death results to one or more of the victims, by death or such other punishment as a military commission under this chapter may direct, and, if death does not result to any of the victims, by such punishment, other than death, as a military commission under this chapter may direct.

(25) Providing material support for terrorism.—

(A) Offense.—Any person subject to this chapter who provides material support or resources, knowing or intending that they are to be used in preparation for, or in carrying out, an act of terrorism (as set forth in paragraph (24)), or who intentionally provides material support or resources to an international terrorist organization engaged in hostilities against the United States, knowing that such organization has engaged or engages in terrorism (as so set forth), shall be punished as a military commission under this chapter may direct.

(B) Material support or resources defined.—In this paragraph, the term "material support or resources" has the meaning given that term in section 2339A(b) of title 18. . . .

(28) Conspiracy.—Any person subject to this chapter who conspires to commit one or more substantive offenses triable by military commission under this chapter, and who knowingly does any overt act to effect the object of the conspiracy, shall be punished, if death results to one or more of the victims, by death or such other punishment as a military commission under this chapter may direct, and, if death does not result to any of the victims, by such punishment, other than death, as a military commission under this chapter may direct. . . .

### Sec. 5. Treaty Obligations not Establishing Grounds for Certain Claims.

(a) In General—No person may invoke the Geneva Conventions or any protocols thereto in any habeas corpus or other civil action or proceeding to which the United States, or a current or former officer, employee, member of the Armed Forces, or other agent of the United States is a party as a source of rights in any court of the United States or its States or territories. . . .

### Sec. 6. Implementation of Treaty Obligations.

(a) Implementation of Treaty Obligations.—

(1) In general.—The acts enumerated in subsection (d) of section 2441 of title 18, United States Code, as added by subsection (b) of this section, and in subsection (c) of this section, constitute violations of

common Article 3 of the Geneva Conventions prohibited by United States law.

(2) Prohibition on grave breaches. — The provisions of section 2441 of title 18, United States Code, as amended by this section, fully satisfy the obligation under Article 129 of the Third Geneva Convention for the United States to provide effective penal sanctions for grave breaches which are encompassed in common Article 3 in the context of an armed conflict not of an international character. No foreign or international source of law shall supply a basis for a rule of decision in the courts of the United States in interpreting the prohibitions enumerated in subsection (d) of such section 2441.

(3) Interpretation by the President. —

(A) As provided by the Constitution and by this section, the President has the authority for the United States to interpret the meaning and application of the Geneva Conventions and to promulgate higher standards and administrative regulations for violations of treaty obligations which are not grave breaches of the Geneva Conventions.

(B) The President shall issue interpretations described by subparagraph (A) by Executive Order published in the Federal Register.

(C) Any Executive Order published under this paragraph shall be authoritative (except as to grave breaches of common Article 3) as a matter of United States law, in the same manner as other administrative regulations.

(D) Nothing in this section shall be construed to affect the constitutional functions and responsibilities of Congress and the judicial branch of the United States. . . .

## NOTES AND QUESTIONS

1. ***Unlawful Enemy Combatants.*** As we noted above, some scholars have argued that "unlawful enemy combatant" is not a legal term of art; it is a term invented by the Bush administration. *See* Peter Jan Honigsberg, *Chasing "Enemy Combatants" and Circumventing International Law: A License for Sanctioned Abuse*, 12 UCLA J. Intl. L. & For. Aff. (forthcoming 2007), *available at* http://ssrn.com/abstract=942058. Congress has now codified the term. But is the definition clear? Would it include members of Hezbollah if they were to conduct a terrorist attack against the United States? What about a permanent resident alien not affiliated with al Qaeda who conducts an attack on a subway in New York? What about members of a Colombian drug gang who attack a patrol of Colombian soldiers and their U.S. military advisors? What are the "hostilities" contemplated by the MCA? The War Powers Resolution, 50 U.S.C. §1541-1548 (2000), declares that the constitutional powers of the President as Commander in Chief may be exercised to introduce U.S. armed forces into "hostilities" only pursuant to a declaration of war, a specific statutory authorization, or a national emergency created by an attack on the United States, its territories or

possessions, or its armed forces. *Id.* §1541(c). Must the "hostilities" contemplated by the MCA definition also be authorized by Congress absent an attack?

2. ***Clear Statement?*** In Greene v. McElroy, 360 U.S. 474, 507 (1959), the Supreme Court declared that it will not assume that Congress or the President has authorized an action of "doubtful constitutionality" implicating individual rights, absent a clear statement, in order to ensure that such actions are the product of "careful and purposeful consideration by those responsible for enacting and implementing our laws." On the other hand, defenders of presidential power have argued that statutes delegating or limiting national security or foreign affairs authority "must be construed . . . to avoid any potential conflict between [the statute] and the President's Article II authority as Commander in Chief." *See, e.g.,* Letter from William E. Moschella (Asst. Attorney General) to The Honorable Pat Roberts, Chairman, S. Select Comm. on Intelligence et al., Dec. 22, 2005, at 4, *available at* http://www.fas.org/irp/agency/doj/fisa/doj122205.pdf (*supra* p. 157). The latter view poses "a clear statement principle of its own — a principle that requires an explicit statement from the national legislature if it seeks to cabin the President's power to protect national security in a time of war." Cass R. Sunstein, *Clear Statement Principles and National Security: Hamdan and Beyond,* 2007 S. Ct. Rev. (forthcoming), *available at* http://ssrn.com/abstract=922406. Which rule — a clear statement of authorization or a clear statement of limitation — does the *Hamdan* majority apply? *See id.* ("the prevailing view in *Hamdan* seems to be captured in a single idea: *If the President seeks to depart from standard adjudicative forms through the use of military tribunals, the departure must be authorized by an explicit and focused decision from the national legislature*") (emphasis in original). Which rule did the Court apply in Hamdi v. Rumsfeld, 542 U.S. 507 (2004) (*supra* p. 359)? Can the decisions be reconciled? *See* Sunstein, *supra* (perhaps, because detention of enemy combatants is more of an incident of the use of military force than is the adjudication of their guilt or innocence).

3. ***Regularly Constituted Court and Common Article 3.*** Is a military commission a "regularly constituted court" for purposes of Common Article 3? Does the finding in 10 U.S.C. §948b(f) establish that it is? Even if that provision is not conclusive, could any unlawful enemy combatant invoke Common Article 3, in light of 10 U.S.C. §948b(g) and MCA §5(a)? Are *these* provisions conclusive? Even if the courts retain the power to decide these questions for themselves, would an executive order interpreting Common Article 3 (or any other part of the Geneva Conventions) be "authoritative (except as to grave breaches of Common Article 3) as a matter of United States Law," as Congress asserted in MCA §6(a)(3)(C)? Does "authoritative" mean controlling on the courts? *See id.* §6(a)(3)(D). In short, which branch has the final say in interpreting treaties of the United States? In interpreting customary international law? If your answer is the courts, what weight should they give the President's "authoritative" interpretation?

Leaving both Congress's and the President's judgments to one side, is the MCA military commission "regularly constituted"? It is constituted by statute, of course. But four justices in *Hamdan* also pointed to another benchmark of "regularity" — "an acceptable degree of independence from the executive. . . ." 126 S. Ct. at 2804 (Kennedy, J., concurring in part). *See* Ellmann, *supra* p. 585. Does the MCA military commission have that degree of independence? What is it about the MCA military commission that gives it more independence than the *Hamdan* military commission had?

4. ***Due Process.*** As noted above, p. 586, it is not clear whether aliens tried by U.S. military commissions abroad have due process rights. Assuming that they do or that they are entitled to equivalent procedural rights by international law, do the MCA's provisions for use of statements obtained by torture, 10 U.S.C. §948r(b)-(c), satisfy due process? What about the provision for admission of hearsay evidence, 10 U.S.C. §949a(2)? *See generally* Eun Young Choi, *Veritas, Not Vengeance: An Examination of the Evidentiary Rules for Military Commissions in the War Against Terrorism*, 42 Harv. C.R.-C.L. L. Rev. 139 (2007). What about the provision for closing hearings, 10 U.S.C. §949d(d)? *See infra* pp. 618-626 (regarding constitutionality of closed special interest immigration proceedings). The provision for introduction of classified evidence, 10 U.S.C. §949d(f)(2)? *See supra* pp. 530-540 (regarding CIPA); James Nicholas Boeving, *The Right to Be Present Before Military Commissions and Federal Courts: Protecting National Security in an Age of Classified Information*, 30 Harv. J.L. & Pub. Poly. (forthcoming 2007). The provision for access to discovery and witnesses, 10 U.S.C. §949j? *See supra* pp. 540-555 (regarding access in criminal courts). *See generally* Douglas A. Hass, *Crafting Military Commissions Post-*Hamdan: *The Military Commissions Act of 2006*, 82 Indiana L.J. (forthcoming 2007) (arguing that the MCA fails to uphold the fairness standards expressed by the Court); *cf.* Jennifer K. Elsea, *The Military Commissions Act of 2006: Analysis of Procedural Rules and Comparison with Previous DOD Rules and the Uniform Code of Military Justice* (Cong. Res. Serv. RL33688), Oct. 12, 2006.

5. ***War (and Other) Crimes Triable by Military Commission.*** Recall that the Supreme Court held that conspiracy was not a crime traditionally cognizable by military commission but also that Congress had not used its power to "define and punish" (U.S. Const. art. I, §8, cl. 10) in order to make conspiracy a war crime. It has now, in 10 U.S.C. §950v(b)(28). But Congress has also made providing material support a crime triable by military commission. *Id.* §950v(b)(25). Does this mean that any alien who supplies material support to a foreign terrorist organization can now be tried by military commission instead of a criminal court? What is the limiting factor, if any, in the material support provision of the MCA? Is it limiting enough?

Recall that there was speculation that the government might drop its prosecution of the so-called "twentieth hijacker," Zacarias Moussaoui, and try him instead by military commission, and that it actually did drop its case against material support defendant al-Marri and placed him in military detention. See *supra* p. 554-555. Does the MCA now supply statutory authority for forum switches? If Congress intended to authorize military trial of aliens arrested in the United States for giving material support to foreign terrorist organizations engaged in hostilities with the United States, is this provision constitutional? *Cf. Milligan, supra* p. 349.

6. **Why Not Before?** For better or for worse, the MCA is a comprehensive delegation of authority for the use of military commissions to try alien "unlawful enemy combatants" in the war on terror. It arguably moots most questions of inherent executive authority, locating the President's authority at its apex in that his authority now "includes all that he possesses in his own right plus all that Congress can delegate." Youngstown Sheet & Tube Co. v. Sawyer, 343 U.S. 579, 635 (1952) (Jackson, J., concurring). Moreover, it resolves some difficult policy issues that the Military Order of November 13, 2001, and its progeny either left open or vacillated about.

What, if anything, does this experience teach about the relative competencies of the political branches? Which branch should make counterterrorism law or policy when there is time for either branch to act? Should the President have sought statutory authority before 2006? Should Congress have waited for him to ask? How would you judge the relative performance of the branches in providing for military trial of alien terrorist suspects? How would you describe the role of the Supreme Court in producing the MCA? *Compare* Ellmann, *supra* p. 585 ("It seems fair to say that besides telling us that the President does not have a blank check, the Court [in *Hamdan*] is also saying that Congress needs to get back in the check-writing business before the courts will permit what otherwise appear to be breaches of human rights."), *with* Yoo, *supra* p. 587 (the Court engaged in a misguided "power grab" that required and justified "a sharp rebuke" by Congress).

# CHAPTER 19

# *TRYING SUSPECTED TERRORISTS AS "SPECIAL INTEREST" IMMIGRANTS*

All 19 of the September 11 hijackers were aliens who had entered the United States legally. Although it is often said that this country is founded on the toil of immigrants, Americans—even some who are themselves immigrants or descendants of immigrants—have frequently perceived threats to national security from legal and illegal immigrants alike. The Alien and Sedition Acts are best known for the Sedition Act, but the Alien Act authorized the President

> at any time during the continuance of this act, to *order* all such *aliens* as he shall judge dangerous to the peace and safety of the United States, or shall have reasonable grounds to suspect are concerned in any treasonable or secret machinations against the government thereof, to depart out of the territory of the United States. . . . [An Act Concerning Aliens, Act of June 25, 1798, 1 Stat. 570, 571 (emphasis in original).]

The widely disliked Alien Act was not renewed, but aliens were made excludable or removable for security reasons under various later laws. *See generally* Michael John Garcia, *Immigration: Terrorist Grounds for Exclusion and Removal of Aliens* (Cong. Res. Serv. RL32564) 3, Sept. 5, 2006.

Almost 200 years after passage of the Alien Act, Congress for the first time expressly added terrorism as a ground for exclusion or deportation. *See* Immigration Act of 1990, Pub. L. No. 101-649, §§601, 602, 104 Stat. 4978, 5069-5070, 5081. In the ensuing years, antiterrorism provisions of the immigration laws were strengthened repeatedly, most notably in the USA Patriot Act, Pub. L. No. 107-56, 115 Stat. 272 (2001), and the REAL ID Act of 2005, Pub. L. No. 109-13, Div. B, 119 Stat. 231, 302.

In Part A of this chapter we explore a case of immigrants threatened with denial of asylum and denial of withholding of deportation on grounds that they engaged in terrorist activity. This case rehearses many of the definitional questions introduced in Chapter 1.

Special interest immigrant proceedings pose unique procedural questions because of the unusual legal status of immigrants. This status reflects Congress's express constitutional power to legislate in the immigration field, the fact that aliens often have loyalties different from those of U.S. citizens, and the risk that aliens may flee the country. One such question is whether, contrary to the prevailing law in criminal courts, secret evidence can be used as a basis for deporting special interest immigrants. We explore this question in Part B.

Another important question is whether deportation proceedings against special interest immigrants may be closed to the public. We explore this question in Part C.

In this chapter we necessarily address only a few of our complex and frequently revised immigration laws that touch on national security. Other aspects of the subjects are explored, for example, in Stephen H. Legomsky, *Immigration and Refugee Law and Policy* 843-914 (4th ed. 2005); *supra* pp. 307-310 (describing civil detention of immigrants in PENTTBOM investigation).

## A.  ARE ALL TERRORISTS A DANGER TO NATIONAL SECURITY?

Presently, an alien is inadmissible or deportable on terror-related grounds if he:

- has engaged in a terrorist activity [defined to include soliciting funds or providing material support for terrorist activity or a terrorist organization];
- is known or reasonably believed by a consular officer, the Attorney General, or the Secretary of Homeland Security to be engaged in or likely to engage in terrorist activity upon entry into the United States;
- has, under circumstances indicating an intention to cause death or serious bodily harm, incited terrorist activity;
- is a representative of (1) a designated or nondesignated terrorist organization [see *supra* pp. 12-21]; or (2) any political, social, or other group that endorses or espouses terrorist activity;
- is a member of (1) any designated terrorist organization . . . , or (2) any nondesignated terrorist organization, unless the alien can demonstrate by clear and convincing evidence that the alien did not know, and should not reasonably have known, that the organization was a terrorist organization;
- is an officer, official, representative, or spokesman of the Palestine Liberation Organization;
- endorses or espouses terrorist activity or persuades others to endorse or espouse terrorist activity or support a terrorist organization; . . .
- has received military-type training, from or on behalf of any organization that, at the time the training was received, was a terrorist organization. [Garcia, *supra*, at 5-6, *citing* 8 U.S.C.A. §1182(a)(3)(B)(i) (West 2005).]

Although some of these terrorism-related grounds for exclusion or deportation raise substantive legal questions similar to those presented by criminal counterterrorist prosecutions, see *supra* pp. 471-493, the following case raises an even more basic question of the relationship of terrorist activity to our national security.

## CHEEMA V. ASHCROFT

United States Court of Appeals, Ninth Circuit, 2004
383 F.3d 848

NOONAN, Circuit Judge. . . . Cheema is a Sikh, born in India in 1958. He is a lawyer and a member of the Sikh Lawyers Association. In 1987, he helped to organize an enormous rally to protest the government of India's decision to divert water from the Punjab. Shortly after this public event, Indian police arrested Cheema, beat him with a wooden stick, and stretched his legs apart until the muscles began to break. He was released ten days later without charges.

In the aftermath in 1987, Cheema gave food and shelter to Gurjeet Singh and Charanjit Singh Channi, whom he describes as leaders in the All India Sikh Student Federation, an organization he describes as nonviolent. The government in its brief characterizes these two men as "well-known terrorists," although its citations to the record showing them to be leaders do not support the characterization of them as terrorists. In January 1989, Cheema was arrested and questioned as to their whereabouts. [Cheema was allegedly tortured, released, re-arrested, tortured again, and released again.] . . .

In August 1990, Cheema fled to Canada and, two months later, entered the United States. He joined the Sikh Youth of America, described by him as supporting the Sikh movement for an independent Khalistan and "very much against any kind of violence." He was elected general secretary of this organization in 1991. Later in 1991, he helped organize the Khalistan Affairs Center, a lobbying office in the United States for the Sikh cause of independence from India. . . .

[Subsequently, Cheema met and worked with Daljit Singh Bittu, who directed a militant wing of a Sikh student organization and was wanted by India for bank robbery and assassination. Cheema raised money in the United States for families that had suffered in the Punjab and individuals injured while trying to cross the border between Pakistan and India, and he told donors to send the money to Bittu. In 1993, Cheema also called the head of the militant Khalistan Commando Force, Paramjit Singh Panjwar, after two bomb blasts in the Punjab, to ask if Panjwar was responsible. When he denied involvement, Cheema told the media. Later, Cheema raised money for the Sikh Defense Fund, which offered legal assistance to Sikhs detained in North America. His wife, Rajwinder Kaur, also sent money from the United States to aid Sikh widows and orphans.]

### Proceedings

On arrival in the United States in May 1993, Cheema and his wife were paroled into the country, but not admitted. [Subsequently they applied for asylum and withholding of deportation under the statute and for relief under the Convention Against Torture [CAT]. See *supra* p. 465. The immigration judge who heard their application relied in part on classified evidence, and ruled against Cheema, but in favor of his wife.] . . .

. . . [Relying solely on the non-classified evidence of record, the Board of Immigration Appeals] held that Cheema had engaged in terrorist activity "by soliciting funds for individuals and groups, i.e. Bittu and Panjwar, that he knew or reasonably should have known or at least had reason to believe had committed terrorist activity;" and that Cheema had given material support to Bittu and Panjwar by connecting calls to them from Sikh militants. The Board further found that his wife had engaged in terrorist activity "by sending money to various Sikh groups . . . she knew or reasonably should have known or had reason to believe had committed or planned to commit terrorist activity."

Contrary to the conclusions of the immigration judge, the Board held that these findings barred withholding of deportation, because the acts of financial support for terrorist persons or groups in India and the facilitation of telephone calls from such persons in India were acts such as to "necessarily endanger the lives, property and welfare of United States citizens and compromise the defense of the United States." The Board also held that the petitioners could not be granted withholding of deportation under CAT but only deferral of removal. . . .

## Analysis

We do not find it necessary to consider the government's use, in the case before the Immigration Judge, of classified material not made available to the petitioners. For the purposes of this decision, we accept the Board's disavowal of consideration of this material.

### A. Statutory Framework

1. *Withholding of Deportation.* INA §241(a)(4)(B) renders deportable "[a]ny alien who has engaged, is engaged, or at any time after entry engages in any terrorist activity (as defined in §212(a)(3)(B)(iii))."

"Terrorist Activity" is defined in INA §212(a)(3)(B)(iii) as:

> [T]o commit an act that the actor knows, or reasonably should know, affords material support, including a safe house, transportation, communications, funds, transfer of funds or other material financial benefit, false documentation or identification, weapons (including chemical, biological, or radiological weapons), explosives, or training—
>
>    (aa) for the commission of a terrorist activity;
>    (bb) to any individual who the actor knows, or reasonably should know, has committed or plans to commit a terrorist activity;
>    (cc) to a terrorist organization described in clause (vi)(I) or (vi)(II); or
>    (dd) to a terrorist organization described in clause (vi)(III), unless the actor can demonstrate that he did not know, and should not reasonably have known, that the act would further the organization's terrorist activity.

*Id.*

Notwithstanding a determination of terrorist activity an alien may be eligible for withholding of deportation or asylum. INA §243, 8 U.S.C. §1253, reads:

(h) Withholding of deportation or return.

(1) The Attorney General shall not deport or return any alien (other than an alien described in section 241(a)(4)(D)) to a country if the Attorney General determines that such alien's life or freedom would be threatened in such country on account of race, religion, nationality, membership in a particular social group, or political opinion.

(2) Paragraph (1) shall not apply to any alien if the Attorney General determines that — . . .

(D) there are reasonable grounds for regarding the alien as a danger to the security of the United States.

. . . For purposes of subparagraph (D), an alien who is described in §241(a)(4)(B) [governing terrorist activity] shall be considered to be an alien for whom there are reasonable grounds for regarding as a danger to the security of the United States. . . .

The statute imposes a two-part analysis: (1) whether an alien engaged in a terrorist activity, and (2) whether there are not reasonable grounds to believe that the alien is a danger to the security of the United States. Having determined that Cheema and his wife engaged in terrorist activity, the Board turned to the second question of whether there are reasonable grounds for regarding them to be "a danger to the security of the United States."

In construing the phrase "danger to the security of the United States," the Board looked to several different definitions of the phrase "national security" but chose not "to adopt any of these definitions wholesale." Instead, the Board created its own test: an alien poses a danger to the security of the United States where the alien acts "in a way which 1) endangers the lives, property, or welfare of United States citizens; 2) compromises the national defense of the United States; or 3) materially damages the foreign relations or economic interests of the United States." We accept for the purposes of this appeal the Board's interpretation of the sense of "national security." . . .

## B. Substantial Evidence

1. *Withholding of deportation.* Under the INA, aliens are rendered ineligible for withholding of deportation if "there are reasonable grounds for regarding them as a danger to the security of the United States." INA §243(h)(2)(D). Aliens who have engaged in terrorist activity are considered a danger to the security of the United States subject to a discretionary waiver. We review whether substantial evidence supports both the finding of terrorist activity and the determination that the alien is a danger to the security of the United States. We may reverse the Board's findings of fact if we are "compelled to conclude to the contrary." 8 U.S.C. §1252(b)(4)(B).

Rajwinder Kaur's actions do not constitute terrorist activity under §212(a)(3)(B)(iii), much less does substantial evidence demonstrate that she is a danger to the security of the United States. The only evidence regarding her donations or activities is her statement that she had "sent money on one or two occasions to . . . women . . . that were widowed or to children that were orphaned." No evidence supplies a link between the donations and any specific organization, let alone Sikh militant organizations. Given that the Board accepted Rajwinder Kaur's testimony as credible, the Board's conclusion that her donations to Indian widows and orphaned children "obviously" and "inherently" posed a danger to the security of the United States stretches speculation to its breaking point. . . .

. . . Not a scrap of evidence shows her to have engaged in terrorist activity as defined in INA §212(a)(3)(B)(iii).

The Board chose to construe some of Cheema's acts as terrorist activity as defined by the INA. Money that he raised did appear to reach Sikh resistance organizations in India. Unfavorable inferences were drawn from his telephone conversations with Sikh militants known to engage in terrorist activities. We are unable to say that we are compelled to reach contrary conclusions. The question remains whether substantial evidence supports the Board's conclusion that there are "reasonable grounds" for regarding Cheema as a danger to our national security.

The Board chose the first criterion of national security, that is, whether Cheema "endangers the lives, property, or welfare of United States citizens." The Board did not address the alternative criteria relating to national defense or foreign relations and economic interests. Our review is limited to the Board's stated grounds for the national security finding. *See SEC v. Chenery Corp.,* 332 U.S. 194, 196 (1947). Our task is to consider whether this conclusion is supported by the requisite substantial evidence.

The Board stated only its conclusion: "It is clear that those who engage in terrorism within the United States, even when that terrorism is not directly aimed at the United States, necessarily endanger the lives, property, and welfare of United States citizens and compromises our national defense." According to the Board, it is "self-evident" that such activities "inherently involve this country in [foreign] conflicts without our leave or agreement" and "create the very real possibility that such conflicts will be brought home to use by their warring factions." . . .

Substantial evidence is required to link the finding of terrorist activity affecting India with one of the criteria relating to our national security. With the extensive resources of the Executive Branch, including the resources of the Departments of Defense, State, Justice, Treasury and others, the INS is in a unique position to provide such evidence. It has not done so. . . .

Contrary to the government's assertion, it is by no means self-evident that a person engaged in extra-territorial or resistance activities — even militant activities — is necessarily a threat to the security of the United States. One country's terrorist can often be another country's freedom-fighter. The Contras in Nicaragua, for instance, used terrorist tactics in an attempt to overthrow the ruling Sandinista government. It would be difficult to conclude, however, without specific evidence, that supporters of the Contras within the United States compromised national defense. The United States itself opposed the Sandinista regime and sent money to assist the Contras. Similarly, the Solidarity Movement that was instrumental in ending Communism in Eastern

Europe was labeled by the Soviet Union as subversive and dangerous, but it can hardly be said that contributors to the Solidarity Movement posed a threat to the lives and property in the United States. We cannot conclude automatically that those individuals who are activists for an independent Tibet are necessarily threats to the United States because they have been labeled by China as insurgents. Without further evidence, it does not follow that an organization that might be a danger to one nation is necessarily a danger to the security of the United States.

History, indeed, is to the contrary. At least since 1848, the year of democratic revolutions in Europe, the United States has been a hotbed of sympathy for revolution in other lands, often with émigrés to this country organizing moral and material support for their countrymen oppressed by European empires such as those of Austria, Britain and Russia. In the twentieth century, active revolutionaries such as De Valera and Ben Gurion worked in the United States for the liberation of their homelands. More recently, foreign anti-Communists living in the United States were active in encouraging and aiding movements against Communist tyranny in the Soviet Union and China. Much of this revolutionary activity would fall under the definition of terrorist activity as the Board interprets the statute. None of it had consequences for the lives and property of American citizens or the national defense, and the slight strains occasionally put on our foreign relations were more than offset by the reputation earned by the United States as a continuing cradle for liberty in other parts of the world.

That terrorist activity affecting a country struggling with strife cannot be equated automatically with an impact on the security of the United States is dramatically illustrated by the case of Nelson Mandela. In 1961, Mandela organized a paramilitary branch of the African National Congress, Umkhonto we Sizwe (MK) or "Spear of the Nation," to conduct guerrilla warfare against the ruling white government. Anthony Sampson, Mandela: The Authorized Biography, Knopf (1999) at 150. He then went into hiding to carry out the MK's mission: "to make government impossible," and began arranging for key leaders and their volunteers to go abroad for training in guerrilla warfare. Sampson at 151, 158. Mandela was convicted by the South African government of treason in 1964 and sentenced to life in prison. In 1986, Congress passed the Comprehensive Anti-Apartheid Act, stating that its goal was to pressure the South African government to release Nelson Mandela from prison. 22 U.S.C. 5011 §101(b)(2) (1986); Sampson at 177. It would not be sensible to conclude that Congress, in aiding a man convicted of treason by his own government, endangered the security of the United States or that the alien supporters of Mandela in this country were all deportable as terrorists endangering our national security.

To be clear, aliens who engage in terrorist activity *may* indeed affect this nation's security, but we cannot conclude that they always do so. Evaluation of this issue requires evidence, not speculation. If the INS, with the impressive resources of the federal government at its disposal, had provided reasons, backed by evidence, for finding Cheema and Rajwinder Kaur to be a threat to the national security of the United States, we would have a different case. But the Board simply does not provide those reasons.

Because the Board erred in determining whether Cheema was a "danger to the security of the United States," we remand to the Board to make that determination using the correct inquiry.

2. *Asylum.* Because we are compelled to conclude that there is no evidence that Kaur engaged in terrorist activity, the Board erred in determining that Kaur is barred from the relief of asylum. . . .

For the reasons stated, Cheema's petitions for withholding of deportation and asylum are REMANDED; the deferral of removal and denial of full relief for him under CAT is AFFIRMED. Rajwinder Kaur's petitions for withholding and for full relief under CAT are GRANTED, and her petition for asylum is REMANDED for the exercise of discretion.

RAWLINSON, Circuit Judge, dissenting: I must respectfully dissent. Our review of asylum rulings made by the BIA has been curtailed in recent years. We may now reverse BIA's factual findings made in the context of ruling on an asylum application only if a contrary finding is *compelled* by the evidence. We must also defer to the BIA's interpretation of immigration law.
Here is what the evidence in this case showed:

- The State Department has identified the Khalistan Commando Force (KCF), headed by Paramjit Singh Panjwar, and the Sikh Student Federation Faction (SSF) headed by Daljit Singh Bittu, as "terrorist Sikh organizations."
- These organizations have engaged in robbery, murder, bombings, kidnappings, threats and general mayhem.
- Bittu has variously been sought for the assassination of relatives of India's Vice-President, the assassination of an Indian Army General, and the largest bank robbery in India's history.
- Bittu distributed weapons to various terrorist organizations, after receiving money from a source in the United States.
- The KCF has taken responsibility for a massacre of bus passengers, who were machine-gunned after the bus was forced from the road, and for a series of car bombings that left 300 dead and 1,200 injured.
- Panjwar and Bittu are described by the Petitioner, Cheema, as close personal friends on whose behalf he has raised thousands of dollars in the United States.
- Cheema has acted as a communications link to Bittu and Panjwar by routing telephone calls through his home in the United States, and thereby avoid[ed] detection by Indian authorities.
- Cheema served as a communications link during the kidnapping of the Romanian ambassador by Sikh terrorists.
- Cheema provided food and shelter to terrorists while they were fugitives from the police.
- Cheema's wife functioned in his stead during his absence.

It is not difficult to connect the dots from Cheema and his wife to Panjwar to Bittu and back again. The BIA's finding that Cheema materially supported terrorist activity is bolstered by substantial evidence, including Cheema's own testimony.

A finding that Cheema provided material support to major international terrorists in turn substantiates the BIA's finding that Cheema and his wife threaten the security of this country. Car bombings, assassinations of government officials, massacres — world wars have begun with less impetus. *See Zenith Radio Corp. v. Matsushita Elec. Indus. Co.*, 494 F. Supp. 1190, 1219 (E.D. Pa. 1980) ("On June 28, 1914, the assassination in Sarajevo of Archduke Franz Ferdinand of Austria-Hungary set off a chain of events that within a few months embroiled all Europe in World War I."); *see also* M. Cherif Bassiouni, *World War I: "The War to End All Wars" and the Birth of a Handicapped International Criminal Justice System*, 30 Denv. J. Intl. L. & Poly. 244, 244 (2002) ("The trigger for [World War I] was an incident that occurred in the volatile Balkans on June 28, 1914, in which Archduke Franz Ferdinand and his wife were assassinated by Gavrilo Princip as they rode in a car in Sarajevo.").

Contrary to the majority's apparent view, our country should not become a haven for those who desire to foment international strife from our shores. I would deny the petition.

## NOTES AND QUESTIONS

1. *Material Support Redux.* The court found that Cheema's wife had not engaged in terrorist activity by sending money to Sikh widows and orphans. Can sending money to widows and orphans *ever* be terrorist activity or material support for terrorist activity? *See* 18 U.S.C. §2339B (2000 & Supp. IV 2004), *supra* p. 479. Why didn't the court find that this activity constituted material support to terrorism?

2. *Danger to U.S. Security.* There was no evidence that Cheema was in any way connected to terrorist activity aimed at the United States or at U.S. persons or property. How, then, could his activities pose a danger to U.S. security? Would it also be a danger to U.S. security for Irish immigrants in Boston to send money to militants in Northern Ireland, or for Iranian immigrants to send money to violent dissident groups in Iran? Does your analysis supply any support for the proposition that *any* terrorist activity or material support for terrorist activity conducted from the United States, regardless of where the terrorist attacks occur, is a danger to U.S. security? *See* United States v. Duggan, 743 F.2d 59, 74 (2d Cir. 1984) (construing the Foreign Intelligence Surveillance Act and finding that "international terrorism conducted from the United States, no matter where it is directed, may well have a substantial effect on United States national security"). Or is any terrorist activity, wherever conducted, necessarily a threat to U.S. national security?

The Board chose to define "security" as implicating "lives, property, or welfare of United States citizens," and the court confined its review to this stated ground for the Board's decision. Suppose the Board had, instead, found that Cheema's activity was a danger to security defined in terms of "national defense or foreign relations and economic relations." Would the court have reversed a decision on this ground?

In any case, which branch is most competent to decide whether activity constitutes such a danger? Why isn't the court bound by the executive branch's conclusion?

3. **Classified Evidence.** The immigration judge initially decided the case in part on the basis of classified evidence not shown to Cheema or his wife. The Board of Immigration Appeals decided without relying on such evidence. Recall from our exploration of the foreign terrorist organization designation process that sometimes the courts can avoid relying on such evidence by finding sufficient support for the challenged government action in the public record. See *supra* p. 15. Suppose, however, that the Board did not do so and therefore looked to the classified evidence as well. Would that be fair to Cheema? Would it be constitutional? See the following case.

## B.   USING SECRET EVIDENCE AGAINST TERRORIST SUSPECTS

### AMERICAN-ARAB ANTI-DISCRIMINATION COMMITTEE v. RENO

United States Court of Appeals, Ninth Circuit, 1995
70 F.3d 1045

D.W. NELSON, Circuit Judge: [Barakat and Sharif, resident aliens, applied for legalization of their status under the immigration laws. They were denied because the Immigration and Naturalization Service (INS), using undisclosed classified information, found them excludable under a statute that provides for the exclusion of aliens who advocate or teach or are members of organizations which advocate or teach the duty, necessity, or propriety of unlawfully assaulting or killing officers of government or unlawfully damaging property. *See* 8 U.S.C. §1182(a)(28)(F), explanatory notes for 1990 amendments.[1] The classified information purported to link Barakat and Sharif to the Popular Front for the Liberation of Palestine (PFLP). Barakat and Sharif then sued in district court to challenge the use of secret information and won an injunction. This appeal followed.] . . .

#### B.   The Due Process Challenge to the Use of Classified Information . . .

##### 2.   Appropriateness of the Permanent Injunction

###### *a. Applicability of due process protections to aliens*

Aliens who reside in this country are entitled to full due process protections. The Government does not dispute that the Due Process Clause protects Barakat and Sharif, but it contends that reliance on undisclosed information to determine legalization satisfies the demands of due process.

---

1. The Immigration and Nationality Act has been amended almost annually, rendering most case citations to the Act obsolete. At this writing, the INA excludes aliens who have engaged in "terrorist activities." 8 U.S.C.A. §1182(a)(3)(B) (West 2005).

### b. Statutory and regulatory authority for summary process . . .

At the time that Barakat and Sharif applied for legalization, the INS regulations required that all issues of statutory eligibility for immigration benefits, including legalization, be determined solely on the basis of information in the record disclosed to the applicant. However, after a three-year delay, the INS finally issued Notices of Intent to Deny to Barakat and Sharif in March 1991, pursuant to amended regulations, effective upon publication as interim rules in January 1991, that extended the confidential use of classified information to statutory entitlement determinations. The INS claimed that the information's "protection from unauthorized disclosure is required in the interests of national security, as provided in [the interim regulations]."

The Government cites section 235(c) of the Immigration and Nationality Act, 8 U.S.C. §1225(c) (as amended), as authority for use of the undisclosed classified information in the legalization determination. That statute establishes the powers of INS officers to inspect aliens "seeking admission or readmission," 8 U.S.C. §1225(a), to temporarily detain aliens who are not entitled to enter "at the port of arrival," 8 U.S.C. §1225(b), and to exclude aliens on the particular finding by the Attorney General that confidential information supports that exclusion, 8 U.S.C. §1225(c) (allowing summary process for exclusion).[2] We do not, however, accept the proposition that denying a resident alien legalization is the same thing as "exclusion."

Use of summary process in settings other than exclusion raises troubling due process concerns. *See, e.g.*, Kwong Hai Chew [v. Colding], 344 U.S. 590 [(1953)] (barring the INS from using summary process to exclude a resident alien returning from abroad, because he was entitled to a hearing as of constitutional right). Thus, even reentering permanent resident aliens, who enjoy few rights because of the admitted power of Congress over entry into the country, are entitled to additional due process safeguards when subjected to the summary exclusion process. Rafeedie v. INS, 880 F.2d 506, 512 (D.C. Cir. 1989), *on remand*, 795 F. Supp. 13, 20 (D.D.C. 1992) (applying the *Mathews* balancing test[3] to determine that subjecting a returning resident alien, who

---

[2. This section of the INA still, at this writing, provides for the "removal without further hearing" of certain aliens on security grounds, if, on review of the removal order, the Attorney General "is satisfied on the basis of confidential information that the alien is inadmissible [on security grounds] and, after consulting with appropriate security agencies of the United States Government, concludes that disclosure of the information would be prejudicial to the public interest, safety, or security. . . ." 8 U.S.C. §1225(c)(1)-(2) (2000).]

[3. In Mathews v. Eldridge, 424 U.S. 319 (1976), the Supreme Court explained that the process constitutionally due before the government deprives a person of life, liberty, or property is determined by balancing (1) the private interest that will be affected by the government action; (2) the risk of erroneous deprivation of that interest through the procedures the government is using, as well as the probable value of additional or substitute procedures; and, finally, (3) the government's interest in the action and in avoiding the additional administrative or fiscal burdens which additional or substitute procedures would impose. *Mathews* balancing is now commonly used to decide procedural due process once a person has shown that government action implicates a private interest protected by the Due Process Clause. *See, e.g.*, Najjar v. Reno, 97 F. Supp. 2d 1329, 1352-1360 (S.D. Fla. 2000) (applying *Mathews* balancing to decide process due in hearings in which the government relied on undisclosed classified information to deny bail to a detained alien alleged to be a supporter of a terrorist organization).]

was accused of being a PFLP officer, to summary exclusion proceedings utilizing secret information violated due process). . . .

### c. The Mathews balancing test

**(1) The Private Interest Affected.** Aliens who have resided for more than a decade in this country, even those whose status is now unlawful because of technical visa violations, have a strong liberty interest in remaining in their homes. Similarly, the denial of legalization impacts the opportunity of an alien to work, which also raises constitutional concerns. The statute provides an entitlement not subject to denial according to the discretion of the Attorney General, as long as the eligibility requirements are satisfied. 8 U.S.C. §1255a(a). Thus, the district court did not err in finding that the private interests affected are truly substantial.

**(2) The Risk of Erroneous Deprivation and Value of Safeguards.** There is no direct evidence in the record to show what percentage of decisions utilizing undisclosed classified information result in error; yet, as the district court below stated, "One would be hard pressed to design a procedure more likely to result in erroneous deprivations." *See, e.g.,* Goss v. Lopez, 419 U.S. 565, 580 (1975) (finding that "the risk of error is not at all trivial" in summary discipline in school settings). Without any opportunity for confrontation, there is no adversarial check on the quality of the information on which the INS relies. *See* Knauff v. Shaughnessy, 338 U.S. 537, 551 (1950) (Jackson, J., dissenting) ("The plea that evidence of guilt must be secret is abhorrent to free men, because it provides a cloak for the malevolent, the misinformed, the meddlesome, and the corrupt to play the role of informer undetected and uncorrected.") (citation omitted).

Although not all rights of criminal defendants are applicable to the civil context, the procedural due process notice and hearing requirements have "ancient roots" in the rights to confrontation and cross-examination. Greene v. McElroy, 360 U.S. 474, 496 (1959).

> Certain principles have remained relatively immutable in our jurisprudence. One of these is that where governmental action seriously injures an individual, and the reasonableness of the action depends on fact findings, the evidence used to prove the Government's case must be disclosed to the individual so that he has an opportunity to show that it is untrue.

*Id.* As judges, we are necessarily wary of one-sided process: "democracy implies respect for the elementary rights of men . . . and must therefore practice fairness; and fairness can rarely be obtained by secret, one-sided determination of facts decisive of rights." Anti-Fascist Committee v. McGrath, 341 U.S. 123, 170 (1951) (Frankfurter, J., concurring). "It is therefore the firmly held main rule that a court may not dispose of the merits of a case on the basis of *ex parte, in camera* submissions." Abourezk v. Reagan, 785 F.2d 1043, 1061 (D.C. Cir. 1986). Thus, the very foundation of the adversary process assumes that use of undisclosed information will violate due process because of the risk of error. We conclude that the district court did not err in finding that there is an exceptionally high risk of erroneous deprivation when undisclosed information is used to determine the merits of the admissibility inquiry.

**(3) The Governmental Interest.** The Government seeks to use undisclosed information to achieve its desired outcome of prohibiting these individuals whom it perceives to be threats to national security from remaining in the United States while protecting its confidential sources involved in the investigation of terrorist organizations. Yet the Government has offered no evidence to demonstrate that these particular aliens threaten the national security of this country. In fact, the Government claims that it need not. It relies on general pronouncements in two State Department publications about the PFLP's involvement in global terrorism and on the President's recent broad Executive Order prohibiting "any United States persons" from transacting business with the PFLP. *See* Exec. Order No. 12947 (January 23, 1995) (finding "that grave acts of violence committed by foreign terrorists that disrupt the Middle East peace process constitute an unusual and extraordinary threat to the national security, foreign policy, and economy of the United States"). We take judicial notice of these government documents on appeal for the limited purpose of assessing the strength of the Government's interest, yet we find these data insufficient to tip the *Mathews* scale towards the Government. These aliens have been free since the beginning of this litigation almost eight years ago, without criminal charges being brought against them for their activities. According to the district court, the government's *in camera* submission targets the PFLP: although it indicates that the PFLP advocates prohibited doctrines and that the aliens are members, it does not indicate that either alien has personally advocated those doctrines or has participated in terrorist activities.

If Barakat and Sharif engage in any deportable activities, the government is not precluded from contesting their legalization or from instituting deportation on the basis of non-secret information. If the Government chooses not to reveal its information in order to protect its sources, the only risk it faces is that attendant to tolerance of Barakat's and Sharif's presence so long as they do not engage in deportable activities. Thus, although the Government undoubtedly has a legitimate interest in protecting its confidential investigations, it has not demonstrated a strong interest in this case in accomplishing its goal of protecting its information while prohibiting these aliens' legalization.

The Government's attempt to bolster its interest by relying on permitted uses of undisclosed information is misguided. Although the courts have allowed the Government to keep certain information confidential, the exceptions to full disclosure are narrowly circumscribed. For example, a formal claim of a "state secrets privilege" may prevent discovery and shield the use of materials against the Government in tort litigation for damages. [*Abourezk*, 785 F.2d at 1061]; *see also* United States v. Reynolds, 345 U.S. 1, 6-7 (1953) (in a tort suit against the Government, permitting nonproduction of an Air Force accident investigation report because of national security concerns); Ellsberg v. Mitchell, 709 F.2d 51 (D.C. Cir. 1983) (in a constitutional tort suit for damages against officials, allowing the Government to withhold production of wiretap information), *cert. denied*, 465 U.S. 1038 (1984). However, the failure to disclose information prevents its use in the adversary proceeding: the effect of upholding the privilege is "that the evidence is unavailable, as though a witness had died." *Ellsberg*, 709 F.2d at 64. Even in those rare cases when the privilege operates as a complete shield to the government and results in the dismissal of a plaintiff's suit, the information is simply unavailable and may not be used by either side. Here, the Government does not seek to shield state information from disclosure in the adjudication of a tort claim against it; instead, it seeks to use secret information as a sword against the aliens.

Because of the danger of injustice when decisions lack the procedural safeguards that form the core of constitutional due process, the *Mathews* balancing suggests that use of undisclosed information in adjudications should be presumptively unconstitutional. Only the most extraordinary circumstances could support one-sided process. We cannot in good conscience find that the President's broad generalization regarding a distant foreign policy concern and a related national security threat suffices to support a process that is inherently unfair because of the enormous risk of error and the substantial personal interests involved. "[T]he fact that a given law or procedure is efficient, convenient, and useful in facilitating functions of government, standing alone, will not save it if it is contrary to the Constitution." [Immigration and Naturalization Service v.] Chadha, 462 U.S. 919, 944 (1983). Therefore, we find that the district court did not err in deciding that use of undisclosed classified information under these circumstances violates due process. . . .

Affirmed in part, reversed and remanded in part [on other grounds].

## NOTES AND QUESTIONS

1. *The State Secrets Privilege.* Proposed Federal Rule of Evidence 509 (which Congress rejected for reasons not relevant to our study) described in pertinent part the common law privilege for "state secrets" as follows: "The government has a privilege to refuse to give evidence and to prevent any person from giving evidence upon a showing of reasonable likelihood of danger that the evidence will disclose a secret of state. . . ." 26 Charles Alan Wright & Kenneth W. Graham, *Federal Practice and Procedure* 416 (1992). The rule defined "state secret" as "a governmental secret relating to the national defense or the international relations of the United States." *Id.* at 415. The privilege was recognized by the Supreme Court in United States v. Reynolds, 345 U.S. 1, 6 (1953), but otherwise has been only generally articulated by lower court decisions. *See generally* Stephen Dycus et al., *National Security Law* 1037-1045 (4th ed. 2007); Louis Fisher, *In the Name of National Security: Unchecked Presidential Power and the Reynolds Case* (2006).

   How would an immigration judge or court determine whether state secrets were involved in a deportation case? Usually a party in litigation who invokes an evidentiary privilege has the obligation to lay a foundation sufficient for other parties and the court to assess the applicability of the privilege. *See, e.g.,* Fed. R. Civ. P. 26(b)(5). The threshold for the government's invocation of the state secrets privilege is generally lower, and once it has been invoked, courts have often been reluctant to second-guess the asserted need it has been for protecting the contested information. *See, e.g.,* Halkin v. Helms, 690 F.2d 977 (D.C. Cir. 1982).

2. ***Statutory Authorization for Using Secret Evidence.*** The rights of aliens in immigration proceedings traditionally depended on their status (e.g., resident or nonresident, entering or reentering, etc.), the nature of the proceeding (e.g., exclusion, removal, suspension of deportation, etc.), and the corresponding statutes and INS regulations. In Jay v. Boyd, 351 U.S. 345 (1956), cited by the government to support its use of secret evidence in *American-Arab Anti-Discrimination Committee*, the Supreme Court found implied authority in INS regulations for the Attorney General to use undisclosed "confidential information" to make the entirely discretionary decision whether to suspend an alien's deportation. Why is *Jay* not controlling in the instant case? In neither case was there express statutory or regulatory authority for using undisclosed classified information against the alien. If the statute is silent or ambiguous about authority to use secret evidence, how should the court resolve the ambiguity? *See* Greene v. McElroy, 360 U.S. 474, 507 (1959) (Court will not assume that Congress or the President has authorized an action of "doubtful constitutionality" implicating individual rights, absent a clear statement, in order to ensure that such actions are the product of "careful and purposeful consideration by those responsible for enacting and implementing our laws"). Does footnote 2, *supra*, p. 611 make a difference in your analysis? Note that *Greene* was decided after *Jay*. Is *Jay* still good law?

3. ***The Risk of Inaccuracy from Using Secret Evidence.*** Boyd, from Jay v. Boyd, *supra*, had permanently resided in the United States since 1914 and had never engaged in any misconduct during his 65 years, although he had *legally* been a member of the Communist Party from 1935 to 1940. He alleged on information and belief that the "confidential information" the Attorney General used against him was that his name had appeared on a list circulated by an organization deemed subversive by the Attorney General. The majority opinion dealt only with the issue of statutory and regulatory authority, asserting in a footnote without elaboration that "the constitutionality of [the regulation] as herein interpreted gives us no difficulty." *Jay*, 351 U.S. at 357 n.21.

It gave dissenters Warren, Black, Frankfurter, and Douglas great difficulty, however. Justice Black asked:

> What is meant by "confidential information"? According to officers of the Immigration Service it may be "merely information we received off the street"; or "what might be termed as hearsay evidence, which could not be gotten into the record . . ."; or "information from persons who were in a position to give us the information that might be detrimental to the interests of the Service to disclose that person's name . . ."; or "such things, perhaps, as income-tax returns, or maybe a witness who didn't want to be disclosed, or where it might endanger their life, or something of that kind. . . ." No nation can remain true to the ideal of liberty under law and at the same time permit people to have their homes destroyed

and their lives blasted by the slurs of unseen and unsworn infor-
mers. There is no possible way to contest the truthfulness of anonymous accusations. The supposed accuser can neither be identified
nor interrogated. He may be the most worthless and irresponsible
character in the community. What he said may be wholly malicious,
untrue, unreliable, or inaccurately reported. In a court of law the
triers of fact could not even listen to such gossip, much less decide
the most trifling issue on it. [*Id.* at 365.]

Illustrating these points, a former Director of Central Intelligence, representing a group of detained Iraqis, found "serious errors" in previously secret
evidence used against his clients, including mistranslations, ethnic and
religious stereotyping, and rumors derived from intergroup rivalry. *See*
Susan M. Akram, *Scheherezade Meets Kafka: Two Dozen Sordid Tales of
Ideological Exclusion*, 14 Geo. Immigr. L.J. 51, 87-88 (1999).

    *Jay* was decided not only before Greene v. McElroy but also before the
explosion of due process decisions in the Supreme Court, including Mathews v.
Eldridge (*supra* p. 611 n.3). In light of these cases, should the constitutionality of the procedure used against Boyd now give judges any difficulty? How
would it fare under a *Mathews* balancing analysis? *See generally* Michael J.
Whidden, *Unequal Justice: Arabs in America and United States Antiterrorism Legislation*, 69 Fordham L. Rev. 2825, 2845-2849, 2874-2879 (2001);
Akram, *supra*, at 51-52; Michael Scaperlanda, *Are We That Far Gone?
Due Process and Secret Deportation Proceedings*, 7 Stan. L. & Poly. Rev.
23, 27-29 (1996).

    The risk of inaccuracy from using secret evidence also may be illustrated
by a case described by the Washington Post as "the only criminal case since
the Sept. 11 attacks in which secret evidence was presented against the
defendant." *See* Dale Russakoff, *N.J. Judge Unseals Transcript in Controversial Terror Case*, Wash. Post, June 25, 2003, at A3. Reportedly local (non-
federal) prosecutors convinced a state judge during a bail hearing that
evidence against a defendant whom they alleged had ties to terrorists was
so sensitive that the defendant could not be allowed to see it. Months later,
an appellate judge ruled that prosecutors had not shown the defendant to be
a security risk, and the trial judge then unsealed the bail hearing transcript.
*Id.*; Robert Hanley & Jonathan Miller, *4 Transcripts Are Released in Case
Tied to 9/11 Hijackers*, N.Y. Times, June 25, 2003, at B5; Jennifer
V. Hughes, *Supposed Links to Terrorism Revealed,* The Record, June 25,
2003, at A01. Most of the evidence consisted of testimony by a detective
about what he had heard from FBI agents about the defendant. Federal
authorities, however, contradicted or denied knowledge of some of this
information after release of the transcripts, and the defendant's attorney
dismissed it as "slanderous, hearsay, double- and triple-hearsay, evidence
which he claimed he could have rebutted if only he and the defendant had
been allowed to see it." Russakoff, *supra*. "To think that they kept me in jail
on this," the defendant said, after being held for six months as a suspected
terrorist. *Id.* The state dropped all but one of 25 counts of selling fraudulent
documents to Hispanic immigrants (none tied to terrorism).

4. *The Probable Value of Additional Process.* Short of unconditionally disclosing all the evidence to Barakat and Sharif, what additional procedures, if any, would satisfy due process? Would supplying them with an unclassified one-page summary of the evidence suffice? *See* Kiareldeen v. Reno, 71 F. Supp. 2d 402 (D.N.J. 1999) (rejecting this alternative because the summary failed to identify a single source and was barely two pages long). Would a more detailed summary, which the judge checked ex parte and in camera for accuracy and completeness against the classified information, satisfy? *See* Najjar v. Reno, 97 F. Supp. 2d 1329, 1359 (S.D. Fla. 2000) (suggesting such a procedure on remand). Should immigration judges have security clearances to perform this function? Should we require the alien's counsel to be cleared as well? Alternatively, would an independent verification of the information internal to the Department of Justice but without disclosure to or participation of the defendant or his counsel suffice? *See Hearing on H.R. 2121 Before the H. Judiciary Subcomm. on Immigration and Claims*, 106th Cong. 47 (2000) (prepared testimony of Larry R. Parkinson, General Counsel, FBI, explaining that "[b]efore any final decision is made to use classified information in immigration proceedings, the information and the case are subjected to rigorous review at high levels of all affected Justice Department components to ensure that it is necessary and appropriate to use the information.").

5. *The Alien Terrorist Removal Court.* The 1996 Anti-Terrorism and Effective Death Penalty Act established a special alien terrorist "Removal Court" (ATRC) as another way of removing alien terrorists from the United States. *See* 8 U.S.C. §§1531-1537 (2000 & Supp. IV 2004). Article III judges are appointed to the ATRC, and the alien is represented by counsel, but only by one who has been selected from a specially cleared panel. The government may submit classified evidence to the court in camera and ex parte, "and neither [an] alien [who is not a permanent resident] nor the public shall be informed of such evidence or its sources" except by an unclassified summary approved by the court as "sufficient to enable the alien to prepare a defense." *Id.* §1534(e)(3). If the court cannot give such approval, the removal hearing is terminated unless the court also finds that the alien's continued presence in the United States, and the provision of a summary to the alien, would both cause "serious and irreparable harm to the national security or death or serious bodily injury to any person." *Id.* §1534(e)(3)(D). Thus, the ATRC is authorized to remove a nonpermanent resident alien suspected terrorist on the basis of secret evidence of which he is completely uninformed. How would such a removal fare under the *Mathews* balancing test? *Compare* Jennifer A. Beall, *Are We Only Burning Witches? The Antiterrorism and Effective Death Penalty Act of 1996's Answer to Terrorism*, 73 Ind. L.J. 693, 705-708 (1998) (contending that it would fail), *and* David B. Kopel & Joseph Olson, *Preventing a Reign of Terror: Civil Liberties Implications of Terrorism Legislation*, 21 Okla. City U.L. Rev. 247, 332-335 (1996) (same), *with* Scaperlanda, *supra* p. 616, at 225-229 (contending that it would pass). Note that, apart from the Foreign Intelligence Surveillance Court, the United States last used a secret court to prosecute and condemn to death German saboteurs in World War II. *Ex Parte Quirin*, 317 U.S. 1 (1942), *supra* p. 353.

*See* Sam Skolnik, *Death Sentences Behind Closed Doors*, Legal Times, Dec. 20, 1999, at 20.

It may be that constitutional doubts about the extraordinary Star Chamber quality of this special court are why the government has never used it. Another reason may be that ordinary criminal prosecutions of terrorists in open court have generally been successful, as the *Bin Laden* case, *supra* p. 494, demonstrates. But a less benign explanation for the neglect of the ATRC to date may simply be that administrative immigration proceedings using secret evidence have afforded a simpler solution. Although the Attorney General has imposed some internal departmental review procedures, see *supra* Note 4,

> there remains no statutory or regulatory obligation for the INS to disclose an unclassified summary, for cleared counsel to be permitted to see the testimony, nor (in some cases) for judicial review by Article III judges before exhausting administrative remedies. The INS administrative use of classified information, outside the ATRC, is thus easier and simpler since fewer rights are afforded the alien. The non-ATRC use of classified information is the faster—albeit less legitimate—approach. [Juliette Kayyem, *Whatever Happened to the Alien Terrorist Removal Court?*, ABA Natl. Security L. Rep. 3 (Mar.-Apr. 2000).]

*See also* Whidden, *supra* p. 616, at 2846 (contending that AEDPA "signaled to the INS that there was political support to apply INS secret evidence proceedings more aggressively"). If this is correct, then opinions like *American-Arab Anti-Discrimination Committee* may perversely encourage recourse to the ATRC, unless, of course, it too is found wanting by their due process analysis.

## C.  PUBLIC ACCESS TO REMOVAL HEARINGS

It is difficult to think of a principle that sets our democracy apart more clearly from most others than our commitment to openness and accountability in government. The Framers understood the critical need for an informed electorate. James Madison famously remarked, "Knowledge will forever govern ignorance, and a people who mean to be their own governors, must arm themselves with the power knowledge gives. A popular government without popular information or the means of acquiring it, is but a prologue to a farce or a tragedy or perhaps both."[4] This nation's founders also appreciated the informing role of the press. As Justice Stewart pointed out in the *Pentagon Papers Case*, "a press that is alert, aware, and free most vitally serves the basic purpose of the First Amendment. For without an informed and free press there cannot be an enlightened people."[5]

---

4. Letter from James Madison to W. T. Barry, Aug. 4, 1822, *in* IX The Writings of James Madison 103 (G.P. Hunt ed., 1910).

5. New York Times v. United States, 403 U.S. 713, 728 (1971) (Stewart, J. concurring).

In some circumstances, however, it is not in the public interest to disclose what the government is up to. If everyone could know everything, our enemies might use some of that knowledge against us. In this democracy we have therefore struck a bargain with ourselves to surrender some knowledge — and with it the power that knowledge gives — to our elected representatives, with the understanding that they will use it to keep us safe.

The exact terms of this bargain have always been controversial and are subject to ongoing renegotiation. But there is general agreement that national security should not be used to justify concealment of government activities that offend bedrock American principles — principles such as fairness, due process, and humane treatment.

Nevertheless, since September 11, 2001, the government has struggled, in the name of national security, to keep almost all information about its detention and interrogation of terrorist suspects secret. The government has also made efforts to close immigration hearings when aliens targeted for deportation are suspected of involvement in terrorism. These proceedings are neither strictly judicial nor strictly administrative. And while they are nominally civil, they may lead to sanctions that are criminal in nature. Such distinctions have complicated decisions about whether to open these proceedings to the public and the media.

The government's ability to close immigration hearings is circumscribed, at least to some degree, by the First Amendment to the United States Constitution, which provides in part, "Congress shall make no law . . . abridging the freedom of speech, or of the press. . . ." While neither a public nor a press right of access to government information is apparent in this language, Professor Emerson argued that

> [t]he public, as sovereign, must have all information available in order to instruct its servants, the government. As a general proposition, if democracy is to work, there can be no holding back of information; otherwise, ultimate decisionmaking by the people, to whom that function is committed, becomes impossible. Whether or not such a guarantee of the right to know is the sole purpose of the first amendment, it is surely a main element of that provision and should be recognized as such. [Thomas I. Emerson, *Legal Foundations of the Right to Know*, 1976 Wash. U. L.Q. 1, 14.]

Yet the Supreme Court declared in a 1978 jail access case that "[n]either the First Amendment nor the Fourteenth Amendment mandates a right of access to government information or sources of information within the government's control." Houchins v. KQED, Inc., 438 U.S. 1, 15 (1978). Concerning the media, the Court remarked earlier that "the First Amendment does not guarantee the press a constitutional right of special access to information not available to the public generally." Branzburg v. Hayes, 408 U.S. 665, 684 (1972).

In 1980, however, the Court recognized a right of the press to attend criminal trials. Richmond Newspapers v. Virginia, 448 U.S. 555 (1980). Then in a similar case two years later, the Court observed that "the First Amendment serves to ensure that the individual citizen can effectively participate in and contribute to our republican system of self-government." Globe Newspapers v. Superior Court, 457 U.S. 596, 604 (1982). More recently, in a case involving records of a criminal proceeding, the Supreme Court explained that public access to "governmental processes" will be granted: (1) when "there is a tradition of accessibility" — that is, when "the place and process have historically been open to the press and general public"; (2) when "public access plays a significant positive role in the functioning of the particular process"; and (3) when there is no showing that "closure is essential to preserve higher values and is narrowly tailored to serve that interest." Press-Enterprise Co. v. Superior Court, 478 U.S. 1, 8-9 (1986). See Eugene Cerruti, *"Dancing in the Courthouse": The First Amendment Right of Access Opens a New Round,* 29 U. Rich. L. Rev. 237 (1995); *see also* Timothy B. Dyk, *Newsgathering, Press Access, and the First Amendment,* 44 Stan. L. Rev. 927 (1992) (arguing that the press should enjoy greater access to government information than the public).

Despite the broad language in *Press-Enterprise,* there is considerable uncertainty about the scope of the First Amendment right of access, and the Supreme Court has not addressed the issue again. *Compare* WPIX, Inc. v. League of Women Voters, 595 F. Supp. 1484, 1489 (S.D.N.Y. 1984) ("Under the first amendment, press organizations have a limited right of access to newsworthy events."), *with* Foto USA, Inc. v. Board of Regents, 141 F.3d 1032, 1035 (11th Cir. 1998) ("There is no First Amendment right of access to public information."). Some courts have expressed doubt about the existence of a broader right of access but applied the *Press-Enterprise* criteria anyway. *See, e.g.*, Capital Cities Media, Inc. v. Chester, 797 F.2d 1164 (3d Cir. 1986) (finding no tradition of public access to agency records).

Against this background, two appellate courts recently reached different conclusions about the scope and applicability of a First Amendment right of access to immigration deportation hearings.

## NORTH JERSEY MEDIA GROUP, INC. v. ASHCROFT

United States Court of Appeals, Third Circuit, 2002
308 F.3d 198, *cert. denied,* 538 U.S. 1056 (2003)

BECKER, Chief Judge. This civil action was brought in the District Court for the District of New Jersey by a consortium of media groups seeking access to "special interest" deportation hearings involving persons whom the Attorney General has determined might have connections to or knowledge of the September 11, 2001 terrorist attacks. This category was created by a directive issued by Michael Creppy, the Chief United States Immigration Judge, outlining additional security measures to be applied in this class of cases, including closing hearings to the public and the press. Named as defendants in the suit were Attorney General John Ashcroft and Chief Judge Creppy. . . .

As we will now explain in detail, we find that the application of the *Richmond Newspapers* [Richmond Newspapers, Inc. v. Virginia, 448 U.S. 555 (1980)] experience and logic tests does not compel us to declare the Creppy Directive unconstitutional. . . .

### III. Under *Richmond Newspapers*, Is There a First Amendment Right to Attend Deportation Hearings? . . .

#### A. The "Experience" Test

##### 1. Is there an historical right of access to government proceedings generally?

In *Richmond Newspapers,* 448 U.S. at 575, the Supreme Court acknowledged the State's argument that the Constitution nowhere explicitly guarantees the public's right to attend criminal trials, but it found that right implicit because the Framers drafted the Constitution against a backdrop of long-standing popular access to criminal trials. . . . Likewise, in *Publicker* [Industries, Inc. v. Cohen, 733 F.2d 1059 (3d Cir. 1984),] at 1059, we found a First Amendment right of access to civil trials because at common law, such access had been "beyond dispute."

The history of access to political branch proceedings is quite different. The Government correctly notes that the Framers themselves rejected any unqualified right of access to the political branches for, as we explained in *Capital Cities Media*[, Inc. v. Chester, 797 F.2d 1164 (3d Cir. 1986)], at 1168-1171, the evidence on this point is extensive and compelling. . . .

This tradition of closing sensitive proceedings extends to many hearings before administrative agencies. For example, although hearings on Social Security disability claims profoundly affect hundreds of thousands of people annually, and have great impact on expenditure of government funds, they are open only to "the parties and to other persons the administrative law judge considers necessary and proper." 20 C.F.R. §404.944. Likewise, administrative disbarment hearings are often presumptively closed. . . .

Faced with this litany of administrative hearings that are closed to the public, the Newspapers . . . submit that, despite frequent closures throughout the administrative realm, deportation proceedings in particular boast a history of openness sufficient to meet the *Richmond Newspapers* requirement. . . .

##### 2. Is the history of open deportation proceedings sufficient to satisfy the Richmond Newspapers "experience" prong?

For a First Amendment right of access to vest under *Richmond Newspapers,* we must consider whether "the place and process have historically been open to the press and general public," because such a "tradition of accessibility implies the favorable judgment of experience." *Press-Enterprise II,* 478 U.S. at 8. Noting preliminarily that the question whether a proceeding has been "historically open" is only arguably an objective inquiry, we nonetheless find that based on both Supreme Court and Third Circuit precedents, the tradition of open deportation hearings is too recent and inconsistent to support a First Amendment right of access.

The strongest historical evidence of open deportation proceedings is that since the 1890s, when Congress first codified deportation procedures, "[t]he governing statutes have always expressly closed *exclusion* hearings, but have *never* closed deportation hearings." (Newspapers' Br. at 30-31.) In 1893, the Executive promulgated the first set of immigration regulations, which expressly stated that exclusion proceedings shall be conducted "separate from the public." *See* Treasury Dept., *Immigration Laws and Regulations* 4 (Washington D.C., Gov't Printing Office 1893). Congress codified those regulations in 1903 and, since that time, it has repeatedly reenacted provisions closing exclusion hearings. In contrast, although Congress codified the regulations governing deportation proceedings in 1904 and has reenacted them many times since, it has never authorized the general closure that has long existed in the exclusion context. . . .

. . . [T]here is also evidence that, in practice, deportation hearings have frequently been closed to the general public. From the early 1900s, the government has often conducted deportation hearings in prisons, hospitals, or private homes, places where there is no general right of public access. Even in recent times, the government has continued to hold thousands of deportation hearings each year in federal and state prisons. Moreover, hearings involving abused alien children are closed by regulation no matter where they are held, and those involving abused alien spouses are closed presumptively. *See* 8 C.F.R. §3.27(c).

We ultimately do not believe that deportation hearings boast a tradition of openness sufficient to satisfy *Richmond Newspapers*. . . .

### IV. Does the *Richmond Newspapers* "Logic" Prong, Properly Applied, Support a Right of Access?

Even if we could find a right of access under the *Richmond Newspapers* logic prong, absent a strong showing of openness under the experience prong, a proposition we do not embrace, we would find no such right here. The logic test compels us to consider "whether public access plays a significant positive role in the functioning of the particular process in question." *Press-Enterprise II*, 478 U.S. at 8. . . .

. . . Under the reported cases, whenever a court has found that openness serves community values, it has concluded that openness plays a "significant positive role" in that proceeding. But that cannot be the story's end, for to gauge accurately whether a role is positive, the calculus must perforce take account of the flip side — the extent to which openness impairs the public good. We note in this respect that, were the logic prong only to determine whether openness serves some good, it is difficult to conceive of a government proceeding to which the public would not have a First Amendment right of access. For example, public access to *any* government affair, even internal CIA deliberations, would "promote informed discussion" among the citizenry. It is unlikely the Supreme Court intended this result.

In this case the Government presented substantial evidence that open deportation hearings would threaten national security. . . .

The Government's security evidence is contained in the declaration of Dale Watson, the FBI's Executive Assistant Director for Counterterrorism and Counterintelligence. Watson presents a range of potential dangers, the most pressing of which we [d]escribe here.

First, public hearings would necessarily reveal sources and methods of investigation. That is information which, "when assimilated with other information the United States may or may not have in hand, allows a terrorist organization to build a picture of the investigation." (Watson Decl. at 4.)

Even minor pieces of evidence that might appear innocuous to us would provide valuable clues to a person within the terrorist network, clues that may allow them to thwart the government's efforts to investigate and prevent future acts of violence. *Id.*

Second, "information about how any given individual entered the country (from where, when, and how) may not divulge significant information that would reveal sources and methods of investigation. However, putting entry information into the public realm regarding all 'special interest cases' would allow the terrorist organization to see patterns of entry, what works and what doesn't." *Id.* That information would allow it to tailor future entries to exploit weaknesses in the United States immigration system.

Third, "[i]nformation about what evidence the United States has against members of a particular cell collectively will inform the terrorist organization as to what cells to use and which not to use for further plots and attacks." *Id.* A related concern is that open hearings would reveal what evidence the government lacks. For example, the United States may disclose in a public hearing certain evidence it possesses about a member of a terrorist organization. If that detainee is actually involved in planning an attack, opening the hearing might allow the organization to know that the United States is not yet aware of the attack based on the evidence it presents at the open hearing. *Id.*

Fourth, if a terrorist organization discovers that a particular member is detained, or that information about a plot is known, it may accelerate the timing of a planned attack, thus reducing the amount of time the government has to detect and prevent it. If acceleration is impossible, it may still be able to shift the planned activity to a yet-undiscovered cell. *Id.* at 7.

Fifth, a public hearing involving evidence about terrorist links could allow terrorist organizations to interfere with the pending proceedings by creating false or misleading evidence. Even more likely, a terrorist might destroy existing evidence or make it more difficult to obtain, such as by threatening or tampering with potential witnesses. Should potential informants not feel secure in coming forward, that would greatly impair the ongoing investigation. *Id.* . . .

Finally, Watson represents that "the government cannot proceed to close hearings on a case-by-case basis, as the identification of certain cases for closure, and the introduction of evidence to support that closure, could itself expose critical information about which activities and patterns of behavior merit such closure." (Watson Decl. at 8-9.) Moreover, he explains, given judges' relative lack of expertise regarding national security and their inability to see the mosaic, we should not entrust to them the decision whether an isolated fact is sensitive enough to warrant closure.

The Newspapers are undoubtedly correct that the representations of the Watson Declaration are to some degree speculative, at least insofar as there is no concrete evidence that closed deportation hearings have prevented, or will prevent, terrorist attacks. But the *Richmond Newspapers* logic prong is unavoidably speculative, for it is impossible to weigh objectively, for example, the community benefit of emotional catharsis against the security risk of disclosing the United States' methods of investigation and the extent of its knowledge. We are quite hesitant to conduct a judicial inquiry into the credibility of these security concerns, as national security is an area where courts have traditionally extended great deference to Executive expertise. *See, e.g., Zadvydas v. Davis,* 533 U.S. 678, 696 (2001) (noting that "terrorism or other special circumstances" might warrant "heightened deference to the judgments of the political branches with respect to matters of national security"). *See also Dep't of the Navy v. Egan,* 484 U.S. 518, 530 (1988) (noting that "courts traditionally have been reluctant to intrude upon the authority of the Executive in military and national security affairs"). The assessments before us have been made by senior government officials responsible for investigating the events of September 11th and for preventing future attacks. These officials believe that closure of special interest hearings is necessary to advance these goals, and their concerns, as expressed in the Watson Declaration, have gone unrebutted. To the extent that the Attorney General's national security concerns seem credible, we will not lightly second-guess them.

We are keenly aware of the dangers presented by deference to the executive branch when constitutional liberties are at stake, especially in times of national crisis, when those liberties are likely in greatest jeopardy. On balance, however, we are unable to conclude that openness plays a positive role in special interest deportation hearings at a time when our nation is faced with threats of such profound and unknown dimension.

### V. Conclusion . . .

Because we find that open deportation hearings do not pass the two-part *Richmond Newspapers* test, we hold that the press and public possess no First Amendment right of access. . . .

[The opinion of SCIRICA, Circuit Judge, dissenting, is omitted.]

## NOTES AND QUESTIONS

1. ***Closing the Door on Democracy?*** In a Sixth Circuit case on identical facts that was decided at almost the same moment, the court reached a dramatically different result. Detroit Free Press v. Ashcroft, 303 F.3d 681 (6th Cir. 2002). Concerning the "experience" prong of the *Richmond Newspapers* test, the court found that deportation hearings have historically been open. Moreover, said the court,

> to paraphrase the Supreme Court, deportation hearings "walk, talk, and squawk" very much like a judicial proceeding. Substantively, we look to other proceedings that have the same effect as deportation. Here, the only other federal court that can enter an order of removal is a United States District Court during sentencing in a criminal trial. *See* 8 U.S.C.A. §1228(c) (2002). At common law, beginning with the Transportation Act of 1718, the English criminal courts could enter an order of transportation or banishment as a sentence in a criminal trial. As *Richmond Newspapers* discussed in great length, these types of criminal proceedings have historically been open. *Richmond Newspapers,* 448 U.S. at 564-74. [303 F.3d at 702.]

As for the "logic" prong, the Sixth Circuit panel declared that public access "undoubtedly enhances the quality of deportation proceedings." *Id.* at 703.

First, public access acts as a check on the actions of the Executive by assuring us that proceedings are conducted fairly and properly. In an area such as immigration, where the government has nearly unlimited authority, the press and the public serve as perhaps the only check on abusive government practices.

Second, openness ensures that government does its job properly; that it does not make mistakes. . . .

Third, after the devastation of September 11 and the massive investigation that followed, the cathartic effect of open deportations cannot be overstated. They serve a "therapeutic" purpose as outlets for "community concern, hostility, and emotions." . . .

Fourth, openness enhances the perception of integrity and fairness. "The value of openness lies in the fact that people not actually attending trials can have confidence that standards of fairness are being observed. . . ." . . .

Fifth, public access helps ensure that "the individual citizen can effectively participate in and contribute to our republican system of self-government." *Globe Newspaper,* 457 U.S. at 604. "[A] major purpose of [the First Amendment] was to protect the free discussion of governmental affairs." *Id.* Public access to deportation proceedings helps inform the public of the affairs of the government. Direct knowledge of how their government is operating enhances the public's ability to affirm or protest government's efforts. When government selectively chooses what information it allows the public to see, it can become a powerful tool for deception. . . . [303 F.3d at 703-705.]

Finding a First Amendment right of access, the Sixth Circuit panel then decided that "the Creppy directive is neither narrowly tailored, nor does it require particularized findings [in individual cases]. Therefore, it impermissibly infringes on the Newspaper Plaintiffs' First Amendment right of access." *Id.* at 705. The court punctuated its ruling with this widely quoted passage:

In our democracy, based on checks and balances, neither the Bill of Rights nor the judiciary can second-guess government's choices. The only safeguard on this extraordinary governmental power is the public, deputizing the press as the guardians of their liberty. "An informed public is the most potent of all restraints upon misgovernment[.]" Grosjean v. Am. Press Co., 297 U.S. 233, 250 (1936). "[They] alone can here protect the values of democratic government." New York Times v. United States, 403 U.S. 713, 728 (1971) (per curiam) (Stewart, J., concurring).

Today, the Executive Branch seeks to take this safeguard away from the public by placing its actions beyond public scrutiny. Against non-citizens, it seeks the power to secretly deport a class if it unilaterally calls them "special interest" cases. The Executive Branch seeks to uproot people's lives, outside the public eye, and behind a closed door. Democracies die behind closed doors. The First Amendment, through a free press, protects the people's right to know that their government acts fairly, lawfully, and accurately in deportation proceedings. When government begins closing doors, it selectively controls information rightfully belonging to the people. Selective information is misinformation. The Framers of the First Amendment "did not trust any government to separate the true from the false for us." Kleindienst v. Mandel, 408 U.S. 753, 773 (1972) (quoting Thomas v. Collins, 323 U.S. 516, 545 [(1945)] (Jackson, J., concurring)). They protected the people against secret government. [303 F.3d at 683.]

2. ***The Judicial Role in Terrorism Cases.*** How would you compare the general attitudes of the Third and Sixth Circuit courts about their roles in cases concerned with terrorism? Should the *North Jersey Media* court have been more skeptical about government assertions of danger from opening deportation hearings? What about claims that some "special interest" cases involved aliens associated with al Qaeda or with the September 11 hijackers? Should the court have demanded proof of these assertions?

3. ***The Public's Interest in Openness.*** In evaluating "whether public access plays a significant positive role in the functioning of the particular process in question," the two courts had very different ideas about the public interests involved. Which court do you think struck the better balance between the public's interest in openness and the risk to national security, and why?

4. ***Public Access to Special Interest Immigration Proceedings in Limbo.*** Because of the importance of these two cases, as well as the sharp split between the circuits, many were surprised by the Supreme Court's decision to deny certiorari in the *North Jersey Media* case. What, if anything, do you think this portends for First Amendment–based access to information about counterterrorism activities generally and about immigration matters in particular? If the Court eventually does resolve the split in the circuits, how should it rule? Does (and should) your answer take into account the passage of time since 9/11? Does your answer consider the disclosure in the media of some controversial secret government initiatives, like the Terrorist Surveillance Program? See *supra* p. 157. The cumulative effect of government secrecy on checks and balances?

# PART VI

# MANAGING TERRORIST ATTACKS

*20*

# *RESPONDING TO A WMD ATTACK*

America will become increasingly vulnerable to hostile attack on our homeland, and our military superiority will not protect us. . . . States, terrorists, and other disaffected groups will acquire weapons of mass destruction, and some will use them. Americans will likely die on American soil, possibly in large numbers.[1]

This grim prediction appeared in a 1999 federal commission report. It was tragically prescient, as the events of September 11, 2001, made clear. Long before the terrorist attacks on the World Trade Center and the Pentagon, however, the U.S. government had begun to develop extensive plans for a response to such an unhappy development. In earlier chapters we examined the elaborate federal apparatus for detecting and interdicting terrorist threats. Here we consider what to do if those prophylactic efforts fail.

Planning by all levels of government for a response to a WMD attack has evolved rapidly since September 11, 2001. In this chapter we approach that response functionally. We begin in Part A with a broad look at planning in advance of an attack. In Part B we consider a range of issues that an actual bioterrorist attack would present. Next, in Part C, we examine the roles of first responders — firefighters, police officers, EMTs, and others — who would necessarily be first on the scene after such an attack. The federal government is invariably a "second responder" in such an emergency. Its plans and authorities are assessed in Part D. Finally, in Part E we look at various restrictions on personal liberties (isolation, quarantine, vaccination) that may be required by the response to a WMD attack.

It should be noted that almost all the legal and practical issues considered in this chapter may be raised by government responses to other great emergencies, such as hurricanes or influenza pandemics. Such emergencies may, of course, pose serious threats to national security.

---

1. United States Commn. on National Security/21st Century (Hart/Rudman Commission), *New World Coming: American Security in the 21st Century* 141 (1999).

## A.  THINKING THE UNTHINKABLE: PLANNING A RESPONSE TO A TERRORIST ATTACK

Is planning for a response to a terrorist attack a good idea, given the need for flexibility in responding to a great national crisis? Is it worth the considerable effort currently being devoted to it, especially considering the relatively low probability of an attack with chemical, biological, or radiological weapons? Is any conceivable plan likely to be effective in reducing the loss of life and property in light of the creativity of terrorists who would use airliners as weapons of mass destruction? If we do engage in planning, is there any reason to think that a future President will feel constrained by any plans if she is convinced that the threat of a terrorist attack is real or if an attack has already created panic in the population?

Concerning the need for flexibility, legislatures and bureaucrats constantly engage in planning about a wide range of issues. These plans lend an element of predictability to government and enable us to lead more orderly and productive lives while at the same time leaving room for adjustments to accommodate currently unpredictable developments. Planning for the response to a terrorist attack is no different in principle from, say, zoning, involving as it does the same difficult judgments about just how much government officials should be constrained in the future by decisions we make today.

In the crisis precipitated by a terrorist attack, will plans that we make now be followed? We might hope that the President would do whatever is reasonably necessary to protect us — perhaps even declaring martial law or relying on some claim to inherent emergency power. Yet the potential for mischief — or mistake — is great. The President might exercise such awesome authority on the basis of erroneous information or when other less drastic alternatives are available. There could be no assurance of how that authority would be exercised or for how long. Unlike a declared war against a foreign state, a "war" against terrorists may have no clear end point: "emergency" authority for the "duration" could last indefinitely. A President might even use the crisis as a pretext for advancement of unrelated goals. Without a clear response plan in place, it would be more difficult to hold him accountable for his actions, at least until some time later.

One reason for planning, then, is that the more carefully we plan ahead and the more diligently we rehearse those plans, the more likely it is that in a great crisis the President will see adherence to the plan as a reasonable option, and the more nearly the President's response will reflect deliberate choices we make now about how to strike the proper balance between physical security and civil liberties.

Another reason to plan carefully for a great emergency — especially for a terrorist attack — is that an effective response will require the cooperation of the public. During the Cold War, Americans became very familiar with this occasional radio and TV message:

> This is a test. This station is conducting a test of the Emergency Broadcasting System. This is only a test.
> [A tone is broadcast to trigger special receivers or alert listeners.]

> This is a test of the Emergency Broadcast System. The broadcasters of your area in voluntary cooperation with Federal, state, and local authorities have developed this system to keep you informed in the event of an emergency. If this had been an actual emergency, the Attention Signal you just heard would have been followed by official information, news, or instructions. This concludes this test of the Emergency Broadcast System.[2]

Without ever mentioning the possibility of a nuclear attack, the message reminded us of the direst possible national emergency. But we were not told under what circumstances short of an actual attack the Emergency Broadcast System might be activated. Neither was it revealed what sort of instructions might be broadcast, or upon whose authority.

To achieve the necessary cooperation, members of the public must expect and understand that: (1) a program exists to deal effectively with the crisis, (2) the plan is legitimate, and (3) someone is in charge to execute the plan. Analyzing a simulated terrorist attack using a smallpox virus, a House sub-committee warned that the "slightest indication of ill preparation, confusion, or conflict among local, State, and Federal agencies — particularly federal — will lead our nation's citizens into a state of chaos and contribute to anarchy."[3] Public confidence will require public education (more than the Emergency Broadcast System tests or the single page the Federal Emergency Management Agency (FEMA) used to put in phone books to explain what to do in the event of a nuclear attack). It will also take reliable communications during an actual crisis. Moreover, citizen involvement in the planning process may promote public acceptance and actually improve the quality of the plan.

A third reason for planning is to "deter terrorism through a clear public position that our policies will not be affected by terrorist acts."[4] This goal can only be achieved if the "clear public position" is credible. In other words, a potential terrorist has to be convinced that his destructive acts will not precipitate a collapse of basic government structures and convinced as well that the American people will not lose faith in their government even in the worst of times. Needless to say, the potential terrorist will be persuaded only if the American people are.

## NOTES AND QUESTIONS

1. ***Balancing Security and Liberty.*** Finding the right balance between security and liberty in planning a response to a threatened or actual terrorist attack is especially daunting, because it is complicated by uncertainty about the timing and character of such an attack. Whom should we entrust with the responsibility for striking that balance? What do you know about the

---

2. Federal Communications Commn., EBS Checklist 9 (1987). Although the warning system is still operational, it was not activated on September 11, 2001. Americans turned instead to CNN and broadcast media for information about the attacks.

3. *Combating Terrorism: Federal Response to a Biological Weapons Attack: Hearing Before the Subcomm. on National Affairs, Veterans Affairs, and Intl. Relations of the H. Comm. on Government Reform,* 107th Cong. 4 (2001).

4. Presidential Decision Directive 39 (PDD-39), *U.S. Policy on Counterterrorism* 3, June 21, 1995, *available at* http://www.fas.org/irp/offdocs/pdd39.htm (partially redacted).

practical capabilities of the executive and legislative branches, respectively, that recommend them for the job?

2. ***Transparency in Planning.***  Planning for a response to a terrorist attack has always been conducted behind closed doors, and details of the plans themselves are closely guarded. Obviously, every detail cannot be made public, lest terrorists exploit those plans in mounting an attack. But where should the line be drawn between what to publicize and what to keep secret? And who should draw the line? Can you describe a planning process that would provide needed security and yet some measure of public accountability? What are the implications of these questions for democratic government?

## B.  A WORST-CASE SCENARIO

### Thomas V. Inglesby, Rita Grossman & Tara O'Toole, A Plague on Your City: Observations from TOPOFF

32 Clinical Infectious Diseases 436 (2001), *available at* http://www.journals.uchicago.edu/CID/journal/issues/v32n3/001347/001347.html

**May 17**: An aerosol of pneumonic plague (*Yersinia pestis*) bacilli is released covertly from a fire extinguisher at a benefit concert in the Denver Performing Arts Center.

**May 20**: The Colorado Department of Public Health and Environment receives information that increasing numbers of persons began seeking medical attention at Denver area hospitals for cough and fever during the evening of May 19th. By early afternoon on May 20, 500 persons with these symptoms have received medical care, and 25 of those have died.

The Health Department notifies the CDC [Centers for Disease Control and Prevention] of the increased volume of sick. Plague is identified first by the state laboratory and subsequently confirmed in a patient specimen by the CDC lab at Ft. Collins. A public health emergency is declared by the State Health Officer, who immediately requests support from DHHS's Office of Emergency Preparedness. The Governor's Emergency Epidemic Response Committee assembles to respond to the unfolding crisis.

Thirty-one CDC staff are sent to Denver. Hospitals and clinics around the Denver area that just a day earlier were dealing with what appeared to be an unusual increase in influenza cases are now recalling staffs, implementing emergency plans, and seeking assistance in determining treatment protocols and protective measures. By late afternoon, hospital staff are beginning to call in sick, and antibiotics and ventilators are becoming more scarce. Some hospital staff have donned respiratory protective equipment.

The CDC and the FBI are notified by Denver police that a dead man has been found with terrorist literature and paraphernalia in his possession; his cause of death is unknown.

The Governor issues an executive order that restricts travel — including bus, rail and air travel — into or out of 14 Denver Metro counties, and commandeers all antibiotics that can be used to prevent or treat plague. At a press conference, the Governor informs the public that there is a plague outbreak in Denver as a result of a terrorist attack, and he announces his executive order. Citizens are instructed to seek treatment at a medical facility if feeling ill or if they have been in contact with a known or suspected case of plague. Those who are well are directed to stay in their homes and avoid public gatherings. The public is told that the disease is spread from person to person only "if you are within 6 feet of someone who is infected and coughing," and told that dust masks are effective at preventing the spread of disease.

Confirmed cases of plague are identified in Colorado locations other than Denver. Patient interviews suggest that most victims were at the Performing Arts Center days earlier. It is announced that the Governor is working with the President of the United States to resolve the crisis and that federal resources are being brought in to support of state agencies. By the end of the day, 783 cases of pneumonic plague have occurred, and 123 persons have died.

**May 21**: Broadcast media report that a "national crash effort" is underway to move large quantities of antibiotics to the region, as the CDC brings in its "national stockpile," but the quantity of available antibiotics is uncertain. The report explains that early administration of antibiotics is effective in treating plague but that antibiotics must be started within 24 hours of developing symptoms. A news story a few hours later reports that hospitals are running out of antibiotics.

A shipment from the National Pharmaceutical Stockpile (NPS) arrives in Denver, but there are great difficulties moving antibiotics from the airport to the persons who need it for treatment and prophylaxis. Out-of-state cases begin to be reported. The CDC officially notifies bordering states of the epidemic. Cases are reported in England and Japan. Both Japan and the World Health Organization request technical assistance from the CDC.

A number of hospitals in Denver are full to capacity and by the end of the day are unable to see or admit new patients. Thirteen hundred ventilators from the NPS are flown to Colorado. Bodies in hospital morgues are reported to have reached critical levels. The U.S. Surgeon General flies to Colorado to facilitate communications. Many states now are requesting supplies from the NPS. By the end of the day, 1,871 plague cases have been diagnosed throughout the U.S. and abroad. Of these, 389 persons have died.

**May 22**: Hospitals are under-staffed and have insufficient antibiotics, ventilators, and beds to meet demand. They cannot manage the influx of sick patients into the hospitals. Medical care is "beginning to shut down" in Denver.

Officials from the Health Department and the CDC have determined that a secondary spread of disease is occurring. The population in Denver is encouraged to wear face masks. The CDC advises that Colorado state borders be cordoned off in order to limit further spread of plague throughout the U.S. and other countries. Colorado officials express concern about their ability to get food and supplies into the state. The Governor's executive order is extended to prohibit travel into or out of the state of Colorado. By noon, there are 3,060 U.S. and international cases of pneumonic plague, 795 of whom have died.

The following day, May 23, 2000, this frightening exercise, called TOPOFF (the acronym stands for "top officials"), was terminated. It had been organized by the Justice Department to test the ability of top officials at all levels of government to respond to a bioterrorist attack. Among the sobering results was the revelation that local health services—medical personnel, hospitals, and pharmaceutical supplies—were not nearly prepared to treat an outbreak of an infectious disease on such a large scale. Communications among local, state, and federal officials were unreliable. And responses were slowed by cumbersome decision-making processes or by a perception that no one was in charge. Other conclusions are described below.

The unfolding situation precipitated a series of increasingly stringent containment measures. By the end of the first day, [a travel advisory was issued] . . . that restricted travel in 16 Denver Metro counties. . . . Some people, in fact, were reported to be racing out of the state. As part of the travel advisory, persons were advised to stay home unless they were close contacts of diagnosed cases or were feeling sick; in the case of the latter they were directed to seek medical care. . . . [T]he police and National Guard admitted . . . that they would be unable to keep people at home. . . . [B]y the end of the exercise, "people had been asked to stay in their homes for 72 hours. . . . How were they were supposed to get food or medicine?"

Throughout the unfolding epidemic, determining what information the public should be given and how quickly was an important and difficult issue. . . . It was clear that the public message itself would affect the capacity to control the epidemic, in that worried or panicked people might not seek the care they needed or, alternatively, might dangerously crowd health care facilities.

Balancing the rights of the uninfected with the rights of the infected was considered a critical issue. One observer commented that a citizen might be expected to respond to the series of advisories by saying, "You've told me I should just stay in my home, now you have an obligation to give me antibiotics." But there were not enough antibiotics to do this. . . .

Sometime into the exercise, (notional) civil unrest broke out. People had not been allowed to shop. Stores were closed. Food ran out because no trucks were being let into the state. Rioting began to occur. Gridlock occurred around the city, including around health care facilities. The use of snow-plows was proposed as a way of clearing the road of cars. Given the constraints of the exercise, it was not possible to gauge the true extent of social disorder that a bioterrorist attack might evoke, but most observers and participants agreed that serious civil disruption would be a genuine risk in such a crisis.

The wide spectrum of disease containment measures which were considered or implemented illustrated the uncertainty surrounding what measures would, in fact, be feasible and effective. One senior health participant said that sufficient legal powers seemed to exist to carry out the decisions that were being made, and noted that legal authorities were not the problem. The critical issue was having access to the necessary scientific, technical, practical and political expertise, and having sufficient reliable and timely information available (e.g., the number and location of sick persons, etc.) to make sound decisions about how to contain the epidemic. . . .

. . . Perhaps the most striking observation overall is the recognition that the systems and resources now in place would be hard-pressed to successfully manage a bioweapons attack like that simulated in TOPOFF. . . . [*Id.*]

While the TOPOFF exercise was underway in Denver in May 2000, simulated terrorist attacks were also occurring in Portsmouth, New Hampshire (positing the use of a chemical weapon) and Washington, D.C. (radiological weapon). Another exercise in June 2001, simulating an attack using smallpox virus, reached similar conclusions, including this one: "Inherent conflicts already exist and will become exacerbated between health and law enforcement officials, military officials, etc. Priority to save victims and protect potential victims was given to the medical community, usurping law enforcement's jurisdiction in investigative matters." *Combating Terrorism: Federal Response to a Biological Weapons Attack*, *supra* p. 631, at 2-3. The smallpox exercise is described in *Dark Winter: Bioterrorism Exercise, Andrews Air Force Base, June 22-23, 2001* (n.d.), *at* http://www.upmc-biosecurity.org/website/events/2001_darkwinter/dark_winter.pdf.

A subsequent exercise, in May 2003, is described in Dept. of Homeland Security, *Top Officials (TOPOFF) Exercise Series: TOPOFF 2—After Action Summary Report* (Dec. 19, 2003). It featured a simulated radiological attack in Seattle, a dispersal of plague bacilli in Chicago, a cyber attack, and terrorism threats in other locations. One conclusion was that "additional clarity . . . would be helpful" regarding authorities and resources available to the federal government. *Id.* at 4. Unlike the earlier TOPOFF exercise, however, in TOPOFF 2 participants were notified well in advance. The resulting lack of unpredictability and spontaneity may have reduced its value as either a test of preparedness or an aid in planning. A similar TOPOFF 3 exercise was conducted in early 2005. It involved 27 federal, 30 state, and 44 local departments and agencies, plus 156 private sector organizations. *See* Dept. of Homeland Security, Office of Inspector General, *A Review of the Top Officials 3 Exercise* (OIG-06-07), Nov. 2005; Eric Lipton, *Fictional Doomsday Team Plays Out Scene After Scene*, N.Y. Times, Mar. 26, 2005, at A11.

In 2005, the Department of Homeland Security (DHS) worked with other federal agencies to develop 15 all-hazards scenarios for use in homeland security preparedness activities. The scenarios represent high consequence terrorist attacks that might be caused by foreign or state-sponsored terrorists, domestic groups, or even single disgruntled individuals. *See* Dept. of Homeland Security/Homeland Security Council, *National Planning Scenarios* (Version 20.1 Draft, Apr. 2005), *available at* http://media.washingtonpost.com/wp-srv/nation/nationalsecurity/earlywarning/NationalPlanningScenariosApril2005.pdf.

## NOTES AND QUESTIONS

1. *Varying Effects of Terrorist Weapons.* Terrorist attacks using biological or radiological weapons might be carried out covertly (as in TOPOFF), with the results not manifesting themselves in health effects until days or even weeks later. By contrast, an attack using chemical weapons, high explosives, or (as on September 11) a civilian airliner would be immediately apparent. Can you describe other practical differences in attacks using different kinds of WMD that would complicate efforts by government officials to minimize

the resulting harm, restore essential public services, maintain public order, and prevent another attack? What different legal issues would be raised?

2. **Assessing the Emergency.** The escalating crisis in the TOPOFF exercise shows the importance of rapid recognition of the nature of an emergency. According to a recent DHS study,

> ER physicians, local hospital staff, infectious disease physicians, medical examiners, epidemiologists, and other public health officials should rapidly recognize the seriousness of the incident. Although laboratory methods to suspect preliminary diagnosis of the plague are available at many local public and private laboratories, there may be delayed recognition of the plague since most hospital ER and laboratory personnel in the United States and Canada have limited or no experience in identifying and/or treating plague.
>
> . . . A rapid onset with large numbers of persons presenting at ERs with pneumonia should create high suspicion of a terrorist incident utilizing the plague. Detection of the plague should also initiate laboratory identification of the plague strain and a determination of the potentiality of known antimicrobial drug resistance. . . . [*National Planning Scenarios, supra,* at 4-4.]

The CDC has developed a standard protocol for reporting possible outbreaks of diseases that might be weaponized by terrorists. *Interim Recommended Notification Procedures for Local and State Public Health Department Leaders in the Event of a Bioterrorist Incident,* Feb. 1, 2001, *at* http://www.bt.cdc.gov/EmContact/Protocols.asp. If a local health official suspects that an outbreak of common symptoms might have been caused by a biological weapon, the official must inform the state's Health Department, which will then notify CDC. If a terrorist source is confirmed or thought by the State Health Department to be probable, the FBI and other predetermined response partners are to be notified. The CDC reporting protocol is not mandatory, however, and state and local governments have adopted it with some variations that might cause delay or confusion in a crisis. Is there any justification for the variations?

3. **First Response.** As soon as a bioterrorist attack is detected, a concerted, immediate response will be required to limit the loss of life. What measures would the first responders to such an attack take? A DHS study includes this partial catalog:

> Persons with primary aerosol exposure to plague need to receive antibiotic therapy within 24 hours in order to prevent near certain fatality. The potential secondary person-to-person spread by fleeing victims will be a challenge. Epidemiological assessments, including contact investigation and notification, will be needed. Actions of incident-site personnel tested after the attack include hazard identification and site control, establishment and operation of the [federal] Incident Command System (ICS), isolation and treatment of exposed victims, mitigation efforts, obtainment of PPE [personal protective equipment] and prophylaxis for responders, site remediation

and monitoring, notification of airlines and other transportation providers, provision of public information, and effective coordination with national and international public health and governmental agencies. . . .

Evacuation and treatment of some victims will be required. Self-quarantine through shelter-in-place may be instituted. . . .

Tens of thousands of people will require treatment or prophylaxis with ventilators and antibiotics. Plague prompts antimicrobial prophylaxis of exposed persons, responders, and pertinent health care workers. Thousands will seek care at hospitals with many needing advanced critical care due to pneumonia caused by plague. Exposed persons will also need to be informed of signs and symptoms suggestive of plague as well as measures to prevent person-to-person spread. PPE (e.g., masks) for responders and health care providers should be available. Mobilization of the Strategic National Stockpile for additional critical supplies and antibiotics will be necessary. Public information activities will be needed to promote awareness of potential signs and symptoms of plague. Proper control measures will include the need for rapid treatment; contact tracing; and, potentially, self-quarantine through shelter-in-place or other least restrictive means. Actions of incident-site personnel tested after the attack include protective action decisions, recognition of the hazard and scope, providing emergency response, communication, protection of special populations, treating victims with additional ventilators at hospitals, providing patient screening clinics, and providing treatment or drug distribution centers for prophylactic antibiotics. Mortuary requirements, animal-based surveillance to monitor potential spread of plague via natural methods, and veterinary services also will need to be considered. Since this is an international incident, the U.S. Department of State's Bureau of Consular Affairs will need to be involved in order to assist foreign populations residing in the United States, foreign nationals in the United States, or U.S. citizens exposed or ill abroad. [*National Planning Scenarios, supra*, at 4-6.]

Who should be expected to perform all these tasks? What legal problems can you foresee in implementing these measures?

4. *Civil Unrest.* In the TOPOFF exercise, civil unrest (notionally, but predictably) broke out after a day or two. Can you suggest ways to avoid domestic violence in the wake of a terrorist attack? If such unrest is unavoidable, what government entity should be charged with responsibility for restoring order?

5. *Getting the Word Out.* The federal government has maintained a nationwide alert system since the earliest days of the Cold War. *See* Linda K. Moore, *Emergency Communications: The Emergency Alert System (EAS) and All-Hazard Warnings* (Cong. Res. Serv. RL32527), Sept. 13, 2006 (describing organization, technology, and protocols for use but little about

the content of messages). But it was not activated on September 11, 2001. When word began to spread about the attacks on the World Trade Center and the Pentagon, Americans turned immediately to their televisions for news. They were rewarded with days of nonstop pictures, government press releases, and expert speculation about what had happened.

Can you think of ways to increase the likelihood that emergency warnings and instructions will be heeded by members of the public? If an attack affects a wide area, as a chemical or radiological weapon might, or involves an infectious biological agent, like plague, do you suppose the government might want to regulate media coverage? Should it be able to impose limits on the dissemination of news? If so, can you say under what circumstances?

6. ***Preventing Another Attack.*** A WMD attack would obviously trigger massive intelligence efforts and criminal investigations. One objective would be to bring to justice those responsible for the attack. Another objective would be to prevent a subsequent attack. Who would be in charge of these activities, and what means would be employed? How would the criminal and intelligence investigations be coordinated with immediate measures to protect the public health?

7. ***Secondary Effects.*** A WMD attack like the one described in TOPOFF is likely to have widespread ripple effects, including disruptions of the nation's financial infrastructure.

> As the financial world . . . begins to realize the likelihood of an epidemic, a sell-off occurs in the markets. There is a high absentee rate at banks, other financial institutions, and major corporations. Adding to these complications is the fact that bank and other financial customers may be staying home, afraid to venture into public places and trying instead to conduct business on the phone. As a result, the phone systems at financial institutions may become completely tied up, with far fewer transactions than normal occurring. Automatic teller machines (ATMs), especially drive-up machines, may run out of cash before they can be replenished. The fear of plague has raised memories of the anthrax incidents of 2001, which may cause many citizens to be afraid to open their mail. [*National Planning Scenarios, supra*, at 6.]

How could these kinds of impacts be limited?

## C.  FIRST RESPONDERS: ROLES AND AUTHORITIES

If terrorists launch an attack in the United States using chemical, biological, radiological, or nuclear weapons or high explosives, local police, EMTs, hospital and other public health personnel, firefighters, and HAZMAT teams will be the first responders — seeking to contain the damage, ministering to the injured, and collecting evidence for a criminal prosecution. *See* Sydney J. Freedberg Jr., *Beyond the Blue Canaries*, Natl. J., Mar. 10, 2001.

Our consideration of the roles and authorities of first responders is framed by the response to the September 11, 2001, terrorist attack on the Pentagon.

Although that attack was overshadowed by the more dramatic catastrophe at the World Trade Center, the reaction of state and local officials in Virginia and surrounding areas demonstrated that intergovernmental planning and cooperation can pay off during a crisis.

### THE 9/11 COMMISSION REPORT: FINAL REPORT OF THE NATIONAL COMMISSION ON TERRORIST ATTACKS UPON THE UNITED STATES

Pages 311-315 (2004)

If it had happened on any other day, the disaster at the Pentagon would be remembered as a singular challenge and an extraordinary national story. Yet the calamity at the World Trade Center [on September 11, 2001] included catastrophic damage 1,000 feet above the ground that instantly imperiled tens of thousands of people. The two experiences are not comparable. . . .

The emergency response at the Pentagon represented a mix of local, state, and federal jurisdictions and was generally effective. It overcame the inherent complications of a response across jurisdictions because the Incident Command System, a formalized management structure for emergency response, was in place in the National Capital Region on 9/11.

Because of the nature of the event — a plane crash, fire, and partial building collapse — the Arlington County Fire Department served as incident commander. Different agencies had different roles. The incident required a major rescue, fire, and medical response from Arlington County at the U.S. military's headquarters — a facility under the control of the secretary of defense. Since it was a terrorist attack, the Department of Justice was the lead federal agency in charge (with authority delegated to the FBI for operational response). Additionally, the terrorist attack affected the daily operations and emergency management requirements of Arlington County and all bordering and surrounding jurisdictions.

At 9:37, the west wall of the Pentagon was hit by hijacked American Airlines Flight 77, a Boeing 757. The crash caused immediate and catastrophic damage. All 64 people aboard the airliner were killed, as were 125 people inside the Pentagon (70 civilians and 55 military service members). One hundred six people were seriously injured and transported to area hospitals. . . .

Local, regional, state, and federal agencies immediately responded to the Pentagon attack. In addition to county fire, police, and sheriff's departments, the response was assisted by the Metropolitan Washington Airports Authority, Ronald Reagan Washington National Airport Fire Department, Fort Myer Fire Department, the Virginia State Police, the Virginia Department of Emergency Management, the FBI, FEMA, a National Medical Response Team, the Bureau of Alcohol, Tobacco, and Firearms, and numerous military personnel within the Military District of Washington.

Command was established at 9:41. At the same time, the Arlington County Emergency Communications Center contacted the fire departments of Fairfax County, Alexandria, and the District of Columbia to request mutual aid. The incident command post provided a clear view of and access to the crash site, allowing the incident commander to assess the situation at all times.

At 9:55, the incident commander ordered an evacuation of the Pentagon impact area because a partial collapse was imminent; it occurred at 9:57, and no first responder was injured.

At 10:15, the incident commander ordered a full evacuation of the command post because of the warning of an approaching hijacked aircraft passed along by the FBI. This was the first of three evacuations caused by reports of incoming aircraft, and the evacuation order was well communicated and well coordinated.

Several factors facilitated the response to this incident, and distinguish it from the far more difficult task in New York. There was a single incident, and it was not 1,000 feet above ground. The incident site was relatively easy to secure and contain, and there were no other buildings in the immediate area. There was no collateral damage beyond the Pentagon.

Yet the Pentagon response encountered difficulties that echo those experienced in New York. As the "Arlington County: After-Action Report" notes, there were significant problems with both self-dispatching and communications: "Organizations, response units, and individuals proceeding on their own initiative directly to an incident site, without the knowledge and permission of the host jurisdiction and the Incident Commander, complicate the exercise of command, increase the risks faced by bonafide responders, and exacerbate the challenge of accountability." With respect to communications, the report concludes: "Almost all aspects of communications continue to be problematic, from initial notification to tactical operations. Cellular telephones were of little value. . . . Radio channels were initially oversaturated. . . . Pagers seemed to be the most reliable means of notification when available and used, but most firefighters are not issued pagers."

It is a fair inference, given the differing situations in New York City and Northern Virginia, that the problems in command, control, and communications that occurred at both sites will likely recur in any emergency of similar scale. The task looking forward is to enable first responders to respond in a coordinated manner with the greatest possible awareness of the situation.

## NOTES AND QUESTIONS

1. *Who Are the First Responders?* Which officials and private citizens were actually the first responders in the 9/11 attack on the Pentagon? What agencies and jurisdictions did they represent? Pursuant to what authority did they operate? Given the gravity, scale, and complexity of the consequences, coordination of the various responses was critically important. Who did the coordinating, and how well was it done?

2. *Regional Cooperation.* Pentagon responders from various agencies and jurisdictions had prior experience working together in different settings, and they benefited from the existence of an incident command center. This permitted regional coordination that was extremely beneficial. Mutual aid agreements — formal, prenegotiated, inter-jurisdictional pacts — also allowed most of the first responders to share a common radio frequency, so they could receive assignments by radio and get to work immediately upon arrival. *9/11 Commission Report, supra,* at 315.

Almost all states have approved a congressionally authorized compact of mutual assistance, and a number of states have entered into such compacts. *See* Emergency Management Assistance Compact, Pub. L. No. 104-321, 110 Stat. 3877 (1996). The compact

> resolve[s] potential legal and financial obstacles that states might otherwise encounter as they provide assistance to the stricken state (or states). The compact sets out the responsibilities of the signatory states, provides authority to officials responding from other states (except the power of arrest) equal to that held by residents of the affected state, assures reciprocity in recognizing professional licenses or permits for professional skills, and provides liability protection (in certain areas) to responders from other states. The compact requires that signatory states develop plans to evacuate civilian population centers. [Keith Bea, *The Emergency Management Assistance Compact (EMAC): An Overview* (Cong. Res. Serv. RS21227)1, Aug. 18, 2006.]

Some states have entered into other mutual assistance agreements as well. *Id.* at 3. See *also* 42 U.S.C.A. §5196(h)(2)(A) (West Supp. 2006) (authorizing the head of FEMA to "assist and encourage the states to negotiate and enter into interstate emergency preparedness compacts"); Pub. L. No. 109-295, §§646(f), 661, 120 Stat. 1355, 1426, 1432-1433 (2006). Regional mechanisms for response to disasters, or the lack thereof, were the focus of reports assessing the response in 2005 to Hurricane Katrina. *See* The White House, *The Federal Response to Hurricane Katrina: Lessons Learned*, Feb. 2006, *available at* http://www.whitehouse.gov/reports/katrina-lessons-learned/; *A Failure of Initiative: Final Report of the Select Bipartisan Committee to Investigate the Preparation for and Response to Hurricane Katrina*, H.R. Rep. No. 109-377 (2006), *available at* http://katrina.house.gov/full_katrina_report.htm.

What advantages do such regional response structures offer? Do you see any practical or legal obstacles to their creation or implementation? Regional authorities may sometimes lack the staff, enforcement powers, and resources needed to respond. And even if they can issue "orders," state and local laws may prevent subregional authorities from complying without state and local authorization by executive order or even legislation, especially if the regional "order" requires one state to expend resources and manpower in another. How can these obstacles be overcome?

3. *State and Local Response Plans.* What plans do you think cities, counties, and states have made in preparation for terrorist attacks? How would you find out about such plans? If a city is unable to respond fully to a terrorist attack, a state might provide assistance to that city. What rules would govern such assistance? Who would be in charge of the state assets deployed to a city under attack? A review and assessment of the status of catastrophe and evacuation planning for all states, as well as major cities and urban areas, may be found at Dept. of Homeland Security, *Nationwide Plan Review—Phase 2 Report*, June 16, 2006, *available at* http://www.dhs.gov/xlibrary/assets/Prep_NationwidePlanReview.pdf;

Keith Bea, L. Cheryl Runyon & Kae M. Warnock, *Emergency Management and Homeland Security Statutory Authorities in the States, District of Columbia, and Insular Areas: A Summary* (Cong. Res. Serv. RL32287), Mar. 17, 2004.

# D.  SECOND RESPONDERS: THE FEDERAL ROLE

From 1950, when the Soviet Union tested its first atomic weapon, until the end of the Cold War, the American people lived in constant fear of a nuclear attack. (That fear has now abated despite the fact that Russia and the United States still maintain more than 6,000 strategic nuclear weapons each on high alert.) For more than 40 years, the Civil Defense Act of 1950, ch. 1228, 64 Stat. 1245 (1951), as amended, directed the creation of a program to minimize the effects of such an attack on the civilian population and to deal with the resulting emergency conditions. Included in the program were planning for continuity of government, recruitment of emergency personnel, stockpiling of critical materials, and provision of warning systems and shelters. The act purported to give the President broad powers in a civil defense emergency — for example, to take property "without regard to the limitation of any existing law," *id.* §303(a), 64 Stat. 1252, and to provide the government with immunity from suits for damages to property, death, or personal injury based on its actions during such an emergency. *Id.* §304, 64 Stat. 1253. The civil defense program, administered since 1979 by FEMA, was supposed to convince the American people and the Soviet leadership that the United States could not only survive a nuclear war, but could also win one.

Among the plans developed by FEMA under the Civil Defense Act was one called "Crisis Relocation." The plan called for evacuation to the countryside of 145 million Americans living in big cities or near key military bases in anticipation of a nuclear attack. In each of 400 target areas the exodus would be guided by instructions printed in local telephone directories. According to the plan, evacuees would be welcomed by their rural hosts and housed in schools, churches, and other public buildings until the trouble blew over. As recently as 1981, FEMA asserted that a "moderate-cost, balanced civil defense program . . . could enable survival of roughly 80 percent of the U.S. population in a heavy attack." FEMA, U.S. Crisis Relocation Planning (P&P-7 1981). Critics of the plan were numerous; some warned that as soon as word of an impending attack got out, target populations would evacuate spontaneously and chaotically. *See, e.g., Counterfeit Ark: Crisis Relocation for Nuclear War* (Jennifer Leaning & Langley Keyes eds., 1984). Presumably, some of these plans have been or will be recycled for possible use if terrorists attack again using weapons of mass destruction.

The Civil Defense Act also provided for federal responses to natural disasters, such as floods and hurricanes. The Act was augmented in 1974 by the Robert T. Stafford Disaster Relief and Emergency Assistance Act (Stafford Act), 42 U.S.C.A. §§5121-5206 (West 2003 & Supp. 2006), as amended. That statute provides broadly for federal assistance to states affected by various disasters. In 1994, the Civil Defense Act was repealed, then partially reenacted as an amendment to the Stafford Act. National Defense Authorization Act for

Fiscal Year 1995, Pub. L. No. 103-337, §§3411, 3412, 108 Stat. 2663, 3100-3111 (1994). A House Armed Services Committee report declared at the time, ironically, that "the program has lost its defense emphasis. . . . Rather, the chief threats today come from tornadoes, earthquakes, floods, chemical spills, and the like." H.R. Rep. No. 103-499, at 5 (1994), *reprinted in* U.S.C.C.A.N. 2091, 2182-2183.

The Stafford Act may be invoked in the event of a presidentially declared major disaster or emergency, including "any natural catastrophe . . . or, regardless of cause, any fire, flood, or explosion," or on "any occasion for which, in the determination of the President, Federal assistance is needed to supplement State and local efforts and capabilities to save lives and to protect property and public health and safety, or to lessen or avert the threat of a catastrophe." 42 U.S.C. §§5122, 5170, 5191(a). While the President's declaration will usually be based on a state governor's request for help, the President may act without such a request when "the primary responsibility for response rests with the United States." *Id.* §5191(b). Moreover, the President may direct the Department of Defense (DOD) to perform any emergency work "essential for the preservation of life and property" for up to ten days. *Id.* §5170b(c). President Clinton declared an emergency under the Stafford Act on April 19, 1995, in response to the terrorist bombing that day of the Alfred P. Murrah Federal Building in Oklahoma City. He ordered FEMA to direct and coordinate responses by other federal agencies and to provide needed federal assistance. 60 Fed. Reg. 22579 (May 8, 1995). *See also* 60 Fed. Reg. 21819 (May 3, 1995) (declaring a "major disaster" and providing public and individual assistance). The Stafford Act was also invoked on September 11, 2001, when President Bush declared a "major disaster" in the State of New York in order to make available various forms of public and individual assistance, 66 Fed. Reg. 48682-01; and the Act was invoked on August 27, 2005, for Louisiana, Mississippi, and Alabama in anticipation of Hurricane Katrina. The White House, *Statement of Federal Emergency Assistance for Louisiana*, Aug. 27, 2005. *See generally* Keith Bea, *Federal Stafford Act Disaster Assistance: Presidential Declarations, Eligible Activities, and Funding* (Cong. Res. Serv. RL33053), Aug. 29, 2005.

In July 2002, the White House Office of Homeland Security published the *National Strategy for Homeland Security, available at* http://www.whitehouse.-gov/homeland/book/. In line with earlier recommendations, this document recognized a need to "clarify lines of responsibility for homeland security in the executive branch, . . . mobilize our entire society, . . . and manage risk and allocate resources judiciously." *Id.* at 3. It called for planning to defend against terrorist attacks using conventional weapons as well as weapons of mass destruction, cyber attacks, and new or unexpected tactics. To accomplish these goals, it proposed the establishment of a new Department of Homeland Security (DHS), which would assume primary responsibility for intelligence and warning of a domestic attack, border and transportation security, domestic counterterrorism, protection of critical infrastructure, and response and recovery from any future terrorist attack. DHS would also respond to natural disasters and consolidate emergency activities into one "genuinely all-discipline, all-hazard plan." *Id.* at 42.

The new department was created later the same year with passage of the Homeland Security Act of 2002, Pub. L. No. 107-296, 116 Stat. 2135 (2002) (codified at 6 U.S.C. §§101-557 and scattered sections of other titles). The Act merges all or portions of 22 federal agencies and 170,000 employees into DHS. Included are the Coast Guard, Customs Service, Transportation Security Administration, FEMA, the Secret Service, parts of the Immigration and Naturalization Service, and a long list of less well-known federal entities. The startup of this huge new enterprise is traced in Harold C. Relyea, *Homeland Security: Department Organization and Management — Implementation Phase* (Cong. Res. Serv. RL31751), Jan. 3, 2005.

One of the principal goals of DHS is to provide a unified federal response to a terrorist incident as well as to natural disasters. DHS is now the focal point for communications between and among federal, state, and local agencies, and it is supposed to provide an authoritative voice of the government in keeping the public informed about emergency responses.

In February 2003, the White House published Homeland Security Presidential Directive/HSPD-5, entitled *Management of Domestic Incidents*. The Directive is meant to "ensure that all levels of the government across the Nation have the capability to work efficiently and effectively together, using a national approach to domestic incident management," *id.* ¶(3), and it declares that the Secretary of Homeland Security is the "principal Federal official for domestic incident management." *Id.* at ¶(4). On the other hand, the Secretary of Health and Human Services (HHS) shares responsibility with DHS for biological incidents, *see* Sarah A. Lister, *An Overview of the U.S. Public Health System in the Context of Emergency Preparedness* (Cong. Res. Serv. RL31719) 22, May 17, 2005, while the Attorney General is given lead responsibility for criminal investigations of terrorist threats or acts within the United States and is directed to "coordinate the activities of other members of the law enforcement community to detect, prevent, preempt, and disrupt terrorist attacks against the United States." HSPD-5 at ¶(8). In addition, the Defense Department may provide military support to civil authorities in a domestic incident but always under the command of the Secretary of Defense. *Id.* at ¶(9). The DHS responsibilities are triggered when a federal agency acting under its own authority has requested DHS assistance; when State and local resources are overwhelmed and federal assistance has been requested by state and local authorities; when more than one federal agency has become involved in responding to the incident; or when the President directs the Secretary to assume management of the incident. *Id.* at ¶(4).

HSPD-5 also ordered the creation of a National Incident Management System (NIMS) to provide a flexible national framework within which governments at all levels and private entities could work together to manage domestic "incidents." The NIMS was rolled out a year later. Dept. of Homeland Security, *National Incident Management System*, Mar. 1, 2004, *available at* http://www.dhs.gov/xlibrary/assets/NIMS-90-web.pdf.

Finally, HSPD-5 called for development of a National Response Plan (NRP) to replace existing national emergency response plans. The new NRP was published in January 2005. Dept. of Homeland Security, *National Response Plan*, Dec. 2004, *available at* http://www.dhs.gov/xlibrary/assets/NRP_FullText.pdf.

Like earlier plans, it provides for a coordinated, all-hazards approach to "incident management," spelling out in broad terms the roles of all relevant elements of the national government and calling for communications and operational coordination by offices within DHS. The NRP also sets out a framework for federal interaction with state, local, and tribal governments and with the private sector in an emergency. In addition, it includes 12 Emergency Support Functions (ESFs), described in annexes to the NRP, that supply details on the mission, policies, and concept of operations of the federal agencies involved in support to state and local agencies.

A related document, *National Preparedness* (HSPD-8), Dec. 17, 2003, "describes the way Federal departments and agencies will prepare for ... a response [to a terrorist attack or major natural disaster], including prevention activities during the early stages of a terrorism incident."

Federal emergency planning is extensively described and evaluated in Henry B. Hogue & Keith Bea, *Federal Emergency Management and Homeland Security Organization: Historical Developments and Legislative Options* (Cong. Res. Serv. RL33369), June 1, 2006; Keith Bea, *Organization and Mission of the Emergency Preparedness and Response Directorate: Issues and Options for the 109th Congress* (Cong. Res. Serv. RL33064), Sept. 7, 2005; *Nationwide Plan Review — Phase 2 Report, supra* p. 641, at 70-78.

## NOTES AND QUESTIONS

1. ***Adequacy of Emergency Response Authority.*** Federal plans for responses to terrorist attacks and other catastrophes are described here in very general terms. In part that is because such plans, as well as the organizations that draw them up, have changed dramatically since September 11, 2001, and are continuing to evolve rapidly. Some current details may be found on the Web site of the Department of Homeland Security, at http://www.dhs.gov/index.shtm.

   Do you think there is adequate authority to execute existing plans? To do whatever else might be required? How will a federal official in charge of responding to a terrorist attack determine whether she has the authority she thinks she needs? Can you suggest a strategy for making it more likely that such an official would act only within the limits of her authority?

2. ***Assigning Agency Responsibilities.*** If the inherent unpredictability of these crises makes it impossible to anticipate every appropriate response, it is at least important to have an agreement about who will have overall responsibility for making necessary decisions based on contemporaneous information. The NRP is supposed to reflect that agreement and to indicate which agencies will be responsible for discharging what federal responsibilities in any given crisis.

   In the aftermath of Hurricane Katrina, however, White House investigators of the flawed federal response to the storm found that, while the NRP is sufficiently "flexible and scalable" to meet any threat or event, "the specific triggers" for the NRP and its components "are unclear." *The Federal Response to Hurricane Katrina, supra* p. 641, at 14. DHS Secretary Michael Chertoff declared Katrina to be an incident of national significance (INS) on August 30, 2005, when two of the four triggering criteria listed in HSPD-5 ¶(4), noted above, had been met. *Id.* Yet there reportedly was confusion about whether the INS was triggered earlier by the President's emergency declaration under the Stafford Act. And according to the White House report, the NRP failed to articulate what actions should be taken by which agencies once an INS was declared. The lack of clear guidance was said to compromise the response. *Id.* at 15. If instead of a hurricane the City of New Orleans had been struck by a bioterrorist attack, the federal response presumably would have been equally ineffectual. Can you guess why it has been so difficult to make federal plans more detailed and concrete? Assigned roles of various federal agencies are described in Keith Bea, *Organization and Mission of the Emergency Preparedness and Response Directorate: Issues and Options for the 109th Congress* (Cong. Res. Serv. RL33064), Sept. 7, 2005. Extensive efforts to reorganize and improve the federal response capability are spelled out in Sarah A. Lister & Frank Gottron, *The Pandemic and All-Hazards Preparedness Act (P.L. 109-417): Provisions and Changes to Preexisting Law* (Cong. Res. Serv. RL33589), Jan. 25, 2007; Keith Bea et al., *Federal Emergency Management Policy Changes After Hurricane Katrina: A Summary of Statutory Provisions* (Cong. Res. Serv. 33729), Dec. 15, 2006.

3. *Critical Infrastructure Protection.* In 2003, President Bush signed *Critical Infrastructure Identification, Prioritization, and Protection* (HSPD-7), Dec. 17, 2003, setting out policy for protection of the nation's telecommunications, finance, transportation, postal, and other vital services. These services have become highly automated and interdependent, and they may be especially vulnerable to cyber attacks. Every federal agency is charged by the directive with assessing the vulnerability of its own critical infrastructures and taking appropriate precautions.

   Homeland Security Act §201(d)(5) charged DHS to "develop a comprehensive national plan for securing the key resources and critical infrastructure of the United States." The plan, including a letter agreement signed by heads of various relevant federal agencies, was completed on June 30, 2006. Dept. of Homeland Security, *National Infrastructure Protection Plan* (2006). Private sector operators — banks, public utilities, airlines, Internet service providers, and others — are enlisted in the effort to guard against terrorist attacks that could dramatically interrupt the routine of daily life as well as threaten national security. What legal and practical challenges do you think might be presented by this collaboration between government and non-government entities?

4. *Secrecy in Planning.* As recently as 1988, the President had prepared and made ready for immediate signature a series of 48 Presidential Emergency Action Documents (PEADs), some of them Top Secret "option documents," others standby executive orders dealing with border controls, detention of aliens, mobilization for a conventional war, and other matters. These were premised not on the Civil Defense Act or the Stafford Act but on the President's "implied authority." Many more recent emergency planning documents are either partly or entirely classified. Should the content of these documents, or in some instances the very existence of the documents, be

made public? What are the practical consequences of keeping them secret? What are the implications for constitutional government?

5. ***Coordination with First Responders.*** Federal planning documents call for the national government to furnish guidance to state and local authorities in planning responses to man-made and natural disasters and to provide direct assistance to those authorities when they are overwhelmed. The documents also call for federal agencies to maintain control in a crisis over uniquely federal functions. Can you tell from the authorities reviewed so far exactly how federal agencies would work with or support state and local authorities and first responders in responding to a WMD attack or massive natural disaster? If first responders are necessarily first on the scene, when, to what extent, and upon whose orders would responsibility for overall management of an incident shift to federal control? How long would that federal primacy continue? Do you think it is important to try to answer these questions in advance of a crisis?

6. ***Communications in a Crisis.*** How would you rate the importance of ensuring clear and reliable communications in a terrorist crisis among the relevant federal, state, and local government agencies? What about providing authoritative current information and instructions to the public? Are the two tasks related? Considering the terrorist attack scenario set forth earlier in this chapter, can you describe strategies for achieving both of these objectives? *See* Linda K. Moore, *Emergency Communications Legislation, 2002-2006: Implications for the 100th Congress* (Cong. Res. Serv. RL 33747), Dec. 14, 2006.

7. ***A Military Role?*** Each state's National Guard has elements trained and equipped to assist, under the direction of the state governor, in the response to a WMD attack or a large natural disaster. See *infra* p. 694. At the federal level, the Stafford Act, the NRP, and other planning documents assign the Defense Department a supporting role in responding to a terrorist attack, including one involving a weapon of mass destruction. Should the military be given a larger role, or even lead agency responsibility? Consideration was given to such proposals in the wake of the flawed response to Hurricane Katrina. *See* David E. Sanger, *Bush Wants to Consider Broadening of Military's Powers During Natural Disasters*, N.Y. Times, Sept. 27, 2005, at A1. Do you think either state or federal governments could mount a fully effective response to such a calamity without the assistance of military forces? These questions are explored in Chapter 21.

# E.   QUARANTINES AND OTHER COMPULSORY RESPONSES

Terrorist attacks using some kinds of weapons of mass destruction would present government responders with challenges not encountered with high explosives or a hostage-taking. A chemical, nuclear, or radiological weapon might require exclusion of persons from a contaminated area. If a biological weapon were used, public health officials might need to prevent infected persons, whether sick or asymptomatic, from spreading the disease to others by isolating them, especially if the infectious agent had been altered to make it drug- or vaccine-resistant. They might also have to be given medicine. Others who might have been exposed to the disease could require vaccination or need to have their movements restricted. *See* Edward A. Fallone, *Preserving the Public Health: A Proposal to Quarantine Recalcitrant AIDS Carriers*, 68 B.U. L. Rev. 441, 460-461 (1988). The federal government has authority to impose interstate and foreign quarantines and take other protective measures, while state and local health departments may exercise quarantine and isolation authority as part of the first response to a terrorist attack. These overlapping authorities, as well as some practical concerns, are examined here.

## 1.  STATE AND LOCAL RESPONSES TO A TERRORIST ATTACK

### JEW HO v. WILLIAMSON

Circuit Court, N.D. California, 1900
103 F. 10

MORROW, Circuit Judge. . . . On the 28th day of May, 1900, the board of health of the city and county of San Francisco adopted [a] resolution [noting nine deaths due to bubonic plague in a San Francisco district and requesting the board of supervisors to authorize quarantine of the district.] . . .

Thereafter . . . the board of supervisors passed [an] ordinance: . . .

> . . . "The board of health . . . is hereby authorized and empowered to quarantine persons, houses, places, and districts within this city and county, when in its judgment it is deemed necessary to prevent the spreading of contagious or infectious diseases." . . .

. . . [O]n the 29th day of May, 1900, at a special meeting of the board of health, a resolution was passed, which . . . provided as follows:

> "And whereas, after a careful and minute investigation had during a period of three months last past, and from the result of investigation made by Drs. Kellogg, bacteriologist to the board of health, Montgomery, of the University of California, Ophulf, of the Cooper Medical College, and J.J. Kinyoun, of the U.S. marine hospital service, each and all of whom have reported to this board that bubonic plague has existed in the district hereafter mentioned, and that nine deaths have occurred within said period within said district from said disease; and whereas, this board has reason to believe and does believe that danger does exist to the health of the citizens of the city and county of San Francisco by reason of the existence of germs of the said disease remaining in the district hereafter mentioned: Now, therefore, be it resolved: That the health officer be and is hereby instructed to place in quarantine until further notice that particular district of the city bounded north by Broadway, northeast by Montgomery avenue, east by Kearney, south by California, and west by Stockton streets; and that the chief of police is hereby requested to furnish such assistance as may be necessary to establish and maintain said quarantine. . . ."

Thereafter, on May 31, 1900, the board of supervisors passed another ordinance . . . [which] provided for the establishment of quarantine regulations in the district named, and directed the chief of police to furnish such assistance as might be necessary to establish and maintain this quarantine.

The complainant in this case, Jew Ho, alleges . . . that he resides . . . within the limits of said quarantined district, and is engaged in the business of conducting a grocery store, as the proprietor and manager thereof, at his said place of residence, and that a great number of the patrons and customers of his said business reside at various places in the city and county of San Francisco outside the boundaries of said quarantined district, and are now, and ever since the 29th day of May, 1900, have been, prevented and prohibited by the defendants from visiting, patronizing, and dealing with the complainant in his said grocery store; that the complainant has been prevented and prohibited since the said 29th day of May, 1900, from selling his goods, wares, and merchandise, and from otherwise carrying on the business in which he is engaged. . . . The complainant alleges that there is not now, and never has been, any case of bubonic plague within the limits of said quarantined district, nor any germs or bacteria of bubonic plague, and that other diseases caused the illness and death of the persons claimed by defendants to have died of the bubonic plague within the 30 days next preceding the filing of this complaint. . . . The prayer of the bill is that an injunction be granted, enjoining and restraining the defendants from interfering with the personal rights and privileges of the complainant. . . .

It is . . . contended that the acts of the defendants in establishing a quarantine district in San Francisco are authorized by the general police power of the state, intrusted to the city of San Francisco. The defendants rely upon a number of cases in support of this asserted jurisdiction and authority. . . .

The case of Lawton v. Steel, 152 U.S. 133 (1894), had relation to a regulation concerning the fisheries. The court said with respect to the police power of the state:

> "The extent and limits of what is known as the 'police power' . . . [are] universally conceded to include everything essential to the public safety, health, and morals, and to justify the destruction or abatement by summary proceedings of whatever may be regarded as a public nuisance. Under this power it has been held that the state may order the destruction of a house falling to decay, or otherwise endangering the lives of passers-by; the demolition of such as are in the path of a conflagration; the slaughter of diseased cattle; the destruction of decayed or unwholesome food; the prohibition of wooden buildings in cities; the regulation of railways and other means of public conveyance, and of interment in burial grounds; the restriction of objectionable trades to certain localities; the compulsory vaccination of children; the confinement of the insane or those afflicted with contagious diseases; the restraint of vagrants, beggars, and habitual drunkards; the suppression of obscene publications and houses of ill fame; and the prohibition of gambling houses and places where intoxicating liquors are sold. Beyond this, however, the state may interfere wherever the public interests demand it; and in this particular a large discretion is necessarily vested in the legislature to determine, not only what the interests of the public require, but what measures are necessary for the protection of such interests.

To justify the state in thus interposing its authority in behalf of the public, it must appear — First, that the interests of the public generally, as distinguished from those of a particular class, require such interference; and, second, that the means are reasonably necessary for the accomplishment of the purpose, and not unduly oppressive upon individuals. The legislature may not, under the guise of protecting the public interests, arbitrarily interfere with private business, or impose unusual and unnecessary restrictions upon lawful occupations. In other words, its determination as to what is a proper exercise of its police powers is not final or conclusive, but is subject to the supervision of the courts." . . .

Affidavits have been filed on behalf of the complainant in this case, — one of them by Dr. J.I. Stephen. . . .

I read that affidavit for the purpose of showing the method adopted by the board of health for the suppressing of this so-called plague, namely, the quarantining of a large territory in the city of San Francisco, — some 10 or 12 blocks, — in which there are located about 10,000 people. It must necessarily follow that, where so many have been quarantined, the danger of the spread of the disease would not diminish. The purpose of quarantine and health laws and regulations with respect to contagious and infectious diseases is directed primarily to preventing the spread of such diseases among the inhabitants of localities. In this respect these laws and regulations come under the police power of the state, and may be enforced by quarantine and health officers, in the exercise of a large discretion, as circumstances may require. The more densely populated the community, the greater danger there is that the disease will spread, and hence the necessity for effectual methods of protection. To accomplish this purpose, persons afflicted with such diseases are confined to their own domiciles until they have so far recovered as not to be liable to communicate the disease to others. The same restriction is imposed upon victims of such diseases found traveling. The object of all such rules and regulations is to confine the disease to the smallest possible number of people; and hence when a vessel in a harbor, a car on a railroad, or a house on land, is found occupied by persons afflicted with such a disease, the vessel, the car, or the house, as the case may be, is cut off from all communication with the inhabitants of adjoining houses or contiguous territory, that the spread of the disease may be arrested at once and confined to the least possible territory. This is a system of quarantine that is well recognized in all communities, and is provided by the laws of the various states and municipalities: That, when a contagious or infectious disease breaks out in a place, they quarantine the house or houses first; the purpose being to restrict the disease to the smallest number possible, and that it may not spread to other people in the same locality. It must necessarily follow that, if a large section or a large territory is quarantined, intercommunication of the people within that territory will rather tend to spread the disease than to restrict it. . . . If we are to suppose that this bubonic plague has existed in San Francisco since the 6th day of March, and that there has been danger of its spreading over the city, the most dangerous thing that could have been done was to quarantine the whole city, as to the Chinese, as was substantially done in the first instance. [In an omitted portion of the opinion, the court found that the quarantine was enforced against members of the Chinese community but not against others.] The next most dangerous thing to do was to quarantine any considerable portion of the city, and not restrict intercommunication within the quarantined district. The quarantined district comprises 12 blocks. It is not claimed that in all the 12 blocks of the quarantined district the disease has been discovered. There are, I believe, 7 or 8 blocks in which it is claimed that deaths have occurred on account of what is said to be this disease. In 2 or 3 blocks it has not appeared at all. Yet this quarantine has been thrown around the entire district. The people therein obtain their food and other supplies, and communicate freely with each other in all their affairs. They are permitted to go from a place where it is said that the disease has appeared, freely among the other 10,000 people in that district. It would necessarily follow that, if the disease is there, every facility has been offered by this species of quarantine to enlarge its sphere and increase its danger and its destructive force. . . . The court cannot but see the practical question that is presented to it as to the ineffectiveness of this method of quarantine against such a disease as this. So, upon that ground, the court must hold that this quarantine is not a reasonable regulation to accomplish the purposes sought. It is not in harmony with the declared purpose of the board of health or of the board of supervisors. . . .

There is one other feature of this case, and that is as to whether or not the bubonic plague has existed in this city, and whether it does now exist. . . .

The evidence of Dr. Stephen and these other physicians shows that, at most, there have been 11 deaths in the quarantined district which on autopsy have disclosed some of the symptoms of the bubonic plague. But there has been no living case under the examination of the physicians from which a clinical history has been obtained, and it does not appear that there has been any transmission of the disease from any of those who have died. From all of which the court infers that the suspected cases were not contagious or infectious, or, if contagious and infectious, they were but sporadic in their nature, and had no tendency to spread or disseminate in the city. If it were within the province of this court to determine this issue, I think, upon such testimony as that given by these physicians, I should be compelled to hold that the plague did not exist and has not existed in San Francisco. But this testimony is contradicted by the physicians of the board of health. They have furnished the testimony of reputable physicians that the bubonic plague has existed, and that the danger of its development does exist. In the face of such testimony the court does not feel authorized to render a judicial opinion as to whether or not the plague exists or has existed in this city. Indeed, that is one of the questions that courts, under ordinary circumstances, are disposed to leave to boards of health to determine, upon such evidence as their professional skill deems satisfactory. If they believe, or if they have even a suspicion, that there is an infectious or contagious disease existing within the city, it is unquestionably the duty of such boards to act and protect the city against it, not to wait always until the matter shall be established to the satisfaction of all the physicians or all the persons who may examine into the question. It is the duty of the court to leave such question to be determined primarily by the authority competent for that purpose. . . .

. . . [T]his quarantine cannot be continued, by reason of the fact that it is unreasonable, unjust, and oppressive, and therefore contrary to the laws limiting the police powers of the state and municipality in such matters . . . . The counsel for complainant will prepare an injunction, which shall, however, permit the board to maintain a quarantine around such places as it may have reason to believe are infected by contagious or infectious diseases, but that the general quarantine of the whole district must not be continued, and that the people residing in that district, so far as they have been restricted or limited in their persons and their business, have that limitation and restraint removed. . . .

## JACOBSON V. MASSACHUSETTS

United States Supreme Court, 1905
197 U.S. 11

Mr. Justice HARLAN delivered the opinion of the court. This case involves the validity, under the Constitution of the United States, of certain provisions in the statutes of Massachusetts relating to vaccination.

The Revised Laws of that commonwealth, chap. 75, §137, provide that "the board of health of a city or town, if, in its opinion, it is necessary for the public health or safety, shall require and enforce the vaccination and revaccination of all the inhabitants thereof, and shall provide them with the means of free vaccination. Whoever, being over twenty-one years of age and not under guardianship, refuses or neglects to comply with such requirement shall forfeit $5."

An exception is made in favor of "children who present a certificate, signed by a registered physician, that they are unfit subjects for vaccination." §139.

Proceeding under the above statutes, the board of health of the city of Cambridge, Massachusetts, on the 27th day of February, 1902, adopted the following regulation: "Whereas, smallpox has been prevalent to some extent in the city of Cambridge, and still continues to increase; and whereas, it is necessary for the speedy extermination of the disease that all persons not protected by vaccination should be vaccinated; and whereas, in the opinion of the board, the public health and safety require the vaccination or revaccination of all the inhabitants of Cambridge; be it ordered, that all the inhabitants of the city who have not been successfully vaccinated since March 1st, 1897, be vaccinated or revaccinated."

Subsequently, the board adopted an additional regulation empowering a named physician to enforce the vaccination of persons as directed by the board at its special meeting of February 27th.

The above regulations being in force, the plaintiff in error, Jacobson, was proceeded against by a criminal complaint in one of the inferior courts of Massachusetts. The complaint charged that on the 17th day of July, 1902, the board of health of Cambridge, being of the opinion that it was necessary for the public health and safety, required the vaccination and revaccination of all the inhabitants thereof who had not been successfully vaccinated since the 1st day of March, 1897, and provided them with the means of free vaccination; and that the defendant, being over twenty-one years of age and not under guardianship, refused and neglected to comply with such requirement. . . .

The defendant . . . asked numerous instructions to the jury, among which were the following:

> That §137 of chapter 75 of the Revised Laws of Massachusetts was in derogation
> of the rights secured to the defendant by . . . the 14th Amendment of the

Constitution of the United States, and especially of the clauses of that amendment providing that no state shall make or enforce any law abridging the privileges or immunities of citizens of the United States, nor deprive any person of life, liberty, or property without due process of law, nor deny to any person within its jurisdiction the equal protection of the laws. . . .

Each of defendant's prayers for instructions was rejected . . . . A verdict of guilty was thereupon returned.

The case was then continued for the opinion of the Supreme Judicial Court of Massachusetts [,which] . . . sustained the action of the trial court . . . .

We come, then, to inquire whether any right given or secured by the Constitution is invaded by the statute as interpreted by the state court. The defendant insists that his liberty is invaded when the state subjects him to fine or imprisonment for neglecting or refusing to submit to vaccination; that a compulsory vaccination law is unreasonable, arbitrary, and oppressive, and, therefore, hostile to the inherent right of every freeman to care for his own body and health in such way as to him seems best; and that the execution of such a law against one who objects to vaccination, no matter for what reason, is nothing short of an assault upon his person. But the liberty secured by the Constitution of the United States to every person within its jurisdiction does not import an absolute right in each person to be, at all times and in all circumstances, wholly freed from restraint. There are manifold restraints to which every person is necessarily subject for the common good. On any other basis organized society could not exist with safety to its members. Society based on the rule that each one is a law unto himself would soon be confronted with disorder and anarchy. Real liberty for all could not exist under the operation of a principle which recognizes the right of each individual person to use his own, whether in respect of his person or his property, regardless of the injury that may be done to others. This court has more than once recognized it as a fundamental principle that "persons and property are subjected to all kinds of restraints and burdens in order to secure the general comfort, health, and prosperity of the state; of the perfect right of the legislature to do which no question ever was, or upon acknowledged general principles ever can be, made, so far as natural persons are concerned." Hannibal & St. J. R. Co. v. Husen, 95 U.S. 465, 471 (1877). . . .

Applying these principles to the present case, it is to be observed that the legislature of Massachusetts required the inhabitants of a city or town to be vaccinated only when, in the opinion of the board of health, that was necessary for the public health or the public safety. The authority to determine for all what ought to be done in such an emergency must have been lodged somewhere or in some body; and surely it was appropriate for the legislature to refer that question, in the first instance, to a board of health composed of persons residing in the locality affected, and appointed, presumably, because of their fitness to determine such questions. To invest such a body with authority over such matters was not an unusual, nor an unreasonable or arbitrary, requirement. Upon the principle of self-defense, of paramount necessity, a community has the right to protect itself against an epidemic of disease which threatens the safety of its members. It is to be observed that when the regulation in question was adopted, smallpox, according to the recitals in the regulation adopted by the board of health, was prevalent to some extent in the city of Cambridge, and the disease was increasing. If such was the situation — and nothing is asserted or appears in the record to the contrary — if we are to attach any value whatever to the knowledge which, it is safe to affirm, is common to all civilized peoples touching smallpox and the methods most usually employed to eradicate that disease, it cannot be adjudged that the present regulation of the board of health was not necessary in order to protect the public health and secure the public safety. Smallpox being prevalent and increasing at Cambridge, the court would usurp the functions of another branch of government if it adjudged, as matter of law, that the mode adopted under the sanction of the state to protect the people at large was arbitrary, and not justified by the necessities of the case. . . .

Whatever may be thought of the expediency of this statute, it cannot be affirmed to be, beyond question, in palpable conflict with the Constitution. Nor, in view of the methods employed to stamp out the disease of smallpox, can anyone confidently assert that the means prescribed by the state to that end [have] no real or substantial relation to the protection of the public health and the public safety. Such an assertion would not be consistent with the experience of this and other countries whose authorities have dealt with the disease of smallpox. And the principle of vaccination as a means to prevent the spread of smallpox has been enforced in many states by statutes making the vaccination of children a condition of their right to enter or remain in public schools. . . .

. . . The matured opinions of medical men everywhere, and the experience of mankind, as all must know, negative the suggestion that it is not possible in any case to determine whether vaccination is safe. Was defendant exempted from the operation of the statute simply because of his dread of the same evil results experienced by him when a child, and which he had observed in the cases of his son and other children? Could he reasonably claim such an exemption because "quite often," or "occasionally," injury had resulted from vaccination, or because it was impossible, in the opinion of some, by any practical test, to determine with absolute certainty whether a particular person could be safely vaccinated?

It seems to the court that an affirmative answer to these questions would practically strip the legislative department of its function to care for the public health and the public safety when endangered by epidemics of disease. . . .

. . . We are unwilling to hold it to be an element in the liberty secured by the Constitution of the United States that one person, or a minority of persons, residing in any community and enjoying the benefits of its local government, should have the power thus to dominate the majority when supported in their action by the authority of the state.

. . . Until otherwise informed by the highest court of Massachusetts, we are not inclined to hold that the statute establishes the absolute rule that an adult must be vaccinated if it be apparent or can be shown with reasonable certainty that he is not at the time a fit subject of vaccination, or that vaccination, by reason of his then condition, would seriously impair his health, or probably cause his death. No such case is here presented. It is the [case] of an adult who, for aught that appears, was himself in perfect health and a fit subject of vaccination, and yet, while remaining in the community, refused to obey the statute and the regulation adopted in execution of its provisions for the protection of the public health and the public safety, confessedly endangered by the presence of a dangerous disease.

We now decide only that the statute covers the present case, and that nothing clearly appears that would justify this court in holding it to be unconstitutional and inoperative in its application to the plaintiff in error.

The judgment of the court below must be affirmed.

*It is so ordered.*

Mr. Justice BREWER and Mr. Justice PECKHAM dissent.

## NOTES AND QUESTIONS

1. ***Reconciling the Cases.*** Can the outcomes in *Jew Ho* and *Jacobson* be reconciled? Can you extract from the two decisions principles to guide state and local decision makers seeking to impose a health-related detention, quarantine, or forced vaccination program in response to a terrorist threat? Does your answer depend on differences in the respective physical procedures or in the seriousness of the impositions they place on members of the public?

   In what respects was the San Francisco quarantine legally insufficient? Why was the *Jew Ho* court competent to decide the reasonableness of the quarantine but not whether the plague existed in San Francisco? Could the San Francisco regulation have been revised to cure its defects while still serving its public health objective? If so, how?

2. ***Quarantine Authority.*** The Supreme Court has long recognized the authority of the government to erect quarantines — both to confine persons and to exclude them — in order to prevent the spread of contagious or infectious diseases. For example, in a recent case approving the confinement of a violent sexual predator, the Court declared that

   > we have never held that the Constitution prevents a State from civilly detaining those for whom no treatment is available, but who nevertheless pose a danger to others. A State could hardly be seen as furthering a "punitive" purpose by involuntarily confining persons afflicted with an untreatable, highly contagious disease. [Kansas v. Hendricks, 521 U.S. 346, 366 (1997).]

   And while the Court has called the constitutional right to travel from one state to another "firmly imbedded in our jurisprudence," Saenz v. Roe, 526 U.S. 489, 498 (1999), other courts have held that the right may be curtailed in an emergency. *See, e.g.*, Smith v. Avino, 91 F.3d 105 (11th Cir. 1996) (upholding a curfew in South Florida in the wake of Hurricane Andrew). *See generally* Kathleen S. Swendiman & Jennifer K. Elsea, *Federal and State Quarantine and Isolation Authority* (Cong. Res. Serv. RL33201), Dec. 12, 2005; 16B Am. Jur. 2d *Constitutional Law* §617 (1998).

3. ***Erring on the Side of Caution?*** How widely may government officials establish a cordon around an area suspected of containing infected persons or hazardous chemicals? More generally, how should doubts be resolved about the possible exposure of individuals to a contagious disease? A due process case involving a quarantine of poultry to combat avian influenza may be instructive. In Empire Kosher Poultry, Inc. v. Hallowell, 816 F.2d 907 (3d Cir. 1987), the court said that evidence of disease need not be shown before the quarantine is erected, since tests might not immediately reveal the existence of infection. Moreover, said the court, a broad buffer zone could be established to prevent the inadvertent movement of infected poultry out of the quarantine area.

4. ***Enforcing a Quarantine.*** One analysis of the federal TOPOFF exercise, *supra* p. 632, calls the quarantine of large groups of people "impractical," citing concern about the level of force needed for enforcement:

> Not only were local officials uncertain about their statutory author-ity to proceed with a quarantine, they believed that the public would probably not cooperate with compulsory orders to commandeer property, restrict movement of people, or forcibly remove them to designated locations. Traditionally, governments have counted upon the public to comply with public health orders on the basis that the good of the community overrides the rights of the individual. These days, however, citizens get angry at forced evacuations for such visible calamities as hurricanes, floods, and wildfires, not to mention a stay-at-home order for a microscopic killer that they may doubt is in their midst. Police also questioned whether their colleagues would recognize the authority of the public health officer to declare a quarantine or would even stick around to enforce the order. Finally, some wondered whether there were enough local and state police to quarantine a large metropolitan area in the first place. [Amy E. Smithson & Leslie-Anne Levy, *Ataxia: The Chemical and Biological Terrorism Threat and the U.S. Response* 269 (Henry L. Stimson Center 2000).]

According to one police captain, "If police officers knew that a biological agent had been released, 99 percent of the cops would not be here. They would grab their families and leave." *Id.* at 270 n.225. Do these practical problems have legal solutions?

5. ***Commerce Clause Limits?*** Are state or local quarantine restrictions poten-tially vulnerable to legal challenge under the dormant Commerce Clause? As early as Gibbons v. Ogden, 22 U.S. 1 (1824), the Supreme Court recognized that quarantine laws may be construed as "laws of commerce." *Id.* at 25. In Compagnie Francaise de Navigation a Vapeur v. State Board of Health, 186 U.S. 380 (1902), however, the Court rejected a charge that a quarantine of the City of New Orleans unduly burdened commerce because it prevented the landing of passengers from a French ship there. The Court stated that "the health and quarantine laws of the several states are not repugnant to the Constitution of the United States, although they affect foreign and domestic commerce . . . until Congress has acted under the authority conferred upon it

by the Constitution." *Id.* at 391. Although state and local health laws that do not favor residents over nonresidents have generally been upheld when challenged under the Commerce Clause, the possibility remains that a state or local restriction could be viewed as unconstitutionally burdensome on interstate or foreign commerce. *See* Erwin Chemerinsky, *Constitutional Law: Principles and Policies* §5.3 (3d ed. 2006).

6. *Federal/State Conflicts.* According to one analysis, in the event of a bioterrorist attack, "[a]lmost certainly, a clash would occur between public health and legal officials at the local, state, and national levels about the measures necessary and the entity with jurisdiction to act." Smithson & Levy, *supra*, at 269. Why might that be so? How could such conflicts be avoided?

Legally, if state or local efforts come directly into conflict with federal measures, the former presumably would have to give way under the Supremacy Clause. Federal preemption would be based on a federal right to regulate. Can you describe limits to the federal government's power to respond to a terrorist attack using a biological weapon? How about a chemical or radiological weapon? Would your answer turn on whether a biological agent was contagious? Can you think of constitutional provisions other than the Commerce Clause that would enable preemptive federal action?

7. *Other Constraints on Individual Liberties.* In addition to quarantines, involuntary evacuations, and forced inoculations, government responses to a WMD attack might include compulsory physical examinations to determine whether individuals are infected with a contagious disease, inspections of private property, and reviews of personal medical records. The Court has held that searches of individuals not related to a criminal prosecution will not offend the Fourth Amendment if the state's interest in the result is sufficiently compelling. *See, e.g.,* Vernonia Sch. Dist. 47J v. Acton, 515 U.S. 646, 653 (1995) (upholding random drug tests of student athletes, when "special needs, beyond the normal need for law enforcement, make the warrant and probable-cause requirement impracticable"); National Treasury Employees Union v. Von Raab, 489 U.S. 656 (1989) (approving drug tests of Customs Service employees); *supra* pp. 152, 213 (discussing the "special needs" exception to the Fourth Amendment; *cf.* Ferguson v. City of Charleston, 532 U.S. 67 (2001) (rejecting nonconsensual drug testing of obstetrics patients when results were to be given to police). In Camara v. Municipal Court of San Francisco, 387 U.S. 523, 539 (1967), the Court observed that warrantless inspections are "traditionally upheld in emergency situations." In the wake of a bioterrorist attack, the government's interest in examining individuals and their property would be strong and immediate. Do you think it would outweigh individual privacy interests? *See* Barry Kellman, *Biological Terrorism: Legal Measures for Preventing Catastrophe,* 24 Harv. J. L. & Pub. Poly. 417, 478-485 (2001).

In a portion of the *Jew Ho* decision omitted here, the Court noted that one reason for striking down the San Francisco quarantine regulation was its enforcement in a racially discriminatory manner against members of the Chinese community. The health crisis, or purported crisis, furnished a pretext for discrimination with other motivations. This was "the administration of a law 'with an evil eye and an unequal hand,'" in violation of the Fourteenth Amendment to the U.S. Constitution. 103 F. at 24, quoting Yick Wo v. Hopkins, 118 U.S. 356 (1886). Recall that in Korematsu v. United States, 323 U.S. 214 (1944), noted *supra* p. 391, involving the exclusion and internment of 120,000 Japanese-Americans during World War II, the Supreme Court was far more credulous in accepting government assertions that racial discrimination was required by military necessity.

In Wong Wai v. Williamson, 103 F. 1 (1900), a companion case to *Jew Ho*, the court struck down a San Francisco compulsory vaccination program aimed at combating plague but enforced only against Chinese residents. Apart from the explicitly race-based administration of the program, the court found, based on expert testimony, that the vaccine could itself be life-threatening if given to a person already exposed to the plague; it was only effective before exposure. Absent the racial criterion, do you think the court would have been willing to scrutinize closely the efficacy of the drug? Should either the efficacy of a drug or the risk it poses to an individual be considered today in a program of compulsory inoculation? Or is this a "special needs" case, like those noted above, in which concerns for public safety would trump individual rights?

## 2. A MODEL STATE RESPONSE: THE MSEHPA?

The *Jew Ho* and *Jacobson* cases may be seen as representative of antiquated state quarantine and vaccination laws, many of which are several decades old, do not reflect current disease or treatment science, and are often targeted at particular diseases. *See* Lawrence O. Gostin, *The Law and the Public's Health: A Study of Infectious Disease Law in the United States*, 99 Colum. L. Rev. 59, 102-106 (1999).

Spurred by the 9/11 and anthrax attacks in 2001, states and cities began to reconsider a range of emergency response issues, including quarantine and isolation authorities. The Model State Emergency Health Powers Act (MSEHPA) (draft Dec. 21, 2001), *at* http://www.publichealthlaw.net/MSEHPA/MSEHPA2.pdf, was drawn up in 2001 by public health experts at Georgetown and Johns Hopkins Universities. *See* Center for Law & the Public's Health, *Model State Public Health Laws* (n.d.), *at* http://www.publichealthlaw.net/Resources/Modellaws.htm.

The MSEHPA borrows from various state laws and provides a template for sweeping state authorities that may be invoked in a public health emergency. It authorizes governors to declare a "public health emergency" after consulting with public health authorities, or in the absence of such consultation "when the situation calls for prompt and timely action." §401. A "public health emergency" is defined as "an occurrence or imminent threat" of illness that is "believed to be caused" by bioterrorism or other disasters and poses "a high probability" of a large number of deaths, serious or long-term disabilities, or widespread exposure "that poses a significant risk of substantial harm to a large number of people in the affected population." §104(m). During a public health emergency, a governor may suspend any statute concerning state government procedures or any agency rule or orders "to the extent that strict compliance with the same would prevent, hinder, or delay necessary action" in response to the public health emergency. §403(a)(1). The public health emergency "shall" be terminated by a governor by executive order "upon finding that the occurrence of an illness or health condition that caused the emergency no longer poses a high probability of a large number of deaths in the affected population . . . or a significant risk of substantial future harm to a large number of people in the affected population." §405(a). Otherwise, a public health emergency will terminate automatically after 30 days unless renewed by the governor or terminated earlier by majority vote of both chambers of a state legislature. §405(b), (c).

In addition, during a public health emergency, the MSEHPA authorizes state officials to close, evacuate, or decontaminate "any facility" or to decontaminate or destroy "any material" where "there is a reasonable cause to believe that it may endanger the public health." §501. Public health authorities are also given power to condemn or assume control over private property, control and manage health care facilities, and control routes and modes of transportation "if such action is reasonable and necessary to respond to the public health emergency." §502.

The MSEHPA includes these provisions concerning vaccination, treatment, isolation, and quarantine:

## MODEL STATE EMERGENCY HEALTH POWERS ACT

Draft Dec. 21, 2001
http://www.publichealthlaw.net/MSEHPA/MSEHPA2.pdf

### Article VI. Special Powers During a State of Public Health Emergency: Protection of Persons

### Section 603. Vaccination and treatment.

During a state of public health emergency the public health authority may exercise the following emergency powers over persons as necessary to address the public health emergency —

(a) Vaccination. To vaccinate persons as protection against infectious disease and to prevent the spread of contagious or possibly contagious disease.

(1) Vaccination may be performed by any qualified person authorized to do so by the public health authority.

(2) A vaccine to be administered must not be such as is reasonably likely to lead to serious harm to the affected individual.

(3) To prevent the spread of contagious or possibly contagious disease the public health authority may isolate or quarantine, pursuant to Section 604, persons who are unable or unwilling for reasons of health, religion, or conscience to undergo vaccination pursuant to this Section.

(b) Treatment. To treat persons exposed to or infected with disease.

(1) Treatment may be administered by any qualified person authorized to do so by the public health authority.

(2) Treatment must not be such as is reasonably likely to lead to serious harm to the affected individual.

(3) To prevent the spread of contagious or possibly contagious disease the public health authority may isolate or quarantine, pursuant to Section 604, persons who are unable or unwilling for reasons of health, religion, or conscience to undergo treatment pursuant to this Section.

### Section 604. Isolation and quarantine.

(a) Authorization. During the public health emergency, the public health authority may isolate . . . or quarantine . . . an individual or groups of individuals. . . . The public health authority may also establish and maintain places of isolation and quarantine, and set rules and make orders. Failure to obey these rules, orders, or provisions shall constitute a misdemeanor.

(b) Conditions and principles. The public health authority shall adhere to the following conditions and principles when isolating or quarantining individuals or groups of individuals:

(1) Isolation and quarantine must be by the least restrictive means necessary to prevent the spread of a contagious or possibly contagious disease to others and may include, but are not limited to, confinement to private homes or other private and public premises.

(2) Isolated individuals must be confined separately from quarantined individuals.

(3) The health status of isolated and quarantined individuals must be monitored regularly to determine if they require isolation or quarantine.

(4) If a quarantined individual subsequently becomes infected or is reasonably believed to have become infected with a contagious or possibly contagious disease he or she must promptly be removed to isolation.

(5) Isolated and quarantined individuals must be immediately released when they pose no substantial risk of transmitting a contagious or possibly contagious disease to others.

(6) The needs of persons isolated and quarantined shall be addressed in a systematic and competent fashion, including, but not limited to, providing adequate food, clothing, shelter, means of communication with those in isolation or quarantine and outside these settings, medication, and competent medical care.

(7) Premises used for isolation and quarantine shall be maintained in a safe and hygienic manner and be designed to minimize the likelihood of further transmission of infection or other harms to persons isolated and quarantined.

(8) To the extent possible, cultural and religious beliefs should be considered in addressing the needs of individuals, and establishing and maintaining isolation and quarantine premises.

(c) Cooperation. Persons subject to isolation or quarantine shall obey the public health authority's rules and orders; and shall not go beyond the isolation or quarantine premises. Failure to obey these provisions shall constitute a misdemeanor.

(d) Entry into isolation or quarantine premises.

(1) Authorized entry. The public health authority may authorize physicians, health care workers, or others access to individuals in isolation or quarantine as necessary to meet the needs of isolated or quarantined individuals.

(2) Unauthorized entry. No person, other than a person authorized by the public health authority, shall enter isolation or quarantine premises. Failure to obey this provision shall constitute a misdemeanor.

(3) Potential isolation or quarantine. Any person entering an isolation or quarantine premises with or without authorization of the public health authority may be isolated or quarantined pursuant to Section 604(a).

## Section 605. Procedures for isolation and quarantine.

During a public health emergency, the isolation and quarantine of an individual or groups of individuals shall be undertaken in accordance with the following procedures.

(a) Temporary isolation and quarantine without notice.

(1) Authorization. The public health authority may temporarily isolate or quarantine an individual or groups of individuals through a written directive if delay in imposing the isolation or quarantine would significantly jeopardize the public health authority's ability to prevent or limit the transmission of a contagious or possibly contagious disease to others. . . .

(4) Petition for continued isolation or quarantine. Within ten (10) days after issuing the written directive, the public health authority shall file a petition pursuant to Section 605(b) for a court order authorizing the continued isolation or quarantine of the isolated or quarantined individual or groups of individuals.

[Section 605(b) permits the public health authority to petition for isolation or quarantine with notice to affected individuals and a hearing within five days, with a ten-day extension possible in "extraordinary circumstances." The court will grant the state's petition if a preponderance of the evidence shows that isolation or quarantine is "reasonably necessary to prevent or limit that transmission of a contagious or possibly contagious disease to others."]

## NOTES AND QUESTIONS

1. *Status of State Legislation.* According to the Center for Law and the Public's Health, as of April 2006, 37 states and the District of Columbia have enacted legislation that includes provisions from or closely related to the MSEHPA. A table documenting state legislative activity is available at http://www.publichealthlaw.net/Resources/Modellaws.htm.

2. *Compulsion of People.* Does the MSEHPA respond to the problems confronted by the courts in *Jew Ho* and *Jacobson*? Review the provisions of Article VI of the MSEHPA, above. What is the difference between isolation and quarantine? What practical difference does it make whether a person is subject to an isolation or a quarantine order? How useful are the conditions and principles set forth in §604(b) in deciding whether to impose isolation or quarantine? Are the public health needs and rights of affected individuals and other persons adequately served? Are the proposed procedures constitutional? Finally, who would actually enforce the quarantine, and how?

3. *Commandeering Resources.* Article V of the MSEHPA, briefly summarized above, provides sweeping powers for a state public health authority to commandeer private resources during a public health emergency. In addition to the authority to close, evacuate, or decontaminate facilities or materials and to gain access to and control of facilities, private property, and transportation modes, state officials would be given control over the procurement, rationing, and distribution of health care supplies. §501-505. The model act anticipates that "just compensation" would be paid to any owner for property lawfully taken during the public health emergency. §506. Under what circumstances would the provisions of Title V be implemented? If enacted, would these provisions violate the Takings Clause of the U.S. Constitution? Would they be wise? How would you advise a state legislature interested in providing for these contingencies to ensure against the abuse of such powers?

4. *A Needed Set of Correctives?* Would you advise state legislatures to enact some version of the MSEHPA? What provisions would you say are most controversial, and why? Some scholars have claimed that the model act is unnecessary and is an overreaction to the need for incremental public health law reform. LSU Program in Law, Science, and Public Health, *White Paper #2: Legislative Alternatives to the Model State Emergency Health Powers Act (MSEHPA)*, Apr. 21, 2003, *available at* http://biotech.law.lsu.edu/blaw/bt/MSEHPA_review.htm.

## 3.  THE FEDERAL RESPONSE TO A BIOTERRORIST ATTACK

The federal responsibility for biological incidents is shared by several agencies, as noted earlier. Overall coordination is supposed to be provided by DHS. The Department of Health and Human Services (HHS), acting through the CDC, will play a leading role, based on its specialized experience and expertise. *See generally* Sarah A. Lister, *The Public Health and Medical Response to Disasters: Federal Authority and Funding* (Cong. Res. Serv. RL33579), Aug. 4, 2006. Some of the statutory and regulatory authorities relevant to that role are set out below.

## PUBLIC HEALTH SERVICE ACT

42 U.S.C.A. §§201-300aaa-13 (West 2003 & Supp. 2006),
as amended

### §243. General Grant of Authority For Cooperation. . . .

(c) Development of plan to control epidemics and meet emergencies or problems resulting from disasters; . . .

(1) The Secretary [of Health and Human Services (the "Service")] is authorized to develop (and may take such action as may be necessary to implement) a plan under which personnel, equipment, medical supplies, and other resources of the Service and other agencies under the jurisdiction of the Secretary may be effectively used to control epidemics of any disease or condition and to meet other health emergencies or problems. . . .

### §264. Regulations to Control Communicable Diseases

(a) Promulgation and Enforcement by Surgeon General. The Surgeon General, with the approval of the Secretary, is authorized to make and enforce such regulations as in his judgment are necessary to prevent the introduction, transmission, or spread of communicable diseases from foreign countries into the States or possessions, or from one State or possession into any other State or possession. For purposes of carrying out and enforcing such regulations, the Surgeon General may provide for such inspection, fumigation, disinfection . . . and other measures, as in his judgment may be necessary.

(b) Apprehension, detention, or conditional release of individuals. Regulations prescribed under this section shall not provide for the apprehension, detention, or conditional release of individuals except for the purpose of preventing the introduction, transmission, or spread of such communicable diseases as may be specified from time to time in Executive orders of the President upon the recommendation of the Secretary, in consultation with the Surgeon General. . . .

(d)(1) Apprehension and examination of persons reasonably believed to be infected. Regulations prescribed under this section may provide for the apprehension and examination of any individual reasonably believed to be infected with a communicable disease in a qualifying stage and (A) to be moving or about to move from a State to another State; or (B) to be a probable source of infection to individuals who, while infected with such disease in a qualifying stage, will be moving from a State to another State. Such regulations may provide that if upon examination any such individual is found to be infected, he may be detained for such time and in such manner as may be reasonably necessary. . . .

HHS has adopted the following regulations to implement this statutory authority:

### INTERSTATE QUARANTINE

42 C.F.R. part 70 (2006)

#### §70.2 Measures in the Event of Inadequate Local Control.

Whenever the Director of the Centers for Disease Control and Prevention determines that the measures taken by health authorities of any State or possession (including political subdivisions thereof) are insufficient to prevent the spread of any of the communicable diseases from such State or possession to any other State or possession, he/she may take such measures to prevent such spread of the diseases as he/she deems reasonably necessary, including inspection. . . .

#### §70.5 Certain Communicable Diseases; Special Requirements.

The following provisions are applicable with respect to any person who is in the communicable period of cholera, plague, smallpox, typhus or yellow fever, or who, having been exposed to any such disease, is in the incubation period thereof:

(a) Requirements relating to travelers.

(1) No such person shall travel from one State or possession to another, or on a conveyance engaged in interstate traffic, without a written permit of the Surgeon General or his/her authorized representative. . . .

#### §70.6 Apprehension and Detention of Persons with Specific Diseases.

Regulations prescribed in this part authorize the detention, isolation, quarantine, or conditional release of individuals, for the purpose of preventing the introduction, transmission, and spread of the communicable diseases listed in an Executive Order setting out a list of quarantinable communicable diseases, as provided under section 361(b) of the Public Health Service Act [42 U.S.C. §264(b)]. Executive Order 13295, of April 4, 2003, contains the current revised list of quarantinable communicable diseases, and may be obtained at http://www.cdc.gov, or at http://www.archives.gov/federal-register/. If this Order is amended, HHS will enforce that amended order immediately and update this reference.

## NOTES AND QUESTIONS

1. *Who's in Charge?* Can you tell from the authorities we have examined who will be responsible for coordinating and implementing all these federal, state, and local laws in a great crisis?
2. *Responding to Listed Pathogens.* The HHS regulations set out above have been amended several times since September 11, 2001, to expand the list of infectious agents for which the CDC may erect quarantines or detain

persons. The executive order incorporated by reference in §70.6 lists cholera, diphtheria, infectious tuberculosis, plague, smallpox, yellow fever, and viral hemorrhagic fevers (including Lassa, Marburg, and Ebola). It also lists severe acute respiratory syndrome (SARS). Not listed are tularemia, botulism, and other contagions that could be weaponized and used by terrorists. A more recent order aimed at halting the spread of bird flu adds "influenza caused by novel or reemergent influenza viruses that are causing, or have the potential to cause, a pandemic." Exec. Order No. 13,375, 70 Fed. Reg. 117,299 (Apr. 1, 2005). CDC issued an extensive and controversial proposed revision to these regulations on November 30, 2005. Dept. of Health and Human Serv., *Control of Communicable Diseases*, 70 Fed. Reg. 71,892-01.

In May 2006, the Homeland Security Council issued its *Pandemic Influenza Implementation Plan, available at* http://www.whitehouse.gov/homeland/nspi_implementation.pdf. At 233 pages, it sets out fairly elaborate guidance for U.S. planning in areas of primary federal responsibility, international efforts, controls of borders and transportation, protection of human and animal health, and public safety, emphasizing the roles of state and local governments wherever possible. *See also* U.S. Dept. of Health and Human Serv., *HHS Pandemic Influenza Plan*, Nov. 2005, *available at* http://www2a.cdc.gov/phlp/docs/PHLP_HHSPandemicInfluenzaPlan.pdf; Sarah A. Lister, *Pandemic Influenza: Domestic Preparedness Efforts* (Cong. Res. Serv. RL331450), Nov. 10, 2005. Because a bird flu pandemic would present many of the legal and practical problems posed by a terrorist attack using plague or some other contagious disease, the *Implementation Plan* probably reflects the latest government thinking about large-scale, integrated planning for both kinds of catastrophe.

3. *Responding to Anthrax.* What measures need to be undertaken by federal officials to address the threat posed by terrorists sending anthrax spores through the mail, as happened in the aftermath of the September 11, 2001, attacks? Recall that anthrax is extremely dangerous but not communicable. Can you explain how various federal agencies might cooperate in this effort? Do HHS and CDC have the authority they need to be helpful? A Defense Department-sponsored report concluded that the anthrax letter attacks "revealed weaknesses in almost every aspect of U.S. biopreparedness and response." David Heyman, *Lessons from the Anthrax Attacks: Implications for U.S. Bioterrorism Preparedness* viii, Apr. 2002, *available at* http://www.fas.org/irp/threat/cbw/dtra02.pdf. *See also* Keith Rhodes, *Diffuse Security Threats: Information on U.S. Domestic Anthrax Attacks* (GAO-03-0323T), Dec. 10, 2002, *available at* pp. 808-822 of another report found at http://www.fas.org/irp/congress/2002_rpt/911rept.pdf; Gen. Acct. Off., *Bioterrorism: Public Health Responses to Anthrax Incidents of 2001* (GAO-04-152), Oct. 2003.

4. *Responding to Smallpox.* Reflecting growing fears that supplies of smallpox virus might fall into the hands of terrorists, the CDC has published a plan for responding to an outbreak of a disease thought to have been eradicated in the 1970s. *See CDC Smallpox Response Plan and Guidelines (Version 3.0)*, Nov. 26, 2002 (with updates), *at* http://www.bt.cdc.gov/agent/smallpox/response-plan/index.asp. The plan calls for employment of

a "ring" strategy to isolate confirmed and suspected smallpox cases, vaccinate persons who may have come into contact with them, and keep all possible contacts under close surveillance. The size of a ring is to be determined
by state and federal health officials. A different CDC directive declares, "No
one will be forced to be vaccinated, even if they have been exposed to smallpox. . . . [However, to] prevent smallpox from spreading, anyone who has
been in contact with a person with smallpox but who decides not to get
the vaccine may need to be isolated for at least 18 days. . . . People
placed in isolation will not be able to go to work." Centers for Disease Control
and Prevention, *What You Should Know About a Smallpox Outbreak,*
Dec. 29, 2004, *at* http://www.bt.cdc.gov/agent/smallpox/basics/outbreak.asp.
A companion document provides guidance for state and local government
planners. *CDC Guidance for Post-Event Smallpox Planning,* Dec. 16, 2002,
*at* http://www.bt.cdc.gov/agent/smallpox/prep/post-event-guidance.asp.

5. ***Federal Authority to Constrain Persons.*** HHS's enabling legislation
states that an "individual believed to be infected with a communicable disease
in a communicable stage" may be "apprehended and examined." 42 U.S.C.
§264(d). If found to be infected, the individual may then be "detained for such
time and in such manner as may be reasonably necessary." *Id.* Do you think
this language is meant to give the CDC authority to quarantine an entire
city? To require vaccinations? What is the relationship between the HHS/
CDC authorities and state law, whether or not a state has adopted something
like the MSEHPA? *See* Kathleen S. Swendiman & Jennifer K. Elsea, *Federal
and State Quarantine and Isolation Authority* (Cong. Res. Serv. RL33201),
Dec. 12, 2005.

6. ***Enforcing a Quarantine.*** HHS and CDC have no police force of their own
to enforce a federal quarantine. How would such a quarantine be enforced?
For one possible answer, see *infra* pp. 691-697.

7. ***Intrastate Quarantine.*** According to some commentators, no statutory
authority exists for a federally mandated quarantine *within* a single
state. *See, e.g.,* National Commission on Terrorism (Bremer Commission),
*Countering the Changing Threat of International Terrorism* 27 (2000).
Considering the language of the Public Health Service Act and its implementing regulations, set out above, do you think these doubts are justified?
Statutory and constitutional bases and limits for both state and federal
public health regulations dealing with bioterrorism threats are briefed
extensively in proposed CDC regulations, Dept. of Health and Human
Serv., *Control of Communicable Diseases,* 70 Fed. Reg. 71,892-01, 71,893-
71896 (Nov. 30, 2005).

8. ***Triage vs. Equal Protection.*** The CDC maintains the Strategic National
Stockpile (SNS) program. Within 12 hours of a terrorist attack, the Stockpile
can deliver "push packages" containing needed pharmaceuticals and other
medical supplies anywhere in the country. *See* CDC, *Strategic National
Stockpile,* Apr. 14, 2005, *at* http://www.bt.cdc.gov/stockpile/. Inventories
are nevertheless limited, and they might not be adequate to treat every
person affected by an outbreak of some diseases. For example, as of
March 2006, 5.5 million doses of antiviral drugs were on hand in case of
pandemic influenza, while another 20 million doses were on order. *See*

Press Release, Dept. of Health and Human Serv., *HHS Buys Additional Antiviral Medication As Preparations for Potential Influenza Pandemic Continue*, Mar. 1, 2006, *available at* http://www.hhs.gov/news/press/2006pres/20060301.html. Who do you think should receive such limited supplies first? Who should be empowered to choose among potential recipients? Would it be a good idea to decide such questions in advance of a terrorist attack or pandemic? If so, how?

# CHAPTER 21

# THE MILITARY'S DOMESTIC ROLE IN COUNTERTERRORISM

Until recently the Defense Department had organized itself almost exclusively to fight a conventional war far from America's shores. In part this reflected the absence of the sort of domestic threats that have emerged in the last decade or so. It also demonstrated the public's antipathy toward any sort of military involvement in domestic life. During the Vietnam War, the Supreme Court noted "a traditional and strong resistance of Americans to any military intrusion into civilian affairs." Laird v. Tatum, 408 U.S. 1, 15 (1972). *See* W. Kent Davis, *Swords Into Plowshares: The Dangerous Politicization of the Military in the Post-Cold War Era,* 33 Val. U. L. Rev. 61, 64-77 (1998). Thus, for most of our history the military's domestic role has consisted primarily of preparations for foreign wars and of occasional support for civilian authorities in curbing civil unrest and fighting the "war on drugs."

On September 11, 2001, however, the military's role, like so much else in this country, began to change. The following day the President described the terrorist attacks as "acts of war." The battlefield in this war obviously extends to the U.S. homeland. We saw earlier that the military may be used to detain and try "enemy combatants." Should troops be deployed even more broadly on this new front? If so, should their Rules of Engagement (ROE) be different from those that guide military operations abroad? What legal authorities exist or would have to be created to accommodate these needed changes?

In Part A of this chapter we address the deep-seated American tradition of avoiding entanglement of the military in civilian life, as reflected in laws designed to limit that entanglement. Part B concerns the domestic intelligence role of the military in counterterrorism. Finally, in Part C we examine the military's role in responding to a terrorist attack on the homeland.

# A.  THE TRADITIONAL ROLE OF THE MILITARY IN AMERICAN SOCIETY

The domestic use of troops has been a fact of life and a matter of controversy at least since President Washington called out the militia to put down the Whiskey Rebellion in 1794. Many other Presidents have deployed federal military forces to help keep the peace, to aid local governments in natural disasters, and to enforce federal and state laws. State governors have called out their militias even more often, especially in the first three decades of the twentieth century. From the earliest days of the Republic, however, Americans have resisted any involvement by military forces in domestic matters.

## 1.  THE POSSE COMITATUS ACT AS A BACKGROUND PRINCIPLE

Could the President deploy troops to enforce a quarantine in the event of a bioterrorist attack like the one outlined in the TOPOFF exercise, *supra* p. 632? Could the troops detain looters? Could they shoot people trying to break out of the quarantine? Fortunately, we have not yet had to face the kind of crisis that would require answers. But in planning for the next terrorist attack, we urgently need answers. The following decision may provide some guidance.

### BISSONETTE V. HAIG

United States Court of Appeals, Eighth Circuit, 1985
776 F.2d 1384, *aff'd*, 800 F.2d 812 (8th Cir. 1986) (en banc),
*aff'd*, 485 U.S. 264 (1988)

ARNOLD, J. This is an action for damages caused by defendants' alleged violations of the Constitution of the United States. . . .

This case arises out of the occupation of the village of Wounded Knee, South Dakota, on the Pine Ridge Reservation by an armed group of Indians on February 27, 1973. On the evening when the occupation began, members of the Federal Bureau of Investigation, the United States Marshals Service, and the Bureau of Indian Affairs Police sealed off the village by establishing road-blocks at all major entry and exit roads. The standoff between the Indians and the law enforcement authorities ended about ten weeks later with the surrender of the Indians occupying the village. . . .

In their amended complaint, plaintiffs allege . . . that they were unreasonably seized and confined in the village of Wounded Knee contrary to the Fourth Amendment and their rights to free movement and travel. Second, they claim that they were unreasonably searched by ground and aerial surveillance. In both cases, plaintiffs assert that the seizures and searches were unreasonable because "Defendants accomplished or caused to be accomplished those actions by means of the unconstitutional and felonious use of parts of the United States Army or Air Force . . . ." This case comes to us on appeal from a dismissal for failure to state a claim, and we therefore accept for present purposes the factual allegations of the complaint.

These allegations must be viewed against the background of the Posse Comitatus Act of 1878, 18 U.S.C. §1385, which plaintiffs claim was violated here. The statute provides:

### §1385.  Use of Army and Air Force as Posse Comitatus[1]

Whoever, except in cases and under circumstances expressly authorized by the Constitution or Act of Congress, willfully uses any part of the Army or the Air Force as a posse comitatus or otherwise to execute the laws shall be fined not more than $10,000 or imprisoned not more than two years, or both.

## A

The first two sets of claims raise the question whether a search or seizure, otherwise permissible, can be rendered unreasonable under the Fourth Amendment because military personnel or equipment were used to accomplish those actions. We believe that the Constitution, certain Acts of Congress, and the decisions of the Supreme Court embody certain limitations on the use of military personnel in enforcing the civil law, and that searches and seizures in circumstances which exceed those limits are unreasonable under the Fourth Amendment.

. . . Reasonableness is determined by balancing the interests for and against the seizure. Usually, the interests arrayed against a seizure are those of the individual in privacy, freedom of movement, or, in the case of a seizure by deadly force, life. Here, however, the opposing interests are more societal and governmental than strictly individual in character. They concern the special threats to constitutional government inherent in military enforcement of civilian law. That these governmental interests should weigh in the Fourth Amendment balance is neither novel nor surprising. In the typical Fourth Amendment case, the interests of the individual are balanced against those of the government. That some of those governmental interests are on the other side of the Fourth Amendment balance does not make them any less relevant or important.

Civilian rule is basic to our system of government. The use of military forces to seize civilians can expose civilian government to the threat of military rule and the suspension of constitutional liberties. On a lesser scale, military enforcement of the civil law leaves the protection of vital Fourth and Fifth Amendment rights in the hands of persons who are not trained to uphold these rights. It may also chill the exercise of fundamental rights, such as the rights to speak freely and to vote, and create the atmosphere of fear and hostility which exists in territories occupied by enemy forces.

The interest in limiting military involvement in civilian affairs has a long tradition beginning with the Declaration of Independence and continued in the Constitution, certain Acts of Congress, and decisions of the Supreme Court. The Declaration of Independence states among the grounds for severing ties with

---

[1. The Latin term "posse comitatus" means, literally, "power or authority of the county," but it connotes a body of persons summoned by a sheriff to assist in preserving the peace or enforcing the law. The persons summoned to assist the sheriff might, of course, be either civilian or military.]

Great Britain that the King "has kept among us, in times of peace, Standing Armies without Consent of our Legislature . . . [and] has affected to render the Military independent of and superior to the Civil power." These concerns were later raised at the Constitutional Convention. Luther Martin of Maryland said, "when a government wishes to deprive its citizens of freedom, and reduce them to slavery, it generally makes use of a standing army."

The Constitution itself limits the role of the military in civilian affairs: it makes the President, the highest civilian official in the Executive Branch, Commander in Chief of the armed services (Art. II, §2); it limits the appropriations for armed forces to two years and grants to the Congress the power to make rules to govern the armed forces (Art. I, §8, cl. 14); and it forbids the involuntary quartering of soldiers in any house in time of peace (Third Amendment).

Congress has passed several statutes limiting the use of the military in enforcing the civil law [including the Posse Comitatus Act and the Insurrection Act, addressed *infra*]. . . .

The Supreme Court has also recognized the constitutional limitations placed on military involvement in civilian affairs. A leading case is Ex parte Milligan, 71 U.S. 2, 124 (1866). . . . More recently, in Laird v. Tatum, 408 U.S. 1, 15-16 (1972), statements the Court made in dicta reaffirm these limitations. . . .

The governmental interests favoring military assistance to civilian law enforcement are primarily twofold: first, to maintain order in times of domestic violence or rebellion; and second, to improve the efficiency of civilian law enforcement by giving it the benefit of military technologies, equipment, information, and training personnel. These interests can and have been accommodated by Acts of Congress to the overriding interest of preserving civilian government and law enforcement. At the time of the Wounded Knee occupation, Congress had prohibited the use of the military to execute the civilian laws, except when expressly authorized. 18 U.S.C. §1385. And it had placed specific limits on the President's power to use the national guard and military in emergency situations. 10 U.S.C. §§331-335. For example, under 10 U.S.C. §332, the President may call upon the military only after having determined that domestic unrest makes it "impracticable to enforce the laws of the United States by the ordinary course of judicial proceedings," and under 10 U.S.C. §334, he may do so only after having issued a proclamation ordering the insurgents to disperse. Those steps were not taken here.

We believe that the limits established by Congress on the use of the military for civilian law enforcement provide a reliable guidepost by which to evaluate the reasonableness for Fourth Amendment purposes of the seizures and searches in question here. Congress has acted to establish reasonable limits on the President's use of military forces in emergency situations, and in doing so has circumscribed whatever, if any, inherent power the President may have had absent such legislation. This is the teaching of Youngstown Sheet & Tube Co. v. Sawyer, 343 U.S. 579 (1952). . . .

**B**

. . . [T]he use of military force for domestic law-enforcement purposes is in a special category, and . . . both the courts and Congress have been alert to keep it there. In short, if the use of military personnel is both unauthorized by any statute, and contrary to a specific criminal prohibition, and if citizens are seized or searched by military means in such a case, we have no hesitation in declaring that such searches and seizures are constitutionally "unreasonable." We do not mean to say that every search or seizure that violates a statute of any kind is necessarily a violation of the Fourth Amendment. But the statute prohibiting (if the allegations in the complaint can be proved) the conduct engaged in by defendants here is, as we have attempted to explain, not just any Act of Congress. It is the embodiment of a long tradition of suspicion and hostility towards the use of military force for domestic purposes.

Plaintiffs' Fourth Amendment case, therefore, must stand or fall on the proposition that military activity in connection with the occupation of Wounded Knee violated the Posse Comitatus Act.

In United States v. Casper, 541 F.2d 1275 (8th Cir. 1976) (per curiam), cert. denied, 430 U.S. 970 (1977), . . . the District Court had found on a stipulated record that the following activities did not violate the Act: the use of Air Force personnel, planes, and cameras to fly surveillance; the advice of military officers in dealing with the disorder; and the furnishing of equipment and supplies. We affirmed "on the basis of the trial court's thorough and well-reasoned opinion." 541 F.2d at 1276.

. . . Therefore, unless plaintiffs now allege that the defendants took actions that went beyond those alleged in the *Casper* case, the actions alleged in the complaint now before us cannot violate the Act.

In *Casper*, quoting from Judge VanSickle's opinion for the District Court, 419 F. Supp. at 194, we approved the following standard for determining whether a violation of the Posse Comitatus Act had occurred:

> Were Army or Air Force personnel used by the civilian law enforcement officers at Wounded Knee in such a manner that the military personnel subjected the citizens to the exercise of military power which was regulatory, proscriptive, or compulsory in nature, either presently or prospectively?

541 F.2d at 1278. . . .

When this concept is transplanted into the present legal context, we take it to mean that military involvement, even when not expressly authorized by the Constitution or a statute, does not violate the Posse Comitatus Act unless it actually regulates, forbids, or compels some conduct on the part of those claiming relief. A mere threat of some future injury would be insufficient. . . .

. . . We of course have no way of knowing what plaintiffs would be able to prove if this case goes to trial, but the complaint, considered simply as a pleading, goes well beyond an allegation that defendants simply furnished supplies, aerial surveillance, and advice. It specifically charges that "the several Defendants maintained or caused to be maintained roadblocks and armed patrols constituting an armed perimeter around the village of Wounded Knee . . . ." Defendants' actions, it is charged, "seized, confined, and made prisoners (of plaintiffs) against their will . . . ." These allegations amount to a claim that defendants' activities, allegedly in violation of the Posse Comitatus Act, were "regulatory, proscriptive, or compulsory," in the sense that these activities directly restrained plaintiffs' freedom of movement. No more is required to survive a motion to dismiss. . . .

As to the second set of claims, . . . plaintiffs charge that they were searched and subjected to surveillance against their will by aerial photographic and visual search and surveillance. As we have already noted, *Casper* holds that this sort of activity does not violate the Posse Comitatus Act. It is therefore not "unreasonable" for Fourth Amendment purposes. . . .

## NOTES AND QUESTIONS

1. *Elements of a Posse Comitatus Act Violation.* What exactly constitutes use of the armed forces "as a posse comitatus or otherwise to execute the laws"? To the "regulatory, proscriptive, or compulsory" standard set forth in *Bissonette*, we may add criteria from other cases growing out of the Wounded Knee incident: whether there was "direct, active" use of the military in civil law enforcement, United States v. Red Feather, 392 F. Supp. 916, 923 (D.S.D. 1975), or whether the use of the Army or the Air Force "pervaded the activities" of the civil law enforcement officers. United States v. Jaramillo, 380 F. Supp. 1375, 1379 (D. Neb. 1974), *appeal dismissed*, 510 F.2d 808 (8th Cir. 1975).

Are you now prepared to say what particular military activities in aid of law enforcement are forbidden? Do you think the Posse Comitatus Act should be amended to make it easier to predict when the Act would apply? If so, how?

The Posse Comitatus Act is described generally in Jennifer Elsea, *The Posse Comitatus Act and Related Matters: A Sketch* (Cong. Res. Serv. RS20590), June 6, 2005; Sean J. Kealy, *Reexamining the Posse Comitatus Act: Toward a Right to Civil Law Enforcement*, 21 Yale L. & Poly. Rev. 383 (2003); Matthew Carlton Hammond, Note, *The Posse Comitatus Act: A Principle in Need of Renewal*, 75 Wash. U. L.Q. 953 (1997).

2. *Judicial Remedies for Violations.* There apparently never has been a criminal prosecution of anyone for violation of the Posse Comitatus Act. *See* Paul Jackson Rice, *New Laws and Insights Encircle the Posse Comitatus Act*, 104 Mil. L. Rev. 109, 111 (1984). Violations of the Posse Comitatus Act have, however, often been asserted as a defense to charges under other criminal statutes. For example, in *Red Feather* and *Jaramillo, supra*, individuals at Wounded Knee were charged with interfering with a "law enforcement officer lawfully engaged in the lawful performance of his official duties." *See* 18 U.S.C. §231(a)(3) (2000). The defendants argued that the federal marshals and FBI agents were not performing their duties lawfully, within the meaning of the statute, because they enlisted military forces as a posse comitatus. *See also* United States v. Mendoza-Cecelia, 963 F.2d 1467, 1478 n.9 (11th Cir.), *cert. denied*, 506 U.S. 964 (1992).

Others apprehended by the military while attempting to smuggle drugs into the United States have argued that the evidence obtained in their arrests was inadmissible at trial. However, the federal courts have consistently refused to exclude such evidence in the absence of widespread and repeated Posse Comitatus Act violations. *See, e.g.*, Hayes v. Hawes, 921 F.2d 100, 104 (7th Cir. 1990); *see also* Timothy J. Saviano, Note, *The Exclusionary Rule's Applicability to Violations of the Posse Comitatus Act*, Army Law., July 1995, at 61.

In Bissonette v. Haig, the appellants sought damages for infringement of their constitutional rights resulting from Posse Comitatus Act violations. Do such statutory violations give rise to a private cause of action separate and apart from any possible constitutional injury? *See* Robinson v. Overseas Military Sales Corp., 21 F.3d 502 (2d Cir. 1994); Lamont v. Haig, 539 F. Supp. 552 (W.D.S.D. 1982).

3. ***Which Military Services Are Covered?*** The Posse Comitatus Act expressly refers only to the Army and Air Force, and several cases have found that the Act does not restrict Navy law enforcement efforts. *See, e.g., Mendoza-Cecelia, supra*, 963 F.2d at 1477-1478; *but cf.* United States v. Chon, 210 F.3d 990 (9th Cir. 2000). Nevertheless, Navy regulations have long prohibited the use of the Navy and Marine Corps as a posse comitatus, with certain exceptions, as a matter of Defense Department policy. *See* SECNAVINST 5820.7B (Mar. 28, 1988).

Several courts have held that unfederalized National Guard forces are not subject to the strictures of the Posse Comitatus Act. *See, e.g.,* United States v. Gilbert, 165 F.3d 470 (6th Cir. 1999). Moreover, Congress has explicitly approved the states' use of the militia for "drug interdiction and counter-drug activities," so long as they remain under state control. 32 U.S.C. §112 (2000 & Supp. IV 2004).

## 2. EXCEPTIONS TO THE POSSE COMITATUS ACT

Recall that the Posse Comitatus Act prohibition applies "except in cases and under circumstances expressly authorized by the Constitution or Act of Congress." 18 U.S.C. §1385 (2006). The most important exception to the Act is a set of five statutes, referred to collectively as the Insurrection Act. It provides, in part:

### INSURRECTION ACT

10 U.S.C. §§331-335 (2000), as amended by Pub. L. No. 109-364, §1076, 120 Stat. 2083, 2404 (2006)

#### §332. Use of Militia and Armed Forces to Enforce Federal Authority

Whenever the President considers that unlawful obstructions, combinations, or assemblages, or rebellion against the authority of the United States, make it impracticable to enforce the laws of the United States in any State or Territory by the ordinary course of judicial proceedings, he may call into Federal service such of the militia of any State, and use such of the armed forces, as he considers necessary to enforce those laws or to suppress the rebellion.

### §333.   Major public emergencies; interference with State and Federal law

(a) Use of Armed Forces in Major Public Emergencies—

(1) The President may employ the armed forces, including the National Guard in Federal service, to—

(A) restore public order and enforce the laws of the United States when, as a result of a natural disaster, epidemic, or other serious public health emergency, terrorist attack or incident, or other condition in any State or possession of the United States, the President determines that—

(i) domestic violence has occurred to such an extent that the constituted authorities of the State or possession are incapable of maintaining public order; and

(ii) such violence results in a condition described in paragraph (2); or

(B) suppress, in a State, any insurrection, domestic violence, unlawful combination, or conspiracy if such insurrection, violation, combination, or conspiracy results in a condition described in paragraph (2).

(2) A condition described in this paragraph is a condition that—

(A) so hinders the execution of the laws of a State or possession, as applicable, and of the United States within that State or possession, that any part or class of its people is deprived of a right, privilege, immunity, or protection named in the Constitution and secured by law, and the constituted authorities of that State or possession are unable, fail, or refuse to protect that right, privilege, or immunity, or to give that protection; or

(B) opposes or obstructs the execution of the laws of the United States or impedes the course of justice under those laws. . . .

(b) Notice to Congress—The President shall notify Congress of the determination to exercise the authority in subsection (a)(1)(A) as soon as practicable after the determination and every 14 days thereafter during the duration of the exercise of that authority.

### §334.   Proclamation to Disperse

Whenever the President considers it necessary to use the militia or the armed forces under this chapter, he shall, by proclamation, immediately order the insurgents or those obstructing the enforcement of the laws to disperse and retire peaceably to their abodes within a limited time.

---

Section 331 provides for federal military assistance in putting down an insurrection against a state government. Section 335 makes the statutes applicable to Guam and the Virgin Islands.

## MILITARY COOPERATION WITH LAW ENFORCEMENT OFFICIALS ACT

10 U.S.C. §§371-382 (2000 & Supp. IV 2004),
as amended by Pub. L. No. 109-304, §17(a)(1), 120 Stat. 1484, 1706 (2006)

### §371. Use of information collected during military operations

(a) The Secretary of Defense may, in accordance with other applicable law, provide to Federal, State, or local civilian law enforcement officials any information collected during the normal course of military training or operations that may be relevant to a violation of any Federal or State law within the jurisdiction of such officials.

(b) The needs of civilian law enforcement officials for information shall, to the maximum extent practicable, be taken into account in the planning and execution of military training or operations.

(c) The Secretary of Defense shall ensure, to the extent consistent with national security, that intelligence information held by the Department of Defense and relevant to drug interdiction or other civilian law enforcement matters is provided promptly to appropriate civilian law enforcement officials. . . .

### §375. Restriction on direct participation by military personnel

The Secretary of Defense shall prescribe such regulations as may be necessary to ensure that any activity (including the provision of any equipment or facility or the assignment or detail of any personnel) under this chapter does not include or permit direct participation by a member of the Army, Navy, Air Force, or Marine Corps in a search, seizure, arrest, or other similar activity unless participation in such activity by such member is otherwise authorized by law. . . .

### §382. Emergency situations involving chemical or biological weapons of mass destruction

(a) In general. — The Secretary of Defense, upon the request of the Attorney General, may provide assistance in support of Department of Justice activities relating to the enforcement of section 175 or 2332c of title 18 during an emergency situation involving a biological or chemical weapon of mass destruction. Department of Defense resources, including personnel of the Department of Defense, may be used to provide such assistance if—

(1) the Secretary of Defense and the Attorney General jointly determine that an emergency situation exists; and

(2) the Secretary of Defense determines that the provision of such assistance will not adversely affect the military preparedness of the United States.

(b) Emergency situations covered. — In this section, the term "emergency situation involving a biological or chemical weapon" means a circumstance involving a biological or chemical weapon of mass destruction —

(1) that poses a serious threat to the interests of the United States; and

(2) in which —

(A) civilian expertise and capabilities are not readily available to provide the required assistance to counter the threat immediately posed by the weapon involved;

(B) special capabilities and expertise of the Department of Defense are necessary and critical to counter the threat posed by the weapon involved; and

(C) enforcement of section 175 or 2332c of title 18 would be seriously impaired if the Department of Defense assistance were not provided.

(c) Forms of assistance. — The assistance referred to in subsection (a) includes the operation of equipment ... to monitor, contain, disable, or dispose of the weapon involved or elements of the weapon. ...

(d) Regulations. — (1) The Secretary of Defense and the Attorney General shall jointly prescribe regulations concerning the types of assistance that may be provided under this section. Such regulations shall also describe the actions that Department of Defense personnel may take in circumstances incident to the provision of assistance under this section.

(2)(A) Except as provided in subparagraph (B), the regulations may not authorize the following actions:

(i) Arrest.

(ii) Any direct participation in conducting a search for or seizure of evidence related to a violation of section 175 or 2332c of title 18.

(iii) Any direct participation in the collection of intelligence for law enforcement purposes.

(B) The regulations may authorize an action described in subparagraph (A) to be taken under the following conditions:

(i) The action is considered necessary for the immediate protection of human life, and civilian law enforcement officials are not capable of taking the action.

(ii) The action is otherwise authorized under subsection (c) or under otherwise applicable law. ...

————————————

Other sections of the 1981 act, as amended, deal variously with the use of military equipment and facilities, training and advising civilian law enforcement officials, maintenance and operation of equipment, reimbursement, the use of Coast Guard personnel for law enforcement, and impacts on military preparedness. References to sections 175 and 2332c of title 18 concern prohibitions on the possession or use of biological or chemical weapons, respectively. 18 U.S.C. §2332c has been replaced by 18 U.S.C. §229 (2000).

Additional exceptions to the Posse Comitatus Act are considered in the following Notes and Questions.

## NOTES AND QUESTIONS

1. *The Insurrection Act.* The Insurrection Act had its origin in a 1792 law invoked by President Washington in suppressing the Whiskey Rebellion. The history of its component parts is traced in Stephen I. Vladeck, Note, *Emergency Power and the Militia Acts*, 114 Yale L.J. 149, 159-167 (2004). In 1827 the Supreme Court indicated that the President had broad discretion in determining when to use these statutes in calling forth the militia, and that his determination was not subject to judicial review. Martin v. Mott, 25 U.S. (12 Wheat.) 19, 29-32 (1827). *See also* Luther v. Borden, 48 U.S. (7 How.) 1, 43-45 (1849); *The Prize Cases*, 67 U.S. (2 Black) 635, 668 (1863).

   Since that time the Insurrection Act has been invoked for a variety of purposes, including the breaking of the Pullman Strike in 1894. More recently, it has been used to help integrate public schools and universities, to control racial unrest, to collect intelligence about citizens, and to enforce a variety of state and federal laws. It was invoked in 1992 to send federalized California National Guard troops, as well as active duty soldiers from Fort Ord and Marines from Camp Pendleton, to Los Angeles to help control rioting in the wake of the Rodney King trial verdict. Exec. Order No. 12,804, 57 Fed. Reg. 19,361 (May 1, 1992); Proclamation No. 6427, 57 Fed. Reg. 19,359 (May 1, 1992).

   One part of the Insurrection Act, 10 U.S.C. §333, was amended in late 2006, reportedly because of a desire to "clarify" the President's authority. Previously, §333 provided in significant part:

   > The President, by using the militia or the armed forces, or both, or by any other means, shall take such measures as he considers necessary to suppress, in a State, any insurrection, domestic violence, unlawful combination, or conspiracy, if it . . .
   >      (2) opposes or obstructs the execution of the laws of the United States or impedes the course of justice under those laws. . . .

   The change was prompted, at least in part, by apparent confusion surrounding the deployment of federal troops in Louisiana in the aftermath of Hurricane Katrina in 2005. See *infra* p. 695. Do you think the new language, *supra* p. 676, makes it clearer when the President can employ troops domestically to help enforce the law? Does the 2006 amendment expand or restrict the President's authority?

   Can you think of any domestic emergency that could not be addressed by the President using troops if one of the provisions of the Insurrection Act were invoked? Would the unwillingness of a state governor to ask for assistance ever be a bar to such use? Could troops so deployed make searches and arrests, direct traffic, or enforce quarantines? Could they shoot people trying to escape a quarantine?

2. *The Military Cooperation with Law Enforcement Officials Act.* A dramatic surge in illicit drug traffic and related criminal activity during the 1970s and 1980s led President Reagan to declare a "war on drugs." *See* Christopher Simpson, *National Security Directives of the Reagan and Bush Administrations* 640-641 (1995). Congress responded in 1981 by enacting the

Military Cooperation with Law Enforcement Officials Act, excerpted above, which allows the military to furnish equipment, facilities, and training to civilian law enforcement agencies, and to share relevant intelligence. 10 U.S.C. §§371-373. The Act also authorizes military personnel to operate equipment to intercept vessels or aircraft for law enforcement purposes. *Id.* §374. But the Act expressly forbids "direct participation by a member of the Army, Navy, Air Force, or Marine Corps in a search, seizure, arrest, or other similar activity unless . . . otherwise authorized by law." *Id.* §375. In separate legislation, the Defense Department was designated lead agency for the detection and monitoring of aerial and maritime shipments of illicit drugs into the United States. 10 U.S.C. §124 (2000). And in 1998 Congress expanded the permitted uses of military personnel to operate loaned equipment to include enforcement of terrorism laws. Pub. L. No. 105-277, Div. B, tit. II, §201, 112 Stat. 2681, 2681-567 (1998) (amending 10 U.S.C. §374).

Do you think this legislation added to powers already enjoyed by the President under the Insurrection Act? If not, why did Congress bother to pass it?

3. ***Other Statutory Exceptions.*** Another exception to the Posse Comitatus Act is found in H.R.J. Res. 1292, Pub. L. No. 90-331, 82 Stat. 170 (1968), which directs federal agencies (including the Department of Defense) to assist the Secret Service in the performance of its protective duties. This authority was used by President Johnson to deploy troops in Chicago during the Democratic National Convention in 1968 and by President Nixon to control antiwar demonstrations on several occasions. Congress has also approved emergency military assistance in enforcing a prohibition on the unauthorized possession or use of nuclear material. 18 U.S.C. §831(d), (e) (2000).

4. ***Constitutional Exceptions.*** The Posse Comitatus Act includes an exception for "circumstances expressly authorized by the Constitution." See *supra* p. 671. One possible express constitutional exception may be found in Article IV, Section 4, which provides, "The United States shall guarantee to every State in this Union a Republican Form of Government, and shall protect each of them against Invasion; and on Application of the Legislature, or of the Executive (when the Legislature cannot be convened) against domestic Violence." Can you describe the limits of the President's power to use troops for law enforcement under this provision?

Defense Department regulations entitled "Employment of Military Resources in the Event of Civil Disturbances" refer to two "constitutional exceptions" to the Posse Comitatus Act "based upon the inherent legal right of the U.S. Government — a sovereign national entity under the Federal Constitution — to insure the preservation of public order and the carrying out of governmental operations within its territorial limits, by force if necessary." 32 C.F.R. §215.4(c)(1) (2006). One exception is described as emergency authority to take

> prompt and vigorous Federal action, including use of military forces, to prevent loss of life or wanton destruction of property and to restore governmental functioning and public order when sudden and unexpected civil disturbances, disasters, or calamities seriously

endanger life and property and disrupt normal governmental functions to such an extent that duly constituted local authorities are unable to control the situations. [*Id.* §215.4(c)(1)(i).]

The other is for "protection of Federal property and functions." *Id.* §215.4(c)(1)(ii). *See also* DOD Dir. 5525.5, *DoD Cooperation with Civilian Law Enforcement Officials* (Dec. 20, 1989), at Encl. 4 §E4.1.2.3. President Johnson apparently believed that he was exercising such inherent powers when he ordered the military to suppress rioting in Washington, D.C. following the assassination of Dr. Martin Luther King Jr. in 1968. *See* Proclamation No. 3840, 33 Fed. Reg. 5495 (Apr. 9, 1968). This regulatory authority closely resembles one for "Immediate Responses," 32 C.F.R. §185.4(e) (2006), noted *infra* p. 694. The powers claimed in the regulations are not "expressly" set out in the constitutional text, of course.

Has Congress "occupied the field" by its enactment of the Posse Comitatus Act and its exceptions, precluding inconsistent exercise by the President of his inherent constitutional powers? Could Congress do so?

5. ***Law Enforcement or War Fighting?*** José Padilla was confined in a military brig for more than three years as an "enemy combatant" before finally being charged with criminal offenses related to terrorism. See *supra* pp. 380-393. In responding to his petition for a writ of habeas corpus, one court remarked:

> Padilla argues also that his detention by the military violates the Posse Comitatus Act. . . . First, it is questionable whether that statute is enforceable in a habeas corpus proceeding to secure release from custody. *Cf.* Robinson v. Overseas Military Sales Corp., 21 F.3d 502, 511 (2d Cir. 1994) (no private right of action to enforce Posse Comitatus Act). Moreover, the statute bars use of the military in civilian law enforcement. Padilla is not being detained by the military in order to execute a civilian law or for violating a civilian law, notwithstanding that his alleged conduct may in fact violate one or more such laws. He is being detained in order to interrogate him about the unlawful organization with which he is said to be affiliated and with which the military is in active combat, and to prevent him from becoming reaffiliated with that organization. Therefore, his detention by the military does not violate the Posse Comitatus Act. [Padilla v. Bush, 233 Fed. Supp. 2d 564, 588 n.9 (S.D. N.Y. 2002), *rev'd in part*, Padilla v. Rumsfeld, 352 F.3d 695 (2d Cir. 2003).]

Do you think the military can avoid application of the Posse Comitatus Act simply by characterizing a person it suspects of criminal activity as an "enemy combatant"? If you think the designation of enemy combatants might be subject to abuse, can you suggest some realistic process for distinguishing between law enforcement and war fighting, at least for this purpose? Or can you articulate some other principled basis for limiting the military's role in activities that involve both law enforcement and war fighting? What are the implications of the Military Commissions Act of 2006, *supra* p. 587, in answering these questions?

## B.  THE MILITARY'S INTELLIGENCE ROLE IN HOMELAND SECURITY

Since the earliest days of the Republic, military intelligence units have supported domestic uses of military force. Chief Justice Marshall reportedly said of Washington, "A general must be governed by his intelligence and must regulate his measures by his information. It is his duty to obtain correct information . . . ." *Quoted in* Tatum v. Laird, 444 F.2d 947, 952-953 (D.C. Cir. 1971), *rev'd*, 408 U.S. 1 (1972). In principle, domestic intelligence collection for force protection or as part of DOD's homeland defense mission has never been controversial.

But military intelligence personnel have also been used at times to collect personal information about Americans who pose no real threat to national security. In this part of the chapter we look first at military intelligence activities at home during the Vietnam War, then turn to recent developments ostensibly related to the war on terrorism.

### 1.  MILITARY DOMESTIC SURVEILLANCE DURING THE VIETNAM WAR

Domestic military intelligence activity reached a peak in the late 1960s, when the Pentagon compiled data on more than 100,000 politically active Americans in an effort to quell civil rights and anti-Vietnam War demonstrations and to discredit protestors. The Army deployed 1,500 plainclothes agents to watch demonstrators, infiltrate organizations, and circulate blacklists. Military officials claimed that they were preparing for the use of troops to put down insurrections. *See* Christopher H. Pyle, *Military Surveillance of Civilian Politics, 1961-1971* (1986). In 1976, the Church Committee, looking into a variety of intelligence community abuses, called the Army program "the worst intrusion that military intelligence has ever made into the civilian community." S. Select Comm. to Study Governmental Operations with Respect to Intelligence Activities, *Improper Surveillance of Private Citizens by the Military* [*Church Committee Report*], S. Rep. No. 94-755, Book III, at 792 (1976). Public disclosure of this activity precipitated the following case.

---

### LAIRD v. TATUM

United States Supreme Court, 1972
408 U.S. 1

Mr. Chief Justice BURGER delivered the opinion of the Court. Respondents brought this class action in the District Court seeking declaratory and injunctive relief on their claim that their rights were being invaded by the Department of the Army's alleged "surveillance of lawful and peaceful civilian political activity." The petitioners in response describe the activity as "gathering by lawful means . . . (and) maintaining and using in their intelligence activities . . . information relating to potential or actual civil disturbances (or) street demonstrations." . . .

The President is authorized by 10 U.S.C. §331[2] to make use of the armed forces to quell insurrection and other domestic violence if and when the conditions described in that section obtain within one of the States. Pursuant to those provisions, President Johnson ordered federal troops to assist local authorities at the time of the civil disorders in Detroit, Michigan, in the summer of 1967 and during the disturbances that followed the assassination of Dr. Martin Luther King. Prior to the Detroit disorders, the Army had a general contingency plan for providing such assistance to local authorities, but the 1967 experience led Army authorities to believe that more attention should be given to such preparatory planning. The data-gathering system here involved is said to have been established in connection with the development of more detailed and specific contingency planning designed to permit the Army, when called upon to assist local authorities, to be able to respond effectively with a minimum of force. As the Court of Appeals observed,

> In performing this type function the Army is essentially a police force or the back-up of a local police force. To quell disturbances or to prevent further disturbances the Army needs the same tools and, most importantly, the same information to which local police forces have access. Since the Army is sent into territory almost invariably unfamiliar to most soldiers and their commanders, their need for information is likely to be greater than that of the hometown policeman.
>
> No logical argument can be made for compelling the military to use blind force. When force is employed it should be intelligently directed, and this depends upon having reliable information — in time. As Chief Justice John Marshall said of Washington, "A general must be governed by his intelligence and must regulate his measures by his information. It is his duty to obtain correct information; . . . ." So we take it as undeniable that the military, *i.e.*, the Army, need a certain amount of information in order to perform their constitutional and statutory missions. 444 F.2d at 952-953 (footnotes omitted).

The system put into operation as a result of the Army's 1967 experience consisted essentially of the collection of information about public activities that were thought to have at least some potential for civil disorder, the reporting of that information to Army Intelligence headquarters at Fort Holabird, Maryland, the dissemination of these reports from headquarters to major Army posts around the country, and the storage of the reported information in a computer data bank located at Fort Holabird. The information itself was collected by a variety of means, but it is significant that the principal sources of information were the news media and publications in general circulation. Some of the information came from Army Intelligence agents who attended meetings that were open to the public and who wrote field reports describing the meetings, giving such data as the name of the sponsoring organization, the identity of speakers,

---

2. "Whenever there is an insurrection in any State against its government, the President may, upon the request of its legislature or of its governor if the legislature cannot be convened, call into Federal service such of the militia of the other States, in the number requested by that State, and use such of the armed forces, as he considers necessary to suppress the insurrection." . . .

the approximate number of persons in attendance, and an indication of whether any disorder occurred. And still other information was provided to the Army by civilian law enforcement agencies. . . .

Our examination of the record satisfies us that the Court of Appeals properly identified the issue presented, namely, whether the jurisdiction of a federal court may be invoked by a complainant who alleges that the exercise of his First Amendment rights is being chilled by the mere existence, without more, of a governmental investigative and data-gathering activity that is alleged to be broader in scope than is reasonably necessary for the accomplishment of a valid governmental purpose. We conclude, however, that, having properly identified the issue, the Court of Appeals decided that issue incorrectly.

In recent years this Court has found in a number of cases that constitutional violations may arise from the deterrent, or "chilling," effect of governmental regulations that fall short of a direct prohibition against the exercise of First Amendment rights. In none of these cases, however, did the chilling effect arise merely from the individual's knowledge that a governmental agency was engaged in certain activities or from the individual's concomitant fear that, armed with the fruits of those activities, the agency might in the future take some other and additional action detrimental to that individual. Rather, in each of these cases, the challenged exercise of governmental power was regulatory, proscriptive, or compulsory in nature, and the complainant was either presently or prospectively subject to the regulations, proscriptions, or compulsions that he was challenging. . . .

The decisions in these cases fully recognize that governmental action may be subject to constitutional challenge even though it has only an indirect effect on the exercise of First Amendment rights. At the same time, however, these decisions have in no way eroded the "established principle that to entitle a private individual to invoke the judicial power to determine the validity of executive or legislative action he must show that he has sustained, or is immediately in danger of sustaining, a direct injury as the result of that action . . . ." Ex parte Levitt, 302 U.S. 633 (1937).

The respondents do not meet this test; their claim, simply stated, is that they disagree with the judgments made by the Executive Branch with respect to the type and amount of information the Army needs and that the very existence of the Army's data-gathering system produces a constitutionally impermissible chilling effect upon the exercise of their First Amendment rights. That alleged "chilling" effect may perhaps be seen as arising from respondents' very perception of the system as inappropriate to the Army's role under our form of government, or as arising from respondents' beliefs that it is inherently dangerous for the military to be concerned with activities in the civilian sector, or as arising from respondents' less generalized yet speculative apprehensiveness that the Army may at some future date misuse the information in some way that would cause direct harm to respondents. Allegations of a subjective "chill" are not an adequate substitute for a claim of specific present objective harm or a threat of specific future harm. . . .

. . . [Plaintiffs] would have the federal courts as virtually continuing monitors of the wisdom and soundness of Executive action; such a role is appropriate for the Congress acting through its committees and the "power of the purse"; it is not the role of the judiciary, absent actual present or immediately threatened injury resulting from unlawful governmental action. . . .

The concerns of the Executive and Legislative Branches in response to disclosure of the Army surveillance activities — and indeed the claims alleged in the complaint — reflect a traditional and strong resistance of Americans to any military intrusion into civilian affairs. That tradition has deep roots in our history and found early expression, for example, in the Third Amendment's explicit prohibition against quartering soldiers in private homes without consent and in the constitutional provisions for civilian control of the military. Those prohibitions are not directly presented by this case, but their philosophical underpinnings explain our traditional insistence on limitations on military operations in peacetime. Indeed, when presented with claims of judicially cognizable injury resulting from military intrusion into the civilian sector, federal courts are fully empowered to consider claims of those asserting such injury; there is nothing in our Nation's history or in this Court's decided cases, including our holding today, that can properly be seen as giving any indication that actual or threatened injury by reason of unlawful activities of the military would go unnoticed or unremedied.

*Reversed.*

Mr. Justice Douglas, with whom Mr. Justice Marshall concurs, dissenting.

## I

If Congress had passed a law authorizing the armed services to establish surveillance over the civilian population, a most serious constitutional problem would be presented. There is, however, no law authorizing surveillance over civilians, which in this case the Pentagon concededly had undertaken. The question is whether such authority may be implied. One can search the Constitution in vain for any such authority. . . .

. . . [W]e have until today consistently adhered to the belief that "[i]t is an unbending rule of law, that the exercise of military power, where the rights of the citizen are concerned, shall never be pushed beyond what the exigency requires." Raymond v. Thomas, 91 U.S. 712, 716.

It was in that tradition that Youngstown Sheet & Tube Co. v. Sawyer, 343 U.S. 579, was decided, in which President Truman's seizure of the steel mills in the so-called Korean War was held unconstitutional. As stated by Justice Black:

> The order cannot properly be sustained as an exercise of the President's military power as Commander in Chief of the Armed Forces. The Government attempts to do so by citing a number of cases upholding broad powers in military commanders engaged in day-to-day fighting in a theater of war. Such cases need not concern us here. Even though "theater of war" be an expanding concept, we cannot with faithfulness to our constitutional system hold that the Commander in Chief of the Armed Forces has the ultimate power as such to take possession of private property in order to keep labor disputes from stopping production. This is a job for the Nation's lawmakers, not for its military authorities. *Id.* at 587. . . .

The act of turning the military loose on civilians even if sanctioned by an Act of Congress, which it has not been, would raise serious and profound constitutional questions. Standing as it does only on brute power and Pentagon policy, it must be repudiated as a usurpation dangerous to the civil liberties on which free men are dependent. For, as Senator Sam Ervin has said, "this claim of an inherent executive branch power of investigation and surveillance on the basis of people's beliefs and attitudes may be more of a threat to our internal security than any enemies beyond our borders." Privacy and Government Investigations, 1971 U. Ill. L.F. 137, 153.

## II

The claim that respondents have no standing to challenge the Army's surveillance of them and the other members of the class they seek to represent is too transparent for serious argument. The surveillance of the Army over the civilian sector — a part of society hitherto immune from its control — is a serious charge. It is alleged that the Army maintains files on the membership, ideology, programs, and practices of virtually every activist political group in the country, including groups such as the Southern Christian Leadership Conference, Clergy and Laymen United Against the War in Vietnam, the American Civil Liberties Union, Women's Strike for Peace, and the National Association for the Advancement of Colored People. The Army uses undercover agents to infiltrate these civilian groups and to reach into confidential files of students and other groups. The Army moves as a secret group among civilian audiences, using cameras and electronic ears for surveillance. The data it collects are distributed to civilian officials in state, federal, and local governments and to each military intelligence unit and troop command under the Army's jurisdiction (both here and abroad); and these data are stored in one or more data banks.

Those are the allegations; and the charge is that the purpose and effect of the system of surveillance is to harass and intimidate the respondents and to deter them from exercising their rights of political expression, protest, and dissent "by invading their privacy, damaging their reputations, adversely affecting their employment and their opportunities for employment, and in other ways." Their fear is that "permanent reports of their activities will be maintained in the Army's data bank, and their 'profiles' will appear in the so-called 'Blacklist' and that all of this information will be released to numerous federal and state agencies upon request."

Judge Wilkey, speaking for the Court of Appeals, properly inferred that this Army surveillance "exercises a present inhibiting effect on their full expression and utilization of their First Amendment rights." 444 F.2d 947, 954. That is the test. The "deterrent effect" on First Amendment rights by government oversight marks an unconstitutional intrusion, Lamont v. Postmaster General, 381 U.S. 301, 307. Or, as stated by Mr. Justice Brennan, "inhibition as well as prohibition against the exercise of precious First Amendment rights is a power denied to government." *Id.* at 309. . . .

The present controversy is not a remote, imaginary conflict. Respondents were targets of the Army's surveillance. First, the surveillance was not casual but massive and comprehensive. Second, the intelligence reports were regularly and widely circulated and were exchanged with reports of the FBI, state and municipal police departments, and the CIA. Third, the Army's surveillance was not collecting material in public records but staking out teams of agents, infiltrating undercover agents, creating command posts inside meetings, posing as press photographers and newsmen, posing as TV newsmen, posing as students, and shadowing public figures.

Finally, we know from the hearings conducted by Senator Ervin that the Army has misused or abused its reporting functions. Thus, Senator Ervin concluded that reports of the Army have been "taken from the Intelligence Command's highly inaccurate civil disturbance teletype and filed in Army dossiers on persons who have held, or were being considered for, security clearances, thus contaminating what are supposed to be investigative reports with unverified gossip and rumor. This practice directly jeopardized the employment and employment opportunities of persons seeking sensitive positions with the federal government or defense industry."[10]

Surveillance of civilians is none of the Army's constitutional business and Congress has not undertaken to entrust it with any such function. . . .

[Dissenting opinion of Mr. Justice BRENNAN, with whom Mr. Justice STEWART and Mr. Justice MARSHALL join, omitted.]

## NOTES AND QUESTIONS

1. *Military vs. Non-Military Intelligence.* Does the domestic collection of intelligence by the military differ in any constitutionally significant way from collection by, say, the FBI? Can you say how?
2. *Standing to Sue.* The *Laird* Court decided that the plaintiffs' claim was nonjusticiable because they could not demonstrate standing to sue, which would have required a showing of "actual present or immediately threatened injury." What kind of injury did they claim to have suffered? Do you think Vietnam War protesters' fears of reprisal by government agencies were justified? Have you ever felt reluctant to speak out, to join a group, or even to attend a meeting because you worried that your statements or actions might be officially noted and used against you? If so, was the effect of your reluctance different in any constitutionally significant way from the effect of a direct government ban on your expression or association?
3. *Relevance of the Posse Comitatus Act?* According to the *Laird* majority, the Army was "essentially a police force" when it collected domestic intelligence, ostensibly in planning for a response to civil unrest. Did the Army's surveillance program therefore run afoul of the Posse Comitatus Act? Why do you suppose the Court did not refer to the Act? If it had, do you think its constitutional analysis would more nearly have resembled that of the *Bissonnette* court?
4. *Effect of the Insurrection Act?* The *Laird* Court cites 10 U.S.C. §331, one provision of the Insurrection Act (see *supra* p. 675), as authority for the

---

10. Hearings on Federal Data Banks, Computers and The Bill of Rights, before the Subcommittee on Constitutional Rights of the Senate Committee on the Judiciary, 92d Cong., 1st Sess. (1971).

deployment of military forces to help control rioting in several American cities in 1967 and 1968. The Court did not point to that same authority for the Army's surveillance program, which extended over a number of years. Could the Court have done so?

5. *Post-Vietnam Reforms.* In 1976, the Church Committee responded to the abuses outlined in *Laird* by proposing a "precisely drawn legislative charter" that would, *inter alia,* "limit military investigations to activities in the civilian community which are necessary and pertinent to the military mission, and which cannot feasibly be accomplished by civilian agencies." *Church Committee Report, supra,* Book II, at 310-311. The committee apparently believed that military intelligence units could make no unique contributions to the domestic security efforts of the FBI, local law enforcement, and other civilian agencies. Its proposal also may have reflected concern about conducting domestic intelligence collection under a military chain of command, whose priority is completion of its military mission, rather than under the Attorney General, whose priority is law enforcement.

Congress did not enact the charter suggested by the Church Committee, but it did pass the Privacy Act in 1974, 5 U.S.C. §552a (2000 & Supp. IV 2004), and the Foreign Intelligence Surveillance Act (FISA) in 1978, 50 U.S.C. §§1801-1862 (2000 & Supp. IV 2004), as amended by Pub. L. No. 109-177, 120 Stat. 204 (2006). See *supra* pp. 119-157. Both measures limit the collection, retention, and sharing of information about how individuals exercise rights guaranteed by the First Amendment, as well as information not relevant to the mission of an agency. But serious doubts exist about the efficacy of these laws in safeguarding personal privacy. *See, e.g.,* William C. Banks, *And the Wall Came Tumbling Down: Secret Surveillance After the Terror,* 57 U. Miami L. Rev. 1147 (2002); Steven W. Becker, *Maintaining Secret Government Dossiers on the First Amendment Activities of American Citizens: The Law Enforcement Activity Exception to the Privacy Act,* 50 DePaul L. Rev. 675 (2000); Technology and Privacy Advisory Comm., *Safeguarding Privacy in the Fight Against Terrorism (TAPAC Report)* 25-26 (Mar. 2004).

The Defense Department's own rules now limit the domestic collection and use of personal information. For example, DOD Dir. 5200.27, *Acquisition of Information Concerning Persons and Organizations Not Affiliated with the Department of Defense* (Jan. 7, 1980), includes the following restrictions:

> 5.2. No information shall be acquired about a person or organization solely because of lawful advocacy of measures in opposition to Government policy. . . .
>
> 5.5. There shall be no covert or otherwise deceptive surveillance or penetration of civilian organizations unless specifically authorized by the Secretary of Defense, or his designee. . . .
>
> 5.7. No computerized data banks shall be maintained relating to individuals or organizations not affiliated with the Department of Defense, unless authorized by the Secretary of Defense, or his designee. . . .

6.3. Access to information obtained under the provisions of this Directive shall be restricted to Governmental Agencies that require such information in the execution of their duties. . . .

*See also* DOD Dir. 5240.1-R, *Procedures Governing the Activities of DoD Intelligence Components That Affect United States Persons* (Dec. 1982); Army Reg. 381-10, *U.S. Army Intelligence Activities* (Nov. 22, 2005), *available at* http://www.fas.org/irp/doddir/army/ar381-10.pdf.

Do these limitations on domestic intelligence collection address the concerns expressed by the Church Committee and by the dissenters in *Laird*? Are additional reforms needed?

## 2. DOMESTIC USE OF MILITARY INTELLIGENCE FOR COUNTERTERRORISM

Several developments in the wake of 9/11 point to an expanding domestic role for the military intelligence agencies, which include the Defense Intelligence Agency and intelligence operations within each of the service branches. *See generally* Stephen Dycus, *The Role of Military Intelligence in Homeland Security*, 64 La. L. Rev. 779 (2004). The Department of Homeland Security's Directorate for Information Analysis and Infrastructure Protection (IAIP) receives, analyzes, and disseminates data about possible domestic terrorist threats from government and private sources, including the military's intelligence components. The National Counterterrorism Center (NCTC), *supra* p. 262, performs many of the same functions. Military intelligence personnel work in both of these agencies, where they become both suppliers and recipients of personal information, some of which may have no clear relevance to the Pentagon's homeland defense mission. Congress has also approved the creation of an Under Secretary of Defense for Intelligence, 10 U.S.C. §137 (Supp. IV 2004), who is supposed to provide "more coordinated, better focused intelligence support for pressing national concerns like homeland security." Dept. of Defense, *Report to Congress on the Role of the Department of Defense in Supporting Homeland Security* 3, Sept. 2003.

In 2002, DOD created the Northern Command (NORTHCOM), based in Colorado, to assist in homeland defense. *See generally* http://www.northcom. mil. Like IAIP and NCTC, NORTHCOM receives and "fuses" intelligence and law enforcement information from various sources, then redistributes it widely to federal, state, and local agencies. Unlike the two civilian agencies, however, NORTHCOM also collects domestic data directly, utilizing a Pentagon organization called Counterintelligence Field Activity (CIFA). *See* DOD Dir. 5105.67, *DoD Counterintelligence Field Activity* (Feb. 19, 2002). CIFA is charged to maintain "a domestic law enforcement database" and to develop a data mining capability.

One CIFA activity, Threat and Local Observation Notice (TALON), is officially described as "much like . . . a 'neighborhood watch' program in which concerned citizens or DoD personnel report suspicious activities." Letter to

Hon. Duncan Hunter from Robert W. Rogalski, Dep. Under Secretary of Defense (Counterintelligence and Security), Jan. 27, 2006. TALON has engaged in surveillance and data collection regarding domestic political activities, for example, compiling records on the Quakers and others who protested the Iraq War. *See, e.g.,* Robert Block & Jay Solomon, *Pentagon Steps Up Intelligence Efforts Inside U.S. Borders,* Wall St. J., Apr. 27, 2006, at 1. It has also monitored demonstrations against military recruitment on university campuses aimed at DOD's "don't ask, don't tell" policy of excluding homosexuals from military ranks. *See Pentagon Releases Documents Acknowledging Surveillance of Gay Groups,* Servicemembers Legal Defense Network, Apr. 11, 2006 (and linked documents), *at* http://www.sldn.org/templates/press/record.html?record=2859. *See also* Robert Block & Gary Fields, *Is Military Creeping Into Domestic Spying and Enforcement?,* Wall St. J., Mar. 9, 2004, at B1 (describing CIFA agent's effort to get videotape of law school conference attended by "three Middle Eastern men" who made "suspicious remarks"). In early 2006, DOD reportedly deleted 1,131 files improperly stored in the TALON data base, out of some 13,000 entries, of which 2,821 involved American citizens. *See* Walter Pincus, *Protestors Found in Database; ACLU Is Questioning Enemies in Defense Dept. System,* Wash. Post, Jan. 17, 2007, at A8. But it is not known what became of information shared with other agencies before it was deleted from the TALON data base.

In June 2005, the Defense Department published *Strategy for Homeland Defense and Civil Support,* declaring that DOD expected to "reorient its intelligence capabilities" to enable it to, *inter alia,* "[c]ollect homeland defense threat information from relevant private and public sector sources, consistent with US constitutional authorities and privacy law," and to "[d]evelop automated tools to improve data fusion, analysis, and management, to track systematically large amounts of data, and to detect, fuse, and analyze aberrant patterns of activity, consistent with US privacy protections." *Id.* at 21. This last is an apparent reference to a data-mining system like DARPA's much maligned Total Information Awareness program. See *supra* pp. 203. The document pledges that DOD will work to "diminish existing cultural, technological, and bureaucratic obstacles to information sharing" among federal agencies, with state, local, and tribal governments, with private entities, and with "key foreign partners." *Id.* at 23.

Even more broadly, the White House has reportedly considered a proposal to expand CIFA's mission to include investigation of crimes within the United States, such as treason, espionage, and foreign or terrorist sabotage, as well as clandestine operations against potential threats at home. *See* Walter Pincus, *Pentagon Expanding Its Domestic Surveillance Activity,* Wash. Post, Nov. 27, 2005, at A6. Further evidence of DOD's expanding domestic intelligence role can be seen in its use of "noncompulsory" national security letters to collect banking and credit information about hundreds of Americans and others from U.S. financial institutions. *See* Eric Lichtblau & Mark Mazzetti, *Military Expands Intelligence Role in U.S.,* N.Y. Times, Jan. 13, 2007, §1, at 1; DOD Instr. 5400.15, *Guidance on Obtaining Information from Financial Institutions* (Dec. 7, 2004), at Encl. 5. (The use of national security letters by the FBI is described *supra* pp. 178-199.)

## NOTES AND QUESTIONS

1. *Legal Limits.* Do you think that current domestic intelligence activities outlined here, including the role of military personnel in DHS's IAIP Directorate and in the NCTC, fall within the limits imposed by the Posse Comitatus Act? Do they conform to DOD's own rules?

   If the Posse Comitatus Act is implicated, do any of its constitutional or statutory exceptions apply? Consider in this regard 10 U.S.C. §371, *supra* p. 677. It directs DOD to give "civilian law enforcement officials any information collected during the normal course of military training or operations that may be relevant to a violation of any Federal or State law," and it declares that the "needs of civilian law enforcement officials for information shall, to the maximum extent practicable, be taken into account in the planning and execution of military training or operations." *Id.* §371(a), (b). In light of this provision, are there any meaningful constraints on military intelligence collection?

2. *Implications for Civil Liberties.* As the military plays a larger domestic intelligence role, how would you weigh possible enhancements in security against possible losses in privacy and related liberties? What civil liberties safeguards apply to civilian intelligence activities that do not apply to the military? Are your answers affected by the availability of new data-mining technology described *supra* pp. 202-204?

## C.  THE MILITARY'S ROLE IN RESPONDING TO DOMESTIC TERRORIST ATTACKS

Even before September 11, it was assumed that, for practical reasons, the military would be prominently involved in responding to a substantial terrorist attack at home. Several qualities recommend it for such a role. No other agency of government has as much equipment, training, and experience in the use of force as the Defense Department does (although some worry that such force may not be sufficiently refined for use at home). No other agency has such a durable communications system. And no other agency, especially if the National Guard is counted among its forces, is so widely dispersed around the country in places where its services may be urgently needed.

### 1.  LEADING OR SUPPORTING ROLE?

Some feel that DOD should be assigned an operational leadership role in responding to a terrorist attack on the American homeland. In the view of one national commission,

> The Department of Defense's ability to command and control vast resources for dangerous, unstructured situations is unmatched by any other department or agency. According to current plans, DoD involvement is limited to supporting the agencies that are currently designated as having the lead in a terrorism

crisis, the FBI and the Federal Emergency Management Agency (FEMA). But, in extraordinary circumstances, when a catastrophe is beyond the capabilities of local, state, and other federal agencies, or is directly related to an armed conflict overseas, the President may want to designate DoD as lead federal agency. This may become a critical operational consideration in planning for future conflicts. Current plans and exercises do not consider this possibility. [National Commission on Terrorism (Bremer Commn.), *Countering the Changing Threat of International Terrorism* 28 (2000).]

*See also* Fred C. Iklé, *Defending the U.S. Homeland: Strategic and Legal Issues for DOD and the Armed Services* (1999). Another study advocates planning ahead for what it views as inevitable DOD primacy in the most extreme circumstances. Ashton B. Carter, John M. Deutch & Philip D. Zelikow, *Catastrophic Terrorism: Elements of a National Policy* (1998).

Not everyone agrees that handing the reins over to the military would be wise, however. According to a different national commission, the President should "always designate a Federal civilian agency other than the Department of Defense (DoD) as the Lead Federal Agency." Advisory Panel to Assess Domestic Response Capabilities for Terrorism Involving Weapons of Mass Destruction (Gilmore Commn.), *Toward A National Strategy for Combating Terrorism* 28 (2000). The Gilmore Commission worried that "[m]any Americans will not draw the technical distinction between the Department of Defense — the civilian entity — and the U.S. Armed Forces — the military entity," leading to the perception that "the military" is in charge. *Id.* Responding to a suggestion that "active-duty forces should be given complete authority for responding to catastrophic disasters," one National Guard official called that a "policy of domestic regime change." Robert Block, *Local and Federal Authorities Battle to Control Disaster Relief,* Wall St. J., Dec. 8, 2005, at 1.

Thus far, government planners have prescribed a supporting role for the military. *Homeland Security Presidential Directive/HSPD-5,* Feb. 28, 2003, names the Secretary of Homeland Security as "principal Federal official for domestic incident management," and assigns "lead responsibility for criminal investigations of terrorist acts" to the Attorney General. Current plans generally call for use of the armed forces only when they could be uniquely helpful in responding to a serious emergency: "DOD provides [Defense Support of Civil Authorities] in response to requests for assistance during domestic incidents to include terrorist attacks, major disasters, and other emergencies. . . . DSCA normally is provided when local, State, and Federal resources are overwhelmed. . . ." Dept. of Homeland Security, *National Response Plan* 41, Dec. 2004.

The Defense Department's own regulations have long described its powers in the midst of a great domestic emergency as subordinate. For example, DOD Dir. 3025.1, *Military Support to Civil Authorities* §4.4.4.2 (Jan. 15, 1993), provides that "DOD resources are provided only when response or recovery requirements are beyond the capabilities of civil authorities (as determined by FEMA or another lead Federal agency for emergency response)." *See generally* Dept. of the Army, *Stability Operations and Support Operations* (FM 3-07), Feb. 20, 2003; DOD Dir. 3025.15, *Military Assistance to Civil Authorities* (Feb. 18, 1997).

In mid-2005, a new DOD policy document appeared that may signal a significantly more expansive domestic role. Dept. of Defense, *Strategy for Homeland Defense and Civil Support*, June 2005. "Our adversaries consider US territory an integral part of a global theater of combat," it declares. "We must therefore have a strategy that applies to the domestic context the key principles that are driving the transformation of US power projection and joint expeditionary warfare." *Id.* at 1. The new policy envisions an "active, layered" defense that could deal with "simultaneous, mass casualty attacks." *Id.* at 7, 10. It also calls for significantly expanded domestic intelligence capabilities. *Id.* at 21-23. Finally, while recognizing that "[d]omestic security is primarily a civilian law enforcement function," the strategy declares that when "directed by the President, the Department will execute land-based military operations to detect, deter, and defeat foreign terrorist attacks within the United States." *Id.* at 26. Still, the Pentagon is careful to distinguish between "homeland defense (HD)," such as domestic air defense, for which DOD is the lead agency, and "homeland security." Jt. Pub. 3-26, *Homeland Security*, Aug. 2, 2005, at v-vi, *available at* http://www.fas.org/irp/doddir/dod/jp3_26.pdf. "Except for HD missions," it says, "DOD will serve in a supporting role for domestic incident management." *Id.* at viii.

## 2.  CONTROLLING AUTHORITIES

A "sense of Congress" provision in the Homeland Security Act of 2002 notes that existing laws, including the Insurrection Act and the Stafford Act, "grant the President broad powers that may be invoked in the event of domestic emergencies, including an attack against the Nation using weapons of mass destruction, and these laws specifically authorize the President to use the Armed Forces to help restore public order." 6 U.S.C. §466(a)(5) (Supp. IV 2004).

The Stafford Act, 42 U.S.C.A. §§5121-5207 (West 2003 & Supp. 2006), as amended, gives the President authority to use any federal agency, including the Defense Department, to assist state governments in disaster relief operations, *id.* §5192, or specifically to use the armed forces to perform work "essential for the preservation of life and property." *Id.* §5170b(c). It has not been construed to permit the use of those forces to maintain law and order, however. *See* Jennifer K. Elsea, *The Use of Federal Troops for Disaster Assistance* (Cong. Res. Serv. RS22266) 4, Sept. 16, 2005.

Several statutory exceptions to the Posse Comitatus Act, especially the Insurrection Act, 10 U.S.C. §§331-335, *supra* p. 675, give the President wide latitude to use troops for almost any purpose, including law enforcement, in the aftermath of a terrorist attack or natural disaster. The military may turn over to law enforcement officials any information collected during "the normal course of . . . military operations," and in fact the military must take law enforcement needs into account in planning and executing its operations. 10 U.S.C. §371. Treating any attack site as a crime scene, this measure could allow troops to assist in gathering evidence for a criminal prosecution, although a related provision bars any "direct participation" by military personnel in a "search, seizure, arrest, or other similar activity" unless otherwise authorized by law. 10 U.S.C. §375. And during an "emergency situation involving a biological or chemical weapon of mass destruction," military personnel may assist the Department of Justice in the collection of intelligence or in searches or seizures, if it is "necessary for the immediate protection of human life," and civilian law enforcement officials cannot do it. 10 U.S.C. §382. *See also* 18 U.S.C. §831(e) (emergency situation involving nuclear materials). *See generally* Charles Doyle & Jennifer Elsea, *Terrorism: Some Legal Restrictions on Military Assistance to Domestic Authorities Following a Terrorist Attack* (Cong. Res. Serv. RS21012), May 27, 2005.

Without reference to any specific enabling legislation, DOD regulations describing "immediate response authority" say that local military commanders may act in an emergency to "save lives, prevent human suffering, or mitigate great property damage." 32 C.F.R. §185.4(e) (2006). *See also id.* at §215.4(c)(1), noted *supra* p. 680, and §501.2(a). This authority was cited when the military furnished medevac aircraft, ambulances, bomb detection dog teams, and various personnel to assist civilian officials following the Oklahoma City bombing in 1995. The regulations would also permit evacuation, restoration of essential public services, and traffic control. *See* Jim Winthrop, *The Oklahoma City Bombing: Immediate Response Authority and Other Military Assistance to Civil Authority (MACA)*, Army Law., July 1997, at 3. Do you think this authority should be spelled out in legislation?

## 3. ORGANIZING FOR A RESPONSE

In 2002, the Defense Department's new NORTHCOM assumed responsibility for DOD's homeland defense efforts and for provision of military support to civil authorities. *See* Scott Shepherd & Steve Bowman, *Homeland Security: Establishment and Implementation of the United States Northern Command* (Cong. Res. Serv. RS21322), Feb. 10, 2005. NORTHCOM manages military responses to all kinds of threats, from terrorism to hurricanes, it works closely with the Department of Homeland Security, and it directs the activities of the Joint Task Force-Civil Support. Details of NORTHCOM's organization and responsibilities, as well as those of various DOD components, are spelled out in considerable detail in *Report to Congress on the Role of the Department of Defense in Supporting Homeland Security, supra* p. 689; Dept. of Defense, *The DoD Role in Homeland Security: Defense Study and Report to Congress,* July 2003.

The National Guard, with some 450,000 personnel, has a special role to play in the response to a terrorist attack. The nearly 5,000 Army and Air National Guard units scattered across the country have essentially the same relevant training and equipment as active duty military elements, and they have extensive experience in firefighting, rescue, evacuation, and cleanup after storms and floods. The importance of the Guard's role and the need for close coordination of the Guard's activities with those of active duty military forces are spelled out in *Failure of Initiative: Final Report of the [House] Bipartisan Committee to Investigate the Preparation for and Response to Hurricane Katrina,* Feb. 15, 2006 [hereinafter *Failure of Initiative*], at 218-224, 228-231. Unless and until they are federalized by the President's order, however, Guard forces operate under the command of state governors. In this posture, as we have seen, *supra*

p. 675, the Posse Comitatus Act does not apply. Thus, there may be an incentive to delay placing these forces under federal command in order to preserve the maximum flexibility in their use. *See generally* the National Guard Bureau home page *at* http://www.ngb.army.mil/; William C. Banks, *The Normalization of Homeland Security After September 11: The Role of the Military in Counter-terrorism Preparedness and Response*, 64 La. L. Rev. 735, 762-768 (2004).

The Pentagon has directed Guard forces to provide training and equipment for at least 55 specialized teams of 22 persons each who would be ready on a moment's notice for deployment to the scene of a chemical or biological weapons attack. Equipped with a mobile analytical laboratory and reliable communications gear, a team would assist state and local personnel in identifying dangerous agents, evacuating victims, and controlling access to affected areas. Initially called Rapid Assessment and Initial Detection (RAID) teams, in 2000 they were given the more prosaic name Weapons of Mass Destruction Civil Support Teams, to emphasize their supporting role. *See* GlobalSecurity. org, *Weapons of Mass Destruction Civil Support Teams*, Apr. 13, 2007, *at* http://www.globalsecurity.org/military/agency/army/wmd-cst.htm; 10 U.S.C. §12310(c) (2000), as amended.

In the aftermath of the September 11 terrorist attacks, National Guard troops, armed and in uniform, were used as extra security at airports across the country. While these personnel were at least nominally under state control, they had to undergo uniform federal training for their new assignments, and their salaries were paid by the federal government. Other National Guard forces were used to beef up security at border crossings into Mexico and Canada.

## 4.  LESSONS FROM HURRICANE KATRINA

*Homeland Security Presidential Directive/HSPD-8*, Dec. 17, 2003, sets "a national domestic all-hazards preparedness goal" for "improved delivery of Federal preparedness and assistance to State and local governments" in response to "domestic terrorist attacks, major disasters, and other emergencies." The Pentagon, in particular, is directed to furnish "information describing the organizations and functions within the Department of Defense that may be utilized to provide support to civil authorities during a domestic crisis."

When Hurricane Katrina hit New Orleans in 2005, local police and other first responders were overwhelmed. The governor of Louisiana immediately asked the White House for 40,000 soldiers to help in the recovery effort. The White House delayed sending any active-duty military forces for five days, however, and then it deployed only 7,200 troops. Apparently it was felt that the President would have had to federalize Louisiana National Guard forces and invoke the Insurrection Act, then maintain federal control of Guard troops to perform law enforcement duties there — to stop looting and other lawlessness. While the Justice Department's Office of Legal Counsel advised that federal military forces could be sent in, even over the objections of local officials, the President reportedly wanted to avoid the perception that he was seizing command from a female Southern governor of another party. *See* Eric Lipton, Eric Schmitt & Thom Shanker, *Political Issues Snarled Plans for Troop Aid*, N.Y. Times, Sept. 5, 2005, at A1. The eventual deployment of military forces, said to be the largest in this country since the Civil War, is described in useful detail in *Failure of Initiative, supra*, at pp. 201-238.

Paradoxically, the President almost immediately suggested a need for expanded authority for the use of federal troops in such an emergency. Asked whether DOD should play a larger role, the President responded,

> Clearly, in the case of a terrorist attack that would be the case, but is there a natural disaster which — of a certain size that would then enable the Defense Department to become a lead agency in coordinating and leading the response effort? That's going to be a very important consideration for Congress to think about. [*President's Remarks During Hurricane Rita Briefing in Texas*, Sept. 25, 2005.]

A follow-on study, *The Federal Response to Hurricane Katrina: Lessons Learned*, Feb. 2006, declared that "DOD capabilities must be better identified and integrated into the Nation's response plans." *Id.* at 54. Moreover, it suggested, in "extraordinary circumstances" it will be "appropriate for the Department of Defense to lead the Federal response." *Id.* at 94. DOD and DHS were directed to revise the National Response Plan to reflect this expanded role. *Id.*

Meanwhile, the government has undertaken planning for a response to an avian influenza pandemic sometime in the future. One worst-case estimate puts deaths in the United States at 1.9 million people. *See* Ceci Connolly, *U.S. Plan for Flu Pandemic Revealed*, Wash. Post, Apr. 16, 2006, at A1. That figure apparently presumes that the spread of the virus can be sharply limited, since mortality among people infected with the virus has been roughly 50 percent. In an October 4, 2005, press conference, President Bush indicated that troops might be used to enforce quarantines in the event of a bird flu outbreak. The government's *Implementation Plan for the National Strategy for Pandemic Influenza*, May 2006, at 29, 160, however, describes DOD's role only in very general terms as supportive. *See generally* Sarah A. Lister, *Pandemic Influenza: Domestic Preparedness Efforts* (Cong. Res. Serv. RL33145) 21-23, Nov. 10, 2005; Kathleen S. Swendiman & Jennifer K. Elsea, *Federal and State Quarantine and Isolation Authority* (Cong. Res. Serv. RL33201) 16-20, Dec. 12, 2005.

## NOTES AND QUESTIONS

1. *How the Military Can Help.* Review carefully the description of the first TOPOFF exercise set forth *supra* p. 632. What useful role could military forces have played in responding to the notional bioterrorist attack?

   Do you agree that we should try to use other agencies whenever possible? If military forces are deployed in such an emergency, who should make the decisions about when and how to use them? What lessons can be learned from the federal response to Hurricane Katrina?

2. *Effect of the Posse Comitatus Act in Various Settings.* One recent study suggests that "[t]here are currently adequate laws and structures in place to facilitate the use of the military in relief efforts in the event of a major catastrophe of whatever kind." ABA Standing Comm. on Law & National

Security et al., *Hurricane Katrina Task Force Subcommittee Report* 23, Feb. 2006. Do you agree?

3. ***Cooperation Between DOD and Other Agencies.*** Based on the brief description of authorities and plans set out above, how would you rate the chances for a strong, efficient collaboration between the Departments of Defense and Justice in responding to a terrorist attack? What about DOD and FEMA? When the Principal Deputy Assistant Secretary of Defense (Homeland Defense) was asked in August 2005 whether he knew of a document issued by the Department of Homeland Security (DHS) that would help DOD determine the requirements for military assistance to civilian authorities, he replied, "To my knowledge, no such document exists." *See Failure of Initiative*, *supra* p. 694, at 203. What would you recommend to improve the chances of collaboration? *See generally* Jeffrey D. Brake, *Terrorism and the Military's Role in Domestic Crisis Management: Background and Issues for Congress* (Cong. Res. Serv. RL30938), Jan. 27, 2003.

4. ***The National Guard's Role.*** How did you react to the presence of armed National Guard troops at airport security checkpoints? Do you think such personal reactions have any legal significance? Is the use of unfederalized National Guard forces in law enforcement consistent with the policies underlying the Posse Comitatus Act?

What advantages or disadvantages can you see to utilizing Guard forces under the control of state governors, rather than federalizing them, to respond to a terrorist attack? How, if at all, is your answer affected by the fact that Guard personnel in every state receive the same training and equipment prescribed by the Pentagon?

# D. MARTIAL LAW: WHEN PLANNING FAILS

If, in the event of an actual or threatened terrorist attack or a large natural disaster, the execution of federal emergency plans fails to restore order, or if such plans are perceived as inadequate, martial law might be invoked as the option of last resort. Such a drastic step might seem advisable because of the military's extensive, coherent organization, its tradition of discipline, its robust communications systems, and its training in the use of force. Martial law could be declared by the President as Commander in Chief of U.S. armed forces, by a state governor as head of an unfederalized national guard, or by a military officer in the field. Without specific guidance from higher authority, military leaders would then be governed only by rules fashioned by them to fit the situation. The content of the rules and the duration of their enforcement would, by definition, be impossible to predict. So, necessarily, would be the effect on Americans' civil liberties.

In the middle of the eighteenth century, Blackstone described martial law as

> temporary excrescences bred out of the distemper of the state, and not any part of the permanent and perpetual laws of the kingdom. For martial law, which is built upon no settled principles, but is entirely arbitrary in its decisions, is . . . in truth and reality no law, but something indulged rather than allowed as a law. [2 William Blackstone, *Commentaries* *413.]

A century later, in a Civil War era case, the Supreme Court, in dicta, described the circumstances under which martial law might be invoked.

## EX PARTE MILLIGAN

United States Supreme Court, 1866
71 U.S. (4 Wall.) 2

[The opinion is set forth *supra* p. 349.]

## NOTES AND QUESTIONS

1. *The Necessity for Martial Law.* In an earlier case growing out of a rebellion in Rhode Island, the Court indicated that

   > a State may use its military power to put down an armed insurrection, too strong to be controlled by the civil authority. The power is essential to the existence of every government, essential to the preservation of order and free institutions, and is as necessary to the States of this Union as to any other government. [Luther v. Borden, 48 U.S. (7 How.) 1, 44-45 (1849).]

   In litigation arising in New Orleans after that city had been captured by the Union Army in 1862 and placed under martial law, the Court declared that "[m]artial law is the law of military necessity in the actual presence of war." United States v. Diekelman, 92 U.S. (2 Otto) 520, 526 (1876). And in his concurring opinion in the Youngstown Sheet & Tube Co. v. Sawyer (*Steel Seizure Case*), 343 U.S. 579, 650 n.19 (1952), Justice Jackson was careful to exclude from his discussion of emergency powers based on necessity, "as in a very limited category by itself, the establishment of martial law."

   The governor of Hawaii declared martial law immediately after the Japanese attack on Pearl Harbor, as he was authorized to do by the Hawaii Organic Act §67, ch. 339, 31 Stat. 141, 153 (1900). Testing a military tribunal's power to try civilians for ordinary criminal offenses, the Court observed that "the term 'martial law' carries no precise meaning. The Constitution does not refer to 'martial law' at all and no Act of Congress had defined the term. It has been employed in various ways by different people and at different times." Duncan v. Kahanamoku, 327 U.S. 304, 315 (1946). Then, struggling to avoid describing the limits of executive or legislative power, the Court found that in using the term "martial law," Congress had not intended to authorize the supplanting of civilian courts by military tribunals. The story is retold in fascinating detail in Harry N. Scheiber & Jane L. Scheiber, *Bayonets in Paradise: A Half-Century Retrospect on Martial Law in Hawai'i, 1941–1946*, 19 U. Haw. L. Rev. 477 (1997).

2. *Standby Martial Law?* In June 1955, the government conducted a massive civil defense exercise to simulate responses to a nuclear attack. To almost everyone's surprise, President Eisenhower hypothetically declared nationwide martial law, suspended the writ of habeas corpus, and authorized military commanders to stop the functioning of local courts. His action

was widely criticized as unnecessary and improper. *See, e.g.,* Robert S. Rankin & Winfried R. Dallmayr, *Freedom and Emergency Powers in the Cold War* 56-60 (1964). Nevertheless, throughout much of the Cold War the government had in place a comprehensive secret plan, called "Plan D," for responding to the threat of a nuclear attack. One element of that plan, Presidential Emergency Action Directive No. 21, apparently included a draft executive order declaring martial law.

In 1987, the Miami Herald reported that Lt. Col. Oliver North and FEMA had drafted a new emergency plan calling for suspension of the Constitution, imposition of martial law, appointment of military commanders to run state and local governments, and detention of dissidents and Central American refugees. Alfonso Chardy, *Reagan Advisors Ran "Secret" Government*, Miami Herald, July 5, 1987, at 1. *See* Jules Lobel, *Emergency Power and the Decline of Liberalism*, 98 Yale L.J. 1385, 1420 (1989) (noting that Lt. Col. North denied drawing up such a plan).

Do you think the President should carry a draft order declaring martial law with her at all times? If so, do you think the terms of the order and criteria for its execution, or at least the fact of its existence, should be publicized?

3. ***Conditions for Martial Law.*** One scholar argues that the Insurrection Act, 10 U.S.C. §§331-335, delegates to the President the power to impose martial law. Vladeck, *supra* p. 679, at 152-153. If Congress has so conferred this power on the President, it has done no more to clarify the circumstances under which the power might be exercised. The Defense Department, on the other hand, has adopted regulations to cover such an eventuality:

> Martial law depends for its justification upon public necessity. Necessity gives rise to its creation; necessity justifies its exercise; and necessity limits its duration. The extent of the military force used and the actual measures taken, consequently, will depend upon the actual threat to order and public safety which exists at the time. In most instances the decision to impose martial law is made by the President. . . . However, the decision to impose martial law may be made by the local commander on the spot, if the circumstances demand immediate action, and time and available communications facilities do not permit obtaining prior approval from higher authority. [32 C.F.R. §501.4 (2006).]

How do these regulatory criteria for invocation of martial law compare with those articulated by the Supreme Court in Ex parte Milligan? Would it be possible, or wise, to try to develop more specific guidelines? Could you draft the guidelines? Is there any way to challenge the legitimacy of the DOD regulations before they can be used — or even afterward?

4. ***Planning to Avoid Martial Law.*** As a practical matter, do you think any statutory or regulatory prescriptions could deter the President or military officials from declaring martial law in the wake of a terrorist attack involving a weapon of mass destruction or in the aftermath of a great natural disaster? Can you think of any way to limit the resort to martial law in such a crisis?

# VII

# NONCRIMINAL SANCTIONS AGAINST TERRORISTS AND THEIR SPONSORS

# *22*
# *PUBLIC SANCTIONS*
# *AGAINST TERRORISTS*
# *AND THEIR SPONSORS*

Because the threat of terrorism is so grave and so complex, the United States has adopted a variety of strategies to combat it. In earlier chapters we examined the use of military force against terrorists and their state sponsors. We then considered ways to detect such threats before they could be carried out and ways to detain and interrogate individuals suspected of involvement in terrorist activities. We also reviewed the use of criminal sanctions to punish and deter terrorism, as well as the use of immigration laws to exclude or remove aliens suspected of terrorism. In the next chapter we address suits for civil damages to punish and deter terrorists and to compensate their victims to some extent.

In this chapter we consider additional measures that do not involve the use of force. First we take up efforts by sovereign states, acting in concert, to address the shared threat of terrorism. We then turn to U.S. government economic sanctions intended to dissuade potential terrorists and deny them the resources they need to carry out their deadly mission.

## A. INTERNATIONAL SANCTIONS

### 1. DEVELOPING A CONSENSUS AMONG NATIONS TO FIGHT TERRORISM

#### a. The United States Reaches Out

If it was not apparent earlier, the events of September 11, 2001, made it abundantly clear that in the fight against terrorism the United States cannot go it alone. United States officials immediately began reaching out to other nations around the globe for assistance in gathering intelligence about terrorist suspects and apprehending persons believed to be connected with the attacks, freezing their financial assets, and mounting a military response against

Osama bin Laden's sponsors in Afghanistan. *See generally* Sean D. Murphy, *International Law, the United States, and the Non-Military "War" Against Terrorism*, 14 Eur. J. Intl. L. 347 (2003).

The United States also asked for help from international organizations. Shortly after the attacks on September 11, the U.N. Security Council passed a resolution calling on "all States to work together urgently to bring to justice the perpetrators, organizers, and sponsors of these terrorist attacks." S.C. Res. 1368, U.N. Doc. S/RES/1368 (Sept. 12, 2001). On the evening of the 11th, the NATO Council announced:

> The NATO nations unanimously condemn these barbaric acts committed against a NATO member state. The mindless slaughter of so many innocent civilians is an unacceptable act of violence without precedent in the modern era. It underscores the urgency of intensifying the battle against terrorism, a battle that the NATO countries — indeed all civilised nations — must win. All Allies stand united in their determination to combat this scourge. [NATO Press Release PR/CP (2001) 122, Sept. 12, 2001.]

These resolutions were followed by commitments to cooperate in actions to combat terrorism, as outlined below.

The United States continues to rely on help from other nations, as well as from international organizations. Among many examples since 9/11, the United States and Russia announced a bilateral agreement in 2006 to improve accounting for and physical protection of nuclear materials held by each nation, and to detect and interdict illicit trafficking in such materials. *See* The White House, *Fact Sheet: The Global Initiative to Combat Nuclear Terrorism*, July 15, 2006; *see also* The White House, *Global Initiative to Combat Nuclear Terrorism*, Nov. 1, 2006 (announcing that 13 nations had joined the initiative). And the Group of Eight (G8) (leading economic states) agreed in 2005 to develop travel document security standards, strengthen controls over shoulder-fired anti-aircraft missiles, and adopt other counterterrorism measures. *See G8 Statement on Counter-Terrorism*, July 8, 2005, *at* http://usinfo.state.gov/ei/Archive/2005/Jul/08-375735.html. Other formal and informal collaborative measures are described below.

#### b.  International Commitment to Counterterrorism

Terrorist attacks at home are nothing new in many nations. Algeria, Colombia, France, Germany, Great Britain, India, Indonesia, Israel, Italy, the Philippines, Russia, Spain, and Sri Lanka are just a few of the states afflicted with this scourge in recent years. Individual nations around the globe have developed their own programs for combating terrorism. Some of these are described in annual reports by the U.S. State Department, now called *Country Reports on Terrorism, available at* http://www.state.gov/s/ct/rls/crt/.

These individual nations have also agreed to cooperate in the fight against terrorism. This agreement can be seen in the following resolution of the United Nations General Assembly:

# UNITED NATIONS GLOBAL COUNTER-TERRORISM STRATEGY

G.A. Res. 60/288, U.N. Doc. A/RES/60/288 (Sept. 20, 2006)

*The General Assembly,*

*Guided* by the purposes and principles of the Charter of the United Nations and *reaffirming* its role under the Charter, including on questions related to international peace and security, . . .

*Reaffirming* that acts, methods and practices of terrorism in all its forms and manifestations are activities aimed at the destruction of human rights, fundamental freedoms and democracy, threatening territorial integrity, security of States and destabilizing legitimately constituted Governments, and that  the international community should take the necessary steps to enhance cooperation to prevent and combat terrorism,

*Reaffirming also* that terrorism cannot and should not be associated with any religion, nationality, civilization or ethnic group, . . .

*Affirming* Member States' determination to continue to do all they can to resolve conflict, end foreign occupation, confront oppression, eradicate poverty, promote sustained economic growth, sustainable development, global prosperity, good governance, human rights for all and rule of law, improve intercultural understanding and ensure respect for all religions, religious values, beliefs or cultures, . . .

*Adopts* the present resolution . . . as the United Nations Global Counter-Terrorism Strategy. . . .

## Plan of Action

We, the States Members of the United Nations, resolve:

1. To consistently, unequivocally and strongly condemn terrorism in all its forms and manifestations, committed by whomever, wherever and for whatever purposes, as it constitutes one of the most serious threats to international peace and security.

2. To take urgent action to prevent and combat terrorism in all its forms and manifestations and, in particular:

> (a) To consider becoming parties without delay to the existing international conventions and protocols against terrorism, and implementing them, and to make every effort to reach an agreement on and conclude a comprehensive convention on international terrorism;
>
> (b) To implement all General Assembly resolutions on measures to eliminate international terrorism, and relevant General Assembly resolutions on the protection of human rights and fundamental freedoms while countering terrorism;
>
> (c) To implement all Security Council resolutions related to international terrorism. . . .

3. To recognize that international cooperation and any measures that we undertake to prevent and combat terrorism must comply with our obligations under international law, including the Charter of the United Nations and

relevant international conventions and protocols, in particular human rights law, refugee law and international humanitarian law.

## I. Measures to Address the Conditions Conducive to the Spread of Terrorism

We resolve to undertake the following measures aimed at addressing the conditions conducive to the spread of terrorism, including but not limited to prolonged unresolved conflicts, dehumanization of victims of terrorism in all its forms and manifestations, lack of rule of law and violations of human rights, ethnic, national and religious discrimination, political exclusion, socio-economic marginalization, and lack of good governance, while recognizing that none of these conditions can excuse or justify acts of terrorism. . . .

## II. Measures to Prevent and Combat Terrorism

We resolve to undertake the following measures to prevent and combat terrorism, in particular by denying terrorists access to the means to carry out their attacks, to their targets and to the desired impact of their attacks. . . .

## III. Measures to Build States' Capacity to Prevent and Combat Terrorism and to Strengthen the Role of the United Nations System in this Regard

We recognize that capacity-building in all States is a core element of the global counter-terrorism effort, and resolve to undertake the following measures to develop State capacity to prevent and combat terrorism and enhance coordination and coherence within the United Nations system in promoting international cooperation in countering terrorism. . . .

## IV. Measures to Ensure Respect for Human Rights for All and the Rule of Law as the Fundamental Basis of the Fight Against Terrorism

We resolve to undertake the following measures, reaffirming that the promotion and protection of human rights for all and the rule of law is essential to all components of the Strategy, recognizing that effective counter-terrorism measures and the protection of human rights are not conflicting goals, but complementary and mutually reinforcing, and stressing the need to promote and protect the rights of victims of terrorism. . . .

---

Omitted here are detailed prescriptions for achieving these stated goals. An even more elaborate agenda for U.N. action is spelled out in The Secretary General, *Uniting Against Terrorism: Recommendations for a Global Counter-Terrorism Strategy*, U.N. Doc. A/60/825 (Apr. 27, 2006). Other U.N. General Assembly resolutions reflecting the same shared concern for the common threat of terrorism date back more than three decades.

It would be a mistake to assume that such resolutions have no practical value. It is true they tend to be cast in very broad, even aspirational, terms, and that they are understood to have no binding effect on member states. Yet while Resolution 60/288, set out above, was adopted without a roll-call vote, states often vote against such measures, suggesting that the resolutions are taken seriously. And although General Assembly resolutions may not represent a perfect consensus among nations, they both reflect and influence public opinion worldwide. They show a commitment to a common purpose and an agreement to cooperate in achieving that purpose. In Resolution 60/288, for example, members of the world community agree not only to attack terrorists directly, but also to abide by basic humanitarian principles in doing so, while at the same time addressing the root causes of terrorism. Such resolutions often mark the beginning of a collaborative process that eventually leads to changes in international and domestic laws.

Of particular importance here are resolutions expressing approval of conventions aimed at combating terrorism. These "United Nations conventions" may then be opened for signature and ratification by all states. Such conventions are described further *infra* pp. 711-717.

A range of U.N. initiatives to fight terrorism are described on a U.N. Web site entitled *UN Action to Counter Terrorism*, at http://www.un.org/terrorism/. Similar efforts by NATO are spelled out at North Atlantic Treaty Organisation, *NATO and the Fight Against Terrorism*, Apr. 3, 2007, at http://www.nato.int/ issues/terrorism/index.html. Resolutions by other international organizations, including the Organization of American States (OAS), the European Union (EU), and the Association of Southeast Asian Nations (ASEAN), are listed at U.S. Dept. of State, *International Terrorism Resolutions* (n.d.), at http:// www.state.gov/s/ct/intl/c4353.htm.

## 2.  COMPULSORY ACTIONS BY INTERNATIONAL ORGANIZATIONS

On October 15, 1999, the U.N. Security Council adopted a resolution "deploring the fact that the Taliban continues to provide safe haven to Usama bin Laden and to allow him . . . to use Afghanistan as a base from which to sponsor international terrorist operations." S.C. Res. 1267, U.N. Doc. S/RES/1267. Resolution 1267 set out limited measures designed to isolate the Taliban physically and financially. Its effect may have been blunted, however, by a trading agreement between the Taliban and neighboring Iran. *See* Pamela Constable, *Iran Opening Eases Choke Hold of U.N. Sanctions on Afghans,* Wash. Post, Dec. 22, 1999, at A25. A little over a year later, the Security Council adopted this more aggressive resolution:

### UNITED NATIONS SECURITY COUNCIL, RESOLUTION 1333

U.N. Doc. S/RES/1333 (Dec. 19, 2000)

*The Security Council,* . . .
*Acting* under Chapter VII of the Charter of the United Nations,
1. *Demands* that the Taliban . . . cease the provision of sanctuary and training for international terrorists and their organizations, take appropriate effective measures to ensure that the territory under its control is not used for terrorist installations and camps, or for the preparation or organization of terrorist acts against other States and their citizens, and cooperate with international efforts to bring indicted terrorists to justice;

2. *Demands also* that the Taliban . . . without further delay . . . turn over Usama bin Laden to appropriate authorities in a country where he has been indicted . . . or to appropriate authorities in a country where he will be arrested and effectively brought to justice;

3. *Demands further* that the Taliban should act swiftly to close all camps where terrorists are trained within the territory under its control . . .

5. *Decides* that all States shall:

(a) Prevent the direct or indirect supply, sale, and transfer to the territory of Afghanistan under Taliban control . . . of arms and related materiel of all types . . .

(b) Prevent the direct or indirect supply, sale, and transfer to the territory of Afghanistan under Taliban control . . . of technical advice, assistance, or training related to the military activities of the armed personnel under the control of the Taliban; . . .

8. *Decides* that all States shall take further measures:

(a) To close immediately and completely all Taliban offices in their territories . . .

(c) To freeze without delay funds and other assets of Usama bin Laden and individuals and entities associated with him . . .

9. *Demands* that the Taliban, as well as others, halt all illegal drugs activities and work to virtually eliminate the illicit cultivation of opium poppy, the proceeds of which finance Taliban terrorist activities; . . .

11. *Decides also* that all States are required to deny any aircraft permission to take off from, land in, or over-fly their territories if that aircraft has taken off from, or is destined to land at, a place in the territory of Afghanistan . . . unless the particular flight has been approved in advance . . . on the grounds of humanitarian need, including religious obligations such as the performance of the Hajj, or on the grounds that the flight promotes discussion of a peaceful resolution of the conflict in Afghanistan. . . .

---

If these resolutions created hardship for the Taliban, they nevertheless failed to dislodge bin Laden. Immediately following the terrorist attacks on September 11, the Security Council passed a resolution calling on "all States to work together urgently to bring to justice the perpetrators, organizers, and sponsors of these terrorist attacks." S.C. Res. 1368, U.N. Doc. S/RES/1368 (Sept. 12, 2001). Two weeks later, the Security Council adopted another resolution that directed all States to criminalize the financing of terrorist activities, to freeze terrorists' assets, to suppress the recruitment of members by terrorist groups, to eliminate the supply of weapons to terrorists, to tighten border controls, and to cooperate in exchanges of information and in the investigation and prosecution of terrorists. S.C. Res. 1373, U.N. Doc. S/RES/1373 (Sept. 28, 2001). This resolution echoed the language of the United Nations International Convention for the Suppression of the Financing of Terrorism, *opened for signature* Jan. 10, 2000, S. Treaty Doc. No. 106-49, excerpted below, which was approved earlier by the U.N. General Assembly, G.A. Res. 54/109, U.N. Doc. A/RES/54/109

(Dec. 9, 1999), but not yet in force. *See* Ilias Bantekas, *The International Law of Terrorist Financing*, 97 Am. J. Intl. L. 315, 325-327 (2003). Since then, the Security Council has adopted more than a dozen additional resolutions in the same vein, including some addressing the threat of weapons of mass destruction. They are available at *UN Action to Counter Terrorism: Security Council Resolutions* (updated regularly), *at* http://www.un.org/terrorism/sc-res.html.

The Security Council resolutions described here differ from U.N. General Assembly resolutions in at least two important respects. First, their adoption requires the approval (or at least abstention) of all five permanent members of the Security Council. Second, such resolutions are binding on all member states, which agree in Article 25 of the U.N. Charter to "accept and carry out the decisions of the Security Council."

On a parallel front, the day after the terrorist attacks on the World Trade Center and the Pentagon, the NATO Council decided that if "this attack was directed from abroad against the United States, it shall be regarded as an action covered by Article 5 of the [North Atlantic] Treaty, which states that an armed attack against one or more of the Allies in Europe or North America shall be considered an attack against them all." NATO Press Release (2001) 124, Sept. 12, 2001. This determination paved the way for cooperation among NATO member states — for example, in allowing military overflights, a privilege denied to the United States by France in 1986 when U.S. planes based in Great Britain were used to strike Libya following the terrorist bombing of a Berlin discotheque (see *supra* p. 60). Eventually, it led to the deployment of NATO troops in Afghanistan, where in August 2003 they took over command of the International Security Assistance Force (ISAF). For details see NATO/OTAN, *International Security Assistance Force* (updated regularly), *at* http://www.nato.int/isaf/.

Binding resolutions of international organizations may sometimes be much more narrowly targeted and, perhaps, more successful as a result. One example is a series of U.N. Security Council resolutions aimed at Libya. When all signs pointed to Libyan complicity in the bombing of PanAm flight 103 over Lockerbie, Scotland in 1988, demands for the surrender of two Libyan intelligence agents for trial in the United States or the United Kingdom were repeatedly rebuffed by Muammar el-Qadhafi. In an effort to encourage cooperation, the United States adopted unilateral economic sanctions against Libya. But to tighten the screws on Qadhafi more fully, the U.N. Security Council approved a resolution on March 31, 1992, that ordered all states to deny take-off and landing rights to aircraft bound to or from Libya (except for humanitarian flights) and to cut off shipments of arms, technical advice, and military training to Libya. S.C. Res. 748, U.N. Doc. S/RES/748. A year and a half later, the Security Council raised the stakes by directing all states to freeze any funds and financial resources owned or controlled by the Libyan government (although the freeze did not apply to proceeds from the sales of petroleum or agricultural products) and to stop shipments of petroleum pipeline or refining equipment to Libya. S.C. Res. 883, U.N. Doc. S/RES/883 (Nov. 11, 1993). These sanctions were suspended when Qadhafi finally turned the two Libyan suspects over for trial before a Scottish court sitting in the Netherlands. *See* S.C. Res.

1192, U.N. Doc. S/RES/1192 (Aug. 27, 1998). One of the defendants was convicted and sentenced to life in prison; the other was acquitted. *See* John P. Grant, *The Lockerbie Trial: A Documentary History* (2004); Michael P. Scharf, *The Lockerbie Trial Verdict*, ASIL Insight, Feb. 2001, *at* http://www.asil.org/insights/insigh61.htm; John Lancaster & Alan Sipress, *A Muted Victory Against Terror*, Wash. Post, Feb. 1, 2001, at A1. The U.N. sanctions were subsequently lifted when Libya accepted responsibility for the actions of its officials, agreed to compensate the families of the victims, and pledged not to support international terrorism. S.C. Res. 1506, U.N. Doc. S/RES/1506 (Sept. 12, 2003). Related unilateral sanctions imposed by the United States were continued for a time, then lifted as well. See *infra* p. 719.

## NOTES AND QUESTIONS

1. ***Efficacy of Binding International Organization Sanctions.*** U.N. Security Council sanctions aimed at Afghanistan and the Taliban regime did not lead to the capture of Osama bin Laden or to prevention of the terrorist attacks of September 11. A U.S. official earlier suggested possible reasons:

   > Today's terrorist threat comes primarily from groups and loosely-knit networks with fewer ties to governments. Bin Laden's organization operates on its own, without having to depend on a state sponsor for material support. He possesses financial resources and means of raising funds — often through narcotrafficking, legitimate "front" companies, and local financial support. Today's non-state terrorists benefit from the globalization of communication, using e-mail and Internet websites to spread their message, recruit new members, raise funds, and connect elements scattered around the world. [*Hearings Before the Subcomm. on Near E. and S. Asian Affairs of the S. Foreign Relations Comm.*, 106th Cong. (Nov. 2, 1999) (testimony of Ambassador Michael A. Sheehan, coordinator for counterterrorism, U.S. Dept. of State), *quoted in* Sean D. Murphy, *Efforts to Obtain Custody of Osama Bin Laden*, 94 Am. J. Intl. L. 366, 367 (2000).]

   Taking these developments into account, can you think of international economic measures that might have been more effective? Can you guess why they were not used?

2. ***Accepting and Carrying Out the Resolutions.*** Because they concern commitments under the U.N. Charter, which is a multilateral treaty, U.N. Security Council resolutions or parts of such resolutions that are intended to be binding on member states have the same force in international law as other treaty obligations. Article 8(c) of Resolution 1333, above, directing states to freeze funds and other assets of bin Laden, is an example. They may in fact have greater force, since Article 103 of the U.N. Charter gives Security

Council resolutions priority over other international obligations. *See* Michael Wood, *The UN Security Council and International Law* (Hersch Lauterpacht Memorial Lecture), Nov. 7, 2006, *available at* http://www.lcil. cam.ac.uk/Media/lectures/pdf/2006_hersch_lecture_1.pdf.   Implementation of Resolution 1373, *supra*, is monitored and reported by the U.N. Counter-Terrorism Committee, *see* Security Council, *Counter-Terrorism Committee* (n.d.), *at* http://www.un.org/sc/ctc/, although the committee lacks enforcement authority. How would you expect the obligations in such resolutions to be enforced against states not in compliance?

Additional international agreements aimed specifically at curbing terrorism are described immediately below. Such conventions typically rely on party states either to take some affirmative action or to refrain from acting, or to adopt implementing laws and regulations. Examples of this kind of implementing action by the United States are found in Part B, below.

## 3.   TREATIES SPECIFICALLY ADDRESSING TERRORISM

There currently are 13 major multilateral treaties, dating back to 1963, that specifically address international terrorism. *See* UN Action to Counter Terrorism, *International Instruments to Counter Terrorism* (n.d.), *at* http://www.un.org/terrorism/instruments.html. Two that figure prominently in our history are the Convention for the Suppression of Unlawful Seizure of Aircraft, Dec. 16, 1970, 22 U.S.T. 1641, and the International Convention Against the Taking of Hostages, Dec. 17, 1979, T.I.A.S. 11081. Both of these treaties and their implementing legislation are described in United States v. Yunis, 924 F.2d 1086 (D.C. Cir. 1991). The most recent such treaty at this writing is the International Convention for the Suppression of Acts of Nuclear Terrorism, *opened for signature* Sept. 14, 2005, G.A. Res. 59/290, annex, U.N. Doc. A/RES/ 59/290 (Apr. 13, 2005).

These treaties are generally concerned with particular terrorist acts, such as hostage takings, aircraft hijackings, bombings, and attacks on diplomats. Most of them require signatory states to pass laws criminalizing the terrorist acts addressed, and then either to prosecute violators or to extradite them to other states having jurisdiction over them. *See* Donald Musch, *International Terrorism Agreements: Documents and Commentary* (2004); H. Comm. on Intl. Relations, 106th Cong., *International Terrorism: A Compilation of Major Laws, Treaties, Agreements, and Executive Documents* (Comm. Print 2000). It should be noted that these treaties have been adopted despite the failure of nations so far to agree on a single, comprehensive definition of the term "terrorism."

One important recent multilateral treaty seeks to thwart terrorists by cutting off the funds they need to operate. International Convention for the Suppression of the Financing of Terrorism, *opened for signature* Jan. 10, 2000, S. Treaty Doc. No. 106-49. It echoes and implements some of the U.N. General Assembly and Security Council resolutions described above. The treaty is in turn implemented by domestic statutes and other measures, as set out in

Part B. This convention was approved by the U.N. General Assembly, G.A. Res. 109, U.N. Doc. A/RES/54/109 (Dec. 9, 1999), and signed by the United States on January 10, 2000, but it did not enter into force until April 10, 2002, long after the attacks on the World Trade Center and the Pentagon.

### INTERNATIONAL CONVENTION FOR THE SUPPRESSION OF THE FINANCING OF TERRORISM

*opened for signature* Jan. 10, 2000, S. Treaty Doc. No. 106-49

### Article 2

1. Any person commits an offence within the meaning of this Convention if that person by any means, directly or indirectly, unlawfully and wilfully, provides or collects funds with the intention that they should be used or in the knowledge that they are to be used, in full or in part, in order to carry out:

(a) An act which constitutes an offence within the scope of and as defined in one of the treaties listed in the annex [listing nine of the eleven other terrorism treaties in existence]; or

(b) Any other act intended to cause death or serious bodily injury to a civilian, or to any other person not taking an active part in the hostilities in a situation of armed conflict, when the purpose of such act, by its nature or context, is to intimidate a population, or to compel a government or an international organization to do or to abstain from doing any act. . . .

4. Any person also commits an offence if that person attempts to commit an offence as set forth in paragraph 1 of this article.

5. Any person also commits an offence if that person:

(a) Participates as an accomplice in an offence as set forth in paragraph 1 or 4 of this article;

(b) Organizes or directs others to commit an offence as set forth in paragraph 1 or 4 of this article;

(c) Contributes to the commission of one or more offences as set forth in paragraphs 1 or 4 of this article by a group of persons acting with a common purpose. Such contribution shall be intentional and shall either:

(i) Be made with the aim of furthering the criminal activity or criminal purpose of the group, where such activity or purpose involves the commission of an offence as set forth in paragraph 1 of this article; or

(ii) Be made in the knowledge of the intention of the group to commit an offence as set forth in paragraph 1 of this article.

### Article 3

This Convention shall not apply where the offence is committed within a single State, the alleged offender is a national of that State and is present in the territory of that State and no other State has a basis under article 7, paragraph 1, or article 7, paragraph 2, to exercise jurisdiction, except that the provisions of articles 12 to 18 [relating to cooperation and mutual assistance among states, extradition, and treatment of prisoners] shall, as appropriate, apply in those cases.

### Article 4

Each State Party shall adopt such measures as may be necessary:

(a) To establish as criminal offences under its domestic law the offences set forth in article 2;

(b) To make those offences punishable by appropriate penalties which take into account the grave nature of the offences.

### Article 5

1. Each State Party, in accordance with its domestic legal principles, shall take the necessary measures to enable a legal entity located in its territory or organized under its laws to be held liable when a person responsible for the management or control of that legal entity has, in that capacity, committed an offence set forth in article 2. Such liability may be criminal, civil or administrative. . . .

### Article 6

Each State Party shall adopt such measures as may be necessary, including, where appropriate, domestic legislation, to ensure that criminal acts within the scope of this Convention are under no circumstances justifiable by considerations of a political, philosophical, ideological, racial, ethnic, religious or other similar nature.

### Article 7

1. Each State Party shall take such measures as may be necessary to establish its jurisdiction over the offences set forth in article 2 when:

(a) The offence is committed in the territory of that State;

(b) The offence is committed on board a vessel flying the flag of that State or an aircraft registered under the laws of that State at the time the offence is committed;

(c) The offence is committed by a national of that State.

2. A State Party may also establish its jurisdiction over any such offence when:

(a) The offence was directed towards or resulted in the carrying out of an offence referred to in article 2, paragraph 1, subparagraph (a) or (b), in the territory of or against a national of that State;

(b) The offence was directed towards or resulted in the carrying out of an offence referred to in article 2, paragraph 1, subparagraph (a) or (b), against a State or government facility of that State abroad, including diplomatic or consular premises of that State;

(c) The offence was directed towards or resulted in an offence referred to in article 2, paragraph 1, subparagraph (a) or (b), committed in an attempt to compel that State to do or abstain from doing any act; . . .

4. Each State Party shall likewise take such measures as may be necessary to establish its jurisdiction over the offences set forth in article 2 in cases where the alleged offender is present in its territory and it does not extradite that person to any of the States Parties that have established their jurisdiction in accordance with paragraphs 1 or 2. . . .

### Article 8

1. Each State Party shall take appropriate measures, in accordance with its domestic legal principles, for the identification, detection and freezing or seizure of any funds used or allocated for the purpose of committing the offences set forth in article 2 as well as the proceeds derived from such offences, for purposes of possible forfeiture.

2. Each State Party shall take appropriate measures, in accordance with its domestic legal principles, for the forfeiture of funds used or allocated for the purpose of committing the offences set forth in article 2 and the proceeds derived from such offences. . . .

### Article 10

1. The State Party in the territory of which the alleged offender is present shall, in cases to which article 7 applies, if it does not extradite that person, be obliged, without exception whatsoever and whether or not the offence was committed in its territory, to submit the case without undue delay to its competent authorities for the purpose of prosecution, through proceedings in accordance with the laws of that State. Those authorities shall take their decision in the same manner as in the case of any other offence of a grave nature under the law of that State. . . .

### Article 11

1. The offences set forth in article 2 shall be deemed to be included as extraditable offences in any extradition treaty existing between any of the States Parties before the entry into force of this Convention. . . .

### Article 12

1. States Parties shall afford one another the greatest measure of assistance in connection with criminal investigations or criminal or extradition proceedings in respect of the offences set forth in article 2, including assistance in obtaining evidence in their possession necessary for the proceedings.

2. States Parties may not refuse a request for mutual legal assistance on the ground of bank secrecy. . . .

### Article 14

None of the offences set forth in article 2 shall be regarded for the purposes of extradition or mutual legal assistance as a political offence or as an offence connected with a political offence or as an offence inspired by political motives. . . .

### Article 18

1. States Parties shall cooperate in the prevention of the offences set forth in article 2 by taking all practicable measures, *inter alia*, by adapting their

domestic legislation, if necessary, to prevent and counter preparations in their respective territories for the commission of those offences within or outside their territories, including: . . .

(b) Measures requiring financial institutions and other professions involved in financial transactions to utilize the most efficient measures available for the identification of their usual or occasional customers, as well as customers in whose interest accounts are opened, and to pay special attention to unusual or suspicious transactions and report transactions suspected of stemming from a criminal activity. For this purpose, States Parties shall consider:

(i) Adopting regulations prohibiting the opening of accounts the holders or beneficiaries of which are unidentified or unidentifiable, and measures to ensure that such institutions verify the identity of the real owners of such transactions; . . .

(iii) Adopting regulations imposing on financial institutions the obligation to report promptly to the competent authorities all complex, unusual large transactions and unusual patterns of transactions, which have no apparent economic or obviously lawful purpose, without fear of assuming criminal or civil liability for breach of any restriction on disclosure of information if they report their suspicions in good faith;

(iv) Requiring financial institutions to maintain, for at least five years, all necessary records on transactions, both domestic or international.

2. States Parties shall further cooperate in the prevention of offences set forth in article 2 by considering:

(a) Measures for the supervision, including, for example, the licensing, of all money-transmission agencies;

(b) Feasible measures to detect or monitor the physical cross-border transportation of cash and bearer negotiable instruments. . . .

---

The convention on terrorism financing was submitted by President Clinton to the U.S. Senate for its approval on October 3, 2000. *See Message from the President of the United States Transmitting International Convention for the Suppression of the Financing of Terrorism*, Oct. 3, 2000, *available at* 2000 U.S.T. LEXIS 131. The Senate gave its advice and consent to ratification on December 5, 2001, and it was ratified by President Bush on June 25, 2002. Statement by the President, *Enactment of Implementing Legislation for International Terrorism Conventions*, June 25, 2002. Some of the domestic legislation required by the convention was enacted the same day. Pub. L. No. 107-197, §§201-301, 116 Stat. 721, 724-728. That measure amended the material support statute, 18 U.S.C. §2339C, set forth in part *supra* p. 480. *See generally* Bantekas, *supra* p. 709, at 323-327.

The multilateral treaties entered into so far do not, of course, address every issue raised by the threat of international terrorism. Moreover, not all nations are parties to all of the treaties. (State signatories to each treaty are listed at Office of the Coordinator for Counterterrorism, U.S. Dept. of State, *International Conventions and Protocols on Terrorism*, Apr. 28, 2006.) Moreover, treaty provisions (e.g., the requirement to enact criminal laws) may be difficult to enforce. These difficulties lie behind current efforts to develop a comprehensive convention on international terrorism. *See* United Nations Global Counter-Terrorism Strategy, *supra* p. 705, at Plan of Action ¶2(a).

## NOTES AND QUESTIONS

1. *Covered Activities?* What activities are proscribed by the Convention for the Suppression of the Financing of Terrorism? How does the definition of "covered acts" compare with the definitions of "terrorism" reviewed in Chapter 1? Does the definition cover advocacy (e.g., a speech at a fund-raiser for Hamas)?

2. *Enforcement.* Why might a state that has signed the Convention for the Suppression of the Financing of Terrorism subsequently decide not to abide by its terms, yet not withdraw from the Convention? Does the Convention do everything it can to minimize the influence of domestic politics in compliance?

   How can the Convention be enforced against a states that either doesn't enact implementing domestic law or, having done so, fails to apply that law to individuals or organizations within its jurisdiction that engage in forbidden activities? What about a state party that refuses to cooperate with other states as required by the Convention?

   Is the Convention self-enforcing — that is, may it be invoked to provide relief in domestic courts? Can you see why states might be reluctant to join such a convention if it were self-enforcing?

3. *Treaty Tactics.* Consider the range of obligations undertaken by Convention signatories. Is it clear what the states parties have agreed to do? Why would a state consent to some fairly onerous obligations in the Convention, when the state might otherwise seek to abate terrorist threats on its own and in a fashion that better serves its own idiosyncratic interests?

4. *Treaty as a Tactic.* Compare the terms of the Convention set out above with U.N. Security Council Resolution 1333, *supra* p. 707. Which type of measure can be adopted more quickly in response to unfolding events? *See* Wood, *supra* p. 711, at ¶ 25 ("Normal treaty-making procedures may be too slow. . . ."). Which is more narrowly targeted, and why? Which is more likely to achieve its goals, and why?

   On September 28, 2001, the U.N. Security Council for the first time ever called upon states to "[b]ecome parties as soon as possible to the relevant international conventions and protocols relating to terrorism, including the International Convention for the Suppression of the Financing of Terrorism of 9 December 1999." S.C. Res. 1373, ¶3(d), U.N. Doc S/RES/1373.

5. *Domestic Law to Implement the Convention.* How would you expect the treaty obligations described above to be translated into domestic legislation? Who would champion them in Congress? Who would oppose them, and why? Which of the obligations could be met without new legislation? Some answers to these questions can be found in Part B, below.

## 4.   OTHER FORMS OF INTERNATIONAL COOPERATION

The bulk of practical day-to-day cooperation among nations in fighting ter-rorism is not the product of any formal agreements or resolutions, and indeed may not be written down anywhere. Instead, cooperation comes from states acting out of recognized self-interest in response to formal but often private diplomatic communications. It is also the product of informal relationships among military, intelligence, and law enforcement agencies and diplomatic corps based on shared interests and the personal relationships of officials within those agencies. The weeks after September 11, for example, saw Defense Secretary Rumsfeld, Secretary of State Powell, and other U.S. officials travel-ing around the world in an effort to gain support for the U.S. use of force in Afghanistan and to arrange ad hoc alliances with Afghanistan's neighbors— Pakistan, Russia, the former Soviet Republics of Uzbekistan and Tajikistan, and even Iran. These states were asked to assist by sharing intelligence and strengthening border controls, and in some instances by permitting the basing of U.S. military forces on their territories.

While such informal cooperation among officials of various nations may profoundly affect national security, it may also significantly affect civil liber-ties. Thus, it may make sense to document these cooperative actions and, at least under some circumstances, to make the records available to the public. On the other hand, the prospect of public exposure might sometimes make such informal agreements more difficult to reach.

## B.   DOMESTIC PUBLIC SANCTIONS

Domestic public sanctions are some the most important tools of U.S. foreign policy, and they figure prominently in the war against terrorism. A number of them implement U.S. obligations found in treaties or U.N. Security Council resolutions, as noted above. Chief among these are measures designed to exert economic pressure. They may deny terrorists the material resources they need to carry out their attacks, and they hit the terrorists' state sponsors where it really hurts—in the pocketbook.

As the world's greatest economic power, the United States has considerable influence, even acting alone, over states that might provide financial support or safe haven for terrorists.

> With respect to nation-states, economic sanctions fall into six categories: restrictions on trading, technology transfer, foreign assistance, export credits and guarantees, foreign exchange and capital transactions, and economic access. Sanctions may include a total or partial trade embargo, embargo on financial transactions, suspension of foreign aid, restrictions on aircraft or ship traffic, or abrogation of a friendship, commerce, and navigation treaty. [Raphael Perl, *Terrorism, the Future, and U.S. Foreign Policy* (Cong. Res. Serv. IB95112) 9, Apr. 11, 2003.]

In addition, the United States has direct control over assets belonging to some terrorists, terrorist groups, or state sponsors of terrorism. *See generally* Barry

E. Carter, *International Economic Sanctions: Improving the Haphazard U.S. Legal Regime,* 75 Cal. L. Rev. 1159 (1987); Stanley J. Marcuss, *Grist for the Litigation Mill in U.S. Economic Sanctions Programs,* 30 Law & Poly. Intl. Bus. 501 (1999).

In this part of the chapter we review several legal tools for wielding economic power to combat terrorism.

## 1. DESIGNATION OF FOREIGN TERRORIST ORGANIZATIONS

The Antiterrorism and Effective Death Penalty Act of 1996, §302(a), Pub. L. No. 104-132, 110 Stat. 1214, 1248 (codified as amended at 8 U.S.C. §1189(a) (Supp. IV 2004)), authorizes the Secretary of State to designate an entity as a "foreign terrorist organization" or FTO. We reviewed the procedure for designating FTOs in Chapter 1.

The severe impact of the Secretary's designation has provoked extensive litigation. In Chapter 15 we considered criminal sanctions for "material support" of an FTO. In Chapter 19 we reviewed the consequences for an alien associated with a designated organization who seeks to travel to or remain in the United States.

## 2. INTERNATIONAL ECONOMIC EMERGENCY POWERS ACT (IEEPA)

Another powerful economic weapon in the U.S. arsenal is the 1977 International Economic Emergency Powers Act (IEEPA). 50 U.S.C. §§1701-1707 (2000 & Supp. III 2003), as amended by Pub. L. No. 109-177, §402, 120 Stat. 192, 243 (2006). The Act authorizes the President to address "any unusual or extraordinary threat, which has its source in whole or substantial part outside the United States, to the national security, foreign policy, or economy of the United States" by declaring a national emergency and regulating "any property in which any foreign country or a national thereof has any interest." *Id.* §§1701(a), 1702(a)(1)(B). It was first used by President Carter to block Iranian assets worth about $12 billion when state-sponsored terrorists took 52 Americans hostage in the U.S. embassy in Tehran in 1979. *See* Dames & Moore v. Regan, 453 U.S. 654 (1981).

The IEEPA was invoked by President Reagan in 1986 as tensions increased between the United States and Libya, see *supra* p. 60, to block all trade and travel between the two countries (except for humanitarian supplies), as well as extensions of credit to Libya, and to block all Libyan property within the United States. Exec. Order No. 12,543, 51 Fed. Reg. 875 (Jan. 7, 1986); Exec. Order No. 12,544, 51 Fed. Reg. 1235 (Jan. 8, 1986). These measures were aimed especially at cutting off commerce in Libyan oil and gas and Libyan access to petroleum refining equipment. They were continued throughout the crisis over the bombing of PanAm flight 103 over Lockerbie, Scotland in 1988, see *supra* p. 709, and finally were lifted in 2004. *See* Exec. Order No. 13,357, 69 Fed. Reg. 56665 (Sept. 20, 2004).

President Clinton invoked the IEEPA in 1995 and again in 1998 to prohibit transactions with "terrorists who threaten to disrupt the Middle East peace process." Exec. Order No. 12,947, 60 Fed. Reg. 5079 (1995); Exec. Order No. 13,099, 63 Fed. Reg. 45167 (1998). On July 4, 1999, he issued Executive Order No. 13,129, 64 Fed. Reg. 36759, declaring a national emergency, freezing all Taliban assets in the United States, and banning all commerce except for humanitarian assistance with that part of Afghanistan controlled by the Taliban. The order preceded by several months U.N. Security Council Resolution 1267, noted above, which directed all member states to freeze Taliban financial resources. *See generally* Robert M. Chesney, *The Sleeper Scenario: Terrorism-Support Laws and the Demands of Prevention*, 42 Harv. J. on Legis. 1, 4-21 (2005) (describing the use of IEEPA and the development of related material-support laws).

Almost two weeks after the terrorist attacks on September 11, 2001, President Bush invoked the IEEPA in the following order.

## EXECUTIVE ORDER NO. 13,224, BLOCKING PROPERTY AND PROHIBITING TRANSACTIONS WITH PERSONS WHO COMMIT, THREATEN TO COMMIT, OR SUPPORT TERRORISM

66 Fed. Reg. 49,079 (Sept. 23, 2001)

By the authority vested in me as President by the Constitution and the laws of the United States of America, including the International Emergency Economic Powers Act (50 U.S.C. 1701 et seq.) (IEEPA), the National Emergencies Act (50 U.S.C. 1601 et seq.) . . . and in view of United Nations Security Council Resolution (UNSCR) 1214 of December 8, 1998, UNSCR 1267 of October 15, 1999, UNSCR 1333 of December 19, 2000, and the multilateral sanctions contained therein . . .

I, GEORGE W. BUSH, President of the United States of America, find that grave acts of terrorism and threats of terrorism committed by foreign terrorists, including the terrorist attacks in New York, Pennsylvania, and the Pentagon committed on September 11, 2001, acts recognized and condemned in UNSCR 1368 of September 12, 2001, and UNSCR 1269 of October 19, 1999, and the continuing and immediate threat of further attacks on United States nationals or the United States constitute an unusual and extraordinary threat to the national security, foreign policy, and economy of the United States, and in furtherance of my proclamation of September 14, 2001, Declaration of National Emergency by Reason of Certain Terrorist Attacks, hereby declare a national emergency to deal with that threat. I also find that because of the pervasiveness and expansiveness of the financial foundation of foreign terrorists, financial sanctions may be appropriate for those foreign persons that support or otherwise associate with these foreign terrorists. I also find that a need exists for further consultation and cooperation with, and sharing of information by,

United States and foreign financial institutions as an additional tool to enable the United States to combat the financing of terrorism.

I hereby order:

Sec. 1. . . . [A]ll property and interests in property of the following persons that are in the United States or that hereafter come within the United States, or that hereafter come within the possession or control of United States persons are blocked:

(a) foreign persons listed in the Annex to this order;

(b) foreign persons determined by the Secretary of State, in consultation with the Secretary of the Treasury and the Attorney General, to have committed, or to pose a significant risk of committing, acts of terrorism that threaten the security of U.S. nationals or the national security, foreign policy, or economy of the United States;

(c) persons determined by the Secretary of the Treasury, in consultation with the Secretary of State and the Attorney General, to be owned or controlled by, or to act for or on behalf of those persons listed in the Annex to this order . . .

(d) . . . persons determined by the Secretary of the Treasury, in consultation with the Secretary of State and the Attorney General:

(i) to assist in, sponsor, or provide financial, material, or technological support for, or financial or other services to or in support of, such acts of terrorism or those persons listed in the Annex to this order or determined to be subject to this order; or

(ii) to be otherwise associated with those persons listed in the Annex to this order or those persons determined to be subject to subsection 1(b), 1(c), or 1(d)(i) of this order.

Sec. 2. . . . (a) any transaction or dealing by United States persons or within the United States in property or interests in property blocked pursuant to this order is prohibited, including but not limited to the making or receiving of any contribution of funds, goods, or services to or for the benefit of those persons listed in the Annex to this order or determined to be subject to this order. . . .

Sec. 4. I hereby determine that the making of donations [of articles, such as food, clothing, and medicine, intended to be used to relieve human suffering] by United States persons to persons determined to be subject to this order would seriously impair my ability to deal with the national emergency declared in this order . . . and hereby prohibit such donations as provided by section 1 of this order. . . .

Sec. 6. The Secretary of State, the Secretary of the Treasury, and other appropriate agencies shall make all relevant efforts to cooperate and coordinate with other countries, including through technical assistance, as well as bilateral and multilateral agreements and arrangements, to achieve the objectives of this order, including the prevention and suppression of acts of terrorism, the denial of financing and financial services to terrorists and terrorist organizations, and the sharing of intelligence about funding activities in support of terrorism. . . .

Executive Order No. 13,224 expanded the coverage of earlier orders to include persons "associated with" designated terrorist groups, and to allow the United States to deny access to its markets for foreign banks that refuse to freeze terrorist assets. *See* White House Office of Communications, *Fact Sheet: Executive Order on Terrorist Financing*, Sept. 24, 2001; *see generally* Nina J. Crimm, *High Alert: The Government's War on the Financing of Terrorism and Its Implications for Donors, Domestic Charitable Organizations, and Global Philanthropy*, 45 Wm. & Mary L. Rev. 1341, 1355-1394 (2004). The annex referred to in Section 1 of the order contained, by year's end, the names of 168 individuals and organizations, from Osama bin Laden and al Qaeda to the Al-Hamati Sweets Bakeries, with an address in Yemen. *See* Office of the Coordinator for Counterterrorism, U.S. Dept. of State, *Comprehensive List of Terrorists and Groups Identified Under Executive Order 13224*, Dec. 31, 2001. A current list, updated regularly, containing hundreds of additional names, may be found at Office of Foreign Assets Control, U.S. Dept. of the Treasury, *Terrorism: What You Need to Know About U.S. Sanctions*, at http://www.treasury.gov/offices/enforcement/ofac/programs/terror/terror.pdf.

The IEEPA was amended by the USA Patriot Act to allow the President to confiscate the property of "any foreign person, foreign organization, or foreign country that he determines has planned, authorized, aided, or engaged in . . . hostilities or attacks against the United States." Pub. L. No. 107-56, §106, 115 Stat. 272, 278 (2001) (adding 50 U.S.C. §1702(a)(1)(C)). *See* Bethany Kohl Hipp, Comment, *Defending Expanded Presidential Authority to Regulate Foreign Assets and Transactions*, 17 Emory Intl. L. Rev. 1311 (2003).

The effectiveness of economic restrictions using the IEEPA is uncertain, because

> much of the flow of terrorist funds takes place outside of formal banking channels (in elusive "hawala" chains of money brokers). Alternatively, a wide variety of international banks in the Persian Gulf is used to manipulate and transfer funds through business fronts owned by Osama bin Laden. Furthermore, much of Al Qaeda's money is believed to be held not in banks but in untraceable assets such as gold and diamonds. Also, some observers have noted that lethal terrorist operations are relatively inexpensive. Current estimates of the cost of carrying out the September 11 attacks range from $300,000 to $500,000. [Perl, *supra* p. 718, at 9.]

*See also* Crimm, *supra* (suggesting that by discouraging contributions to legitimate Muslim charities such restrictions may thwart efforts to alleviate conditions that breed terrorism).

Still, those restrictions sometimes hit home. The Justice Department recently announced a settlement with Chiquita Brands International, Inc., to pay a $25 million fine for its violations of an IEEPA ban on transactions with a right-wing paramilitary organization called the United Self-Defense Forces of Colombia (AUC), listed as an FTO in 2001. Chiquita reportedly paid the AUC some $1.7 million in protection money. *See* Dept. of Justice, *Chiquita Brands International Pleads Guilty*, Mar. 19, 2007. Consider also the following case.

## HUMANITARIAN LAW PROJECT v. UNITED STATES DEPT. OF TREASURY

United States District Court, Central District of California, 2006
463 F. Supp. 2d 1049, *motion for reconsideration granted*, 2007 WL 1229194
(Apr. 20, 2007)

COLLINS, District Judge. . . . This case is the latest in a series of challenges that Plaintiffs have raised to measures taken by the Federal Government in the wake of the September 11, 2001 attacks on this Country. [Another decision in the series is reproduced *supra* p. 480.] Plaintiffs are five organizations and two United States citizens seeking to provide support to the lawful, nonviolent activities of the Partiya Karkeran Kurdistan (Kurdistan Workers' Party) ("PKK") and the Liberation Tigers of Tamil Eelam ("LTTE"). The PKK and the LTTE have been designated as foreign terrorist organizations [under 8 U.S.C. §1189(a)].

The PKK is a political organization representing the interests of the Kurds in Turkey, with the goal of achieving self-determination for the Kurds in Southeastern Turkey. Plaintiffs allege that the Turkish government has subjected the Kurds to human rights abuses and discrimination for decades. The PKK's efforts on behalf of the Kurds include political organizing and advocacy, providing social services and humanitarian aid to Kurdish refugees, and engaging in military combat with Turkish armed forces.

The LTTE represents the interests of Tamils in Sri Lanka, with the goal of achieving self-determination for the Tamil residents of Tamil Eelam in the Northern and Eastern provinces of Sri Lanka. Plaintiffs allege that the Tamils constitute an ethnic group that has for decades been subjected to human rights abuses and discriminatory treatment by the Sinhalese, who have governed Sri Lanka since the nation gained its independence in 1948. The LTTE's activities include political organizing and advocacy, providing social services and humanitarian aid, defending the Tamil people from human rights abuses, and using military force against the government of Sri Lanka.

Plaintiffs seek to aid the PKK and the LTTE in the following ways: (1) they seek to provide training in human rights advocacy and peacemaking negotiations, as well as to provide legal services in aid of setting up institutions for providing humanitarian aid and in negotiating a peace agreement; (2) they seek to provide humanitarian aid directly to the PKK and LTTE; (3) they seek to provide engineering services and technological support to help rebuild the infrastructure in tsunami-afflicted areas; and (4) they seek to provide psychiatric counseling for survivors of the tsunami. . . .

In this case . . . Plaintiffs for the first time challenge Executive Order 13224, signed by President George W. Bush on September 23, 2001 pursuant to the emergency powers vested in him by the International Emergency Economic Powers Act ("IEEPA"). . . .

Plaintiffs challenge five aspects of the EO and its accompanying Regulations. First, they contend that the EO's ban on "services" is unconstitutionally vague because it fails to adequately notify the public, and Plaintiffs specifically, of the conduct to which the ban applies. Furthermore, they argue that the ban on "services" is overbroad because it encompasses a substantial amount of protected speech. Second, they assert that the EO Regulations are vague because they contain no definition of the term "specially designated terrorist group," thereby giving the President unfettered discretion to designate which individuals and groups fit within that term. Third, Plaintiffs contend that the President's designation authority, as exercised in the EO itself and as distinct from the designation authority delegated to the secretary of treasury, is unconstitutionally vague. Fourth, Plaintiffs contend that the EO's ban on being "otherwise associated with" a terrorist group is vague and overbroad, as it punishes individuals and groups for exercising their First Amendment right to freedom of association. [A fifth challenge, alleging that the Regulations' licensing provision violated the First and Fifth Amendments, was dismissed on standing grounds.] . . .

### A. Plaintiffs' Challenge to the EO's Ban on "Services"

#### 1. Vagueness

A challenge to a statute based on vagueness grounds requires the court to consider whether the statute is "sufficiently clear so as not to cause persons 'of common intelligence . . . necessarily [to] guess at its meaning and [to] differ as to its application.'" *United States v. Wunsch*, 84 F.3d 1110, 1119 (9th Cir. 1996) (quoting *Connally v. General Constr. Co.*, 269 U.S. 385, 391 (1926)). Vague statutes are void for three reasons: "(1) to avoid punishing people for behavior that they could not have known was illegal; (2) to avoid subjective enforcement of the laws based on 'arbitrary and discriminatory enforcement' by government officers; and (3) to avoid any chilling effect on the exercise of First Amendment freedoms." *Foti v. City of Menlo Park*, 146 F.3d 629, 638 (9th Cir. 1998). . . .

#### a. Vague as applied

. . . "An as-applied challenge contends that the law is unconstitutional as applied to the litigant's particular speech activity, even though the law may be capable of valid application to others." [*Foti,* 146 F.3d at 629.] . . .

Here, the EO's ban on "services" is not vague as applied to Plaintiffs' proposed conduct.[3] On the contrary, it unquestionably applies to each of the activities in which Plaintiffs seek to engage. First, the Regulations' prohibition on providing "educational" and "legal" "services" unequivocally prohibits Plaintiffs from providing training in human rights advocacy and peacemaking negotiations, as well as providing legal services in setting up institutions to provide humanitarian aid and in negotiating a peace agreement. Second, while not covered by the Regulations' definition of "services," the EO itself explicitly

---

3. The Regulations define "provision of services" as follows: . . .

    (b) Example: U.S. persons may not, except as authorized by or pursuant to this part, provide legal, accounting, financial, brokering, freight forwarding, transportation, public relations, educational, or other services to a person whose property or interests in property are blocked pursuant to §594.201(a).

31 C.F.R. §594.406.

bars Plaintiffs from providing humanitarian aid to the PKK and LTTE. *See* EO §4.[4] . . .

In contrast, the EO's ban on "services" does not apply to Plaintiffs' efforts to independently support the PKK or LTTE in the political process. Nothing in the EO Regulations' definition of "services" prohibits independent political activity; instead, the Regulations prohibit Plaintiffs from providing "services" to an SDGT. This prohibition would not, for example, prohibit Plaintiffs from vocally supporting the activities of the PKK or the LTTE. Indeed, the Government readily concedes this fact. . . .

. . . Accordingly, their vagueness challenge to the EO as applied to their proposed activity fails.

### b. Vague on its face . . .

A plaintiff may . . . successfully challenge a statute as vague on its face when the statute impinges on constitutionally protected activity and gives unfettered discretion to law enforcement officers to determine whether a given person's conduct violates the statute. . . .

Additionally, a person may challenge a statute as vague on its face when the statute "clearly implicates free speech rights." *Cal. Teachers Ass'n* [v. State Bd. of Educ., 271 F.3d 1141 (9th Cir. 2001)], at 1149. But even where a statute clearly implicates free speech rights, the statute will nevertheless survive a facial vagueness attack as long as "it is clear what the statute proscribes 'in the vast majority of its intended applications.'" *Gospel Missions* [of America v. City of Los Angeles, 419 F.3d 1042 (9th Cir. 2005),] at 1047 (quoting *Cal. Teachers Ass'n,* 271 F.3d at 1151). Indeed, even where a law implicates First Amendment rights, the Constitution must tolerate a certain amount of vagueness. *Cal. Teachers Ass'n,* 271 F.3d at 1151. . . .

Here . . . the EO's ban on "services" is not vague on its face. First, Plaintiffs' allegations aside, the EO's ban on "services" does not give "unfettered authority" to designate a person or group as an SDGT. While the Regulations' definition of "services" may not be exact, it does not permit subjective standards of enforcement. . . . [T]he word "services" is, by and large, a word of common understanding and one that could not be used for selective or subjective enforcement. Although instances may arise where it is unclear whether the EO prohibits some conduct, this does not mean that the EO provides unfettered discretion as to what constitutes "services." . . .

Second, the EO's ban on "services," while conceivably vague as to some hypothetical conduct, will nevertheless be clear in the vast majority of its intended applications. In the vast majority of cases, any given individual would be able to distinguish when he or she was providing a "service" to a designated terrorist group, as opposed to engaging in independent activity.

---

4. As a general rule, the IEEPA does not authorize the Executive to regulate or prohibit humanitarian aid, even if the Executive declares an emergency under §1702(a). 50 U.S.C. §1702(b)(2). But this general rule is inapplicable where, among other situations, the Executive determines that providing humanitarian aid "would seriously impair his ability to deal with any national emergency declared under section 1701 of this title . . . or would endanger Armed Forces of the United States which are engaged in hostilities or are in a situation where imminent involvement in hostilities is clearly indicated by the circumstances." *Id.* . . .

Tellingly, Plaintiffs cite no examples, other than their own proposed conduct, where the EO would be vague as to its intended applications. But as explained earlier, Plaintiffs' proposed conduct is clearly prohibited by the Executive Order. And to the extent that Plaintiffs contend that the EO's ban on "services" might be interpreted to preclude independent advocacy or activity, such an interpretation would be unreasonable. On the contrary, as explained earlier, the Government concedes that the EO's ban on "services" does not prohibit independent activity or advocacy. . . .

In short, given the clarity of the EO's ban on "services" in the vast majority of its intended applications, it is unlikely to inhibit a substantial amount of First Amendment activity. As such, facial invalidation is not warranted. *See Cal. Teachers,* 271 F.3d at 1152.

## 2. Overbreadth

"The First Amendment doctrine of overbreadth is an exception to [the] normal rule regarding the standards for facial challenges." *Virginia v. Hicks,* 539 U.S. 113, 118 (2003). Under the overbreadth doctrine, a "showing that a law punishes a 'substantial' amount of protected free speech, 'judged in relation to the statute's plainly legitimate sweep, suffices to invalidate all enforcement of that law, until and unless a limiting construction or partial invalidation so narrows it as to remove the seeming threat or deterrence to constitutionally protected expression.'" *Id.* at 118-19 (internal quotation marks and citations omitted). . . .

. . . Plaintiffs have failed to establish that the EO's ban on "services" is substantially overbroad. Indeed, it is content-neutral and serves the legitimate purpose of deterring groups and individuals from providing services to foreign terrorist organizations.[11] "Further, the [EO's] application to protected speech is not 'substantial' [either] in an absolute sense or relative to the scope of [its] plainly legitimate applications. The Court, therefore, declines to apply the 'strong medicine' of the overbreadth doctrine, finding instead that as-applied litigation will provide a sufficient safeguard for any potential First Amendment violation." *Humanitarian Law Project* [v. Gonzales], 380 F. Supp. 2d [1134 (C.D. Cal. 2005),] at 1153.

## B. Plaintiffs' Vagueness Challenge to the Term "Specially Designated Terrorist Group"

Next, Plaintiffs challenge the term "specially designated global terrorist" [SDGT,] as used in both the EO and its Regulations. Plaintiffs note that this term is nowhere to be found in the IEEPA. . . .

. . . First . . . the Regulations define the term "specially designated terrorist group." Specifically, the Regulations define "specially designated terrorist group" as "any foreign person or person listed in the Annex or designated pursuant to Executive Order 13224 of September 23, 2001." 31 C.F.R. §594.310. Moreover, even if it lacked a definition, the term "specially designated terrorist

---

11. Although Plaintiffs argue that the EO's ban on "services" is content-based, this argument lacks merit. The ban does not distinguish between "good" or "bad" services; rather, it prohibits the provision of all services to SDGTs.

group" is nothing more than shorthand for groups or individuals designated under the EO, as opposed to groups designated under other executive orders. Thus . . . this term is not vague.

Second, Plaintiffs' argument overlooks the limited circumstances under which the IEEPA affords the Executive any power. Indeed, before the Executive may take any action under the IEEPA, he or she must first declare a national emergency. And furthermore, any action the Executive takes under the IEEPA's grant of authority must relate to that identified emergency. This, coupled with the limited circumstances described below under which a person may be designated under the EO, ensures that the designating authorities are not afforded "unfettered discretion" in designating groups or individuals as SDGTs.

Third, the EO provides adequate criteria for designating an individual or group as an SDGT. In particular, the EO requires the secretary of the treasury to make specific findings before designating any group or individual as an SDGT. EO §1(b)-(d)(ii). For example, the secretary of the treasury may designate a person as an SDGT if the secretary determines that the person has committed, or poses a significant risk of committing, acts of terrorism that "threaten the security of United States nationals or national security, foreign policy, or [the] economy of the United States." EO §1(b). Additionally, the secretary of the treasury may designate a person as an SDGT if the secretary determines that the person is "owned or controlled by, or . . . act[s] for or on behalf of" other SDGTs. EO §1(c). Finally, the secretary of the treasury may designate a person as an SDGT if the secretary determines that the person has assisted in, has sponsored, or has provided "financial, material, or technological support for, or financial or other services to or in support of," acts of terrorism or other SDGTs. EO §1(d)(i). These provisions of the EO . . . set forth adequate criteria for the secretary of the treasury to exercise his discretion in designating individuals and groups as SDGTs. . . .

Accordingly, Plaintiffs' challenges to the term "specially designated terrorist group" and to the EO's designation procedure both fail.

### [C]. Plaintiffs' Vagueness Challenge to the President's Designation Authority

Plaintiffs point out that in addition to the designation authority that the President delegated to the secretary of the treasury, in the EO the President himself designated twenty-seven groups and individuals as SDGTs. Plaintiffs contend that regardless of the merits of the designation authority delegated to the secretary of treasury, this Presidential designation authority is unconstitutional. Specifically, they contend that these designations were made without any explanation of the criteria used, and that the EO provides no process by which the groups can challenge their designations. In addition, the President retains the authority to make similar designations at any time in the future, thus subjecting Plaintiffs to the risk that they too are subject to being similarly designated. Accordingly, Plaintiffs contend that the President's designation authority is unconstitutionally vague.

Plaintiffs present a strong facial challenge to the President's designation authority. Indeed, the EO provides no explanation of the basis upon which these twenty-seven groups and individuals were designated, and references no findings akin to those the secretary of treasury is required to make.

In addition, the procedures for challenging designations made by the secretary of treasury are not clearly available with regard to designations made by the President. In short, the criteria and processes discussed above that apply to the delegated designation authority, and that help ensure its constitutionality, do not appear to apply to the President's designation authority. Rather, the President's designation authority is subject only to his unfettered discretion. Finally, nothing in the EO appears to divest the President of his authority to make additional designations.

The Government has offered no argument demonstrating how the President's designation authority is constrained in any manner. Rather, the Government contends only that Plaintiffs' fear of punishment derives from their association with groups that were designated not by the President, but by the secretary of state pursuant to delegated authority. However, this attempt to challenge Plaintiffs' standing fails to meet Plaintiffs' argument, which is that they may be subject to designation under the President's authority for any reason, including for associating with the PKK and the LTTE, for associating with anyone listed in the Annex, or for no reason. . . .

Accordingly, the President's designation authority is unconstitutionally vague.

### [D].   Plaintiffs' Challenge to the EO's Ban on Being "Otherwise Associated With" an SDGT

Plaintiffs also challenge the constitutionality of the EO provision proscribing groups and individuals from being "otherwise associated with" an SDGT. *See* EO §1(d)(ii). This "otherwise associated with" provision, according to Plaintiffs, is overbroad because it directly impinges on their First Amendment right to freedom of association. . . . Furthermore, they assert that the provision is so vague that it could punish independent activity and encourage arbitrary enforcement. Relatedly, Plaintiffs posit that the term "otherwise associated" is so inherently vague that an average person of reasonable intelligence could not determine which conduct falls within the provision's proscriptions and which does not. . . .

### [2]. Vague on Its Face

. . . [T]he Court finds that the prohibition on being "otherwise associated with" an SDGT on its face unconstitutionally intrudes upon activity protected by the First Amendment.

First, the term "otherwise associated" is not itself susceptible of a clear meaning. Nor does the provision mitigate the vagueness of the term by supplying any definition. Indeed, as Plaintiffs point out, the provision contains no definition of the term whatsoever. Accordingly, the provision lends itself to subjective interpretation. *See Coates* [v. City of Cincinnati], 402 U.S. [611 (1971),] at 612-614.

Second, and relatedly, unlike the term "services," discussed [*supra*], the "otherwise associated with" provision contains no definable criteria for designating individuals and groups as SDGTs. Thus, the provision on its face gives the Government unfettered discretion in enforcing it.

Accordingly, the "otherwise associated with" provision is unconstitutionally vague on its face.

### [3]. Overbreadth

As discussed above, a law is overbroad if it punishes a substantial amount of protected conduct judged in relation to the statute's legitimate sweep, until and unless the law is narrowed to remove the threat.

Plaintiffs argue persuasively that the "otherwise associated with" provision is unconstitutionally overbroad because it punishes mere association with an SDGT. It is axiomatic that the Constitution forbids punishing a person for mere association. . . .

Here, it is facially clear, and the Government offers no argument to the contrary, that the "otherwise associated with" provision imposes penalties for mere association with an SDGT. There is nothing in the provision purporting to limit its application only to those instances of association also involving activity, let alone activity that furthers or advances an organization's illegal goals. . . .

Accordingly, the "otherwise associated with" provision is unconstitutionally overbroad. . . .

### Conclusion

For the reasons stated above, . . .

2. The Court finds that the President's authority to designate SDGTs under Executive Order 13224 is unconstitutionally vague on its face. The Court therefore GRANTS Plaintiffs' Motion for Summary Judgment on this ground. . . .

4. The Court finds that Executive Order 13224, §1(d)(ii), the "otherwise associated with" provision, is unconstitutionally vague on its face and overbroad. The Court therefore GRANTS Plaintiffs' Motion for Summary Judgment on this ground. . . .

Accordingly, Defendants, their officers, agents, employees, and successors are ENJOINED from (1) designating any of the Plaintiffs as SDGTs pursuant to the President's authority under Executive Order 13224 to make such designations; and (2) enforcing Executive Order 13224, §1(d)(ii), against any of the Plaintiffs by blocking their assets or subjecting them to designation as SDGTs for being "otherwise associated with" the PKK or the LTTE.[18] The Court declines to grant a nationwide injunction.

*It is so ordered.*

## NOTES AND QUESTIONS

1. ***Comparing the FTO Cases.*** The plaintiffs in *Humanitarian Law Project* (HLP) mounted both facial and as-applied challenges to Executive Order

---

18. This Court's injunction does not enjoin the enforcement of any other portions of the Executive Order against Plaintiffs.

No. 13,224 and its implementing regulations, alleging violations of their First Amendment rights of association and Fifth Amendment due process rights. The arguments here are similar to those in the other FTO cases we have studied, People's Mojahedin Organization of Iran v. Department of State, *supra* p. 13, United States v. Afshari, *supra* p. 16, Humanitarian Law Project v. Reno, *supra* p. 480, and United States v. Al-Arian, *supra* p. 485. In the other cases, the FTO designation process and the particular designations enjoyed mixed reviews. Here the court found that the authority for designation under the executive order is unconstitutional in some respects.

What distinguishes the result here from the earlier results? Is the language of the enabling statutes different in some constitutionally significant way? Is the language of the executive order here significantly different from that of the statutes in the other cases? Does the court apply the First and Fifth Amendments differently here?

2. ***Prior Notice of Sanctions.*** In §10 of Executive Order No. 13,224, President Bush declared that "because of the ability to transfer funds or assets instantaneously, prior notice to such persons of measures to be taken pursuant to this order would render these measures ineffectual." But does due process require such notice? Consider the holdings in National Council of Resistance of Iran v. Dept. of State, 251 F.3d 192, 209 (D.C. Cir. 2001) (Secretary of State must provide advance notice to an organization before placing it on the FTO list unless doing so would "impinge upon the security and other foreign policy goals of the United States"); People's Mojahedin Organization of Iran v. Dept. of State, 327 F.3d 1238, 1242 (D.C. Cir. 2003), *supra* p. 13, ("Due Process Clause requires only that process which is due under the circumstances of the case").

3. ***Criteria for Designation.*** Under Executive Order No. 13,224, economic sanctions may be imposed upon persons, organizations, or states determined, for example, "to have committed, or to pose a significant risk of committing, acts of terrorism." What additional constitutional challenges might be mounted against these criteria?

4. ***The Persistent Challenge of Vagueness.*** The HLP court finds that the term "services" in the executive order is not unconstitutionally vague, since the effect of the ban would be "clear in the vast majority of its intended applications." 463 F. Supp. 2d at 1063. Indeed, as the court observes, "Plaintiffs cite no examples, other than their own conduct, where the EO would be vague as to its intended applications." *Id.* If you conclude that enforcement against taxi drivers and pizza delivery personnel are not "intended applications," can you say with reasonable certainty what kinds of interactions with an organization or its members would place one in legal jeopardy? How would you compare the court's analysis on this point with that of the court in Humanitarian Law Project v. Reno, *supra* p. 480?

Prompted by the decision in the principal case, the Treasury Department's Office of Foreign Assets Control issued a new regulation, 31 C.F.R. §594.316, defining the term "otherwise associated with" in §1(d)(ii) of Executive Order No. 13,224, as follows:

The term "to be otherwise associated with," as used in [31 C.F.R.] §594.201(a)(4)(ii), means:

(a) To own or control; or

(b) To attempt, or to conspire with one or more persons, to act for or on behalf of or to provide financial, material, or technological support, or financial or other services, to.

The government then moved for reconsideration of the decision, arguing that the new definition cured the unconstitutional vagueness and overbreadth of the term, and asked the court to lift its injunction. The court did so. Humanitarian Law Project v. United States Dept. of Treasury, 2007 WL 1229194 (C.D. Cal. Apr. 20, 2007), at *3-6. Do you think the new regulatory language addresses the concerns expressed by the court earlier? The court also found, upon reconsideration, that the plaintiffs lacked standing to challenge the President's authority to designate SDGTs. *Id.* *6-8.

## 3. OTHER DOMESTIC ECONOMIC SANCTIONS AGAINST STATE SPONSORS OF TERRORISM

One provision of the Antiterrorism and Effective Death Penalty Act of 1996, Pub. L. No. 104-132, §321(a), 110 Stat. 1214, 1254 (codified at 18 U.S.C. §2332d (2000 & Supp. IV 2004)), makes it a crime for U.S. persons, except in accordance with Treasury Department regulations, to engage in financial transactions with the governments of states designated by the Secretary of State under §6(j) of the Export Administration Act of 1979, 50 U.S.C. app. §2405(j) (2000), as amended by Pub. L. No. 108-458, §7102(c)(1), 118 Stat. 3637, 3776 (2004), as supporting international terrorism. As of early 2007, five states were so designated: Cuba, Iran, North Korea, Sudan, and Syria. *See* U.S. Dept. of State, *State Sponsors of Terrorism* (n.d.), *available at* http://www.state.gov/s/ct/c14151.htm.

The Secretary of State's designation also allows the President to restrict or prohibit exports of sensitive technology, including some computers, to such states. 50 U.S.C. App. §2405(j). Such a restriction could be especially painful for a developing nation. The Defense Department is barred from providing financial assistance to designated states, to states identified in the Secretary of State's annual *Country Reports on Terrorism, supra* p. 704, as "providing significant support for international terrorism," or to states that the President determines grant "sanctuary from prosecution to any individual or group that has committed an act of international terrorism; or otherwise supports international terrorism." 10 U.S.C. §2249a (2000). In addition, the Arms Export Control Act bars government exports, and provides civil and criminal penalties for transfers by U.S. persons, of munitions to states that the Secretary of State determines have "repeatedly provided support for acts of international terrorism." 22 U.S.C. §2780 (2000 & Supp. IV 2004). The Foreign Assistance Act employs the same language to bar certain other kinds of U.S. government aid. 22 U.S.C. §2371 (2000). More narrowly, the Iran Sanctions Act of 1996, Pub. L. No. 104-172, 110 Stat. 1541 (as amended), *reprinted at* 50 U.S.C. §1701 note (2000), as amended by the Iran Freedom Support Act, Pub. L. No. 108-458, 120 Stat. 1344 (2006), requires the President to impose sanctions for certain investments that would enhance Iran's ability to develop its petroleum resources or weapons of mass destruction. And currency transfers that could be helpful to terrorists are targeted by provisions of the USA Patriot Act that address money laundering. Pub. L. No. 107-56, §§301-377, 115 Stat. 272, 296-342 (2001). *See* Michael Shapiro, *The USA Patriot Act and Money Laundering*, 123 Banking L.J. 629 (2006).

We noted earlier that the President had invoked the IEEPA to impose economic sanctions on Libya from 1986 to 2004. See *supra* p. 719. He also directed the Secretary of State to designate Libya as a state sponsor under the Export Administration Act, the Foreign Assistance Act, and the Arms Export Control Act, then lifted that designation in Presidential Determination No. 2006-14, 71 Fed. Reg. 31909 (May 12, 2006).

There is considerable redundancy among the various statutory sanctions, of which only some are mentioned here, and several of them provide for waiver by the President if, for example, he determines that it is "in the national security interests of the United States to do so." 10 U.S.C. §2249a(b) (2000).

## NOTES AND QUESTIONS

1. *Unilateral Executive Power to Impose Sanctions?* All of the economic sanctions we have examined have been based on statutory authority, or at least on authority delegated to the President by Congress. (The Supreme Court's decision in Dames & Moore v. Regan, noted *supra* p. 718, belongs in this category, as it rests on Congress's acquiescence or on the "general tenor" of legislation in the area. *Dames & Moore* involved the President's suspension of private claims against Iran following the 1979 seizure of American hostages in Tehran.) But could the President impose some new sanctions without congressional approval? Professor Carter, recalling Justice Jackson's concurring opinion in the *Steel Seizure Case,* points out that statutory authorities for such sanctions "are both comprehensive and specific. . . . If the President were to act contrary to one of the limits on his discretion or if he were to operate outside the statutory procedures, his power would be at 'its lowest ebb,' and a court might refuse to uphold his act." Carter, *supra* p. 718, at 1245-1246. What arguments could the President make to support such a unilateral initiative?

2. *Unintended Consequences.* One criticism of wide-ranging U.S. economic sanctions is that "persons having a relatively limited connection to the United States are unwillingly made 'foot soldiers' in U.S. 'wars' against perceived enemies." Cindy G. Buys, *United States Economic Sanctions: The Fairness of Targeting Persons from Third Countries,* 17 B.U. Intl. L.J. 241, 242 (1999). Others argue that those most vulnerable to the effects of economic sanctions are also those least able to respond to them — namely, the poorer citizens of the sanctioned states. *See, e.g.,* Alan Einismann, Note, *Ineffectiveness at its Best: Fighting Terrorism with Economic Sanctions,* 9 Minn. J. Global Trade 229 (2000). *See also* Sarah H. Cleveland, *Norm Internalization and U.S. Economic Sanctions,* 26 Yale J. Intl. L. 1 (2001). How would you respond to these criticisms?

# CHAPTER 23

# *SUING TERRORISTS AND THEIR SPONSORS*

In this concluding chapter we consider the use of a familiar legal device—the tort suit—to counter terrorism. Successful suits in tort may produce some measure of justice for victims of terrorism in the form of judgments for damages. Even if those judgments don't eventually provide economic relief for the plaintiffs, they condemn the terrorists or their sponsors as outlaws, and they may make it much more difficult for terrorists to finance their activities by exposing their assets to attachment.

The intersection of relevant domestic and international laws figures prominently in this study. In Part A we examine several domestic statutes, one of them incorporating international law, that establish causes of action for damages and jurisdiction in federal courts. In Part B we take up the issue of state sovereignty in suits against state sponsors of terrorism. Finally, in Part C we review briefly the frustrations successful plaintiffs have experienced in trying to collect on their judgments.

## A. SUING TERRORISTS AND THEIR NON-STATE SPONSORS

Civil damages suits for terrorist acts are authorized by several statutes, including the Antiterrorism Act, 18 U.S.C. §2333 (2000) (ATA), the Alien Tort Statute (ATS) (also known as the Alien Tort Claims Act), 28 U.S.C. §1350 (2000), and the Torture Victim Protection Act, 28 U.S.C. §1350 note (2000) (TVPA). Application of the ATA is illustrated in the following case, and of the other statutes in the Notes that follow it.

### BOIM v. QURANIC LITERACY INSTITUTE AND HOLY LAND FOUNDATION FOR RELIEF AND DEVELOPMENT

United States Court of Appeals, Seventh Circuit, 2002
291 F.3d 1000

ROVNER, Circuit Judge. In this case of first impression, the parents of a young United States citizen murdered in Israel by Hamas terrorists have sued several individuals and organizations for the loss of their son. Two of the organizational defendants moved to dismiss the complaint, and the district court denied the motion. In this interlocutory appeal, we are asked to consider the viability of a claim brought under the never-tested 18 U.S.C. §2333, which allows U.S. nationals who have been injured "by reason of an act of international terrorism" to sue therefor and recover treble damages. We affirm the district court's denial of the defendants' motion to dismiss.

## I. . . .

David Boim was the son of Joyce and Stanley Boim, who are United States citizens. David held dual citizenship in the United States and Israel. In 1996, the Boims were living in Israel, where seventeen-year-old David was studying at a yeshiva. On May 13, 1996, David was murdered as he waited with other students at a bus stop near Beit El in the West Bank. He was struck by bullets fired from a passing car, and was pronounced dead within an hour of the shooting. His two attackers were later identified as Amjad Hinawi and Khalil Tawfiq Al-Sharif. The Palestinian Authority apprehended Hinawi and Al-Sharif, and temporarily imprisoned them in early 1997. They were released shortly thereafter, apparently pending trial. Al-Sharif subsequently killed himself and five civilians and injured 192 other people in a suicide bombing in Jerusalem on September 4, 1997. Two other suicide bombers joined him in this action. Hinawi, who confessed to participating in the shooting of David Boim, was eventually tried for David's murder by a Palestinian Authority court and was sentenced to ten years' imprisonment on February 17, 1998.

Both Hinawi and Al-Sharif were known members of the military wing of Hamas. The Boims describe Hamas as an extremist, Palestinian militant organization that seeks to establish a fundamentalist Palestinian state. The group is divided into two branches, one political and one military. The military branch receives orders and material support from the political branch. Hamas seeks to advance its political objectives through acts of terrorism and works to undermine the Middle East peace process through violent attacks on civilians. . . . The Boims believe that Hamas has command and control centers in the United States, Britain and several Western European countries. The leaders of these control centers coordinate fund-raising efforts from sympathetic parties in these various countries and then launder and channel the money to Hamas operatives in Gaza and the West Bank. They also arrange for the purchase of weapons and for the recruitment and training of military personnel. They work with local commanders in the West Bank and Gaza to plan terrorist attacks. Hamas was designated a terrorist organization by President William Jefferson Clinton in 1995 by Executive Order [pursuant to the International Emergency Economic Powers Act (IEEPA). See *supra* p. 718.]. In 1997, Hamas was designated a foreign terrorist organization pursuant to 8 U.S.C. §1189. [See *supra* pp. 12-13.]

The Boims allege that Hamas' military wing depends on foreign contributions, with approximately one-third of its multi-million dollar annual budget coming from fund-raising in North America and Western Europe. The Boims believe that the Quranic Literacy Institute ("QLI") and the Holy Land Foundation for Relief and Development ("HLF"), along with other defendants not involved in this appeal, are the main fronts for Hamas in the United States. They allege that these organizations' allegedly humanitarian functions mask their core mission of raising and funneling money and other resources to Hamas operatives in support of terrorist activities. . . .

The Boims bring their suit against HLF, QLI and other organizational and individual defendants pursuant to 18 U.S.C. §2333. They charge that all of the defendants are civilly liable for David's murder. They name Hinawi and Al-Sharif as the persons who actually killed David, but allege that the other defendants aided, abetted and financed Hinawi and Al-Sharif. They assert that the organizational defendants provided material support or resources to Hamas as those terms are defined in 18 U.S.C. §§2339A and 2339B [set forth *supra* p. 479]. The Boims seek compensation for the extreme physical pain David suffered before his death, and for the cost of his funeral and the loss of accretion to his estate due to his death at age seventeen. They also seek damages for their own extreme mental anguish and loss of the society of their son. They ask for $100,000,000 compensatory damages, $100,000,000 punitive damages, plus costs and attorney's fees, and request the trebling of damages pursuant to the statute. . . .

## II.

The district court . . . correctly certified three issues for [interlocutory] appeal:

(1) Does funding, *simpliciter*, of an international terrorist organization constitute an act of terrorism under 18 U.S.C. §2331?
(2) Does 18 U.S.C. §2333 incorporate the definitions of international terrorism found in 18 U.S.C. §§2339A and 2339B?
(3) Does a civil cause of action lie under 18 U.S.C. §§2331 and 2333 for aiding and abetting international terrorism? . . .

The Boims seek to recover against HLF and QLI pursuant to 18 U.S.C. §2333, which provides, in relevant part:

> Any national of the United States injured in his or her person, property, or business by reason of an act of international terrorism, or his or her estate, survivors, or heirs, may sue therefor in any appropriate district court of the United States and shall recover threefold the damages he or she sustains and the cost of the suit, including attorney's fees.

18 U.S.C. §2333(a). "International terrorism," in turn, is a defined term:

> [T]he term "international terrorism" means activities that—
>   (A) involve violent acts or acts dangerous to human life that are a violation of the criminal laws of the United States or of any State, or that would be a criminal violation if committed within the jurisdiction of the United States or of any State;
>   (B) appear to be intended—
>     (i) to intimidate or coerce a civilian population;
>     (ii) to influence the policy of a government by intimidation or coercion; or

(iii) to affect the conduct of a government by assassination or kidnapping; and

(C) occur primarily outside the territorial jurisdiction of the United States, or transcend national boundaries in terms of the means by which they are accomplished, the persons they appear intended to intimidate or coerce, or the locale in which their perpetrators operate or seek asylum.

18 U.S.C. §2331(1). . . .

## A.

The plaintiffs' first theory is that the simple provision of funds to Hamas by QLI and HLF constitutes an act of international terrorism because it "involve[s] violent acts or acts dangerous to human life." The Boims liken payments to Hamas to murder for hire: the person who pays for the murder does not himself commit a violent act, but the payment "involves" violent acts in the sense that it brings about the violent act and provides an incentive for someone else to commit it. The Boims urge us to adopt a very broad definition of "involves" that would include any activity that touches on and supports a violent act. They argue that David's murder was indisputably a violent act, and we have no quarrel with that premise. But they further argue that the provision of money or in-kind services to persons outside the country who set up the infrastructure used to recruit and train David's murderers, buy their weapons, and compensate their families also "involves" violent acts. The defendants, in turn, urge us to read the statute to hold liable only those who actually commit a violent act.

. . . The controversy here centers on the definition of international terrorism, and in particular on the definition of the word "involve," which is susceptible to many meanings. The statutory definition of international terrorism in section 2331(1) is drawn *verbatim* from the Foreign Intelligence Surveillance Act, 50 U.S.C. §1801(c) ("FISA"). No court has yet expounded on the meaning or scope of "international terrorism" as it is used in FISA either, so we are not aided by that origin. . . .

The government, in its very helpful *amicus curiae* brief, delineates some of the legislative history of sections 2331 and 2333. That history, in combination with the language of the statute itself, evidences an intent by Congress to codify general common law tort principles and to extend civil liability for acts of international terrorism to the full reaches of traditional tort law. In particular, the statute itself contains all of the elements of a traditional tort: breach of a duty (i.e., committing an act of international terrorism); injury to the person, property or business of another; and causation (injured "by reason of"). Although the statute defines the class of plaintiffs who may sue, it does not limit the class of defendants, and we must therefore look to tort law and the legislative history to determine who may be held liable for injuries covered by the statute. . . .

The statute clearly is meant to reach beyond those persons who themselves commit the violent act that directly causes the injury. The Senate report on the bill notes that "[t]he substance of [an action under section 2333] is not defined by the statute, because the fact patterns giving rise to such suits will be as varied and numerous as those found in the law of torts. This bill opens the courthouse door to victims of international terrorism." S. Rep. 102-342, at 45 (1992). This same report also remarks that the legislation, with "its provisions for compensatory damages, treble damages, and the imposition of liability *at any point along the causal chain of terrorism*," would "interrupt, or at least imperil, the flow of money." *Id.* at 22 (emphasis added). . . .

But to the extent that the Boims urge a reading of the statute that would lead to liability for merely giving money to Hamas, a group which then sponsored a terrorist act in the manner the Boims have alleged, we agree with the district court, the defendants and the government that those allegations would be inadequate. To say that funding *simpliciter* constitutes an act of terrorism is to give the statute an almost unlimited reach. Any act which turns out to facilitate terrorism, however remote that act may be from actual violence and regardless of the actor's intent, could be construed to "involve" terrorism. Without also requiring the plaintiffs to show knowledge of and intent to further the payee's violent criminal acts, such a broad definition might also lead to constitutional infirmities by punishing mere association with groups that engage in terrorism, as we shall discuss later in addressing the First Amendment concerns raised here.

Additionally, the statute itself requires that in order to recover, a plaintiff must be injured "by reason of" an act of international terrorism. . . . Foreseeability is the cornerstone of proximate cause, and in tort law, a defendant will be held liable only for those injuries that might have reasonably been anticipated as a natural consequence of the defendant's actions. Restatement (2d) of Torts, §§440-447. In the circumstances of this case, the Boims cannot show that David Boim was injured "by reason of" the defendants' payments to Hamas in the traditional tort sense of causation unless they can also show that murder was the reasonably foreseeable result of making the donation. To hold the defendants liable for donating money without knowledge of the donee's intended criminal use of the funds would impose strict liability. Nothing in the language of the statute or its structure or history supports that formulation. . . . [T]he complaint cannot be sustained on the theory that the defendants themselves committed an act of international terrorism when they donated unspecified amounts of money to Hamas, neither knowing nor suspecting that Hamas would in turn financially support the persons who murdered David Boim. In the very least, the plaintiffs must be able to show that murder was a reasonably foreseeable result of making a donation. Thus, the Boims' first theory of liability under section 2333, funding *simpliciter* of a terrorist organization, is insufficient because it sets too vague a standard, and because it does not require a showing of proximate cause.

**B.**

The Boims' second theory of liability is that the defendants' violation of sections 2339A and 2339B, the criminal counterparts to section 2333, gives rise to civil liability under section 2333. The Boims further contend that sections 2339A and 2339B demonstrate Congress' intent to include the provision of material support to terrorist organizations in the definition of international terrorism for the purposes of section 2333. . . .

HLF and QLI, of course, protest the district court's conclusion that funding may form the basis for a section 2333 civil action if the funding meets the standards for criminal liability under sections 2339A or 2339B. . . .

. . . [T]he Congressional record for section 2333 indicates an intention to cut off the flow of money in support of terrorism generally. Sections 2339A and 2339B further this goal by imposing criminal liability for financial support of terrorist activities and organizations. The fact that Congress imposed lesser criminal penalties for the financial supporters indicates perhaps that they found the financiers less dangerous or less culpable than the terrorists they finance, but it does not in any way indicate that Congress meant to limit civil liability to those who personally committed acts of terrorism. On the contrary, it would be counterintuitive to conclude that Congress imposed criminal liability in sections 2339A and 2339B on those who financed terrorism, but did not intend to impose civil liability on those same persons through section 2333. . . .

. . . Because Congress intended to impose criminal liability for funding violent terrorism, we find that it also intended through sections 2333 and 2331(1) to impose civil liability for funding at least as broad a class of violent terrorist acts. If the plaintiffs could show that HLF and QLI violated either section 2339A or section 2339B, that conduct would certainly be sufficient to meet the definition of "international terrorism" under sections 2333 and 2331. Such acts would give rise to civil liability under section 2333 so long as knowledge and intent are also shown, as we shall discuss shortly in the context of aiding and abetting.

We hasten to add that, although proof of a criminal violation under sections 2339A or 2339B might satisfy the definition of international terrorism under section 2333, such proof is not necessary to sustain a section 2333 claim. As we discuss in the context of aiding and abetting, we believe Congress intended for civil liability for financing terrorism to sweep more broadly than the conduct described in sections 2339A and 2339B. . . . For civil liability, section 2333 requires that the plaintiff be injured "by reason of" the act of international terrorism. Because we believe Congress intended to import standard tort law into section 2333, causation may be demonstrated as it would be in traditional tort law. Congress has made clear, though, through the criminal liability imposed in sections 2339A and 2339B, that even small donations made knowingly and intentionally in support of terrorism may meet the standard for civil liability in section 2333. Congress' goal of cutting off funding for terrorism would be seriously compromised if terrorist organizations could avoid liability by simply pooling together small donations to fund a terrorist act. . . .

**C.**

We turn next to the Boims' theory that HLF and QLI may be held civilly liable under section 2333 for aiding and abetting an act of international terrorism. Under this theory, the Boims urge us to find that aiding and abetting a violent act is conduct that "involves" a violent act as that word is used in section 2331(1). . . . Because 18 U.S.C. §2 criminalizes aiding and abetting the commission of a felony, the Boims maintain there is no doubt Congress intended to include liability for aiding and abetting in section 2333. The government, in its *amicus* brief, adds that the language and legislative history of section 2333 indicate an intent by Congress to import into section 2333 civil tort law principles as expressed in the Restatement Second of Torts, and as applied in the cases. Under that jurisprudence, according to the government, aiding and abetting liability should be applied under section 2333. . . .

. . . [T]he language of section 2333 tracks the traditional elements of tort law as expressed in the Restatement, and the legislative history expressly references tort principles in setting out the perimeters of Congress' intent.

. . . Congress also expressed an intent in section 2333 to make civil liability at least as extensive as criminal liability. The statute defining "international terrorism" includes activities that "involve violent acts or acts dangerous to human life that are a violation of the criminal laws of the United States or of any State, or that would be a criminal violation if committed within the jurisdiction of the United States or of any State." 18 U.S.C. §2331(1). This language, embracing activities that "involve" violent acts, taken at face value would certainly cover aiding and abetting violent acts. Remember, too, the criminal laws include 18 U.S.C. §2, which creates liability for aiding and abetting violations of any other criminal provisions. By incorporating violations of any criminal laws that involve violent acts or acts dangerous to human life, Congress was expressly including aiding and abetting to the extent that aiding and abetting "involves" violence. As we discussed earlier, "involve" is a rather broad word. If we were to interpret "involve" literally, we would be attributing almost unlimited liability to any act that had some link to a terrorist act. Congress could not have meant to attach unlimited liability to even remote acts; it must have meant something else. As we have seen from the language and legislative history of section 2333, that something else is traditional tort and criminal liability. Aiding and abetting, which is surely subsumed in the definition of acts that "involve" certain criminal violations, is a well known and well defined doctrine. That Congress did not use the words "aid and abet" in the statute is not determinative when it did use words broad enough to include all kinds of secondary liability. . . .

Finally, if we failed to impose liability on aiders and abettors who knowingly and intentionally funded acts of terrorism, we would be thwarting Congress' clearly expressed intent to cut off the flow of money to terrorists at every point along the causal chain of violence. . . . Congress' purpose here could not be met unless liability attached beyond the persons directly involved in acts of violence. The statute would have little effect if liability were limited to the persons who pull the trigger or plant the bomb because such persons are unlikely to have assets, much less assets in the United States, and would not be deterred by the statute. Also, and perhaps more importantly, there would not be a trigger to pull or a bomb to blow up without the resources to acquire such tools of terrorism and to bankroll the persons who actually commit the violence. Moreover, the organizations, businesses and nations that support and encourage terrorist acts are likely to have reachable assets that they wish to protect. The only way to imperil the flow of money and discourage the financing of terrorist acts is to impose liability on those who knowingly and intentionally supply the funds to the persons who commit the violent acts. For all of these distinguishing reasons, we [think] that aiding and abetting liability is both appropriate and called for by the language, structure and legislative history of section 2333.

**D.**

The defendants raise two First Amendment objections to this section 2333 action against them. First, they argue that the Boims seek to hold them liable for their mere association with Hamas. Harking back to a line of cases involving the Communist party, HLF and QLI contend that, when an organization has both legal and illegal aims, a person may not be punished for mere membership in or association with that organization, but may be held civilly liable only if he or she possesses the specific intent to further the organizations' illegal purposes. Second, they contend that, to the extent the Boims' claim is founded on a violation of section 2339B, it cannot withstand First Amendment scrutiny because section 2339B fails to account for the intent and the associational rights of the contributors who donate money for humanitarian purposes. . . .

*1.*

HLF and QLI begin their argument with the well-established proposition that the Constitution protects against the imposition of liability based solely upon association with a group. . . .

. . . The arguments of the defendants . . . beg the question, though, because section 2333 does not seek to impose liability for association alone but rather for involvement in acts of international terrorism. The defendants nonetheless object that the definition of acts of international terrorism is so broad that they might be held liable for involvement in terrorist activity when all they intended was to supply money to fund the legitimate, humanitarian mission of Hamas or other organizations. . . .

. . . When activity protected by the First Amendment is present, damages are restricted to the direct consequences of the illegal violent conduct and may not include the consequences resulting from associated peaceful picketing or other protected First Amendment activity. [The Supreme Court has] summarized the rule to be applied:

> Civil liability may not be imposed merely because an individual belonged to a group, some members of which committed acts of violence. For liability to be imposed by reason of association alone, it is necessary to establish that the group itself possessed unlawful goals and that the individual held a specific intent to further those illegal aims.

[NAACP v. Claiborne Hardware Co., 458 U.S. 886 (1982)], at 920.

We have already held that the Boims may prevail on their claim by showing, among other things, that the defendants aided and abetted David's murder. This requires them to prove that the defendants knew of Hamas' illegal activities, that they desired to help those activities succeed, and they engaged in some act of helping the illegal activities. If the Boims are able to prove the defendants aided and abetted terrorist acts, liability would not offend the principles announced in *Claiborne Hardware*. The Boims have alleged that HLF and QLI supplied money to Hamas to fund terrorist operations, that they are "front" organizations with ostensibly legitimate purposes which are actually engaged in fund-raising and money laundering in support of terrorist activities. They have alleged that HLF and QLI provided the money to purchase the weapons and train the men who killed David Boim. HLF and QLI, of course, deny these allegations and argue that as a factual matter, Hamas is primarily a humanitarian organization, and that any money supplied to Hamas by QLI and HLF was intended to fund humanitarian efforts, not terrorism. This is a classic factual dispute, not suitable for resolution on a motion to dismiss for failure to state a claim. If the Boims are able to prove their allegations, that HLF and QLI provided legitimate-looking fronts for raising money to support the terrorist operation that resulted in David Boim's murder, their claim will not run afoul of the First Amendment. The Boims are not seeking to hold HLF and QLI liable for their mere association with Hamas, nor are they seeking to hold the defendants liable for contributing money for humanitarian efforts. Rather, they are seeking to hold them liable for aiding and abetting murder by supplying the money to buy the weapons, train the shooters, and compensate the families of the murderers. That Hamas may also engage in legitimate advocacy or humanitarian efforts is irrelevant for First Amendment purposes if HLF and QLI knew about Hamas' illegal operations, and intended to help Hamas accomplish those illegal goals when they contributed money to the organization. . . .

### III.

In short, we answer the three questions certified by the district court as follows: funding, *simpliciter*, of a foreign terrorist organization is not sufficient to constitute an act of terrorism under 18 U.S.C. §2331. However, funding that meets the definition of aiding and abetting an act of terrorism does create liability under sections 2331 and 2333. Conduct that would give rise to criminal liability under section 2339B is conduct that "involves" violent acts or acts dangerous to human life, and therefore may meet the definition of international terrorism as that term is used in section 2333. Finally, as we have set forth the elements of an action under section 2333, civil liability for funding a foreign terrorist organization does not offend the First Amendment so long as the plaintiffs are able to prove that the defendants knew about the organization's illegal activity, desired to help that activity succeed and engaged in some act of helping. The plaintiffs have not yet had an opportunity to develop the facts of their case. Today we hold that dismissal would be premature at this stage of the litigation because we can envision a set of facts in support of the claim they have alleged that would entitle them to relief.

*Affirmed.*

## NOTES AND QUESTIONS

1. **Who May Sue?** Section 2333 does not allow suit by everyone victimized by an act of international terrorism. Who may sue? Are only U.S. nationals eligible?
2. **Who Can Be Sued and for What?** Section 2333 creates a right to sue, but it does not expressly identify who can be sued or on what theory of liability. What exactly is the theory of liability, and who could be liable? Consider three possibilities.

First, and most obviously, §2333 plaintiffs could sue the primary actors who directly committed the acts of international terrorism (as defined by §2331(1)) that injured them. The Boims argued that the Quranic Literacy Institute and the Holy Land Foundation had themselves committed acts of international terrorism and thus were liable as primary tortfeasors. Why did the court reject this theory?

On the other hand, can you see why it is unlikely that Congress meant to restrict liability only to such primary tortfeasors? David Boim was killed in a drive-by shooting. But many §2333 plaintiffs may be victims of suicide terror attacks. Giving plaintiffs a "remedy" only against successful suicide terrorists would be a cruel joke. In either case, moreover, the primary tortfeasors are unlikely to have assets.

Second, §2333 may authorize suit also against defendants whose violations of statutes criminalizing material support for terrorist or foreign terrorist organizations proximately caused the acts that injured the plaintiffs. This theory expands §2333 liability to include secondary liability. How did the court rule on this theory and why?

Third, §2333 may extend liability to *any* defendant who would be liable under common law tort principles. *Restatement (Second) of Torts* §876 (1979) provides,

> For harm resulting to a third person from the tortious conduct of another, one is subject to liability if he
>
> (a) does a tortious act in concert with the other or pursuant to a common design with him, or
>
> (b) knows that the other's conduct constitutes a breach of duty and gives substantial assistance or encouragement to the other so to conduct himself, or
>
> (c) gives substantial assistance to the other in accomplishing a tortious result and his own conduct, separately considered, constitutes a breach of duty to the third person.

This theory of §2333 liability would thus open the door to secondary liability for conspiracy (§876(a)) and aiding and abetting (§876(b)), as well as for violation of the material support statutes (§876(c)). How did the court rule on this theory and why?

3. *Scienter for Civil Liability.* Why did the court refuse to find §2333 liability for "funding *simpliciter*"? What is necessary to make funding more than "*simpliciter*"?

If some degree of scienter is the answer, how much? Note that the degree of scienter may depend on the precise theory of liability. For common law aiding and abetting, what scienter does the court require? *But see* Linde v. Arab Bank, PLC, 384 F. Supp. 2d 571, 584 (E.D.N.Y. 2005) (finding that defendant's general awareness of its role and knowing and substantial assistance is enough, citing the *Restatement*). What degree of scienter for violation of the material support statutes? Is the court's finding consistent with the language of the statutes themselves? See *supra* pp. 479-480.

4. *Tracing Responsibility.* How far up the causal chain does secondary liability for a terrorist act extend? In *Linde, supra,* U.S. nationals injured

by terrorist attacks in Israel sued under the ATA, claiming that Arab Bank knowingly provided banking services for Hamas and other terrorist organizations and knowingly disbursed funds to terrorists and the families of "martyrs." The court decided that these allegations sufficed to avoid dismissal. Can individual donors to a terrorist organization be held liable? Suppose the organization is dual purpose (like Hamas): it conducts terrorist acts, but it also provides social services, and the donor wishes to support the latter? How about the person who delivers pizza to the organization's headquarters? The lawyer who provides advice about the legality of the organization's activities?

5. ***First Amendment Defenses.*** The defendants in *Boim* raise important, familiar First Amendment concerns. We have seen the same issues analyzed in cases involving criminal responsibility (*see, e.g.*, United States v. Rahman, 189 F.2d 88 (2d Cir. 1999), *supra* p. 471) and the blocking or forfeiture of assets (*see, e.g.*, Humanitarian Law Project v. United States Dept. of Treasury, 463 F. Supp. 2d 1049 (C.D. Cal. 2006), *supra* p. 722). How did the *Boim* court respond to these First Amendment issues in this setting? Citing NAACP v. Claiborne Hardware Co., the court finds that civil liability can be imposed for association with Hamas only on a showing that a member knew of its unlawful goals and had a *specific intent* to further them. If the defendant is a bank or commercial entity that claims no association with Hamas, however, should this scienter requirement apply?

6. ***Alien Tort Statute.*** Aliens injured by acts of terrorism are not entitled to sue under the Antiterrorism Act invoked in *Boim*, unless they are heirs or survivors of an American victim, since that statute provides relief only for a "national of the United States . . . or his or her estate, survivor, or heirs." But they may seek recovery under the Alien Tort Statute (ATS) (sometimes called the Alien Tort Claims Act), 28 U.S.C. §1350 (2000). The ATS establishes original jurisdiction in federal courts for "any civil action by an alien for a tort only, committed in violation of the law of nations or a treaty of the United States." In Sosa v. Alvarez-Machain, 542 U.S. 692 (2004), the Supreme Court held that the ATS only creates subject matter jurisdiction, not a cause of action for violations of international law. It then read "tort . . . committed in violation of the law of nations" narrowly to include only those few torts that were recognized at the time of the Act's passage in 1789 (violation of safe conducts, infringement of the rights of ambassadors, and piracy), as well as any newer claim that "rest[s] on a norm of international character accepted by the civilized world and defined with a specificity comparable to the features of [these three] 18th-century paradigms. . . ." *Id.* at 725.

Does a claim of injury from terrorism meet this demanding test? In two recent cases excerpted *supra* pp. 21-35, the courts reached opposite answers. *Compare* Almog v. Arab Bank, PLC, 471 F. Supp. 2d 257, 285 (E.D.N.Y. 2007) ("organized, systematic suicide bombings and other murderous attacks against innocent civilians for the purpose of intimidating a civilian population are a violation of the law of nations for which this court can and does recognize a cause of action under the ATS"), *with* Saperstein v. Palestinian Authority, 2006 WL 3804718, *7 (S.D. Fla. Dec. 22, 2006) ("politically motivated terrorism has not reached the status of a violation of the law of nations").

7. ***Torture Victim Protection Act.*** The Torture Victim Protection Act (TVPA), 28 U.S.C. §1350 note (2000), creates a cause of action for an individual (or her successor) who, *inter alia*, is the victim of an extra-judicial killing by "an individual [acting] under actual or apparent authority, or color of law, of any foreign nation." Thus, in In re Terrorist Attacks on September 11, 2001, 392 F. Supp. 2d 539, 565-566 (S.D.N.Y. 2005), the court dismissed TVPA claims against several organizations that were potentially liable under the ATA because they were not "individuals" and against several individuals because they were not acting under "color of state law."

8. ***RICO.*** In In re Terrorist Attacks on September 11, 2001, *supra*, the plaintiffs sought recovery for violation of the Racketeer Influenced and Corrupt Organizations Act, 18 U.S.C. §§1961-1968 (2000 & Supp. IV 2004), as amended, alleging that various defendants who were "employed by or associated with [an] enterprise engaged in . . . foreign commerce" undertook to "conduct or participate, directly or indirectly, in the conduct of such enterprise's affairs through a pattern of racketeering activity." *Id.* §1962(c). The court found that to state a claim for recovery under RICO, a plaintiff must show that the defendant was "a participant 'in the operation or management of the enterprise itself.'" 392 F. Supp. 2d at 565. What is the likelihood that a plaintiff will be able to make the necessary proof in a case growing out of a terrorist attack?

9. ***Extraterritorial Jurisdiction and Forum Non Conveniens.*** Finding a viable theory of liability and identifying eligible defendants are not the only obstacles to civil liability by any means. Usually the defendants in a claim arising from an act of international terrorism will be foreign, and the act itself, by definition, will have occurred abroad. *See* 18 U.S.C. §2333(1) (2000) (defining international terrorism, in relevant part, as activities that "occur primarily outside the territorial jurisdiction of the United States. . . ."). On what jurisdictional basis did Congress proscribe such acts and make them subject to civil liability? See *supra* pp. 493-503. If an act was conducted entirely abroad, on what basis could a U.S. court exercise personal jurisdiction over the defendants? (Hint: the Quranic Literacy Institute and Holy Land Foundation were both based in and operated within the United States.) Finally, the law of forum non conveniens establishes that if a plaintiff has an adequate alternative foreign forum that would be more convenient in light of the location of evidence and witnesses, forum interest, and other practical factors, then a U.S. court can dismiss the suit. *See* Gene R. Shreve & Peter Raven-Hansen, *Understanding Civil Procedure* §6.02[1] (2002). Why wouldn't application of this doctrine result in dismissal of most ATA or ATS claims? The answer for ATA claims lies in part in §2334, which prohibits a forum non conveniens dismissal of a §2333 claim unless the "foreign court is *significantly* more convenient and appropriate" and "that foreign court offers a remedy which is *substantially the same* as the one available in the courts of the United States." 18 U.S.C. §2334(d)(2)-(3) (emphasis added).

10. *Availability of Evidence.* Even if all of the foregoing obstacles can be overcome, a successful plaintiff may have to prove not only that a defendant was involved somehow in a terrorist attack but also that the defendant had the requisite scienter. The plaintiff might also have to be able to describe a defendant's role in association with others in a terrorist enterprise. These proofs could require access to information in government hands, some of which might be classified, or the testimony of individuals in government custody. When a plaintiff engages in discovery to gain access to such information or seeks to introduce it into evidence, it may be blocked if the government invokes its state secrets privilege. For example, this privilege was used to bar the deposition of a former FBI analyst in a damages suit by 9/11 victims. Burnett v. Al Baraka Investment & Development Corp., 323 F. Supp. 2d 82 (D.D.C. 2004). *See generally* Stephen Dycus et al., *National Security Law* 1037-1045 (4th ed. 2007). In the alternative, a court might decide that the risk of exposing sensitive information at trial is so great that the trial simply cannot go forward, leaving the plaintiff without any way to vindicate her claim. *See generally id.* at 1045-1050.

# B. SUING STATE SPONSORS OF TERRORISM

Until fairly recently the long-recognized general immunity of foreign states from suit in U.S. courts presented an insurmountable obstacle to recovery from a state sponsor of terrorism. That immunity has been codified, yet limited by certain exceptions, in the Foreign Sovereign Immunities Act (FSIA), 28 U.S.C. §§1330, 1602-1611 (2000 & Supp. IV 2004), as amended. *See generally* Jennifer K. Elsea, *Suits Against Terrorist States by Victims of Terrorism* (Cong. Res. Serv. RL31258), June 7, 2005. One exception, long thought to provide relief for terrorists' victims, is addressed in the following case.

## CICIPPIO-PULEO V. ISLAMIC REPUBLIC OF IRAN *Overturned by NDAA 2008*

United States Court of Appeals, District of Columbia Circuit, 2004
353 F.3d 1024

HARRY T. EDWARDS, Circuit Judge: This case involves a lawsuit brought against the Islamic Republic of Iran ("Iran") under the terrorism exception, 28 U.S.C. §1605(a)(7), to the Foreign Sovereign Immunities Act ("FSIA"), 28 U.S.C. §§1330, 1602-11 (2000). . . .

### I. Background

**A. Facts**

On the morning of September 12, 1986, Joseph. J. Cicippio was kidnaped in Beiruit, Lebanon, by the terrorist group Hizbollah, an agent of Iran's Ministry of Information and Security ("MOIS"). At the time of his abduction, Mr. Cicippio was comptroller of the American University of Beirut. Hizbollah held him hostage for 1,908 days. During that time, he was randomly beaten, confined in rodent- and scorpion-infested cells, and bound by chains. He suffered from numerous medical problems emanating from the inhumane treatment that he experienced during his captivity. . . .

In 1996, Joseph Cicippio filed suit against Iran under the "terrorism exception" to the FSIA, 28 U.S.C. §1605(a)(7), and the Flatow Amendment, 28 U.S.C. §1605 note. His lawsuit was joined by his wife, Elham Cicippio, two other hostage victims, and the wife of one of the other victims. The Iranian defendants did not respond to the complaint and were found in default. The case was tried *ex parte* and, on August 27, 1998, the District Court rendered a judgment for Joseph Cicippio in the amount of $20 million in damages for lost wages and opportunities and compensatory damages for pain and suffering and mental anguish, and $10 million for Mrs. Cicippio in damages for loss of her husband's society and companionship and mental anguish. *See Cicippio* [v. Islamic Republic of Iran, 18 F. Supp. 2d 62 (D.D.C. 1998),] at 64, 70. Iran never entered an appearance in the case and no appeal was taken from the judgment of the District Court.

The instant case arises from a lawsuit brought in 2001 by Joseph Cicippio's seven adult children and seven siblings against Iran and MOIS for the intentional infliction of emotional distress and loss of solatium they sustained as a result of Mr. Cicippio's ordeal. The suit was [also] based on claims purporting to arise under §1605(a)(7) and the Flatow Amendment. . . . On January 10, 2002, the Cicippios filed a motion for summary judgment. . . .

## B. The Statutory Framework

The FSIA provides that "[s]ubject to existing international agreements to which the United States is a party at the time of enactment of this Act a foreign state shall be immune from the jurisdiction of the courts of the United States and of the States except as provided in sections 1605 to 1607 of this chapter." 28 U.S.C. §1604. Under the FSIA, foreign states enjoy immunity from suit in U.S. courts unless Congress waives immunity under an enumerated exception. In 1996, as part of the comprehensive Antiterrorism and Effective Death Penalty Act ("AEDPA"), Congress enacted the "terrorism exception" to the FSIA, waiving the immunity of foreign states and their agents in any case

> in which money damages are sought against a foreign state for personal injury or death that was caused by an act of torture, extrajudicial killing, aircraft sabotage, hostage taking, or the provision of material support or resources (as defined in section 2339A of title 18) for such an act if such act or provision of material support is engaged in by an official, employee, or agent of such foreign state while acting within the scope of his or her office, employment, or agency . . .

28 U.S.C. §1605(a)(7). This provision only waives the immunity of a foreign state defendant that has been specifically designated by the State Department as a "state sponsor of terrorism," 28 U.S.C. §1605(a)(7)(A), and does not apply if

> (i) the act occurred in the foreign state against which the claim has been brought and the claimant has not afforded the foreign state a reasonable

opportunity to arbitrate the claim in accordance with accepted international rules of arbitration; or

(ii) neither the claimant nor the victim was a national of the United States (as that term is defined in section 101(a)(22) of the Immigration and Nationality Act) when the act upon which the claim is based occurred.

28 U.S.C. §1605(a)(7)(B).

Five months after the passage of AEDPA, Congress enacted a separate provision, titled *Civil Liability for Acts of State Sponsored Terrorism*, which created a private right of action against officials, employees, and agents of foreign states for the conduct described in §1605(a)(7). *See* Omnibus Consolidated Appropriations Act of 1997, Pub. L. No. 104-208, Div. A, Title I, §101(c) [Title V, §589], 110 Stat. 3009-172 (codified at 28 U.S.C. §1605 note). This provision is known as the "Flatow Amendment," in recognition of the family of Alisa Flatow, a woman who died as the result of a terrorist bombing in Israel. *See Flatow v. Islamic Republic of Iran,* 999 F. Supp. 1, 12 (D.D.C. 1998). The Flatow Amendment provides:

> (a) An official, employee, or agent of a foreign state designated as a state sponsor of terrorism designated under §6(j) of the Export Administration Act of 1979 [§2405(j) of the Appendix to Title 50, War and National Defense] while acting within the scope of his or her office, employment, or agency shall be liable to a United States national or the national's legal representative for personal injury or death caused by acts of that official, employee, or agent for which the courts of the United States may maintain jurisdiction under §1605(a)(7) of title 28, United States Code for money damages which may include economic damages, solatium, pain, and suffering, and punitive damages if the acts were among those described in §1605(a)(7).

28 U.S.C. §1605 note.

It is undisputed that the Flatow Amendment permits U.S. nationals to pursue a private right of action for terrorism against officials, employees, and agents of designated foreign states acting in their personal capacities. At issue here is whether §1605(a)(7) and the Flatow Amendment similarly provide a cause of action against a *foreign state*.

## C. The District Court's Judgment

The District Court assumed that plaintiffs' factual allegations were true, but denied . . . their motion for summary judgment. The court also *sua sponte* dismissed the Cicippios' complaint under Federal Rule[] of Civil Procedure 12(b)(6) . . . concluding that "the FSIA, as amended, does not confer subject matter jurisdiction upon it to entertain claims for emotional distress and solatium brought by claimants situated as are these plaintiffs upon the allegations of their complaint." Noting that a foreign state is "liable in the same manner and to the same extent as a private individual under like circumstances," 28 U.S.C. §1606, the District Court held that the plaintiffs could not recover under the prevailing common law rule governing third party claims for outrageous conduct causing severe emotional distress. . . .

### E. The Appearance of the United States as *Amicus Curiae*

On November 6, 2003, the court issued the following order soliciting the views of the United States:

> It is **ORDERED**, on the court's own motion, and in accordance with 28 U.S.C. §517, that the United States of America file, by December 1, 2003, a statement of its current position on the question whether the Foreign Sovereign Immunities Act, 28 U.S.C. §§1602-11 (2003), allows a cause of action for torture and hostage taking against foreign states, or only authorizes statutory claims against state officials, employees, or agents as specified in the Flatow Amendment, 28 U.S.C. §1605 (note) (2000). . . .

### II. Analysis . . .

### B. The Limited Cause of Action under the Flatow Amendment

. . . The question here is whether the Flatow Amendment, which does not refer to "foreign state," may be construed, either alone or in conjunction with section 1605(a)(7), to provide a cause of action against a foreign state.

This issue was flagged in *Price v. Socialist People's Arab Jamahiriya,* 294 F.3d 82 (D.C. Cir. 2002), where we observed that

> [t]he FSIA is undoubtedly a jurisdictional statute which, in specified cases, eliminates foreign sovereign immunity and opens the door to subject matter jurisdiction in the federal courts. There is a question, however, whether the FSIA creates a federal cause of action for torture and hostage taking *against foreign states.*

*Id.* at 87. Since *Price,* some district court opinions in this circuit have held or assumed that the Flatow Amendment creates a cause of action against foreign states. *See Cronin v. Islamic Republic of Iran,* 238 F. Supp. 2d 222, 231 (D.D.C. 2002) (holding that the Flatow Amendment provides a cause of action against a foreign state). [Cites to other such cases omitted.]

This court, however, has never affirmed a judgment that the Flatow Amendment, either alone or in conjunction with section 1605(a)(7), provides a cause of action against a foreign state. The issue was raised in *Bettis v. Islamic Republic of Iran,* 315 F.3d 325, 333 (D.C. Cir. 2003), but the appeal was resolved on other grounds. In *Roeder v. Islamic Republic of Iran,* 333 F.3d 228 (D.C. Cir. 2003), the court noted that, "[i]n view of the Flatow amendment's failure to mention the liability of foreign states, it is 'far from clear' that a plaintiff has a substantive claim against a foreign state under the Foreign Sovereign Immunities Act," *id.* at 234 n.3, but that appeal was also decided on other grounds.

We now hold that neither 28 U.S.C. §1605(a)(7) nor the Flatow Amendment, nor the two considered in tandem, creates a private right of action against a foreign government. Section 1605(a)(7) merely waives the immunity of a foreign state without creating a cause of action against it, and the Flatow Amendment only provides a private right of action against officials, employees, and agents of a foreign state, not against the foreign state itself. Because we hold that there is no statutory cause of action against Iran under these provisions, we affirm the District Court's judgment without deciding whether the evidence presented by the plaintiffs is sufficient to recover for intentional infliction of emotional distress or loss of solatium.

There is a clearly settled distinction in federal law between statutory provisions that waive sovereign immunity and those that create a cause of action. It cannot be assumed that a claimant has a cause of action for damages against a government agency merely because there has been a waiver of sovereign immunity. *See FDIC v. Meyer,* 510 U.S. 471, 483-84 (1994). As the Supreme Court has noted:

> The first inquiry is whether there has been a waiver of sovereign immunity. If there has been such a waiver, as in this case, the second inquiry comes into play—that is, whether the source of substantive law upon which the claimant relies provides an avenue for relief.

*Id.* at 484.

The Supreme Court has also made it clear that the federal courts should be loathe to "imply" a cause of action from a jurisdictional provision that "creates no cause of action of its own force and effect . . . [and] imposes no liabilities." *See Touche Ross & Co. v. Redington,* 442 U.S. 560, 577 (1979). "The ultimate question is one of congressional intent, not one of whether this Court thinks that it can improve upon the statutory scheme that Congress enacted into law." *Id.* at 578. In adhering to this view, the Supreme Court has declined to construe statutes to imply a cause of action where Congress has not expressly provided one.

Unsurprisingly, the Supreme Court has applied the distinction between immunity and liability in interpreting the FSIA itself, explaining that "[t]he language and history of the FSIA clearly establish that the Act was not intended to affect the substantive law determining the liability of a foreign state or instrumentality." *First Nat'l City Bank v. Banco Para El Comercio Exterior de Cuba,* 462 U.S. 611, 620 (1983). With this case law to guide us, there can be little doubt of the outcome in this case.

The language of section 1605(a)(7) and the Flatow Amendment—the only provisions upon which plaintiffs rely—is clear. In declaring that "[a] foreign state shall not be immune from the jurisdiction of courts of the United States or of the States . . . ," 28 U.S.C. §1605(a)(7) merely abrogates the immunity of foreign states from the jurisdiction of the courts in lawsuits for damages for certain enumerated acts of terrorism. It does not impose liability or mention a cause of action. The statute thus confers subject matter jurisdiction on federal courts over such lawsuits, but does not create a private right of action.

As noted above, the Flatow Amendment imposes liability and creates a cause of action. But the liability imposed by the provision is precisely limited to "an official, employee, or agent of a foreign state designated as a state sponsor of terrorism." "Foreign states" are not within the compass of the cause of action created by the Flatow Amendment. In short, there is absolutely nothing in section 1605(a)(7) or the Flatow Amendment that creates a cause of action against foreign states for the enumerated acts of terrorism.

We also agree with the United States that, insofar as the Flatow Amendment creates a private right of action against officials, employees, and agents of foreign states, the cause of action is limited to claims against those officials in their *individual,* as opposed to their official, capacities:

> As the Supreme Court repeatedly has explained, an *official*-capacity claim against a government official is in substance a claim against the government itself. . . . By definition, a damages judgment in an official-capacity suit is enforceable against the state itself (and only against the state). Thus, to construe the Flatow Amendment as permitting official-capacity claims would eviscerate the recognized distinction between suits against governments and suits against individual government officials. . . . [T]he text of the Flatow Amendment and Section 1605(a)(7), as well as all relevant background interpretive principles . . . foreclose any such construction.

Br. for the United States as *Amicus Curiae* at 17.

The plaintiffs and *amicus curiae* dispute both the meaning and relevance of the legislative history of the FSIA or the Flatow Amendment in support of their competing arguments to the court. The legislative history is largely irrelevant, however, because the statutory language is clear — nothing in section 1605(a)(7) or the Flatow Amendment establishes a cause of action against *foreign states.* And . . . there is nothing in the legislative history that raises any serious doubts about the meaning of the statute. . . .

There is nothing anomalous in Congress's approach in enacting the Flatow Amendment. As we noted in *Price,* the passage of §1605(a)(7) involved a delicate legislative compromise. While Congress sought to create a judicial forum for the compensation of victims and the punishment of terrorist states, it proceeded with caution, in part due to executive branch officials' concern that other nations would respond by subjecting the American government to suits in foreign countries. *See Price,* 294 F.3d at 89. . . .

Clearly, Congress's authorization [in the Flatow Amendment] of a cause of action against officials, employees, and agents of a foreign state was a significant step toward providing a judicial forum for the compensation of terrorism victims. Recognizing a federal cause of action against foreign states undoubtedly would be an even greater step toward that end, but it is a step that Congress has yet to take. And it is for Congress, not the courts, to decide whether a cause of action should lie against foreign states. Therefore, we decline to imply a cause of action against foreign states when Congress has not expressly recognized one in the language of section 1605(a)(7) or the Flatow Amendment.

Although we affirm the District Court's dismissal of plaintiffs' complaint for failure to state a claim under section 1605(a)(7) and the Flatow Amendment, we will nonetheless remand the case. The Cicippios' suit was filed in the wake of judgments in favor of Mr. and Mrs. Cicippio and other hostage victims, so they may have been misled in assuming that the Flatow Amendment afforded a cause of action against foreign state sponsors of terrorism. We will therefore remand the case to allow plaintiffs an opportunity to amend their complaint to state a cause of action under some other source of law, including state law. . . .

## NOTES AND QUESTIONS

1. ***The FSIA Exception for Terrorist Acts.*** The first suit following enactment of the 1996 terrorism exception in the FSIA and the Flatow Amendment was Alejandre v. Republic of Cuba, 996 F. Supp. 1239 (S.D. Fla. 1997), which sought damages against the Cuban government for shooting down a pair of unarmed civilian planes in 1996. Another case was based on Libya's then-alleged involvement in the 1988 destruction of PanAm flight 103 over Lockerbie, Scotland. Rein v. Socialist People's Libyan Arab Jamahiriya, 995 F. Supp. 325 (E.D.N.Y. 1998). Still another grew out of the 1995 suicide bombing of a tourist bus in the Gaza Strip that killed a Brandeis University junior studying abroad. Flatow v. Islamic Republic of Iran, 999 F. Supp. 1 (D.D.C. 1998). Courts in these and other cases either assumed or held that §1605(a)(7) and the Flatow Amendment provided a cause of action against state sponsors of terrorism and their agents and instrumentalities. *See, e.g.,* Smith v. Islamic Emirate of Afghanistan, 262 F. Supp. 2d 217, 228 (S.D.N.Y. 2003) ("While not free from doubt, the better view in my opinion is that the Flatow Amendment likely provides a cause of action against a foreign state.").

   Private suits against state sponsors of terrorism, including the earlier suit by Joseph Cicippio and his wife mentioned in the principal case, have resulted in large default judgments against the defendant states. By mid-2005, awards in at least 32 cases totaled just under $7 trillion. *See* Elsea, *supra* p. 745, at 47-49.

2. ***Personal Jurisdiction Over State Sponsors.*** The *Flatow* court declared that 28 U.S.C. §1605(a)(7) satisfied Due Process Clause requirements for the establishment of personal jurisdiction over a foreign state for the claim in that case. *Flatow,* 999 F. Supp. at 19-23. If you represented the government of Iran in such a suit, however, what objections might you raise to the court's personal jurisdiction over your client? *See* Kevin Todd Shook, Note, *State Sponsors of Terrorism Are Persons, Too: The Flatow Mistake,* 61 Ohio St. L.J. 1301 (2000). *But see* Lee M. Caplan, *The Constitution and Jurisdiction Over Foreign States: The 1996 Amendment to the Foreign Sovereign Immunities Act in Perspective,* 41 Va. J. Intl. L. 369 (2001); Joseph W. Glannon & Jeffrey Atik, *Politics and Personal Jurisdiction: Suing State Sponsors of Terrorism Under the 1996 Amendments to the Foreign Sovereign Immunities Act,* 87 Geo. L.J. 675 (1999).

3. ***Who May Sue?*** The FSIA provides that a court shall decline to hear a suit under §1605(a)(7) in which "neither the claimant nor the victim was a national of the United States." *Id.* §1605(a)(7)(B)(ii). Does this leave any recourse in U.S. courts for injured aliens against state sponsors of terrorism? Are there other limitations on standing to sue?

4. ***Who May Be Sued and for What?*** The *Cicippio* court interpreted the language of FSIA's terrorism exception narrowly, holding that neither the Flatow Amendment nor §1605(a)(7), nor the two together, create a cause of action against a foreign state. The court said it based its holding mainly on the language of the two provisions, adding that "it is for Congress, not the courts, to decide whether a cause of action should lie against foreign states." 353 F.3d at 1036. Six months later another D.C. Circuit panel affirmed the

holding in *Cicippio*. Acree v. Republic of Iraq, 370 F.3d 41, 58-59 (D.C. Cir. 2004), *cert. denied*, 544 U.S. 1010 (2005). Unless a plaintiff can point to a different cause of action, the practical effect of these decisions is to cut off entirely recovery for state sponsorship of terrorism.

Might the court have misconstrued Congress's intent? Quoting the lower court, the Court of Appeals cited only a fragment of 28 U.S.C. §1606 to justify its dismissal under Rule 12(b)(6) because the plaintiffs could not recover under familiar common law rules. But 28 U.S.C. §1606 provides more fully, "As to any claim for relief with respect to which a foreign state is not entitled to immunity under section 1605 . . . of this chapter, the foreign state shall be liable in the same manner and to the same extent as a private individual under like circumstances. . . ." Can you read this language to mean that the cause of action created by §1606 is defined by reference to §1605, not to some other body of law? If you can, why do you think the court did not do so?

In the *Cicippio* court's view, the purpose of the Flatow Amendment was to create a limited cause of action when none existed under §1605(a)(7). But, according to one commentator, the Flatow Amendment was meant to expand an existing cause of action under §1605(a)(7) to provide otherwise unavailable punitive damages against state officials. Ruthanne M. Deutsche, *Suing State-Sponsors of Terrorism Under the Foreign Sovereign Immunities Act: Giving Life to the Jurisdictional Grant After Cicippio-Puleo*, 38 Intl. Law. 891, 901-903 (2004) (pointing to evidence in the legislative history).

The court in Boim v. Quranic Literary Institute, *supra* p. 733, pointed out that Congress has adopted several measures indicating its belief that economic sanctions may provide an effective deterrent against terrorism. These measures include statutes authorizing private tort suits against terrorists and their non-state sponsors and criminal sanctions for material support. Indeed, the *Boim* court read the criminal material support statutes as evidence of Congress's broad commitment to utilize such sanctions as a way to punish and deter terrorism, and it used that reading to construe the statute authorizing private suits broadly. Can you square the *Boim* court's analysis with the *Cicippio* court's construction of §1605(a)(7)?

Suit against a government official, agent, or employee of a state sponsor of terrorism under the Flatow Amendment, according to the *Cicippio* court, can only be maintained if the defendant was acting in his "personal" capacity. 353 F.3d at 1035-1036. A claim against an individual acting in his official capacity is "in substance a claim against the government itself." *Id.* at 1034. In other words, the plaintiffs' only recourse was against Iranian officials acting *ultra vires* — as outlaws. The identification of responsible individual Iranian agents and proof of their lack of authorization, however, could be nearly impossible. That is because the information needed to make such proofs, if it exists, is most likely held by the government, which would resist its disclosure by invoking the state secrets privilege. And the proofs, if they could be made, would ironically have to show a *lack* of state sponsorship of terrorism.

5. ***Effect of the Cicippio Decision?*** The *Cicippio* court's decision that neither §1605(a)(7) nor the Flatow Amendment creates a cause of action came after a

long series of successful suits in the D.C. Circuit and elsewhere either deciding or assuming otherwise, as noted above. Why do you suppose a matter of such fundamental importance was not raised and resolved much earlier? What are the implications of the decision for other suits against state sponsors of terrorism?

6. *A Role for the U.S. Government?* Why did the *Cicippio* court order the government to submit an amicus brief outlining its position on the key issue in the case? According to one commentator, "participation of the executive branch in cases interpreting the Flatow Amendment and in other cases with serious foreign policy implications is appropriate and beneficial for both the courts and the government." Joseph Keller, *The Flatow Amendment and State-Sponsored Terrorism*, 28 Seattle U. L. Rev. 1029, 1032 (2005). What contribution could the government make to the appropriate resolution of such private suits?

The government's opposition to passage of §1605(a)(7) in 1996 is well documented. *See, e.g.,* Price v. Socialist People's Libyan Arab Jamahiriya, 294 F.3d 82, 89 (D.C. Cir. 2002) ("[S]uch legislation . . . had been consistently resisted by the executive branch."). In its amicus brief in *Cicippio*, the government expressed the same opposition, arguing that "the imposition of liability for acts of state sponsored terrorism is an area of law with serious ramifications for the United States Government's conduct of foreign affairs."  Brief for the United States as *amicus curiae* at 4, *Cicippio, supra.* Having lost the legislative battle, should the government now play an active role in discouraging this kind of litigation because of possible negative impacts on U.S. interests? Does the FSIA make any provision for such intervention?

Roeder v. Islamic Republic of Iran, 333 F.3d 228 (D.C. Cir. 2003), involved a suit by hostages seized by Iran at the U.S. embassy in Tehran in 1979. The United States was allowed to intervene as of right. The government argued, successfully, that §1605(a)(7) did not abrogate an existing executive agreement that barred claims against Iran arising out of the hostage taking. (The executive agreement was upheld in Dames & Moore v. Regan, 453 U.S. 654 (1981).)

Do these cases raise any doubt about the desirability of private tort litigation against international terrorism, or its consistency with an effective counterterrorist policy? If so, isn't one answer that Congress has already resolved that doubt by enacting the ATA and ATS remedies? Does the ATA provision authorizing the Attorney General to seek a stay of any §2333 civil action that he thinks interferes with a criminal prosecution shed any light on this question? *See* 18 U.S.C. §2336(c).

7. *Other Possible Causes of Action.* Following the lead of the *Cicippio* decision, the court in *Acree, supra,* 370 F.3d at 43, dismissed a suit against Iraq, finding that the plaintiffs had failed to offer "any other coherent alternative causes of action" (other than the Flatow Amendment) to give effect to the jurisdictional grant provided in §1605(a)(7). But is relief available under some alternative cause of action if the conditions set out in §1605(a)(7) are met? Might 18 U.S.C. §2333, reproduced *supra* p. 735, create such a cause of action? *See Price, supra,* 294 F.3d at 87 ("it is possible that such an action could be brought under the 'international terrorism' statute,

18 U.S.C. §2333(a)"). Might the ATS do so? For an argument that federal common law, incorporating principles of domestic tort law and customary international law, provides such a cause of action, see Deutsch, *supra*, at 907-915.

8. ***Punitive Damages.*** Some courts have awarded punitive damages against both state sponsors of terrorism and against their officials and agents. *See, e.g.,* Sutherland v. Islamic Republic of Iran, 151 F. Supp. 2d. 27, 52 (D.D.C. 2001) (finding the defendants guilty of "outrageous conduct" and concluding that a very large award might have a significant deterrent effect on the defendants' behavior). Total punitive damages awards in such cases now amount to more than $5.5 billion. *See* Elsea, *supra* p. 745, at 1 n.4. In fashioning awards in cases like these do you think a court ought to take into account complex diplomatic and foreign policy concerns? If so, how?

9. ***Goosey Gander: Suits Against the United States for Its Alleged Sponsorship of Terrorism.*** Before passage of the terrorism exception to FSIA in 1996, "Executive branch officials feared that the proposed amendment to FSIA might cause other nations to respond in kind, thus potentially subjecting the American government to suits in foreign countries for actions taken in the United States." *Price, supra,* 294 F.3d at 89. Their fears may have been justified.

> At least two of the States affected by the FSIA exception appear to have enacted legislation allowing their citizens to file suit against the United States for violations of human rights or interference in the countries' affairs. Cuba reportedly allows such suits for violations of human rights; and two judgments assessing billions of dollars in damages against the U.S. have apparently been handed down. Iran reportedly has authorized suits against foreign States for intervention in the internal affairs of the country and for terrorist activities resulting in the death, injury, or financial loss of Iranian nationals; and at least one judgment for half a billion dollars has been handed down against the U.S. [Elsea, *supra,* at 45.]

Should the prospect of such retaliation influence courts' interpretation of domestic law?

## C.  COLLECTING THE JUDGMENT

Getting a judicial award for damages resulting from a terrorist act is one thing. Getting paid may be quite another. If assets belonging to a terrorist or his sponsor can be located, of course, those assets are in principle subject to attachment to satisfy a judgment. The FSIA provides that the commercial assets of a state sponsor of terrorism may be attached even if those assets were not involved in the terrorist act that gave rise to the judgment. 28 U.S.C. §1610(b)(2).

But successful plaintiffs have been frustrated in efforts to collect on their judgments when defendants' assets were blocked or even forfeited by the U.S. government. Recall that various resolutions of the U.N. Security Council, see *supra* pp. 707-710, as well as the International Convention for the Suppression of the Financing of Terrorism, *supra* p. 712, require the freezing or seizure of terrorists' assets. The President has blocked such assets under authority provided by the International Economic Emergency Powers Act (IEEPA), *supra* p. 718, and the Trading With the Enemy Act, 50 U.S.C. App. §§1-39, 41-44 (2000). Not surprisingly, these blockings and seizures have been extremely controversial.

Suits against Iran and Cuba, for example, resulted in very large judgments against both states, as noted above. Both Iran and Cuba had substantial assets in the United States, yet those assets were either blocked by the Treasury Department or otherwise held by the U.S. government. With one modest exception the President refused to release them.

Congress acted in 1998 to make the blocked assets available to satisfy the judgments, but it also authorized the President to continue blocking in the interest of "national security," and the President immediately did so. *See* Presidential Determination No. 99-1, *Determination to Waive Requirements Relating to Blocked Property of Terrorist-List States,* 63 Fed. Reg. 59201 (Oct. 21, 1998). Two years later Congress passed the Victims of Trafficking and Violence Protection Act of 2000, Pub. L. No. 106-386, §§2002-2003, 114 Stat. 1464, 1541-1546 (2000), directing the Treasury Secretary to pay compensatory damage awards in certain final and pending suits against Iran and Cuba out of blocked assets and other funds held by the government. The President then released Iranian and Cuban assets worth more than $476 million to make those payments. 65 Fed. Reg. 70382 (Nov. 22, 2000) and 65 Fed. Reg. 78533 (Dec. 15, 2000). Then in 2002 Congress acted yet again to add to the list of cases for which compensatory damages awards could be paid out of blocked assets. Pub. L. No. 107-228, §686, 116 Stat. 1350, 1411 (2002).

Subsequently, in late 2002 Congress passed and President Bush signed into law the Terrorism Risk Insurance Act, Pub. L. No. 107-297, 116 Stat. 2322. That Act includes the following provision:

> Notwithstanding any other provision of law, and except as provided in subsection (b), in every case in which a person has obtained a judgment against a terrorist party on a claim based upon an act of terrorism, or for which a terrorist party is not immune under section 1605(a)(7) of title 28, United States Code, the blocked assets of that terrorist party (including the blocked assets of any agency or instrumentality of that terrorist party) shall be subject to execution or attachment in aid of execution in order to satisfy such judgment to the extent of any compensatory damages for which such terrorist party has been adjudged liable. [*Id.* §201(a), 116 Stat. 2337.]

Subsection (b) states that the President may waive this provision "in the national security interest" to prevent the attachment of embassies and other properties subject to the Vienna Convention on Diplomatic Relations or the Vienna Convention on Consular Relations.

Nevertheless, immediately after the invasion of Iraq in 2003 President Bush confiscated and vested title in the United States to frozen Iraqi assets worth some $1.73 billion, changing them from "blocked" assets to U.S. assets, and preventing their attachment to satisfy judgments obtained after the invasion for Iraq's earlier support of terrorism. The confiscated assets would be used, according to the President, in the postwar reconstruction of Iraq. Exec. Order No. 13290, 68 Fed. Reg. 14307 (Mar. 20, 2003). Congress then passed yet another measure allowing the President to bar attachments of Iraqi property. Pub. L. No. 108-11, §1503, 117 Stat. 559, 579 (2003).

This dizzying political back-and-forth parallels efforts by the executive branch to dissuade courts from awarding judgments against state sponsors of terrorism, as noted above. The history of competing efforts by the two political branches, often played out in the courts, is carefully traced in Elsea, *supra* p. 745.

## NOTES AND QUESTIONS

1. *A Disagreement About Tactics.* Does it strike you as odd that Congress has sought compensation for victims of terrorists from their state sponsors, while the President has persistently thwarted the victims' efforts to collect on their judgments? What possible reasons could the President have for blocking recovery from available assets? In the case of Iraqi assets the Administration wanted to use those resources to help rebuild the war-torn state, as noted above. Concerning other states' blocked assets, Presidents Clinton and Bush have indicated that persons other than the successful litigants have meritorious claims that need to be satisfied (for example, exiled Cubans whose property was confiscated by Fidel Castro) and that the blocked assets served as a powerful diplomatic tool in negotiations with the state owners. *See* Daniel E. Reitz, Comment, *Raising a Paper Tiger: Public Law No. 105-277 §117(d) and the Gutting of the State Sponsored Terrorism Exception to the Foreign Sovereign Immunities Act,* 69 U. Cin. L. Rev. 357 (2000); Sean P. Vitrano, Comment, *Hell Bent on Awarding Recovery to Terrorism Victims: The Evolution and Application of the Antiterrorism Amendments to the Foreign Sovereign Immunities Act,* 19 Dick. J. Intl. L. 213 (2000). Who should decide national priorities in allocating such assets? Can you describe a program that would accommodate the concerns of both political branches?

2. *Whose Property Is Subject to Attachment?* In Ministry of Defense and Support for the Armed Forces of the Islamic Republic of Iran v. Elahi, 546 U.S. 450 (2006), a successful plaintiff in a suit against Iran under 28 U.S.C. §1605(a)(7) and the Flatow Amendment sought to attach an arbitration award obtained by Iran's Ministry of Defense against a third party in separate litigation. The Iranian Ministry of Defense claimed that it was not an "agency or instrumentality" of the state whose property would be subject to attachment if the "state engaged in commercial activity in the United States," 28 U.S.C. §1610(b), but was instead an integral part of the state, whose property could be attached only if that property sought to be attached were "used for a commercial activity in the United States." *Id.* §1610(a). The Supreme Court ruled that attachment could not be allowed before settling the question of the status of the Ministry of Defense.

# CONSTITUTION OF THE UNITED STATES

We the People of the United States, in Order to form a more perfect Union, establish Justice, insure domestic Tranquility, provide for the common defence, promote the general Welfare, and secure the Blessings of Liberty to ourselves and our Posterity, do ordain and establish this Constitution for the United States of America.

## Article I

*Section 1.* All legislative Powers herein granted shall be vested in a Congress of the United States, which shall consist of a Senate and House of Representatives.

*Section 2.* The House of Representatives shall be composed of Members chosen every second Year by the People of the several States, and the Electors in each State shall have the Qualifications requisite for Electors of the most numerous Branch of the State Legislature. . . .

The House of Representatives shall chuse their Speaker and other Officers; and shall have the sole Power of Impeachment.

*Section 3.* The Senate of the United States shall be composed of two Senators from each State, [chosen by the Legislature thereof,][1] for six Years; and each Senator shall have one Vote. . . .

The Senate shall have the sole Power to try all Impeachments. When sitting for that Purpose, they shall be on Oath or Affirmation. When the President of the United States is tried, the Chief Justice shall preside: And no Person shall be convicted without the Concurrence of two thirds of the Members present.

Judgment in Cases of Impeachment shall not extend further than to removal from Office, and disqualification to hold and enjoy any Office of honor, Trust or Profit under the United States: but the Party convicted shall nevertheless be liable and subject to Indictment, Trial, Judgment and Punishment, according to Law.

---

1. Changed by the Seventeenth Amendment to read "elected by the people thereof."

*Section 4.* The Times, Places and Manner of holding Elections for Senators and Representatives, shall be prescribed in each State by the Legislature thereof; but the Congress may at any time by Law make or alter such Regulations, except as to the Places of chusing Senators.

The Congress shall assemble at least once in every Year, and such Meeting shall [be on the first Monday in December,][2] unless they shall by Law appoint a different Day.

*Section 5.* . . . Each House shall keep a Journal of its Proceedings, and from time to time publish the same, excepting such Parts as may in their Judgment require Secrecy; and the Yeas and Nays of the Members of either House on any question shall, at the Desire of one fifth of those Present, be entered on the Journal. . . .

*Section 6.* The Senators and Representatives shall receive a Compensation for their Services, to be ascertained by Law, and paid out of the Treasury of the United States. They shall in all Cases, except Treason, Felony and Breach of the Peace, be privileged from Arrest during their Attendance at the Session of their respective Houses, and in going to and returning from the same; and for any Speech or Debate in either House, they shall not be questioned in any other Place.

. . . [N]o Person holding any Office under the United States, shall be a Member of either House during his Continuance in Office.

*Section 7.* All Bills for raising Revenue shall originate in the House of Representatives; but the Senate may propose or concur with amendments as on other Bills.

Every Bill which shall have passed the House of Representatives and the Senate, shall, before it becomes a Law, be presented to the President of the United States; If he approve he shall sign it, but if not he shall return it, with his Objections to that House in which it shall have originated, who shall enter the Objections at large on their Journal, and proceed to reconsider it. If after such Reconsideration two thirds of that House shall agree to pass the Bill, it shall be sent, together with the Objections, to the other House, by which it shall likewise be reconsidered, and if approved by two thirds of that House, it shall become a Law. . . . If any Bill shall not be returned by the President within ten Days (Sundays excepted) after it shall have been presented to him, the Same shall be a Law, in like Manner as if he had signed it, unless the Congress by their Adjournment prevent its Return, in which Case it shall not be a Law.

Every Order, Resolution, or Vote to which the Concurrence of the Senate and House of Representatives may be necessary (except on a question of Adjournment) shall be presented to the President of the United States; and before the Same shall take Effect, shall be approved by him, or being disapproved by him, shall be repassed by two thirds of the Senate and House of

---

2. Changed by section 2 of the Twentieth Amendment to read "begin at noon on the 3d day of January."

Representatives, according to the Rules and Limitations prescribed in the Case of a Bill.

*Section 8.* [1] The Congress shall have Power To lay and collect Taxes, Duties, Imposts and Excises, to pay the Debts and provide for the common Defence and general Welfare of the United States; but all Duties, Imposts and Excises shall be uniform throughout the United States;

[2] To borrow Money on the credit of the United States;

[3] To regulate Commerce with foreign Nations, and among the several States, and with the Indian Tribes;

[4] To establish an uniform Rule of Naturalization . . . ;

[9] To constitute Tribunals inferior to the supreme Court;

[10] To define and punish Piracies and Felonies committed on the high Seas, and Offenses against the Law of Nations;

[11] To declare War, grant Letters of Marque and Reprisal, and make Rules concerning Captures on Land and Water;

[12] To raise and support Armies, but no Appropriation of Money to that Use shall be for a longer Term than two Years;

[13] To provide and maintain a Navy;

[14] To make Rules for the Government and Regulation of the land and naval Forces;

[15] To provide for calling forth the Militia to execute the Laws of the Union, suppress Insurrections and repel Invasions;

[16] To provide for organizing, arming, and disciplining, the Militia, and for governing such Part of them as may be employed in the Service of the United States, reserving to the States respectively, the Appointment of the Officers, and the Authority of training the Militia according to the discipline prescribed by Congress; . . .

[18] To make all Laws which shall be necessary and proper for carrying into Execution the foregoing Powers, and all other Powers vested by this Constitution in the Government of the United States, or in any Department or Officer thereof.

*Section 9.* . . . [2] The Privilege of the Writ of Habeas Corpus shall not be suspended, unless when in Cases of Rebellion or Invasion the public Safety may require it. . . .

[3] No Bill of Attainder or ex post facto Law shall be passed. . . .

[7] No Money shall be drawn from the Treasury, but in Consequence of Appropriations made by Law; and a regular Statement and Account of the Receipts and Expenditures of all public Money shall be published from time to time.

[8] No Title of Nobility shall be granted by the United States: And no Person holding any Office of Profit or Trust under them, shall, without the Consent of the Congress, accept of any present, Emolument, Office, or Title, of any kind whatever, from any King, Prince, or foreign State.

*Section 10.* [1] No State shall enter into any Treaty, Alliance, or Confederation; grant Letters of Marque and Reprisal; coin Money; emit Bills of Credit;

make any Thing but gold and silver Coin a Tender in Payment of Debts; pass any Bill of Attainder, ex post facto Law, or Law impairing the Obligation of Contracts, or grant any Title of Nobility. . . .

[3] No State shall, without the Consent of Congress, lay any Duty of Tonnage, keep Troops, or Ships of War in time of Peace, enter into any Agreement or Compact with another State, or with a foreign Power, or engage in War, unless actually invaded, or in such imminent Danger as will not admit of delay.

## Article II

*Section 1.* The executive Power shall be vested in a President of the United States of America. He shall hold his Office during the Term of four Years, and, together with the Vice President, chosen for the same Term, be elected, as follows . . .

Before he enter on the Execution of his Office, he shall take the following Oath or Affirmation: — "I do solemnly swear (or affirm) that I will faithfully execute the Office of President of the United States, and will to the best of my Ability, preserve, protect and defend the Constitution of the United States."

*Section 2.* The President shall be Commander in Chief of the Army and Navy of the United States, and of the Militia of the several States, when called into the actual Service of the United States; he may require the Opinion, in writing, of the principal Officer in each of the executive Departments, upon any Subject relating to the Duties of their respective Offices, and he shall have Power to grant Reprieves and Pardons for Offenses against the United States, except in Cases of Impeachment.

He shall have Power, by and with the Advice and Consent of the Senate, to make Treaties, provided two thirds of the Senators present concur; and he shall nominate, and by and with the Advice and Consent of the Senate, shall appoint Ambassadors, other public Ministers and Consuls, Judges of the supreme Court, and all other Officers of the United States, whose Appointments are not herein otherwise provided for, and which shall be established by Law: but the Congress may by Law vest the Appointment of such inferior Officers, as they think proper, in the President alone, in the Courts of Law, or in the Heads of Departments. . . .

*Section 3.* He shall from time to time give to the Congress Information of the State of the Union, and recommend to their Consideration such Measures as he shall judge necessary and expedient; he may, on extraordinary Occasions, convene both Houses, or either of them, and in Case of Disagreement between them, with Respect to the Time of Adjournment, he may adjourn them to such Time as he shall think proper; he shall receive Ambassadors and other public Ministers; he shall take Care that the Laws be faithfully executed, and shall Commission all the Officers of the United States.

*Section 4.* The President, Vice President and all civil Officers of the United States, shall be removed from Office on Impeachment for, and Conviction of, Treason, Bribery, or other high Crimes and Misdemeanors.

## Article III

*Section 1.* The judicial Power of the United States, shall be vested in one supreme Court, and in such inferior Courts as the Congress may from time to time ordain and establish. The Judges, both of the supreme and inferior Courts, shall hold their Offices during good Behaviour, and shall, at stated Times, receive for their Services, a Compensation, which shall not be diminished during their Continuance in Office.

*Section 2.* The judicial Power shall extend to all Cases, in Law and Equity, arising under this Constitution, the Laws of the United States, and Treaties made, or which shall be made, under their Authority; — to all Cases affecting Ambassadors, other public Ministers and Consuls; — to all Cases of admiralty and maritime Jurisdiction; — to Controversies to which the United States shall be a Party; — to Controversies between two or more States; — [between a State and Citizens of another State; — ] between Citizens of different States, — between Citizens of the same State claiming Lands under Grants of different States, [and between a State, or the Citizens thereof, and foreign States, Citizens or Subjects.][3]

In all Cases affecting Ambassadors, other public Ministers and Consuls, and those in which a State shall be Party, the supreme Court shall have original Jurisdiction. In all the other Cases before mentioned, the supreme Court shall have appellate Jurisdiction, both as to Law and Fact, with such Exceptions, and under such Regulations as the Congress shall make.

The Trial of all Crimes, except in Cases of Impeachment, shall be by Jury; and such Trial shall be held in the State where the said Crimes shall have been committed; but when not committed within any State, the Trial shall be at such Place or Places as the Congress may by Law have directed.

*Section 3.* Treason against the United States, shall consist only in levying War against them, or in adhering to their Enemies, giving them Aid and Comfort. No Person shall be convicted of Treason unless on the Testimony of two Witnesses to the same overt Act, or on Confession in open Court.

The Congress shall have Power to declare the Punishment of Treason, but no Attainder of Treason shall work Corruption of Blood, or Forfeiture except during the Life of the Person attainted.

## Article IV . . .

*Section 4.* The United States shall guarantee to every State in this Union a Republican Form of Government, and shall protect each of them against Invasion; and on Application of the Legislature, or of the Executive (when the Legislature cannot be convened) against domestic Violence. . . .

## Article VI . . .

This Constitution, and the Laws of the United States which shall be made in Pursuance thereof; and all Treaties made, or which shall be made, under the

---

3. The bracketed material in this section is changed by the Eleventh Amendment.

Authority of the United States, shall be the supreme Law of the Land; and the Judges in every State shall be bound thereby, any Thing in the Constitution or Laws of any State to the Contrary notwithstanding.

The Senators and Representatives before mentioned, and the Members of the several State Legislatures, and all executive and judicial Officers, both of the United States and of the several States, shall be bound by Oath or Affirmation, to support this Constitution; . . . .

## AMENDMENTS TO THE CONSTITUTION OF THE UNITED STATES OF AMERICA

### Amendment I

Congress shall make no law respecting an establishment of religion, or prohibiting the free exercise thereof; or abridging the freedom of speech, or of the press, or the right of the people peaceably to assemble, and to petition the Government for a redress of grievances.

### Amendment II

A well regulated Militia, being necessary to the security of a free State, the right of the people to keep and bear Arms, shall not be infringed.

### Amendment III

No Soldier shall, in time of peace be quartered in any house, without the consent of the Owner, nor in time of war, but in a manner to be prescribed by law.

### Amendment IV

The right of the people to be secure in their persons, houses, papers, and effects, against unreasonable searches and seizures, shall not be violated, and no Warrants shall issue, but upon probable cause, supported by Oath or affirmation, and particularly describing the place to be searched, and the persons or things to be seized.

### Amendment V

No person shall be held to answer for a capital, or otherwise infamous crime, unless on a presentment or indictment of a Grand Jury, except in cases arising in the land or naval forces, or in the Militia, when in actual service in time of War or public danger; nor shall any person be subject for the same offence to be twice put in jeopardy of life or limb, nor shall be compelled in any criminal case to be a witness against himself, nor be deprived of life, liberty, or property, without due process of law; nor shall private property be taken for public use without just compensation.

## Amendment VI

In all criminal prosecutions, the accused shall enjoy the right to a speedy and public trial, by an impartial jury of the State and district wherein the crime shall have been committed; which district shall have been previously ascertained by law, and to be informed of the nature and cause of the accusation; to be confronted with the witnesses against him; to have compulsory process for obtaining witnesses in his favor, and to have the assistance of counsel for his defence. . . .

## Amendment VIII

Excessive bail shall not be required, nor excessive fines imposed, nor cruel and unusual punishments inflicted.

## Amendment IX

The enumeration in the Constitution of certain rights shall not be construed to deny or disparage others retained by the people.

## Amendment X

The powers not delegated to the United States by the Constitution, nor prohibited by it to the States, are reserved to the States respectively, or to the people. . . .

## Amendment XIV

***Section 1.*** All persons born or naturalized in the United States and subject to the jurisdiction thereof, are citizens of the United States and of the State wherein they reside. No State shall make or enforce any law which shall abridge the privileges or immunities of citizens of the United States; nor shall any State deprive any person of life, liberty, or property, without due process of law; nor deny to any person within its jurisdiction the equal protection of the laws. . . .

# Table of Cases

*Principal cases are set in italics. Cases cited in the authors' text, notes, and questions are set in Roman type.*

# INDEX